LSAT®
PrepTests 62–71
Unlocked

Exclusive Data, Analysis & Explanations for
10 Actual, Official LSAT PrepTests Volume V

KAPLAN

PUBLISHING

New York

LSAT® is a registered mark of the Law School Admission Council, Inc.

© 2017 by Kaplan, Inc.

Published by Kaplan Publishing, a division of Kaplan, Inc.
750 Third Avenue
New York, NY 10017

ISBN: 978-1-5062-2343-8
10 9 8 7 6 5 4 3 2 1

Kaplan Publishing print books are available at special quantity discounts to use for sales promotions, employee premiums, or educational purposes. For more information or to purchase books, please call the Simon & Schuster special sales department at 866-506-1949.

Table of Contents

Introduction

About This Book

This book contains complete explanations to every question from officially released LSAT PrepTests 62 through 71, along with exclusive data and analysis of test taker performance and question difficulty on each one of these LSAT exams. It is the perfect companion to these tests individually, or to the LSAC's bundle of these tests released under the title *10 Actual, Official LSAT PrepTests Volume V.*

Whether you are taking a prep course or studying on your own, taking officially released LSATs is an essential component of successful preparation. LSAT students are fortunate that LSAC (the organization that develops and administers the test) typically releases three LSATs—the test forms given in June, in the Fall, and in December—each year. It probably goes without saying that practice with recent LSATs is especially valuable, and the tests covered by this book range from the test administration in December 2010 through the one in December 2013. At the time of this book's release, *10 Actual, Official LSAT PrepTests Volume V* is the most recent bundle of 10 tests released by LSAC.

While practice tests are necessary, LSAT experts will tell you that simply taking and scoring tests isn't sufficient to maximize your score improvement. You need to know why you missed questions, and how to get to the right answers even more efficiently. That's where this companion comes in. For each of the 10 tests explained and analyzed here, Kaplan provides exclusive data about how test takers perceived the tests' difficulty. We then compare that to actual student performance on the test, and we identify each test's 10 most difficult questions and categorize the difficulty of all of the test's questions. You'll also see how representative each test is of the LSAT's most recent trends and learn about anything that makes a particular test administration unique or unusual. Finally, you get complete explanations for every question, game, and passage in the test, including explanations for every wrong answer.

Start by reading the section called "Introduction: How to Use Kaplan LSAT Explanations," so that you get familiar with Kaplan's methods, strategies, and terminology. Then, after taking any of the practice tests covered by this volume, put your practice experience in context by reading the test's "Inside Story" page. Finally, review your performance on any question, game, or passage from the test. Kaplan's LSAT experts encourage you to review every question—even those you got right—to learn how top LSAT scorers use patterns to approach the exam effectively and efficiently.

No matter how you choose to use the information and explanations included in this book, Kaplan is here to encourage and support your study and practice. For over 70 years, our commitment has been to raising scores for every test taker. So, here's to good luck, and, more importantly, good preparation.

How to Review a PrepTest

Taking full-length practice LSAT tests is an essential part of comprehensive preparation for this important exam. Not only do practice tests contain examples of all the questions, games, and passages used by the testmaker, but by taking practice LSATs, you also get a feel for the timing restrictions that make each section of the LSAT so challenging. Moreover, when you take full-length exams, you approximate the endurance and stamina demands of Test Day.

The LSAT is unique among the major post-graduate admissions exams in that the LSAC (the organization that creates and administers the LSAT) releases three previously administered, official LSAT tests each year. To help our students get the most out of these valuable practice resources, Kaplan has a team of LSAT experts who evaluate each test, and write comprehensive explanations for every question (indeed, for every answer choice) immediately after the exam's release. Now, for the first time, we are making these explanations available to everyone who is serious about his or her LSAT preparation.

Here are a few tips for the best way to use the explanations.

1. Learn the Kaplan Methods for Each Section

Every official LSAT contains two sections of Logical Reasoning, and one section each of Logic Games (or Analytical Reasoning, as the LSAC calls it) and Reading Comprehension. Test takers who train with Kaplan learn simple but highly effective methods for the questions, games, and passages in these sections. Thus, our explanations are written so that they follow the steps of those methods consistently. As you review the questions in the test, the explanations here will not only explain why a particular answer is correct, it will show you how an LSAT expert efficiently untangles the question, and how she can demonstrate that all four other answers are incorrect.

The Kaplan Methods for each type of scored section are outlined for each section later in this chapter. The methods are somewhat intuitive, so you'll get the gist of each one pretty quickly. In addition, you'll learn about some of the specific strategies Kaplan students learn in class. Keep an eye out for those strategies again as you review the questions in your test.

Terminology and Definitions

In our comprehensive LSAT prep courses, Kaplan students learn a sweeping vocabulary of terms, categories, and distinctions for the question types, patterns of reasoning, flaws, conclusions, and rhetorical devices employed by the testmaker. If you are not currently in a Kaplan LSAT prep course, you may come across terms with which you're unfamiliar, or unsure how to understand in the context of the test. For such terms, we've created a glossary that you can find at the back of this book.

2. Evaluate Timed Practice Differently than Untimed Practice

We'll stipulate that you have already completed the test. Why else would you be looking at the explanations? Now, a couple of questions: First, did you take the LSAT under strict, timed conditions? If you did, review questions in context. Were you running out of time near the end of the section? Did you have to guess? Did you spend far too long to get one or two questions correct, thus costing yourself the opportunity to try other questions? Many of the explanations in this book will give you strategies for answering questions more efficiently and effectively, as well as always explaining how to answer them correctly. Speed and confidence can be important to your score on Test Day—in some cases, as important as expertise.

If you did not time yourself, or if you gave yourself extra time to complete the LSAT, review the questions to assess your mastery of LSAT skills. There is nothing wrong with untimed practice. Indeed, Kaplan's expert LSAT instructors encourage their students to engage in untimed, mastery practice whenever the students learn a new question type. When you are reviewing a test on which you took extra time, your focus should be on assessing how you did on each step of each question, and especially on how well you executed the skills rewarded by the LSAT.

3. Note the Question Difficulty

At the beginning of each section of explanations, you will see a list of the questions in that section of the test. For each question, we provide the question type and a difficulty rating of between 1 star (easiest) and 4 stars (hardest). Pay attention to the difficulty level of the questions you got right and those you missed.

Because our students take official, released LSAT tests for practice during their courses, we at Kaplan have hundreds of thousands of data points on the questions in these released tests. We can accurately determine the difficulty of every question on each exam, and even determine which incorrect answers gave students the most trouble, and which ones they dismissed easily.

Here's how the star ratings work. Four-star questions are the 10 most difficult questions on the test. Typically these are answered correctly by one-third of students or less. The next 20 questions in difficulty are assigned a 3-star rating. The next 30 get a 2-star rating. And, the rest (the easiest 40 or 41 questions on the exam) are given a 1-star rating. On most LSATs, the 1-star questions are answered correctly by 70 percent of students or more.

The difficulty ratings help you assess your performance in two important ways. First, when you miss a 4-star or 3-star question, you're in good company. These questions are difficult for most students. Study the explanation to a 4- or 3-star question carefully, and note the strategic approaches that allows LSAT experts to solve these tough verbal and reasoning puzzles. On the other hand, when you miss a 1- or 2-star question, focus on where you may have misinterpreted the instructions or some key piece of information. While these questions are not too hard for most students, even top scorers occasionally miss 1- and 2-star questions, usually because of same kinds of oversights you'll see cleared up in the explanations in this book.

The second way difficulty ratings can help you is by providing insight into your score. Here is a chart showing how raw score (the number of correct answers a test taker generates) translates into scaled score (the 120 to 180 score law schools see on your score report) and into percentile (the percentage of test takers who scored below you on a given exam).

Raw Score (#correct)	Scaled Score	Percentile
92	172	99th
85	167	95th
81	164	90th
74	160	80th
67	156	70th
63	154	60th
58	151	50th
55	149	40th
50	146	30th
45	143	10th
39	139	10th

How raw score (number of questions correct) translates into scaled score and percentile ranking PrepTest 77 (December 2015)

Because the LSAC score report is comparing you to all those who took your test, and to the cohort of applicants likely to apply to law school at the same time you do, the translation from raw score to scaled score and percentile change slightly from test to test. The previous chart, however, provides a good estimate of scoring on most recent LSATs. As you can see, on most tests, you could miss nine of the ten 4-star questions and still score a 172, placing you in the 99th percentile, and giving you a score competitive at any law school in the country. Were you to miss all of the 4- and 3-star questions, you would still get 71 correct answers, producing a scaled score around 158, better than 75 percent of test takers. To place above the 50th percentile (or, to score over 151, if you like), you'll need to get about 58 correct answers, that's all of the 1-star and not quite a majority of the 2-star questions. Now, most test takers get a mixture of easier and harder questions right, and even top scorers occasionally mess up and miss a 1-star question. But, take note of what happens once you are scoring over the 50th percentile: adding between five and ten correct answers to your performance can move your percentile score up ten points or more, making your application stronger than those of thousands of other test takers.

4. Recognize Patterns in the LSAT and in Your Performance

As a standardized test, the LSAT is nothing if not predictable. You won't know the content of the questions or passages you'll see on your official exam, of course, but repeated practice can reveal patterns that will help you improve your performance. As you review multiple tests, you will begin to see that certain question types recur with greater or lesser frequency. Moreover, each question type is amenable to a handful of expert strategies, which are often outlined in the explanations in this book. Beyond the patterns associated with question strategies and correct answers, you'll see that even the incorrect answers regularly fall into a handful of definite types as well. Whenever this is the case, the Kaplan explanations will highlight and articulate the incorrect answer pattern.

Use these patterns and categories to help assess your own performance. Ask yourself the following questions, and answer honestly. Do you regularly struggle with a particular Logic Reasoning question type? Is a certain pattern in Logic Games easier for you? Does another game type trip you up? Do some topics or question types in Reading Comprehension give you more trouble than others? Throughout the test, are there incorrect answer types to which you are routinely susceptible?

In our comprehensive Kaplan LSAT prep courses, we provide tools that help all of our students identify their individual strengths and weaknesses, and then we provide personalized instruction to help them maximize their potential on the test. If you are preparing on your own, identifying the patterns that impact your performance (for better or worse) will require more time and attention, but don't skip this important part of review. Determine your areas of greatest opportunities for improvement, and focus on them as you continue your practice. That leads directly to the next tip.

5. Apply What You Learn

This is the most significant tip of all. Taking a practice LSAT is important. If you complete your practice test under timed, test-like conditions, it will give you a great snapshot of your performance as it stands now. But, to get a genuine understanding of your strengths and opportunities—and, more importantly, to improve your performance—you need to take and review multiple tests.

The greatest value of these explanations is that you can use each practice test to evaluate your performance. That will point you in the right direction the next time you practice. Don't be content with getting a question right. Review the explanation until you are satisfied that you can get a similar question right the next time you see one, and that you can get it right as quickly and efficiently as you'll need to under the time constraints of the test. When you get a question wrong, don't simply read the correct answer and think, "Oh, I get it now." Make sure you know how you misread or misunderstood the question, and why the particular incorrect answer you chose was tempting.

Practice and review the LSAT consistently with the help of expert explanations, and you will improve.

Logical Reasoning Method and Strategies

The Kaplan Method for Logical Reasoning has four steps. The order of Steps 1 and 2 may surprise you a little bit.

LOGICAL REASONING METHOD

1. Identify the Question Type
2. Untangle the Stimulus
3. Predict the Correct Answer
4. Evaluate the Answer Choices

Every Logical Reasoning question has three easily identifiable parts: the stimulus, the question stem, and five answer choices. The **stimulus** is the paragraph or short dialogue at the top of the question; it may contain an argument or a set of statements. Beneath the stimulus is the **question stem**; it gives the test taker her task, e.g., identify an assumption in the argument, pick the answer that makes the argument stronger or weaker, describe a flaw in the author's reasoning, or choose the answer that follows from the statements in the stimulus. Underneath the question stem, there are five **answer choices**, exactly one of which fulfills the task called for by the question stem; the other four answer choices are demonstrably incorrect.

The Kaplan Method for Logical Reasoning takes the most efficient and strategic route through the questions. You will see this Method reflected in the explanations to every Logical Reasoning question.

Step 1: Identify the Question Type

Begin with the question stem. Find out what your task is. That way, you'll know what to look for as you are analyzing the stimulus. The explanations will show you how an expert approaches the stimulus differently depending on the question type found in the question stem.

LOGICAL REASONING STRATEGY

Identify the Question Type

As you review your test, take note of the task, or question type, for every Logical Reasoning question. You'll soon notice that certain question types are more prevalent. Moreover, you'll begin to see how LSAT experts approach the same question types consistently to maximize their accuracy and speed. Note: Every question type is defined in the glossary.

Step 2: Untangle the Stimulus

Once you understand your task, read the stimulus actively, focusing on the sentences or statements that will help you choose the correct answer.

LOGICAL REASONING STRATEGY

Effectively Analyze Arguments

In questions that ask you to analyze an **argument**, you will want to first locate and paraphrase the author's **conclusion**, meaning the assertion or opinion about which the author is trying to convince the reader. After identifying the conclusion, focus on the author's **evidence**, the statements or premises the author offers in support of the conclusion. Many questions require that you then determine the author's **assumption**(s), the unstated premise(s) that logically connect the evidence to the conclusion.

The explanations will outline expert argument analysis whenever it is relevant, but here's a simple demonstration. Imagine a stimulus with this simple argument:

This raspberry lemonade is a very sour drink. Therefore, it will not pair well with the pasta dish.

Here, the author's conclusion is that the raspberry lemonade will not pair well with the pasta dish. His evidence is that the raspberry lemonade is quite sour. From this, you can determine that the author assumes that very sour drinks will not pair well with the pasta dish. You may agree or disagree with the author; the LSAT doesn't care about that. The test will reward you for being able to untangle and analyze the explicit (conclusion and evidence) and implicit (assumption) parts of the author's argument. You'll see argument analysis demonstrated in a majority of the Logical Reasoning explanations.

LOGICAL REASONING STRATEGY

Effectively Catalog Statements

In cases where the stimulus does *not* contain an argument, the LSAT typically rewards you either for making a valid inference based on the stimulus, or for resolving an apparent paradox described in the stimulus. Because there is usually no argument in these stimuli, LSAT experts approach them differently, but no less strategically.

In non-argument-based questions, experts note five patterns:

Concrete statements/assertions: The statement "All students at State U must complete Composition 102" is far stronger, and thus more likely to lead to valid deductions, than a statement such as "Some students at State U have taken Professor Manning's archaeology seminar."

Shared terms: When two statements share a term, they often combine to produce valid deductions. For example, if the author tells you that "Project X receives government funding," and then tells you that "projects which receive government funding are subject to annual review," you can infer that Project X is subject to annual review.

Keywords: Words that highlight how an author thinks two statements relate to one another can be helpful in making inferences. Consider what you can infer about a fictional politician named Carson in the following sentence: "The population of Crow County is quite conservative, *but* Carson is likely to be elected Commissioner." That's quite different than what we could infer were the author to say: "The population of Crow County is quite conservative, *and so* Carson is likely to be elected Commissioner."

By the way, every Paradox question stimulus will contain a contrast Keyword, highlighting the two seemingly contradictory statements at issue.

Conditional statements: Also known as Formal Logic, conditional (or "If-then") statements are powerful tools for making valid inferences. Consider a statement such as "If Rebecca auditions for the role of Desdemona, then Jonas will audition for the role of Hamlet." This makes Jonas's audition necessary for Rebecca's. If this stimulus went on to say, "Jonas will not audition for the role of Hamlet," then you can deduce that Rebecca will not audition for the role of Desdemona. Note: Formal Logic is discussed further at the end of this chapter.

Uncertain statements: Statements containing terms such as *some, several,* and *most* are less concrete than those containing *all, every,* or *none.* LSAT experts, however, learn to recognize patterns to produce valid deductions. One of these patterns, fairly common on the LSAT, is a pair of "most" statements. For example, if a stimulus states that "Most members of the water polo team are in-state students," and tells you that "Most members of the water polo team are scholarship athletes," an LSAT expert will deduce that "At least one in-state student is a scholarship athlete."

Untrained test takers instinctively read the stimulus first, after all, it is at the top of the question. When they next read the question stem, however, they often have to reread the stimulus now that they know their task. The Kaplan Method for Logical Reasoning eliminates this redundancy. The strategies outlined here help the well-trained test taker zero in on the relevant, helpful statements in the stimulus.

Step 3: Predict the Correct Answer

After untangling the stimulus, an LSAT expert will pause very briefly to paraphrase what the correct answer must say. This allows the expert to evaluate the answer choices more efficiently and effectively.

Without pausing to "pre-phrase" the correct answer, a test taker is likely to read answer choice (A), and then to reread the stimulus. If still unsure whether choice (A) is correct, this untrained test taker will do the same thing with choices (B), and (C), and so on. This reading, rereading, and comparing of answer choices is far too time consuming, and can make you more confused about the question than you were to begin with.

An LSAT expert, armed with a strong prediction, evaluates the answer choices by asking, "Does this answer choice match my prediction?" If the answer is "No," she crosses it out. If the answer is "Yes," she can confidently circle it and move on to the next question.

LOGICAL REASONING STRATEGY

Accurately Predict Correct Answers

Different Logical Reasoning question types (e.g., Assumption, Strengthen/Weaken, Flaw, Inference) reward different skills. LSAT experts learn to predict correct answers accurately and in the ways that best fit the different question stem tasks.

Here are some of the ways LSAT experts treat the prediction step differently in the most common Logical Reasoning questions.

Assumption questions: In the simplest arguments, it's easy to spot (and to state) the author's assumption. For example, if an author concludes that "Socrates is mortal" because of evidence that "Socrates is human," then this author is assuming (correctly, in fact) that "Humans are mortal." On the LSAT, however, arguments are usually a bit more complex than that. Moreover, the LSAT may ask for an assumption *necessary* to the author's argument, or for an assumption *sufficient* to establish the author's conclusion. In the explanations, you'll see how LSAT experts predict the correct answer differently depending on the Assumption question stem.

Strengthen/Weaken questions: In these questions, the correct answer states a fact that makes the author's conclusion more or less likely to follow from the author's evidence. That's different than saying that the answer will prove or disprove the argument. For example, if an author argues that "The new public tennis courts will not be built because MegaCorp has withdrawn its offer to fund the new public tennis courts," the author assumes that *only* MegaCorp's funding would make the construction of new courts possible. To weaken that argument, the test will provide a correct answer that names a potential alternate source of funding. That is the LSAT expert's prediction: "The correct answer here will point out another way to pay for the construction." The LSAT expert does not try to guess which source the test will choose (a tax levy, a bond issue, a wealthy philanthropist, a private tennis club), but he knows with confidence that the one correct answer will provide an alternative source and that the four incorrect answers will not.

Flaw questions: It is common for some Flaw questions to be among the toughest questions on a given LSAT. That's because they ask you to describe an error in the author's reasoning. The answer choices often contain abstract wording and avoid reference to the subject matter of the stimulus. For a Kaplan-trained LSAT expert, however, Flaw questions can be among the easiest for predicting what the correct answer will contain. That's because there are a handful of Flaw types that the testmaker uses again and again. Some of them will sound familiar (ad hominem, circular reasoning, correlation versus causation, unrepresentative samples, equivocation) even if you can't easily define them at this point. Of course, the explanations will always point out these common flaw types when they appear in questions or in answer choices, and definitions of every flaw type appear in the glossary.

Inference questions: These are often the hardest questions in which to accurately predict the correct answer. After all, there are sometimes dozens of things you could infer from a series of three or four statements. When you are preparing to evaluate the answer choices in Inference questions, pay careful attention to the question stem. Does it ask for a correct answer that "must be true" given the statements in the stimulus, or does it ask for the one that is "most strongly suggested" by the statements in the stimulus? Beyond that, keep an eye out for the patterns discussed above in the strategy labeled "Effectively Catalog Statements." If you are given two statements that share a common term, or if you spot conditional statements, you can be fairly certain that the testmaker wants you to use those tools to reach the correct answer.

Step 4: Evaluate the Answer Choices

In the discussion of Step 3, you saw how an LSAT expert uses a solid prediction of the correct answer to confidently evaluate each answer choice. Test takers who truly master the Logical Reasoning Method become so confident that, if choice (C) is clearly the correct answer, they may not check choices (D) and (E) at all, or if they do, they do so quickly, just to confirm that they are clearly incorrect. In the explanations in this book, we always present the correct answer first to reinforce the strategies of predicting and evaluating. In addition, we discuss each wrong answer thoroughly, even though you (if you follow the Method) may not need such thorough analysis on Test Day.

LOGICAL REASONING STRATEGY

Spot Common Wrong Answer Patterns

The LSAT is so standardized, that particular types of incorrect answers appear over and over throughout the test. Spotting these common wrong answer types will make you more efficient throughout the Logical Reasoning section.

The most common wrong answer type is Outside the Scope, an answer that introduces a fact or consideration irrelevant to the argument or statements in the stimulus. Other important wrong answer types include 180 and Extreme. A 180 incorrect answer states exactly the opposite of what the correct answer must say. These 180 answers can be effective "traps" for an inattentive test taker. If the correct answer must weaken an argument, for example, it's not uncommon for one or more of the wrong answers to effectively strengthen the argument. Extreme wrong answers stay within the scope of the stimulus, but overstate what the correct must say. If you can infer, for example, that at least one in-state student is a scholarship athlete, one of the wrong answers might state that "most in-state students are scholarship athletes."

NOTE: There are a handful of other incorrect answer patterns. Whenever an answer choice fits one of the these patterns, the explanations will make note of the pattern, and the term describing the incorrect answer type will be defined in the glossary.

In our comprehensive LSAT prep courses, Kaplan students learn and practice the Logical Reasoning Method over several class sessions, and in dozens of additional *LSAT Channel* lessons and homework assignments. If you are not in a Kaplan course, we still want you to improve your LSAT score as much as possible. That's why we make the Logical Reasoning Method the foundation of every question's explanation, and why we always highlight and explain the strategies outlined here.

Logic Games Method and Strategies

Every Logic Games section contains four games, each with five to seven questions. To finish the section within the allotted 35 minutes, you need to average around 8 and 1/2 minutes per game. That's a tall order, one most test takers are not able to fill. The Kaplan Method for Logic Games is designed to attain the maximum combination of speed and accuracy within this section.

> **LOGIC GAMES METHOD**
>
> 1. Overview
> 2. Sketch
> 3. Rules
> 4. Deductions
> 5. Questions

You may find it striking that the LSAT expert completes four steps in this Method before turning her attention to the questions. That seems counter-intuitive. Don't we want to get to the questions as quickly as possible? As you study the logic games explanations in this book, however, you'll see that the expert's approach, which involves organizing the game's information first, allows her to answer the questions much more efficiently, sometimes in a matter of seconds. These explanations will demonstrate the enormous power of patience in logic games, and will convince you of the value of consistently applying the Method to every game you encounter.

To understand what each step involves, let's first define the parts of a logic game as they appear in the test booklet. To conduct your overview of the game, you'll examine the game's **setup**, the short description of the game's situation, entities (the people or things you're asked to arrange in the game), and action (the game's task). Beneath the setup, the testmaker always includes some **rules**, which are listed in indented text. These rules provide restrictions on how the entities may behave within the game's action and framework. After that, you'll see the game's **questions**. In most games, one or more of the questions will begin with a hypothetical "If" condition. Such a condition acts like an additional rule, but it applies *only* to that individual question. Keep your Master Sketch with the rules that apply throughout the game separate from your scratchwork on individual questions containing new "If"s that are unique to that question.

Step 1: Overview

The goal here is to have a clear mental picture of your task. Ideally, you could describe your job within the game in a single sentence, e.g., "I will be dividing eight students into two teams of four with no overlap," or "From among seven books, I will select four and reject three." Be as precise as you can without overstating the limitations imposed by the setup. Make sure, for example, that the game asks you to choose "exactly four books" and not "at least four books." In logic games, every word is important.

> ## LOGIC GAMES STRATEGY
>
> ### Ask the SEAL Questions to Conduct Your Overview
>
> To make sure that they have a strong grasp of the game's layout and task, LSAT experts ask four questions, known to Kaplan students by the acronym SEAL, from the first letter of each word.
>
> What is/are the …
>
> **Situation**—What is the real-world scenario being described? What is the deliverable information—an ordered list, a calendar, a chart showing what's matched up?
>
> **Entities**—Who or what are the "moving parts," the people or things I'm distributing, selecting, sequencing, or matching?
>
> **Action**—What is the specific action—distribution, selection, sequencing, matching, or a combination of those—that I'm performing on the entities?
>
> **Limitations**—Does the game state parameters (e.g., select exactly four of the seven, sequence the entities one per day) that determine or restrict how I'll set up and sketch the game?
>
> Throughout Kaplan Logic Games explanations, the LSAT experts will often break down their Overviews just like this. Be sure you see what they see before you move into the complicated rules and deductions.

Step 2: Sketch

Based on your Overview, create a simple framework in which you record and organize the game's information, rules, and limitations. The testmaker uses just a handful of game types, so as you review your work and study the expert's sketches in the explanations, learn to identify the most common actions and the sketches typically associated with them. Here are two good rules of thumb: 1) Always list out the entities in abbreviation (e.g., M O P T W Y) above your sketch framework, and 2) make your framework as simple and easy to copy as possible (since you will want to repeat it when a question offers you a new "If" condition).

> ## LOGIC GAMES STRATEGY
>
> ### Learn the Standard Sketch for Each Game Type
>
> Every game needs a Master Sketch. It provides a framework into which you can build the rules and restrictions that will allow you to answer the questions. Fortunately, the LSAT uses the same game types test after test, and you can learn some standard patterns that will save you time and frustration on Test Day. Here's how LSAT experts typically set up the most common game actions.
>
> **Strict Sequencing**—These games ask you to arrange or schedule entities in numbered positions, or on specific days or times. A series of numbered slots (either horizontal or vertical) usually suits this task.

A B C D E F

——— ——— ——— ——— ——— ———
 1   2   3   4   5   6

Loose Sequencing—These games are similar to Strict Sequencing, but here, the setup does not provide numbered slots or days of the week. Instead, all of the rules describe the relative position of two or more entities. The rules can be combined to show all of the known relationships among the entities.

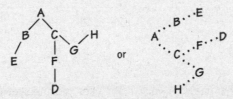

Selection—These games ask you to choose or select a smaller group of entities out of a longer list. All you really need here is a roster of all the entities. Then, you can circle those selected and cross out those rejected.

A̶ B̶ Ⓒ D E̶ F Ⓖ

Matching—These games ask you to match up members of one group with those of another, or to assign certain attributes to some members and different attributes to others. A list or grid fits the bill here.

x y z

A | B | C | D | E | F

or

	A	B	C	D	E	F
x						
y						
z						

Distribution—These games give you a group of entities and ask you to break it up into smaller groups (two or three smaller groups is most common, but you will see four on occasion).

LMNOPRS

1	2	3
———	———	———
———	———	———
		———

For every game, the Kaplan explanations will show the LSAT expert's initial sketch framework and explain how she chose it. Then, you'll see how the expert develops the sketch to accommodate the rules and deductions provided by the game. Study the sketches carefully and make sure you see why the expert chose the one she did.

Now, some games may have twists or special requirements that require you to vary or add to these standard sketches, and Hybrid games combine two or three of the standard actions together. Don't let these exceptions deter you from learning the standard sketches. Once you know the common patterns, it will be easier to see how LSAT experts can account for the unique features of any game within them.

Step 3: Rules

Once you have created a sketch framework, you will then analyze and sketch each rule. Make sure to consider what each rule does and does not determine. Again, every word in Logic Games is important. A rule stating that "A gives his presentation on a day earlier than the day on which B gives his presentation" is different than one stating that "A gives his presentation on the day immediately before the day on which B gives his presentation," and both are distinct from the rule "A gives his presentation on the day immediately before or the day immediately after the day on which B give his presentation." As you review the explanations, pay careful attention to how the LSAT expert sketched out each rule to make sure you didn't over- or under-determine the rule's scope.

LOGIC GAMES STRATEGY

Build Rules Directly into the Sketch Framework

Always seek to depict rules in the most concrete, helpful way possible. If you can, build them right into the sketch, so that you can see their impact on the setup and the entities.

When you encounter a rule that establishes exactly where an entity should go, your instinct will rightly be to place that entity right into your sketch framework. Consider, for example, a game that asks you to sequence six entities—A, B, C, D, E, and F—into six numbered positions—1 through 6. If you get a rule that says "D will be placed in Position 4," you'll just jot down "D" on top of that slot in your framework. Perfect! The entity can't move, and you'll always see where it is.

With other types of rules, however, many test takers do not add them to the sketch in the most helpful way. When analyzing Logic Games rules, LSAT experts always consider what the rules does and does not restrict. Sometimes, the negative implications of a rule are stronger than its affirmative ones. For example, consider a game that asks you to sequence six entities—A, B, C, D, E, and F—into six numbered positions—1 through 6. A typical rule for that game might say: C must be placed before A. You could jot down something like "C ... A," but that doesn't tell you anything concrete. You cannot easily place that into your sketch framework. The negative implications of that rule, however, are very strict: C absolutely cannot go in position 6, and A absolutely cannot go in position 1. If you write something like "~ C" directly underneath slot 6 and "~ A" underneath slot 1 in your sketch, you will have a very clear visual depiction of this rule.

Throughout the Kaplan explanations, take time to study how LSAT experts draw and depict the rules. It's okay if your drawings don't look identical to those in the explanations, but you're sure to encounter a few instances in which the expert's sketch makes a lot of sense, and teaches you a few new tactics for handling games and their rules.

Step 4: Deductions

This is the step that most untrained test takers miss, but it is also the step that can transform your performance on a game. Deductions arise when you are able to combine rules and restrictions to determine additional information. Logic games reward test takers for being able to quickly and accurately determine what must, can, and cannot be true about the entities in the game, and deductions can increase your brain's processing power enormously. Take the simplest kind of deduction, accounting for "Duplications," in other words, entities mentioned in more than one rule. Here's the scenario:

In a game that asks you to arrange six entities (call them A, B, C, D, E, and F) into six hour long spots from 1 pm through 6 pm, you have two rules:

> B gets an earlier spot than C.
> D gets a later spot than C.

Combining those two rules (B ... C and C ... D) produces a three-entity list (B ... C ... D). That's pretty routine, but consider the implications. You now know that D will never take 1 pm or 2 pm, that C will never take 1 pm or 6 pm, and that B will never take 5 pm or 6 pm.

Most deductions are more elusive than that, and some are even more powerful in their effects on the entities within the game. As you review your work and study the explanations, pay attention to the deductions made by the LSAT experts. Especially in games where you feel that you really struggled, discovering that there was an available deduction that you missed can make the entire game clearer and more comprehensible.

LOGIC GAMES STRATEGY

Use the BLEND Checklist to Make All Available Deductions

One of the hardest things to learn to do in logic games is to make all of the deductions quickly, and then to be confident enough that there are no more deductions that you can move on to tackle the question set. To help with this difficult task, Kaplan's LSAT experts have created a mnemonic of the five most common deduction-producing patterns seen in the rules and restrictions. We call it BLEND, for the first letter of each item in the list. Check for these patterns, and you'll be sure you don't overlook an available deduction, and you'll know when there are no more deductions to be found.

Blocks of Entities: When a rule forces two or more entities to occupy adjacent spaces in a list, or to be placed together in a group, check to see where space is available for them, and where they may prevent other entities from appearing.

Limited Options: When a rule (or combination of rules) restricts the entire game to just two or three patterns, LSAT experts will often create dual sketches to depict the game. Pay careful attention to Limited Options in the explanations. They aren't always easy to spot, but when they occur, they make the questions much, much easier to answer.

Established Entities: When a rule (or combination of rules) restricts an entity to just one space in a list, or forces the entity to be placed into a particular group, note it. This is powerful not only because you have firmly placed one entity, but also because that entity's placement may prevent others from being assigned to the same position or group.

Number Restrictions: When rules and limitations within a game restrict the number of entities that may be placed into a particular group, it makes the game much easier to solve. Being asked to split up seven students into two teams doesn't tell you much, but deducing that Team A must have three students and Team B must have four tells you a lot.

Duplications: When an entity appears in two rules, it allows the rules to be combined. We just described the simple B … C + C … D = B … C … D type of duplication, but duplications can be far more sophisticated, and may appear in any type of logic game.

In the explanations to every game, the expert will note when one or more of these patterns appears, and the term will appear in the glossary in case you've forgotten how it's defined.

Step 5: Questions

We alluded to the fact that logic games reward you for being able to determine what must, can, and cannot be true about the placement of the entities within the game. Scan the questions from any logic games section, and you'll see multiple variations asking "Which one of the following is an acceptable arrangement/could be true/must be false/etc.?" Throughout the explanations, you'll see how an LSAT expert uses the Master Sketch (including the additional deductions he's made) to make short work of these questions.

Quite often, the question stem opens with a New-"If" condition, but then asks one of these same questions given the new constraint or limitation. In most cases, LSAT experts tackle these with new "mini-sketches" so that they can make the new condition concrete. This strategy is discussed briefly below.

LOGIC GAMES STRATEGY

Use "Mini-sketches" to Take Control of New-"If" Questions

One "rookie mistake" that untrained test takers will make in Logic Games is to create a Master Sketch for a game and then try to use it for all of the game's New-"If" questions. Let's say a game has five questions, and when our untrained test taker comes to Question 2, he sees that it begins with a new "If" condition. He then adds the new restrictions into his overall Master Sketch and works out the implications. That's great for that one question, but here are a few reasons why it's a bad strategy for the rest of the game:

Subsequent questions will either have different New-"If" conditions, or they will have no new conditions at all. That means that to use his Master Sketch again, the untrained test taker will have to erase all of the work he did on Question 2. At a minimum, that will be messy and will take up some time. The bigger risk is that the test taker will forget exactly which of the deductions he made at the beginning of the game, and which he made specifically for Question 2. He could wind up inadvertently leaving some of Question 2's work in the sketch, or erasing some of the initial deductions he'd made. Either way, he's now in danger of missing all the subsequent questions associated with the game.

Additionally, if our untrained test taker effectively erases the work in the sketch that was unique to Question 2, he will no longer have that work to refer to. In the next strategy note, you'll learn how LSAT experts sometimes consult their work on earlier questions to help answer later ones. If you are building-erasing-rebuilding your sketch as you go, you won't have a record of the work you've done throughout the question set. ·

LSAT experts avoid these pitfalls by creating a Master Sketch containing the setup, rules, and deductions for the overall game. And, then, they leave it alone. They can consult the Master Sketch for questions without New-"If" conditions. For each New-"If" question, however, they quickly copy the Master Sketch and label it with the question number of the New-"If" question. They add the question's new "If" condition to this copy, and work out the question's implications there. When they move on, they leave that question's work as a reference, just in case it helps them on a subsequent question.

As you review, study the new "mini-sketches" that experts make for New-"If" questions. You'll learn not only how they got a particular question right, but also how they effectively manage an entire game.

There are a handful of relatively rare Logic Games question types, but well-trained test takers can use the same sketches and techniques to answer them, as well. At times, test takers who have truly mastered the Logic Games Method will even use their work on one or two questions to help them quickly answer another. That's why it is valuable to review an entire game, from Step 1 all the way through the last question, even when you only missed one or two of the questions along the way. Your review will not only reveal where you went off track on the questions you missed, it also will likely show you how you could have handled the entire game more quickly and confidently.

LOGIC GAMES STRATEGY

Use Previous Work to Determine what Could be True

The LSAT always provides enough information to answer every question. That's comforting to know, but open-ended questions that ask you what could be true or must be false in a game without giving you any new conditions or constraints can be very time consuming. For most students, their instincts tell them to try out every answer choice one by one.

LSAT experts know to keep track of the work they do on every question, and when they can use it to help them solve these open-ended questions. If they see that an open-ended question will be very time consuming, or will require them to test every answer choice, they often skip that question temporarily. After working through the other questions in the set, they'll come back to the open-ended question.

Here's how it works. Let's say a question asks "Which one of the following must be false?" You check your Master Sketch, but you don't see anything there that definitively rules out one of the answer choices. Work through the rest of the questions for the game. Along the way, you'll likely encounter one question that asks for an "acceptable arrangement" of entities. You'll probably also have two or three questions with New-"If" conditions, and you'll solve those by creating "mini-sketches" that reveal some additional "acceptable arrangements." Now, the expert test taker uses critical thinking: "Since the correct answer to the open-ended question must be false, all four of its wrong answers could be true." Then, he can check any acceptable arrangement he has discovered or created along the way. Any answer choice for the "must be false" question that appears in an acceptable arrangement is an incorrect answer, and he can cross it out. Sometimes, you may be able to eliminate all four wrong answers in this way.

Students in Kaplan's comprehensive LSAT prep courses drill with the Logic Games Method in class and throughout their homework. They are assigned chapters in Kaplan's LSAT treatise "LSAT Premier" that go over the strategies, tactics, and techniques associated with each step of the Method. They practice it on dozens of real LSAC-released logic games in Kaplan's exclusive Qbank, a library of over 2,000 official LSAT questions. As you review your work in these explanations, follow along with the LSAT experts who make the Logic Games Method their template for accuracy and speed in this section.

Reading Comprehension Method and Strategies

For many students, Reading Comprehension is the section of the LSAT in which they find it most difficult to improve their scores. This is due, in part, to how familiar Reading Comprehension feels. In one way or another, you have been tested from grade school through college on how well you understood or remembered something that you had read. Learning to read actively and strategically, in the way rewarded by the LSAT, takes some getting used to. Kaplan's Reading Comprehension Method is designed to make your performance on this section of the test just as efficient and effective as our Logic Games Method can on that section.

READING COMPREHENSION METHOD

1. Read the Passage Strategically
2. Analyze the Question Stem
3. Research the Relevant Text
4. Predict the Correct Answer
5. Evaluate the Answer Choices

Given that you have four passages (and their accompanying questions) to complete in 35 minutes, time is precious in Reading Comprehension. LSAT experts will usually complete Step 1 for a passage in around 3 to 4 minutes. That leaves between 4 to 5 minutes to tackle the questions, using Steps 2 through 5 for each one. Here's what each step accomplishes.

Step 1: Read the Passage Strategically

LSAT Reading Comprehension passages are excerpts of around 450 to 500 words, typically from academic writing in fields covered by social science, natural science, humanities, and law. The writing is dense, and the topics are rarely, if ever, familiar to the casual reader. This content is pretty intimidating, and students often compound the problem by trying to read and remember the details and facts in these arcane passages.

But, here's what LSAT experts know: The LSAT is far more interested in *how* and *why* the author wrote the passage than it is in *what* the author said about the details. Here's why. Imagine if you saw this question on the LSAT.

> In which of the following years did George Washington lead Continental Army troops across the Delaware River?

This is a question that rewards knowledge, not reading comprehension. If you happen to know the answer, you could get this question right even without the passage. Law schools need to evaluate your skill level in comprehension and analysis. So, the LSAT asks questions more like these.

> The author of the passage would most likely agree with which one of the following statements about Washington's military leadership?

The author includes a reference to Washington's crossing of the Delaware in order to

The primary purpose of the fourth paragraph of the passage is

To answer LSAT questions, you need to read for the passage's structure, and the author's opinions, and not just for names or dates or facts. Anticipating the kinds of questions that the test asks, LSAT experts read actively, interrogating the author as they proceed. When the author offers an opinion, the expert looks for where and how the author supports it. If the author describes two theories, the expert looks for the author's evaluation of them, or for language in which the author prefers one theory over the other. An LSAT expert's reading is never passive or wayward.

READING COMPREHENSION STRATEGY

Use Keywords to Read Effectively

Given the LSAT's emphasis on opinion and purpose, Kaplan has compiled a list of Keywords that indicate text that is likely to be relevant in answering LSAT questions. These include terms that indicate an author's point of view, her reason for including a detail or illustration, and words that show contrast or correspondence between two things or ideas. LSAT experts circle or underline these Keywords when they encounter them in the passage, and they use Keywords to effectively paraphrase or summarize chunks of text.

To see why Keywords are so helpful, try to answer the following question:

Type X coffee beans grow at very high altitudes. Type X coffee beans produce a dark, mellow coffee when brewed.

With which one of the following statements would the author most likely agree?

> o. Coffee beans that grow at high altitudes typically produce dark, mellow coffee when brewed.
> o. Coffee beans that grow at high altitudes typically produce light, acidic coffee when brewed.

You cannot answer that question from the text alone. It contains only facts. To understand the author's point of view, and thus to answer the LSAT question about it, you need for the author to supply Keywords that logically connect the facts in a specific way. Observe:

> Type X coffee beans grow at very high altitudes, *but* produce a *surprisingly* dark, mellow coffee when brewed.

Now, choice (2) is the correct answer on the LSAT. Choice (1) is clearly incorrect. But, what if the author had written the following?

> Type X coffee beans grow at very high altitudes, *and so* produce a dark, mellow coffee when brewed.

Now, it's choice (1) that is supported by the passage. Notice that the facts did not change at all, but when the author changes the Keyword, the correct answer on the LSAT changes. Keywords indicating a passage's structure or an author's point of view are not the kinds of words you typically pay attention to when you are reading for school, so you need to train yourself to spot them, and use them, on the LSAT.

Throughout the Kaplan LSAT explanations for Reading Comprehension, LSAT experts will show you the Keywords and phrases that they circled or underlined in the passage text. Then, as they explain individual questions associated with a passage, they will demonstrate how they refer back to those Keywords to research the passage, predict correct answers, and evaluate the answer choices. The categories of Keywords are defined in the glossary.

By circling or underlining Keywords, and then jotting down succinct notes in the margin next to the passage, an LSAT expert creates a "Roadmap" of the passage. This helps the expert quickly research the text when one of the questions refers to a detail, illustration, or argument in the passage.

While a Roadmap of Keywords and margin notes is helpful on most questions, there are a typically a few questions accompanying each passage that call for broader answers, such as the author's "primary purpose" or the passage's "main idea." To prepare for these questions, an LSAT expert also summarizes the "big picture" of the passage as she reads. Keeping in mind the kinds of questions that the LSAT asks, these summaries must go beyond mere subject matter to encompass how and why the author wrote the passage. Big picture summaries are described in the following strategy note.

READING COMPREHENSION STRATEGY

Summarize the Passage's Big Picture

In addition to circling Keywords and jotting down notes in the margins next to the passage, LSAT experts also mentally summarize passages as they strategically read LSAT Reading Comprehension passages. To do this efficiently, experts will usually break down the passage's big picture into Topic, Scope, Purpose, and Main Idea. You'll see these "big picture" terms referenced throughout Kaplan's LSAT explanations, and for most passages, the discussion following the Sample Roadmap will paraphrase the expert's summaries for you.

The Topic means the overall subject matter. It almost always appears in the first paragraph. At this high level, the subject matter is likely to be familiar to you, even if you don't know much about it.

The Scope refers to the aspect of the Topic that interests this author. For example, if the Topic is George Washington, the Scope could be Washington's economic policies, Washington's education, or Washington's service as a general in the Continental Army. Usually, you will have some idea of the Scope from the passage's first paragraph, although occasionally, it may not be entirely clear until the second (or even third) paragraph. The Scope must be narrower than the Topic, and it is important that you recognize *the author's* Scope and avoid imposing your thoughts about a Topic onto the passage.

Identifying the author's purpose is central to your LSAT success. To put your finger on why the author is writing the passage, look to the passage's structure. Does the author begin by describing someone else's idea or theory about the subject? If so, the author's purpose may be to *rebut* the other thinker's idea. On the other hand, the author might go on to *explain* how this other person's theory influenced subsequent ideas on the subject. In another passage structure common on the

LSAT, the author opens with a description of an event or phenomenon. She might go on to *evaluate* the importance of the phenomenon, or she might *advocate* for a particular kind of response to it. Notice that all of the italicized words here are verbs, and learn to paraphrase the author's Purpose as a verb in your own summaries. Remember, you want to capture *why* and *how* the author examines a subject, and not only *what* she says about it.

If you have summarized the Topic, Scope, and Purpose accurately, you can usually combine them into a fairly clear statement of the passage's Main Idea. For example, if the Topic is George Washington, the Scope is Washington's time as commander of the Continental Army, and the author's Purpose is to *illustrate* how his military career influenced his political career, then the Main Idea might be something like: "Washington's generalship trained him to be consultative and decisive in political battles with Congress." In the most academic passages on the LSAT, you may encounter a one-sentence thesis statement or summary that makes the Main Idea explicit, but more often, you will need to paraphrase the Main Idea by combining the Topic, Scope, and Purpose you have identified from the passage structure and the author's point of view.

As you review Reading Comprehension sections using these explanations, you'll see how LSAT experts handle "main idea" and "primary purpose" questions using the kinds of big picture strategies we've just discussed.

In Reading Comprehension, Step 1 should take you around 3–4 minutes. Think of your passage Roadmap much as you would your Master Sketch in a logic game. It highlights and organizes the most important information in the passage, and it gets you ready to answer the questions.

Step 2: Analyze the Question Stem

Reading Comprehension passages are usually accompanied by 5–8 questions. Start your analysis of each question by identifying two things: the question type and any clues that will help you research the passage text. Kaplan always identifies the question type at the start of every question's explanation. The question types are defined in the glossary, as well.

As we've already alluded to, some Reading Comprehension questions ask about the "big picture." Kaplan calls these Global questions, and if you've summarized the Topic, Scope, Purpose, and Main Idea of the passage, you won't need do any further research. Just use your summaries to predict the correct answer.

Other question types focus on the specifics of what the author said. Occasionally, you'll encounter a Detail question. These usually begin with a phrase such as "According to the passage …" making it clear that the correct answer is something stated in the passage. The LSAT also often tests details through Logic Function questions. These question stems cite the detail from the passage and then ask *why* the author included the detail or *how* he used it. A common phrasing for this question type is: "The author refers to *xxx* (lines 24–26) in order to." Use the detail, and any line or paragraph reference to research the text. Keywords before or after the detail ("*but* xxx is different" or "xxx is *especially important because*") will often demonstrate the author's reason for including it, and will help you predict the correct answer.

By far, the most common question type in Reading Comprehension is the Inference question. These ask you for something that the passage implies, but does not state explicitly. Inference question stems can be open-ended ("With which one of the following statements would the author of the passage most likely agree?") or they may include references to a detail in the passage ("Based on the information presented in the passage, which one of the following economic policies would

Washington have been most likely to endorse?"). Whenever a research clue is present, use it to pinpoint the relevant text in the passage. For example, the "economic policies" mentioned in the second Inference question stem would likely take you to a particular paragraph, and maybe even to a particular line in the passage about Washington.

A handful of questions in the Reading Comprehension section will mimic the skills tested in the Logical Reasoning section. A Reading Comprehension question could, for example, ask you to strengthen an argument made by the author, or to identify a method of argument parallel to one in the passage. To manage these questions, LSAT experts employ the skills they've learned for the comparable question types in the Logical Reasoning section. This is a good reminder that you should review complete tests, even when you're primarily concerned with just one or two sections.

Step 3: Research the Relevant Text

Don't answer LSAT Reading Comprehension questions on a whim. Whenever you are able to research the passage, do so. But, be careful. Don't passively re-read the passage, or go on a "fishing expedition" for details you don't remember.

An LSAT expert uses the research clues that he finds in question stems in conjunction with his strategic reading Roadmap to put his finger right on the relevant text in the passage. Moreover, the expert always seeks out Keywords that indicate *why* the author included a detail, or *how* the author used it in the passage. In some questions, the LSAT testmaker will include wrong answers that use words or phrases directly from the passage, but that distort what the author had to say about those words or phrases. The following strategy examines how LSAT experts use research effectively and efficiently.

READING COMPREHENSION STRATEGY

Use Research Clues to Answer Questions Efficiently

Most LSAT test takers are pretty good readers. Given unlimited time, a lot of test takers could probably get all of the Reading Comprehension questions correct. Of course, the LSAT does not give you unlimited time. Indeed, the 35-minute time limit may be your biggest obstacle to Reading Comprehension success.

LSAT experts combat the test's time constraints by very effectively avoiding pointless re-reading. There are five kinds of research clues they recognize in question stems that help them zero in on the relevant text and predict the correct answer.

> **Line References**—Experts research around the referenced detail, looking for Keywords that indicate why the referenced text has been included and how it is used.
> **Paragraph References**—Experts consult their Roadmaps to check the paragraph's scope, and its function in the passage.
> **Quoted Text** (sometimes accompanied by a line reference)—Experts check the context of the quoted term or phrase, and they consider what the author meant by it.
> **Proper Nouns**—Experts check for the context of the person, place, or thing in the passage; they check for whether the author made a positive, negative, or neutral evaluation of it; and they consider why the author included it.

> **Content Clues**—Experts take note when question stems mention terms, concepts, or ideas highlighted in the passage, knowing that these almost always refer to something that the author emphasized, or about which the author expressed an opinion.

If you struggle to maintain your accuracy while trying to complete the Reading Comprehension in time, pay attention to how Kaplan's LSAT experts explain their work in Step 3. It could really change the way you take the test.

Step 4: Predict the Correct Answer

Once you have researched the passage (or, for Global questions, once you have paused to consider your big picture summaries of the passage), take a moment to paraphrase (or "pre-phrase," if you like that term) what the correct answer must contain. Taking a few seconds to predict the correct answer can save you a lot of time as you move through the answer choices. Just as they do in Logical Reasoning explanations, the Kaplan experts who write the Reading Comprehension explanations will always share their predictions with you in their analysis of Step 4. Pay careful attention to this step if you want to improve your speed and accuracy in Reading Comprehension.

Step 5: Evaluate the Answer Choices

Every question on the LSAT has one correct answer and four demonstrably incorrect ones. This is especially important to remember in Reading Comprehension because comparing answer choices back to the text can lead to endless re-reading and wasted time. Armed with a solid prediction (or, at a minimum, with a clear idea of the author's purpose and point of view), evaluate the choices boldly. If (A) does not contain what the correct answer must say, cross it out and move on. Those who master the Reading Comprehension Method often become so confident that once they spot the correct answer, they do not even need to read the rest of the answer choices. In the Kaplan explanations, we always explain why every wrong answer is wrong, even when the correct answer is (A). On Test Day, however, you will be well served by the ability to predict and evaluate consistently.

READING COMPREHENSION STRATEGY

Spot Common Wrong Answer Patterns

LSAT experts use the standardized nature of the LSAT to their advantage in Reading Comprehension (just as they do in Logical Reasoning) by anticipating certain types of wrong answers that occur over and over again.

Many of the wrong answer types in this section are the same ones associated with Logical Reasoning questions. You will see a fair share of Outside the Scope wrong answers, and in Reading Comprehension Global questions particularly, you will see incorrect answers that go beyond the scope, encompassing more than what the author included in her Purpose or Main Idea. You will also see Extreme and 180 incorrect answers similar to those in Logical Reasoning.

Two incorrect answers types that are more common in Reading Comprehension than they are in Logical Reasoning are the Distortion and Half-Right/Half-Wrong answer choices. Distortion incorrect answers are those that stay within the scope of the passage, but then twist what the author has said in a way that misstates the author's position or point of view. Half-Right/Half-Wrong answer choices are those that start off well, matching the passage up to a point, but then incorrectly characterize or contradict the passage in their second half.

Whenever an answer choice fits into one of the common wrong answer categories, the Reading Comprehension explanations will point it out. If there is a incorrect answer type that doesn't make sense to you, check out its description in the glossary.

Students in Kaplan's comprehensive LSAT prep courses make Reading Comprehension a regular part of their practice. They understand that they have to. After all, improvement in Reading Comprehension requires diligent practice. Kaplan instructors encourage both un-timed and timed practice so that students can learn the skills and strategies rewarded by the Reading Comprehension section, and then evaluate them under test-like conditions. In addition to having access to hundreds of released LSAT Reading Comprehension passages, Kaplan students also hone their skill set with *LSAT Channel* lessons covering the full range of ability levels, from Fundamentals to Advanced. Even if Reading Comprehension is your strongest section initially, practice and review it throughout your LSAT prep. Steady improvement in this tough section will lead to a higher score on the exam.

A Note About Formal Logic on the LSAT

In college and university Philosophy departments, Formal Logic is an enormous topic that may cover several semesters and hours and hours of difficult reading. Its reputation as a formidable and intimidating subject is well deserved. The LSAT, however, tests only a small sliver of Formal Logic, a sliver that can be mastered with a few hours of expert instruction and diligent practice.

The aspect of Formal Logic tested on the LSAT is restricted to **conditional statements** (also called "If-then" statements). You'll see them from time to time in Logic Games, and multiple times in Logical Reasoning on every test. Here's a brief introduction to how you will see Formal Logic described and discussed in these explanations.

Conditional Statements: Sufficiency and Necessity

A conditional statement is defined by having a **sufficient** clause and a **necessary** clause. That's a hifalutin' way of saying it has an "If" clause and a "then" clause. Here's a simple example:

If this car is running, then it has gasoline in its gas tank.

That means that gasoline in the gas tank is necessary for this car to run. So, the necessary clause follows "then." That's always the case. Now, notice that the clause "this car is running" is sufficient to establish that the car has gasoline in its gas tank. The "If" clause is always sufficient (that is, it is enough by itself) to establish the truth of the necessary (or "then") clause.

In the explanations, the LSAT expert will often abbreviate Formal Logic by using an arrow for the "then" clause, like this:

If   car running   →   has gas

Translating Conditional Statements

There are many ways to express conditional logic in the English language, and the LSAT uses them all. For example, on the test, the previous conditional statement might be expressed in any of the following ways:

This car will run only if it has gasoline in its gas tank.
This car will not run unless it has gasoline in its gas tank.
Only if this car has gasoline in its gas tank will this car run.
If this car does not have gasoline in its gas tank, then this car will not run.

From the perspective of Formal Logic these are all equivalent statements. They all present exactly the same relationship of a sufficient term to a necessary term. LSAT experts learn to recognize conditional statements and to quickly and accurately translate them into the "If-then" format. You'll see this skill demonstrated several times in the explanations to any LSAT test.

The final version of our statement about the car ("If this car does not have gasoline in its gas tank, then this car will not run") is also known as the contrapositive of the original statement. Being able to formulate the contrapositive of any conditional statement is a crucial skill for LSAT success.

Contrapositives

The logic underlying contrapositives is simple. Since the term that follows "then" is necessary for the term that follows "If," when you negate the necessary term, you must also negate the sufficient term. In other words, when you remove something that is necessary, you can't have the thing it's necessary for. So, to abbreviate our previous example:

If   *NO gas*   →   *car NOT running*

If our original statement is true, then this one must be true as well. And, that's it. To form the contrapositive of a conditional statement, reverse *and* negate its sufficient and necessary terms.

Be careful, though, because if you reverse without negating, or if you negate without reversing, you will create illogical statements (and the LSAT will punish illogical statements with wrong answers). For example, here's what we would get by negating our original statement's terms without reversing them too:

If   *car NOT running*   →   *NO gas*

But that could be wrong, couldn't it? If the car is not running, it might have a dead battery, or a broken transmission, or it might even be turned off. In any of those cases, it might have gasoline in its gas tank.

Similarly, here's what we'd get by reversing without negating:

If   *has gas*   →   *car running*

Again, the mistake is obvious in our simple example. Having gasoline is necessary for the car to run, not sufficient for it to run. It could have a full tank of gas, but if its battery is dead, it would not be running.

To see why contrapositives are important on the LSAT, consider a Logic Games rule: "If Katherine is selected, then Malik will be selected." It's easy to translate and jot down:

If   *K*   →   *M*

That will be helpful any time you know that Katherine is selected in the game. But, here's what the test is likely to ask: "If Malik is not selected, then which one of the following must be true?" An LSAT expert may even anticipate a question like this one because as soon as he sees the original conditional statement among the rules, he will also note its contrapositive by reversing and negating the original terms:

If   *NOT M*   →   *NOT K*

There's no doubt that if Malik is not selected, then it must be true that Katherine is not selected either.

Conditional Statements with Multiple Terms

From time to time, the LSAT will include conditional statements that have more than one term in the sufficient clause, in the necessary clause, or in both. For the most part, these work just the same as the previous example, but there is one important additional note we need to make about contrapositives in conditional statements with multiple terms. To see this, let's add a term to the necessary clause of our original statement:

If	*car running*	→	*has gas AND has charged battery*

This statement now has two terms in the necessary clause, and *both* are necessary: If this car is running, then it has gasoline in its gas tank AND it has a charged battery. Because both conditions are necessary, the negation of either one will cause the car not to run. Thus, the contrapostive would read:

If	*NO gas OR NO charged battery*	→	*car NOT running*

When we reverse and negate to form the contrapositive, we must also change the "and" linking the two necessary terms to "or." This will always work, regardless of whether the "and" or the "or" are found initially in the sufficient clause or in the necessary clause. We can illustrate this with another Logic Games rule. Imagine that the test tells you the following: "If Juliana and Nestor attend the dance, then Patricia will not attend the dance." That is, if J and N are *both* there, P will not be. Here's that rule in Formal Logic shorthand:

If	*J AND N*	→	*NOT P*

Now, to form the contrapositive, reverse and negate the terms, and change the "and" to an "or":

If	*P*	→	*NOT J OR NOT N*

That might look funny initially, but it is absolutely true based on the original statement. Patricia will not go to the dance if both Juliana and Nestor go. So, knowing that Patricia *is* at the dance is sufficient to establish that at least one of the other two is absent.

Any time you see a conditional statement, you can form its contrapositive correctly by reversing and negating the terms, and changing "and" to "or" or vice versa.

Combining Conditional Statements

The LSAT often rewards your ability to combine conditional statements to reach valid deductions that may not be apparent at first. The most obvious example is when they give you two statements like these:

If	*A*	→	*B*
If	*B*	→	*C*

From this, we can pretty easily deduce the following:

If	*A*	→	*B*	→	*C*

And, thus:

$$\textit{If} \quad A \quad \rightarrow \quad C$$

When the example is that straightforward, the deduction is pretty easy to see. However, on the LSAT, the testmaker will sometimes add a step or two. Imagine that you see these rules in a logic game:

Danny will audition for any play that Carla directs.

Danny will not audition for a play unless Rebekkah also auditions for that play.

First, you will need to translate those sentences into Formal Logic abbreviations:

$$\textit{If} \quad C_{dir} \quad \rightarrow \quad D_{aud}$$

$$\textit{If} \quad \sim R_{aud} \quad \rightarrow \quad \sim D_{aud}$$

Now, the result of the first statement (its necessary clause) is that Danny auditions. The trigger (or sufficient clause) of the second sentence is that Rebekkah does *not* audition. Right now, you can't combine those statements. But look what happens when you formulate the contrapositive of the second sentence:

$$\textit{If} \quad D_{aud} \quad \rightarrow \quad R_{aud}$$

Now, the trigger (the sufficient clause) of the second statement is that Danny auditions. Thus:

$$\textit{If} \quad C_{dir} \quad \rightarrow \quad D_{aud} \quad \rightarrow \quad R_{aud}$$

So, when combined, those statements allow you to deduce that Rebekkah also auditions for any play that Carla directs.

The skill of combining conditional statements doesn't only appear in Logic Games. In fact, it's far more common in Logical Reasoning questions. Wherever they encounter Formal Logic on the test, LSAT experts are adept at spotting conditional statements, translating them into the "If-then" format, formulating their contrapositives, and combining them to reach deductions.

For students in a comprehensive LSAT prep program, they regularly practice Formal Logic in and out of class, in their books, and their homework assignments, and they hone their skills watching Formal Logic *LSAT Channel* sessions. Whenever you encounter Formal Logic in these explanations, the LSAT expert will explain the analysis thoroughly, using abbreviations like those you've seen here. Always give Formal Logic an extra careful review.

Taking a Kaplan LSAT Course: A Personalized Experience

Preparation for the LSAT is a combination of two things: instruction and practice—lots of it. And every student is different, with different strengths, weaknesses, goal scores, and dream schools. That means every student has different needs. So Kaplan customizes the LSAT preparation experience for you. You get the right instruction and the right practice at the right time for you. Here's how we do it:

Personalized Instruction: Core Curriculum + *The LSAT Channel*

First, Kaplan customizes instruction. There's not one long "one-size-fits all" course for you to sit through. There is a core curriculum—10 sessions in our In Person or Live Online classes, including 3 full-length, proctored practice tests—that everyone attends. The core sessions cover the key concepts for each and every question type. If you are enrolled in our Self-Paced program, this material is presented in short, digestible chapters.

But how do we personalize it? We recently introduced a new innovation called *The LSAT Channel*. It's nightly, live-streamed, live online instruction with Kaplan's best teachers, and features over 100 unique one-hour episodes on every LSAT topic imaginable. If you're rocking Logical Reasoning, you can attend advanced episodes tailored for you. If you're struggling in, let's say, Hybrid Logic Games, you can attend foundations episodes to go deeper into the basics. *The LSAT Channel* provides unique, customizable, niche live instruction (lots and lots of it), and all of the *LSAT Channel* lessons are also available in an On Demand archive for viewing whenever you want.

Personalized Practice: PrepTest Library, Explanations, Qbank & Smart Reports

Second, Kaplan customizes practice. The LSAT has not changed substantially since 1991, and you'll have access to every officially released LSAT PrepTest. That's over 80 exams and 8,000 questions. Plus, you'll have detailed answers and explanations to each. But additionally, we give you an online tool called Qbank where you can create customized quizzes to practice questions in the specific areas where you need the most help.

How will you know what to do? Kaplan's scoring analytics tool, Smart Reports, evaluates your performance on practice tests to tell you exactly where you need help and where you need to focus your time.

Personalized Promise: Kaplan's Higher Score Guarantee

And finally, you can be confident in your decision to prep with Kaplan, as our courses feature the industry-leading Higher Score Guarantee. If you are not ready to take the LSAT for any reason or are unhappy with your score, you can repeat your course and have continued access to your resources for free—no questions asked. And if for whatever reason your score does not improve, even though you've done the required work, you'll receive a full tuition refund. You'll have the confidence to rock the LSAT on Test Day.

Kaplan LSAT Course Options

All of the benefits of a Kaplan comprehensive course are available in four different ways:

> Private Tutoring – Get the attention you need from a personal tutor
> In Person – Learn in a real classroom taught by an expert, Kaplan-trained instructor.
> Live Online – Get the convenience of a live classroom in the comfort of your home.
> Self-Paced – Study at your own pace in a location that's convenient for you.

Free LSAT Events

Kaplan regularly hosts free, live online LSAT events for prospective law students to learn more about the test and the admissions process. Find LSAT Practice Tests, Preview Classes, Free *LSAT Channel* Previews, Admissions Seminars, and more.

PrepTest 62

The Inside Story

PrepTest 62 was administered in December 2010. It challenged 42,096 test takers. What made this test so hard? Here's a breakdown of what Kaplan students who were surveyed after taking the official exam considered PrepTest 62's most difficult section.

Hardest PrepTest 62 Section as Reported by Test Takers

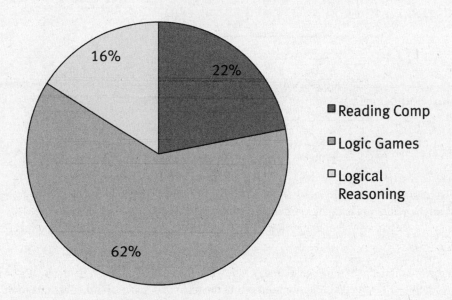

Based on these results, you might think that studying Logic Games is the key to LSAT success. Well, Logic Games is important, but test takers' perceptions don't tell the whole story. For that, you need to consider students' actual performance. The following chart shows the average number of students to miss each question in each of PrepTest 62's different sections.

Percentage Incorrect by PrepTest 62 Section Type

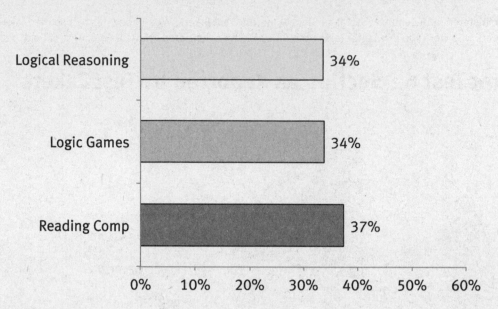

Actual student performance tells a quite different story. On PrepTest 62, Logical Reasoning and Logic Games were basically equal in difficulty, and Reading Comprehension was actually more difficult than either of the other section types. [NOTE: Several LSATs administered during 2010 and 2011 had very challenging Reading Comprehension sections, so tests from this time period provide great RC practice opportunities.]

Maybe students overestimate the difficulty of the Logic Games section because it's so unusual, or maybe it's because a really hard Logic Game is so easy to remember after the test. But the truth is that the testmaker places hard questions throughout the test. While more than 60 percent of test takers rated Logic Games as the hardest section, in actuality, that section contained only two of PrepTest 62's hardest questions. Here were the locations of the 10 hardest (most missed) questions in the exam.

Location of 10 Most Difficult Questions in PrepTest 62

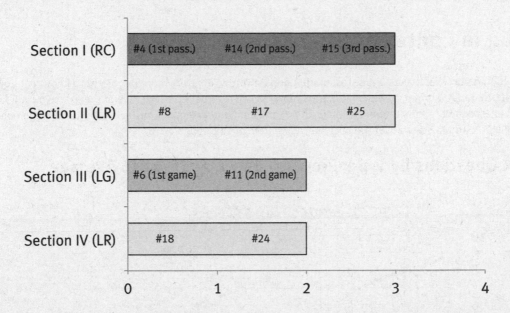

The takeaway from this data is that, to maximize your potential on the LSAT, you need to take a comprehensive approach. Test yourself rigorously, and review your performance on every section of the test. Kaplan's LSAT explanations provide the expertise and insight you need to fully understand your results. The explanations are written and edited by a team of LSAT experts, who have helped thousands of students improve their scores. Kaplan always provides data-driven analysis of the test, ranking the difficulty of every question based on actual student performance. The 10 hardest questions on every test are highlighted with a 4-star difficulty rating, the highest we give. The analysis breaks down the remaining questions into 1-, 2-, and 3-star ratings so that you can compare your performance to that of thousands of other test takers on all LSAC material.

Don't settle for wondering whether a question was really as hard as it seemed to you. Analyze the test with real data, and learn the secrets and strategies that help top scorers master the LSAT.

7 Can't–Miss Features of PrepTest 62

- PrepTest 62 contained 102 Questions! The last time that happened was—get ready for this—October of 1992 on PrepTest 6, the test that was administered a week before the first debate … between President George H. W. Bush and Arkansas Governor Bill Clinton!
- It's not terribly uncommon for Point at Issue questions to be missing from a test, but it's still noteworthy when a Logical Reasoning question type is entirely absent as it was on this test—as Point at Issue questions were on PrepTest 62.
- The second LR section featured two Paradox EXCEPT questions. The last time there were two in the same section was back on PrepTest 47 (October 2005).
- The four games in PrepTest 62's Logic Games section consist of just two actions: the section has two Strict Sequencing games, one Matching game, and one Sequencing/Matching Hybrid game.
- A lot of students struggled with the second game in this section, the one asking you to pick colors for three stained glass windows. That's especially unfortunate because this game was accompanied by *seven* questions. Check out the explanations for that game to see how LSAT experts set up this Matching game in which the windows are not explicitly numbered or labeled.
- In its Reading Comprehension section, PrepTest 62 featured only three Global questions. At the time of this test's release, that was only the third time there was such a paucity of Global questions. The most recent time it had occurred previously was PrepTest 43 (June 2004).

- The most famous LSAT test taker in cinematic history is almost certainly Elle Woods from *Legally Blonde*. And, in case you've forgotten, Elle got a 179! Well, the week before PrepTest 62 was administered, Reese Witherspoon (accompanied by her canine co-star "Bruiser") got her star on Hollywood's Walk of Fame.

PrepTest 62 in Context

As much fun as it is to find out what makes a PrepTest unique or noteworthy, it's even more important to know just how representative it is of other LSAT administrations (and, thus, how likely it is to be representative of the exam you will face on Test Day). The following charts compare the numbers of each kind of question and game on PrepTest 62 to the average numbers seen on all officially released LSATs administered over the past five years (from 2012 through 2016).

Number of LR Questions by Type: PrepTest 62 vs. 2012–2016 Average

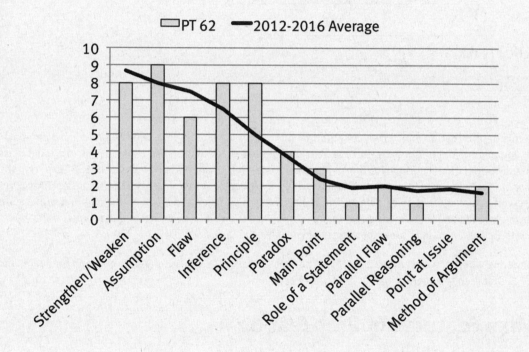

KAPLAN

Number of LG Games by Type: PrepTest 62 vs. 2012–2016 Average

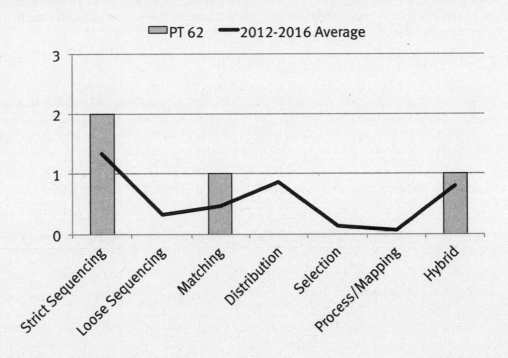

Number of RC Questions by Type: PrepTest 62 vs. 2012–2016 Average

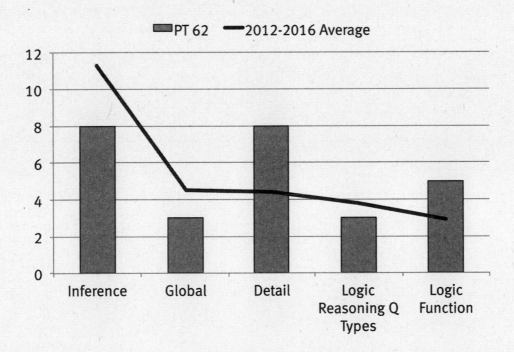

There isn't usually a huge difference in the distribution of questions from LSAT to LSAT, but if this test, or any of its specific sections, seems harder (or easier) to you than another you've taken, compare the number of questions of the types on which you, personally, are strongest and weakest. And then, explore within each section to see if your best or worst question types came earlier or later.

Students in Kaplan's comprehensive LSAT courses have access to every released LSAT, and to an online Q-Bank with thousands of officially released questions, games, and passages. If you are studying on your own, you have to do a bit more work to identify your strengths and your areas of opportunity. Quantitative analysis (like that in the charts shown here) is an important tool for understanding how the test is constructed, and how you are performing on it.

Section I: Reading Comprehension
Passage 1: Earthquake-Dating by Lichenometry

Q#	Question Type	Correct	Difficulty
1	Global	A	★
2	Detail	C	★★
3	Logic Function	E	★
4	Inference	B	★★★★
5	Logic Function	B	★
6	Logic Reasoning (Assumption)	E	★★
7	Detail	D	★
8	Inference	D	★★

Passage 2: Custom-Made Medical Illustrations as Evidence

Q#	Question Type	Correct	Difficulty
9	Logic Reasoning (Parallel Reasoning)	A	★★★
10	Inference	E	★
11	Detail	E	★★
12	Detail	D	★
13	Inference	C	★★
14	Logic Function	B	★★★★

Passage 3: Dental Caries and Archaeology

Q#	Question Type	Correct	Difficulty
15	Global	A	★★★★
16	Detail	B	★★
17	Inference	A	★★
18	Detail	B	★★★
19	Inference	D	★
20	Inference	C	★★
21	Logic Reasoning (Method of Argument)	D	★★

Passage 4: The Fiction of Sarah Orne Jewett

Q#	Question Type	Correct	Difficulty
22	Detail	D	★★
23	Inference	C	★★
24	Logic Function	B	★★★
25	Global	E	★★
26	Logic Function	E	★★★
27	Detail	C	★★

Passage 1: Earthquake-Dating by Lichenometry

Step 1: Read the Passage Strategically

Sample Roadmap

line #	Keyword/phrase	¶ Margin notes
1	To study	
2	usually	
4	Using	
5	they measure	
6–8		Seismologists use RC dating to study ancient earthquakes
8	Since	
11	can show	
16	recently ... called lichenometry	Bell/Brandon invent lichenometry
18	based on	
21	Instead	
24		Def.
26		How it works
29	for example	
31	Hence	
33	If	
38	since	
40	distinct advantages	
41		Lichenometry advantages
45	Additionally,	
46		More accurate dates
50	however,	
51	requires	but sites have to be just right
53	best used	
55	minimize	

Discussion

The general **Topic**—the study of earthquakes that occurred long ago—presents itself immediately, and the author wastes no time in telling us what seismologists "usually" do when researching past quakes. A detailed description of the traditional method of radiocarbon dating is presented, fleshing out paragraph 1. Even though it isn't fully clear by the end of the first paragraph, you can expect the **Scope** of the passage to involve alternative earthquake-dating methods.

Why? A discussion of how something is *usually* done is often followed by how it can be done differently. Furthermore, having so much specific information about a scientific method right in the first paragraph signals a classic LSAT RC pattern. It is common for a passage to describe one theory or method, present an alternative, and close with the author's assessment. The savvy reader will recognize this typical structure quickly. Even if the details about the scientific methods are conceptually difficult, focusing on the passage structure helps ensure a strategic initial read-through.

Sure enough, paragraph 2 introduces lichenometry, an alternative method of dating earthquakes, recently developed by geologists Bull and Brandon. The Keyword *instead* contrasts this new method to the old carbon dating technique: the old method requires analyzing fault-line sediments, but this new method measures lichens growing on rocks that became exposed during an earthquake. The remainder of the paragraph explains in detail what lichens are and how their constant growth rate provides useful evidence of when rockfalls caused by seismic activity have occurred.

All of this information has been presented in a neutral manner, so the author's opinion and Purpose have yet to be revealed. Predictably, this changes at the outset of paragraph 3: the author states that the new method, lichenometry, has "distinct advantages" over the old method of radiocarbon dating. Why? Because the old method is less precise, "accurate only to within plus or minus 40 years," due to the amounts by which the carbon 14 isotope naturally varies, especially over the past 300 years. In contrast, lichenometry can accurately date an earthquake within 10 years, but there are caveats. Note the author's caution, stating this accuracy rate as Bull and Brandon's "claim" and outlining the specific requirements of sites amenable to lichenometry. Even though the author opened the paragraph with a strong endorsement of the new method, there is no hint of anything extreme or any suggestion that the old method does not still have its uses. Indeed, the passage closes with information about lichenometry's limitations. It's now clear that the **Purpose** of the passage was to introduce and evaluate the new method, with the **Main Idea** being that lichenometry is an alternative method for dating earthquakes that is advantageous under certain circumstances.

1. (A) Global

Step 2: Identify the Question Type

A Global question couldn't be any more straightforward to identify than this. A strategic reading of the passage should conclude with a summation of the Main Idea.

Step 3: Research the Relevant Text

The entire passage must be taken into account.

Step 4: Make a Prediction

The correct answer will express that the new dating method of lichenometry is useful and has certain advantages over the old method of radiocarbon dating, but it won't be extreme.

Step 5: Evaluate the Answer Choices

(A) is accurate in content and tone.

(B) is a Distortion. Although the passage discusses lichenometry's limitations, the author was careful to note that accuracy rates were "claimed"—not "proven"—by Bull and Brandon.

(C) is wrong in many ways. It is Extreme, as lichenometry is never named the "most reliable" method in the passage. Whether this method is being embraced by "most" seismologists studying past earthquakes is never mentioned, making the answer choice Out of Scope. And the only mention of which method is usually used is made in the first paragraph, where radiocarbon dating, not lichenometry, wins.

(D) is a Distortion. With its specific site requirements, lichenometry is not "easily" applied, and whether or not the new method has revolutionized the study of earthquakes is never stated nor implied, and it certainly is not the focus of the passage.

(E) is a classic Extreme trap. Although the passage discusses some limitations of radiocarbon dating, it never calls the method "unreliable," nor does the passage call for it to be abandoned.

2. (C) Detail

Step 2: Identify the Question Type

The phrase "the passage provides information" indicates a Detail question.

Step 3: Research the Relevant Text

The question does not offer any content clues, line references, or other hints. Each answer choice must be assessed, one by one, for justification based on the passage contents. This is potentially a time-consuming task, so, although it's often wise to tackle Detail questions early in the set, this may be one to save for later.

Step 4: Make a Prediction

With nothing to go on, it really isn't possible to make a prediction without evaluating each answer choice. These answer choices are presented *Jeopardy!* style: as questions. But the mantra "1 Right/4 Rotten" still applies: only one question is answered by the passage contents.

Step 5: Evaluate the Answer Choices

(C) finds its support at the very end of the passage. Lines 57–58 state that shade and wind "promote faster lichen growth." This clearly tells us some of the conditions which encourage lichens to grow at a more rapid rate than usual.

(A) poses a question tangential to the lichen growth rates discussed in paragraph 2 and the need for their accurate calibration mentioned in paragraph 3, but the passage never explains how scientists measure these rates. The choice is Out of Scope.

(B) is likewise Out of Scope, glancing off the issue of variable intensities of radiation striking the upper atmosphere, indeed mentioned in lines 44–45. However, the passage never delves into how scientists determine the intensity.

(D) is a Distortion. Although the passage mentions near the end that lichenometry is *best* used to measure earthquakes less than 500 years old, it does not say a thing about any earthquakes actually identified using lichenometry.

(E) offers a question that is completely Out of Scope, asking about other uses for radiocarbon dating.

3. (E) Logic Function

Step 2: Identify the Question Type

"[T]he author's primary purpose" might initially suggest another Global question, but this stem doesn't ask about the entire passage. Instead, it's focused on why the author used one particular piece of information, which makes it a Logic Function question.

Step 3: Research the Relevant Text

This stem provides the starting point: lines 29–30. However, remember that context is key. The surrounding lines will help clarify the purpose.

Step 4: Make a Prediction

The information at lines 29–30 serves as an example supporting the previous assertion that lichens grow at a slow and steady rate over long periods of time. The example of just 9.5 millimeters of growth per 100 years most definitely conveys remarkably slow growth over many years' time.

Step 5: Evaluate the Answer Choices

(E) is the only answer choice that addresses the relationship between time and lichen growth.

(A) is a Faulty Use of Detail, attaching the example cited in the question stem to an earlier comment. But the growth rate of a species doesn't say anything about how quickly it establishes itself on newly exposed rock surfaces in the first place.

(B) may seem right: it's hard to imagine anything slower than 9.5 mm per century. But this, too, is a Faulty Use of Detail trap. How that specific variety of lichen's growth rate compares to those of other species is never mentioned, and it's not safe to assume that there aren't even slower varieties.

(C) is a potential trap for the student who fails to research the relevant text and works from memory. But the discussion about how environmental conditions can alter lichens' growth rates happens at the end of the passage, well after the phrase in question.

(D) also refers to a later portion of the passage, irrelevant to the part cited in the question stem.

4. (B) Inference

Step 2: Identify the Question Type

The "strongly supported" language is that of a classic Inference question.

Step 3: Research the Relevant Text

The open-ended wording of the question stem offers nothing to work with. A strategic test taker will often save such a labor-intensive question for last.

Step 4: Make a Prediction

Every answer choice must be reviewed. Although a specific prediction is impossible to form, remember that the correct answer *must be true* based on the contents of the passage. If the answer is a maybe, it's wrong.

Step 5: Evaluate the Answer Choices

(B) draws on information in the very first sentence of the passage: seismologists dig along visible fault lines to find evidence of past shifts and use radiocarbon dating to estimate when those shifts occurred. If no faults lines are evident, then it must be true that this process would be hampered.

(A) relies on a Faulty Use of Detail to lure test takers. Predicting the likelihood and location of future earthquakes is mentioned as a usage of radiocarbon dating at the end of paragraph 1, but the predictive value of lichenometry is not discussed.

(C) is Outside the Scope. The scope of the passage is limited to discussion of just these two methods of dating earthquakes, not all possible methods, so (C) has no basis in the passage and cannot be taken as true.

(D) is a Distortion of the figures mentioned in paragraph 3.

(E) is Extreme, though it might have held some appeal, based on the information at the end of the passage. But note the contrast between the author's qualified statement ("minimize the influence") and the unconditional tone of the answer choice ("The usefulness *is* limited"). The answer goes too far in delimiting the usefulness of lichenometry and therefore must be rejected.

5. (B) Logic Function

Step 2: Identify the Question Type

This is another question seeking the author's primary purpose in placing a specific portion of the passage—here, the first paragraph, in context of the entire passage. That gives this Logic Function question something of a Global slant.

Step 3: Research the Relevant Text

A good passage map will note that the first paragraph introduced the first of two methods discussed by the passage: radiocarbon dating, the usual method employed by researchers to determine when past earthquakes occurred.

Step 4: Make a Prediction

The first paragraph introduces a conventional method, against which a recently developed technique will be compared. The correct answer will state this.

Step 5: Evaluate the Answer Choices

(B) accurately matches the prediction.

(A) is a Distortion. Radiocarbon dating is not examined on a step-by-step basis in the rest of the passage.

(C) is a Distortion. The passage never calls radiocarbon dating outdated.

(D) is Outside the Scope. It fails because lichenometry is not a traditional procedure and it is the only one other than radiocarbon dating that is discussed in the passage. "Other traditional procedures" are never mentioned in the passage.

(E) is another Distortion. Don't be tempted by the known limitations of radiocarbon dating accuracy mentioned at the beginning of paragraph 3. Stick to the prediction.

6. (E) Logic Reasoning (Assumption)

Step 2: Identify the Question Type

A relatively rare Assumption RC question is signaled by the final words of the question stem.

Step 3: Research the Relevant Text

The stem points to lines 50–58, the discussion of lichenometry's inherent limitations.

Step 4: Make a Prediction

As with any LR Assumption question, the task here is to identify the conclusion and evidence and then determine the gap between them. The conclusion is complex: "sites must be selected to minimize the influence of snow avalanches and other disturbances that would affect normal lichen growth, and conditions like shade and wind that promote faster lichen growth must be factored in." Why? Because "using lichenometry requires ... accurate calibration of lichen growth rates." Can such conditions be accurately factored in? Bull and Brandon seem to assume so.

Step 5: Evaluate the Answer Choices

(E) nicely articulates Bull and Brandon's assumption, and this choice can be double-checked with the Denial Test. After all, if the extent to which conditions like shade and wind affected the growth of lichen could *not* be determined, then Bull and Brandon's assertion that these conditions *must be* factored in would create an impossibility.

(A) is Outside the Scope and has no such effect. In fact, its subject matter—the accuracy of lichenometry relative to other methods used to date earthquakes more than 500 years old—is also irrelevant to Bull and Brandon's statements about site selection.

(B) is likewise Outside the Scope as the mention of radiation intensity hitting Earth's upper atmosphere in paragraph 3 does not include any information about how it is measured, nor is it particularly salient to the information in lines 50–58.

(C) is Extreme and Outside the Scope. There is no information in the passage about what types of rocks are or are not able to host lichens, and whether or not they are limited only to mountainous rock formations has no bearing on the considerations Bull and Brandon suggest for lichenometry site selection.

(D) can be eliminated using the Denial Test. Whether or not its claim is true may *seem* pertinent to site selection, but it is not really a factor upon which Bull and Brandon's insistence that site selection be conducted rigorously relies. If rockfalls studied in lichenometry do tend to be subject to more frequent snowfalls and avalanches, then the care in site selection demanded by Bull and Brandon is warranted. If not, care is still required. While perhaps not totally irrelevant, the issue is not *central* to the geologists' point and thus not the assumption underlying their argument.

7. (D) Detail

Step 2: Identify the Question Type

This Detail question is heralded by the words "[t]he passage indicates ... "

Step 3: Research the Relevant Text

Use the content clues to focus your research. The reliability of radiocarbon dating is discussed in paragraph 3.

Step 4: Make a Prediction

Lines 41–48 explain that the precision of radiocarbon dating is hampered by naturally occurring inconsistencies in the amount of carbon 14, depending on the varying intensity of radiation striking Earth's upper atmosphere.

Step 5: Evaluate the Answer Choices

(D) paraphrases the prediction succinctly.

(A) is Outside the Scope. The passage mentions no difficulty in radiocarbon dating due to the quantity of different organic materials.

(B) is also Outside the Scope. The passage does not indicate that the amount of organic materials used in radiocarbon dating is what may make it unreliable.

(C) might play on your memory of the fourth question of the passage, but is Outside the Scope. Invisible fault lines were not discussed within the actual passage. Researching the relevant text in the passage, and forming a strong prediction, make this answer choice easily dismissible.

(E) brings up radiation striking the upper atmosphere, which the passage does state is a factor in the carbon 14 variation. However, there's no direct indication or even a suggestion that the striking of the upper atmosphere hasn't always happened.

8. (D) Inference

Step 2: Identify the Question Type

Though wordy, the phrases "given the information in the passage" and "likely be most applicable" are harbingers of an Inference question.

Step 3: Research the Relevant Text

The only clue in the question stem is that lichenometry might be applicable to something other than earthquake dating. Review paragraph 2 for the principles underlying lichenometry.

Step 4: Make a Prediction

Although a very specific prediction is neither easy to form nor advisable, characterize the answer as something that must be true based on what the passage states about lichenometry: it requires measuring the size of lichens growing on rocks exposed by a natural event in order to determine the date at which that event occurred.

Step 5: Evaluate the Answer Choices

(D) offers the only scenario that provides conditions amenable to new lichen colonization and subsequent growth.

(A) can be ruled out because lichenometry involves analyzing lichens on *exposed* rock surfaces.

(B) fails the "Must Be True" standard. The potential for lichen growth on a fossilized skeleton—while plausible—is not guaranteed by anything in the passage, and this skeleton from thousands of years ago, is well outside the 500 year window in which lichenometry is best suited.

(C) cannot involve lichenometry because the submerged beach would not have any remaining *exposed* rock surfaces. Furthermore, lichenometry is best used for events within the last 500 years, and **(C)** is about an *ancient* beach.

(E) is eliminated because lichenometry is about measuring the age of something based on the predictable size of lichen growth. Nothing in the passage provides evidence that technique could measure rainfall rates.

KAPLAN

Passage 2: Custom-Made Medical Illustrations as Evidence

Step 1: Read the Passage Strategically

Sample Roadmap

line #	Keyword/phrase	¶ Margin notes
1	While … long allowed	Custom med. illust. in court?
3	the issue	
4	legitimate	
5	ongoing debate and misinformation	debate
6	opponents … argue … while	
11	such as	Con 1: med textbook pictures adequate
14	so	
16	Another line of complaints	Con 2: custom pictures misrepresent
19	Even	
20	believing	
25	But this is mistaken … Even if	Au = but pictures must be vetted by experts
28	unless	
30	It has also	
31	subtly distort	Con 3: custom illust. distort issue
32	even if	
33	But	
34	and	
36	Unlike	Au = but prof illustrators strive for simple, accurate
40	include only	
46	For example,	too complex is bad
50		Au = custom illust. valuable
53	are especially valuable	
55		informs expert test'y
59	Since	Most users not experts, so pictures useful

Discussion

Custom-made medical illustrations make for a rather discrete **Topic**, with the **Scope** of the passage focusing on "whether they have a legitimate place in the courtroom." The author readily presents a point of view by referring to some of the rhetoric as "misinformation" and goes on to begin listing some of the points made by opponents of customized drawings. Paragraph 1 concludes with the first of these points: in most cases, generic illustrations from medical textbooks can be adequate.

Paragraph 2 introduces a second complaint about using custom-made medical drawings as evidence that "stems from the belief" (more language that hints at the author's disagreement) that such illustrations present a biased picture. The author rebuts this viewpoint, arguing that such illustrations would not be admitted as evidence without testimony from a medical expert to verify their accuracy.

A third objection to customized illustrations is presented in paragraph 3: these drawings might distort issues with various illustrative techniques. Again the author provides a rebuttal, noting that professional medical illustrators strive for accuracy. The author goes on to point out that custom-made drawings can provide more clarity for jurors and judges by omitting irrelevant anatomical details that would be a part of generic illustrations. By now it is quite clear that the author's **Purpose** is to defend the use of custom-made medical illustrations as evidence in legal cases.

The final paragraph reinforces the author's contention that custom-made medical illustrations are valuable, providing visual explanations for very complex data. In the end, the reader has no doubt of the author's **Main Idea:** contrary to criticism, custom-made medical illustrations are a useful tool for litigators trying to explain complicated medical terminology.

9. (A) Logic Reasoning (Parallel Reasoning)

Step 2: Identify the Question Type

We may expect to see a Global question as the first problem of the set, but not so here, which is a reminder that nothing is guaranteed on the LSAT. Indeed, there's not a single Global question about this passage. Here we are faced with a Parallel Reasoning question, indicated by the phrase "which of the following is most analogous ..."

Step 3: Research the Relevant Text

The question stem demands an analogy to the role "custom-made medical illustrations play in personal injury cases." The author describes this role in several places; the Roadmap should guide you to the discussions in the second half of the passage, especially at lines 53–55. There, the author states

that these illustrations "provide visual representations of data whose verbal description would be very complex."

Step 4: Make a Prediction

The correct answer will refer to another item that would provide a clear visual explanation for something that requires a complex verbal description.

Step 5: Evaluate the Answer Choices

(A) describes illustrations that accompany a technical oral presentation. Perfect!

(B) suggests a visual tool to avoid, not accompany, verbal descriptions. That's off the mark.

(C) is incorrect because drawings as analytical tools for psychologists are not related to the illustrative drawings used to clarify testimony.

(D) describes a graphic that doesn't offer any value as a visual explanation for a verbal presentation.

(E) is off because preliminary sketches don't provide any clarification of complex information.

10. (E) Inference

Step 2: Identify the Question Type

Inference questions are commonly "based on the passage" and often ask about what is "most likely."

Step 3: Research the Relevant Text

The question stem's only content clue is about medical textbook illustrations. These are discussed twice in the passage; the brief mention at line 10, however, does not really provide insight into the author's opinion of textbook drawing. The useful portion of the passage for this question is found at the end of paragraph 3: lines 36–49.

Step 4: Make a Prediction

The answer must be true based on the passage and should reflect the author's contention that medical textbook illustrations may be too detailed and complex compared to custom-made illustrations, which provide only relevant information.

Step 5: Evaluate the Answer Choices

(E) relates to the prediction nicely, and is supported by lines 44–46, which state that deleting complex details from textbooks can eliminate confusion.

(A) is a 180. Color use is discussed in the third paragraph, but custom-made illustrations are said to sometimes even avoid using color, which is another way of saying they, and not medical textbooks, are the ones that rely less on color use.

(B) is a Faulty Use of Detail, twisting the comment at the end of the second paragraph, which refers to custom-made drawings, not to medical textbooks.

(C) is Out of Scope, for the passage does not say anything about who creates the illustrations for either medical textbooks or custom-made drawings.

(D) is a Distortion. It recalls the information presented around lines 19–21. However, those lines only suggest that *some* lawyers may believe that, not *most*, making this answer also Extreme.

11. (E) Detail

Step 2: Identify the Question Type

This Detail question is identified by the phrase "the passage states."

Step 3: Research the Relevant Text

Don't rely on your memory: check the passage (at lines 28–29) to verify what it says about medical experts in relation to custom-made medical illustrations.

Step 4: Make a Prediction

The passage says that custom-made illustrations are "inadmissible as evidence... unless a medical expert" is present to testify to their accuracy. The correct answer will paraphrase this.

Step 5: Evaluate the Answer Choices

(E) is the expected paraphrase.

(A) is a Distortion. Medical experts confirm the accuracy of an illustration but wouldn't necessarily have any say about admissibility.

(B) is another Distortion: "temper the impact" implies a level of influence the passage does not ascribe to medical experts.

(C) a 180. According to the passage, illustrations clarify the words of experts, not the other way around.

(D) is Out of Scope, as experts' advice to attorneys is never discussed in the passage.

12. (D) Detail

Step 2: Identify the Question Type

"According to the passage" is a hallmark Detail question phrase.

Step 3: Research the Relevant Text

The question stem offers a content clue: we need to check the passage for any discussion about the differences between medical textbook and custom-made illustrations. This can be found in the third paragraph.

Step 4: Make a Prediction

The information at lines 36–41 provides the most specific comparison between the illustrations in medical textbooks and those that are custom-made: the former are highly detailed, whereas the latter can be designed to include only pertinent information related to the lawsuit.

Step 5: Evaluate the Answer Choices

(D) restates the prediction and is therefore correct.

(A) makes an incorrect assertion (that medical textbook illustrations do not accurately represent human anatomy) and is also Out of Scope, as the accuracy of textbook drawings is never discussed.

(B) is a Distortion of the discussion of color at the beginning of the third paragraph. It is also Extreme: while the passage says custom illustrators sometimes eschew the use of color, it does not say that they "must" avoid it.

(C) is Out of Scope; the objectivity or subjectivity of drawings is never discussed.

(E) is a 180, since the whole point of custom-made illustrations is to make complex concepts easier to understand for nonmedical people in the court.

13. (C) Inference

Step 2: Identify the Question Type

This author's attitude problem is an Inference question variant.

Step 3: Research the Relevant Text

The content clue in this question points to the final paragraph, where expert testimony is discussed (lines 55–63).

Step 4: Make a Prediction

The passage says, without reservation or other commentary, that expert medical testimony is often very technical and might be difficult for people without medical training to visualize. The correct answer will be true based on this information, and it will reflect an author attitude that is neither critical nor laudatory toward medical experts.

Step 5: Evaluate the Answer Choices

(C) has a neutral tone and mentions the limitations of a strictly verbal presentation, making it the correct answer.

(A) questions the effectiveness of testimony and mentions the difficulty of explaining medical data, which is a Distortion of the author's assertion that illustrations can be instructive by supplementing complex testimony that might be difficult to translate mentally into visual imagery.

(B) is incorrect because the author shows no "disdain" toward the experts.

(D) implies an accusation, never stated by the author, that experts are *trying* to overwhelm judges and jurors.

(E) is Extreme in its use of the term *intolerance*.

14. (B) Logic Function

Step 2: Identify the Question Type

Two types of questions ask about authorial purpose: Global questions pertain to the overall passage, but this question homes in on just one paragraph, making it a Logic Function question.

Step 3: Research the Relevant Text

The third paragraph is the subject of this question. Remember to consider it in context: the preceding paragraph discussed the suggestion that customized drawings are biased—the second of three critical points discussed by the passage. The third paragraph goes on to list the third and final objection to custom-made medical illustrations: that they might distort issues. The author then argues against this criticism and praises custom-made illustrations as useful for their ability to include only those aspects of physiology relevant to the case. This paves the way for the final paragraph, which further advocates the use of customized illustrations in the courtroom.

Step 4: Make a Prediction

The correct answer will focus on structure and context and reflect this paragraph's treatment of a point of contention against customized illustrations.

Step 5: Evaluate the Answer Choices

(B) properly identifies the author's reply to another objection. Note how this answer compares the objection discussed in the third paragraph to the objection in the previous paragraph—they're both variations on distorting information. This underscores the importance of researching the context of a content clue.

(A) calls for an argument that isn't actually made in the third paragraph. Because this idea is somewhat in line with the passage's overall purpose, it might tempt a test taker who failed to follow Steps 3 and 4.

(C) overemphasizes the reference to medical textbook illustrations, making this wrong answer a Distortion.

(D) is too vague. While the paragraph does add some detail about the controversy, that's not its primary purpose.

(E) is too narrow, focusing only on the discussion contained in the latter portion of the paragraph.

Passage 3: Dental Caries and Archaeology

Step 1: Read the Passage Strategically

Sample Roadmap

line #	Keyword/phrase	¶ Margin notes
Passage A		
1	strongly linked	Cavities linked to carbs
3	provide ...	
4	clues	
6	several factors,	clue of agri. development
8	In particular,	
9	since	
11	Many ... have demonstrated the link	North Am. ex.
14	differed between	
15	primarily	
17	heavily dependent	More agri = more cavities
19	frequently	
23	however	Exception: gatherers who ate acorns & cavity-causing plants
25	For example	
29	And	
31	notably	

line #	Keyword/phrase	¶ Margin notes
Passage B		
32		Thai ex.
35	appear to	Group went from H/G to Agri
36	Evidence indicates	
37	increasingly dependent on	
39	suggests	Agri = ↓ health
40	results in	
43	may result	
45		Cavities more freq – why
48	thus	
49	However,	
50	also result in	
51		Thai group ate grains/rice
54	also included	
55	Since	should show cavities
58	Yet	
60	is slightly greater	But cavities ↓
61	do not indicate	
63	unexpected ... is more likely	
64	although	Prob b/c diet was varied; yams < rice
65	varied enough	
66	Furthermore	

KAPLAN

Discussion

Passage A introduces the link between dental caries (tooth decay) and carbohydrate-rich agricultural diets. This Topic, it turns out, is useful to researchers trying to determine when a population transitioned from relying on hunting and gathering to farming, especially because of the way carbohydrates stick to teeth, as the first paragraph mentions.

In the second paragraph, the connection between caries and carbohydrates is demonstrated with an example of work done by Leigh, who studied teeth (found through archaeology) for decay. The use of dental decay evidence to assess carbohydrate consumption by various populations is the passage's **Scope**, and the **Purpose** is to discuss various archaeological examples that demonstrate the relationship between diet and dental caries. The second paragraph concludes with the author's **Main Idea**: generally, the more a population depends on agriculture, the higher its rate of caries formation will be.

The third paragraph of passage A presents two exceptions to this general rule, attributing the high caries rate to particular foods prevalent in the gathered diets of these nonagricultural populations.

Passage B introduces Ban Chiang, an archaeological site in Thailand, and asserts in the first paragraph that the population interred there over a span of two millennia shifted from hunting, gathering, and cultivating to an increasingly agriculture-dependent lifestyle. This shift is the **Topic**. Note the relation of this information to that in passage A, which said that the link between caries and agricultural diets provides clues about such a transition.

The beginning of passage B's second paragraph echoes this, and then this paragraph explains in greater detail how starchy foods or changes in tooth wear affect the development of caries. So, the **Scope** is how the dental health of the Ban Chiang inhabitants can be used to determine when their shift to agriculture occurred.

Returning to Ban Chiang, the third paragraph instructs that its population ate carbohydrates as part of a varied diet all along. In line with the theory presented in passage A as well as in passage B's second paragraph, increased reliance on foods like yams and rice should result in more caries. Now the author's **Purpose** is clear: to examine what the dental health of the Ban Chiang remains say about their diet and shift to agriculture.

The final paragraph reveals the **Main Idea**: the Ban Chiang remains defy expectations by demonstrating somewhat decreased caries. To conclude, the author offers a theory about the surprising data, suggesting that the Ban Chiang population ate a continually varied diet, even with increased use of agriculture, and perhaps in later years consumed fewer yams (the sweeter and more damaging carbohydrate) in favor of more rice.

Both passages focus on the use of dental evidence as a tool for understanding historical populations' diets and lifestyles and, more specifically, how dental caries is linked to increased reliance on agriculture.

15. (A) Global

Step 2: Identify the Question Type

Global questions in Comparative Reading passages can address just one or, as here, both of the passages.

Step 3: Research the Relevant Text

No specific text should be reviewed for a Global question: consider the passages in their entireties and, because the question stem asks it, focus on what is true of both.

Step 4: Make a Prediction

Both passages study past populations, exploring the link between dental caries and reliance on agriculture. The correct answer will reflect this.

Step 5: Evaluate the Answer Choices

(A) matches the prediction, dental evidence being the "archaeological record."

(B) touches on something mentioned early in passage B (line 40), but passage A never mentions overall health.

(C) is potentially tempting but too narrow, focusing only on one type of society. The passages do discuss the effects of carbohydrate-rich foods on caries formation but not just in strictly agricultural societies.

(D) is Out of Scope, because the "first agricultural society" is never in either passage.

(E) is likewise Out of Scope, because the extent to which carbohydrates could be obtained is never discussed.

16. (B) Detail

Step 2: Identify the Question Type

When a question mentions specific things "discussed" in a passage, that's a Detail question.

Step 3: Research the Relevant Text

Comparative Detail questions require checking both passages for the relevant information. This question stem points out the last paragraph of passage A, but the first, third, and last paragraphs of passage B should also be consulted.

Step 4: Make a Prediction

The right answer will reflect the contrast between the two populations. Those discussed at the end of passage A were nonagricultural societies that ate gathered foods, but the Ban

Chiang people were increasingly reliant on agriculture and always ate some cultivated foods.

Step 5: Evaluate the Answer Choices

(B) does the job perfectly.

(A) is a 180. The populations in the last paragraphs of passage A did in fact eat cariogenic foods, including plenty of carbohydrates.

(C) is another 180 and is also Extreme because the Ban Chiang's diet was "varied," not *primarily* carbohydrates.

(D) is Out of Scope, as tooth wear is not discussed in passage A.

(E) is a Distortion and a 180. Although Ban Chiang peoples were agriculturally dependent, food "processing" is not mentioned anywhere in passage B. Furthermore, the first group mentioned in passage A did consume "highly processed stone-ground flour."

17. (A) Inference

Step 2: Identify the Question Type

The phrase "strongly supports" is a typical Inference question marker.

Step 3: Research the Relevant Text

Comparative Reading question sets rarely include a question like this one, focusing on only one passage. Passage B mentions fiber and grit at line 47, but, for context, start a bit earlier, around line 42.

Step 4: Make a Prediction

The answer must be true based on the information given. The passage states that reducing fiber and grit would diminish tooth wear, suggesting that fiber and grit actually contribute to tooth wear. While some tooth wear helps prevent caries by eliminating surface food traps, too much wear exposes dental pulp, which could promote caries.

Step 5: Evaluate the Answer Choices

(A) is correct.

(B) is Out of Scope. The typical consumption of fiber and grit is never mentioned.

(C) is also Out of Scope, because the nutritional value of fiber and grit is never discussed.

(D) presents a combined Faulty Use of Detail/180 trap through its mention of fissures. It's suggested that fiber and grit actually remove fissures, not form them.

(E) is another Faulty Use of Detail, attempting to trigger memory about sticky carbohydrates mentioned elsewhere in the passage.

18. (B) Detail

Step 2: Identify the Question Type

The question asks about something "mentioned" in both passages. This is a Detail question that requires careful research.

Step 3: Research the Relevant Text

The question asks for stated evidence that supports the prevailing view regarding the effect of carbohydrates on caries. Research evidence for this view is provided in the second paragraph of both passages.

Step 4: Make a Prediction

The evidence used in passage A is Leigh's study, which found little caries in primarily meat-eating populations and much caries in agricultural ones. The studies mentioned in passage B as evidence (lines 41–42) indicate the uncommonness of caries in pre-agricultural societies. So, both passages provide evidence of populations that don't rely primarily on agriculture and display low levels of caries.

Step 5: Evaluate the Answer Choices

(B) matches the prediction perfectly.

(A) mentions highly processed foods, a topic never discussed in passage B.

(C) is incorrect because fiber and grit are discussed only in passage B.

(D) is incorrect because tooth wear is discussed only in passage B.

(E) is incorrect because overall health is discussed only in passage B.

19. (D) Inference

Step 2: Identify the Question Type

"Most likely" signals an Inference question.

Step 3: Research the Relevant Text

There is little in this question stem to guide specific research: both passages say a lot about dental caries throughout.

Step 4: Make a Prediction

Because of the lack of a strong content clue, this question requires the time-consuming task of checking each answer choice against the passages. The answer must be true for both passages.

Step 5: Evaluate the Answer Choices

(D) is justified by text in the final paragraphs of both passage A and passage B. In each case, anomalies in the usual correlation between agricultural dependence and dental caries are described.

(A) is a very broad statement that distorts both passages' central idea about dental caries incidence—especially given the exceptional cases provided that defy expected predictions.

(B) brings up difficulties with dental caries detection—an issue not mentioned in either passage. This choice is thus Out of Scope.

(C) serves up a 180, getting the story backward.

(E) could not be an idea with which both authors agree since only passage B discusses tooth wear.

20. (C) Inference

Step 2: Identify the Question Type

The "passage suggests" language means this is an Inference question.

Step 3: Research the Relevant Text

The question stem offers one clue: "carbohydrate-rich foods." These are mentioned in passage A's first and third paragraphs and in passage B in the final two paragraphs.

Step 4: Make a Prediction

As with the previous question, there is a lot of information about carbohydrate-rich foods in both passages. Instead of trying to predict the one piece of information the correct answer will use, go through the answers and check them against both passages. The correct answer will be true according to both passages.

Step 5: Evaluate the Answer Choices

(C) reflects the varying cariogenic potential of different carbohydrates, as provided at lines 28–31 in passage A and lines 67–68 of passage B.

(A) incorrectly compares the cariogenic potential of wild carbohydrates to that of cultivated ones; neither passage makes this comparison

(B) is wrong because passage B never mentions substantial processing.

(D) brings up tooth wear, which is not discussed in passage A.

(E), like **(A)**, incorrectly suggests a comparison between wild and cultivated carbohydrates with respect to cariogenic potential.

21. (D) Logic Reasoning (Method of Argument)

Step 2: Identify the Question Type

The question asks to relate evidence from one passage to a generalization stated in the other. Such Comparative Reading questions are similar to Method of Argument problems found in Logical Reasoning.

Step 3: Research the Relevant Text

The stem provides one specific reference to lines 20–22: this is the assertion that a population more dependent on agriculture is more likely to demonstrate a higher rate of caries formation. The Ban Chiang population's caries formation is revealed in the final paragraph of passage B.

Step 4: Make a Prediction

The Ban Chiang population defied expectations by demonstrating decreased caries frequency when it was more agriculturally reliant, contrary to the claim from passage A in question.

Step 5: Evaluate the Answer Choices

(D) is the accurate summation.

(A) is a 180.

(B), though less extreme than **(A)**, is also a 180.

(C) fails because it ignores the clear connection between the generalization and the "unexpected finding" in passage B.

(E) is Extreme. While the Ban Chiang result is an exception to the generalization, it doesn't necessarily disprove it.

Passage 4: The Fiction of Sarah Orne Jewett

Step 1: Read the Passage Strategically

Sample Roadmap

line #	Keyword/phrase	¶ Margin notes
1	Recent criticism	Recent crit
2	notable	
3		Jewett = 19th c. dom. nov.
5	resemble ... focus	
7	relegated	
8	differs markedly	Au = but she's diff.
11		less about child care
13	chief source of drama ... By contrast	
15	Even more strikingly ... while	
17		Jewett not religious
19	almost wholly secular	
20	do not merely	Soc/cult changes part of diff.
21	personal	
22	attribute to them	
24	But ... while	
25	can be	
26	argued ... ultimately	Au: But big diff is Jewett has diff view of it
29	is based	
33	not uncommon	
36	didactic ... absent from	old dom. now was multi-purpose; not Jewett
38	fiction as an ...	
39	autonomous sphere with value in and of itself	
42	but it became the ...	late 19th c. novel as work of art
43	dominant one ... later	
45	pure art:	
49	Thus ... unlike	So, Jewett trying to make self-contained "art"
50	not as a means to an end but as an ...	
51	end in themselves ... fundamental difference ... should	
52	be	

Discussion

The work of fiction writer Sarah Orne Jewett is the **Topic** of this passage. How to classify Jewett's writing is the **Scope**. The author begins by stating that critics have sought to align Jewett with domestic novelists of an earlier era, but quickly reveals a contrary opinion by noting how Jewett's work differs "markedly" from that of the mid-nineteenth-century writers. The subsequent discussion and support for this alternative view serves as the author's **Purpose**. The rest of the first paragraph introduces two primary differences between Jewett's work and domestic novels: (1) the role of children, prominent in domestic novels and absent in Jewett's, and (2) religiosity, which is a strong part of domestic novels but hardly present in Jewett's work.

In the second paragraph, the author attempts to account for these differences, acknowledging that societal changes could be a factor but quickly turning to the central idea: that the nature and purpose of fiction writing itself had shifted by the end of the nineteenth century. Domestic novels, the passage states, had many functions, serving to provide instruction and promote beliefs. But by Jewett's time, literature had become more esoteric.

The third paragraph expounds on this notion further, tracing the changing conception of fiction and underscoring the author's **Main Idea**: that Jewett's works were not intended as "means to an end but as an end in themselves" (lines 50–51) and that this "fundamental difference" should be a factor in classifying Jewett's novels differently from the domestic literature that had been written for different reasons.

22. (D) Detail

Step 2: Identify the Question Type

When a question asks which answer choice is best answered by the passage, it's a Detail question.

Step 3: Research the Relevant Text

The format of this question requires each answer choice to be researched for its merits. Work quickly, but be sure to justify the answer you choose on the basis of text written in the passage.

Step 4: Make a Prediction

The one correct answer will be something that is addressed within the text of the passage.

Step 5: Evaluate the Answer Choices

(D) finds its justification in the final lines of the passage: the conception of fiction as pure art is discussed at line 45, leading to the assertion that Jewett's intent was for her fiction to be read for its own sake.

(A) raises the topic of male writers, which is Out of Scope for this passage.

(B) raises another Out of Scope topic: post-1860s domestic novels.

(C) is a Distortion/Faulty Use of Detail found in the second paragraph. The passage's mention of migration to urban centers was relative to fiction of the later nineteenth century, not that of the 1850s. Moreover, the passage doesn't mention *how* it affected fiction, just that it did.

(E) is Out of Scope because of its mention of U.S. regions.

23. (C) Inference

Step 2: Identify the Question Type

"It can be inferred …" is a dead giveaway for an Inference question.

Step 3: Research the Relevant Text

The question stem provides both a content clue and a line reference. Go right to the beginning of the passage to double-check: the recent criticism is an effort to categorize Jewett as a domestic fiction writer.

Step 4: Make a Prediction

Despite the specific references to the first words of the passage, the question demands understanding of an attitude that unfolds in the next couple of lines. The author initially admits that Jewett's works and domestic novels do resemble one another. However, the *but* that ends line 7 signals the author's ultimate opinion, supported throughout the passage: the literary critics who attempt to align Jewett with domestic fiction writers are wrong.

Step 5: Evaluate the Answer Choices

(C) is in line with the author's view that casting Jewett as a domestic novelist is a mistake.

(A) is a 180. The author clearly believes that the recent criticism is incorrect.

(B) is also a 180, with distorted reasoning to support it.

(D) is more tempting, but casting the current criticism as reliant on a too-narrow view of the proper goals of fiction distorts the passage's commentary. Nothing states, that the recent criticism about Jewett is necessarily "dominant," nor does the passage state what that criticism relies upon. The goals of fiction also aren't discussed pejoratively, so casting goals as "proper" is inappropriate, as well.

(E) is incorrect because it is Extreme to state that there is "*no* reasonable support" for the critics' position. Indeed, the author acknowledges that Jewett's work "does resemble" the domestic fiction genre, right in the second sentence of the passage.

24. (B) Logic Function

Step 2: Identify the Question Type

A question asking why an author used a certain word is always a Logic Function question.

Step 3: Research the Relevant Text

The stem directs the research here: seek out the word *continuum* at line 30 and then search around it for context.

Step 4: Make a Prediction

The "continuum" in question is described as including various writings that share a common goal, Domestic fiction, and fiction in general, is seen as part of that group. Therefore, the correct answer will get across the idea that this continuum groups fiction with these other writings as a conglomerate.

Step 5: Evaluate the Answer Choices

(B) reflects fiction as part of a range of written works and is correct.

(A) reaches to a past unmentioned in the passage. It is Out of Scope.

(C) is Out of Scope because the format of domestic novel publication is never mentioned in this article.

(D) is tempting if the concept of "continuum" is taken out of context. However, it does not match the prediction, and it offers a broad platitude that distorts the one evolution in fiction discussed in the passage.

(E) confuses the word *continuum* with *continuity* and will not tempt test takers who follow the Reading Comprehension Method by seeking a match to a strategically researched prediction.

25. (E) Global

Step 2: Identify the Question Type

Any question asking about the passage as a whole is a Global question. It's unusual for Global questions to be buried in the middle of the set, which provides a good reminder that an initial scan of all the questions is always wise. The strategic test taker will have tackled this problem first.

Step 3: Research the Relevant Text

A good Roadmap helps answer Global questions, which test understanding of the complete passage.

Step 4: Make a Prediction

The author exposes a trend in literary criticism toward categorizing the work of a particular author and then argues against this view.

Step 5: Evaluate the Answer Choices

(E) succinctly and accurately states the prediction.

(A) is Extreme due to its language of "radical redefinition."

(B) is a Distortion. The passage neither really proposes an evaluation of a particular style of writing nor finds Jewett's work as paradigmatic of anything.

(C) is Out of Scope, because nothing is said in the passage about any "long-held assumptions" about any group of writers.

(D) is another Distortion, as there is no weighing of merits, nor are the two conceptions of fiction discussed by the passage necessarily "opposing," as suggested by the proposed answer.

26. (E) Logic Function

Step 2: Identify the Question Type

When a question asks about the structure of a paragraph, it's classified as a Logic Function problem.

Step 3: Research the Relevant Text

This question names the second paragraph, which contains a discussion attempting to explain the differences between mid-nineteenth-century domestic fiction and the work of author Jewett.

Step 4: Make a Prediction

The paragraph begins by suggesting a few possible reasons for the differences, acknowledges the plausibility of these factors, but then proposes another explanation: the differing conceptions of fiction. The correct answer will trace this structure.

Step 5: Evaluate the Answer Choices

(E) accurately describes both the structure and the tone of paragraph 2.

(A) is Extreme. Nothing is really rejected by the author, and there's certainly no suggestion of *violence* of any sort.

(B) is likewise Extreme and even a 180; while the passage does mention differing hypotheses to explain the difference between fictional works of two eras, the hypotheses are shown to overlap rather than be incompatible.

(C) uses wording that is inaccurate and incomplete. Stick to your prediction to avoid such traps.

(D) takes quite a while to state something completely fanciful. Nothing in the paragraph follows what's described by the answer choice, which seems designed to tire the test taker with its convoluted language.

27. (C) Detail

Step 2: Identify the Question Type

This wordy question stem might be difficult to categorize quickly: the term "most reasonably" could be construed as the language of an Inference question. However, the question really wants you to identify something that was directly discussed in the passage, making it a Detail question.

Step 3: Research the Relevant Text

"Conceptions of fiction" are first discussed in the second paragraph. Start at line 25 to review the content and its context.

Step 4: Make a Prediction

The right answer will reflect the key phrase that the differences between Jewett's writing and that of earlier domestic novelists "ultimately reflect different conceptions of the nature and purpose of fiction." Those differences are described in the first paragraph, which should also be double-checked before any answer gets a commitment.

Step 5: Evaluate the Answer Choices

(C) reflects the key differences between the domestic novelists, and Jewett's work and is a question that is answered by the author's hypothesis about differing conceptions of fiction's aims. It's a winner.

(A) is a Distortion of the information about Jewett's writing: although the passage states that Jewett's work did not feature children and religious themes, it does not go so far as to say she was *unwilling* to include such themes.

(B) is a Faulty Use of Detail that hangs on the information presented in the early lines of paragraph 2, when migration from rural to urban communities is mentioned. However, it is not mentioned as a subject matter of Jewett or the domestic novelists, and its use in this answer choice is incorrect.

(D) poses a valid question but one that is beyond the scope of this passage.

(E) is a similar Distortion to **(A)**: the passage does not say that Jewett was "unable" to write about religion and children, merely that she did not do so.

Section II: Logical Reasoning

Q#	Question Type	Correct	Difficulty
1	Principle (Identify/Inference)	D	★
2	Strengthen	E	★
3	Assumption (Sufficient)	B	★
4	Strengthen	E	★
5	Flaw	C	★
6	Inference	A	★
7	Parallel Flaw	C	★
8	Flaw	A	★★★★
9	Assumption (Sufficient)	C	★
10	Main Point	B	★
11	Flaw	A	★
12	Assumption (Necessary)	E	★
13	Principle (Parallel)	D	★
14	Method of Argument	B	★★
15	Assumption (Sufficient)	B	★★
16	Strengthen	E	★★★
17	Assumption (Sufficient)	A	★★★★
18	Principle (Apply/Inference EXCEPT)	D	★★
19	Inference	D	★★★
20	Paradox	C	★★★
21	Inference	E	★★★
22	Weaken	D	★★★
23	Principle (Identify/Strengthen)	C	★★
24	Inference	E	★★
25	Assumption (Necessary)	A	★★★★
26	Principle (Identify/Strengthen)	E	★

1. (D) Principle (Identify/Inference)

Step 1: Identify the Question Type

The question asks you to identify the broad principle illustrated by the facts and findings of a study. Find the answer choice that accurately matches the key element(s) of the principle.

Step 2: Untangle the Stimulus

In the study, children were taught the word *stairs* while going up and down stairs. Later, when the children saw a person climbing a ladder, they called the ladder "stairs." Your task is to determine the principle behind the children's application of the word *stairs* to the ladder.

Step 3: Make a Prediction

The key element of the principle must hinge on the children's use of the word *stairs* for any object used to climb up and down, even objects that are not referred to as such. Since the ladder was used to climb up and down, the children identified it in the same way as the stairs.

Step 4: Evaluate the Answer Choices

(D) matches this prediction perfectly and is thus the correct answer. Essentially, this choice indicates that when young children learn a word for an object that is used in a specific way, the children might incorrectly apply that word to another object with the same use.

(A) is a Distortion. It wrongly states that the children learned the word *stairs* without seeing the object.

(B) is Outside the Scope. Nothing indicates how children *best* learn words, only how they learned and applied a word in this study.

(C) is also Outside the Scope. No facts are given about relative ease of learning.

(E), like **(B)**, is Outside the Scope because the stimulus is not focused on how children *best* learn words.

2. (E) Strengthen

Step 1: Identify the Question Type

The stem asks for the answer choice that "most strengthens the argument," so the correct answer will consist of an additional fact that will make the conclusion more likely to follow from the evidence.

Step 2: Untangle the Stimulus

The Keyword *since* alerts us to evidence offered in support of the conclusion, which follows the comma. Since many people who live to 100 years and older engage in unhealthy behavior that often shortens life spans, the author concludes that long life is likely to be a genetic predisposition. The argument takes a big unsupported leap: from the fact that these people live longer than their behavior should permit to the

conclusion that genetics is the explanation. What's needed is some factual evidence for the genetic predisposition.

Step 3: Make a Prediction

Think critically about facts that would support genetics as a contributing factor to longevity. Perhaps consider studies suggesting the existence of a longevity gene or longevity as a family trait. Be flexible in predicting strengtheners—keep the conclusion in mind and look only for facts that support it.

Step 4: Evaluate the Answer Choices

(E) is the correct answer because it supports the conclusion that genetics is a factor by establishing longevity as a trait shared by siblings.

(A) is Outside the Scope. The stimulus says nothing about the relative impacts of these various unhealthy behaviors, and this choice doesn't provide any basis for the conclusion that longevity is genetic.

(B), like **(A)**, provides an irrelevant conflation of behaviors but no support for the conclusion.

(C) goes Outside the Scope in much the same way that **(A)** and **(B)** do. Don't get distracted by extraneous details and miss the point.

(D) is Outside the Scope. The argument is about why people live long lives. The behavior of people who don't live long lives has no bearing on the conclusion.

3. (B) Assumption (Sufficient)

Step 1: Identify the Question Type

The question asks for an assumption that, if true, will support the conclusion; i.e., a sufficient assumption. Unlike a necessary assumption, a sufficient assumption doesn't have to be true, so the Denial Test may not be useful. But if the assumption is true, it acts as a strengthener to support the conclusion.

Step 2: Untangle the Stimulus

The Keyword [*s*]*o* signals the crux of this argument. The conclusion, which follows the comma in the last clause, is that medication M will most likely be produced in capsule form. The word *since* preceding this conclusion indicates part of the evidence—the company cannot manufacture M in soft-gel form. We are also told that any medication that tastes unpleasant is usually manufactured in one of three forms: capsule, tablet, or soft-gel. M cannot be manufactured in tablet form (or in soft-gel form); therefore, it will be manufactured in capsule form.

Step 3: Make a Prediction

To predict the assumption, be alert for a mismatch between the terms of the conclusion and the terms of the evidence. The scope of the conclusion—what the conclusion is about—is how medication M will be produced. The scope of the evidence is how unpleasant-tasting medications are produced. The shift in scope between evidence and conclusion needs some justification if the argument is to be convincing. That justification comes from the assumption that M is an unpleasant-tasting medication.

Step 4: Evaluate the Answer Choices

(B) matches the prediction perfectly by simply establishing that M tastes unpleasant. Therefore, if it can't be produced in two of the three usual forms in which unpleasant-tasting medications are made, then it will probably be produced in the only remaining form.

(A) is Outside the Scope. Liquid form is not discussed as an option.

(C) is Outside the Scope. Manufacture in multiple forms is not an issue. The argument is about M being produced as a capsule.

(D) is Outside the Scope. This is about M, not most medications. The facts state that the manufacturer cannot create a soft-gel, so the soft-gel form is not an issue here.

(E) is an Irrelevant Comparison. Nothing in the argument makes a comparison of taste between capsule and other forms.

4. (E) Strengthen

Step 1: Identify the Question Type

The question asks us to find an answer choice that supports the "industry analysts' prediction." The information in the question stem not only tells you that you are finding a strengthener but also alerts you to what conclusion needs to be supported.

One quick note: This question could have been presented equally effectively as a Paradox question. This reminds us of how closely related the question types are and how they rely on the same kinds of reasoning.

Step 2: Untangle the Stimulus

The prediction is that Morris will soon own a majority of the shares of the newspaper. However, no support for the prediction is provided. The facts only state that Morris wants to own a majority, but the company that currently owns a majority refuses to sell its shares. Even so, analysts predict that Morris will soon get the shares.

Step 3: Make a Prediction

To make the prediction more likely to come true, some fact is needed to ensure that Azedcorp will abandon its "steadfast" refusal and sell its shares. Don't waste time speculating why Azedcorp won't sell—the correct answer will clearly give a reason to expect Azedcorp will sell its shares.

Step 4: Evaluate the Answer Choices

(E) gives a fairly certain reason to expect that Azedcorp will sell its shares. **(E)** is therefore correct.

(A) is no help. Even if Azedcorp owns no other newspaper stock, no reason is given for it to sell its *Daily* shares. This could even provide a reason to hold the shares and perhaps weaken the prediction.

(B) doesn't help. The evidence states that Azedcorp has steadfastly refused to sell. There is no reason to believe that a "recent" offer of more money has changed or will change that refusal.

(C) doesn't help either. Even if Morris is the only interested buyer, no reason is provided for Azedcorp to sell to her if it doesn't want to sell.

(D) is Out of Scope. The prediction is about what Morris will own, not what she currently owns. This fact contributes nothing to the analysts' prediction.

5. (C) Flaw

Step 1: Identify the Question Type

The question states that the argument in the stimulus is flawed. This means that the evidence does not support the conclusion. The answer choice will describe why.

Step 2: Untangle the Stimulus

The conclusion, indicated by the Keyword [*t*]*herefore*, is that eliminating lead paint from homes will end the problem of childhood lead poisoning. The reason given is that cases of lead poisoning have decreased since the ban of lead paint and leaded gasoline; however, there are still homes that contain lead paint.

Step 3: Make a Prediction

To predict this flaw, notice the extreme language in the conclusion that lead poisoning will "finally be eradicated"; i.e., completely eliminated. Why? Because the lead paint will be gone. The author of this argument is making the assumption that there are no sources of hazardous lead other than the lead paint. This is the classic flaw of overlooked possibility.

Step 4: Evaluate the Answer Choices

(C) tells us that the argument "fails to consider" other potential sources of lead. This is exactly what was predicted.

(A) is a Distortion. The conclusion does not rely on the percentage of houses that have lead paint, but rather on the fact that eliminating lead paint from any homes that have it will eradicate the poisoning hazard.

(B) is awkwardly worded in order to confuse. To paraphrase; **(B)** states that the argument assumes its conclusion; i.e., is circular. That is not the flaw here.

(D) is Outside the Scope. The argument is about eliminating lead poisoning by eliminating lead paint. The economic feasibility of doing so is not an issue.

(E) is Extreme and Outside the Scope. The argument does not rely on children living in the homes and certainly not in *all* of the homes.

6. (A) Inference

Step 1: Identify the Question Type

The question "which one of the following must be true?" asks us to draw an inference from the statements in the stimulus.

Step 2: Untangle the Stimulus

Read the stimulus for what is true: (1) soft drink labels do not contain exact caffeine content; (2) if exact caffeine content were listed, it would be easier to limit caffeine intake, but not eliminate it; (3) if it were easier to limit intake, many people would do so, and limiting intake would improve their health.

Step 3: Make a Prediction

When reading a sequence of likely consequences like this, look for the most definite statements of fact rather than struggling to make a prediction. The correct answer could be a number of things, so best to take stock of what you know.

The most definite statements are that (1) exact caffeine content is not provided on soft drinks, (2) caffeine intake wouldn't be eliminated by content labeling, and (3) many people would limit intake if caffeine content was labeled and this would improve their health.

Step 4: Evaluate the Answer Choices

(A) follows directly from the last statement. "At least some" on the LSAT means "at least one," and this is consistent with "many."

(B) is Outside the Scope. We know what content labeling enables people to do. We do not know what effect the absence of content labeling has. (Maybe people could limit their intake without the information or get the information another way.)

(C) is Outside the Scope. The facts provide us with no information about the difficulties of eliminating caffeine intake other than the fact that content labeling doesn't help.

(D) is a 180. The facts state that content labeling does not help eliminate caffeine intake.

(E) could be true, but not necessarily. Some people's health might not improve as a result of content labeling, but it doesn't follow that some people's health would worsen.

7. (C) Parallel Flaw

Step 1: Identify the Question Type

Since the question is looking for an argument with similar reasoning to the stimulus, this is a Parallel Reasoning question. Furthermore, the stimulus and the correct answer will both be flawed—in the same way.

Step 2: Untangle the Stimulus

MacNeil concludes that she will never be able to afford any one of the collector's works because the collection is one of the most valuable ever assembled. Characterize the conclusion as a negative prediction about a piece of something based on something known about the whole.

Step 3: Make a Prediction

The flaw in the argument is a classic flaw: attributing a characteristic of the whole to each of the parts. MacNeil assumes that because the collection as a whole is highly valuable, each of the art pieces that make it up must be highly valuable. The correct answer will make the same mistake.

Step 4: Evaluate the Answer Choices

(C) is the correct choice because it commits the same flaw in the same way—because something is true about the whole (the paragraph is long), it must also be true about its individual parts (the sentences that make it up must be long).

(A) is not parallel. It commits the same flaw of whole-versus-part. However, the flaw is not committed in the same way—a characteristic of an individual word (part) is attributed to the entire book (whole).

(B) is not flawed. *Unanimously* means everyone. All members of the council voted for the plan.

(D) is not parallel. It attributes a characteristic of the members of a company (part) to the company itself (whole).

(E) is not parallel. It attributes a defining feature of the individual atoms (part) to the molecule that they are part of (whole).

8. (A) Flaw

Step 1: Identify the Question Type

"The reasoning in the argument is flawed … " Characterize the flaw and look for the answer choice that describes it.

Step 2: Untangle the Stimulus

The first sentence gives us an argument made by a critic of space exploration. The word *But* at the start of the next sentence signals the author's disagreement. The conclusion is that the critic exaggerates the risk of sending explorers to Mars. The reason is that every stage of the long journey has a backup system, so any given stage of the journey has a low probability of failure resulting in death.

Step 3: Make a Prediction

The words "at any given stage" should alert you to watch for a scope problem. The conclusion is about the risk of the whole "long and complicated journey." The evidence is about the risk at any given stage of the trip. The author is assuming that because each stage by itself has a low risk of failure, the risk is correspondingly low over the entire duration of the trip.

Step 4: Evaluate the Answer Choices

(A) fits the prediction.

(B) is Outside the Scope. The author does not conclude that something cannot occur. He merely concludes the risk is exaggerated.

(C) is a Distortion. Get past the abstract language in this answer choice by asking what the argument concludes "*must* be true." The conclusion is that the risk is exaggerated. The conclusion is not based on any evidence that the risk is *probably* exaggerated

(D) is Outside the Scope. The conclusion isn't about whether something will or won't work.

(E) is Outside the Scope. The author does not attack the adequacy of the critic's argument. He offers factual evidence to refute it.

9. (C) Assumption (Sufficient)

Step 1: Identify the Question Type

The question asks for an assumption that, if true, will support the conclusion; i.e., a sufficient assumption. Unlike a necessary assumption, a sufficient assumption doesn't have to be true, so the Denial Test may not be useful. But if the assumption is true, it acts as a strengthener to support the conclusion.

Step 2: Untangle the Stimulus

This stimulus is wordy, so use careful strategic reading to simplify it. The Keyword *however* signals the author's point, and the word *Because* provides the evidence leading up to that point. Paraphrasing, the conclusion is simply that the retrospective studies described cannot be reliable. The reason is that these studies depend upon the subjects' own reports about their pasts.

Step 3: Make a Prediction

Look for the mismatch between evidence and conclusion. The scope of the conclusion is the unreliability of these retrospective studies. The scope of the evidence is the nature of the information the studies rely upon. To draw a conclusion about reliability based upon the source of information, the author is assuming that the source is unreliable; i.e., the subjects won't provide reliable reports.

Step 4: Evaluate the Answer Choices

(C) is wordy, but it fits the prediction. Rather than say "in retrospective studies," it describes the study at length; and rather than say the subjects' reports are "unreliable," it says they are "highly susceptible to inaccuracy." Good paraphrasing skills really come in handy in selecting this correct answer choice.

(A) is Outside the Scope. The argument is not about what's needed to make a study reliable or not. The conclusion is that it cannot be reliable, and the evidence provides a factual reason why.

(B) is a Distortion. The word *unless* indicates that there is a condition under which the study could be made reliable. However, the conclusion of the argument is an unqualified assertion that the studies cannot be reliable.

(D) is Outside the Scope. The argument is not about what would make the study reliable.

(E) is a restatement of the evidence. Retrospective studies must use the subjects' own reports about their past. We are told this in the argument, so it is not the assumption.

10. (B) Main Point

Step 1: Identify the Question Type

This question simply asks for the conclusion of the argument. Keywords can often help, but be ready to paraphrase.

Step 2: Untangle the Stimulus

First, the author tells us that new passenger planes will have extra space for shops and lounges in addition to passenger seating. The next sentence begins with the Keyword [*h*]*owever*, which signals that the author is going to make a contrasting point—the space will more likely be used for seating. The last sentence elaborates on why this might be true—the increase in passengers and the need for bigger jets.

Step 3: Make a Prediction

The conclusion is signaled by the Keyword [*h*]*owever* and sums up the author's opinion about the first sentence—the extra space will more likely be used for passenger seating than for shops and lounges.

Step 4: Evaluate the Answer Choices

(B) fits the prediction precisely.

(A) is not the conclusion but rather a fact that the author of the argument is taking issue with. The word *However* that starts the next sentence tells us this.

(C) restates one of the facts that explain why the space will more likely be used for passengers. This is evidence, not the conclusion.

(D), like **(C)**, restates a piece of evidence.

(E) is an inference drawn from the evidence, but it is not the main conclusion. If the number of passengers will triple and the airports won't be able to accommodate enough normal-sized planes, it follows that more passengers will fly in the gigantic planes. **(E)** states an implicit subsidiary conclusion that provides support for the main conclusion—that the extra space on these planes will be used for passenger seating.

11. (A) Flaw

Step 1: Identify the Question Type

"Error in reasoning" identifies this as a Flaw question. In this Dialogue/Response stimulus, we are asked to identify the reasoning error in the reporter's response to the scientist.

Step 2: Untangle the Stimulus

The scientist states that in a study testing two athlete's foot medications, M and N, only the people who were given M were cured. Because of the word *only*, we can translate this into Formal Logic:

If	cured	→	medication M

Be careful with the confusing wording. The word *only* signals the necessary condition, but it can sometimes be difficult to determine which word *only* modifies, especially when the passive voice is used. In this case, the sense of the statement is that only those who were given medication M were cured. Taking M is the necessary condition.

The reporter responds by stating that this means anyone who wasn't cured didn't get medication M. In other words:

If	~ cured	→	~ medication M

This improper contrapositive is the key to the reporter's error.

Step 3: Make a Prediction

This is a classic flaw of confusing sufficient and necessary conditions. The reporter misinterprets the scientist's statement to say that anyone who wasn't cured didn't take M. Using the logic of the contrapositive, anyone who took M was cured. In other words, *M always cured athlete's foot*. However, the scientist actually said that people who were cured took M. This doesn't preclude the possibility that some people who *weren't* cured took M as well!

Sufficient/Necessary flaws can be expressed in a number of ways: sufficient/necessary, can/must, overlooked possibility. Be flexible when reading answer choices.

Step 4: Evaluate the Answer Choices

(A) fits the prediction. The reporter mistakes the fact that M can cure athlete's foot to mean it must always cure athlete's foot.

(B) is Outside the Scope. The reporter draws no conclusions about the population as a whole. His conclusion is simply about the results of the study.

(C) is Outside the Scope. The availability of M outside of the study is not an issue.

(D) is a Distortion. The reporter states a conclusion about people who were not cured, not about people who were cured.

(E) is another Distortion, as it is concerned with how people might be cured.

12. (E) Assumption (Necessary)

Step 1: Identify the Question Type

The question asks for an assumption that the argument depends upon; i.e., a necessary assumption. When in doubt, the Denial Test might help.

Step 2: Untangle the Stimulus

The conclusion is signaled by the word *However*. Contrary to the experts' belief that the plesiosauromorph lurked and ambushed its prey, the author concludes that it hunted by chasing its prey over long distances. The support for this is the shape of the dinosaur's fins, which were similar to the wing shape of birds that specialize in flying long distances.

Step 3: Make a Prediction

The argument states that because the dinosaur's fin was shaped like the wings of birds that specialize in flying long distances, the dinosaur must have swum long distances. This reasoning by analogy only works if the shape of the dinosaur's fin relates to its behavior in water the same way the bird's wing shape relates to its behavior in the air.

Step 4: Evaluate the Answer Choices

(E) fits the prediction precisely. The Denial Test confirms: If the shape of the marine animal's fin did not affect its swimming in the same way the shape of the bird's wing affects its flying, the argument would fail to convince.

(A) is Outside the Scope of the argument. The argument draws a conclusion about how the plesiosauromorph behaved based upon the shape of its fin. Evolutionary ancestors are not the issue.

(B) is Outside the Scope. The argument draws a conclusion about plesiosauromorph behavior based on the shape of its fin. Whether or not its fins were unique is not the issue.

(C) is Outside the Scope of the argument. While this fact may give support to the conclusion that the plesiosauromorph chased its prey over long distances, it has nothing to do with the argument in the stimulus, which draws its conclusion from the shape of the dinosaur's fins. **(C)** is, therefore, not a necessary assumption for this argument.

(D) is Out of Scope. Even if most animals that chase their prey are specialized for long-distance swimming, as this choice says, some animals that are specialized for long-distance swimming might still lurk and ambush. This answer doesn't lead to the conclusion that this particular dinosaur chased prey over long distances. However, it should also be noted that the resemblance of the plesiosauromorph's fin to the wing of a bird that is specialized for long-distance flying does not necessarily mean that the dinosaur was specialized for long-distance swimming. **(D)** makes the same assumption that the argument makes.

13. (D) Principle (Parallel)

Step 1: Identify the Question Type

This Principle question asks us to find a specific factual situation in an answer choice that follows the same principle that underlies the factual situation presented in the stimulus. We must first read to identify the principle, and then apply it to the answer choices.

Step 2: Untangle the Stimulus

The facts state that buying screensavers to save money can backfire and actually end up costing more money than is saved. The reason is that the interesting graphics will cause users of the program to waste time. Generalize these facts to a broader rule of thumb that might apply to a different situation.

Step 3: Make a Prediction

Generalize the screensaver program to any technology used to save costs, and generalize the employees who use the program to any human affected by the money-saving technology. Then, the underlying principle would become this: there may be unanticipated human costs associated with using the money-saving technology.

Step 4: Evaluate the Answer Choices

(D) fits the prediction nicely. It states that a security system used to reduce losses by theft (money-saving technology) can cost more in customer goodwill (human costs) than it saves.

(A) is Outside the Scope. This choice states that money may not be saved if a product is chosen based on user preferences. In the principle, money *is* saved, but it may be offset by other unanticipated costs.

(B) is Outside the Scope. The principle is not about saving money in the long run.

(C) is Outside the Scope. This choice makes a comparison of the times it takes to perform two alternative activities. This does not match the elements of the principle, which deal with the hidden costs of one alternative.

(E) is Outside the Scope. This choice compares the relative costs of choosing between two alternative products. The principle makes no such comparisons.

14. (B) Method of Argument

Step 1: Identify the Question Type

In this Dialogue/Response question, you are asked about the music critic's response to the music professor's argument. This is a Method of Argument question. Generalize and characterize the way in which the critic reasons.

Step 2: Untangle the Stimulus

The music professor concludes (Keyword: [*t*]*hus*) that rap is extremely individualistic and nontraditional because rap musicians work alone and do not learn through a formal process. The word *But* at the beginning of the critic's response signals disagreement, so read to characterize how the critic rebuts the argument. He does not disagree with the professor's evidence; i.e., he doesn't dispute that rap musicians work alone or that they don't use formal learning. Instead, he presents facts that suggest rap (1) has a traditional appeal, (2) has developed into its own tradition, and (3) often conforms to audience preferences and therefore is not purely individualistic.

Step 3: Make a Prediction

All of the answer choices begin with *challenges*. Predict what the critic is challenging and how he is making the challenge. The critic is challenging both points of the professor's conclusion. He does this by offering three new facts about rap and rap musicians.

Step 4: Evaluate the Answer Choices

(B) fits the prediction. The critic offers three observations not considered by the professor in order to counter the conclusion that rap is individualistic and nontraditional.

(A) doesn't work because the critic does not challenge any of the professor's stated premises. The critic's evidence consists of new facts.

(C) doesn't work. The critic does not challenge the professor's grounds (evidence); he challenges the conclusion. In addition, this choice presents a Distortion of the professor's argument—he is not using rap to generalize about a broader context. The context is about rap.

(D) doesn't work either. The critic does not offer alternative explanations for the professor's evidence. In fact, he does not address the professor's evidence at all.

(E) is incorrect because, again, the critic does not challenge the evidence that the music professor gives. Furthermore, the professor does not make any claims about tradition in his evidence, making **(E)** a Distortion.

15. (B) Assumption (Sufficient)

Step 1: Identify the Question Type

The question asks for an assumption that, if true, will support the conclusion; i.e., a sufficient assumption. Unlike a necessary assumption, a sufficient assumption doesn't have to be true, so the Denial Test may not be useful. If the sufficient assumption is true, it acts like a strengthener to support the conclusion.

Step 2: Untangle the Stimulus

Complicated stimuli require careful strategic reading. Use the Keywords to follow the reasoning. "Smith argues" gives us somebody's theory. The word *But* signals the author's disagreement. The word *Thus* signals a conclusion. But this is followed by the words "This, in turn, suggests." The final conclusion then, is in this last sentence: "Smith herself is not aware of the true meaning of her own words." This is supported by a subsidiary conclusion (signaled by *Thus*)—if Smith's theory is correct, we can use Smith's social circumstances to discover at least some of the meaning of her statements. Smith's theory, given in the first sentence, is that understanding the true meaning of an author's statements requires insight into the author's social circumstances.

Step 3: Make a Prediction

Look for the mismatch between the scope of the evidence and the scope of the conclusion. The author explicitly assumes that Smith's theory is correct, in which case the evidence is as follows: to understand her own true meaning, Smith must have insight into her own social circumstance. The conclusion is this: Smith is unaware of the true meaning of her words. The conclusion is likely true if Smith lacks insight into her social circumstances.

Quick note on sufficient assumptions: the conclusion that Smith is unaware of her true meaning does not *require* that she lack awareness of her social circumstances. There could be other reasons why she is unaware. However, given her own theory, a lack of insight helps to conclude that she is unaware. This demonstrates the difference between a sufficient assumption and a necessary assumption.

Step 4: Evaluate the Answer Choices

(B) fits the prediction perfectly. By her own theory, if Smith lacked insight into her own social circumstances, it would follow that she could not understand her own meaning.

(A) is Outside the Scope. The argument does not address "intended meaning," and the relative importance of different kinds of meaning is not an issue.

(C) is Outside the Scope. The argument is not concerned with Smith's intended meaning, only with her awareness of her true meaning.

(D) is a Distortion. It is not Smith's theory that lacks insight. The theory is about the relationship of lack of insight to lack of understanding.

(E) is Outside the Scope. "Intended meaning" plays no role in this argument.

16. (E) Strengthen

Step 1: Identify the Question Type

"Most strengthens" identifies a Strengthen question. The correct answer choice will contain a fact that will make the conclusion more likely to be true.

Step 2: Untangle the Stimulus

The words "This shows that" takes us right to the conclusion: "snoring can damage the throat." The evidence for this is that tissue biopsies show that people who snore frequently are more likely to have serious abnormalities in their throat muscles than people who snore infrequently or never.

Step 3: Make a Prediction

This is a classic Cause and Effect argument pattern. When the conclusion is that X (snoring) causes Y (throat damage), keep the classic assumptions in mind: (1) Y didn't cause X; (2) something else didn't cause Y; or (3) the correlation isn't coincidental. Since this is a Strengthen question, scan the answer choices for a fact that confirms that throat damage didn't cause the snoring or a fact that eliminates the likelihood of any other cause of the throat damage.

Step 4: Evaluate the Answer Choices

(E) fits the prediction with a clear statement that the throat abnormalities were not the cause of the snoring. This doesn't prove that the snoring caused the abnormalities, but it improves the likelihood, and that's all that's needed for an LSAT strengthener.

(A) is a possible 180. If true, this fact might cast doubt on the conclusion by questioning the reliability of the evidence. In any event, it's not a strengthener.

(B) is Outside the Scope. Why the patients were being treated has no bearing on the findings of the biopsies.

(C) is Outside the Scope. The argument is the causal relationship between frequent snoring and throat damage; other characteristics of the patients are not at issue.

(D) is an Irrelevant Comparison. The argument is about people who had throat surgery and snore. Whether these people were more or less likely to snore than anyone else is irrelevant.

17. (A) Assumption (Sufficient)

Step 1: Identify the Question Type

The question asks for an assumption that, if true, will support the conclusion; i.e., a sufficient assumption. Unlike a necessary assumption, a sufficient assumption doesn't have to be true, so the Denial Test may not be useful. If the sufficient assumption is true, it acts like a strengthener to support the conclusion.

Step 2: Untangle the Stimulus

This is a short argument, but short doesn't necessarily mean simple! As always, think critically as you read. The Keyword *for* in the second clause identifies the evidence. So, the argument starts with the conclusion in the first clause: one should never sacrifice health to acquire money.

The reason is that you can't obtain happiness without health.

If	happiness	→	health
If	~ health	→	~ happiness

In other words, if acquiring money sacrifices your health, don't do it, because you need your health to obtain happiness.

Step 3: Make a Prediction

This argument relies on Formal Logic. The signal for this is the word *without*, which establishes a necessary relationship between health and happiness. However, the complexity of the terms might make the use of Formal Logic confusing to start out. Instead, start by looking for the terms in the conclusion that must be tied with the terms of the evidence. Once the relevant terms are identified, Formal Logic might help.

The author recommends against the acquisition of money if it means sacrificing health in the conclusion, based upon evidence that sacrificing health makes happiness unobtainable. The assumption that ties this together would be that one should never acquire money if it makes happiness unobtainable. In Formal Logic:

If	makes happiness unobtainable	→	~ acquire money

Step 4: Evaluate the Answer Choices

(A) fits the prediction. This answer is essentially a contrapositive form of the prediction made above. Translating the Formal Logic demonstrates:

If	acquire money	→	~ make happiness unobtainable

(B) is a Distortion. Health and money are not alternative requirements for happiness; only health is needed. In this argument, money can only detract from happiness (if it sacrifices health), not create it.

(C) is Outside the Scope. The argument is not about the conditions under which health is to be valued. Rather, it is about the conditions under which one should or should not acquire money.

(D) is a Distortion. First, "being wealthy" is not necessarily synonymous with acquiring money. Even if it were, the argument does not assume that acquiring money makes one unhappy. The assumption, like the argument itself, is conditional—if it makes happiness unobtainable, then don't do it!

(E) is a Distortion, as well as an Irrelevant Comparison. The argument rests on the assertion that without health, happiness cannot be obtained. The fact that health is necessary for happiness does not mean it's conducive to happiness, nor does it have anything to do with the comparative benefits of health and money.

18. (D) Principle (Apply/Inference EXCEPT)

Step 1: Identify the Question Type

This is an unusual Principle question—two principles are presented in the Dialogue/Response stimulus. The task is to identify both Vanessa's and Jo's principles. Since this is also an EXCEPT question, the facts in four of the answer choices will be consistent with both of the principles. The correct answer choice will violate one or both.

Step 2: Untangle the Stimulus

Vanessa states that all computer code must be written by two programmers working together at the same workstation in order to avoid writing code only one programmer could understand. Jo states an exception to this rule: highly productive programmers should work alone because they work best alone.

Step 3: Make a Prediction

Four of the answer choices will be fact patterns that are consistent both with Vanessa's rule that programmers work in pairs and with Jo's exception that highly productive programmers work alone. The correct answer will most likely describe average or below-average programmers working alone or highly productive programmers working in pairs.

Step 4: Evaluate the Answer Choices

(D) is the correct answer because it violates Jo's principle. Yolanda and Mike are both very productive programmers who have been assigned to work together at the same workstation. By Jo's principle, they should work alone.

(A) is consistent with both principles. Olga and Kensuke both have average productivity, and therefore they should be, and are, assigned together. How they feel about it is not relevant.

(B) is consistent with both principles. John is not one of the most productive programmers even though he is experienced.

Therefore, his assignment to work with Tyrone, an underproductive novice, is consistent with Vanessa's principle without violating Jo's exception.

(C) is consistent with both principles. Chris is not one of the most productive programmers. Since he is more productive than Jennifer, Jennifer is not among the most productive, either. Therefore, assigning them together is consistent with Vanessa's principle without violating Jo's exception.

(E) is consistent with both principles. Kevin and Amy are both average, and they have been assigned together in order to avoid having their idiosyncrasies appear in the code.

19. (D) Inference

Step 1: Identify the Question Type

The question "which one of the following must be true?" identifies this as an Inference question. Read the statements in the stimulus and determine what must be true based upon them.

Step 2: Untangle the Stimulus

Look for the statements in the stimulus that provide the most certain facts. The first two statements provide facts about "most" pet stores in the city. Most stores sell birds, and of those, most also sell fish. This may not be much help in determining what must be true, since *most* is an ambiguous word on the LSAT. However, the next sentence states two certain facts: any store that sells fish, but not birds, sells gerbils; and if a store is independently owned, it does not sell gerbils.

Step 3: Make a Prediction

The wording of the last two statements confirms that Formal Logic will be the key to connecting the statements in this stimulus and arriving at an inference:

> *If*   **fish AND ~ birds**   →   **gerbils**

and

> *If*   **independently owned**   →   **~ gerbils**

To make an inference by joining these statements, make the contrapositive of the second statement:

> *If*   **gerbils**   →   **~ independently owned**

Using "gerbils" as the common term, join the statements to reveal:

> *If*   **fish AND ~ birds**   →   **~ independently owned**

Therefore, we know that no independently owned pet store in the city sells tropical fish but not exotic birds.

When evaluating answer choices in Formal Logic Inference questions, remember: given a sufficient condition, the necessary condition can be inferred; but given a necessary condition, nothing can be inferred!

Step 4: Evaluate the Answer Choices

(D) is the exact prediction.

(A) is a Distortion. This answer reverses the sufficient and necessary terms of the proper inference.

> *If*   **~ independently owned**   →   **~ birds**

In the facts of the stimulus, "not independently owned" is a necessary condition following from the fact "the store sells gerbils." An inference cannot be drawn from a necessary condition.

(B) is Outside the Scope. No facts link stores that sell both fish and birds with stores that sell gerbils. The only connection with stores that sell gerbils given is with stores that sell fish but not birds. This statement may or may not be true.

(C) is Outside the Scope. The word *some* to qualify stores that sell gerbils takes this answer choice beyond the facts given, since the only facts we are given about stores that sell gerbils pertain to all of them. This statement may or may not be true.

(E) is Outside the Scope. No facts allow any inference about independently owned stores that do not sell fish. The facts state that independently owned stores don't sell gerbils, and from this it follows that they don't sell "fish but not birds." But no inference can be drawn about those that do not sell fish.

20. (C) Paradox

Step 1: Identify the Question Type

The words "helps to explain" identify this as a Paradox question. The long question stem requires careful reading to establish what needs explaining. The astronomer has resolved a conflict between the ages of stars and the age of the universe by his estimates of star distances. The task is to explain why his estimates resolved the conflict.

Step 2: Untangle the Stimulus

First, the conflict is explained: earlier estimates of star distances meant that some stars were older than the universe, which is impossible. This astronomer estimates that the stars are actually farther away, which also means they are brighter. This, he claims, resolves the age conflict.

Step 3: Make a Prediction

Paradox questions are closely related to the Assumption family of questions. Usually the reason a fact seems unexplained or paradoxical is because the author of the stimulus is overlooking something or taking something for granted, much like an arguer making an assumption. Looking for the mismatched terms can help to locate what is needed to explain the facts.

In this stimulus, the astronomer leaps from the fact that stars are farther and brighter to the fact that they are no longer older than the universe. Farther and brighter, therefore, translates into younger in his argument. Look for a fact that links the brightness of a star with its age.

Step 4: Evaluate the Answer Choices

(C) is exactly the fact needed. The astronomer's estimates place the stars farther away, which makes them brighter. If brighter stars are younger stars, then this explains why the stars are no longer estimated to be older than the universe.

(A) is Outside the Scope. The ages of the stars relative to everything else in the universe does nothing to explain why the astronomer now has a more realistic estimate of their ages than before.

(B) is a 180. If more bright stars indicate a younger universe, this fact would make the conflict between the age of the stars and the age of the universe worse.

(D) is a valid inference that follows from the astronomer's statements about stellar brightness. However, it provides no information about the age of the stars, which is what is needed to explain how the astronomer resolved the conflict in the ages of the stars and the universe.

(E) is Outside the Scope. The number of stars that astronomers are able to see has no bearing on the distance and age estimates of the stars that are the subject of the astronomer's conflict.

21. (E) Inference

Step 1: Identify the Question Type

The words "Which of the following … supported by the information above" identify this as an Inference question. The facts in the stimulus make one of the answer choices true. Summarize the facts.

Step 2: Untangle the Stimulus

First, two facts about most large nurseries: they sell raspberries primarily to commercial growers, and all of their plants are guaranteed to be free of disease. *However* signals a contrasting fact: a shipment of raspberries from Wally's Plants had a common virus.

Step 3: Make a Prediction

We have no facts to indicate whether Wally's Plants is a large nursery. If it's not, no inferences are possible. If it is, then selling raspberries with a common virus might be a violation of its guarantee. However, the facts state only that "most" large nurseries have guarantees, which may or may not

include Wally's. This stimulus has lots of wiggle room. Don't waste time trying to formulate a firm prediction. Instead, think critically about the scope of the facts and be alert to the qualifying language. Elimination will likely be the primary strategy in a question such as this.

Step 4: Evaluate the Answer Choices

(E) must be true. It starts with the condition that Wally's Plants is a large nursery. This condition is necessary to make any inference, since the only facts given are about large nurseries. If Wally's is a large nursery, and "most" large nurseries guarantee their plants, it's accurate to say that Wally's diseased raspberries "probably" weren't what they were guaranteed to be. (*Most* on the LSAT means more than half, and *probably* means more likely than not.)

(A) is a Distortion. This choice presents two hypothetical conditions, neither of which permits an inference to be drawn. Nothing can be inferred from the fact that Johnson is a commercial grower, and nothing can be inferred from the fact that Wally's is not a large nursery. Joining them with an *and* doesn't help.

(B) is a Distortion. Paraphrase to identify the sufficient and necessary terms: If the plants weren't as guaranteed (i.e., weren't disease-free), then Johnson is probably not a commercial grower. (Or the contrapositive; if Johnson is likely to be a commercial grower, then the plants are disease-free.)

Nothing in the stimulus makes "commercial grower" a necessary condition following from diseased plants. Nor does it make "disease-free" a necessary condition following from "commercial grower."

(C) is a Distortion. The facts state that most large nurseries sell primarily to commercial growers. The LSAT uses the word *most* to mean more than half and the word *probably* to mean more likely than not, so it can be properly inferred that Johnson is probably a commercial grower. However, the contrapositive doesn't work when using this kind of semi-Formal Logic. It cannot be inferred that if Johnson is not a commercial grower, then Wally's is probably not a large nursery. Large nurseries sell to noncommercial growers as well, just not as many.

(D) is Outside the Scope. No facts suggest that Johnson is or is not a commercial grower, so no inference can be drawn from that. Also, the extra term *well-run* is not an element of the facts given.

22. (D) Weaken

Step 1: Identify the Question Type

The question asks for an answer choice that weakens the argument. The correct answer will provide a fact that makes the conclusion less likely to be true.

Step 2: Untangle the Stimulus

The word *so* takes us to a recommendation, which is this manager's conclusion: they should try "it" (i.e., a new marketing campaign for their newest product). The support for this recommendation is that although a new marketing campaign would not guarantee success, it is one chance to save the product.

Step 3: Make a Prediction

An argument is best weakened by undermining the central assumption. The conclusion is that they should launch a new marketing campaign. The evidence is that it could save the new product. The manager concedes it might not work. But more than that, he overlooks the possibility that a new marketing campaign could have drawbacks or costs that offset the benefit of saving the new product.

This argument follows a common LSAT pattern for Strengthen/ Weaken questions. The conclusion is a recommendation, and the evidence is a statement of the advantages of doing it. In this kind of one-sided argument, the assumption is that there are no disadvantages that outweigh the stated advantages.

To weaken this argument, look for facts that suggest a disadvantage to the proposed marketing campaign.

Step 4: Evaluate the Answer Choices

(D) fits the prediction by stating how the proposed campaign would have an adverse effect on the company overall.

(A) is a 180. If the new product is that important, this answer choice provides further support for trying the campaign to save it.

(B) is Outside the Scope. The argument isn't about the likelihood of the product failing (the manager concedes it could fail). It's about whether a potential solution should be tried.

(C) is Outside the Scope. The manager states that the campaign has a chance to succeed, even if there are no guarantees.

(E) is Outside the Scope. The argument is about the new product, not the other products. No facts suggest a link between the success of the new product and failure of the other products, or vice versa.

23. (C) Principle (Identify/Strengthen)

Step 1: Identify the Question Type

This Principle question asks for a broad rule that helps "justify" the consumer advocate's argument. That makes this akin to a Strengthen question, which means using argument-based skills to untangle the stimulus.

Step 2: Untangle the Stimulus

The words "So even though" signal a conclusion coming: the use of TMD has not been shown to be an acceptable practice, even though it poses a minimal risk to most of the population. The advocate's reason for concluding that it falls short of acceptability rests on two points: people don't actually ingest it in the manner that is considered safe, and as a result, a minority segment of the population is put at risk.

Step 3: Make a Prediction

This is a Principle question. Look for a general statement of the advocate's two criteria for acceptability: if a substance is used in an unanticipated way and puts some people at risk, it is not acceptable.

Step 4: Evaluate the Answer Choices

(C) fits the prediction by including both of the advocate's criteria for acceptability. The correct answer to a Principle question provides a 1:1 match of all of the relevant elements stated in the principle.

(A) is Outside the Scope. The possibility of risk at low doses is not an element of the principle here.

(B) is a 180. The argument is about ingestion of the pesticide on peaches, and the facts state that the majority of the population doesn't eat peaches and, therefore, doesn't ingest the TMD on them.

(D) is a Distortion. The argument mentions small children as an aside to add some emotional appeal to the statement that a minority of the population is at risk. The argument isn't about the obligation to protect small children, regardless of the conditions.

(E) is Outside the Scope. Putting pesticides on peaches is not a measure taken to protect people. The argument is not about a protective measure backfiring and causing more harm.

24. (E) Inference

Step 1: Identify the Question Type

The question asks for an answer choice that can be rejected based upon the facts in the stimulus. Therefore, the answer choice must be untrue. This is a "must be false" Inference question. Look for facts that contradict the facts in the stimulus. Wrong answer choices "could be true."

Step 2: Untangle the Stimulus

Two facts are given: the first states that the goal of the new anti-smoking law was to protect workers from secondhand smoke in their workplaces. The second says that the law cannot be interpreted to "ever" prohibit smoking in private homes. Four of the answer choices will be consistent with these known facts about the law. The correct choice will contradict the facts and, therefore, can be rejected.

Step 3: Make a Prediction

Don't waste time trying to formulate a firm prediction for an Inference question of this type. Instead, think critically about the scope of the facts and be sensitive to extreme wording, such as the word *ever*. Knowing the intent of the lawmakers, an inference can be made about whom the law will protect if it is interpreted and enforced as intended. Knowing what the law can *never* be interpreted to prohibit, an inference can be made about whom the law does not protect.

Step 4: Evaluate the Answer Choices

(E) must be false. The workplaces of domestic workers are private homes, but the facts clearly state that the law doesn't ever prohibit smoking in private homes. The extreme word *ever* allows for no exceptions. Therefore, this law cannot protect domestic workers who go into private homes. This is the answer that should be rejected.

(A) could be true. There is no basis for determining how the law will be interpreted. The facts only give one way in which it cannot be interpreted. It's possible that other aspects of the law could be misinterpreted.

(B) could be true. The intent of the lawmakers was to protect workers from a known health risk. It can be inferred from this that the people who supported the law believed it would significantly impact the health of many workers.

(C) is true. The law prohibits smoking in workplaces. No provision is given for protection outside the workplace.

(D) could be true. The fact that the law unambiguously omits prohibition of smoking in private homes could be a reflection of a general belief that smoking in one's own home is a fundamental right.

25. (A) Assumption (Necessary)

Step 1: Identify the Question Type

The question asks for an assumption that the argument depends upon; i.e., a necessary assumption. When in doubt, the Denial Test might help.

Step 2: Untangle the Stimulus

The Keyword [*s*]*o* begins the president's conclusion: to increase the number of applicants, the university needs to raise tuition and fees. The support for this is given in the president's explanation for why the applicant pool has been shrinking: low tuition and fees could lead prospective students to the conclusion that the quality of the education at that institution is low.

Step 3: Make a Prediction

Notice the mismatch in the terms of the evidence and conclusion signaled by the words "possible explanation" and "need to"—the president states a necessary solution to a problem based upon one possible explanation for the

problem. The president is taking his speculation as fact. This is a classic argument pattern: what could be true is true.

Step 4: Evaluate the Answer Choices

(A) fits the prediction. The president is assuming his explanation of why applications are low applies to this case, which leads to his conclusion that tuition needs to be raised.

If an answer choice is worded in a way that isn't immediately clear, the Denial Test will confirm the choice. Restate **(A)** in the negative: If the proposed explanation does not apply in this case (students don't equate low tuition with low quality), then the president's conclusion that they need to raise tuition is undermined.

(B) is a Distortion. The president speculates that students may believe this to be true, but the president himself doesn't necessarily assume it's true.

(C) is a Distortion, confusing a necessary condition for a sufficient one. The president states that if they wish to increase the applicant pool, they need to raise tuition and fees. By this reasoning, raising tuition would be necessary to achieve the goal, but he doesn't assume it will guarantee it.

(D) is Outside the Scope. The existence of an *additional* explanation adds nothing to the president's reasoning. His conclusion that tuition needs to be raised to attract applicants is based solely on his explanation.

If this answer choice had said "alternative explanation" rather than "additional explanation," then it would have been another way of expressing the correct assumption given already in **(A)**. Careful reading avoids traps like this.

(E) is Outside the Scope. The argument is about what is needed to correct the problem of a shrinking applicant pool and speculates that low tuitions are the cause of the problem. Past failure to increase tuition may explain why tuitions are low, but the president's argument doesn't need an explanation for the low tuition in order to make his point.

26. (E) Principle (Identify/Strengthen)

Step 1: Identify the Question Type

This Principle question asks for a broad rule that helps "justify" the reasoning in the editorial. That makes this akin to a Strengthen question, which means using argument-based skills to untangle the stimulus.

Step 2: Untangle the Stimulus

First, a suggestion is presented. The Keyword [*b*]*ut* in the second sentence signals the editor's rebuttal of the suggestion and gives the conclusion: water should not be supplied by private, for-profit companies. Support is given by the next sentence (beginning with the Keywords [*a*]*fter all* ...): clean water is essential to health, and promoting health is not the primary purpose of a private company.

Step 3: Make a Prediction

Connecting the evidence and conclusion, a general statement of the principle underlying this argument would be this: if a company's primary purpose is not to promote health, then it should not be hired to perform a service that is necessary to human health.

Step 4: Evaluate the Answer Choices

(E) restates the prediction in its contrapositive form.

(A) is Outside the Scope. The condition that a government agency be included plays no role in this argument.

(B) is Outside the Scope. Concluding that a private, for-profit company should not supply the water does not suggest that a government should. Also, the company's willingness or ability to supply the water is not under consideration.

(C) is a Distortion. The argument merely states that promoting health is not the company's primary purpose. The editor is not asserting that the private company *could* not consistently supply clean water. At most he's suggesting that maybe it won't if that's not its primary purpose.

(D) is a Distortion. In answer choices that rely on "something" or "a thing," or on vague pronouns, paraphrase by substituting in the appropriate noun to see if the answer makes sense. In this case, "clean water" is the noun. While the editor states that clean water is essential for human health, he then discusses the purpose of the private companies—not the purpose of clean water.

Section III: Logic Games

Game 1: Motel Service Appointments

Q#	Question Type	Correct	Difficulty
1	Acceptability	D	★
2	"If" / Must Be True	D	★
3	Must Be True	E	★★
4	Must Be False (CANNOT Be True)	E	★
5	"If" / Must Be True	B	★
6	Rule Substitution	A	★★★★

Game 2: Stained Glass Windows

Q#	Question Type	Correct	Difficulty
7	Acceptability	B	★
8	Must Be False (CANNOT Be True)	C	★★
9	"If" / Could Be True	B	★★
10	"If" / Could Be True	B	★★
11	"If" / Could Be True	A	★★★★
12	Could Be True	C	★★
13	"If" / Must Be True	E	★★★

Game 3: Management Skills Conference

Q#	Question Type	Correct	Difficulty
14	Acceptability	C	★
15	"If" / Must Be True	A	★★★
16	Complete and Accurate List	A	★★★
17	"If" / Could Be False	D	★★★
18	"If" / Could Be False	E	★★★

Game 4: Testifying Witnesses

Q#	Question Type	Correct	Difficulty
19	Acceptability	B	★
20	"If" / Could Be True	E	★
21	"If" / Must Be True	A	★
22	Must Be False (CANNOT Be True)	A	★★
23	Must Be False (CANNOT Be True)	D	★★

Game 1: Motel Service Appointments

Step 1: Overview

Situation: Scheduling service appointments at a motel

Entities: The six services: G, L, P, S, T, W

Action: Strict Sequencing. Arrange the six services in order from earliest to latest.

Limitations: The six services are spread out over six days. This limitation ensures a straightforward sequencing game with no blanks or ties.

Step 2: Sketch

Scan the rules to check whether this game is Strict or Loose. Rules 3 and 4 are concrete, so draw the basic Strict Sequencing sketch—list the entities and draw six slots.

G L P S T W

1	2	3	4	5	6

Step 3: Rules

Rule 1 is a basic loose sequencing rule, so pause for a moment and make sure you orient it correctly: "earlier" in this game means to the *left*. Water and landscaping can't be last and first, respectively.

W...L

1	2	3	4	5	6
~L					~W

Rule 2 is another loose sequencing rule. Since two services are scheduled after power, it can't be fifth or sixth, and neither gas nor satellite can be first.

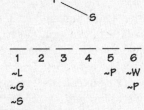

1	2	3	4	5	6
~L				~P	~W
~G					~P
~S					

Rules 3 and 4 tell you where services *can't* go, so make those notations in your Master Sketch:

G ≠ 2,3
S ≠ 2,3
T ≠ 2,3,6

1	2	3	4	5	6
~L	~G	~G		~P	~W
~G	~S	~S			~P
~S	~T	~T			~T

Step 4: Deductions

The Big Deduction in this game rests on the critical concept of *turning negatives into positives*. Whenever you learn that an entity can't go in a slot, ask yourself: Where *can* it go? What *does* go in that slot? In this game, there are four days from which three entities are stricken. Since there are only six entities in the game, deduce that each of those days must have one of the other three entities:

W...L

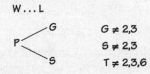

G ≠ 2,3
S ≠ 2,3
T ≠ 2,3,6

1	2	3	4	5	6
~L	~G	~G		~P	~W
~G	~S	~S			~P
~S	~T	~T			~T

Step 5: Questions

1. (D) Acceptability

For Acceptability questions, start with the rules and apply them to the choices.

To test Rule 1, look for the choice that schedules water *later* than landscaping. That's **(C)**—eliminate it.

Next, eliminate **(A)** for violating Rule 2: gas can't be scheduled before power.

For Rule 3, look for the choice that has either gas, satellite, or telephone on the second or third day. **(E)** puts telephone second, so cross it out.

Rule 4 states that telephone can't be last, quickly eliminating **(B)**. Circle **(D)** and move on.

2. (D) "If" / Must Be True

The new information in this choice effectively extends Rule 3 to the fourth day. Draw a new sketch for this "If" question, then consider what you know about the entities it mentions: gas, satellite, and telephone. All of a sudden, gas and satellite are squeezed out of the first four days, forcing them to be fifth and six. That leaves just one day for the telephone appointment: the first day.

T __ __ __ G/S S/G

L/P/W

Since this is a Must Be True question, the right choice must be true *all* of the time. That means it has to match what's in your sketch, and the only thing you know for certain is that telephone is first. Scan the choices for this fact: it's in **(D)**, so circle it and move on. The remaining choices talk about other entities, each of which could go in multiple days.

3. (E) Must Be True

The correct answer to a Must Be True question is one that's *always* true in your Master Sketch. But your Master Sketch hasn't placed any entities, and the choices themselves don't offer concrete relationships. When you encounter a situation like this, don't panic—*skip the problem* and do it at the end of the game. The sketches you draw for other problems may make the choices easier to eliminate.

(E) is the only choice that fits all of your sketches and confirms the Master Sketch. Since water can't be sixth and gas can't be first, second, or third, the only way to put gas earlier than water is to put gas fourth and water fifth. But doing that would force landscaping sixth, leaving no space for satellite. Thus, no matter where water goes, it's earlier than gas.

(A) fails because landscaping is later than telephone when telephone comes first, which happens in the second and fifth questions of the game, and the acceptable list in the first question.

(B) fails in the second question, whose sketch allows landscaping to be scheduled earlier than power.

(C) is tempting because all of your main sketches feature telephone going first. However, the Master Sketch allows telephone to go as late as fifth, in which case gas could be fourth and satellite sixth.

(D) is tempting for the same reason as **(C)**—telephone always seems to end up first—but if you place telephone fourth or fifth, water would be forced to precede it.

Here's a quick sketch that shows **(C)** and **(D)** can be false: W L P G T S

4. (E) Must Be False (CANNOT Be True)

First, translate the phrase "CANNOT be" so that you're clear on the task: the correct choice can *never* happen. That means if a choice can happen even once, it's incorrect.

Next, consider what you know about the fourth through sixth days. You know that the fifth and sixth days prohibit some entities, but when you scan the choices for a clear violation, you'll see there isn't one. Thus, you must think about the rest of the sketch. The most concrete piece of information at your disposal is the fact that power, landscaping, and water are your only candidates for the second and third days, Thus, if two of them appear elsewhere, you'll run out of legal entities for days 2 and 3.

Scan the choices again: **(E)** uses water and landscaping in the second half of the sketch, which means that an illegal entity will go in either the second or third day. Circle **(E)** and continue.

For completeness, here's an acceptable list of entities for each of the other choices:

(A): TWPGSL

(B): TWPLSG

(C): TWLPSG

(D): PWLTSG

5. (B) "If" / Must Be True

This question is very similar to the second question: draw a sketch with the new information, then pick the choice that matches what is *always* true in the sketch. The time you took to turn negatives into positives in Step 4 pays off here in a big way: If gas and satellite aren't sixth, then the only appointment that can be sixth is landscaping. Scan the choices: there's your deduction in **(B)**.

If you skipped the third question, it's worth your while to draw the new sketch. The fourth and fifth days are the only places gas and satellite can go, forcing the telephone appointment to again be first.

$$T \quad P/W \quad W/P \quad G/S \quad S/G \quad L$$

(D) incorrectly places telephone fourth, and **(A)**, **(C)**, and **(E)** all make claims about entities whose exact placement is uncertain.

6. (A) Rule Substitution

Any question that asks you to substitute a rule is a great candidate to skip on sight and revisit later. These problems can take a long time. In this scenario, if you skipped the third question, you'd go back to complete that, then move on to the next game.

When you do tackle a Rule Substitution question, look at your Master Sketch and identify the exact effects of the rule being replaced. With Rule 4 in effect, telephone can't be sixth, which means it must be either first, fourth, or fifth. Furthermore, by striking telephone from the sixth slot, Rule 4 forces either landscaping, gas, or satellite to be sixth. Look for the rule that replicates these effects.

(A) correctly mimics the rule. If telephone comes before gas or satellite, then it can't be sixth, but it could still be first, fourth, or fifth. The only concern is that if telephone is fifth, then gas or satellite would be sixth, which seems to add a new restriction by prohibiting landscaping from going sixth. However, under the rules as written, this restriction is already in place: If telephone is fifth and landscaping is sixth, then gas and satellite run out of places to go.

(B) adds a new restriction by forcing telephone *directly* before gas or satellite. Under the rules as written, this doesn't have to happen if telephone is first.

(C) appears to work because it stops telephone from going sixth. However, the current rules allow—and in fact force—landscaping to be scheduled *before* telephone when telephone is either fourth or fifth.

(D) is also tempting because it stops telephone from going sixth. However, as in **(B)**, the word *immediately* adds an incorrect restriction. Under the rules as written, if telephone is fourth or fifth, it can be immediately before satellite instead of gas.

(E) is incorrect because it precludes landscaping from going sixth.

Game 2: Stained Glass Windows

Step 1: Overview

Situation: An artist creating stained glass windows

Entities: The five colors of glass—G, O, P, R, Y—and the three windows

Action: Matching. Match the colors of glass to the windows. This is a Matching game, rather than a Distribution game, because each color can be repeated.

Limitations: Each color must be used at least once, and each window must have at least two colors.

Step 2: Sketch

Draw three windows, with space for the colors underneath. Add two slots under each window to remind you that each window must have at least two colors.

G O P R Y *at least once*

1	2	3
—	—	—
—	—	—

Note that while labeling the windows 1, 2, and 3 is convenient for your own purposes, the game doesn't actually "care" which window gets which colors—the windows aren't named in either the setup or the rules. This is a useful pattern to notice in some Matching/Distribution games, as it allows you to add more to your Master Sketch than may at first seem possible.

Step 3: Rules

Rule 1 says that green and purple will be together exactly once, so you can actually draw this Block of Entities right into your Master Sketch.

G / P × 1

1	2	3
G / P	—	—
	—	—

Rule 2 means that two windows will have rose and the third won't. Since you're not sure whether or not the green and purple window will have rose, you can't draw this rule into the Master Sketch just yet. Instead, make a note in the entity list that you'll have two roses.

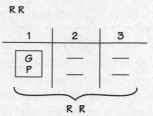

R R

1	2	3
G / P	—	—
	—	—

R R

Rule 3 expresses a Formal Logic relationship, so begin by translating it:

Y → ~G and ~O

G or O → ~Y

This rule lends itself to interpretation. Basically, this rule prevents a window from having both yellow and green, and both yellow and orange. It's the kind of interpretation that supports the "think first, then draw" approach.

Never YG
Never YO

Interestingly, this is the rare Formal Logic rule that you can work directly into your sketch. Yellow has to go somewhere, but it can't go in window 1 because it would clash with green. Place yellow in one of the remaining windows and note that green and orange can't join it.

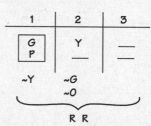

R R

1	2	3
G / P	Y	—
	—	—
~Y	~G	
	~O	

R R

Rule 4 is another Formal Logic rule that will eventually make it into the Master Sketch. First, translate it:

~P → O

~O → P

Always O or P or both

This is a useful pattern of Formal Logic rule to recognize on the LSAT. If the *absence* of one entity forces the *presence* of another, then you can deduce right away that at least one of the entities must be present. This is a huge deduction in this game, because it means that orange or purple (or both) must be in every window. Since orange can't go in the yellow window, purple must go there. Draw all of this into your Master Sketch.

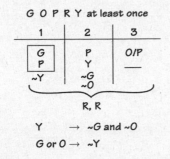

Step 4: Deductions

Since you've already drawn three of the four rules into the Master Sketch, there's not a lot of deducing to be done. Notice, however, that one rule in particular is worth focusing on before you move on to the problems: there are exactly two rose windows (Rule 2). This is the only rule you haven't taken care of yet, so this will be your go-to rule when you make new deductions in the problems.

Step 5: Questions

7. (B) Acceptability

For Acceptability questions, start with the rules and apply them to the choices.

Starting with Rule 1, **(C)** has two *green* and purple windows (there can be only one), so cross it out.

Checking Rule 2, **(E)** has only one rose window, so it's gone.

To test Rule 3, make sure neither orange nor green are ever paired with yellow. This happens in window 2 of **(D)**, so eliminate it.

Rule 4 means that every window must have either purple or orange, and window 2 in **(A)** doesn't. Circle **(B)** and move on.

8. (C) Must Be False (CANNOT Be True)

The word *cannot* in all capital letters signals that the correct choice must be false, whereas the wrong choices could all be true. The biggest clue in this stem, however, is the word *complete*. Rule 4 forces every window to have purple or orange, so before you do any more work, scan the choices to see if any of them fail to have one of the required colors. **(C)** does! Circle it and move on.

For completeness, **(A)**, **(D)**, and **(E)** could be the complete combinations of window 3, while **(B)** could be the complete combination of window 1.

9. (B) "If" / Could Be True

The word *if* signals that you have new information and perhaps will need a new sketch. Remember what you noticed in Step 4: Rule 2 is the key rule to think about in this game, since it's the only one not already in your sketch. If exactly two windows have two colors, then the two rose windows can't be both windows 1 and 2. If they were, then only window

3 could have two colors. Thus, window 3 must have rose, and the other rose window is either 1 or 2.

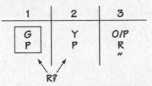

You're looking for the possibility that could be true, so cross out any choice that violates your new sketch. Again, note the word *complete*—no other colors are present.

(B) is the only choice that works: orange and rose could be the complete combination of window 3. Every other choice violates the new sketch you've drawn.

10. (B) "If" / Could Be True

This problem is very similar to the previous one. Once again, the "If" signals new information and a new sketch, and again, you'll pick the choice that could be true while crossing out the ones that violate your sketch. Window 3 is the only one that could have just rose, purple, and orange, so draw this out:

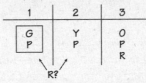

(B) is the only choice that could work. If the second rose window is window 2, then green, purple, and orange could be the complete combination of window 1. The fact that each combination is "complete" causes all the other choices to violate your sketch for this problem.

11. (A) "If" / Could Be True

This problem is just like the last two: draw a new sketch and pick the choice that could be true. This time, you're told that orange is used more often than green. Since orange can't go into window 2, two is the most orange windows you could have, which means there's only one green window. Orange has to go in windows 1 and 3, and window 1 must be the only green window. Draw this out:

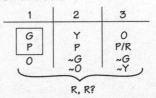

Notice that Rule 2—the key rule—is unaffected by the new information. The two rose windows could still go anywhere. **(A)** works if windows 1 and 2 are the two roses and purple goes in window 3. The remaining complete lists don't fit anywhere in your new sketch.

12. (C) Could Be True

Since there's no new information, consult your Master Sketch. Green, yellow, and orange are each stricken from at least one window, and rose goes in exactly two windows. That leaves only one color, purple, that could go in all three windows. Circle **(C)**.

13. (E) "If" / Must Be True

You need the choice that's *always* true, so you'll cross out the choices that could be true or false. The new piece of information is that rose and orange can't go together, so consider how this affects your Master Sketch. As with the third question of the game, begin by thinking where rose can go. Orange is already stricken from window 2, so if windows 1 and 3 contain rose, orange won't be allowed anywhere. This would violate a limitation of the game, so one of the rose windows must be window 2.

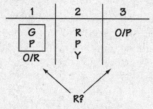

Notice now that window 2 is complete—three of the five colors are in it, and the other two aren't allowed to be. Scan the choices to see if you've hit the jackpot with purple, yellow, and rose—**(E)** says you have.

(A) may be tempting because window 1 is purple and green, but that window isn't complete—orange or rose must still be added to it because two windows must be rose and there is the limitation that every color, including orange, must be used at least once. Given the new "If" in this question, that means every window will contain either orange or rose.

(B) can be avoided by putting rose in window 1.

(C) can be avoided by not putting green in window 3.

(D) can be avoided by not putting purple in window 3.

Game 3: Management Skills Conference

Step 1: Overview

Situation: Employees at a management skills conference

Entities: Four employees—Q, R, S, T—and five talks—Fb, Gs, Hp, Io, Ls

Action: Strict Sequencing. Determine which two talks each employee attends. This requires scheduling each employee twice within the five successive talks. Here, the twist on Strict Sequencing is that more than one employee can attend the same talk. This game could also be viewed as a Sequencing/Matching Hybrid game. Regardless of how the game is classified though, the sketch would be the same.

Limitations: Each employee attends exactly two talks, and each talk holds a maximum of two employees. Start thinking about Numbers: either one talk goes unattended while the other four are full, or three of the talks are full while the other two get a person each. In numeric terms, the distribution is either 2-2-2-2-0 or 2-2-2-1-1 (not necessarily in that order, though).

Step 2: Sketch

Sequencing tends to be a dominant action when it appears in Hybrid games, so let it serve as the backbone of your sketch. Arrange the talks in order and leave space below for the employees, but don't draw any slots—as you saw in Step 1, it's possible for a talk to be empty. Don't make a notation that makes you think any of the talks *must* have an employee in them.

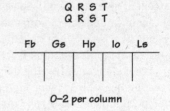

Step 3: Rules

Rule 1 limits the placement of Quigley. Make a note below Feedback and Handling People that Quigley can never attend them.

Q ≠ Fb, Hp

Fb	Gs	Hp	Io	Ls
~Q		~Q		

Rule 2 works the same way—mark that Rivera never attends Goal Sharing or Handling People.

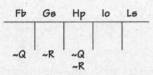

Q ≠ Fb, Hp

Fb	Gs	Hp	Io	Ls
~Q	~R	~Q		
		~R		

Rule 3 can be notated in the simplest way: simply put, Spivey and Tran are never together.

S̶T̶

Rule 4 brings in the Sequencing element of the game. Make sure your notation captures that information. Since no employee can attend the same talk twice, one of Tran's two talks must be earlier than the other one. That talk will have Quigley in attendance, forming a Block of Entities.

T₁Q

Rule 5 works identically to Rule 4. Make a Block of Entities with Rivera's first talk and one of Spivey's.

R₁S

Step 4: Deductions

Any time a game has a Block of Entities, think critically about where it can go. This simple step frequently reaps big deductions. In this game, you have a block each from Rules 4 and 5. Tran's first talk, with Quigley in tow, must be either in Goal Sharing or Information Overload. Feedback and Handling People don't work because Quigley can't attend them, and Leadership doesn't work because Tran's first talk can't be the last talk of the conference—if she attends Leadership, that's her *second* talk, not her first. Similarly, Rivera's first talk, which she'll attend with Spivey, can only be Feedback or Information Overload.

Now another classic LSAT concept comes to light: any time you find yourself saying, "It's either this ... or that," immediately think Limited Options. Blocks make great Limited Options because placing a block usually fills a significant portion of the game. In this case, placing a block of two workers accounts for fully a quarter of the game. So, Limited Options are definitely worth doing. Either block will work, but Rivera's is slightly better because her placement is more constrained than Tran's. Draw the two possibilities, noting that if Rivera's first talk is the fourth of the conference, then her second talk must be Leadership, the only talk left.

I)

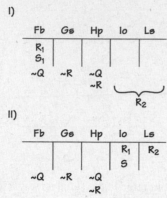

II)

Now consider what else you can deduce in each option. Quigley and Rivera are still limited as before, which is significant in Option II: with Information Overload full, Quigley must attend Goal Sharing and Leadership.

II)

Option II is starting to fill up, but Tran and Quigley's Block of Entities remains unaccounted for. The only way Tran can partner up with Quigley is to attend Goal Sharing. In that case, since Information Overload and Leadership are already full, Tran must attend Handling People for her second talk.

II)

The only thing left is Spivey's other talk. Since she can't go with Tran and everything else is full, she must attend Feedback. The entire sketch is complete.

II)

Option I is still open, but you've solved the entire game in Option II. That's the power of combining Blocks of Entities and Limited Options deductions.

Step 5: Questions

14. (C) Acceptability
For Acceptability questions, start with the rules and apply them to the choices.

The easiest rule to test is Rule 3: Spivey never attends a talk with Tran. **(A)** violates this rule.

Rules 1 and 2 are the next easiest to test. No choice violates Rule 1, but Rivera attends Handling People in **(B)**, violating Rule 2.

To test Rule 4, find Tran's first talk and make sure Quigley attends it, too. **(D)** violates this rule.

Finally, to test Rule 5, find Rivera's first talk and make sure Spivey is there. **(E)** breaks this rule.

Circle **(C)** and move on.

15. (A) "If" / Must Be True
New "Ifs" in a game with Limited Options often limit you to one option or the other. Check for that first, then draw a new sketch if necessary. Handling People can only be empty in Option I. Looking immediately for a choice that *must be true* in that option, you hit the jackpot in **(A)**: Rivera attending Feedback is drawn right into your sketch. Circle it and move on.

The incorrect choices are all statements that may or may not be true in Option I. **(B)** is wrong because Rivera could avoid Leadership by attending Information Overload instead. **(C)** fails because Spivey could attend either Goal Sharing or Leadership for her other talk. **(D)** and **(E)** don't work because Tran's block with Quigley could be in either Goal Sharing or Information Overload but doesn't *necessarily* need to be in one or the other, and Tran's second talk can dodge both by being Leadership.

16. (A) Complete and Accurate List
Always translate Complete and Accurate List questions into simpler phrasing. This one asks, in so many words, "Which talks could Rivera and Spivey attend together?" Your Limited Options are excellent here. Rivera and Spivey attend Feedback together in Option I and Information Overload in Option II. Any choice missing one or the other is wrong, so cross out **(C)** and **(D)**. The rules prohibit Rivera from attending Goal Sharing, so that eliminates **(B)**. The difference between **(A)** and **(E)** is Leadership, which Rivera and Spivey could attend together in Option I. Circle **(A)** and move on.

17. (D) "If" / Could Be False
Always check the new "If" to see whether it limits you to one option or the other, then draw a new sketch if necessary. Quigley must attend Leadership with Rivera in Option II, so redraw the Option I sketch with Quigley attending Leadership by herself. The rest of the sketch fills in nicely: If Rivera can't join Quigley in Leadership, then the only other place for her is Information Overload. Putting her there leaves Goal Sharing as the only available talk for Tran's block with Quigley. Finally, since Spivey and Tran can't be together, they must be split across Handling People and Information Overload.

Fb	Gs	Hp	Io	Ls
R₁	T₁	S/T₂	R₁	Q₂
	Q₁		S/T₂	

You've filled the whole sketch, so take a moment to characterize the answer choices to make sure you don't lose the point with a small mistake. On a Could Be False question, the correct answer could be true or false, but the incorrect answers can *never* be false. Thus, cross out the choices that *must be true*.

(A), **(B)**, **(C)**, and **(E)** directly match information in your sketch and therefore must be true. Only **(D)** could be false: Spivey could attend Information Overload instead, leaving Handling People for Tran. Circle **(D)** and go to the last problem.

18. (E) "If" / Could Be False

This problem works out almost identically to the previous one. As always, check how the new "If" limits your options and draw a new sketch if needed. In Option II, Rivera attends Information Overload with Spivey, so she can only be there by herself in Option I. This forces Tran's block with Quigley into Goal Sharing, and Quigley's second session only fits in Leadership. As before, since Spivey and Tran can't be together, they must be split across the two remaining sessions: Handling People and Leadership.

Fb	Gs	Hp	Io	Ls
R₁	T₁	S₂/T₂	R₂	Q₂
S₁	Q₁			S₂/T₂

Once again, the right choice could be true or false, while the incorrect choices must be true. **(A)**, **(B)**, **(C)**, and **(D)** match your sketch directly, so they must be true. Only **(E)** could be false: Tran could attend either Handling People or Leadership. Circle **(E)** and advance to the next game.

Game 4: Testifying Witnesses

Step 1: Overview

Situation: Witnesses testifying at a trial

Entities: Six witnesses—M, R, S, T, U, W

Action: Strict Sequencing. Arrange the witnesses in the order they testify

Limitations: The witnesses testify only one at a time and only once each, ensuring that this Sequencing game doesn't contain any curveballs.

Step 2: Sketch

Scan the rules to determine whether this Sequencing game is Strict or Loose. Since Rules 1 and 3 form Blocks of Entities, draw a Strict Sequencing sketch: list the six entities and draw a slot for each.

```
         M R S T U W
        ___ ___ ___ ___ ___ ___
         1   2   3   4   5   6
```

Step 3: Rules

Rule 1 says that Sanderson forms a Block of Entities with either Tannenbaum or Ujemori.

$$\boxed{ST} \; or \; \boxed{TS}$$

Rule 2 provides a loose sequencing relation. Before sketching it, take care to note that "earlier" in this game is to the left and "later" is to the right. Also note that no relationship is provided between Ramirez and Wong.

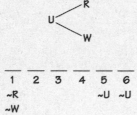

```
        ___ ___ ___ ___ ___ ___
         1   2   3   4   5   6
        ~R              ~U  ~U
        ~W
```

Rule 3 is worded differently from Rule 1, but it restricts the game in a similar way.

$$\boxed{TM} \; or \; \boxed{WM}$$

Step 4: Deductions

The vagueness and small quantity of rules suggest that this is a deduction-free game, but work through BLEND just in case. Beginning with Blocks of Entities, note that Sanderson can't be last and Mangione can't be first. Rule 2 demonstrates that Ujemori can be neither fifth nor sixth, while neither Wong nor Ramirez can go first. However, since no block is definite, you can't place anything further. No entities are Established or provide an avenue for Limited Options, and since this is a Sequencing game, there's nothing you can do with Numbers.

Finally, there is some entity Duplication among the rules, but the relationships are too vague to pin anything down.

Don't worry when a game offers few deductions: as long as you know you haven't missed anything, you can be confident that the problems will give you the information you need to solve them.

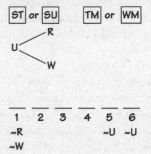

```
        ___ ___ ___ ___ ___ ___
         1   2   3   4   5   6
        ~R              ~U  ~U
        ~W
```

Step 5: Questions

19. (B) Acceptability

For Acceptability questions, start with the rules and apply them to the choices.

Checking Rule 1, **(D)** puts Ramirez after Sanderson, which is illegal. **(A)** and **(E)** put Ramirez before Ujemori, violating Rule 2. Finally, **(C)** violates Rule 3 by sticking Ramirez right before Wong.

Circle **(B)** and move on.

20. (E) "If" / Could Be True

A new "If" means a new sketch. Draw Tannenbaum in the first spot, then revisit the rules that talk about him: Rules 1 and 3. Rule 3 yields nothing useful, but according to Rule 1, Sanderson must now be in a block with Ujemori. Combine Rules 1 and 2 and examine your sketch:

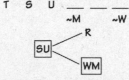

```
         T   S   U  ___ ___ ___
                    ~M      ~W
```

Four of the entities are related and there are only five slots left, so your options are limited. Ramirez and Wong can go no earlier than fourth, and Sanderson-Ujemori must either go second-third or third-fourth. Before scanning the choices, characterize them. On a "Could Be True" question, a choice is correct if it's true even once. Thus, the wrong choices will all be statements that are *never* true.

(A) and **(B)** break the game by putting Ramirez and Wong too early in the lineup, while **(C)** and **(D)** don't work because they place Sanderson and Ujemori too late. **(E)** is the only choice that could work—circle it and move on.

21. (A) "If" / Must Be True

Once again, it's time to redraw your sketch and make deductions from the new information. Place Sanderson fifth and look at the rules that mention him. Only Rule 1 does, which would place either Tannenbaum or Ujemori sixth. However, Ujemori can't go there without breaking Rule 2, so that means Tannenbaum must be sixth.

Now that Tannenbaum's been placed, look at the rules that talk about *him*. You've already worked Rule 1 into the sketch, so check out Rule 3. Tannenbaum can no longer precede Mangione, so Wong has to. This allows you to combine Rules 2 and 3.

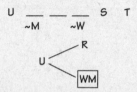

Three witnesses must come after Ujemori, but there are only four slots open. The only way everyone will fit is if Ujemori goes first. Circle **(A)** and move on.

22. (A) Must Be False (CANNOT Be True)

The question asks you what CANNOT work, so the correct choice is a statement that must be false. By contrast, the four wrong choices will be statements that could be true at least once.

This is a great problem to skip and do later because it offers no new information on a game with sparse deductions. Specifically, your Master Sketch tells you nothing whatsoever about slots 3 and 4. Fortunately, when you do come back and start to test the choices, you can stop after **(A)**. If Tannenbaum comes *after* Mangione, then the only way to satisfy Rule 3 is to place Mangione after Wong. Since **(A)** puts Mangione third, Wong is forced to testify second, which would put Ujemori first (to satisfy Rule 2). However, that leaves no room for Sanderson to precede Tannenbaum or Ujemori, violating Rule 1. Since the question asks for the choice that breaks the game, don't bother checking the other choices. Circle **(A)** and approach the final problem.

For completeness, here are acceptable lists for **(B)** through **(E)**:

(B): UWRSTM

(C): TMSURW

(D): SUTRWM

(E): TSUWMR

23. (D) Must Be False (CANNOT Be True)

This problem is very similar to the previous one, except that your Master Sketch provides some information about the first slot. Once again, you'll cross out the choices that could be true and circle the one that breaks the game.

(A), **(B)**, **(C)**, and **(E)** don't cause the game to break. **(D)**, however, makes it impossible to satisfy Rule 1. Thus, it is the correct answer.

For completeness, here are acceptable lists for **(A)**, **(B)**, **(C)**, and **(E)**:

(A): SUTMRW

(B): TMSURW

(C): TSUWMR

(E): UWSTMR

Section IV: Logical Reasoning

Q#	Question Type	Correct	Difficulty
1	Main Point	C	★
2	Principle (Identify/Inference)	D	★
3	Strengthen	A	★
4	Role of a Statement	C	★
5	Weaken	B	★
6	Inference	A	★
7	Paradox	C	★
8	Inference	C	★★
9	Parallel Flaw	C	★
10	Flaw	B	★
11	Inference	B	★
12	Main Point	D	★★
13	Flaw	C	★★
14	Weaken	E	★★★
15	Principle (Identify/Strengthen)	D	★
16	Assumption (Sufficient)	B	★★
17	Paradox (EXCEPT)	D	★★★
18	Assumption (Sufficient)	D	★★★★
19	Flaw	B	★★★
20	Principle (Identify/Strengthen)	E	★
21	Method of Argument	A	★
22	Strengthen	E	★★★
23	Assumption (Necessary)	D	★★★
24	Inference	C	★★★★
25	Parallel Reasoning	C	★★★
26	Paradox (EXCEPT)	D	★★

1. (C) Main Point

Step 1: Identify the Question Type

The phrase "main conclusion" signals a Main Point question. Bracket the conclusion and circle the choice that summarizes it.

Step 2: Untangle the Stimulus

The contrast Keyword [*h*]*owever* in the sixth line offers up the author's conclusion: Camouflage is not the reason for the fish's bright colors.

Next, unravel the stimulus piece by piece to paraphrase the evidence. The first sentence poses the question of why the fish that live near coral reefs are so colorful. The next sentence offers "One suggestion," a tip-off that this is likely NOT what the author thinks. If the author believed the suggestion, she would simply say it; she would not preface it as "one suggestion." After an explanation of the suggestion and some evidence—maybe the bright colors help fish camouflage themselves against the reef, which is, "after all," what a lot of animals do to avoid predators—you see the contrast Keyword [*h*]*owever*, confirming that the author disagrees. The stimulus ends with evidence—the corals themselves are only colored with dull browns and greens.

Step 3: Make a Prediction

Main Point questions yield themselves easily to prediction because once you've found the conclusion, you're done with Step 3. The author thinks that the camouflage suggestion is wrong. Look for the choice that paraphrases it.

Step 4: Evaluate the Answer Choices

(C) matches your prediction perfectly. It even borrows the phrase "The suggestion ... is mistaken" from the stimulus.

(A) is a Distortion. The author is not trying to convince you that the suggestion exists—that's part of the evidence introduced in the stimulus. Rather, the author's trying to convince you that this hypothesis is wrong.

(B) is another Distortion, this time because it refers to the evidence for the mistaken suggestion. That piece of evidence may be one reason to believe in the suggestion, but the presence of that relationship is not what the author wants to prove.

(D) restates evidence for the author's conclusion, not the conclusion itself. The lack of color in a reef is why the author thinks the camouflage suggestion is a bad one.

(E), like **(D)**, restates a piece of evidence for the author's conclusion.

2. (D) Principle (Identify/Inference)

Step 1: Identify the Question Type

The word *propositions* signals that this is a Principle question, but since Principle questions come in many flavors, your work isn't done. Specifically, note that you need to identify the principle, or general idea, that the stimulus adheres or "conforms" to. Additionally, the stem mentions "reasoning," which tells you that the stimulus will contain an argument. Get ready to bracket the conclusion and look for evidence.

Step 2: Untangle the Stimulus

The evidence Keyword *because* in the last sentence signals evidence, which means that the conclusion will soon follow; the author wants to convince you that the survey's responses are ambiguous. Her evidence is that the statement used in the survey was ambiguous.

The survey, introduced in the first sentence, evaluated how many teenagers believe in telekinesis. This is really just background information though, because the entire argument is contained in the last sentence. The contrast Keyword [*b*]*ut* suggests that the author isn't a fan of this survey statement, hinting at the negative conclusion.

Step 3: Make a Prediction

Notice that the evidence gives information about the statement teenagers were responding to, whereas the conclusion makes a claim about the responses themselves. Here we see a subtle shift in scope: the author takes for granted that responses to an ambiguous question are themselves ambiguous. This is the general idea ("proposition") to which the argument conforms, so look for a choice that paraphrases it.

Step 4: Evaluate the Answer Choices

(D) matches your prediction by providing the link between ambiguous ("poorly phrased") questions and ambiguous responses. Notice that the correct choice is the only one that doesn't use extreme language.

(A) is Extreme and Out of Scope. The author never mentions uncontroversial statements or their usefulness.

(B) is also Extreme and Out of Scope. It doesn't matter whether every statement is ambiguous ("amenable to several interpretations"); what matters is whether responses to such statements are also ambiguous.

(C) is yet another Extreme, Out of Scope choice. The author doesn't care what makes things unambiguous; she cares about what makes things ambiguous.

(E) is yet another Extreme choice, with its use of the word *always*. In addition, this choice is Out of Scope because it tells you nothing about ambiguity. Furthermore, whether statements can or can't always have naturalistic interpretations is irrelevant.

3. (A) Strengthen

Step 1: Identify the Question Type

The word "strengthens" tells you the question type (Strengthen) and your task: find a piece of information that supports the conclusion.

Step 2: Untangle the Stimulus

The conclusion Keyword phrase "[t]his shows that" in the final sentence signifies the author's main point: Genes are responsible for perfect pitch. Paraphrase the author's evidence: A study comparing people who have perfect pitch and people who don't found that those with perfect pitch are much more likely to have relatives who have it, too.

Step 3: Make a Prediction

This argument tests the concepts of representativeness and causality. The author claims that genes cause perfect pitch, so the classic alternative would be that something else causes perfect pitch. Indeed, the evidence—a survey, signaling representativeness—does nothing to refute this possibility. The survey compares two groups of people: those with perfect pitch and those without. For the survey to be representative, the two groups would have to be alike in all relevant respects except the one being tested, namely, whom they're related to. The author never guarantees this.

Since your job is to strengthen the argument, look for information that makes it more than likely that genes caused one group to have perfect pitch and the other not to.

Step 4: Evaluate the Answer Choices

(A) strengthens (though it doesn't prove) the argument by removing the possibility that perfectly pitched people are more likely to submit their relatives to music training, causing them to acquire perfect pitch as well. Thus, without that possibility, it's more likely genes are responsible.

(B) is Out of Scope. The personal qualities of the researchers have no bearing on the argument.

(C) is a subtle Distortion. It talks about the effect of having perfect pitch, when the argument is interested in the cause.

(D) is a 180. It weakens the argument by presenting the possibility that people with perfectly pitched relatives might get their perfect pitch from music training, not from genes.

(E) is Out of Scope. It tells you a consequence of music training, but it doesn't say that anyone in the argument does or doesn't have such training. Since the argument itself never mentions music training at all, **(E)** has no bearing on the argument.

4. (C) Role of a Statement

Step 1: Identify the Question Type

The word *role*, followed by the citation of a particular statement, gives away the question type: Role of a Statement. Find the conclusion and evidence and then think carefully about the role played by the quoted statement.

Step 2: Untangle the Stimulus

The conclusion Keyword phrase "[t]his suggests that" in the final sentence signifies the author's conclusion: The predatory dinosaur was chasing the grazing dinosaur. Since this is not the statement in question, the role of the statement is not the author's conclusion. Instead, it must be part of the evidence.

Now determine how the statement is used as evidence. The argument begins with some background information about the two dinosaurs: the dinosaurs' tracks show that the predatory one had matched the stride of the grazing one. Note this statement carefully, because it's the one whose role the question asks you to identify. This statement is important because matching stride is exactly what modern predators do when they chase their prey.

Step 3: Make a Prediction

This stimulus provides an argument by analogy: modern predators match the prey's stride when they hunt, so that's probably what the dinosaur predator did, too. The statement whose role you're identifying sets up the analogy. If the predatory dinosaur hadn't matched stride with the grazing dinosaur, then the analogy wouldn't apply.

Step 4: Evaluate the Answer Choices

(C) is a great match. It correctly cites the analogy as a piece of evidence, and it rightly claims that the statement sets up ("provides the basis for") the analogy.

(A) is Out of Scope and a Distortion. The "scientific importance" isn't relevant, and the statement is part of the evidence.

(B) distorts the statement by calling it a "hypothesis," when in fact it's evidence used to support the analogy. And it's certainly never rejected—it plays a key role in establishing the conclusion.

(D) is Out of Scope. A "possible objection" appears nowhere in the argument, and the statement isn't "counteracting" anything.

(E) is a Distortion. The conclusion is the final sentence of the stimulus, whereas the statement appearing elsewhere is part of the evidence.

5. (B) Weaken

Step 1: Identify the Question Type

The word *weakens* tells you that this is a Weaken question. Bracket the conclusion, find the evidence, and predict what kind of information would undermine the link between the two.

Step 2: Untangle the Stimulus

The conclusion Keyword phrase "[t]his shows that" in the final sentence signals the arrival of the author's voice: Sunscreen isn't likely to reduce your risk of getting skin cancer. The author's belief is based on the evidence that we've seen more and more skin cancer cases in the last 25 years, despite our increased use of sunscreen.

Step 3: Make a Prediction

The only evidence offered in this argument is a piece of research, which should have made you think representativeness. The conclusion talks about getting skin cancer in general, whereas the research is limited to the past 25 years. To weaken the argument, look for a choice that shows how the 25-year limit makes the research insufficient to establish a general claim about the effect of sunscreen on skin cancer.

Step 4: Evaluate the Answer Choices

(B) matches the prediction perfectly. It undermines the argument by highlighting the limitation of the 25-year window. If skin cancer is the result of sunburns that occurred before the widespread use of sunscreen, then the effect of sunscreen on skin cancer is impossible to determine.

(A) is Out of Scope. For it to weaken the argument, you have to assume that the most expensive brands are effective at preventing cancer and any cheaper brands are not. Choices that require additional information to strengthen or weaken a conclusion are never right answers to these types of questions on the LSAT.

(C) is Out of Scope because dermatologists are irrelevant to the argument. The use of their research can't hurt or help the study, because nothing is known about them.

(D) is also Out of Scope. The evidence clearly states that the overall skin cancer rate has gone up, so it is unimportant who is or isn't able to reduce their own risk of getting the disease.

(E) is an Irrelevant Comparison. It doesn't matter who uses sunscreen most regularly; what matters is whether those people, having used the sunscreen, are less likely to get skin cancer or not. **(E)** doesn't provide this information.

6. (A) Inference

Step 1: Identify the Question Type

You need to find the choice that "follows logically" from the stimulus, signaling an Inference question. Don't look for a conclusion or evidence; there's no argument here. Instead, accept the stimulus as fact and look for the choice that must be true. In contrast, the four wrong answer choices could be false or need not be true.

Step 2: Untangle the Stimulus

The words *Any* and *if* in the first sentence tip you off that Formal Logic is at play. Translate that sentence for clarity:

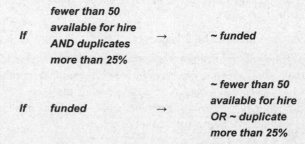

Next, you learn that the proposed department will in fact duplicate more than 25 percent of the material in an existing department. Reading strategically, notice that if this department also has fewer than 50 people available each year for hire, then it won't be funded. However, the author doesn't say that. Surprisingly, the author states that the department will be funded.

Step 3: Make a Prediction

Although many Inference answers are hard to predict, prediction is not impossible. In fact, Inference questions containing Formal Logic reward you nicely for doing so.

In Step 2, you saw that if the new department had fewer than 50 hiring positions per year, then it wouldn't get funded. But it is getting funded, so you can deduce that there must be 50 or more yearly hiring positions (the contrapositive).

Step 4: Evaluate the Answer Choices

(A) states your prediction exactly. When this kind of thing happens on Test Day, circle **(A)** and move on. Don't even consider the remaining answer choices.

(B) is Outside the Scope. You know nothing about departments other than Anthropology.

(C) distorts the information. Not duplicating more than 25 percent of the material makes it more likely a department will get funded, not less. This is a common way for the LSAC to test how well you understand the stimulus.

(D) distorts a piece of information. The stimulus says, effectively, that A duplicates 25 percent of B, while **(D)** claims that B duplicates 25 percent of A. The stimulus offers no way to find out how much of the new department the existing one duplicates.

(E) is a 180. It contradicts, rather than follows logically from, the stimulus. If this choice were true, then the new department would not get funded, but you know from the stimulus that the department will get funded.

7. (C) Paradox

Step 1: Identify the Question Type

The word *explain* indicates a Paradox question. Figure out what seems strange about the researcher's findings, and then come up with something that would explain that inconsistency.

Step 2: Untangle the Stimulus

Begin by paraphrasing the argument. The researcher tracked the beak size of two groups of birds. Both groups were the same species, but one group was wild while the other was captive. Whereas the captive birds' beak size didn't change, the wild birds' beaks got smaller over time.

Step 3: Make a Prediction

The author's dilemma is that the beak size changed for one group but not the other, even though they're the same species. However, the familiar pattern of representativeness pops up in this problem—perhaps as something the author is overlooking here. Since the stimulus presents statistical information about two groups, it's foreseeable that some difference between the wild group and the captive group will explain the different outcome. Perhaps something different about the wild birds made their beaks more inclined to shrink, or something different about the captive birds made their beaks less inclined to shrink.

Step 4: Evaluate the Answer Choices

(C) is an excellent match that rewards a thorough analysis. It presents a feature that explains why the wild birds' beaks would have shrunk but not those of the captive birds.

(A) is a tempting choice. It appears to explain why the study would have reported smaller beak sizes for the wild birds. But the flaws with this choice are extremely illustrative.

First, the answer choice requires you to make an unwarranted assumption. The stimulus doesn't say that the researchers obtained the beak sizes by capturing and measuring the birds. So the ease of doing either is irrelevant. Second, note that the stimulus never compares the beak size of wild birds to the beak size of captive birds. It compares the size of wild beaks at the end of the study to the size of wild beaks at the beginning of the study, and does the same for the captive beaks. So, even if the error in **(A)** did cause the researchers' data to report the wild birds' beaks as smaller than they really are, it still doesn't explain why the beak size decreased over

the course of the study. If it was easier to catch small-beaked birds at the start of the study, this would also be true at the end of the study.

(B) has the same flaws as **(A)**, and it's a 180. If anything, this choice makes the stimulus even more puzzling, as the greater ease of catching large-beaked wild birds (if you accept the flawed reasoning) should have made the beak size increase, not shrink.

(D) doesn't explain the paradox. The birds' body sizes are irrelevant to the apparent paradox.

(E) doesn't explain the paradox, either. The choice doesn't tell you whether the repeated beaks were small or large, so it doesn't explain the apparent findings without an additional assumption. If anything, it points out a flaw in the data collection: measuring the same beak more than once unfairly skews the data toward that bird's beak size.

8. (C) Inference

Step 1: Identify the Question Type

Since the stimulus "supports" one of the choices, you're looking at an Inference question. Summarize the evidence and look for the choice supportable by those statements.

Step 2: Untangle the Stimulus

When untangling a dense stimulus for an Inference question, work carefully to understand all of the information to find the right choice.

The first sentence introduces the topic—storytelling—and tells you that it's a "universal aspect of both past and present cultures." This actually means that storytelling is an aspect of all cultures that have existed thus far.

Note that the second sentence is lengthy. But it rewards the strategic reader for noticing that over half the sentence is preceded by the illustration Keywords *such as*. So, the sentence contains one idea followed by a series of examples. In a nutshell, cultures all across the globe and human history produce stories about the same themes.

Step 3: Make a Prediction

This stimulus contains surprisingly little information, so stick tight to what's there when evaluating the answer choices: all cultures tell stories, and all of their stories have many themes in common.

Step 4: Evaluate the Answer Choices

(C) barely deviates from the stimulus at all. Since there's so little information and the correct choice must be true, there's almost no wiggle room. If all cultures write stories about the same things, then all cultures must have at least some "concerns and interests" in common.

(A) is wrong because the author never says where storytellers get their themes. Storytellers might borrow from each other, or they could come up with the same ideas independently.

(B) is impossible to know for sure because the stimulus tells you nothing about what storytellers do or don't understand.

(D) is a strike because the stimulus doesn't tell you anything about the relative importance of anything.

(E) fails because the stimulus offers no guidance on the best way to understand a culture.

9. (C) Parallel Flaw

Step 1: Identify the Question Type

The phrase "similar in reasoning" indicates a Parallel question, and the fact that the original reasoning is "questionable" tells you that you're looking at a Parallel Flaw question. Find and characterize the flaw in the argument, then pick the choice that has the same flaw.

Step 2: Untangle the Stimulus

The little word *so* in the third line signals the conclusion: it's likely that Jackie's first child wasn't born early. When doing Parallel questions, don't forget to use the shortcut: characterize the conclusion, then look at each choice's conclusion and eliminate the ones whose types don't match. In this problem, the shortcut actually eliminates all of the incorrect answer choices.

This conclusion is a qualified ("likely") assertion of fact about something that happened in the past.

Note the ostensible conditional statement in the argument. If the first child is early, then the second child is likely to be as well. Take care to note that the first sentence is not a Formal Logic rule because of the qualifier *likely*. Thus, a first child's being born early is not sufficient to guarantee anything, and a second child's being born early is not a requirement for anything.

The flaw, of course, is that the author treats this statement as valid Formal Logic, attempting to invoke the contrapositive. Also note that the author applies "likely" to the result in both statements; he doesn't carry it over when he flips the terms. So, he concludes that Jackie's first child was likely born before its due date on the basis of knowing that her second child was not born before its due date.

Step 3: Make a Prediction

This argument follows a common pattern of LSAT reasoning in which the evidence combines a rule and a fact to produce the conclusion. The flaw has to do with the fact that the rule isn't actually a rule, but you should still sketch out the author's reasoning in the abstract to make the parallel argument easier to spot:

If	X (Child 1 early)	→	Y likely (Child 2 early)

Fact: ~Y (Child 2 early)

Thus,

If	~Y (Child 2 early)	→	~X likely (Child 1 early)

Apart from the fact that the Formal Logic rule isn't valid, this argument otherwise correctly forms the contrapositive. Thus, look for the choice that also tries to apply the contrapositive from a conditional statement but doesn't recognize that the conditional statement is qualified. The conclusion should be in the form of a qualified assertion of fact.

Step 4: Evaluate the Answer Choices

(C)'s argument matches your prediction to the letter. Using the conclusion type shortcut, **(C)** is the best place to start because it's the only choice whose conclusion is a qualified assertion of fact about the past. Hawkman I and Hawkman II are analogous to the first and second children, respectively, and the author concludes that the first Hawkman probably wasn't a hit because the second Hawkman wasn't. The quasi-rule is that if the first movie is a hit, then its sequel is likely to be as well. In the abstract, the arguments translates as

If	X (original a hit)	→	Y likely (sequel a hit)

Fact: ~Y (Hawkman II a hit)

Thus,

If	~Y (sequel a hit)	→	~X likely (original a hit)

(A) is incorrect because its conclusion is a qualified prediction. Also, this choice makes a bad contrapositive: it negates the sufficient and necessary conditions without flipping them.

(B) is incorrect because its conclusion expresses a qualified necessary/sufficient relationship ("anyone … is probably … "). Furthermore, it contains a fake rule but doesn't have a fact to pair it with.

(D) also has a qualified prediction conclusion. Interestingly, this choice is actually a sound argument. By being likely to fail, Pallid Starr meets the sufficient condition for the given rule. Sound logic can never be the correct answer to a Parallel Flaw question.

(E)'s conclusion is yet another qualified prediction. Also, it uses a rule that's true Formal Logic, whereas the original stimulus contained information that was only likely rather than definite. The flaw with this choice is the classic error of confusing necessity with sufficiency: If Tai has gone sailing, then the weather must be nice; but if the weather is nice, then you don't know anything. Remember that *only* always signals the necessary piece of a Formal Logic relationship.

10. (B) Flaw

Step 1: Identify the Question Type

The word *vulnerable* signals a Flaw question. Identify the conclusion, summarize the evidence, and then predict the flaw.

A quick scan of the answer choices tells you that the author has (1) taken something for granted, (2) failed to adequately address something, or (3) overlooked a possibility. Keep these potential flaws in mind as you read the stimulus.

Step 2: Untangle the Stimulus

This argument features the conclusion Keyword [*h*]*ence*, which makes finding the conclusion a snap: it's likely that primitive life has evolved on Europa. Perhaps a shocking claim, but the author has evidence: there's liquid water on Europa, and you need liquid water for life to evolve.

Step 3: Make a Prediction

Any time you see the word *only* in a Flaw question, check for the classic sufficiency/necessity mix-up. Doing so makes short work of this problem. The word *only* tells you that water is necessary for life, but the author acts as though water is sufficient for life: from the fact that there is water, she concludes that there must be life.

Using the potential flaws identified earlier, prephrase your answer. Perhaps the author is taking for granted that something necessary for life to evolve is sufficient for life to evolve. Or perhaps the author is failing to adequately address that other things might be necessary for life to evolve. Finally, perhaps the author is overlooking the possibility that other things are necessary for life to evolve. All three statements describe the same flaw, so be somewhat flexible in how the correct answer choice might be worded.

Step 4: Evaluate the Answer Choices

(B) says, in so many words, "Water might not be sufficient for life." Circle it and move on.

(A) accuses the author of taking something "for granted," but the thing being taken for granted in **(A)** is logically true. If a condition is necessary for the evolution of life, then life indeed could not evolve anywhere that condition isn't met. In any case, the argument talks about a place that does have water, so places where "this condition does not hold"—that is, places that don't have water—are irrelevant.

(C) is tempting because the author does take for granted that life would have evolved "if, but only if" liquid water was present. But that's not what **(C)** says. It instead connects the presence of life to the evolution of life, and the author doesn't care about the presence of life, only its evolution.

(D) talks again about there not being water, which has no bearing on the argument because Europa does have water.

(E) is Extreme yet tempting, because it appears to cast doubt on the data submitted by the spacecraft. If there's no liquid water on Europa, then life couldn't have evolved there. However, the author doesn't take for granted that "no" conditions besides liquid water could have caused the data. She states that the data "strongly suggest" the presence of liquid water, implicitly acknowledging that the presence of water may be a mistaken interpretation. Furthermore, she qualifies her conclusion with the word *likely*. Although unjustified certainty is a classic pattern of flawed reasoning on the LSAT, this author has carefully avoided that error.

11. (B) Inference

Step 1: Identify the Question Type

The fact that the correct choice is "strongly supported" by the "statements above" signals an Inference question. Summarize all of the information in the stimulus, make any deductions you can, and then test the choices to see which one must be true.

Step 2: Untangle the Stimulus

The stimulus opens with some bad news: unless an antibiotic kills bacteria completely, the bacteria will "inevitably" become more resistant to it. Identify the Formal Logic, and then jot down a translation:

If	~ eliminate	→	greater resistance
If	~ greater resistance	→	eliminate

The contrast Keyword [*h*]*owever* in the second sentence introduces more bad news: at the moment, there is no antibiotic that can kill bacteria X completely. The Keyword *no* tells you that you can translate this statement to Formal Logic as well:

If	current antibiotic	→	~ eliminate X
If	eliminate X	→	~ current antibiotic

Step 3: Make a Prediction

When you have multiple Formal Logic rules in an Inference stimulus, look for ways to combine them. Here, you can predict that if a current antibiotic is used against X, it won't eliminate X, which in turn means that X will become more resistant to it:

If	current antibiotic	→	~ eliminate X →	greater resistance

Step 4: Evaluate the Answer Choices

(B) matches your prediction perfectly. It combines the two Formal Logic relationships as in Step 3.

 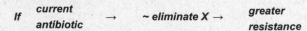

(A) is Outside the Scope. It makes a claim about the likelihood of developing an antibiotic that can kill X. However, the fact that X currently beats all of our antibiotics doesn't mean that we won't be able to develop a stronger one. The stimulus doesn't provide any information one way or the other.

(C) also talks about the feasibility of completely killing X, which is Outside the Scope. In particular, the stimulus offers no information about the effects of combining two antibiotics.

(D) distorts the information in the stimulus. X is a bacterial species, so it will grow more resistant to antibiotics over time, but that's not the same thing as becoming more "virulent."

(E) is Outside the Scope but tempting because it talks about X, antibiotics, and resistance, all of which were discussed in the stimulus. However, the stimulus offers no information about the antibiotics that have been used against X. In fact, as far the as the stimulus is concerned, no antibiotics might ever have been used against X at all.

12. (D) Main Point

Step 1: Identify the Question Type

The phrase "main conclusion" signals a Main Point question. Identify the conclusion and combine multiple statements in the argument, if necessary to complete a summary of it.

Step 2: Untangle the Stimulus

The contrast Keyword *however* in the second sentence highlights the author's strong opinion: "Such criticism ... is never sincere." To give context to the conclusion, search the first sentence to see what criticism the author is referring to. The opening line states that politicians often criticize their opponents for expressing their views in an unclear way.

Step 3: Make a Prediction

When a Main Point question features a conclusion with a pronoun phrase ("such criticism"), refer to additional portions of the stimulus to paraphrase the author's main idea. The author believes it is not sincere to criticize your political opponents for expressing their views in a muddled way.

Step 4: Evaluate the Answer Choices

(D) is an excellent match to your prediction. Don't be thrown by the long sentence: the outlying structure "A politician criticizing ... is being insincere" tells you that you're on the right track, and the middle three lines reiterate the first sentence of the stimulus.

(A) is a subtle Distortion. The author doesn't claim that incomprehensible people are insincere; in fact, she suggests that no politician is truly incomprehensible. The people she calls insincere are the ones who accuse people of being incomprehensible.

(B) is Out of Scope. The author's conclusion is about people who are not sincere; what it would take to establish that someone is sincere misses the mark of the argument.

(C) is also Out of Scope. The author criticizes a particular brand of criticism but never mentions criteria for "refraining from" or "engaging in" criticism in general.

(E) is a classic Distortion. It summarizes the last sentence of the stimulus, which is the author's evidence, not her conclusion.

13. (C) Flaw

Step 1: Identify the Question Type

The phrase "vulnerable to criticism" foretells that there's already something wrong with the argument, heralding a Flaw question. Break down the argument into evidence and conclusion, then characterize the error in the author's reasoning.

Step 2: Untangle the Stimulus

The conclusion Keyword phrase "[t]his variation establishes" signals the author's main point. Note it is densely written and requires some unraveling. Symptoms of mental illness are affected by some organic factors, and these factors, the author concludes, aren't spread equally around the world. This sentence also gives the strategic reader a clue that the central piece of evidence is some kind of "variation." Catching such clues helps you confirm that you've identified the components of an argument correctly.

The opening sentence introduces the idea that mental illness symptoms are affected by organic factors. The emphasis Keyword *surprising* and the contrast Keyword *however* in the second sentence signal that something interesting is about to come up, and this is where the author introduces the "variation" that serves as the primary piece of evidence: Among people with mental illnesses, the incidence of symptoms is very different in different countries.

Step 3: Make a Prediction

To find the assumption (and corresponding flaw) in this argument, pay careful attention to the terms used in the evidence and conclusion. The evidence shows that there is variation in the incidence of symptoms, while the conclusion claims a variation in the organic factors that affect the symptoms. Organic factors do affect the symptoms, but the author never states that they're the only things that affect the symptoms. Something else besides organic factors could affect the incidence of symptoms, too. The author has overlooked that possibility, and that's your prediction.

Step 4: Evaluate the Answer Choices

(C) satisfies your prediction. It points out that cultural factors, which the author overlooked, affect the incidence of symptoms ("how mental illnesses manifest themselves").

(A) is Out of Scope. While the author indeed never specifies how many mental illnesses she's discussing, the number of mental illnesses doesn't matter. What matters is whether the symptoms of those illnesses, however many there are, can be affected by anything besides organic factors.

(B) is a Faulty Use of Detail and also a 180. Brain compounds, which are tagged by the illustration Keywords *such as* in the stimulus, are just one example of organic factors. Even if the author has neglected to consider something about brain compounds, there may be other organic factors that do what the author needs them to do. Furthermore, the possibility that organic factors vary from culture to culture actually strengthens the author's claim that organic factors are spread unevenly around the world.

(D) is Extreme and a Distortion. The author doesn't have to assume that something is true of *any* change in brain chemistry, since her evidence doesn't hinge on brain chemistry changes. For that matter, notice that the *changes* mentioned in this choice are actually a distortion of the word *variation* in the stimulus. The *variation* in the stimulus refers to different places having different numbers of symptoms, not changes in the symptoms themselves.

(E) is Extreme. The author doesn't have to assume anything about all "mental phenomena" or all "physical phenomena," just mental illness symptoms and organic factors, respectively. Furthermore, it doesn't matter whether mental phenomena could or couldn't be "manifestations" of anything else.

14. (E) Weaken

Step 1: Identify the Question Type

The word *weakens* tells you that this is a Weaken question. Analyze the argument and then predict what would make the conclusion less likely to be true.

Step 2: Untangle the Stimulus

The Keyword [*t*]*herefore* highlights the argument's conclusion. The author predicts that privatizing national parks will benefit park visitors. The evidence is that privatizing telecommunications benefited consumers by increasing competition among phone companies. Since privatization worked for the telecommunications industry, the author predicts it will work for national parks as well.

Step 3: Make a Prediction

This argument tests knowledge of classic LSAT patterns. The conclusion is a prediction, so think critically about under what circumstances the prediction would fail. Since the argument relies on an analogy between the national park system and the phone industry, predict that the analogy doesn't hold up. If the national park system is sufficiently different from the phone industry, then a plan that worked for one wouldn't necessarily work for the other.

Step 4: Evaluate the Answer Choices

(E) rewards your excellent prediction. Privatization worked well for the phone industry because it increased competition; if privatizing parks will not produce as much competition, then the author's prediction is less likely to come true.

(A) is Out of Scope. It doesn't matter whether privatization is or isn't "politically expedient"; what matters is whether or not it benefits park visitors.

(B) is Out of Scope. Again, the question is whether or not privatization benefits consumers. Whether or not it causes other problems is irrelevant.

(C) is Out of Scope. Park visitors could benefit from a proposal with or without knowing what's going on behind the scenes.

(D) is an Irrelevant Comparison. While it may sound hostile to the author's argument that privatizing parks will benefit fewer people than privatizing telecommunications, this might just be because the number of people who go to parks is smaller than the number of people who use phones. In that case, privatization could still benefit the people who do use parks.

15. (D) Principle (Identify/Strengthen)

Step 1: Identify the Question Type

The word *principles* signals a Principle question, but since Principle questions come in many flavors, don't stop there. This problem asks you to select the principle that would "justify the reasoning" in the stimulus, so treat it like a Strengthen question. Find the conclusion and evidence and then predict the principle that would plug the gap between them.

Step 2: Untangle the Stimulus

The opinion Keyword *should* in the last line points out the author's conclusion: Fake jewels should have as much value as real ones. Unravel the rhetorical question in the preceding sentence to find the author's evidence: The two types of jewels deliver an equal amount of "aesthetic pleasure."

Step 3: Make a Prediction

This argument features a classic scope shift. The author shifts from "aesthetic pleasure" in the evidence to "value" in the conclusion. Thus, she takes for granted that if two things provide equal aesthetic pleasure, then they're also equally valuable.

Step 4: Evaluate the Answer Choices

(D) paraphrases the prediction perfectly. It's the only choice that even tries to connect "value" to "aesthetic pleasure."

(A) is Out of Scope. What jewelers should or shouldn't collect has no effect on the author's claim that fake jewels are as valuable as real ones.

(B) is Out of Scope. "Market demand" has no bearing on the argument.

(C) is Out of Scope but is perhaps more tempting because of the negative phrasing. It says, more simply, that fans of diamonds might get different amounts of aesthetic pleasure from them. However, it doesn't say which kind of diamond (real or fake) delivers more pleasure and so has no bearing on the argument.

(E) is an interesting Distortion. It offers a restriction on when jewelers should buy counterfeit jewels, which does nothing to justify the reasoning in the argument.

16. (B) Assumption (Sufficient)

Step 1: Identify the Question Type

The phrase "is assumed" signals a Sufficient Assumption question. Find the conclusion and evidence and then predict a missing link that would plug the gap between them.

Step 2: Untangle the Stimulus

The Keyword [*t*]*hus* in the last sentence points out the author's conclusion: There are more engraving than non-engraving etching tools. The remainder of the stimulus is evidence. First, all engraving tools are either pin-tipped or bladed. Next, some bladed tools are used for engraving and some aren't, but all pin-tipped tools are used for engraving. It seems reasonable, then, to suppose that engraving tools are more common than etching tools.

Step 3: Make a Prediction

What the author has forgotten is that there might be a lot more bladed tools than pin-tipped ones. For example, if there are 1,000 bladed tools and only 10 pin-tipped ones, then there could well be a lot more nonengraving tools. Only one of those 1,000 bladed tools might be used for engraving, in which case you'd have 999 nonengraving tools and only 11 engraving ones.

The author must take for granted, then, either that there are at least as many pin-tipped tools as bladed tools or that the majority of bladed tools are used for etching. Either assumption is sufficient to prevent the prevalence of more bladed tools than pin-tipped ones.

Step 4: Evaluate the Answer Choices

(B) matches one of your predictions exactly, point for point.

(A) is a challenging Out of Scope attempt. Just because all engraving tools are also etching tools doesn't mean that nonengraving tools aren't etching tools. Thus, the counterexample scenario you found in Step 3 could still occur.

(C) is also Out of Scope. It removes the possibility that a tool would have both a blade and a pin-tip, but this possibility isn't what causes the argument as written to fail—it's the possibility that there are many more bladed tools than pin-tipped ones and that most of the bladed tools aren't used for engraving. This choice doesn't address that possibility.

(D) is a 180. If the majority of bladed tools are not used for engraving, then a minority of them are. But the author wants to prove that more tools are used for engraving, not less. Notice that if you removed the word *not* from this choice to make it read, "The majority of bladed etching tools are used for engraving," then it would be correct.

(E) restates the evidence. If all pin-tipped tools are used for engraving and bladed tools are the only other kind, then you can already deduce from the stimulus that all non-engraving tools must be bladed. It adds no new information, so it can't possibly be a missing piece of evidence.

17. (D) Paradox (EXCEPT)

Step 1: Identify the Question Type

You can identify this Paradox question from the phrase "resolve the apparent discrepancy." The word *EXCEPT* at the end of the stem means you want the choice that doesn't explain the seeming contradiction in the stimulus. Look for a choice that either makes the paradox more confusing or has no bearing on it at all.

Step 2: Untangle the Stimulus

The author compares the results of two studies. In the first, adults who ate a lot of beta-carotene were much less likely to die of cancer or heart disease than their non-beta-carotene-eating counterparts. The seeming paradox is that in the second study, adults who took beta-carotene supplements got no health benefits, cancer related or otherwise, at all.

Step 3: Make a Prediction

Since this is an EXCEPT question, the wrong choices are easier to predict than the correct one. Since the stimulus revolves around studies, check for representativeness. There are quite a few differences between the two studies, so get ready to cross out choices that explain how some or all of the following could have accounted for the seemingly contradictory results:

- The first study surveyed 1,500 people; the second surveyed 20,000.
- The first study lasted 24 years; the second lasted 12.

○ The first group got their beta-carotene from food, while the second group took supplements.

Step 4: Evaluate the Answer Choices

(D) fails to hit on any of the representativeness issues you caught in Step 3. Even if only half the subjects in the second study took actual beta-carotene supplements, that's still 10,000 people who should have been less likely to get cancer or heart disease. However, the stimulus reports that "no" benefits were present. Since this choice doesn't explain why beta-carotene gave health benefits to one group and not another, it's the right choice.

(A) explains why the difference between getting beta-carotene naturally and getting it through supplements is significant, thereby explaining the paradox.

(B) explains the paradox by exposing the weakness of the second study's 12-year limit.

(C), like **(A)**, explains why getting beta-carotene naturally would yield health benefits, while getting it through supplements would not.

(E) resolves the paradox by attacking the representativeness of the first study alone. If the people who didn't get beta-carotene also happened to be the ones who smoked, then it was probably the smoking, rather than the lack of beta-carotene, that caused them to be more likely to die of cancer or heart disease. In that case, beta-carotene doesn't actually do anything, and the outcome of the second study—in which the people who got beta-carotene saw no improvement to their health—is not surprising.

18. (D) Assumption (Sufficient)

Step 1: Identify the Question Type

The phrase "if … assumed" signifies a Sufficient Assumption question. Find the gap between the evidence and conclusion and then predict a missing piece of information that affirms the conclusion.

Step 2: Untangle the Stimulus

The argument features no conclusion or evidence Keywords, so use the One Sentence Test to find the author's opinion. It's the conditional statement in the first sentence: if aliens exist outside our solar system, we're not going to find them anytime soon unless they're at least as smart as we are. Translate the Formal Logic:

| If | find aliens soon | → | aliens as smart as us |
| If | aliens ~ as smart as us | → | ~ find aliens soon |

The remainder of the argument states why: our spaceships can't reach planets beyond our solar system, and aliens

below our intelligence level won't be able to communicate with us across space.

Step 3: Make a Prediction

Though the argument seems sensible, it features a subtle but definite scope shift: the conclusion talks about finding aliens, whereas the evidence talks about communicating with them. Just because we can't communicate with aliens doesn't mean we can't find them. The author rules out one alternative—landing a ship on an alien planet—but never states that it's the only alternative. Thus, the author takes for granted that the only way to find aliens is to communicate with them or send spacecraft to their planet. Look for some variation of this assumption in the choices.

Step 4: Evaluate the Answer Choices

(D) rewards your hard work in Step 3. It says, in so many words, that talking with aliens and landing a ship on their planet are the only possible ways to find them.

(A) is Out of Scope. It talks about aliens within our solar system, whereas the argument is concerned with aliens outside our solar system.

(B) is also Out of Scope. It provides information about aliens who are as intelligent as we are, but it fails to explain why the aliens have to be as intelligent as we are in the first place.

(C) fails because it merely expands on a piece of evidence. The author already said that our ships can't reach planets outside our solar system, and this choice extends that restriction to planets within our solar system as well. However, the fact remains that we might not need ships to find aliens at all.

(E) shares the same flaw as **(B)**. By stating what's true about equally intelligent aliens, it fails to address the author's assumption that the aliens need to be as intelligent as we are in the first place.

19. (B) Flaw

Step 1: Identify the Question Type

The word *vulnerable* signals a Flaw question, and the stem also offers a hint as to the type of flaw: the author has overlooked a possibility. Find the author's conclusion and evidence, then predict what was overlooked.

Step 2: Untangle the Stimulus

The Keyword [s]*ince* in the last sentence signals evidence, and the structure of the sentence indicates that the last phrase of the stimulus is the conclusion: bulging or slipped disks ("these conditions") can't possibly lead to serious back pain. The evidence is that a large number of people had such disks yet never experienced serious back pain.

Step 3: Make a Prediction

This problem rewards your solid grasp on the concepts of sufficiency and necessity. The evidence proves that bulging or slipped disks aren't sufficient by themselves to cause serious back pain. However, they might still contribute to serious back pain by acting in concert with something else. This is what the author has overlooked.

Step 4: Evaluate the Answer Choices

(B) is a perfect match to your prediction.

(A) is Out of Scope. It highlights a classic flaw, but not the one in this argument. It says, in so many words, that something can be sufficient without being necessary. However, bad disks are not sufficient to produce serious back pain.

(C) is a Distortion. It talks about an effect occurring in the absence of a phenomenon, whereas the argument talks about a phenomenon (bad disks) occurring in the absence of an effect (back pain).

(D), like **(A)**, pokes at the wrong classic flaw. It attacks the representativeness of the survey, but the author's flaw isn't that her conclusion makes a claim about a sample the evidence is unrepresentative of. The flaw is that she misapplies the study's results due to her misunderstanding of sufficiency.

(E) offers a Distortion similar to **(C)**. It discusses the likelihood of a factor occurring in the presence of an effect, whereas the argument talks about the likelihood of an effect (back pain) occurring in the presence of a factor (bad disks).

20. (E) Principle (Identify/Strengthen)

Step 1: Identify the Question Type

Don't stop after the word *principles* that signals that you're working on a Principle question. Analyze the entire stem to determine which flavor of Principle question this is. Since you have to "justify the conclusion" of the stimulus, this Principle question is acting as a Strengthen question. Find the conclusion and evidence, then predict and bolster the assumption.

Step 2: Untangle the Stimulus

The evidence Keyword [*f]or* in the last sentence suggests that the conclusion is in the previous line: T's manufacturer is partly to blame for the illnesses, even though it didn't know that T was unsafe. The author's reasoning, given in the last line, is that the manufacturer could have prevented the illnesses if it had investigated T before letting people handle it.

Step 3: Make a Prediction

On any Strengthen or Strengthen-like problem, expect a scope shift from the evidence to the conclusion. This argument certainly delivers: the evidence talks about being able to prevent something, whereas the conclusion talks about being to blame for something. To justify this reasoning, the author must believe that having the ability to affect an outcome makes one responsible for that outcome. Look for this principle in the choices.

Step 4: Evaluate the Answer Choices

(E) is a match. If the consequences of a manufacturer's actions are preventable, then the manufacturer has the ability to affect them. And the choice says the manufacturer is responsible for those consequences if that's the case, which is your prediction.

(A) is Out of Scope. Medical compensation is irrelevant to the argument.

(B) is Extreme. It's perfect except for the word *only*. The author takes for granted that manufacturers are responsible for preventable consequences, not that they aren't responsible for any other kind.

(C) is a subtle Distortion. It holds manufacturers responsible for health risks "of which they are aware," but the author makes no such restriction: she thinks manufacturers are responsible for any health risk that could have been avoided, whether the manufacturer was aware of it or not.

(D) is a 180. Whether or not an outcome is preventable is far from irrelevant; in fact, the Illnesses' preventability is the author's very basis for holding T's manufacturer responsible for them.

21. (A) Method of Argument

Step 1: Identify the Question Type

The tell for this short stem is "proceeds," signaling a Method of Argument question. Don't worry about the author's assumptions here; focus instead on how the author reasons.

Step 2: Untangle the Stimulus

This argument is a straightforward series of facts culminating in a conclusion tagged by the Keyword *therefore*. The author concludes that Phoenix will get the contract. The contract can only go to Phoenix or Cartwright, and the author has just learned that Cartwright won't get it.

Step 3: Make a Prediction

Method of Argument problems call for you to generalize the author's reasoning. The author presents two possibilities, asserts that one is false, and concludes that the other must therefore be true. Look for a choice that summarizes this strategy.

Step 4: Evaluate the Answer Choices

(A) is a perfect summary of both the argument and your prediction.

(B) is a 180. The author's inference is based on a claim that an event will not occur, not that it will.

(C) is also a 180. The author supports, not refutes, a claim that something is inevitable (Phoenix getting the contract) by establishing the impossibility, not possibility, of an alternative event (Cartwright getting the contract).

(D) fails because the author bases her conclusion on a single event, not on "an established pattern" of several events.

(E), like the other wrong choices, incorrectly characterizes the author's evidence. The author bases her claim on a single concrete fact (Cartwright not getting the contract); at no point does she offer a "general statistical statement."

22. (E) Strengthen

Step 1: Identify the Question Type

The word *supports* marks this as a classic Strengthen stem. Find the evidence and conclusion and then predict what would make the conclusion more likely. The stem offers a bonus by telling you that you're supporting "the researchers' hypothesis," so you know what the conclusion will be.

Step 2: Untangle the Stimulus

The researchers' hypothesis appears in the last sentence: children are less likely to develop allergies if they're exposed to germs as infants. The researchers base this hypothesis on the fact that allergies are less common among children from larger families.

Step 3: Make a Prediction

Like many Strengthen stimuli, this one features a couple of gaps between the evidence and the conclusion. First, the conclusion talks about germs, which don't appear in the evidence at all. Instead, the evidence talks about growing up in a large family. The author must take for granted that growing up in a large family exposes you to more germs.

It so happens that this is a pretty reasonable assumption—being around lots of people does, presumably, expose one to more germs. Thus, consider what else the author takes for granted: she must believe that it's the increased exposure to germs—and not some other quality of children from larger families—that accounts for the lack of allergies. Consider both of the author's assumptions when you evaluate the choices.

Step 4: Evaluate the Answer Choices

(E) provides a match for your second assumption. Entering day care is like growing up in a larger family: children in day care are surrounded by more people and thus get exposed to more germs. **(E)** compares children from small families who entered day care and those who did not, and finds that those who did were less likely to get allergies. This corroborates the

author's assumption that being exposed to more germs is the key distinguishing quality of children who don't get allergies.

(A) is a Distortion. If allergies increase when average family size decreases, then that would seem to support the author's argument. Notice, however, that this actually confirms the author's evidence, not her conclusion. To support the link between the evidence and the conclusion, you either need to show that being around more people exposes one to more germs or that the increased exposure to germs—and not some other difference between children from large families and children from small ones—is the cause of the difference in allergy incidence.

(B) is a perfect 180. It weakens the hypothesis by presenting a factor other than germ exposure that makes children from large families less likely to get allergies.

(C) is an Irrelevant Comparison. The author is concerned with the factors that make people more or less likely to develop allergies; the relative deadliness of allergies and germs is beside the point.

(D) is a 180 similar to **(B)**. It states that hereditary factors play an important role in determining allergy incidence among children, making it less likely that germ exposure makes any difference.

23. (D) Assumption (Necessary)

Step 1: Identify the Question Type

The word *assumption* clearly marks this as an Assumption question. Bracket the conclusion, find the evidence, and then predict what the author left out.

Step 2: Untangle the Stimulus

The little but significant Keyword [*s*]*o* in the last sentence signifies the conclusion: Some of Hollywood's earliest movies will perish. The evidence points out that transferring movies from unstable to stable material is laborious and expensive, and that there's no way we'll be able to save all the movies currently on unstable material before some of them disintegrate.

Step 3: Make a Prediction

Even the most difficult and reasonable-seeming arguments have a scope shift somewhere, and this argument is no exception. The conclusion brings up "films from the earliest years of Hollywood," which the evidence never mentions; instead, the evidence talks about preserving movies in general. Thus, the author must take for granted that Hollywood's earliest movies need preserving in the first place.

Step 4: Evaluate the Answer Choices

(D) fits the bill. The author must assume that "some" (at least one) of Hollywood's earliest movies still exist on unstable material. If none of them do, then none of them need saving, and the argument falls apart.

(A) is Extreme and Out of Scope. The author doesn't have to assume that our current technology for preserving movies will never get an update, because the evidence already asserts that we won't be able to finish preserving every movie before some of them disintegrate. On Assumption questions, choices that directly argue with the evidence are always wrong.

(B) is an Irrelevant Comparison that fails for a similar reason to **(A)**. It doesn't matter if there are cheaper ways to preserve movies because, again, the evidence already assures you that some movies will be lost. Avoid choices that argue with the evidence.

(C) is a Distortion. At first glance, it appears to match your prediction by stating that not many of Hollywood's earliest movies have already been moved to stable film. It would seem, then, that a lot of films from the earliest years of Hollywood still require preservation. This isn't actually true, however, due to the fuzziness of the phrase "not many." On the LSAT, "many" and "not many" mean exactly the same thing, as the term "many" is subjective. One out of 100 infants getting a life-threatening disease might be considered "many," for example. Thus, if there are 100 early Hollywood movies that need saving, then 99 of them could already have been saved as far as "not many" is concerned.

For this choice to work, you have to assume that "not many" represents a substantial majority of Hollywood's earliest movies, and choices that require such an assumption are never right on the LSAT.

(E) is another Irrelevant Comparison. What matters is whether or not any of Hollywood's earliest movies will be lost; the relative popularity of the perished movies has no bearing on the argument.

24. (C) Inference

Step 1: Identify the Question Type

Your task is to "logically complete" the stimulus, so this is an Inference question. Wrap your head around the given information and then find the choice that it logically supports.

Step 2: Untangle the Stimulus

This stimulus deals with the old wives' tale that weather affects arthritis. A study found no correlation between various features of the weather and arthritic flare-ups. The researchers also surveyed the people who believed in the myth and found that these people gave "widely varying" estimates of how long it takes for the pain to kick in after the supposed arthritis-inducing weather occurs.

Step 3: Make a Prediction

Since there's no correlation between weather and arthritis pain, and since the people who believe in a correlation can't seem to agree on when the pain starts after the weather changes, the study points to one thing: arthritis isn't actually affected by the weather. Look for some version of this conclusion in the choices.

Step 4: Evaluate the Answer Choices

(C) is your match. If the correlation is being imagined, then it's not real.

(A) is a Distortion. The fact that there were "widely varying accounts of the time delay" between weather changes and the arrival of bad pain is given as evidence that there was no connection between the weather and the pain, not that some people were more quickly affected by the weather than others. According to the stimulus, the weather doesn't affect arthritis at all.

(B) may be true, but it's Out of Scope. It offers no information about people's assessments of pain "intensity."

(D), like **(A)**, is a Distortion. It claims that weather in some way affects arthritis, which contradicts the entire point of the stimulus.

(E) is Extreme and also contradicts the stimulus. The author makes a claim about the links between weather and arthritis (there aren't any), so she surely doesn't believe that scientific investigation into the matter is "impossible."

25. (C) Parallel Reasoning

Step 1: Identify the Question Type

The stem asks you to compare the reasoning of the stimulus to the reasoning in the choices, heralding a Parallel question. Characterize the conclusion and use the conclusion type shortcut to eliminate some choices; then characterize the whole argument if more than one choice remains.

Step 2: Untangle the Stimulus

The word *so* in the last sentence tags the conclusion: if you're looking for a job, move to a city with high-tech businesses. This conclusion expresses a Formal Logic relationship about what people with a certain goal ought to do, so the correct choice's conclusion must do the same. The author's evidence is that cities with high-tech businesses tend to have healthy economies and cities with healthy economies tend to have many job openings.

Step 3: Make a Prediction

Processing the lengthy choices in a Parallel problem can be challenging, so strip the argument to its barest abstract elements. In a nutshell, the author argues as follows:

X tends to have Y.

Y tends to have Z.

So, if you want Z, do X.

Look for the choice that has the same structure.

Step 4: Evaluate the Answer Choices

(C) fits the structure you predicted:

X (antique dealers) tend to have Y (authenticated antiques).

Y (authenticated antiques) tend to be Z (valuable).

So, if you want Z (valuable antiques) do X (buy them from an antique dealer).

(A) has the correct type of conclusion, but it has four variables instead of three: old antiques, being valuable, antique dealers, and authenticated ages. Antiques whose ages have been authenticated are not necessarily old.

(B) also has the right type of conclusion, but it is riddled with scope shifts. The evidence talks about antique dealers who authenticate the ages of their antiques, whereas the conclusion talks about antique dealers in general. Furthermore, the author shifts from antiques being plentiful to their being valuable.

(D) is eliminated by its conclusion type. The conclusion makes a statement about what people do, not what they ought to do.

(E), unlike **(A)** and **(B)**, has too few variables. The first sentence is background filler that doesn't actually support the conclusion, and the entire argument is contained in the last line: X (antique dealers) have lots of Y (valuable antiques), so people who want Y should head over to X.

26. (D) Paradox (EXCEPT)

Step 1: Identify the Question Type

The word *explain* signals a Paradox question. Since the stem ends with *EXCEPT*, look for the choice that *doesn't* resolve the seeming contradiction in the stimulus.

Step 2: Untangle the Stimulus

The stimulus presents the findings of a study that looked at poverty and malnourishment among old and young people. In the 66 and older group, more people were malnourished than impoverished; in the 65 and younger group, the opposite was true—more people were impoverished than malnourished. In other words, some people in the older group had enough money to buy food yet were malnourished, while some people in the younger group were very poor yet *weren't* malnourished. This is the paradox.

Step 3: Make a Prediction

On a Paradox EXCEPT question, the wrong choices are easier to predict than the correct one. Since the study looked at two different groups, predict that some difference between the

two groups accounts for the study's results. Specifically, cross out any choice that explains either of the following:

1. How old people can be malnourished without being poor

2. How young people can be poor without being malnourished

Step 4: Evaluate the Answer Choices

(D) is the only choice that doesn't highlight a relevant difference between the two groups. It states that both groups are equally likely to be impoverished, but this doesn't explain how old people can be malnourished without being impoverished or how young people can be impoverished without being malnourished.

(A) explains the paradox in a roundabout way. If doctors incorrectly diagnose malnutrition among older patients, then many more old people are malnourished than was reported by the study.

(B) explains the paradox more directly. If older people take medications that increase their need for nutrients, then the medications might cause malnutrition regardless of the patient's wealth.

(C) explains the paradox in yet another way: if older people are more likely to lose their appetite, then they won't eat as much, which may cause them to become malnourished even if they have the means to feed themselves.

(E) provides one more biological explanation for older people's malnutrition: interference with their digestion.

PrepTest 63

The Inside Story

PrepTest 63 was administered in June 2011. It challenged 26,812 test takers. What made this test so hard? Here's a breakdown of what Kaplan students who were surveyed after taking the official exam considered PrepTest 63's most difficult section.

Hardest PrepTest 63 Section as Reported by Test Takers

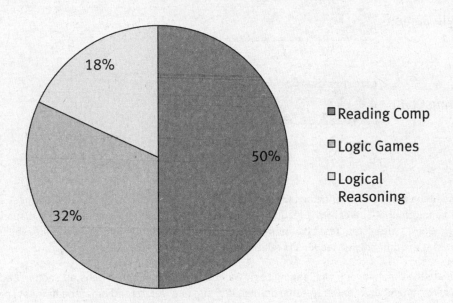

PrepTest 63 is an outlier. It marks the only time since 2010 that at least half of students considered Reading Comprehension the hardest section on the LSAT. Indeed, it is one of only three LSAT administrations during that time that Reading Comprehension was the top vote-getter in the survey. Were you to base your opinion only on these results, you might think that studying Reading Comp is the key to LSAT success. Well, Reading Comp is important, but test takers' perceptions don't tell the whole story. For that, you need to consider students' actual performance. The following chart shows the average number of students to miss each question in each of PrepTest 63's different sections.

Percentage Incorrect by PrepTest 63 Section Type

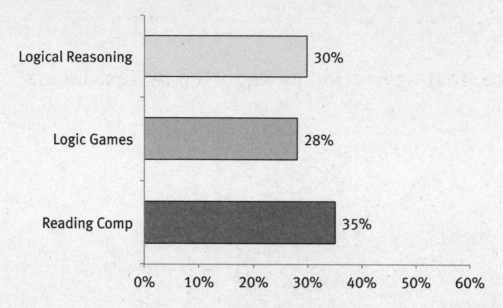

Actual student performance tells quite a different story. On average, Reading Comprehension was the toughest section, but not nearly by the overwhelming margin that "perceived difficulty" suggests. On most exams, we see a similar disparity between the perceived difficulty of Logic Games and actual test taker performance in that section. On almost every released LSAT, actual performance results show that the difficulty of sections is relatively equal.

Maybe students overestimate the difficulty of a challenging Logic Games or Reading Comprehension section because a very hard game or passage is so easy to remember after the test. In contrast, it's much harder to remember the hardest Logical Reasoning questions when there are a total of 50 or 51 LR questions on the test. The truth is that the testmaker places hard questions throughout the test, and students striving for a top score want to be prepared for all of them. As tough as the Reading Comprehension section was on PrepTest 63, it contained only three of the exam's ten hardest questions, while five of the ten hardest were in Logical Reasoning. Here were the locations of the 10 hardest (most missed) questions in the exam.

Locations of 10 Most Difficult Questions in PrepTest 63

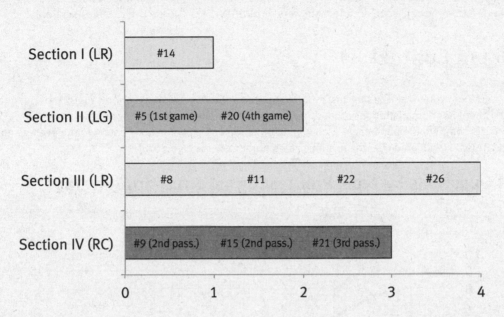

The takeaway from this data is that, to maximize your potential on the LSAT, you need to take a comprehensive approach. Test yourself rigorously, and review your performance on every section of the test. Kaplan's LSAT explanations provide the expertise and insight you need to fully understand your results. The explanations are written and edited by a team of LSAT experts, who have helped thousands of students improve their scores. Kaplan always provides data-driven analysis of the test, ranking the difficulty of every question based on actual student performance. The 10 hardest questions on every test are highlighted with a 4-star difficulty rating, the highest we give. The analysis breaks down the remaining questions into 1-, 2-, and 3-star ratings so that you can compare your performance to that of thousands of other test takers on all LSAC material.

Don't settle for wondering whether a question was really as hard as it seemed to you. Analyze the test with real data, and learn the secrets and strategies that help top scorers master the LSAT.

7 Can't–Miss Features of PrepTest 63

- In Logical Reasoning, PrepTest 63 was light on Assumption Family questions, with Assumption, Flaw, and Strengthen/ Weaken questions combined accounting for only 21 questions. That marked the lowest total since PrepTest 43 (June 2004) which had just 20.
- For an unusual LR question stem check out Section 3, Question 22: "From which one of the following sets of facts can the conclusion be properly drawn using the principle?" It's a one-of-a-kind Apply the Principle question that functions like a Sufficient Assumption question.
- Although they were once pretty common, this test featured a Weaken EXCEPT question for the first time since PrepTest 50 (September 2006).
- PrepTest 63's Logic Games section featured *three* Strict Sequencing games. The final game of the LG section is an excellent example of how the LSAT can put a twist on Sequencing tasks. The setup is a sequence of six positions, but arranged vertically, and there are only three entities used (which can repeat) to take up the six slots. To date, there has never been another game that used both of those variations simultaneously.
- This was the first test since PrepTest 46 (June 2005) in which none of the games really involved a conditional rule that was worth noting in Formal Logic. There is a Distribution rule about entities that can't be together and a Sequencing rule about an entity that goes first or last, but nothing that corresponds to standard "If-then" statement.

- On PrepTest 63, the Comparative Reading set of passages was the fourth set for just the second time ever as of the release of this test.
- If you're looking for an automobile club or some consumer protection, you'll find three consecutive correct answers of (A)(A)(A) in LR and three consecutive correct answers of (B)(B)(B) in this test's Logic Games section!

PrepTest 63 in Context

As much fun as it is to find out what makes a PrepTest unique or noteworthy, it's even more important to know just how representative it is of other LSAT administrations (and, thus, how likely it is to be representative of the exam you will face on Test Day). The following charts compare the numbers of each kind of question and game on PrepTest 63 to the average numbers seen on all officially released LSATs administered over the past five years (from 2012 through 2016).

Number of LR Questions by Type: PrepTest 63 vs. 2012–2016 Average

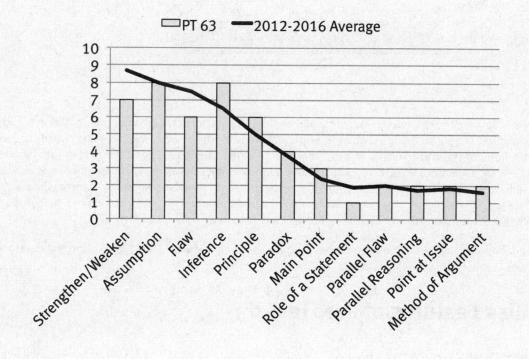

KAPLAN

Number of LG Games by Type: PrepTest 63 vs. 2012–2016 Average

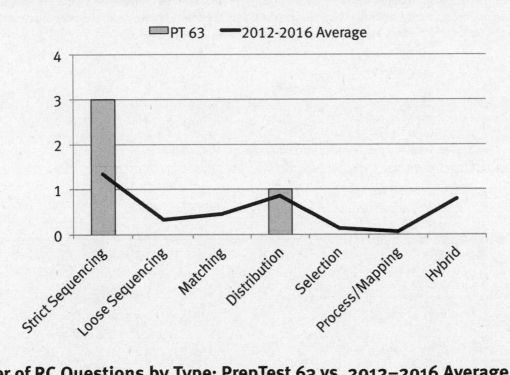

Number of RC Questions by Type: PrepTest 63 vs. 2012–2016 Average

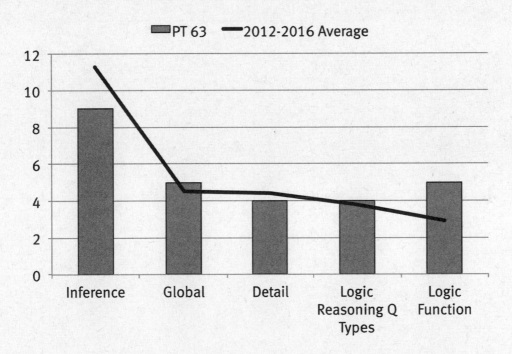

There isn't usually a huge difference in the distribution of questions from LSAT to LSAT, but if this test seems harder (or easier) to you than another you've taken, compare the number of questions of the types on which you, personally, are strongest and weakest. And then, explore within each section to see if your best or worst question types came earlier or later.

Students in Kaplan's comprehensive LSAT courses have access to every released LSAT, and to an online Q-Bank with thousands of officially released questions, games, and passages. If you are studying on your own, you have to do a bit more work to identify your strengths and your areas of opportunity. Quantitative analysis (like that in the charts shown here) is an important tool for understanding how the test is constructed, and how you are performing on it.

Section I: Logical Reasoning

Q#	Question Type	Correct	Difficulty
1	Inference	C	★
2	Weaken	B	★
3	Flaw	C	★
4	Paradox	D	★
5	Assumption (Necessary)	B	★
6	Inference	A	★★
7	Weaken (EXCEPT)	B	★★★
8	Main Point	E	★★
9	Inference	D	★
10	Assumption (Sufficient)	A	★★
11	Principle (Identify/Strengthen)	D	★
12	Inference	B	★
13	Main Point	D	★
14	Point at Issue	D	★★★★
15	Principle (Identify/Strengthen)	C	★
16	Strengthen	D	★
17	Method of Argument	C	★
18	Strengthen	E	★★
19	Assumption (Necessary)	C	★★
20	Inference	B	★★★
21	Parallel Reasoning	E	★★★
22	Principle (Identify/Strengthen)	B	★★
23	Flaw	B	★★
24	Parallel Flaw	E	★★★
25	Flaw	A	★★

1. (C) Inference

Step 1: Identify the Question Type

The question stem asks you to fill in the blank that ends the stimulus, so it's an Inference question. Based on what's given, try to predict the logical ending of the argument.

Step 2: Untangle the Stimulus

The stimulus is essentially a recommendation to grow stinging nettles next to potato plants to boost the potato plants' yield. Stinging nettles attract insects that kill potato plant pests, but they also attract aphids that are potentially harmful to potato plants. Despite the mixed evidence, the author ends by leaving the recommendation unchanged.

Step 3: Make a Prediction

If the author ends the passage by upholding the recommendation despite the aphid issue, then he must believe that the benefits of planting stinging nettles outweigh the problems with aphids. Since this is an Inference question, you don't need to predict the answer exactly. But you can approach the answer choices with a flexible prediction—in this case, a reason why aphids aren't enough of a problem to dissuade gardeners from planting stinging nettles.

Step 4: Evaluate the Answer Choices

(C) matches this prediction. If the aphids attracted by stinging nettles aren't the kinds that harm potato plants, then the author's recommendation stands.

(A) doesn't convince us that the aphids won't be prohibitively harmful to the potato plants, so it doesn't give us a reason to follow the author's recommendation.

(B) misses the mark because the issue isn't the risk of damage to stinging nettles; it's the risk of damage to potato plants.

(D) introduces other potentially harmful organisms, but those organisms fall Outside the Scope of the argument, which hinges on whether the advantages of stinging nettles outweigh the disadvantages.

(E) also introduces an Out-of-Scope concept: food plants other than potato plants.

2. (B) Weaken

Step 1: Identify the Question Type

Anytime a question stem asks for the answer that "calls into question" an author's conclusion, it's seeking a weakener.

Step 2: Untangle the Stimulus

The zookeeper's conclusion is that Jocko kept silent strategically in order to keep the other chimps away from his food. The zookeeper bases this conclusion on an experiment. When Jocko was given a large quantity of bananas, he uttered a bark that drew the other chimps, who stole his food. The next day, Jocko was given just one banana and kept silent.

Step 3: Make a Prediction

The most straightforward way to weaken an argument is to undermine its central assumption. Here, the zookeeper assumes that Jocko *strategized* to keep quiet in order to guard his food. That means the zookeeper is likewise assuming that difference in the quantity of food Jocko was given didn't make the difference in his decision to utter a food bark. He assumes Jocko didn't think, "Hey, here's a bunch of bananas; I'll call the others," versus "Oh, a single banana—no reason to call out." If quantity does make a difference, then it could account for Jocko's decision not to bark the second time.

Step 4: Evaluate the Answer Choices

(B) directly attacks the author's assumption. If Jocko kept silent because the quantity of food was small on the second day, then he wasn't deliberately trying to keep the other chimps from stealing his food, and the zookeeper's conclusion is in doubt.

(A) doesn't affect the argument. There's no evidence as to whether bananas are Jocko's favorite food. Furthermore, the type of food didn't change from one day to the next.

(C) also has no effect. Why the chimps took Jocko's food on the first day is unimportant, since the zookeeper is making an argument about Jocko's motivation for keeping silent.

(D), even if true, doesn't hurt the argument. Whether or not the noises are signals has no effect on the zookeeper's explanation for Jocko's silence.

(E), like **(A)**, deals with food preference, which is Outside the Scope.

3. (C) Flaw

Step 1: Identify the Question Type

The word "flaw" in the question stem tells you this is a Flaw question. Look for an unacceptable disconnect between evidence and conclusion.

Step 2: Untangle the Stimulus

The argument concludes that the publishing business bases its trends on false assumptions about public tastes. The only evidence is a survey of journalism students in which most preferred serious stories to the more trivial coverage that seems to dominate their field.

Step 3: Make a Prediction

When an argument in a Flaw question is based entirely on a survey, look for issues of representativeness. Here, instead of consulting a randomly chosen sample of the public at large, the survey only consults journalism students—a population that would have a distinct point of view about current trends in their own field. So the conclusion (about the "interests of the public") relies on an unrepresentative sample in the evidence.

Step 4: Evaluate the Answer Choices

(C) matches the prediction perfectly.

(A) is off because the argument isn't causal at all.

(B) misses the mark because the author never discusses anyone's intentions, let alone any "effects" produced.

(D) accuses the author of attacking the argument's opponents, but no such attacks occur.

(E) doesn't happen in the argument, either. The author does support the conclusion of the argument; it's just that there are problems with the reliability of the support.

4. (D) Paradox

Step 1: Identify the Question Type

This is a Paradox question because it asks for the answer that "accounts for" something unexplained in the stimulus.

Step 2: Untangle the Stimulus

In a Paradox stimulus, focus on the claims or statements that appear to be at odds. Here, you learn that electric bug zappers apparently work very well to control flying pests. However, pest control experts advise people to use insect-eating birds or insecticide sprays instead of bug zappers.

Step 3: Make a Prediction

Once you define the paradox, don't waste too much time trying to predict the exact language of the correct answer. Just make sure you know what the correct choice must explain. Here, go into the answer choices prepared to select the answer that explains why pest controllers would discourage using bug zappers despite their effectiveness at killing flying pests. There must be some other consideration that trumps that effectiveness.

Step 4: Evaluate the Answer Choices

(D) provides that consideration. If the insects killed by the bug zappers are generally more beneficial than those killed by birds and insecticides, then that explains why pest control experts would be reluctant to use zappers.

(A) doesn't provide any new information about the bug zappers that would justify the pest control experts' recommendation. It just provides a potential benefit about birds (i.e., they are likely to remain in the area if given certain things).

(B) is an Irrelevant Comparison. It doesn't give a reason not to use bug zappers, and it certainly doesn't show any advantage to using birds or insecticides.

(C) is far Outside the Scope of the stimulus because it deals with electricity use and light sources, which presumably have no effect on the usefulness of bug zappers as insect killers.

(E), like **(A)**, doesn't provide any new information about the bug zappers that would justify the pest control experts' recommendation. It just provides a potential benefit of the insecticides (i.e., they are not harmful to people, birds, or pets).

5. (B) Assumption (Necessary)

Step 1: Identify the Question Type

The question stem asks for the assumption that the argument "depends on." The right answer will therefore be an unspoken piece of evidence that must be true for the conclusion to follow from the evidence.

Step 2: Untangle the Stimulus

The conclusion is signaled by *hence*: Rocks placed in Japanese gardens should vary widely in appearance, just as they do in nature. This is because Japanese gardens should be designed to show harmony with nature.

Step 3: Make a Prediction

Notice the key term *harmony* in the evidence. In order to make her recommendation, the gardener assumes that choosing rocks that make the garden appear natural is a way to display harmony with nature.

Step 4: Evaluate the Answer Choices

(B) is a good match for the prediction. It must be true in order for the argument to be valid. If **(B)** is untrue—if imitating nature doesn't help to achieve harmony with nature—then there's no reason to follow the gardener's recommendation.

(A) goes wrong with "every key value" because the argument is concerned with just one value—displaying harmony with nature.

(C) is Extreme. Perhaps there are other criteria as well for selecting rocks. The gardener's just recommending a course of action to meet one criterion.

(D) is a Distortion of the argument. The gardener isn't equating *expressing* harmony with being natural. She's assuming that *imitating* nature helps realize the ideal of harmony.

(E) is not necessary for the argument to be valid. It doesn't connect the standard of harmony with the gardener's recommendation for rock selection.

6. (A) Inference

Step 1: Identify the Question Type

This is an Inference question since it asks you to find the answer choice that must be true based on the statements in the stimulus.

Step 2: Untangle the Stimulus

Don't be intimidated by the jargon; you need no outside knowledge for Inference questions. Here's what the stimulus says. Vacuum tubes can resist greater amounts of heat than can semiconductor parts. This would make vacuum tubes preferable to semiconductors in digital circuits, but they'd also need to be comparable to semiconductors in all other ways. (The Keywords "only if" signal a necessary condition in Formal Logic.) However, vacuum tubes and semiconductors are not comparable in one major way: current capacity.

Step 3: Make a Prediction

Sometimes for Inference questions, you can put a prediction together based on the stimulus. If vacuum tubes aren't comparable to semiconductors in every way, then the tubes don't meet a necessary condition for being preferable to semiconductors. Hence, vacuum tubes aren't preferable to semiconductors in digital circuits.

Step 4: Evaluate the Answer Choices

(A) says that current vacuum tubes can't beat semiconductors for digital circuits.

(B) is a Distortion. There's no indication that the difference in current capacity is the only thing standing in the way of using vacuum tubes in digital circuits or that there is any hope that vacuum tubes will be able to match the current capacity of digital circuits.

(C) fails for the same reason as **(B)**. There could be other factors (shape and size, for instance) that make vacuum tubes unsuitable for use in digital circuits.

(D) is Outside the Scope; it discusses applications other than digital circuits, which the stimulus doesn't discuss.

(E) is Extreme (a common wrong answer type in Inference questions). Vacuum tubes could have advantages over semiconductors other than those discussed in the stimulus.

7. (B) Weaken (EXCEPT)

Step 1: Identify the Question Type

The question stem indicates that four of the answer choices will weaken the argument; the one correct answer will either strengthen the argument or have no effect on it.

Step 2: Untangle the Stimulus

The argument claims to have found the cause of the Athens epidemic: the Ebola virus. The symptoms mentioned in accounts of the epidemic (particularly the unique symptom of hiccups) are consistent with the symptoms of the disease caused by the Ebola virus.

Step 3: Make a Prediction

Don't try to predict all four weakeners; that would be a waste of time. Instead, look to eliminate any answer that introduces a fact severing the link between the Ebola virus and the Athenian epidemic.

Step 4: Evaluate the Answer Choices

(B) says that hiccups don't always accompany Ebola infection, but that doesn't weaken the argument. According to the evidence, hiccups are associated with Ebola and were "experienced by *many* victims" of the Athenian epidemic. So, hiccups need not be present in every single Ebola infection in order for the argument to work. **(B)** is therefore the correct answer.

(A) hurts the argument because it suggests that the Athenians did not report suffering certain symptoms consistent with Ebola infection.

(C) makes it nearly impossible for the Ebola virus to have afflicted the Athenians, since it takes away the virus's method of transmission.

(D) suggests that the contagiousness of the Athenian epidemic was not consistent with an Ebola epidemic, thus undermining the argument.

(E) also undermines the argument by pointing out a difference in duration between Ebola epidemics and the one that afflicted Athens.

8. (E) Main Point

Step 1: Identify the Question Type

Since the question stem asks you to identify the conclusion of the argument, it's a Main Point question. Find the choice that best states the argument's final conclusion or overall main idea.

Step 2: Untangle the Stimulus

The letter begins with the author blaming the editor for unfairly criticizing a claim made by environmentalists. The author then cites the editor's evidence for the critique and proceeds to introduce a fact the editor didn't account for in the critique.

Step 3: Make a Prediction

When predicting the correct answer to a Main Point question in which the stimulus argument doesn't have strong Keywords signaling the conclusion, look for a statement of the author's point of view. That statement comes in the first sentence, a value judgment. The main point is that the editor did not provide enough evidence for a fair critique of the environmentalists' claim. Everything else in the argument, especially the last sentence, is intended to support that point.

Step 4: Evaluate the Answer Choices

(E) matches the prediction. The editorialist tried to use the constant level of the wolf population as evidence that the environmentalists' claim was exaggerated. According to the letter writer, though, the environmentalists' claim is correct and only owing to their actions has the wolf population remained constant.

(A) is a paraphrase of the letter writer's evidence—it's a fact that he introduces to undermine the editor's use of the wolf population data—but it's not his overall conclusion.

(B) is off because the author's point isn't to state that the number of wolves killed each year is the same as the number born. In fact, the letter attempts to defend the environmentalists, who argue that *more* wolves are killed than are born each year. The letter's point is that the editorial attacking the environmentalists used poorly interpreted data.

(C) isn't the main point because the author never makes any recommendations on how to maintain the wolf population.

(D) isn't actually a claim made by the author. The author never attacks the studies but rather the editorialist's use of those studies to disprove environmentalists' claim about the killing of wolves.

9. (D) Inference

Step 1: Identify the Question Type

The phrase "properly inferred" in the question stem tells you this is an Inference question. Find the choice that must be true if the scientist's statements are true.

Step 2: Untangle the Stimulus

The scientist describes a correlation. From the mid-1990s into the next decade, every time a microchip's computing speed doubled, the cost of producing that microchip also doubled. And for several decades, the number of microchip transistors, and hence the chips' computing speed, has doubled every year and a half.

Step 3: Make a Prediction

Notice in the stimulus that computing speed doubles as a result of a doubling in the number of transistors and that (at least from the mid-1990s into the 2000s) a doubling in computing speed triggers a doubling in the cost of producing the microchips. Thus, during that same time period, a doubling in cost must have accompanied a doubling in the number of transistors.

Step 4: Evaluate the Answer Choices

(D) matches the prediction and must be true. Just as expected, it makes the link between cost doubling and

transistor doubling during the decade starting in the mid-1990s.

(A) is a Distortion. It confuses necessity and sufficiency. According to the passage, doubling the number of transistors results in a doubling of speed. There's no claim that doubling the number of transistors is the only way to accomplish the gain in speed.

(B), with its discussion of the retail cost of computers, is Outside the Scope. Without knowing how that retail cost was affected by the increases in microchip production costs, **(B)** cannot be inferred.

(C), also Outside the Scope, focuses on the efforts of computer engineers. Nothing can be deduced from the stimulus about those engineers or their efforts.

(E) makes an unwarranted prediction. There's no way to know from the stimulus what engineers will be able to achieve.

10. (A) Assumption (Sufficient)

Step 1: Identify the Question Type

The question stem asks for the answer choice that, if assumed, makes the conclusion follow from the evidence. The right answer, in other words, will be an assumption *sufficient* to make the argument valid. Look for the conclusion–evidence gap as you read the argument.

Step 2: Untangle the Stimulus

Ms. Sandstrom wrote a newspaper column that resulted in people doing damage to the Mendels' farm. The Keyword *thus* signals the conclusion: Ms. Sandstrom should pay for the damage—*if* she could have expected that her column would cause damage to the Mendels' farm.

Step 3: Make a Prediction

That "If" condition is important. It's what leads the author to conclude that Ms. Sandstrom is liable for damages. If it's a rule that people ought to pay for damage that they could have reasonably expected to occur as a result of their actions, then the author's conclusion follows logically.

Step 4: Evaluate the Answer Choices

(A) matches the prediction to the letter.

(B) doesn't make the conclusion follow. The Mendels' claim is that Ms. Sandstrom *could have* reasonably expected her action to lead to damage, not that she definitely and actually did expect it to.

(C), even if true, doesn't help establish that Ms. Sandstrom is responsible for the damages, and that's the conclusion the correct answer must help establish.

(D) misses the point. Even if Ms. Sandstrom knew that her column could incite people to damage the farm, her expectations have to be connected to an obligation to pay in order for the conclusion to follow.

(E), like **(D)**, fails to connect the evidence to an obligation to pay. Even if the Mendels believe that Ms. Sandstrom could have formed expectations about the consequences of her action, that still does not guarantee the conclusion.

11. (D) Principle (Identify/Strengthen)

Step 1: Identify the Question Type

The question stem seeks a policy that justifies an action in the stimulus. That makes this a Principle question, since the right answer will be a broad, lawlike rule that supports the argument.

Step 2: Untangle the Stimulus

The University of Williamstown revoked Meyer's PhD, presumably because his employer uncovered that Meyer committed scientific fraud by falsifying data. In a later investigation, the university found no evidence that he had also falsified data in his doctoral thesis, but it didn't change its decision to revoke his PhD.

Step 3: Make a Prediction

The only wrongdoing that the university was able to confirm was Meyer's scientific fraud. On that basis alone, it revoked the PhD. So it must be a rule at the university that if someone has a PhD from the university and commits scientific fraud, the university will revoke the degree. Whether the fraud was associated with the candidate's thesis is, apparently, irrelevant.

Step 4: Evaluate the Answer Choices

(D) matches the prediction. It's strong enough to justify the school's action based on the evidence the university had.

(A) doesn't apply in this case because Meyer wasn't found to have committed academic fraud while at the university.

(B) falls short on two counts. First, Meyer hasn't been proven guilty of academic fraud. Second, Meyer isn't an applicant—he has already earned his PhD.

(C) doesn't apply because Meyer isn't a current student whom the university decided to expel. He's an alumnus whom the university stripped of a degree.

(E) doesn't justify the university's decision because Meyer isn't a candidate for employment there.

12. (B) Inference

Step 1: Identify the Question Type

The key phrase "most strongly supported by the … statements" indicates an Inference question. Find the answer choice that must be true based on the stimulus.

Step 2: Untangle the Stimulus

The aerobics instructor says kickboxing is risky because of the likelihood of injury while overextending. She goes on to say that overextension is highly likely when beginners try to match the kicks of more experienced kickboxers.

Step 3: Make a Prediction

The last sentence tells you that beginners are very likely to overextend while trying to match the kicks of more experienced practitioners. The second-to-last sentence says that overextending leads to injuries. Putting those two together, you can determine that beginners risk injury when trying to match the kicks of more experienced kickboxers. Be prepared for the correct answer to say something to this effect. As always, though, any statement that must be true based on the instructor's statements would be the correct answer here.

Step 4: Evaluate the Answer Choices

(B) follows directly from the stimulus. If beginners are likely to be injured by mimicking the high kicks of more skilled kickboxers, then avoiding such mimicry would reduce the likelihood of injury.

(A) distorts the stimulus. Beginners are likely to injure themselves trying to match the skilled kickboxers, but that doesn't mean that skilled kickboxers can't themselves be injured, especially since the stimulus says that overextension "often leads to … injuries."

(C) is also a Distortion. Trying to match more skilled kickboxers is presented is a likely way for beginners to engage in the kind of overextension that leads to injury. The stimulus does not say it's the only way a beginner could be injured while kickboxing.

(D) is Outside the Scope. Other forms of exercise that don't involve high kicks aren't discussed in the stimulus.

(E) is Extreme. Beginners *risk* injury while overextending, but this doesn't mean that *most* beginners definitely experience injury that way.

13. (D) Main Point

Step 1: Identify the Question Type

Since the question is seeking the argument's "overall conclusion," it's a Main Point question.

Step 2: Untangle the Stimulus

The first sentence provides background for the argument. The second predicts the impact the penalty will have on the company. The third sentence provides the author's point of view about the trial. The last sentence (beginning with "after all") justifies that point of view, giving what the author considers the benefits of the trial.

Step 3: Make a Prediction

Two sets of evidence Keywords (*since* and *after all*) follow the statement that the trial was worthwhile. So the idea that the trial was worthwhile is the author's conclusion. Everything else in the argument exists to support this idea.

Step 4: Evaluate the Answer Choices

(D) is an accurate paraphrase of the prediction.

(A) misses the mark because it tries to paraphrase the author's evidence, not her main point. The fact that the trial exposed information that competitors used to pressure the company is *why* the author considers the trial valuable.

(B) virtually restates the last sentence of the argument. This entire sentence provides reasons why the trial was worthwhile. It's part of the evidence, not the conclusion.

(C) isn't the main conclusion because the author argues that the trial was still valuable despite a penalty that's unlikely to affect the company's behavior.

(E) isn't stated by the author anywhere in the argument and isn't even inferable.

14. (D) Point at Issue

Step 1: Identify the Question Type

Since the question asks you what two speakers disagree over, it's a Point at Issue question. Predict the area of disagreement between the speakers or use the Decision Tree to eliminate answers.

Step 2: Untangle the Stimulus

Waller says that if extrasensory perception (ESP) existed, people would accept it because it would be demonstrable by anyone who actually possessed it. Chin says that nothing can be demonstrated to satisfy all skeptics, so the public will never accept ESP, since skepticism dominates public opinion.

Step 3: Make a Prediction

Waller and Chin appear to disagree over whether public opinion can be used as an indicator of ESP's existence. Chin, unlike Waller, seems to think that whether or not ESP really existed, people would still be skeptical. If you weren't able to make this prediction, however, you could have used the Decision Tree. Test each answer choice by asking whether both speakers have opinions about that answer choice and whether those opinions differ. Both of those are necessary conditions for the right answer.

Step 4: Evaluate the Answer Choices

(D) matches the prediction and stands up to the Decision Tree. It's the only choice about which both Waller and Chin have opinions. Waller believes that the public's failure to believe in ESP is good reason to deny its existence, and Chin doesn't.

(A) is not something both speakers have a clearly defined opinion about. Waller appears to believe that ESP isn't real because, if it were, it would be demonstrated. Chin, however, doesn't assert that ESP exists; rather, he claims that a failure to convince the public is not a reason to conclude that it doesn't exist. Indeed, he says that convincing the public will be impossible in any event.

(B) is definitely something Chin has an opinion on—he'd say you can't convince them—but Waller doesn't weigh in on the likelihood of winning over the skeptics.

(C) isn't discussed in the stimulus. Neither Waller nor Chin speaks about the strength of the case against ESP.

(E) appears to be something Waller and Chin implicitly agree on. Neither one seems to believe that the public has yet embraced ESP as a real phenomenon.

15. (C) Principle (Identify/Strengthen)

Step 1: Identify the Question Type

The question stem tells you that the answer choices are all broad principles, one of which will strengthen the argument.

Step 2: Untangle the Stimulus

The counselor concludes that Hagerle owes her a sincere apology comparable to the one Hagerle gave the physician. The Keyword *because* signals the counselor's evidence: Hagerle told the same lie to both her and the physician, and he's already sincerely apologized to the physician.

Step 3: Make a Prediction

The counselor assumes that Hagerle should sincerely apologize for an offense if it's an offense for which he's already sincerely apologized to someone else. The answer that validates this assumption will be correct.

Step 4: Evaluate the Answer Choices

(C) validates the assumption and therefore strengthens the argument.

(A) sounds nice, but it doesn't support the argument because the counselor's argument hinges on whether or not she is *owed* an apology.

(B) requires both the counselor and the physician to be owed an apology. But the issue isn't whether the physician, too, is owed an apology—he's already received one. The issue is whether the counselor is owed an apology because of the one Hagerle gave to the physician.

(D) gets into the issue of whether Hagerle is capable of apologizing sincerely, which is a different issue from whether Hagerle owes an apology to the counselor.

(E) is Extreme ("all others to whom the lie was told") and also doesn't deal with the person who was lied to being owed an apology, which is central to the argument.

16. (D) Strengthen

Step 1: Identify the Question Type

The language in the question stem makes it clear that the right answer will strengthen the argument; that is, it will make the conclusion more likely to follow from the evidence.

Step 2: Untangle the Stimulus

The argument concludes that Weston's population will show a decline over the last decade. The evidence is the survey of address changes, which shows that twice as many households moved out of the city as moved into the city.

Step 3: Make a Prediction

The argument initially may sound unassailable, but there's a difference between the number of households and the number of people. The argument assumes that each household moving out of Weston had, on average, more than half the number of people than each household moving in or being added to the size of existing households. Any answer choice validating this will strengthen the argument.

Step 4: Evaluate the Answer Choices

(D) directly matches the prediction. If the majority of households leaving Weston had more people than the majority of those moving into Weston, then the next census will, if it's accurate, report a decline in Weston's overall population.

(A) doesn't add anything new to the argument, so it has no effect.

(B) doesn't help the argument for two reasons. First, the author is predicting a population loss, not a gain. Second, the argument provides no history of what was reported in previous census data, so the effect of **(B)** on the argument can't be determined.

(C) weakens the argument by suggesting that the address change survey had underreported the number of people moving into the city.

(E) gets into the motivation of those who left Weston, but that's Outside the Scope of the argument.

17. (C) Method of Argument

Step 1: Identify the Question Type

The key phrase "argument does which one of the following" is an indicator of a Method of Argument question.

Step 2: Untangle the Stimulus

The conclusion of the psychologist's argument comes right after *but*: People should not necessarily try to prevent themselves from making cognitive errors while predicting the effect an event will have on their happiness. The psychologist supports this conclusion by pointing to a different scenario. People make visual errors concerning parallel lines, but no one would reasonably agree to surgery merely to prevent herself from making such errors.

Step 3: Make a Prediction

In a Method of Argument question, focus on how the argument is structured, not on its specific content. In order to reach his conclusion, the psychologist makes an analogy to a similar situation in which one would more clearly choose not to follow the course of action she discourages.

Step 4: Evaluate the Answer Choices

(C) matches the prediction by describing an argument by analogy.

(A) is off because there's no claim in the argument that any event is inevitable. Moreover, the psychologist cites no alternative event in making his argument.

(B) is wrong because the psychologist doesn't argue against any theories—only a specific course of action.

(D) distorts the purpose of the analogy. The psychologist's point is not to prove that predicting events is like looking at parallel lines. He takes the similarity of the events for granted in order to support his recommendation against trying to avoid cognitive errors.

(E) inaccurately describes the psychologist's use of the visual analogy as a generalization. It's an example of a specific situation in which the action he discourages would be unreasonable.

18. (E) Strengthen

Step 1: Identify the Question Type

The question stem tells you that the stimulus will contain a principle and an application of it. Your task is to find the answer justifying the application.

Step 2: Untangle the Stimulus

The stimulus establishes the principle: An art auction house is guilty of misrepresentation if it describes items in order to intentionally mislead bidders. The application claims that Healy's is guilty because it described a modern vase as dating from the eighteenth century.

Step 3: Make a Prediction

In order for Healy's action to constitute misrepresentation (according to the principle), its description of the vase would have to be a deliberate attempt to mislead bidders. Any answer choice that demonstrates this will certainly strengthen the case against Healy's.

Step 4: Evaluate the Answer Choices

(E) does just what the prediction called for. If Healy's decided, without doing research, to describe the vase as an eighteenth-century just to increase its auction price, that sounds a lot like a deliberate attempt to mislead.

(A) doesn't help because it does nothing to demonstrate a deliberate attempt on the part of Healy's to mislead bidders. The correct answer must address Healy's actions and motives.

(B) introduces a comparison to similar pottery without drawing a direct line between it and an attempt by Healy's to misrepresent the attributes of the vase. The actions of the bidders are likewise irrelevant.

(C), if true, shows that Healy's is in violation of its own stated policy, but that doesn't support the idea that Healy's is guilty of deliberately misleading bidders in a way applicable to the principle.

(D) suggests that Healy's may have behaved in a way that goes against the beliefs of some of its employees. But that's not the same as the principle's description of misrepresentation.

19. (C) Assumption (Necessary)

Step 1: Identify the Question Type

The question stem asks for an assumption required by the argument. The Denial Test may help if you're stuck.

Step 2: Untangle the Stimulus

The anthropologist's conclusion is that our prehistoric ancestors did not interbreed with Neanderthals. The only evidence for this is the fact that our DNA is different from Neanderthals' DNA.

Step 3: Make a Prediction

But what if Neanderthals' DNA was similar to that of our prehistoric ancestors? If so, then the author can't use that evidence to establish that conclusion. So the anthropologist assumes that our prehistoric ancestors had DNA that was no more similar to Neanderthals' DNA than is ours.

Step 4: Evaluate the Answer Choices

(C) matches the prediction. The author must assume that the DNA of contemporary humans and our *Homo sapiens* ancestors can both be distinguished from the DNA of Neanderthals.

(A) would need to be true if the anthropologist were arguing that prehistoric human ancestors *did* interbreed with Neanderthals. But that's the opposite of the conclusion.

(B) makes the Irrelevant Comparison between testing the DNA of remains and testing that of living species. Further, if **(B)** is true, then it's harder for the anthropologist to use the DNA of Neanderthal remains as evidence.

(D) doesn't have to be true for the argument to work. Even if human ancestors and Neanderthals were in the same geographic area, they still could have avoided interbreeding. So **(D)** doesn't pass the Denial Test.

(E) is Extreme. The anthropologist says there is a significant difference between the two species' DNA. So, the argument would still be valid even if some similarities were due to something other than inbreeding.

20. (B) Inference

Step 1: Identify the Question Type

This is an Inference question since it asks you to accept the stimulus as true and find the answer choice that must be true based on it.

Step 2: Untangle the Stimulus

This stimulus is littered with Formal Logic Keywords (*if, unless*), so lay out each of the statements using Formal Logic notation. The first sentence provides two statements:

If	more consumers downtown	→	profits increase
If	cost of living decreases	→	more consumers downtown

And the last sentence provides one more:

If	profits increase	→	downtown traffic congestion must have decreased

Step 3: Make a Prediction

The Formal Logic statements can be connected as a logical chain:

If	cost of living decreases	→	more consumers	→	profits increase	→	congestion decreases

Don't try to predict the content of an answer in this Inference question. Instead, move into the answer choices and select the one that is in line with your Formal Logic translations and/or their contrapositives.

Step 4: Evaluate the Answer Choices

(B) must be true based on the Formal Logic. Cost of living decreases will lead to an increase in consumers, which the first sentence of the stimulus tells us will increase the profits of businesses. Remember that the correct answer to an Inference question need not synthesize *all* of the statements in the stimulus; it simply must be true based on one or more of them.

(A) gets the logical chain backward. Decreases in traffic congestion don't guarantee anything according to the stimulus (they're *necessary* for increased downtown business profits).

(C), like **(A)**, reverses the chain of logic.

(D), like **(A)** and **(C)**, also reverses the chain of logic.

(E) confuses the sufficient and necessary conditions in the first sentence. The only thing an increase in profits guarantees is that traffic congestion has decreased.

21. (E) Parallel Reasoning

Step 1: Identify the Question Type

The phrase "pattern of reasoning … most similar to" always indicates a Parallel Reasoning question. Find the answer choice that uses the same kind of evidence to reach the same kind of conclusion as the stimulus.

Step 2: Untangle the Stimulus

The conclusion comes at the end of the argument. Any domestic long-distance call that doesn't cost 10 cents a minute must cost 15 cents a minute. The evidence is that any domestic long-distance call starting between 9 am and 5 pm costs 15 cents a minute and all other domestic long-distance calls cost 10 cents.

Step 3: Make a Prediction

The Keyword *any* indicates that you can use Formal Logic to abstract the stimulus. The structure of the argument is essentially as follows:

If	**X**	→	**Y**
If	**~X**	→	**Z**

So,

If	**~Z**	→	**Y**

The right answer choice may rearrange these elements, but it will have all and only those elements. (By the way, the logic here is sound. Take the contrapositive of the second piece of evidence—If ~ Z → X—and combine it with the first piece of evidence—If Z → Y—and you'll see that they unequivocally establish the conclusion.)

Step 4: Evaluate the Answer Choices

(E) is a match. Replace "extensive lab work" with X, "conducted in a laboratory" with Y, and "conducted in a normal classroom" with Z, and the structure will match the stimulus exactly.

(A) has a different structure: If X → Y; If ~ X → Z; thus, If ~ X → ~ Y. So, this is parallel up until both terms of the conclusion.

(B) has a different structure: If X → Y; If ~ X → Z; thus, If ~ Z → X. This is parallel up until the necessary term of the conclusion.

(C) has a different structure: If X → Y; If ~ X → Z; thus, If Z → ~ Y. This is parallel up until the conclusion, which negates the Y term instead of the Z term.

(D) has a different structure: If X → Y; If ~ X → Z; thus, If X → ~ Z. This has parallel evidence, but the conclusion is not parallel for either term.

22. (B) Principle (Identify/Strengthen)

Step 1: Identify the Question Type

The question stem identifies a Principle question. The answer choices all state principles; the correct one will strengthen ("helps to justify") the argument.

Step 2: Untangle the Stimulus

The argument concludes that the child who pushed another child was wrong to do so if his intent was to hurt that child. The evidence for this is that the pusher knows the difference between right and wrong.

Step 3: Make a Prediction

In order for the evidence to establish the conclusion, the argument must assume that someone who knows the difference between right and wrong should not carry out an action intending to harm someone else. Look for the answer choice that validates this assumption.

Step 4: Evaluate the Answer Choices

(B) validates the assumption directly, thereby justifying the argument's conclusion on the basis of its evidence.

(A) makes the understanding of right and wrong necessary for an action to be wrong when—to fit the argument at hand—it should be sufficient.

(C) says that if an act is wrong, then there's intent to harm. This reverses the terms of the conclusion but does nothing to strengthen the connection of the evidence to the conclusion.

(D) falls Outside the Scope of the argument because the conclusion is that the child's behavior was wrong if the child actually intended to cause harm. This is a principle about negligence, not intent.

(E) discusses a person who doesn't know the difference between right and wrong. It doesn't help this argument since the author stipulates that the pusher clearly knows that difference.

23. (B) Flaw

Step 1: Identify the Question Type

The phrase "reasoning flaw" indicates a Flaw question. Find the logical disconnect in the argument.

Step 2: Untangle the Stimulus

The researcher concludes that certain makes of car must be more common than other makes in certain areas of the nation. The evidence is an experiment in which people overestimated the frequency of their car among the nation's car owners. The results of the experiment are consistent with the researcher's conclusion.

Step 3: Make a Prediction

Anytime an author sticks her neck out and concludes that something *must* be true, there had better be proof. But the results of the experiment don't prove the researcher's conclusion; they're merely consistent with it. The correct answer will explain that the author overestimated the strength of the evidence, drawing too certain a conclusion.

Step 4: Evaluate the Answer Choices

(B) is in line with the prediction. The classic flaw here is Possible Versus Certain.

(A) isn't a flaw. Whether or not the subjects knew the actual statistics doesn't matter; the point is that they overestimated them and what that overestimation indicates about the researcher's hypothesis.

(C) doesn't describe the researcher's flaw because the variety of regions from which the subjects were drawn doesn't actually matter.

(D) accuses the researcher of building her argument on an inherent contradiction when no such contradiction exists. The evidence is all consistent; it just isn't strong enough to justify so certain a conclusion.

(E) gets it backward. The researcher actually extracts a generalization from the results of a particular experiment.

24. (E) Parallel Flaw

Step 1: Identify the Question Type

This is a Parallel Flaw question. The stem tells you that the right answer will have not only the same logical structure as the stimulus but also the same logical flaw.

Step 2: Untangle the Stimulus

The conclusion in the last sentence is an assertion of fact: most parking tickets in college towns are issued to students. The evidence is that more of them are issued when students are around than when students aren't around.

Step 3: Make a Prediction

That evidence doesn't necessarily establish the conclusion, however. Just because tickets are issued more often when students are merely *around* doesn't mean that most tickets are issued to students. Maybe more police officers are patrolling when students are around, after all. You're looking for the answer choice that makes the same flawed assumption—that most instances of an event happen to a certain group just because the event happens more often when that group is around. To put this into classic flaw terms, the author mistakenly imputes causation to a situation that may have an alternate cause or might be mere coincidence.

Step 4: Evaluate the Answer Choices

(E) is perfectly parallel. Just replace "snacks" with "parking citations" and "other people's children" with "students," and you'll have an argument identical to the one in the stimulus, right on down to the flaw.

(A) is flawed, to be sure. But it's flawed because it makes a scope shift from popcorn in the evidence to all snacks in the conclusion and because it assumes without warrant that children buy the additional snacks purchased in movie theaters.

(B) concludes with a comparison of two houseplants ("greener than"), which isn't the same as the assertion of fact that concludes the stimulus.

(C) shares the same kind of conclusion as the stimulus, but it doesn't commit a clear flaw. The argument in **(C)** just assumes that studying makes one studious.

(D) is wrong because it doesn't conclude anything about a majority of instances the way that the stimulus does. The conclusion here is a comparison. This choice also commits a different flaw, a scope shift between a wide variety of available products and a greater number of purchases.

25. (A) Flaw

Step 1: Identify the Question Type

The stem indicates that the argument is "vulnerable to criticism," so you know already that it's flawed. Your task is to determine how and choose the answer that accurately describes the flaw.

Step 2: Untangle the Stimulus

The counselor's conclusion is signaled by *therefore*: harsh criticism is the only thing that will bring about personal change. The evidence follows a logical chain: people need a motive to change, and harsh criticism provides a motive by virtue of being unpleasant.

Step 3: Make a Prediction

The word *only* in the conclusion signals some Formal Logic—specifically, it signals the necessary condition. The counselor concludes that harsh criticism is necessary for change, since harsh criticism provides one thing—a motive—that is also necessary for change. You can see this relationship in Formal Logic notation:

Evidence 1:

| If | change | → | motive |

Evidence 2:

| If | harsh criticism | → | unpleasant | → | motive |

Conclusion:

If   change   →   harsh criticism

Notice that the author has concluded that harsh criticism is necessary for the motive required to change, when the evidence merely shows that harsh criticism is sufficient for that motive. One needs a motive and harsh criticism is one such motive, but it may not be the only one. This classic Necessity Versus Sufficiency flaw shows up time and again on the LSAT, so learn to recognize it.

Step 4: Evaluate the Answer Choices

(A) matches the prediction. It happens to use the exact terms—*necessary* and *sufficient*—you saw previously, but it could substitute *enough* or *guarantee* for *sufficient*, or *needed* for *necessary*, and still be the right answer.

(B) isn't a possibility the argument needs to address, since the counselor confines the argument to what's necessary for change. She doesn't compare different goals of criticism or suggest that motivating change is its only use.

(C) isn't an assumption the counselor makes. The counselor just focuses on the need for motive and what will provide the motive, not on whether motive always produces a change.

(D) isn't the flaw because the counselor doesn't draw any distinctions between doing things and avoiding them.

(E) implies circular reasoning, an offense the counselor hasn't committed. The counselor makes the case for harsh criticism not by merely refuting an argument but by providing additional (albeit flawed) logic.

Section II: Logic Games

Game 1: Judicial Appointments to Appellate and Trial Courts

Q#	Question Type	Correct	Difficulty
1	Acceptability	E	★
2	Must Be False (CANNOT Be True)	B	★
3	Must Be False (CANNOT Be True)	A	★
4	"If" / Must Be True	C	★
5	Rule Substitution	E	★★★★

Game 2: Skydiving Team

Q#	Question Type	Correct	Difficulty
6	Acceptability	B	★
7	Must Be True	D	★
8	"If" / Could Be True EXCEPT	C	★
9	"If" / Must Be False	D	★★
10	"If" / Could Be True EXCEPT	A	★

Game 3: Company's Vehicles Being Serviced

Q#	Question Type	Correct	Difficulty
11	Acceptability	B	★
12	Must Be False (CANNOT Be True)	E	★
13	"If" / Must Be True	C	★★
14	"If" / Could Be True EXCEPT	E	★★★
15	"If" / Could Be True	A	★★★
16	"If" / Must Be True	B	★★
17	Partial Acceptability	B	★★

Game 4: Street Entertainer with Boxes and Balls

Q#	Question Type	Correct	Difficulty
18	"If" / Could Be True	B	★★
19	"If" / Could Be True	C	★★
20	Must Be True	E	★★★★
21	Must Be True	A	★★★
22	"If" / Could Be True	C	★★
23	"If" / Must Be True	D	★★

Game 1: Judicial Appointments to Appellate and Trial Courts

Step 1: Overview

Situation: Judges appointed to one of two courts

Entities: Seven judges—H, J, K, L, M, O, P

Action: Distribution. Your task is to sort the judges by the court to which each is appointed.

Limitations: Each judge is appointed to only one court. The appellate court has three open slots, and the trial court has six open slots. That's nine slots for only seven judges, so there will be two slots that remain unfilled.

Step 2: Sketch

Since this is a Distribution game, list the entities and draw a table with two columns, one for each of the two courts. Since you know how many spots are open at each court, draw in slots to represent them.

```
    H J K L M O P
      appellate   |   trial
    — — —         |  — — —
                  |  — — —
```

Step 3: Rules

Rule 1 places Li in the appellate court. Put that right into the sketch.

```
      appellate   |   trial
    L — —         |  — — —
                  |  — — —
```

Rule 2 places Kurtz in the trial court. Add that to the sketch too.

```
      appellate   |   trial
    L — —         |  K — —
                  |  — — —
```

Rule 3 forbids Hamadi and Perkins serving on the same court. Since there are only two courts, this means that one of them will serve on the appellate court and the other will serve on the trial court. Fill in one slot in each court.

```
      appellate   |   trial
    L H/P __       |  K P/H __
                  |  — — —
```

Jefferson, McDonnell, and Ortiz are Floaters—they don't appear in any of the rules.

Step 4: Deductions

There aren't any Blocks of Entities (though Hamadi and Perkins are an anti-block or "impossible pair," since they can't be placed together). It wouldn't help to draw any Limited Options since the game doesn't break down into an either/or situation. Kurtz and Li are Established Entities, but they have little immediate impact beyond taking one space in each court. In this game, as in any Distribution game, you should investigate the Number Restrictions. The appellate court now has a minimum of two judges and a maximum of three judges. The trial court must therefore have at least four judges and at most five. (One of the slots in the trial court will not be filled; you can erase it or cross it out.) There aren't any Duplications, since none of the entities appears in more than one rule.

```
      appellate   |   trial
    L H/P __       |  K P/H __
                  |  — —    xx
        2–3       |    4–5
```

Step 5: Questions

1. (E) Acceptability

Check each rule and eliminate any choice(s) that violates it.

(A) violates Rule 1 because it has Li on the trial court. **(C)** violates Rule 2 because it has Kurtz on the appellate court. Finally, **(B)** and **(D)** both violate Rule 3 by having Hamadi and Perkins on the same court.

Circle **(E)** and move on.

2. (B) Must Be False (CANNOT Be True)

(B) is the only choice here that cannot be true (i.e., must be false). Your sketch shows that there isn't room on the appellate court for both McDonnell and Ortiz. This is why it helps to fill a slot with "H/P" according to Rule 3.

All the other choices are possible. **(D)** even appears in the correct answer to the Acceptability question.

3. (A) Must Be False (CANNOT Be True)

(A) is demonstrably false due to space restrictions based on the Numbers. You'd need four slots in the appellate court to make **(A)** happen.

All the other choices are possible. **(B)** and **(C)** occur in the correct answer for the Acceptability question.

4. (C) "If" / Must Be True

Incorporate the information from the new "If" clause into a new sketch:

```
      appellate   |   trial
    L H/P O        |  K H/P __
                  |  — —    xx
```

Now the appellate court is full, so the remaining Floaters (Jefferson and McDonnell) must go into the trial court.

```
      appellate   |   trial
    L H/P O        |  K H/P J
                  |  M  xx  xx
```

(C), therefore, is correct. **(B)** must be false, and **(A)**, **(D)**, and **(E)** (all involving Hamadi or Perkins, who can move between courts) are merely possible.

5. (E) Rule Substitution

This question type can be tough, so it's a good one to leave for later in the game. The right answer will force you to do what Rule 3 does, which is to place Hamadi and Perkins in different courts.

(E) is the winner here. Kurtz and Li are already on different courts (Rules 1 and 2 are still enforced), so what **(E)** really means is that you can't have Hamadi and Perkins together on the appellate court or on the trial court. That's equivalent to Rule 3.

(A) doesn't do the trick, since it would allow you to place both Hamadi and Perkins on the trial court.

(B) means that you'd have to have at least one of Hamadi and Perkins on the trial court, but just as with **(A)**, you'd still be able to place both of them on the trial court.

(C) prevents you from appointing both Hamadi and Perkins to the same court as Jefferson, but they could still be on the same court as each other.

(D) says that if Hamadi is on the appellate court, then Perkins is on the trial court. This rule, however, would still allow both of them to be on the trial court.

Game 2: Skydiving Team

Step 1: Overview

Situation: A team of people skydiving from a plane one at a time

Entities: Six team members—L, O, P, T, W, Z

Action: Strict Sequencing. Your task is to determine the order in which the team members dive from the plane.

Limitations: Team members dive one time each and one at a time.

Step 2: Sketch

The rules and questions make reference to specific positions in the diving order, so a Strict Sequencing setup (with numbered dashes) makes the most sense.

```
        L  O  P  T  W  Z
       __ __ __ __ __ __
        1  2  3  4  5  6
```

Step 3: Rules

Rule 1 places Trevino before Weiss in the diving order, but that's not specific enough to go into the sketch, so jot it down nearby:

```
            T...W
```

Rule 2 gives you only two options for positioning Larue: 1 or 6. Revisit that restriction in a moment, when you get to the Deductions step.

Rule 3 restricts Weiss and Zacny from diving last:

```
        L  O  P  T  W  Z
       __ __ __ __ __ __
        1  2  3  4  5  6
                       WZ
```

Rule 4 means that Pei must follow only one of Ohba and Larue. And because team members dive one at a time, Pei will follow one of Ohba and Larue and precede the other:

```
        O...P...L  or  L...P...O
```

Step 4: Deductions

Several entities are arranged in loose blocks: Trevino always precedes Weiss, and Pei must be positioned between Ohba and Larue. Speaking of Larue, the restrictions placed on this entity create Limited Options:

```
                OPTION I
        L
       __ __ __ __ __ __
        1  2  3  4  5  6
                       WZ

                OPTION II
                         L
       __ __ __ __ __ __
        1  2  3  4  5  6
                       WZ
```

This makes Larue an Established Entity. But you can go further with some of the other slots, too. Since Trevino must always precede Weiss, Trevino can't ever dive last, and Weiss

can't dive first. Furthermore, since Weiss can't go last, Trevino can't go fifth. And since Pei must dive between Ohba and Larue, Pei can't dive either first or last.

In Option I, this leaves only Ohba to dive last. Furthermore, since Trevino precedes Weiss, Weiss can't dive second:

```
                OPTION I
        L                       O
       __ __ __ __ __ __
        1  2  3  4  5  6
        PW  W          T    WZ
                            TP

                OPTION II
                            L
       __ __ __ __ __ __
        1  2  3  4  5  6
        PW             T    WZ
                            TP
```

In Option II, there's no way for Pei to dive after Larue, so Pei will have to dive after Ohba, meaning Ohba can't dive fifth.

The final Master Sketch:

```
                OPTION I
        L                       O
       __ __ __ __ __ __
        1  2  3  4  5  6
        PW  W          T    WZ
           T...W            TP

                OPTION II
                            L
       __ __ __ __ __ __
        1  2  3  4  5  6
        PW             TO   WZ
         T...W    O...P     TP
```

Step 5: Questions

6. (B) Acceptability

As always for Acceptability questions, eliminate incorrect answers rule by rule. **(B)** turns out to be correct.

(C) fails because Trevino doesn't precede Weiss (Rule 1). **(E)** is out because Larue isn't diving first or last (Rule 2). **(A)** is out because it has Weiss diving last (Rule 3). **(D)** is incorrect because Pei is diving before Ohba and Larue (Rule 4).

7. (D) Must Be True

Count on deductions to provide answers to a straightforward "Must Be True" question. You know that Trevino can't dive last, since she must precede Weiss. And since Weiss is explicitly barred from diving last, Trevino can't dive fifth either. So **(D)** must be true. Notice that Trevino was barred from diving fifth or sixth in both options as they're shown in your Master Sketch.

All of the other choices could be false. In fact, **(B)** and **(E)** are false in the correct answer from the Acceptability question. **(A)** will be false in any Option II arrangement, since Larue dives last in that case. **(C)** could be false in Option II, where Pei could dive fifth.

KAPLAN

8. (C) "If" / Could Be True EXCEPT

First, characterize the right answer. You're seeking the answer that must be false.

Larue diving last puts you in Option II.

̶	̶	̶	̶	̶	L
1	2	3	4	5	6
P̶W̶				T̶O̶	W̶Z̶
	T...W		O...P		T̶P̶

In this option, Ohba can't dive fifth, since Ohba must precede Pei. Therefore, **(C)** is false and the correct answer. All the other choices are possible in Option II.

9. (D) "If" / Must Be False

For this question, eliminate any choice that could be true. The new "If" creates a Block of Entities: T ... WZ. However, this new "If," unlike most, doesn't restrict you to just one option. In Option I, the WZ block can dive third and fourth or fourth and fifth. If Weiss and Zacny dive third and fourth, then Trevino must dive second and Pei must dive fifth:

L	T	W	Z	P	O
1	2	3	4	5	6

If Weiss and Zacny dive fourth and fifth, then Trevino and Pei will dive second and third, in either order:

L	T/P	P/T	W	Z	O
1	2	3	4	5	6

(A), **(B)** and **(E)** are therefore possible—eliminate all three.

In Option II, the WZ block can dive second and third. In that case, Trevino would dive first, leaving Ohba to dive fourth and Pei to dive fifth:

T	W	Z	O	P	L
1	2	3	4	5	6

This doesn't break any rules, so **(C)** is also possible. **(D)** is the last answer standing and is correct. Under the condition from this question's stem, Pei can dive second, third, or fifth but never fourth.

10. (A) "If" / Could Be True EXCEPT

Once again, the question stem asks us to find the choice that must be false. The new "If" means that we're in Option I. Add Trevino into the second slot:

L	T	̶	̶	̶	O
1	2	3	4	5	6
P̶W̶	W̶			T̶	W̶Z̶
	T...W				T̶P̶

In this case, since Ohba must dive last, then **(A)** is false and therefore correct. None of the other choices is prevented by the rules.

Game 3: Company's Vehicles Being Serviced

Step 1: Overview

Situation: A company's six vehicles being serviced during a certain week, Monday through Saturday

Entities: Six vehicles—H, L, P, R, S, V

Action: Strict Sequencing. Your task is to determine the day on which each vehicle is serviced.

Limitations: Each vehicle is serviced exactly one time during the week, and exactly one vehicle is serviced each day.

Step 2: Sketch

The rules all relate the entities to each other, so expect to sketch a lot of loose relationships. However, there may be certain deductions and new "If" clauses in the questions for which a strict setup with dashes will be useful.

Step 3: Rules

Rule 1 confirms that the hatchback cannot be serviced on Saturday.

Mo	Tu	We	Th	Fr	Sa
					H̶

Rule 2 establishes a relative order for the roadster, van, and hatchback: V...R...H.

Rule 3 means that you must see one of PV/VP or PS/SP somewhere in the sketch. Pay attention to "but not both" at the end of the rule, though.

Rule 4 means that either the sedan will be earlier than the pickup and later than the limousine, or vice versa: L...S...P or P...S...L.

All the entities appear at least once in the rules, so there are no Floaters.

Step 4: Deductions

There are no solid blocks here. As for Limited Options, it turns out that some of the days are very restricted. Since the rules prevent the van, roadster, hatchback, and sedan from being serviced on Saturday, then the only two vehicles that could go there are the limo and the pickup. It's worthwhile to sketch both, since placing each of them may reveal something about other entities.

With the limo on Saturday, the only way to satisfy Rule 4 is to have the pickup before the sedan. To preserve the loose orderings from Rules 2 and 4, neither the sedan, the roadster, nor the hatchback can go on Monday, and the hatchback can't go on Tuesday. Conversely, the pickup, van, and roadster can't go on Friday, and the van can't go on Thursday:

OPTION I

P/V				H/S	L
Mo	Tu	We	Th	Fr	Sa
R̶S̶H̶	H̶			V̶	P̶R̶V̶	H̶R̶V̶S̶

V...R...H   P...S   PV/VP or PS/SP (NOT both)

With the pickup on Saturday, either the van or the sedan will have to go on Friday (Rule 3); you have to place either the van or the sedan next to the pickup. But Rule 2 means the van can't go on Friday, so that day has to belong to the sedan:

OPTION II

V/L			L/H	S	P
Mo	Tu	We	Th	Fr	Sa
R̶H̶	H̶	V̶	V̶R̶		H̶R̶V̶S̶

V...R...H   PV/VP or PS/SP (NOT both)

These Limited Options also provide you with some Established Entities, since you now know that Friday's vehicle must be either the sedan or the hatchback.

Step 5: Questions

11. (B) Acceptability

In all Acceptability questions, use the rules to eliminate the answer choices. Rule 1 is violated by **(C)**, which places the hatchback on Saturday. Rule 2 is violated by **(A)**, which places the roadster later in the week than the hatchback. **(D)** violates Rule 3, since it doesn't have the pickup next to either the van or the sedan. Finally, Rule 4 is violated by **(E)**, which places the sedan earlier than both the pickup and the limo. This leaves **(B)** as the only acceptable answer.

12. (E) Must Be False (CANNOT Be True)

Questions like this one, which doesn't have a new "If" clause, often reward deductions you've already made. Since the van must precede the roadster and the hatchback, and since the hatchback must precede at least one vehicle, there must be at least three vehicles serviced after the van. So the latest day to service the van is Wednesday. This makes **(E)** correct. All of the other choices feature vehicles that could be serviced on either Friday or Saturday in one of the Limited Options.

13. (C) "If" / Must Be True

When a new "If" clause tells you what isn't true, investigate the possibilities. Ask yourself, "What could be true in this case?" The roadster, hatchback, and sedan already can't be serviced on Monday, since they each must follow at least one other vehicle. And your options show you that the vehicle serviced on Monday must be the pickup, the limo, or the van. With the "If" clause eliminating the pickup and limo, the van must be the vehicle serviced on Monday. So **(C)** must be true and is correct.

14. (E) "If" / Could Be True EXCEPT

With any LSAT Logic Games question (and especially with an EXCEPT question), characterize the answer choices first. The correct answer is the one that must be false; the four wrong answers could be true. Now incorporate the "If" clause. If the limo isn't serviced on Saturday, then you're in Option II, where the sedan is serviced on Friday and the pickup is serviced on Saturday. Therefore, **(E)** must be false. All the other choices are possible in Option II; just check the sketch.

15. (A) "If" / Could Be True

If the sedan is earlier than the pickup, then you must be in Option II again. In this option, only **(A)** is possible. All the other choices must be false.

16. (B) "If" / Must Be True

This question is already answered by your analysis of Rule 4. If the limo is serviced on Saturday, then the sedan is definitely serviced earlier than the limo, and you're in Option I. Therefore, the sedan must be serviced after the pickup, making **(B)** undeniably true.

17. (B) Partial Acceptability

This question doesn't give you any new information, so you need to consider both options. First of all, the options tell you that Friday's vehicle has to be the hatchback or the sedan, so **(A)** and **(E)** won't work. All the remaining choices have the hatchback on Friday, so compare them against Option I. In this option, the limo is on Saturday, so it can't be on Wednesday. This eliminates **(C)** and **(D)**, leaving **(B)** as the only choice that could be true.

Game 4: Street Entertainer with Boxes and Balls

Step 1: Overview

Situation: A street entertainer with six boxes that have balls of one of three colors inside

Entities: Six boxes, numbered 1 through 6; balls of three different colors (green, red, white)

Action: Strict Sequencing. Your task is that of the "onlookers" mentioned in the setup, to determine the color of the ball inside each box.

Limitations: Each box contains only one ball.

Step 2: Sketch

Since the opening paragraph tells you that the boxes are numbered from bottom to top, set up a Strict Sequencing sketch reflecting that:

```
6
5
4
3
2
1
```

As you get started with the rules, prepare to determine how many of the six balls are red, how many are green, and how many are white.

Step 3: Rules

Rule 1 says that the number of red balls must be greater than the number of white balls. You'll explore those number possibilities further in Step 4.

Rule 2 says there must be at least one green ball lower than the lowest red ball. Make sure you don't read more into this rule than what is here. There could be a green ball above a red one in the sequence, but there must be at least one green one lower than the lowest red.

Rule 3 creates a block: A green ball will appear immediately above a white ball at some point in the sequence.

Step 4: Deductions

Rule 3 established one Block of Entities:

```
┌───┐
│ G │
│ W │
└───┘
```

The most important element of BLEND here is probably the Number Restrictions. The rules confirm that there is at least one of each color in the boxes. Since there are only six balls, and there must be more red balls than white, the number of white balls can only be one or two.

If there are two white balls, then there must be three red balls, leaving one green ball. If there is only one white ball, then there could be two red balls, leaving three green balls; there could be three red balls, leaving two green balls; or

there could be four red balls, leaving one green ball. So four ratios are possible:

R	G	W
3	1	2
2	3	1
3	2	1
4	1	1

In that last ratio (with four red balls), the green and white balls must form the GW block, and since there must be a green ball below the lowest red ball, the GW block will occupy boxes 1 and 2:

```
6    R
5    R
4    R
3    R
2    G
1    W
```

Step 5: Questions

18. (B) "If" / Could Be True

As expected, the Numbers are important right off the bat. As you saw in the Deductions, if there are two white balls, there must be three red balls and one green ball. That one green ball must be lower than all three red balls (Rule 2) and directly above a white ball (Rule 3), so it can only be placed in box 2 or box 3. **(B)** is therefore correct.

19. (C) "If" / Could Be True

Again, start with the Numbers. The "If" clause establishes that there are at least two green balls. Since they are in boxes 5 and 6, those green balls can't be below any red balls, so there will have to be one more green ball to satisfy Rule 2. That makes three green balls, so there will be two red balls and one white ball (Rule 1). The red balls can either be in boxes 3 and 4 or boxes 2 and 3. They have to be next to each other to leave room for the GW block:

```
6    G    G
5    G    G
4    R    W
3    R    R
2    G    R
1    W    G
```

This means that only **(C)** is possible.

20. (E) Must Be True

The question asks you to identify the box that must share a color with at least one other box—in other words, the box that could not contain a unique color. The Numbers tell you that if a box does not share a ball color with any other box, then that box must contain either a green ball or a white ball (there are always at least two reds). Box 6 can't have the only green ball, since at least one green ball must be lower than the lowest red ball (Rule 2). And box 6 can't have the only white ball, since there must be a GW block somewhere in the sketch (Rule 3). So **(E)** is correct.

A quick strategic point: This and the subsequent "Must Be True" question can be great questions to do late in the game. Your sketches for "If" questions show that boxes 4 and 5 can contain a unique color, so eliminate **(C)** and **(D)**.

21. (A) Must Be True

The correct answer must be true, meaning that all four wrong answers could be false. **(A)** can't be false. If you try to make box 4 the lowest possible box containing a green ball, then red balls will fill boxes 5 and 6 (and according to Rule 2, those would be the only red balls). This means that in order to satisfy Rule 1, you'll have to have more green balls somewhere in boxes 1 through 3.

This is a great question to do later in the game, after you've amassed sketches from the "If" questions—and since four of the six questions are "If" questions, they'll produce a lot of helpful info. Particularly, the sketches from subsequent two "If" questions show that **(B)** through **(E)** can be false in at least one instance. Therefore, all four choices can be ellminated.

22. (C) "If" / Could Be True

The "If" clause puts red balls in boxes 2 and 3. From that, you know that a green ball must be in box 1 (Rule 2):

```
6
5
4
3        R
2        R
1        G
```

Since the correct answer could be true, the green ball in box 1 eliminates **(A)** and **(B)**. You still need to incorporate the GW block (Rule 3). This block can go into boxes 5 and 6 or boxes 4 and 5. And the remaining box must contain either a red ball or a green ball so that red balls will outnumber white balls:

```
6      G      G/R
5      W      G
4      G/R    W
3      R      R
2      R      R
1      G      G
```

This eliminates **(D)** and **(E)**, leaving **(C)** as the only possibility.

23. (D) "If" / Must Be True

The new "If" establishes three balls, all of the same color. Because of the number restrictions that follow from Rule 1, that color must be either red or green:

```
6
5
4      R      G
3      R      G
2      R      G
1
```

In the first case, box 1 must contain a green ball (Rule 2), leaving boxes 5 and 6 for the GW block. In the second case, the remaining boxes will contain two red balls and one white ball (Rule 1), which must be in box 1 to create the GW block:

```
6      G      R
5      W      R
4      R      G
3      R      G
2      R      G
1      G      W
```

In either case, **(D)** is true. Each of the other choices is false in at least one of these scenarios.

Section III: Logical Reasoning

Q#	Question Type	Correct	Difficulty
1	Role of a Statement	E	★
2	Flaw	D	★
3	Principle (Identify/Inference)	E	★
4	Point at Issue	A	★
5	Inference	D	★
6	Assumption (Necessary)	D	★
7	Inference	B	★
8	Paradox	B	★★★★
9	Weaken	C	★
10	Main Point	A	★
11	Assumption (Necessary)	B	★★★★
12	Paradox	A	★
13	Inference	B	★
14	Flaw	B	★★
15	Assumption (Necessary)	E	★
16	Weaken	E	★★★
17	Assumption (Sufficient)	D	★★★
18	Flaw	A	★★★
19	Method of Argument	C	★★
20	Parallel Reasoning	E	★★
21	Strengthen	B	★★★
22	Principle (Apply/Assumption)	A	★★★★
23	Principle (Identify/Strengthen)	C	★★★
24	Assumption (Sufficient)	A	★★★
25	Parallel Flaw	A	★★★
26	Paradox	A	★★★★

1. (E) Role of a Statement

Step 1: Identify the Question Type

The question provides a claim and asks why it was offered by the commentator, making this a Role of a Statement question. Separate the argument into evidence and conclusion and determine the function of the claim in question.

Step 2: Untangle the Stimulus

This stimulus has two arguments. First, Acme Engines states its case. A train wreck was caused when a poorly placed switch was hit by an engineer's knee. Acme claims that it's not responsible because it was supposedly unaware of the problem. As for relocating the same switch in other locomotives, Acme insists it was merely trying to remedy an inconvenience.

The commentator, however, is not buying the story. Instead, the commentator asserts that Acme *is* responsible. As evidence, the commentator cites the cost to Acme of relocating the switch in its other locomotives (this is the statement the question is asking about). The commentator suggests that Acme would not have spent $500,000 just to fix an inconvenience.

Step 3: Make a Prediction

The claim about the cost of the switch relocation is part of the commentator's evidence against Acme. By saying that the cost seems too high to fix a simple inconvenience, the commentator suggests an ulterior motive on Acme's part. In concluding that Acme is responsible, the commentator suggests that Acme *was* aware of the problem beforehand and the claim of "fixing an inconvenience" is just an excuse.

Step 4: Evaluate the Answer Choices

(E) fits the commentator's intentions in bringing up the questionable cost.

(A) exonerates the train's engineer, but the commentator is only concerned with Acme's responsibility.

(B) distorts the commentator's intention. He likely believes that relocating the switch could have helped avoid the wreck; his point, though, is that Acme knew the switch problem existed.

(C) is wrong because the cause of the accident is mentioned in the argument's first sentence.

(D) is wrong because the commentator isn't questioning the danger of the switch. In fact, by claiming that Acme is responsible, he acknowledges that the knee switch was a problem. **(D)** is a point that Acme would like to make and, thus, a 180.

2. (D) Flaw

Step 1: Identify the Question Type

The question asks why the author's reasoning is "flawed," making it easy to recognize as a Flaw question. Break the argument into conclusion and evidence and describe why or how the evidence doesn't properly lead to the conclusion.

Step 2: Untangle the Stimulus

The artist starts off with her conclusion: almost everyone in her country wants to be an artist, even if they have to work other jobs too. Her evidence is that almost everyone she knows wants to make a living as an artist, even though they already have other jobs.

Step 3: Make a Prediction

It takes a great leap of logic to make a claim about an entire country's ambitions based on the dreams of a few dishwashers and store clerks that one knows personally. This is a classic unrepresentative sample: drawing a conclusion about a large population from a sample that's too small and/or may not represent the characteristics of the larger population in the conclusion.

Step 4: Evaluate the Answer Choices

(D) perfectly expresses the representativeness issue.

(A) suggests circular reasoning, but the artist's evidence doesn't depend on her conclusion. Her evidence comes from what she's been told by people she knows.

(B) distorts the argument. The artist doesn't base her conclusion about the whole population on what's true of *each* person in the country—only what's true about the handful of people she knows.

(C) suggests that the artist backs up her conclusion by citing a widely held viewpoint. However, the evidence is only about people she knows—hardly enough people to qualify as "widely held." **(C)** distorts the argument; the conclusion, not the evidence, asserts that the view is widely held.

(E) might be tempting, since the artist does shift from evidence about people's hopes of "making a living" as an artist to a conclusion about wanting to "be an artist" even if they have to support themselves with "day jobs." The language use is a little fuzzy, but in order to make a living as an artist, one would have to be an artist. So, if people say they want to make a living as artists, then it's valid to conclude they want to *be* artists. This distinction is not needed in context of the argument.

3. (E) Principle (Identify/Inference)

Step 1: Identify the Question Type

A "proposition" is a general statement, also known on the LSAT as a principle. The stimulus will provide a specific illustration and the question will ask you to identify the principle—the broader rule of thumb—that conforms to the given situation.

Step 2: Untangle the Stimulus

The author mentions two types of keyboards: the qwerty and the Dvorak. The qwerty is the current standard and has been since the typewriter was invented. The Dvorak seems to be a better alternative, allowing for faster typing. The author claims, however, that the numerous costs associated with changing over (e.g., money and time) outweigh the advantage of faster typing, making a switch impractical.

Step 3: Make a Prediction

The correct answer will follow the same logic, only broadening the scope so as to apply not just to keyboards. In essence, the author is saying that the costs of switching away from a standard practice can outweigh the tangible benefits of an alternative, making the switch impractical.

Step 4: Evaluate the Answer Choices

(E) correctly identifies the greater practicality of sticking with a standard over switching to an alternative.

(A) starts off great, since the Dvorak keyboard would improve speed. However, there's no suggestion that accuracy would be sacrificed.

(B) is a 180, since the standard here (the qwerty keyboard) is *less* efficient than the alternative.

(C) distorts the argument, suggesting that the reason for sticking with the standard is a *dislike* of change. However, the author cites money, time, and frustration as factors in the decision.

(D) also distorts the argument. The switch to the alternative would entail both emotional and financial considerations, but the author doesn't describe one or the other as more significant.

4. (A) Point at Issue

Step 1: Identify the Question Type

Asking for the "point of disagreement," this is a standard Point at Issue question. Identify the main point of each author and determine where they conflict with each other. Remember to use the Decision Tree if you're unsure about an answer.

Step 2: Untangle the Stimulus

Sam starts out by arguing that, even though mountain lions and bighorn sheep are protected species, we shouldn't interfere in their predator–prey relationship simply to save the sheep. Just let nature take its course.

Meli isn't on the same page. Meli seems intent on protecting the bighorn sheep, even if that means stepping in and reducing the mountain lion population.

Step 3: Make a Prediction

Clearly, Sam and Meli have different agendas. Both seem eager to protect the endangered sheep, but Sam is resigned to the position that humans must stay out of the situation, while Meli insists that humans must act, even to the point of stunting the mountain lion population. The correct answer will address their conflict over how much action humans should take to save the sheep.

Step 4: Evaluate the Answer Choices

(A) correctly identifies the issue: How much do humans need to be involved in the situation? Plus, it satisfies the decision tree: 1) Sam has an opinion about the answer choice—he agrees that humans shouldn't intervene; 2) Meli has an opinion about the answer choice—she disagrees and feels we *should* intervene; 3) their views on this choice are diametrically opposed.

(B) makes a distinction between saving an entire species and saving a few individual animals, a distinction not made by either author. This answer is Outside the Scope of the argument.

(C) is Outside the Scope of both authors' positions, since neither one discusses which species is "easier" to preserve.

(D) discusses the effect of limiting the mountain lion population. Meli makes that suggestion but never implies that it would kill off the lions entirely.

(E) mentions what would happen if we didn't limit the mountain lion population. According to Sam, who doesn't want to interfere, we would then "hope the bighorns survive." He expresses no opinion on whether the bighorns will survive, so he can't be said to disagree with this answer choice.

5. (D) Inference

Step 1: Identify the Question Type

The question stem describes the stimulus as a set of statements and calls for a correct answer "inferred" from those statements. This is an Inference question all the way. Simply catalog and combine the information provided and look for logical deductions that can be made.

Step 2: Untangle the Stimulus

The parent here is against pushing rigorous work onto very young children for the sake of making the nation more competitive. While rigorous work is okay for secondary school kids, the parent asserts, younger students should have curricula that address their developmental needs. Rigorous work for these primary school students would provide only short-term gains and cause the children to burn out.

Step 3: Make a Prediction

There's no Formal Logic here, so the correct answer will merely be consistent with the ideas presented without distorting or exaggerating the parent's claims or including anything the parent didn't mention. Boiling everything down, the correct answer will follow from the idea that rigorous work is bad for primary school students and wouldn't help them with the developmental needs that their curriculum should address.

Step 4: Evaluate the Answer Choices

(D) exactly matches the parent's concern.

(A) mentions increasing rigorous work in secondary school, but the parent is only concerned with *not* increasing it in primary school. Even though the parent says that rigorous work makes sense in secondary school, that's far short of suggesting it should be increased.

(B) is Outside the Scope, since the parent never addresses the developmental needs of secondary school students—only that of primary school students.

(C) sets a requirement for being more competitive, which seems to be of no concern to the parent. The parent is much more concerned with doing what's best for the kids than with making the nation competitive.

(E) suggests that rigorous study in primary school is necessary to the nation becoming more competitive. Given the parent's stance *against* rigorous study in primary school (including a note at the end saying it may ultimately work against us), there's no support for this answer.

6. (D) Assumption (Necessary)

Step 1: Identify the Question Type

The question directly asks for the assumption, making it easy to identify. The word *depends* indicates the assumption is required, meaning that you can use the Denial Test can to confirm the correct answer. Start by identifying the evidence and conclusion; then look for what the author failed to mention.

Step 2: Untangle the Stimulus

The author discusses the evaluation of a company's bus drivers. While drivers complain that being observed while driving affects them, the author concludes that the best drivers will still be the best drivers while being supervised. The evidence is that all bus drivers are affected by having a supervisor on board.

Step 3: Make a Prediction

Since all drivers are affected, the author implies fairness—everybody has the same disadvantage. The best stay the best, and the worst stay the worst. However, if two people are both affected, they aren't necessarily affected *equally*. One person may be severely affected and the other only mildly affected. In order for this argument to work, the author must assume that the effect of being observed is roughly equal for all drivers.

Step 4: Evaluate the Answer Choices

(D) matches the prediction exactly. Using the Denial Test, if the bus drivers *aren't* affected in the same way, then the best drivers may be more affected, leading to results that don't line up as neatly as the author suggests.

(A) is irrelevant. Even if there is another effective evaluation method, that doesn't affect the author's argument about *this* method.

(B) is Outside the Scope. The argument isn't about the supervisor's judgments. It's only about the drivers' performance.

(C) mentions the effect on *most* drivers ("slightly worse"), but that leaves room for other drivers to be more greatly affected or even to have their performance improved by observation. That would go against the author's assumption.

(E) is irrelevant. Again, even if there is another way to perform assessments—indeed, even if the other way is better—it doesn't affect the author's argument about *this* evaluation.

7. (B) Inference

Step 1: Identify the Question Type

This stem asks you to find something "supported" by the "information" given. That means you're looking for an inference. Accept the statements in the stimulus as facts and look for one answer that is absolutely accurate based on those facts.

Step 2: Untangle the Stimulus

According to the author, economic growth increases demand for new technologies. While few businesses provide new technologies, lots of people want them. Despite all that, a rapid acceleration of new technologies can actually hurt both the businesses that provide them and the people who buy them.

Step 3: Make a Prediction

There's a strong paradox element in this set of facts. To see how the facts fit together, combine the first and last statements. Since economic growth increases demand for new technologies, and accelerating technological change can hurt suppliers and buyers, then it's safe to say that economic growth can (oddly enough) hurt people in the new technology business. The correct answer will play off that deduction.

Step 4: Evaluate the Answer Choices

(B) makes the connection that economic growth can ultimately hurt technology business.

(A) is an Irrelevant Comparison. Though it is reasonable to think that technological change would help technology companies, there's nothing in the stimulus that allows you to compare them with other companies. Moreover, the information in the stimulus says that change can cause new technology businesses to fail.

(C) distorts the logic of the first sentence. While growth can create demand for technology, that doesn't mean the causality can necessarily be reversed (i.e., technology doesn't necessarily stimulate economic growth).

(D) is another Irrelevant Comparison and a potential 180. Economic growth stimulates demand for new technologies, which the last line says can cause buyers to fail, not prosper. Even for those companies that do prosper, you can't conclude that they prosper more during periods of economic growth.

(E) is Extreme. While the demand for technology *can* cause business to fail, it doesn't *have* to. Moreover, the author discusses only businesses in the technology sector. While more of those businesses might fail, there may be fewer failures in other sectors, potentially creating a decrease in *overall* business failures.

8. (B) Paradox

Step 1: Identify the Question Type

Being asked to "resolve" a "discrepancy" is a common request of Paradox questions. The stimulus will provide information that seems to be contradictory. The correct answer will explain away the mystery.

Step 2: Untangle the Stimulus

According to the energy analyst, heavy usage of air conditioners due to a current heat wave is causing power outages. A solution is proposed: ask residents to cut back on using their air conditioners at home. While that seems like a viable solution, the analyst suggests otherwise, saying that blackouts would still occur even if people agreed to cut back. So the mystery is this: if air conditioners are causing the blackouts, why would there still be blackouts if people reduced their use of air conditioners at home?

Step 3: Make a Prediction

The key here is to consider an overlooked possibility. The solution offered is only a partial solution: cutting back on using air conditioners *at home*. However, if air conditioners are still used frequently at offices, stores, or other locations,

then cutting back on residential usage wouldn't fully resolve the problem.

Step 4: Evaluate the Answer Choices

(B) adequately addresses what the proposed solution overlooks. If most air-conditioning was outside the home, then heavy air conditioner usage could still cause blackouts.

(A) is tempting but irrelevant. The author says explicitly that "air conditioner use has overloaded the … power grid." Presumably, the other drains on the electrical system are there all the time. Increased air conditioner use (due to the heat wave) has overloaded the system. Why reducing that wouldn't prevent blackouts is still a mystery with **(A)**.

(C) provides an alternative solution, but it doesn't explain why the analyst feels the proposed solution won't work.

(D) is irrelevant since the analyst's claim is based on the event that residents *do* reduce their usage.

(E) is irrelevant since the analyst's assertion is only applicable while the heat wave continues ("blackouts will probably occur unless the heat wave abates").

9. (C) Weaken

Step 1: Identify the Question Type

This question is simply asking for something that weakens the argument. Start by identifying the conclusion and evidence. Then, look for the answer that makes the author's central assumption less likely.

Step 2: Untangle the Stimulus

According to the author, there are two types of relaxation training: short-term and long-term. The author concludes that the more expensive long-term training is unnecessary for most people. The evidence is that, in patients using either training type, anxiety diminishes in the short run.

Step 3: Make a Prediction

This is a classic case of an author ignoring potential benefits. Since the long-term training is more expensive than short-term training and offers the same short-term results, the author assumes there are no other benefits to long-term training that would make it preferable. In particular, since the argument is focused only on short-term results, the author overlooks potential ongoing benefits of the long-term training. If such benefits exist, then long-term training *could* be warranted, going against the author's argument.

Step 4: Evaluate the Answer Choices

(C) provides exactly the kind of long-term benefit that would warrant taking long-term training over short-term training: a reduced chance that anxiety will resurface.

(A) simply provides alternatives to both short-term and long-term training. However, that would still make long-term training unwarranted, thus strengthening the author's point.

(B) contains a common LSAT trap, tempting you to confuse *generally* and *always*. According to the author, long-term training is "generally" more expensive. That's not the same as saying it's "always" more expensive. The author's use of the word *generally* allows for some exceptional cases like the ones mentioned in **(B)**. Therefore, this doesn't truly affect the argument.

(D) is a 180. If just the thought of treatment helps, then the more expensive long-term training certainly seems unwarranted, as the author claims.

(E) is a 180, since it provides more reasons why short-term training seems the better alternative.

10. (A) Main Point

Step 1: Identify the Question Type

The question asks for the editorialist's "conclusion," otherwise known as the Main Point. Use the One-Sentence Test to determine the one sentence that most strongly expresses the editorialist's opinion.

Step 2: Untangle the Stimulus

This Is a common pattern for arguments in Main Point stimuli: the argument presents one point of view and then contradicts it. The editorialist first presents the opinion of consumerism critics: advertising convinces people that they *need* something when they really just *want* it. The editorialist's rebuttal starts with the word *however*. The editorialist claims that the criticism rests on an unclear distinction between wants and needs, since the two ideas are often hard to distinguish.

Step 3: Make a Prediction

The editorialist's argument starts at the word *however*, with the immediate claim that the critics are relying on a fuzzy distinction between wants and needs. The last sentence just serves as evidence for why that distinction isn't as clear as the critics think.

Step 4: Evaluate the Answer Choices

(A) correctly expresses the editorialist's position: The critics rely on a fuzzy use of the terms *wants* and *needs*.

(B) plays around with the critics' point of view but completely ignores the editorialist's argument against their fuzzy distinction between wants and needs. It uses the words of the stimulus but distorts its meaning.

(C) mentions a judgment the editorialist never makes. While the critics may be making an unfair distinction, the editorialist never goes so far as to say that there's nothing wrong with advertising.

(D) is a Distortion. The editorialist never calls the critics out for ignoring certain necessities.

(E) is Extreme. The fuzzy distinction is only discussed in the context of advertising. The editorialist doesn't state or suggest that it is "often" an issue.

11. (B) Assumption (Necessary)

Step 1: Identify the Question Type

The question doesn't hide the fact that you're looking for an assumption. However, it's helpful to note that the assumption is required by the argument, meaning the Denial Test may come in handy. Start by identifying the conclusion and evidence and then determine the "disconnect" between them.

Step 2: Untangle the Stimulus

The author concludes that people who use the Web for medical advice can do themselves more harm than good. The evidence is that people can't tell the difference between valid information and quackery (i.e., invalid information). Further complicating things is that quackery is easier to read, making it more appealing to people without a medical background.

Step 3: Make a Prediction

The evidence is about the mixed information people find on the Web, and the conclusion is about what's bad for people. The assumption merely connects these two concepts: relying on information that may be invalid can be more harmful than beneficial.

Step 4: Evaluate the Answer Choices

(B) matches the prediction exactly: someone who doesn't rely on valid information when trying to diagnose an illness can do more harm than good. This choice is actually a conditional Formal Logic statement. When translated (by replacing *unless* with *if not*), it reads:

$$\text{If} \quad \begin{array}{l}\textit{people don't rely}\\ \textit{exclusively on valid} \rightarrow\\ \textit{info}\end{array} \quad \begin{array}{l}\textit{they can do more}\\ \textit{harm than good}\end{array}$$

This perfectly matches the prediction.

(A) seems reasonable, but it is irrelevant to the argument. The conclusion is already limited to those who rely on the Web to self-diagnose. Whether people surfing for medical information are *typically* trying to self-diagnose doesn't affect the argument.

(C) brings up the possibility of medically informed people who *can* discriminate properly among the various sources of information. This is Outside the Scope of the stimulus, which is limited to those who "often" can't distinguish and are thus "likely" to do themselves harm.

(D), when reworded, states: If something is not clearly written, then people assume it's invalid. This could add weight to the argument, but it isn't *required* by the argument. If you deny **(D)** (i.e., if people assumed that unclear information is valid), it doesn't address people's assumptions when information *is* clearly written, which is the author's concern. Moreover, this choice doesn't connect the evidence to the conclusion, which is what the assumption must do.

(E) distorts the logic of the argument. The author's argument is that, if information can be either valid or quackery, then it can do more harm than good. This answer states if people *don't* rely on quackery, then they *won't* do more harm—a logically distinct argument. One could rely on valid information and still do harm. Finally, this answer discusses relying on quackery *instead* of valid info; the argument suggests that people can't distinguish between the two.

12. (A) Paradox

Step 1: Identify the Question Type

When a question asks you to explain something, it's typically a Paradox question. In this case, the paradox revolves around why kids find it easier to catch a ball thrown quickly. The stimulus will provide information about why this is unusual. The correct answer will resolve the discrepancy.

Step 2: Untangle the Stimulus

The author states that adults usually throw balls slowly to children, since children haven't fully developed their coordination. However, despite this lack of coordination, children actually find it easier to catch balls thrown more quickly.

Step 3: Make a Prediction

So why are fastballs easier to catch if the kids haven't fully developed their coordination? While you may not be able to predict an exact solution, you know the correct answer will identify a reason why kids can catch fast balls more easily than slow balls.

Step 4: Evaluate the Answer Choices

(A) helps explain this discrepancy. If quickly thrown balls trigger self-defense mechanisms, then the kids might be reacting instinctively despite their lack of coordination. At slower speeds, when self-defense isn't employed, the child wouldn't have that intuition and would thus be impaired by the lack of coordination.

(B) is a 180. If slower balls are less obscured, one would think they would be easier to catch. Yet the author says the opposite is happening.

(C) is irrelevant because the paradox is about children's abilities, not adults'. Plus, if adults find slowly thrown balls

easier to catch, it's even harder to understand why kids would be different.

(D) is Outside the Scope since the paradox involves children catching balls, not throwing them.

(E) suggests that there may be speeds that are *too* fast for children, but that still offers no explanation for why somewhat faster balls are easier to catch than slower balls.

13. (B) Inference

Step 1: Identify the Question Type

The stimulus is described as a set of "statements" that will "support" the correct answer. This is an Inference question. (A Strengthen question would go the other way around; i.e., use the correct answer to support the argument in the stimulus.) Combine the information given to make valid deductions and find the one answer that must follow from the stimulus.

Step 2: Untangle the Stimulus

The author presents a similarity between genetic profiles and fMRIs: Both contain private information. However, there is a difference. A patient's face can be recognized from an fMRI, while you would need a label or a record to determine whom a genetic profile belongs to.

Step 3: Make a Prediction

Summing up, both a genetic profile and an fMRI can reveal private information. The images in an fMRI could be used to reveal a person's identity, which couldn't be done with a genetic profile without access to labels or records. The correct answer will most likely address this potential breach in privacy, a risk of fMRIs but not of genetic profiles.

Step 4: Evaluate the Answer Choices

(B) is supported. If there were no labels or records, the fMRI could still reveal a person's identity through images, while the genetic profile would remain anonymous.

(A) seems reasonable since providers could just use the images from the fMRI to ID patients instead of labels. However, there's a significant difference between saying the labels aren't needed and saying they're not important. Perhaps the labels could provide other important information (e.g., date of birth) that the images alone can't. And the cost of using the skull information to create a facial image could be prohibitively expensive.

(C) is unsupported since genetic profiles can only be linked to somebody using labels or records. There's no suggestion that those labels and records aren't also kept private.

(D) distorts the information given. While both are described as containing private information, nothing suggests that most of that information is the same between them.

(E) seems tempting, since people would seem to have a reason to be more concerned. However, there's nothing to suggest that they actually *are* more concerned. After all, if patients aren't aware of the discrepancy, then they probably wouldn't recognize any need for concern.

14. (B) Flaw

Step 1: Identify the Question Type

Despite being asked for the council member's "technique" (a typical sign of Method of Argument), the technique is described as "questionable," which means there's a Flaw in the argument. While some Method of Argument skills can be useful here, the ultimate approach would be to break the argument into its evidence and conclusion to understand why the reasoning isn't logically sound.

Step 2: Untangle the Stimulus

The council member recommends using an abandoned shoe factory as emergency shelter instead of the courthouse, as others have suggested. The council member's evidence is simply that the courthouse proponents have given no evidence to support their suggestion.

Step 3: Make a Prediction

Notice that, for her part, the council member fails to provide any evidence that the abandoned factory would be a good shelter. Instead, the council member simply rejects an alternative due to a lack of evidence. (Talk about hypocrisy!) The correct answer to this classic Flaw question will point out that the author rejects an alternative solution merely based on lack of evidence.

Step 4: Evaluate the Answer Choices

(B) points out this mistake. The council member accepts her own claim (use the shoe factory) simply because the opposing members don't have enough evidence to back up their solution (use the courthouse).

(A) is a Distortion. The council member does exploit a lack of evidence. However, she uses a lack of evidence in *favor* of a view (i.e., no evidence in favor of the courthouse) as proof that the view is *not* correct (i.e., the courthouse *shouldn't* be used). She doesn't say, "The opponents haven't offered evidence against the shoe factory."

(C) is mistaken because the council member doesn't attack her opponents personally, just their lack of evidence.

(D) is Outside the Scope since there is no appeal to fear.

(E) is a 180 since the argument being attacked (using the courthouse) *is* held by some council members.

15. (E) Assumption (Necessary)

Step 1: Identify the Question Type

The question comes right out and asks for the assumption. Be sure to break the argument down into its evidence and conclusion and look for the disconnect between the two. Also, since this argument "relies" on the assumption, the Denial Test can be used if needed.

Step 2: Untangle the Stimulus

The author opens with the conclusion: James misled the Core Curriculum Committee (CCC) into thinking the Anthropology Department chair endorsed the proposal. His evidence is what the department chair actually said. The chair *did* endorse the proposal, but with a condition—that the draft include every recommendation that would be in the final proposal.

Step 3: Make a Prediction

The author's conclusion that James misled the CCC suggests that James didn't actually get the department chair's endorsement. James had to meet a requirement to get the department chair's endorsement. To suggest that James didn't get the endorsement, the author must be assuming James failed to meet the requirement. In other words, James must not have included in the draft every recommendation he would ultimately make to the CCC.

Step 4: Evaluate the Answer Choices

(E) expresses the missing piece of the puzzle. If the proposal didn't include all recommendations, then James wouldn't have satisfied the department chair's requirement. That means no endorsement, allowing the author to conclude James wasn't truthful in saying he had the chair's backing.

(A) focuses on whether or not the CCC will *implement* the proposal's recommendations. That's Outside the Scope of the argument, which is about whether James got the endorsement or not.

(B) is irrelevant. All that matters is whether or not the department chair endorsed *this* proposal.

(C) provides a motive for James to mislead the CCC, but it doesn't confirm the author's accusation that he actually was misleading.

(D) might be tempting. If he acted under the assumption that the department chair would simply approve all his recommendations, then James could have amended his draft thinking he wouldn't lose the endorsement. However, there's no evidence that he actually did this, so it doesn't confirm the author's conclusion.

16. (E) Weaken

Step 1: Identify the Question Type

The stem directly asks for something that will weaken the argument. Start by identifying the evidence and the conclusion, then find an answer that contradicts the author's central assumption.

Step 2: Untangle the Stimulus

The author tells you that Travaillier Corporation has recently hired people with experience in the bus tour industry. The company is hiring these folks despite having a clientele primarily interested in air travel. From that, the author concludes that Travaillier must be trying to attract new customers.

Step 3: Make a Prediction

The author assumes that Travaillier would not promote bus tours in addition to flights to current customers. In other words, he assumes that bus tours will be marketed exclusively to new customers. Any answer that suggests the bus tours are for current customers will weaken that assumption. For example, just because Travallier's current customers prefer to travel by air doesn't mean they wouldn't want to take a bus tour when they reach their destination.

Step 4: Evaluate the Answer Choices

(E) works by suggesting that Travaillier is attempting to expand by promoting the new services (i.e., the bus tours) to current customers—not necessarily new customers.

(A) is irrelevant because it's already given that current customers aren't changing their preferences. If anything, a history of difficulty in changing customer preferences would tend to strengthen the author's argument that the new employees are part of an effort to attract new customers.

(B) discusses other travel companies' failures, which have no bearing on whom Travaillier is or isn't trying to entice.

(C) might seem plausible, given that the new employee's air package experience would be useful for current customers. However, if the bus tours are still unappealing to current customers, then that aspect of the new employee's experience would work in favor of the author's argument. The wording of this choice also leaves open the possibility that all but one of the new hires has no air travel experience. That, too, would strengthen the author's argument.

(D) is Outside the Scope because it discusses not only other travel agencies but also high-spending customers, neither of which is relevant to the author's argument.

17. (D) Assumption (Sufficient)

Step 1: Identify the Question Type

The question is plainly asking for what's "assumed," making this an Assumption question. Start by identifying the evidence and the conclusion. According to the question, the conclusion will be valid *if* the correct answer is assumed, meaning the assumption is sufficient to form a valid argument. The Denial Test will not necessarily help on this question.

Step 2: Untangle the Stimulus

The educator wastes no time stating the conclusion: traditional classroom education is ineffective. The evidence is that the traditional classroom isn't a social process and you must have a social process to develop students' insights. The last sentence simply describes the nonsocial aspects of the traditional classroom: outside-the-group teachers with artificial, rigid interactions.

Step 3: Make a Prediction

If you need a social process to develop students' insights, then the traditional classroom can't develop students' insights (since it's not a social process). However, that doesn't justify calling the traditional classroom "ineffective." To do that, the author would have to assume that developing students' insights is required for education to be effective.

Step 4: Evaluate the Answer Choices

(D) completes the argument perfectly. If insight development is needed for effective education, and traditional classrooms don't develop insight, then the author's conclusion that those classrooms are ineffective is valid.

(A) mentions "genuine education," a concept never discussed in the argument.

(B) distorts the logic. In abbreviated Formal Logic terms, this answer states:

$$\text{If} \quad \begin{array}{c} \sim \textit{rigid AND} \\ \sim \textit{artificial} \end{array} \quad \rightarrow \quad \textit{effective}$$

However, to complete the argument, the author would need the statement to read:

$$\text{If} \quad \begin{array}{c} \textit{rigid AND artificial} \\ \textit{(like traditional} \\ \textit{classroom)} \end{array} \quad \rightarrow \quad \sim \textit{effective}$$

So, **(B)** negates that statement but doesn't reverse its terms, thus it is not the correct contrapositive.

(C) makes a connection between social processes and rigidness/artificiality. However, it does not validate calling a type of education ineffective.

(E) brings up nontraditional classrooms, which are Outside the Scope of this argument.

18. (A) Flaw

Step 1: Identify the Question Type

Saying an argument is "vulnerable to criticism" is classic LSAT language for saying there's a Flaw. Break down the argument into the conclusion and evidence and look for an answer that indicates why the evidence doesn't properly lead to the conclusion.

Step 2: Untangle the Stimulus

The argument starts off with evidence about how avoiding fat can reduce the risk of heart disease. Moreover, one can avoid fat by avoiding dairy products. The author uses this information to conclude that avoiding dairy products can help you stay healthy.

Step 3: Make a Prediction

The facts can be connected to show that avoiding dairy (which helps you avoid fat) can lower the risk of heart disease. However, the author makes a giant leap in suggesting that this would help maintain good health overall. While avoiding heart disease is definitely a great thing, there's more to good health than simply avoiding heart problems. The correct answer will expose the author's failure to consider other factors that contribute to good health. In classic Flaw question terms, the author has committed a fatal scope shift, from "heart disease" in the evidence to "good health" in the conclusion.

Step 4: Evaluate the Answer Choices

(A) points out the author's mistake. The author ignores that, even though a certain practice (eating dairy) can have negative consequences (increased risk of heart disease), eliminating that practice (avoiding dairy) may also have *other* negative consequences for one's health.

(B) suggests that there may be ways to maintain good health (or reduce heart problems) other than avoiding dairy. However, other solutions are not the issue here. This doesn't address the real flaw, that the recommendation (avoiding dairy) might not work.

(C) may be tempting, since the author does assume that we should eliminate dairy foods owing to their risks. But that's not the problematic assumption in the argument. The author's flaw comes from overlooking a possible upside to including dairy that could improve a person's overall health.

(D) is wrong because heart disease *is* relevant to good health—it's just not the *only* thing relevant.

(E) is wrong because the author never goes so far as to say anything will "necessarily occur." The argument hinges on loose language like "probability ... is increased" and "less likely."

19. (C) Method of Argument

Step 1: Identify the Question Type

The words *proceeds by* indicate that question is asking *how* the professor constructs the argument, meaning that you're looking for the Method of Argument. Use Keywords to determine structure and focus on how the author *does* what he sets out to do, not on what the author *says*.

Step 2: Untangle the Stimulus

The professor makes an argument about forming an idea about your environment. You can't base your idea on one fleeting perception because each individual perception is limited to just one individual perspective. The professor supports this argument by making a similar argument about history: you can't form a view of the past based on one history book because each book reflects that author's biases.

Step 3: Make a Prediction

The professor backs up an argument about picturing one's environment with a comparable argument about constructing a view of the past. The correct answer will reflect the professor's use of an analogy or comparison to make the argument.

Step 4: Evaluate the Answer Choices

(C) is a match, since it perfectly describes the author's support for one argument via its resemblance to another argument.

(A) does match the author's use of comparison, but he doesn't suggest that either argument is flawed. Indeed, the author appears to consider both arguments valid. They both recommend, with no sense of flawed logic, avoiding the use of individual, single-perspective experiences to form larger pictures of the world.

(B) mentions "absurd consequences." While using a single glimpse of one's environment would lead to an inaccurate conception, the professor doesn't imply an *absurd* conception would result.

(D) is wrong because the author never describes or defines anything as having two closely related characteristics.

(E) is wrong because it suggests that individual perspectives and authors' biases are types of human cognition; that's not supported by the stimulus in any way.

20. (E) Parallel Reasoning

Step 1: Identify the Question Type

Since the question asks for a pattern of reasoning "similar" to the one in the stimulus, this is Parallel Reasoning. The correct answer must match the logical structure of the stimulus—including the conclusion type and any Formal Logic.

Step 2: Untangle the Stimulus

The argument is based on the past and present: to date, the city council has passed into law most proposals endorsed by the Citizens League. The author uses this evidence to predict that future proposals endorsed by the Citizens League will also be likely to pass. Note that the conclusion is a "soft" prediction—something will *probably* happen.

Step 3: Make a Prediction

The argument uses a majority of past results to predict that future occurrences will likely match those results. The correct answer must also make a prediction that suggests a likely continuation of past results. In general terms, if most items that have historically met a particular criterion (endorsed by the Citizens League) produced a particular result (passed by city council), then future items that meet that criterion will probably produce the same result.

Step 4: Evaluate the Answer Choices

(E) matches at every level: if most items that have historically met a particular criterion (stone artifacts at the site) produced a particular result (domestic tool), then future items that meet that criterion will probably produce the same result.

(A) falls apart in the conclusion, which suggests that only "most" grants will be awarded to biologists. The original argument concludes that "any" future proposal will be passed. That's not logically the same. Also, this argument shifts from evidence about Vasani grants in general to a conclusion about just those grants awarded to academics; no comparable shift in scope happens in the original argument.

(B) is a different argument, applying a characterization of individual items (trees) to larger groups (species of trees). Also, the conclusion is not a prediction. It is an assertion of fact about *most* species, which is logically different from the original argument about *any* future proposal.

(C) does make a prediction. There's also evidence of how most items that have historically met a criterion (local newspaper editor) produced a particular result (unsympathetic). However, the conclusion is about sympathetic employees, not people who meet the initial criterion (future editors). To be parallel, the conclusion here would need to read, "Thus, any future editors will probably be unsympathetic to local farmers, too."

(D) also makes a prediction. Again, there's evidence of how most items that have met a criterion (past the deadline) produced a particular result (rejected). However, this argument concludes that those people will not make the same mistake again, changing the historical pattern rather than continuing it.

21. (B) Strengthen

Step 1: Identify the Question Type

The stem unambiguously asks for something that will strengthen the argument. After breaking down the argument into its evidence and conclusion, determine what the chemist is assuming and find an answer that validates the chemist's assumption.

Step 2: Untangle the Stimulus

The chemist starts with a lot of evidence about a particular weed killer. Its molecules come in two forms: one that kills weeds and one that has no effect. In different soils, the molecules are concentrated differently. Because of this, the molecules will vary in effectiveness from one soil to the next. Thus, the chemist concludes that the data regarding the weed killer's effectiveness are probably misleading.

Step 3: Make a Prediction

Think about what would make the data misleading. According to the chemist's evidence, the data should show different levels of effectiveness depending on the different concentration of molecules in the soil. Anything that suggests the data aren't representing these potential fluctuations would validate the accusation of being misleading.

Step 4: Evaluate the Answer Choices

(B) raises questions about the validity of the data. If the data come almost exclusively from evenly concentrated soil, then they ignore the various other conditions in which one molecule can be more concentrated than the other (which alters the weed killer's effectiveness). This validates the chemist's claim that the data are probably misleading.

(A) is Outside the Scope. Whether any weed killer with molecules in two forms will exhibit the same pattern (one that kills weeds and one that doesn't) is beside the point. The weed killer in this argument has that pattern, as you already know from the evidence.

(C) suggests that most soil conditions favor one molecule over the other. However, if that's the case, then it's possible that the weed killer is designed for that kind of soil, raising no concerns about the data.

(D) is a 180. If the data cover a wide variety of soils, then it seems to address the concerns about varying effectiveness. This would lend more credibility to the data, contrary to the chemist's point.

(E) discusses the reasonable idea that *if* the data focused on only one form of the molecule, then that would be misleading. However, there's no indication that the data do that. If the data focused on both molecules, there's no argument to be made.

22. (A) Principle (Apply/Assumption)

Step 1: Identify the Question Type

The question stem tells you that there's a principle in the stimulus. When the principle (the broad rule) is in the stimulus, the LSAT often asks you to apply that principle to a specific situation in the correct answer. However, in this case, the author has already applied the principle to a circumstance and drawn a conclusion. What this question is asking for is something that, if true, would allow the author to reach that conclusion. Therefore, this stem is posing a task quite similar to asking for the author's assumption.

Step 2: Untangle the Stimulus

The principle involves some Formal Logic. If an officer has an exemplary record, that officer is eligible for a Mayor's Commendation. Otherwise (i.e., if the officer *doesn't* have an exemplary record), the officer isn't eligible. Furthermore, if the officer is eligible and exceeded expectations by saving someone's life, then the officer should receive the award. The author uses this set of rules to conclude that Officer Franklin should receive a Mayor's Commendation but Officer Penn should not.

Step 3: Make a Prediction

There are two parts to the conclusion here that need validation. First, what would have to be true to conclude that Franklin should receive the award? According to the principle, Franklin would first have to be eligible (that is, he would have to have an exemplary record), and then he would have to have saved someone's life in an action above and beyond the call of duty. Second, why deny Penn the commendation? There could be many reasons, but the clearest would be that Penn lacks an exemplary record, meaning that he's not even eligible. The correct answer needs to confirm that both Franklin and Penn have the appropriate circumstances.

Step 4: Evaluate the Answer Choices

(A) gets everything right. With his exemplary record, Franklin is eligible for the award. And, because he exceeded expectations to save the child's life, the principle states that he should receive the award. Despite exceptional efforts, Penn doesn't have an exemplary record. According to the principle, that denies him eligibility for the award.

(B) distorts the logic with Penn. With exemplary records, both officers are eligible for the award. Franklin's actions are sufficient to give him the award. Penn, on the other hand, didn't exceed expectations. Nonetheless, the failure to meet one sufficient condition does not logically warrant denying him the award. This treats the sufficient condition of exceeding expectations as if it were necessary.

(C) falls apart right off the bat. Without an exemplary record, Franklin is ineligible for the award, contradicting the conclusion.

(D) makes no mention of either officer's record, so there's no way to tell if either one is eligible for the award.

(E) also distorts the logic with Penn. Exemplary records make both officers eligible for the award. Franklin's actions are sufficient to give him the award. Penn, on the other hand, didn't exceed expectations and didn't save any lives. Nonetheless, the failure to meet these sufficient conditions does not logically warrant denying him the award. This treats the sufficient conditions of exceeding expectations and saving a life as if they were necessary.

23. (C) Principle (Identify/Strengthen)

Step 1: Identify the Question Type

The question stem directly asks for a principle. More specifically, you're looking to identify a principle among the answer choices, which means the correct answer will be broader in scope than the stimulus. Since the principle will be used to "justify" the argument, this question rewards the same skills as a Strengthen question. Break the argument down into evidence and conclusion and find the principle that validates the author's assumption.

Step 2: Untangle the Stimulus

The essayist begins by stating life is easier to enjoy if you can make choices that match your personal beliefs and see those choices accepted by others. One way to accomplish this is to choose friends and associates who share your beliefs. Based on these ideas, the essayist concludes that you shouldn't be denied the freedom to make those choices.

Step 3: Make a Prediction

Since the concept of preserving freedom is only introduced in the conclusion, the essayist must be making an assumption regarding that concept. What the essayist wants to preserve is the freedom to choose friends and associates, which according to the evidence enables us to see our choices accepted by others, making it easier to enjoy life. So, from a broader perspective, the author feels that we should not deny people the freedom to do something that would ultimately make life easier to enjoy.

Step 4: Evaluate the Answer Choices

(C) perfectly captures the heart of the essayist's argument. The freedom that the essayist claims would make life less difficult is the freedom to choose our associates. And if no one should be denied that kind of freedom, then the essayist's conclusion is valid.

(A) distorts the reasoning. This choice just ensures that you can make the initial lifestyle choices, but the main thrust of the argument is about choosing friends so that you can see your choices validated. Adding **(A)** to the argument doesn't help the author justify his conclusion that no one should be denied the freedom to associate.

(B) seems nice, but it doesn't address whether or not we're free to choose those associates. It's possible to associate with people who share your beliefs even if you're not free to choose your associates.

(D) goes Extreme in many ways. The evidence never states that enjoying life *depends* on having friends who share your beliefs (rather, an enjoyable life is "less difficult" in such cases). Furthermore, the essayist isn't concerned about being the denied the ability to *have* such associates, only the ability to *choose* them.

(E) is too weak, saying that an individual should have the right to choose friends if it makes life easier to enjoy. However, the essayist assumes that since freedom of association makes it easier for some people to enjoy their lives, *no one* should be denied that right.

24. (A) Assumption (Sufficient)

Step 1: Identify the Question Type

The stem outright asks for an assumption. For this question, it's important to note that the assumption is not required. It is merely something that, when added to the evidence, will allow the conclusion to be properly drawn. So, it's imperative to find the gap between the evidence and conclusion and close that gap with the correct answer.

Step 2: Untangle the Stimulus

The physician describes a series of potential causal events. A deficiency in vitamin D, which is needed to absorb calcium, is often the cause of calcium deficiency in older people. That calcium deficiency, in turn, often leads to higher blood pressure. However, a glass of milk provides the calcium needed to avoid a deficiency. So, the physician concludes that drinking milk can lower these older peoples' blood pressure.

Step 3: Make a Prediction

Since a calcium deficiency often causes higher blood pressure, it seems to make sense that increasing calcium intake could help prevent higher blood pressure. However, there's still the issue of the vitamin D, which the physician claimed is "needed" for the body to absorb the calcium. So, even if people increase their calcium, a lack of vitamin D would make the body incapable of absorbing that calcium, and thus the calcium deficiency (and resulting blood pressure) wouldn't be prevented. However, if the physician assumes that the milk also gives people the needed vitamin D, then the possibility of lowering blood pressure returns.

Step 4: Evaluate the Answer Choices

(A) provides a perfect assumption. If the milk provides the needed vitamin D, then the calcium provided by the milk can be absorbed, and calcium deficiency can be prevented. And that means taking away a cause of high blood pressure.

(B) offers evidence that there's nothing in milk that will increase blood pressure. However, without knowing about the vitamin D, there's still not enough evidence to conclude that the calcium will be absorbed. And if the calcium can't be absorbed, it can't reduce high blood pressure.

(C) offers evidence that the milk won't cause a deficiency in vitamin D. However, it still doesn't account for whether older people will get the needed vitamin D elsewhere. If they don't, then the calcium in the milk is still irrelevant.

(D) confirms that calcium and vitamin D together can regulate blood pressure, but that still doesn't validate whether the milk recommended by the physician contains that helpful combination.

(E) merely makes the evidence about vitamin D deficiency "frequently" causing calcium deficiency more definite. However, it still doesn't warrant any conclusion about the milk because it fails to address whether the people will have the needed vitamin D.

25. (A) Parallel Flaw

Step 1: Identify the Question Type

The stem is looking for an argument with reasoning "similar to" that in the stimulus. Furthermore, the reasoning is described as "flawed." So, start by identifying the flaw in the original argument, then find the answer that contains the exact same flaw.

Step 2: Untangle the Stimulus

The philosopher claims that, in a fair tax system, each person would pay taxes proportional to the value of society's service to that person's interests. The most objective way to determine how much society serves a person's interests involves that person's wealth. From this, the philosopher concludes that a person's income should be the only factor in determining a person's tax rate.

Step 3: Make a Prediction

The philosopher makes two mistakes. The major flaw is that the evidence discusses the *best* factor for making a decision while the conclusion suggests it's the *only* factor that matters. In addition, the best factor described is "wealth." However, the conclusion limits that to "income," as if there's no other factor that contributes to wealth. The correct answer will commit both errors. In summary, there's evidence that using some factor (wealth) is the best way to measure something (how well someone is served by society), which will be used for another purpose (determining a tax rate). The conclusion claims that one aspect of that factor (income) should be the only criterion used.

Step 4: Evaluate the Answer Choices

(A) commits both flaws in the same way. There's evidence that using some factor (speed) is the best way to measure something (danger of cars), which will be used for another purpose (determining a car tax). The conclusion claims that one aspect of that factor (acceleration) should be the only criterion used.

(B) does not provide a *best* way to accomplish anything, and it doesn't have a conclusion about one solution being the *only* solution.

(C) also doesn't provide a best way to accomplish anything. It does use the phrase "solely in proportion," which does mirror the stimulus. However, in the stimulus that sole criterion is used as part of the conclusion, but in **(C)** it is used as part of the evidence.

(D), like **(B)**, has nothing about a *best* way to do something and nothing about using a *sole* criterion.

(E) has a recommendation conclusion about what should be the "highest priority," which is close but not entirely parallel to using a *sole* criterion. **(E)** also fails to mention a best way to do something in the evidence.

26. (A) Paradox

Step 1: Identify the Question Type

Since the stem asks for a fact that will "explain" something "surprising," this is a Paradox question. There will be two ideas that seem to contradict one another. The correct answer will solve the mystery of how those ideas can coexist.

Step 2: Untangle the Stimulus

Two statistics from a recent poll are presented. The first is that almost half the city's residents believe the mayor is guilty of certain ethic violations. Yet the second shows that, somehow, just over half the residents consider his performance good or excellent. That assessment of the mayor's performance remains unchanged from what it was before the accusations of ethics violation.

Step 3: Make a Prediction

The mystery is this: How can the mayor continue to have such a high performance rating if so many people find him guilty of ethics violations? The answer lies in the numbers. Just under half feel he's guilty, and just over half think he's doing great. If almost half the residents feel he's guilty, then the rest of the residents (a little over half) don't feel that way—and that's roughly the same percentage who continue to rate his performance good or excellent. In other words, the situation makes sense if those who believe he's guilty have always rated his performance as poor, while the remaining population (a slight majority) don't believe he's guilty and continue to rate him as good.

Step 4: Evaluate the Answer Choices

(A) resolves the numbers perfectly. If there's a near-perfect correlation between the people who find him guilty (almost half) and those who have always thought his performance was poor, then the remaining people (slightly more than half) would not believe he's guilty and would continue to rate him as good or excellent.

(B) discusses people's opinions of Walker's opponents, who have no bearing on the statistics provided.

(C) is irrelevant because it doesn't change the fact that almost half the population finds him guilty.

(D) again brings up an opponent who has no bearing on the statistics provided.

(E) mentions how Walker defended himself, but that doesn't change the fact that almost half the city still believes he's guilty, nor for that matter does it explain why he still has a high approval rating in spite of that.

Section IV: Reading Comprehension
Passage 1: "Tradition" and Sea Otter Pelts

Q#	Question Type	Correct	Difficulty
1	Global	A	★★
2	Logic Function	C	★★★
3	Detail	E	★★
4	Inference	B	★
5	Inference	A	★★
6	Logic Function	E	★★★
7	Logic Reasoning (Principle)	C	★★★

Passage 2: Kate Chopin

Q#	Question Type	Correct	Difficulty
8	Global	B	★
9	Inference	A	★★★★
10	Detail	C	★★
11	Inference	A	★
12	Logic Function	C	★
13	Inference	C	★★★
14	Global	B	★
15	Logic Reasoning (Principle)	D	★★★★

Passage 3: Ocean Floor Discoveries

Q#	Question Type	Correct	Difficulty
16	Global	C	★★★
17	Logic Function	D	★
18	Detail	A	★★
19	Inference	C	★★★
20	Logic Reasoning (Strengthen)	B	★★
21	Inference	A	★★★★

Passage 4: Objectivist Historians

Q#	Question Type	Correct	Difficulty
22	Global	B	★★
23	Detail	C	★
24	Inference	B	★★
25	Inference	B	★
26	Logic Function	D	★★
27	Logic Reasoning (Method of Argument)	E	★★

Passage 1: "Tradition" and Sea Otter Pelts

Step 1: Read the Passage Strategically

Sample Roadmap

line #	Keyword/phrase	¶ Margin notes
1	a powerful	Alaska—"traditional" impt. legal concept
2	wide variety… relating …	
3	to	
5	privileges and exemptions	
7	But in spite	
8	is rarely defined	Not well defined
9	Instead	
13	One of the most prevalent	common def—continuing & regular
14	is based …	
15	on	
16	not only … but also	
17	continuity and regularity … But … recent	2 new cases show problems
19	illustrate … problems	
21	initially	1910—sea otter hunting banned
23	continued	
24	but it also included	1972—MMPA exemptions
28	subsequently	
29	defining	
31	Not covered	later—FWS regs "within living memory"
33	because	
35		1986 case—Ct. upheld FWS
37	but	1991 case
38	Then	
41	After hearing	new evidence
44	reconsidered	sea otter used pre-Russians
45	now held	
46	"strained …	
47	interpretation" … and that	
48	excessively …	new ruling: FWS too restrictive
49	restrictive	
52	does not mean	"living memory" rule not common sense
54	It defies common sense	
55	only	

Discussion

It's common for LSAT Reading Comprehension selections to contrast a traditional view with a more recent development, but here *tradition*, as that term is defined in Alaskan law, is the **Topic** of the passage. In paragraph 1, the author introduces tradition as a "powerful legal concept," used in both state and federal law to justify certain privileges. Midway through the paragraph, the contrast Keyword *but* signals that the author will discuss issues with the term. "In spite of its prevalence," tradition isn't well defined. And, the author says, this makes for "problematic and inconsistent" legal rulings.

Certainly, the author will discuss the problems further, but the specific Scope of the passage is narrower still. Paragraph 2 opens by giving two dimensions of the legal definition of *tradition*. It refers to practices that are "long-standing" and continuous. The author will "illustrate the problems" that accompany this definition with two recent cases that involved Alaska Natives' use of sea otter pelts. This illustration, the focus of the remaining paragraphs, constitutes the author's **Purpose**. And indeed, the sea otter cases define the passage's **Scope**.

Before describing the facts of the cases, the author uses paragraph 3 to outline the statutory background. The discussion is chronological. In 1910, the Fur Seal Treaty banned sea otter hunting. In 1972, the Marine Mammal Protection Act (MMPA) sustained the ban but exempted Alaska Natives who were using sea otter pelts for "traditional native handicrafts." At some point after that (the passage just says "subsequently"), Fish and Wildlife Service (FWS) regulations defined *traditional* in a way that no longer protected the sea otter hunters, stating that Alaska Natives hadn't produced sea otter handicrafts "within living memory."

The two cases described in paragraph 4 both occurred after the FWS regulations had interpreted *traditional* to exclude sea otter pelt items. In the first, in 1986, FWS agents seized sea otter pelt items made by an Aleut woman. The court upheld the FWS regulations. In the second case, from 1991, the same woman joined a Tlingit man who sued the government to recover seized sea otter pelt clothing items. Two things made the outcome different this time. First, the two Native plaintiffs presented evidence to show that Alaskan Native people had made extensive use of sea otter pelts prior to Russian occupation in the 1700s. Second, the court decided that the regulation limiting the "traditional" exemption to crafts made "within living memory" was overly restrictive. The 1991 court found that defining *traditional* in a way that applies to only a short period of time "defies common sense." By the end of this paragraph, you can state the **Main Idea** succinctly: two cases involving items made from otter pelts illustrate the courts' reinterpretation of the term *traditional* as it applies to Alaskan natives.

1. (A) Global

Step 2: Identify the Question Type

This is a straightforward Global question stem calling for the author's "main point."

Step 3: Research the Relevant Text

You need not reread the passage. Simply use your Purpose and Main Idea summaries to articulate the big picture.

Step 4: Make a Prediction

The statement of the Main Idea given above will work nicely as a prediction. Make sure you look for a choice that makes clear that the author is using the two cases as *examples* or *illustrations* of how the courts have looked at the term *traditional*.

Step 5: Evaluate the Answer Choices

(A) fits perfectly. The answer simply paraphrases the term *traditional* into the phrase "the legal concept of tradition."

(B) contradicts the passage. In fact, the two Alaskan natives won their cases by showing that, although the use of sea otter pelts had not been practiced for a long time, native people had used sea otter pelts in the more distant past.

(C) distorts the passage by asserting a "wave" of legal cases. Moreover, it misses the battles over the term *traditional* altogether.

(D) is too broad. The passage stays tightly focused on the term *traditional*, not other legal terms. Also, the passage shows that the legal concept of tradition has been fought over and reinterpreted in recent decades, not "long taken for granted."

(E) is too vague, and it introduces a value judgment—that the law is insufficiently concerned with native people—that the author doesn't make in the passage. Finally, while the first paragraph states that both state and federal laws grant certain exemptions based on "traditional use," the passage doesn't focus on any challenges to state laws.

2. (C) Logic Function

Step 2: Identify the Question Type

This question asks why the 1991 court criticized the FWS interpretation of *traditional*. With its line reference and research clues, this stem helps you get the point efficiently.

Step 3: Research the Relevant Text

You should know from your Roadmap's margin notes that the 1991 court overturned the FWS interpretation. The court's reasoning appears at lines 49 through 58. The court found the "living memory" rule too restrictive. The fact that circumstances intervened that prevented the native people from using certain items, the court said, doesn't make those items less traditional. Essentially, the court concluded that the FWS interpretation just doesn't follow a commonsense definition of *traditional*.

Step 4: Make a Prediction

Look for the correct answer to paraphrase the court's reasoning. The court said the FWS interpretation is "strained" because it doesn't follow the commonsense understanding of the word *traditional*.

Step 5: Evaluate the Answer Choices

(C) does justice to the court's reasoning. The commonsense definition of the term *traditional* is mangled by the FWS's "living memory" clause.

(A) distorts the passage and the 1991 court's decision. How the natives understood the term is beside the point. At any rate, it's the natives' interpretation that carried the day.

(B) is a subtle Distortion. Although dictionaries would, presumably, contain "commonsense" definitions of words, the passage doesn't tell you that the court referred to dictionary definitions in its decision.

(D) is a 180. The court's decision holds that the FWS's interpretation led the FWS to describe a practice as nontraditional when, in fact, it was traditional.

(E) is another Distortion. The entire battle over the term *traditional* concerns the attempt to designate which practices are and are not covered by the term. The 1991 court, however, didn't overturn the FWS interpretation because it failed to make such designations.

3. (E) Detail

Step 2: Identify the Question Type

The stem's opening phrase—"According to the passage"—tells you that the correct answer paraphrases a statement the author made. The Content Clue helps you research this Detail question in paragraph 4.

Step 3: Research the Relevant Text

The detail this question is looking for is the evidentiary basis of the 1991 court's ruling. That will be contained in paragraph 4. More precisely, the basis for the court's decision will appear before the court's ruling is stated. So, look for the answer to this question between lines 41 and 46.

Step 4: Make a Prediction

The testimony at trial proved that Alaskan Natives had used sea otter pelts in the 1700s, prior to Russian occupation. The passage said that, in light of that testimony, the court "reconsidered" the legal definition of *traditional*. The correct answer, then, will paraphrase the evidence about sea otter pelt use in the past.

Step 5: Evaluate the Answer Choices

(E) gets it right. The phrasing of this choice is vague, but the testimony was the basis for the court's decision.

(A) distorts the court's rationale. In fact, the court thought the FWS's interpretation too narrow. Moreover, this choice involves the court's reasoning, not the basis for its holdings.

(B) is tempting, but it's a Faulty Use of Detail wrong answer. The commonsense interpretation is what the court said the FWS should use. But the court's decision applied the "correct" definition to the facts from the testimony to conclude that sea otter pelts were, in fact, *traditional* use items.

(C) is a double Distortion. First, the court's ruling overturned the FWS interpretation. Second, adherence to the *intent* of the FWS regulations isn't mentioned at all.

(D) is another Faulty Use of Detail. The Fur Seal Treaty (mentioned in paragraph 3, by the way) initially banned sea otter hunting altogether. The MMPA later made an exemption for traditional use. And finally, the FWS regulations used the "living memory" definition to limit the exemption. It's an enormous stretch to make a new interpretation of the Treaty the basis for the 1991 court's decision.

4. (B) Inference

Step 2: Identify the Question Type

The stem is calling for what the "passage most strongly suggests" about the 1986 court's beliefs. That makes this an Inference question. The correct answer will follow from what the passage said about the 1986 court.

Step 3: Research the Relevant Text

The 1986 case gets only a few lines in the passage. The correct answer will come from lines 35 through 38. All you're told is that the court upheld the FWS regulations. Those were described in paragraph 2. The FWS regulations used the "living memory" definition of traditional, meaning that a practice wasn't traditional unless it had been done consistently up to a time recent enough that living people could recall it.

Step 4: Make a Prediction

The correct answer may be worded in a number of ways, but it will say that the court agreed with the FWS's "living memory" interpretation.

Step 5: Evaluate the Answer Choices

(B), with somewhat roundabout language, matches the prediction. By agreeing with the FWS regulations, the 1986 court made continued and recent practice central criteria for finding use of an item to be *traditional*.

(A) is off base. Nothing in the passage suggests that the 1986 court used any kind of balancing criteria.

(C) is a Faulty Use of Detail. It was the 1991 court that drew upon a "commonsense" test to overturn the FWS definition of *traditional*.

(D) simply misstates the "living memory" exception. To be considered "traditional," items had to be commonly produced prior to 1972 but also produced recently enough to be "within living memory." The 1986 court made no effort to encourage the term be used in any other way.

(E) is a 180. The 1986 court found against the native Alaskan plaintiff and upheld the federal government's definition.

5. (A) Inference

Step 2: Identify the Question Type

This is an open-ended Inference question. The correct answer will be a statement that must be true based on the passage.

Step 3: Research the Relevant Text

There are no research clues in the question stem, but a scan of the answer choices shows that most refer to dates and events mentioned in the passage. Make sure to get your chronology straight as you research individual choices.

Step 4: Make a Prediction

It's not a good use of time to comb through the entire passage and extract all the dates and events. Refer to the answer choices. The correct answer will follow from the passage (and your research can confirm it). The wrong answers will all distort the passage, contradict the author, or range beyond the scope of the passage.

Step 5: Evaluate the Answer Choices

(A) is true based on paragraph 2. The Fur Seal Treaty of 1910 banned the hunting of sea otters. The MMPA, in 1972, allowed for the taking of protected marine mammals for traditional practices.

(B) is a 180. The fact that the MMPA didn't mention sea otters *explicitly* is what led to all the agency regulations and court cases that take up the rest of the passage.

(C) is Outside the Scope. In paragraph 4, you learn that Alaskan Natives hunted sea otters and made goods from their pelts prior to Russian occupation. The passage doesn't go into detail about the politics behind the Russian decision to prevent the native people from hunting.

(D) is Outside the Scope. The year 1972 was the year of the MMPA. The ecological status of sea otters that year isn't mentioned in the passage.

(E) is Extreme. Nothing in the passage suggests that Alaskan Natives hunted sea otters more than other marine mammals in the pre–Russian occupation years.

6. (E) Logic Function

Step 2: Identify the Question Type

Logic Function questions ask for the answer that says why the author included a detail or how a detail functions within the passage. The detail referenced in this stem is "the Fur Seal Treaty (line 22)."

Step 3: Research the Relevant Text

All that the sentence mentioning the Fur Seal Treaty says is that it banned the hunting of sea otters in 1910. Its location at the start of paragraph 2, however, tells you why the author included it. This treaty kicked off the whole controversy over whether Alaskan Natives traditionally used sea otter pelts.

Step 4: Make a Prediction

The correct answer will reflect the fact that the Fur Seal Treaty was the triggering event for all the legal rules and cases involving the term *traditional*.

Step 5: Evaluate the Answer Choices

(E), with its phrase "help explain the evolution," is the best match for the prediction. The Fur Seal Treaty itself didn't get into *traditional* exemptions, but it paved the way for all the subsequent legislation and litigation that did.

(A) is Outside the Scope. The Fur Seal Treaty was the earliest federal ban, but nothing in the passage suggests that the sea otter was endangered, let alone "on the verge of extinction," at that time.

(B) misrepresents the author's purpose. The author doesn't go into how many animals were covered by the treaty, nor is there any reason for him to want to establish such a fact in the passage.

(C) is a Distortion and Outside the Scope of the passage. First, there's nothing to suggest that the Fur Seal Treaty is "well-known." Second, while it's true that the treaty is a legal precedent, that's not the author's purpose in mentioning it.

(D) involves a Faulty Use of Detail (the Russian occupation is mentioned in paragraph 4) and goes Outside the Scope (no part of the author's purpose involves assigning blame for the overhunting of sea otters).

7. (C) Logic Reasoning (Principle)

Step 2: Identify the Question Type

This is a somewhat unusual question stem for the Reading Comprehension section, but the task is similar to a common Logical Reasoning question type: Principle. Here, you're asked to apply the 1991 court's ruling to other cases (in the answer choices). The correct answer will be a case to which the ruling is relevant. Notice that this means all four wrong answers will be Outside the Scope because the ruling won't be relevant to the cases they describe.

Step 3: Research the Relevant Text

Research the 1991 case in paragraph 4. In it, the court overturned the "within living memory" exception in the FWS regulations. The court based its decision on testimony that showed that Alaskan Natives had long ago used a practice but had been forced by historical circumstances to discontinue its use. The court found the practice to be *traditional* within the legal sense of the word.

Step 4: Make a Prediction

The correct answer will cite a case in which traditional peoples used a certain practice until outside forces intervened and caused them to give it up.

Step 5: Evaluate the Answer Choices

(C) is dead on: a traditional practice (a handicraft) was common until industrialization forced out the animals necessary for it.

(A) misses the piece about an outside force causing the native people to discontinue the traditional practice.

(B) doesn't fit the scenario at all. The 1991 court didn't consider endangered status. Moreover, this choice doesn't involve a practice being discontinued due to historical circumstances.

(D) doesn't have anything about discontinuing a traditional practice, and it introduces a criterion (the number of people who were expert in the practice) neither the passage nor the 1991 court (as far as you know) addresses.

(E) would fit with the FWS "within living memory" exemption because of the elders who still practice the traditional handicraft. The 1991 court would have little to say about this case.

Passage 2: Kate Chopin

Step 1: Read the Passage Strategically

Sample Roadmap

line #	Keyword/phrase	¶ Margin notes
3	Born in ...	
4	1850 ... sentimental novels	Chopin's childhood—sentimental novels
6	In these works	
9	Later	Chopin's 1st model: local colorists
12	local colorists	
13	After 1865	decline of women's culture
14	"women's culture"	
17	1870s	
18	1880s	local colorists' approach
20	Like	
22	However	
23		colorists' reaction to losing "women's culture"
29	Unlike	
31	But	Chopin used style, not subj. matter, of local colorists
39	however ... 1890s	1890: Chopin moves from local colorists' model to New Women
43	New Women writers	
45		form/content of New Women's work
48	Instead of	
50	experimented	
52		Chopin used NW's impress. in *The Awak.*

Discussion

Paragraph 1 establishes the **Topic** (Kate Chopin's literary development) and the **Scope** (how it was influenced by 19th-century women's literary movements). The author begins by discussing the style of novel prevalent in Chopin's childhood—the sentimental novel. The paragraph ends by introducing a group—the local colorists—after whom Chopin first modeled her fiction.

Paragraph 2 describes the style and subject matter of the local colorists. These writers were attracted to the new aspects of society that began to open up to women after 1865, and their regional stories clinically observed women's lives. But as traditional aspects of female experience continued to fade, the local colorists became nostalgic and treated house, garden, and the entire domestic milieu as a mythic environment.

Paragraph 3 discusses how the colorists affected Chopin. Chopin didn't use the colorists' subject matter (she focused her work on "loneliness, isolation, and frustration"), but she did adopt their unaffected style to depict extreme states. Chopin, however, avoided what she saw as the excesses of the sentimental novels of her childhood.

Paragraph 4 introduces Chopin's break with the local colorists—by the 1890s she was already being influenced by a different movement, the New Women. The next three sentences describe features of the New Women's writing: freedom and innovation, a modification of the sentimental form to make room for fantasy and parable, and experimentation with impressionistic methods. The author ends by noting that Chopin adopted this impressionism and expanded on it in *The Awakening*.

Since the author never expresses a strong point of view, the Purpose and Main Idea should reflect this neutrality. The author's **Purpose** is to describe literary movements in the nineteenth century and how they influenced Chopin's writing. The **Main Idea** is that Chopin's literary style was influenced by an aversion to the excesses of sentimental novels, an adoption of the conventions of the local colorists, and a commitment to the impressionistic style pioneered by the New Women.

8. (B) Global

Step 2: Identify the Question Type

The scope of the question stem is the passage as a whole—it asks you to "summarize the content"—so this is a Global question.

Step 3: Research the Relevant Text

There's no text to research for a Global question like this. Instead, the Roadmap and your summaries of the Topic, Scope, Purpose, and Main Idea will guide you to a prediction.

Step 4: Make a Prediction

From your analysis of the passage during Step 1, you can determine the passage's Main Idea: the work of the local colorists and the New Women contributed stylistically to Chopin's literary development as she tried to distance herself from the excesses of the novels popular in her youth.

Step 5: Evaluate the Answer Choices

(B) is the best match for this prediction.

(A) goes wrong on two counts. First, the passage says that Chopin was *stylistically* influenced by the work of the New Women, not that she borrowed material from them. Second, Chopin didn't show an interest in recapturing the atmosphere of the sentimental novels.

(C) misrepresents the passage's focus. *The Awakening* isn't the topic of the passage, and the author doesn't compare it to other works of nineteenth-century fiction.

(D) contradicts paragraph 3, which says that Chopin borrowed from the literary conventions of the local colorists. Furthermore, the "elevated, romantic language" mentioned in **(D)** was a feature of the sentimental novels, not of Chopin's work.

(E) introduces elements not mentioned in the passage (e.g., "struggling to develop") and also contradicts the idea expressed in paragraph 3 that Chopin embraced the local colorists' conventions.

9. (A) Inference

Step 2: Identify the Question Type

Since the question stem asks for the answer choice with which Chopin "would ... have been most likely to agree," this is an Inference question.

Step 3: Research the Relevant Text

Look for places where the author discusses Chopin's point of view, particularly as it relates to the local colorists (who are discussed in paragraphs 2 and 3). Paragraph 3 says she explored themes that were unlike those of the local colorists. Lines 38 through 40 are more specific, saying that Chopin didn't share the colorists' nostalgia for the past and began to move beyond them by the 1890s.

Step 4: Make a Prediction

The correct answer is likely to be supported by lines 38 through 40. Look for the answer that must be true if Chopin wasn't devoted to the subject matter of the local colorists.

Step 5: Evaluate the Answer Choices

(A) is directly supported by the passage. If Chopin diverged from the local colorists in terms of subject matter, then she would agree that they were misguided in their nostalgia for "women's culture."

(B) is a 180. Chopin adopted the colorists' dispassionate manner of storytelling, so she wouldn't disparage it.

(C) is off because the passage doesn't suggest that either Chopin or the author believes that the local colorists inspired the work of the New Women.

(D) is at odds with paragraph 2, which says that the local colorists were attracted to new realms opening up to women. And Chopin didn't seem to mind the local colorists' regional focus.

(E) distorts the passage. The local colorists did in fact use scientific detachment (lines 21–22), but it was Chopin who sought to portray extreme psychological states.

10. (C) Detail

Step 2: Identify the Question Type

The phrase "according to the passage" indicates a Detail question.

Step 3: Research the Relevant Text

Chopin's adoption of the conventions of other writers is discussed mainly in paragraphs 3 and 4. In paragraph 3, the passage says Chopin borrowed the "uninflected" style of the local colorists. In paragraph 4, the author says she borrowed the "impressionistic approach" of the New Women.

Step 4: Make a Prediction

Look for the correct answer to mention either a detached, uninflected style (taken from the local colorists) or impressionism (taken from the New Women).

Step 5: Evaluate the Answer Choices

(C) matches the information in paragraph 3 perfectly.

(A) was a feature of the sentimental novels Chopin grew up with (lines 6–9), but this feature was presumably one of the "excesses" (line 34) that Chopin sought to avoid.

(B) was a feature of the later work of the local colorists, but Chopin didn't follow the colorists into this thematic territory (see lines 29–30).

(D) is mentioned in line 48 as a feature of the local colorists' work, but Chopin and the New Women diverged from this in favor of a more impressionistic style (lines 49–57).

(E) is mentioned in lines 29–30, but this appears to be thematic territory that Chopin alone wanted to explore since it differs from what the local colorists were interested in.

11. (A) Inference

Step 2: Identify the Question Type

The stem asks you what "women's culture" "most probably refers to," so you'll need to put it together based on the text. That makes this an Inference question.

Step 3: Research the Relevant Text

You're given a line reference, so go back to line 14 and read around it for context. In this sentence, the author says "women's culture" dissolved as women entered educational, professional, and political realms. Later in paragraph 2, the author says that the local colorists mourned "women's culture" by imbuing the home and garden with mythic significance.

Step 4: Make a Prediction

Based on these two references, you can deduce that the expression of "women's culture" had to do with domesticity or the household.

Step 5: Evaluate the Answer Choices

(A) matches the prediction.

(B) is Outside the Scope of the discussion of "women's culture."

(C), similar to **(B)**, is Outside the Scope of the discussion of "women's culture."

(D) is a 180 because it is contradicted by lines 13–16.

(E), similar to **(D)**, is contradicted by lines 13–16.

12. (C) Logic Function

Step 2: Identify the Question Type

The phrase "in order to" signals a Logic Function question. What the author says about the sentimental novels is less important than *why* the author says it.

Step 3: Research the Relevant Text

Take the line reference and go back to paragraph 1, but read before and after lines 3–9 for context. The preceding sentence says that Chopin's literary development took her through several phases of fiction. The sentence beginning at line 9 discusses Chopin's inspiration after she'd grown up and started writing fiction of her own.

Step 4: Make a Prediction

The author mentions the sentimental novels in order to describe the literary environment in which Chopin grew up so that we can see where her literary development came from.

Step 5: Evaluate the Answer Choices

(C) matches the prediction.

(A) is a Distortion of the passage. The author says that Chopin used the works of the local colorists as her models, not the authors of these sentimental novels.

(B) is wrong because Chopin's departure from the local colorists isn't discussed until paragraph 4, and that departure had nothing to do with the sentimental novelists.

(D) conflates a couple of details that have nothing to do with lines 3–9. The "excesses" mentioned in **(D)** are those of the sentimental novelists (line 34), but the "nostalgic tendencies" are those of the local colorists (lines 38–39).

(E) is not an aim of the author in this passage. In lines 3–9, the author is describing the literary form that was prevalent *before* Chopin began to write. Also, it's an overstatement to say that lines 3–9 prove that sentimental novels were "flourishing."

13. (C) Inference

Step 2: Identify the Question Type

If a question stem asks what the passage "suggests," then it's an Inference question.

Step 3: Research the Relevant Text

The New Women are mentioned only in paragraph 4, where the author says that their work was characterized by a pursuit of freedom and innovation and by experimentation with impressionistic methods. *The Awakening* is mentioned beginning in line 52, where the author says Chopin "embraced this impressionistic approach more fully."

Step 4: Make a Prediction

Those lines point up the main difference between the New Women's work and *The Awakening*: Chopin committed more fully to the impressionistic techniques that the New Women merely experimented with.

Step 5: Evaluate the Answer Choices

(C) is consistent with the related statements mentioned in the prediction.

(A) seems to be a similarity between the work of the New Women and *The Awakening*, since the New Women were just as interested as Chopin in exploring female consciousness (lines 49–52).

(B) is something the New Women did (lines 44–47), but the author doesn't say that Chopin accomplished or avoided this in *The Awakening*.

(E) contradicts the passage, which says that *The Awakening* was unified differently, not *more* unified (line 55).

(D) is also something the New Women did (lines 44–47). However, no mention is made of whether Chopin also relied on fantasy in *The Awakening*.

14. (B) Global

Step 2: Identify the Question Type

"Primary purpose" is a classic key phrase that indicates a Global question. Answering these questions is precisely why you summarize the Purpose of the passage in Step 1.

Step 3: Research the Relevant Text

There are no specific lines to research, but make your prediction in line with your analysis of the passage in Step 1.

Step 4: Make a Prediction

The author's tone is neutral throughout; the Purpose is to explain how movements in women's fiction in the nineteenth century informed Kate Chopin's literary development.

Step 5: Evaluate the Answer Choices

(B) matches this prediction to a T.

(A) is Outside the Scope of the passage. The author doesn't make a comparison between Chopin's life story and events in *The Awakening*.

(C) also misrepresents the author's focus. Chopin is not being used as an example; the passage is about her specifically, not about nineteenth-century women's fiction in general.

(D) gets the author's tone wrong. The author never presents or counters any outside opinions.

(E) is off because the author never compares Chopin to any other writers, especially not in terms of their relative worth.

15. (D) Logic Reasoning (Principle)

Step 2: Identify the Question Type

The question stem tells you that the answer choices are all "generalizations," or principles. The right answer will be a principle illustrated by the work of the New Women.

Step 3: Research the Relevant Text

The New Women are discussed in paragraph 4, where the author says that they modified the sentimental form to allow for fantasy and parable. They also, according to the passage, experimented with an impressionistic style to explore previously unexplored parts of the female consciousness.

Step 4: Make a Prediction

You might be able to draw a couple of generalizations from this information, but the right answer will probably deal with the idea that groups of writers can alter their form or style to suit new content that they've chosen to explore.

Step 5: Evaluate the Answer Choices

(D) is supported directly by lines 49 through 52. The New Women experimented with impressionism in order to depict aspects of the female experience that the passage says were "hitherto unrecorded."

(A) is an Irrelevant Comparison. Although the New Women "pursued innovation" within the genre of the novel, there's nothing in the passage that indicates their works actually effected social change.

(B) is Outside the Scope. The New Women weren't concerned with effecting social change.

(C) is not supported because the passage doesn't suggest that the New Women were responding to changes in social customs. Furthermore, it would be Extreme to say such changes "inevitably" lead to changes in literary techniques.

(E) displays a Faulty Use of Detail. It was Chopin and the local colorists, not the New Women, who used an uninflected manner to depict their characters' states.

Passage 3: Ocean Floor Discoveries

Step 1: Read the Passage Strategically

Sample Roadmap

line #	Keyword/phrase	¶ Margin notes
1	Until the 1950s	1950s: ocean floor theories face new discoveries
3	But	
4	new discoveries	1st disc: magnetic var.
5	First	
7	because	why basalt has normal/reversed polarity
12	although	
16		magnetite in basalt records polarity when magma cools
25		2nd disc: mid-ocean ridge
26	other great oceanic ...	
27	discovery of the 1950s:	
30		features of ridge (stripes w/diff polarity)
33	Scientists theorized that	
34		theory: ridge built by ocean floor spreading
39	this process	
40	built the mid-ocean ridge	
41	several	support for theory
42	First	
44	Further	
45	Finally ... because	
50		correl. btwn ages of magnetic reversals and magnetic striping pattern in rock

Discussion

The first two sentences introduce the **Topic** (ocean floor geology) and hint at the **Scope** (new discoveries about the ocean floor in the 1950s). Scientists previously thought that the ocean floor's geology remained unchanged, but they began to modify that theory in the 1950s. One of the two major discoveries leading to this modification was of the magnetic variations in oceanic basalt. Basalt contains magnetite, which records the magnetic polarity of the earth at the time the basalt hardens from magma.

Paragraph 2 introduces the second big discovery: the global mid-ocean ridge. Then the author describes a key feature of the ridge—stripes of rock that alternate polarities are laid out on either side of the ridge. Then, the author introduces scientists' theory explaining the ridge. According to this theory, ridge crests are where new magma erupts onto the ocean floor and hardens into new crust. The new rock pushes older rock away from the ridge crest, continually building and rebuilding the mid-ocean ridge and accounting for the alternating polarity over millions of years.

Paragraph 3 describes the evidence supporting the ocean floor–spreading theory. The Keywords in the succeeding sentences (*first, further, finally*) serve as a guide to help you navigate the three pieces of evidence: The rocks become progressively older the farther away you get from the crest; the youngest rocks have normal polarity; and the ages of the earth's polarity reversals and the magnetic striping pattern have a "remarkable" correlation.

By now the author's **Purpose** should become more apparent: to describe the discoveries that led scientists to change their commonly held ideas about the geology of the ocean floor. And the **Main Idea** is that the discovery of the magnetic variations in oceanic rock and of the global mid-ocean range caused scientists to revise their theories about the ocean floor's geology.

16. (C) Global

Step 2: Identify the Question Type

Any question stem that seeks the "main idea" of the passage is a Global question.

Step 3: Research the Relevant Text

You don't need to research a specific part of the passage. Just rely on your understanding of Topic, Scope, Purpose, and Main Idea to handle Global questions.

Step 4: Make a Prediction

The correct answer will reflect the Main Idea that new discoveries during the 1950s changed scientists' minds about the geology of the ocean floor.

Step 5: Evaluate the Answer Choices

(C) matches this prediction and captures the thrust of the entire passage. Specifically, the two significant discoveries were the ocean floor's "odd magnetic variations" (paragraph 1) and the "global mid-ocean ridge" (paragraph 2).

(A) is off because the passage doesn't discuss theories regarding how the ocean floor was originally formed.

(B) distorts the discoveries discussed in the passage. The discovery of basalt's magnetic properties and the discovery of the magnetic striping on either side of the mid-ocean ridge are two separate discoveries. More importantly, this choice is too narrow and focused on details to offer the passage's "main idea."

(D) overinflates the importance of a specific detail and then distorts it to boot. The passage says that basalt's reversed polarity *on land* causes distorted compass readings. But more importantly, this detail isn't the author's main point.

(E) doesn't reflect the scope of the passage. The discovery of the mid-ocean global ridge is only mentioned as one discovery that led to a modification of scientists' theories about the ocean's geology.

17. (D) Logic Function

Step 2: Identify the Question Type

The phrase "in order to" indicates a Logic Function question. The stem is asking *why* the author chose to characterize the correlation as "remarkable."

Step 3: Research the Relevant Text

The last sentence of the passage is long—it stretches from line 45 to line 56. This last sentence is part of a paragraph that provides evidence for scientists' theory about ocean floor spreading.

Step 4: Make a Prediction

The author calls the correlation "remarkable" to show that it is worthy of notice because it provides particularly strong support for the ocean floor–spreading theory.

Step 5: Evaluate the Answer Choices

(D) is a great match for the prediction. This answer demonstrates the importance of margin notes that capture the purpose of a paragraph or important sentence.

(A) misrepresents the author's use of *remarkable*. The ocean floor spreading of "several centimeters per year" (lines 53–54) isn't necessarily the same as "an extremely slow rate." More to the point, *remarkable* isn't used as an adjective for *rate*; it modifies "correlation."

(B) doesn't go far enough. The use of *remarkable* doesn't explain the existence of the mid-ocean ridge; it supports a theory about how the mid-ocean ridge was built by ocean floor spreading.

(C) is Outside the Scope because the passage doesn't provide any information comparing the current strength of the magnetic field to what it was previously believed to be.

(E) isn't supported by the passage, which doesn't say anything about the regularity of the intervals at which the earth's magnetic field reversed itself. The reference you're being asked about simply says that the reversals match the striping pattern.

18. (A) Detail

Step 2: Identify the Question Type

The question stem begins with "according to the passage," so this is a Detail question. Targeted research of the passage will be essential.

Step 3: Research the Relevant Text

"Magnetite grains" are a Content Clue. Magnetite is mentioned in paragraph 1. The grains are specifically discussed in lines 17 through 23.

Step 4: Make a Prediction

These facts will form the basis of your prediction: Magnetite grains align themselves with the earth's magnetic field, and when magma cools, that alignment is frozen.

Step 5: Evaluate the Answer Choices

(A) is correct. Since magnetite orientation is set at the time magma hardens, the grains that were set recently match the earth's current polarity.

(B) is wrong because nothing in the passage says that some magnetite grains don't align themselves with the earth's magnetic field.

(C) is Outside the Scope because the passage doesn't discuss other types of rock where magnetite may or may not be found.

(D) is wrong because the author never discusses the size of the grains.

(E), like **(D)**, is wrong because the author never discusses the size of the grains.

19. (C) Inference

Step 2: Identify the Question Type

The stem asks for the answer choice "most likely to be true" based on the passage, so this is an Inference question.

Step 3: Research the Relevant Text

The reversals of the earth's magnetic polarity are discussed primarily in three places: lines 19–20 (magnetite grains record whenever the earth has reversed polarity), lines 30–33 (alternating stripes of oceanic basalt reflect normal and

reversed polarity), and lines 47–56 (the correlation between the ages of the earth's polarity reversals and the pattern of stripes in oceanic basalt).

Step 4: Make a Prediction

Consider the question stem as you form your prediction. It asks you to apply information from the passage to a new fact: the time between reversals in the Earth's polarity varies greatly. If the stripes of basalt reflect those reversals, then some will be wider and some narrower, reflecting the different lengths of time between reversals.

Step 5: Evaluate the Answer Choices

(C) must be true based on the passage. The magnetic stripes record how long the earth's polarity was at a certain orientation. So it makes sense that if the time intervals fluctuate greatly, then the stripes will vary greatly in width.

(A) is unsupported. The passage says that magnetite distorts compass readings on land, but there's no information allowing you to determine whether compass distortions are more pronounced at the peaks of the mid-ocean ridge.

(B) cannot be inferred because nothing in the passage establishes a relationship between the fluctuation of time intervals and the pattern of the mid-ocean ridge winding its way around the earth. Taking it as far as the baseball comparison puts this answer completely Outside the Scope.

(D) is an Irrelevant Comparison, since a reversal in the earth's polarity would presumably affect continental rock and oceanic rock equally.

(E) is also unsupported. Within any given stripe, you can conclude that the polarity of the basalt is unchanged, but that doesn't necessarily mean that all the basalt in a given stripe is the same age. After all, the stem suggests that some polarity reversals may take a very long time. All of the basalt formed during that time will have the same magnetite orientation.

20. (B) Logic Reasoning (Strengthen)

Step 2: Identify the Question Type

The stem asks you to find the answer choice that best supports a theory in the passage. This question resembles a Strengthen question from the Logical Reasoning section.

Step 3: Research the Relevant Text

The main support for the ocean floor–spreading theory is provided in paragraph 4. The author cites three main lines of evidence: the rocks nearest the ridge crest are the youngest, those youngest rocks have the same polarity as the earth does currently, and the ages of the earth's magnetic reversals correlate with the ocean floor's magnetic striping pattern.

Step 4: Make a Prediction

You're looking for a fact that would make it more likely that the ocean floor–spreading theory is valid. Such a fact would probably augment one of the main pieces of evidence or, in any case, make it more believable that the mid-ocean ridge is created by rock rising through weak zones in the ocean floor.

Step 5: Evaluate the Answer Choices

(B) would further solidify the "remarkable correlation" between the ages of the earth's magnetic reversals and the pattern of magnetic stripes. If **(B)** is true, then scientists can point to something other than continental and oceanic rock to establish a timeline for the reversals.

(A), if anything, just shows that other types of rock may also exhibit variations in polarity.

(C) would just show that basalt is present under the sea and on land. That doesn't bolster any of the evidence offered in support of the ocean floor–spreading theory.

(D) can't have any effect on the theory unless we know the relationship between peak height and the spreading of the ocean floor, and the passage doesn't establish such a relationship.

(E) has no effect on the theory. Whether or not other types of volcanic rock are found on the ocean floor, it's the magnetite found in basalt that provides evidence for the theory.

21. (A) Inference

Step 2: Identify the Question Type

Since the stem asks for the answer that the passage most strongly supports, this is an Inference question. The correct answer must be true based on information in the passage.

Step 3: Research the Relevant Text

The question stem provides no clues to help you do your research. The right answer may be broad or specific, but it will certainly be in line with the passage and with your understanding of Topic, Scope, Purpose, and Main Idea.

Step 4: Make a Prediction

It's impossible to predict the answer to this Inference question with no clear references in the stem to guide your research. However, as with any Inference question, the right answer is the one that must be true based on the passage.

Step 5: Evaluate the Answer Choices

(A) must be true based on the passage. The author says that new magma (which cools to form basalt) comes up through weak zones along the ridge crest. This causes the ocean floor to "move away from the spreading center," so it makes sense that the farther away you get from the center (that is, the closer you get to the shores of landmasses), the older the rock will be.

(B) contradicts the passage. The author says at the end of paragraph 1 that once magma cools to form basalt, its polarity is "locked in," suggesting that basalt doesn't reverse its polarity.

(C) is a comparison unsupported by the passage. The author tells you that compass readings become distorted on land, but you have no information about the relative frequency of the distortion on land as compared to at sea.

(D) is unsupported because the passage never says anything about the strength or weakness of the magnetic field over time.

(E) might seem reasonable at first, but if the earth's magnetic field has reversed polarity several times, then a rock formed today will match the polarity of a rock formed two reversals ago, four reversals ago, and so on. In fact, based on the passage, **(E)** is untrue.

Passage 4: Objectivist Historians

Step 1: Read the Passage Strategically

Sample Roadmap

line #	Keyword/phrase	¶ Margin notes
Passage A		
1	Central	historical objectivity
2	ideal of objectivity	
3	include	
5	and above all	characteristics
7	According to	
8	:	judge on faithfulness to facts
9	should be	
11	it should be	
13	does not mean ... as	not relativist
14	claim	
16	see their role as that	obj. hist—Sh'd never have "agendas"; no propaganda
17	neutral ... must never	
18	or, worse	
19	should	
22	Thus	get rid of politics, loyalties
23	must purge	
24	primary allegiance	

line #	Keyword/phrase	¶ Margin notes
Passage B		
28	requires of	requirements to separate hist from propaganda
30	do such things	
33	Yet objectivity … should not be	objectivity ≠ neutral
35	compatible with	
37	but only	can have political view
39	most compellingly … embodied	
43	precisely because	powerful args: articulate opposing view
44	so as …	
45	to	
46	not those of … but …	respectfully dissent
47	those	
49	To	don't just talk to those who agree with you
50	one must first … Those so	
52	can never	
53	but	
54	Such	
56	even	this kind of arg. more persuasive
58	is the highest fruit	
59	neutrality	
60	plays no part … Authentic … bears no resemblance	don't be like "equal time" newscast
64	irrespective	

Discussion

Both authors define what they consider "objective" history scholarship. While neither passage appears to have been written in response to the other, the two authors' conclusions are sharply at odds, though they profess to have many of the same goals and motivations. Keeping track of where the two passages agree and disagree will be paramount as you attack the question set.

The first sentence of passage A introduces the **Topic** (of both passages, as it turns out): the ideal of objectivity, which is central to historical scholarship. The remainder of the short first paragraph lists three principles this author believes define objectivist history. "[A]bove all," says the author, is "a distinction between history and fiction." As a strategic reader, you know this will be a close approximation of the passage's **Scope**, and you can anticipate that this author will develop and define what he means by *fiction* or, conversely, *fact*.

The second paragraph does, indeed, give the author's view of historical "facts," which he sees as "prior to and independent of interpretation." In this view, historical interpretation should be judged on how well it accounts for the facts. And we shouldn't take differing interpretations as evidence that the facts lack fixed meaning. In other words, the point isn't that the facts are ambiguous; it's that some historical theories are better at getting them right.

The third paragraph has a cautionary message for historians who aspire to objectivity: don't advocate for a side or write propaganda. The author praises "balance and evenhandedness," which he says are tainted by political, partisan, or biased positions. At the end, he tells historians to abandon all "external loyalties."

The author's **Purpose** and **Main Idea** should be clear from paragraphs 2 and 3. He is trying to define objectivist history and outlines the dos and don'ts for historians striving for objectivity. He believes that this is achieved by a single-minded devotion to the facts and by cutting oneself off from political (or any other outside) loyalties.

If you asked the author of passage B for her **Purpose**, the answer would sound quite similar to that of passage A's author: to define objectivist history and give guidelines for how to accomplish it. As you'll see, though, her **Main Idea** for how to accomplish that is almost diametrically opposed.

In paragraph 1 of passage B, the author separates historical scholarship from propaganda. To achieve the former, she says, the historian must give up wishful thinking and, in essence, make peace with uncomfortable truths. So far, the two authors might approve of one another.

In paragraph 2, however, passage B's author makes a sharp break with the thinking of passage A's author. Passage B's author says that objectivity has nothing to do with neutrality and is "perfectly compatible with strong political commitment." As a strategic reader on the LSAT, you know you'll need to understand this difference of opinion clearly. The second paragraph in passage B is long, but don't skim over it. Get the author's point and understand her support for it. She equates objectivity with what she calls the "*powerful argument*." (Her italics act as a kind of emphasis Keyword.) To make such an argument, the historian has to understand the opponents' view fully and articulate it clearly and sensitively. If the historian can't see the other side, she says, he'll never do more than preach to the choir.

In the third paragraph, passage B's author reasserts her earlier point in light of what she's said about the "*powerful argument*." Writing history in this way is truly objectivist but not at all neutral. It's "more faithful to complexity of historical interpretation" than the kind of neutrality passage A's author would endorse, she says. She ends with a comparison to modern newscasts, which give equal airtime to both sides regardless of merit. That's completely at odds with her definition of objectivity.

22. (B) Global

Step 2: Identify the Question Type

This question stem is really calling for the Scope shared by both passages. That makes it a Comparative Reading twist on the typical Global question.

Step 3: Research the Relevant Text

There's no need to read or reread the text of the passage. Just consider what each author's goals are by recalling your Topic, Scope, Purpose, and Main Idea summaries.

Step 4: Make a Prediction

Both authors believe they know what objectivist history is and how historians can go about accomplishing it. Although they have different answers, they're both trying to answer the same question: What are the dos and don'ts for the objectivist historian?

Step 5: Evaluate the Answer Choices

(B) gets it right. It focuses on what the historians should avoid, but both authors are clearly trying to answer this question.

(A) is Outside the Scope because neither author expresses any particular interest in recent scholarship. These authors are talking about historians generally.

(C) also is Outside the Scope because neither author discusses or speculates about the origins of the objectivist ideal.

(D) also goes Outside the Scope. Although the scholars would likely agree that relativist history is unsound, this question isn't a focus for either author. Passage A disparages the relativists explicitly (lines 14–15), but passage B doesn't even bring them up.

(E) offers a question tangential to these two passages and is Outside the Scope. Both authors are likely as concerned with why the interpretation of historical events differs from author to author during the same time period as they are with why interpretations change over time.

23. (C) Detail

Step 2: Identify the Question Type

This question asks for a Detail that appears in both passages. Specifically, the right answer will give a requirement both authors believe appropriate for historians' work.

Step 3: Research the Relevant Text

Most of the authors' requirements (and recommendations, criteria, etc.) are different, so focus only on what they share. Most likely, that will be a detail from paragraph 1 of passage B; after that, passage B breaks sharply from the position in passage A.

Step 4: Make a Prediction

Both authors consider themselves proponents of objectivism. To that end, both think facts and evidence should trump preconceived ideas or preferred interpretations.

Step 5: Evaluate the Answer Choices

(C) gets it right. It's a good paraphrase for passage A at lines 10–11 and for passage B at lines 31–32.

(A) is Outside the Scope of both passages. Neither author encourages borrowing from other disciplines.

(B) distorts both authors' positions. The author of passage B tells historians that they must understand and articulate opposing views, but she doesn't say they need to borrow their rivals' methodologies. Passage A says little, if anything, about methodology other than it must hold adherence to the facts above all else.

(D) is a Distortion of passage B. In her charge to objectivists, this author argues that they must lay out their argument in a way "that reveals by its every twist and turn its respectful appreciation of the alternative arguments it rejects." That's quite different than a point-by-point *refutation* of the opponents' objections.

(E) accurately reflects the position of passage B that **(D)** mangles. The problem with this choice is that passage A's author makes no mention of such a requirement.

24. (B) Inference

Step 2: Identify the Question Type

The phrase "most likely" identifies this as an Inference question. But note, too, its similarity to Point at Issue

questions from the Logical Reasoning section. The correct answer must be something both authors express an opinion about, and their opinions must be diametrically opposed.

Step 3: Research the Relevant Text

There's no specific research clue, so use your summaries of the two authors' Topic, Scope, Purpose, and Main Idea to predict the correct answer.

Step 4: Make a Prediction

The number one disagreement between the two authors is whether an objectivist historian writes from a political or social point of view. This central difference of opinion must be expressed in the right answer.

Step 5: Evaluate the Answer Choices

(B) is simple and to the point. Passage A's author states that the objectivist must reject all political agendas (lines 20–21); passage B's author says straight out that true objectivism is "perfectly compatible with strong political commitment" (lines 34–35).

(A) uses the term *detachment* vaguely. Depending on how it's defined (or to what it's applied), it's possible for both authors to agree with this statement.

(C) misses the concerns of both authors. Neither makes a claim about whether current historians are more or less objective than those of the past.

(D) is a statement with which both authors would disagree. It's a statement, in other words, on which they share the same view.

(E) is Outside the Scope. Again, neither author expresses any opinion about differences or similarities among historians over time.

25. (B) Inference

Step 2: Identify the Question Type

When a Reading Comprehension question asks about the author's attitude (or, in this case, authors' attitudes), treat it as an Inference question. The correct answer will follow from the statements in the passage(s). Make sure to focus on emphasis/opinion Keywords as you research.

Step 3: Research the Relevant Text

There's no specific research clue, so use your summaries of the two authors' Topic, Scope, Purpose, and Main Idea to predict the correct answer.

Step 4: Make a Prediction

This question asks you what the two authors have in common, specifically as they consider "objectivity." You know from your initial strategic reading that both consider themselves advocates of objectivism and that both are writing to tell historians how to achieve it. Use that to eliminate answers that distort or contradict the authors' positions or to identify the correct answer.

Step 5: Evaluate the Answer Choices

(B) is a statement both authors would heartily endorse. Both consider objectivism admirable and important to good historical work. They just have different ideas of what it means in practice.

(A) seems probable; after all, both scholars place pretty high demands on historians. But the problem with **(A)** as an answer choice is that it simply receives no support from the passages. Neither author speculates on how hard his or her requirements are to fulfill.

(C) reflects an attitude of passage A's author, but it contradicts what passage B's author says at lines 34–35.

(D) comes out of nowhere. Neither author expresses an attitude about historians as self-evaluators.

(E), once again, tries to get you to think there's a commentary about past and present historians in these passages. But there isn't, and **(E)** is Outside the Scope.

26. (D) Logic Function

Step 2: Identify the Question Type

Logic Function questions reference a detail—in this case, one mentioned in both passages—and ask you *why* the author included it or *how* it's used in the argument. Make sure you're predicting an answer that fits with what the question stem is asking.

Step 3: Research the Relevant Text

Passage A mentions propaganda in paragraph 3, at line 18. This author contrasts it with neutrality and casts it as the extreme form of advocacy. Passage B mentions propaganda in paragraph 1, at line 28. Passage B's author says that for historians to avoid becoming propagandists, they have to forego wishful thinking, accept uncomfortable truths, and live up to the standards of logic and evidence.

Step 4: Make a Prediction

For both authors, propaganda is the opposite of objective history. And for both, it's the embodiment of the "wrong" approach to history. The correct answer may express this in any number of ways, but it will get at the gist of this shared opinion.

Step 5: Evaluate the Answer Choices

(D) is the best match for the prediction. Passage A (with "or, worse, propagandist") is more explicit about characterizing propaganda as an extreme, but given the list of crimes against scholarship that passage B associates with propaganda, it's fair to say the second author would consider it an extreme, too.

(A) cannot be either author's purpose in referencing propaganda. Neither passage features a claim by anyone from a rival school.

(B) is well Outside the Scope of either passage. Neither author compares historians to scholars in other fields.

(C), not only fails to reflect a view expressed by either author, but it also makes the rather absurd assumption that propaganda ever had credit to lose.

(E) does not describe a function shared by both authors, even though the author of passage B contrasts propaganda with history, another type of writing she might consider "persuasive."

27. (E) Logic Reasoning (Method of Argument)

Step 2: Identify the Question Type

This question stem is similar to a Method of Argument question in the Logical Reasoning section. There, you must pick the choice that accurately describes the author's argumentative strategy. The Comparative Reading twist here is that the right answer will reflect a strategy used by both authors.

Step 3: Research the Relevant Text

There's no specific detail to research, but your Roadmap and big-picture summaries should help you predict what the right answer will say.

Step 4: Make a Prediction

For both authors, outlining the dos and don'ts of objectivism was part of their Purpose. The correct answer is likely to say that both authors examine what historians must do for their work to be objective and caution against the mistakes that could lead them to fail.

Step 5: Evaluate the Answer Choices

(E) picks up on the second half of the prediction. Although they disagree about what the obstacles are, both authors are firmly committed to exposing those obstacles and instructing historians to avoid them.

(A) is Outside the Scope. Neither author actually cites examples of either good or bad (in their minds, objective or unobjective) historical work.

(B), like many of the incorrect answers in this question set, imputes a comparison between past and present historians that neither author makes.

(C) cannot reasonably describe a strategy that either uses, because neither author cites an opposing argument.

(D) introduces a comparison with scholars from other fields, but neither author makes any claims about how scholars in other fields work or whether their approaches are objective.

PrepTest 64

The Inside Story

PrepTest 64 was administered in October 2011. It challenged 45,169 test takers. What made this test so hard? Here's a breakdown of what Kaplan students who were surveyed after taking the official exam considered PrepTest 64's most difficult section.

Hardest PrepTest 64 Section as Reported by Test Takers

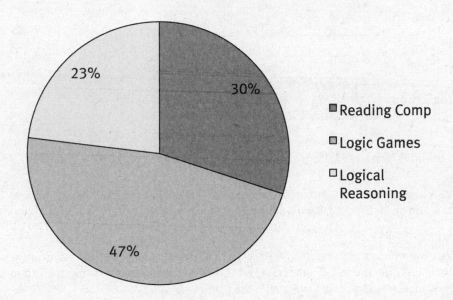

Based on these results, you might think that studying Logic Games is the key to LSAT success. Well, Logic Games is important, but test takers' perceptions don't tell the whole story. For that, you need to consider students' actual performance. The following chart shows the average number of students to miss each question in each of PrepTest 64's different sections.

Percentage Incorrect by PrepTest 64 Section Type

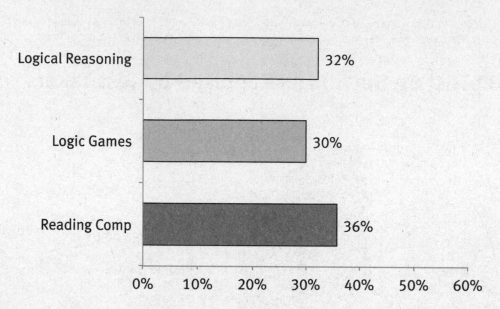

Actual student performance tells quite a different story. On average, students were almost equally likely to miss questions in all three of the different section types, and on PrepTest 64, Reading Comprehension and Logical Reasoning were somewhat higher than Logic Games in actual difficulty.

Maybe students overestimate the difficulty of the Logic Games section because it's so unusual, or maybe it's because a really hard Logic Game is so easy to remember after the test. But the truth is that the testmaker places hard questions throughout the test. Here were the locations of the 10 hardest (most missed) questions in the exam.

Location of 10 Most Difficult Questions in PrepTest 64

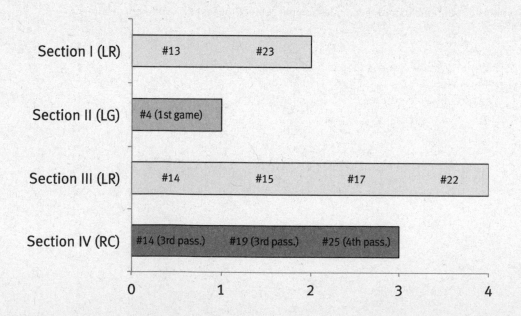

The takeaway from this data is that, to maximize your potential on the LSAT, you need to take a comprehensive approach. Test yourself rigorously, and review your performance on every section of the test. Kaplan's LSAT explanations provide the expertise and insight you need to fully understand your results. The explanations are written and edited by a team of LSAT experts, who have helped thousands of students improve their scores. Kaplan always provides data-driven analysis of the test, ranking the difficulty of every question based on actual student performance. The 10 hardest questions on every test are highlighted with a 4-star difficulty rating, the highest we give. The analysis breaks down the remaining questions into 1-, 2-, and 3-star ratings so that you can compare your performance to that of thousands of other test takers on all LSAC material.

Don't settle for wondering whether a question was really as hard as it seemed to you. Analyze the test with real data, and learn the secrets and strategies that help top scorers master the LSAT.

7 Can't–Miss Features of PrepTest 64

- There weren't many Principle Questions in PrepTest 64's two Logical Reasoning section—just three total, the fewest since PrepTest 40 (June 2003).
- Most LR questions with Principle/Application stimuli are not Principle questions, but rather Strengthen questions. On this test, though, both Principle/Application stimuli were actually Flaw questions (Section 1, Question 24; Section 3, Question 2).
- PrepTest 64 had a lot of Assumption Family questions, in fact, the Assumption Family scored a double-double, with 10 Strengthen/Weaken questions *and* 10 Flaw questions. The last time that happened was way back on PrepTest 48 (December 2005).
- Limited Options abound! All four games in the LG section can be approached using the Deduction of Limited Options.
- Be careful in Reading Comprehension here, especially on Question 3. Usually the LSAT puts words like EXCEPT and LEAST in all caps, but this time the word *least* is set in lowercase.
- Although most Global questions ask for the author's Purpose or passage's Main Idea, they occasionally ask for the *organization* of the passage. Not only did PrepTest 64 feature the first Global-Organization question since PrepTest 56 (December 2008), but it featured *two* of them--the first time that had happened since PrepTest 45 (December 2004).
- Although some tests are somewhat unbalanced for the frequency that each answer appears as the correct answer, PrepTest 64's Reading Comp and Logic Games sections were as even as possible: Each answer (A) through (E) shows up as the correct answer five or six times in RC and four or five times in LG.

PrepTest 64 in Context

As much fun as it is to find out what makes a PrepTest unique or noteworthy, it's even more important to know just how representative it is of other LSAT administrations (and, thus, how likely it is to be representative of the exam you will face on Test Day). The following charts compare the numbers of each kind of question and game on PrepTest 64 to the average numbers seen on all officially released LSATs administered over the past five years (from 2012 through 2016).

Number of LR Questions by Type: PrepTest 64 vs. 2012–2016 Average

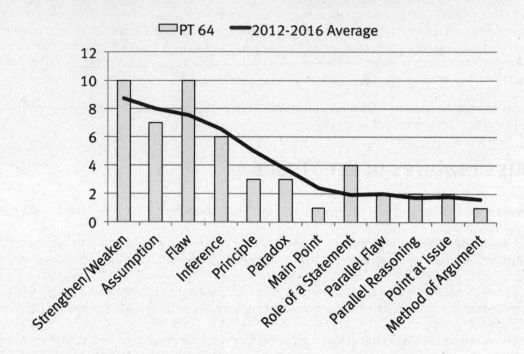

Number of LG Games by Type: PrepTest 64 vs. 2012–2016 Average

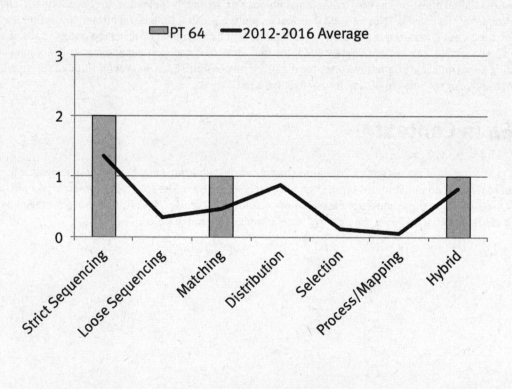

Number of RC Questions by Type: PrepTest 64 vs. 2012–2016 Average

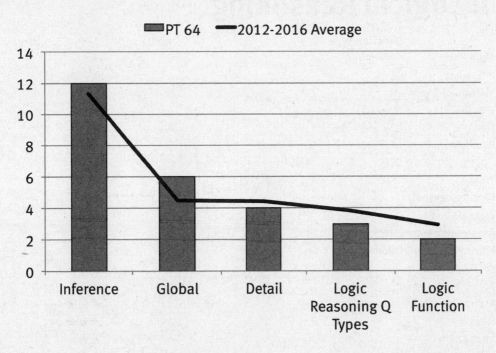

There isn't usually a huge difference in the distribution of questions from LSAT to LSAT, but if this test seems harder (or easier) to you than another you've taken, compare the number of questions of the types on which you, personally, are strongest and weakest. And then, explore within each section to see if your best or worst question types came earlier or later.

Students in Kaplan's comprehensive LSAT courses have access to every released LSAT, and to an online Q-Bank with thousands of officially released questions, games, and passages. If you are studying on your own, you have to do a bit more work to identify your strengths and your areas of opportunity. Quantitative analysis (like that in the charts here) is an important tool for understanding how the test is constructed, and how you are performing on it.

Section I: Logical Reasoning

Q#	Question Type	Correct	Difficulty
1	Main Point	C	★
2	Inference	C	★
3	Method of Argument	B	★
4	Weaken	A	★
5	Flaw	A	★
6	Paradox	E	★
7	Flaw	C	★
8	Weaken	B	★
9	Parallel Flaw	B	★★
10	Weaken	A	★★
11	Assumption (Sufficient)	E	★
12	Principle (Identify/Strengthen)	D	★
13	Weaken	D	★★★★
14	Role of a Statement	A	★★
15	Assumption (Necessary)	B	★★★
16	Flaw	A	★★★
17	Strengthen	A	★★
18	Inference	B	★★
19	Flaw	C	★
20	Inference	D	★★★
21	Parallel Reasoning	E	★★
22	Strengthen	B	★★★
23	Assumption (Sufficient)	D	★★★★
24	Flaw	E	★★★
25	Role of a Statement	B	★★★

1. (C) Main Point

Step 1: Identify the Question Type

The phrase "most accurately states the conclusion of the argument" identifies this Main Point question. Look for Keywords that signal the conclusion in the argument, watch out for subsidiary conclusions, and be prepared to combine statements to paraphrase the author's main point.

Step 2: Untangle the Stimulus

The argument is chock full of Keywords to guide your search for the author's main point. The first statement starts with "[s]ometimes it is advisable," a good indication that the author will counter with something that complicates this advice. Sure enough, the next statement begins with "[b]ut": It's a good idea to get a second medical opinion, but it can be awkward for both doctors and patients. The word *since* indicates that everything following the second sentence serves as supporting evidence. Stay focused on the author's main point.

Step 3: Make a Prediction

Combining the first and second statements yields a great prediction of the author's main point: seeking a second opinion can be awkward for patients and physicians.

Step 4: Evaluate the Answer Choices

(C) matches the prediction perfectly, as "those involved" refers to patients and physicians.

(A) misses the mark. The author never discusses the difference between optional and necessary second opinions. As far as you can tell from the stimulus, his opinion covers both instances.

(B) goes wrong in two ways. Like (A), it goes Outside the Scope by distinguishing necessary second opinions. In addition, the feelings of the physicians who give first and second opinions are part of the argument's evidence, not the author's main point.

(D) incorrectly identifies a piece of evidence in the argument as the author's main point.

(E), like (D), incorrectly identifies a piece of evidence in the argument as the author's main point.

2. (C) Inference

Step 1: Identify the Question Type

The phrase "must also be true" identifies this as an Inference question. Catalog and paraphrase the statements in the stimulus. Keep your eyes open for Formal Logic and/or terms that allow statements to be combined.

Step 2: Untangle the Stimulus

This series of facts indicates that although there has been a substantial jump in the number of Florida panthers since the 1970s, it's still not enough for the population to be self-sustaining. In addition, the last piece of information states that the panthers' current habitat is at capacity, unable to support any more panthers.

Step 3: Make a Prediction

Think about how that last sentence can be connected to the others. In their current habitat, the panther population cannot increase to the numbers required for the panthers to be self-sustaining. Work through the answer choices for a statement that must be true on the basis of these statements.

Step 4: Evaluate the Answer Choices

(C) must be true on the basis of the stimulus. Since their current habitat is at capacity, the panthers will need to move to a different, larger habitat to increase and become self-sustaining.

(A) is Outside the Scope. Only the capacity, not the quality (marginal or otherwise), of the panthers' current habitat is discussed.

(B) twists the logic of the stimulus. If the panther population is to become self-sustaining, then reaching a population of 250 is necessary. You can't tell from what's given whether reaching a population of 250 is sufficient to guarantee that the panthers will be self-sustaining.

(D) is Extreme. Although the Florida panthers have reached capacity in their current habitat, there remains the possibility that they could move to a different habitat and increase in number.

(E) need not be true based on the stimulus. While the population of panthers has increased, there's no mention of whether this was due to a larger habitat.

3. (B) Method of Argument

Step 1: Identify the Question Type

The phrase "argument proceeds by" indicates a Method of Argument question. Focus on how the author moves through the argument rhetorically. Don't get too caught up in the content. The correct answer is likely to be abstract and descriptive.

Step 2: Untangle the Stimulus

The sentence "But this is not so," midway through the argument flags the conclusion. To understand how the author makes his point, consider his opponents' argument. The opponents fight efforts to create more equality because they assume egalitarianism will lead to homogeneity. The author rejects this assumption, giving evidence that we can increase both equality and diversity.

Step 3: Make a Prediction

Think in the abstract. The author is attacking the critics' presumption that promoting common interests must result in "bland uniformity" by explaining that it can also result in increased diversity. So, the author refutes the critics' view by attacking the truth of their central assumption.

Step 4: Evaluate the Answer Choices

(B) matches the prediction perfectly. The author rebuts the critics' objection to egalitarianism by attacking their assumption that the advancement of common interest will result in bland uniformity.

(A) is Outside the Scope. The author never discusses the consequences that would result from accepting the critics' view.

(C) is Outside the Scope. The author says nothing about the motives of the critics and certainly doesn't suggest that they're self-interested. Perhaps they're legitimately, if mistakenly, concerned about a loss of diversity.

(D) is an Irrelevant Comparison. The topic of group versus individual distinctions is never broached by the author.

(E) is a double Distortion. The critics don't offer a counterexample, and the phrase "universal claim" doesn't really fit the "[e]fforts" they're criticizing.

4. (A) Weaken

Step 1: Identify the Question Type

The phrase "constitutes the logically strongest counter to the … argument" indicates a Weaken question. The correct answer choice will be a fact that weakens the physician's assumption. Identify the physician's conclusion, paraphrase her evidence, and identify her central assumption. Then look for a fact that would make that assumption less likely.

Step 2: Untangle the Stimulus

The conclusion is signaled by the phrase "[t]his shows that." The physician believes that magnetic fields are likely to alleviate some back pain. Her evidence is the results of the experiment. Fifty participants with chronic back pain were split into two groups, one with magnets and one that got no treatment at all. More people in the group treated with magnets reported that they felt better than did people in the second group, very few of whom indicated a reduction in pain. Pay close attention to the fact that the second group received no treatment at all.

Step 3: Make a Prediction

On its face, this argument seems to make sense. But the key here is to notice that the author is attributing the reduction in pain to the magnets and not to the fact that the first group received some treatment rather than no treatment. The author is assuming that the first group's positive results were due to

the magnets, not to a placebo effect. The argument will be weakened if anything other than the magnets might have caused the test group's improvement.

Step 4: Evaluate the Answer Choices

(A) provides an alternative reason for the differing results among the two groups. The first group, who knew they were receiving experimental treatment, may have believed it was helping regardless of whether it actually helped. This choice describes the placebo effect in a nutshell.

(B) is an Irrelevant Comparison. Whether treatments other than magnets are even more effective is never discussed.

(C) is an Irrelevant Comparison. The argument is entirely about back pain. Whether magnets are or are not effective for pain in other areas of the body doesn't affect the validity of the physician's argument.

(D) is Outside the Scope. What the designers of the experiment believed is immaterial to the validity of the experiment's results.

(E) is Outside the Scope. The physician never discusses the cause of the back pain. It's possible that some types of back pain aren't relieved by magnets, but this is consistent with the physician's conclusion: Magnets are "probably effective at relieving some back pain."

5. (A) Flaw

Step 1: Identify the Question Type

There are two things to note in this question stem. First, "[t]he argument is flawed" indicates that this is a Flaw question. Second, "fails to consider the possibility" gives you the type of flaw. Approach the argument looking for what the author has overlooked or taken for granted. The answer choices here will be content specific, so the correct answer must match the scope of the argument.

Step 2: Untangle the Stimulus

As with any Flaw question, start with the conclusion. Here, it's signaled by "[w]e can conclude from this that … " The author believes that, rather than improving dogs' behavior, discipline actually makes it worse. The author's evidence is that kennel club members who often discipline their dogs report more misbehavior than those who don't discipline their dogs as much.

Step 3: Make a Prediction

The author is making a causal argument. While misbehavior and discipline are correlated, the author is taking for granted that the discipline is causing the misbehavior. But it's just as likely that the reverse may be true. So, the author is overlooking the possibility that the dogs are being disciplined more often because they misbehave more often.

Step 4: Evaluate the Answer Choices

(A) provides the alternative the author has overlooked. The members discipline their dogs more because of the dogs' misbehavior, not the other way around, as the author assumes.

(B) is Outside the Scope. The author says nothing about what dogs are thinking about or learning from their owners' reactions to misbehavior. It's not a problem with the argument.

(C) is Outside the Scope. The cause of misbehavior in other animals is never mentioned, so it cannot be a problem with the argument.

(D) is an Irrelevant Comparison. The argument is strictly limited to kennel club members' frequent discipline of their dogs. Their skill in raising dogs compared to nonmembers is never discussed.

(E) is an Irrelevant Comparison for reasons similar to those in **(D)**. Whether kennel club members are more likely than nonmembers to discipline their dogs is immaterial to the argument.

6. (E) Paradox

Step 1: Identify the Question Type

The phrase "resolve the apparent discrepancy" indicates a Paradox question. Isolate the seemingly inconsistent facts in the stimulus and determine why the author thinks there's a problem. The correct answer will be fact that helps explain or reconcile the apparent contradiction.

Step 2: Untangle the Stimulus

The Keyword [*y*]*et* signals where the problem comes in. The author is confused about how the number of tornadoes recorded annually has tripled in the past 50-odd years when, during the same period, the climatic causes of tornadoes have not changed.

Step 3: Make a Prediction

Remember that every paradox is resolvable. The correct answer will offer a fact that clears up the discrepancy. Here, the author overlooks the difference between the number of tornadoes reported and the number actually happening. So, to resolve the paradox, look for an answer choice that explains how there can be an increase in the number of tornadoes reported in light of the stability of the weather conditions.

Step 4: Evaluate the Answer Choices

(E) provides a reason that more tornadoes are being recorded. Authorities have more assistance in detecting tornadoes now than in the past. Perhaps the same number of tornadoes was occurring in 1953, but limitations on detection resulted in significantly fewer being recorded.

(A) is Outside the Scope. The author is strictly concerned with the increase in the number of tornadoes recorded from 1953 to the present. The knowledge of causes prior to this time frame has no affect on the argument.

(B) is Outside the Scope. Tornado intensity has no bearing on why the number of tornadoes recorded has increased so significantly.

(C) is too narrow. The fact that the increased rate of tornado reporting has, apparently, slowed very recently, doesn't help explain the enormous increase over the past 50-odd years.

(D) is Outside the Scope. Damage caused by tornadoes, let alone the amount of damage, is immaterial to resolving the problem in the stimulus. Perhaps more homes have been built in "Tornado Alley" during that time. That would mean more property damage even if the number of tornadoes was the same.

7. (C) Flaw

Step 1: Identify the Question Type

The phrase "the argument is flawed" indicates that this is a Flaw question. Start with the conclusion, paraphrase the evidence, then predict where the author's logic has gone wrong.

Step 2: Untangle the Stimulus

The phrase "[f]rom these examples, it is clear that … " confirms that the author's conclusion is in the last sentence. It's quite broad: Eventually, nutritionists will view any food as healthful. The author cites two foods, chocolate and olive oil, each with an earlier report deeming that food unhealthy and a recent report indicating its positive health effects.

Step 3: Make a Prediction

The problem with the argument is the author makes a broad claim ("almost any food") on the basis of two examples. The author may be right, but the evidence is insufficient (too small a sample, too narrow a selection) to properly support the claim.

Step 4: Evaluate the Answer Choices

(C) picks up on the predicted problem with the author's argument. The claim is an overly broad generalization about almost any food on the basis of a few instances (chocolate and olive oil). This is referred to as an "unrepresentative sample" flaw.

(A) is Outside the Scope. The bias of the source of the reports is not at issue in the argument. Even if the reports are completely valid, they are still insufficient to support such a broad claim.

(B) is not a flaw in the argument. Actually, the general rule would seem to apply to these two instances, but that's beside the point. The argument uses the examples to support the rule, not the other way around.

(D) is Outside the Scope. This is too broad. For the author's conclusion to be valid, positive results need to be reported for almost all foods. All nutritional results need not be reported. A hundred studies might say, "Soy is healthful," but the author needs only one.

(E) may seem to hurt the author's conclusion, but there are two reasons it doesn't. First, the author's conclusion is that almost all foods will be reported to be healthy. This allows for some (or many) foods to be reported as unhealthy. Furthermore, the author cites two examples of foods that were originally reported as unhealthy. So, even if many foods are currently reported to be unhealthy, they still could be reported as healthy later.

8. (B) Weaken

Step 1: Identify the Question Type

The phrase "would provide evidence against" indicates a Weaken question. Use the extra information in the stem. Specifically, it tells you that the correct answer will provide a fact that works against the bottom-up theory presented in the argument.

Step 2: Untangle the Stimulus

The entire stimulus is merely a description of the bottom-up theory. The author never weighs in on whether it's valid or not. The core of the bottom-up theory has to do with the food chain: It rests primarily on the availability of edible plants, since herbivores eat edible plants and predators eat herbivores. Thus, the number of predators has a small effect on the ecosystem compared to the availability of edible plants.

Step 3: Make a Prediction

Think about the type of evidence that works against the bottom-up theory. Anything that shows that predators are a key factor in the ecosystem, or that edible plants are not, would undermine the theory.

Step 4: Evaluate the Answer Choices

(B) provides a fact that shows the detrimental effect of eliminating predators from an ecosystem. This choice undermines the bottom-up theory in just the way you predicted.

(A) is a 180. The effort to increase the monkey population failed because the edible plants they fed upon were nearly extinct. That supports the bottom-up theory.

(C) is a 180. The substantial decrease in the edible plants on Jaevix Island was followed by a substantial decrease in the island's ants and anteaters, exactly as the bottom-up theory would predict.

(D) is a 180. Because the availability of edible plants on Lisdok Island did not change (a new fern took the place of the old one), there was no effect on the population of herbivores. That's right in line with the bottom-up theory.

(E) is a 180. In spite of an outside threat (extensive hunting), the pig population remained unchanged as the availability of edible plants increased. This is consistent with the bottom-up theory.

9. (B) Parallel Flaw

Step 1: Identify the Question Type

The phrase "most closely parallels" coupled with "flawed reasoning" indicates this is not just a Parallel Reasoning question but a Parallel Flaw question. Analyze the argument as a whole, approaching it like a Flaw question stimulus. The correct answer choice will exhibit the same pattern of reasoning with the same flaw.

Step 2: Untangle the Stimulus

This argument is based on a conditional, Formal Logic rule. Depict it in the abstract:

Evidence:

If	X (child develops healthy bones)	→	Y (diet includes enough calcium)

Conclusion:

If	~ X (child does not develop healthy bones)	→	~ Y (diet does not include enough calcium)

Step 3: Make a Prediction

Once you've broken the argument down into the abstract, the flaw becomes clear. There are a number of ways to describe this flaw: the author treats a sufficient condition as if it were necessary; the author negates the logic without reversing the terms, and so on. The bottom line for this Parallel Flaw question is that the correct answer will display exactly the same pattern: it will offer a conditional statement as evidence and then negate, but not reverse, the terms in the statement in its conclusion.

Step 4: Evaluate the Answer Choices

(B) exhibits the same flawed pattern of reasoning as the stimulus:

Evidence:

If	X (cake tastes good)	→	Y (cake contains the right amount of flour)

Conclusion:

If | ~ X (cake does not taste good) | → | ~ Y (cake does not contain the right amount of flour)

(A) has no flaw in the logic of its argument. The conclusion is a correctly formed contrapositive of the conditional statement in the evidence:

Evidence:

If | X (firm crust) | → | Y (baked at right temperature)

Conclusion:

If | ~ Y (not baked at right temperature) | → | ~ X (does not have a firm crust)

(C) is incorrect because there's no conditional statement present in the evidence. Rather, the conclusion is a prediction based on past events.

(D) has a causal relationship in its opening statement that might be interpreted along the lines of "If yeast or baking powder → sweet rolls will rise." But the two sufficient terms already make this different from the stimulus. The conclusion here—that you can swap the sufficient ingredients for one another—also has no parallel In the stimulus.

(E) contains a conditional statement in its evidence, but the conclusion is unrelated. The evidence concerns the number of contestants in each category, while the conclusion discusses the likelihood of winning in each category.

10. (A) Weaken

Step 1: Identify the Question Type

The phrase "most seriously undermines the reasoning" indicates that this is a Weaken question. The correct answer will provide a fact that makes the author's assumption less likely to follow from his evidence.

Step 2: Untangle the Stimulus

The conclusion is signaled by the phrase "[t]his shows that …" There, the author makes a comparison: social inertia is a greater determinant of human behavior than is the desire for comfort and safety. As evidence, the author gives examples of workers who, despite miserable conditions, resisted technological innovations.

Step 3: Make a Prediction

The author is making a causal argument: social inertia is causing our behavior. To use the evidence in the argument to reach his conclusion, the author must assume that only social inertia causes people to resist technological innovation. The author rules out comfort and safety as motives, but there could be other reasons (besides social inertia, comfort, or safety) to resist technological change. An answer choice that

introduces another potential reason to resist technological innovation will weaken this causal argument.

Step 4: Evaluate the Answer Choices

(A) presents an alternative reason for the workers' opposition: even though working conditions were terrible, laborers believed technological innovation could cost them their jobs.

(B) is a 180; it strengthens the author's argument. Reluctance to take on new challenges (e.g., innovative technology) would be a sure sign of social inertia.

(C) is Outside the Scope. A few counterexamples don't damage the author's reasoning. Remember, he concludes that social inertia is a greater influence than the desire for comfort and safety. The author's many examples could still carry the day, and what's more, nothing in **(C)** indicates that the innovations workers embraced were designed to improve comfort or safety.

(D) is Outside the Scope. The speed at which people best adapt to innovation tells you nothing about their reasons for being for or against it in the first place.

(E) is Outside the Scope. Whether or not people correctly believe that technological innovations lead to increased worker productivity has no bearing on whether the author is correct in identifying the primary influences on human behavior.

11. (E) Assumption (Sufficient)

Step 1: Identify the Question Type

The phrase "if assumed" identifies this as an Assumption question type. Furthermore, the "If" indicates that you are looking for a sufficient assumption. The correct answer choice here can be broad, as long as it guarantees that the argument's conclusion follows from its evidence. Also, the phrase "the psychologist's conclusion" should draw your attention to the psychologist's argument in the stimulus first.

Step 2: Untangle the Stimulus

The phrase "a psychologist argued that … " flags the psychologist's conclusion. The psychologist believes that flattery of supervisors is not the reason workers are promoted. The evidence is that flattery is too obvious.

Step 3: Make a Prediction

The psychologist's central assumption is that supervisors' decisions to promote workers are not influenced by blatant or obvious behavior. In other words, flattery couldn't influence their decision because they know it's happening.

Step 4: Evaluate the Answer Choices

(E) provides the assumption as predicted. If the statement here is added to the psychologist's argument, its conclusion follows unequivocally from its evidence.

(A) is Outside the Scope. The degree to which supervisors expect to be flattered is immaterial to the psychologist's argument that flattery is ineffective because it's obvious.

(B) is irrelevant. Regardless of the official guidelines, flattery could be an additional factor in who gets promotions.

(C) is Outside the Scope. The psychologist is focused on whether flattery, when obvious to the flattered person, is effective. The effects of flattery that is not noticed are never discussed.

(D) is at best Outside the Scope and at worst a 180. If anything, supervisors taking flattery as sincere appreciation might be more inclined to promote the flatterer. The assumption needed to link the evidence and conclusion in this argument is that obvious behaviors don't successfully influence supervisors.

12. (D) Principle (Identify/Strengthen)

Step 1: Identify the Question Type

The word *principles* tips you off that this is a Principle question. More importantly, this Principle question mimics a Strengthen question, as evidenced by the phrase "helps to justify the reasoning." Attack it the same way you would a Strengthen question, but keep in mind that the correct answer will be phrased as a broad rule, able to support the specific case in the stimulus and others like it.

Step 2: Untangle the Stimulus

The Keyword [*h*]*owever* indicates the author's opinion. The author contends that potential harm doesn't justify the government in silencing groups promoting diets of uncooked meat. The author reasons that government wouldn't silence political groups merely because of potential harm, either.

Step 3: Make a Prediction

The broader principle underlying the author's analogy between political groups and the raw meat advocates is that the government should not silence groups simply because they support positions that could be harmful to some people. Look for an answer choice that matches the prediction.

Step 4: Evaluate the Answer Choices

(D) is a perfect match to the prediction. If this principle is valid, the author's analogy is stronger, and so too is his conclusion.

(A) is Outside the Scope. The degree of societal support that a group's message enjoys is irrelevant to the author's conclusion that the government is not justified in censoring a

group's message. An answer must address "potential harm" to be within this argument's scope.

(B) is Extreme. The author doesn't give blanket approval to any government action so long as it benefits society. If anything, the author is advocating that the government should be restrained from acting in cases of possible societal harm.

(C) is Outside the Scope. The author is not concerned with why groups advocate their positions. The author is solely concerned with when the government should be prohibited from silencing those groups because of the potential effects of their positions.

(E) is Outside the Scope. The argument in the stimulus is focused on whether the government is justified in taking a certain action. What "[o]ne" should encourage the government to do is tangential to the point of irrelevance.

13. (D) Weaken

Step 1: Identify the Question Type

The phrase "would most weaken the ... argument" indicates that this is a Weaken question. The correct answer will call into question the medical researcher's argument.

Step 2: Untangle the Stimulus

As indicated by the phrase "[t]his indicates that ... ," the medical researcher concludes that stretching before jogging does not help to prevent injuries. The evidence is a scientific study that showed no significant difference between the number of injuries sustained by joggers who stretched before exercising and those who didn't.

Step 3: Make a Prediction

Think critically about the assumption. The author is assuming that the two groups of runners are alike in every other way or, said the other way around, that the only relevant difference between the two is that one group stretched and the other didn't. But what if the stretchers were more injury prone to begin with? Or what if they stretched because they'd been injured in the past? If the stretchers are more susceptible to injury, then the author's assumption would be weaker.

Step 4: Evaluate the Answer Choices

(D) provides a potential weakener to the medical researcher's argument. Runners who are more prone to injury are more likely to stretch. If a group more prone to injury is showing the same injury rate as one unlikely to be injured, perhaps stretching is preventing injuries.

(A) is an Irrelevant Comparison. The medical researcher is only concerned with comparing the two groups in the study; she wants to determine whether stretching makes a difference in injury rates. This choice might allow you to draw the conclusion that being part of a study prevents injury, but it's irrelevant to the researcher's argument.

(B) is Outside the Scope. There's nothing in the argument to indicate that difficulty in stretching is relevant to the question of whether stretching helped or didn't help prevent injury.

(C) is both Outside the Scope and a 180. How the injuries occur is immaterial. In addition, this statement would seem to strengthen the medical researcher's claim that stretching does not affect likelihood of injury.

(E) fails for two reasons. First, if jogging is not one of the "certain forms of exercise," this statement is irrelevant to the argument. Second, the argument is about preventing injuries, not reducing their severity.

14. (A) Role of a Statement

Step 1: Identify the Question Type

The phrase "[t]he claim that … plays which one of the following roles" indicates a Role of a Statement question. Using Keywords and the argument's structure, determine whether the statement in question is the conclusion or part of the evidence.

Step 2: Untangle the Stimulus

The statement in the question stem is found at the beginning of the second sentence, with the pronoun [*t*]*his* replacing "superconductor development," the subject of the first sentence. The structure here allows you to see that the author intends for the second sentence to follow from the first. The word *for* after the claim you're characterizing indicates that what follows is further evidence for the claim. In short, the author argues that superconductor development will help with productivity because similar developments did so in the past, as evidenced by reduced shipping costs and less energy lost in transit.

Step 3: Make a Prediction

So, the phrase "[t]his [superconductor development] will probably improve industrial productivity," is the author's conclusion. Find the answer choice that identifies the statement in the question stem as the conclusion.

Step 4: Evaluate the Answer Choices

(A) correctly identifies the statement in the question stem as the conclusion, with the argument's first sentence and everything following the claim provided as evidence.

(B) incorrectly refers to the claim as a generalization, when the claim discusses a specific benefit of a specific action. Also, the opening statement (about transporting energy) leads to (i.e., is evidence for) the claim in question; it's not an illustration.

(C) incorrectly identifies the statement in the question stem as an assumption. Remember that an assumption is a

missing piece of evidence; it will never appear in the argument.

(D) incorrectly identifies the statement in the question stem as evidence.

(E) also incorrectly identifies the statement in the question stem as evidence.

15. (B) Assumption (Necessary)

Step 1: Identify the Question Type

The phrase "an assumption on which the argument depends" identifies this as an Assumption question. Specifically, it is asking for an assumption necessary to the argument. So the correct answer choice must be a statement that, if not true, would make the argument invalid. Watch out for answer choices that are too broad.

Step 2: Untangle the Stimulus

Start with the conclusion. Although there are no Keywords, the phrase midway through the argument meets the One-Sentence Test: this charge is unfair. Specifically, the author takes issue with the view that Colette's novels are indifferent to important moral questions. In support, the author shows that the emotional crises put forth in Collette's novels raise important moral questions.

Step 3: Make a Prediction

The author takes the mere appearance of crises involving moral questions as a sign that Colette was actively concerned (i.e., was not indifferent) about those questions. So, the author must be assuming that putting forth such emotional crises in the way Colette does shows that she wasn't indifferent to the moral questions they raise.

Step 4: Evaluate the Answer Choices

(B) is correct, but its negative wording may be hard to identify as a match to the assumption as predicted. The Denial test helps here. If a novel that puts forth those emotional crises in the way Colette's did does have to be indifferent, then the author's refutation of the critics would fall apart. Think of it like this: the assumption "X makes you stronger" always entails the assumption "X does not have to make you weaker." Likewise, the assumption "this kind of novel is not indifferent" always entails "this type of novel does not have to be indifferent."

(A) is Outside the Scope. The author never discusses Colette's literary achievements or the critic's failure to acknowledge them appropriately.

(C) is a Distortion. The issue is not whether the novel must concern itself with moral questions to deserve praise. Rather, the author merely explores whether the complaint that Colette's novels were indifferent is fair.

(D) is a Distortion. The vividness of Colette's language is only discussed as background filler in the first sentence. Its purpose in the argument ends there.

(E) is a Distortion. The author is not concerned with whether Colette's purpose in presenting the said emotional crises was to explore important moral questions. Rather, the author merely wants to point out that her novels are not indifferent to such questions. The Denial Test can help here. Even if it wasn't Colette's explicit purpose to explore moral questions, the novels she wound up writing might not be indifferent to them. This would be like saying that since Victor Hugo didn't intend for *Les Miserables* to become a Broadway play, the novel isn't suitable for adaptation.

16. (A) Flaw

Step 1: Identify the Question Type

The phrase "[t]he reasoning in the argument is flawed" indicates that this is a Flaw question. Start by identifying the conclusion and the evidence, then look for an answer that expresses why they aren't adequately connected.

Step 2: Untangle the Stimulus

The strong conclusion Keyword [*t*]*hus* signals the author's main point. Social theorists who believe that people are motivated purely by self-interest must also believe that democracy is a lost cause. Use the first sentence for context: there is an implication that government by consent is impossible if one only cares about oneself. The evidence, signaled by the Keyword *since*, confirms that consent is required for democracy.

Step 3: Make a Prediction

The author's argument depends upon whether the social theorists believe the implication identified in the first sentence. If they do, the conclusion holds. If they don't, the conclusion may not necessarily be true. So, the author has mistakenly inferred that the social theorists believe consent is impossible if everyone is out for himself or herself.

Step 4: Evaluate the Answer Choices

(A) is abstractly worded but matches the prediction exactly. Simply knowing that the social theorists hold the belief that people are concerned only with their self-interest is not enough to know that the theorists necessarily believe the implication that government by consent is therefore impossible. Provided that they believe consent to be possible, you need not conclude that they believe democracy impossible.

(B) is not a flaw present in the argument. The author confines her argument to "social theorists who believe that people are concerned only with their self-interest." In this case, the group would be composed of just these people. So, the

distinction between group and individual is meaningless in this argument.

(C) is the reverse of **(B)** yet is still wrong. The author never talks about characteristics of one member of a group being imparted to the whole. The author addresses the group of social theorists with a particular idea; she doesn't cite an individual social theorist and assume all social theorists must believe the same thing he does.

(D) is not a flaw present in the argument. The author never attacks the social theorists personally. Rather, she strictly limits her critique to what she believes are the logical consequences of the theorists' views.

(E) is not a flaw present in the argument. The truth or falsity of the theorists' conclusion is never discussed, just the implications of their beliefs. This answer choice would apply to an argument such as "My friend said my boat would capsize because it was so windy. My boat didn't capsize, so it must not be possible for wind to capsize a boat."

17. (A) Strengthen

Step 1: Identify the Question Type

The phrase "most helps to justify the reasoning" indicates a Strengthen question. Remember that the correct answer to a Strengthen question will make the author's central assumption more likely. It can, in some cases, be as clear cut as saying that the author's assumption is true. Don't be thrown off by the phrase "if assumed" in the question stem.

Step 2: Untangle the Stimulus

Start with the conclusion in the opening sentence. Although there's an absence of conclusion Keywords, recommendations (indicated here by the phrase "should have") typically satisfy the One-Sentence Test for recognizing the author's opinion. The archaeologist believes that the mosaics should never have been removed. The evidence is that we had exhausted all information they could provide, and their removal could mislead future archaeologists who won't know the mosaics have been removed on purpose.

Step 3: Make a Prediction

Whenever the author recommends against a course of action, the author might be overlooking other reasons justifying the action. In this example, the author is assuming that once the archaeologists had all their information, there were no other reasons for removing the mosaics. To support the conclusion, that needs to be true. The correct answer could state affirmatively, "Only archeological considerations matter," or it could rule out the importance of one or more alternative considerations.

Step 4: Evaluate the Answer Choices

(A) matches the prediction. The fact that the author overlooked any nonarchaeological reasons for removing the mosaics is now immaterial. Removing a potential weakener will always strengthen an argument.

(B) is Outside the Scope. Whether or not archaeologists could detect that Zeugma had been flooded has no bearing on the argument as to whether the mosaics ought to have been left behind. If anything, knowing that the site had been flooded would be a clue that the mosaics had been removed on purpose. That would weaken the author's concern about confusing future archeologists.

(C) is Outside the Scope. The archaeologist never addresses whether removing the mosaics compromised the archaeologists' ability to identify the materials used to make the mosaics. In fact, she insists that archaeologists already had all the information they needed. Given the information in the argument, the materials may be just as easy to identify in their new location.

(D) is irrelevant. Note the language the author uses in the evidence: future archaeologists "might be misled by their absence." The author allows for this to be a rare occurrence. So, **(D)** has no bearing on the argument either way.

(E) Is Outside the Scope. The environmental impact of removing the mosaics is never at issue in the argument. In fact, the author only addresses archaeological concerns for removing the mosaics. If this choice said that removing artifacts causes environmental harm, the author could add that as another argument for her conclusion, but it wouldn't justify the reasoning in the argument she's already made.

18. (B) Inference

Step 1: Identify the Question Type

Because the stem asks for something that can be "properly inferred," this can be easily identified as an Inference question. Be sure to accept all the given information as true, combine statements, and find the one answer that must directly follow.

Step 2: Untangle the Stimulus

The opening statement tells you that engineers have created a better traffic flow on the (oddly named) Krakkenbak Bridge. This is followed by some Formal Logic. If the city hadn't invested in computer modeling technology, the increased traffic flow wouldn't have happened. Furthermore, if traffic flow on the bridge hadn't increased, the city wouldn't have resolved its financial predicament.

Step 3: Make a Prediction

The Formal Logic statements can be combined to form one string of logic:

$$\text{If} \quad \begin{array}{c} \sim \text{ investment} \\ \text{in modeling} \\ \text{technology} \end{array} \rightarrow \begin{array}{c} \sim \text{increased} \\ \text{traffic flow} \end{array} \rightarrow \begin{array}{c} \sim \text{resolution} \\ \text{to financial} \\ \text{problems} \end{array}$$

The correct answer will conform to this string of logic or its contrapositive.

Step 4: Evaluate the Answer Choices

(B) is a perfect match to the logic. From the first Formal Logic statement, you know that not investing in modeling technology would have prevented the increased traffic flow. In turn, from the last statement, you can determine that this would have prevented the city from resolving its financial predicament.

(A) goes Outside the Scope by discussing competing computer modeling software. The Formal Logic in the stimulus doesn't specify a specific computer modeling package. Even if the city chose a different software package, it might still have resolved the traffic flow problem and, in turn, the financial predicament.

(C) distorts the information. While there was an increase in traffic flow (i.e., the movement of cars), that doesn't mean there were more cars.

(D) is Extreme. This choice discusses the effect of not making computer modeling technology a top priority. However, to increase the traffic flow, the city merely had to invest in such technology; nothing in the stimulus says it was the highest budgetary priority.

(E) mentions the mayor's motives for pushing computer modeling technology. However, while the technology did help with traffic flow, there's no evidence that this was the reason for the mayor's advocacy. Maybe he was just doing his buddy at the software firm a favor and got lucky.

19. (C) Flaw

Step 1: Identify the Question Type

The question asks why the argument is "flawed," making this easy to identify as a Flaw question. In addition, the stem already indicates the general flaw: the court analyst fails to consider something—the most common mistake Logical Reasoning authors make on the LSAT. After breaking the argument down into its evidence and conclusion, consider alternative explanations that the court analyst overlooked.

Step 2: Untangle the Stimulus

The court analyst starts off immediately with the conclusion: DNA tests shouldn't be allowed in court for criminal cases. The evidence has two parts: (1) Controversy exists regarding the reliability of DNA tests, and (2) it is unreasonable to use tests when the scientific community does not agree about how reliable the tests are.

Step 3: Make a Prediction

The author uses some vague language, and as a result his argument gets a little fuzzy. Based on the last sentence, if there were no widespread agreement about the reliability of DNA tests, then the court analyst could rightfully claim that they should be disallowed. However, the court analyst merely mentions controversy, without explaining fully the basis of that controversy. He assumes that the controversy is divisive enough to prevent widespread agreement about DNA tests' general reliability. So, without much information about that controversy, the court analyst overlooks the possibility that the controversy is trivial and doesn't rise to the level of widespread disagreement about the reliability of DNA tests in general.

Step 4: Evaluate the Answer Choices

(C) hits upon exactly what the court analyst overlooks: a trivial controversy regarding the exact reliability of DNA testing, a controversy that wouldn't affect an overall agreement about DNA's general reliability.

(A) is Outside the Scope of the argument. The court analyst is concerned with what courts should do, not what they can do (i.e., have the authority to do).

(B) is a Distortion, implying that the court analyst believes absolute certainty to be the benchmark for measuring evidence. However, the court analyst pushes merely for widespread agreement, not absolute certainty.

(D) is a slight, but fatal, Distortion of the argument. The author calls for the scientific community to agree on reliability but doesn't say anything about scientific witnesses. Furthermore, the last thing the analyst overlooks is the fact that data should not be admitted without agreement over its reliability; that's the gist of the court analyst's whole point.

(E) is Outside the Scope, discussing noncriminal cases, which are of no relevance to the court analyst's argument.

20. (D) Inference

Step 1: Identify the Question Type

Since the question asks for an answer that "must be true" based on the given statements, this is an Inference question. Don't expect a complete argument. Simply translate any Formal Logic and look for statements or ideas that can be logically combined to make deductions.

Step 2: Untangle the Stimulus

The author provides information about special discount coupons for Frequent Viewers club members at a place called VideoKing. The information states the two ways that members can get the coupons: (1) Members who have rented more than ten videos in the past month can only get the coupon where they last rented a video, and (2) members who have not rented more than ten videos in the past month can only get the coupon at the Main Street location.

Then there's information about Pat, who it should be noted is not described as a Frequent Viewers club member. Pat has not rented more than 10 videos in the past month, and she can get the coupon at the Walnut Lane location.

Step 3: Make a Prediction

Pat's case is rather curious. She hasn't rented more than 10 videos in the past month. If she were a Frequent Viewers club member, she would only be able to get the coupon at the Main Street location. However, she can get it at Walnut Lane. This gives us two important pieces of information. First, Pat is definitely not a Frequent Viewers club member (otherwise she would be forced to get her coupon at Main Street). Second, knowing that she's not a member and that she can get the coupon, we know that these coupons must be available to some nonmembers as well (restrictions unknown). The correct answer will play off one or both of these deductions.

Step 4: Evaluate the Answer Choices

(D) is correct. Since Pat can get the coupon and she isn't a member (given that she doesn't have to follow the rules ascribed to members), it must be true that some nonmembers can get the coupon.

(A) reverses the Formal Logic of the stimulus. While Main Street is the only location where members who've rented fewer than ten times can get the coupon, that doesn't mean these are the only people who can get the coupon at Main Street. Just consider the case of a member who has rented more than ten times in the past month and whose last rental was from Main Street.

(B) doesn't follow from the stimulus. The only individual you learn about is Pat, who isn't a member. There may or may not be members who've rented fewer than 10 times.

(C) contradicts the logic. The conditions are mutually exclusive—members can't satisfy both (you can't both rent and not rent more than ten videos)—and each condition allows for picking up the coupon at only one location.

(E) doesn't follow because Pat isn't a club member. Since no rules are provided for nonmembers, there's no way to tell if she can get the coupon at locations other than Walnut Lane.

21. (E) Parallel Reasoning

Step 1: Identify the Question Type

Since the question asks for a line of reasoning "similar to" that in the stimulus, this is Parallel Reasoning. Look for ways to compare the structure of the arguments, including the type of conclusion and how the author forms the evidence.

Step 2: Untangle the Stimulus

The argument starts by discussing two options that game show winners have for making prize decisions: they choose either the prize that's more expensive or the one that's more familiar. Then, the author applies this principle to one winner, named Ed. He is equally unfamiliar with both his prize options. So, the author concludes Ed will choose the more expensive prize.

Step 3: Make a Prediction

The correct answer will match the structure of the stimulus logic using a new scenario. Be sure to consider how the argument works in broad terms. In this case, the structure is as follows: some actors (game show winners) will choose one of two courses of actions (choose either the more expensive or the more familiar prize). One particular actor (Ed) cannot choose one course of action (no prize is more familiar), so he will choose the other (choose the more expensive prize). The correct answer will match this structure.

Note, this question is also susceptible to the strategy of merely comparing conclusion types. The original stimulus concludes with a certain prediction ("will thus choose"). Only **(E)** does the same ("it will try"). **(A)** and **(B)** conclude with assertions of fact ("did not receive," "would not have been standing"). **(C)** concludes with a comparison ("Y is the more eccentric"). And **(D)** concludes with a qualified prediction ("will probably not enter"). In this question, accurately assessing and comparing conclusions is sufficient to identify the one correct answer choice.

Step 4: Evaluate the Answer Choices

(E) matches the structure of the stimulus perfectly: Some group of entities (rabbits) have two courses of action (double back or flee for cover). One particular entity (rabbit in the film) can't perform one of those actions (there is no cover), so that entity will perform the other action (double back).

(A) does provide a group of entities (academic writers) with two courses of action (advance or royalties). However, the specific entity described (Professor al-Sofi) already received an advance, so one of the actions was already taken. Not a match.

(B) also provides a group of entities (children) with two courses of action (Rocket or Mouse). However, again, the specific entity described (Janine) already chose one of those actions. Not a match. Moreover, nothing in the evidence justifies the length of the wait specified in the conclusion here.

(C) starts off with Formal Logic that is unlike anything in the stimulus. Plus, there's no choice between two courses of action. Not a match.

(D) provides a group of entities (students) with two courses of action (physics or art). However, the specific entity described

(Miyoko) declines them both, which never happens in the original stimulus. Not a match.

22. (B) Strengthen

Step 1: Identify the Question Type

The question outright asks for something that "strengthens" the given argument. As you would in any Strengthen question, identify the conclusion and the evidence in the argument, then find an answer that validates any assumption the author makes.

Step 2: Untangle the Stimulus

The microbiologist provides some information about bacteria in sewage sludge. Those bacteria exposed to heavy metals in the sludge have adapted and can now resist heavy-metal poisoning. These same bacteria also happen to be resistant to antibiotics. The microbiologist concludes that the exposure to heavy metals is somehow responsible for the resistance to antibiotics.

Step 3: Make a Prediction

This is a classic case of suggesting causation based on the evidence of a correlation. In other words, the microbiologist assumes that just because these bacteria exposed to heavy metals happen to resist antibiotics, the exposure to heavy metals must be the cause of their ability to resist antibiotics. This kind of argument also assumes that no other factor could have caused the result, in this case, the resistance to antibiotics. The correct answer will strengthen the likelihood of causation and/or discount other factors that could affect the bacteria.

Step 4: Evaluate the Answer Choices

(B) works perfectly. By removing heavy metals from the equation and keeping everything else the same, this answer suggests that nothing else in the sludge is building up the bacteria's resistance to antibiotics, which in turn suggests that heavy metals definitely seem to be a significant factor, as the microbiologist concludes. Notice that the bacteria described in this choice function exactly as does a control group in a scientific experiment. When everything is kept the same between test and control groups except the hypothesized causal agent, the experiment can confirm or disconfirm the hypothesis more convincingly.

(A) is tempting because it suggests that bacteria not resistant to antibiotics are free of exposure to heavy metals. This might appear to strengthen the connection between the two, but this answer fails to account for another significant factor: the sludge. If these nonresistant bacteria are found outside of sewage sludge, then it's possible that another ingredient (apart from heavy metals) in sewage sludge contributes to antibiotic resistance.

(C) is a 180. This statement weakens the argument by showing that the microbiologist has the causality reversed. This answer suggests that the bacteria are resistant to antibiotics before they get into the sludge and that their antibiotic resistance contributes to their resistance to heavy-metal poisoning.

(D) correlates the concentrations of heavy metals and antibiotics, but it does nothing to strengthen the connection between bacteria's exposure to heavy metals and their resistance to antibiotics.

(E) is a 180. This choice weakens the argument considerably by showing that the presence of heavy metals and sewage sludge is irrelevant. The resistance to heavy-metal poisoning and antibiotics would still exist without such exposure.

23. (D) Assumption (Sufficient)

Step 1: Identify the Question Type

This question directly asks for something that is "assumed." As with any Assumption question, start by identifying the conclusion and evidence, then look for an answer that logically connects the two.

Step 2: Untangle the Stimulus

The ethicist takes umbrage with the common wedding promise to love "until death do us part." According to the ethicist, the word *love* is used to represent a feeling, and people can't control their feelings. Thus, it makes no sense to promise unending love since that feeling could potentially change and we'd be unable to stop that from happening. From this rather unromantic notion, the ethicist concludes with a recommendation: such promises should not define the word *love* in a way that represents love as a feeling.

Step 3: Make a Prediction

With a recommendation, an author must assume that the evidence provided is sufficient reason to justify the recommendation. In this case, the ethicist recommends not defining *love* as a feeling when making promises. The evidence is that such usage ultimately makes no sense. Therefore, the author's assumption is that the nonsensical result of defining *love* as a feeling is enough to warrant recommending against using such a definition.

Step 4: Evaluate the Answer Choices

(D) perfectly connects the ethicist's claim (the interpretation of *love* in such promises makes no sense) to her concluding recommendation (don't make such an interpretation or definition).

(A) is not an assumption, because the ethicist already states this when saying "feelings are not within one's control." That makes this statement a repeat of the evidence, not an

assumption. An assumption is unstated information that allows the evidence to lead logically to the conclusion.

(B) is Outside the Scope. This choice may be tempting, since the ethicist does seem to have a problem with making promises we can't control. However, the argument (and the ethicist's conclusion) is ultimately about how people define the word *love*, not the kinds of promises people should or should not make.

(C) doesn't help because the ethicist merely wants to avoid a feelings-based definition. Whether other legitimate definitions exist is irrelevant. The author already qualifies his argument by saying, "If *love* here refers to a feeling ... ."

(E) sounds reasonable based on the ethicist's claim that "a promise to do something not within one's control makes no sense." However, it's not an assumption because it doesn't further any connection to the ultimate conclusion, which is about whether the word *love* should be defined as a feeling in the context of a wedding vow.

24. (E) Flaw

Step 1: Identify the Question Type

"[V]ulnerable to criticism" is classic LSAT language indicating the argument has a Flaw. Here, the author tries to apply the logic of a principle to reach the conclusion. While your skills in Principle questions will be helpful, stay focused on the ultimate question: finding the flaw. That means identifying why the evidence (which includes the stated principle) doesn't logically support the main conclusion.

Step 2: Untangle the Stimulus

The principle given here involves some Formal Logic: if a food product has an ingredient potentially upsetting to most of that product's consumers, then the food's label should list that ingredient. The author then tries to apply this logic to Crackly Crisps, which has some genetically engineered ingredients. However, the author says that most Crackly Crisps consumers would not be concerned about those ingredients. So, the author concludes, there's no need to list those ingredients on the Crackly Crisps label.

Step 3: Make a Prediction

This is a classic misapplication of Formal Logic. In shorthand, the principle reads:

If	**ingredient is potentially upsetting**	→	**label should list the ingredient**

You're then told that most Crackly Crisps consumers wouldn't be upset about the genetic ingredients. However, the Formal Logic only tells us about ingredients that would upset those customers. Upsetting consumers is merely a sufficient condition, not a necessary one. In other words, if the ingredient is potentially upsetting, then it must be on the label. However, ingredients that aren't potentially upsetting may also have to be on the label. The correct answer will point out this confusion between sufficiency and necessity.

Step 4: Evaluate the Answer Choices

(E) is wordy, but it accurately describes the Formal Logic flaw. There is a claim that, if a certain condition is met (ingredients can upset customers), then a certain action (putting ingredients on a label) should be taken. And the author mistakenly confuses that to mean that if the condition isn't met (won't upset customers), the action need not be taken (no need to put ingredients on the label).

(A) is Outside the Scope since the principle only pertains to consumers of the product in question. Consumers in general are of no relevance to this argument.

(B) is also Outside the Scope since the principle is not about the actual safety of the ingredients. It's only about consumer concern.

(C) is Outside the Scope since the author makes no value judgment, let alone one that contradicts the principle.

(D) is an Irrelevant Comparison of consumer willingness to buy foods with some ingredients listed to their willingness to buy foods with all ingredients listed; this concept that is not addressed by this argument.

25. (B) Role of a Statement

Step 1: Identify the Question Type

The phrase "plays which of the following roles" is enough to peg this as a Role of a Statement question. The question asks about a claim that the town can reduce spending on trash removal by having residents sort their own garbage. Once you've found that claim, break the argument down into its conclusion and evidence and determine how the claim in the question stem factors into the argument.

Step 2: Untangle the Stimulus

The claim in question appears right at the top: Have residents sort their own garbage, and the town can save money on trash removal. However, the editorial's author notes a problem: while some residents may agree to the request, a lot of residents will resent the suggestion and refuse to do it. Thus, the author concludes that the current voluntary system should be retained. It won't really cost that much more, and it will save the hassle of having unhappy residents.

Step 3: Make a Prediction

The author's conclusion is that the current voluntary system is a better system for trash collection. The evidence is that the alternative (make residents sort their own garbage) can lead to resentment. So the question is: Why does the author

mention the potential to save money in the first place? It's a benefit of the proposal that he eventually shoots down. The author appears to be ceding a valid point for that alternative before bringing up the overriding concerns that ultimately make it less convincing. The correct answer will admit that the author makes this concession while maintaining opposition to the proposal it supports.

Step 4: Evaluate the Answer Choices

(B) correctly identifies the author's intention in using the claim highlighted in the question stem. The potential to save money is a fact that supports a proposal (tell residents to sort their garbage), which is an alternative to what the editorial defends as preferable (keep garbage sorting voluntary).

(A) distorts the author's intention. The claim in question is that money can be saved. The editorial provides overriding considerations but never demonstrates that the claim is false. The author never says the city can't save money this way.

(C) is a 180. The editorial is refuting the suggestion that residents should be told to sort their own garbage. The potential to save money is a benefit of this idea, not a difficulty for it.

(D) is another 180. The editorial provides evidence that overrides the claim in question; it certainly doesn't rely on that claim.

(E) is off because the editorial's conclusion is to stick to the current system. The claim in question is made by the editorialist's opponents.

Section II: Logic Games

Game 1: New Employee Parking Spaces

Q#	Question Type	Correct	Difficulty
1	Acceptability	E	★
2	"If" / Could Be True	B	★
3	Completely Determine	C	★
4	How Many	D	★★★★
5	"If" / Could Be True	A	★
6	"If" / Must Be True	E	★

Game 2: Ambassador Assignments to Countries

Q#	Question Type	Correct	Difficulty
7	Acceptability	B	★
8	Could Be True	A	★★
9	"If" / Could Be True	E	★
10	"If" / Must Be True	A	★★
11	Must Be False (CANNOT Be True)	C	★★
12	Rule Substitution	D	★★★

Game 3: Bicycle Testers

Q#	Question Type	Correct	Difficulty
13	Acceptability	C	★
14	"If" / Must Be True	E	★★★
15	Could Be True EXCEPT	D	★★
16	Must Be False (CANNOT Be True)	C	★★★
17	"If" / Could Be True	B	★★★
18	Must Be False (CANNOT Be True)	D	★★★

Game 4: Top, Middle, and Bottom Bookcase Shelves

Q#	Question Type	Correct	Difficulty
19	Partial Acceptability	B	★
20	Completely Determine	A	★★
21	Must Be True	A	★★
22	"If" / Partial Acceptability	D	★★
23	"If" / Must Be True	C	★★

Game 1: New Employee Parking Spaces

Step 1: Overview

Situation: New employees assigned to numbered parking spaces

Entities: Six new employees—R, S, T, V, X, Y

Action: Strict Sequencing. Assign each employee a numbered parking space.

Limitations: Each employee is assigned to only one space, and each space will have exactly one employee.

Step 2: Sketch

The opening paragraph and rules make reference to the numbered spaces, so a Strict Sequencing setup (with numbered dashes) makes the most sense.

$$\frac{R\ S\ T\ V\ X\ Y}{1\quad 2\quad 3\quad 4\quad 5\quad 6}$$

Step 3: Rules

Rule 1 places Young in a higher-numbered space (i.e., farther to the right) than Totowa. Since you can't place this into the Master Sketch directly, jot it down nearby:

T . . . Y

Rule 2 does the same for Xu and Souza:

S . . . X

Rule 3 puts Robertson to the right of Young:

Y . . . R

Rule 4 restricts Robertson to one of the first four spaces.

Finally, it's worth noting that V is a Floater, since V isn't mentioned in any of the rules.

Step 4: Deductions

There aren't any strictly defined Blocks of Entities, but several of the employees are ordered in loose sequencing arrangements. Notice that Young is duplicated in Rules 1 and 3, so those rules can be connected:

T . . . Y . . . R

Robertson is also a Duplication, in Rules 3 and 4. Since Robertson's parking space must be to the right of Totowa's and Young's, Robertson can't be any further to the left than space #3. This, in combination with Rule 4, means that only spaces #3 and #4 are available to Robertson. This forms the basis of Limited Options:

Opt. I

$$\frac{R\ S\ T\ V\ X\ Y}{1}\ \frac{R}{2}\ \frac{}{3}\ \frac{}{4}\ \frac{}{5}\ \frac{}{6}$$

Opt. II

$$\frac{R\ S\ T\ V\ X\ Y}{1}\ \frac{}{2}\ \frac{}{3}\ \frac{R}{4}\ \frac{}{5}\ \frac{}{6}$$

In the first option (Robertson in space #3), Totowa and Young will have to park in spaces #1 and #2, respectively. And Xu's space must always be to the right of Souza's, with Vaughn floating:

Opt. I

$$\frac{T}{1}\ \frac{Y}{2}\ \frac{R}{3}\ \frac{S/V}{4}\ \frac{}{5}\ \frac{V/X}{6}$$

S...X   ✗   S̶

In the second option (Robertson in space #4), Totowa and Young aren't locked into specific parking spaces. The relative orders of the entities still remain, though. Totowa takes either space #1 or space #2, and Young takes either space #2 or space #3. Since Totowa and Young must have lower-numbered spaces than Robertson, and since Souza must have a lower-numbered space than Xu, there isn't room for Xu in spaces #1-#3:

Opt. II

T...Y
$$\quad\ \frac{}{1}\ \frac{}{2}\ \frac{}{3}\ \frac{R}{4}\ \frac{}{5}\ \frac{}{6}$$
S...X   X̶Y̶   X̶   X̶T̶   T̶Y̶   Y̶T̶S̶

Step 5: Questions

1. (E) Acceptability
Check each rule and eliminate choices that violate it.

(A) violates Rule 1 because it has Young in a lower-numbered space than Totowa. **(C)** violates Rule 2 because it has Xu in a lower-numbered space than Souza. **(D)** violates Rule 3 since it has Robertson in a lower-numbered space than Young. Finally, **(B)** violates Rule 4 by having Robertson in space #5.

Circle **(E)** and move on.

2. (B) "If" / Could Be True
The new "If" extends the loose T ... Y ... R block to include Souza. If Totowa is in a higher-numbered space than Souza, then you're in Option II, and Souza must be in space #1:

$$\frac{S}{1}\ \frac{T}{2}\ \frac{Y}{3}\ \frac{R}{4}\ \frac{}{5}\ \frac{}{6}$$

This means that every choice except **(B)** must be false. Vaughn and Xu are interchangeable in spaces #5 and #6, so **(B)** could be true.

3. (C) Completely Determine
The correct answer here, if true, will result in only one arrangement of parking spaces for the six employees. In such questions, look for answer choices that nail down Floaters—such as **(C)**. Vaughn can only take space #3 in Option II. Rules 1 and 3 mean that Totowa must then take space #1 and Young must take space #2. And since Xu's

space must be higher numbered than Souza's, Xu is in #6, and Souza is in #5:

$$\frac{T}{1} \quad \frac{Y}{2} \quad \frac{V}{3} \quad \frac{R}{4} \quad \frac{S}{5} \quad \frac{X}{6}$$

That's the only acceptable arrangement with V taking space #3, so **(C)** is correct. All of the other choices leave at least two of the spaces undetermined.

4. (D) How Many

This question asks for the number of entities restricted to exactly two spaces. Go down the list of entities and check the possibilities for each. Robertson has to take either space #3 or #4, based on your deductions. Totowa must take either #1 or #2, since Totowa must have a lower-numbered space than both Young and Robertson. Similarly, Young must take space #2 or #3. And since there isn't enough room for Xu in the spaces with lower numbers than Robertson's, Xu must take either space #5 or #6. Vaughn could take any of three spaces—#4, #5, or #6—in Option I. Souza could take any of five spaces—#4 or #5 in Option I and any space from #1 through #3 in Option II. So four of six employees—R, T, X, and Y—are restricted to just two acceptable spaces, making **(D)** correct.

5. (A) "If" / Could Be True

This new "If" puts you in Option II because in Option I, there isn't room for Young to take a parking space numbered higher than Souza's. Redraw Option II now that Young has to have a higher-numbered space than both Souza and Totowa. Souza and Totowa are interchangeable, but Young must, to comply with Rule 3 under this question's conditions, take space #3. Vaughn and Xu remain interchangeable at the far right:

$$\frac{S/T}{1} \quad \frac{T/S}{2} \quad \frac{Y}{3} \quad \frac{R}{4} \quad \frac{V/X}{5} \quad \frac{X/V}{6}$$

Therefore, **(A)** is the only one that could be true. All the other choices must be false in this case.

6. (E) "If" / Must Be True

Here's where you see immediate payoff from your Limited Options. If Robertson is assigned space #3, then you're looking at Option I. In this Option, Young is always assigned space #2, which means that **(E)** must be true. All of the other choices are merely possible or, in the case of **(B)**, flat-out false.

Game 2: Ambassador Assignments to Countries

Step 1: Overview

Situation: Ambassadors assigned to three countries

Entities: Five ambassador candidates—J, K, L, N, O

Action: Selection/Distribution Hybrid. Your task is to choose three of five ambassador candidates and assign them to one country each.

Limitations: Each country gets only one ambassador, and no ambassador is assigned to more than one country. You know that in any acceptable arrangement, two candidates are rejected.

Step 2: Sketch

Since the initial action is Selection, make a list of the candidates. Be prepared to circle any candidates who are assigned and cross out the ones who aren't. Once you have determined the country to which an ambassador is assigned, you can abbreviate its name under that ambassador's initial.

Step 3: Rules

Rule 1 establishes that exactly one of Kayne and Novetzke is always assigned to an ambassadorship, though it doesn't specify the country.

Rule 2 is a Formal Logic rule that connects Kayne's assignment to Jaramillo's:

$$\text{If } \textcircled{J} \rightarrow \textcircled{K}$$
$$\text{If } \cancel{K} \rightarrow \cancel{J}$$

That contrapositive has important implications, since rejecting two entities means selecting all of the other three. We'll look more closely at this in Step 4.

Rule 3 is more Formal Logic:

$$\text{If } O_{Ven} \rightarrow K_{not\ Yem}$$
$$\text{If } K_{Yem} \rightarrow O_{not\ Ven}$$

Rule 4 establishes that Zambia is the only country to which Landon can be assigned. You can list Zambia under Landon's initial, but don't circle it.

Step 4: Deductions

Blocks of Entities aren't an issue here because no two ambassadors can be assigned to the same country. You can use the either/or nature of Rule 1, however, to create Limited Options, since selecting either Kayne or Novetzke has a ripple effect on the other entities. If Kayne is assigned, Novetzke cannot be:

Opt. I

$$\text{J} \quad \textcircled{K} \quad \text{L} \quad \cancel{N} \quad \text{O}$$
$$\quad\quad \text{Zam}$$

Conversely, if Novetzke is selected, Kayne cannot be. This triggers Rule 2, so Jaramillo won't be assigned either. Thus, the three ambassadors will be Landon, Novetzke, and Ong.

Landon will have to go to Zambia, and the other two can each go to either Venezuela or Yemen:

Opt. II

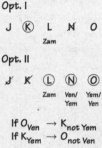

$$\cancel{J} \quad \text{K} \quad \textcircled{L} \quad \textcircled{N} \quad \textcircled{O}$$
$$\quad\quad \text{Zam} \quad \text{Ven/} \quad \text{Yem/}$$
$$\quad\quad\quad\quad \text{Yem} \quad \text{Ven}$$

There aren't any Established Entities, except for Kayne or Novetzke, exactly one of whom must always be assigned. The Numbers are settled, since three of five candidates will always be assigned, one to each of three countries. So, the final Master Sketch should look like this:

Opt. I

$$\text{J} \quad \textcircled{K} \quad \text{L} \quad \cancel{N} \quad \text{O}$$
$$\quad\quad \text{Zam}$$

Opt. II

$$\cancel{J} \quad \text{K} \quad \textcircled{L} \quad \textcircled{N} \quad \textcircled{O}$$
$$\quad\quad \text{Zam} \quad \text{Ven/} \quad \text{Yem/}$$
$$\quad\quad\quad\quad \text{Yem} \quad \text{Ven}$$

$$\text{If } O_{Ven} \rightarrow K_{not\ Yem}$$
$$\text{If } K_{Yem} \rightarrow O_{not\ Ven}$$

Armed with these Options, you can make short work of the questions.

Step 5: Questions

7. (B) Acceptability

As always, eliminate incorrect answer choices rule by rule.

(D) fails because Kayne and Novetzke are both given ambassadorships (violates Rule 1). **(A)** is out because Jaramillo is assigned to an ambassadorship but Kayne is not (violates Rule 2). **(E)** is out because it has Ong in Venezuela and Kayne in Yemen (violates Rule 3). **(C)** is wrong because Landon is assigned to a country other than Zambia (violates Rule 4). **(B)** is therefore correct.

8. (A) Could Be True

The question asks for the pair of candidates who could both be rejected. As you evaluate the choices, determine the three candidates who would be given ambassadorships and consider whether the implications lead to a violation of the rules.

If, as **(A)** says, Jaramillo and Novetzke are rejected, then Kayne, Landon, and Ong are selected. This doesn't violate any rules, so it could be true and is therefore correct. Note that this is perfectly compatible with Option I.

(B) and **(E)** would result in both Kayne and Novetzke being assigned to ambassadorships, which violates Rule 1. If Kayne is rejected, then the other rejected candidate must be Jaramillo (see Option II), so **(C)** and **(D)** aren't possible.

9. (E) "If" / Could Be True

Ong can be assigned to Venezuela in either Option. In Option I, that means that Kayne must become ambassador to Zambia (Kayne must be selected in Option I, and assigning him to Yemen would violate Rule 3 in this case). With Kayne assigned to Zambia, Landon (who cannot take a post other than Zambia) will be rejected, and Jaramillo will be selected and assigned to Yemen:

Opt. I

Ⓙ Ⓚ K̶ N̶ Ⓞ
Yem Yem Zam Ven
    Zam

None of the answers contains Jaramillo and Kayne.

With Ong assigned to Venezuela in Option II, the other two ambassadors would be Landon, assigned to Zambia, and Novetzke, assigned to Yemen:

Opt. II

J̶ K Ⓛ Ⓝ Ⓞ
    Zam Yem Ven

Landon and Novetzke are the pair in **(E)**, the correct answer.

10. (A) "If" / Must Be True

The "If" clause in this question stem limits you to Option I; if Kayne is assigned, Novetzke cannot be. What's more, assigning Kayne to Yemen triggers the contrapositive of Rule 3. With Kayne assigned to Yemen, Ong cannot be assigned to Venezuela, meaning that Ong is assigned to Zambia or isn't assigned at all.

In the first case, with Ong assigned to Zambia, Landon can't be assigned, so Jaramillo will have to be assigned (specifically, to Venezuela, the only remaining unassigned country):

Opt. I

Ⓙ Ⓚ L̶ N̶ Ⓞ
Ven Yem Zam   Zam

In the second case, Ong joins Novetzke as an unassigned candidate, leaving Jaramillo and Landon to be assigned. Landon must go to Zambia, so Jaramillo is left to go to Venezuela:

Opt. I

Ⓙ Ⓚ Ⓛ N̶ Ø
Ven Yem Zam

Either way, Jaramillo must go to Venezuela, so **(A)** is correct.

11. (C) Must Be False (CANNOT Be True)

Make sure to characterize the answer choices. The correct one here cannot be true.

The Limited Options lead you directly to **(C)** as the impossible answer. If Novetzke is assigned to an ambassadorship, you're looking at Option II, in which Landon is assigned, always to Zambia. So Novetzke can only be assigned to Venezuela or Yemen.

Landon or Ong could be denied an ambassadorship in Option I, so **(D)** and **(E)** could be true. And there's nothing stopping Jaramillo or Kayne from going to Zambia in Option I, as long as Landon isn't assigned an ambassadorship, so **(A)** and **(B)** are both possible.

12. (D) Rule Substitution

It's impossible to predict the wording that the right answer will use, but you know that it will establish exactly the same restriction that Rule 2 establishes: Jaramillo is assigned to an ambassadorship only if Kayne is also.

(A) reverses the terms in Rule 2's Formal Logic without negating them. That doesn't result in an equivalent statement since it's not the complete contrapositive.

(B) introduces Landon and Ong, but it doesn't lead to Jaramillo's assignment being necessary for Kayne's.

(C) links Ong with Kayne, but it doesn't link either one with Jaramillo.

(D) would mean that if Jaramillo is assigned, then Novetzke is not, which in turn means (according to Rule 1) that Kayne would have to be. This preserves the effect of Rule 2, so **(D)** is correct.

(E) means that if Ong is assigned, Novetzke is not, which means that Kayne is assigned. But none of this logic involves Jaramillo.

Game 3: Bicycle Testers

Step 1: Overview

Situation: Four riders testing four bicycles during a two-day study for a cycling magazine

Entities: Four bicycles—F, G, H, J—and four testers—Reynaldo, Seamus, Theresa, Yuki

Action: Matching. Your task is to determine which bicycle each person tests on day 1 and which on day 2.

Limitations: Each rider tests exactly one bicycle on each day; no rider can test the same bicycle on both days. Thus, each bicycle is tested exactly two times, by different riders each time.

Step 2: Sketch

Create a small table with the bicycles as rows and the days as columns. You'll fill in the tester for each bike on each day as the rules, deductions, and questions dictate:

Rey, Sea, The, Yuk

	1	2
F		
G		
H		
J		

Note that the bicycles are depicted with single letters (as per the game's setup) and the riders are abbreviated. That way the two types of entities are visually distinct.

Step 3: Rules

Rule 1 prevents Reynaldo from ever testing F. Note that in F's row.

	1	2
F		Rey
G		
H		
J		

Rule 2 prohibits Yuki from testing J. Note that as well.

	1	2
F		Rey
G		
H		
J		Yuk

Rule 3 means that Theresa must be present exactly once in the H row.

	1	2
F		Rey
G		
H		The (once)
J		Yuk

Rule 4 means that one row must have Yuki on the first day and Seamus on the second day. Depict them as a Block of Entities:

Yuk	Sea

Step 4: Deductions

You can consider Yuki on day 1 and Seamus on day 2 as a Block of Entities in Rule 4. Because Theresa has to test H and Yuki can't test J, this Yuki-Seamus block can only test bicycles F or G. This forms the basis of Limited Options:

Opt. I:

	1	2	
F	Yuk	Sea	Rey
G			
H		The (once)	
J		Yuk	

Opt. II:

	1	2	
F	Sea/The	Yuk	Rey
G	Yuk	Sea	
H	Rey/The	The/Rey	The (once)
J		Yuk	

For Option II, once the Yuki-Seamus block is assigned to bicycle G, there are some further deductions. Based on Rule 1, the only remaining bicycles for Reynaldo to test are H on one day and J on the other day. This means that the two testers for bicycle H are definitely Reynaldo and Theresa. With bicycles G and H accounted for, the only bicycle available for Yuki to test on Day 2 is bicycle F, because she cannot test bicycle J based on Rule 2.

Beyond this, there isn't much you can fill in. There are no Established Entities. Theresa's testing H exactly once is close, but you've already shown that in each option. The Numbers are already worked out: four riders test two distinct bicycles each. The only Duplication is Yuki (in Rules 2 and 4), but you've already used the implications of that to create the Limited Options sketch. You'll have to wait until certain conditions are established, such as the day on which Theresa tests H, to fill in the gaps.

Step 5: Questions

13. (C) Acceptability

Go rule by rule and eliminate any choice that violates the terms of a rule. Rule 1 is violated by **(A)**, which has Reynaldo testing F. Rule 2 is violated by **(D)**, which has Yuki testing J. Rule 3 is violated by **(B)**, since it doesn't have Theresa testing H at all. Finally, Rule 4 is violated by **(E)**, since the bicycle tested by Yuki on day 1 is tested by Theresa (not Seamus) on day 2. **(C)** is the correct answer.

14. (E) "If" / Must Be True

If Theresa tests G on the second day, she will test H on the first day (Rule 3). That means you're looking at Option I, since the Yuki-Seamus block would have to test F on days 1 and 2. That allows you to finish the entire sketch. Since Yuki cannot test J, she'll test H on day 2:

	1	2	
F	Yuk	Sea	Rey
G		The	
H	The	Yuk	The (once)
J		Yuk	

Now, the only bike available to Rey on day 2 is J, and since riders test different bikes each day, Rey will test G on day 1. The last spot to fill in is J on day 1, which must be tested by Seamus:

	1	2	
F	Yuk	Sea	Rey
G	Rey	The	
H	The	Yuk	The (once)
J	Sea	Rey	Yuk

Since Yuki can't ever test J, she'll test H on day 2, making **(E)** correct. The completed mini sketch reveals all of the other choices to be false in this case.

15. (D) Could Be True EXCEPT
Your Limited Options from Rule 4 tell you that Yuki must test either F or G on the first day. So right away, **(D)** cannot be true.

It's worth noting that your previous work helps you eliminate answers as well. For example, the correct answer to the Acceptability question (the first question in the set) shows that **(A)** and **(E)** are permissible and can therefore be eliminated.

16. (C) Must Be False (CANNOT Be True)
The incorrect answer choices aren't readily apparent from previous work in this case, so there's not much to do here short of trying out answers. But even in this situation, strategy is important. Start by testing choices that involve move restricted entities such as bicycle F, because the Limited Options sketch has nearly every assignment nailed down for that bicycle.

In **(B)**, Seamus tests F on day 1, that is something that could be true based on Option II, so it is not the correct answer. **(C)** lists Theresa on bicycle F on day 2. However, the Limited Options show that the only possible riders of bicycle F on day 2 are Seamus (Option I) or Yuki (Option II). So, **(C)** must be false and is therefore the correct answer. All of the remaining choices are possible.

17. (B) "If" / Could Be True
The correct answer here will be acceptable under the new "If" condition. That means the four wrong answer choices must be false. If Theresa tests J on the first day, she'll have to test H on the second day (Rule 3). So **(C)** and **(E)** are impossible. Also, Seamus can't test J at all, since testing J on the second day

would require Yuki to test J on the first day (Rule 4) and Yuki is never allowed to test J (Rule 2). So eliminate **(D)** as well. With Theresa, Seamus, and Yuki all prevented from testing J on day 2, the only rider left to test J on day 2 is Reynaldo:

	1	2	
F		Rey	
G			
H		The	The (once)
J	The	Rey	Yuk

This means Reynaldo isn't free to test G on day 2, so **(A)** also won't work. Only **(B)** remains and is therefore correct.

18. (D) Must Be False (CANNOT Be True)
The correct answer choice for this question must be false. That means you will eliminate any choice that could be true. **(A)** and **(B)** can be eliminated; they are shown to be acceptable in the completed sketches for the two "If" questions, the second and fifth questions in the set, respectively. Note also that **(B)** occurs in the correct answer to the Acceptability question (the first question in the set).

(C) would have to happen in Option I, but this doesn't create any problems as long as Theresa tests H on one day and J on the other:

	1	2	
F	Yuk	Sea	Rey
G	Rey	Yuk	
H	The/Sea	Rey/The	The (once)
J	Sea/The	The/Rey	Yuk

(D) would also have to happen in Option I. Since Seamus's day 2 must be the same as Yuki's day 1 (Rule 4), Seamus would test G on day 1 in this scenario. That would put Theresa on G for day 2 in this answer choice. Theresa still has to test H (Rule 3), so she would do that on day 1. This means Reynaldo will have to test J on day 1 and H on day 2. But this would force Yuki to test J on day 2, in violation of Rule 2:

	1	2	
F	Yuk	Sea	Rey
G	Sea	The	
H	The	Rey	The (once)
J	Rey	Yuk	Yuk

(D) is impossible and, therefore, the correct answer.

Game 4: Top, Middle, and Bottom Bookcase Shelves

Step 1: Overview

Situation: Books on a bookcase with three shelves

Entities: Eight books—F, G, H, I, K, L, M, O

Action: Strict Sequencing. Your task is to place eight books among three shelves, taking into account that particular books must be on higher or lower shelves than certain other ones. The higher/lower aspect is what makes it a Sequencing game. However, it is also reasonable to perceive it as a Distribution game in which the eight books are allocated to the three shelves. Regardless of the classification, you'll arrive at the same general Master Sketch.

Limitations: Each of three shelves must contain at least two books. Since there are only eight books total, this means that no shelf can contain more than four books.

Step 2: Sketch

List the three shelves vertically, along with a list of the books. Be prepared to add dashes for each shelf as you work out the number of books it can contain:

```
       F G H I K L M O

Top:
Mid:
Bttm:
(2–4 books each)
```

Step 3: Rules

Rule 1 requires the bottom shelf to contain more books than the top shelf. Combined with the Numbers limitation from the opening paragraph, this yields some important restrictions. The top shelf must contain exactly two books, and the bottom shelf must contain three or four. This means the middle shelf will contain two or three books:

```
Top:   __  __   2
Mid:   __  __  (__)  2–3
Bttm:  __  __  __  (__)  3–4
```

Rule 2 places I firmly on the middle shelf:

```
Top:   __  __   2
Mid:   I   __  (__)  2–3
Bttm:  __  __  __  (__)  3–4
```

Rule 3 places K somewhere above F. So F cannot be on the top shelf, and K cannot be on the bottom shelf:

```
Top:   __  __   2              F̶  K
Mid:   I   __  (__)  2–3
Bttm:  __  __  __  (__)  3–4   K̶  F
```

Rule 4 places O somewhere above L. So L cannot be on the top shelf, and O cannot be on the bottom shelf:

```
Top:   __  __   2              F̶L̶  K  O
Mid:   I   __  (__)  2–3
Bttm:  __  __  __  (__)  3–4   K̶O̶  F  L
```

Rule 5 establishes a Block of Entities that must be on a shelf together: F-M.

Finally, G and H are Floaters, not mentioned in any of the rules.

Step 4: Deductions

The Block of Entities from Rule 4 is crucial. Whenever a game has a block, the placement of that block can significantly restrict the game's action. Since F cannot be on the top shelf thanks to Rule 3, the F-M block is either on the middle shelf or the bottom shelf. If F and M are on the middle shelf with I, then K must be on the top shelf (Rule 3) along with O (Rule 4) and no other books. Therefore, all the remaining books—G, H, and L—must go on the bottom shelf so that the bottom shelf can have more books than the top shelf.

```
       Opt. I
Top:   K   O
Mid:   I   F   M
Bttm:  G   H   L
```

If the F-M block is on the bottom shelf, then the Numbers can work out in two ways. The middle shelf and bottom shelf can have three books each, or the middle shelf can have two books, leaving four for the bottom shelf.

```
       Opt. II
Top:   __  __          F̶L̶  K   O
Mid:   I   __
Bttm:  F   M   __      K̶O̶  F   L


Top:   __  __          F̶L̶  K   O
Mid:   I   __
Bttm:  F   M   __  __  K̶O̶  F   L
```

Either way, the remaining rules remain intact.

Step 5: Questions

19. (B) Partial Acceptability

Check the answer choices against the rules, referring to the Limited Options sketch where it's helpful.

Neither K nor O can be on the bottom shelf based on Rules 3 and 4, so **(C)** and **(D)** are wrong. Rule 1 establishes that the bottom shelf has to have three or four books, so **(A)** is out. Finally, Rule 5 creates the F-M block, and **(E)** has M on the bottom shelf without F, so eliminate it. Only **(B)** remains; it's possible in Option II and therefore correct.

20. (A) Completely Determine

Your Options make short work of this question. You already have a fully determined arrangement of the books in Option I, which is based on F and M being placed together on the middle shelf with I. So, as **(A)** says, if I and M are on the same shelf, then F is also on that shelf. K and O will have to be on the top shelf to fulfill Rules 3 and 4, leaving the remaining three books for the bottom shelf. As soon as you see that this choice puts you into Option I, you can be confident that it completely determines the placements.

Any of the remaining choices would have to happen in Option II, and none of them would fully restrict all the books to only one shelf.

21. (A) Must Be True

Since there's no "If" clause here, the correct answer must be true in both options. In Option I, **(A)** is definitely true. In Option II, M is on the bottom shelf, and O can't be on the bottom shelf (Rule 4). So O has to be somewhere above M, proving **(A)** correct. None of the other choices has to be true in both options.

22. (D) "If" / Partial Acceptability

If G is on the top shelf, you have to be looking at Option II (G is on the bottom in Option I, after all). In Option II, F and M are both on the bottom shelf, so **(E)** is impossible.

Now it comes down to the Numbers. If the middle shelf has only two books, then the bottom shelf will have four. In this case, the only books that can join F and M on the bottom shelf are H and L. This leaves K and O to be split up between the top and middle shelves:

```
Top:   G   K/O          FL   K   O
Mid:   I   O/K                :   :
Bttm:  F   M   H   L   KO   F   L
```

So if the middle shelf has two books, neither **(A)** nor **(B)** can be the complete and accurate list you're looking for. If the middle shelf has three books, then the one book to join F and M on the bottom shelf must be H or L:

```
Top:   G   __          FL   K   O
Mid:   I   __  __            :   :
Bttm:  F   M   H/L   KO   F   L
```

Therefore, both those books can't be on the middle shelf. **(C)** is therefore wrong. Only **(D)** remains as a possibility. And it could be a complete and accurate list of books for the middle shelf as follows:

```
Top:   G   O          FL   K   O
Mid:   I   K   L            :   :
Bttm:  F   M   H   KO   F   L

                 H
```

23. (C) "If" / Must Be True

The new "If" extends the ordering in Rule 4. O must be higher than L, so if L is higher than H, O will have to be on the top shelf, L on the middle shelf, and H on the bottom shelf. This can only happen in Option II, where F and M are on the bottom shelf.

```
Top:   O   __          FL   K   O
Mid:   I   L   (__)          :   :
Bttm:  F   M   H   (__)   KO   F   L
```

Therefore, H and M will have to be on the same shelf, and **(C)** is correct.

Section III: Logical Reasoning

Q#	Question Type	Correct	Difficulty
1	Inference	B	★
2	Flaw	E	★
3	Inference	C	★
4	Flaw	B	★
5	Point at Issue	D	★
6	Flaw	D	★
7	Point at Issue	B	★
8	Paradox	D	★
9	Strengthen	A	★
10	Role of a Statement	D	★
11	Flaw	E	★★
12	Assumption (Necessary)	C	★
13	Paradox	A	★
14	Flaw	A	★★★★
15	Weaken	B	★★★★
16	Role of a Statement	D	★★★
17	Strengthen	B	★★★★
18	Principle (Apply/Inference)	B	★★
19	Assumption (Necessary)	D	★★
20	Principle (Apply/Inference)	C	★★★
21	Assumption (Sufficient)	A	★★★
22	Inference	C	★★★★
23	Parallel Flaw	E	★★★
24	Strengthen	B	★★
25	Parallel Reasoning	D	★★
26	Assumption (Sufficient)	E	★★★

1. (B) Inference

Step 1: Identify the Question Type

The question asks for something that logically fills in the blank at the end of the stimulus. Since the last sentence begins with the word [*t*]*hus*, the blank will represent a logical conclusion, supported by the rest of the stimulus. In other words, the test is asking you an Inference question, and the right answer will follow unequivocally from the information given. Look for ways to combine the statements and find an answer that follows from those facts.

Step 2: Untangle the Stimulus

The author provides information about "hot spots," places teeming with different species called "endemic" species. Commercial development threatens those areas, and endemic species (such as the ones in those areas) are the types of species most likely to become extinct. The author then starts to make a recommendation to environmental organizations with limited resources, groups that want to preserve species but can't fight every possible battle. And that's where the argument stops.

Step 3: Make a Prediction

So, what would the author recommend to these organizations? They want to preserve species but have to choose their battles selectively. Since "hot spots" contain not just any species but numerous species of the kind that most often become extinct, it would follow that those areas are where environmental efforts will have the greatest impact. The correct answer will finish the author's recommendation by calling for environmental organizations to concentrate on those areas.

Step 4: Evaluate the Answer Choices

(B) is the perfect recommendation, since these habitats will allow organizations to help a large number of threatened species all at once.

(A) doesn't address the hot spots. By being so open-ended, this recommendation would allow organizations to select battles over a single species rather than battles in areas (e.g., hot spots) that could help multiple species.

(C) distorts the author's idea. It's not that all endemic species should be treated equally. It's that hot spots are where you can find more of them and thus have the opportunity to save more than you could in other areas.

(D) is a pessimistic viewpoint that is not expressed by the author. Just because most extinctions involve endemic species, that doesn't mean most endemic species will become extinct. That's like saying most houses on my street have basements, so most houses with basements are on my street.

(E) is counterproductive. If organizations are limited to how many battles they can wage, then expanding the definition of "hot spot" would just create more options from which to choose. Moreover, expanding the definition would mean including more low-value areas as "hot spots."

2. (E) Flaw

Step 1: Identify the Question Type

"[V]ulnerable to criticism" is classic LSAT language indicating that the argument has a Flaw. Here, the author tries to apply a principle to reach the conclusion. While your skills in Principle questions will be helpful, stay focused on the ultimate task: finding and describing the flaw. That means identifying why the argument's evidence (which includes the principle) does not logically support its conclusion.

Step 2: Untangle the Stimulus

The principle provides some Formal Logic: If you sell something you know is defective but claim that it works just fine, you're committing fraud. The author then provides a supposed example, in which Wilton sells a bike to Harris without much knowledge about its condition. Wilton said the bike was fine, but Harris later discovered defective brakes. Based on the principle, the author concludes that Wilton committed fraud.

Step 3: Make a Prediction

There's one major problem with the author's application. The principle states that fraud occurs when someone sells a defective product as safe but knows the product is defective. However, Wilton didn't know about the defect. Therefore, the principle doesn't apply. The correct answer will describe the author's failure to make this key distinction.

Step 4: Evaluate the Answer Choices

(E) exposes the author's mistake. Wilton, without proper knowledge, asserted the bike was in good working condition. But that's not the same as asserting it was fine while knowing it was defective (which is what constitutes fraud).

(A) is Outside the Scope because fraud only entails knowledge of the defect, not whether the seller makes an effort to fix the defect.

(B) brings up the selling price of the bike, which is irrelevant to determining whether fraud occurred.

(C) is inaccurate, since *defective* is used consistently to mean "faulty" or "not working properly."

(D) discusses Harris's belief about what Wilton was saying, but the buyer's belief of the seller's claim is irrelevant to the principle. All that matters for a determination of fraud is what Wilton said and whether he was deliberately misleading Harris.

3. (C) Inference

Step 1: Identify the Question Type

The question is asking for something that would logically fill in the blank at the end of the argument. Since the last sentence begins with the word [*t*]*herefore*, the blank will contain a conclusion supported by the rest of the stimulus. That means that this is an Inference question; you're looking for something directly supported by the statements given. Look for ways to combine the statements given as evidence and find an answer that follows directly from those facts.

Step 2: Untangle the Stimulus

The author states that boat engines make noises at various frequencies, some of which are the same as those of screams and squeals killer whales use to communicate. While the killer whales don't seem bothered by the boats, louder engine noises can damage their hearing.

Step 3: Make a Prediction

According to the last claim, killer whales are susceptible to hearing damage because they continue to behave normally when the boats are around. This is unfortunate because, as stated previously, killer whales communicate through screams and squeals. Losing their hearing would suggest that their communication would also be impaired. The correct answer will likely make the connection between the boat noise and the potential for killer whales to lose their communication abilities.

Step 4: Evaluate the Answer Choices

(C) sums up everything perfectly. The noises can cause hearing damage, which would make it harder to hear screams and squeals, which would ultimately affect the killer whales' ability to communicate.

(A) makes an irrelevant and unsupported comparison between younger and older killer whales.

(B) goes contrary to the evidence, which states that killer whales "do not seem to behave differently around running boat engines."

(D) suggests that killer whales would prefer areas that are less likely to hurt them. While that sounds reasonable, the evidence suggests otherwise. Apparently, killer whales don't avoid areas with boats, since they don't behave any differently in the presence of boats.

(E) mentions the ability to find food, which is entirely outside the argument's scope.

4. (B) Flaw

Step 1: Identify the Question Type

The stem asks why the journalist's argument is "flawed," making this a Flaw question. Separate the argument into its

evidence and conclusion and find the answer that expresses why the evidence doesn't adequately support the conclusion.

Step 2: Untangle the Stimulus

The journalist got quite a scoop: a list of companies accidentally sent by a trade group that has long kept its membership list secret. What's more, a trade group representative confirmed that everyone on the list is indeed a member. Browsing through this list, the journalist notes an omission: Bruch Industries. Its absence from the list leads the journalist to conclude that Bruch Industries is not a member of the trade group.

Step 3: Make a Prediction

The problem here is that, while the list is described as 100 percent accurate, there's nothing to confirm that the list is complete. In other words, while every company on the list is indeed a member, there may be other members that aren't on the list. In that case, Bruch Industries might still be a member, even though its name doesn't appear on the journalist's list. The correct answer will indicate this oversight on the journalist's part.

Step 4: Evaluate the Answer Choices

(B) identifies the problem just right. If this journalist's document doesn't list every member, then Bruch Industries could still be a member despite its absence from the document.

(A) is irrelevant since the journalist's argument is about whether or not Bruch Industries is a member, not whether or not it wants to be.

(C) is also irrelevant. How the list got out in the first place has no bearing on the journalist's mistaken argument about Bruch Industries' membership.

(D) doesn't make sense in the context of the journalist's argument, since the journalist believes that Bruch Industries is not a member. The journalist does not imply that the company is trying to keep its membership status a secret.

(E) is tempting since the journalist does rely on the representative's confirmation. However, nothing suggests that the representative has something to hide or that his information is inaccurate. More importantly, the representative confirmed only that the list is accurate, not that it's complete. The journalist's logical flaw is that he takes the list's completeness for granted.

5. (D) Point at Issue

Step 1: Identify the Question Type

A question that asks for something two speakers "disagree" over is a Point at Issue question. This question stem states further that this disagreement is about today's children's stories. Summarize both speakers' arguments and look for an answer with which one speaker would agree and the other speaker would disagree. Remember that you can use the Decision Tree to test any answer about which you're unsure.

Step 2: Untangle the Stimulus

Peter starts by claiming that today's children's stories lack clearly immoral characters. He then argues that children's stories should have such characters because children need to learn about consequences of bad behavior. Yoko immediately starts off with a contradiction of Peter's initial claim. She feels that today's children's stories do have clearly immoral characters. It's just that today's characters aren't as frightening, which she suggests is better.

Step 3: Make a Prediction

Yoko's immediate contradiction of Peter's opening claim seems to be a clear source of disagreement. While Peter thinks today's stories lack clearly immoral characters, Yoko believes otherwise, even if the characters are less frightening than they used to be. The correct answer will capture these contrasting opinions about the presence of immoral characters.

Step 4: Evaluate the Answer Choices

(D) expresses exactly what Peter and Yoko disagree over in terms of today's children's stories. Use the Decision Tree: (1) Does Peter have an opinion about this answer? Yes, as he claims right off the bat. (2) Does Yoko have an opinion about this answer? Yes, as she rebuts it at the start of her argument. (3) Do they have different opinions? Yes! Peter feels today's stories don't have such characters, and Yoko feels they do.

(A) doesn't work because Peter makes no comment about whether the stories are frightening. He only cares that kids learn about consequences.

(B) also brings up the idea of these stories being less frightening, which only Yoko discusses. Again, Peter speaks only to the learning of consequences.

(C) is Outside the Scope of both arguments since neither Peter nor Yoko mentions anything about overall quality.

(E) is exactly what Peter believes, but Yoko expresses no opinion about the concept of consequences.

6. (D) Flaw

Step 1: Identify the Question Type

The phrase "vulnerable to criticism" is a common way the LSAT indicates there's a Flaw in the argument. Break the resident's argument down into its evidence and conclusion; then find the answer that describes why the evidence doesn't adequately support the conclusion.

Step 2: Untangle the Stimulus

The resident starts right off with her conclusion: too much algae is hurting the smaller fish in the local pond. The evidence is the resident's observations that a large number of dead smaller fish has always been accompanied by an unusually large presence of algae.

Step 3: Make a Prediction

This is a causal argument. Mistaken ascription of causality is one of the most commonly tested types of flawed logic on the LSAT. The evidence provides a mere correlation: dead smaller fish appear at the same time as lots of algae. The conclusion implies that the algae caused the smaller fish to die. Causal arguments typically contain one or more of three flaws: (1) The causality could be reversed (i.e., the small fish dying could have somehow led to the increase in algae); (2) there may be other overlooked causes (i.e., something else harmed the fish); or (3) the correlation may just be coincidental, and the two events had no effect on each other. The correct answer will express one of these three possible flaws.

Step 4: Evaluate the Answer Choices

(D) fits the second potential flaw: overlooked alternative causes. If a third factor was involved, then the algae itself may have had nothing to do with the fish dying.

(A) makes an Irrelevant Comparison between smaller and larger fish. This argument only concerns smaller fish.

(B) also makes an Irrelevant Comparison to smaller fish in other environments, which have no bearing on this argument.

(C) is irrelevant because the argument is only concerned about what's harming the smaller fish. Fish of other sizes don't matter.

(E) suggests that fish could also be hurt by unusually small amounts of algae, but that doesn't indicate any problem with the argument that large amounts of algae hurt fish. Plenty of things can harm living creatures through over- and under-abundance.

7. (B) Point at Issue

Step 1: Identify the Question Type

Since the question asks for something over which the two speakers "disagree," this a Point at Issue question. Summarize both speakers' arguments and look for an answer with which one speaker would agree and the other would disagree. Remember that you can use the Decision Tree to test any answer about which you're unsure.

Step 2: Untangle the Stimulus

Tanner starts out by arguing that people should demand debates before political elections. Tanner's reasoning is that debates allow voters to determine better which candidate will do best in office. Saldana has a different perspective on debates. Saldana argues that debates are good for those candidates with better debating skills. Because of this, Saldana concludes that the debates won't help voters tell who is most qualified for office.

Step 3: Make a Prediction

Tanner and Saldana definitely don't see eye to eye on the benefits of debates. Tanner feels that they help voters find the best-suited candidate, while Saldana feels they merely reward good speakers and don't help voters find the most qualified candidate. The correct answer will concentrate on their conflicting opinion about debates helping to find the best candidate.

Step 4: Evaluate the Answer Choices

(B) is exactly the point over which Tanner and Saldana disagree. Use the Decision Tree: (1) Does Tanner have an opinion about this answer? Yes, as mentioned in his evidence. (2) Does Saldana have an opinion about this answer? Yes, as she describes in her conclusion. (3) Do they have different opinions? Yes! Tanner feels voters can better determine who's more qualified through debates, and Saldana feels they *can't.*

(A) is off because only Saldana makes any reference to debating skills and is thus the only one of the two speakers who has an opinion about this answer.

(C), like **(A)**, focuses on debating skills, a topic that Tanner does not weigh in on.

(D) is a Distortion. Tanner is the only one of the two speakers to discuss which candidates are qualified, and Saldana is the only one to mention debating skills. However, no one correlates debating skills with qualification.

(E) also distorts the issue. Tanner and Saldana are arguing about whether people can, from debates, learn which candidate is most qualified, not whether the debates will affect the outcome of the elections.

8. (D) Paradox

Step 1: Identify the Question Type

When a question asks you to explain a situation, it's a Paradox question. According to the question stem, the stimulus will describe a phenomenon, which you can anticipate will appear to be inexplicable or contradictory. Once you've identified the apparent conflict, look for the answer that dispels the mystery without changing the facts.

Step 2: Untangle the Stimulus

The author presents a study with unusual results: Highways with the greatest number of cars, and hence the ones with the most traffic, are actually the least likely locales for fatal accidents.

Step 3: Make a Prediction

With more cars and more traffic, you'd expect such roads to be more dangerous. However, contrary to expectations, these roads are actually the safest (in terms of percentage of fatal accidents). How is that possible? While you may be able to come up with some ideas, the only prediction you need is that the correct answer will explain why these roads are actually safer or why roads with fewer cars are more dangerous. Be very cautious about incorrect answer choices that are Outside the Scope; the stimulus is about the fatal accident rate, not the overall accident rate.

Step 4: Evaluate the Answer Choices

(D) provides a possible explanation for the conundrum. If most serious accidents occur when drivers travel at high speeds, then fatal accidents (the kind at issue here) are more likely to happen on roads where people can reach those high speeds. High-traffic roads are described as the most congested, a condition that would slow down drivers. This would take away some of the danger, explaining the lower rate of fatal accidents.

(A) is, at worst, a 180. Drivers on high-traffic roads would have more cars to keep track of and would therefore seem more likely to be distracted. If distractions lead to accidents, this would make the low fatal accident rate of such roads even more unusual. Note, too, that this choice doesn't indicate anything about the likelihood of fatal car accidents. Thus, at best, it is Outside the Scope.

(B) informs you of which roads have the highest rate of accidents, but it does nothing to explain why that's the case. You're left with exactly the same paradox to resolve.

(C) provides irrelevant information. The destination of drivers has no bearing on why they get into accidents.

(E) suggests that heavily traveled roads can have the same percentage of trucks as any other road. Having the same mix of traffic does nothing to explain why they would have lower rates of fatal accidents.

9. (A) Strengthen

Step 1: Identify the Question Type

The word *strengthen* in the question stem makes this as clearly worded a Strengthen question as you're going to find. Start by breaking down the argument into its evidence and conclusion. The correct answer will validate the assumption that connects those two pieces.

Step 2: Untangle the Stimulus

The author starts out with some information about jurisdictions where lawmakers have decided that the penalties for theft and bribery should be equal. Based on this, the author concludes that lawmakers believe these crimes produce an equal amount of harm.

Step 3: Make a Prediction

The author makes a pretty blatant scope shift in this argument. The evidence is merely about the two crimes resulting in equal penalties. The conclusion is that these crimes are viewed as producing equal harm. The author must be assuming that lawmakers assign punishments for crimes on the basis of what they perceive to be the harm from the crime. The correct answer will make that assumption more likely or valid.

Step 4: Evaluate the Answer Choices

(A) justifies the author's argument by confirming the connection between the penalties lawmakers assign for a crime and the harm that lawmakers feel results from that crime.

(B) brings up how lawmakers would determine the legality of certain acts, which is Outside the Scope of this argument. The author is concerned with penalties for crimes already deemed illegal.

(C) mentions that lawmakers might increase penalties after a particularly harmful case involving a particular crime. (You might imagine them responding to a public outcry.) Even if that's true, it doesn't strengthen this argument, which concludes that lawmakers must be equating the harm of theft and that of bribery.

(D) may be tempting, as it is consistent with the idea that both crimes result in equal harm. However, it does not strengthen the author's argument, which tries to show that mandating equal penalties indicates that lawmakers perceive equal harm.

(E) wanders off course by suggesting how effective such an equal-penalty system could be. However, the efficacy of such a system is not relevant to the argument at hand.

10. (D) Role of a Statement

Step 1: Identify the Question Type

The stem asks you to decide how a particular statement "figures in the argument." That language signals that this is a Role of a Statement question. Decide why the author has included the statement we should "learn the lessons of history" and find the choice that describes that role.

Step 2: Untangle the Stimulus

The first sentence tells you almost everything you need to know. The author ascribes the admonition from the question stem to other people, and the Keyword *but* indicates clearly that the author does not agree that we should try to "learn the lessons of history." The author goes on to describe learning from history as an impossible task. He adds that, even if we could learn from history, we'd never be able to apply what we'd learned. What a pessimist!

Step 3: Make a Prediction

The statement that we should "learn the lessons of history" is a claim that the author sets out to debunk. Look for an answer choice that says something like: "It is a position against which the author argues."

Step 4: Evaluate the Answer Choices

(D) is the correct answer. The author argues that because learning and benefiting from history's lessons is impossible, it isn't something that people should try to do. The statement referenced in the question stem is one that the author wants to discredit.

(A) is incorrect because the author doesn't believe that the inability to learn and apply history's lessons is a problem that humans can ever "resolve."

(B) incorrectly states that the statement referenced in the stem is compatible with the author's conclusion. The two statements are totally opposed.

(C) is incorrect because the author does not "take for granted"—or *assume*—that we should not learn the lessons of history. Rather, the author makes an argument, supported by relevant evidence, that we should not learn those lessons.

(E) is a 180. The statement in the stem is not the author's assumption; it is a claim that the author disagrees with. Remember, on the LSAT, "assumption" always refers to an unstated premise.

11. (E) Flaw

Step 1: Identify the Question Type

"[V]ulnerable to criticism on the grounds … " is classic Flaw language. Analyze the argument, identifying its conclusion and evidence, and what the author is taking for granted. Use that to look for the answer choice that describes why the conclusion does not logically follow from the evidence.

Step 2: Untangle the Stimulus

After reading through the stimulus, identify and bracket the conclusion: "Sigerson's proposal [that we should outlaw certain campaign contributions] is dishonest." A Keyword, *because*, points to the evidence: Sigerson has, in the past, accepted many contributions of the very sort he's now trying to ban. But Sigerson's acceptance of these donations doesn't prove that he is a hypocrite or a liar. Perhaps he has accepted these donations reluctantly and only out of necessity. It could be that after participating in, and even benefiting from, a corrupt system, Sigerson is more determined than ever to clean it up. It isn't "dishonest" to argue that something you've done in the past should be outlawed in the future.

Step 3: Make a Prediction

The argument is flawed because the author makes the dubious assumption that a person cannot honestly argue that something he has done in the past should, going forward, be illegal.

Step 4: Evaluate the Answer Choices

(E) calls the author out for ignoring the difference between Sigerson's past behavior and his proposed legislation, which would affect only the future behavior of politicians like himself. It's correct.

(A) describes an error of Formal Logic. The author's argument, however, doesn't involve any conditional statements. **(A)** is also Outside the Scope; the author never argues that Sigerson's proposal should or shouldn't be adopted—only that Sigerson's advocacy is "dishonest."

(B) does not describe the author's evidence correctly; the author never claims that Sigerson has made an "inadequate argument" on behalf of the proposed legislation. Also, the author never rejects the proposal; his argument involves the honesty of its proponent.

(C) is Outside the Scope. "[O]ther city politicians" have nothing to do with this argument, which is only about the possible dishonesty of a single politician, Sigerson.

(D) inaccurately indicates that the author accuses Sigerson of being "unfamiliar with the issues." Quite to the contrary, the author impugns Sigerson for personal actions related to the issue.

12. (C) Assumption (Necessary)

Step 1: Identify the Question Type

The word *assumption* tells you that this is, of course, an Assumption question. More specifically, it's asking for a necessary assumption, one the argument "requires." Remember that you can use the Denial Test on "necessary" Assumption questions.

Step 2: Untangle the Stimulus

The conclusion comes at the very end of the stimulus: "[S]ome books published by Garden Path are flawed." The evidence, highlighted by the Keyword [s]*ince*, is just above: A gardening book is flawed if it does not explain the basics of composting. All the author tells us about Garden Path's books is that some of them "do not explain the difference between hot and cold composting."

Step 3: Make a Prediction

In order to draw the conclusion that Garden Path books are inadequate from the evidence that they fail to explain the basics of composting, the author must assume that "the basics of composting" include an explanation of "hot and cold composting." Look for an answer that states that an explanation of composting basics must distinguish between hot and cold composting.

Step 4: Evaluate the Answer Choices

(C) matches the prediction perfectly. Without this assumption, the author cannot draw her conclusion about Garden Path books from the evidence given. This is the correct answer.

(A) can be eliminated based solely on the way it ends. The author doesn't make any assumptions about books that are not flawed. The author argues, instead, that certain books are flawed. Perhaps all gardening books are flawed!

(B) is Outside the Scope; the author does not argue for or against any gardening practices.

(D) confuses a necessary condition with a sufficient condition. The author of the stimulus assumes that a book that explains the basics must explain the difference between hot and cold. In other words: understanding hot and cold is necessary to understanding the basics. **(D)** reverses this Formal Logic statement, saying that understanding the hot/cold distinction is sufficient to understand the basics.

(E), like **(A)**, goes against the grain of the author's argument: the author argues that certain books are flawed, not that they aren't flawed. It's easy to imagine a book that gets composting right but is deeply flawed about sunlight, water, and fertilizer, isn't it? The author neither claims nor assumes that every book describing composting basics is perfect.

13. (A) Paradox

Step 1: Identify the Question Type

The phrase "does most to explain" indicates that your task here is to resolve a paradox, mystery, or discrepancy. In other words, this is a Paradox question. As you read the stimulus, find the apparent contradiction or seeming inconsistency.

Step 2: Untangle the Stimulus

The Keyword [b]*ut* highlights the paradox. Astronomers have discovered that they badly undercounted the number of galaxies that exist in the universe, yet they had not underestimated the universe's "total mass." The correct answer must explain how both of these facts can be true at the same time.

Step 3: Make a Prediction

If the astronomers got the mass right, but the galaxy count wrong, it could be that galaxies have less mass than scientists had previously believed. Or perhaps galaxies just have very little mass compared to the universe as a whole, so that finding five times as many galaxies doesn't much change the total mass. Think of it like this: if you had a very heavy pocket full of coins with what you thought was 50 quarters and 1 dime, you could discover you had five times more dimes than you thought you had, but it wouldn't make much difference to the weight in your pocket.

Step 4: Evaluate the Answer Choices

(A) resolves the paradox in just the way you expected. Galaxies account for a "tiny percentage of the universe's total mass." Thus, the difference between 10 billion and 50 billion galaxies would not make much of a difference in calculating total universal mass. **(A)** is correct.

(B) does not address the underlying paradox. The accuracy of the astronomers' estimates is beside the point. The mystery is why one part of their estimate of the universe's makeup (number of galaxies) changed so dramatically while the other part (overall mass) did not.

(C) gives a reason why astronomers have revised their initial estimate of the number of galaxies in the universe, but it does not explain why an increase of 40 billion galaxies would not lead to a dramatic increase in total mass.

(D) is Outside the Scope. The author never discusses "[t]heories about how galaxies are formed."

(E) is similar to **(B)**, in that it invites you to question the accuracy of the astronomers' estimates. But deciding that the astronomers estimate the universe's total mass in different ways does not resolve the seeming incongruity between quintupling the number of galaxies and leaving the estimate of total mass more or less unchanged.

14. (A) Flaw

Step 1: Identify the Question Type

The phrase "expresses a flaw in the argument's reasoning" is a classic Flaw prompt. The correct answer will describe why the newspaper subscriber's evidence fails to logically lead to her conclusion.

Step 2: Untangle the Stimulus

Paraphrase the newspaper subscriber's conclusion: Arnot's plan to fix social ills by fundamentally changing government will not work. As evidence, the subscriber notes that one of Arnot's assumptions—that government can be trusted—is dubious. The subscriber assumes that any conclusion based on a dubious premise is false.

Step 3: Make a Prediction

A conclusion can be valid even if one of the premises used to support it is bad. Consider, for instance, this argument: "Michael Jordan was a great basketball player because he starred in a movie with Bugs Bunny." This is a lousy argument—it depends on the silly assumption that appearing in a cartoon can make a person a great athlete—but the conclusion that Michael Jordan was a great basketball player is nevertheless true. You can think of thousands of similar examples. Look for an answer choice that states that a conclusion can be correct even if some arguments in favor of it are poor.

Step 4: Evaluate the Answer Choices

(A) gives you just what we're looking for. The newspaper subscriber has improperly discarded a conclusion just because "an inadequate argument has been given for it." Even if government cannot be trusted, Arnot might be right that fundamentally changing government can eliminate social ills. Perhaps the fundamental changes even address the problem of untrustworthiness.

(B) says, essentially, that the author is treating a necessary condition as a sufficient condition. But the stimulus does not include conditional statements, nor does it demonstrate any Formal Logic errors.

(C) is a Distortion; it gets the subscriber's problem backward. This choice states that the subscriber overlooks the possibility that one can make a good argument in favor of a bad conclusion. Actually, she rejected what might be a good conclusion on the basis that it had bad evidence.

(D) accuses the newspaper subscriber of twisting Arnot's words. Nothing in the stimulus, however, gives us any reason to suspect that the subscriber has mischaracterized Arnot's position.

(E) describes equivocation, a flaw commonly seen on the LSAT. But the newspaper subscriber doesn't use "government" in a deceptive or inconsistent way, so **(E)** is incorrect.

15. (B) Weaken

Step 1: Identify the Question Type

This stem is a standard Weaken prompt. Look for a fact that makes the author's central assumption less likely to be true.

Step 2: Untangle the Stimulus

Begin by bracketing and paraphrasing the conclusion: the city council made a good move in hiring a long-term economic development adviser. The reason for this cheerful assessment comes at the end of the stimulus. Other cities that have invested in this sort of planning have benefited greatly from it. So, the author assumes that what was true of those other cities will be true of his, as well.

Step 3: Make a Prediction

In making his argument, the columnist never establishes the similarity between his own city and these other, successful cities. If there are significant differences, the author's assumption that the economic adviser's impact will be similar in his city is severely compromised. The correct answer will introduce an important difference between the columnist's city and the cities that have successfully invested in economic development advisers.

Step 4: Evaluate the Answer Choices

(B) provides one of those differences you were looking for. If the columnist's city has a significantly smaller population and economy than the other cities he cites, it's possible that an economic development adviser will not have the effect that the columnist anticipates.

(A) is Outside the Scope. The columnist uses car maintenance as an illustrative analogy. This argument is not about auto repairs; it is about the city council's hiring of an economic development adviser.

(C) is incorrect for the same reason as **(A)**; the particulars of auto maintenance are a red herring, irrelevant to strengthening or weakening the argument.

(D) is irrelevant. Even if few city councils want to spend the money to hire advisers, the columnist's city has apparently made the choice to do so. The argument is about how good that choice will turn out to be.

(E) is Outside the Scope. The columnist never argues that hiring the adviser will yield immediate returns. The point of his argument is that hiring the adviser will prove to be the right choice over the long run.

16. (D) Role of a Statement

Step 1: Identify the Question Type

The phrase "describes the role played … by the statement" indicates that this is a Role of a Statement question. Find out why the author mentions that cell phone use is especially upsetting on planes.

Step 2: Untangle the Stimulus

The key to this question is to correctly identify and bracket the conclusion. Rearrange the order of the statements so that they flow logically to the author's final point:

Airplanes are usually packed pretty tight. So, on airplanes, you can't get up and move if the person next to you is being annoying. Thus, an annoying cell phone user would be even more upsetting on an airplane than he would on a bus or train. And annoying cell phone users are pretty bad on buses and trains. Therefore, proposals to allow cell phone use on airplanes are a bad idea.

Now, it's pretty clear that the statement that cell phones are likely to be more annoying on airplanes than they are on buses and trains is an intermediate conclusion. It follows from the fact that you can't get up and move away from annoying cell phone use on the plane, and it supports the author's ultimate conclusion that cell phones should not be allowed on planes.

Step 3: Make a Prediction

The correct answer will say, in some way, that the statement mentioned in the stem is an intermediate conclusion, supported by other evidence in the argument but used to support the author's main point.

Step 4: Evaluate the Answer Choices

(D) correctly describes the statement in the stem as an intermediate conclusion: one supported by evidence and also serving as evidence. **(D)** is the winner.

(A) is incorrect. The claim that airplane cell phone use is especially irritating is not the editorialist's final conclusion. The main conclusion is that the "recent proposals" are "ill-advised."

(B) is a 180. The editorialist agrees with the statement mentioned in the stem; he isn't trying to rebut it.

(C) says, essentially, that the statement referenced in the stem serves as evidence in support of an intermediate conclusion used in support of the main conclusion. That's not quite right. The statement mentioned in the stem is an intermediate conclusion, serving as immediate evidence in support of the author's main point.

(E) states incorrectly that the statement in the stem serves merely to put the editorialist's argument in context. The statement mentioned in the stem actually plays a more significant role than that; it is the most important evidence that the author offers in support of his conclusion.

17. (B) Strengthen

Step 1: Identify the Question Type

"[M]ost helps to support" is a standard Strengthen prompt. Bracket the conclusion, paraphrase the evidence, and articulate the author's assumption. Then, predict a fact that would make the assumption more likely to be true.

Step 2: Untangle the Stimulus

The conclusion (note the Keyword *evidently*) is the first sentence of the stimulus: The brain's own immune cells are responsible for the deteriorating cognition that Alzheimer's sufferers experience. The author supports this claim with two pieces of evidence. First, anti-inflammatory drugs slow mental decline. Second, the brain's immune cells, in attacking protein deposits, also destroy healthy cells. The first part of the evidence is what is slightly perplexing: What's the relevance of the anti-inflammatory drugs? In order for this information about the drugs to support the author's thesis, it must be true that anti-inflammatory drugs reduce the number of immune cells in the brain or slow their effects in some way. That's the author's assumption.

Step 3: Make a Prediction

A good Strengthen answer will suggest that "anti-inflammatory drugs, such as acetylsalicylic acid," destroy or limit the function of "microglia—the brain's own immune cells."

Step 4: Evaluate the Answer Choices

(B) connects the evidence and conclusion in just the right way, and it's the correct answer here. "Acetylsalicylic acid" is an anti-inflammatory drug. If this acid reduces the number of immune cells and simultaneously slows mental decline in Alzheimer's patients, the author's claim that immune cells are causing declines in cognition is more convincing.

(A) is Outside the Scope. According to the author, the problem is that, in an attempt to eliminate the protein BA buildup, the brain releases immune cells that poison and impair the surrounding brain cells. Why the protein buildup occurs in the first place is irrelevant.

(C) simply reiterates something the author already told you: microglia attack harmful protein buildups. But simply repeating the evidence doesn't strengthen the author's reasoning.

(D) is a 180; it weakens the argument. If the protein buildups impair cognitive function, it seems possible that the proteins, and not the immune cells fighting them, are the cause of Alzheimer's patients' worsening cognition.

(E), like **(A)**, is Outside the Scope. This argument is about whether a specific symptom can be traced to microglia. It makes no difference whether immune cells also create problems for people who do not suffer from Alzheimer's.

18. (B) Principle (Apply/Inference)

Step 1: Identify the Question Type

The word *principles* tells you that this is a Principle question. But what type of Principle question is it? The stem says that the lawyer's stimulus will state some "principles." Those principles will then "support" one of the answer choices. In other words, this is an Apply the Principle question.

Step 2: Untangle the Stimulus

The presence of Formal Logic Keywords suggests that you should diagram this stimulus. Recall, also, that Apply the Principle questions often involve conditional statements. The stimulus articulates two rules about when accessing computer files without permission is or is not justified.

The first sentence includes the necessity key phrase "only if." Diagram it as:

If	OK to access without permission	→	computer typically used in business ops
If	computer ~ typically used in business ops	→	~ OK to access without permission

The second sentence includes the sufficiency Keyword [*If*. The phrase "in addition" is significant; in your diagram, translate it as "and."

If	grounds to believe computer has evidence AND computer typically used in business ops	→	OK to access without permission
If	~ OK to access without permission	→	~ grounds to believe computer has evidence OR computer ~ typically used in business ops

Step 3: Make a Prediction

The answer choices will, in essence, present different "cases." The correct answer will contain a case that can be decided on the basis of one or both of the rules above. So, the right answer will start with one of the Formal Logic triggers in the stimulus (from one of the rules or from one of their contrapositives) and will arrive at the appropriate necessary condition.

Step 4: Evaluate the Answer Choices

(B) provides both of the triggers in the second statement (the consulting firm's computer was used in business, and it was reasonably believed to contain legal evidence) and arrives at the correct result: the behavior of the police was justified. Note that it does not matter whether the computer actually contained any useful evidence. Having reasonable grounds for believing that a computer typically used for business contains evidence is enough to justify access.

(A) does not include one of the sufficient conditions given in the stimulus. Even if the store owner's computer is commonly used in the store's operations, Sunok's behavior might still be unjustified. Frequent business use of a computer is a necessary condition for unauthorized access, not a sufficient condition. There's nothing to suggest that the computer contains data usable as evidence against the computer's owner, and Sunok was not given permission by the computer's owner to access the computer.

(C) ends with the conclusion that a computer search was not justified. In the Formal Logic diagrams, only one condition triggers the conclusion "not justified"; if a computer is not regularly used in business, then an unauthorized search is not okay (the contrapositive of the first rule). Natalie's computer is commonly used in business, so the conclusion in **(C)** is unsupported.

(D), like **(A)**, incorrectly treats regular business use as a sufficient, rather than a necessary, condition. Only if the customs officials had reasonable grounds for thinking the computer contained useful evidence could we be sure that the search was justified. **(D)** states that the officials suspected the importer of smuggling, but it doesn't say they had reason to suspect that the computer contained evidence. The officials' actions may have been impermissible.

(E) is similar to **(C)**. Note that, in the stimulus, the only trigger that leads to "not justified" is "not used in business." The computer in **(E)** is used in business, so the stimulus gives you no reason to conclude that an unauthorized search would not be allowed. Note that neither rule restricts the type of files that may be accessed once the search is under way.

19. (D) Assumption (Necessary)

Step 1: Identify the Question Type

The phrase "assumption required" means that this is an Assumption question seeking an assumption necessary for the argument's conclusion to follow from its evidence. The Denial Test is available here.

Step 2: Untangle the Stimulus

A great Keyword—*therefore*—highlights the author's conclusion: "biological catalysts" reduce the cost of leather tanning. The evidence comes in the previous two sentences. When waste disposal is taken out of the equation, both tanning methods (biological catalysts and the conventional process) cost the same. The biological method, however, produces 20 percent less waste. The author's assumption is that less waste means cheaper waste disposal.

Step 3: Make a Prediction

You've identified the author's assumption, but be careful. This assumption may be unwarranted. A tablespoon of radioactive waste, for instance, might be costlier to dispose of than a ton of paper waste. Perhaps biological catalysts create less waste but more expensive waste. The correct answer will suggest that the smaller amount of waste created by the "biological catalyst" method leads to smaller waste disposal costs.

Step 4: Evaluate the Answer Choices

(D) is a very weak statement. It doesn't tell us that disposing of biological waste is cheaper than the alternative; it merely states that biological waste isn't "significantly more" expensive to get rid of. But remember that weak statements, when negated, usually create strong statements. Try the Denial Test here. Negating **(D)** produces this statement: "Disposal of tanning waste produced with biological methods costs significantly more ...." If this is true, then the author's conclusion is unsustainable. The statement in **(D)** is thus a necessary assumption, and **(D)** is the correct answer.

(A) is Outside the Scope. The quality of the leather goods is not relevant to this discussion—only the cost of tanning.

(B) is also Outside the Scope. It states that biological catalysts cost less by weight than do alternatives like calcium

oxide. But this doesn't really add anything important to the discussion; the author has already told us that biological catalysts are cheaper when waste disposal is left out of the picture. What you need to know is the cost of waste disposal, and **(B)** doesn't shed any light on that part of the process. To confirm that **(B)** is not the right answer, try the Denial Test. **(B)**, negated, reads: "The biological catalysts ... are equally costly or more costly, by weight, than [alternatives]." This statement does not destroy, or even weaken, the author's argument. After all, you don't know whether you use a greater or lesser weight of biological catalysts than you would of conventional ones. According to the evidence, waste disposal aside, the process involving biological catalysts is less expensive.

(C) is similar to **(B)**; it gives specific information about why, when you subtract waste disposal costs, biological catalysts are cheaper than the alternatives. But why biological catalysts are cheaper is irrelevant, and **(C)** is Outside the Scope.

(E), which focuses on labor costs, is also Outside the Scope. The assumption necessary to the argument has only to do with waste disposal costs.

20. (C) Principle (Apply/Inference)

Step 1: Identify the Question Type

This stem explicitly indicates a Principle question. More importantly, the phrases "principle stated above" and "the following arguments" tell you that the specific example in the correct answer will logically apply the principle in the stimulus. This question acts almost exactly like an Inference question, in which the correct answer must be true based on the statements in the stimulus.

Step 2: Untangle the Stimulus

The entire stimulus is a conditional, Formal Logic statement. Diagram it. "[I]f" highlights the sufficient condition. There are actually two sufficient conditions in this case, either of which is enough to prove that one should not play a practical joke on someone. Here's the rule in "If-then" form:

If	joke shows contempt OR joker believes it could cause harm	→	~ play joke
If	[okay to] play joke	→	joke ~ show contempt AND joker ~ believe it could cause harm

Note that the joke player's subjective perception of risk is what's important; the objective threat posed by the joke does not play a part in this rule. Also, notice that both parts of the restriction—the part dealing with contempt and the part dealing with harm—apply only to the person whom the joke is being played on. If I play a harmless joke that doesn't show contempt for you, but *does* make cruel fun of '80s pop sensation Rick Astley, the joke might be acceptable under the rule in the stimulus.

Step 3: Make a Prediction

The right answer will do one of three things: (1) state that a joke shows contempt and conclude that the joke should not be played; (2) state that the joker believes the joke will threatens harm and conclude that the joke should not be played; or (3) state that a joke is acceptable to play and conclude from that fact that the joke does not show contempt for its target and also that the joker does not believe the joke will threaten harm.

Step 4: Evaluate the Answer Choices

(C) is correct. In the scenario described in (C), the author believes that a joke might bring significant harm. The author concludes from this that the joke should not be played. That matches the principle from the stimulus perfectly.

(A) is a subtle trap answer. It uses the phrase "should have realized that [the joke] would bring" harm. That's different from believing, at the time of playing the joke, that it would bring harm. The principle diagrammed doesn't have anything to do with the things the joker should know. It deals only with what the joker actually believes.

(B) can be eliminated as soon as you notice that it concludes that it is okay to play a particular joke. "Okay to play a joke" is not a necessary, or resulting, condition according to the stimulus, so there's no way that (B) is correctly applying the principle. Even if a joke is harmless and not at all contemptuous, there could be many other reasons that it's not okay to play it on someone. It might be silly or irritating, and that could be a reason not to play it.

(D), like (A), includes a scope shift. "Show contempt for someone" is not the sufficient condition given in the stimulus. Instead, the stimulus forbids jokes that "show contempt for that person," the person on whom the joke is being played. (D) is incorrect.

(E) deals with actual harm, not the joker's subjective expectation of harm. Without knowing whether the joker in (E) believed he'd significantly harm the target of the joke, you can't say whether the joke was okay under the principle in the stimulus.

21. (A) Assumption (Sufficient)

Step 1: Identify the Question Type

The stem phrase "if assumed" makes this question an Assumption question. More specifically, the question calls for a "sufficient" assumption, an unstated premise that, when

added to the evidence, guarantees that the author's conclusion is "properly drawn."

Step 2: Untangle the Stimulus

Bracket the very last part of this stimulus; that's the conclusion: "Checkers's motive in refusing to accept the coupons was simply to hurt Marty's pizza." The evidence is that accepting the coupons would have cost Checkers nothing and would have made some Checkers customers happy. Since the conclusion is about Checkers's motive, the author must be assuming that if Checkers refused to do something that would have cost nothing and made some customers happy, the reason must have been to hurt the competitor.

Step 3: Make a Prediction

The author assumes that, under the circumstances described in the stimulus, there are no reasons other than malice toward Marty's that would prevent Checkers from accepting a coupon issued by Marty's. The answer may be phrased affirmatively or negatively, so look for either "no alternative reason exists for Checkers to refuse the coupons" or "a motivation to hurt Marty's business is the only reason for Checkers to refuse the coupons."

Step 4: Evaluate the Answer Choices

(A) matches the prediction closely, and it is the correct answer. Any pizza place that refuses a competitor's coupon in the situation described in the stimulus "is motivated solely by the desire to hurt that competitor." In other words, there are no alternative explanations for Checkers's behavior.

(B) says that "[a]ny" company wishing to harm a competitor would act as Checkers did. But it doesn't say that only a company wishing to harm a competitor would. In Formal Logic terms, (B) treats the desire to harm as a sufficient condition, whereas the author assumes that it's a necessary condition. Remember, he assumes that there's no other reason for Checkers's actions.

(C) is Outside the Scope. The behavior of other companies is irrelevant, unless it somehow sheds light on the motives of Checkers. The statement in (C) reveals nothing about Checkers's motives, so it certainly isn't sufficient to establish the professor's conclusion.

(D) is Outside the Scope as well. It may be true that accepting coupons from Marty's would benefit Marty's, but this doesn't prove that Checkers declined the coupons out of a desire to hurt Marty's. Keep in mind that Checkers's motive is what's significant here.

(E) begins badly and ends worse. According to the stimulus, accepting the coupons would have benefited some of Checkers's customers. What's more, the professor's conclusion is that Checkers's motive was to harm Marty's, not to benefit its own customers.

22. (C) Inference

Step 1: Identify the Question Type

The phrase "[t]he science writer's statements, if true …" indicates that this is an Inference question. The phrase "most strongly support" tells you to look for a statement that must be true based on the stimulus.

Step 2: Untangle the Stimulus

In an Inference stimulus, there's no need to bracket a conclusion or look for a missing piece of evidence. Instead, take an inventory of the facts given in the stimulus with the presumption that everything in the stimulus is absolutely true. In simplified form, this stimulus says: scientists tend to be highly successful in solving the problems they "have been called upon to solve." Because of this, people think that scientists can solve any problem. But it turns out that scientists are calling upon themselves (or arranging for others to call on them) to solve the problems they eventually address. The upshot is that scientists aren't asked to solve problems they can't solve.

Step 3: Make a Prediction

The correct answer will follow from the information in the stimulus. It's unlikely that you can predict the precise language of the correct answer, but you know that it will be in line with the fact that scientists' remarkable success is related to the fact that they're called on to solve only those problems for which scientific solutions are feasible.

Step 4: Evaluate the Answer Choices

(C) says what the stimulus strongly implies: if scientists weren't cherry-picking missions for themselves, their success rate would likely be less "astounding" than it currently is. (C) makes the point that the science writer has been driving at and is the correct answer.

(A) gets the logic backward. The science writer says that when scientists are called on to solve a problem, the problem is one for which the scientists can formulate a solution. He doesn't suggest that every time scientists can formulate a solution for problem, they'll be called on to solve that problem. There are plenty of problems that scientists could probably solve but for which solutions aren't in anyone's economic or social interest.

(B) is Extreme. The author says that scientists "typically" select the problems they solve and are "almost" never asked to solve problems outside their purview. The "[a]ny" at the start of this answer simply isn't supported by the stimulus.

(D) indicates that most of the problems scientists are working on are ones "that politicians and business leaders want solved;" this has no support in the stimulus. The passage says nothing about what politicians and business leaders desire, nor does it mention what percentage of scientific

missions address their desires as opposed to the desires of medical professionals, city planners, environmentalists, and so on.

(E), due to the use of the word *only*, makes a very strong claim: Nothing apart from the problem selection process—not scientific skill, not rigor, not brilliance, not luck—plays even a tiny role in science's success rate. That's a pretty harsh assessment, one that finds no support in the science writer's argument.

23. (E) Parallel Flaw

Step 1: Identify the Question Type

"Pattern of flawed reasoning … is most similar …" is classic Parallel Flaw question language. Identify the flawed reasoning pattern in the stimulus argument and find the one answer choice that commits precisely the same mistake.

Step 2: Untangle the Stimulus

A Keyword, [*t*]*hus*, indicates the conclusion: most mechanics understand circuits. The evidence comes in two more "most" statements: (1) Most mechanics are experienced, and (2) most experienced mechanics understand circuits. To see why this evidence fails to prove the conclusion, pick some percentages that fit the stimulus. *Most* means "more than half." If "most mechanics are experienced," then it's possible that, say, only 51 percent of mechanics are experienced. If "most experienced mechanics understand circuits," it's possible that 51 percent of experienced mechanics—or around 26 percent of all mechanics—understand circuits. Twenty-six percent is not "most" mechanics, so the author's conclusion is unwarranted by the evidence he presents.

Step 3: Make a Prediction

The correct answer, mimicking the flawed logic in the stimulus, will say something that fits this pattern: most Xs are Ys. Most Ys are Zs. Thus, most Xs are Zs.

Step 4: Evaluate the Answer Choices

(E), in simplified form, reads like this: most (Xs) snow-removal companies (are Ys) do lawns. Most (Ys) companies that do lawns (are Zs) hire summer workers. Thus, most (Xs) snow-removal companies (are Zs) hire summer workers. This is exactly the pattern detected in the stimulus, and thus (E) is the correct answer.

(A) doesn't include any "most" statements. There's no way that this argument is parallel to the one in the stimulus.

(B) is a Distortion. The first statement, "the most common species … are migratory," does not mean "most birds are migratory." For example, 99 percent of birds could be nonmigratory, as long as the most common species account for 1 percent of all birds and are migratory species. Thus, (B) does not open with a "most Xs are Ys" statement; already, it is not parallel to the argument in the stimulus.

(C) is incorrect. Most (Xs) drivers who don't like to go fast (are NOT Ys) are not sports car buyers. Most (Zs) speeding tickets (are Ys) are issued to sports car drivers. This is already not parallel.

(D) is incorrect. Most (Xs) nature photographers (are NOT Ys) are not photographers who like portraits. Most (Ys) portrait photographers (are Zs) like dignitaries. Already, this argument has deviated from the pattern we observed in the stimulus.

24. (B) Strengthen

Step 1: Identify the Question Type

"Which of the following statements ... most strengthens the argument" is standard Strengthen language. Analyze the argument in the stimulus, noting its conclusion and paraphrasing its evidence. Then, look for the answer choice that makes the author's central assumption more likely to be true.

Step 2: Untangle the Stimulus

The evidence appears at the end of the stimulus: people who believe they can succeed tend to do better than those who doubt their own abilities. From this, the author concludes that if you want to do well, you should act as though you believe you can succeed. There's a scope shift here; genuinely believing in one's abilities is different from acting as though one believes In one's abilities. The author assumes that acting as though you have self-confidence will help you in the same way that being confident would.

Step 3: Make a Prediction

The correct answer will state a fact that makes it more likely that acting confident will yield benefits comparable to those of being confident.

Step 4: Evaluate the Answer Choices

(B) fits the prediction nicely. If real confidence follows from pretended confidence, then people who pretend to be confident should ultimately enjoy the same benefits that confident people do. **(B)** is the correct answer.

(A) is Outside the Scope. The stimulus is talking about people who don't believe in themselves but fake it. The fact that confidence-inspiring people are themselves confident doesn't help the argument.

(C) mentions nothing about the effects of faking confidence, so it's Outside the Scope.

(D) tells you that a lot of people who act confident really are confident. Maybe that's because they show their genuine confidence to the world. The fact in this choice makes it no more likely that pretending to be confident will have benefits.

(E) affirms what the stimulus suggested, that self-doubt doesn't necessarily help you succeed. But the author's argument is that pretending to be confident does help, and **(E)** doesn't reveal any useful information about that connection.

25. (D) Parallel Reasoning

Step 1: Identify the Question Type

The stem asks you to identify an argument with a "pattern of reasoning most similar to that" in the stimulus. In other words, this is a Parallel Reasoning question. With answer choices as long as those in this question, start by comparing the conclusion in the stimulus to the conclusions in the answers. Eliminate any choices in which the conclusions are different in type or strength. Then, compare the evidence in the remaining answer choices against that in the stimulus if need be.

Step 2: Untangle the Stimulus

The conclusion comes at the very end of the stimulus: a strike is likely. The evidence is just above: past experience indicates that the union is unlikely to agree to terms that would prevent the strike.

Step 3: Make a Prediction

The correct answer will have a conclusion that predicts an outcome is likely. It will base this on evidence that past behavior indicates that a relevant party will not take a course of action that could prevent the bad result.

Step 4: Evaluate the Answer Choices

(D) has a conclusion that matches the soft prediction in the stimulus: Lopez "probabl[y]" won't win the marathon. That's because his sponsors "are known" (from past experience) to be poor at keeping their athletes hydrated. This argument follows the pattern we identified in the stimulus. So, **(D)** is the correct answer.

(A) has a conclusion that is too strong—"we can be sure." And its evidence makes no reference to past history. It cannot be parallel to the argument in the stimulus.

(B) has a conclusion, like that in **(A)**, that is too strong—"will donate." Moreover, its evidence is a single decision, not a pattern of past conduct.

(C) has a conclusion that is different from the one in stimulus. The author of **(C)** is not predicting a bad result. Instead, this conclusion is a value judgment that a particular course of action wouldn't be a good idea. Because the conclusions in the stimulus and **(C)** are not parallel, the arguments as a whole cannot be parallel.

(E) is similar to **(A)** and **(B)**. The conclusion here is too strong ("will not"), and the evidence is not a record of past behavior.

26. (E) Assumption (Sufficient)

Step 1: Identify the Question Type

This Assumption question stem asks for a premise that would guarantee the validity of the argument in the stimulus. The question falls in the "Sufficient Assumption" category.

Step 2: Untangle the Stimulus

A Keyword, [*t*]*herefore*, highlights the conclusion: consumers who don't acquire detailed product information are behaving rationally. The evidence comes in two parts. First, acquiring product info is a pain in the neck. Second, it is irrational to put yourself through the trouble of acquiring that info *unless* you believe that the benefits of getting it will be great enough to justify the cost and effort. Notice that the author never says whether information-ignoring consumers actually believe that the benefits of their inaction outweigh its costs. The author assumes that these consumers believe that the benefits do not outweigh the headaches.

Step 3: Make a Prediction

The correct answer must state that information ignorers expect that the benefits involved in acquiring detailed product information will not outweigh the costs and difficulties.

Step 4: Evaluate the Answer Choices

(E) matches the prediction almost word for word and is correct. If you add this statement to the evidence in the stimulus, the argument's conclusion must follow.

(A) starts off on the wrong foot with the sufficient condition "[r]ational consumers who do not expect that the benefits outweigh the cost." The author's assumption is that those who don't bother to gather information expect the costs to outweigh the benefits. So, **(A)** doesn't tell you what the information ignorers believe, it tells you what rational consumers do.

(B) contains [*w*]*henever*, which is a sufficiency Keyword. In simplified form, **(B)** says: "If it's rational to ignore info, then it's irrational to acquire it." That allows you to add to the conclusion, but it doesn't link the argument's evidence to the conclusion. For that, you need to know what those who forego detailed information believe about the information's value. The conditional statement in **(B)** doesn't provide any link between the argument's evidence and conclusion, much less a sufficient assumption.

(C) contains a scope shift, one you might have seen coming. The stimulus says that consumers expect that the costs outweigh the benefits. This answer choice says that the costs actually do outweigh the benefits, but it doesn't say that consumers expect this to be the case. The statement in **(C)** is therefore Outside the Scope.

(D) gets the connection backward. The argument assumes that those ignore detailed information don't expect it to be valuable and concludes that these consumers are, therefore, rational. **(D)** tells you what rational consumers expect about the value of information, but it doesn't make any connection to those who don't bother to get information. So, this choice doesn't allow you to draw a conclusion about the rationality of those who ignore information.

Section IV: Reading Comprehension
Passage 1: Utility and Criminal Deterrence

Q#	Question Type	Correct	Difficulty
1	Global	D	★
2	Logic Function	B	★
3	Inference	E	★★
4	Logic Reasoning (Parallel Reasoning)	B	★
5	Global	A	★
6	Inference (EXCEPT)	C	★★

Passage 2: Mexican-American Proverbs

Q#	Question Type	Correct	Difficulty
7	Global	B	★
8	Logic Function	A	★
9	Detail	E	★★
10	Inference	B	★★
11	Inference	D	★★★
12	Inference	D	★★★

Passage 3: Evolutionary Psychology and Altruism

Q#	Question Type	Correct	Difficulty
13	Global	E	★★
14	Logic Reasoning (Method of Argument)	B	★★★★
15	Detail	C	★★
16	Detail	A	★
17	Logic Reasoning (Method of Argument)	E	★★
18	Inference	D	★★
19	Inference	C	★★★★

Passage 4: Dostoyevsky and the Radicals

Q#	Question Type	Correct	Difficulty
20	Global	E	★
21	Inference	B	★
22	Detail	A	★★
23	Inference	C	★★
24	Global	C	★★
25	Inference	C	★★★★
26	Inference	A	★★★
27	Inference	D	★★★

Passage 1: Utility and Criminal Deterrence

Step 1: Read the Passage Strategically

Sample Roadmap

line #	Keyword/phrase	¶ Margin notes
1	most effective	criminal deterrence
2	such as ... as opposed to	
3	such as ... currently	
4	On one side	
6	a product of	
8	suggest	√ one side: change beliefs, econ'y rehab
12	On the other side	
14	primarily	√ other side: ↑ fines/penalties law enforcem't deter
15	suggest	
17	the best	
18	However	
21	surprisingly	
22	complementary	actually complementary util. max reconciles
24	which holds	util. max reconciles
30	weighing them	balancing test
31	and then	
32	Using this ... framework,	criminal = rational dec.
35	According	
37	if	
40	Within this framework	
41	For instance	↑ ing costs/neg. deter
44	result in	↓ ing util./ ↓ chance of criminal choice
48	thereby	
50	such as	↑ non-crim. good also ↓ util. of crime
53	All else being equal	
54	will effectively	
55	This	
56	demonstrates	
57	the optimal ...	optimal approach includes both
58	approach	

Discussion

This passage opens directly with the **Topic**: a debate over effective deterrence of deliberate crimes. The author first makes sure you know the difference between "deliberate" crimes (planned or thought-out crimes such as fraud) and "impulsive" crimes (emotionally motivated crimes of passion). Next, the author lays out the two sides of the debate about how best to prevent deliberate crimes. The first side sees crime as a social problem and emphasizes social measures, such as increasing economic access for disadvantaged people and rehabilitating those who've been convicted of crimes, to deter it. The other side sees crime as the result of personal choice and calls for negative deterrence: increased law enforcement and stronger punishments. The author ends paragraph 1 with an unexpected twist that happens to outline the **Scope** of the passage as well: when crime is viewed through the lens of economics, the two sides of the debate over deterrence are "surprisingly complementary." As a strategic reader, you now know the author's **Purpose** as well: she'll explain the economic principle at work and how she sees it resolving the debate over deterrence.

In paragraph 2, the author explains the economic principle she says resolves the deterrence debate. Called "utility maximization," it holds that rational decision makers will choose courses of action that will give them the greatest overall satisfaction. It works as a kind of balancing test. People facing choices, the principle holds, will weigh the chances of a positive outcome and their expected gain against the chances of a negative outcome and their possible loss. When this principle is applied to deliberate crimes, says the author, it shows that the choice to commit a crime is a rational decision.

Even before beginning paragraph 3, you know that here the author will explain how the utility maximization principle resolves the debate over deterring deliberate crime. First, the author lays out how the potential criminal weighs the incentives (what he has to gain from the crime if it works) against the disincentives (the chances of getting caught and the severity of the punishment). It's because of this balancing, the author says, that both sides of the deterrence debate are valid. The negative deterrents make the disincentives to crime stronger. When the potential criminal realizes he's more likely to be caught or that punishment is likely to be greater, his rational choice will be against committing the crime. Likewise, when social measures make it possible to get benefits without committing crimes, the positive incentives are decreased. The author closes with a summary of her **Main Idea**: the principle of utility maximization shows that the strongest deterrent will include policies that decrease incentives and increase disincentives to those who consider committing deliberate crimes.

1. (D) Global

Step 2: Identify the Question Type

This straightforward Global question calls for the author's "main point." Use your summary of the author's Main Idea to predict the correct answer.

Step 3: Research the Relevant Text

Here, the author stated an explicit conclusion at the end of the passage. Like your Main Idea summary, the correct answer will paraphrase the passage's final sentence.

Step 4: Make a Prediction

The passage's Main Idea is that the principle of utility maximization shows that the strongest deterrent will include policies that decrease incentives and increase disincentives to those who consider committing deliberate crimes. Use that as your prediction of what the correct answer will say.

Step 5: Evaluate the Answer Choices

(D) paraphrases the author's conclusion and the passage's Main Idea. It uses the gloss "both sides in the debate" instead of going into detail about incentives and disincentives, but it's the only answer that accurately summarizes the passage's big picture.

(A) is incomplete. While it accurately describes the author's application of the utility maximization principle to criminal behavior, it leaves out the entire discussion of how this shows that both sides of the deterrence debate have merit.

(B) is a Distortion of the first paragraph's description of the two sides in the deterrence debate. The first side in the debate believes crime is caused by external forces (the "influence of societal norms and institutions," lines 6–7), while the other side believes crime is a matter of personal choice (lines 14–15). But the author's point is *not* that legal scholars have discovered that both sides are right about what motivates criminal behavior; it's that utility maximization shows that the most effective deterrence includes elements of both sides' recommendations.

(C) is a classic Distortion wrong answer. The author never says that utility maximization can quantify the effects of each side's deterrence measures; she simply says that the best deterrence efforts should include policies from both sides.

(E) is also a Distortion of the passage. This choice mashes together the application of utility maximization from paragraph 2 with the first side's explanation of what motivates deliberate crime from lines 14–15. The author never implies that being able to see criminal behavior as the choice of rational decision makers means that social forces have no influence. In fact, the author believes that utility maximization shows that both sides in the debate make valid points.

2. (B) Logic Function

Step 2: Identify the Question Type

The phrase "in order to" identifies this as a Logic Function question, asking why the author mentioned "crimes of passion" in the first paragraph. Your Roadmap has everything you need to answer this question efficiently.

Step 3: Research the Relevant Text

The Keyword phrase "such as" right before "crimes of passion" tells you that the author uses such crimes as an example of "impulsive crimes," which, in turn, she contrasts with deliberate crimes, the prevention of which is the Topic of the passage.

Step 4: Make a Prediction

The correct answer will put the reference to crimes of passion in context, noting that the author is using the reference to contrast impulsive and deliberate crimes.

Step 5: Evaluate the Answer Choices

(B) matches the prediction and explains precisely why the author mentioned "crimes of passion." By giving an example of crimes that are not deliberate, she helps define what is deliberate.

(A) is a 180. Crimes of passion are not deliberate; they're impulsive. That's the point of the author's example.

(C) is a Distortion of the author's Purpose. Although she's interested in examining the best ways to deter deliberate crimes, she never says other types cannot be deterred.

(D) is premature. The author will not begin explaining the two sides of the debate until line 4, in the sentence that follows the quote in this question's stem. What's more, the two sides are debating how to deter deliberate crimes, and crimes of passion are offered as an example of impulsive crimes.

(E), like **(D)**, jumps the gun on what the author is discussing. In the sentence that follows the reference to crimes of passion, the author will tell you that the first side of the debate argues that society influences the likelihood of deliberate crimes. But, as the Keywords indicate, the author contrasts crimes of passion with deliberate crimes.

3. (E) Inference

Step 2: Identify the Question Type

This question stem asks what the passage "suggests," making this an Inference question. Make sure to note the word *least*. Here, the four incorrect answer choices will follow from the passage, while the correct answer will not. Note, too, that this question has the flavor of Parallel Reasoning. The four incorrect answer choices describe situations in which someone uses the utility maximization principle laid out in the passage to make a rational decision. The correct answer will either describe someone who rejects utility maximization or simply acts in some other way.

Step 3: Research the Relevant Text

The author defines the economic principle of utility maximization in paragraph 2. At lines 25–28, she tells you that, under the principle, a rational actor will seek to maximize "anticipated overall satisfaction." The remainder of the paragraph explains that this means a kind of balancing test between the likelihood and value of success versus the likelihood and detriment of failure.

Step 4: Make a Prediction

As you evaluate the choices, reject answers in which the person described seeks maximum "expected utility" by weighing the potential benefits and detriments of a course of action. While the decisions described in the answer choices all deal with potentially illegal activity, the point is not what kind of action the actor is thinking about; it's whether he's using the utility maximization rationale to make his decision.

Step 5: Evaluate the Answer Choices

(E) has a worker choosing violent action based on emotion and frustration. This sounds more like a "crime of passion" than a rational decision based on assessing expected utility. That makes it the right answer to this question that asks for the answer that "least" follows from the passage.

(A) is wrong because the actor is making a rational decision according to the utility maximization principle. He's deemed the potential downside to be very unlikely.

(B) is wrong because the motorist's choice is rational in light of utility maximization. While speeding would get her to the destination faster, she's judged the potential downside as very likely.

(C) is wrong because, although the industrialist's action may be reprehensible, it is rational from the perspective of utility maximization. Even if he were caught, the fine he'd pay is less than the cost of cleaning up his plant's pollution.

(D) is wrong because, although the government official may be desperate, she's making a rational utility maximization decision. She's choosing to solicit bribes because she's judged the potential upside to be worth the risk of prosecution.

4. (B) Logic Reasoning (Parallel Reasoning)

Step 2: Identify the Question Type

This question mimics Parallel Reasoning questions from the Logical Reasoning section by asking for the answer "most similar" to the reasoning of the legal scholars described in the passage. Research the way the legal scholars use the utility maximization principle and then find the answer in which someone uses the same kind of reasoning in an argument.

Step 3: Research the Relevant Text

The author describes how legal scholars have used utility maximization at the end of the first paragraph. In lines 18–22, you learn that legal scholars borrowed the principle from the field of economics and applied it to the debate over deterrence. It's also relevant that the legal scholars used utility maximization to show that two things that appeared contradictory were actually complementary.

Step 4: Make a Prediction

Based on your research, you know that the correct answer will describe a scholar from one field borrowing an established principle from a different field to resolve an apparent discrepancy within his own field. Don't concern yourself with the subject matter in the answer choices; look for a similar use of a principle borrowed from another field of study.

Step 5: Evaluate the Answer Choices

(B) is the only choice that matches the legal scholars' use of utility maximization. Here, an art professor borrows the rules of optics from physics in order to show that lines that appear to diverge are actually parallel.

(A) is a Distortion of the passage. Here, the astronomer borrows the paradox, not to resolve a discrepancy, but rather as a metaphor to describe a discovery made in her field. The legal scholars in the passage don't use utility maximization as a metaphor.

(C) is too vague to qualify as parallel with the situation in the passage. The botanist borrows a quotation, not a rule or principle from another field of scholarship. And she does so in order "to make a point." There's no way to tell whether that point is comparable to the legal scholars' resolution of two seemingly opposed views.

(D) has tempting language, but it doesn't match the passage. You may have been attracted to the similarity between legal scholars and judges, but that turns out to be nothing more than distraction. The judge simply applies evidence from a scholarly field to justify his ruling. This is not analogous to a scholar from one subject using principles from another to resolve a discrepancy.

(E) misses the point of the passage entirely. This choice doesn't have scholars or professors borrowing principles or rules from scholars in other fields. Moreover, the mediator here uses a borrowed quotation to "set a [positive] tone" for a bargaining session. That's quite different from resolving a scholarly debate.

5. (A) Global

Step 2: Identify the Question Type

This is a Global question because the correct answer must describe the entire passage. Unlike correct answers in the more common "main point" or "primary purpose" Global questions, the correct answer here will describe the passage's organization. Use your Roadmap to summarize the steps the author takes paragraph by paragraph.

Step 3: Research the Relevant Text

Looking at your margin notes, you see that paragraph 1 introduced the debate over deterrence and told you that legal scholars have applied an economic principle to it; paragraph 2 describes the principle; and paragraph 3 describes how the principle shows that both sides of the debate have merit and that the two sides' recommendations can be used together.

Step 4: Make a Prediction

The answer choices are relatively brief, so you know that the correct answer will be a very high-level summary of the passage. Expect the right answer to say something like: "The author describes both sides of a debate and shows how the introduction of a principle has reconciled them."

Step 5: Evaluate the Answer Choices

(A) matches the outline of the passage made in the prediction. It's the only choice that accurately states that the author introduces and resolves a debate.

(B) is a Distortion. In the passage, the economic principle shows that the two sides of the debate are compatible; it doesn't "decide between them."

(C) is a 180. In the passage, the principle shows that both sides of the debate have value; it doesn't "discredit them."

(D) is a Distortion of the passage, getting the relationship between the principle and the sides of the debate backward. The solutions offered in the debate don't instantiate (give concrete evidence of support for) the principle. Rather, the principle illustrates how the solutions offered in the debate can be used together.

(E) mangles the order of the passage and its use of the principle. In the passage, the author introduces the two sides of the debate before she brings up the principle. Also, the principle reconciles the two sides of the debate and does not highlight their differences.

6. (C) Inference (EXCEPT)

Step 2: Identify the Question Type

The word *suggests* identifies this as an Inference question. The "EXCEPT" at the end of the question stem means that the correct answer will not follow from the text; it may contradict the passage or simply be outside its scope. All four wrong answer choices, on the other hand, will be true based on what's in the passage.

Step 3: Research the Relevant Text

There's no specific reference clue in the stem to guide your research to a specific paragraph or detail. Use your Scope, Purpose, and Main Idea summaries to eliminate wrong answer choices or to identify the right answer (the one that contradicts or distorts the author's points or misses her Scope entirely).

Step 4: Make a Prediction

With an Inference EXCEPT question, it may be easier to predict what the incorrect answer choices will say than to predict what the correct answer will contain. A quick glance at the answer choices shows that all five speculate about what will happen to the crime rate under different circumstances. The four incorrect answer choices, then, will all correctly apply the lessons of utility maximization to the deterrence of deliberate crime. It's likely to increase when prospective criminals determine crime will pay more than obeying the law does or when they expect punishment to be unlikely or light. It's likely to go down when those same people expect poor returns on their criminal activity or anticipate being caught more easily or punished more severely.

Step 5: Evaluate the Answer Choices

(C) contradicts the passage and is thus the right answer to this Inference EXCEPT question. If those considering crime expect diminished returns from lawful activity, the economic principle would predict an increase in crime.

(A) follows directly from the passage. Decreasing expected utility (or, if you like, increasing the negatives) should reduce crime rates, according to the author.

(B) agrees with the utility maximization principle. Since increasing the lawful opportunities available to those considering crime will lower the crime rate, ending programs to assist criminals in finding a way to gain legitimate utility would likely increase crime.

(D) applies the reasoning in the passage correctly. If expected utility from lawful activity decreases, individuals are more likely to find crime a rational opportunity.

(E) is a straightforward implication of utility maximization as the author applies it to deliberate crime. When law enforcement increases, rational decision makers are more likely to decide crime is not worth the risk, thus driving the crime rate down.

Passage 2: Mexican-American Proverbs

Step 1: Read the Passage Strategically

Sample Roadmap

line #	Keyword/phrase	¶ Margin notes
2	rich and varied	Mex-Am proverbs
3	as well as	
4	refers	def.
7	great majority	
9	though ... did not	
10	in fact	
11	exact equivalents	Mex. proverbs from Sp./Europe
13	individual	
14	varies depending on	Each use is particular
16	Nonetheless ... important	
19	often serve a didactic purpose	but soc'l function: educate
20	important	
21	":"	
22	more ...	more in Mex-Am than Eng.
23	prominent ... than	
29	a particularly frequent	Ev.
30	":"	
31	most frequently used ... for example	esp'ly peer relations
34	derives from	
36	or from	preserve trad comm/family
37	especially	
40	Another dimension	Another function: ethnicity
42	consciousness of ethnicity	
45	Even	even non-instruct'n'l keeps culture
47	nevertheless serve	
49	links to	
50	are established and maintained	↑ Mex-Am ID and trad'n
51	thus	
52	thereby	

Discussion

In its very first sentence, this passage uses positive emphasis/opinion Keywords—"rich and varied" and *vital*—to introduce the **Topic**: Mexican American proverbs and their use. As a strategic reader, you can anticipate that the author will continue to celebrate these proverbs as he further defines the **Scope** of the passage, exploring the variety of proverbs and their function. First, though, he uses the rest of paragraph 1 to give you a little more background. Lines 4–8 define the term *proverb*, a saying that carries a message or nugget of wisdom. Note the location of this definition in your margin notes. The rest of paragraph 1 tells you where Mexican American proverbs came from. While they came to Mexico from Spain, many proverbs are actually from a common pool of European proverbs and have "exact equivalents" in English.

Paragraph 2 is long, so use Keywords to identify the pieces of text that will be important for the LSAT, places where the author makes clear his purpose or point of view. A number of emphasis Keywords—*important, prominent, particularly, frequently*, and *especially*—highlight the author's takeaways. The bulk of the paragraph is about "one important function" (line 20), the "didactic" (that is, instructional or educational) use of proverbs in Mexican American communities. In fact, the author tells you, this particular use of proverbs is "much more prominent" (lines 22–23) in Mexican American traditions than it is in their English-speaking counterparts. The author provides evidence that Mexican American parents use proverbs for all kinds of instruction, but he focuses on their "particularly frequent" (line 29) use for regulating children's peer-group relationships. The author finds this point so important that he illustrates it with an example (lines 31–33). (This should put you, the strategic reader, on alert for an LSAT question about why the author includes the example or how he uses it in the text.) The author concludes paragraph 2 by offering a couple of possible sociological reasons for the emphasis on peer-group relationships.

Paragraph 3 kicks off with "[a]nother dimension," telling you the author will be exploring another function of proverbs in the Mexican American community: They "serve to foster a consciousness of ethnicity." Knowing and using these proverbs, says the author, allows for distinct identity within a multicultural milieu. He emphasizes that even nondidactic proverbs make users and hearers aware of folklore and traditional culture and "thus provide" (line 51) ties to Mexican heritage that make young people feel more familiar with and connected to Mexican tradition. In this passage the author has no critics or opponents, so his **Purpose** is simply "to tell" or "to explain." And the **Main Idea** is what he's explaining: proverbs are important in Mexican American culture, because parents use them to instruct children and they keep people aware of Mexican traditions and ethnic identity.

7. (B) Global

Step 2: Identify the Question Type

This standard Global question stem calls for the "main point of the passage." Use your summary of the Main Idea to predict the correct answer.

Step 3: Research the Relevant Text

There's no need to re-read the passage here. As a strategic reader, you've already summarized the author's Main Idea.

Step 4: Make a Prediction

Use the Main Idea summary to identify the correct answer. Remember that the correct answer must correspond to the entire passage and that one or more of the wrong answer choices, while not distorting the passage, may focus too narrowly on details or subpoints. The Main Idea summary as stated previously was "Proverbs are important in Mexican American culture, because parents use them to instruct children and they keep people aware of Mexican traditions and ethnic identity."

Step 5: Evaluate the Answer Choices

(B) matches the prediction and accurately summarizes the main point of the passage. This choice notes the prominence of proverbs in Mexican American culture and accurately paraphrases both of the functions the author talked about.

(A) misstates one of the author's points; he says Spanish proverbs were similar to those in other European traditions. This choice also omits any mention of the didactic or ethnic identity functions of proverbs, which the author spends most of the passage discussing.

(C) is too narrow. It accurately paraphrases the end of paragraph 1, but that's not enough to count as the "main point of the passage."

(D) comes entirely from paragraph 2. This choice is too narrow to constitute the "main point of the passage."

(E) distorts the author's Purpose. The passage is intended to outline the use of proverbs in the Mexican American community, not to use Spanish-language proverbs as an illustration of how proverbs are used cross-culturally.

8. (A) Logic Function

Step 2: Identify the Question Type

If you read the passage strategically, this Logic Function question should have come as no surprise. It asks why the author offers the example at lines 32–33. Consult your Roadmap, and you can predict the correct answer perfectly.

Step 3: Research the Relevant Text

A glance at paragraph 2 reminds you that the saying quoted at lines 32–33 is one of the proverbs "most frequently used" by parents to instruct adolescents about peer-group relationships, which are a "particularly frequent focus" of proverbs in the Mexican American community.

Step 4: Make a Prediction

The illustration Keywords *for example* (line 31) tells you how to phrase your prediction. The author quotes the proverb to illustrate how Mexican American parents use proverbs to instruct children about peer-group relationships.

Step 5: Evaluate the Answer Choices

(A) is a perfect match for the prediction and an ideal expression of the author's reason for quoting the proverb in the text. It's in there to illustrate how proverbs are used to provide instruction about peer-group relationships.

(B) is Outside the Scope. The author isn't discussing the *tone* of Mexican American proverbs at this point (or indeed, anywhere) in the passage.

(C) is a Faulty Use of Detail. The link between proverbs and "traditional wisdom" comes later in paragraph 2 (line 38), where the author gives reasons why Mexican American parents may be concerned about their children's peer-group relationships. The Keywords that introduce the proverb in the text ("for example," line 31), however, makes it clear that the proverb is included to illustrate what the author said just *before* it.

(D) is a Faulty Use of Detail and a Distortion of the author's purpose in quoting the proverb. In paragraph 1, the author tells you that many Spanish proverbs have English-language equivalents and, of course, tells you that the proverb at lines 32–33 is "roughly translated" into English. But the author did not include the proverb in the passage "in order to" illustrate the ease of translation, so this choice doesn't correctly answer the question stem.

(E) misstates the author's reason for including the proverb. At no point in the passage does the author express an opinion on how effective proverbs are as instructional tools.

9. (E) Detail

Step 2: Identify the Question Type

The wording of this Detail question stem is a little unusual; it provides for answers in the form of questions. But the correct answer is a question that can be answered directly by information the "passage provides." So, use the answer choices to research the text and eliminate the four answers that cannot be determined from the passage.

Step 3: Research the Relevant Text

There are no research clues in this question stem. You'll need to use the answer choices to target details in the passage that would answer the question posed by the correct answer choice.

Step 4: Make a Prediction

Although you can't predict the wording of the correct answer—after all, the passage provides information that could answer several questions—you know that it will be within the Scope of the passage and will not contradict or distort the author's Main Idea. Moreover, a quick glance at the answer choices reveals that most or all deal with similarities and differences among Mexican American, Spanish-language, and English-language proverbs. Paragraphs 1 and 2 will help you identify the right answer or eliminate the wrong ones.

Step 5: Evaluate the Answer Choices

(E) is a question the passage answers. Lines 22–24 tell you directly that didactic use of proverbs is more common in Mexican traditions than it is in English-speaking ones. This is the correct answer.

(A) is a Distortion. In paragraph 1, you learn that the "great majority" of Mexican proverbs came from Spain. Many of these, it turns out, are proverbs that existed in other languages as well. But the passage never tells you where else Mexican proverbs may have originated. You can't answer the question in this choice from information in the passage.

(B) is Outside the Scope. The author never discusses the origins of English-language proverbs beyond saying that some came from a common European pool. You can't tell from the passage whether any came to English from Mexican American sources.

(C) is a Distortion. In paragraph 2, the author tells you that instructional proverbs are more common in Mexican than in English-language traditions. But be careful: that says nothing about what is in the English-language proverbs.

(D) is Outside the Scope. The author simply doesn't discuss the proverbs of any ethnic group or community other than Mexican Americans. You can't answer this choice's question from information in the passage.

10. (B) Inference

Step 2: Identify the Question Type

"[M]ost strongly suggests" is common Inference question language. The correct answer will be true based on the passage. The research clue is "the use of proverbs," which tells you the correct answer will come from paragraphs 2 or 3.

Step 3: Research the Relevant Text

Review your margin notes rather than diving into a deep re-reading of all this text. As you should have noted, the opening sentence of paragraph 2 announces the author's overall view of proverb use: It "varies depending on the individual speaker and … social context." From there, the author goes into the didactic, or instructional, use of proverbs by Mexican Americans. The author emphasizes the importance of peer-group relationships in this use context. Paragraph 3 tells about another use of proverbs: fostering ethnic identity and group membership.

Step 4: Make a Prediction

The correct answer will follow from one of the points you noted in the Research step. Don't re-read two-thirds of the passage before evaluating the answer choices. Your Roadmap will allow you to eliminate wrong answer choices and zero in on the one choice that must be true based on the passage.

Step 5: Evaluate the Answer Choices

(B) is correct. It follows from the very first sentence of paragraph 2 and is consistent with everything in paragraphs 2 and 3. The use of the qualifier "at least in part" ensures that the wording of the choice is not too extreme.

(A) is a 180. This answer flies in the face of what you learn about Mexican American parents near the end of paragraph 2. Proverbs are used to instruct children because the parents "sense that traditional, community-approved norms are threatened" (lines 34–35).

(C) is Extreme. While peer-group relationships are "a particularly frequent focus" of didactic proverbs, the passage does say not it constitutes the most frequent use of proverbs in Mexican American communities overall.

(D) is Outside the Scope. Paragraph 3 tells you that proverbs do serve "as vehicle for the transmission of ... the Spanish language" (lines 47–48), but this is an unintended effect of nondidactic use. Nowhere does the passage state or imply that proverbs are used for the purpose of language instruction.

(E) is a Distortion of the passage. Between paragraphs 2 and 3, the author notes that proverbs have more than one function. But that doesn't mean that the user *intends* for proverbs to have multiple consequences. Indeed, the author states that those proverbs without an "explicitly didactic purpose *nevertheless* serve" additional social functions (lines 46–47, emphasis added).

11. (D) Inference

Step 2: Identify the Question Type

This is an open-ended Inference question stem. The correct answer will be true based on the author's position in the passage.

Step 3: Research the Relevant Text

There is no clue in the question stem to guide your research. Use your Purpose and Main Idea summaries to get a handle on what the author says. The right answer will agree with the author's point of view, while the wrong answer choices will distort or contradict the author or miss the passage's Scope.

Step 4: Make a Prediction

As stated at the end of Step 1, the author's Purpose and Main Idea are to explain that proverbs are important in Mexican American culture and that parents use them to instruct children and keep people aware of Mexican traditions and ethnic identity. If you need to go back to the passage text, use individual answer choices as research clues.

Step 5: Evaluate the Answer Choices

(D) gets explicit support from the end of paragraph 2. At lines 34–39, the author explains why Mexican American parents use proverbs to regulate their children's peer-group relationships: the parents "sense that traditional, community-approved norms are threatened ... [and] need to appeal to traditional wisdom to bolster their authority."

(A) is a Distortion of paragraph 1. The majority of Mexican proverbs originated in Spain, and "many" of those are part of the common European tradition. That's not enough to conclude that *most* Mexican American proverbs are part of the wider tradition.

(B) is a Distortion of paragraph 2. There, you learn that Mexican American parents are more likely to use proverbs didactically than are English-speaking parents. That's a far cry from saying that they "emphasize the value of traditional wisdom" more than "other parents in the United States."

(C) is another Distortion of the information in paragraph 1. There, the author tells you that many of Mexican proverbs that originated in Spain are part of the common European proverb pool. He makes no comparison between the overall number of Spanish-language proverbs and the overall number of pan-European proverbs.

(E) is a 180. According to line 11, many European proverbs have "exact equivalents" in more than one language. Moreover, the author offers an English translation of the proverb at lines 32–33 to illustrate his point about peer-group instruction, thus suggesting he finds the translation accurate enough to be understood.

12. (D) Inference

Step 2: Identify the Question Type

This is an open-ended Inference question stem. The correct answer will follow from statements in the passage, but there is no specific research clue pointing you to a reference or detail.

Step 3: Research the Relevant Text

There is no clue in the question stem to guide your research. Use your Purpose and Main Idea summaries to get a handle on what the author says. The right answer will agree with the author's point of view, while the incorrect answer choices will distort or contradict the author or miss the passage's Scope.

Step 4: Make a Prediction

As stated at the end of Step 1, the author's Purpose and Main Idea are to explain that proverbs are important in Mexican American culture and that parents use them to instruct children and keep people aware of Mexican traditions and ethnic identity. If you need to go back to the passage text, use individual answer choices as research clues.

Step 5: Evaluate the Answer Choices

(D) is the correct answer choice. Like the correct answer to this passage's first Inference question, it is supported explicitly by the first sentence of paragraph 2. That sentence (lines 13–16) makes the point that even when the words of the proverb are identical, its meaning is shaped by who says it and in what context.

(A) contains a Faulty Use of Detail and is a Distortion of the author's point. The author notes that one didactic use of proverbs is "the inculcation of table manners" (lines 27–28), but he doesn't connect that to how proverbs serve to foster consciousness of ethnicity, let alone to say that ethnic identification is the proverb's "primary purpose" in that instance.

(B) is Extreme. The author discusses only the Mexican American community and its use of proverbs. The passage does not support the claim that proverbs in any community have an ethnic identity function.

(C) is Outside the Scope. The author doesn't compare or contrast Mexican Americans' use of proverbs with that of Spanish-language speakers anywhere else in the world.

(E) is a Distortion of the author's emphasis in paragraph 2. While the author does say that peer-group relationships are a "particularly frequent focus" of didactic proverb use in Mexican American families, he doesn't say that this topic is not of concern in other American communities or that parents in these communities don't try to teach their children about its importance in their own ways.

Passage 3: Evolutionary Psychology and Altruism

Step 1: Read the Passage Strategically

Sample Roadmap

line #	Keyword/phrase	¶ Margin notes
Passage A		
1		ev. psych
2–5		def.
6	thereby	
9	thorny … :	So, why altruism?
12	?	
13	probably lies in	Auth: prob'ly ident'y and empathy
15	could have … arisen in response to	
16		poss. orig.
20	thereby	could have helped kin
23	for example	
25	may thus	explains beh'v'r
27	Since	
30	Later	
31		from kin, extended to local groups
Passage B		
35	conspiracy …	ev. psych
36	theory	genes "conspire to reproduce"
38	Indeed	
39	Thus	
43	appear persuasive	Ex. child care and monogamous families
44		
50	take this as evidence	
52	?	is ev. psych right?
53	Maybe yes, maybe no	Auth: not sure
54	needs … handled with great care	
56		multiple motives for beh'v'r
58	*only* if	
59	But … vanishingly … :	ev. psych overlooks alt. causes
63	but so too	
64	Not all of … motives	maybe ppl. just care about kids
65	instrumental	

Discussion

In the first paragraph of passage A, the author introduces the **Topic**: the field of evolutionary psychology and a "thorny" issue—altruism—its practitioners have tried to explain. Evolutionary psychology, the author tells you, explains human behavior by looking at how a behavior increases a person's reproductive success, thus spreading the gene that causes the behavior. This approach makes it tricky for evolutionary psychologists to explain altruism, a behavior in which the actor uses his own energy to preserve the life of someone else.

The beginning of paragraph 2 announces the **Scope**—the "answer probably lies in"—and sets up the rest of passage A, which will outline evolutionary psychology's hypothesis for why humans are altruistic. The keys to altruism, according to evolutionary psychology, are "identification and empathy." These began because they made it more likely that a person would help his or her kin, people with whom the actor shared genetic material. The paragraph ends with the example of a mother helping a child, even at risk to herself.

Paragraph 3 explains how these behaviors expanded to general human behavior. Early in human evolution, people "lived in small, kin-based groups." At that time, altruism would certainly have benefitted others with whom the altruistic individual shared genes. Later, as humans lived in larger groups, people grew to behave altruistically toward unrelated people as well. It's worth noting that the author of passage A doesn't critique or evaluate evolutionary psychology or its altruism hypothesis. His **Purpose** is best described as "to explain" or "to outline." The **Main Idea** is what he's explaining: Evolutionary psychology hypothesizes that altruism grew out of identification with and empathy toward kin and grew to include others.

You know right off that the author of passage B takes a negative view of the same **Topic**: evolutionary psychology. She calls it "a kind of conspiracy theory." That's strong language relative to the typically academic prose used in LSAT Reading Comprehension. Pay close attention to see what she means by this provocative statement. As she explains in the rest of paragraph 1, evolutionary psychology explains behavior due to influences of which people are unaware (the goal of genes to propagate themselves). So, she says, evolutionary psychology casts genes in the role of conspirators. As a strategic reader, you should note two things. First, of course, is the author's negative tone. Second, the author has not, to this point, said anything about altruism. Always, in Comparative Reading, you want to keep track of both passages' Scopes. Questions will reward you for noting the similarities and differences.

The second author's skeptical tone continues in paragraph 2: Evolutionary psychology's explanations can "appear persuasive on the face of it." She is going to tell us why we

should doubt them when we dig a little deeper, but she doesn't do so yet. The rest of paragraph 2 simply goes through an evolutionary psychology argument: Humans evolved monogamy "because of our interest in propagating our genes." She ends the paragraph with a question that establishes this passage's **Scope**: "Are they [the evolutionary psychologists] right?"

Paragraph 3 states and supports the author's answer to the question: "Maybe yes, maybe no." As the paragraph progresses, the author's **Purpose** becomes clear: to *caution against* hasty acceptance of evolutionary psychology's hypotheses. The author presents her evidence several ways—abstractly, at lines 60–61; with a concrete example, at lines 61–64; and just sort of conversationally, at lines 64–66. But her point boils down to one basic premise: Unless we find a behavior that "would be reasonable *only* if" people have an interest in propagating their genes, we cannot be sure that the evolutionary psychology explanations are right. Passage B's **Main Idea** is this: Don't be hasty in accepting evolutionary explanations for behaviors that might have multiple causes or influences.

The two passages are similar in Topic and Scope; both examine evolutionary psychology's explanation of certain aspects of human behavior (specifically, altruism in passage A and monogamy in passage B). But the Purposes are quite different: passage A just explains or outlines evolutionary psychology's explanation (there's a tacit acceptance of the theory), while passage B cautions against embracing evolutionary psychology's approach. The two authors seem to have a similar understanding of evolutionary psychology, but the author of passage B is explicitly unconvinced by its findings.

13. (E) Global

Step 2: Identify the Question Type

This is a sort of "mini" Global question, asking for the "main point" of passage A. Use your Main Idea summary to predict the correct answer.

Step 3: Research the Relevant Text

There is no gain in re-reading for Global questions, provided that you summarized the passage during your initial strategic read. Here, you should have had something along the lines of the Main Idea summary above: Evolutionary psychology hypothesizes that altruism grew out of identification with and empathy toward kin and grew to include others.

Step 4: Make a Prediction

Use the Main Idea to identify the correct answer or to eliminate those that contradict or distort the passage and those that venture outside the Scope or are too narrow.

Step 5: Evaluate the Answer Choices

(E) paraphrases the first passage's outline of the evolutionary psychology explanation for altruistic behavior, just as you predicted.

(A) is too narrow. It accurately states why the author of passage A called altruism a "thorny" issue in paragraph 1, but it doesn't include anything about the theory's explanation for altruism.

(B) is a Distortion of the passage. Nothing indicates that there is "[n]ew evidence" in the study of altruism and genetic success.

(C) is a 180. The passage suggests that altruism spread as people moved from living in small, kin-based societies to larger, more diverse ones. If anything, that suggests that altruism continues to be an evolutionarily adaptive behavior.

(D) is a Distortion of passage A's Purpose. The author doesn't acknowledge or engage critics of evolutionary psychology. This author seems to tacitly accept evolutionary psychology—it "has taught us" (line 1)—but there's no way to say that the passage's main point is that its critics are wrong.

14. (B) Logic Reasoning (Method of Argument)

Step 2: Identify the Question Type

Treat this one like a Method of Argument question from the Logical Reasoning section. The correct answer will describe *how* the two passages approach the Topic differently.

Step 3: Research the Relevant Text

There's no need to re-read in order to get a handle on this question. You know from summarizing each passage's Purpose and Main Idea that the author of passage A tacitly accepts the theory of evolutionary psychology and wants to outline one of its hypotheses, while the author of passage B is skeptical about the basis of the theory and wants to caution against accepting its findings.

Step 4: Make a Prediction

Use your summaries from Step 3 to identify the correct answer or to eliminate those that contradict or distort what the two authors said.

Step 5: Evaluate the Answer Choices

(B) accurately reflects the difference between the two authors' approaches. Passage A seems comfortable with the foundations of evolutionary psychology, while the author of passage B is far more skeptical.

(A) is Outside the Scope. It's unclear what **(A)** means by "logical implications." Both authors examine the practical application of evolutionary psychology theory to specific instances of human behavior. If anything, the author of passage B has more concerns about logical inconsistencies in the theory's ascription of causality to genetic self-

propagation than does the author of passage A. However you interpret this answer choice, it doesn't match the approaches of the two authors.

(C) is a 180. It's the author of passage B who says not all motives are "instrumental" (line 65), suggesting that some behaviors have explanations other than genetic reproductive success.

(D) is a Distortion. Nothing suggests that the author of passage B is skeptical of "evolutionary theory in general." It's a specific application of evolutionary theory to human behavior that she's concerned about.

(E) also distorts the Scope and Purpose of passage B. Its author doesn't impute any bad intentions to evolutionary psychologists. She just thinks there's a good chance they came up with wrong answers.

15. (C) Detail

Step 2: Identify the Question Type

This Detail question asks for a specific example used in passage B.

Step 3: Research the Relevant Text

A quick check of your Roadmap should show a margin note next to paragraph 2 identifying the only example that passage uses: monogamous families. The entirety of paragraph 3 is then given over to why the author thinks evolutionary psychology's explanation for monogamy is questionable.

Step 4: Make a Prediction

Your research produced a simple, accurate prediction of what the correct answer must say: monogamous families.

Step 5: Evaluate the Answer Choices

(C) matches the prediction and is correct. Evolutionary psychology's explanation for the practice of monogamy is the only example that passage B critiqued.

(A) is a Distortion. That early humans lived in small societies is a fact that evolutionary psychology uses in its explanation, not a behavior it attempts to explain.

(B) is a Distortion. The slow maturation of human infants is a biological fact noted by the evolutionary psychologists in their explanation; it's not a behavior they attempt to explain.

(D) is what the author of passage B accuses evolutionary psychologists of doing. It's not an example of something the evolutionary psychologists try to explain.

(E) is what the author of passage B offers as an alternative explanation (rather than gene propagation) for why certain human behaviors may exist.

16. (A) Detail

Step 2: Identify the Question Type

You know this is a Detail question right from the opening phrase: "According to passage A … ." The correct answer here will contain something passage A cites as a cause of certain human behaviors.

Step 3: Research the Relevant Text

The author explains evolutionary psychology in paragraph 1. It holds that certain human behaviors evolved because the genes of individuals with those behaviors were more likely to spread into future generations. The rest of passage A is a detailed outline of how the theory is applied to a specific behavior: altruism. The underlying cause—gene propagation—is no different here.

Step 4: Make a Prediction

Throughout passage A, human behaviors are explained through evolutionary psychology. That is, behaviors evolved because those who had them were more genetically "successful."

Step 5: Evaluate the Answer Choices

(A) matches the prediction and is correct. This is the only choice that gets at the foundation of the evolutionary psychology theory.

(B) gets cause and effect backward. Altruism (unselfish action) is the behavior that evolved because the genes of those who practiced it were more likely to spread.

(C) is Outside the Scope. The passage doesn't give improved health of a person who behaves in a particular way as the reason for that behavior's evolution. Indeed, it suggests that the altruistic person would put herself at risk in order to help ensure the survival of others, which is why altruism has been a "thorny" problem for evolutionary psychology.

(D) is Outside the Scope. Passage A simply doesn't mention food-gathering ability.

(E) is a Distortion of the altruism example. The author says altruism was likely adaptive because humans lived in small, mutually dependent groups, not because it "prompted" them to live in such groups.

17. (E) Logic Reasoning (Method of Argument)

Step 2: Identify the Question Type

When the testmaker asks you how one argument or passage relates to another, you should think about the responding author's method of argument. In other words, you can word your prediction as "She proceeds by … ." Pay attention to Keywords and use them to describe how the passage or selection in question responds to the other one.

Step 3: Research the Relevant Text

While passage B may not have been written in response to passage A, it certainly tackles the same subject matter—evolutionary psychology theory—as does the first passage. A glance at your Roadmap makes clear that passage B tries to make you skeptical of the approach embraced by passage A. Passage B's third paragraph gives the reasons for doubt: Evolutionary psychology overlooks alternative explanations/causes for behaviors it attempts to explain.

Step 4: Make a Prediction

The correct answer will have to say that passage B calls into question the theory in passage A by pointing out what passage B's author takes to be faulty causal reasoning.

Step 5: Evaluate the Answer Choices

(E) uses somewhat generic language, but it correctly describes how passage B responds to the types of arguments made in passage A. "[R]elies on questionable reasoning" is simply a paraphrase for "uses faulty logic."

(A) is a 180. passage B's author wants to undermine the certainty about evolutionary psychology found in arguments like those in passage A.

(B) is Extreme. Passage B never claims that evolutionary psychology's finding are "clearly false." Indeed, after posing the question "Are they right?" at the end of paragraph 2, passage B's author responds with "Maybe yes, maybe no."

(C) is a Distortion of passage B's approach. The author of the second passage never says evolutionary psychologists are poor observers; rather, she suggests they may draw unwarranted conclusions from their observations.

(D) is a radical Distortion. passage B gives (at lines 56–59) the type of evidence that could confirm evolutionary psychology's findings. The author of passage B considers such cases "vanishingly rare," but that is not the same as saying she finds evolutionary psychology "vacuous" or unconfirmable.

18. (D) Inference

Step 2: Identify the Question Type

This question stem has shades of several other question types found on the LSAT. It takes the designation Inference because the correct answer is a statement that follows from what's said in passage B. But the correct answer is also something directly asserted in passage A (making this a bit like a Detail question), and it will serve to exemplify the reference to "conspiracy theory" in passage B (which is similar to what a Logic Function question might ask). Most important, use all of the research clues and make sure you are predicting the answer based on the question being asked.

Step 3: Research the Relevant Text

Passage B calls evolutionary psychology a "conspiracy theory" because it explains behavior by means of a cause (gene propagation) of which the person performing the behavior is unaware. Thus, the genes are "conspiring" behind the scenes. While the author of passage A would likely not appreciate the negative tone of passage B's characterization, he certainly doesn't disagree that those performing certain behaviors are unaware of underlying genetic mechanisms. Indeed, he concludes both paragraphs 2 and 3 by noting that apparently selfless behaviors are caused by genes "promoting their own self-propagation."

Step 4: Make a Prediction

The correct answer will almost certainly involve the "unseen" genetic self-interest causing outwardly selfless behavior by individuals. This is precisely the type of explanation passage B's author distrusts as a "conspiracy theory."

Step 5: Evaluate the Answer Choices

(D) fits the prediction to a T. It is an assertion from passage A (see lines 24–26), and it exemplifies the type of explanation passage B characterizes as a "conspiracy theory."

(A) is a Distortion of passage B's use of "conspiracy theory." The phrase is used to characterize what passage B's author considers questionable reasoning and findings of evolutionary psychologists, not the fact that they seek to use an evolutionary approach to studying human behavior.

(B) is a Faulty Use of Detail. This answer choice is an assertion made in passage A, but it has no relationship to what the author of passage B would call a "conspiracy theory," in which a hidden mechanism is cited as the cause of ostensible behavior.

(C) is another Faulty Use of Detail. The statement in this answer choice is simply an example of altruistic behavior. It's not related to evolutionary psychology's explanation for that behavior, which is what passage B called a "conspiracy theory."

(E) is yet another Faulty Use of Detail. This is simply a fact about early humans that figures into the evolutionary psychology explanation for altruism, but it has nothing to do with the "conspiratorial" underpinnings of the hypothesis that concern the author of passage B.

19. (C) Inference

Step 2: Identify the Question Type

The stem explicitly identifies this as an Inference question, but note the particular Comparative Reading task involved here. The correct answer will be an assumption in the argument laid out in passage A that the author of passage B considers flawed. This question is a cornucopia of LSAT tasks

and reasoning that will really reward the well-trained test taker who can leverage a variety of LSAT skills.

Step 3: Research the Relevant Text

Passage B's author makes quite clear what he thinks would make evolutionary psychology's finding valid. At lines 56–59, she says a behavior can be decisively explained by an interest when the behavior is reasonable *only* in light of the actor having that interest. Applying that rather abstract language to evolutionary psychology, passage B's author means, "For gene propagation to decisively explain a human behavior, you have to show that the behavior is reasonable *only if* there's an interest in gene propagation; if there's another possible interest in play, I'm not buying that explanation."

Step 4: Make a Prediction

Now, you can put your Formal Logic skills to work. "Only if" is a signal of necessity. So, passage B's author is saying, "An interest in gene propagation must be necessary to the behavior in order for gene propagation to be a convincing explanation." Now, remember what the question stem asks for: an assumption passage B's author would consider flawed. Since passage B's author considers an interest in gene propagation necessary to a behavior's explanation, she would consider an argument that says gene propagation is sufficient to explain a behavior as logically flawed. "Necessity versus Sufficiency" is, of course, one of the classic flaws you learn for the Logical Reasoning section, and this question is a great example of just how integrated LSAT skills are throughout the test.

Step 5: Evaluate the Answer Choices

(C) hits the nail on the head. The key is the phrase "it is sufficient to show," which highlights what passage B's author would consider a logical flaw: By treating evidence sufficient to show that genetic success is responsible for a given behavior as if it were necessary for the behavior, the evolutionary psychologists are overlooking alternative explanations that are just as likely. You may have noted that this choice uses the phrase "reproductive success" in place of "gene propagation" from the prediction above, but the passage tells you that genes are propagated by way of reproductive success.

(A) is Outside the Scope. Evolutionary psychology, as far as you can tell from the passage, doesn't concern itself with physical characteristics. So this is neither an assumption of the argument in passage A nor something the author of passage B would consider flawed.

(B) is a "double Distortion," mangling both passages A and B. First, the evolutionary psychology argument in passage A wouldn't consider any early behavior to be "orchestrated by ... genes." Behaviors might be completely random. They survive as "continuing" human behaviors because they benefit the genes. Moreover, passage B's author is concerned that evolutionary psychologists misuse evidence sufficient to show the genetic advantage of a behavior, not that they inappropriately assume gene propagation to be necessary for a behavior to occur.

(D) is Outside the Scope. Neither the evolutionary psychologists discussed in passage A nor the author of passage B opines on explanations of animal behavior.

(E) is Outside the Scope. Evolutionary psychologists probably do make the assumption stated in this answer choice, but the squabble between them and the author of passage B is over their explanation of behaviors that have not been eliminated over time.

Passage 4: Dostoyevsky and the Radicals

Step 1: Read the Passage Strategically

Sample Roadmap

line #	Keyword/phrase	¶ Margin notes
1	Dostoyevsky's time	
3	One position maintained	two opp. views in Russian lit crit
4	while ... radical ...	
5	view maintained ... only if	
9		Dos takes 3rd view
11	But	diff. btw Dos/radicals re: reality
13	since	
17	meaningless	
18		Dos view of reality—shaped by indiv.
22	another sphere	contains sphere of fantastic
26		Dos: rad view contradictory
33	contradiction in terms	
35	But	
36–40		Dos defines "artistic"
42		rad. view: art must be useful
44	unsatisfactory	
47		Dos: impossible to measure usefulness
51	because	

Discussion

The first sentence of the passage establishes the **Topic**: Russian literary criticism in Dostoyevsky's time. The subsequent sentences (lines 3–9) hint at **Scope**: Dostoyevsky's reaction to two opposing critical views. The first view holds that art supersedes everyday reality. Dostoyevsky, the author says, rejected this view outright—"reality was literature's crucial source" (lines 10–11). The second view (that of the radicals) claimed that art has to depict reality and effect social change. Dostoyevsky was closer to the radicals, but he split with them because he had a "deeper" understanding of reality (lines 11–13). The author gives two reasons for this assessment: Dostoyevsky made no theoretical distinction between reality and fantasy, and he saw reality as much more than "the merely tangible." As a strategic reader, you should anticipate that the next two paragraphs will deal with these critical distinctions.

Paragraph 2 elaborates on Dostoyevsky's understanding of reality and how fantasy relates to it. For Dostoyevsky, reality is shaped by individual experience, so that two people may have different experiences of reality. Lines 21–25 describe how the fantastic was a component of Dostoyevsky's concept of reality. Fantasy, he believed, is essential to the novelist's concerns.

Paragraph 3 draws a distinction between Dostoyevsky and the radical critics with regard to art's political role. The radicals believed that art's political purposes subsume any consideration of form. Dostoyevsky, not surprisingly, disagrees. The second half of the paragraph is devoted to Dostoyevsky's definition of what makes a literary work "artistic" in the first place: Characters and images must be clearly portrayed, and in the end, the artistic quality of a work boils down to "simply the ability to write well."

Paragraph 4 introduces still another point at issue between the radicals and Dostoyevsky: the requirement that art should be "useful" to society. To Dostoyevsky, attempting to qualitatively measure a work's usefulness is futile and unreliable.

The author's **Purpose** is to contrast Dostoyevsky's view of literature with those of the other two "camps" of Russian literary thought, particularly the ideas of the radical critics. And the **Main Idea**, which fulfills that Purpose, is that Dostoyevsky disagreed with the radicals when it came to the nature and role of reality in literature and whether or not "usefulness" is important in art.

20. (E) Global

Step 2: Identify the Question Type

The scope of the question stem is the passage as a whole—it asks you for the "main point." Therefore, this is a Global question.

Step 3: Research the Relevant Text

There's no text to research for a Global question like this. Instead, your Roadmap and understanding of the author's Purpose and Main Idea will guide you to a prediction.

Step 4: Make a Prediction

During your strategic reading of the passage during Step 1, you summarized the passage's Main Idea: that Dostoyevsky's literary view differed from that of the radicals concerning how reality should be depicted, whether art must serve a political purpose above all else, and whether art should be useful.

Step 5: Evaluate the Answer Choices

(E) is the best match for the prediction. This choice fits the passage's Scope perfectly and matches the author's list of contrasts between Dostoyevsky and the radicals.

(A) mischaracterizes Dostoyevsky's point of view. He didn't borrow from the two views mentioned in paragraph 1; his view was distinct and in opposition to both views.

(B) is a 180. Dostoyevsky never claimed, according to the passage, that literature should be removed from reality (lines 10–11). Moreover, had he held that view, it wouldn't have opposed the position of first group of critics (lines 3–4).

(C) doesn't incorporate the entirety of paragraphs 2 and 3, which detail other points of disagreement between Dostoyevsky and the radicals. This choice's statement that Dostoyevsky and the radicals differed "solely" over the issue of usefulness is a Distortion of the passage.

(D) is true according to the passage but too narrow to constitute the Main Idea. It doesn't take into account paragraphs 3 and 4, which move away from ideas about the depiction of reality to concerns about the nature and usefulness of art itself.

21. (B) Inference

Step 2: Identify the Question Type

This is an Inference question, since it asks for an answer choice that Dostoyevsky would have characterized as artistic. You'll have to take what's in the passage and carry it one logical step further.

Step 3: Research the Relevant Text

According to your Roadmap, Dostoyevsky defines what makes a work "artistic" in paragraph 3 (lines 36–41 specifically). He is quoted as saying that artistry rests in the ability of an author to communicate thoughts through characters and images so that the reader can perceive those thoughts.

Step 4: Make a Prediction

The correct answer will be supported by lines 36–41. Look for the answer that matches Dostoyevsky's mention of fictionalizing one's thoughts through characters and images.

Step 5: Evaluate the Answer Choices

(B) matches Dostoyevsky's definition almost to the letter, since it expresses an author's ideas through characters and events. **(B)** is therefore correct.

(A) doesn't work because it doesn't fictionalize the author's thoughts but rather the experiences of other people.

(C) sounds too much like what the radical critics value—communicating a political view. No such requirement is stated in Dostoyevsky's view. The use of allegory is irrelevant to Dostoyevsky's view as well.

(D) Isn't artistic because the author of an autobiographical essay isn't fictionalizing his or her thoughts through character and image, as Dostoyevsky describes. As far as you know from the passage, a work's subject matter is not Dostoyevsky's concern.

(E) contains fictional characters, but the characters don't necessarily express the author's thoughts. They debate social problems, which again speaks more to the radical critics' view than Dostoyevsky's.

22. (A) Detail

Step 2: Identify the Question Type

The phrase "according to the passage" is a strong indication of a Detail question. You're looking for a belief of Dostoyevsky that contrasts with that of the radicals with regard to realism.

Step 3: Research the Relevant Text

The author details the differences between Dostoyevsky's and the radicals' view of reality in paragraph 2. For Dostoyevsky, "reality" is shaped by individual experience and contains within it the sphere of fantasy.

Step 4: Make a Prediction

The correct answer will paraphrase one of the two views you just researched.

Step 5: Evaluate the Answer Choices

(A) is a direct paraphrase of lines 17–20, where you learn that Dostoyevsky thought individual experience could shape the perception of reality.

(B) is a 180. Dostoyevsky was a realist, although not a radical (lines 10–15). Moreover, he thought "fully realized artistic works" could serve a political view (lines 33–34).

(C) is a Faulty Use of Detail wrong answer choice. It paraphrases the view of the first camp of Russian literary theorists (lines 3–4), a view not ascribed to Dostoyevsky.

(D), like **(B)**, is a Distortion based on the wrong part of the passage. Dostoyevsky's view left room for realism to serve sociopolitical purposes, just not at the expense of the artistic merit of a literary work.

(E) is a 180. Lines 10–11 say that Dostoyevsky agreed that reality is "literature's crucial source."

23. (C) Inference

Step 2: Identify the Question Type

The stem asks you to define a vocabulary term as it is used in the context of the passage, so it's essentially an Inference question.

Step 3: Research the Relevant Text

The word *useful* is a commonly used word. But don't make the mistake of simply predicting a dictionary definition of the term. Research the meaning in the passage. The term *useful* is first mentioned in paragraph 1 (line 9) and then used in that way throughout paragraph 4.

Step 4: Make a Prediction

Lines 5–9 are where the term *useful* is actually defined. According to the radicals, art is useful only if it is based in concrete reality and helps to create social change. Find a match for this definition in the choices.

Step 5: Evaluate the Answer Choices

(C) is the best match for the way the author uses *useful* in the passage.

(A) introduces the element of the fantastic, a concept defined and defended in the passage by Dostoyevsky, not the radicals. The term "useful" is not associated with fantasy anywhere in the passage.

(B) is the basis of Dostoyevsky's definition of what makes a literary work "artistic" as described in paragraph 3. The definition of *useful*, on the other hand, was in the context of the radicals' view of literature.

(D), like **(A)**, is part of Dostoyevsky's view about the writer's task, so **(D)** has nothing to do with the radicals' definition of "useful" art.

(E) misses the mark because the radicals weren't interested in theoretical advances through literature but rather social advances.

24. (C) Global

Step 2: Identify the Question Type

One subtype of Global question asks you to describe the organization of the passage. Like any other Global question, though, it can be identified by its focus on the passage as a whole. Expect the answer choices to a "descriptive" question, like this one, to be generic, outlining the rhetorical flow of the passage, not its content.

Step 3: Research the Relevant Text

Your Roadmap is the best place to go to form a prediction on a question like this. The right answer should encompass what the author does paragraph by paragraph.

Step 4: Make a Prediction

Paragraph 1 outlines three viewpoints—those of the two opposing camps and then that of Dostoyevsky. Then each subsequent paragraph discusses a specific point at issue between Dostoyevsky and the second of the two opposing camps (the radical critics).

Step 5: Evaluate the Answer Choices

(C) matches the organization of the passage. While Dostoyevsky disagreed with both groups of critics, the author spends the bulk of passage distinguishing Dostoyevsky from the radicals.

(A) is wrong because the first of the three positions is not explained in detail; it gets only two of the passage's 52 lines.

(B) incorrectly claims that Dostoyevsky's view is differentiated in detail from both of the other two views. The author sums up Dostoyevsky's split from the first view in one short sentence (lines 10–11) but spends three paragraphs outlining Dostoyevsky's disagreements with the radicals.

(D) imputes author opinion when the tone of the passage is neutral. The author never offers a value judgment about any of the three positions in the passage.

(E) is wrong for the same reasons as **(D)**.

25. (C) Inference

Step 2: Identify the Question Type

Two main signals identify this as an Inference question: the word *inferred* and the phrase "Dostoyevsky would most likely have agreed with … "

Step 3: Research the Relevant Text

Dostoyevsky's view of the first group of critics is found at lines 10–11 in paragraph 1.

Step 4: Make a Prediction

The first position (lines 3–4) holds that art should be elevated above reality, but later in the paragraph (lines 10–11), the author describes Dostoyevsky as a realist who held that reality should be the primary source of all literature. This difference will inform the correct answer.

Step 5: Evaluate the Answer Choices

(C) is consistent with the prediction and uses almost the same language as the passage.

(A) is a 180; Dostoyevsky strongly disagreed with the first group of critics. It also distorts the passage, because the view

that art should contain an element of the fantastic is ascribed only to Dostoyevsky and not to the critics in lines 3–4.

(B) is also a 180; again, Dostoyevsky strongly disagreed with the first group of critics. This choice also claims that the first group takes a position on reality that the passage does not associate with these critics.

(D) is not a claim made by the first group of critics in lines 3–4. Furthermore, Dostoyevsky actually believed that fantasy was an important element of reality.

(E) is not the view presented in lines 3–4 but rather part of the radical critics' view, which is also opposed to the first group's position.

26. (A) Inference

Step 2: Identify the Question Type

The question stem asks what Dostoyevsky "would most likely agree with," so this is an Inference question. Notice the reference clue—"about works of literature"—and use that to guide your research.

Step 3: Research the Relevant Text

In this case, all the choices have to do with the relationship between literature serving a political view and literature being well written. So paragraph 3 will contain the text that forms the basis of the correct answer.

Step 4: Make a Prediction

According to lines 33–34, Dostoyevsky believed that only fully realized artistic works could serve any goals, political or otherwise. Then, in lines 40–41, Dostoyevsky claims that artistry is the ability to write well. So the right answer will likely combine these two ideas in a manner consistent with paragraph 3.

Step 5: Evaluate the Answer Choices

(A) matches the prediction. According to lines 33–34, "[o]nly fully realized works could fulfill their goals," and according to the rest of the paragraph, fully realized works are well written.

(B) improperly reverses the Formal Logic. Dostoyevsky's claim from lines 33–34 is that being fully artistically realized is necessary for a work to serve its goals. **(B)** has it the other way around.

(C) is a Distortion. Dostoyevsky's view would hold that if a work isn't well written, it can't serve a political view. But that isn't the same as saying that a poorly written work will always attempt to serve a political view.

(D) is a 180. Dostoyevsky claims that high quality of writing is a precondition of a work meeting its goals. High-quality writing was Dostoyevsky's greatest concern, but the passage never says he rejected political views in artistic works.

(E) also distorts Dostoyevsky's view. He bases the quality of a work primarily on its artistic merit. Serving a political view is secondary and doesn't necessarily disqualify a work from being well written.

27. (D) Inference

Step 2: Identify the Question Type

The word *suggests* indicates an Inference question. Here, the correct answer gives a step the radicals could have taken to make Dostoyevsky less critical of their position. To get the right answer, understand what Dostoyevsky disliked about the radicals' view and find an answer that would bring them more in line with Dostoyevsky's goals.

Step 3: Research the Relevant Text

You know from your Roadmap that Dostoyevsky disagreed with the radicals over the nature of reality, the importance of artistic quality, and the requirement that art be "useful." That's a lot, but the right answer will bring the radicals into line with Dostoyevsky on one of those points.

Step 4: Make a Prediction

The radicals have three main requirements for art and literature: that they depict reality "as it is" (paragraph 2), that they serve a particular political position (paragraph 3), and that they be "useful" to society. Dostoyevsky took issue with each of these requirements, so he would probably soften his view if any of these requirements was relaxed.

Step 5: Evaluate the Answer Choices

(D) is supported directly by paragraph 3. The radical critics insisted that art must serve a political view and subordinate any artistic concerns. However, Dostoyevsky claimed that the artistic merit of a work was the chief determinant of its value.

(A) is a 180, since Dostoyevsky believed that fantasy and reality must be "intimately bound" (lines 23–25).

(B) is also a 180. Lines 30–33 say that the radical critics were already putting clarity of purpose ahead of formal concerns, and that this was something with which Dostoyevsky did not agree.

(C) also misses the mark. Dostoyevsky apparently believed that reality was the crucial source of literature, so if, as **(C)** says, the radicals were to advocate eliminating aspects of it from literary works, Dostoyevsky would object even more strongly to their views.

(E) is wrong because Dostoyevsky seemed to have a problem with the demand itself, not with the radicals' explanation of it.

PrepTest 65

The Inside Story

PrepTest 65 was administered in December 2011. It challenged 35,825 test takers. What made this test so hard? Here's a breakdown of what Kaplan students who were surveyed after taking the official exam considered PrepTest 65's most difficult section.

Hardest PrepTest 65 Section as Reported by Test Takers

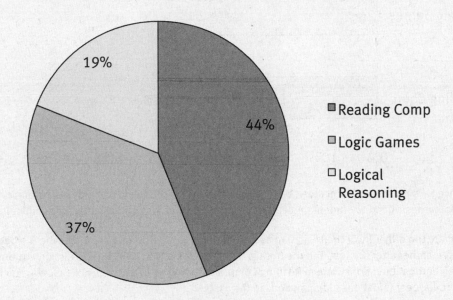

Based on these results, you might think that studying Reading Comp is the key to LSAT success. Well, Reading Comp is important, but test takers' perceptions don't tell the whole story. For that, you need to consider students' actual performance. The following chart shows the average number of students to miss each question in each of PrepTest 65's different sections.

Percentage Incorrect by PrepTest 65 Section Type

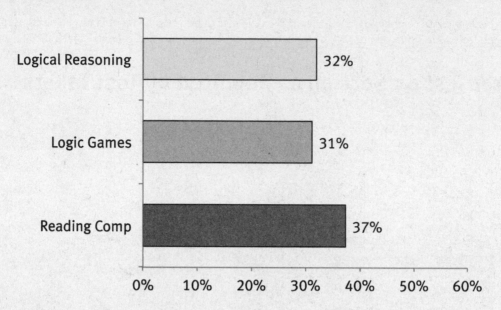

Actual student performance tells quite a different story. While Reading Comp was indeed the hardest section on PrepTest 65, Logical Reasoning was the second hardest, despite student perception that Logic Games was significantly more difficult.

Maybe students overestimate the difficulty of the Logic Games section because it's so unusual, or maybe it's because a really hard Logic Game is so easy to remember after the test. But the truth is that the testmaker places hard questions throughout the test. On PrepTest 66, four of the ten hardest questions were in Reading Comp, but four were in the Logical Reasoning sections, as well. Here were the locations of the 10 hardest (most missed) questions in the exam.

Location of 10 Most Difficult Questions in PrepTest 65

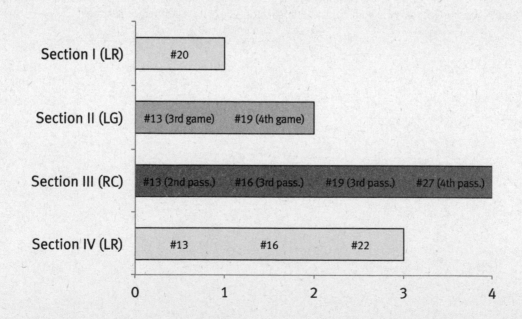

The takeaway from this data is that, to maximize your potential on the LSAT, you need to take a comprehensive approach. Test yourself rigorously, and review your performance on every section of the test. Kaplan's LSAT explanations provide the expertise and insight you need to fully understand your results. The explanations are written and edited by a team of LSAT experts, who have helped thousands of students improve their scores. Kaplan always provides data-driven analysis of the test, ranking the difficulty of every question based on actual student performance. The ten hardest questions on every test are highlighted with a 4-star difficulty rating, the highest we give. The analysis breaks down the remaining questions into 1-, 2-, and 3-star ratings so that you can compare your performance to that of thousands of other test takers on all LSAC material.

Don't settle for wondering whether a question was really as hard as it seemed to you. Analyze the test with real data, and learn the secrets and strategies that help top scorers master the LSAT.

7 Can't-Miss Features of PrepTest 65

- In the second Logical Reasoning section, Question 15 provides a stimulus that ends in "since sometimes ___." That's followed by an unusual Strengthen/Weaken question stem: "The conclusion of the argument is most strongly supported if which one of the following completes the passage?"
- In the first LR section, Question 3 is an Evaluate the Argument question, with the correct answer being the one that LEAST helps to evaluate the argument. At the time of this test's release, it was only the third such question ever. The most recent one prior to PrepTest 65 had been on PrepTest 45 (December 2004).
- PrepTest 65's Logic Games section had a Selection game, the first test to have one since PrepTest 59 (December 2009). Moreover, it was a Selection game with three subcategories of entities—desserts, main courses, and side dishes—the first such game since PrepTest 50 (September 2006) which had parents, and students, and teachers, oh my!
- At the time of its release, this was just the second test that had a Law passage as the Comparative Reading passage (the first was on PrepTest 56 (December 2008). This would kick off quite a trend, however, as six of the next eight LSATs after PrepTest 65 featured a Comparative Reading passage with a Law topic.
- The fourth passage features a pretty unique set of questions including a Global-Organization question, an Inference LEAST question, an Inference question about a hypothetical, and an LR-style Parallel Reasoning question.
- On PrepTest 65, you needed to read past the first answer a lot because (A) was the correct answer only twice among the test's 23 LG questions and only eight times among its 51 LR questions.
- PrepTest 65's Reading Comp section was pretty tough, but with passages on blackmail and digital security, maybe it was priming test takers to go see *Girl With the Dragon Tatoo*, which came out the same month the test was given.

PrepTest 65 in Context

As much fun as it is to find out what makes a PrepTest unique or noteworthy, it's even more important to know just how representative it is of other LSAT administrations (and, thus, how likely it is to be representative of the exam you will face on Test Day). The following charts compare the numbers of each kind of question and game on PrepTest 65 to the average numbers seen on all officially released LSATs administered over the past five years (from 2012 through 2016).

Number of LR Questions by Type: PrepTest 65 vs. 2012-2016 Average

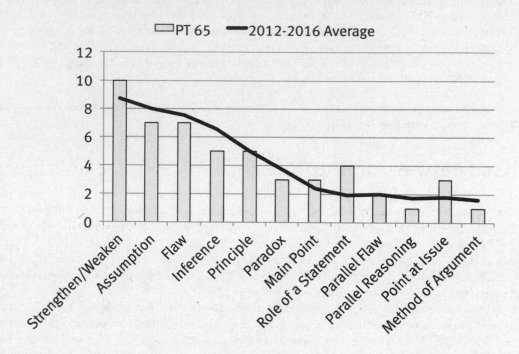

Number of LG Games by Type: PrepTest 65 vs. 2012-2016 Average

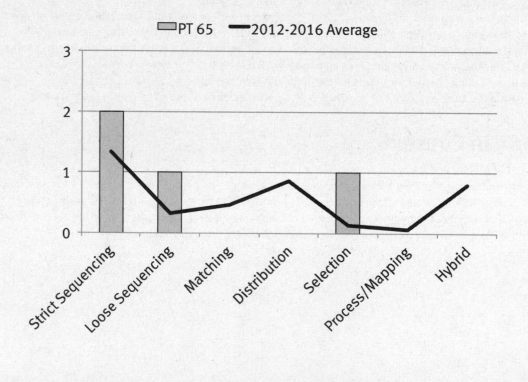

Number of RC Questions by Type: PrepTest 65 vs. 2012-2016 Average

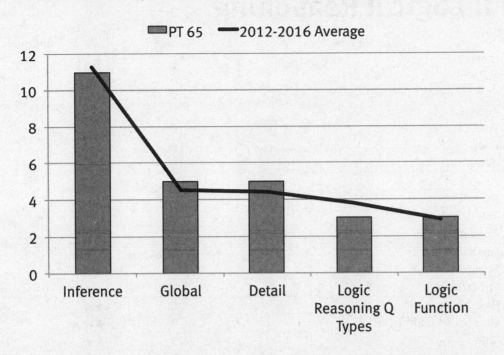

There isn't usually a huge difference in the distribution of questions from LSAT to LSAT, but if this test seems harder (or easier) to you than another you've taken, compare the number of questions of the types on which you, personally, are strongest and weakest. And then, explore within each section to see if your best or worst question types came earlier or later.

Students in Kaplan's comprehensive LSAT courses have access to every released LSAT, and to an online Q-Bank with thousands of officially released questions, games, and passages. If you are studying on your own, you have to do a bit more work to identify your strengths and your areas of opportunity. Quantitative analysis (like that in the charts here) is an important tool for understanding how the test is constructed, and how you are performing on it.

Section I: Logical Reasoning

Q#	Question Type	Correct	Difficulty
1	Strengthen	B	★
2	Main Point	A	★
3	Strengthen/Weaken (Evaluate the Argument)	B	★
4	Inference	C	★
5	Weaken	D	★
6	Principle (Parallel)	A	★★
7	Inference	D	★
8	Flaw	A	★
9	Main Point	C	★
10	Role of a Statement	B	★
11	Parallel Flaw	A	★★
12	Paradox	C	★★
13	Strengthen	E	★★
14	Strengthen	B	★★
15	Flaw	C	★★
16	Assumption (Sufficient)	B	★★★
17	Flaw	D	★★
18	Assumption (Necessary)	B	★★★
19	Strengthen	C	★★★
20	Flaw	D	★★★★
21	Assumption (Necessary)	D	★
22	Role of a Statement	E	★★
23	Point at Issue	E	★★
24	Principle (Identify/Strengthen)	C	★
25	Inference	D	★★★

1. (B) Strengthen

Step 1: Identify the Question Type

The phrase "most strengthens the argument" indicates a Strengthen question. Remember that the correct answer to a Strengthen question will bolster the credibility of the author's conclusion based specifically on the evidence he gives.

Step 2: Untangle the Stimulus

Start with the conclusion in the final sentence. The contrast Keyword [*b*]*ut* along with the phrase "so the research suggests" indicate the conclusion. The author believes a diet need not be low in fat to guard against heart attacks. The evidence is that two groups of men and women who had previously suffered heart attacks (and thus were at risk of a second) were each given different diets: a Mediterranean-type diet, which includes a "fair amount" of fat, or a traditional Western diet with an explicit low-fat modification. The study found that the Mediterranean-type dieters had a significantly lower risk of a second heart attack than did those who followed the low-fat Western diet.

Step 3: Make a Prediction

You want an answer that will make the author's seemingly paradoxical assertion (that diets don't have to be low in fat to be heart-healthy) more likely. Look for a choice that presents a reason why diets such as the Mediterranean diet can still be effective in preventing heart attacks.

Step 4: Evaluate the Answer Choices

(B) matches the prediction. That the kinds of oils in the fat of the Mediterranean diet have beneficial health effects explains why the people who followed that diet have a lower risk of a second heart attack.

(A) is irrelevant. Eliminating almost all fat from one's diet does not apply to either group of dieters in this scenario, especially the Mediterranean dieters, the ones whose improved health the correct answer must explain.

(C) is Outside the Scope. Whether or not the Mediterranean dieters enjoyed the food or made any subsequent lifestyle changes does not explain why they exhibited positive health effects during the time frame of the study.

(D) Is Outside the Scope. It is unknown whether the Mediterranean dieters (or those on the low-fat Western diet, for that matter) began an exercise regimen or participated in anything else that might have accounted for their positive results.

(E) is Outside the Scope. The original argument doesn't mention any additional treatments. Stay within the scope of the argument. Focus on something about the diet itself that brought about the result.

2. (A) Main Point

Step 1: Identify the Question Type

The phrase "most accurately expresses the overall conclusion" identifies this Main Point question. Watch out for conclusion Keywords, which may indicate subsidiary conclusions, and be prepared to combine statements into a paraphrase of the author's main point. If necessary, use the One-Sentence Test.

Step 2: Untangle the Stimulus

The argument is chock full of Keywords to help guide your search for the author's main point. The first statement leads off with "[s]ome people," a good indication that the author finds their point of view problematic. Sure enough, the next sentence begins with [*b*]*ut*, a contrast Keyword. In this case, the author points out a problem with green flowers. The next sentence begins with [*t*]*hus*, but conclusion Keywords rarely signal the actual conclusions of Main Point questions. The final sentence yields the author's ultimate recommendation: Florists should stock up on white carnations before St. Patrick's Day.

Step 3: Make a Prediction

The author's main point is the opinion that the rest of the stimulus is there to support; to wit, the recommendation that florists stock up on white carnations before St. Patrick's Day.

Step 4: Evaluate the Answer Choices

(A) matches the prediction almost verbatim, with "[i]t is a good idea" mirroring the recommendation language in the conclusion.

(B) restates the evidence that author presents to introduce the initial difficulty—green flowers are rare.

(C) incorrectly identifies a piece of background evidence in the argument as the author's main point.

(D) incorrectly identifies as the main point the author's primary support (evidence). This tells us *why* florists should stock white carnations; the main point is *that* they should.

(E) also incorrectly identifies a piece of evidence as the author's main point. The Keyword [*t*]*hus* may make this a tempting choice, but it is actually a subsidiary conclusion that leads to the author's ultimate Conclusion.

3. (B) Strengthen/Weaken (Evaluate the Argument LEAST)

Step 1: Identify the Question Type

Read seemingly unfamiliar question stems carefully. The phrase "would be LEAST useful in evaluating the argument" makes your task clear: look for the answer choice that is least relevant to the argument. The four incorrect answer choices will all have some bearing, good or bad, on the argument's validity.

Step 2: Untangle the Stimulus

As always with argument-based questions, analyze the author's conclusion and evidence. The conclusion is signaled by the Keyword *therefore*, with the first half of the last sentence offered as the author's primary support. Even though low-wattage bulbs are more expensive, we should all use them because they offer "enormous" advantages. Note how vague that conclusion is.

Step 3: Make a Prediction

Having a handle on the scope of the argument (low-wattage bulbs versus normal bulbs) will make it easier to spot relevant information in the answer choices. You know there are enormous advantages to low-wattage bulbs, but you have no idea what those advantages are. Don't forget to characterize your answer choices in question stems containing "LEAST" or "EXCEPT." Four answer choices will provide some information about those advantages. The correct answer choice will shed no light on the matter. Work through the answer choices for a statement that is irrelevant to the author's cost-benefit analysis.

Step 4: Evaluate the Answer Choices

(B) is not useful in evaluating the author's argument recommending that consumers use low-wattage bulbs. The home lighting industry's profits, or lack of profits, from low-wattage bulbs are immaterial to whether the consumer should or should not buy the bulbs.

(A) is relevant information. The cost of burning low-wattage bulbs compared to normal bulbs could affect the consumer's benefits.

(C) is relevant information. The cost of buying low-wattage bulbs compared to normal bulbs would factor into the consumer's decision-making process.

(D) is relevant information. Reviews by low-wattage bulb users would, indeed, make the author's argument stronger or more suspect.

(E) is relevant information. The durability of low-wattage bulbs compared to normal bulbs would influence whether they should be used or not.

4. (C) Inference

Step 1: Identify the Question Type

The phrase "most logically completes the passage" identifies this as an Inference question. You're looking for what the author would say based on the statements already provided. Work through the stimulus and paraphrase the statements. The answer choice will be the logical "fill-in-the-blank" conclusion.

Step 2: Untangle the Stimulus

The author begins with the argument that although fencing in swimming pools to prevent kids from drowning is a good idea, it's more important to teach children to swim. Then the author draws an analogy based on the same principle. Yes, we should prevent children from consuming the soft drinks and candies advertised during their favorite TV shows, but what's an even better idea? That's what you need to predict.

Step 3: Make a Prediction

Think about how that last sentence can be connected to the others. The author is not against precautionary safety measures. Rather, the author is *also* in favor of teaching children skills that will allow them to protect themselves. Once you've paraphrased the argument, don't waste time predicting every possible inference. Work through the answer choices for a statement that must be true on the basis of the statements about the swimming pool.

Step 4: Evaluate the Answer Choices

(C) concludes the author's argument logically, aptly completing the analogy. As teaching children to swim might obviate the need for the fence around the swimming pool, so educating children to make smart health choices would obviate a prohibition on drinks and candies.

(A) is Outside the Scope. Teaching children the benefits of TV-watching would not give them skills that would allow them to avoid the dangers of sugared drinks and sweets.

(B) twists the logic of the stimulus. The author isn't attacking television advertisements. Rather, the author argues that children's access to the items *shown* on those ads should be restricted. In addition, the focus of the author's swimming pool analogy is on empowering children, so the statement that finishes the stimulus must have that same focus.

(D) is irrelevant. The author limits the scope of the argument to drinking/eating habits. Physical activity in general goes too far.

(E) twists the logic of the stimulus. Again, the critique is not of television itself. Additionally, the focus is on increased safety, not increased entertainment.

5. (D) Weaken

Step 1: Identify the Question Type

The phrase "most seriously weakens" indicates you are dealing with a Weaken question here. Identify the conclusion, paraphrase the evidence, predict the central assumption, and then look for a fact that attacks that central assumption.

Step 2: Untangle the Stimulus

The Keyword *therefore* signals the conclusion. The author believes that the TV program is noticeably skewed in favor of those against the planned freeway. The author's evidence is the 2:1 ratio of interviews with people against the freeway project to interviews with those in favor of it.

Step 3: Make a Prediction

On its face, the author's point seems to make sense. But the key here is to notice that the author attributes the unequal numbers of interviews opposing and favoring the proposed freeway to the press bias and nothing else. That's the central assumption. Perhaps something else, such as the actual opinion of the affected parties, led to the overwhelming lack of support.

Step 4: Evaluate the Answer Choices

(D) provides an alternative reason for the lack of support among the interviewees. The number of interviews accurately represents the public's opinion. If anything, this choice makes it appear that the interviews were slightly *over*-inclusive of those who favor the freeway.

(A) is Outside the Scope. Whether viewers knew about the controversy has no bearing on whether the program was indeed skewed.

(B) is Outside the Scope. Viewer expectations of bias do not affect whether an actual bias exists.

(C) is Outside the Scope. The author focuses on the *number* of interviews that were for or against the proposed freeway project. The degree of passion for either side is immaterial.

(E) is a 180 and could actually strengthen the argument. The TV station owner's potential gain from disseminating objections to the freeway project might encourage a bias.

6. (A) Principle (Parallel)

Step 1: Identify the Question Type

The word *principle* makes it clear that this is a Principle question. This particular Principle question mimics a Parallel Reasoning question, as evidenced by the phrase "most closely conforms." First, identify the principle behind the argument in the stimulus. Then, search for the answer choice that follows the same reasoning and correctly applies that same principle.

Step 2: Untangle the Stimulus

The contrast Keyword [*b*]*ut* indicates the author's opinion. Evan urges us to stay away from seafood for the same moral reasons vegetarians stay away from other meats. His moral test rests on vegetarians' belief that it is wrong to inflict pain on animals in order to get food. Likewise, Evan believes, since we don't know for sure whether sea creatures can experience pain, we should be safe and avoid eating them.

Step 3: Make a Prediction

The broader principle underlying Evan's argument is that one should abstain from any behavior that could possibly have

negative consequences. Essentially, this is a "better safe than sorry" argument. Look for an answer choice that matches the prediction.

Step 4: Evaluate the Answer Choices

(A) is a perfect match to the predicted principle. Since neither the author nor Farrah knows if the author repaid Farrah, the money should be handed over now. Farrah remaining unpaid would be a negative consequence. Again, better safe than sorry.

(B) is Outside the Scope. In the original argument, the author advocates a course of action ("we should ... refrain") based on a lack of knowledge. In this answer choice, the author anticipates a possible consequence ("we should expect") of the lack of knowledge.

(C) is Outside the Scope. This argument entails no lack of knowledge. Rather, the author recommends against a course of action because of known negative consequences.

(D) is Outside the Scope. While there would be potential benefits from updating the security system, the author does not discuss any possible negative consequences, nor does the author encourage action in order to avoid them.

(E) is Outside the Scope. The conclusion that Allende's experiences did not negatively affect her view of life does not promote any sort of action to prevent possible negative consequences. This argument's conclusion is an assertion of fact, not parallel to the recommendation that concludes the stimulus.

7. (D) Inference

Step 1: Identify the Question Type

The phrase "most logically completes the final sentence" identifies this as an Inference question. Work through the stimulus and paraphrase the statements. The correct answer choice will logically conclude the last sentence and will not be broader than the stimulus' scope.

Step 2: Untangle the Stimulus

The economist's reasoning draws an analogy between government intervention in the free market and the administration of drugs. The author argues that since most drugs are both dangerous *and* helpful, their potential to help must outweigh their potential for danger in the course of their intended use. Your task is to figure out how that reasoning analogously supports the only acceptable way for the government to intervene in the free market.

Step 3: Make a Prediction

Think about how that last sentence can be connected to the others. As with the administration of drugs, the benefits of government intervention must outweigh the costs.

Step 4: Evaluate the Answer Choices

(D) logically concludes the author's reasoning. It uses the same "balancing test" approach, implying that intervention would be better than nonintervention.

(A) is Outside the Scope. The point at issue is not the approval rating that government action would generate, but whether actual benefits surpass actual costs.

(B) is a Distortion. In the analogy the author acknowledges that there may be harmful effects. However, he is not concerned with *how* harmful the effects will be, but rather whether such effects will be less than the expected advantages.

(C) is Out of Scope. There is no discussion about exacerbating existing problems. Even if that were to happen, it is only part of the information to be considered. The author is concerned with whether harmful effects will outweigh expected advantages.

(E) is too broad and need not be true based on the stimulus. The author never discusses the reason for the government intervention or the unavailability of other solutions.

8. (A) Flaw

Step 1: Identify the Question Type

The phrase "the reasoning … is flawed" identifies this question as a Flaw. You can look for common flaw types, or break down the author's conclusion, evidence, and assumption, and then evaluate how the author's reasoning goes wrong.

Step 2: Untangle the Stimulus

As with any Flaw question, start with the conclusion, signaled here by "this shows that." The author believes that considering the nutritional information on food products leads to (read "causes") healthy eating behavior. The author's only piece of evidence is a correlation: fat content in the diets of those who consider nutrition labels is much lower than it is in the diets of those who do not.

Step 3: Make a Prediction

The author is making a causal argument. The author is taking for granted that the reading of the labels is causing the positive health behavior. On the basis of the evidence, though, it's just as likely that the reverse may be true, and that healthy behavior is encouraging a greater attention to nutrition labels. Alternatively, something else could be causing the healthy behavior, or the correlation between healthy behavior and label reading could simply be coincidental.

Step 4: Evaluate the Answer Choices

(A) provides the proper flaw type. It's not clear which is causing which, so the author can't justifiably assume causation one way or another.

(B) is Outside the Scope. The author's claim incorporates all people (those who do read labels and those who don't), so representativeness is not at issue.

(C) is Outside the Scope. The evidence merely states a phenomenon, making no claim of necessity or sufficiency either way. The author then concludes without warrant that there is a causal connection.

(D) is incorrect. The author actually assumes there is only one explanation.

(E) is Outside the Scope. The stimulus mentions a result (that the proportion of fat calories is lower in those who read labels) but doesn't discuss *why* those who read labels do so. Presumably they want to be healthy or lose weight, but the author doesn't state this and certainly draws no conclusion about this group's intentions.

9. (C) Main Point

Step 1: Identify the Question Type

The phrase "expresses the conclusion" identifies this Main Point question. Watch out for subsidiary conclusions, and be prepared to combine statements into a paraphrase of the author's main point.

Step 2: Untangle the Stimulus

Evaluate the stimulus as though you were Roadmapping a Reading Comprehension passage. The first statement tells you about the position of "[s]ome paleontologists," a good indication that the author will disagree with their viewpoint. Sure enough, the next statement begins with *however*, a contrast Keyword, confirming the author's disagreements with the hypothesis in the first statement. The evidence starts with the Keyword *because*. All of the following statements are support for the author's contention in the second statement. Stay focused on the author's main point.

Step 3: Make a Prediction

Combining the first and second statement yields a great prediction of the author's main point: it is unlikely that *Apatosaurus* could gallop.

Step 4: Evaluate the Answer Choices

(C) matches the prediction perfectly.

(A) misses the mark. *Why* the *Apatosaurus* couldn't gallop—its legs would have broken—is evidence the author uses to support the main point: *that* the *Apatosaurus* probably couldn't gallop.

(B), like **(A)**, incorrectly identifies a piece of evidence as the author's main point. That the *Apatosaurus's* leg bones could not support galloping supports the idea that the dinosaur couldn't gallop, not the other way around.

(D) is phrased conditionally, whereas the author's argument is not. Moreover, this choice distorts the entirety of the argument rather than paraphrasing its conclusion.

(E) is Outside the Scope. It is implied by the argument, but not the author's main point. If the author had only one sentence to make his takeaway point, this would not be it.

10. (B) Role of a Statement

Step 1: Identify the Question Type

The phrase "role played in the argument" indicates that this is a Role of a Statement question. Using Keywords or other methods to identify conclusions, determine whether the statement in question is evidence or conclusion.

Step 2: Untangle the Stimulus

The statement in the question stem is found at the end of the last sentence—but the conclusion appears in the second sentence. There are no Keywords to indicate the conclusion, but all the rest of the argument, including the statement in question, supports it. You can add in your own conclusion Keywords to see if your classification of evidence and conclusion makes sense.

Step 3: Make a Prediction

The phrase "[t]his advance could help reduce the high incidence of anemia in the world's population" is the author's conclusion. This is not the statement in question. Therefore, the statement must be part of the evidence. If necessary, you can always go back to the stimulus to help you pinpoint more specifically how the statement is being used.

Step 4: Evaluate the Answer Choices

(B) correctly identifies the statement in the question stem as part of the evidence.

(A) incorrectly identifies the statement as the conclusion.

(C) incorrectly identifies the statement in the question stem as a claim the author is refuting. The author isn't arguing against anything, and in fact, he needs the statement in question to advance his point.

(D) incorrectly identifies the statement as a qualification of the conclusion. The conclusion is not restricted in any way.

(E) incorrectly identifies the statement in the question stem as an example ("illustrates") of an unstated principle. The statement at issue is factual in nature, offered to show that the author's conclusion is plausible. It's not an illustration of anything, certainly not of an implicit general rule.

11. (A) Parallel Flaw

Step 1: Identify the Question Type

The phrase "reasoning most similar to" coupled with "exhibits a flaw" indicates this is a Parallel Flaw question. Approach the argument as you would a Flaw question. As you identify the conclusion and evidence and pinpoint the relevant gap between the two, keep common flaw types in mind. The correct answer choice will exhibit the same pattern of reasoning and the same flaw as the stimulus.

Step 2: Untangle the Stimulus

This is a very short stimulus: only two sentences. The Keyword [*t*]*herefore* indicates the conclusion. The Inspector concludes that whoever stole the guest's diamonds must have worn gloves. The inspector's evidence is that only the owner's fingerprints are present at the scene of the crime.

Step 3: Make a Prediction

Evaluate where the inspector's reasoning goes wrong. The evidence suggests a likely suspect: the owner. Yet the inspector overlooks that plausible explanation for the missing jewels and instead fashions an alternate theory. The correct answer will have the same reasoning: a plausible explanation for something is discarded without reason.

Step 4: Evaluate the Answer Choices

(A) exhibits the same flawed pattern of reasoning as the stimulus. It's possible—even likely, given that the campers have eaten nothing else—that food from the camp cafeteria caused the illness, but the author disregards this explanation for no apparent reason.

(B) There is no flaw in the logic of this argument. The conclusion is correctly reasoned based on the evidence. Notice the tentative phrasing of the conclusion. By using the word *might*, the author both remains open to alternative reasons for the second prototype's poor performance and devises a conclusion nearly impossible to disprove.

(C) uses past experience to draw a qualified (*likely*) conclusion, but the logic doesn't add up. Even though each swimmer has more losses than wins, it is still necessary for one swimmer (the best of the worst, so to speak) to win. However, this argument doesn't overlook an obvious explanation for an occurrence, so it's not a match.

(D) exhibits the same category of flaw (overlooked possibilities) as that seen in the stimulus. However, this choice doesn't reject a possibility strongly supported by the evidence; it overlooks all other possibilities.

(E) is the wrong type of flaw. The stimulus does not contain a faulty analogy.

12. (C) Paradox

Step 1: Identify the Question Type

The word *explain* indicates that this is a Paradox question. Summarize the seemingly inconsistent facts in the argument (there will usually be a sentence for each), and then look for an answer that makes sense of the mystery.

Step 2: Untangle the Stimulus

Remember: paradox questions don't contain a conclusion, so don't spend time looking for one. Two pieces of evidence are presented, with the implied conclusion being, "Isn't that weird?" Here, the first sentence states that shrimp species at 11 reefs differ markedly from one another. But that surprises the author, because the currents in that area are so conducive to interbreeding.

Step 3: Make a Prediction

Remember, every paradox is resolvable. You don't need to come up with a specific prediction to a Paradox question, because the possibilities could be endless. For this question, the correct answer choice will explain why there are no signs of interbreeding despite ocean currents that allow the shrimp to interbreed.

Step 4: Evaluate the Answer Choices

(C) explains why the shrimp do not appear to be interbreeding. When not breeding, they might be carried around among the various reefs. But before breeding, the shrimp migrate back to their original reef and breed with their own genetic kind. This would explain the lack of interbreeding despite the encouraging conditions.

(A) is Outside the Scope. The level of genetic differences between shrimp and other marine species has no bearing on why the shrimp populations themselves remain genetically distinct from reef to reef.

(B) is Outside the Scope. Each individual shrimp's genetic makeup is not at issue. The paradox centers on why the populations remain unique at each reef.

(D) is a 180. This deepens the paradox. If the majority of breeding-age shrimp have moved away from home, then it is even harder to explain why there is no sign of interbreeding between populations.

(E) is Outside the Scope. If many of the baby shrimp are swept into the ocean, that might lead to a diverse population in the deep, but it doesn't explain why there is no interbreeding back at the coral reefs.

13. (E) Strengthen

Step 1: Identify the Question Type

The phrase "most strengthens the argument" indicates a Strengthen question. Remember, the correct answer to a

Strengthen question can be the argument's central assumption. Look for the answer choice that makes the conclusion more likely to logically flow from the evidence presented.

Step 2: Untangle the Stimulus

Start with the conclusion in the final sentence, signaled by the Keyword [*t*]*hus*. The author believes that growing salt-tolerant plants via seawater irrigation should be beneficial for desert regions, even though the farms would produce more if they pumped fresh water. The evidence is that pumping in seawater into farms near sea level is noticeably cheaper than pumping in fresh water.

Step 3: Make a Prediction

The author presents both a benefit (pumping seawater is cheaper) and a cost (yields will diminish) yet still concludes that seawater agriculture is the way to go. The author must be assuming that the benefits will outweigh the costs, a common assumption on the LSAT. To support the conclusion, the correct answer choice needs to shore up the author's assumption by proving the benefit or eliminating any other potential costs.

Step 4: Evaluate the Answer Choices

(E) matches the prediction. If pumping water is one of the largest expenditures, then the seawater irrigation becomes the more attractive (i.e., cheaper) option.

(A) doesn't strengthen the argument. The nutritional value may differ between halophytes and conventional plants, but it's unclear which side the difference favors (or if one side is even favored at all).

(B) is Outside the Scope. The fact that some halophytes need salt doesn't mean farmers would benefit from growing them.

(C) is a 180. If large expenditures would be necessary to find the prime agricultural halophytes, then it might not be cost-beneficial for farmers to attempt to grow them.

(D) is irrelevant. "Different" is not necessarily better or worse. Based on the information presented, it's impossible to know whether those costs are a point for or against halophytes.

14. (B) Strengthen

Step 1: Identify the Question Type

The phrase "most justifies the above application" indicates a Strengthen question. Even if you identified this as a Principle question, your task is still the same: find the answer that supports the application of the principle in the stimulus. In other words, make sure that the scenario presented fits all the conditions of the principle.

Step 2: Untangle the Stimulus

First, paraphrase the principle. If an insurance policy is written so that a reasonable person wouldn't read it, then the policyholder's reasonable expectations of coverage should legally trump the actual written language. Then summarize how the principle is applied. Here, Celia should be covered for hail damage even though her policy doesn't technically cover it.

Step 3: Make a Prediction

For the application to be valid, Celia's case must meet all of the principle's criteria. The correct answer will likely expand on the situation in the stimulus, showing that the principle's criteria were indeed fulfilled. Notice that the word *reasonable* is introduced as a litmus test for both the policy's text and the policyholder's expectations.

Step 4: Evaluate the Answer Choices

(B) matches the prediction. Celia's policy was written unreasonably, while her expectations for coverage were reasonable.

(A) doesn't go far enough. Yes, Celia reasonably expected coverage for hail damage. However, only one condition has been met. The answer choice does not indicate whether the policy was written such that a reasonable person wouldn't read it thoroughly.

(C) isn't enough. This is what **(A)** was missing: proof that a reasonable person would not read the insurance policy. Unfortunately, it isn't clear whether Celia's expectations were reasonable or not. Both sets of criteria must be met for the application to be valid.

(D) is Outside the Scope. **(B)** and **(D)** are almost identical except **(D)** mixes up the standards. The coverage issue rests on what Celia herself, not a reasonable person in general, would have reasonably expected. The reasonableness of reading the policy depends on what a reasonable person would have done in Celia's position, not what Celia actually did. **(D)** gets it backwards.

(E) makes the same mistake as **(C)**. It fails to mention Celia's expectations of coverage.

15. (C) Flaw

Step 1: Identify the Question Type

The phrase "the researcher's argument is flawed" indicates that this is a Flaw question. In addition, the phrase "fails to consider that" gives you a helpful hint. Apparently, the author has erroneously overlooked an alternative or a key fact that goes against the conclusion. Start with the conclusion, paraphrase the evidence, and then predict what the author has overlooked.

Step 2: Untangle the Stimulus

The Keyword [*t*]*herefore* confirms that the author's conclusion is the last sentence. The author surmises that the number of deaths per year would decrease by half provided medicine could prevent all iatrogenic disease. The author defines iatrogenic "disease" as resulting from medical treatments or hospitalization, and offers evidence showing that more people die from iatrogenic disease than die of all other causes combined.

Step 3: Make a Prediction

The author mistakenly assumes that the eradication of iatrogenic disease is sufficient to decrease the number of annual deaths by half. But keep in mind that those who suffer from iatrogenic causes are people hospitalized for surgeries or treatments for other diseases or conditions. In essence, the author must be assuming that a significant portion of those who die from iatrogenic disease would not die from the conditions that put them in the hospital in the first place.

Step 4: Evaluate the Answer Choices

(C) indicates that eradicating iatrogenic disease may not have the effect the author expects. If people who would have died from iatrogenic disease instead die shortly thereafter from something else, then the number of deaths per year won't decrease by half.

(A) is Outside the Scope. It seems likely that preventing non-iatrogenic diseases would reduce the rate of iatrogenic disease. After all, fewer people would likely be hospitalized. This, however, points out no flaw in the argument about reducing the death rate by eliminating iatrogenic disease.

(B) is Outside the Scope. Whether or not invasive or damaging medical treatments are causing iatrongenic disease is unclear. Additionally, the fact that some treatments can be improved isn't enough. The author's condition is that *all* iatrogenic disease be prevented.

(D) is irrelevant. If the author's condition is met and iatrogenic disease is completely eliminated, then people could no longer die from it. Whether this is accomplished in one way or in 100 ways is beside the point.

(E) is irrelevant. The fact that every non-iatrogenic disease carries a risk of iatrogenic disease means nothing to the argument. The author's conclusion is conditional: deaths will decrease *if* iatrogenic disease can be prevented. This answer choice may make it more difficult for the author's condition to be met in the real world, but his logic (if iatrongenic disease is prevented, then deaths will go down) remains intact.

16. (B) Assumption (Sufficient)

Step 1: Identify the Question Type

The word *assumed* identifies this as an Assumption question. Furthermore, the "If" indicates that you are looking for a sufficient assumption. There may be several assumptions that would be sufficient to ensure that the conclusion follows logically from the evidence, but only one answer choice will state such an assumption.

Step 2: Untangle the Stimulus

The Keyword [s]o flags the activist's conclusion. It's a recommendation. The activist believes at least one city council member should vote against the proposal. The activist's reasoning is that all city council members should do one of two things (abstain or vote against the proposal), yet if no council members vote, then the city's voters will decide.

Step 3: Make a Prediction

The activist encourages one dissenting vote because complete abstention would lead to a public vote. The activist must find such an outcome in some way distasteful. Look for an answer that says the activist assumes the matter must be kept out of the hands of the city's voters.

Step 4: Evaluate the Answer Choices

(B) provides the assumption as predicted. If the proposal shouldn't be put to a public vote, then the activist's conclusion that one city council member has to vote against the proposal makes sense.

(A) is Extreme. The activist notes that one way to get the proposal into the hands of the city voters is through a complete abstention by the city council. But what the city's voters will then decide on the proposal is unknown.

(C) is Outside the Scope. The activist isn't making a prediction of how city council members will or will not vote. He's recommending that at least one member vote "No." Additionally, the activist limits the argument's scope to the city council members doing one of two things: abstaining or voting against.

(D) is Outside the Scope. This is a faulty contrapositive of the activist's conditional second statement. This answer choice negates without reversing. The stimulus tells you what will happen if all council members abstain, not what will happen if not every member of the city council abstains. It's possible the matter could still go to the voters.

(E) distorts the conclusion. The activist specifies that *at least one* member should vote against the proposal. More than one (perhaps even all) could decide to vote no and the activist would still be satisfied.

17. (D) Flaw

Step 1: Identify the Question Type

The phrase "argument is flawed" indicates that this is a Flaw question. In addition, the phrase "fails to consider the possibility" signals that the author has committed a common flaw: overlooked alternatives. Start with the conclusion,

paraphrase the evidence, and then determine what the author has overlooked.

Step 2: Untangle the Stimulus

The conclusion Keyword [t]hus signals the author's main point: Gloomy financial news reports do not harm the economy by negatively affecting consumer confidence (media critics who believe they do are mistaken). The evidence, signaled by the Keyword [b]ut, confirms that studies show that spending trends correlate with people's confidence in their own finances.

Step 3: Make a Prediction

The economist's conclusion argues that negative news reports on the state of the economy as a whole don't actually harm the economy. But the author's evidence focuses on people's confidence in their *own* economic situation. The gap is between personal and general. The economist assumes that no relationship exists between how people feel about the overall economy and how they feel about their own finances. In essence, the economist overlooks a possible causal relationship.

Step 4: Evaluate the Answer Choices

(D) matches the prediction. It confirms that there is a causal relationship. If people have a pessimistic view of the economy overall, that leads to a pessimistic view of their own finances. As a result, they won't spend money and the economy will suffer, which is the outcome the critics predicted. They weren't mistaken after all.

(A) reverses the critics' logic and thus is irrelevant. The issue is economic news affecting personal confidence, not personal confidence affecting how economic news is interpreted. The economist's argument isn't flawed by its failure to consider the possibility of this other effect.

(B) is irrelevant. The accuracy of the news reports is not at issue. Inaccurate reports could still affect consumer confidence, possibly more than accurate ones, depending on what the reporter says.

(C) is Outside the Scope. The critics and the economist focus on the people who do pay attention to economic reports. There is no discussion of people who ignore the news.

(E) is irrelevant. The conclusion is about whether news reports affect the economy by shaking consumer confidence. How the *speed* of economic downturns affects individuals' actual situations is beside the point.

18. (B) Assumption (Necessary)

Step 1: Identify the Question Type

The phrase "requires the assumption" identifies this as an Assumption question. In addition, the word *requires* indicates that you're looking for a necessary assumption. You can use the Denial Test to check or eliminate answers.

Step 2: Untangle the Stimulus

Start by identifying the conclusion. The Keywords [c]*learly, therefore* signal the author's main point. The zoologist splits the majority of wild large mammal species in existence today into only two groups: those difficult to domesticate and those not worth domesticating. Why? Because people in the past would have already tried to domesticate any wild mammal that seemed to be a worthwhile candidate. Note that the conclusion is about present-day wild animals, while the evidence is about past attempts to domesticate them.

Step 3: Make a Prediction

The author must assume that those past attempts were adequate, or as good as contemporary people could achieve. In other words, the author assumes that conditions remain the same. If he didn't—that is, if you deny his assumption—there could be animals that are now easier or more worthwhile to domesticate. Look for an answer choice that supports the idea that past and current domestication processes are sufficiently similar.

Step 4: Evaluate the Answer Choices

(B) matches the predicted assumption. The Denial Test helps here. If it *is* much easier today to domesticate wild large-mammal species than it was in the past, the author's conclusion no longer holds true. In that case, the fact that past domestication attempts had failed would not be good evidence that current attempts could not succeed.

(A) merely restates the evidence in the second statement of the argument, so it can't be the unstated assumption.

(C) is Outside the Scope. The zoologist is concerned with species in existence today, not those that have already gone extinct.

(D) is a Distortion. This answer choice uses terms from the argument but gets the logic wrong. The zoologist never discusses the relationship between feasibility and the worthiness of domesticating wild animal species.

(E) is a Distortion. The author is not concerned with which animal species were the easiest to domesticate in the past.

19. (C) Strengthen

Step 1: Identify the Question Type

The phrase "strengthen the reasoning" indicates a Strengthen question. Remember that the correct answer to a Strengthen question can be either the central assumption itself or a fact that makes the assumption more likely to be true.

Step 2: Untangle the Stimulus

Start by finding the conclusion. The conclusion Keyword [h]*ence* in the final sentence signals the conclusion. It's a claim of causality: this year's abnormally large bird population is the result of last year's mild winter. The evidence is that due to the mild temperatures, a significant number of birds did not visit feeders and fewer than expected migrated.

Step 3: Make a Prediction

To strengthen a claim of causation, look for a scenario that either supports the causal relationship or rules out a possible alternative cause. To support the conclusion in this case, pick the answer choice that either directly or indirectly connects the mild temperatures to the bird population increases, making the phenomenon less likely to have been caused by anything else.

Step 4: Evaluate the Answer Choices

(C) matches the prediction. The fact that because they were able to avoid feeders, the birds were less susceptible to predators this past winter provides an indirect reason for the booming population. If fewer birds were killed, it logically follows that the population is larger than normal.

(A) is irrelevant. This answer indicates that the two things are sometimes correlated (notice that the choice does not say "usually" or even "often occur") and does not further the author's claim of causation.

(B) is irrelevant. There is no indication that the different mating behaviors affect population size either negatively or positively.

(D) is a 180. If this is true, then it would make more sense for the number of birds visiting the feeders to be higher, not lower, than usual. A lack of food would more likely have a negative effect on the size of the bird population.

(E) is Outside the Scope. The author is not concerned with why birds visit feeders; rather, he uses the fact that fewer birds visited feeders as evidence that the weather caused the increased bird population.

20. (D) Flaw

Step 1: Identify the Question Type

The phrase "a flaw in the ... reasoning" indicates that this is a Flaw question. Start with the conclusion, paraphrase the evidence, and then determine where the author's logic has gone wrong. That will be your prediction of the correct answer.

Step 2: Untangle the Stimulus

The Keyword [t]*herefore* confirms that the journalist's conclusion is in the last sentence. The journalist opines that a small observational study is more likely to have dramatic findings than a large randomized trial is. As evidence, she notes that the news media tend to report solely on those studies with dramatic findings, and do, in fact, report more frequently on small (yet somewhat unreliable) observational studies.

Step 3: Make a Prediction

The problem with the argument is that the author overlooks any alternative reasons for why the smaller studies are more often featured on the news than large randomized trials are. The author may be right, but the evidence she gives is insufficient to necessarily support her claim.

Step 4: Evaluate the Answer Choices

(D) picks up on the predicted problem with the author's argument. If small studies are far more common than large trials, then there is a logical alternative reason for the small studies' frequent appearance on the news.

(A) is Outside the Scope. Although the journalist does mention the unreliability risk associated with small studies, she does not discuss—let alone impugn—the motives behind the studies' fallibility.

(B) is not a flaw in the argument. The author notes that newspapers report most often on studies with dramatic findings (as well as on small observational studies that can be unreliable), but she never indicates that those studies with dramatic findings aren't based on strong scientific evidence.

(C) is Outside the Scope. The journalist doesn't confuse the two separate claims. She accepts both as true and uses them to draw a conclusion (admittedly, a potentially flawed one) comparing the findings of small observational studies to those of large clinical trials.

(E) points out a common causal flaw: ignoring that cause and effect may be reversed. This flaw, however, doesn't apply in this case. It doesn't make sense that reporting on a study could retroactively cause the study's findings to become dramatic-sounding.

21. (D) Assumption (Necessary)

Step 1: Identify the Question Type

The phrase "requires the assumption" identifies this as a Necessary Assumption question, which means that if you deny the correct answer, the author's conclusion will fall apart. Identify the relevant gap between the evidence and conclusion.

Step 2: Untangle the Stimulus

The Keyword [*t*]*herefore* flags the author's conclusion. The author believes government incentives (which, in an effort to slow global warming, encourage farmers to plant trees) are hastening the effects of global warming. The incentives are based on the fact that vegetation absorbs carbon dioxide and

prevents it from trapping heat. The author's evidence for his belief that the incentives are backfiring is a recent study which found that trees absorb and store carbon dioxide less effectively than native grasses do.

Step 3: Make a Prediction

As you formulate the assumption, pay attention to the relevant evidence: the comparison between trees and native grasses. For the author to conclude that the incentives to plant more trees are actually hastening global warming, then the trees must, in some way, be harming or eliminating their more effective counterparts: native grasses.

Step 4: Evaluate the Answer Choices

(D) provides the assumption as predicted. If trees replace a viable area for native grasses, that would be counterproductive to slowing global warming. In other words, if the farmers are *not* removing native grasses for tree-planting, then the author has no grounds on which to critique the incentives.

(A) is irrelevant. As long as trees absorb more carbon dioxide than they emit, they remain a valid solution. This choice gives you no reason to believe otherwise.

(B) is irrelevant. The point isn't why farmers will or won't plant trees, but that getting them to do so is counterproductive to the incentives' goal.

(C) is Outside the Scope. Although the lack of viability for native grasses is mentioned, deforestation never comes up in the author's argument. The author discusses planting trees, not cutting them down.

(E) is Outside the Scope. Whether governments are or are not promoting native grasses has no effect on the author's argument that incentives encouraging tree-planting are harmful.

22. (E) Role of a Statement

Step 1: Identify the Question Type

The phrase "the role played ... by the claim" indicates this is a Role of a Statement question. Using Keywords, determine whether the statement in question is evidence or conclusion, and then go back and refine your categorization as necessary.

Step 2: Untangle the Stimulus

The statement in question is the third sentence of the stimulus, and that sentence is immediately preceded by the conclusion. There is no conclusion Keyword, but the answer to a rhetorical sentence is usually the author's main point. Here, the author argues that the position of a car driver's seat probably has a significant effect on safe driving. The rest of the stimulus, including the statement with which you are concerned, is the evidence.

Step 3: Make a Prediction

As noted, the statement immediately follows the author's conclusion. Find the answer choice that identifies the statement cited in the question stem as support for the conclusion.

Step 4: Evaluate the Answer Choices

(E) correctly identifies the statement in the question stem as a piece of evidence in support of the conclusion.

(A) incorrectly identifies the statement in the question stem as the conclusion.

(B) incorrectly identifies the statement as counteracting the evidence. However, there is no conflict within the stimulus. Rather, the continuation Keyword [_li_kewise] shows that the statement in question flows easily to the rest of the evidence.

(C) is incorrect. The statement does not show a causal relationship (it "affects," but does not cause), nor does the stimulus present any observed phenomena that the statement could explain.

(D) incorrectly identifies the statement from the question stem as evidence refuted by the author. To the contrary, it is used by the author to support his main point.

23. (E) Point at Issue

Step 1: Identify the Question Type

The phrase "disagree over" signals a Point at Issue question. Use the Decision Tree to determine what the physician and the trampoline enthusiast are arguing about.

Step 2: Untangle the Stimulus

Paraphrase each argument. The physician argues that trampolines should be used only under professional supervision because they are dangerous and they cause thousands of injuries every year. The trampoline enthusiast argues that every exercise carries risk, even when carried out under professional supervision; trampoline use is no exception.

Step 3: Make a Prediction

It appears that the physician and the trampoline enthusiast are arguing over whether professional supervision makes any sort of appreciable difference in guarding against the risks inherent in trampoline activity. Using this prediction, you can apply the Decision Tree as you work through the answer choices. The correct answer choice will produce a "Yes" to each of the following questions: (1) Does the physician discuss the subject matter of the answer choice? (2) Does the trampoline enthusiast discuss the subject matter of the answer choice? (3) Do they have differing opinions on this topic?

Step 4: Evaluate the Answer Choices

(E) matches the prediction. This answer choice yields affirmative responses to all steps of the Decision Tree.

(A) is Outside the Scope. The physician and the trampoline enthusiast may well agree that the number of trampoline injuries is "significant." Their argument is over whether this necessitates professional supervision.

(B) is Outside the Scope. Neither speaker distinguishes injuries suffered on home trampolines from injuries that occur on trampolines in gyms or elsewhere.

(C) is Outside the Scope. Neither the physician nor the trampoline enthusiast cites the number of trampoline users, so neither is comparing the number of users to the number of trampoline-related injuries; nor does the physician discuss the rate of injuries over time.

(D) is Outside the Scope. This is an assumption implicit in the physician's argument, but the trampoline enthusiast might well agree with it. The trampoline enthusiast never says (or suggests) that professional supervision would _not_ help reduce the number of injuries, just that risks exist even _with_ supervision.

24. (C) Principle (Identify/Strengthen)

Step 1: Identify the Question Type

The word _principles_ is a great tip-off to Principle-type questions. In addition, this Principle question mimics the Strengthen question type, as evidenced by the phrase "most helps to justify the reasoning"—so attack it the same way you would a Strengthen question. Look for an answer that would make the editorialist's conclusion more likely to follow from his evidence. Just be sure the correct answer can support a broader application than the specific example cited in the argument.

Step 2: Untangle the Stimulus

The contrast Keyword _but_ indicates the editorialist's opinion. The author contends, contrary to some critics, that the recent coverage of the politician's nephew's personal problems was good journalism. The author presents two reasons why the coverage was commendable: (1) It was accurate, and (2) it attracted more viewers than normal due to interest in the subject matter.

Step 3: Make a Prediction

The editorial's assumption (generalized into a principle) is that accurate and interesting reports equal good journalism. Remember, one way to strengthen an argument is to find an answer choice that states the unexpressed assumption. If the assumption is true, the conclusion is more likely to follow from the evidence. Look for an answer choice that matches the prediction.

Step 4: Evaluate the Answer Choices

(C) is a perfect match to the predicted principle. Indeed, if the statement in this choice is true, then the editorialist's conclusion is confirmed.

(A) is Outside the Scope. Although one of the local television stations criticized the reporting, the author of the editorial gives no criteria for when journalism deserves to be criticized. Conversely, the author of the editorial indicates the journalism in question *did* provide information people want, and thus is good journalism.

(B) is also Outside the Scope. The journalism discussed *did not* misrepresent the facts. Statements about what constitutes bad journalism cannot help justify this argument about what constitutes good journalism.

(D) reverses the logic of the argument. The author states that the coverage was accurate and interesting, and therefore was good journalism. In other words, the author assumes that providing accurate information that people want is sufficient to produce good journalism. But that doesn't mean that *all* good journalism is on subjects or figures of popular interest.

(E) is Outside the Scope. The stimulus only provides a conclusion about journalism that is accurate and interesting. It doesn't offer information about journalism that is inaccurate or uninteresting.

25. (D) Inference

Step 1: Identify the Question Type

The phrase "must be true" identifies this as an Inference question. Work through the stimulus and paraphrase the statements. Combine any Formal Logic.

Step 2: Untangle the Stimulus

In any Inference stimulus, you should work with the strongest statements first, since they're most likely to lead to clear deductions. Here, that means translating and contraposing the conditional Formal Logic statements. The first sentence contains one Formal Logic statement and the third sentence contains two. Skip the second sentence for the moment.

First Sentence:

If	coffeehouse OR restaurant	→	public place

If	~ public place	→	~ coffeehouse AND ~ restaurant

Third Sentence:

If	~ comfortable public place	→	~ well designed

If	well-designed	→	comfortable public place

If	comfortable public place	→	spacious interior

If	~ spacious interior	→	~ comfortable public place

Step 3: Make a Prediction

The second statement (which only addresses "[m]ost public places") is not concrete enough to form a single, strict connection to the other statements. However, "comfortable public place" is a term shared by both statements in the third sentence. This allows you to combine those statements and make a deduction about public places:

If	well-designed	→	comfortable	→	spacious interiors

Now, keep in mind that the first sentence told you that all coffeehouses and restaurants are public places. Work through the answer choices to find an answer choice that follows unequivocally from this chain of logic.

Step 4: Evaluate the Answer Choices

(D) must be true on the basis of the statements. Since coffeehouses and restaurants are public places, it follows (from the combined third-sentence statements) that well-designed coffeehouses or restaurants are comfortable and thus have spacious interiors.

(A) reverses the logic in the last statement. It reverses the terms in the statement without negating them. The fact that all comfortable restaurants have spacious interiors doesn't mean that all restaurants with spacious interiors are comfortable—any more than saying "All of my books are in English" means "All books in English are mine."

(B) is a Distortion. Artwork is but one necessary component of most well-designed public places. That doesn't ensure that having artwork means the place is necessarily well-designed.

(C) is Extreme. Knowing that most well-designed public places feature artwork tells us nothing about the types of establishment they are. Maybe the public places with art are restaurants, libraries, or schools.

(E) reverses the logic in the last statement. Again, this answer does not correctly negate the terms in order to form a proper contrapositive. While all non-spacious public places are not well-designed (because they are uncomfortable), this tells you nothing about public places that *are* spacious. Some may be well-designed and others not, for reasons entirely separate from spaciousness.

Section II: Logic Games

Game 1: Piano Recital

Q#	Question Type	Correct	Difficulty
1	Acceptability	D	★
2	"If" / Could Be True	A	★
3	Must Be False (CANNOT Be True)	C	★
4	Completely Determine	E	★★
5	How Many	B	★★

Game 2: Crafts Presentations

Q#	Question Type	Correct	Difficulty
6	Acceptability	C	★
7	"If" / Could Be True	D	★
8	"If" / Could Be True	E	★★
9	Must Be False (CANNOT Be True)	B	★★
10	"If" / Must Be True	B	★
11	Must Be False (CANNOT Be True)	C	★

Game 3: Luncheon Foods

Q#	Question Type	Correct	Difficulty
12	Acceptability	B	★
13	Must Be True	D	★★★★
14	"If" / Must Be False (CANNOT Be True)	E	★
15	"If" / Could Be True	D	★★★
16	"If" / Must Be True	A	★★

Game 4: TV Scheduling

Q#	Question Type	Correct	Difficulty
17	Acceptability	B	★
18	"If" / How Many	B	★★
19	"If" / Could Be True EXCEPT	D	★★★★
20	"If" / Must Be True	E	★★★
21	"If" / Could Be True	C	★★★
22	Must Be False (CANNOT Be True)	B	★★★
23	Rule Substitution	C	★★★

Game 1: Piano Recital

Step 1: Overview

Situation: Piano students scheduled to perform in a recital

Entities: Five students—Fernando, Ginny, Hakim, Juanita, Kevin

Action: Loose Sequencing. Your task is to put the pianists in order from first to last.

Limitations: Each student performs exactly once. The students perform one at a time.

Step 2: Sketch

In any Sequencing game, first scan the rules to find out whether the game involves Strict or Loose Sequencing. Here, the first and second rules are loose while the third creates a block. There wouldn't be any harm in drawing five empty slots, but this game probably won't require them. Just list the entities and plan to combine the rules later to form a vertical, weblike Loose Sequencing diagram.

F G H J K

Step 3: Rules

Rule 1 states that Ginny performs earlier than—i.e., above—Fernando. Note that this rule does not say how many (or how few) other pianists perform in between these two.

Rule 2 puts Kevin before both Hakim and Juanita. Note that this does not specify a relationship between Hakim and Juanita.

K
⁄ \
H J

Rule 3 creates a block; Hakim and Fernando must perform consecutively, in either order.

$\boxed{H \atop F}$ or $\boxed{F \atop H}$

Step 4: Deductions

Because there are two ways in which Hakim and Fernando may be ordered, Limited Options make sense here. In the first sketch, place Fernando immediately before, or above, Hakim. In the second sketch, place Fernando immediately after, or below, Hakim. Additionally, the H-F block allows you to combine the loose sketches from the first two statements. Rules 1 and 2 mean both Ginny and Kevin perform before the F-H block. Juanita is after Kevin. Notice that the first pianist will always be Ginny or Kevin. The last pianist could be Hakim, Fernando, or Juanita.

The finalized Master Sketch should look similar to this.

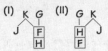

Step 5: Questions

1. (D) Acceptability

On Acceptability questions, eliminate wrong answers by testing the rules against each choice. Rule 1 says Ginny must perform before Fernando, which eliminates **(E)**. Rule 2 states that Kevin performs before both Hakim and Juanita. This eliminates both **(A)** and **(B)**. Rule 3, which states that Hakim and Fernando must perform consecutively, eliminates **(C)**. That leaves **(D)** as the correct answer.

2. (A) "If" / Could Be True

This question includes an "If" statement: Juanita must appear before Ginny. Redraw your sketch.

In both Options, Ginny appears before the Fernando-Hakim block. And Kevin must always perform earlier in the schedule than Juanita.

You're looking for a statement that could be true, i.e., a statement that is correct in one or both of the mini-sketches. Kevin, Juanita, and Ginny all have determined places (1, 2, and 3, respectively). Because this question asks for what *could* be true (and not what *must* be), the correct answer will likely involve one of the two undetermined entities: Fernando or Hakim. Start with **(A)**, which includes Fernando. Fernando performs fourth in the first sketch, so the statement in **(A)** could be true and is correct. You're ready to move on. For the record: Ginny cannot perform second, so **(B)** must be false. **(C)**, which involves Hakim, the other undetermined entity, is also impossible, since Hakim appears fourth or fifth in the sketches. Juanita must perform second in both sketches, so **(D)** must be false. Kevin must perform first, so **(E)** must be false as well.

3. (C) Must be False (CANNOT Be True)

This question doesn't add any new information, so use your master sketch to answer it. The correct answer must be false, meaning that the four incorrect answers could each be true. Note that it may be worthwhile to tackle this question after answering any "If" questions so that you can make use of previous sketches. The two mini-sketches from the previous question for instance, eliminate **(B)** and **(D)**. Those sketches show that Ginny can perform third and Hakim fourth, and Juanita can perform second and Ginny third.

(A) states that Fernando cannot perform immediately before Juanita. That's possible in Option II of the Master Sketch, where Fernando follows Hakim.

(C) posits that Hakim performs immediately before Ginny. That isn't possible in Option I or Option II because G must come before the F-H block. The statement must be false. Therefore, **(C)** is the correct answer. For the record, **(E)** is incorrect because Kevin could perform immediately before Hakim in Option II.

4. (E) Completely Determine

This question asks you to identify a statement that, if true, completely settles the order of the five performances. The most unsettled entities are Fernando and Hakim because their order could go either way. You'll want to determine their placement for sure, but notice that either F or H appears in every answer choice. That means there isn't an easy way to decide which answer choices to test first. In this case, it's best to just go in order. You can eliminate **(A)** right out of the gate; Option I in the Master Sketch makes it clear that placing Fernando right before Hakim does not fully determine the order of the other entities.

(B) creates a G-F-H block, but because Juanita could perform before or after that block, the order of all entities is still not determined.

(C) creates an F-H-J block, but the order of Ginny and Kevin is still up in the air, so **(C)** is not the answer you're looking for.

(D) produces a J-H-F block. Again, though, it's unknown whether Ginny or Kevin comes first.

According to this process of elimination, **(E)** must be the correct answer. If you'd like to confirm that **(E)** is right, create a K-F-H block. According to Rule 1, Ginny must come before Fernando. Rule 2 states that Kevin performs before Juanita. Therefore, a K-F-H block produces this sketch:

The order is completely determined, and **(E)** is the correct answer.

5. (B) How Many

The correct answer to this question cites the number of pianists who could perform fourth. There are only five performers, so just check the Master Sketch and count how many could take the fourth slot.

Both options (and several previous sketches) show that Fernando and Hakim can perform fourth. Therefore, we can eliminate **(A)** right off the bat. Now consider the other entities. What about Ginny? In both Options, she must perform before Fernando and Hakim, which means the latest she could perform is third. Eliminate **(E)**. The same analysis eliminates Kevin; so eliminate **(D)**, too. That leaves only Juanita. If Juanita performs before the F-H block, then (like Kevin and Ginny) Juanita's latest possible position is third. If she performs after the F-H block, then she must perform fifth, because both Ginny and Kevin must come before that block. Thus, Juanita can never go fourth. The correct answer is **(B)**: Two pianists, Fernando and Hakim, could occupy the fourth slot.

Game 2: Crafts Presentations

Step 1: Overview

Situation: Art teachers giving presentations on a variety of subjects at a craft studio's open house

Entities: Six subjects—needlework, origami, pottery, stenciling, textile making, woodworking; categorized by teacher—Jiang, Kudrow, Lanning

Action: Strict Sequencing. Your task is to determine the order of the presentations.

Limitations: The presentations are given one at a time. Jiang presents needlework and origami. Kudrow presents pottery, stenciling, and textile making. Lanning's only presentation is on woodworking.

Step 2: Sketch

First, create a list of entities that shows which presentations are connected to each teacher. Use full-sized letters for the teachers and subscript for the presentations.

Glance at the rules to determine whether the sketch should be a Loose or Strict Sequencing sketch. Because Rule 1 is a restriction rather than a relative placement of entities, seeing its impact will be easier with a Strict Sequencing sketch with six slots. Draw the slots and number them, left to right, from 1 to 6.

$$J_n \ J_o \ K_p \ K_s \ K_t \ L_w$$
$$\overline{} \ \overline{} \ \overline{} \ \overline{} \ \overline{} \ \overline{}$$
$$1 \quad 2 \quad 3 \quad 4 \quad 5 \quad 6$$

Step 3: Rules

Rule 1 is a Strict Sequencing rule that forbids Kudrow to give consecutive presentations. This actually restricts three presentations: pottery, stenciling, and textile making. None of them can be placed next to each other. You can make a note of this rule for now; in the Deductions step, its effect will become more tangible.

$$\text{Never} \ \underline{K} \ \underline{K}$$

Rule 2 places Kudrow's stenciling presentation before (or to the left of) Jiang's origami presentation.

$$K_s \ldots J_o$$

Rule 3 places Kudrow's textile-making presentation before Lanning's woodworking presentation.

$$K_t \ldots L_w$$

Step 4: Deductions

Rule 1 is powerful. Because Kudrow must give three non-consecutive presentations, the presenters' order is somewhat restricted. Kudrow's middle presentation must be flanked on both sides by one of Jiang's or Lanning's presentations. Determine the acceptable arrangements for Kudrow's presentations. If Kudrow presents third, then she must present first, and also fifth or sixth. If Kudrow presents fourth,

then she must present first or second and also sixth. Because those are the only ways to validly distribute Kudrow's three presentations, Limited Options are your best bet.

(I)
$$\underline{K} \ \underline{} \ \underline{K} \ \underline{} \ \underline{} \ \overset{K}{\underline{\wedge}}$$
$$1 \quad 2 \quad 3 \quad 4 \quad 5 \quad 6$$

(II)
$$\overset{K}{\underline{\wedge}} \ \underline{} \ \underline{} \ \underline{K} \ \underline{} \ \underline{K}$$
$$1 \quad 2 \quad 3 \quad 4 \quad 5 \quad 6$$

In Option I, note that Kudrow's first two presentations could be pottery, stenciling, or textile making. Kudrow's third presentation is more restricted. If Kudrow is in slot 5, she could present pottery, stenciling, or textile making. If she is sixth, then she must present pottery because stenciling must precede origami, and textile making must come before woodworking.

(I)
$$\underline{K} \ \underline{} \ \underline{K} \ \underline{} \ \underline{} \ \overset{K}{\underline{\wedge}}$$
$$1 \quad 2 \quad 3 \quad 4 \quad 5 \quad 6$$
$$ \overset{\displaystyle s}{t}$$

In Option II, begin with the last slot. Kudrow must present sixth, and since Rules 2 and 3 forbid stenciling or textile making from being placed last, the last slot must be pottery. The fourth presentation could be stenciling or textile making. If Kudrow goes first, that presentation could also be stenciling or textile making. However, look at what happens if Kudrow goes second. Neither woodworking nor origami can go first because each follows another presentation. That leaves only needlework, demonstrated by Jiang.

(II)
$$\overset{K}{\underline{\wedge}} \ \underline{} \ \underline{} \ \underline{K} \ \underline{} \ \underline{K_p}$$
$$1 \quad 2 \quad 3 \quad 4 \quad 5 \quad 6$$
$$\overset{\displaystyle \not{o}}{\not{w}} \qquad \text{If} \ \frac{K}{2} \rightarrow \frac{J_n}{1}$$

The finalized Master Sketch should look similar to this.

(I)
$$\underline{K} \ \underline{} \ \underline{K} \ \underline{} \ \underline{} \ \overset{K}{\underline{\wedge}}$$
$$1 \quad 2 \quad 3 \quad 4 \quad 5 \quad 6$$
$$ \overset{\displaystyle s}{t}$$

(II)
$$\overset{K}{\underline{\wedge}} \ \underline{} \ \underline{} \ \underline{K} \ \underline{} \ \underline{K_p}$$
$$1 \quad 2 \quad 3 \quad 4 \quad 5 \quad 6$$
$$\overset{\displaystyle \not{o}}{\not{w}} \qquad \text{If} \ \frac{K}{2} \rightarrow \frac{J_n}{1}$$

$$K_s \ldots J_o$$
$$K_t \ldots L_w$$

Step 5: Questions

6. (C) Acceptability

With any Acceptability question, test the rules against the answer choices, eliminating any choice that violates the rules. Rule 1, which forbids Kudrow from giving consecutive presentations, means that pottery, stenciling, and textile making can never appear next to each other in a valid sketch. **(A)** has pottery and textile making side by side; eliminate it. **(E)** has textile making and stenciling first and second; eliminate that choice as well. Rule 2 states that stenciling must be presented before origami. **(D)**, which places stenciling after origami, is therefore incorrect. Rule 3, finally, requires that textile making be presented before woodworking. **(B)**, however, places textile making last, so it is wrong. That leaves only **(C)**, which is the correct answer.

7. (D) "If" / Could Be True

Start by drawing a mini-sketch to account for the condition in the question stem. If textile making (which is presented by Kudrow) is fifth, then we must be in Option I. Re-sketch that Option, and place Kt in the fifth slot.

$$\text{(I)} \quad \frac{K}{1} \quad \frac{}{2} \quad \frac{K}{3} \quad \frac{}{4} \quad \frac{K_t}{5} \quad \frac{}{6}$$

Textile making must be presented before Lanning presents woodworking, so woodworking must be sixth. The second and fourth demonstrations must be Jiang's. Either needlework or origami can go there. No other deductions can be made.

$$\text{(I)} \quad \frac{K}{1} \quad \frac{J}{2} \quad \frac{K}{3} \quad \frac{J}{4} \quad \frac{K_t}{5} \quad \frac{L_w}{6}$$

You now have enough information to answer the question. The correct answer is the only one that could be true in the mini-sketch. Woodworking is presented last, so **(A)** and **(E)** are both impossible. Pottery and stenciling (both demonstrated by Kudrow) must be presented first and third, in either order. **(B)** and **(C)**, therefore, can't be true. That leaves **(D)**. Stenciling could come third and origami fourth. That would force pottery into the first slot and needlework into the second slot. That creates an acceptable arrangement, so **(D)** is the correct answer.

8. (E) "If" / Could Be True

Start by accounting for the "If" condition in a mini-sketch. Needlework can only be presented first in Option II. Redraw that Option, adding Jn to the first slot.

$$\text{(II)} \quad \frac{J_n}{1} \quad \frac{K}{2} \quad \frac{}{3} \quad \frac{K}{4} \quad \frac{}{5} \quad \frac{K_p}{6}$$

That's all you need to attack the answer choices. The correct answer is the only one acceptable in the mini-sketch. Stenciling and textile making will be presented second and fourth, in either order, so **(B)**, **(C)**, and **(D)** are all impossible. The last slot is taken up by Kudrow's pottery presentation, so **(A)** is false as well. **(E)** is the only answer choice left and is a valid possibility in the mini-sketch. If woodworking is third, then textile making must be second. That leaves stenciling in the fourth slot and origami in the fifth. Select **(E)** and keep moving.

$$\text{(II)} \quad \frac{J_n}{1} \quad \frac{K_t}{2} \quad \frac{L_w}{3} \quad \frac{K_s}{4} \quad \frac{J_o}{5} \quad \frac{K_p}{6}$$

9. (B) Must Be False (CANNOT Be True)

The correct answer here will list a pair of spaces that cannot *both* be taken by Jiang. If an answer choice lists a pair of spaces acceptable for Jiang, eliminate it. It turns out (not surprisingly) that this question can be answered using the Limited Options in the Master Sketch.

Start at the top. Jiang could go first and third in Option II, so eliminate **(A)**. But Jiang can never take the first and fourth places. In Option I Kudrow is first, and in Option II Kudrow is fourth, so Jiang can't be both first and fourth. Thus, **(B)** is the correct answer. For the record: Option II allows Jiang to present first and fifth, or second and third, so you can eliminate **(C)** and **(D)**. Finally, **(E)** is incorrect since Jiang could present second and fourth in Option I.

10. (B) "If" / Must Be True

Start your work here by recording the "If" condition from the question stem in a mini-sketch. Needlework can be sixth only in Option I. Redraw this option, with Jn in the sixth slot.

Because textile making must be presented before woodworking, and stenciling must come before origami, the only subject left for Kudrow's last presentation in the fifth slot is pottery.

$$\text{(I)} \quad \frac{K}{1} \quad \frac{}{2} \quad \frac{K}{3} \quad \frac{}{4} \quad \frac{K_p}{5} \quad \frac{J_n}{6}$$

With this placement, you have enough information to answer the question. The correct answer must be true in the mini-sketch. Because pottery is fifth (not coincidentally, this is the one firm deduction you made), the statement in **(B)** must be true and is correct.

On Test Day, you would select **(B)** and keep moving; but for practice, check out the other answer choices. Kudrow's presentations, in the first and third slots, must be textile making and stenciling, in either order. According to Rules 2 and 3, textile making must come before woodworking, and stenciling before origami. Thus, deciding the order of stenciling and textile making completes the sketch. These are the two possible outcomes:

$$\text{(I)} \quad \frac{K_s}{1} \quad \frac{J_o}{2} \quad \frac{K_t}{3} \quad \frac{L_w}{4} \quad \frac{K_p}{5} \quad \frac{J_n}{6}$$

$$\quad \frac{K_t}{1} \quad \frac{L_w}{2} \quad \frac{K_s}{3} \quad \frac{J_o}{4} \quad \frac{K_p}{5} \quad \frac{J_n}{6}$$

Origami can be second, so **(A)** could be false. Stenciling could come first, and textile making third, so **(C)** and **(D)** could be false as well. Woodworking, finally, could be the second craft demonstrated, so **(E)** does not have to be true.

11. (C) Must Be False (CANNOT Be True)

Before you draw new sketches for an open-ended question like this, remember to check both the Master Sketch and your previous mini-sketches. Since the correct answer cannot be the subject of the second presentation, eliminate the four choices naming subjects that can be presented second. In this case, the two options in the Master Sketch tell us everything we need to know. **(A)** has needlework, a subject that could be the second presentation in either option. Go back and test **(A)** with a sketch only if none of the other answers is a clear winner. **(B)** is origami, another subject that could be the second presentation in both options. Move on to **(C)**, pottery, a subject presented by Kudrow. In Option I, Kudrow cannot present second. In Option II, Kudrow presents pottery sixth, in order to accommodate Rules 2 and 3. In neither option can pottery come second. **(C)** is the correct answer. To confirm, **(D)** is incorrect because textile making could be second in Option II (the acceptable full arrangement would be Jn-Kt-Lw-Ks-Jo-Kp). Finally, **(E)** is incorrect because woodworking could be second in either option provided textile making is presented first.

Game 3: Luncheon Foods

Step 1: Overview

Situation: A luncheon organizer selecting five foods to serve

Entities: Eight foods—desserts F and G; main courses N, O, P; and side dishes T, V, W. Of these, F, N, T are served hot; the other dishes are served cold

Action: Selection. Your task is to choose five of the eight possible menu items; you'll reject the other three.

Limitations: Exactly five foods will be selected for the menu and three left off. F, N, and T are the only hot foods.

Step 2: Sketch

The diagram for a selection game is just the list of entities. As foods are selected, circle them. As foods are excluded, cross them off the list. For this game, it makes sense to create a list that breaks the entities into three visually distinct categories. Make a note above or below the sketch to remind yourself that exactly five foods will be chosen and three excluded. In another note, make a list of the three hot foods: F, N, and T.

Hot: F, N, T

dessert	main	sides
F G	N O P	T V W

Step 3: Rules

Rule 1 states that at least one food from each of the three categories must be selected. Add a note just below the sketch.

$\geq$ 1 ea. category

Rule 2 says the selection must include at least one of the hot foods (F, N, and T). Add that note beneath the sketch.

$\geq$ 1 hot (F, N, T)

Rule 3 is the first of three Formal Logic rules. If P or W is included, then both are included. The contrapositive is that if either P or W is excluded, both are excluded. If you drew this rule as a pair of arrow diagrams, that's fine, but there's a simpler way to express it because it leads to just two possibilities: either both P and W are selected, or both P and W are excluded.

P W or P̸ W̸

Rule 4 is straightforward Formal Logic. If G is in, then O is in. Write out the contrapositive as well: if O is excluded, then G is excluded.

If G → O
If O̸ → G̸

Rule 5 is the last of the game's Formal Logic rules. If N is selected, V must be excluded. The contrapositive is that if V is included, N must be excluded. There's a simpler way to express this rule, as well. Because selecting one always means rejecting the other, N and V can never be selected together.

If N → V̸
If V → N̸
or
Never N V

Step 4: Deductions

Because you know that exactly five foods will be selected, and that P and W must be selected or rejected as a block, you may be tempted to try Limited Options here. Look, however, at the questions. The first question is an Acceptability question and is likely to serve as a quick and easy point. The last three questions are all "If" questions and will provide information you can easily plug into a mini-sketch. The only open-ended question is the second question of the set which you should leave for last. The most efficient approach, then, is to jump right into the question set.

The finalized Master Sketch should look similar to this.

Hot: F, N, T

dessert	main	sides	$\geq$ 1 ea. category
F G	N O P	T V W	$\geq$ 1 hot (F, N, T)

P W or P̸ W̸

If G → O
If O̸ → G̸

Never N V

Step 5: Questions

12. (B) Acceptability

On Acceptability questions, check each rule against the answer choices and eliminate answers that violate a rule. Rule 1, which requires the inclusion of at least one food from each category, is not violated by any of the answer choices. Rule 2's requirement that a hot food (F, N, or T) be selected eliminates **(E)**.

Rule 3 states that P and W are both in or both out, so get rid of **(D)**, which includes P but not W. Rule 4's logic is violated in **(C)**, which includes G but not O. And Rule 5, which says that N and V can never be selected together, eliminates **(A)**. **(B)** is the last choice standing and is correct.

13. (D) Must Be True

Because this question is open-ended, you might choose to leave it for last and use the sketches you make for the three subsequent "If" questions to help eliminate answer choices. (**(A)**, for instance, can be eliminated by the sketch for the second to last question of the set which shows that both F and T can be excluded from a valid selection.) For now, just take the choices in order. The correct answer is the only one in which at least one of the foods mentioned must be included in any acceptable sketch. In other words, for each of the four wrong answers, you can eliminate both foods mentioned and still make an acceptable selection of five luncheon items.

(D) turns out to be the right answer. If you eliminate O and P, you cannot create an acceptable menu of five foods. Rejecting O requires you to reject G (Rule 4), and rejecting P requires you to reject W (Rule 3). That leaves only four food choices, but the luncheon needs five. Since you cannot complete an acceptable selection without at least one of O and P, **(D)** is correct.

Here's why the other four choices are incorrect:

(A) If you reject F and T, which are both hot foods, then you must include N (Rule 2). Including N requires you to reject V (Rule 5). That leaves five foods—G, N, O, P, and T—which constitute an acceptable selection. Since you do not need either F or T to create an acceptable menu, **(A)** is incorrect.

(A) F G N O P T V W

(B) Rejecting G and O doesn't trigger any other rules and leaves six foods available. Since five foods are needed for the luncheon, both P and W must be included (see Rule 3). Since N and V cannot both be included (Rule 5), this leaves two acceptable arrangements.

(B) F G N O P T V W
F G N O P T V W

(C) N and T are both hot foods, so with them rejected, you must include F (Rule 2). There are five more foods to choose from. In order to get a total of five foods for the luncheon, you must include both P and W (see Rule 3). At this point, G, O, and V remain. There are two acceptable ways to complete the luncheon selection.

(C) F G N O P T V W
F G N O P T V W

(E) Eliminating V and W triggers Rule 3, so P must be rejected as well. That leaves five foods: F, G, N, O, and T. This selection contains at least one food from each category and has all three hot foods, so there's no problem with Rules 1 and 2. You accommodated Rule 3 by rejecting both P and W. Rule 4 is fine here as both G and O are included. Since V is out, Rule 5 is not violated, either. You can make an acceptable selection without V and W, so **(E)** is incorrect.

(E) F G N O P T V W

14. (E) "If" / Must Be False (CANNOT Be True)

This question provides a helpful "If" statement: O is selected, and both N and P are rejected because they are the other two main courses. Put this information into a mini-sketch and continue making deductions. Rule 3 states that if P is excluded, W is excluded as well, so cross out W. At this point, exactly five foods—F, G, O, T, and V—remain, so your selection is complete.

F G N O P T V W

The question asks for the food that cannot be selected under these conditions. The correct answer is **(E)**; you know from the mini-sketch that W is out. All four incorrect answers present foods that must be selected in this case.

15. (D) "If" / Could Be True

Begin your work on "If" questions by incorporating the question stem's condition into a mini-sketch. This one says to exclude F. G must therefore be selected, since one food from each group must be selected (Rule 1) and G is the only other dessert. If G is selected, then O is selected as well (Rule 4).

F G N O P T V W

Five foods remain. Of them, you must select three and reject two. P and W act as a block and must be selected together or rejected together. If you reject both P and W, you'd have to include both N and V in order to select five foods. That violates Rule 5. Therefore, P and W must both be selected.

F G N O P T V W

With G, O, P, and W all selected, there is room for only one more food. Desserts, main courses, and side dishes are all represented, but every valid selection must also include one or more of the hot foods, F, N, and T. F is already out—so either N or T must be chosen. There is no room for V, which must be excluded. At this point, you have two acceptable selections:

F G N O P T V W
F G N O P T V W

Now turn to the answer choices. The correct choice could be true; all four incorrect answers must be false. **(A)** is impossible, because two main courses, O and P, have already been selected. **(B)** is also incorrect, since W, a side dish, is already part of the selection. **(C)** must be false because there is room for only one hot food: either N or T, but not both. **(D),** however, is a statement that could be true; main courses N, O, and P could all be selected under this question's conditions. Sure enough, **(E)** is impossible because one of the three side dishes, V, is already crossed out. **(D)** is the correct answer.

16. (A) "If" / Must Be True

This question provides a generously detailed "If" statement. Incorporate these conditions into a mini-sketch. Select T and V, and reject the other side dish, W.

F G N O P T V W

Because W is gone, P must be rejected as well (Rule 3), and because V is selected, N must be excluded (Rule 5). But a main course is required (Rule 1), so O must be selected. Finally, a valid selection must include five foods, so select F and G as well.

F G N O P T V W

The question asks for a pair of entities that must be selected.
(A) lists F and G and is correct. All the other answer choices
include one rejected entity.

Game 4: TV Scheduling

Step 1: Overview

Situation: A TV programmer scheduling shows to fill a three-hour programming block

Entities: Five shows: an hour-long program, *Generations*; and four half-hour programs: *Roamin'*, *Sundown*, *Terry*, *Waterloo*

Action: Strict Sequencing. Your task is to order the television programs within the three-hour block.

Limitations: The five programs are shown one at a time, back to back, within a three-hour period beginning at 1:00 pm. Each is shown exactly once.

Step 2: Sketch

This game includes 30-minute shows and hour-long shows. Therefore, the ideal sketch will include six half-hour slots, but will also break the diagram into three larger parts, one for each hour.

Since an hour-long program fills two slots in the diagram, represent *Generations*—the hour-long program—as a block of two Gs.

$$\boxed{G\ G}\ R\ S\ T\ W$$

$$\underline{\quad}\ \ \underline{\quad}\ \ \Big|\ \ \underline{\quad}\ \ \underline{\quad}\ \ \Big|\ \ \underline{\quad}\ \ \underline{\quad}$$
$$1\quad 1{:}30\quad\ \ 2\quad 2{:}30\quad\ \ 3\quad 3{:}30$$

Step 3: Rules

Rule 1 says that *Generations* must begin at 1:00, 2:00, or 3:00. Because all of the other shows are 30 minutes long, this rule means that *Generations* will be either the first, the third, or the fifth program on the schedule.

$$\underline{\quad}\ \ \underline{\quad}\ \ \Big|\ \ \underline{\quad}\ \ \underline{\quad}\ \ \Big|\ \ \underline{\quad}\ \ \underline{\quad}$$
$$1\quad 1{:}30\quad\ \ 2\quad 2{:}30\quad\ \ 3\quad 3{:}30$$
$$\boxed{G\ G}$$

Rule 2 forbids *Terry* from beginning at 1:00, 2:00, or 3:00. Add restrictions underneath those slots.

$$\underline{\quad}\ \ \underline{\quad}\ \ \Big|\ \ \underline{\quad}\ \ \underline{\quad}\ \ \Big|\ \ \underline{\quad}\ \ \underline{\quad}$$
$$1\quad 1{:}30\quad\ \ 2\quad 2{:}30\quad\ \ 3\quad 3{:}30$$
$$\cancel{T}\qquad\quad\ \cancel{T}\qquad\quad\ \cancel{T}$$
$$\boxed{G\ G}$$

Rule 3 is a loose sequencing rule that schedules *Roamin'* earlier than *Sundown*.

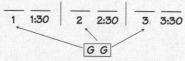

$$R\ .\ .\ .\ S$$

Rule 4 is an unusual sequencing rule. Either *Waterloo* is immediately before *Terry*, or *Terry* is some time before *Waterloo*. Keep this block in mind throughout the game. If there isn't space for *Waterloo* and *Terry* to sit side by side, then *Terry* must come earlier than *Waterloo*.

$$\boxed{W\ T}\ \text{ or }\ T\ .\ .\ .\ W$$

Step 4: Deductions

Add restrictions to your sketch to reflect the fact that *Sundown* cannot go first and *Roamin'* cannot go last. You may be tempted to try Limited Options using the *Generations* block—but be careful. If *Generations* goes first, for example, *Terry* can air at 2:30 or 3:30. *Waterloo* and *Terry* could still appear in either order—and we haven't even gotten to *Roamin'* and *Sundown*. In short, placing *Generations* does not necessarily lead to powerful deductions that you can build into the sketch. Instead of trying to figure out all of the game's possibilities now, begin with the Acceptability question, and then work through the "If" questions. Sketches from those are likely to make answering the remaining questions easier.

The finalized Master Sketch should look similar to this.

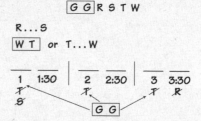

$$\boxed{G\ G}\ R\ S\ T\ W$$

$$R\ .\ .\ .\ S$$
$$\boxed{W\ T}\ \text{ or }\ T\ .\ .\ .\ W$$

$$\underline{\quad}\ \ \underline{\quad}\ \ \Big|\ \ \underline{\quad}\ \ \underline{\quad}\ \ \Big|\ \ \underline{\quad}\ \ \underline{\quad}$$
$$1\quad 1{:}30\quad\ \ 2\quad 2{:}30\quad\ \ 3\quad 3{:}30$$
$$\cancel{T}\qquad\qquad\cancel{T}\qquad\qquad\cancel{T}\ \ \cancel{R}$$
$$\cancel{S}\qquad\qquad\qquad\boxed{G\ G}$$

Step 5: Questions

17. (B) Acceptability

Check the rules one by one and eliminate any answer choice that violates a rule. Rule 1 requires *Generations* to begin at 1:00, 2:00, or 3:00—which means that the show must appear first, third, or fifth in the sequence of programs. **(C)** incorrectly has *Generations* running fourth in the selection, meaning that it would begin at 2:30. Cross off **(C)**. Rule 2 states that *Terry* must begin at 1:30, 2:30, or 3:30. **(A)** has *Terry* starting at 3:00, so eliminate it. Rule 3 requires *Roamin'* to be broadcast earlier than *Sundown*, so eliminate **(E)**, which has *Sundown* third and *Roamin'* fourth. Finally, Rule 4 states that *Waterloo* must come either immediately before *Terry* or at some point after Terry. **(D)** has *Waterloo* first and *Terry* fourth, so it doesn't work. **(B)** is the correct answer.

18. (B) "If" / How Many

In this "If" question, *Waterloo* must occupy the first slot. Build that into a mini-sketch. According to Rule 4, because *Waterloo* comes before *Terry* (as it must in this case), *Terry* must come immediately after *Waterloo*. Place *Terry* in the 1:30 time slot. There are now two places where the G-G block can go: the 2:00 hour or the 3:00 hour. Don't waste time trying to visualize these outcomes in your head; sketching them out takes 10 seconds, tops. The two remaining entities, *Roamin'* and *Sundown*, fill the remaining two slots. Due to Rule 3, *Roamin'* must air earlier than *Sundown*.

$$\underline{W} \ \underline{T} \ | \ \underline{G} \ \underline{G} \ | \ \underline{R} \ \underline{S}$$

$$\underline{W} \ \underline{T} \ | \ \underline{R} \ \underline{S} \ | \ \underline{G} \ \underline{G}$$

There are exactly two ways that the shows could be programmed validly under this question's conditions. **(B)** is the correct answer.

19. (D) "If" / Could Be True EXCEPT

On any "If" question, start by placing the new "If" condition into a mini-sketch. If *Roamin'* is the second program, it could air at 1:30 (after a half-hour show) or at 2:00 (after *Generations*). Thus, there are three places where the G-G block could appear in the sketch. If *Roamin'* airs at 1:30, *Generations* could air at 2:00 or 3:00. If *Generations* is first, during the 1:00 hour, then *Roamin'* would air at 2:00. While it may seem as though drawing three mini-sketches is time-consuming, it is by far the fastest and most accurate approach to this question.

$$\underline{} \ \underline{R} \ | \ \underline{G} \ \underline{G} \ | \ \underline{} \ \underline{}$$

$$\underline{} \ \underline{R} \ | \ \underline{} \ \underline{} \ | \ \underline{G} \ \underline{G}$$

$$\underline{G} \ \underline{G} \ | \ \underline{R} \ \underline{} \ | \ \underline{} \ \underline{}$$

Roamin' must always air before *Sundown*. In the first two sketches, then, it is impossible to place *Waterloo* and *Terry* side by side. That means, according to Rule 4, *Terry* must air before *Waterloo*. In the first two sketches, *Terry* must air first—but Rule 2 forbids that. Therefore, the top two sketches are invalid.

$$\cancel{\underline{T}} \ \underline{R} \ | \ \underline{G} \ \underline{G} \ | \ \cancel{\underline{S/W}}$$

$$\cancel{\underline{T}} \ \underline{R} \ | \ \cancel{\underline{S/W}} \ | \ \cancel{\underline{G} \ \underline{G}}$$

$$\underline{G} \ \underline{G} \ | \ \underline{R} \ \underline{} \ | \ \underline{} \ \underline{}$$

Now, in the remaining sketch (where *Generations* is at 1:00 and *Roamin'* at 2:00), there are two slots *Terry* could fill: 2:30 and 3:30. If *Terry* airs at 2:30, then *Sundown* and *Waterloo* may be shown in either order in the last two slots. If *Terry* airs at 3:30, then Rule 4 requires *Waterloo* air at 3:00. *Sundown* is left to fill the last vacant slot, at 2:30.

$$\underline{G} \ \underline{G} \ | \ \underline{R} \ \underline{T} \ | \ \underline{S/W}$$

$$\underline{G} \ \underline{G} \ | \ \underline{R} \ \underline{S} \ | \ \underline{W} \ \underline{T}$$

The question asks for a statement that must be false. That means all four incorrect answers are acceptable. **(A)** is not the right choice, since *Sundown* could air third. **(B)** is also incorrect; *Sundown* could be the fourth program when *Waterloo* airs at 3:30. Eliminate **(C)**, since *Terry* is indeed the fifth program when it airs last at 3:30. The last two choices, **(D)** and **(E)**, both have to do with *Waterloo*. According to the sketches, *Waterloo* can only air fourth or fifth. Therefore, the

statement in **(E)** could be true, but the one in **(D)** must be false. **(D)** is the correct answer.

20. (E) "If" / Must Be True

Here's another "If" question. This one states that *Sundown* airs third. There are two ways that this might happen. First, *Sundown* could air at 2:00, after two half-hour shows. In that case, the G-G block would fill the last two half-hour slots (during the 3:00 hour). Alternatively, *Sundown* could air at 2:30, after *Generations* and one half-hour-long program. In this case, the G-G block would take up the first two slots (during the 1:00 hour).

$$\underline{} \ \underline{} \ | \ \underline{S} \ \underline{} \ | \ \underline{G} \ \underline{G}$$

$$\underline{G} \ \underline{G} \ | \ \underline{} \ \underline{S} \ | \ \underline{} \ \underline{}$$

Rule 3 requires *Roamin'* to air earlier than *Sundown*. In the top sketch, *Roamin'* must air at 1:00 or 1:30. In the bottom sketch, *Roamin'* airs at 2:00.

$$\overset{R}{\underline{\diagup\!\diagdown}} \ | \ \underline{S} \ \underline{} \ | \ \underline{G} \ \underline{G}$$

$$\underline{G} \ \underline{G} \ | \ \underline{R} \ \underline{S} \ | \ \underline{} \ \underline{}$$

Rule 4 states that either *Waterloo* airs immediately before *Terry*, or *Terry* airs earlier than *Waterloo*. In the top sketch, there isn't room for a W-T block. Therefore, *Terry* must air earlier than *Waterloo*. This means that *Waterloo* can only air at 2:30. And because *Terry* cannot begin on the hour, *Terry* must be shown at 1:30, leaving *Roamin'* to fill the empty slot at 1:00.

$$\underline{R} \ \underline{T} \ | \ \underline{S} \ \underline{W} \ | \ \underline{G} \ \underline{G}$$

In the bottom sketch, because of the rule forbidding *Terry* to begin on the hour, *Terry* must air at 3:30. *Waterloo* fills the open slot at 3:00.

$$\underline{G} \ \underline{G} \ | \ \underline{R} \ \underline{S} \ | \ \underline{W} \ \underline{T}$$

This question asks you to identify a statement that must be true. **(A)** could be false; *Generations* is dead last in the first of the two sketches. According to the sketches, *Roamin'* can go first or second, which means both **(B)** and **(C)** could be false. And, since *Terry* is the second program to air in the top sketch, **(D)** could be false. That leaves only **(E)**. And indeed, *Waterloo* is fourth in both versions of the mini-sketch. In the top sketch, *Waterloo* airs at 2:30, after *Roamin'*, *Terry*, and *Sundown*. In the bottom sketch, *Waterloo* airs at 3:00, after *Generations*, *Roamin'*, and *Sundown*. **(E)** must be true, and it is the correct answer.

21. (C) "If" / Could Be True

If *Generations* is the third program aired, then it must begin at 2:00, following two half-hour shows that air during the 1:00 hour. That leaves two slots open for *Terry*: 1:30 and 3:30. If *Terry* airs at 1:30, then the first program could be either *Roamin'* or *Waterloo*. If *Roamin'* airs first, then the last two programs are *Waterloo* and *Sundown*, in either order. If

Waterloo is first, then, due to Rule 3, *Roamin'* must air at 3:00 and *Sundown* at 3:30. If *Terry* airs at 3:30, then *Waterloo* must air at 3:00, according to Rule 4. *Roamin'* would then air at 1:00, and *Sundown* at 1:30.

T @ 1:30

<u>R</u> <u>T</u> | <u>G</u> <u>G</u> | <u>S/W</u>

or

<u>W</u> <u>T</u> | <u>G</u> <u>G</u> | <u>R</u> <u>S</u>

T @ 3:30

<u>R</u> <u>S</u> | <u>G</u> <u>G</u> | <u>W</u> <u>T</u>

The question asks for a statement that could be true. **(A)** and **(B)** are both false, since *Roamin'* must air first or fourth. *Sundown* could air fourth in the top sketch (in the event that *Roamin'* starts at 1:00), so **(C)** is the correct answer. For the record, **(D)** is false, since *Terry* must air either second or fifth. **(E)** is false as well, since *Waterloo* can air only first, fourth, or fifth.

22. (B) Must Be False (CANNOT Be True)

If you handle the "If" questions first, this open-ended question becomes a free point. The sketches from the previous question show that **(A)**, **(C)**, and **(D)** are all acceptable. The sketches from the fourth question of the set show that **(E)**, too, describes a valid outcome. **(B)**, which does not appear in any valid sketch drawn to this point, is the winner by default.

To see why **(B)** cannot work, create a W-R block. Under Rule 4, *Terry* must air earlier in the schedule than the new W-R block. *Roamin'* must always air earlier than *Sundown*. Under Rule 2, *Terry* must start on the half-hour. Because three programs now come later than *Terry* in the sequence, the only time available to *Terry* is 1:30. However, that leaves no place for the G-G block. The diagram is not valid, confirming that **(B)** is correct.

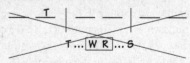

23. (C) Rule Substitution

This question asks you to identify a rule that has the exact same effect as Rule 1. Rule 1 states that the G-G block must start on the hour, i.e., at 1:00, 2:00, or 3:00. That leads to the deduction that *Generations* must air first (during the 1:00 hour), third (during the 2:00 hour, after two half-hour shows), or fifth (during the 3:00 hour, after all four half-hour shows). **(C)** says the same thing in a roundabout way; if *Generations* cannot air second or fourth, then it must air first, third, or fifth. If you swapped Rule 1 for the statement in **(C)**, the game wouldn't change at all. And that means **(C)** is the correct answer.

Section III: Reading Comprehension
Passage 1: Latina Autobiography in the 1980s

Q#	Question Type	Correct	Difficulty
1	Global	B	★
2	Detail	D	★
3	Logic Function	E	★
4	Detail	A	★★
5	Inference	B	★
6	Inference	A	★★
7	Logic Reasoning (Weaken)	D	★★★

Passage 2: The Archivist's Dilemma

Q#	Question Type	Correct	Difficulty
8	Global	A	★
9	Detail	C	★★
10	Inference	A	★★
11	Logic Function	B	★★
12	Inference	D	★★
13	Inference	E	★★★★

Passage 3: Blackmail in Two Legal Contexts

Q#	Question Type	Correct	Difficulty
14	Global	C	★
15	Inference	B	★★★
16	Inference	A	★★★★
17	Detail	A	★★★
18	Inference	E	★★
19	Logic Reasoning (Parallel Reasoning)	D	★★★★

Passage 4: Restoring Europe's Farmland

Q#	Question Type	Correct	Difficulty
20	Global	A	★
21	Global	E	★
22	Detail	B	★★
23	Inference	D	★★★
24	Logic Function	E	★★
25	Inference (LEAST)	B	★★★
26	Inference	C	★★★
27	Logic Reasoning (Parallel Reasoning)	B	★★★★

Passage 1: Latina Autobiography in the 1980s

Step 1: Read the Passage Strategically

Sample Roadmap

line #	Keyword/phrase	¶ Margin notes
1	proliferation	
5	also	3 notable Latina autobios
6	prominence … notable	Latina autobio prominent
12		innovative -Mix language -Many identities
13	innovative	mix lang
14	each	many identities
17		-Mixed structure/genres
20	without,	
21	preference	
22		Frontera: narr/poetry together
26	likewise	War Yrs: events out of sequence
28	not	
29	but rather	
32	departure	female vs. male autobios
33	important difference	
35	departs even further	*Home Alive*: 2 voices together
39	not	
40	but rather	
42	While	
43	may seem … fragmentary … confusing,	
44	in fact	
47	":"	intentional exper.
50	Rather	
52	revolutionized	Effect on autobio genre
55	In doing so,	Auth–high level of respect for these female authors
55	for too long	

Discussion

The **Topic**—U.S. Latina writers—is set by line 4, as the author mentions the proliferation of their work in the 1980s. In the second sentence, the author narrows in on the end of the decade and also the **Scope**—Latina writers' foray into autobiography. The author ends the paragraph by citing three notable autobiographies by these writers, so you can expect the rest of the passage to discuss the features of these works and why they deserve prominence.

Paragraph 2 describes the many ways in which these authors' works were innovative. They cross linguistic boundaries, and they address the multifaceted identities of their authors. This innovation, according to the author, becomes apparent when one examines the structure of the works, which mix content from many different genres.

Paragraph 3 devotes itself to a discussion of each autobiography in turn. Lines 22–25 discuss features of Anzaldua's work (*Borderlands/La Frontera*), which juxtaposes poetry and narrative. Lines 25–34 discuss Moraga's autobiography (*Loving in the War Years*), which mixes genres (note the author's use of *likewise*, in line 26, linking this work to *Borderlands*) and departs from chronological ordering. The author even cites a critic who says that this departure represents a chief distinction between autobiographies written by women and those written by men. Lines 35–45 discuss the Moraleses' work (*Getting Home Alive*), which combines the voices of two different authors. The author ends the paragraph by pointing out that this feature might seem confusing and haphazard, but is actually a deliberate experiment.

Finally, Paragraph 4 shows the effects of these Latina writers' choices on the genre of autobiography. Keywords such as *revolutionized* and "redrawing the boundaries" illustrate the extent to which the author believes these writers have affected their genre. This confirms the author's **Purpose**: to describe the revolutionary techniques of these Latina autobiographers; and **Main Idea**: that these writers deliberately combined and experimented with different genres and conventions to suit their needs.

1. (B) Global

Step 2: Identify the Question Type

Any question asking you for the "main point of the passage" is a Global question.

Step 3: Research the Relevant Text

For a Global question, don't go back to a specific part of the passage. Instead, consult your understanding of Topic, Scope, Purpose, and Main Idea from Step 1.

Step 4: Make a Prediction

The Main Idea of the passage is that in the 1980s, Latina writers altered the genre of autobiography to suit their needs. These authors were better able to communicate the complexity of their identities by changing the structure and form of the medium in which they worked.

Step 5: Evaluate the Answer Choices

(B) is the best match for this prediction. It addresses how these writers changed the genre to make it suit their goals.

(A) is off because nothing in the passage indicates that the specific writers discussed—Moraga, Anzaldua, or the Moraleses—were formerly writing mostly poetry and fiction. The passage's first sentence mentions that Latina writers in general wrote poetry and fiction.

(C) makes a distinction between traditional and nontraditional Latina autobiographers, a distinction the author never makes. Indeed, the author mentions no traditional Latina autobiographies at all.

(D) distorts the goals of the Latina writers. Their blend of genres wasn't for its own sake; it existed because these writers needed to express all facets of their identities.

(E) focuses on the acknowledgments of literary critics, which is only secondary in the passage. It's a point too minor to constitute the author's Main Idea.

2. (D) Detail

Step 2: Identify the Question Type

The phrase "according to the passage" at the beginning of the question stem indicates that this is a Detail question. Use the clues in the question stem to find the relevant text.

Step 3: Research the Relevant Text

The question stem refers to a "motivating factor" in the Latina writers' decisions. This should lead you to paragraph 2. Line 17 says "this effort manifests itself … " so look to the previous sentence to determine what exactly their effort was.

Step 4: Make a Prediction

Lines 13–17 say that the Latina autobiographers intended to "confront traditional linguistic boundaries" and "address the politics of multiple cultural identities." Note, too, that the author reiterates this same goal at the end of paragraph 3, in lines 47–49. Expect the correct answer to paraphrase these ideas.

Step 5: Evaluate the Answer Choices

(D) does just that, paraphrasing the goals articulated in paragraph 2 with almost the exact language used in lines 47–49.

(A) is a 180; the Latina writers abandoned chronological ordering, which the author of the passage says is a hallmark of traditional autobiography.

(B) is wrong because the author never mentions any genres that the Latina writers wanted to avoid; rather, it seems that these writers were casting the net wide to incorporate any genre that suited their needs.

(C) mentions overt political expression, which isn't something the Latina writers avoided. As a matter of fact, the author says (in paragraph 2) that one of the Latina autobiographers' goals was to "address the politics" of cultural identity, and (in paragraph 3) that Cherrie Moraga organized her autobiography "in terms of her political development."

(E) is a Distortion. The beginning of paragraph 3 mentions that Gloria Anzaldua juxtaposed narrative sequences and poetry, but this isn't to say that the Latina writers believed that poetry could not be used for narrative.

3. (E) Logic Function

Step 2: Identify the Question Type

The question stem is essentially asking for the purpose of the author's discussion of *Getting Home Alive*, making this a Logic Function question.

Step 3: Research the Relevant Text

Getting Home Alive is discussed primarily in lines 35–45. The author chooses to discuss *Getting Home Alive* last out of the three autobiographies in the passage. The discussion begins by saying that *Getting Home Alive* "departs even further from the conventions typical of autobiography" and ends by saying that the book is "a fully intentional and carefully designed experiment with literary structure."

Step 4: Make a Prediction

The author is using *Getting Home Alive* as an example of the Latina autobiographers' departure from common structural conventions, one that really pushed the experimental boundaries.

Step 5: Evaluate the Answer Choices

(E) matches this prediction. This answers choice's phrase "extent of ... experimentation" matches the author's expression "departs even further."

(A) is Outside the Scope. The author distinguishes Getting Home Alive on the basis of how far it departed from traditional autobiography, but never delineates certain types of experimental autobiography.

(B) cites a different part of paragraph 3—the part in which the author discusses *Borderlands/La Frontera*.

(C) is a 180; the author mentions the Moraleses' use of multiple voices to set their memoir apart from other autobiographies, even those written by Latina authors.

(D) is a Distortion. The author does say that the structure of *Getting Home Alive* may confuse some readers, but the author isn't making a general point about Latina autobiographies confusing readers.

4. (A) Detail

Step 2: Identify the Question Type

The language in the question stem is direct ("the passage indicates"), so this is a Detail question. The correct answer will be stated in the passage in black and white.

Step 3: Research the Relevant Text

The stem doesn't point you to a specific place to research, since Latina autobiographies are discussed throughout the passage. But since the question stem doesn't reference a specific autobiography, go to where they're all discussed as a whole: paragraphs 1, 2, and 4.

Step 4: Make a Prediction

If you are facing a vague Detail question, don't spend too much time trying to make a prediction. Instead, know that before you select the correct answer you need to be able to point to where it's mentioned or paraphrased in the passage. Use your Roadmap, Keywords, and margin notes to research the answer choices.

Step 5: Evaluate the Answer Choices

(A) is the only one directly stated in the passage. Lines 17–21 confirm that the blending of other genres is central to the distinctiveness of these autobiographies. Moreover, in paragraph 3 you learn that *Borderlands/La Frontera* contains poetry (line 25), that *Loving in the War Years* is "characterized by a mixture of genres" (lines 26–27), and that *Getting Home Alive* also employs poems (line 39).

(B) is Outside the Scope. The passage does not indicate that each autobiography quotes from these sources.

(C) is Outside the Scope. Only the discussion of *Borderlands/La Frontera* mentions anything about the author's cultural background, and even that discussion does not indicate the *ways* it impacted the author.

(D) is a Distortion. Only *Getting Home Alive* is listed as having more than one author.

(E) is Outside the Scope. Although paragraph 2 talks about what methodologies were used by each author, there is not an *explanation of why* each author chose that methodology.

5. (B) Inference

Step 2: Identify the Question Type

Any question asking about the author's attitude toward something discussed in the passage is an Inference question.

Step 3: Research the Relevant Text

Getting Home Alive is discussed in lines 35–45, so consult those lines first. The author describes the work's features in lines 35–42, but the following sentence is where the author's opinion of the work emerges.

Step 4: Make a Prediction

The author claims that the Moraleses' choice of order within the text might seem confusing and haphazard but is in fact a very deliberate experiment. The correct answer will be consistent with that view.

Step 5: Evaluate the Answer Choices

(B) is fully consistent with the author's view. The author makes a point of mentioning that the work may seem "fragmentary and confusing" because she expects that to be readers' initial impression.

(A) is completely Outside the Scope because the author never discusses *Getting Home Alive* in relationship to other works by its authors.

(C) is Outside the Scope. It concerns how *Getting Home Alive* will be received by academics—a concern the author of the passage doesn't have. Furthermore, it is doubly wrong because it implies that the author takes a dim view of *Getting Home Alive*, which clearly isn't the case.

(D), like **(C)**, is Outside the Scope. The author is not concerned with how *Getting Home Alive* will be treated by scholars. It then compounds its mistake by inaccurately suggesting that the author makes a prediction about the book's future critical reception.

(E) is a Distortion. The author never claims that *other critics* have come around to the idea that the Latina authors expanded the possibilities for the genre of autobiography.

6. (A) Inference

Step 2: Identify the Question Type

Since the question stem asks you to determine what the author "most likely intends" rather than what she states directly, this is an Inference question.

Step 3: Research the Relevant Text

The stem directs you to line 51. Read the entire sentence containing that line, in which the author claims that the Latina writers of the 1980s eschewed the existing guidelines that previous autobiographers have followed.

Step 4: Make a Prediction

Among the innovations with which the author credits the Latina authors are: mixing genres and structures, presenting events outside a chronological order, and combining multiple voices within a single work. If those are indeed innovations, then the author must believe that the conventions are:

sticking to a single genre, presenting events in chronological order, and maintaining a single voice. Expect one of these to be in the answer choices.

Step 5: Evaluate the Answer Choices

(A) is a direct match, focusing specifically on the standard of chronological sequence.

(B) is a principle that, according to paragraph 2, the Latina writers actually followed, so it wouldn't represent a parameter from which they strayed.

(C) distorts the passage. The author does mention Moraga's use of her political development as a frame for her work, but this is not how the author claims that she departed from convention. It's quite likely that a traditional autobiography—say, that of Winston Churchill or Thomas Jefferson—would have had political overtones.

(D) is also a Distortion. Writers like Anzaldua and the Moraleses did not separate their work by genre, so **(D)** wouldn't represent a principle that these writers abandoned. Indeed, the passage implies that traditional autobiography did not even include these other genres, let alone that it blended them together with narrative.

(E) may also be an implicit principle that the Latina autobiographers follow, since they mix several genres while presenting their personal experiences.

7. (D) Logic Reasoning (Weaken)

Step 2: Identify the Question Type

The question stem asks for the answer that "undermines" a claim made by the author. This resembles a Weaken question from the Logical Reasoning section.

Step 3: Research the Relevant Text

The stem directs you to lines 50–55, where the author asserts that the Latina writers "revolutionized the genre of autobiography" and made the genre "more amenable to the expression of their own experiences."

Step 4: Make a Prediction

You need not predict the correct answer verbatim. However, you know that the right answer will suggest that the Latina autobiographers didn't revolutionize the genre or that their authorial choices weren't so innovative after all.

Step 5: Evaluate the Answer Choices

(D) does just that. If certain 19th-century autobiographies contained some of the same innovations that the author claims were pioneered by the Latina writers of the 1980s, then the innovations didn't originate with the Latina writers, and the author's claims are severely weakened.

(A), if anything, strengthens the author's claim by suggesting that chronologically linear autobiographies were less *en* *vogue* after the Latina writers of the 1980s came onto the scene. Perhaps the Latina writers did revolutionize the genre.

(B) doesn't affect the author's claim. The author doesn't argue that the Latina autobiographers made their style of autobiography more pervasive in Latina writing generally. Moreover, the degree of critical acclaim these works received is Outside the Scope of this passage.

(C) also has no effect. The author's argument doesn't require that chronologically linear autobiographies went completely extinct after the 1980s.

(E) discusses non-autobiographical material, which is Outside the Scope of the author's claim about the genre of autobiography. Critical reception is also irrelevant to the author's argument.

Passage 2: The Archivist's Dilemma

Step 1: Read the Passage Strategically

Sample Roadmap

line #	Keyword/phrase	¶ Margin notes
1	While	Problem for archivists—losing info fast
3	greater than ever.	
4	great concern	
6	while	
7	increased exponentially,	
8	decreased almost as rapidly	
10	for example	Ex. old material still preserved
13	whereas	Ex. newer media degrading
16	but	
19	seem	Possible solution: computers
23	But	
24		Issue: tech obsolete quickly
26	For example	
29	because	
30		Examples of tech issues
31	And	
33	Yet	
35		Time running out
37	Even if	
41		Archivists must decide quickly what to save based on value judgment
43	Ideally, … should	
46	for example … because	
49	But	
50	only	
53	Undoubtedly	
54	danger … not so much	Danger—so much material, no time to make all necessary value judgments
56	but rather	
58	virtually impossible	

Discussion

The first two sentences of paragraph 1 establish the **Topic**—archivists; and the **Scope**—how archivists deal with the loss of vital information. The next sentence introduces a major problem: Much more information is being preserved, but the media on which that information is recorded degrades more rapidly. The rest of the paragraph is devoted to examples of this phenomenon, from clay tablets to books to photographs to videotapes, in declining order of durability. It turns out that newer media are actually more susceptible to degradation than older media.

LSAT authors rarely introduce a problem without discussing possible solutions, so it's no surprise that paragraph 2 begins by introducing the solution of computer technology. The Keywords "seem to offer ... an answer" suggest that the author is hesitant. Reading on, you learn that computer technology indeed is not a perfect solution; the breakneck pace of technological progress can rapidly make a storage system obsolete (the example of optical computer disks is used to stress this point). The author ends paragraph 2 by pointing out another complication: Time is quickly running out.

The author begins the final paragraph by saying that even without the challenges that computer technology presents, the time crunch will force archivists to make tough decisions quickly about what to save and what to throw away. Those decisions will have to be based on the value of the information being saved. The writings of Homer and Virgil are introduced as examples of works that have survived because of an enduring belief in their value. The passage ends with a warning ("[t]he danger now"): because of the volume of records on unstable media, archivists won't be able to make those decisions quickly enough.

The author's **Purpose** is to discuss a major problem facing archivists, and the passage's **Main Idea** is that archivists' work is becoming more difficult because the volume of information being stored is increasing, but the durability of storage media is decreasing.

8. (A) Global

Step 2: Identify the Question Type

Whenever the question stem asks for the main point of a passage, it's a Global question.

Step 3: Research the Relevant Text

Without a specific place in the passage to consult, base your prediction on your broader understanding of Topic, Scope, Purpose, and Main Idea that you developed during Step 1.

Step 4: Make a Prediction

The Main Idea of the passage is that archivists are facing the enormous challenge of preserving vital information on unstable media even as the volume of information being stored continues to increase.

Step 5: Evaluate the Answer Choices

(A) matches this prediction perfectly. It reflects the Scope and Main Idea of the entire passage.

(B) doesn't match the author's concerned tone. In fact, this choice is a 180. The entire passage details a problem currently facing archivists, but **(B)** makes it sound like the problem is already being solved.

(C) misses the main point. The author does detail the limited shelf lives of different media, but the passage concerns the difficulties that this presents, rather than simply comparing them.

(D) is a Distortion. "[P]reserving vital records and documents" is the core of the archivists' charge, but they face difficulty because storage media are not durable, not because the media are of limited capacity.

(E) is wrong because the author doesn't make a value judgment on the information chosen by archivists to store. The point of the passage is that such a judgment is increasingly urgent for archivists to make.

9. (C) Detail

Step 2: Identify the Question Type

This is a Detail question because the correct answer here is a question answered by information stated directly in the passage.

Step 3: Research the Relevant Text

The stem has no clues to help you research, so save this step for when you're evaluating the answer choices.

Step 4: Make a Prediction

The passage ostensibly provides information to answer hundreds of questions, so instead of making a prediction, go into the choices, prepared to find the part of the passage that answers the question in the correct choice.

Step 5: Evaluate the Answer Choices

(C) is answered by lines 26–29, which say that optical storage disks were the cutting edge of technology in the 1980s. Thus, **(C)** is correct.

(A) is not answered. Lines 45–46 say that printed versions of Virgil and Homer survive, but these lines don't say whether they're printed on parchment.

(B) is a Distortion. The passage doesn't even say *that* acidic paper is less stable than digital storage tape.

(D) is not answered. Lines 9–11 tell you that the clay tablets on which Mesopotamia's laws were recorded still exist, but these lines don't tell you how many of the tablets survive.

(E) is also unanswered. You know from lines 49–52 that copies of Plato's works turned up, but there's no information as to their original medium.

10. (A) Inference

Step 2: Identify the Question Type

The phrase "most strongly suggests" indicates an Inference question.

Step 3: Research the Relevant Text

The stem doesn't direct you to a specific place to research. That makes this vague question a good one to answer later in the set, especially when the author doesn't express a strong point of view.

Step 4: Make a Prediction

Without a clear place to research, your Inference will have to be based on—or consistent with—the author's Main Ideas. Keep in mind that the correct answer is the one that must be true based on the passage.

Step 5: Evaluate the Answer Choices

(A) must be true based on the passage. The last sentence of paragraph 2 says that archivists, even the ones who are resistant to computer technology, are "running out of time."

(B) flies in the face of the author's tone throughout the passage. Lines 33–36 and 40–43 indicate that the author believes archivists have to make quick decisions about what to keep and what to discard.

(C) is unsupported because the author never argues for nondigital methods of storage.

(D) is an Irrelevant Comparison. The author's concern revolves around the media on which records are stored, not whether the records are in the form of images or text.

(E) is a correlation the author never addresses. Nothing in the passage suggests that the durability of a storage system depends on how much information is stored within that system.

11. (B) Logic Function

Step 2: Identify the Question Type

The question stem asks you to find the author's "primary purpose" for mentioning a specific fact, so this is a Logic Function question.

Step 3: Research the Relevant Text

The stem directs you to lines 19–23, which are at the beginning of paragraph 2. The paragraph begins, "Computer technology would seem to offer archivists an answer."

Step 4: Make a Prediction

Your Roadmap tells you that these lines are intended to present a possible fix for the dilemma outlined in the first paragraph—the loss of vital information over time.

Step 5: Evaluate the Answer Choices

(B) matches this prediction. The adjective *ostensible* matches the author's tone ("would seem to offer ... an answer").

(A) fails because lines 19–23 are not argumentatively related to the first sentence of the passage. Later in the paragraph, when the author discusses the declining durability of storage media, there is support for the first sentence's claim that "the potential for losing this information is now greater than ever." But this question is asking about the opening of paragraph 2.

(C) is incorrect because lines 19–23 don't argue a point. Further, the idea that computer storage might be a solution for archivists isn't refuted by the passage's final sentence, which identifies a current danger for archivists.

(D) is incorrect because lines 19–20 mention that computer technology "would seem to offer ... an answer," so the author isn't continuing to offer problems.

(E) doesn't make sense because the author is using lines 19–23 to respond to paragraph 1, not paragraph 3.

12. (D) Inference

Step 2: Identify the Question Type

Two clues point to this being an Inference question: "passage provides the most support" and "inferring." Find the answer choice that must be true based on the passage.

Step 3: Research the Relevant Text

There are no clues to help your research, so be prepared for the correct answer to be supported by any part of the passage.

Step 4: Make a Prediction

You may not be able to predict the precise answer, but armed with the author's Purpose and Main Idea, you can evaluate the answer choices. Be ready to select the answer that must be true.

Step 5: Evaluate the Answer Choices

(D) can be inferred from two statements in the passage. Lines 15–18 say that photographs last 40 years and videotapes last 20 years. Lines 31–33 mention that some varieties of digital storage tape are safe for only 10 years.

(A) is Outside the Scope because it mentions vulnerability to theft or unauthorized use, which the author never discusses.

(B) distorts the passage. Digital storage tape might be more recent than optical disks, but nothing in the passage suggests that information was transferred from one medium to the other.

(C) is Outside the Scope. The author says that archivists are reluctant to adopt computer-based methods of storage, but not necessarily because of the cost.

(E) need not be true. Just because the amount of information stored is increasing doesn't automatically mean that archivists consider a larger portion of it essential.

13. (E) Inference

Step 2: Identify the Question Type

The looser language of the question stem ("the passage - suggests") indicates an Inference question.

Step 3: Research the Relevant Text

The stem doesn't have any major clues for research, so finding the answer will rely on your broad understanding of the big ideas in the passage.

Step 4: Make a Prediction

The correct answer is hard to predict exactly, but it will be consistent with some part of the passage. Before selecting an answer, find the lines where the author implies it. Additionally, evaluate the answer choices with the author's Purpose and Main Idea in mind. Eliminate any choices that contradict or distort the passage.

Step 5: Evaluate the Answer Choices

(E) can be inferred primarily from paragraph 3. Lines 43–44 say that ideally, archivists will decide what to keep and what to discard based on a value judgment of each document. Therefore, archivists' value judgments determine what remains from the past, which in turn will determine how future generations understand the past.

(A) contradicts the beginning of paragraph 3, in which the author allows for the development of new and more viable electronic storage systems.

(B) also contradicts paragraph 3. In lines 40–43, the author stresses the need for archivists to make decisions about what to keep and what to discard. If the author agreed with **(B)**, there would be no need to make such decisions.

(C) is Outside the Scope of the passage. Nothing the author says indicates that the general public has been deceived as to the durability of electronic storage.

(D) is a Distortion. Archivists have to make the distinction between essential and dispensable information *more quickly* now, according to the passage, but the author doesn't suggest that making this distinction is a new concern for archivists.

Passage 3: Blackmail in Two Legal Contexts

Step 1: Read the Passage Strategically

Sample Roadmap

line #	Keyword/phrase	¶ Margin notes
Passage A		
1		blackmail unique
2	unique … ":" … no one has	
3	heart of the problem	
5		paradox: 2 legal acts illegal together
9	But	
12	So	
13	lack of a successful theory	
14	damaging consequences … ":"	statutes overly broad
16	Consequently	
20	however	
21	key	blackmail wrong b/c triangular
24	depends	
27	For example,	Ex. blackmailing criminal bad for state
29	Thus,	
30	because	
Passage B		
32	not necessary	Rome—blackmail got no special law
36	not	
38	assumption … true enough, it seems	principle—is harm caused?
39	harmed if	If harmed by revealed info = unlawful
41	And if	
42	then	
45		Revealer needed good reason for revealing
48	In short	
49	was not, … sufficient	Truth of assertion not sufficient for revealing
50	Granted,	
52	But … even if it were true,	
54	only if … legitimate	OK to reveal only if in pubic interest
56	Just	
57	because … did	
58	not mean	

Discussion

Passage A begins by introducing the **Topic** that will likely be common to both passages: the legal conception of blackmail. Passage A, however, deals exclusively with blackmail in Canadian and U.S. common law. The author goes on to introduce a paradox: Blackmail, an illegal action, results from the combination of two actions, each of which is legal when taken individually. Paragraph 1 ends with a question that nails down the passage's **Scope**: why the combination of these two legal actions is illegal.

LSAT authors rarely pose rhetorical questions, so expect to find an answer at some point in the passage. For now, paragraph 2 deals with the consequences of the blackmail paradox. The current laws on the books outlaw behavior that "no one believes is criminal" and that isn't prosecuted by jurists "precisely as written."

Paragraph 3 is where the author attempts to resolve the paradox. This resolution is the author's **Purpose**. Lines 21–22 are the crux of the author's view. Blackmail is wrong because it is triangular. The power of the blackmailer depends on a third party who may affect the blackmail victim if the information comes to light. An example is given in line 27: if someone blackmails a criminal, the blackmailer's leverage comes from knowing that the state would be interested in prosecuting the victim if it knew of the crimes. The Keyword *thus* (line 29) wraps it up, and provides the **Main Idea**: blackmail is illegal because the blackmailer misuses a third party for his or her own gain.

Right away, passage B establishes its own **Scope**: blackmail as handled by classical Roman jurists. The author starts by pointing out that the Romans didn't conceive of blackmail as a unique crime. In Roman law, what mattered was whether an action caused harm and not whether it was legal or illegal on its face.

The Romans assumed (lines 38–40) that a blackmail victim would be harmed if his shameful secrets were revealed. Because of this, the act of blackmail constituted a harm and was therefore unlawful. (Don't worry about Latin legalese like *prima facie*, which simply means "at first look" or "on its face." Your grasp of a Reading Comp passage will never fully depend on knowing terms like this.) Therefore, the blackmailer had to show positive cause for revealing the information.

The final paragraph deals in terms with which you are hopefully becoming more familiar: Formal Logic terms. Notice "sufficient" in line 49 and "only if" in line 54. The author provides a necessary condition for the revelation of shameful information to be lawful: there must be an overriding public interest in the information, and the revelation must be for a legitimate purpose. Just because the information is true

doesn't mean a blackmailer can lawfully reveal (or threaten to reveal) it.

Both passages examine the legal idea of blackmail, but the **Purpose** of passage A is to examine and resolve the paradox of blackmail in Canadian/U.S. common law, whereas the **Purpose** of passage B is to discuss how the Romans treated blackmail legally. The **Main Ideas** of the passages show their divergence. Passage A maintains that blackmail is a unique and paradoxical crime that is illegal because it misuses a third party for the blackmailer's benefit. Passage B holds that blackmail wasn't a unique crime to the Romans and that it was illegal because it caused harm to the blackmail victim (unless there was a compelling state interest in the information).

14. (C) Global

Step 2: Identify the Question Type

The phrase "central topic" makes this a Global question.

Step 3: Research the Relevant Text

In Step 1, you determined the Topic, Scope, Purpose, and Main Idea of each passage. Use that to form the basis of your prediction.

Step 4: Make a Prediction

The two passages deal with how different legal systems handle the crime of blackmail.

Step 5: Evaluate the Answer Choices

(C) matches the prediction perfectly. Passage A deals with contemporary North American approaches to blackmail; passage B takes on the Roman legal system's understanding of the same crime.

(A) is incorrect because passage B doesn't deal with triangular transactions at all. Further, this choice is too broad to capture what passage A discusses.

(B) mentions free speech, which also isn't discussed in passage B.

(D) is too broad for both passage A (which focuses specifically on Canadian and U.S. law) and passage B (which focuses on classical Roman law). Neither passage takes a broad historical view.

(E) is off because each passage manages to explain the illegality of blackmail in a particular legal context.

15. (B) Inference

Step 2: Identify the Question Type

If a question asks about what an author means by using a particular phrase, it's an Inference question.

Step 3: Research the Relevant Text

The question stem directs you to line 29. The sentence ending in line 29 begins with "For example," so it's wise to read the previous sentence as well to see what this sentence is illustrating.

Step 4: Make a Prediction

The author's point in this part of the passage is that a blackmail victim pays money to avoid harm from a third party. In the criminal example the author gives, the third party is the state, which would certainly prosecute the blackmail target if it learned of the target's crimes. So "the state's chip" is the state's responsibility to investigate and prosecute crime.

Step 5: Evaluate the Answer Choices

(B) matches the prediction. The author of passage A considers the "third party" (as the state would be in this case) to suffer harm from the blackmail scheme, so he must consider the state's interest in prosecuting crime to be "legitimate."

(A) is wrong because the determination of what actions are crimes is already a settled matter, one in which a blackmailer couldn't intervene.

(C) is moot because in a blackmail situation the crime has already occurred.

(D) is Extreme and too broad. The passage doesn't suggest that the government relies only on private citizens. Further, the example used by the author doesn't just concern "important" information; it also has to do with crime.

(E) is a Distortion. The blackmailer in question doesn't need to have witnessed the crimes of the blackmail victim. The blackmailer just needs to have knowledge of the crimes.

16. (A) Inference

Step 2: Identify the Question Type

The words "most strongly supported by ... the passage" indicate an Inference question since the right answer will be the one that must be true based on the author's words.

Step 3: Research the Relevant Text

The stem doesn't give you a specific place to research, so the entirety of both passages is in play. Remember, however, that the correct answer will not contradict or distort the Purpose and Main Idea of the relevant passage.

Step 4: Make a Prediction

Without a clear reference to a specific portion of the passage, this question is nearly impossible to predict with any precision. Use your Roadmap and be prepared to find specific lines in the passage to support the answer choice that must be true.

Step 5: Evaluate the Answer Choices

(A) must be true. The author of passage B says in line 33 that the Romans needed no special category for blackmail. Also, lines 52–56 describe the narrow protection afforded those who revealed shameful information, so presumably the Romans didn't assume a blanket right to free speech.

(B) goes too far. That the Romans didn't have a specific provision outlawing blackmail doesn't suggest anything about the extent to which the crime was committed as compared to modern times.

(C) is much too broad. The passages' scope concerns only how these two legal systems handled blackmail. You can't infer anything about how these legal systems dealt with freedoms in general. Remember: the correct answer must be based on the passages, not on your own "outside" knowledge.

(D) is a 180 because it's a justification for the illegality of blackmail under Roman law. Passage A claims that blackmail is illegal in Canadian and U.S. common law because it involves misusing state power for one's own gain.

(E) is also a 180. Lines 27–31 acknowledge that public authorities have an interest in learning about crimes. It is precisely this interest that blackmailers exploit for their purposes.

17. (A) Detail

Step 2: Identify the Question Type

When a question stem asks you to determine which answer choice is true or untrue as stated in the passage, it's a Detail question. Note the Comparative Reading twist here, requiring you to research both passages.

Step 3: Research the Relevant Text

You'll need to carefully research both passages, since the correct answer will be true of Canadian and U.S. law in passage A and untrue of Roman law in passage B.

Step 4: Make a Prediction

There are certain broader points that you already know would be true in passage A but not in passage B (e.g., blackmail is illegal because it misuses the power of a third party such as the state), but finer points of divergence could appear in the answer choices, so stay flexible.

Step 5: Evaluate the Answer Choices

(A) is confirmed in passage A by lines 4–6 and is contradicted in passage B by lines 33–37, which say that Roman law considered blackmail one single action and based its consideration of blackmail on its potential to cause harm, not on its surface legality or illegality.

(B) is stated in passage A (lines 21–22), but it's also presumably true in passage B. The Romans also conceived of blackmail as possibly involving three parties: the victim, the perpetrator, and the public authorities.

(C) is actually untrue in passage A, which says that most blackmail laws are not meant to be enforced precisely as written (lines 16–19).

(D) is stated in passage A (lines 25–26), but it's not contradicted by passage B.

(E) is a 180. The first sentence of passage A says that blackmail is "unique among major crimes" in Canadian and U.S. common law; the first sentence of passage B says that blackmail had no special category in Roman law.

18. (E) Inference

Step 2: Identify the Question Type

This is an Inference question because you have to base your answer on "what can be inferred from the passages."

Step 3: Research the Relevant Text

It's tough to pinpoint specific parts of the passages to research, but focus on each passage's discussion of what makes blackmail illegal. Passage A discusses the wrongness of blackmail in lines 20–31; paragraphs 2 and 3 of Passage B discuss why blackmail was illegal in classical Roman law.

Step 4: Make a Prediction

It's tough to predict the exact content of the correct answer here, but always be sure to characterize the correct answer. The illegality of blackmail under Roman law turns on its potential to cause harm to the status or reputation of the victim.

Step 5: Evaluate the Answer Choices

(E) is a revelation of shameful information that holds no legitimate interest for public authorities. Thus, it would violate Roman law. However, there is no specific third party being misused, so it doesn't fall under the triangular incorrectness articulated in passage A. **(E)** is correct.

(A) is Outside the Scope because it involves bribery, which is distinct from blackmail in that no party is revealing, or threatening to reveal, wrongdoing.

(B) is wrong because Roman law protected the revelation of information that was in the public interest. Embezzlement is a crime that would be reasonably within that interest.

(C) constitutes perjury, which would presumably be illegal in both Roman and Canadian/U.S. legal systems. Furthermore, no blackmail is involved here.

(D), like **(B)**, involves information of potentially criminal wrongdoing that would be within the public interest.

19. (D) Logic Reasoning (Parallel Reasoning)

Step 2: Identify the Question Type

This question resembles a Parallel Reasoning question since it asks you to find the answer choice that contains a relationship "analogous to" a relationship in the passage.

Step 3: Research the Relevant Text

There's no specific place to research the answer to this question, so the answer will likely rely on your broader understanding of the main points in both passages.

Step 4: Make a Prediction

You won't be able to predict the content of the correct answer, but you should characterize the relationship between Canadian/U.S. and Roman conceptions of blackmail. Broadly stated, passage A says that Canadian and U.S. common law have a special category for blackmail, whereas Roman law treats blackmail as one of a class of actions that cause harm instead of having a separate category for it.

Step 5: Evaluate the Answer Choices

(D) is a perfect match. Canadian and U.S. common law make a special case out of blackmail, but Roman law does not.

(A) has one country with no legal requirement whatsoever, but this mischaracterizes the relationship between the passages because the legal systems in the passages have restrictions against blackmail.

(B) is wrong because Roman law didn't outlaw blackmail in more instances than did Canadian and U.S. common law.

(C) is wrong because none of the legal systems in the passages permitted blackmail, and the Canadian/U.S. conception of blackmail is not necessarily more legally permissive than that of classical Roman law.

(E) is off because it has one country legally permitting racing-grade motorcycles, but classical Roman law didn't legally permit blackmail at all.

Passage 4: Restoring Europe's Farmland

Step 1: Read the Passage Strategically

Sample Roadmap

line #	Keyword/phrase	¶ Margin notes
2	problems	
6	difficult …however	Restoring land damaged by farming is difficult
7	because	
8	Moreover	
12	While	
14	impractical	
15	And while	
17		Will restore naturally, but study investigating how to accelerate process artificially
18	investigating the possibility	
22		study methods
30		Results
37		Adding beneficial microorg
42	better	
43	but still not as well as	
45	concluded … this is because	
47	while … for example …beneficial	Why microorg help
50	are lacking. … results	
51	suggest	
52	hinges	
53	In other words,	
55	now believe	Planting seeds and "sowing" in microorg is key to boosting diversity

Discussion

In paragraph 1, the author Introduces the **Topic**: farmland in Europe; and quickly narrows to **Scope**: problems with overproduction of that land. One problem in particular captures the author's attention: How can we restore a natural balance of flora to land that has been overworked? Lines 5–12 detail some difficulties in solving this problem: the land has been stripped of nutrients, highly fertilized, and overrun by thistles. The author then goes on to present a quick solution (removing and replacing the topsoil), but tells you that this solution isn't practical. By the end of the paragraph, the author mentions that a study is underway to determine whether humans can accelerate the process of reestablishing biodiversity on this land.

Paragraph 2 describes the study's methodology—a former cornfield was divided into identical plots, some control and some variable—and gives some initial results three years into the study. On control plots, thistles dominated. On plots where a diverse set of flora was sown, thistles disappeared.

Paragraph 3 continues to detail the results of the study. Some of the plots of land were enriched with beneficial microorganisms, and those plots better supported seedlings than did plots that were not enriched. Line 45 introduces an explanation for this: land farmed for many years contains a lot of harmful organisms and not very many beneficial organisms. This explanation leads to the author's ultimate recommendation: the sowing of native plant seeds should be accompanied by the introduction of beneficial microorganisms into the soil.

This recommendation reveals the author's **Purpose**: to lay out a strategy for restoring a natural balance to overworked farmland; and **Main Idea**: natural balance can be restored by introducing both native seeds and beneficial microorganisms to damaged land.

20. (A) Global

Step 2: Identify the Question Type

The "central idea" of the passage is equivalent to its Main Idea, making this a Global question.

Step 3: Research the Relevant Text

With no specific lines to research, use your Roadmap and the Topic, Scope, Purpose, and Main Idea summaries you made during Step 1.

Step 4: Make a Prediction

You already predicted the Main Idea during Step 1. The right answer may use slightly different words, but it will express the same idea: that sowing native seeds and helpful microorganisms simultaneously could be a viable way to restore farmland.

Step 5: Evaluate the Answer Choices

(A) matches this prediction. The term *two-pronged* clearly refers to using native seeds and beneficial microorganisms simultaneously.

(B) is too general and misrepresents the study, which achieved a favorable balance of flora in the damaged farmland after only three years.

(C) is Outside the Scope. The author never argues for a change in farming practices. The passage focuses only on how to recover the original biodiversity of the farmland.

(D) blows up a small point made at the end of paragraph 1 and tries to pass it off as the main idea of the passage. If **(D)** were the author's main point, there would be no need to discuss the study and its implications.

(E) ignores the author's focus on possible solutions to reestablish natural diversity in farmland.

21. (E) Global

Step 2: Identify the Question Type

This question is Global because its stem asks for the organization of the passage as a whole.

Step 3: Research the Relevant Text

Your Roadmap is the best place to go for your prediction to an "organization" question.

Step 4: Make a Prediction

Paragraph 1 describes a dilemma facing European farmers. Paragraph 2 details a study that investigates a possible solution to the dilemma. Paragraph 3 discusses the study's results and makes a recommendation based on those results.

Step 5: Evaluate the Answer Choices

(E) matches the prediction exactly. This is the only choice that opens with the presentation of a problem and ends with a recommendation.

(A) completely ignores paragraph 1 and claims that the author judges the study's results, which the author does not do.

(B) is off because the author doesn't present a hypothesis in the beginning of the passage, and contradictory evidence is never introduced.

(C), like **(A)**, ignores paragraph 1. Furthermore, the author never discusses the likely effectiveness of the course of action given.

(D) is incorrect because the author discusses only one study, and the only possible "goal" discussed (that of restoring a natural environmental balance to farmland) is never revised.

22. (B) Detail

Step 2: Identify the Question Type

This is a Detail question because it concerns what the passage mentions directly, or "offers," rather than what it implies or suggests.

Step 3: Research the Relevant Text

The explanation that the question stem seeks is in paragraph 3—specifically, in lines 44–50, which begin with "researchers have concluded that this is because … "

Step 4: Make a Prediction

According to the passage, soil that has been out of production for 20 years contains beneficial microorganisms that help strengthen plant roots against attacks by disease-causing organisms.

Step 5: Evaluate the Answer Choices

(B) is a perfect match. This choice focuses on the problems of the overworked land rather than the advantages in the fallow land, but the nature of this question is comparative, so accurately describing either of the soils' conditions will provide the correct answer.

(A) is mentioned in lines 7–8, which is not the part of the passage explaining the study's results.

(C) is mentioned in the same part of the passage—lines 8–12.

(D) is a 180. The soil from the land that is out of production actually contains beneficial organisms.

(E) also goes against the passage, which says that soil taken from out-of-production land contains organisms that defend roots against attack.

23. (D) Inference

Step 2: Identify the Question Type

Any question asking you to determine what is "most likely to be true" based on the passage is an Inference question. Despite this wording, know that you're seeking the answer that *must* be true.

Step 3: Research the Relevant Text

The stem directs you to the first paragraph, where the author discusses replacing topsoil as the quickest solution to restore heavily fertilized land (lines 12–14).

Step 4: Make a Prediction

Some Inference questions, such as this one, can be reasonably predicted. If replacing topsoil is indeed a way to fix the problems associated with heavily fertilized land, then the soil used to replace the topsoil will probably not be heavily fertilized.

Step 5: Evaluate the Answer Choices

(D) is consistent with the prediction

(A) is Extreme. Nothing suggests that the new soil will be totally free of thistles—just that the thistles won't take over.

(B) is, if anything, a 180. Fungi are mentioned in paragraph 3 as beneficial to native plant diversity, so presumably, new topsoil would be helped by fungi.

(C) is unsupported because the topsoil is being replaced in order to remove the fertilizer and restore the nutrients. The number of seeds of native herbs and grasses already in this soil is unimportant.

(E) also doesn't need to be true. The replacement soil could have been used to grow any crop, as long as that soil is not heavily fertilized and/or depleted of nutrients.

24. (E) Logic Function

Step 2: Identify the Question Type

The words "primarily serves to" indicate a Logic Function question, since the question is focused on *why* the author makes a certain reference.

Step 3: Research the Relevant Text

Context is key in Logic Function questions. Read the entire sentence containing lines 16–17. The sentence says that while people generally believe that land will restore its own biodiversity, a study is being performed to see if the process can be accelerated.

Step 4: Make a Prediction

The belief in lines 16–17 provides context for the Netherlands study. The study came about because the natural restoration process is slower than many people would prefer.

Step 5: Evaluate the Answer Choices

(E) is the best match. The general belief serves as an impetus to the study seeking to accelerate the natural process.

(A) is a Distortion. The Netherlands study doesn't attempt to discredit the belief that land will gradually restore itself; it attempts to determine whether human intervention can hasten that process.

(B) is Outside the Scope. The author never discusses any arguments in favor of or against intense agricultural production.

(C) is wrong because the author suggests no such thing. If anything, the author suggests that agricultural overproduction has very serious consequences—hence the efforts to reverse those consequences as quickly as possible.

(D) is wrong because the author discusses the problems associated with overproduction earlier in the paragraph. Furthermore, perceptions of the reasons behind the problems are outside the passage's scope.

25. (B) Inference (LEAST)

Step 2: Identify the Question Type

This might have been a hard question to classify. But since it requires you to put together different pieces of information from the passage to determine something that isn't stated directly, it's an Inference question. Pay attention to the "LEAST" in the stem; you'll need to find a circumstance in which one *wouldn't* carry out a study similar to the Netherlands study.

Step 3: Research the Relevant Text

This question can be tough to research, but a clue can be found near the first mention of the Netherlands study in paragraph 1.

Step 4: Make a Prediction

The Netherlands study came about as a way to attempt to accelerate the slow process by which nature reestablishes diversity in farmland. But the study wouldn't be necessary if the author's "quick fix" from lines 12–14 (removing and replacing topsoil) were feasible.

Step 5: Evaluate the Answer Choices

(B) matches the prediction. The study is prompted, in part, by the infeasibility of the "quickest way" to solve the overfertilization problem: removing and replacing the topsoil (see lines 12–15).

(A) is a problem associated with agricultural overproduction. The Netherlands study was specifically designed to try to address this type of problem, so there's no reason not to use its methods in these circumstances.

(C), like **(A)**, is a problem associated with agricultural overproduction. So it would be a legitimate circumstance to use the methods from the Netherlands study.

(D) would also motivate a researcher to carry out Netherlands-like methods in order to return the field to a state in which it could support something other than thistles and weeds.

(E) is Outside the Scope. The use of fields adjacent to the field in question should have no effect on the methods used to restore the field in question to natural diversity.

26. (C) Inference

Step 2: Identify the Question Type

The phrase "can be inferred" is the clearest possible indication of an Inference question.

Step 3: Research the Relevant Text

In this Inference question, the stem is quite specific. The disease organisms in lines 46–47 are mentioned as a reason why seeds sown in unenriched plots didn't do as well as seeds sown in plots enriched with beneficial microorganisms.

Step 4: Make a Prediction

With the disease microorganisms out of the way, more native plants could probably thrive—if the results of the study are valid. Look for something similar in the answer choices.

Step 5: Evaluate the Answer Choices

(C) matches this prediction perfectly. This answer presents a fairly straightforward paraphrase of the text referred to in the question stem.

(A) seems to get the passage backward. In overworked fields, the number of disease organisms is high and population of mycorrhiza is low. Nothing suggests that the rate of mycorrhiza would go even lower.

(B) also distorts the passage. Eliminating disease organisms wouldn't totally eradicate thistles; it would just allow native plants to thrive so that thistles wouldn't dominate the land.

(D) is another Distortion. The passage doesn't suggest that the presence of disease organisms keeps the population of beneficial microorganisms down.

(E) is unsupported. Getting rid of these disease organisms would not necessarily pave the way for other disease organisms to thrive.

27. (B) Logic Reasoning (Parallel Reasoning)

Step 2: Identify the Question Type

The phrase "most analogous to" makes this question resemble a Parallel Reasoning question from the Logical Reasoning section.

Step 3: Research the Relevant Text

The process for curtailing the spread of thistles is described in lines 35–44, and the author's recommendation is in the last sentence of the passage.

Step 4: Make a Prediction

You can't predict the content of the right answer, but you know that it will describe a similar process: plant native seeds, and then protect those native plants from being overrun with thistles by adding protective microorganisms.

Notice that all the choices begin the same way. This helps you see that "prevent Party A from winning a majority of seats in the legislature" is parallel to "curtail the spread of thistles." Remember this as you evaluate each choice.

Step 5: Evaluate the Answer Choices

(B) is the parallel answer. Just as the newspaper prevents Party A's dominance by strengthening its rivals against attacks, the process in paragraph 3 prevents the dominance of thistles by strengthening the native plants against attack.

(A) would be correct if researchers could somehow convert thistles into a more diverse set of native plants. But nothing in **(A)** parallels the researchers' attempt to defend the native plants from attacks by diseases.

(C) would be parallel if researchers attempted to rid the land of factors they knew were beneficial for thistle growth. But the researchers never dealt directly with thistles; instead, they supported the native plants, whose success would keep the thistles from growing out of control.

(D) would be parallel if researchers attacked the thistles directly. But since the researchers indirectly halted the thistles' spread by supporting the native plant population, **(D)** is not parallel.

(E) would be parallel if researchers figured out a way to get the thistles to destroy themselves. But with no mention of strengthening the native plants, **(E)** can't be parallel.

Section IV: Logical Reasoning

Q#	Question Type	Correct	Difficulty
1	Paradox	C	★
2	Assumption (Necessary)	E	★
3	Weaken	D	★
4	Point at Issue	B	★
5	Principle (Identify/Strengthen)	B	★
6	Inference	E	★
7	Strengthen/Weaken (Evaluate the Argument)	A	★
8	Flaw	C	★
9	Inference	E	★
10	Paradox	D	★
11	Flaw	D	★
12	Role of a Statement	C	★★
13	Assumption (Necessary)	E	★★★★
14	Main Point	E	★★
15	Strengthen	E	★★
16	Method of Argument	A	★★★★
17	Parallel Reasoning	C	★★
18	Principle (Identify/Inference)	B	★
19	Weaken (EXCEPT)	B	★★
20	Assumption (Necessary)	D	★★★
21	Role of a Statement	E	★★★
22	Assumption (Sufficient)	A	★★★★
23	Principle (Identify/Assumption)	B	★★★
24	Parallel Flaw	A	★★★
25	Point at Issue	C	★★
26	Flaw	E	★★★

1. (C) Paradox

Step 1: Identify the Question Type

The word *explain* reveals that this is a Paradox question. In this case, the paradox revolves around the comparatively greater decline of sugar maples. Identify the seemingly contradictory information, and then search for an answer that resolves the mystery.

Step 2: Untangle the Stimulus

The stimulus states that three different trees (spruce, fir, and sugar maple) all need calcium to survive and that acid rain diminishes calcium levels in the soil. However, when subjected to acid rain, sugar maples exhibit more signs of calcium deficiency than spruces or firs do.

Step 3: Make a Prediction

This makes sense if something different about sugar maples makes them more susceptible (or something about spruces and firs makes them more immune) to calcium issues caused by acid rain. It's not necessary to predict exactly what that something is, but know that the correct answer will resolve the paradox by expressing such a key difference.

Step 4: Evaluate the Answer Choices

(C) distinguishes sugar maples from the other species in a relevant way. A mineral compound found in soil is unaffected by acid rain. When calcium levels in the soil are low, spruces and firs can extract the calcium they need from that compound; sugar maples can't.

(A) brings up other ways the soil might be damaged by acid rain but doesn't address any difference between sugar maples and the other two types of trees. It's Outside the Scope of the paradox.

(B) is a 180. If sugar maples deteriorate *less* rapidly than spruces or firs, then it's even more mysterious why they would be the trees showing more signs of decline.

(D) makes an irrelevant distinction among different seasons instead of distinguishing the characteristics of sugar maples from those of other trees.

(E) expresses a difference between sugar maples and the other trees. However, the paradox in the stimulus concerns spruces and firs in "such forests," i.e., forests exposed to the acid rain. That spruces and firs are found in other forests as well is Outside the Scope of the paradox.

2. (E) Assumption (Necessary)

Step 1: Identify the Question Type

The question asks directly for the argument's assumption. Start by identifying the author's conclusion and evidence, and determine the central assumption (the unstated premise, if you will) that will connect those two pieces of the argument.

Since the assumption is "required," you can, if need be, use the Denial Test to confirm or eliminate answers.

Step 2: Untangle the Stimulus

The Keyword [h]*owever* indicates the author's opinion. He doubts that the syndicated columnists described in the opening sentence will achieve their goal of swaying readers' votes. His evidence (indicated by the Keyword *for*) is that most voters have already formed opinions before the columnists' work appears.

Step 3: Make a Prediction

While voters may have formed opinions before reading the columnists' arguments, this evidence doesn't say that new information or arguments couldn't persuade them to change their minds. In order for the author to conclude that columnists won't persuade voters, he must assume that voters will maintain their points of view even after the release of the columnists' work.

Step 4: Evaluate the Answer Choices

(E) expresses exactly the author's assumption. The Denial Test confirms that this is a necessary assumption. After all, if people *could* be persuaded to change their minds, then the author has no solid reason why columnists couldn't succeed at persuading voters. His conclusion would fall apart.

(A) is irrelevant. According to the author, "nearly all who will vote" have already made up their minds. Influencing the undecided would have, at best, a negligible effect.

(B) suggests that columnists could accidentally have an effect opposite to their intentions. While this may strengthen the idea that they would be unsuccessful, it's hardly a *necessary* assumption. Even if they *didn't* have an adverse effect, they could still have no effect at all.

(C) might strengthen the argument by suggesting that voters probably wouldn't expose themselves to columns that could sway their opinions. However, it's not necessary for the author to assume this. It may well be that decided voters will read opposing views and still not change their minds.

(D) makes an irrelevant distinction between frequent and infrequent column readers, and thus doesn't adequately address the main issue: that almost all voters have already made a decision.

3. (D) Weaken

Step 1: Identify the Question Type

The question directly asks for something that "weakens" the consultant's argument. Start by identifying the conclusion and evidence. Once you've grasped the central assumption, look for an answer that contradicts or undermines that assumption.

Step 2: Untangle the Stimulus

The travel industry consultant introduces a new strategy of some airlines: making business-class seats roomier. The consultant's argument starts after the contrast Keyword *but*, concluding that airlines should focus on the comfort of leisure travelers rather than business travelers. The evidence (signaled by *because*) is that leisure travelers account for the vast majority (80%) of tickets sold.

Step 3: Make a Prediction

Eighty percent is certainly a substantial proportion of tickets sold, but the number of tickets sold is merely one factor in determining what is best for the airline. The consultant assumes that airlines should make decisions solely on what affects the people who buy the greatest number of tickets. The correct answer will challenge this assumption by raising an overlooked consideration—most likely one that would validate the airlines' approach in catering to business travelers.

Step 4: Evaluate the Answer Choices

(D) brings up a relevant overlooked alternative. Leisure travelers may buy more tickets, but business travelers actually bring in more money. In that case, it would be prudent to keep the higher-revenue customers happy.

(A) doesn't work. There's nothing here to indicate that business travelers will feel less valued if the airlines make leisure travelers more comfortable. And if business travelers continue to use the airline, the consultant's argument could still be valid.

(B) is Outside the Scope. The argument is only about the airlines that are focusing on business class and neglecting leisure travelers.

(C) is too narrow to be a relevant "weakener." Initially, it may seem to weaken the consultant's argument because if leisure travelers aren't concerned about comfort, then airlines shouldn't worry about focusing on it. But the argument is about comfort in general, not limited to "sleeping in comfort" or "long flights." Moreover, the fact that these particular comforts aren't the "primary" concern for leisure travelers doesn't mean they aren't high on the list.

(E) is a 180, suggesting that leisure travelers are less interested in comfort than in ticket prices. Moreover, this answer choice does nothing to suggest that it is important for airlines to take care of the business traveler.

4. (B) Point at Issue

Step 1: Identify the Question Type

When a question asks for something two people "disagree about," it wants the Point at Issue. Summarize both speakers' arguments, and then look for an answer with which one

speaker would agree and the other would disagree. You can use the Decision Tree to confirm your choice.

Step 2: Untangle the Stimulus

Gaby starts right off with her conclusion: schoolchildren should make their own decisions about what to learn, receiving minimal guidance from teachers. She feels this will enable the students to become more successful in life. Logan disagrees, arguing that schoolchildren should acquire fundamental knowledge and that this can be accomplished only through systematic instruction from qualified teachers.

Step 3: Make a Prediction

Gaby and Logan have distinct ideas as to which educational system most benefits children: Gaby suggests children make decisions with minimal teacher involvement; Logan suggests a more fundamental program with intensive teacher involvement. The correct answer will focus on this difference in learning environment.

Step 4: Evaluate the Answer Choices

(B) correctly addresses the learning environment issue. Use the Decision Tree. Gaby certainly has an opinion on the extent of teachers' direction (teachers' involvement should be minimal), as does Logan (teachers should be heavily involved), and those two opinions are absolutely different.

(A) is not addressed by Gaby, who expresses no opinion on how best to acquire fundamental knowledge.

(C) is a clever 180. Both Gaby and Logan agree that qualified teachers are important. Gaby says children should be supported by experienced teachers, even if their guidance is minimal; Logan says children need systematic instruction from qualified teachers.

(D) is Outside the Scope. Neither speaker discusses the fostering of creativity.

(E) is also Outside the Scope because neither speaker addresses children's *interest* in fundamental subjects. Gaby talks only about appealing to their interests (which may or may not include fundamental subjects), while Logan urges the teaching of fundamentals regardless of students' interest.

5. (B) Principle (Identify/Strengthen)

Step 1: Identify the Question Type

The question asks for a *principle* that would support the judge's argument, making it a Principle question that mimics a Strengthen question. Furthermore, the question states that the principle is "assumed" by the judge, so your skills in identifying assumptions will also come in handy. The correct answer will be a broader version of the specific assumption underlying the judge's reasoning.

Step 2: Untangle the Stimulus

In this particular case, a plaintiff has requested an order allowing her to question each of three defendants separately, with the other defendants and their respective legal counsel removed from the room. However, the judge concludes (signaled by *therefore*) that the request cannot be granted. The evidence is that two of the defendants have the same legal counsel and the court will not order either to get new legal counsel.

Step 3: Make a Prediction

Consider the problem at hand. There are three defendants (call them A, B, and C), two of whom (say, A and B) have the same lawyer. The plaintiff requests that when Defendant A is deposed, Defendants B and C be removed, along with their lawyers. However, if that were to happen, Defendant B would be escorted out with his lawyer—who happens also to be Defendant A's lawyer. In that case, Defendant A would be left without legal counsel. By denying the plaintiff's request, the judge assumes that leaving Defendant A to answer questions without legal counsel is unacceptable. The correct answer will generalize this assumption.

Step 4: Evaluate the Answer Choices

(B) is a perfect match. If defendants in general have the right to legal counsel while being questioned, then the judge is right in denying the plaintiff's request since it would allow the questioning of two defendants without legal counsel present.

(A) is Outside the Scope. The plaintiff's request involves questioning the defendants. The legal counsel isn't forced to reveal anything.

(C) is Outside the Scope. No information is provided about self-incrimination. Indeed, nothing indicates that this is even a criminal matter.

(D) is also Outside the Scope since the argument never mentions rights that are denied the defendants but afforded to the plaintiff.

(E) distorts the argument by affirming the defense counsel's right to question the plaintiff—a concept that is irrelevant to the judge's decision.

6. (E) Inference

Step 1: Identify the Question Type

The phrase "properly inferred" indicates this is an Inference question. Accept each statement as valid and look for ways to combine statements that use the same terms and concepts. The correct answer will be directly based on this information.

Step 2: Untangle the Stimulus

The entire stimulus is a long string of causes and effects. Coastal estuaries are susceptible to pollution by nutrient-rich sewage, which leads to overnutrified waters, which leads to an increase in algae, which means more food for microorganisms toxic to fish, which means lots of dead fish. In fact, note the strength of the final result: "*most* fish in the estuary" may be killed.

Step 3: Make a Prediction

The correct answer will be consistent with this unfortunate chain of events. Be wary of answers that reverse the chain of events or negate its terms without reversing them (violating the proper laws of Formal Logic).

Step 4: Evaluate the Answer Choices

(E) perfectly summarizes initial cause to ultimate result. Overnutrifying the waters would lead to algae, then microorganisms, and ultimately the death of most of the fish in that estuary. This answer gets even the strength of the result correct.

(A) is Outside the Scope inasmuch as the stimulus only discusses the effect of sewage pollution. Other forms of pollution may be more or less harmful.

(B) isn't directly supported. According to the stimulus, algae provide food to microorganisms that are toxic to fish. However, you're given no information about reproduction rates or other types of microorganisms.

(C) is Extreme. While the stimulus doesn't mention other ways sewage can harm fish, it certainly doesn't suggest that toxic microorganisms are the *only* source of danger from the sewage.

(D) distorts the stimulus by negating the logic. Nutrient-rich sewage will lead to abundant algae, but something else might do so as well. In Formal Logic terms, nutrient-rich sewage is sufficient to increase algae but may not be necessary for that increase.

7. (A) Strengthen/Weaken (Evaluate the Argument)

Step 1: Identify the Question Type

In an unusual but not all that uncommon twist on Strengthen/Weaken questions, this question asks for a piece of information that would help you "evaluate" the argument. First, identify the conclusion and evidence; then, identify the central assumption. The correct answer choice poses a question relevant to the assumption. In other words, the hypothetical response to that question will make the conclusion either more or less likely to be true based on the given evidence.

Step 2: Untangle the Stimulus

The question asks about the archaeologists' hypothesis (clearly identified by the word *hypothesize*). They conclude that the massively heavy stones found in the prehistoric city of Tiwanaku, quarried 90 kilometers away across a lake, were transported to Tiwanaku on reed boats. The evidence is that recent experimenters, using local materials and traditional techniques to build reed boats, successfully transported a 9-ton stone.

Step 3: Make a Prediction

The experimenters' success shows that a reed boat built today *can* transport the massive stones. However, Tiwanaku was a prehistoric city, perhaps thriving at a time well before the same local materials were available or the traditional techniques for building reed boats were devised. The archaeologists must assume that the people at Tiwanaku had access to the same materials *and* techniques the recent experimenters used. The correct answer will address either of these two concerns.

Step 4: Evaluate the Answer Choices

(A) adequately questions the existence of traditional reed boat–building techniques in ancient Tiwanaku. If those techniques were in use back then, then the archaeologists' experiment is further validated. However, if those techniques didn't come into use until after Tiwanaku was deserted, the experiment is not applicable.

(B) is irrelevant since the hypothesis is about how the stones were transported to Tiwanaku, not whether they were also used near the quarry site.

(C) is also irrelevant since the hypothesis is about a prehistoric city, not present-day society.

(D) is Outside the Scope because the hypothesis addresses only the transport of the andacite stones. Perhaps other, larger stones were quarried near Tiwanaku with no need for elaborate transport.

(E) poses a question that wouldn't affect the argument regardless of the answer. All that matters is whether such a raft could transport such a heavy stone. Whether the raft lasted years or for just one trip, the task would be complete.

8. (C) Flaw

Step 1: Identify the Question Type

"Vulnerable to criticism" is classic LSAT language indicating there's a flaw in the reasoning. Start by identifying the conclusion and evidence. Once you determine the central assumption, look for an answer that explains why that assumption is questionable.

Step 2: Untangle the Stimulus

The *therefore* at the end indicates the union member's conclusion: The labor union shouldn't strike now, despite what some members feel. The union member has two pieces of evidence: Striking would take money from the strike fund, and the union would suffer a major financial loss by being heavily fined.

Step 3: Make a Prediction

This is a common argument structure tested on the LSAT: an author recommends against a course of action, but presents only the negative impacts of taking the action. The author of such an argument overlooks potential benefits that could outweigh the negatives. In this case, the union member argues against striking because of possible financial losses. However, the benefits resulting from an effective strike could be more valuable than any immediate financial hit. The correct answer will identify this overlooked possibility.

Step 4: Evaluate the Answer Choices

(C) identifies the classic flaw. Although it's true that the union could lose money, the author doesn't consider whether potentially more valuable benefits may result.

(A) misses the point of the argument. The union member argues against the strike because it will deplete the strike fund and result in a fine. Nothing suggests that he would change his mind if a depleted strike fund were the only concern. There's simply no reason to accuse him of overlooking this possibility.

(B) is Outside the Scope. While it's true that the union member doesn't quantify the financial loss, knowing that the loss would be "major" is sufficient for the argument.

(D) is incorrect because the union member brings up finances merely as *one* factor—in his mind, apparently, the decisive factor. That doesn't necessarily imply that the union member assumes it's the most important.

(E) is irrelevant. Even if there will *never* be a better opportunity to strike, the resulting financial loss could still be enough to deter the action.

9. (E) Inference

Step 1: Identify the Question Type

The stem describes the stimulus as "statements," not as an argument. These statements, it says, will "strongly support" the correct answer. That means the correct answer is a valid inference. Translate any Formal Logic, combine statements by looking for common terms, and then determine what must be true.

Step 2: Untangle the Stimulus

The stimulus starts off with some Formal Logic: for birds or mammals to contract West Nile virus, they must be bitten by an infected mosquito:

If	contract W.N. virus	→	mosquito bite
If	~ mosquito bite	→	~ contract W.N. virus

Mosquitoes can get the virus from biting infected animals—although it's important to note that this isn't the *only* way for mosquitoes to get the virus. The stimulus then offers some random history about the virus (which feels like fodder for trap answers). However, the last line offers some important information: humans can catch the virus, but in humans it's never strong enough to infect a biting mosquito.

Step 3: Make a Prediction

There's Formal Logic here that can be connected. The last line states that some humans have become infected. According to the first line, this can happen only through mosquito bites, so some humans have definitely been bitten by infected mosquitoes. However, the last line states that humans can't infect mosquitoes. In other words, if mosquitoes get the West Nile virus, it can't be from biting an infected human. So the combination of all this information is: any animal (including a human) that contracts the disease must have been bitten by a mosquito, which in turn must have become infected by a source other than humans. Don't spend a lot of time predicting one particular answer. Just look for something that directly follows from this information.

Step 4: Evaluate the Answer Choices

(E) must be true. As stated in the final sentence of the stimulus, humans can't carry enough of the West Nile virus to infect a biting mosquito. Therefore, an infected mosquito, bird, or nonhuman mammal must have brought the disease to North America.

(A) is unsupported. If enough infected mosquitoes bit humans, West Nile virus most certainly could become common.

(B) is unsupported because only infected mosquitoes can transmit the virus. The area with the highest density of mosquitoes could be teeming with *un*infected mosquitoes.

(C) is unsupported. While humans can't transmit the virus back to mosquitoes, humans may well show symptoms of infection.

(D) is an unsupported comparison. The virus may have originated in Africa, but nothing in the stimulus indicates that it affects more people there. Remember that the correct answer to an Inference question must be supported *by the statements in the stimulus* alone.

10. (D) Paradox

Step 1: Identify the Question Type

When a question asks you to "resolve" a discrepancy, there's a paradox in need of explanation. Look for two seemingly contradictory ideas in the stimulus, and find an answer that reconciles the apparent conflict between them.

Step 2: Untangle the Stimulus

The first claim is that people have tried to reduce their fat intake by cutting down on red meat. However, on average,

those who cut back on red meat actually consumed *more* fat than those who didn't cut back.

Step 3: Make a Prediction

The central mystery is how people could cut a fatty food from their diets yet still consume more fat. The correct answer will explain where that extra fat comes from. The most likely explanation is that these people replaced the red meat with another high-fat food.

Step 4: Evaluate the Answer Choices

(D) provides a perfect explanation. Those who reduced the amount of red meat in their diets ate more of other foods that are even *higher* in fat. That would explain why they're now worse off than the people who stuck with red meat.

(A) makes an Irrelevant Comparison. The paradox involves a comparison between the fat intakes of those who cut back on red meat and those who didn't. It has nothing to do with how many people made the dietary change or when they did it.

(B) doesn't resolve the paradox because the reason *why* people made the decision to cut back on red meat (some may have done it for health reasons, others for financial ones) doesn't explain why those who reduced their red meat consumption are now eating more fat.

(C) is a 180. If the people who cut back on red meat are eating just as much of other fatty foods as everyone else, then where that extra fat is coming from is even more curious.

(E) is irrelevant to the paradox. Even if red meat isn't as fatty as previously thought, it still doesn't explain why the people who eat less red meat consume more fat overall.

11. (D) Flaw

Step 1: Identify the Question Type

The question asks for the "reasoning error" in Tom's argument, which is another way of asking for the flaw. Moreover, while Tom's argument may have several flaws, the question specifically asks for the flaw pointed out by Rolanda's response. Be sure to read all parts of the conversation for context.

Step 2: Untangle the Stimulus

Rolanda starts the discussion by recommending that she and Tom rent the Oak Avenue house. Her evidence is that it has the largest yard they've seen in Prairieview. Tom counters by disputing the yard size. Tom argues that it's not the biggest yard they've seen. His evidence is that the section within 20 feet of the street actually belongs to the city. Rolanda fires back by saying the same 20-foot restriction holds for all the other homes in Prairieview.

Step 3: Make a Prediction

Tom's argument assumes that taking 20 feet off the Oak Avenue yard means that the yard is technically smaller than it looks. However, by pointing out that the restriction applies to all of the other yards they've seen in the city, Rolanda suggests that Tom, mistakenly, is applying the 20-yard restriction only to the Oak Avenue yard. If he were to make the same reduction to all of the yards they've seen in Prairieview, then the Oak Avenue yard would be the biggest.

Step 4: Evaluate the Answer Choices

(D) points out the error that Rolanda has spotted. Tom tried to apply a rule (the property line restrictions) only to the Oak Street house rather than to all relevant houses (all others they've seen in Prairieview).

(A) is Outside the Scope of Tom's argument. His argument is about the actual specs of the Oak Avenue yard, not about the benefits of a particular size.

(B) is a Distortion of the dialogue. Tom doesn't say so explicitly, but he likely assumes that the 20-foot area is *not* available for private use. If he assumed that it was available for him and Rolanda to use, the fact that the city owns the 20-foot strip next to the street likely wouldn't concern him or make him think of the yard as smaller than "it looks."

(C) is a 180. Tom's mistake is actually *not* applying a general rule to yards that the rule *is* intended to cover.

(E) distorts the argument, since Tom never breaks down the yard into parts. Furthermore, if you interpret the "part" to be the Oak Avenue yard and the "whole" to be all yards in Prairieview, then this is a complete 180, as Tom *fails* to apply the same 20-foot rule to all yards.

12. (C) Role of a Statement

Step 1: Identify the Question Type

Since the question provides a claim from the stimulus and asks for the "role played" by that claim, this is a Role of a Statement question. Start by locating the cited claim and making a mark next to it. Then dissect the argument into its conclusion and evidence, and consider where and how the marked claim fits into the argument.

Step 2: Untangle the Stimulus

The cited claim about jazz singers using their voices much as jazz players use horns is the very first sentence. The example of Billie Holiday, who used her voice exactly as described in the claim, follows next. After proposing another claim about a reciprocal effect (horn players mimicking vocal styles), the author reaches the conclusion (indicated by the conclusion Keyword [*so*]): jazz contains mainly horns that sound like voices and voices that sound like horns.

Step 3: Make a Prediction

The example of Billie Holiday supports the statement in question. However, that statement is not the ultimate conclusion. The main conclusion, at the end, is supported by both the initial claim and the converse claim about horns emulating voices. So the correct answer will likely express the dual context of the opening claim: an example supports it, and it supports the final conclusion.

Step 4: Evaluate the Answer Choices

(C) accurately describes the role of the opening claim. Some evidence is provided for it (Billie Holiday), and it's used to support the main conclusion (jazz has voicelike horns and hornlike voices).

(A) distorts the argument's structure. The claim from the question stem is *not* the argument's main conclusion. Moreover, while the cited claim is supported by another statement (the example of Billie Holiday), that statement is not backed up by any other statement.

(B) is off base because the last sentence (as evidenced by the Keyword [*so*]) is also a conclusion—in fact, it's the main one.

(D) goes astray immediately by suggesting there's no evidence for the opening claim. Even though there are no evidence Keywords, the information about Billie Holiday supports the idea that jazz singers use their voices like instruments.

(E) is Half-Right/Half-Wrong. The answer gets the first half right: the claim in question does support a conclusion. However, it supports the main conclusion. It is a subsidiary conclusion; it does not support one.

13. (E) Assumption (Necessary)

Step 1: Identify the Question Type

The question directly asks for the educator's "assumption," making this an Assumption question. Identify the conclusion and evidence; then predict the correct answer, the assumption that will close the gap between the evidence and conclusion. Since the assumption is described as "required," it is a Necessary Assumption question and is susceptible to the Denial Test.

Step 2: Untangle the Stimulus

The educator's conclusion comes as the end, indicated by the Keyword [*therefore*: smaller class sizes probably won't help students perform better. The evidence is that, even though smaller classes allow for more personalized instruction, reducing class sizes would require more teachers. But the region has a shortage of qualified teachers, and underqualified teachers would be unacceptable.

Step 3: Make a Prediction

There's a subtle error in the educator's argument. Qualified teachers are needed for the class-size reduction program to work. The educator merely states that there's a shortage of such teachers *in the region*. In order for the argument to work, the educator must be assuming that the school district can use qualified teachers only from that area.

If you didn't catch that subtle scope shift, two things would still help answer this question. Applying the Denial Test not only validates the correct answer but also helps to eliminate irrelevant and unnecessary answers. Also, in general, when an author predicts something won't happen, rely on the broad assumption that no possible alternative way of accomplishing the intended results is possible.

Step 4: Evaluate the Answer Choices

(E) closes the loophole in the author's argument by eliminating the possibility of hiring people from outside the region. The Denial Test confirms this answer: if qualified teachers *could* be persuaded to relocate to the region, then the school district wouldn't have to rely on underqualified teachers or worry about the regional shortage of qualified teachers. That would destroy the educator's argument that reduction in class sizes wouldn't improve student performance. Thus, he must assume that qualified teachers *can't* be persuaded to relocate.

(A) distorts the educator's argument. The educator is not arguing about whether or not class sizes *should* be reduced (or the conditions under which they should be). Rather, he's speculating on whether or not such a program would work.

(B) is a 180, serving to weaken the argument. The educator's conclusion is that class size reduction probably *wouldn't* work. There's no need to assume that it *would* work for some teachers. You could also argue that this choice is irrelevant: while some teachers would be able to improve their classes, this may not be enough to make the program work district-wide.

(C) makes an Irrelevant Comparison. Students' preferences wouldn't affect the success of class-size reductions, and thus have no bearing on the argument at hand.

(D) is Extreme, falling apart because of the word *any*. This choice claims *no* students would improve if mainly or only underqualified teachers were hired. Use the Denial Test: what if, with underqualified teachers, some students did improve? It wouldn't matter! The educator's conclusion is not about the improvement of individual students but about "overall" improvement—which could still decline despite some individual successes.

14. (E) Main Point

Step 1: Identify the Question Type

When a question asks for the "conclusion drawn," it wants the author's main point. Look for Keywords that distinguish evidence from conclusions, and keep an eye out for contrast Keywords that indicate the author's opinion counters a previously asserted opinion. You'll see this pattern often in Main Point questions.

Step 2: Untangle the Stimulus

The geographer begins by offering some scientific data about what conditions favor tropical storms (in short, warm ocean surfaces). The phrase "for this reason" indicates the data is being used to support a conclusion: Global warming will cause more frequent and harsher tropical storms. However, the Keyword [*b*]*ut* indicates a contrast to that initial conclusion. The geographer argues that bigger and more frequent storms probably won't happen. Why? Because other factors (e.g., unstable winds) will negate the higher temperatures that global warming would cause.

Step 3: Make a Prediction

The first opinion presented (global warming will lead to more frequent and severe storms) came from "early discussions." However, the geographer presents that opinion only to attack it. The contrasting view (that more extreme storms probably *won't* result from global warming) is the geographer's conclusion. The correct answer will paraphrase that view.

Step 4: Evaluate the Answer Choices

(E) accurately expresses the geographer's contrasting viewpoint: global warming won't produce the kinds of storms predicted in the earlier discussions.

(A) is a minor point supported by the initial claim that tropical storms need heat and moisture. That point, however, is just part of the scientific data, which are used to explain the original predictions with which the author disagrees. This is definitely not the geographer's conclusion.

(B) distorts the geographer's claims. While the early discussions predicted that global warming would affect tropical storm development, they never suggested global warming would be the *only* contributing factor.

(C) is Outside the Scope since the geographer doesn't mention reversing global warming, let alone discuss what effects that reversal might produce.

(D) mistakenly identifies the last sentence of the passage as the conclusion. However, this information is the geographer's evidence, supporting his belief that early predictions won't come true.

15. (E) Strengthen

Step 1: Identify the Question Type

While most questions on the LSAT that ask you to fill in the blank are Inference questions (essentially asking for the logical conclusion), this one asks you to fill in the blank with something that will "strongly [support]" the argument. This means you need to fill in a piece of evidence that will strengthen the argument, making this a Strengthen question.

Step 2: Untangle the Stimulus

The author starts by stating the original function and purpose of copyrights: They gave authors a monetary incentive to circulate their ideas. With the Keyword *however*, the author introduces a contrast, concluding that copyright sometimes goes beyond this purpose. The blank at the end must be filled by a missing piece of evidence (indicated by the Keyword *since*) that would support that conclusion.

Step 3: Make a Prediction

At this point, the author has defined the original role of copyright (a financial incentive for authors to circulate ideas) and concluded that copyright sometimes exceeds this role. What's missing is an example or explanation of how copyright sometimes exceeds its original role. The correct answer will state a way in which copyright is sometimes not limited to financially rewarding authors.

Step 4: Evaluate the Answer Choices

(E) does the job. After an author dies, financial incentives for that author would become immaterial. If copyrights still hold past that time, then they must be surpassing the original purpose, as the present author concludes.

(A) offers an alternative to copyright for the circulation of ideas, but doesn't discuss whether or not copyrights sometimes go beyond the original intentions.

(B) suggests that authors don't need the financial incentive copyright offers, but again, the answer choice doesn't address the argument's assertion that copyrights exceed the original purpose behind them.

(C) is irrelevant, since difficulty in finding a publisher has no effect on the purpose of copyrights.

(D) is Outside the Scope. This is an argument about the goals of copyright protection, not its efficacy. If anything, a lack of enforceability probably reduces the purposes a law can reasonably be said to have. In any case, this choice doesn't make the argument any stronger.

16. (A) Method of Argument

Step 1: Identify the Question Type

The word *by* may be small, but it indicates that the question is asking for *how* the economist responds to the critic, not *what* the economist says. The goal of a Method of Argument question is to describe how an argument is made. Focus on the structure of the argument and avoid answers that dwell on the details. Often, in a dialogue stimulus, the second speaker points out a flaw in the first speaker's argument. Your knowledge of common flaw types will help you answer these questions.

Step 2: Untangle the Stimulus

The dialogue starts with a critic who attacks an economist for previously predicting that a recession would occur if economic policies weren't changed. The critic asserts that instead, the country saw economic growth. The economist defends the prediction by stating that economic policies did in fact change and that change prevented the recession.

Step 3: Make a Prediction

The key to answering this question is noticing the conditional aspect of the economist's original prediction: *if* policies were not changed (i.e., if they remained the same), the economy would suffer. The economist introduces evidence showing that policies *were* changed. Therefore, the sufficient condition that would result in a recession wasn't met. The critic's mistake then (a common one surrounding predictions) is assuming that conditions *did* remain the same.

Step 4: Evaluate the Answer Choices

(A), in rather fancy-sounding terms, is exactly what the economist does—shows how the condition (no change in policy) that would have led to the predicted result (recession) didn't happen.

(B) is off because the economist doesn't argue that the recession has yet to happen. By pointing out that economic policies changed, the economist proves original conditions no longer exist and therefore the original prediction will not follow, regardless of how much time passes.

(C) doesn't work because the economist doesn't point out an inconsistency between the *critic's* two statements. The critic's statements are adequately consistent with one another. Instead, the economist argues that the critic misinterpreted the conditions on which the *economist's* prediction was based.

(D) is off because the economist doesn't counter either of the critic's two claims: that the economist made a prediction and that the economy grew. Likely, the economist agrees with both of those claims.

(E) is off because the economist doesn't dispute any facts (he only quibbles with the characterization of his forecast as "bumbling"). Instead, the economist explains that the critic overlooks the conditional aspect of the prediction.

17. (C) Parallel Reasoning

Step 1: Identify the Question Type

The question asks for an argument that is "similar in its reasoning" to the one in the stimulus. That indicates a Parallel Reasoning question. Broaden the structure of the stimulus into generic terms, and use easily comparable structural components to find the one answer that matches the structure piece by piece. Specifically, characterize the conclusion and see if any answer choices can be quickly rejected.

Step 2: Untangle the Stimulus

The author's conclusion begins with the contrast Keyword [*b*]*ut*. The author argues that even though music videos seem to suggest synthesizer pop and punk rock dominated 1970s music, such an impression would be deceptive. The conclusion is an assertion of fact that an impression created by limited or unrepresentative evidence is wrong. The author's evidence is that videos were new in the 1970s and mainly appealed to synth-pop and punk rock musicians.

Step 3: Make a Prediction

The correct answer will take the general idea behind the argument and apply it to a field other than music. In general, the structure is: looking at select historical items (music videos) can give a misleading view of a field (music) because, at the time, those items appealed to only a limited subset of people (cutting-edge musicians).

Step 4: Evaluate the Answer Choices

(C) matches the structure piece for piece—even if it shifts the time frame a little. In the future, looking at select historical items (CD-ROMs) can give a misleading view of a field (publishing) because, at the time, those items appealed to only a limited subset of people (computer game publishers).

(A) is Extreme in its conclusion, which says that our view of early literature can "never be accurate." The original argument states only that music videos could mislead people, not that people's view of 1970s music could never be right.

(B) distorts the structure by talking about memory rather than understanding and by claiming that our memory of 1960s television is *not* distorted. Also, this answer choice doesn't discuss unrepresentative evidence, such as the music videos. It doesn't say, for example, that only comedies from the 1960s continue to be rerun.

(D) presents fallible evidence (silent films) but differs from the stimulus in *why* the evidence is shoddy. Technical problems, not issues of representation, are the culprit here.

(E) goes astray immediately in its conclusion, which is a prediction, not an assertion of fact. In addition, this argument

explains how views could be accurate *despite* questionable evidence, while the original argument was about how people could be misinformed *because* of it.

18. (B) Principle (Identify/Inference)

Step 1: Identify the Question Type

The question asks for the "generalization" illustrated by the stimulus. *Generalization* is another word for principle—a broad rule that can apply to specific circumstances. The correct answer will take the specific example in the stimulus and express it in more generic terms.

Step 2: Untangle the Stimulus

According to the stimulus, certain institutions (e.g., hospitals and universities) can successfully achieve the purpose they proclaim publicly, even though they employ individuals who work there for their own selfish reasons.

Step 3: Make a Prediction

The correct answer will broaden the scope of this idea to apply not just to other institutions, but possibly to groups in general. In short, the correct answer will provide a general rule about how some groups can have a particular quality (a public purpose) even if their members don't share that quality (have their own selfish purposes).

Step 4: Evaluate the Answer Choices

(B) is a clean match. The organizations in the stimulus do have a property (public purpose) not possessed by all their members (some of whom have selfish motives).

(A) is Outside the Scope. The principle in the stimulus is about the relationship between parts (workers) and a whole (institutions), not about the relationship between wholes (which is what social organizations would be in this case).

(C) distorts the information. While this statement may be true, at question are the institutions' and individuals' actual purposes, not their claimed purposes.

(D) is Outside the Scope. Founders' original intentions are irrelevant, as are any consequences beyond those evincing public purposes. Neither original intentions nor additional consequences relate to the fact that institutions and individuals working within them can have different aims.

(E) distorts the stimulus. Even if we assume that the institutions mentioned in the stimulus were created to serve public purposes, nothing there indicates that they serve other purposes "just as effectively." The author simply remarks that they serve public purposes effectively despite the fact that their employees have selfish motives.

19. (B) Weaken (EXCEPT)

Step 1: Identify the Question Type

The question stem suggests that four answers will weaken the consumer advocate's argument. The correct answer will be the one exception. It will be either a 180 and strengthen the argument, or it will be irrelevant and have no effect on the argument. As always with argument-based questions, start by identifying the conclusion and evidence and then determine the central assumption.

Step 2: Untangle the Stimulus

The advocate mentions that some countries irradiate certain foods to make them last longer. The contrast Keyword *however* indicates the consumer advocate's point of contention (in this case, the conclusion): people shouldn't eat irradiated foods. What follows is a list of three reasons to avoid such foods: 1) Irradiated foods are also exposed to radioactive substances; 2) irradiation can diminish vitamins and leave chemical residues; and 3) irradiation produces harmful radiolytic products.

Step 3: Make a Prediction

Don't let scientific jargon like "irradiated," "gamma rays," and "radiolytic" scare you off. At its core, this is a classic LSAT argument. The author recommends against a course of action (in this case, eating irradiated foods) and backs up the recommendation with a series of negative effects. The assumptions are both that the negatives will directly harm consumers and that the negatives outweigh any benefits. Four answers will weaken the author's conclusion by showing how the listed negatives aren't bad enough to merit a change in consumption. One answer either will strengthen the argument by furthering the dangers attributed to irradiated foods or will be entirely irrelevant.

Step 4: Evaluate the Answer Choices

(B) is irrelevant and, therefore, correct. The author doesn't claim that irradiated food is the only cause of cancer and other health problems. Even if there are many other causes, irradiated foods might still be harmful. Thus, the advocate's argument stands unaffected. That makes this the correct answer.

(A) weakens the argument by showing that unique harmful radiolytic products are rarely found in irradiated food.

(C) weakens the argument by showing that irradiation reduces vitamin content in a miniscule number of fruits and vegetables.

(D) weakens the argument by showing that although radiation can leave behind harmful chemicals, the amount of such chemicals found in irradiated food is actually *less* than that occurring naturally.

(E) weakens the argument by showing that people who eat irradiated food don't actually get cancer any more often than the general population.

20. (D) Assumption (Necessary)

Step 1: Identify the Question Type

The question directly asks for the author's assumption. Since it's defined as "required," the Denial Test can be used to check answer choices. Before you get to those, though, be sure to identify the author's conclusion and evidence, and identify the core assumption.

Step 2: Untangle the Stimulus

The author starts right off with the conclusion—a recommendation to use colored paper rather than paint when demonstrating the use of color. The evidence emphasizes a key difference between colored paper and paint. Colored paper easily allows the use of the exact same color over and over so that one can see the precise impact of that color in different contexts. By contrast, paint doesn't allow for this since mixing two paints to get the exact same color is difficult, and paint's textures can distort the color's effect.

Step 3: Make a Prediction

Based on the evidence, the key difference between colored paper and paint involves how helpful they are when comparing colors in different contexts. The color of paper is easily replicated, making it easy to use for such comparisons. With paint, exact color matches are hard to accomplish and the paint texture can throw off the color, making precise comparisons difficult. Look for the scope shift between the evidence and conclusion. The author's recommendation is not about comparing color in different contexts, it's about learning how to use color. For the argument to work, the author must assume that comparing colors in different contexts is an integral part of learning about the use of color.

Step 4: Evaluate the Answer Choices

(D) is a match, connecting the evidence about observing colors in different contexts to the conclusion about learning to use color. If this choice were denied, and observing color across varying context does *not* help students learn about the use of color, then the author's assertion that paper is better because it allows such demonstrations no longer makes sense.

(A) is tempting because the author's problem with paint is that its texture can interfere with the color's effect. This answer choice eliminates a similar problem with paper. However, it doesn't explain *why* colors need to be exactly the same in order for teachers to explain their use. In other words, this answer doesn't connect the evidence (whether the color of paper or paint is more reliable) with the conclusion (that paper is preferable for teaching color use).

It's simply more evidence that paper is superior. Even if differently textured paper would *not* have the same effect in a given context, the author may still be justified in saying paper is preferable to paint.

(B) is off because, again, the answer choice doesn't connect the evidence with the conclusion's mismatched term ("use of color"). This answer choice appears to support the author's predilection for paper, but you can deny it without having an effect on the overall argument. Even if this answer were denied, meaning that a difference in paper color is *not* more difficult to notice than a difference in paint color (perhaps they're equally difficult), paper is still easier to match, and so the author may still have a valid argument.

(C) is irrelevant at best and a 180 at worst. The effect of lighting doesn't have any bearing on whether the colors can be easily replicated for precise comparisons. Furthermore, this answer shows that paper doesn't react as much as paint to changes in light, which could potentially make for less precise comparisons.

(E) is a Distortion because the author's recommendation is to make sure students can make precise comparisons among different contexts, not that students be able to see the differences between compositions using paper and those using paint.

21. (E) Role of a Statement

Step 1: Identify the Question Type

The question cites a claim from the stimulus and asks for its "role in the philosopher's reasoning," making this a Role of a Statement question. Start by finding the cited claim. Then break down the argument into conclusion and evidence, using Keywords and context to note where the cited claim fits into the argument.

Step 2: Untangle the Stimulus

The cited claim is the first sentence, namely that social scientists need data about several societies in order to explain the cause of cultural phenomena. The colon indicates that the next piece will explain what was just said. What follows is a specific example to support this claim: one needs several pieces of information to say that certain climatic or ecological factors caused a particular political structure. First, one must make sure no societies without those climatic or ecological factors have that same political structure. Second, one must make sure that the reverse is also true: no societies *with* the climatic or ecological factors have a different political structure.

Step 3: Make a Prediction

The initial claim (the claim in question) is the philosopher's main point. From there, the philosopher—rightly hesitant about causal

arguments—explains how social scientists can solidify a causal relationship: make sure the cause always produces the expected results, and make sure the result is always brought about by the expected cause. The correct answer will identify the claim as a conclusion and likely will mention how the philosopher backs it up with an example of how to establish causality.

Step 4: Evaluate the Answer Choices

(E) is a perfect match. It identifies the statement in the question stem as a claim the author tries to justify (i.e., the conclusion), and it correctly recognizes the evidence as setting out the requirements for establishing a causal relationship.

(A) immediately falters because the philosopher doesn't address any "problem" with social scientists' need for certainty. Indeed, he seems to be providing helpful guidance for how to achieve relative certainty.

(B) reverses the argument. The cited claim is the general theoretical idea—to explain causality, one needs comparative data—while the rest of the argument contains the support.

(C) starts off perfectly, identifying the opening claim as a general hypothesis. However, the example provided doesn't actually show a causal relationship; it shows what social scientists need in order to *establish* or to *disprove* a causal relationship.

(D) contains multiple Distortions. The philosopher doesn't present the initial claim as a "dilemma." Furthermore, while the data needed certainly seems involved, the philosopher never goes so far as to say that a phenomenon's status as cause or effect is "difficult" to determine.

22. (A) Assumption (Sufficient)

Step 1: Identify the Question Type

The question directly asks for something "assumed" by the scientist, making this an Assumption question. The question does also mention that the assumption will "strongly support" the argument, which seems to indicate a Strengthen question. However, while correct answers to many Strengthen questions can simply be information that makes the conclusion more likely, the correct answer here will actually *be* an assumption that guarantees the conclusion. The approach is the same either way: identify the conclusion and evidence, and then bridge the gap.

Step 2: Untangle the Stimulus

Before drawing a conclusion, the scientist presents the physicists' assertion. Physicists claim that their peer review process prevents fraud in physics. However, biologists, who made the same claim, ultimately were wrong about the effectiveness of their peer review. Biologists learned from their mistake and enhanced their protections against fraud, which averted further major incidents. The scientist concludes by recommending that physicists make similar enhancements in order to ensure progress in the field of physics.

Step 3: Make a Prediction

In attempting to help physicists, the scientist recounts the biologists' history. The moral of the story: physicists may want to reassess their precautionary measures if they truly want to be protected from fraud. The scientist does not, however, limit his conclusion to fraud prevention. He claims that taking the recommended steps would be "conducive to progress." It's a classic scope shift. The scientist assumes (perhaps rightly) that scientific fraud impairs the potential for progress in physics.

Step 4: Evaluate the Answer Choices

(A) resolves the scope shift by connecting the idea of scientific fraud (which the evidence addresses) and progress (which the author brings up in the conclusion).

(B) is irrelevant because it only emphasizes the effectiveness of the biologists' new policy in reducing fraud. It does nothing to show how this is conducive to progress; i.e., it does nothing to connect the evidence to the conclusion.

(C) Initially, this choice seems to support the scientist. If no completely effective peer review system exists, then that removes the possibility that the physicists' system is as effective as they claim. However, the scientist doesn't argue for a system that is "completely effective," just that physicists should increase their safeguards. Furthermore, this still doesn't connect fraud prevention to the progress of the field.

(D) is a 180. If the biologists had a worse system 20 years ago than the physicists have now, then perhaps the enhancements the biologists have made since then merely brought them up to the same level as the physicists. In that case, given the biologists' recent success, the physicists would have no need to change.

(E) is also a 180. If physics has been relatively free of fraud, then there seems to be little reason to recommend making any change to the peer review system.

23. (B) Principle (Identify/Assumption)

Step 1: Identify the Question Type

This question asks for a principle. Since the principle "underlies" the argument, that means you need to identify the principle, rather than apply it. Break the argument down into conclusion and evidence, and pinpoint the assumption. Then rephrase the argument in broader, more general terms.

Step 2: Untangle the Stimulus

The phrase "this shows that" in the last sentence indicates the conclusion. Everything mentioned before shows how the

conclusion is supported, and thus is evidence. The conclusion says that some dogs descended from more recently domesticated wolves than other dogs did. Before reaching that conclusion, the biologist presents the general belief that dogs descended from domesticated wolves. Then comes the primary piece of evidence: Some dog breeds are genetically closer to wolves than they are to most other dog breeds.

Step 3: Make a Prediction

The biologist presents quite a scope shift. The evidence offers a variance in how closely certain dogs are related to wolves. The conclusion then discusses when certain wolves were domesticated. The biologist assumes that a dog that is more closely related to wolves than to other dog breeds must have descended from a more recently domesticated wolf. Stated as a rule, this general assumption serves as the principle underlying the argument.

Step 4: Evaluate the Answer Choices

(B) expresses the principle just right. Since certain dog breeds are genetically closer to wolves than to most other dog breeds, this principle allows for the conclusion that those breeds came from wolves that were more recently domesticated.

(A) distorts the author's assumption in two ways. First, the author is concerned with dog breeds more closely related to wolves than to other dog breeds, not those more closely related to wolves than other breeds *are*. Second, the author takes a close relation to wolves as evidence that the wolves from which a breed originated were more recently domesticated, and not vice versa.

(C) provides more detail about the comparison in the author's evidence, but it doesn't represent the principle on which the author builds the argument. Indeed, denying the statement here would make the author's argument even stronger. This choice says that there are no dog breeds genetically closer to wolves than they are to *all* other dog breed. The biologist's evidence is simply that *some* breeds are closer to wolves than to *most* other dog breeds; he'd be happy to find a breed closer to wolves than it is to any other breed.

(D) is a meaningless tautology. Saying that a dog breed more closely related to wolves than another dog breed is therefore more closely related to wolves than the other dog breed is adds nothing to the argument. This choice doesn't address any aspect of *when* domestication appeared or what it indicates.

(E) is Extreme. It's unclear if dog breeds that are more closely related to each other than they are to wolves came from wolves domesticated long ago. The author only asserts that some dogs are more related to *wolves* than to most *dogs*. The author doesn't present any evidence about dogs that are more closely related to most other *dogs* than to *wolves*.

24. (A) Parallel Flaw

Step 1: Identify the Question Type

A question that asks for an argument "most similar to that" in the stimulus is a Parallel Reasoning question. Moreover, the argument is described as "flawed." Therefore, the correct answer not only has to match the structure of the stimulus piece by piece, but it must commit the exact same error in reasoning.

Step 2: Untangle the Stimulus

Using the word *invariably*, the author presents some Formal Logic right off the bat: if someone is a paleomycologist (i.e., one who studies ancient fungi), then that person knows about all published works of all other paleomycologists. The author then presents Professor Mansour, who is familiar with the published works of one paleomycologist, Professor DeAngelis. From this, the author concludes that Professor Mansour must be a paleomycologist. Go ahead and translate the Formal Logic statements in order to more easily see the error in logic.

First Statement:

If	paleomycologist	→	*familiar with all other paleomycologists' publications*

Second and Third Statements:

If	Mansour	→	*familiar with one paleomycologist's publications*	→	paleomycologist

Step 3: Make a Prediction

This argument makes not one, but two classic flaws in interpreting the Formal Logic. First off, being acquainted with all paleomycologists' works is the necessary result of being an ancient-fungus expert. It is not sufficient for concluding that one is a fungus expert. However, the author, when discussing Professor Mansour, makes this classic error by reversing the terms without negating them. Furthermore, paleomycologists are said to be acquainted with the works of *all* other fungus experts. Mansour is said to be acquainted with the work of only *one* paleomycologist: Professor DeAngelis. The correct answer will also include Formal Logic. It will provide one Formal Logic rule and will then commit the same two errors: treating the necessary condition as sufficient and basing a conclusion on evidence that only partially matches the necessary condition.

Step 4: Evaluate the Answer Choices

(A) gets everything right—in other words, it gets the logic all wrong in the same way the stimulus did. The Formal Logic here is: if one flight is delayed, then all connecting flights are also delayed. Evidence of *one* delayed connecting flight (not *all*) is then used to conclude that the original flight was also a delayed Global Airlines flight. Not only does this reverse the Formal Logic improperly (as happened in the stimulus), but the evidence only partially matches the necessary condition (as also happened in the stimulus). *All* connecting flights need to be delayed, but only one delayed connecting flight is cited here.

(B) is indeed flawed in how it handles the Formal Logic. However, this answer improperly negates the logic without reversing it, rather than reversing it without negating it. Furthermore, choice B doesn't make the same mistake of using partial evidence to reach a conclusion.

(C) doesn't demonstrate flawed Formal Logic. If fuel prices drop, expenses go down and income stays the same. That, as the conclusion indicates, is a recipe for increased profits. The only error here is a lack of information about Global's other revenues and expenditures. That's a lack of information, not an error in reasoning.

(D) mistakenly confuses a possible outcome with a certain outcome. Gavin's tenure means he is *eligible to* participate in the plan, but that doesn't warrant a conclusion that he *does* participate. That flaw, however, doesn't match either of the two flaws in the stimulus.

(E) fails in a couple of respects. Immediately, the parallelism falters when the Formal Logic leads to one of two possible results—something the original argument didn't have. Furthermore, while the evidence does address only part of the necessary condition, it indicates that Global Airlines *doesn't* meet the particular condition (losing passengers), which is also contrary to what happens in the original stimulus.

25. (C) Point at Issue

Step 1: Identify the Question Type

This question asks for what two people "disagree ... about," which is a way of asking for the Point at Issue. Summarize the points of both speakers and look for the one answer with which one speaker would agree and the other speaker would disagree.

Step 2: Untangle the Stimulus

Lutsina has a positive view of futuristic science fiction. By being free from the constraint of presenting current realities, it can be more ambitious in its social visions and is therefore potentially more effective as social criticism than is conventional fiction. Priscilla doesn't view futuristic science fiction writers with such fond eyes. She claims that their ambitious views are more about technology than society, which indicates how current reality stifles their imagination. Because of that, she claims, social criticism is more effective in fiction that presents current realities: conventional fiction.

Step 3: Make a Prediction

Ultimately, Lutsina and Priscilla wind up pushing two different types of fiction as the more effective means of social criticism. Lutsina argues that futuristic science fiction is better for criticism, while Priscilla advocates for conventional fiction. The correct answer will express this point of contention.

Step 4: Evaluate the Answer Choices

(C) gets right to the heart of the argument. Lutsina would definitely agree that futuristic science fiction has more promise for social criticism, while Priscilla would disagree and argue that conventional fiction has more promise.

(A) is not supported. Lutsina would agree with this answer, since she directly states that science fiction writers envisage such social arrangements. However, while Priscilla suggests those writers are, in general, better at imagining radical technology, she may be willing to concede that *some* sci-fi writers have successfully envisioned new social arrangements.

(B) is Outside the Scope. The speakers aren't arguing about fiction writers' skills at writing; they're arguing about the effectiveness of their genres for social criticism.

(D) is not supported. Lutsina would most likely disagree with the statement. However, even though Priscilla mentions that these writers are better at envisioning technology than they are at envisioning social arrangements, that doesn't mean she sees that as a "shortcoming."

(E) is Outside the Scope and Extreme. Lutsina does not contend that science fiction criticizes current social arrangements by *contrasting* them with radically different ones. Priscilla asserts that the *most* effective social criticism comes from accurately portraying current realities, but that doesn't mean she finds contrasts with radically different social arrangements completely ineffective.

26. (E) Flaw

Step 1: Identify the Question Type

The question asks why the argument is "flawed," making this easy to identify as a flaw question. Break the argument down into its conclusion and evidence, and look for an answer that explains why the evidence doesn't adequately back up the conclusion. Keep common flaw types in mind.

Step 2: Untangle the Stimulus

The author makes two arguments. The first is that her volleyball club will have the best team in the city because it has recruited the best players in the city. This subsidiary argument leads to the second one, which is that her club will almost certainly be city champions this year because the best team (which she claims to have) is most likely to win.

Step 3: Make a Prediction

Both of her arguments are flawed. In the first argument, she assumes her group as a team will share the characteristics of its individual members. In other words, she assumes that because the individual players are the best, they will work together as a whole better than any other team. The second argument makes an improper shift from individual comparison to overall assessment. More specifically, being more likely to win than any other team doesn't make the team a near-certain winner of the championship. Say, for example, that there are four teams; if the best team has a 40 percent chance of winning, and each of the other teams has a 20 percent chance of winning, then the best team is more likely to win than each other team individually but still is more likely overall to lose the tournament (60% chance) than win. An answer that indicates either of these points will be correct, as it will demonstrate something that makes the argument flawed.

Step 4: Evaluate the Answer Choices

(E) expresses the flaw in the author's second argument. The author concludes that because an event is the most likely outcome of multiple individual possibilities (her team is more likely to win than is each other team), that event is more likely than not to occur (her team will almost certainly win).

(A) distorts the author's arguments. The author claims her team is the best based on the quality of her individual players, not on competition. Also, there's no indication that competition was used to determine which players are the best.

(B) is off because how good the team and its individual players *is* relevant to the team's quality. There is nothing irrelevant here, just misinterpreted data.

(C) is tempting, since the author does make such a prediction. However, there's nothing wrong with predicting an outcome based on comparing the competitors. The flaw the author commits is taking it to the extreme and asserting her team will "almost certainly" win.

(D) reverses, but fails to negate, the logic of the author's first argument. She assumes that if each individual part of her team is the best, then her team as a whole is the best team, not the other way around.

PrepTest 66

The Inside Story

PrepTest 66 was administered in June 2012. It challenged 25,223 test takers. What made this test so hard? Here's a breakdown of what Kaplan students who were surveyed after taking the official exam considered PrepTest 66's most difficult section.

Hardest PrepTest 66 Section as Reported by Test Takers

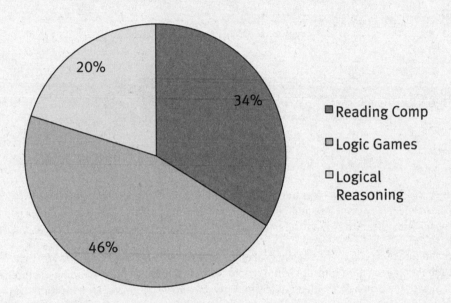

Based on these results, you might think that studying Logic Games is the key to LSAT success. Well, Logic Games is important, but test takers' perceptions don't tell the whole story. For that, you need to consider students' actual performance. The following chart shows the average number of students to miss each question in each of PrepTest 66's different sections.

Percentage Incorrect by PrepTest 66 Section Type

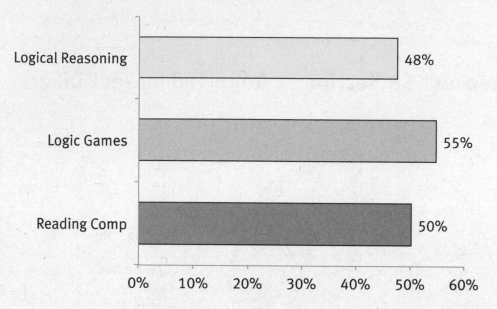

PrepTest 66 was the rare test on which student perceptions of difficulty lined up to their actual results. Logic Games was indeed the most challenging section, narrowly beating out Reading Comprehension. In terms of student performance, Logical Reasoning is almost as hard as the other sections, despite students' perception that the LR sections were by far the easiest.

Maybe students underestimate the difficulty of the Logical Reasoning section because the questions feel the most straightforward. But the truth is that the testmaker places hard questions throughout the test. On PrepTest 67, Reading Comprehension has four of the test's ten hardest questions, with the other six divided equally between LG and LR. Here were the locations of the 10 hardest (most missed) questions in the exam.

Location of 10 Most Difficult Questions in PrepTest 66

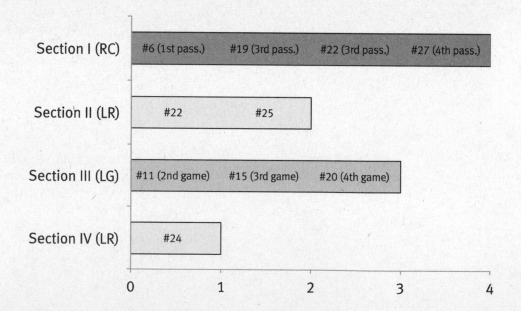

The takeaway from this data is that, to maximize your potential on the LSAT, you need to take a comprehensive approach. Test yourself rigorously, and review your performance on every section of the test. Kaplan's LSAT explanations provide the expertise and insight you need to fully understand your results. The explanations are written and edited by a team of LSAT experts, who have helped thousands of students improve their scores. Kaplan always provides data-driven analysis of the test, ranking the difficulty of every question based on actual student performance. The 10 hardest questions on every test are highlighted with a 4-star difficulty rating, the highest we give. The analysis breaks down the remaining questions into 1-, 2-, and 3-star ratings so that you can compare your performance to that of thousands of other test takers on all LSAC material.

Don't settle for wondering whether a question was really as hard as it seemed to you. Analyze the test with real data, and learn the secrets and strategies that help top scorers master the LSAT.

8 Can't–Miss Features of PrepTest 66

- No more tiny writing! PrepTest 66 was the first released LSAT to give students two pages per logic game. Test takers rejoiced!
- All that space meant extra room for writing out Limited Options sketches. Good thing, too, because all four games here are amenable to a Limited Options deduction.
- Seven times in history a question has been removed from the test for scoring purposes. PrepTest 66 is the only one where the question came from the Logic Games section. So, you'll have an extra 4.2 seconds per question when trying out the LG section.
- Only three Inference Questions in Logical Reasoning marks the single lowest total for that type of question in a single test ever.
- This test did not have a single Role of a Statement question, despite four appearing on each of the two preceding tests.
- In Reading Comprehension, PrepTest 66's longest single passage (Passage 4) had the section's fewest questions (a mere five); its second shortest passage (Passage 3) had the most questions (eight).
- If you're reading this on an eBook, be careful not to bring in any outside knowledge to Passage 1, which is all about Digital Publishing.
- While test takers were holding their breath waiting for their LSAT scores from PrepTest 66, court watchers were holding theirs, too, as this test was administered the same month that the US Supreme Court ruled on challenges to the Affordable Care Act.

PrepTest 66 in Context

As much fun as it is to find out what makes a PrepTest unique or noteworthy, it's even more important to know just how representative it is of other LSAT administrations (and, thus, how likely it is to be representative of the exam you will face on Test Day). The following charts compare the numbers of each kind of question and game on PrepTest 66 to the average numbers seen on all officially released LSATs administered over the past five years (from 2012 through 2016).

Number of LR Questions by Type: PrepTest 66 vs. 2012-2016 Average

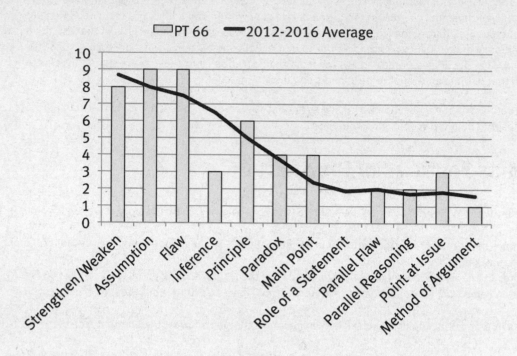

Number of LG Games by Type: PrepTest 66 vs. 2012-2016 Average

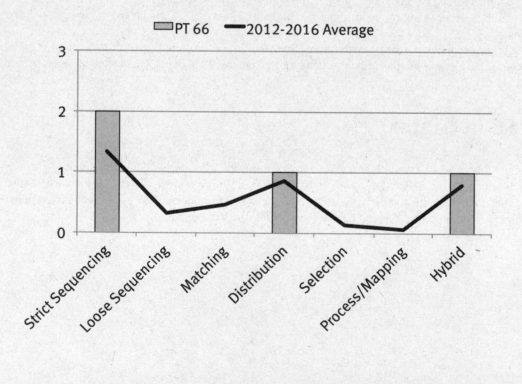

Number of RC Questions by Type: PrepTest 66 vs. 2012-2016 Average

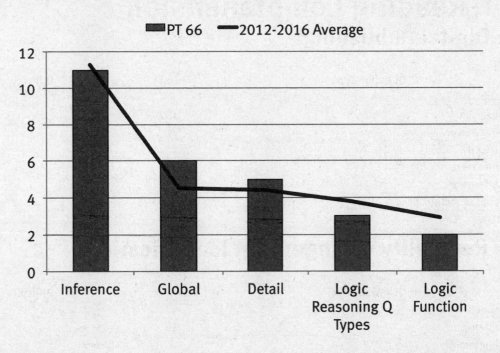

There isn't usually a huge difference in the distribution of questions from LSAT to LSAT, but if this test seems harder (or easier) to you than another you've taken, compare the number of questions of the types on which you, personally, are strongest and weakest. And then, explore within each section to see if your best or worst question types came earlier or later.

Students in Kaplan's comprehensive LSAT courses have access to every released LSAT, and to an online Q-Bank with thousands of officially released questions, games, and passages. If you are studying on your own, you have to do a bit more work to identify your strengths and your areas of opportunity. Quantitative analysis (like that in the charts shown here) is an important tool for understanding how the test is constructed, and how you are performing on it.

Section I: Reading Comprehension
Passage 1: Digital Publishing

Q#	Question Type	Correct	Difficulty
1	Global	E	★★
2	Logic Function	D	★
3	Inference	A	★
4	Detail (EXCEPT)	B	★
5	Inference	A	★★★
6	Inference	C	★★★★
7	Logic Function	B	★★

Passage 2: Reliability of Fingerprint Identification

Q#	Question Type	Correct	Difficulty
8	Global	D	★
9	Inference	B	★★
10	Inference	A	★★
11	Detail	C	★
12	Logic Reasoning (Principle)	E	★
13	Detail	C	★
14	Global	B	★★★

Passage 3: Ellington's Jazz and Morrison's Jazz

Q#	Question Type	Correct	Difficulty
15	Global	E	★★
16	Logic Reasoning (Method of Argument)	B	★
17	Logic Reasoning (Weaken)	B	★
18	Inference	D	★★
19	Global	C	★★★★
20	Inference (EXCEPT)	A	★
21	Inference	D	★★★
22	Detail	E	★★★★

Passage 4: Discovery of Nuclear Fission

Q#	Question Type	Correct	Difficulty
23	Global	B	★
24	Inference	D	★
25	Inference	A	★★
26	Inference	B	★★
27	Detail	E	★★★★

Passage 1: Digital Publishing

Step 1: Read the Passage Strategically

Sample Roadmap

line #	Keyword/phrase	¶ Margin notes
2	widely	T-Digital texts
3	assumed ... lead to	current view: dig. will replace text
6	But ... more likely ... I believe	
8		Auth: disagree ↓
10	Once	we will print dig. texts
11	most	
12	will be able to	
13	practically limitless	
14	even	
16	Also	dig. pub. costs ↓
17	no physical inventory, ... thereby	
21	would make	
24	it is likely	expected to overtake print
25	supplant ... at least rival	
26	although ... some time before	not enough dig. books yet
30	Moreover ... elimination	
31	means	
32	greater proportion	lit agents: ↓ cost = ↑ $ for authors
33	therefore	
34	according to ... a larger ...	
35	share ... Currently	
39	thus be expected ...	
40	to ... significantly bigger	
41	But	Auth: trad. pub. houses = $ in prod. infrastructure
42	heavily	
44	reluctant ... So	
46	unfettered by	startups will launch dig. print
48	will have to	
50	or else	
51	typical	Auth: predict trad. pub will ↓ overhead or lose authors
53	help explain	

Discussion

In paragraph 1, the author introduces the **Topic** of the passage: the future of digital text. Many assume that digital books will replace their print counterparts. The author thinks otherwise, as signaled by [*b*]*ut* at line 6. This Keyword introduces the first of the author's predictions (and the passage's **Scope**) about how digital text will be produced and consumed: the author believes that digital texts will not be consumed digitally but rather will be printed and bound at point-of-sale machines. Lines 10–15 lay out the author's view that the future will feature a nearly limitless on-demand library from which readers can choose to print a wide variety of texts.

Paragraph 2 lists the potential economic advantages of digital publishing over traditional processes. (Note that lines 18–20 include four examples, fertile ground for a detail EXCEPT question). The author uses these claims of efficiency and convenience (line 22–25) as evidence for a second prediction: traditional publishing will face decline or demise. Still ("although" at line 26), the author cautions, point-of-sale printing won't be economically justified until some future date when enough books have been digitized.

The author continues this vision of the future ("[m]oreover" at line 30) in the third paragraph with a discussion of the changing economic model for authors and publishing houses. Here, you find the author's third prediction: the new economic model will result ("therefore" at line 33) in literary agents arguing that the authors they represent should get a greater percentage of profits at the expense of printing houses. The author argues, however ("[b]ut" at line 41), that traditional publishing houses will be reluctant to give up those profits, creating opportunity for upstart digital publishers. As is "typical" when economic models change (line 51), traditional publishers will have to increase efficiency or lose their authors. This risk explains traditional publishers' concern over the future of digital publishing.

The author's **Purpose**—to evaluate the future of digital publishing—reveals the passage's **Main Idea**: as publishing houses evolve to digital texts, changing distribution methods and lower direct costs will necessitate a new model for revenue sharing between publishers and authors.

1. (E) Global

Step 2: Identify the Question Type

Any question asking you for the "main point of the passage" is a Global question.

Step 3: Research the Relevant Text

For a Global question, don't go back to a specific part of the passage. Rather, use your understanding of the Topic, Scope, Purpose, and Main Idea from Step 1 to predict the correct answer.

Step 4: Make a Prediction

The author's main point is expressed in his predictions for the future of digital text publication, a future in which traditional publishers will have to adapt to changing economic forces in the publishing process in order to remain competitive.

Step 5: Evaluate the Answer Choices

(E) is correct because it describes the author's view of digital publishing's evolution, citing the economic factors (including the demands of authors) this author believes will drive competition in the industry.

(A) focuses too narrowly on the final sentence of the passage. While the author believes the publishing industry will evolve in ways typical of a changing economic model, the author's primary goal isn't limited to showing that this is a typical case. **(A)** fails to provide the author's evaluation of the economic factors that are driving the change in digital publishing and includes no allusion to the author's several predictions for the future of publishing.

(B) is a Distortion. The author's primary goal is not to describe the factors hindering the acceptance of digital text but rather to outline the changes expected to occur as it gains prevalence.

(C) includes details from the passage about digital text, including its convenience and increased profitability, but then goes too far in predicting with certainty digital text's impact on authors and their movement among publishing houses.

(D) ignores the author's evaluation of the impact of economic factors on digital publishing. While the author believes point-of-sale machines are a realistic future for the majority of digital publications, the author is concerned with the impact of digital text on traditional publishing, not consumer preferences.

2. (D) Logic Function

Step 2: Identify the Question Type

Whenever the testmaker provides a detail and asks *why* the author has included it (the clue here is "primarily to"), you're being asked a Logic Function question; your task is to identify the author's purpose for including the detail.

Step 3: Research the Relevant Text

The phrase "whole categories of expense" and the line reference (lines 30–31) should direct you to the beginning of the third paragraph. Use your Roadmap to identify the detail's context.

Step 4: Make a Prediction

Zeroing in on Keywords illuminates the quoted words' context: "Moreover" indicates a continuation of the ideas in the previous paragraph in which the author describes the costs eliminated by the move to digital publication. Thus, "whole categories of expense" must refer to the commercial costs of traditional publishing described in the second paragraph.

Step 5: Evaluate the Answer Choices

(D) is correct. It describes the costs previously detailed in paragraph 2.

(A) is Outside the Scope. Authors' profits are discussed later in the passage, but literary agents' fees are never mentioned.

(B) is also Outside the Scope. The costs associated with binding and printing at point-of-sale machines are never mentioned.

(C) contains a Faulty Use of Detail and is a 180 to boot. Keep in mind that line 30 refers to categories of expense that digital publishing will eliminate. Later in paragraph 3, the author says that he expects authors' royalties to increase, so these certainly aren't what "categories of expense" in line 30 refer to.

(E) is also faulty. Line 30 refers to categories of *expense* that will be eliminated by digital publishing. **(E)**, on the other hand, refers to publisher's *profits*. The author believes there will be less unsold inventory after the introduction of digital publishing, but that doesn't make this answer's reference to money from sales relevant to the costs mentioned at line 30.

3. (A) Inference

Step 2: Identify the Question Type

The word *inferred* provides a straightforward clue to this Inference question, and the phrase "author would agree" makes clear that you'll need to focus on the author's point of view.

Step 3: Research the Relevant Text

The stem has no clues to help you research, so be prepared to consult your Roadmap and consider the Purpose and Main Idea to identify strong statements of the author's point of view.

Step 4: Make a Prediction

Because countless inferences must be true based on the author's statements, avoid trying to make too specific a prediction. Instead focus on evaluating the choices, determining which one must be true based on the text.

Step 5: Evaluate the Answer Choices

(A) is the correct answer. In paragraph 3, the author argues that "[u]nder this competitive pressure, traditional publishers will have to reduce their redundant functions ... or else they will lose their authors" (lines 47–51), providing a solid match for **(A)**'s warning.

(B) is Extreme. The author never outlines a "primary threat" to the spread of digital publishing.

(C) is Outside the Scope. While it *could be* true, the author provides no evidence to imply that he believes digital publishing will revitalize retail book sales.

(D) is also Extreme. The author makes no claim that *any* book published digitally will outperform its traditional counterpart.

(E) is Outside the Scope. The author doesn't link reduced *advertising* costs to the transition to digital publishing as **(E)** suggests.

4. (B) Detail (EXCEPT)

Step 2: Identify the Question Type

This is a Detail question because the incorrect choices are directly identified in the passage, while the correct answer is the exception that is not directly mentioned or stated. Having noted the list of four items at the beginning of paragraph 2, you could have anticipated this question.

Step 3: Research the Relevant Text

The list of things "digital publishing will dispense with the need for" appears at the beginning of paragraph 2 ("eliminating the cost of ... " at lines 17–20), so direct your attention to identifying the one answer choice not included in this list.

Step 4: Make a Prediction

The passage directly states that digital publication will eliminate costs related to "warehousing," "shipping," "displaying," and "returning" traditional books. As you assess the choices, use this list to quickly eliminate any of these details.

Step 5: Evaluate the Answer Choices

(B) stands out as the detail never mentioned within the text, and it is the correct answer. The cost associated with book cover design is the only choice not mentioned in the list that appears in lines 17–20.

(A) is the first eliminated cost, mentioned in line 18.

(C) is a second cost savings, described in lines 18–19.

(D) is identified in line 20 as a cost that will be eliminated by digital publishing.

(E) can be eliminated based on lines 19–20.

5. (A) Inference

Step 2: Identify the Question Type

The hypothetical "If … true, then which one of the following would most likely be the case?" indicates that you'll have to identify an inference—something that would be true—based on the information in the passage's opening paragraphs.

Step 3: Research the Relevant Text

First, identify the scenario the question is referencing from the first two paragraphs. It begins most clearly in lines 6–10, in which the author describes "digital files of books [that] will be printed and bound on demand at point of sale by machines that can quickly and inexpensively make single copies … ." In paragraph 2, the author goes on to list costs associated with traditional printing and to predict the decline of the traditional printing industry.

Step 4: Make a Prediction

Many inferences could be based on the author's prediction that point-of-sale printing machines will be the future of digital publishing, but given that the question stem includes the first two paragraphs as reference, anticipate a choice that corresponds to the ways in which the author says the printing industry will change. Evaluate each choice, asking yourself which one is a solid match for the author's point-of-sale printing hypothesis.

Step 5: Evaluate the Answer Choices

(A) is correct and matches the scenario's warehouse demands. If the author's prediction holds true, publishing warehouses will no longer be necessary for storing books but will be used instead to house the materials required to print and bind digital texts at point-of-sale machines.

(B) is Outside the Scope. This choice veers far off course by talking about *used* book sales, something the author doesn't discuss.

(C) also needn't be true in the scenario. The distinction between direct selling by publishers or through intermediaries is irrelevant to the author's prediction regarding point-of-sale machines.

(D) is Outside the Scope. Nothing in the passage indicates that the author's prediction would impact the demand for copyediting or book design services.

(E) is not supported by the author's statements. There's no reason to believe that a shift of binding and printing from publishing houses to point-of-sale machines would affect the demand for book-grade paper.

6. (C) Inference

Step 2: Identify the Question Type

This question stem states explicitly that this is an Inference question. The correct answer will follow from the author's statements.

Step 3: Research the Relevant Text

With no clues in the stem, move on to analyze the choices. However, be strategic. All of the answer choices mention a transition to or acceptance of "the new digital model." Noting this common thread among the choices should help limit your research to paragraph 3, where the author discusses factors impacting the transition to and acceptance of digital publishing.

Step 4: Make a Prediction

Consult your Roadmap for paragraph 3 to target the author's view on eventual transition to the new digital model. According to the author, traditional publishers will be forced to adapt in response to changes in profit structure needed to oblige authors and literary agents as inventory-related costs decline.

Step 5: Evaluate the Answer Choices

(C) correctly matches the author's evaluation of the impetus (or cause) of the transition: the demands of literary agents and the changing profit structure.

(A) incorrectly credits the changing literary tastes of consumers. The author makes no mention of literary genres or changing consumer appetites as factors driving the industry.

(B) is a classic example of a Faulty Use of Detail wrong answer. While the author believes the efficiency and convenience of digital format will ensure its success, the "ease of keeping books 'in print'" is never mentioned as a driving force, and it is certainly not the *primary* factor ensuring eventual acceptance of digital text.

(D) assigns the transition to innovations in marketing, which the author does not mention; this choice is thus Outside the Scope of this passage.

(E) is Outside the Scope because of its suggestion that familiarity with new technologies, and not economic factors, will be the primary cause of the eventual shift to digital publishing.

7. (B) Logic Function

Step 2: Identify the Question Type

The final question of this set—a Logic Function question—asks for the purpose or function of the passage's final sentence, so you'll have to consider the reasons why the author included this statement.

Step 3: Research the Relevant Text

Lines 51–55 provide the final sentence of the passage, but keep in mind the context of paragraph 3 as you make a prediction.

Step 4: Make a Prediction

Use the Keywords in the sentence to understand its general structure. "Such adjustments are typical" gives a perspective outside of the world of publishing, while "and may help explain" attempts to provide the expected reasoning of traditional publishers.

Step 5: Evaluate the Answer Choices

(B) matches the structure of the sentence. It includes both the mention of the broader context indicated in the first part of the statement and the attempt to clarify the traditional publisher's position.

(A) incorrectly credits the author with arguing that traditional publishing isn't modernizing quickly enough, a claim not made in the final sentence.

(C) fails to take into account the context the author provides and erroneously interprets the passage's final sentence as a summary of the author's overall vision.

(D) is Outside the Scope. The author makes no mention of the primary obstacle to digitalization facing traditional publishers.

(E) erroneously interprets the author's evaluation of the causes of traditional publishers' caution as the author's own recommendation for publishers to remain cautious. The author provides no recommendation for a course of action.

Passage 2: Reliability of Fingerprint Identification

Step 1: Read the Passage Strategically

Sample Roadmap

line #	Keyword/phrase	¶ Margin notes
Passage A		
2	challenges	def. challenge f-print ev.
3	claiming	
5	cites	def: no studies
8	claims	def: no error rate
11	and ... asserts	
12	cites	and no uniform standard
16	not	ct. acknowledges but f-print has long history
17	attained ... has been used	
18	have long	
19	While	
20	even more consistent	
21	court sees no reason	ct. will not reject f-prints
24	While	
27	are held to	ct. concedes diff. standards but testing adequate to support f-print ev.
30	regularly subjected	
33	therefore	
35	exceedingly low	
Passage B		
36	lack	F-prints have no shared standard
38	simply	
39	Some examiners use	point-counting vs. holistic approaches
41	but	
43	Others reject	
44	for ... Either ...	
45	way	
47	Although	% of shared "points" unknown and f-prints in ev are incomplete
48	the chance	
50	is unknown	
52	? ... Moreover	
56	?	chance of false "match" unknown
57	yet	
60	little systematic study	error rate unknown
62	? ... Although	
64	more rigorous	best tests show high error rate

Discussion

Passage A begins with an important clue in the first line: this passage discusses a criminal defendant's appeal. The **Topic** of the passage is fingerprint evidence, but already the **Scope** is narrowing to the use of fingerprint evidence in this specific case. LSAT passages, and especially law passages and Comparative Reading passages, frequently contain arguments. In the first paragraph, the author lays out the defendant's conclusion (fingerprint identification theory is untested) and evidence (the lack of relevant studies). Note that his evidence came from the testimony of the fingerprint examiner.

Paragraph 2 elaborates the defendant's position. The defendant continues to press his point about the lack of certainty pertaining to fingerprint evidence. He "claims" (line 8) that no one has established how often fingerprint examiners are mistaken in their findings. As evidence, he "cites" (line 12) the fingerprint examiner at his trial, who testified that experts have not agreed upon a single standard for how many points of comparison are needed for positive identification of a print.

The contrast Keyword [a]lthough at the beginning of paragraph 3 indicates an important turn in the structure of the argument. Here, the author acknowledges that fingerprint evidence falls short of the standards of scientific laws, but she rejects the defendant's conclusion. In defending the court's use of fingerprint evidence, she cites its longevity as a practice and its widespread use. If you had any uncertainty about who wrote this passage, "this court sees" in line 21 should confirm that this was written by the appellate court judge.

In passage A's final paragraph, the judge acknowledges that various examiners rely on different numbers of points of identification, but she holds that proficiency testing, uniform standards, and peer review make the conclusions of fingerprint examiners reliable. The judge concludes with these findings: the lower court properly admitted testimony on the reliability of fingerprint identification. The author's **Purpose** is determined by her role as a judge—to evaluate the lower court's use of testimony on fingerprint evidence in the defendant's trial. The **Main Idea** is expressed in the last sentence: fingerprint evidence is reliable enough for jurors to hear testimony about its low error rate.

Right from its first sentence, passage B sounds as if it could be the argument made by the defendant in the trial discussed in passage A. So, the **Topic** here is much the same as that in passage A, although the **Scope** appears broader, discussing the problems inherent in fingerprint identification rather than its use in a particular trial. In the first paragraph, passage B's author decries the lack of objective standards for determining a fingerprint match. Some examiners count points of similarity between prints, while others take a holistic approach. Either way, says this author, no one agrees on the criteria sufficient to establish a match.

Paragraph 2 is chock-full of both Keywords and rhetorical questions, used here to raise doubts and reinforce the idea that fingerprint identification may be unreliable. The thrust of the argument here is that no one knows the likelihood that two individuals might share a given number of points of similarity between their fingerprints. Even worse ("[m]oreover" at line 52), the fingerprints in many criminal cases are partial and smudged. The paragraph's last sentence sums up the argument: fingerprint examiners can't answer these important questions, so we can't be certain of the value of fingerprint evidence.

Paragraph 3 uses another rhetorical question (how often are the fingerprint examiners wrong?) and ends by suggesting that the error rate may be much higher than examiners admit. By the end of passage B, you can definitively say that the author's **Purpose** is to raise questions about fingerprint identification. The **Main Idea** isn't captured in any one sentence, but you can paraphrase the overall argument by summing up each paragraph in turn: fingerprint identification techniques are not standardized, their reliability is unsubstantiated, and the results are of questionable value.

Both passages are concerned with the reliability of fingerprint identification, but passage A is focused specifically on the use of fingerprints as evidence in criminal trials and its findings pertaining to the defendant's case. Passage B, on the other hand, appears to be written for any interested audience. The two passages clearly take different positions. Passage A concludes that standards for fingerprint identification are reliable enough for use in criminal trials, whereas passage B harbors serious doubts about the reliability of fingerprint evidence. Each author takes pains to acknowledge the other side's arguments, however, be cautious of extreme language in the answer choices.

8.(D) Global

Step 2: Identify the Question Type

The words *main point* identify this as a Global question. Note that this question concerns only passage B.

Step 3: Research the Relevant Text

In Step 1 you already determined that the Main Idea of passage B was that fingerprint identification is of questionable value for several reasons. Use this as the basis of your prediction.

Step 4: Make a Prediction

Passage B questions the value of fingerprint identification because of its lack of standardization, reliability, and substantiation. Expect the right answer to encompass this without necessarily parroting the same wording found in the passage.

Step 5: Evaluate the Answer Choices

(D) matches the prediction nicely. Notice that the correct answer even refers to a "number of … problems," mirroring the list of criticisms noted paragraph by paragraph in your Roadmap.

(A) is far Outside the Scope. Passage B only refers tangentially to the use of fingerprint evidence in criminal law, and it never says anything about defendants or about challenges to faulty evidence in trials.

(B) is Extreme. Passage B is not specifically focused on criminal trials, and while the author raises doubts about the usefulness of fingerprint evidence, he stops short of saying that it is definitely too unreliable to be used.

(C) is a Faulty Use of Detail. The author of passage B does discuss the error rate in the last paragraph, but this is too narrow to be the main point of the passage. Moreover, the author's critique in paragraph 3 is more nuanced than the statement in **(C)**; the author suggests that more systematic study is needed to know the error rate with any certainty.

(E) is Outside the Scope. The author of passage B does not mention a growing consensus of any sort.

9. (B) Inference

Step 2: Identify the Question Type

The words *most likely* make this an Inference question. For this question, your task is to find the answer containing a statement over which the two authors are committed to opposing positions.

Step 3: Research the Relevant Text

This question does not refer you to any specific part of the passages, but you should already have determined in Step 1 that the key point of contention between the passages is over the usefulness and reliability of fingerprint identification.

Step 4: Make a Prediction

The correct answer must be a statement about which the two authors must disagree. Wrong answers will be statements with which one author might agree or about which one author expresses no opinion.

Step 5: Evaluate the Answer Choices

(B) provides a statement over which the two authors would disagree. The author of passage B criticizes the lack of systematic study on fingerprint identification error rates and in his last sentence points to one "rigorous" study that found the error rate may be as high as 34 percent. The judge who wrote passage A isn't as explicit, but she says in her last

sentence that the trial court was correct to accept testimony that the error rate is "exceedingly low."

(A) is a statement with which both authors would agree. The author of passage A applauds uniformity in testing, standards, and peer review in her third paragraph, while the author of passage B argues that there is too little uniformity in his first paragraph. Both, clearly, feel that uniform training is desirable.

(C) might be tempting, but in fact, both authors would agree with this statement. The author of passage A acknowledges explicitly that fingerprint identification has "not attained the status of scientific law," and clearly the author of passage B, less convinced of fingerprint identification's value, would not argue that it has.

(D) is only within the scope of passage B; passage A never opines about examiners who use "holistic methods." Moreover, the author of passage B appears to doubt equally the point-counting and holistic methods, so he can't be said to weigh their "relative merits."

(E) mentions "agencies," which come up in the first line of the fourth paragraph of passage A but are never mentioned by passage B. At any rate, both authors generally agree that specific standards for fingerprint examiners vary.

10. (A) Inference

Step 2: Identify the Question Type

The word *inferred* makes explicit that this is an Inference question. This is a specific, fairly common variation on Inference questions that asks you to determine the author's profession from clues in the text.

Step 3: Research the Relevant Text

In Step 1 you made a Roadmap of passage A, and several Keywords in the passage should have drawn your attention to clues that this passage is part of a judge's decision in a criminal appeal. At line 21, where the author draws the conclusion to paragraph 3's argument, she specifically identifies herself as "this court."

Step 4: Make a Prediction

This author must be an appellate judge who hears criminal appeals.

Step 5: Evaluate the Answer Choices

(A) is a perfect, clear match for the prediction. Passage A's author is the appellate judge ruling on the admissibility of testimony in a lower court.

(B) might be tempting if you read too fast and only saw the references to the defendant's claims in the beginning; however, line 21 clarifies that this was written by the judge who, in fact, rules against the defense in this opinion.

(C) also relies on the possibility that you overlooked the language in line 21 and line 33 indicating that the passage was written from the point of view of the court itself. The decision in passage A upholds the defendant's conviction but does so from the point of view of the judge, not the prosecutor.

(D) is a trap for those who assume that LSAT passages are always written by academics. While many law passages on the LSAT are indeed the work of law professors, passage A is not.

(E), like (D), inappropriately attributes the passage to an academic, thereby ignoring the phrase "this court" in line 21.

11. (C) Detail

Step 2: Identify the Question Type

The phrase "[e]ach passage discusses" marks this as a Detail question. This question asks for something both passages explicitly relate to their evaluations of fingerprint identification reliability.

Step 3: Research the Relevant Text

The difficulty with research for this question is that fingerprint identification reliability is a theme running throughout both passages. Indeed, passage B could be the basis for the defendant's brief as both raise the issues of inadequate testing (lines 4 and 60), error rates among fingerprint examiners (lines 8–12 and 59–65), the lack of agreement on "points of identification" sufficient for a match (lines 12–15 and 37–43), and, more generally still, the lack of uniformity in standards and practices among examiners. Responding to the defendant's argument, the court in passage A also takes up the issue of uniformity in examiner standards and practices, concluding that there is uniformity sufficient to consider fingerprint identification reliable.

Step 4: Make a Prediction

With so many shared points and details, there is no need to form too specific a prediction. Use your Roadmap to evaluate the choices. Only the correct answer will cite a detail that both authors related to fingerprint reliability. The wrong answers here will provide details found in only one of the two passages or references to things not related to reliability in the passages.

Step 5: Evaluate the Answer Choices

(C) mentions the different practices used among different fingerprinting experts. Such differences are mentioned by passage A (at lines 8–15 and 24–28) and by passage B (at lines 39–46) and in both cases are related to the reliability of fingerprint evidence.

(A) mentions a criminal defendant, which was within the scope of passage A but not of passage B. In any event,

passage A does not relate a defendant's ability to poke holes in the prosecution's case to the reliability of fingerprint evidence.

(B) talks about personal integrity, but neither author says anything (positive or negative) about the integrity or ethics of fingerprinting experts, and certainly neither author relates their integrity to the reliability of the evidence they produce.

(D) draws on the mention of partial and smudged prints in passage B, at line 53, but passage A never mentioned this detail, let alone in relation to fingerprint reliability. (A later question in this set will also ask for something shared by both passages and, again, will refer to partial prints in one of the incorrect answers.)

(E) draws on the mention of a "holistic approach" in passage B, at line 44, but passage A never mentions this approach.

12. (E) Logic Reasoning (Principle)

Step 2: Identify the Question Type

The word *principles* makes this a Logic Reasoning question similar to a Principle question from the Logical Reasoning section. Moreover, the phrase "underlies the arguments" tells you that you need to identify a principle that serves as an assumption (connecting conclusion to evidence) in both authors' arguments.

Step 3: Research the Relevant Text

Because this question is asking for an underlying principle of the entire argument of both passages, the big picture is more useful than specifics. In passage A, you noted in the Roadmap that the conclusion comes in the last paragraph: the trial court was correct, or, in other words, fingerprint identification is reliable. The evidence the author gives refers to consistency and uniformity and is found in lines 24–33. In passage B, you summarized the Main Idea as the conclusion that fingerprinting is unreliable. Here, the evidence is essentially the entire passage; you might already have summarized that as "not standardized, of doubtful certainty, and error-prone," or words to that effect.

Step 4: Make a Prediction

This "double principle" question is a challenging variation, but as with any argument-based question, your task is to first identify the gap between the Evidence and the Conclusion. You could say that passage A argues "consistent and uniform, therefore reliable" and that passage B argues "not standardized and uncertain, therefore unreliable." Notice that even as the passages reach opposing conclusions, they both start with the same kind of evidence. Thus, both must assume that consistency, uniformity, and standardization (all roughly synonymous) are correlated with reliability. This might seem obvious, but because it has not been stated explicitly by either author, it is a necessary underlying principle of both passages.

Step 5: Evaluate the Answer Choices

(E) is the only choice that directly connects reliability with standardization.

(A) relies on a Faulty Use of Detail by pulling the phrase "withstood the test of time" directly from passage A. Nothing in passage B suggests this is a principle underlying that author's argument.

(B) discusses "scientific" proof, but this was only a minor point made by passage A and is never mentioned in passage B. Worse still, this choice concentrates on a defendant's rights, a subject the author of passage B goes nowhere near. This can't be a principle underlying either author's argument.

(C) mentions partial prints. The question of how likely partial prints are matched concerns the author of passage B, but this question is never raised in passage A. (It's worth noting that this is the second question in the set to ask for something shared by both passages and use the detail about partial prints in one of the incorrect answers.)

(D) mentions "rigorous" tests, a detail taken from the last paragraph of passage B, but such tests are never mentioned by the author of passage A. In fact, the fourth paragraph of passage A suggests that the judge is convinced by evidence other than rigorous tests that fingerprint examiners have "an extremely low error rate."

13. (C) Detail

Step 2: Identify the Question Type

The word *allude*, meaning to make a casual or indirect reference to, is unusual for an LSAT Reading Comprehension question. You are looking for an allusion made in the text of both passages, so treat this as a Detail question. Don't be surprised, however, if the correct answer feels a bit like an inference since an allusion is an indirect reference.

Step 3: Research the Relevant Text

Your Roadmap can help you to find the place in each passage that discusses the specific method used for fingerprint identification. Passage A mentions "points of identification" in lines 14–15 and "points and characteristics" in lines 27–28. Passage B mentions "point-counting" in lines 39–40 and contrasts this with a "holistic" method in lines 43–44.

Step 4: Make a Prediction

Since passage A never says anything about a holistic approach, your answer must be a paraphrase of the "points of identification" method.

Step 5: Evaluate the Answer Choices

(C) mentions counting shared characteristics, which is a rough paraphrase of the "points" method discussed—*alluded* to—in both passages.

(A) refers to the holistic method, which is mentioned only in passage B.

(B) refers to "computerized databases," which are entirely Outside the Scope of both passages. An answer choice like this one serves as a trap for those who rely on outside knowledge about fingerprinting; television police dramas allude to such databases regularly, but neither passage mentions them.

(D) is a Distortion of the rhetorical question at lines 53–56. The author of passage B doesn't discuss the odds of individuals sharing characteristics as a method of fingerprint identification but rather to question the reliability of the "points of identification" method. At any rate, passage A never alludes to the frequency of individuals sharing rare fingerprint characteristics.

(E) is also Outside the Scope; neither passage mentions computers or techniques for enhancing or clarifying smudged fingerprints. For all you know, these passages may even have been written in the past, long before such image-enhancing technology was available.

14. (B) Global

Step 2: Identify the Question Type

This is a Global question because it asks about both passages as a whole.

Step 3: Research the Relevant Text

Rather than rereading any part of the text, you should review the Scope, Purpose, and Main Idea of each passage.

Step 4: Make a Prediction

The passages differ in a handful of easily identifiable ways. The most obvious is that passage B is far more skeptical of fingerprint evidence than is passage A. Equally important, passage A is written specifically to decide the admissibility of testimony from a fingerprinting expert at the defendant's trial, while passage B critiques the validity of fingerprint identification in general.

Step 5: Evaluate the Answer Choices

(B) matches the second of these predictions. The Scope of passage B is clearly broader than that of passage A.

(A) is a 180. Passage B is clearly more negative; this is a trap for those who read the question stem too quickly and are thinking about the wrong passage.

(C) is a Distortion. Passage B does indeed stop short of explicitly saying that fingerprint evidence should not be used, but it is not tentative or uncertain in tone. It may be that the number of rhetorical questions in the text gives the appearance of tentative opinions, but keep in mind that pointing out how much remains unanswered is this author's goal.

(D) is Outside of Scope; neither passage shows disrespect to other points of view.

(E) is also Outside of the Scope. Both passages rely on the same unstated principle (uniform standards and practices help ensure the reliability of fingerprint identification), but there is no particular difference in the quality of the arguments. If anything, passage B makes the point that current studies and standardization aren't strong enough.

Passage 3: Ellington's Jazz and Morrison's Jazz

Step 1: Read the Passage Strategically

Sample Roadmap

line #	Keyword/phrase	¶ Margin notes
1		music/lit overlap
2	not coexisted without	
6	Nowhere is …	writing has emulated music
7	this truer	ex: Afro-Am art
10	But	
12		Morrison first to use music genre to structure novel
17	not only	jazz is in plot & narr.
18	but, more strikingly	
19	from	
20		shifts in voice
23	to	
24	But	narrator present thru-out
25	both	
26	and	
27	On the one hand	
29	on …	
30	the other hand	
32	In this way	connection to jazz performance
37	was the first to	Ellington used similar techniques
39	Yet	
41		indiv. improve. w/in frame
45		connection to Morrison
50	paradoxically	effect of Morrison's achievement
51	within the fixed scope	
52	By	
55	serves	narrative innovation

Discussion

The author begins by describing a feature of the relationship between music and literature. Literature developed out of sound, and ever since, writers have aspired to creating in words the relationship between form and content found in music. The author believes this phenomenon is seen most clearly in the African American tradition, in which music figures prominently in literature. By now, the **Topic** should be clear—the influence of music on literature.

Despite the tradition among African American writers of using music as metaphor and theme (notice the Keyword [b]ut at line 10), Toni Morrison, in writing her novel *Jazz*, was the first to use a musical genre as the basis for an entire novel's narrative structure. Now you can also correctly guess that the **Scope** is Morrison's use of jazz structures as a narrative influence in her novel. Effective strategic reading means anticipating where the author will go next. Because the author ends paragraph 1 by introducing *Jazz*, you can correctly predict that the next paragraph will discuss the features of *Jazz* that illustrate Morrison's use of jazz, the musical genre, as an organizing force.

And that's exactly what paragraph 2 does. Lines 19–24 mention that Morrison shifts perspectives between different characters. Lines 24–32, though, tell you that through all these shifts, Morrison maintains the presence and authority of the narrator. The paragraph ends by, predictably, tying this feature of Morrison's novel to a feature of jazz band performance.

Paragraph 3 gets even more specific by introducing a particular jazz composer, Duke Ellington. The first two sentences of the paragraph detail the features of his compositions: he wrote for specific musicians, allowing them room to improvise (to express their unique "voices" as Morrison does with her characters) but providing them with a framework in which to perform their solo riffs. The last sentence draws a direct line between this feature and the structure of Morrison's novel.

The author concludes the passage by describing the results of Morrison's choice to simulate the style of jazz in her narrative structure. This is also a good time to distill the **Main Idea**: Morrison expands the possibilities of narrative by creating the paradoxical sense of individual improvisation within a cohesive, deliberate narrative. As for the **Purpose**, while the author is certainly complimentary to Morrison, the passage has a mostly neutral tone. The author has set out to describe Morrison's use of jazz as a structuring principle for her novel and how her literary technique mirrored Ellington's musical work.

15. (E) Global

Step 2: Identify the Question Type

The scope of the question stem is the passage as a whole—it asks you for the "main point"—so this is a Global question.

Step 3: Research the Relevant Text

There's no text to research for a Global question like this. Instead, your Roadmap and understanding of Topic, Scope, Purpose, and Main Idea will guide you to a prediction.

Step 4: Make a Prediction

From your strategic reading of the passage during Step 1, you already know the passage's main idea: *Jazz* exemplifies Morrison's narrative innovation, an innovation comparable to that achieved by Duke Ellington in his jazz music compositions.

Step 5: Evaluate the Answer Choices

(E) is the best match for this prediction.

(A) is never mentioned in the passage. Furthermore, the author suggests that many musical forms (perhaps jazz included) found their way into the themes and plots of many African American novels before Morrison wrote *Jazz*. According to the author, Morrison's great innovation wasn't in subject matter but rather in narrative structure.

(B) is incorrect because the author never says that Morrison describes a musical ensemble performance; rather, the passage's point is that the structure of the novel itself *simulates* a jazz ensemble performance.

(C) is incorrect because the author locates the uniqueness of Morrison's novel, not in its use of jazz as a metaphor, but in its use of jazz as an inspiration for organizing the entire narrative structure.

(D) is a distortion. The passage never says that Morrison was continuing or building on other writers' work when she wrote *Jazz*. Nor does it say that Morrison developed her jazz-like style of narration gradually—for all we know, *Jazz* is the only one of Morrison's novels to employ this style.

16. (B) Logic Reasoning (Method of Argument)

Step 2: Identify the Question Type

This question stem asks you how the first paragraph "proceeds." That makes this a Logic question, since the question is focused more on *how* the passage is written than on *what* it is saying. You'll see the same kind of wording in the stem for a Method of Argument question in the Logical Reasoning section.

Step 3: Research the Relevant Text

Your Roadmap is a powerful tool on a Logic question that asks about the thrust of an entire paragraph. Use your margin notes as you reread key words and phrases from paragraph 1.

Step 4: Make a Prediction

The structure of paragraph 1 progresses from a general discussion of the influence of music on literature to a certain artistic tradition exemplifying this influence to a specific point about Morrison's use of musical structures in one particular novel. The correct answer choice will reflect this progression.

Step 5: Evaluate the Answer Choices

(B) is the best match for this prediction.

(A) is a 180. The author's claim about literature aspiring to the condition of music is illustrated by the African American tradition, not denied by it.

(C) is a Distortion. There's no indication that the author's point about music and literature is a "common claim." Nor can you characterize the author's point about Toni Morrison as an inference.

(D) also distorts the paragraph. The author's initial observation concerns the relationship between two art forms, and that observation is reinforced, not contradicted, by the example of Toni Morrison's *Jazz*.

(E), like (A), is a 180. The author mentions African American writing as an art form that genuinely exemplifies ("[n]owhere is this truer" at lines 6–7) the idea that literature tries to emulate music in making form contribute to content.

17. (B) Logic Reasoning (Weaken)

Step 2: Identify the Question Type

Since the question stem asks for the answer choice that "call[s] into question" the author's claim, this is equivalent to a Weaken question. Approach the question much as you would its counterpart in the Logical Reasoning section.

Step 3: Research the Relevant Text

The stem directs you to lines 10–16, in which the author asserts that in writing *Jazz*, Toni Morrison was the first African American writer to attempt to use elements of a musical genre as an inspiration for structuring an entire novel.

Step 4: Make a Prediction

As you know from Logical Reasoning, a valid weakener can take many forms. But no matter how it's worded, a weakener will make an author's conclusion less likely to be true. So you need the answer choice that suggests that Morrison wasn't the first African American writer to try to structure an entire novel around elements of a musical form.

Step 5: Evaluate the Answer Choices

(B) almost exactly matches the prediction. If (B) is true, then there had been previous attempts by African American novelists to use musical structures as narrative inspiration, and the author's claim would be invalid.

(A) neither supports nor undermines the author, since the claim in question is not that Morrison attempted to organize her novel around the structures of jazz but that she was the first African American writer to make such an attempt.

(C) comes close, but for a novel to "appear as if" its author tried to make the narrative reminiscent of an art form is different for an author to deliberately pattern the narrative after specific musical structures.

(D) suggests that all novels, even those predating *Jazz*, could be interpreted as musical in nature. But even if this is true, it can also still be true that Morrison was the first to consciously attempt to structure a novel around a genre of music.

(E) is an Irrelevant Comparison because it introduces non–African American writers, who have nothing to do with the author's claim.

18. (D) Inference

Step 2: Identify the Question Type

If a question stem asks you to find the answer choice "support[ed]" by information in the passage, it's an Inference question.

Step 3: Research the Relevant Text

Since the question stem mentions Duke Ellington, look to paragraph 3 to provide support for the correct answer.

Step 4: Make a Prediction

Inference questions are almost always tough to predict verbatim, but from paragraph 3 you gathered that Ellington was an innovative composer and the first to write with his musicians' specific "voices" in mind. Ellington allowed his musicians to improvise within his musical frame in the same way that Morrison allowed her characters to "improvise" within her narrative frame. The correct answer will be one that must be true based on the information in this paragraph.

Step 5: Evaluate the Answer Choices

(D) is supported by the first sentence of paragraph 3 (lines 36–39). (D) must be true if Ellington constructed his compositions "with his individual musicians and their unique 'voices' in mind."

(A) can't be inferred from the passage. For all we know, Morrison drew on a different source for inspiration or left Ellington uncredited.

(B) is contradicted by lines 39–42; Ellington allowed his musicians to improvise for as long as they wanted so long as they did so within his musical frame.

(C) is completely unsupported since the author never mentions that Ellington himself appears in the novel.

(E) is similarly unsupported by the passage. The author only refers to Ellington's jazz compositions. Remember not to bring in outside information in an attempt to support an answer choice.

19. (C) Global

Step 2: Identify the Question Type

Remember that Global questions can appear anywhere in the question set, including right in the middle. "[P]rimary purpose" is a dead giveaway to the question type here.

Step 3: Research the Relevant Text

As with any Global question, you will find the answer not by examining a specific line or paragraph in the passage but by consulting your understanding of the big picture gained during Step 1.

Step 4: Make a Prediction

The author's tone, though complimentary to Morrison, is still neutral, and the purpose must reflect that. The author is simply out to describe a feature (the narrative structure) of Morrison's *Jazz* and how it is analogous to a feature of Duke Ellington's music.

Step 5: Evaluate the Answer Choices

(C) matches the prediction.

(A) is too broad. The author might be analyzing and commending one particular achievement made by Morrison in *Jazz*, but that's different from saying that Morrison made a variety of contributions to fiction in general.

(B) is a 180. The author spends the entire passage drawing similarities between Morrison's and Ellington's work, not contrasts.

(D) is also too broad. The author isn't making a comparison between two arts in general, and there's no indication from the author that music and literature are all that dissimilar in the first place.

(E) is Outside the Scope. The author never details or sources Morrison's thematic concerns.

20. (A) Inference (EXCEPT)

Step 2: Identify the Question Type

Any question asking you about the "author's attitude" toward a component of the passage is a variation on an Inference question. But note the word "EXCEPT": here, you need to find the choice that is *not* consistent with the author's attitude toward *Jazz*.

Step 3: Research the Relevant Text

The author's attitude toward *Jazz* is found throughout paragraphs 2 and 4. Opinion Keywords like "linguistic virtuosity" in line 54 show the author's appreciation for the novel.

Step 4: Make a Prediction

In EXCEPT questions, it's often impossible to predict what the odd man out will say. Be prepared to eliminate any answer choice that is not part of the author's discussion of Morrison's novel.

Step 5: Evaluate the Answer Choices

(A) is the exception and therefore the correct answer choice. A glance at lines 6–10 shows that the author is using these lines to discuss African American music in general, not the specific narrative achievement of Morrison's novel *Jazz*.

(B) is from the first sentence of the second paragraph, in which the author not only discusses Morrison's novel but does so with a complimentary tone and an appreciation for Morrison's literary achievement.

(C), like (B), comes from the second paragraph in which the author gives credit to Morrison's writing.

(D) is from the fourth paragraph, which also reflects the author's positive attitude toward *Jazz*.

(E), like (D), comes from the fourth paragraph in which the author praises *Jazz*.

21. (D) Inference

Step 2: Identify the Question Type

Two clues indicate that this is an Inference question: the word *inferred* and the phrase "author would be most likely to believe ... ."

Step 3: Research the Relevant Text

This question stem doesn't point you to a specific place to research. You'll have to use your summaries of the Topic, Scope, Purpose, and Main Idea to guide you initially.

Step 4: Make a Prediction

Because research is difficult, prediction will also be tough. However, you know that the correct answer will be consistent with the author's Main Idea, which is that Morrison's use of Ellington-like jazz structures as a narrative frame for her novel was a literary innovation. Be prepared to find support in the passage for any answer you want to select as correct.

Step 5: Evaluate the Answer Choices

(D) can be inferred because the author points to additional structural similarities between *Jazz* and the work of Duke Ellington, such as the use of bold, lyrical individual voices within a narrator's or composer's carefully defined framework (lines 39–48). (D) is therefore correct.

(A) not only cannot be inferred but is actually a 180 because it contradicts lines 12–15, where the author mentions that no African American writer had previously attempted what Morrison achieved in *Jazz*.

(B) can't be inferred because the author never compares Morrison's depiction of the lives of jazz musicians to depictions by any other writers.

(C) can't be inferred because the author says neither that the narrative voices of Morrison's characters nor that the musicians in Ellington's band ever merge to form an indistinguishable whole.

(E) can't be inferred because the author never mentions any attempt by Morrison to disguise the similarities between her work and Ellington's.

22. (E) Detail

Step 2: Identify the Question Type

Since the correct choice will be a question answered directly by the information in the passage, this is a Detail question. All four incorrect answer choices will be outside the passage's Scope.

Step 3: Research the Relevant Text

You don't have any clues in the question stem to guide your research. When this happens, don't skip research entirely; rather, expect to do your research as you evaluate the choices.

Step 4: Make a Prediction

The passage provides enough information to answer a whole host of questions, so it doesn't make sense to predict here. However, confirm your correct answer by locating the exact lines in the passage that answer it.

Step 5: Evaluate the Answer Choices

(E) is answered by lines 10–16, in which the author says that many African American writers used musicians and music as theme and metaphor in their writing. This feature is shared by *Jazz*, which is connected to music in plot, theme, and narrative structure. **(E)** is therefore correct.

(A) is Outside the Scope because the author confines the discussion to the interplay between music and literature. Visual art is never mentioned.

(B) is Outside the Scope because *Jazz* is the only work by Morrison that the author mentions.

(C) is Outside the Scope because the author never discusses the critical response to *Jazz*.

(D) is Outside the Scope because the author never quantifies how many writers were inspired by Ellington.

Passage 4: Discovery of Nuclear Fission

Step 1: Read the Passage Strategically

Sample Roadmap

line #	Keyword/phrase	¶ Margin notes
1		sci often indirect
3	and	
5	A case in point	ex: disc of nuclear fission
7	Between 1934	
9	and 1939	
13	however	
14	Earlier ... even before	early theory
16	some theoretical physicists	
17	indicating	
18	But	
20	and	neutron exp. not aimed at proving atom-split theory
22	A common view	
26		Meitner, Fermi—similar results
30	numerous similar results	
31	partly because	why results weren't recognized
34	but ... more significantly	
35	because	
37	1938	
39		Hahn cont. work
41	":"	
43	conclusively	Hahn's results
46	even remarked	
49	but	
54	finally recognized the	Meihner makes connection
55	significance	
56	":"	
58	"nuclear fission"	coins new term
60	When	
61		others corroborate

Discussion

The author begins the passage by making a broad point: science often doesn't advance in a smooth, straight line. Scientists often look back after devising a new theory and realize that evidence for that theory has been around for a while. As soon as you see the key phrase "[a] case in point" in line 5, you know that the author is now illustrating this point with an example: the discovery of atom splitting. From 1934 to 1939, scientists generated evidence of nuclear fission without recognizing it as such. So now you know the **Topic** (advances in scientific knowledge) and the **Scope** (the advances that led to the discovery of nuclear fission). As a strategic reader, you know the remainder of the passage will tell the story of how scientists learned to split the atom and about evidence they should have recognized but only discovered *ex post facto*.

The Keyword that begins paragraph 2 ([*e*]*arlier*) signals that the author is providing background for the events that led to scientists splitting the atom. Indeed, there was already by the 1930s a theoretical basis for atom splitting, but many physicists of the time didn't believe that it could happen through neutron bombardment. So the crucial experiments weren't even designed with the aim of atom splitting in mind.

Paragraph 3 is long, so break it up. In lines 26–36, the author discusses the similarity of results among all the different physicists and explains why the products of their experiments weren't readily identified. In the next 10 lines, the author describes Hahn's continuation of Meitner's neutron bombardment research and his discovery of barium as a by-product of the experiments. Finally, lines 46–53 detail Hahn's statistical evidence: the two elements resulting from the experiments turned out to have as many nuclear particles combined as uranium does alone.

Paragraph 4 provides Meitner's conclusion based on her colleague's data: the neutron bombardment had been splitting uranium atoms all along. Then, the author says, after Meitner published her findings, the rest of the scientific community in North America and Europe corroborated them. By now, you should have zeroed in on the author's **Purpose** (to use the discovery of nuclear fission as an example of an indirect path to scientific progress) and **Main Idea**, which is that at times, such as in the 1930s when physicists discovered nuclear fission, scientific progress doesn't follow a smooth trajectory of steadily increasing knowledge.

23. (B) Global

Step 2: Identify the Question Type

The key phrase "primary aim" means that the scope of this question is the entire passage, thereby making this a Global question.

Step 3: Research the Relevant Text

Since "primary aim" is just another way to say "primary purpose," there's no text to research for this question. Instead, use your understanding of the passage's big picture to make a prediction.

Step 4: Make a Prediction

From your strategic reading of the passage during Step 1, you already know the author's Purpose: to use the case of nuclear fission as an example of the haphazard way in which scientific knowledge advances.

Step 5: Evaluate the Answer Choices

(B), which begins with the verb *illustrate*, is the best match for the author's Purpose.

(A) gets the author's tone wrong. The passage doesn't rebut a prevailing view; it simply uses one case to illustrate a general idea about scientific progress. The passage is far more neutral than **(A)** suggests.

(C) distorts the passage. While the author does mention that it took a while for physicists to realize that they had experiments that supported the theory, no comparison is made between the importance of the experiments and that of the theory.

(D), like **(A)**, suggests that the author has a negative tone, and the author never refers to an idea of scientists making "slow" progress. The passage identifies no opponent with whom the author would "take issue."

(E) is incorrect because the author never accuses any of the scientists involved in nuclear fission of being intellectually arrogant. They simply didn't recognize the significance of their experiments.

24. (D) Inference

Step 2: Identify the Question Type

The phrase "most likely reason" indicates an Inference question. You're asked to make a specific inference about the reaction of the theoretical physicists from paragraph 2 to Meitner's findings.

Step 3: Research the Relevant Text

Going back to lines 16–18, you find mention of the theoretical physicists producing calculations that showed the possibility, at least in theory, of nuclear fission. And Meitner's insight regarding the experiments can be found in the last paragraph, where the author mentions that she "finally recognized the significance of the data," which was that she and others "had actually been splitting uranium atoms."

Step 4: Make a Prediction

Now you can put those two parts of the passage together to infer that the theoretical physicists would be pleased that

Meitner confirmed through experimental results what they had only conjectured in theory.

Step 5: Evaluate the Answer Choices

(D) is consistent with the prediction.

(A) doesn't work because nothing in the passage indicates that Meitner was consulting the physicists' calculations in order to arrive at her insight.

(B) is Outside the Scope. The author doesn't say that the theoretical physicists were concerned about the acceptance of their discipline in the world at large or suggest that this is why they would have applauded Meitner's insights.

(C) isn't specific enough. The theoretical physicists weren't making any predictions about nuclear instability in general; they were aiming for a theory to allow for atoms to split apart.

(E) not only isn't related to the theoretical physicists' goals or expectations, but it also goes against the passage; the author says in paragraph 1 that scientists had "compiled increasing evidence" during the years 1934–1939, but the passage suggests that scientists had not been "analyzing the data," at least with respect to atom splitting, during those years.

25. (A) Inference

Step 2: Identify the Question Type

When the test asks you to find the answer choice "most nearly equivalent" to the meaning of a term in the passage, you're dealing with a variation on an Inference question.

Step 3: Research the Relevant Text

The question stem points you to line 62, but you'll have to read around that line for context. According to the passage, "the relevant evidence" had been present in the physics community for some time.

Step 4: Make a Prediction

The evidence in the passage that "had been present for some time" is the same evidence that, in paragraph 1, had gone unrecognized by physicists. That evidence must be the experimental results of neutron bombardment of uranium conducted by separate groups of scientists in the 1930s.

Step 5: Evaluate the Answer Choices

(A) matches the prediction perfectly.

(B) refers to Meitner's research in Sweden after she fled Germany, but it was Hahn's continuation of her neutron bombardment experiments that helped lead to the discovery.

(C) describes evidence that was relevant to the discovery of nuclear fission; however, this isn't the evidence mentioned at line 62. This detail helped Meitner realize that researchers had been unwittingly splitting atoms, while the evidence referred to at line 62 refers to results that "had been present

for some time" and that helped scientists in Europe and America corroborate Meitner's conclusion.

(D), like **(C)**, gives a detail that helped Meitner realize Hahn had been splitting atoms, but that singular event does not match the language from lines 62–63 that the "relevant evidence" had been "present for some time."

(E) is a fact that the author remarks on, but this fact isn't scientific evidence relevant to the discovery of nuclear fission. It's merely a fact describing the context in which the discovery happened.

26. (B) Inference

Step 2: Identify the Question Type

The language of the question stem is relatively uncategorical—"Given the information … which one of the following … would have been most likely"—so you'll need to make an inference here.

Step 3: Research the Relevant Text

You're asked to infer what could have reduced the amount of time it took for physicists to realize that their experiments were actually splitting atoms. Your Passage Map should lead you to paragraph 3, specifically lines 30–36, which detail the reasons why the uranium split remained undiscovered.

Step 4: Make a Prediction

The emphasis Keywords *more significantly* in line 34 lead you to the author's main reason for why the discovery was delayed: physicists expected that all the by-products of the neutron bombardment would be close to uranium in their nuclear composition. So that expectation likely kept them from investigating other possibilities.

Step 5: Evaluate the Answer Choices

(B) is a valid inference.

(A) cannot be inferred because the author never points to different research techniques as a cause for the delayed discovery of nuclear fission.

(C) is a 180. If the physicists weren't aware of the theoretical calculations indicating the possibility of fission, they might actually have taken even more time to realize the implications of their experimental results. Keep in mind that they weren't using neutron bombardment in hopes of splitting the atom.

(D) is incorrect because nothing in the passage suggests that physicists would have made their discovery sooner if more experiments were being done.

(E) is incorrect because the author never suggests that the physicists' discovery was delayed because they chose to use uranium rather than some other substance.

27. (E) Detail

Step 2: Identify the Question Type

"According to the passage" is a phrase that reliably indicates a Detail question.

Step 3: Research the Relevant Text

This might be a tough answer to research, so mine the question stem for as many clues as you can. The author discusses the 1930s physics community at large primarily in paragraph 2, where the author provides background and context; the beginning of paragraph 3, where it's mentioned that many physicists achieved similar experimental results; and the very end of the passage, where it's mentioned that scientists from two continents rushed to corroborate Meitner's findings.

Step 4: Make a Prediction

Because the author states several things about the physics community during the 1930s, don't try to predict a single detail that will appear as the correct answer. Be prepared, however, to confirm the correct answer by locating it in one of the parts of the passage identified in Step 3.

Step 5: Evaluate the Answer Choices

(E) is mentioned directly in lines 30–34.

(A) distorts the passage. The author mentions that the physicists of the 1930s didn't believe that atoms could be split through neutron bombardment, but that's not the same as neglecting the theoretical possibility of splitting atoms.

(B) is never mentioned. No one in the passage reevaluated the calculations of the theoretical physicists in paragraph 2.

(C) is a 180, contradicted by the second half of paragraph 3, in which Hahn discovered that neutron bombardment split uranium into barium and technetium.

(D) is Outside the Scope. The passage mentions no other kinds of atoms that were split in the 1930s.

Section II: Logical Reasoning

Q#	Question Type	Correct	Difficulty
1	Flaw	E	★
2	Assumption (Necessary)	D	★
3	Strengthen (EXCEPT)	D	★
4	Assumption (Necessary)	B	★
5	Weaken	C	★
6	Assumption (Sufficient)	E	★
7	Principle (Identify/Strengthen)	D	★
8	Flaw	B	★
9	Principle (Identify/Inference)	A	★
10	Assumption (Necessary)	A	★★
11	Flaw	E	★★
12	Principle (Identify/Strengthen)	B	★★★
13	Flaw	A	★
14	Inference	C	★
15	Flaw	E	★★
16	Parallel Reasoning	A	★★
17	Strengthen	C	★★★
18	Main Point	A	★★
19	Assumption (Sufficient)	D	★★
20	Point at Issue	D	★★
21	Flaw	A	★★
22	Inference	D	★★★★
23	Paradox	B	★
24	Parallel Flaw	C	★★
25	Method of Argument	E	★★★★

1. (E) Flaw

Step 1: Identify the Question Type

The phrase "is vulnerable to … criticisms" identifies this as a Flaw question. You'll need to break down the author's argument, identifying his conclusion and evidence, and determining his assumption. Then, you must evaluate how the author's reasoning goes wrong. Remember to keep an eye out for common flaw types.

Step 2: Untangle the Stimulus

The author, the mayor, states there are only two choices for dealing with an expected increase in traffic: build an expressway or do nothing. The author goes on to reject the do-nothing plan and concludes that building the expressway is the only option.

Step 3: Make a Prediction

The mayor makes the common error of failing to consider other possibilities. He provides no reason for limiting the city's options to only two choices. Nothing here rules out other options the city council could consider. The city could build a subway system or increase the number of bus routes, for example. Your prediction is straightforward: the argument is flawed because the author evaluates only two possibilities when many others might deserve attention as well.

Step 4: Evaluate the Answer Choices

(E) correctly identifies the logical flaw in general terms that match the prediction.

(A) misidentifies the source of the problem stated in the evidence. The projected severity of the increase in automobile traffic is not at issue. Instead, the focus of the argument is on the options available to accommodate the automobile traffic. The author's mistake is a failure to consider a wider range of those options, not a wider range of projections.

(B) describes a flaw that cannot apply to this argument. The options the author names—to do nothing and to do something—are mutually exclusive. In that regard, the mayor's logic is sound. The problem is that he doesn't consider any other options.

(C) is Outside the Scope. The focus of the argument is how to respond to a projected increase in traffic. The argument is not flawed because the projection might change a decade down the road. It might be wise to consider the long-term effects of a plan, but your task is not to critique the mayor's policy-making; it is to describe how "[t]he reasoning in the mayor's argument" is flawed.

(D) is Outside the Scope. The cost of traffic to the city's economy might be why the city council is evaluating options, but the mayor's argument focuses only on the options available to resolve the city's traffic situation.

2. (D) Assumption (Necessary)

Step 1: Identify the Question Type

The phrase "an assumption required" identifies this as an Assumption question. In addition, the word *required* indicates that you're looking for an assumption necessary for the author's conclusion to follow from her evidence. You can use the Denial Test to check or eliminate answers.

Step 2: Untangle the Stimulus

The author, a museum curator, concludes that an earthenware hippopotamus in the museum's collection was a religious object. The curator's evidence is twofold: (1) the hippopotamus was found in a tomb, upside down, with its legs broken off, and (2) the ancient Egyptians believed that the dead wage war against beasts and that breaking the legs of a representation of an animal would aid the deceased in that war.

Step 3: Make a Prediction

The curator ascribes the breaking of the earthenware hippopotamus's legs to those who placed it into the tomb. Thus, she assumes the hippopotamus was discovered in the same condition as when it was placed in the tomb. This means the author assumes that nothing between burial and discovery caused the hippopotamus's legs to break.

Step 4: Evaluate the Answer Choices

(D) correctly removes the possibility of the legs being broken between the burial and discovery of the hippopotamus. If you deny this answer, saying a natural occurrence caused the legs on the hippopotamus to break, you would ruin the connection between the curator's evidence and her conclusion. The statement in (D) is necessary to the argument.

(A) is Outside the Scope. Whether discovered in a child's tomb or an adult's, the hippopotamus could be a religious object. This statement is not necessary to the author's argument.

(B) is Outside the Scope. The curator tells us that the hippopotamus is an earthenware figure and that it resembles a child's toy. Neither prevents the object from also being a religious object. Distinguishing earthenware objects from toys is not necessary to the curator's argument.

(C) is Extreme. The argument is focused on the condition of the hippopotamus at the time of burial. Ruling out any entry of the tomb after the burial until the archaeologists found the tomb is not necessary to the author's argument. Someone could have entered the tomb without disturbing the hippopotamus or breaking its legs.

(E) is Outside the Scope. The focus of the argument is on the broken legs, not on the fact that the hippopotamus was upside down. This detail is an irrelevant distractor.

3. (D) Strengthen (EXCEPT)

Step 1: Identify the Question Type

The phrase "strengthens the ... argument EXCEPT" identifies this as a variant on a Strengthen question. The word *EXCEPT* indicates that the four incorrect answer choices must strengthen the argument. Thus, the correct answer choice could weaken the argument or fall outside the argument's scope; it just cannot strengthen the argument.

Step 2: Untangle the Stimulus

In this argument, the lawyer's conclusion recommends jury instructions should be in simple, understandable language and not in their current convoluted legalese. The Keyword [s]*ince* identifies the lawyer's evidence: it is more important for jurors to have a basic understanding of their role than to understand the precise details of their role.

Step 3: Make a Prediction

The lawyer believes simpler language will allow juries to have a better basic understanding of their role. In order for this to be true, the precise details and convoluted language currently given to juries must be preventing juries from understanding their basic role. The four incorrect answers will all support this position.

Step 4: Evaluate the Answer Choices

(D) is irrelevant because this answer focuses on a difficulty in articulating the "details," not on how too much detail can reduce a juror's understanding of his role. The author has explicitly stated that understanding details is less important than grasping the basic role, so pointing out that it is hard to express details in simple language doesn't add a fact that makes the argument stronger.

(A) is a strengthener. This answer says jurors understand simpler language better than convoluted language, exactly the point the author is trying to make.

(B) is a strengthener. This answer helps the author's conclusion by confirming that convoluted language prevents jurors from understanding their basic role.

(C) is a strengthener. This answer makes the author's recommendation feasible; it confirms that easily comprehensible language is "adequate" to explain the role of the jurors.

(E) is a strengthener because it eliminates the need of precise details in order for a juror to understand his role.

4. (B) Assumption (Necessary)

Step 1: Identify the Question Type

The phrase "an assumption ... the argument depends" identifies this as an Assumption question. In addition, the word *depends* indicates that you're looking for a necessary

assumption, without which the conclusion cannot follow logically from the evidence. You can use the Denial Test to check or eliminate answers.

Step 2: Untangle the Stimulus

The conclusion Keyword [*t*]*hus* identifies the author's main point: pharmacological intervention will be as effective as "traditional 'talk' methods." The author bases this comparison on the evidence that "talk" therapy produces a chemical change in the brain and that this change leads to improved behavior by the patient.

Step 3: Make a Prediction

To reach his conclusion from the evidence in the argument, the author must limit the effectiveness of "talk" therapy in improving a patient's behavior to only the chemical changes that result from the therapy. Those chemical changes, after all, are what pharmaceuticals can mimic. The author must, in turn, assume that there are no other, nonchemical benefits from "talk" therapy that also contribute to the patient's improved behavior.

Step 4: Evaluate the Answer Choices

(B) matches the prediction by identifying the chemical changes in the patient's brain, resulting from the "talk" therapy, as the only reason for the patient's improved behavior. If you deny this choice, saying that "talk" therapy provides patients with other, nonchemical benefits, the author's argument falls apart.

(A) is Extreme. The author focuses only on neurochemical changes related to "talk" therapy. Extending this reasoning to *all* neurochemical changes is beyond the argument's scope and thus not necessary to the author's reasoning.

(C) is a 180. The evidence in the argument tells us that "talk" therapy has brought about psychological changes (both chemical and behavioral) in patients. **(C)** says the opposite.

(D) is Extreme. This answer goes beyond the argument's scope to claim psychology and neuroscience will become indistinguishable. The author's point is much more limited: that one neurochemical treatment can be as effective as one traditional psychological treatment. The statement in this choice is far too broad to be necessary to the argument.

(E) is an Irrelevant Comparison. Comparing the cost of neurochemical intervention to that of psychological therapy is not necessary to the author's conclusion. Instead of focusing on cost, the comparison should focus on the effectiveness of each treatment.

5. (C) Weaken

Step 1: Identify the Question Type

The phrase "most seriously undermines" indicates that you are dealing with a Weaken question. Identify the conclusion, paraphrase the evidence, determine the central assumption, and then look for a fact that attacks that assumption.

Step 2: Untangle the Stimulus

The author's conclusion is the combination of multiple sentences. The word [b]ut signals the author's view that certain scientists are misguided. The line before gives us what the scientists are misguided about: they consider *H. pylori* a commensal, defined (even earlier in the stimulus) as something that benefits the human body. The evidence for the author's disagreement is a comparison between *H. pylori* and *M. tuberculosis*. Both bacteria, the author says, cause 10 percent of their hosts to get sick, but no one considers *M. tuberculosis* to be a commensal.

Step 3: Make a Prediction

The author's main point is that the scientists are misguided because *H. pylori* and *M. tuberculosis* are alike. To attack this reasoning, the correct answer must show that the two bacteria are dissimilar. The author's only criterion for comparison is that both bacteria infect the same percentage of people who harbor them. From that one consideration, she deduces that since *M. tuberculosis* is not a commensal, *H. pylori* cannot be either. However, this ignores another statement in the stimulus: *H. pylori* strengthens the human immune system. The author offers no evidence that *M. tuberculosis* provides any benefit to the people who harbor it. To maintain her contention that the two bacteria are comparable, the author must assume that *M. tuberculosis* offers some benefit to people who harbor it, just as *H. pylori* does for its hosts. The correct answer will attack that assumption.

Step 4: Evaluate the Answer Choices

(C) is correct. Confirming that *M. tuberculosis* provides no benefit justifies the view of the author's scientific opponents, those who consider *H. pylori*, but not *M. tuberculosis*, to be a commensal.

(A) is Outside the Scope. The ability of antibiotics to treat the negative effects of both bacteria is not relevant to the classification of one or both of the bacteria as commensals.

(B) is a Distortion. The argument focuses on the comparison between *M. tuberculosis* and *H. pylori* bacteria, not between tuberculosis the disease and the ulcers triggered by *H. pylori*.

(D) is an Irrelevant Comparison. The number of people who host a given bacteria does not determine whether that bacteria is a commensal. Instead, the determination hinges on whether the bacteria provides a benefit to an individual who harbors it.

(E) is also irrelevant. The comparison here is the same as that in **(D)**, merely reversing the sizes of the host populations. The number of people who host a given bacteria does not determine whether that bacteria is a commensal. Instead, the

determination hinges on whether the bacteria provides a benefit to an individual who harbors it.

6. (E) Assumption (Sufficient)

Step 1: Identify the Question Type

The word *assumed* identifies this as an Assumption question. Additionally, the question stem tells you that the argument will be complete "If" the assumption is added, so you are looking for an assumption *sufficient* to establish the conclusion from the evidence. Only one answer choice will provide an assumption that makes the conclusion follow inevitably from the evidence here.

Step 2: Untangle the Stimulus

The Keyword [s]o signifies the author's conclusion: there is at least one studio apartment with a scenic view at the Vista Arms apartment building. The author's evidence is that most of the apartments on the upper floors of the building have scenic views.

Step 3: Make a Prediction

Notice that although both the evidence and conclusion discuss apartments with scenic views, only the evidence discusses upper-floor apartments. Similarly, only the conclusion discusses studio apartments. This is the gap that you must bridge. For the author's conclusion to work, he must assume that at least one of the upper-floor apartments with a scenic view is a studio apartment. Look for an answer choice that ensures that there is at least one studio apartment with a scenic view on the upper floors.

Step 4: Evaluate the Answer Choices

(E) matches the prediction and is correct. If *most* of the apartments on the upper floors of the building are studio apartments, and *most* apartments on the upper floors have scenic views, then it must be true that there is *at least one* studio apartment with a scenic view. This makes the author's conclusion a certainty.

(A) is Outside the Scope. Knowing that all of the apartments on the lower floors of the building have scenic views is not sufficient to establish that at least one studio apartment has a scenic view. In fact, this choice fails to mention studio apartments at all.

(B) is irrelevant. Even if all the apartments in the building have scenic views, this choice leaves open the possibility that there are no studio apartments in the building. Also, there is no mention here of apartments on the upper floors.

(C) is irrelevant. If most apartments in the building are studio apartments, there is still no way to know whether any of those studio apartments has a scenic view since this choice does not place any of those studios on the upper floors.

(D) is irrelevant. Even if most of the apartments with scenic views are on the upper floors, there is no mention of studio apartments here and therefore no way to conclude that at least one studio apartment has a scenic view.

7. (D) Principle (Identify/Strengthen)

Step 1: Identify the Question Type

The word *principles* clearly identifies this as a Principle question. In addition, the phrase "most help to justify Mike's reasoning" indicates a task identical to that in Strengthen questions. So, approach this question the same way you would a Strengthen question: look for an answer that would make Mike's conclusion more likely to follow from his evidence. The correct answer will be a principle that supports Mike's assumption.

Step 2: Untangle the Stimulus

Although there are no Keywords that indicate the conclusion, the One-Sentence Test identifies the sentence that states Mike's main point. Here, the first sentence contains Mike's overall conclusion: that it is not wrong for him to use Tom's computer even though Tom did not give him permission to do so. The rest of the stimulus contains Mike's evidence: it's all right for him to use Tom's computer because Tom used Mary's bicycle last week without Mary's permission. In short, Mike states that it is not wrong for him to use Tom's item because Tom treated Mary's property the same way.

Step 3: Make a Prediction

If Mike thinks it is okay to use Tom's computer without asking because Tom used Mary's bicycle without asking, then Mike thinks that it is okay to treat Tom the same way Tom treated someone else. Look for an answer choice with a principle that supports Mike's reasoning.

Step 4: Evaluate the Answer Choices

(D) is the correct answer and matches the prediction. If it is permissible to treat people in a way similar to the way they treated others, then Mike is justified in treating Tom the way Tom treated Mary.

(A) is Outside the Scope. Mike is concerned about whether using Tom's computer without permission would be wrong, not whether doing so would be criminal. The argument does not discuss the idea of theft in any case.

(B) is Outside the Scope. Nothing in the argument concerns when one should tell the truth or when it is acceptable not to.

(C) is a Distortion. Mike justified using Tom's computer without permission because Tom had used Mary's bicycle without permission, not because Tom had used something of Mike's without permission. This choice is close, but it distorts Mike's reasoning.

(E) is Outside the Scope. The argument is not concerned with the relationship between harm and an action being wrong. In any event, there's no way to know whether Tom would be harmed by Mike's action.

8. (B) Flaw

Step 1: Identify the Question Type

The phrase "[t]he reasoning … is most vulnerable to criticism" identifies this as a Flaw question. Break down the argument into conclusion and evidence and think about why Robinson's evidence does not allow his conclusion to be properly drawn.

Step 2: Untangle the Stimulus

Wexell claims that the museum wasted its money purchasing props and costumes from famous stage productions because those items have no artistic significance outside the context of a performance. The Keyword [*s*]*o* indicates Robinson's conclusion: Wexell is wrong—the museum did not waste its money purchasing those items. His evidence is that many of the props and costumes are too old to be used in a performance and displaying these items is the only way to make them available to the public.

Step 3: Make a Prediction

Robinson supports his conclusion that the museum did not waste its money by citing evidence irrelevant to Wexell's argument. Wexell is not concerned about whether these items are available to the public; Wexell's claim is that it is a waste of the museum's money even to have items with no remaining artistic significance. Robinson misses Wexell's point entirely, and you should look for an answer choice that states this flaw.

Step 4: Evaluate the Answer Choices

(B) provides the flaw in Robinson's argument: Robinson raises concerns that are irrelevant to Wexell's overall point. Wexell does not care whether the props and costumes are available to the public, as they have no artistic significance once divorced from the productions for which they were created.

(A) is Outside the Scope. Robinson does not offer any anecdotal, or personal, evidence to support a general claim, so this choice must be wrong.

(C) is Outside the Scope. Robinson does not attack Wexell's person or character; she disagrees with Wexell's conclusion. Robinson's mistake is that she raises an issue irrelevant to Wexell's argument.

(D) is Outside the Scope. Robinson does not claim that Wexell is wrong because Wexell's evidence is insufficient. In fact, Robinson does not even address Wexell's evidence but rather raises her own considerations.

(E) is Outside the Scope. This choice describes the common flaw of Necessity versus Sufficiency. There are no sufficient or necessary conditions here, so the flaw cannot involve confusing the two.

9. (A) Principle (Identify/Inference)

Step 1: Identify the Question Type

The phrase "most closely conforms to … propositions" identifies this as a Principle question. The correct answer will represent the broad principle that underlies the specific situation in the stimulus.

Step 2: Untangle the Stimulus

The stimulus describes a game in which one person must reconstruct a dream by posing yes/no questions to a group of people who purportedly know the dream's narrative. In fact, these people do not know the dream's narrative and are responding to the questions according to some arbitrary rule. So, the person reconstructing the dream is, in reality, creating one. The point of the stimulus is that the person usually is able to construct a dream narrative that is both coherent and ingenious, even though no dream was ever related to the group.

Step 3: Make a Prediction

The broad principle underlying the "dream game" is that a person is able to create a coherent and ingenious narrative about something that did not happen, provided that the person believes it existed and that it had coherence and order.

Step 4: Evaluate the Answer Choices

(A) matches the prediction and states a broad principle to which the "dream game" conforms. Because the person who constructs the dream narrative is told that the dream was related to the group, he presumes that the dream happened and that it had order and coherence.

(B) is an Irrelevant Comparison. The party scenario doesn't involve a person's ability to correctly understand what someone else says. The fact that the dream is fictional doesn't imply that the person asking questions creates a false understanding of the answers she gets, which presumably are no more complicated than "yes" and "no."

(C) is Outside the Scope. The true nature of dreams is irrelevant to the party scenario. In any event, the person in the argument constructs a coherent, ingenious narrative for a dream that never happened.

(D) is Outside the Scope. The scenario here does not involve interpreting someone's actual dream but rather being able to construct a dream narrative based on responses to yes/no questions from a group of people who were allegedly told about a dream.

(E) is Outside the Scope. The party situation in the argument does not involve anyone explaining his behavior to others.

10. (A) Assumption (Necessary)

Step 1: Identify the Question Type

The word *assumption* identifies this as an Assumption question. Additionally, the word *depends* indicates that you are looking for a necessary assumption, one without which the conclusion cannot be logically drawn from the evidence. You can use the Denial Test to check or eliminate answer choices.

Step 2: Untangle the Stimulus

Begin by identifying the author's conclusion. Here, it's at the end of the argument: computers cannot currently be made significantly faster. There are two pieces of evidence. First, computer manufacturers want to make CPU chips smaller, without losing sophistication, because the smaller chips create faster computers. Second, CPU chips cannot be made significantly smaller without decreasing their sophistication.

Step 3: Make a Prediction

The author assumes that there is no way to make computers faster other than by making CPU chips significantly smaller. This must be true for the conclusion to follow, because if there were any other way to make computers faster without decreasing the size of the CPU chip, the conclusion would not necessarily be true. Look for an answer that says making CPU chips smaller is the only way to make computers faster.

Step 4: Evaluate the Answer Choices

(A) matches the prediction perfectly. This choice states that if computers are to be made faster, then their CPU chips must be smaller. Since we know that we cannot make the chips smaller without losing sophistication, computers cannot be currently made faster. This choice states an assumption necessary to the author's argument.

(B) is irrelevant and does not even mention the speed of computers. Knowing the degree to which CPU chips can be made smaller tells you nothing about whether having smaller CPU chips is the only way to increase computer speed.

(C) is irrelevant. Learning that the speed of a CPU chip will decrease if both the size and sophistication of the chip decrease misses the point in the evidence that manufacturers want to develop smaller, but equally sophisticated, CPU chips. At any rate, this does not state that CPU chips *must* be smaller to make computers faster, which is the unstated but necessary assumption in the argument.

(D) is Outside the Scope. Computer manufacturers' beliefs about the feasibility of significantly faster computing are irrelevant to whether smaller CPU chips are necessary for faster computers.

(E) is a 180. This choice provides a way to increase the speed of a CPU chip while maintaining its size. If this is true, then it suggests that computers can be made faster even without decreasing the size of the CPU chip.

11. (E) Flaw

Step 1: Identify the Question Type

The phrase "the reasoning ... is most vulnerable to criticism" identifies this as a Flaw question. Also, the phrase "involves a confusion between" gives you a very helpful hint: in some way, the author has conflated two key elements of the argument. Identify the conclusion, paraphrase the evidence, and keep an eye out for two elements that the author has confused with each other.

Step 2: Untangle the Stimulus

The Keyword *definitely* confirms that the author's conclusion is the last sentence. The author believes the environmentalists' claim is false. In other words, the author claims that pollution is not killing off many amphibian species annually. As evidence, the author points out that biologists have discovered many new species of amphibians in the last year.

Step 3: Make a Prediction

The author offers the number of species the scientists know about as evidence for a claim about the number of species that exist. This shift in scope from evidence to conclusion is unwarranted. Scientists may discover many new species (perhaps the scientists have new tools or methods, or maybe they're just looking in new places) even as many other species are dying off. Remember to phrase your prediction in a way that states the author's "confusion" of what scientists know with what actually exists.

Step 4: Evaluate the Answer Choices

(E) matches the prediction, albeit in slightly more abstract terms. The number of species of amphibians that biologists know about is not the same as the number living on the planet.

(A) is Outside the Scope. The author doesn't confuse a category (amphibians) with its particular examples (certain species of amphibians) or vice versa.

(B) is Outside the Scope. Necessary and sufficient conditions aren't mentioned in this argument in any form.

(C) misses this argument's flaw entirely. The author does not make a causal claim. While the author disputes the environmentalists' claim that pollution is causing extinctions, there is no "confusion between" pollution and extinction in his argument.

(D) mischaracterizes the flaw in two ways. First, the argument contains no correlations, so the author cannot have confused

one with something else. Second, the author disputes a claim that pollution is killing off amphibian species but doesn't confuse this claim with a correlation between those two phenomena.

12. (B) Principle (Identify/Strengthen)

Step 1: Identify the Question Type

The word *principles* identifies this as a Principle question. The phrase "most helps to justify the argument's reasoning" further tells you that this question mimics the Strengthen question type. Find the conclusion and paraphrase the evidence. Use them to predict the correct answer: a general rule that makes the conclusion more likely to follow from the evidence.

Step 2: Untangle the Stimulus

The second, strongly worded sentence is the author's conclusion. She believes that gardeners are mistaken in their beliefs about dried peat moss. In other words, the use of dried peat moss in gardening is not environmentally sound. The author's evidence is the fact that dried peat moss is derived from sphagnum moss, which contributes a substantial amount of oxygen to the atmosphere. In making dried peat, the gardening industry is destroying sphagnum moss faster than the moss can reproduce. (Note that the statement that dried peat moss contains no chemical additives and is renewable is used as evidence by the gardeners, not by the author. Don't let this distract you from finding the rule that connects the author's evidence to her conclusion.)

Step 3: Make a Prediction

Make sure you understand the author's assumption. The key jump in the author's reasoning is between sphagnum moss's contribution of oxygen to the atmosphere and the claim that using dried peat (which destroys sphagnum moss habitat) is environmentally unsound. You need a principle that connects these two elements.

Step 4: Evaluate the Answer Choices

(B) is a perfect match for the prediction. The evidence tells you that dried peat uses up sphagnum moss and reduces the oxygen that enters the atmosphere. **(B)** makes this outcome sufficient to establish that using dried peat is environmentally unsound. If this principle is valid, then the author's argument is solid.

(A) is a Faulty Use of Detail. The references to renewability and chemical additives are taken from the gardeners' argument, not the author's. **(A)** is a statement with which the author would agree, but it is not a principle that helps to justify her reasoning.

(C) is a Distortion. The rain forests are an item of comparison for sphagnum moss, not the actual point of the argument.

Also, the author needs to establish what makes a practice environmentally *un*sound, not what makes it environmentally sound.

(D) is Outside the Scope. No reference is made here to the environmental benefits of any practice, nor is any kind of cost-benefit analysis implied. Also, as with **(C)**, this choice focuses on what makes a practice environmentally sound, not on what makes it environmentally unsound.

(E) is Outside the Scope. The author doesn't mention banning anything.

13. (A) Flaw

Step 1: Identify the Question Type

The word *flawed* clearly identifies this Flaw question. Because this is a Dialogue/Response stimulus, read Brooks's argument first to provide context. Identify Morgenstern's conclusion and evidence and determine the flawed assumption that, in her mind, connects them.

Step 2: Untangle the Stimulus

Morgenstern is telling Brooks to quit his job. Her reasoning is based on the fact that Brooks is already unhappy in his current job and that one consequence of quitting may be the unhappiness that results from not finding another job.

Step 3: Make a Prediction

There are two related flaws in this argument. Morgenstern says that unhappiness is one potential consequence of Brooks not finding another job, but she neglects to mention other potential consequences. For instance, Brooks could end up bankrupt or homeless as well as unhappy, and these might be good reasons not to quit. Also, Morgenstern relies on Brooks's claim that he is unhappy, but she doesn't ask how unhappy he is. To argue that quitting can't make things worse, Morgenstern must overlook the possibility that Brooks might become even more unhappy than he is now. Either of these predictions might show up in the correct answer.

Step 4: Evaluate the Answer Choices

(A) matches the second prediction perfectly. If, by quitting his job, Brooks might become even more unhappy than he is now, he might have good reason not to quit.

(B) is Outside the Scope. Morgenstern isn't simply assuming the conclusion; she is using the potential outcome of unhappiness to evaluate the decision to quit.

(C) is a Distortion. Morgenstern may not be clear on exactly how unhappy Brooks is or could become, but she hasn't distorted the meaning of anything Brooks said.

(D) is Outside the Scope. There is only one type of risk discussed here, the risk of not finding another job.

(E) is Outside the Scope. Morgenstern is only advising Brooks to quit, not making a general argument about other people's job decisions.

14. (C) Inference

Step 1: Identify the Question Type

The phrase "must also be true" identifies this as an Inference question. Work through the stimulus to catalog and paraphrase the statements. Combine any statements containing Formal Logic.

Step 2: Untangle the Stimulus

The first sentence is a pure Formal Logic statement. The second sentence is a bit "fuzzier"; on the LSAT, "most" means "more than 50 percent." Both can be diagrammed as conditional statements.

If	shown at LN	→	Canadian
If	prize winner at LN	→	50% chance of prize at int'l festival

Step 3: Make a Prediction

Start making the links in the chain of logic here. All films shown at Lac Nichoutec Film Festival are Canadian films, so any prize-winning film there is Canadian. Thus, any film from the Lac Nichoutec Festival that went on to win international prizes is Canadian. But there are important limits to what you can deduce here. Nothing in the stimulus tells you how many prize winners the festival produced or how many international film festivals there are. Therefore, it's important to avoid drawing inappropriate inferences. You don't know, for instance, that most international prize winners were from Lac Nichoutec (or from Canada for that matter). Only one choice will be unequivocally true.

Step 4: Evaluate the Answer Choices

(C) must be true. All films at the Lac Nichoutec Film Festival were Canadian, and most of the prize winners also won prizes at international festivals, so *some* Canadian films won prizes at international film festivals.

(A) is a Distortion. This choice draws an inappropriate inference that Canadian entries to international film festivals were limited in some way. Many Canadian films that did not win prizes at Lac Nichoutec, or were not even shown at that festival, could have still been shown at international festivals.

(B) is Extreme, as well as Outside the Scope. The Lac Nichoutec festival might have shown only a tiny fraction of all the films produced this year in Canada, and the stimulus gives you no reason to assume otherwise.

(D) is a Distortion. On the LSAT, *most* means "greater than half" but has no upper limit. It is possible that every single film that won a prize at Lac Nichoutec was also shown at an international festival. Furthermore, the stimulus tells us about films from Lac Nichoutec that won prizes at international festivals, not about films that were simply shown at international festivals.

(E) is also a Distortion. The stimulus tells you nothing about international film festival prize winners from countries other than Canada. Don't quibble that this seems unlikely in real life; the stimulus asks for what must be true *based on "the above statements."* Given only the stimulus here, it is possible that Canadian films swept every international film festival and won every single award.

15. (E) Flaw

Step 1: Identify the Question Type

The phrase "most vulnerable to criticism" indicates that this is a Flaw question. The phrase "overlooks the possibility" also gives you a helpful hint. As you find the conclusion and paraphrase the evidence, watch out for alternative possibilities that the author may have overlooked.

Step 2: Untangle the Stimulus

The strong opinion offered in the second sentence is the conclusion. Since the author says the social critics' claim is absurd, she must believe that the cynicism of contemporary journalism does not undermine society's well-being. As evidence, she says that journalists have always been cynics and that today's journalists are no more cynical than those of previous eras.

Step 3: Make a Prediction

The author's reasoning relies on a subtle shift between evidence about journalistic cynicism and a conclusion about harm to society. Cynical journalism may not be causing any more harm than it did in previous eras, but that doesn't mean it's harmless. To use the wording in the question stem, the author overlooks the possibility that cynical journalism was also harmful to society in the past.

Step 4: Evaluate the Answer Choices

(E) is a perfect match for the prediction. If cynical journalism has always had negative effects on society, then the critics are right and the author is wrong.

(A) is a Distortion. The author is talking about the effects of journalistic cynicism, so the effects of "widespread cynicism" are not relevant. Furthermore, if widespread cynicism were beneficial, this would not undermine the author's claim that it is harmless.

(B) is a Distortion. It might be true that having more information about powerful people's motives can make one more cynical. It might even give a reason why journalists would become cynical, but it doesn't address the effects of

cynicism on society, so the author's argument isn't harmed by overlooking this possibility.

(C) is Outside the Scope. Whether journalists' cynicism is genuine or feigned has no bearing on the effects of their work on society.

(D) is Outside the Scope. Whether the cynical journalists' portrayal of human greed is accurate or inaccurate has no bearing on its effects on society.

16. (A) Parallel Reasoning

Step 1: Identify the Question Type

A question asking for the answer choice with reasoning "most similar to" that in the argument is a Parallel Reasoning question. Analyze the argument and find an answer choice that matches the reasoning piece by piece. Alternatively, characterize the stimulus argument's conclusion and eliminate any answer choices in which the conclusion does not match the conclusion type in the stimulus.

Step 2: Untangle the Stimulus

The Keyword [s]*o* indicates the conclusion: the owners of Uptown Apartments should make improvements to the apartment complex. Note that the conclusion is a recommendation for a course of action. The evidence states that the owners of Uptown Apartments are hesitant to make improvements but that doing so would benefit them by making other properties they own in the area more valuable.

Step 3: Make a Prediction

The correct answer will take the general idea behind the argument and apply it to a new situation. In general, the argument breaks down as follows: although a person may not want to perform some action (the owners of Uptown Apartments do not want to improve the apartment complex), that action (improving the complex) would produce an indirect benefit for the person (the surrounding housing would be more valuable), and so that action (improving the complex) should be performed.

Step 4: Evaluate the Answer Choices

(A) is correct and matches the reasoning in the stimulus. Although a person may not want to perform some action (John does not want to undergo surgery), that action (undergoing surgery) would produce an indirect benefit for the person (John could exercise again), and so that action (undergoing surgery) should be performed.

(B) can be quickly eliminated because its conclusion is not a recommendation for a course of action but is instead a negative evaluation of an action already taken.

(C) is a Distortion. This argument states that because not performing an action (having the mechanic check) could potentially lead to some negative consequence (Max's engine would be ruined), that action should be performed (Max should have the mechanic check for the crack). The evidence about the negative consequences of inaction does not match the evidence in the stimulus. Moreover, nothing here suggests that Max is opposed to the action.

(D) can also be quickly eliminated because its conclusion is not a recommendation. Here, the argument ends with an assertion about the end result of a series of causal links (dental problems → avoiding candy → fruit eating → better diet).

(E) distorts the original argument in several ways. First, the conclusion here is a value judgment ("it is in the long-term interest of the company") rather than a recommendation. Second, nothing suggests initial hesitation on the company's part. Finally, the benefit here is not indirect; the new product would itself become popular.

17. (C) Strengthen

Step 1: Identify the Question Type

The phrase "provides the most support for" identifies this as a Strengthen question. Break down the argument into conclusion and evidence, predict the central assumption, and find an answer choice that validates the president's assumption.

Step 2: Untangle the Stimulus

The president's conclusion is a prediction: implementing the new copy protection will substantially increase sales of Ditalgame's products. He believes this because currently the company's games are subject to widespread illegal copying and the company will soon begin using a new copy protection feature on its games.

Step 3: Make a Prediction

The president claims that Ditalgame will increase sales of its games by implementing the new copy protection because right now the games are subject to illegal copying. Notice his underlying assumption: that people like the games well enough that they will be interested in paying for them once they are prevented from making illegal copies. Look for an answer choice that validates this assumption and makes it more likely to be true that Ditalgame's sales will increase once the new protection is in place.

Step 4: Evaluate the Answer Choices

(C) is correct. If the new copy protection allows people to play a game just long enough to decide they really want it, then the president's prediction that sales of Ditalgame's games will increase is more likely to be true.

(A) is Outside the Scope. How much money Ditalgame spent developing the new copy protection and whether it can recoup those costs are irrelevant to whether the sales of the

company's games will increase once the copy protection is implemented.

(B) is Outside the Scope and fails to mention the new copy feature at all. Knowing that Ditalgame's market share declined even though the market for computer games has grown steadily tells you nothing about whether the new copy protection will lead to increased game sales. If anything, it suggests that the company's games may not be popular enough to attract new buyers.

(D) is Outside the Scope. Knowing that this magazine, popular among people who copy computer games, generally gives favorable reviews to the company's games is not enough to support the prediction that the new copy protection will cause an increase in Ditalgame's game sales. You don't know that these readers have enough money to buy the games or that the protection system will allow them to discover that they really like the games enough to buy them.

(E) is an Irrelevant Comparison. Whether Ditalgame's games are more frequently copied than those of its competitors has nothing to do with whether the new copy protection will lead to an increase in sales of the company's games. After all, the competitors may already have copy protection in place.

18. (A) Main Point

Step 1: Identify the Question Type

The phrase "most accurately expresses the overall conclusion" identifies this as a Main Point question. Focus on Keywords, look out for subsidiary conclusions, and expect to combine statements in the argument to paraphrase the author's main point.

Step 2: Untangle the Stimulus

The first sentence informs you that an economy might be able to function without paper money. The next sentence, highlighted by the Keyword [*I*]*nstead*, explains the alternative: the government would electronically record all transactions. The Keyword [*h*]*owever* in the following sentence indicates a contrast and the columnist's point of view. She states that no society would willingly accept a government that electronically records all transactions, even if it were possible. The Keyword *for* indicates evidence and reinforces the fact that the previous part of the sentence is the columnist's overall point. The reason society would not accept the alternative to paper money is that it gives the government too much power, something people distrust.

Step 3: Make a Prediction

Combining the first two-thirds of the argument provides a great summary of the columnist's main point: a society would not willingly accept a world in which the government would electronically record all transactions instead of using paper money.

Step 4: Evaluate the Answer Choices

(A) matches your prediction perfectly. It accurately combines the first two sentences of the stimulus with the clause following "[h]owever."

(B) mistakes the author's evidence for her conclusion. The author offers societies' distrust of governments with too much power to support her conclusion that people will reject a system in which the government electronically records transactions.

(C) restates the first sentence, which simply introduces a possibility that the columnist goes on to discuss. Her main point is that people will reject the alternative to paper money.

(D), like **(B)**, mistakes the author's evidence for her overall point. The fact that **(D)** applauds societies' reluctance doesn't change its role in the argument.

(E) fails to state the conclusion and actually contradicts the argument. In her first sentence, the author makes clear that she believes it might soon be possible for an economy to function without paper money.

19. (D) Assumption (Sufficient)

Step 1: Identify the Question Type

The word *assumed* identifies this as an Assumption question. Additionally, the question stem tells you that the argument will be complete "If" the assumption is added, so the correct answer will contain an assumption *sufficient* to establish the conclusion. Only one answer choice will provide an assumption that makes the conclusion follow inevitably from the evidence given.

Step 2: Untangle the Stimulus

The Keyword [*t*]*hus* signifies the scientist's conclusion: some interpreters have misconstrued Marxism by treating it as a political program aimed at transforming society. The evidence states that because Marxism describes rigorously a historical movement toward socializing the means of production, it should be considered a scientific theory.

Step 3: Make a Prediction

The scientist argues that because Marxism is a scientific theory, interpreters misconstrue Marxism when they treat it as a political program aimed at social transformation. Notice the shift in terms between conclusion and evidence: the former discusses Marxism as a political program, while the latter describes Marxism as a scientific theory. If the scientist assumes that anything regarded as a scientific theory cannot be a political program, then his conclusion will follow ineluctably from his evidence.

Step 4: Evaluate the Answer Choices

(D) matches your prediction perfectly. If it is true that scientific theories cannot be interpreted to be, or to imply,

political programs, then it must be true that people misconstrue Marxism (a scientific theory) when they treat it as a political program.

(A) is Outside the Scope. Whether the description that Marxism gives of historical phenomenon is as rigorous as it claims to be is irrelevant to whether people misconstrue Marxism by viewing it as a political program. The statement in **(A)** certainly is not sufficient to establish the conclusion in this argument.

(B) is Outside the Scope. The aims of science and people seeking to transform society by political means are irrelevant to the argument, as is whether these aims are compatible with each other.

(C) is a Distortion and fails to mention political programs. We know from the first sentence of the stimulus that a body of thought that rigorously describes a historical movement should be regarded as a scientific theory. Whether *only* bodies of thought consisting purely of rigorous description are scientific theories is irrelevant to whether those theories can be considered political programs.

(E) is a Distortion and fails to mention scientific theories. Whether the means of production will inevitably become socialized regardless of political programs is irrelevant to whether scientific theories can be considered political programs.

20. (D) Point at Issue

Step 1: Identify the Question Type

The phrase "committed to disagreeing with each other … " identifies this as a Point at Issue question. You can use the Decision Tree to identify the issue about which Daniel and Carrie disagree.

Step 2: Untangle the Stimulus

Paraphrase each person's argument. Daniel claims that an action must be performed with the right motivations in order to be morally good, even if that action fulfills a moral obligation. Carrie claims that fulfilling a moral obligation is the only thing that is required for an action to be morally good because people do not consciously control the motivations for their actions.

Step 3: Make a Prediction

The issue between Daniel and Carrie is whether the motivations behind a person's action affect whether that action is morally good. Use this prediction in combination with the Decision Tree as you evaluate each answer choice. The correct answer will produce a "yes" to each of the following questions: (1) Does Daniel discuss the subject matter of the answer choice? (2) Does Carrie discuss the subject matter of the answer choice? (3) Do they have differing opinions on the topic?

Step 4: Evaluate the Answer Choices

(D) matches the prediction and yields affirmative responses to all three questions of the Decision Tree. Daniel agrees with this choice, stating that an action cannot be morally good if it is performed with the wrong motivation. Carrie disagrees because she claims that a person's motivation for performing an action is irrelevant to whether that action is morally good.

(A) is Outside the Scope. Neither person discusses one's moral obligation to attempt actions that are impossible to perform.

(B) is a Distortion. Daniel claims that if an action is good, then it must be performed with the right motivations (i.e., that the right motivation is necessary for an action's moral goodness). Carrie says one's motivations are irrelevant to whether an action is morally good. Neither claims that the right motivation is sufficient to establish an action's moral goodness, and, thus, neither can be said to have an opinion on whether an action performed with the right motivation might not be morally good.

(C) is a Distortion. Daniel and Carrie do not discuss whether fulfilling a moral obligation is itself the motivation for taking an action that results in the fulfillment of a moral obligation. Indeed, neither defines what the "right motivations" would be. Rather, they disagree over whether motivation affects the action's morality.

(E) is a Distortion. Daniel believes that some actions are required by a "sense of duty," but goes on to say that having the right motivation is necessary for an action to be moral. There's not enough information to tell whether he would consider a sense of duty to be the right motivation or whether he would consider such a motivation sufficient to ensure an action's morality. Carrie, meanwhile, dismisses the necessity of motivation. It's impossible to determine whether they would disagree about the statement in **(E)**.

21. (A) Flaw

Step 1: Identify the Question Type

This is a Flaw question. The correct answer will describe how the author's reasoning goes off track. Identify the conclusion and evidence. Use them to determine why the author's assumption is unwarranted.

Step 2: Untangle the Stimulus

The author leads off with his conclusion: the bridge renovation wasted taxpayer money (the mayor lied when he said it didn't). The author believes this because a panel investigated the larger project of which the bridge renovation was a part and concluded that the larger project wasted taxpayer money.

Step 3: Make a Prediction

The flaw here is in equating conclusions about each part of a large project to conclusions about the large project overall. It's possible that the large project was wasteful but the specific task of renovating the bridge was not. The author's argument is equivalent to saying that the guitarist in a band is a poor musician because a critic found the band as a whole to be bad, or saying that a person's spleen is diseased because a doctor concluded that the person is in generally poor health.

Step 4: Evaluate the Answer Choices

(A) describes the author's flaw precisely. Knowing that the larger project was wasteful doesn't mean the specific part of it involving bridge renovation was wasteful.

(B) doesn't match the stimulus. The author does not draw a conclusion about government waste in general; he draws a conclusion about waste in one specific subproject within one larger project.

(C) cites a flaw not found here. Although the author says that the mayor lied about the bridge renovation, he doesn't draw his conclusion on the basis of claims impugning the mayor's character. He cites (just not carefully enough) commission findings to support his point.

(D) describes a circular argument, a description that does not match the argument in the stimulus. The author turns to the commission report as evidence, so he certainly is not presupposing his conclusion. His mistake is in assuming that every subproject was as wasteful as the overall project on which the commission reported.

(E) misses the stimulus entirely. The author does not call either the mayor's or the commission's motives into question.

22. (D) Inference

Step 1: Identify the Question Type

This is a straightforward Inference question stem. The correct answer follows from the statements in the stimulus. Catalog and summarize the stimulus statements and look to combine them to make a valid deduction.

Step 2: Untangle the Stimulus

By way of background, the author explains that in good weather, a certain airport allows one plane per minute to land. In bad weather, however, planes may not land on adjacent runways simultaneously, so the rate is reduced to one plane every two minutes. Note that the stimulus does *not* tell you how many runways the airport has. The stimulus ends with the practical implications of this state of affairs. Airlines make out their flight schedules expecting good weather, so when the landing rate is reduced during bad weather conditions, serious delays result.

Step 3: Make a Prediction

The bulk of this stimulus is factual background. But when the author brings in implications of the landing patterns for airlines using the airport, you're able to make some clearer deductions. Since the bad-weather landing rate is 30 planes per hour, and since this causes serious delays, you can unequivocally infer that the airlines plan for more than 30 planes per hour to land. Be careful not to speculate, however. You do not know that the airlines plan for the maximum rate of 60 planes per hour. Likewise, you don't have enough information to determine exactly how the airport limits landings during bad weather; it may close one runway entirely, or it may allow planes to land alternately (just not simultaneously) on two adjacent runways.

Step 4: Evaluate the Answer Choices

(D) follows directly from the statements in the stimulus. Since delays are caused when the airport limits landings to 30 per hour, airlines must schedule for more than 30 per hour.

(A) is Extreme; the phrase "on any one runway" is not supported by the stimulus. While the total number of landings allowed is cut from 60 to 30 during bad weather, nothing in the stimulus tells you whether that reduction is accomplished by shutting down one runway or by restricting the landings on more than one. Remember, you're not told how many runways there are at this airport.

(B) is Extreme. During good weather, planes may land on the two runways simultaneously, and up to 60 planes may land per hour. That information is not sufficient to establish how often planes are landing on adjacent runways and certainly doesn't support the conclusion that simultaneous landings are "likely" at any given time.

(C) is a 180. Delays result during bad weather, when adjacent runways *cannot* be used simultaneously.

(E) is Outside the Scope. There could be any number of reasons for delays at the airport during good weather. Knowing that there are delays during bad weather doesn't allow you to infer how infrequent they are when the weather is fine.

23. (B) Paradox

Step 1: Identify the Question Type

When the question stem calls for you to explain or resolve an "apparent discrepancy," you're looking at a Paradox question. Read the stimulus to identify the seemingly contradictory statements, then evaluate the answers to find the one choice that helps explain how the two statements may reasonably coexist.

Step 2: Untangle the Stimulus

This lengthy stimulus provides a lot of background on primate social grooming. Usually, you learn, larger primate groups

spend more time in social grooming activities, the purpose of which is to strengthen group bonding. Additionally, primates with bigger brains usually spend more time grooming one another. All of this leads to the paradox: early humans had big brains and lived in big groups, but apart from parents and their children, spent almost no time in social grooming activities.

Step 3: Make a Prediction

The one fact not accounted for in the author's analysis of early human behavior is the role grooming did or did not play in strengthening group bonds. The correct answer will offer some explanation of how early humans kept their large groups together without the activity (social grooming) that seems to serve the bonding function among other primates.

Step 4: Evaluate the Answer Choices

(B) offers the explanation you need. In early human groups, language served to strengthen group bonds. Thus, early humans could live successfully in large groups without the need for social grooming.

(A) is irrelevant to the paradox. It might explain what early humans did with their free time, but it doesn't help explain how they kept large groups cohesive and bonded.

(C) doesn't address the relevant paradox. We need to learn how humans were able to maintain group cohesion, not why they may have had less need than other primates for grooming activities.

(D) doesn't help resolve the paradox of maintaining large groups without the bonding inherent in social grooming. At best, it further complicates the issue by suggesting that large early human groups broke up temporarily only to reform after hunting.

(E) is a 180. The fact that other large-brained primates engage in social grooming makes it that much more confusing that early human groups did not.

24. (C) Parallel Flaw

Step 1: Identify the Question Type

When the stem asks for a correct answer that "most closely resembles ... the argument above," you know you're looking at a Parallel Reasoning question. In this case, you're told that the reasoning in the stimulus and the correct answer will contain the same flaw. Analyze the argument, characterize its flaw, and find the choice with reasoning flawed in exactly the same way.

Step 2: Untangle the Stimulus

This argument makes an error in Formal Logic. The author starts with a conditional statement: if the party had produced sound economic theory *and* had implemented its program, then there would have been a significant decline in inflation.

The next statement contradicts the result of the conditional statement: inflation has not declined (indeed, it's gone up). From this, the author concludes that one part of the two-part sufficient trigger in the conditional statement did not occur: the party did not produce sound economic theories. Notice that the conclusion is silent on whether the party implemented its program (the other half of the two-part sufficient trigger).

Step 3: Make a Prediction

Outlining the Formal Logic in the author's first statement makes the flaw clear and prepares you to evaluate the answer choices.

If	economic theories sound AND program implemented	→ inflation decreases

The appropriate contrapositive would be as follows.

If	inflation ~ decrease	→ economic theories ~ sound OR program ~ implemented

Once we identify the contrapositive, the author's error is clear. She correctly negated the necessary term in the original statement, but in her analysis of the sufficient terms, she forgot to substitute *OR* for *AND*. Having noted the increase in inflation, she could conclude that *at least one of* the two sufficient conditions did not occur, but she gives no reason for saying it was the lack of sound economic theories rather than a failure to implement the party's program. The correct answer will exhibit exactly the same flawed application of Formal Logic: if X and Y, then Z. Not Z; therefore, not X.

Step 4: Evaluate the Answer Choices

(C) hits the nail on the head, making exactly the same mistake as the argument in the stimulus. The author starts with a conditional statement: if X (sell subsidiaries) AND Y (purchase patent) → Z (stock price doubles). She then contradicts the result of the conditional statement: NOT Z (stock price did not improve). From this, she concludes that one of the two parts in the sufficient condition did not occur: therefore, NOT X (not sell subsidiaries). Just as in the stimulus, the conclusion here is silent on Y; we don't know whether the company purchased patents.

(A) is not flawed. Here, either of two sufficient conditions (invasion *or* climate change) would result in architectural change. The author notes that the area's architecture has not changed and correctly concludes that the area has seen no invasion.

(B) contains a fatal Distortion of the original argument. Here, the entire argument is about what may occur in the future

rather than being an analysis of past events. Although the argument has superficial similarities to the stimulus, it is premised on what people "fear," and the workers "promise" not to strike. The conclusion about what they "must think" is too speculative to correspond to an actual increase in inflation and the idea that the party's theories *were*, in fact, unsound.

(D) is flawed, but not in the same way as the stimulus argument. Here, two conditions (battle won *and* rebels freed) were "expected" to result in a show of support for the rebels. From the fact that support for the rebels has materialized, the author concludes that the battle was won. This fails to match the stimulus for two reasons. First, the conditional statement here is about what was *expected* to happen, not necessarily what would happen. Second, and even more important, the reasoning flaw here comes from concluding that winning the battle and freeing the rebels are the *only* reasons the rebels might receive a show of support. The stimulus argument contains no comparable confusion between sufficient and necessary conditions.

(E) is not parallel to the stimulus because this argument contains only one condition (equipment "worth the investment") and then fails to mirror even that one condition in the conclusion ("no improvement on the old"). There's nothing here resembling the stimulus argument's failure to turn *AND* into *OR* as the contrapositive is formed.

25. (E) Method of Argument

Step 1: Identify the Question Type

The phrase "describes the argumentative strategy" identifies this as a Method of Argument question. The correct answer will reflect, likely in abstract terms, the *way* in which the author advances his main point. Note the Keywords and paraphrase how the author attempts to convince his readers.

Step 2: Untangle the Stimulus

The author presents a dilemma. When a group cannot come to an agreement, group members are often called "stubborn, bull-headed, or unyielding." The problem is that these are difficult accusations to prove. The author then announces his main point: if you want to make your accusation stick, he says, go with the term *unyielding*. His reason is that if the person you accuse hasn't yielded on the issue you are debating, she can't very well turn around and say she's not unyielding.

Step 3: Make a Prediction

To prepare yourself to evaluate the answer choices, paraphrase the author's argumentative strategy in abstract terms. Out of three possible accusations, the author recommends the one that puts the accused in a position of trying to deny that her character reflects her actions in this case. Note, too, that the author limits his recommendation to those who want their accusation to stick.

Step 4: Evaluate the Answer Choices

(E) is the choice that accurately describes how the author makes his argument. His recommendation is conditional (if you want your accusation to stick) and it puts the accused person in a position of trying to deny the conclusion (you are unyielding) while accepting the premise (you didn't yield).

(A) is a Distortion. The primary argument advances a reason for choosing one line of attack, not for rejecting the others. Moreover, the author considers all three accusations problematic because they are "abusive, difficult to prove, and rarely help the group reach a resolution." He never claims that they have "no substance in fact."

(B) is Extreme. The primary argument advances a reason for choosing one line of attack, not for rejecting the others. One reason the author considers the three accusations problematic is that they "rarely help the group reach a resolution." That contrasts starkly with the claim here that they make it "virtually impossible ... to reach a consensus."

(C) is Half-Right/Half-Wrong. The author does conditionally advocate for a tactic, but not because he considers it less "offensive" than the alternatives. After all, all three accusations "often seem abusive." Rather, his reason for preferring "unyielding" is that circumstances make the accusation harder to rebut and thus more likely to stick.

(D) is a 180. The author says that all three accusations "rarely help the group reach a resolution." He doesn't claim that the "unyielding" accusation makes consensus any more likely. He simply argues that it's harder than the others for the accused person to deny.

Section III: Logic Games

Game 1: Chemistry Class Lab Sessions

Q#	Question Type	Correct	Difficulty
1	Acceptability	E	★
2	"If" / Must Be True	E	★★
3	"If" / Complete and Accurate List	B	★★★
4	"If" / Could Be True EXCEPT	A	★★★
5	"If" / How Many	C	★★★

Game 2: Shopping Center Businesses

Q#	Question Type	Correct	Difficulty
6	Acceptability	E	★
7	"If" / Could Be True	A	★
8	"If" / Must Be True	C	★★
9	"If" / Must Be True	D	★★★
10	"If" / Must Be True	B	★★
11	Rule Substitution	D	★★★★

Game 3: Software Company Sales Zones

Q#	Question Type	Correct	Difficulty
12	Acceptability	B	★
13	"If" / Could Be True	E	★★★
14	Must Be False	A	★★
15	Partial Acceptability	A	★★★★
16	Must Be False (CANNOT Be True)	D	★
17	Item Removed from Scoring		
18	"If" / Could Be True	A	★★★

Game 4: Wayne & Zara's Piano Solos

Q#	Question Type	Correct	Difficulty
19	Partial Acceptability	C	★★★
20	Minimum	A	★★★★
21	"If" / Must Be True	C	★★
22	"If" / How Many	B	★★★
23	"If" / Could Be True	C	★★★

Game 1: Chemistry Class Lab Sessions

Step 1: Overview

Situation: Six lab assistants scheduled in chemistry lab sessions across three days, with one morning and one afternoon session each day

Entities: Six lab assistants—Julio, Kevin, Lan, Nessa, Olivia, Rebecca

Action: Strict Sequencing. Your task is to assign each assistant to either a morning or afternoon slot on one of three days (Wednesday, Thursday, and Friday).

Limitations: Each lab assistant will be assigned to exactly one lab session. There are six assistants and six sessions. "Each session is led by a different lab assistant," so there will be no empty slots, and no person will be left out.

Step 2: Sketch

Create a table with the days across the top and two dashes underneath each to represent the morning and the afternoon sessions. List the entities across the top.

```
      J  K  L  N  O  R
      Wed  Thu  Fri
AM    ___  ___  ___
PM    ___  ___  ___
```

Step 3: Rules

Rule 1 places Kevin and Rebecca on the same day. This can't be placed into the sketch yet; just jot it out:

$$\frac{K}{R} \text{ or } \frac{R}{K}$$

Rule 2 says that Lan and Olivia are on different days. This also cannot be placed directly in the sketch, so jot it out:

$$\text{NOT } \frac{L}{O}$$
$$\text{NOT } \frac{O}{L}$$

Rule 3 puts Nessa in the afternoon. Write "N" parallel to the afternoon. Use an arrow pointing toward the row to make the impact of the rule clearer.

Rule 4 is a loose sequencing rule, putting Julio's assignment on an earlier day than Olivia's. Jot this out as "J … O" right below the table of days.

At this point, your sketch will appear as follows:

```
      J  K  L  N  O  R
      Wed  Thu  Fri
AM    ___  ___  ___
PM    ___  ___  ___  ←N
```

$$\frac{K}{R} \text{ or } \frac{R}{K} \quad \text{NOT } \frac{L}{O} \quad \text{NOT } \frac{O}{L} \quad J...O$$

Step 4: Deductions

Rule 1 provides you with a Block of Entities. Kevin's and Rebecca's sessions will take up one entire day. Rule 4, meanwhile, reveals that Julio's session and Olivia's sessions will occupy the other two days, with Olivia's session on a day after Julio's. Therefore, the three days, not necessarily in this order, will consist of the following:

$$\frac{K/R}{R/K} \quad \frac{J}{U} \cdots \frac{O/}{/O}$$

Duplications provide further deductions. Olivia is duplicated in Rules 2 and 4, with Rule 2 stating that Lan and Olivia are on different days. This means that the only place left for Lan's assignment is on Julio's day, leaving Nessa's assignment to take the afternoon session on Olivia's day. You now know that the three days, not necessarily in this order, will consist of the following:

$$\frac{K/R}{R/K} \quad \frac{J/L}{L/J} \cdots \frac{O}{N}$$

Now, think about how these blocks can fit into the sketch. Julio's session must occur some day before Olivia's, so Julio cannot be assigned a Friday lab session. Turning this negative deduction into a positive one reveals that Julio must be given a session on either Wednesday or Thursday. This leads to Limited Options. When a Block of Entities fits into a sketch in only two ways, draw out both to have a more complete Master Sketch.

First, if Julio is on Wednesday, you have Option I:

```
           Wed  Thu  Fri
Opt. I     J/L  ___  ___
           L/J  ___  ___
```

Second, if Julio is on Thursday, you have Option II:

```
           Wed  Thu  Fri
Opt. II    ___  J/L  ___
           ___  L/J  ___
```

Option I cannot be filled out any further. You know that between Thursday and Friday, one day will have Kevin and Rebecca and the other will have Olivia and Nessa, but not which is which. Leave this for now. (You may realize that Option I can be broken down into two suboptions—one with Kevin and Rebecca on Thursday and the other with Kevin and Rebecca on Friday. Writing out these suboptions is not necessary, but it may be helpful if you notice and sketch it quickly.)

Option II, however, leads to further deductions. With Julio's session on Thursday, the only place left for Olivia is Friday. Further, since Olivia is paired with Nessa, Nessa takes Friday afternoon (Rule 3), and Olivia takes Friday morning. This leaves Kevin and Rebecca for Wednesday.

The Master Sketch for the two options should look something like this:

```
        Wed  Thu  Fri
Opt. I   J/L  ___  ___        ┌─┐ ⮌ ┌───┐
         L/J  ___  ___        │O│ ╱ │K/R│
                              │N│   │R/K│
                              └─┘   └───┘

        Wed  Thu  Fri
Opt. II  K/R  J/L   O
         R/K  L/J   N
```

Step 5: Questions

1. (E) Acceptability

Use each rule to eliminate the answer choice that violates it. **(C)** violates Rule 1 because Kevin and Rebecca are on different days. **(D)** violates Rule 2 by putting Lan and Olivia on the same day. **(A)** violates Rule 3 by putting Nessa's session in the morning. Finally, **(B)** violates Rule 4 by putting Olivia's session on a day prior to Julio's.

Circle **(E)** and move along.

2. (E) "If" / Must Be True

The question stem condition that Lan is not on Wednesday can be met only in Option II, with Lan on Thursday. It is clear from your Option II sketch that Julio is the other person to lead a Thursday session, so **(E)** is correct.

(A) is incorrect because, in Option II, Rebecca is on Wednesday. **(B)** is incorrect because, in Option II, Olivia is on Friday. **(C)** is incorrect because, in Option II, Nessa is on Friday. **(D)** is incorrect because, in Option II, Kevin is on Wednesday.

3. (B) "If" / Complete and Accurate List

The "If" clause in this question stem places Kevin's session one day before Nessa's. This can take place only in Option I because, in Option II, Kevin's session is two days before Nessa's. Redraw your Option I sketch, placing Kevin's block on Thursday and Nessa's on Friday. It's clear who will teach each day:

```
        Wed  Thu  Fri
Opt. I   J/L  K/R   O
         L/J  R/K   N
```

The only lab assistants who could lead the Thursday afternoon session are Kevin and Rebecca, so **(B)** is correct. All of the other answer choices place an unacceptable person on Thursday.

4. (A) "If" / Could Be True EXCEPT

"Could be true EXCEPT" means that the right answer must be false.

The new "If" condition places Julio and Kevin in morning sessions. This could happen in either option, so redraw both of them, plugging Julio and Kevin into morning slots. In Option I, with Julio leading the Wednesday morning session, Lan takes Wednesday afternoon. Kevin is assigned to either the Thursday morning or Friday morning session. In Option II, Julio's being on Thursday morning means that Lan is on Thursday afternoon. Likewise, in Option II, with Kevin on Wednesday morning (per the "If" condition), Rebecca is on Wednesday afternoon:

```
        Wed  Thu  Fri
Opt. I    J   ___  ___        ⮌
          L   ___  ___        ┌─┐ ╱ ┌─┐
                              │K│   │O│
                              │R│   │N│
                              └─┘   └─┘

        Wed  Thu  Fri
Opt. II   K    J    O
          R    L    N
```

Looking at these two mini sketches, it is clear that **(A)** is false; Lan is always in the afternoon. That makes **(A)** the correct answer in this "could be true EXCEPT" question.

The four incorrect answers all could be true. **(B)** could be true in Option II. **(C)** and **(E)** are possible in either option. **(D)** could be true in Option I.

5. (C) "If" / How Many

Assigning Julio to Thursday afternoon can take place only in Option II. Redraw the Option II sketch and place Julio on Thursday afternoon. This forces Lan to take Thursday morning. The other entities remain unchanged:

```
        Wed  Thu  Fri
Opt. II  K/R   L    O
         R/K   J    N
```

This sketch clearly shows that, in addition to Julio's assignment, three other assistants' exact assignments are also known: Lan on Thursday morning, Olivia on Friday morning, and Nessa on Friday afternoon. The right answer is therefore **(C)**, three.

Beware of the tempting wrong answer **(D)**. While four assistants' positions are known, the question stem asks for assistants *other than* Julio.

KAPLAN

Game 2: Shopping Center Businesses

Step 1: Overview

Situation: Seven businesses in a shopping center arranged in a straight row

Entities: Seven businesses—an optometrist, a pharmacy, two restaurants, a shoe store, a toy store, a veterinarian

Action: Strict Sequencing. Your task is to assign each business to a space, from 1 through 7.

Limitations: "One in each space" tells you each business will be assigned to exactly one space. The only twist is that there are two restaurants.

Step 2: Sketch

Draw seven dashes, one for each slot. Write out the numbers 1 through 7 below the slots. List the entities across the top. To account for the two restaurants, remember to list "R R" among the entity abbreviations.

```
       O P R R S T V
    ___ ___ ___ ___ ___ ___ ___
     1   2   3   4   5   6   7
```

Step 3: Rules

Rule 1 says that the pharmacy is at one end of the row and one of the restaurants is at the other end. This leads to only two possibilities. Either the pharmacy is in space 1 and a restaurant is in space 7, or a restaurant is in space 1 and the pharmacy in space 7. This creates Limited Options, so draw them both out. In Option I, put the pharmacy in space 1 and a restaurant in space 7. In Option II, put a restaurant in space 1 and the pharmacy in space 7.

```
            O P R R S T V
Opt. I   P  ___ ___ ___ ___ ___  R
         1   2   3   4   5   6   7

Opt. II  R  ___ ___ ___ ___ ___  P
         1   2   3   4   5   6   7
```

Rule 2 says that the two restaurants must be separated by at least two businesses. In Option I, this means a restaurant cannot be in spaces 5 or 6. In Option II, a restaurant cannot be in spaces 2 or 3. List out these negatives below the slots:

```
            O P R R S T V
Opt. I   P  ___ ___ ___ R̶ R̶  R
         1   2   3   4   5   6   7

Opt. II  R  ___ ___ ___ ___ ___  P
         1   2   3   4   5   6   7
            R̶   R̶
```

Rule 3 places the pharmacy next to the optometrist or veterinarian. Since the pharmacy is already in your sketch, draw this rule directly into the sketch as well. In Option I, the optometrist or veterinarian must be in space 2; in Option II, the optometrist or veterinarian must be in space 6.

```
            O P R R S T V
Opt. I   P  O/V ___ ___ R̶ R̶  R
         1   2   3   4   5   6   7

Opt. II  R  ___ ___ ___ ___ O/V P
         1   2   3   4   5   6   7
            R̶   R̶
```

Rule 4 creates a negative block—the toy store cannot be next to the veterinarian. This can't be fit into the sketch yet, so jot it beneath the framework:

```
            O P R R S T V
Opt. I   P  O/V ___ ___ R̶ R̶  R
         1   2   3   4   5   6   7

Opt. II  R  ___ ___ ___ ___ O/V P
         1   2   3   4   5   6   7
            R̶   R̶

                NOT T V
                NOT V T
```

Step 4: Deductions

Run through the BLEND checklist to look for any more deductions. You've accounted for the Blocks of Entities, with the pharmacist next to either the optometrist or veterinarian in both options. You created Limited Options based on Rule 1. You placed the Established Entities—P and one R—in both options. The Numbers are accounted for in this game; you won't get any simpler than one business per space. You've accounted for the Duplications—the restaurants (Rules 1 and 2) and the pharmacy (Rules 1 and 3)—through the Limited Options sketch you've been building all along.

Since BLEND reveals nothing else to sketch or deduce, the sketch is complete. Move on to the questions.

The Master Sketch for the two options should look something like this:

```
            O P R R S T V
Opt. I   P  O/V ___ ___ R̶ R̶  R
         1   2   3   4   5   6   7

Opt. II  R  ___ ___ ___ ___ O/V P
         1   2   3   4   5   6   7
            R̶   R̶

                NOT T V
                NOT V T
```

Step 5: Questions

6. (E) Acceptability

Use each rule to eliminate the answer choice that violates it. **(C)** violates Rule 1 by not putting the pharmacy in space 1 or space 7. **(B)** violates Rule 2 by not separating the restaurants by at least two businesses. **(D)** violates Rule 3 by not putting the pharmacy next to either the optometrist or the veterinarian. Finally, **(A)** violates Rule 4 by putting the toy store and veterinarian next to each other.

Circle **(E)** and move along.

7. (A) "If" / Could Be True

The new condition, placing the shoe store in space 2, can only work in Option II. Draw a mini sketch by recopying Option II and put the shoe store in space 2.

Opt. II | R | S | __ | __ | __ | O/V | P
| 1 | 2 | 3 | 4 | 5 | 6 | 7
Ŕ (under 3)

The question asks for what could be true, so any answer choice that is possible is correct. **(A)** could be true because putting the optometrist in space 5 allows the veterinarian to take space 6, which separates it from the toy store in accordance with Rule 4. Since the restaurants must be separated by at least two businesses, the second restaurant lands in space 4, with the toy store in space 3. This arrangement could be true and is therefore correct.

Opt. II | R | S | T | R | O | V | P
| 1 | 2 | 3 | 4 | 5 | 6 | 7

(B) is incorrect because in Option II, a restaurant is in space 1. **(C)** is incorrect because in Option II, a restaurant in space 3 would place the two restaurants too close together, violating Rule 2. **(D)** is incorrect because in Option II, the optometrist or veterinarian must be in space 6. Finally, **(E)** places the veterinarian in space 4, which in Option II would force the optometrist to fill space 6 next to the pharmacist. This cannot work, because it leaves only spaces 3 and 5 for the toy store, and either of those spaces would be next to the veterinarian in violation of Rule 4.

8. (C) "If" / Must Be True

The "If" clause places the veterinarian in space 5, something that can occur in either option. Redraw both options in your mini sketch and plug in the new condition.

Placing the veterinarian in space 5 triggers Rule 1; the optometrist will be next to the pharmacist in both sketches.

In Option I, the only businesses left to place are the toy store, shoe store, and the second restaurant. The toy store must be placed in space 3 to separate it from the veterinarian. This means the second restaurant can only fit in space 4 in order to follow Rule 2. The shoe store takes the only available space, space 6.

In Option II, the second restaurant can only fit in space 4 in order to follow Rule 2. That leaves spaces 2 and 3 for the toy store and shoe store, which can go in either order.

Opt. I | P | O | T | R | V | S | R
| 1 | 2 | 3 | 4 | 5 | 6 | 7

Opt. II | R | T/S | S/T | R | V | O | P
| 1 | 2 | 3 | 4 | 5 | 6 | 7

Use this mini sketch to evaluate the choices; the right answer must be true in both of them. **(C)** is correct because in both options, a restaurant must be in space 4.

(A), **(B)**, **(D)**, and **(E)** are all incorrect because each could occur in only one of the two mini sketches and, therefore, *could* be true but do not have to be true.

9. (D) "If" / Must Be True

The condition placing the optometrist next to the shoe store creates a Block of Entities:

[O S] or [S O]

This block can fit in both options, so draw a mini sketch with both options displayed.

Since the optometrist–shoe store block takes up two spaces, there will be limits on how it can fit. One possibility is that the optometrist sits next to the pharmacy. But this creates difficulties in both options. The three remaining spaces would need to hold the veterinarian, the toy store, and the second restaurant. To abide by Rule 2, the second restaurant would have to take space 4. But this would leave the veterinarian next to the toy store in violation of Rule 4. The optometrist cannot be next to the pharmacy under this question's condition.

Opt. I | P | O | S | R | T/V | V/T | R
| 1 | 2 | 3 | 4 | 5 | 6 | 7
unacceptable

Opt. II | R | T/V | V/T | R | S | O | P
| 1 | 2 | 3 | 4 | 5 | 6 | 7

Thus, the veterinarian will have to take the space next to the pharmacy. Consider the remaining entities. You need to place the toy store, the second restaurant, and the newly formed optometrist–shoe store block. The toy store cannot be next to the veterinarian. Neither can the optometrist–shoe store block because the only open spaces would, in that case, place the second restaurant too close to the fixed restaurant on the end, violating Rule 2. So, in both options, the second restaurant must be next to the veterinarian.

Opt. I | P | V | R | __ | __ | __ | R
| 1 | 2 | 3 | 4 | 5 | 6 | 7

Opt. II | R | __ | __ | __ | R | V | P
| 1 | 2 | 3 | 4 | 5 | 6 | 7

At this point, it doesn't matter how you place the toy store and the optometrist–shoe store block because, in any event, the answer to this question will be the same. If in Option I, for example, the optometrist–shoe store block takes spaces 4 and 5 and the toy store takes space 6, the two businesses on either side of the optometrist–shoe store block are the toy store and a restaurant. If, on the other hand, in Option I the optometrist–shoe store block takes spaces 5 and 6 while the toy store takes space 4, the answer is the same: the two businesses on either side of the optometrist–shoe store block are the toy store and a restaurant. Spaces 2, 3, and 4 in Option II offer exactly the same alternatives. In every acceptable scenario under this question's conditions, the businesses on either side of the optometrist–shoe store block are the toy store and one restaurant, and **(D)** is correct.

(A), **(B)**, **(C)**, and **(E)** are all incorrect because, as the mini sketch for this question demonstrates, only a restaurant and the toy store can surround the optometrist–shoe store block created by the question stem.

10. (B) "If" / Must Be True

The condition placing the shoe store in space 4 works in both options, so redraw mini sketches for each.

In Option I, the unfixed restaurant must be separated from the restaurant in space 7 by at least two businesses (Rule 2), but it cannot be next to the pharmacist (Rule 3), so it can only end up in space 3. This leaves spaces 5 and 6 empty, but the toy store and veterinarian cannot be placed in adjacent spaces (Rule 4). Therefore, the veterinarian must end up in space 2 next to the pharmacist, while the toy store and optometrist occupy spaces 5 and 6 in either order.

In Option II, the same rules apply in mirror-image fashion. The unfixed restaurant must be separated from the restaurant in space 1 by at least two spaces (Rule 2), but it cannot be next to the pharmacist (Rule 3), so it ends up in space 5. This leaves spaces 2 and 3 empty, but the toy store and veterinarian cannot be placed in adjacent spaces (Rule 4). Therefore, the veterinarian must take space 6 next to the pharmacist, while the toy store and optometrist occupy spaces 2 and 3 in either order.

Opt. I	P	V	R	S	O/T	T/O	R
	1	2	3	4	5	6	7

Opt. II	R	O/T	T/O	S	R	V	P
	1	2	3	4	5	6	7

The correct answer must be true. In both options, the pharmacist is next to the veterinarian, so **(B)** is the correct answer.

(A), **(C)**, and **(D)** are possible in either option, but they don't *have* to be true. **(E)** must be false under this question's condition.

11. (D) Rule Substitution

This question asks for a rule that would have the same effect on the game as Rule 2, which states that the restaurants must be separated by at least two other businesses.

To solve, notice that the restaurant is a duplicated entity. It's also mentioned in Rule 1, which puts the pharmacist and one restaurant at opposite ends of the seven available spaces (with five businesses between them). If the unfixed restaurant must be at least two spaces away from the fixed restaurant at one end, then by default, the unfixed restaurant can be no further than two spaces from the pharmacist at the opposite end. This is exactly what **(D)** states, and it is therefore the right answer.

To solve the Equivalent Substitute Rule question, you can also always eliminate any answer choice that goes farther than the

original rule, any answer that doesn't go far enough, and any answer that misses the relevant restriction altogether.

(A) doesn't go far enough. It's true that a restaurant always ends up in spaces 3, 4, or 5, but this rule doesn't take into account the Limited Options. It does not preclude the restaurants from being in spaces 5 and 7 in Option II or in spaces 1 and 3 in Option I; in either of those scenarios, the restaurants would have only one business between them.

(B) goes too far. The mini sketch for the previous question for example, illustrates that the restaurant on the end can be adjacent only to the toy store, so **(B)** doesn't substitute for Rule 2.

(C) doesn't go far enough. With the rule stated in this choice, nothing precludes the two restaurants from having only one business between them, *either* the toy store or the veterinarian.

(E) goes too far. The mini sketch for the previous question for example, illustrates that the optometrist can be next to the shoe store, so **(E)** does not replicate the restrictions in Rule 2.

Game 3: Software Company Sales Zones

Step 1: Overview

Situation: A software company assigning its sales representatives to one of three sales zones

Entities: Seven representatives—Kim, Mahr, Parra, Quinn, Stuckey, Tiao, Udall

Action: Distribution. Your task is to assign each sales representative to a single zone.

Limitations: Each representative is assigned to only one zone. Note there is no limit on how many (or how few) representatives can or will be assigned to each zone.

Step 2: Sketch

Since this is a Distribution game, list the entities and draw a table with three columns, one for each of the three zones. Label the columns 1, 2, and 3. Since you don't know how many spots are open within each zone, hold off on drawing in slots until you can determine more.

K M P Q S T U
1   2   3

Step 3: Rules

Rule 1 places either Parra or Tiao, but not both, in Zone 1. Add a slot for P/T under Zone 1. To designate that you can't have both, add NEVER PT off to the side of your sketch. One will always be in Zone 1, the other will not.

Rule 2 matches Rule 1. Add a slot for T/U under Zone 2 and add NEVER TU to your list of "impossible pairs":

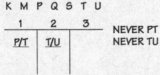

Rule 3 forms a Block of Entities—P and Q—that must be together. Because you haven't placed P or Q yet, record the block next to your sketch:

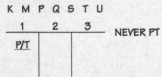

Rule 4 forms another Block of Entities. S and U also must be together. Add this next to your sketch:

Rule 5 provides number restrictions. Zone 3 will always have more sales representatives assigned to it than Zone 2. Shorthand the rule as "z3 > z2." Make this rule more concrete by considering its implications for each zone. Because Rule 2 has placed at least one sales representative in Zone 2, add two slots beneath Zone 3 to designate that it must contain *at least* two sales representatives. Consider the rule's impact on Zone 2, too. Zone 2 can never be assigned more than two sales representatives—if Zone 2 had three or more sales representatives, then Zone 3 would have to have four or more, and there would be an insufficient number of representatives to place T or P in Zone 1.

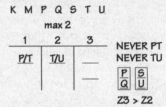

Kim and Mahr are Floaters—they don't appear in any of the rules.

Step 4: Deductions

The placement of the blocks—PQ and SU—will be restricted by the Numbers Restrictions of the game. You'll need two open slots in any zone to which you assign either pair. In Zone 2, the PQ block is impossible because there's only room for one additional sales representative after T or U is assigned to that group. Rule out the PQ block under Zone 2.

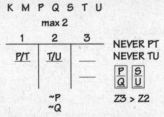

The first two rules are either/or rules: either one scenario or the other, but not both, will happen. These rules are usually strong indicators that Limited Options will be beneficial. Here, since both either/or rules reference Tiao, you can set up a scenario with three options: (I) Tiao is assigned to Zone 1 and Parra is not; (II) Tiao is assigned to Zone 2 and Udall is not; or (III) Tiao is assigned to neither Zone 1 nor Zone 2. The third option leaves Parra in Zone 1 and Udall in Zone 2 and places Tiao in the only available zone, Zone 3.

Don't fret if you didn't immediately set up these options or if you set up Limited Options based on only one of the either/or rules. Logic games in which three options might be useful are rare on the LSAT. Remember, though, that time you spent working on Steps 1–4 of the Logic Games Method will pay off during Step 5—the questions.

Now, with a few Established Entities in each Limited Option, look for and build in additional information about duplicated entities.

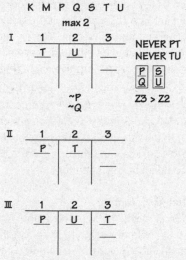

In Option I, Tiao is assigned to Zone 1, so Parra cannot be. Udall is assigned to Zone 2 and will be joined by Stuckey (Rule 4). With the maximum of two sales representatives assigned to Zone 2, use double lines to close that zone. As a result, the PQ block can be assigned to neither Zone 1 nor Zone 2 and will take two slots in Zone 3. Remember that Zone 3 must always have more representatives assigned to it than Zone 2 (Rule 5). Add another slot to Zone 3. At least three sales representatives, including at least one (and maybe both) of the Floaters—Kim or Mahr—will be assigned to Zone 3.

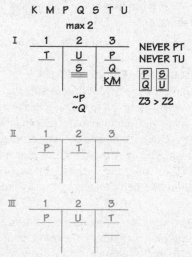

In Option II, Tiao is assigned to Zone 2, and Parra is assigned to Zone 1. Parra, as always, is joined by Quinn in Zone 1 (Rule 3). Tiao's assignment to Zone 2 prohibits Udall (Rule 2) and, in turn, Stuckey (Rule 4) from Zone 2. The SU block will have to be assigned to either Zone 1 or Zone 3.

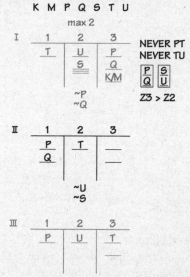

Option III yields the most deductions. Tiao is assigned to Zone 3. Parra is assigned with Quinn (Rule 3) to Zone 1. Udall, accompanied by Stuckey (Rule 4), is assigned to Zone 2. With two representatives assigned to Zone 2, three representatives must be assigned to Zone 3 (Rule 5). The remaining two representatives—Kim and Mahr—must be assigned to Zone 3 with Tiao.

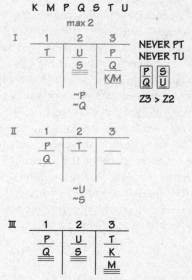

The Master Sketch for all three options should look something like this:

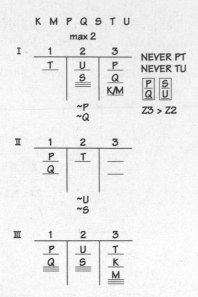

Step 5: Questions

12. (B) Acceptability

Check each rule and eliminate any choice(s) that violates it. **(D)** violates Rule 1 because neither Parra nor Tiao is assigned to Zone 1. **(E)** violates Rule 2 because neither Tiao nor Udall is assigned to Zone 2. **(A)** violates Rule 3 by separating Parra and Quinn. Finally, **(C)** violates Rule 4 because it separates Stuckey and Udall.

Circle **(B)** and move on.

13. (E) "If" / Could Be True

When working with Limited Options, use the "If" clause to guide your prepResearch. For Zone 1 to have more sales representatives than Zone 3 has, Zone 1 will have to be assigned four representatives and Zone 3 two representatives. (Were Zone 1 to have four representatives and Zone 3 two representatives, there would be no representative for Zone 2 in violation of Rule 2. Were Zone 1 to have three representatives and Zone 3 two representatives, Zone 2 would have two representatives, violating Rule 5.) The acceptable situation—Zone 1 with four representatives and Zone 3 with two—is possible only in Option II. A mini sketch reveals that Parra, Quinn, and two others will be assigned to Zone 1; Tiao will be the only entity assigned to Zone 2; and two entities will be assigned to Zone 3.

The correct answer could be true, while the four incorrect answers must be false. **(E)** is the winner here. Udall and Stuckey could be assigned to Zone 3.

(A) and **(B)** are impossible here, as this stem's "If" condition dictates that Tiao alone is assigned to Zone 2. **(C)** and **(D)** are always false in Option II, in which Parra and Tiao are assigned to Zones 1 and 2, respectively.

14. (A) Must Be False

The correct answer must be false in all three options. Notice that each answer choice provides a pair of entities and a specific zone. Number restrictions make **(A)** demonstrably false. Option II is the only one in which Stuckey can be assigned to Zone 1. Adding Stuckey (and Udall, per Rule 4) along with Kim would put five sales reps in Zone 1. This means that Rule 5 would be violated, since now Zones 2 and 3 would have only one representative each. **(A)** is correct.

The remaining choices are all possible. **(B)**, **(C)**, and **(D)** are possible in Option II, in which Zone 3 could be assigned to sales reps Udall and Stuckey along with either Kim or Mahr (or both, for that matter). **(E)** is also possible in Option II. If four sales reps are assigned to Zone 1, Parra, Stuckey, Quinn, and Udall could all be assigned together.

15. (A) Partial Acceptability

This question asks you for a complete and accurate list of sales reps that could be assigned to Zone 3. The word *could* indicates that you're looking for a complete, acceptable assignment for only one of the three zones: Zone 3.

Test **(A)** against the options. Assigning Kim and Mahr as the only sales reps in Zone 3 could only be achieved in Option II. That would place Stuckey and Udall in Zone 1 with P and Q and leave Tiao alone in Zone 3. That's acceptable, so **(A)** is correct.

(B) is incomplete, and **(D)** is inaccurate. Tiao can only be assigned to Zone 3 in Option III. There, the complete and accurate list of assignments for Zone 3 is Kim, Mahr, and Tiao.

(C) is incomplete. Parra and Quinn can only be assigned to Zone 3 in Option I, but that option requires at least one additional representative to join them.

(E) is not acceptable in any of the three options.

16. (D) Must Be False (CANNOT Be True)

This question asks you to identify the sales representative that can never be assigned to the same zone as Quinn. Paired with Parra (Rule 3), Quinn has been placed in each of our options. Notice that **(D)** names the only other entity affirmatively placed in all three options. Since Tiao is never assigned to the same zone as the PQ block, **(D)** is the correct answer. Quinn and Tiao can never be assigned to the same zone.

(A) and **(B)**, Kim and Mahr, name the Floaters in this game and can therefore be eliminated. Either Kim or Mahr could be paired with Quinn in Option I.

(C) and **(E)** can be eliminated because the Stuckey/Udall block, could be paired together with Parra and Quinn in Option II.

17. Item Removed from Scoring
This question was removed from scoring and was not published when the test was released.

18. (A) "If" / Could Be True
Start with the information provided by the new "If" in the question stem. Pairing Mahr and Stuckey together means that Mahr and the SU block must all be in the same zone. That can only take place in Option II and, because of Number Restrictions, only in Zone 3. Redraw the option:

```
        K M P Q S T U
   II    1    2    3
         P    T    U
         Q         S
                   M
              K?
```

Only Kim remains unassigned. As a Floater, Kim could be assigned to any of the three zones. So **(A)**, assigning Kim to Zone 2, could be true.

(B) and **(D)** must be false. Your mini sketch of Option II requires that Mahr, Stuckey, and Udall be assigned to Zone 3. **(C)** is impossible as well; because you're working in Option II, Parra must be assigned to Zone 1. Finally, **(E)** also must be false; Tiao must be assigned to Zone 2 in Option II, contrary to **(E)**.

Game 4: Wayne & Zara's Piano Solos

Step 1: Overview

Situation: Two pianists deciding the order in which they'll perform and the type of music they'll play in each solo for an upcoming recital

Entities: Two pianists—Wayne and Zara—and two types of music—modern and traditional

Action: Sequencing/Matching Hybrid. Your task is to determine the order in which the two pianists will perform and to assign the type of music to be played during each solo.

Limitations: One pianist will perform each solo, one after the other, and each solo must be either a modern or a traditional piece.

Step 2: Sketch

Since this is a Sequencing/Matching Hybrid, create two lists, one for the performers' order and one below it for the type of piece performed in each solo:

```
          1    2    3    4    5
W/Z     ___  ___  ___  ___  ___

mod/trad ___ ___  ___  ___  ___
```

Step 3: Rules

Rule 1 states that the third solo is a traditional piece. Build this directly into your sketch:

```
          1    2    3     4    5
W/Z     ___  ___  ___  ___  ___

mod/trad ___  ___  trad ___  ___
```

Rule 2 states that *exactly* two traditional pieces are consecutive. This creates a Block of Entities that must appear exactly once in the game. Make sure to depict this in a way that indicates that a modern piece must appear in any space right before or after this block. Since the block of two traditional pieces could be in spaces 1 and 2 or spaces 4 and 5, don't mistake this for a block of four entities.

$$\text{mod}\ /\boxed{\text{trad}\ \text{trad}}/\ \text{mod}$$

Rule 3 limits the fourth solo to either Wayne performing a traditional piece or Zara performing a modern piece. This gives rise to a Limited Options sketch:

```
Opt. I    1    2    3    4    5
W/Z     ___  ___  ___   W   ___

mod/trad ___  ___  trad trad ___


Opt. II   1    2    3    4    5
W/Z     ___  ___  ___   Z   ___

mod/trad ___  ___  trad mod  ___
```

$$\text{mod}\ /\boxed{\text{trad}\ \text{trad}}/\ \text{mod}$$

You'll fill in much more under Step 4 but, for now, sketch out the remaining rules.

Rule 4 requires that two different people perform the second and fifth solos. Jot this down:

$$\frac{2}{W}\ \frac{5}{Z}\ \text{ or }\ \frac{2}{Z}\ \frac{5}{W}$$

Rule 5 states that Wayne must perform a modern piece before any traditional piece is played. So you must see a traditional piece before the first time that Wayne plays a traditional piece.

```
              first
              W
Never       ────
         trad ... mod
```

Step 4: Deductions

Now, see what further deductions you can make about each of the Limited Options introduced by Rule 3.

In Option I, the third and fourth pieces are already designated as traditional. According to Rule 2, therefore, the second and fifth pieces must be modern. Moreover, Wayne must play a modern piece prior to any traditional piece being performed, so the first solo must be modern (whether it is performed by Wayne or Zara). Finally, Wayne must perform at least one (and could perform both) of solos 1 and 2.

```
Opt. I   1    2    3    4    5
        ↙W↘
       ___  ___  ___   W   ___
       mod  mod  trad trad mod
```

In Option II, the second solo must be assigned a traditional piece since solos 2 and 3 are the only ones that could contain the block of traditional pieces required by Rule 2. To account for Rule 5, Wayne will need to perform a modern piece in solo 1. No additional deductions are available here.

```
Opt. II   1    2    3    4    5
          W   ___  ___   Z   ___
         mod  trad trad mod ___
```

As you work with these options, remember Rule 4's requirement that solos 2 and 5 have different performers.

The Master Sketch for the two options should look something like this:

```
Opt. I   1    2    3    4    5
             ↙W↘             W
        ___  ___  ___  ___  ___
        mod  mod  trad trad mod


Opt. II  1    2    3    4    5
         W              Z
        ___  ___  ___  ___  ___
        mod  trad trad mod
```

$$\frac{2}{W}\frac{5}{Z} \text{ or } \frac{2}{Z}\frac{5}{W}$$

Step 5: Questions

19. (C) Partial Acceptability

The Limited Options sketch makes evaluating the answer choices here quick and easy. In Option I, the traditional pieces could be solos 3 and 4. In Option II, the traditional pieces could be solos 2 and 3 or solos 2, 3, and 5. The correct answer will have one of those three acceptable groups. Only **(C)**, which matches the Option I traditional pieces, is acceptable.

20. (A) Minimum

This question requires you to determine the minimum number of traditional pieces that Wayne must play. Use the Limited Options sketch to evaluate the choices. In Option I, Wayne must perform one traditional piece (solo 4) but need not perform the other traditional piece. That allows you to eliminate **(C)**, **(D)**, and **(E)**. (You may have noticed that **(E)** would be impossible in either option, since a maximum of three traditional pieces can be performed in any case.)

Now, check Option II. There, Wayne is not required to play any traditional pieces. If Zara plays solo 2 there, Wayne could perform another modern piece as solo 5. Thus, Wayne could play no traditional pieces at all, making **(A)** the correct answer. The arrangement matching **(A)** looks like this:

```
Opt. II  1    2    3    4    5
         W    Z    Z    Z    W
        ___  ___  ___  ___  ___
        mod  trad trad mod  mod
```

21. (C) "If" / Must Be True

On a "must be true" question with Limited Options, the correct choice must be true in *both* options. Start by adding the new information to both options. In both cases, Wayne must perform solos 1 and 2 under this question's "If" condition. Whenever Wayne performs solo 2, Rule 4 requires that Zara play solo 5. Place Zara in solo 5 in both options as well.

```
Opt. I   1    2    3    4    5
         W    W         W    Z
        ___  ___  ___  ___  ___
        mod  mod  trad trad mod


Opt. II  1    2    3    4    5
         W    W              Z    Z
        ___  ___  ___  ___  ___
        mod  trad trad mod
```

Now, check each answer choice until you find one that must be true in both options. **(A)** must be false; Wayne performs solo 1 in both options here. Eliminate it. **(B)** represents something that could be true but not something that must be true. Wayne could perform solo 3 in either option, but so could Zara; eliminate this answer. **(C)** is correct because Zara must perform solo 5 in both options. On Test Day, stop here and move on to the next question.

For practice, check the remaining answer choices. **(D)** and **(E)** could be true, but they do not need to be true. In Option I, solo 2 is modern, but in Option II, it is traditional. Likewise, the fourth solo is a traditional piece in Option I, but it is modern in Option II.

22. (B) "If" / How Many

For solo 5 to be a traditional piece, you must use the arrangement in Option II. (In Option I, solo 5 is always modern.) Draw a mini sketch to illustrate this question's new "If" condition.

```
Opt. II  1    2    3    4    5
         W              Z
        ___  ___  ___  ___  ___
        mod  trad trad mod  trad
```

From this sketch, you can see that the performers for solos 1 and 4 are determined. But no additional rules or restrictions are triggered that would help you nail down the performers for solos 2, 3, or 5 with any certainty. **(B)** must be correct; you can determine the performers for exactly two solos.

23. (C) "If" / Could Be True

The new condition in this question assigns Wayne to solo 5 and has him perform a tradition piece. This can occur only in Option II, so account for this information in a mini sketch. In addition, designate Zara to solo 2 in order to abide by Rule 4.

```
Opt. II  1    2    3    4    5
         W    Z         Z    W
        ___  ___  ___  ___  ___
        mod  trad trad mod  trad
```

Only the performer for solo 3 is undetermined.

The correct answer could be true, meaning that all four wrong answers must be false. This sketch proves that **(C)** is correct. Notice that the correct answer to this Could Be True question involved the only slot in the entire sketch that is not determined.

Wayne performs solo 1, so **(A)** is incorrect. Solo 2 is a traditional piece performed by Zara, so eliminate **(B)** and **(D)**. Lastly, solo 4 is modern in this case, so **(E)** is also wrong.

Section IV: Logical Reasoning

Q#	Question Type	Correct	Difficulty
1	Flaw	A	★
2	Principle (Identify/Strengthen)	C	★
3	Assumption (Necessary)	E	★
4	Weaken	B	★
5	Main Point	B	★
6	Weaken	C	★
7	Assumption (Necessary)	B	★
8	Weaken	D	★★
9	Main Point	A	★★
10	Paradox	A	★★
11	Principle (Identify/Strengthen)	B	★
12	Strengthen	A	★★
13	Parallel Reasoning	D	★
14	Principle (Apply/Inference)	E	★
15	Paradox	B	★★★
16	Strengthen	C	★
17	Assumption (Sufficient)	E	★★★
18	Paradox	E	★★★
19	Point at Issue	D	★★
20	Assumption (Sufficient)	D	★★★
21	Inference	D	★★★
22	Flaw	C	★★
23	Point at Issue	B	★★★
24	Parallel Flaw	D	★★★★
25	Flaw	E	★★
26	Main Point	B	★★

1. (A) Flaw

Step 1: Identify the Question Type

The phrase "most accurately describes a flaw" identifies this as a Flaw question. You'll need to break down the author's argument, identifying his conclusion and evidence and determining his assumption. Then, you must evaluate how the author's reasoning goes wrong. Remember to keep an eye out for common flaw types.

Step 2: Untangle the Stimulus

The author concludes that most people voted against the national referendum even though the official results showed 80 percent of voters were in favor of the referendum. The author believes the official results are incorrect because everyone the author knows voted against the proposal.

Step 3: Make a Prediction

The author makes the common error of failing to consider whether the evidence is representative of the conclusion. Everyone the author knows voted against the referendum, but the author likely knows only a small portion of all the voters. Moreover, the author's acquaintances may well be concentrated in a particular political position or party. Your prediction is clear: the argument is flawed because the author's sample may not represent voters in general.

Step 4: Evaluate the Answer Choices

(A) correctly identifies the logical flaw in general terms that match the prediction.

(B) identifies a flaw that does not apply to this argument. The author does not expect anyone to assume the national results are wrong without any evidence that they are. The author provided evidence—his experience with other voters—to support the position that the results are wrong.

(C) describes a flaw that cannot apply to this argument. The author did not attack the people who released the official results. Instead, the author used his experience with other voters to attack the results.

(D) is Outside the Scope. The author's argument focuses only on the results of the referendum. How people should have voted is not relevant to the scope of this argument.

(E) misidentifies the source of the problem in the evidence. The author does not claim that most people believe the results are wrong. Rather, the author believes the results are wrong based on his experience with people who voted.

2. (C) Principle (Identify/Strengthen)

Step 1: Identify the Question Type

The word *principles* is a clear tip-off that this is a Principle question. In addition, this Principle question mimics the Strengthen question type, as evidenced by the phrase "most

helps to justify the Several of these tables printed out gray instead of black in the hard copy. Print page 326 to see which ones. argument," so attack it the same way you would a Strengthen question. Look for an answer that would make the editorialist's conclusion more likely to follow from her evidence. Just be sure the correct answer can support a broader application than the specific example cited in the argument.

Step 2: Untangle the Stimulus

The author recommends that information on the Internet be regulated. The author acknowledges that unregulated information is usually preferable, but she recognizes that misinformation on the Internet prevents users from knowing when information is accurate. This matters because accurate information is only useful if it can be distinguished from inaccurate information.

Step 3: Make a Prediction

The correct answer will strengthen the connection between the author's recommendation to regulate the Internet and the goal of being able to identify accurate information on the Internet. Since this is a Principle question, we will look for an answer with a broader application.

Step 4: Evaluate the Answer Choices

(C) correctly connects regulation with the ability to distinguish between accurate information and misinformation. This answer choice is also written in general terms, allowing it to serve as the basis for drawing conclusions about cases other than regulation of information on the Internet.

(A) is Extreme. The focus of the argument is regulation providing people with the ability to distinguish accurate information from misinformation. Claiming that people's access will always be restricted by regulation is not necessary for this argument.

(B) is a 180, the opposite of the correct answer. This answer choice discredits regulation as a way to identify accurate information.

(D) is a Distortion. The principle laid out in this choice doesn't account for the author's premise that accurate information needs to be "easily" distinguished from misinformation. Having access to a "vast array of misinformation" would mean making this distinction slower and more difficult.

(E) is a Distortion. The author stated that unregulated information is usually desirable. This answer choice distorts the author's position by claiming that useless, unregulated misinformation is more desirable than accurate, regulated information.

3. (E) Assumption (Necessary)

Step 1: Identify the Question Type

The phrase "an assumption on which the argument relies" identifies this as an Assumption question. In addition, the word *depends* indicates that you're looking for a necessary assumption, without which the conclusion cannot follow logically from the evidence. You can use the Denial Test to check or eliminate answers.

Step 2: Untangle the Stimulus

In this argument, the author concludes that the current club president acted appropriately when inviting Dr. Hines to speak without consulting other club members beforehand. To support this position, the author refers to the actions of a prior president who hired an accountant without consulting other club members beforehand.

Step 3: Make a Prediction

The author believes the current president acted appropriately by not consulting other club members because a prior president acted the same way in hiring an accountant. The author of this argument makes two related assumptions: (1) hiring an accountant is sufficiently similar to inviting a speaker, and (2) the prior president acted appropriately when taking action without consulting the other club members.

Step 4: Evaluate the Answer Choices

(E) correctly states that the prior president acted appropriately in hiring the accountant without first consulting other club members.

(A) doesn't add anything to the argument. This answer choice merely adds similar cases to the prior president's record. It adds to the evidence already provided without linking it in any necessary way to the author's conclusion. The author has already stated that the previous president acted without consulting other club members; an assumption necessary to the argument is that such action was proper.

(B) is Outside the Scope. The focus of the argument is whether the president's actions were appropriate or not. That other members expected to be consulted is not relevant.

(C) is Outside the Scope. The crux of this argument is whether the president behaved appropriately in extending the invitation. Whether Dr. Hines accepts the invitation has no bearing on the appropriateness of his having been invited in the first place.

(D) is a Distortion. The argument's author must assume that the president's discretion is roughly similar in both cases, since he is using the former president's hiring of the accountant to justify the current president's invitation to the speaker, Dr. Hines.

4. (B) Weaken

Step 1: Identify the Question Type

This question stem calls for an answer presenting a fact that would "undermine" the spokesperson's argument. This, then, is a Weaken question. Analyze the spokesperson's argument, determine her central assumption, and predict the kinds of facts that would cast doubt on that assumption.

Step 2: Untangle the Stimulus

The company spokesperson claims that the millions of Filterator X owners who are satisfied with the product's performance prove that the water filter removes chemical contaminants in significant amounts.

Step 3: Make a Prediction

To reach this conclusion from the evidence, the company spokesperson assumes that the millions of satisfied owners are able to determine that the filter does, in fact, significantly reduce the chemical contaminants in their water. The correct answer choice will attack this connection.

Step 4: Evaluate the Answer Choices

(B) is correct. This answer choice attacks the spokesperson's assumption that the claims of satisfied customers are actually evidence that the filter removes contaminants. If the statement in this answer choice is true, more than half of customers are unable to accurately assess the filter's effectiveness.

(A) is Outside the Scope. Evaluating the taste of the water is not relevant to evaluating the effectiveness of the filter at removing chemicals.

(C) is an Irrelevant Comparison. Comparing the likelihood that different groups will buy the filter is beside the point. The argument is clearly focused on the ability of the product to filter water.

(D) is Outside the Scope. The argument is concerned with the ability of the product to filter water. Whether Filterator X owners read the publication attacking the product has no bearing on the conclusion or evidence in the argument.

(E) is Outside the Scope. Even if *Household Products* consistently rates Filterator X negatively, this does not affect the ability of the product to filter water. The argument is centered on whether customer satisfaction is evidence of the product's ability to purify water.

5. (B) Main Point

Step 1: Identify the Question Type

The phrase "most accurately expresses the main point" identifies this Main Point question. Watch out for conclusion Keywords, which may indicate subsidiary conclusions, and be prepared to combine statements into a paraphrase of the author's main point. If necessary, use the One-Sentence Test.

Step 2: Untangle the Stimulus

The argument begins with a famous artist's claim that all great art imitates nature. The next sentence goes further and offers a result if this claim is true; in that case, "any music that is great art will imitate nature." The word [b]ut signals a contrast. The author offers a couple of perfunctory examples of music imitating nature to emphasize the contrary position. Following the contrasting examples, the author makes his final claim: most great music imitates nothing at all.

Step 3: Make a Prediction

To find the main point, you must break down the argument into its parts. The first two sentences provide the foundation for the analysis that follows: a famous artist's claim that all great art imitates nature. The implication of that claim is that all great music must imitate nature. Next, the author gives two examples of how music might meet the artist's criterion, but he asserts at the end that most great music imitates nothing at all. The author's point is to suggest a dilemma: either the artist is incorrect in stating her requirement for great art, *or* what we know as great music must not be great art.

Step 4: Evaluate the Answer Choices

(B) is correct. This answer mirrors the dilemma that ensues from accepting the artist's criterion for great art and trying to apply it to great music. The author's ultimate assertion—that most great music is not mimetic—produces one of the two results in (B) when applied to the artist's principle.

(A) is Extreme. This judgment of music is too strong to reflect the argument here. It's equally likely that the artist's principle is incorrect.

(C) is Outside the Scope. The argument is centered on music, not painting and sculpture, being great art. If (C) were true, it would raise an equally confounding dilemma—one parallel to, but distinct from, this argument's main point.

(D) is irrelevant. Neither the artist nor the author claims that great art must imitate all aspects of nature. It's unclear what effect this statement would have on the argument.

(E) is a 180. This would, one supposes, reflect the famous artist's position. The author takes exception to this by saying that most great music (the argument implies that great music has already been identified) imitates nothing.

6. (C) Weaken

Step 1: Identify the Question Type

This Weaken question requires you to identify the answer choice that provides information to counter Tamara's evidence. Since Tamara is the second speaker in this

Dialogue/Response stimulus, read both speakers' arguments to understand the full context of the issue at hand.

Step 2: Untangle the Stimulus

Patricia cites a paradox of Japan's Tokugawa period: even though ninjas were trained to be assassins, very little ninja activity took place, and most people did not fear ninjas. Tamara rejects Patricia's analysis and argues that many wealthy Japanese constructed intentionally squeaky floors to provide a warning if a ninja was in the house.

Step 3: Make a Prediction

Tamara disputes Patricia's claim by relying on the behavior of wealthy Japanese during the Tokugawa period. For this behavior to be evidence against Patricia's position that *most* Japanese did not fear ninjas, Tamara must assume that wealthy Japanese made up a majority of Japan's population. The correct answer will counter this assumption.

Step 4: Evaluate the Answer Choices

(C) correctly weakens Tamara's assumption by stating that wealthy people made up only a small portion of the Japanese population during the Tokugawa period.

(A) fails to provide enough information to weaken Tamara's position and might even strengthen it. The arguments take different positions as to whether most Japanese feared ninjas. Although there may be other reasons for constructing squeaky floors, one reason was to warn house occupants that ninjas were in the house. If anything, this answer choice suggests that the poor might have feared ninja assassins, too.

(B) is a Distortion. This answer choice confuses the argument's purpose. That squeaky floors may not have been effective at warning homeowners of ninja intruders is irrelevant to the proportion of Japanese who feared ninjas.

(D) is Outside the Scope. This argument is focused on what most Japanese thought of ninjas during the Tokugawa period, not after it.

(E) is Outside of the Scope. The number of ninjas during time periods other than the Tokugawa period has no bearing on the proportion of Japanese who feared ninjas during the Tokugawa period.

7. (B) Assumption (Necessary)

Step 1: Identify the Question Type

The phrase "[t]he Several of these tables printed out gray instead of black in the hard copy. Print page 326 to see which ones. argument requires the assumption" identifies this as an Assumption question. In addition, the word *requires* indicates that you're looking for a necessary assumption, without which the conclusion cannot follow logically from the evidence. You can use the Denial Test to check or eliminate answers.

Step 2: Untangle the Stimulus

The philosopher concludes that to be a moral agent, one must have free will. This conclusion is based on the evidence that one cannot be a moral agent without desiring to conform to a principle.

Step 3: Make a Prediction

The philosopher's conclusion states that free will is necessary to being a moral agent. Her evidence is that a moral agent desires to conform to a principle. The assumption will bridge the gap between evidence and conclusion by stating that free will is necessary for someone to have a desire to conform to a principle.

Step 4: Evaluate the Answer Choices

(B) correctly connects a desire to conform to a principle with having free will. Using the Denial Test on this answer choice would ruin the philosopher's conclusion: if free will weren't necessary for one to desire to conform to a principle, the author couldn't conclude that moral agents have free will based on evidence of their desire to conform to a principle.

(A) is Outside the Scope. By way of background, the author obliquely states that an action's consequences are relevant to the action's morality, but the statement in this answer choice is not necessary to the author's main argument about moral agents.

(C) is a Distortion. This answer choice requires one to consider consequences in order to be free. This is an attempt to link the main argument (about moral agents) to the irrelevant background sentence that introduces the stimulus. This statement is not required for the main argument's conclusion to follow from its evidence.

(D) is a Distortion. This answer choice states that any person who has desires (any desires at all) must be a moral agent. This misses the point of the argument's evidence, which says that no one without a specific desire (the desire to conform to a principle) can be a moral agent. **(D)** alters the argument's terms and mistakes a necessary condition for a sufficient one to boot.

(E) is Outside the Scope. Even if we assume that morally worthy actions are undertaken only by moral agents, this answer choice merely reasserts the evidence. It does nothing to link the evidence to the conclusion, which entails free will.

8. (D) Weaken

Step 1: Identify the Question Type

The phrase "most seriously weakens" indicates that you are dealing with a Weaken question here. Identify the conclusion,

paraphrase the evidence, determine the central assumption, and then look for a fact that attacks that assumption.

Step 2: Untangle the Stimulus

In this argument, the author concludes that publishing a scholarly journal is much more profitable now than it was several years ago. To support this position, the author cites two facts: the costs of publishing a scholarly journal have remained fairly constant, and the subscription rate for libraries has increased dramatically.

Step 3: Make a Prediction

The argument appears reasonable, but the author leaves a crucial question unanswered: What portion of total subscriptions are library subscriptions? The author assumes that the increased price libraries pay to subscribe to scholarly journals is enough to justify the conclusion that publishing a scholarly journal is "much more" profitable than in previous years. The correct answer will attack this assumption.

Step 4: Evaluate the Answer Choices

(D) correctly weakens the assumption by stating that most subscribers are individuals and their subscription rate has remained unchanged. If most subscribers are paying an unchanged rate, then the conclusion that journals are "much more" profitable is doubtful.

(A) is Outside the Scope. How libraries are able to afford the increased rate for journal subscriptions is not relevant to the profits of the journal publishers.

(B) is Outside the Scope. Library budgets are irrelevant to the profits earned by journal publishers.

(C) is Outside the Scope. The argument's focus is on how profitable it is to publish the scholarly journal. This answer choice is focused on what would happen if journals began losing money.

(E) is Outside the Scope because the number of times the journal is published a year does not necessarily impact the journal's profitability. More information would be needed in order for this answer to weaken the argument.

9. (A) Main Point

Step 1: Identify the Question Type

The phrase "most accurately states the argument's overall conclusion" identifies this as a Main Point question. Watch out for conclusion Keywords, which may indicate subsidiary conclusions, and be prepared to combine statements into a paraphrase of the author's main point. If necessary, use the One-Sentence Test.

Step 2: Untangle the Stimulus

An author, Terrence Gurney, believes his books are panned by critics because they are widely popular. The author of the stimulus argument concludes that Gurney is wrong. Her evidence is that Gurney's writing is "flat" and that this is why the critics don't praise his works.

Step 3: Make a Prediction

The argument's conclusion is the sentence in which the author contradicts Gurney: "Surely he is mistaken." To anticipate the correct answer, you need to paraphrase the argument's rebuttal of Gurney's position. The correct answer will say something along these lines: "Popularity is not the reason Gurney fails to receive praise from critics."

Step 4: Evaluate the Answer Choices

(A) correctly summarizes the author's main point: she disagrees with Gurney's supposition that his books' wide appeal is the reason for the poor critical reception of his writing.

(B) is a Distortion. The argument suggests that Gurney's writing is subpar—it's "flat, leaving no lasting impression"—but this is part of the evidence, not the main point.

(C) is a Distortion. This choice accurately sums up the evidence in the argument, not its main point.

(D) is a 180. This is exactly Gurney's point. The argument, however, says that wide appeal is not the reason for the tepid critical response to Gurney's books.

(E) is Outside the Scope. The author does not speculate on how critics should have responded to Terrence's writing. The author only attempts to explain the response Terrence's writings actually received.

10. (A) Paradox

Step 1: Identify the Question Type

The word *explain* indicates that this is a Paradox question. Summarize the seemingly inconsistent facts in the stimulus; then look for an answer that makes sense of the mystery. This question stem provides additional guidance by asking you to explain how lightening could have produced the first amino acids.

Step 2: Untangle the Stimulus

Scientists have shown how an electrical spark or lightning can trigger the production of amino acids, the "building blocks" of life on Earth. Scientists also know that amino acids would have required a "reducing atmosphere," with lots of hydrogen and not much oxygen. But scientists believe that when life began on Earth, the atmosphere had lots of oxygen and not much nitrogen.

Step 3: Make a Prediction

The paradox centers around Earth's atmosphere at the time life began. Amino acids need a hydrogen-rich, oxygen-poor

atmosphere, yet scientists believe that the atmosphere contained a lot of oxygen. The correct answer will explain how the needs of amino acids could have been met under these unfavorable conditions.

Step 4: Evaluate the Answer Choices

(A) is correct. This answer explains that meteorite impacts created a reducing atmosphere at the impact site. If this is true, the scientists' explanation for how life began on Earth could be true, even though Earth's overall atmosphere was rich in oxygen at the time.

(B) is Outside the Scope. The task is to explain how the first amino acid could have survived on Earth, not whether a single amino acid was enough to begin life on Earth.

(C) does not provide enough information to resolve the paradox. We don't know from this answer choice whether Earth's atmosphere was favorable to amino acids at the time life began. The fact that the atmosphere changed subsequent to that time is irrelevant.

(D) is irrelevant. The frequency of lightning does not pertain to the focus of the argument. Frequent lightning would make it more likely for amino acids to form, but the paradox of how they survived in the wrong type of atmosphere remains.

(E) is Outside the Scope. This answer provides an additional way amino acids might have reached Earth, but it doesn't resolve the paradox of how the amino acids survived in an unfavorable atmosphere.

11. (B) Principle (Identify/Strengthen)

Step 1: Identify the Question Type

"Principles" is a clear indicator of a Principle question. You'll find general rules outlined in the answer choices, and you'll have to determine which one would "justify," or strengthen, the specific situation described in the argument. Thus, this question is similar to a Strengthen question.

Step 2: Untangle the Stimulus

The art critic takes issues with Ms. Paulsen's selection to receive the Woerner Journalism Award for criticism. The art critic argues that Ms. Paulsen isn't an appropriate choice because the award shouldn't apply to her criticism of cars. Cars are utilitarian, the art critic believes, and as a result fail to reveal culturally revealing truths. Pay careful attention to the author's evidence in Principle questions to understand the justification given.

Step 3: Make a Prediction

To justify the art critic's reasoning, the answer will provide a general rule that strengthens the reasoning that Ms. Paulsen isn't an appropriate choice. For it to follow from the art critic's evidence that Paulsen was an inappropriate choice, it must be true that criticism, as it applies to the award recipients, matches the art critic's definition. So, the answer will define true criticism as the review of works that reveal important truths about the culture that created them. If works don't do that, then it's inappropriate to call reviews of those works "criticism."

Step 4: Evaluate the Answer Choices

(B) justifies the art critic's position, summing it up in general terms. If objects don't reveal important truths about the culture, then reviews of those objects cannot appropriately be considered to be criticism. This is a one-to-one match with the critic's stance.

(A) is a Faulty Use of Detail. It fails to address the author's primary concern that criticism should review objects that are culturally revealing. This answer choice doesn't justify the critic's argument since, as far as you can tell, he didn't oppose Paulsen's nomination on the grounds that she called cars works of art.

(C) is Outside the Scope. The art critic's justification for excluding Ms. Paulsen's reviews was that the objects of her reviews were not culturally revealing, not that her purpose for writing the review itself was questionable. Whether she intended her writing to reveal truths about her culture is irrelevant.

(D) is Outside the Scope. There's no evidence to suggest that Ms. Paulsen does or does not consider herself to be a critic. Self-assessment as a "critic" is not in question.

(E) is Extreme. The author's argument is meant to exclude the review of non-culturally revealing, utilitarian objects as appropriate criticism. **(E)** expands the definition of criticism to *all* writing that reveals important truths about a culture. This is far beyond the scope the art critic is attempting to define.

12. (A) Strengthen

Step 1: Identify the Question Type

"Most strengthens the manager's argument" indicates that this is a Strengthen question, so you'll need to focus on the manager's conclusion. Remember that the correct answer to a Strengthen question can either support the central assumption or be any fact that makes the conclusion more likely based on the evidence.

Step 2: Untangle the Stimulus

The manager's conclusion is summed up in the final sentence, signaled by [*t*]*hus*. The author believes that the change to unlimited free shipping is likely responsible for the increase in sales. The manager cites the fact that the sales increase happened around the same time as the policy change as evidence of causation. This is the archetypal correlation (evidence)–causation (conclusion) argument pattern.

Step 3: Make a Prediction

To strengthen causal arguments, seek either to increase the likelihood that the stated cause is the actual cause or to show that there's no alternative cause. Any choice that provides evidence drawing a closer link between free shipping and the increase in sales volume will help to justify the conclusion. So, too, will any choice that rules out a potential weakener, whether by denying an alternate cause or countering any suggestion that the correlation is merely coincidental.

Step 4: Evaluate the Answer Choices

(A) is correct. It strengthens the tie between the lure of free shipping and its impact on sales. If similar companies that don't provide free shipping have been seeing a decrease in their sales, the relationship is more likely to be causal. Further, this counters the potential weakener that the increase is typical industry-wide; had all mail-order companies been seeing sales increases regardless of shipping options and costs, then it would be more likely that the timing of the sales increase was just a coincidence.

(B) would, if anything, weaken the argument. Whether the company actively promoted its new policy is irrelevant to the cause of the sales increase. However, if its customers were unfamiliar with or completely unaware of the change, it would make it less likely—not more—that the change in policy was responsible.

(C) is Outside the Scope. The author provides no information about *profits* in the argument, only sales figures. Whether the overall profits for the company have increased or decreased is outside the scope of what caused the increase in *sales*.

(D) is Outside the Scope. No evidence is provided about whether the company's competitors increased or decreased their sales volume as they shifted to unlimited free shipping. The fact that this company waited until well after its competitors decided to do so is equally irrelevant.

(E) is irrelevant. Its shipping policy could put this company in the majority, as this choice suggests, or minority relative to its competition. Neither scenario better explains whether the change in shipping policy was responsible for the recent upward trend in sales.

13. (D) Parallel Reasoning

Step 1: Identify the Question Type

The phrase "most similar to" indicates that you're looking for a pattern of Parallel Reasoning. Generalize the structure of the stimulus in broad terms and use easily comparable parts of the structure to find the one answer that matches the argument piece by piece. Specifically, compare the conclusions to see if any answer choices can be quickly eliminated.

Step 2: Untangle the Stimulus

The author's conclusion is signaled by *but* in the second sentence. Even though the author agrees the chance of a nuclear meltdown is low, the contrast Keyword signals that she evaluates the building of nuclear power plants as "unwise." The author's evidence is that the catastrophic consequences are too high to merit building the plants.

Step 3: Make a Prediction

The correct answer will take the general reasoning of this argument and apply it to an unrelated situation. In general, you're looking for an argument that evaluates a course of action as unwise when the potential negative consequences are great, even if the chance that those damages will occur is low.

Step 4: Evaluate the Answer Choices

(D) is a perfect match for the original argument. The author evaluates a course of action (bungee jumping) as "reckless" because the potential damages are too great ("so extreme") to justify the action, even though the likelihood of injury is small.

(A) gives the wrong reason for the evaluation. Here, the activity (mountain climbing) has quite dangerous consequences (mishaps are "often fatal"). But the author doesn't evaluate the sport as risky *despite* the rarity of accidents. Rather, he argues that it is risky *because of* the number accidents. Since there are few mountain climbers, he says, accidents per climber are more likely than they might seem from the low overall number of accidents.

(B) veers far off track from the original argument. This choice recommends pursuing a course of action (eating veggies) that, while not beneficial in a single instance, nonetheless helps over time. That fails to matches the low-likelihood-but-high-potential-for-catastrophe scenario described in the original argument.

(C) presents a conclusion similar to that in the original argument; here, the author evaluates skydiving as "foolish." That's where the similarities end. Given the precautions that accompany skydiving, the author says the risk of catastrophe is quite low. This author gives skydiving a negative evaluation because it doesn't carry much potential for "rewards."

(E) matches the stimulus author's conclusion and evaluates another low-risk situation—riding in a car without a seat belt—as "unwise." However, the reasoning here is that putting on a seat belt is so easy. The original argument would have been nonsensical had it argued that building nuclear plants is unwise because not building them can be done with minimal effort.

14. (E) Principle (Apply/Inference)

Step 1: Identify the Question Type

The words *principle* and *justify* are common signals of a Principle question. You're asked to determine which of the specific situations in the answer choices is justified by the principle or rule that will be provided by the university president. It may be challenging to predict the specific situation that will match, but strive to fully understand the general rule given in the stimulus.

Step 2: Untangle the Stimulus

The university president's principle is expressed in a straightforward Formal Logic statement. If research in a field of study could potentially unearth insight to help our quality of life, then research institutions should invest in it. Expressed in shorthand:

$$\text{If} \quad \begin{array}{c}\textit{research provides}\\ \textit{insight to improve}\\ \textit{quality of life}\end{array} \rightarrow \textit{invest in research}$$

Step 3: Make a Prediction

The correct answer will describe a specific situation that exemplifies the rule above: research justified because it could provide insight into improving quality of life. Or it could be a match for the contrapositive:

$$\text{If} \quad \sim \textit{invest in research} \rightarrow \begin{array}{c}\textit{research} \sim \textit{provide}\\ \textit{insight to improve}\\ \textit{quality of life}\end{array}$$

Check each answer choice against your understanding of the rule, looking for a one-to-one match. Be rigorous as you test choices. The president's rule tells you that providing insights that could improve the quality of life is *sufficient* to justify investment. This does not tell you that such insights are *necessary* for investment (there could well be other reasons to fund research).

Step 4: Evaluate the Answer Choices

(E) provides a research project in which investment is justified by the fact that it could benefit our quality of life. Because the investigation into mathematical properties of folded structures might provide insight into what causes disease, the institute has funded it. That's in line with the university president's reasoning.

(A) is a Distortion. The president's principle tells you when you must fund research, not when to deny funding. The situation in **(A)** is compatible with the president's principle but isn't justified by it.

(B) is Outside the Scope. The president's principle says that when research provides insights that could improve the quality of life, that research should be funded. It's unclear whether the research described here would provide such insights, so the funding isn't justified by the president's principle.

(C) is also Outside the Scope. The president's principle gives you one criterion sufficient to justify funding, but there could be many others. There's no way to know whether the university acted responsibly in funding the research position listed here, but the president's principle is entirely irrelevant to this decision one way or the other.

(D) is Outside the Scope. The contrapositive of the president's reasoning is that if something does not merit investment, then it must not provide insights that could improve quality of life. Nothing in this choice indicates whether the "poorly understood aspects of economic behavior" targeted by the proposed research would have yielded such insights. Thus, the president's principle cannot be applied to the decision described here.

15. (B) Paradox

Step 1: Identify the Question Type

The word *explain* reveals that this is a Paradox question. In this question, the paradox is in the study's findings, which will seem to contradict some other information. Search for the answer that resolves the irregular results.

Step 2: Untangle the Stimulus

The stimulus defines carpal tunnel syndrome, a nerve disorder, and provides an example of one of its causes: "repetitive motions such as typing." In a recent study, workers with less control over their work were found to have three times the risk of developing carpal tunnel syndrome, even though the groups studied performed similar amounts of typing.

Step 3: Make a Prediction

In Paradox questions, the answer to the mystery is found in the contrast. The correct answer will explain why *even though* they typed the same amount as empowered employees, disempowered employees faced a greater risk of carpal tunnel syndrome. It's not necessary to predict the specific reason, but one choice will resolve the paradox of why one group of workers is getting this nerve disorder at accelerated rates despite equal exposure to the disorder's cause.

Step 4: Evaluate the Answer Choices

(B) provides a fact relevant to why the employees with less control are at a greater risk. The fact that a lack of control induces stress that makes people more susceptible to nerve disorders like carpal tunnel syndrome would explain why the group with more control at work is at a lower risk of contracting the disorder.

(A) is a Faulty Use of Detail. It could be true that office workers with the most control tend to type significantly less. However,

this study compared workers who did *similar amounts of typing*, so those who type the least are irrelevant to this study.

(C) provides a reason that office workers develop carpal tunnel syndrome, but it fails provide any explanation of the difference in risk between the two groups.

(D) is incorrect. Like **(A)**, **(D)** focuses only on those who use keyboards rarely, while the study compared risk levels in office workers who performed similar amounts of typing.

(E) is a 180. While **(E)** provides no information about whether carpal tunnel syndrome could be caused by the repetitive motions that workers with the most control over their work perform, any information from **(E)** would suggest a higher risk to those with the most control over their work, not those with the least control.

16. (C) Strengthen

Step 1: Identify the Question Type

The combination of a Principle/Application stimulus and this stem calling for the answer that justifies the specific application of the principle makes this a variant on the Strengthen question type. Treat the application as a conclusion and the stated principle as evidence. The correct answer will strengthen the assumption that ties the two together. Note that the stem here is very strong—the correct answer "justifies" the application of the principle.

Step 2: Untangle the Stimulus

The principle states that telemarketers should avoid any behavior that will make people dislike the telemarketer's client. The application makes that rule relevant to cases in which the telemarketer calls a person who says he doesn't want to buy the client's product. In that case, the application says that the principle requires the telemarketer not to try to talk the person she's called into buying the product.

Step 3: Make a Prediction

As you would with any Assumption-family question, take note of how the conclusion differs from the evidence. Here, the conclusion (the application) is a blanket prohibition against trying to talk the person into buying the client's product. The evidence (the principle) is about not doing anything that will make a person dislike the client. The correct answer needs to state that trying to talk someone who has already said he doesn't want to buy the client's product into buying that product will make that person dislike the client.

Step 4: Evaluate the Answer Choices

(C) matches the prediction and justifies the application of the principle. In fact, this choice is so strong—"[a]ny employee" and "will engender animosity"—that it is sufficient to justify the application of the principle in the stimulus.

(A) works against the application of the principle. If the telemarketer is likely to have good judgment about whether her attempt to get the person she has called to buy will or will not make the person dislike the client, then the blanket prohibition in the application doesn't make much sense.

(B) is too weak to justify the application. This choice says that some telemarketers may be unsure whether an attempt to sell to a person who has indicated that he doesn't want the client's product would predispose that person to dislike the client. This leaves open the possibility that some telemarketers are likely to discern when their attempts to sell would not make the customer dislike the client. In that case, the blanket prohibition on trying to sell might not be justified.

(D) is Outside the Scope. The principle here involves a requirement to avoid any action that would make a person dislike the client. The likelihood that a person who likes the client might still decline to buy will neither help nor harm the application in the stimulus.

(E) is an Irrelevant Comparison. The stimulus involves actions to be avoided in order to prevent more people from disliking the client. A general rule about who is more likely to purchase neither strengthens nor weakens this application of the principle.

17. (E) Assumption (Sufficient)

Step 1: Identify the Question Type

The word *assumed* explicitly identifies this as an Assumption question. Because the conclusion of this argument will follow "if" the correct answer is added, you're looking here for an assumption sufficient to complete the author's reasoning.

Step 2: Untangle the Stimulus

The author's conclusion is that Pluto is not a true planet. The evidence is that Pluto formed in orbit around another planet (Neptune) and was ejected from that orbit when the planet captured another moon.

Step 3: Make a Prediction

Here, the correct answer will ensure that the conclusion follows from the evidence. The correct answer will make that logical link by stating that the fact that Pluto formed in orbit around Neptune means that Pluto is not a true planet.

Step 4: Evaluate the Answer Choices

(E) The statement here is sufficient to complete the argument. Since Pluto formed in orbit around Neptune, **(E)**'s statement that a planet must form only while in orbit around the sun is enough to establish the author's conclusion that Pluto is not a true planet.

(A) This choice is not helpful to the argument because although Pluto formed as a moon of Neptune, it was subsequently ejected from orbit around Neptune. This choice leaves open the possibility, contrary to the author's conclusion, that Pluto is now a planet.

(B) This statement is necessary, but not sufficient, to establish the author's conclusion. All that you learn from this choice is that two of Pluto's characteristics do not require that it be considered a planet; this is not enough to ensure that Pluto is not a planet.

(C) The conditional language in this choice doesn't help bridge the gap between the author's evidence and conclusion. The counterfactual condition that Pluto would have remained a moon tells us nothing about whether it can now be considered a planet.

(D) This choice might be helpful if size were relevant to determining a body's status. The statement here, however, says that size is irrelevant, so regardless of what we learn about Pluto's size, we're no closer to establishing the author's conclusion that Pluto is not a planet.

18. (E) Paradox

Step 1: Identify the Question Type

Any stem that asks you to *explain, resolve,* or *reconcile* an apparent contradiction is a Paradox question. Read the stimulus strategically to identify the two seemingly incompatible statements.

Step 2: Untangle the Stimulus

The stimulus begins with a piece of background information: early humans needed a high-calorie, sufficiently fatty diet in order to develop anatomically modern brains. The paradox follows. On one hand, the necessary diet was most abundantly and reliably found in shore environments. On the other hand, most brain development actually occurred in humans who lived in savanna and forest habitats.

Step 3: Make a Prediction

The correct answer will explain why brain development happened to a greater extent in environments in which the optimal diet was less abundant and reliable. The correct answer will provide either (1) a disadvantage of the abundant, reliable shore habitat that made it less desirable for early human brain development or (2) an advantage of the savannah and forest environments that compensated—in terms of brain development—for the less than optimal food supply.

Step 4: Evaluate the Answer Choices

(E) contains a fact that helps explain why early human brain development would have happened in the forest and savanna, even though the shore had more abundant and reliable resources. Since brain development requires a high-calorie diet, the fact that gathering food on the shore would burn up more calories helps explain why the shore might not have supported the greatest brain development; after you subtract the calories lost in food acquisition, you might find that *net* calorie intake was lower in shore environments than in the savannah or forest.

(A) doesn't resolve the paradox because it gives no reason why the savannah and forest might have outperformed the shore. Presumably, if **(A)** were true, fat reserves would have lasted longer in every environment.

(B) is irrelevant to the paradox, which is about the environment that would best contribute to brain development.

(C) is an Irrelevant Comparison. The stimulus is clear that, at the time of early human brain development, shore environments had more abundant and reliable food resources than did savannah and forest. How the latter environments compare to their present-day counterparts makes no difference to the situation you're tasked with resolving.

(D) is entirely Outside the Scope. The fact that early human shore environments are newly researched does nothing to resolve the paradox that the greatest brain development was seen in areas lacking the most abundant, reliable resources.

19. (D) Point at Issue

Step 1: Identify the Question Type

The dialogue between the two editors and the question stem asking for the point "they disagree with each other about" tell you that this is a Point at Issue question. The correct answer is the only one about which the two editors express diametrically opposed opinions.

Step 2: Untangle the Stimulus

The editors' disagreement is fairly pointed. Editor Y claims the photograph is good because its composition is attractive. Editor Z agrees that the photo is pretty but contends that it is bad because it doesn't make a statement.

Step 3: Make a Prediction

Since the two editors agree that the photograph is attractive, but disagree about whether it is good, they must disagree on the question of whether attractiveness is sufficient to make a photograph good.

Step 4: Evaluate the Answer Choices

(D) matches the prediction perfectly. Editor Y would agree with the statement in **(D)**, while Editor Z would disagree. The latter editor requires a good photograph to make a statement as well as to be attractive.

(A) contains a statement Editor Z seems likely to agree with, given his thoughts on the photograph under discussion. As

for Editor Y, however, she expresses no opinion on photographs that do or do not make statements.

(B) expresses an opinion with which either editor might agree or disagree. Editor Y seems to consider attractive composition sufficient to make a photograph good, and we know Editor Z does not consider attractiveness sufficient. But the statement in **(B)** amounts to saying that attractiveness is not *necessary* to a photograph's being good. On that question, we have no information revealing either editor's opinion.

(C) presents an opinion with which Editor Z explicitly agrees—he says the photo under discussion is pretty but makes no statement. Editor Y is silent on photos that make statements, so we can't guess her opinion on the statement in **(C)**. She might well agree, so this is not a point at issue between the two editors.

(E) is irrelevant. Editor Z might say that prettiness encompasses more than just attractive composition or might consider the two categories identical. Either way, he'd maintain his point that the photograph is no good since it doesn't make a statement.

20. (D) Assumption (Sufficient)

Step 1: Identify the Question Type

This Assumption question's stem calls for an answer that "if" added to the president's argument would allow his conclusion to be "properly drawn." Said another way, the question is calling for a sufficient assumption.

Step 2: Untangle the Stimulus

The president's argument is made up of a series of conditional (Formal Logic) statements, but they aren't arranged in the most helpful order. The conclusion—signaled by the Keyword [*s*]*o*—is in the middle of the stimulus: without marketing our programs, our school won't be able to maintain its educational quality. The third and first sentences of the stimulus fit together to present the president's evidence: without marketing, the school won't increase enrollment; and if the school doesn't increase enrollment, it will have to decrease spending.

Step 3: Make a Prediction

If you lay out the argument logically, the assumption is clear. Without marketing, the school won't increase enrollment. Without increased enrollment, the school will have to cut spending. Therefore, without marketing, the school won't be able to maintain its educational quality.

The unstated premise that makes the president's conclusion follow directly from the evidence is "If the school has to reduce spending, it will not be able to maintain its educational quality." The wording may change slightly, but the correct answer has to match that prediction's meaning.

Step 4: Evaluate the Answer Choices

(D) matches the prediction and completes the president's argument in a way that makes his conclusion unavoidable based on the evidence.

(A) is a 180. Because increased enrollment is necessary for the school to avoid spending cuts, the president assumes that the school will not maintain its quality *without* an increase in enrollment.

(B) does not link the evidence (spending cuts) to the conclusion (maintain educational quality). Moreover, it makes a mistake with the argument's Formal Logic: an increase in enrollment is necessary, but may not be sufficient, to avoid spending cuts.

(C) does not link the evidence (spending cuts) to the conclusion (maintain educational quality). Moreover, it makes a mistake with the argument's Formal Logic: marketing is necessary, but may not be sufficient, to increasing enrollments.

(E) does not link the evidence (spending cuts) to the conclusion (maintain educational quality). Moreover, it makes a mistake with the argument's Formal Logic: marketing is necessary, but may not be sufficient, to increasing enrollments; increasing enrollments is necessary, but may not be sufficient to avoid spending cuts; thus, marketing is necessary, but may not be sufficient to avoid spending cuts.

21. (D) Inference

Step 1: Identify the Question Type

Because the correct answer "logically follows" from the stimulus statements, this is a straightforward Inference question. The right answer must be true based on the stimulus alone.

Step 2: Untangle the Stimulus

The statements here reflect a pattern used often in LSAT Inference questions. Think of it as presenting a dilemma. If an action is taken (shift sorting to residents), one negative result will result (recyclables go to the dump). If the same action is not taken (don't shift sorting to residents), a different negative result will occur (city goes over on sanitation budget).

Step 3: Make a Prediction

Since the two triggers in the stimulus are just an on/off switch for the same action (shift the sorting requirement or don't shift it), you can conclude that the city is stuck between the horns of the dilemma. The correct answer will lay this out: either the city is going to wind up with more recyclables in its landfill, *or* it's going to exceed its sanitation budget. One or the other of those results will occur.

Step 4: Evaluate the Answer Choices

(D) matches the prediction and lays out the two horns of the dilemma you identified. There is no way for the city to stay within budget without shifting the sorting of recyclables to residents. That shift, in turn, will cause an increase in recyclables that get thrown out with the garbage destined for the city dump.

(A) is too specific. The author's statements make clear that, under the new sorting system, *some* residents will start tossing recyclables out with the garbage. Whether *most* will continue to recycle cannot be established from the statements here.

(B) is a conditional statement that does not follow from the stimulus. The author's statements make clear that, under the new sorting system, some recyclables that are currently put into the recycling would end up at the landfill instead. There's not enough information to say that *all* those who continue to recycle will sort their recycling. Perhaps some will put out their recycling unsorted.

(C) cannot be deduced from the information in the stimulus. We know that without requiring residents to sort their recycling, the city cannot make its overall sanitation budget. But **(C)** deals with two specific totals within the budget: the current annual cost of sorting recycling and the expected annual cost of sending garbage to the landfill. Without more information, those cost categories are irrelevant. It could be that landfill costs are always higher than sorting costs, but if the resident sorting program reduces the sorting costs more than it increases the landfill costs, it would still help the city make its budget.

(E) makes a mistake with the Formal Logic in the stimulus. The last sentence in the stimulus states that implementing resident sorting is necessary for the city to stay within its sanitation budget. **(E)** mistakenly states that implementing resident sorting is sufficient for the city to stay within its budget. Even without taking the time to translate the Formal Logic involved, it should be clear that you cannot deduce the statement in **(E)** without more information: How many new trucks will the city have to buy? Will the population of the city increase? And so on.

22. (C) Flaw

Step 1: Identify the Question Type

This is a Flaw question asking you to describe the "questionable reasoning technique" used in the stimulus. Identify the conclusion and evidence, consider the assumption linking them, and describe the error in reasoning found in the author's assumption.

Step 2: Untangle the Stimulus

The author's conclusion is that meerkat "sentinels" (the meerkats who watch for predators) are acting altruistically (not selfishly). Her evidence is that, even as the sentinel runs for cover to protect itself, it gives a loud bark, which has the effect of warning other foraging meerkats of the predator's presence.

Step 3: Make a Prediction

If your instinctive response to the argument was "How do you know what a sentinel meerkat is thinking?" then you're on the right track. The flaw here—inferring the motive for an action based on the effect of the action—appears regularly on the LSAT. Consider it a variant on the "correlation versus causation" flaw but realize that here, the author is saying, "*Y* was the result of action *X*, so producing *Y* must be the reason for taking action *X*." The correct answer could describe the flaw directly: the author has inferred the sentinel meerkat's motives from the results of its behavior. Alternately, the answer could relate the flaw in terms of overlooked alternatives: although the effect of the sentinel's bark is to warn other meerkats, the reason the sentinel barks (to scare off the predator) is actually selfish.

Step 4: Evaluate the Answer Choices

(C) matches the first, more descriptive, version of the prediction. You can't properly conclude that the motive for an action was altruistic simply because it helped others. To reach the author's conclusion, you need evidence ruling out selfish reasons for the sentinels' barking or evidence that barking puts the sentinels at greater risk.

(A) mischaracterizes the evidence in this argument. The effect of the sentinels' barking (other meerkats take cover) certainly doesn't undermine the conclusion that the barking is altruistic. The problem is that simply noting the effect doesn't establish an altruistic motive either.

(B) describes a circular argument, but the problem here is not that doubting the author's conclusion would cause us to doubt her evidence; indeed, the effects of the sentinels' barking could be tested empirically and independently of the conclusion. The flaw in this argument is that the effect of an action is insufficient to establish the motive for the action.

(D) mischaracterizes the author's conclusion. The author says that the warning effect of the sentinel's bark proves that the sentinel's motivation "is at least in part" altruistic. The author doesn't commit the "all-or-nothing" flaw described in **(D)**.

(E) distorts both parts of the author's argument. First, the author's conclusion asserts a fact; it does not deny the truth of someone else's claim. Second, the author's evidence is an observed effect of an animal's behavior; it is not the accusation that someone else lacks evidence for another claim.

23. (B) Point at Issue

Step 1: Identify the Question Type

The Dialogue/Response stimulus and the task of identifying what the two speakers "disagree with each other over" make this a Point at Issue question. Characterize both arguments and use the Decision Tree tactic to evaluate the answer choices.

Step 2: Untangle the Stimulus

Alex makes a short clear argument: (conclusion) shrimp farming damages the environment because (evidence) investors abandon the farms after turning a quick profit. Jolene does not deny Alex's conclusion, but she somewhat obliquely takes issue with his evidence. She tells us that some shrimp farms are abandoned, not because their investors took their quick profits and ran, but because the farms proved unsustainable. Moreover, well-made shrimp farms require large investments of time and money, so their owners strive to make the farms profitable over time.

Step 3: Make a Prediction

The correct answer is the one in which the two speakers express opposed opinions. Wrong answers may be something on which neither speaker expresses an opinion, something on which only one of the two speakers expresses an opinion, or something on which the two speakers agree. Here, the disagreement is around the issue raised by Alex's evidence—whether shrimp farm investors abandon farms after taking quick profits.

Step 4: Evaluate the Answer Choices

(B) is an issue over which the two speakers would have diametrically opposed views. Alex would say, "Yes, and afterward, the investors abandon them." Jolene would say, "No. Shrimp farms abandoned quickly were not sustainable, and those that prove profitable are designed to produce shrimp for many years."

(A) is Outside the Scope of both arguments. Both speakers cite some shrimp farmers who abandon farms quickly, but neither opines on the percentage of farmers who *eventually* abandon their farms in the long run.

(C) is an issue on which Alex would express clear agreement but on which Jolene is silent. She says nothing against Alex's conclusion but rather challenges his evidence. It's quite possible that she believes shrimp farms damage the environment in other ways.

(D) is a statement with which Alex would clearly agree; indeed, it is a more or less direct paraphrase of his argument. While Jolene says shrimp farms are rarely abandoned because their investors took quick profits, it's unclear whether she believes that abandonment (when it does happen and for whatever reason) results in environmental harm. She might, on that limited point, agree with Alex.

(E) is a point of view we can infer from Alex's statements; he would consider at least those who abandon farms after taking out quick profits to be environmentally irresponsible. Since Jolene doesn't acknowledge shrimp farmers who act like those in Alex's argument, you can't deduce that she considers any of them environmentally irresponsible.

24. (D) Parallel Flaw

Step 1: Identify the Question Type

The phrase "most similar to the reasoning in" is standard to Parallel Reasoning questions. Moreover, in this question, the correct answer will mirror the "flawed reasoning" in the stimulus. Characterize the flaw in the stimulus argument before evaluating the answer choices.

Step 2: Untangle the Stimulus

You can look at the stimulus argument by breaking down its Formal Logic or by characterizing the flawed reasoning more holistically. To understand the Formal Logic, start by translating the observation in the first sentence:

> **If** *evaluation poor* → *~ raise*

To form the contrapositive, reverse and negate the terms:

> **If** *raise* → *evaluation ~ poor*

The thrust of the rule is now clear: a raise is incompatible with a poor evaluation. Now, consider how the author has tried to apply the observation to Lester's case: Lester did *not* get a raise, so he must have gotten a poor evaluation. The application to Lester's situation treats the sufficient condition (poor evaluation) as if it were the only reason (necessary) one would not receive a raise. In fact, there may be any number of reasons Lester didn't get a raise (he may not have been employed long enough, or perhaps only outstanding evaluations got raises while Lester's evaluation was only "good," or …).

The original Formal Logic allows you to deduce from the fact that someone got a raise that the person's evaluation wasn't poor. It doesn't allow you to draw any conclusions about someone who did *not* get a raise.

Step 3: Make a Prediction

Use your outline of the flawed Formal Logic or your generic descriptions of the flaw to find the correct match. The right answer is the only one that will present a Formal Logic rule indicating that two things are incompatible (you can't have X and Y), then assert that one of the incompatible things did not happen (no X), and conclude that the other incompatible thing must have happened (therefore, Y). Likewise, it will be the only one susceptible to the criticism that the author has treated a sufficient condition as a necessary one and, in the

process, overlooked the many other necessary conditions that may apply.

Step 4: Evaluate the Answer Choices

(D) matches the flaws in the stimulus argument precisely, and is correct. In this choice, you see the following: no one both owns and rents (you can't have X and Y); my neighbors do not own (no X), so they must rent (therefore, Y). The original Formal Logic allows you to deduce from the fact that someone owns a house that the person does not rent the house. It doesn't allow you to draw any conclusions about someone who does *not* own a house. Maybe the occupants' uncle owns the house and is letting them stay there rent-free, or maybe they're squatting illegally, or maybe it's one of many other possibilities.

(A) has no flaw. Here, the original condition tells you that owning is incompatible with paying rent. Since the neighbors pay rent, you can accurately conclude that they do not own.

(B) has no flaw. Here, the original condition tells you that owning is incompatible with paying rent. Since the neighbors own, you can accurately conclude that they do not pay rent.

(C) commits a different reasoning error than the stimulus argument does. Here, the Formal Logic says: if NOT rent, then own. The reasoning goes wrong in the application of that rule to the facts. The neighbors, you learn, have not paid any rent. But you're not told whether they just moved in, or whether their payments are deferred for some reason, or whether they signed a lease and are just behind in writing the check. The flaw here is the simple scope shift between "*rent* [their house]" and "not *paid rent on* their house." There's no sufficiency versus necessity problems in this example.

(E) has no flaw. The Formal Logic rule here is quite specific: if NOT own, then pay rent. The application mirrors the rule exactly: the neighbors do NOT own, so they pay rent.

25. (E) Flaw

Step 1: Identify the Question Type

The phrase "vulnerable to criticism" tells you this is a Flaw question. The question stem helps you predict the correct answer by telling you that the correct answer is a consideration overlooked by the author.

Step 2: Untangle the Stimulus

The conclusion is signaled by the phrase "[a]ll of this shows" at the beginning of the final sentence. The author reaches two causal conclusions: not eating enough fiber causes colon cancer, and eating enough fiber prevents it. The evidence is in the stimulus's first sentence: numerous studies have shown a correlation between high-fiber diets and a low incidence of colon cancer. The bulk of the stimulus consists of examples of these studies.

Step 3: Make a Prediction

Causal arguments are vulnerable to three main criticisms: (1) the causal relationship is reversed, (2) the correlation reflects a mere coincidence, or (3) there is an overlooked, alternate cause. The third flaw is in play here, since the question stem tells you to find the overlooked possibility. The correct answer will, therefore, account for the correlation between high-fiber diets and a low incidence of colon cancer but will suggest a cause other than consumption of fiber.

Step 4: Evaluate the Answer Choices

(E) is the only answer that does exactly what the question stem here called for: it suggests an overlooked cause for the low colon cancer rate among those who eat high-fiber diets. If it's true that other healthy stuff in high-fiber foods is actually causing the reduced cancer rates, the author's argument is seriously called into question.

(A) is irrelevant. The author's argument is about what causes and prevents colon cancer, not a prediction that it will increase or that diets will become less healthy.

(B) is Outside the Scope. The relationship between fiber and other types of cancer has no direct bearing on the argument here. The author's argument is certainly not vulnerable to having overlooked the discovery that fiber is a cancer-fighting agent generally, a fact that would, if anything, make his conclusion more likely to be true.

(C) is irrelevant. This author isn't making a prediction about how many people are likely to eat a high-fiber diet or even suggesting that people do so. He's asserting the fact that eating such a diet will prevent colon cancer.

(D) is an Irrelevant Comparison. The stimulus treats cereals and fruits and vegetables as components of high-fiber diets; it makes no distinctions with regard to their cancer-fighting properties.

26. (B) Main Point

Step 1: Identify the Question Type

The question stem calls for the "main conclusion" of the argument, so this is a Main Point question. Keep in mind that the argument may contain subsidiary conclusions supporting the author's ultimate point.

Step 2: Untangle the Stimulus

Typical of Main Point questions, the stimulus here is quite long, so read strategically and use Keywords to help you zero in on the argument's structure. The stimulus begins with a wonderful clue: "[m]any people think." It's likely that the anthropologist's main point will rebut this popular opinion. What these people think is based on a chain of reasoning: humans evolved language; new traits evolve slowly; so, we should find a crude, language-like trait in primates, like chimpanzees, that are closely related to humans. The

author's response comes in the next sentence and logically follows the Keyword *but*. The anthropologist acknowledges that his opponents' argument is reasonable but denies that it gives us any reason to expect a crude, language-like trait in chimpanzees. The anthropologist's evidence follows. Humans and chimpanzees are, indeed, closely related, but humans didn't evolve from chimps. Rather, both likely evolved from a distant common ancestor. The human ancestor with a crude, language-like trait may well have existed after the human and chimpanzee branches had already separated on the evolutionary tree.

Step 3: Make a Prediction

The correct answer must summarize the anthropologist's ultimate conclusion: the reasoning that says a recent predecessor of modern humans had a language-like trait doesn't lead to an expectation that chimpanzees have such a trait. Be careful to avoid answer choices that state the anthropologist's evidence: humans did not evolve from chimpanzees, and the human ancestor with a language-like trait came along after the human and chimpanzee lines of evolution had diverged.

Step 4: Evaluate the Answer Choices

(B) matches the prediction and summarizes the anthropologist's main point succinctly. It's the only answer that really addresses the anthropologist's point of attack: the reasoning that "many people" use does not lead to the expectation they have.

(A) includes some of the anthropologist's evidence but not his main point.

(C) is irrelevant, since it says nothing about whether the chimps' communicative systems are in any way like human language. This answer does not sum up the anthropologist's conclusion that the expectation of "many people" is misguided.

(D) is a gross oversimplification of the anthropologist's evidence (*not* his conclusion) that the evolutionary branch leading to humans developed language-like traits after the branch leading to chimpanzees had diverged.

(E) is a succinct statement of the anthropologist's evidence but *not* of his conclusion, which addresses why the reasoning of "many people" doesn't support their prediction.

PrepTest 67

The Inside Story

PrepTest 67 was administered in October 2012. It challenged 37,780 test takers. What made this test so hard? Here's a breakdown of what Kaplan students who were surveyed after taking the official exam considered PrepTest 67's most difficult section.

Hardest PrepTest 67 Section as Reported by Test Takers

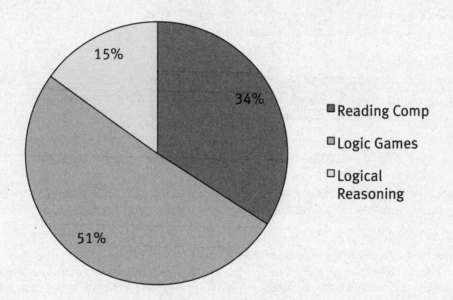

Based on these results, you might think that studying Logic Games is the key to LSAT success. Well, Logic Games is important, but test takers' perceptions don't tell the whole story. For that, you need to consider students' actual performance. The following chart shows the average number of students to miss each question in each of PrepTest 67's different sections.

Percentage Incorrect by PrepTest 67 Section Type

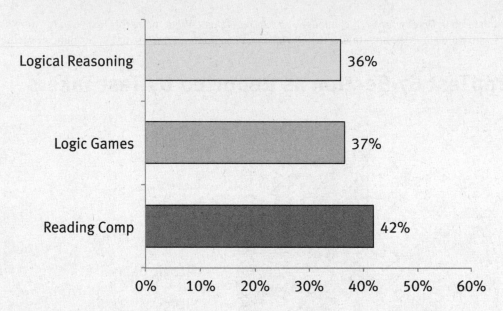

Actual student performance tells quite a different story. On average, students are almost equally likely to miss questions in all three of the different section types, while on PrepTest 67, Reading Comprehension was notably harder than Logic Games in actual difficulty.

Maybe students overestimate the difficulty of the Logic Games section because it's so unusual, or maybe it's because a really hard Logic Game is so easy to remember after the test. But the truth is that the testmaker places hard questions throughout the test. While four of PrepTest 67's 10 toughest questions were from Logic Games (indeed, they were all from one particular game), the other six were distributed among Reading Comprehension and the two Logical Reasoning sections. Here were the locations of the 10 hardest (most missed) questions in the exam.

Location of 10 Most Difficult Questions in PrepTest 67

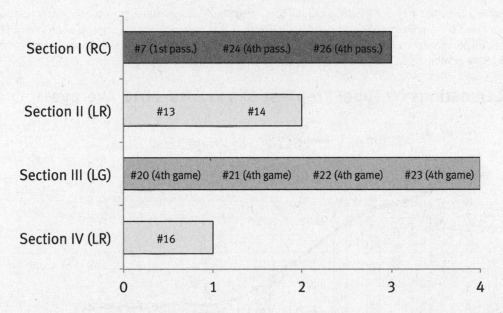

The takeaway from this data is that, to maximize your potential on the LSAT, you need to take a comprehensive approach. Test yourself rigorously, and review your performance on every section of the test. Kaplan's LSAT explanations provide the expertise and insight you need to fully understand your results. The explanations are written and edited by a team of LSAT experts, who have helped thousands of students improve their scores. Kaplan always provides data-driven analysis of the test, ranking the difficulty of every question based on actual student performance. The 10 hardest questions on every test are highlighted with a 4-star difficulty rating, the highest we give. The analysis breaks down the remaining questions into 1-, 2-, and 3-star ratings so that you can compare your performance to that of thousands of other test takers on all LSAC material.

Don't settle for wondering whether a question was really as hard as it seemed to you. Analyze the test with real data, and learn the secrets and strategies that help top scorers master the LSAT.

9 Can't–Miss Features of PrepTest 67

- PrepTest 67's Logical Reasoning sections contain only a single Main Point question, even though there are four on each of PrepTest 66 and PrepTest 68.
- Most recent tests include one Principle/Application style stimulus. PrepTest 67 features three.
- The Logic Games section here featured *two* Matching games for the first time since PrepTest 46 (June 2005).
- The game about Millville's Development Zones (Game 4) is highly unusual. And although it lacks any major deductions the explanations serve up great info on how to efficiently handle the questions.
- Since Rule Substitution questions debuted on PrepTest 57, this was just the second released test to not have one (the other was PrepTest 60).
- PrepTest 67 did, however, feature a rare "Supply the If" question. As of the release date of this test there have only been seven total in LSAT history.
- This was just the third time ever since Comparative Reading debuted in June 2007 that the Comparative Reading set of passages was accompanied by only five questions.
- There are a lot of Logical Reasoning style questions in the RC section: Strengthen, Principle, Method of Argument, and two Parallel Reasoning questions.
- Test takers who needed to blow off a little steam after the test probably went dancing. After all, Psy's "Gangnam Style" was the #1 song the week that PrepTest 67 was originally administered.

PrepTest 67 in Context

As much fun as it is to find out what makes a PrepTest unique or noteworthy, it's even more important to know just how representative it is of other LSAT administrations (and, thus, how likely it is to be representative of the exam you will face on Test Day). The following charts compare the numbers of each kind of question and game on PrepTest 67 to the average numbers seen on all officially released LSATs administered over the past five years (from 2012 through 2016).

Number of LR Questions by Type: PrepTest 67 vs. 2012-2016 Average

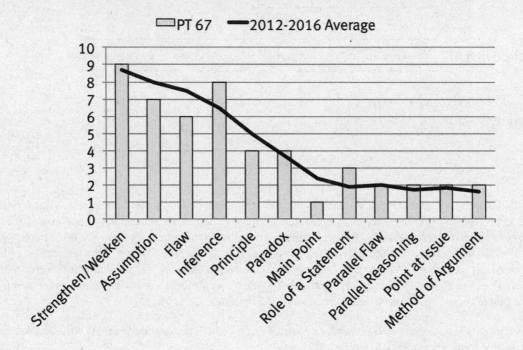

Number of LG Games by Type: PrepTest 67 vs. 2012-2016 Average

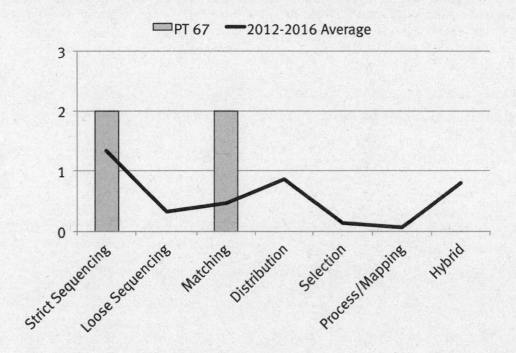

Number of RC Questions by Type: PrepTest 67 vs. 2012-2016 Average

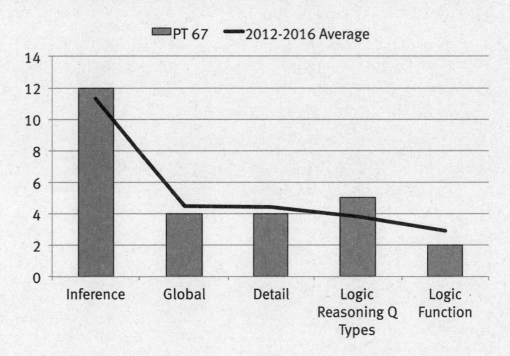

There isn't usually a huge difference in the distribution of questions from LSAT to LSAT, but if this test seems harder (or easier) to you than another you've taken, compare the number of questions of the types on which you, personally, are strongest and weakest. And then, explore within each section to see if your best or worst question types came earlier or later.

Students in Kaplan's comprehensive LSAT courses have access to every released LSAT, and to an online Q-Bank with thousands of officially released questions, games, and passages. If you are studying on your own, you have to do a bit more work to identify your strengths and your areas of opportunity. Quantitative analysis (like that in the charts shown here) is an important tool for understanding how the test is constructed, and how you are performing on it.

Section I: Reading Comprehension
Passage 1: The Biography of Lorenzo Tucker

Q#	Question Type	Correct	Difficulty
1	Global	B	★
2	Logic Function	A	★★
3	Inference	A	★
4	Inference	C	★★
5	Global	E	★
6	Detail	D	★
7	Inference	D	★★★★

Passage 2: The Autobiography of Nisa

Q#	Question Type	Correct	Difficulty
8	Detail	E	★★★
9	Inference	C	★★★
10	Inference	C	★★★
11	Logic Reasoning (Strengthen)	D	★★
12	Inference	E	★★★
13	Logic Reasoning (Parallel Reasoning)	A	★★★
14	Inference	B	★★★

Passage 3: The Effects of Species Invasion

Q#	Question Type	Correct	Difficulty
15	Global	D	★
16	Detail	E	★★★
17	Inference	E	★★
18	Logic Reasoning (Parallel Reasoning)	B	★★
19	Logic Reasoning (Method of Argument)	D	★

Passage 4: The Paradox of Omnipotence

Q#	Question Type	Correct	Difficulty
20	Global	A	★
21	Inference	E	★★
22	Inference	B	★★
23	Logic Reasoning (Principle)	B	★★★
24	Detail	A	★★★★
25	Logic Function	D	★★
26	Inference	C	★★★★
27	Inference	E	★★

Passage 1: The Biography of Lorenzo Tucker

Step 1: Read the Passage Strategically

Sample Roadmap

line #	Keyword/phrase	¶ Margin notes
1	Until my present study	Tucker not discussed til auth's study
2	not	
4	Yet	Long career on and off stage
10	In addition	
13		Also kept relics of Afr-Am entert. hist.
16	help shed new light	
18	insufficient	
19		Source material for study
23	Also ...	
24	examined	
29	primary	Main source: personal interviews
30	however	
33	advantages and disadvantages	
35	greatest advantages	Adv. to studying living people
37	Yet ... caution	
38	since	
40	no matter	
41	the fact is	Disadv: bias
44	therefore	Biographer must verify
46		Unverifiable info not included
48	for the most part	
50	But	Exception: T's personal memories
52	since	
53	So	
55	however	T's memories match hist. ev.
56	it is important to note that	
57	tend to corroborate ... illuminating	
58	valuable	
60	therefore	Study will combine oral, other ev.

Discussion

Paragraph 1 introduces the subject of the author's study: African American entertainer Lorenzo Tucker. Though Tucker is mentioned throughout the passage, the **Topic** of the passage is actually the biography that's been written about him. Lines 4–14 provide information on Tucker's extensive involvement in the entertainment industry. The author concludes the paragraph by mentioning that Tucker's memories and his memorabilia collection form the basis of a study that will illuminate an area of entertainment history that hasn't gotten enough attention from scholars.

Paragraph 2 confirms the **Scope** of the passage—the study's sources and the process by which it was completed. The author drew upon a variety of sources to write the biography, but in lines 29–32 you learn that the main source for the study was a series of interviews the author did with Tucker himself.

In paragraph 3, the author steps back for a general discussion of the pluses and minuses of writing a biography of a living person. The biographer has the benefit of access to the subject's own oral testimony, but because of the subject's personal bias, objectivity can often be lost. To safeguard against this loss, the author is clear: verification is a must.

The author uses paragraph 4 to reassure you that she has included what could be verified and mostly excluded what couldn't be. The exception is Tucker's personal recollections that pertain to his career, but the author mentions that those recollections comport with the historical record. She notes such recollections will be combined with historical evidence to create the biography. By now, you can surmise the author's **Purpose** (to describe the sources and the methodologies used in writing Tucker's career biography) and the **Main Idea** (to write Tucker's biography, the author will combine carefully verified oral evidence and historical evidence in the hopes of repairing a deficiency in the scholarship).

1. (B) Global

Step 2: Identify the Question Type

Since this question stem asks you to summarize the entire passage, this is a Global question. Predict the author's Main Idea.

Step 3: Research the Relevant Text

The entire passage is relevant, but during your summarization of the author's Main Idea, you should have paid close attention to any "conclusion"-like statements the author makes. Lines 59–61 contain the Keyword *therefore*, and this sentence does indeed help summarize the author's main point. Additionally, lines 16–18 explain why the author took on this biography: so far, scholars have neglected this part of U.S. entertainment history.

Step 4: Make a Prediction

The Main Idea you predicted during Step 1 should form the basis of your prediction: the biographer will combine oral and historical evidence to fill a hole in U.S. entertainment history and write Lorenzo Tucker's career biography.

Step 5: Evaluate the Answer Choices

(B) is a match.

(A) labels the author's methods as "innovative" when nothing in the passage indicates this. Furthermore, the author's study cannot correct "misinterpretations" of African American film and theater history, since there hasn't been enough study of the subject in the first place.

(C) focuses on Tucker himself, rather than his biography. It leaves out the vast majority of the passage, in which the author details the sources and methodologies involved in researching Tucker's biography.

(D) misrepresents the focus of the passage. The author mentions the difficulties of writing a contemporary biography of a living person in paragraph 3, but her goal is not to use the Tucker biography as an example of those problems.

(E) is incorrect because according to the author, not only have Tucker's nonperforming contributions been ignored, but Tucker hasn't been discussed in depth at all. This choice also leaves out the whole discussion of the author's own study.

2. (A) Logic Function

Step 2: Identify the Question Type

Any question asking you to determine the author's "purpose" for including a specific detail, quote, or paragraph is a Logic Function question.

Step 3: Research the Relevant Text

In Logic Function questions, context is key. In addition to the lines referenced in the question, you need to read around them to see how they fit into the paragraph and, by extension, the passage as a whole.

Step 4: Make a Prediction

The author says Tucker's memorabilia helped shed new light on an aspect of the entertainment industry that hasn't been discussed enough. So the author mentioned the memorabilia to identify one of the sources she used (along with Tucker's own memories) to write the biography.

Step 5: Evaluate the Answer Choices

(A) is a perfect match for this prediction.

(B) is Outside the Scope. The author never discusses "typical scholarly approaches" to data gathering.

(C) might be correct if the author indicated some kind of deficiency in Tucker's memorabilia or any other consideration that would render them unusable. But since the author borrows from both Tucker's memories and memorabilia for the biography, **(C)** is a Distortion.

(D) mentions "nonprofessional interests and accomplishments," which are Outside the Scope of the passage. The author explicitly refers to the study as a "career biography" (line 61) of Tucker.

(E) is incorrect because, if anything, the author seems to indicate that the range and scope of Tucker's memorabilia collection set him apart from others.

3. (A) Inference

Step 2: Identify the Question Type

This question stem asks you to use the information in the passage to determine the author's attitude in an imaginary scenario. That makes this an Inference question.

Step 3: Research the Relevant Text

The question stem provides an imaginary scenario, but the author does have thoughts about using a person's own recollections in a historical text. Those thoughts are in paragraph 3.

Step 4: Make a Prediction

From the author's use of phrases like "must be approached with caution" in line 37, you can infer that the author would eye the physicist's book cautiously, since the physicist's use of his own recollections could strip the book of its objectivity.

Step 5: Evaluate the Answer Choices

(A) matches the prediction well.

(B) goes against the author's assertion in paragraph 3 that those involved in the events documented in a study will remember those events in their own unique ways.

(C) also contradicts the passage. The physicist's book constitutes exactly the kind of source that the author uses to write about Lorenzo Tucker, so it's unlikely the author would think personal recollections are "rarely" used in scholarly histories.

(D) draws a distinction between writings about entertainment and those about scientific discovery—a distinction this author never discusses.

(E) flies in the face of the author's claim in lines 43–45 that oral narrative requires a great deal of verification.

4. (C) Inference

Step 2: Identify the Question Type

This question stem is full of words and phrases that indicate an Inference question: "passage most strongly supports," "inference," and "author would agree with."

Step 3: Research the Relevant Text

The text that the passage introduces is discussed throughout the passage, but pay close attention to the parts in which the author expresses a point of view, namely the end of paragraph 1 and paragraph 4.

Step 4: Make a Prediction

There's a lot of information about the author's text, so a prediction might be tough to come by. However, you know the author believes this text fills a gap in scholarship (lines 16–19) and that the personal recollections in the study have undergone thorough verification (paragraph 4). The correct answer must be true based on the author's statements.

Step 5: Evaluate the Answer Choices

(C) is directly supported by paragraph 1, specifically its last sentence, which says that the study sheds new light on an area of American entertainment history that hasn't seen enough scholarly attention. This makes **(C)** the correct answer.

(A) isn't supported by the passage. The author considers the study important because it fills a gap in scholarship, so it wouldn't make sense that the author would think the biography unsuitable for academic audiences.

(B) again introduces the unsupported idea that the author's methods are somehow "innovative," an idea that's never alluded to in the passage.

(D) is something the author would disagree with, since a good chunk of the passage is devoted to discussing the difficulty of obtaining objectivity and the consequent need for verification of information obtained in the study.

(E) imputes to the author a desire to use the study's methodology as a template for some broader purpose, which is never advocated in the passage. Additionally, the author focuses on verifying personal recollections, not on verifying memorabilia authenticity.

5. (E) Global

Step 2: Identify the Question Type

This is a Global question because it asks you to find the author's primary concern—in other words, the author's Purpose.

Step 3: Research the Relevant Text

Instead of researching the text itself, consult your understanding of the big picture that you derived in Step 1 to help you make your prediction.

Step 4: Make a Prediction

The author's Purpose is to detail the sources and methods used in creating the career biography of Lorenzo Tucker.

Step 5: Evaluate the Answer Choices

(E) matches this perfectly.

(A) is far too broad and far too slanted. In Global questions, beware of answer choices that misrepresent the author's Scope or tone. The author does not set out to criticize in this passage.

(B) is a Distortion. The author doesn't advocate for her method to be used across the board. The passage is simply an explanation of the method used on a particular project.

(C) is incorrect because while the author likely believes the study is valuable because it fills a gap, she never summarizes any of the study's content.

(D) suggests that the author is using the passage to correct a previous point of view, but nowhere in the passage does the author even introduce, much less challenge, another viewpoint.

6. (D) Detail

Step 2: Identify the Question Type

Because this question stem asks you to identify what the author mentions, this is a Detail question.

Step 3: Research the Relevant Text

The author discusses the study's source material throughout paragraph 2.

Step 4: Make a Prediction

Paragraph 2 says that the author drew from a variety of sources: microfilms, photos, programs, and newspapers housed in libraries; the 10 of Tucker's films still available; and interviews with Tucker's colleagues, contemporaries, and Tucker himself. Expect one of these sources to appear in the answer choices.

Step 5: Evaluate the Answer Choices

(D) is a perfect match for lines 26–29.

(A) is Outside the Scope. There is no mention of critics' reviews.

(B) is a Distortion. Tucker himself collected memorabilia, and the author interviewed many of Tucker's contemporaries, but the passage doesn't mention that the contemporaries themselves collected memorabilia concerning Tucker.

(C) is Outside the Scope. Scripts that Tucker produced are not discussed.

(E) is also Outside the Scope. Union records are never mentioned.

7. (D) Inference

Step 2: Identify the Question Type

The question stem uses the word *inferences* and asks you to find what the passage "supports" regarding the author's study. That makes this an Inference question.

Step 3: Research the Relevant Text

Much of the passage references the author's study, but the paragraphs that specifically discuss the author's sources and methods are paragraphs 2 and 4 (with a little background introduced in paragraph 1), so expect the right answer to be supported by these parts of the passage.

Step 4: Make a Prediction

Because countless inferences can be drawn from these parts of the passage, prediction may be more trouble than it's worth. Instead, proceed to the answer choices and select the one that must be true based on the text.

Step 5: Evaluate the Answer Choices

(D) is supported by two separate pieces of information. Line 5 mentions that Tucker performed in 20 films, and lines 23–26 mention that the author examined 10 of those films—in other words, not a majority of them—to analyze Tucker's acting technique. This is therefore the valid inference and the correct answer.

(A) is a Distortion. The author's study isn't unique in its divergence from previous studies of African American films; instead, it is unique in shedding any light on this aspect of film history at all.

(B) is unsupported by the passage. Nothing in the text indicates that the author was a colleague of Tucker's.

(C) is likewise unsupported. You can't conclude anything about the author's expectations concerning her standing in the scholarly community.

(E) goes Outside the Scope by introducing other scholarly biographies of African American performers, which the author never discusses. Nor does the author ever introduce the study's rhetorical structure; she details just its methods and sources.

Passage 2: The Autobiography of Nisa

Step 1: Read the Passage Strategically

Sample Roadmap

line #	Keyword/phrase	¶ Margin notes
1		Shostak's work has 3 narrative strands
5	challenges ... penchant	
6	first	1st: biog. details
10	second	2nd: metaphor for women's exp.
13	third	3rd: encounter btw Shostak/Nisa
17	corrects	Nisa correct trad. attitudes
18	qualifies	
19	warning	
21	particularly	
22	seemingly	
24	prime	
25	But	
26	makes ...	Nisa's life exp. shows ugly facts
27	us feel ... ugly	
32	undermine the idyllic ...	examples
33	vision ... cherish	
35		Nisa as metaphor for gender issues
39	In fact ... illuminate not ...	
40	just ... but	Exp. of all women illuminated
41	shock	
42	omits	
45		Shostak presents encounters w/ Nisa
48	but	
49	Indeed	Nisa's life shaped into conven. narrative
50	potent	
51	in fact, do not	
52	":" ... for ...	
53	example	
55		Narr. shaped by dialogue b/tw Shostak & Nisa

Discussion

Paragraph 1 introduces the **Topic** (Shostak's autobiography of Nisa) and immediately outlines the three narrative strands that the book weaves together. The features and effects of these three strands are the passage's **Scope**. Part of being an active LSAT reader is anticipating where the author will go next, so as you were reading lines 6–15, hopefully you suspected the rest of the passage would explore each of these three strands in more detail (especially since there are three additional paragraphs).

Paragraph 2 discusses the first strand at length: the details of Nisa's autobiography. These details not only illuminate our understanding of the !Kung, the author says, but they also help correct traditional attitudes about seemingly "simple" cultures. The facts of Nisa's life, of which the author gives several examples, stand in stark contrast to these preconceptions.

Paragraph 3 gets into the second strand: how Nisa's life can be viewed as a metaphor for women's experiences everywhere. This feature of the book is remarkable to the author because most ethnographic studies don't delve into women's views of women.

Paragraph 4 deals with the third strand: the intercultural encounter between Shostak and her subject. The author claims this interaction shapes the otherwise formless details of Nisa's life into a narrative that those steeped in the Western literary tradition would recognize.

By now, you can see that the author's **Purpose** is to discuss the features of Shostak's book, as well as the book's contributions to the field of ethnography. The **Main Idea** is that the three-pronged approach of Shostak to her autobiography of Nisa breaks new ground in ethnography, illuminates women's experiences, and blurs the distinction between ethnographer and subject.

8. (E) Detail

Step 2: Identify the Question Type

There aren't any clear indicators to help you decide on the question type here, but even if you thought this was an Inference question, your process wouldn't have been any different. Your research and prediction is still just as focused.

Step 3: Research the Relevant Text

The first paragraph is where the author contrasts Shostak's approach with that of other ethnographers. Specifically, lines 5–6 state that her work challenges the typical preference ethnographers have for general, anonymous subject matter.

Step 4: Make a Prediction

The author is therefore asserting that Shostak is distinctive because her focus is specific and particular to an individual. The correct answer will be in line with this.

Step 5: Evaluate the Answer Choices

(E) matches this prediction perfectly.

(A) is incorrect because nothing in the passage indicates that Shostak was studying cultures similar to the !Kung. Moreover, the passage doesn't indicate that this kind of extrapolation isn't present in the work of other ethnographers.

(B) is a 180. Lines 16–17 say that Shostak describes Nisa's personality in terms of !Kung ways.

(C) is a Distortion. Shostak contrasts Nisa's experiences with Western stereotypes of Nisa's culture but not with the culture itself.

(D) is Outside the Scope since, while Shostak's book is full of empirical data, the author doesn't claim Shostak gathers it in an attempt to prove a hypothesis, nor would doing so necessarily break with the approach of most ethnographers.

9. (C) Inference

Step 2: Identify the Question Type

Any question that asks for the "author's opinion" is an Inference question. Some Inference questions specifically ask for the author's attitude in this way.

Step 3: Research the Relevant Text

The phrase "women's views of women" leads you to paragraph 3. The last sentence of the paragraph is where you find the author's point of view.

Step 4: Make a Prediction

The author does not mince words in lines 41–43. The author calls it a salutary, or beneficial, "shock" to realize how often ethnographic literature doesn't include women's perspective on women. Therefore, the author must have a negative view of this omission.

Step 5: Evaluate the Answer Choices

(C) correctly characterizes this attitude.

(A) is a 180. The author all but indicts most ethnographic literature for ignoring women's views of women.

(B) is also a 180. If most women ethnographers were already beginning to study the views of women, then the author wouldn't be shocked by Shostak's choice to do so.

(D) starts out well with "[i]t is surprising," but what shocks the author isn't that ethnographers' studies of women don't use information from "individual interviews of women." What shocks the author is much broader—that most ethnographers don't discuss women's views of women at all.

(E) is a Distortion. The author is disappointed that most ethnographers don't study women's views about women in the first place.

10. (C) Inference

Step 2: Identify the Question Type

The phrase "can be inferred" indicates an Inference question.

Step 3: Research the Relevant Text

Line 18 mentions the "received attitudes" corrected by Shostak's work, but a few lines later, you get an actual example from Michel Leiris: the idea that ethnographers project their own happiness onto the societies they study.

Step 4: Make a Prediction

The Leiris quote and the author's use of quotations around the word *simple* in line 18 suggest that the "received attitudes" are oversimplified and whitewashed ideas of life in these societies. The correct answer will be consistent with this.

Step 5: Evaluate the Answer Choices

(C) clearly exemplifies the received attitudes mentioned in the passage. The assumption that seminomadic people live simple, uncomplicated lives is challenged by facts from Nisa's life that show the serious problems she has faced. **(C)** is therefore correct.

(A) is mentioned by the author as a quality of !Kung people but not as an attitude held by ethnographers.

(B) explains why Westerners are inclined to hold these "received attitudes," but it is not an example of the attitudes themselves.

(D) is a 180 because it's an example of a fact that challenges the received attitudes.

(E) draws a comparison between seminomadic women and other women, a comparison that is Outside the Scope. The "received attitudes" are about societies in general, not about just the society's women.

11. (D) Logic Reasoning (Strengthen)

Step 2: Identify the Question Type

The question stem asks you to find the answer that supports a claim made by the author. It therefore resembles a Strengthen question from the Logical Reasoning section.

Step 3: Research the Relevant Text

This contention made by the author is found in paragraph 3. The author claims that Shostak's interest in issues of gender results in Nisa's story answering not only what it is like to be a !Kung woman but also what it is like to be a woman.

Step 4: Make a Prediction

The correct answer to this question will strengthen this argument. It's impossible to know verbatim what this answer will say, but you do know that it will support the link between Nisa's experience and that of women in other cultures.

Step 5: Evaluate the Answer Choices

(D) is a valid strengthener. If another ethnographer finds similarities in the experiences of women from markedly different cultures, then the author's claim that Nisa's experiences are universal is more likely to be true.

(A) is a Distortion. Sympathy isn't the same as shared experience.

(B) shifts the Scope of the argument from comparing women across cultures to comparing men and women.

(C) is Outside the Scope. A discussion of dialogue technique doesn't help support the idea that Nisa's experience can teach us anything about women's experiences elsewhere.

(E) doesn't help the author's argument because while it builds a bridge to other !Kung women, it does not connect Nisa to women of other cultures, a bridge on which the author's claim relies.

12. (E) Inference

Step 2: Identify the Question Type

The phrase "can be inferred" indicates an Inference question.

Step 3: Research the Relevant Text

Fortunately, this question stem points you to a very specific part of the passage. The entire sentence containing the phrase in question is in lines 49–50.

Step 4: Make a Prediction

The author says Shostak employs a potent literary convention by casting her book in the shape of a "life." And the rest of the paragraph goes on to discuss how Shostak uses her encounter with Nisa to help form the biographical narrative. So the convention in question must be the creation of a recognizably distinct narrative, or story.

Step 5: Evaluate the Answer Choices

(E) is a perfect match.

(A) is a Distortion. It's not Shostak's use of "personal revelation" that ties her to Western literary traditions; it's her shaping of the details of Nisa's life into a recognizable story.

(B) is Outside the Scope. "[D]ramatic emphasis" isn't mentioned by the author as a feature of Shostak's approach.

(C) is also Outside the Scope. Shostak's Western literary convention is creating a story; no mention is made of a "comparison."

(D) is yet another Outside the Scope answer. Nisa's story is presented as representative of women's experience, but nothing in the passage suggests that there's anything "poetic" about Shostak's telling of it.

13. (A) Logic Reasoning (Parallel Reasoning)

Step 2: Identify the Question Type

This is a Parallel Reasoning question because it asks for an answer choice most analogous to reasoning from the passage—in this case, Shostak's approach to her work.

Step 3: Research the Relevant Text

Shostak's approach is discussed mainly in paragraph 4. The author says Shostak interweaves Nisa's story with the presentation of their encounter. She records interactions and dialogue between herself and Nisa.

Step 4: Make a Prediction

You don't know exactly what the right answer will say, but you know what to look for: a writer or artist including his or her interaction with the subject in the work itself.

Step 5: Evaluate the Answer Choices

(A) is a match right away.

(B) doesn't match because Shostak isn't presenting her work as written by Nisa herself.

(C) doesn't match because Shostak isn't trying to use Nisa's life to stand in for the lives of all !Kung people.

(D) doesn't match because Shostak isn't using details from her own life story in the work.

(E) doesn't match because Shostak doesn't write about people in many different cultures.

14. (B) Inference

Step 2: Identify the Question Type

The question stem uses the word *inferred* and it asks you to determine what the author believes, so it's an Inference question.

Step 3: Research the Relevant Text

The question stem sends you back to the end of paragraph 4. The quotation in question is from Nisa herself. Note that the part of the sentence containing the quote begins with "Nisa, for example …" So read the preceding sentence to see what the quote is an example of.

Step 4: Make a Prediction

The first part of the sentence says real human lives don't follow neat narratives. So the quote from Nisa is being used as an example to support this idea.

Step 5: Evaluate the Answer Choices

(B) is a match to that prediction.

(A) is incorrect because Nisa's quote is a mere reporting of events, not a demonstration of cultural values.

(C) is a Distortion. The less-than-idyllic nature of nomadic people's lives is discussed mainly in paragraph 2; Nisa's quote at the end of the passage is unrelated to this.

(D) is a 180. The quote from Nisa is an example of life details that do not form a "recognizable story."

(E) is another Distortion. The fourth paragraph as a whole deals with the blurred distinction between ethnographer and subject, but the quote itself is an example of how a person's life doesn't naturally unfold in the shape of a story.

Passage 3: The Effects of Species Invasion

Step 1: Read the Passage Strategically

Sample Roadmap

line #	Keyword/phrase	¶ Margin notes
Passage A		
1	Until recently	Prev. view: invasive species only harm disturbed hab.
2	complacent	
4	Many shared	
6	most vulnerable ... because	
8	however ... realize	New view: pristine hab. harmed too
9	even	
11	problems	
12	high damage	Serious conseq.
13	merit serious concern	
14	profoundly	Effects of invasive species
15	threaten	
16	For example	Example: forests supplant marsh in Fl
18	Yet	
21	Traditionally	
29	Similarly	Example: plants supplant reptiles in Aus.
Passage B		
32	The real threat	Inv. species don't threaten nature, but our idea of it
33	isn't ... but	
36	Rather	
38	Indeed	
40	often increase	Invasions increase biodiv.
44		Invasions don't destroy ecosys.
48	But ... failed	
51	Unlike	
52	for example	Real effect of invasions: neutral change
56	stark:	
57	In actuality	
59	costly damage ... tragic ... But	Only a few species cause damage
61	not	
62	but rather	

Discussion

Passage A starts by outlining the previous view of most conservationists: they felt (as did Charles Elton) that the risk of damage from invasive species was mostly located in disturbed habitats. Then the author shares a recent development: ecologists now agree that ecosystems are threatened indiscriminately by invasive species.

The next paragraph goes on to detail the kind of damage that can be done to ecosystems by invading species. The Florida marshes are used as an extended example: a species of tree from Australia crowded out the native sawgrass, and several species experienced the fallout. The Scotch broom is used as an additional example.

The author of passage B is less panicked than passage A's author. This author claims that any threat posed by species invasion is just to our idea of what nature should be. Whereas passage A sees a threat to biodiversity, passage B points out that introduced species can increase biodiversity. Whereas passage A warns that ecosystems could disappear, passage B says that invading species transform rather than eliminate ecosystems. Passage B ends by pointing out that most introduced species blend into their ecosystems without causing any kind of catastrophic damage.

Now that you've read both passages, you can see that they both share a **Topic** (species invasion) and a **Scope** (its effects on ecosystems). The passages diverge when it comes to Purpose and Main Idea. For passage A, the Purpose is to warn about the deleterious effects of species invasion, and the Main Idea is that ecologists have rightly begun to realize the damage that can be done to many different kinds of ecosystems by species that originated elsewhere. For passage B, the **Purpose** is to counter the idea that species invasion has only negative effects, and the **Main Idea** is that invading species don't always damage their environments—they merely transform them into different environments.

15. (D) Global

Step 2: Identify the Question Type

This question stem is asking for a question that both passages concern themselves with answering. That makes this a Global question, since it focuses on an issue central to both passages.

Step 3: Research the Relevant Text

Your understanding of the big picture will form the basis of your prediction here. Specifically, since the passages share the same Topic and Scope, these will be most useful to you.

Step 4: Make a Prediction

The Scope of both passages is the effects of invasive species on the ecosystems they invade. The right answer will be a question that is within this Scope.

Step 5: Evaluate the Answer Choices

(D) is an exact match.

(A) is incorrect because only passage A touches on the idea that some ecosystems are more vulnerable than others to invasive species.

(B) is not answered by either passage. Both authors agree that some invasive species can be harmful, but no mention is made of how to distinguish harmful species from harmless species. Furthermore, the author of passage A does not even acknowledge the possibility of harmless invasive species.

(C) isn't answered by either passage. Passage A comes closest, since it decries damage caused by introduced species, but no suggestion is made about how to prevent such damage.

(E) is an issue neither passage addresses. Both passages discuss the effects of species invading nonnative ecosystems, but neither author tells you how they're able to do so in the first place.

16. (E) Detail

Step 2: Identify the Question Type

Because this question is asking what one or the other passage "asserts" (rather than something looser like "implies" or "suggests"), this is a Detail question.

Step 3: Research the Relevant Text

Your research here is two pronged: you'll have to find what passage A says about the ecologists and then make sure it's not stated in passage B. Your Roadmap tells you that paragraph 1 of passage A discusses the ecologists.

Step 4: Make a Prediction

According to passage A, the ecologists in question used to be complacent about the effects of invasive species, but now they're waking up to the idea that invasive species can damage all kinds of ecosystems. And sure enough, this assertion is nowhere in passage B.

Step 5: Evaluate the Answer Choices

(E) is a good paraphrase of this prediction.

(A) is a Distortion. Both authors discuss the ecological impact of invasive species. So, research has not been limited to studies on economic impact.

(B) is Outside the Scope. Neither author defines what an ecosystem is, so neither author can be inconsistent with the criteria used to make that determination.

(C) is Half-Right/Half-Wrong. Passage A's author likely agrees with this statement, but so does passage B's author in lines 58–59: "[a] few species do cause costly damage and tragic extinctions." Additionally, the word *most* in the answer choice is Extreme; it is not clear that the number of ecologists that hold this view is over half of all ecologists.

(D) is Outside the Scope. It is unknown what the prevailing view was before Elton's book. Elton introduced the view that disturbed habitats were more vulnerable to invasive species, but no mention is made of whether ecologists were focused on biodiversity only at the local level before Elton's book.

17. (E) Inference

Step 2: Identify the Question Type

The words "would be most likely to agree" indicate an Inference question. Here, you need to infer the opinion of passage B's author about a term used in passage A.

Step 3: Research the Relevant Text

First things first: line 17. In this part of passage A, the author uses *natural* with the word *wild* to describe how the Everglades might appear to the untrained eye. The term is being used there to mean "pristine and undisturbed." Now on to passage B, where the author says in the very first sentence that invasive species aren't harmful to actual nature but rather to our human ideal of nature.

Step 4: Make a Prediction

The author of passage B is thus accusing some individuals (including, ostensibly, the author of passage A) of confusing the two meanings of *nature*—a logical flaw of equivocation, perhaps? The correct answer needs to be consistent with this prediction.

Step 5: Evaluate the Answer Choices

(E) is entirely consistent with this prediction and with passage B's point of view.

(A) makes a distinction that the author of passage B doesn't entertain. The "difference between pristine and disturbed environments" is much more relevant to passage A.

(B) is a Distortion. The author of passage B isn't implying that passage A uses *natural* in ways that contradict each other. Instead, passage B implies that the word *natural* has two senses that need to be distinguished from each other.

(C) is a Distortion. The author certainly wouldn't think that passage A clarifies any difference between *wild* and *natural*—the equivocal way in which *natural* is used is the main source of passage B's critique.

(D) is unsupported, since the author of passage B says nothing to indicate that humans' idea of what constitutes nature is in any way unconventional. He may disagree with

how the term *natural* is being used but not that the alternate definition is unusual to begin with.

18. (B) Logic Reasoning (Parallel Reasoning)

Step 2: Identify the Question Type

This question stem asks for the answer choice "most analogous" to passage B's main point, so it's phrased identically to a Parallel Reasoning question. You'll need to predict passage B's Main Idea and find an answer choice employing the same logic.

Step 3: Research the Relevant Text

Your global understanding of passage B's big picture will be more useful to you than a close reading of any lines in the text. Passage B's Main Idea is that the changes brought to ecosystems by invasive species aren't in themselves negative and aren't the cause for concern that those like the author of passage A think they are.

Step 4: Make a Prediction

You don't know what subject matter the correct answer will use. However, you do know that it will match the broad idea that changes caused to a certain system by elements from another system aren't necessarily a reason for alarm.

Step 5: Evaluate the Answer Choices

(B) matches this sentiment exactly.

(A) would be correct if the change to the piece of clothing happened because of an influence from outside. But since **(A)** is merely concerned with the passage of time, it misses the point of both passages.

(C) distorts passage B's main point. Passage B doesn't assert that species invasion is necessary; it just asserts that when such invasion occurs, its effects aren't necessarily something to bewail.

(D) is Extreme. The author of passage B isn't claiming that the influence of introduced species is necessary for an ecosystem to thrive but only that such influence isn't always a bad thing.

(E) is incorrect because passage B doesn't draw a distinction between synthetic and natural phenomena.

19. (D) Logic Reasoning (Method of Argument)

Step 2: Identify the Question Type

This question asks about the relationship between the passages, so you'll have to determine how each author develops his or her passage. Thus, your process here will be similar to that for a Method of Argument question.

Step 3: Research the Relevant Text

There's no specific place to go to research your answer, but you should pay close attention to the Purpose of each passage and how the Purposes relate to each other (e.g., whether or not passage B is a direct response to passage A).

Step 4: Make a Prediction

On Comparative Reading passages, make sure to take a few seconds during Step 1 to characterize the relationship between the passages, because the questions will focus heavily on this relationship. Here, the author of passage A raises serious concerns about the severity of the effects of invasive species on ecosystems. And the author of passage B characterizes these effects as neither good nor bad but simply evaluated in terms of humans' view of nature.

Step 5: Evaluate the Answer Choices

(D) is the best match here.

(A) is a Distortion. Neither passage is concerned with hypothesizing about the "causes" of species invasion; the passages are divided about how to view its effects.

(B) discusses an assumption central to both passages, but no such assumption exists. And passage B doesn't defend any claim or concept questioned in passage A.

(C) is partially correct in its discussion of passage A, but it mischaracterizes the tone of passage B. The author of passage B is neutral about the effects of species invasion on the ecosystems they invade. Even if the author of passage B views an increase in biodiversity as "beneficial," the word *usually* in this answer choice makes it more Extreme than the author's opinion.

(E) is incorrect because passage A doesn't make any policy proposals and neither does passage B critique any.

Passage 4: The Paradox of Omnipotence

Step 1: Read the Passage Strategically

Sample Roadmap

line #	Keyword/phrase	¶ Margin notes
1	?	
4	or even	
5	But	Paradox of omnip; Sov. has power to limit its own power
6	thereby contradicting	
8	traditionally	
10	considerable	Omnip. can cause prac. diffic.
11	difficulty	
14	confronted	N&W example: Eng/Fr monarchs
17	best	
18	For example	N&W: sov. should try to limit certain actions
20	Yet	Ex: reneging on debts
25		Eng/Fr needed $$ to expand
27	however	
30		Omnip → reput. for not repaying debts
32	Consequently	
34	Not surprisingly	Conseq. higher int. rates for monarchs
38	argue	N&W: Eng. Constit. → Parl. controls $$
40	halted ... faithless	
41	Henceforth	
44	disregard	
45	inability	Crown's credit improves
46	ability	
47	because	
49	Thanks to	N&W: constit. limits sov. power
50	now conventional	
51	benefit	
52	But ... neglect	Auth disagrees
53	fail	
54	For example	
55	did not solve	
56	but just	
57	":"	Paradox of omnip. trans. from Crown to Parliament

Discussion

The author uses paragraph 1 to lay out a theoretical conundrum: if a sovereign has unlimited power, then it also has the power to limit its own power, in which case it would no longer have unlimited power. The author then names the conundrum (and, by extension, the passage's **Topic**): the "paradox of omnipotence."

Paragraph 2 states that the omnipotence paradox has practical consequences. This challenge is the passage's **Scope**. The author introduces two social scientists, North and Weingast, who studied the practical difficulties the paradox of omnipotence caused for English and French monarchs in the 17th and 18th centuries.

Paragraph 3 presents one of North and Weingast's assertions: sometimes, the best thing an omnipotent sovereign can do is to commit itself not to do something. Specifically, an omnipotent sovereign should not renege on financial commitments. While an omnipotent sovereign is in the position to ignore its financial obligations, doing so would affect its standing with creditors.

Paragraph 4 gets even more specific by showing how this scenario played itself out in England and France. Monarchs needed to borrow money to expand their empires, but with no mechanism in place to prevent them from dodging their debts, their credit rating plummeted, and creditors in turn hiked their interest rates.

In paragraph 5, the author presents North and Weingast's argument: the Glorious Revolution turned the situation around in England by giving Parliament the power of the purse. This meant that the Crown couldn't wriggle out of its financial obligations, and creditors became more willing to lend money to the Crown at lower rates.

In the final paragraph, the author presents the now-conventional view (shared by North and Weingast) that constitutional settlements (such as the one ushered in by the Glorious Revolution) solve the omnipotence paradox. But the author disagrees, arguing that instead of solving the problem, the English constitution just transferred the problem from one entity to another. Now, the author argues, Parliament is a sovereign power itself. This settles the author's **Purpose** (to explain the consequences of and evaluate a purported solution to the paradox of omnipotence) and his **Main Idea**—that the omnipotence paradox can have practical consequences for governments, particularly when it comes to lending and borrowing money, and that redistributing power through a constitution isn't a totally effective solution.

20. (A) Global

Step 2: Identify the Question Type

This is a Global question because it asks you to determine the main point of the passage.

Step 3: Research the Relevant Text

The author's main point isn't always stated directly in a certain line or two of the passage. For Global questions, Step 3 more often involves consulting the understanding of the big picture (Topic, Scope, Purpose, Main Idea) that you gained during Step 1.

Step 4: Make a Prediction

The correct answer needs to encapsulate the whole passage while also including the author's point of view. In the author's view, absolute power creates a paradox that has practical implications for sovereigns, and constitutions are not necessarily a solution to the problem (England being a prime example).

Step 5: Evaluate the Answer Choices

(A) matches this prediction.

(B) is too broad. The author isn't making a general point about similarities between theoretical paradoxes and their practical counterparts in politics. The author is making a specific point about a specific paradox, that of sovereign omnipotence.

(C) is too specific. England is used as an example of the paradox of omnipotence, but England is not the overall focus of the passage. And while monarchs did escape the practical problem after the Glorious Revolution, this answer choice ignores the author's argument that the burden was not completely eliminated but was instead transferred to Parliament.

(D) also puts the focus entirely on England and the Glorious Revolution, when the author is just using that country's situation as an example to demonstrate his points. Specifically, this choice only addresses paragraph 6.

(E) would be correct if the passage contained only the first paragraph. However, **(E)** doesn't include anything about the practical consequences of the logical contradiction or about the limits of the constitutional solution.

21. (E) Inference

Step 2: Identify the Question Type

The phrase "passage most strongly supports" is a clear indication of an Inference question.

Step 3: Research the Relevant Text

The question stem mentions "creditors" and "wealthy subjects," so the information at the end of paragraph 4 will yield the correct answer.

Step 4: Make a Prediction

In lines 32–37 in paragraph 4, the author mentions that before the Glorious Revolution of 1688, English and French monarchs abused their unlimited power by reneging on their debts. This led creditors to set higher interest rates for monarchs than for their wealthy subjects. This suggests the creditors considered the wealthy subjects more trustworthy borrowers than their monarchs.

Step 5: Evaluate the Answer Choices

(E) matches the prediction and is a valid inference.

(A) is unsupported by the passage. Just because the wealthy subjects could borrow on more favorable terms doesn't mean creditors saw them as contributing any less than their "fair share."

(B) goes against the passage, since the wealthy subjects had a better credit rating than their monarchs. Arguably, this might have been the view creditors had of the monarchs themselves, but it was not a view the creditors had of the wealthy subjects.

(C) might be true, since the monarchs had a reputation for ignoring property rights when doing so suited their interests (which wealthy subjects likely didn't appreciate), but you can't conclude that **(C)** is unequivocally true based on the passage itself.

(D) is unsupported. The wealthy subjects' lower interest rates don't necessarily indicate they had a grasp of the theoretical conundrum of the paradox of omnipotence.

22. (B) Inference

Step 2: Identify the Question Type

When a question stem uses the phrase "[b]ased on the passage," it's an Inference question.

Step 3: Research the Relevant Text

The question stem gives you a lot to help you research. Paragraph 5 discusses the reforms ushered in by the Glorious Revolution.

Step 4: Make a Prediction

The Glorious Revolution, according to the passage, brought about a constitutional settlement that brought the purse strings under Parliament's control. This stopped the Crown from shirking its debts, which in turn led to the Crown being able to borrow at lower rates. So it's clear the lower rates are at least partially the result of Parliament's ability to defend creditors from any royal abuses.

Step 5: Evaluate the Answer Choices

(B) would therefore be an important matter to settle for any creditor making a decision about lending to the Crown.

(A) is Outside the Scope. Parliament can effectively defend commercial interests whether or not its members are aware of the paradox presented by their unlimited power.

(C) makes an issue out of how recently Parliamentary elections were held, which is totally Outside the Scope of the passage.

(D) also introduces an irrelevant idea—that of the number of laws enacted.

(E) would be correct if the question asked about the period before the Glorious Revolution, when the English monarchies needed (and took) large amounts of capital in order to expand their armies. However, once Parliament began to play a supervisory role and the Crown could no longer dishonor its commitments, the number of its commitments became irrelevant.

23. (B) Logic Reasoning (Principle)

Step 2: Identify the Question Type

The question stem asks for a principle that underlies the author's argument. This resembles a Principle question from the Logical Reasoning section. Use the same techniques that you'd use on that question type here.

Step 3: Research the Relevant Text

The question stem directs you to the last paragraph—specifically, the author's argument, which is contained in lines 52–63.

Step 4: Make a Prediction

This Principle question mimics an Assumption question, since it asks for an idea that "underlies" the argument. The author's conclusion, so to speak, is that the constitutional settlement didn't solve the paradox of omnipotence. His evidence is that the constitutional settlement of the Glorious Revolution simply transferred unlimited power from the Crown to Parliament, so Parliament ended up in the position the Crown originally occupied. The author must be assuming that relocating a problem is not a sufficient solution. Instead, a solution must completely eliminate the issue.

Step 5: Evaluate the Answer Choices

(B) is a good match for this prediction.

(A) distorts the author's argument. The author is concerned with the practical consequences of the original theoretical paradox, but he doesn't judge the solution in practical terms.

(C) is Extreme. The author isn't arguing for completely abolishing the form of the English government. The author merely argues that constitutions don't always solve the problems created by absolute power.

(D) would suggest that the author was fine with Parliament having unlimited legal authority, but the author says that's still part of the problem.

(E) goes too far. The author isn't arguing for an explicit enumeration of all the powers of each branch of government.

24. (A) Detail

Step 2: Identify the Question Type

The phrase "[a]ccording to the passage" indicates a Detail question. Use the clues in the question stem to guide your research.

Step 3: Research the Relevant Text

The author discusses the consequences of the English and French monarchs' absolute power in paragraph 4. Lines 28–37 spell out the answer for you (note the phrase "absence of limitations" in lines 28–29 and the Keyword [*c*]*onsequently* in line 32).

Step 4: Make a Prediction

Because the English and French monarchs had no limits on their power, they could shirk their debts and refuse to honor their commitments. This led to higher interest rates and less favorable borrowing terms.

Step 5: Evaluate the Answer Choices

(A) matches the prediction.

(B) is never mentioned in the passage as a step monarchs took to exercise their power.

(C) is a Distortion. The wealthy subjects had lower interest rates than monarchs, but that doesn't mean they could more easily borrow.

(D) is Outside the Scope. Nothing in the passage compares how much money the monarchs' unrestricted power caused them to borrow to how much they would have borrowed if they did not have that unrestricted power.

(E) is a 180. The monarchs' absolute power meant that they did not have to honor property rights.

25. (D) Logic Function

Step 2: Identify the Question Type

The phrase "in order to" indicates a Logic Function question. Instead of determining what the author says, your task is to determine why he says it.

Step 3: Research the Relevant Text

As with any Logic Function question, you need to read around the lines referenced to get a sense of context. The referenced lines come at the beginning of paragraph 4, in which the author describes the credit crunch the English and French crowns faced.

Step 4: Make a Prediction

However, a glance up at the end of paragraph 2 reveals the real reason why the author mentions the two countries' financial woes—as examples of the practical consequences of having unchecked power. If the countries had not needed to borrow money, in this case to finance their struggles to expand their empires, then they wouldn't have needed to deal with the practical challenge of the paradox of omnipotence.

Step 5: Evaluate the Answer Choices

(D) is a match.

(A) is incorrect because the author never intends to weaken this particular assertion made by North and Weingast.

(B) is a Distortion. The monarchs' need for capital wasn't an example of their low standing with their creditors—it was a function of their struggle to expand their empires.

(C) is another Distortion. The monarchs' need for capital doesn't demonstrate their unlimited power. Their unlimited power allowed them to renege on commitments to repay loans, but it wasn't why they needed the loans of vast amounts of capital to begin with.

(E) attributes to the author a claim that he never makes in the passage. The huge need for capital does not apply to whether sovereigns have honored or broken their commitments—those responses would relate to only after they've received the capital they sought to borrow.

26. (C) Inference

Step 2: Identify the Question Type

This is an Inference question because it's asking you to make a conclusion about a hypothetical situation—denoted by the word [*s*]*uppose*—based on information in the passage. Also, the word *inferred* is a sure signal of an Inference question.

Step 3: Research the Relevant Text

The English Parliament is discussed in paragraphs 5 and 6.

Step 4: Make a Prediction

The author says Parliament began to control the purse strings of the English government after the Glorious Revolution. The author also asserts that, instead of solving the problem of the omnipotence paradox, the Glorious Revolution merely transferred the problem from the Crown to Parliament. So Parliament, after 1688, had unchecked power. The correct answer will be consistent with this information.

Step 5: Evaluate the Answer Choices

(C) is supported by the author's assertion in line 59 that Parliament lacks the power to bind itself. Thus, like the sovereigns before it, Parliament can unmake any of its commitments as easily as it made them. This makes **(C)** the correct answer.

(A) is unsupported. The author never makes a connection between a government's association with other nations and that government's ability to obtain favorable credit terms.

(B) is similar to (A) in that it attempts to link Parliament's creditworthiness to its partnership with other nations. But the passage doesn't support that link.

(D) should be eliminated because the passage indicates only that the commercial interests represented by Parliament want property rights upheld. The passage doesn't provide any information on the views of the commercial interests regarding this kind of commitment.

(E) isn't consistent with the passage. The author already claims that Parliament has absolute sovereignty to do whatever it wants, so it's not likely that joining a multinational body could increase that power.

27. (E) Inference

Step 2: Identify the Question Type

This is an Inference question because it asks you to find the answer choice that those mentioned in the passage would agree or disagree with based on their viewpoints.

Step 3: Research the Relevant Text

Your Roadmap tells you that the author's view is contrasted with that of North and Weingast in paragraph 6 (lines 49–53 to be exact).

Step 4: Make a Prediction

North and Weingast would accept the idea that constitutions solve the paradox of omnipotence, but the author clearly disagrees with that. The correct answer will be consistent with this.

Step 5: Evaluate the Answer Choices

(E) is a direct match for this prediction.

(A) is mentioned in paragraph 5 as part of North and Weingast's argument, but nothing in the passage suggests the author would disagree with this.

(B) is too broad. North and Weingast think that the constitutional settlement took care of the omnipotence paradox in England, but that's not the same as saying they think the paradox of omnipotence no longer exists at all.

(C) is also mentioned at the end of paragraph 5 as support for North and Weingast's argument, but presumably the author doesn't disagree with this.

(D) is mentioned in paragraph 4, but this is something that the author asserts, not something with which he disagrees.

Section II: Logical Reasoning

Q#	Question Type	Correct	Difficulty
1	Weaken	A	★
2	Paradox	A	★
3	Strengthen	B	★
4	Paradox (EXCEPT)	B	★
5	Inference	E	★
6	Assumption (Necessary)	A	★
7	Inference	E	★★
8	Principle (Identify/Strengthen)	E	★
9	Flaw	B	★
10	Point at Issue	D	★
11	Inference	C	★
12	Method of Argument	D	★★
13	Flaw	E	★★★★
14	Assumption (Necessary)	A	★★★★
15	Principle (Identify/Strengthen)	C	★
16	Point at issue	C	★★★
17	Weaken	B	★★
18	Principle (Identify/Strengthen)	D	★★
19	Parallel Reasoning	B	★★
20	Role of a Statement	C	★★★
21	Flaw	D	★★★
22	Role of a Statement	B	★★★
23	Parallel Flaw	B	★★★
24	Inference	D	★
25	Strengthen	C	★★

1. (A) Weaken

Step 1: Identify the Question Type

The phrase "most seriously weaken" indicates you are dealing with a Weaken question. Identify the conclusion, paraphrase the evidence, predict the central assumption, and then look for a fact that attacks that central assumption.

Step 2: Untangle the Stimulus

The author concludes in the first sentence of the argument that the Johnsons should plant peach trees instead of apricot trees. The author acknowledges that apricots are very popular but contrasts this point with two pieces of evidence to support the conclusion: peach trees are cheaper and will bear fruit sooner.

Step 3: Make a Prediction

The author assumes there is no other good reason why the Johnsons would plant apricot trees instead of peach trees. In analyzing the answer choices, look for the answer that will provide a reason why the Johnsons should plant apricot trees instead of peach trees.

Step 4: Evaluate the Answer Choices

(A) correctly provides a reason why apricot trees would be preferable to peach trees: apricots sell for more than peaches.

(B) is a 180. It strengthens the argument by providing a third reason why the Johnsons would want to plant peach trees, stating that peach trees produce fruit for more years than apricot trees.

(C) is incorrect. This answer choice states that the cost to maintain either tree is the same. The correct answer needs to show apricot trees are preferable to peach trees.

(D) is Outside the Scope. To weaken the author's argument, the correct answer must provide a reason why apricot trees should be planted instead of peach trees. This answer choice discusses the growth in the market for apricots but does not discuss how this growth compares to that of the market for peaches, nor does this choice discuss how this trend will carry into the future, when the Johnsons' trees will begin producing fruit.

(E) is Outside the Scope. This answer choice discusses a decrease in peach production but, like **(D)**, does not compare both fruits and so doesn't explain how this decrease impacts which type of tree the Johnsons should plant. If anything, this choice strengthens the argument, because it means peach supply has gone down. But even so, it's possible that demand for peaches has also declined.

2. (A) Paradox

Step 1: Identify the Question Type

The word *explain* indicates that this is a Paradox question. Summarize the seemingly inconsistent facts in the argument and then look for an answer that makes sense of the mystery. This question stem provides additional direction by asking you to explain specifically "the increased rate of population loss."

Step 2: Untangle the Stimulus

When reading the stimulus, you need to identify the contrary positions. A rare variety of camel was endangered because its habitat was used as a place to test weapons. Now the testing has ended, but the camel population is declining even more quickly.

Step 3: Make a Prediction

The correct answer will explain why the population of camels is declining more quickly even though the testing of weapons has ended.

Step 4: Evaluate the Answer Choices

(A) correctly provides a reason why the population of camels is declining even more quickly now. The weapons testing prevented poachers from killing the camels. Now that the testing has ended, the poachers are able to hunt the camels, further reducing their numbers. This explains why the population of camels is decreasing more quickly without the weapons testing.

(B) is an Irrelevant Comparison. The greater damage caused by the weapons testing earlier in the testing period as compared to later in that period does not explain why the population is declining more quickly now that the testing has ended.

(C) is incorrect. By stating that the land was still somewhat dangerous after testing ended, this answer choice would explain why camels continue to die. However, this choice does not explain why the population is declining more quickly now that the testing has ended.

(D) is Outside the Scope. Like **(B)**, this answer choice focuses solely on the time during weapons testing. The focus of the correct answer will be on why the population is declining after the testing has ended.

(E) is Outside the Scope. Again, the focus of the correct answer will be on the time after the testing ended, not during the testing. This answer choice discusses the impact of food scarcity during the weapons testing, which doesn't explain the change in the rate of population decline that has occurred since testing ended.

3. (B) Strengthen

Step 1: Identify the Question Type

The phrase "most strengthens" identifies this as a Strengthen question. Break down the argument into conclusion and evidence, predict the central assumption, and find an answer choice that supports the author's assumption.

Step 2: Untangle the Stimulus

The author's conclusion, signaled by the Keyword [*t*]*hus*, states that reading fewer books and spending more time on each book is better than reading as many as possible. To support this position, the author compares reading a book to traveling to a new place and states that readers read and travelers travel to enlarge their understanding rather than simply to acquire information.

Step 3: Make a Prediction

First, the author believes traveling and reading a book are similar enough to compare them to each other. Second, the author believes it is better to read fewer books and spend more time on each book just as travelers visit fewer places and spend more time in each place. Since he also states that both readers and travelers try to enlarge their understanding rather than simply acquire information, the author assumes that traveling in one location for a longer period of time will result in greater understanding. The correct answer will reinforce the author's assumption.

Step 4: Evaluate the Answer Choices

(B) correctly states that spending additional days in a single location will provide a greater understanding of that place than will staying only a few days there.

(A) is Outside the Scope. Why tourists travel—for business or relaxation, and so on—is beyond the scope of this author's argument. Additionally, this answer choice doesn't address duration of stay.

(C) is an Irrelevant Comparison. This answer choice incorrectly compares visiting a place to reading about a place, whereas the author is simply saying the same principle applies to both. The focus of the argument is on the amount of time it takes to gain a greater understanding about a book or place, not on whether a book or a place promotes greater understanding.

(D) is a Distortion. This answer choice fails to connect understanding a single location with the amount of time spent in that location. It explains why some tourists stay longer, but the author is only concerned with the idea that doing so increases understanding.

(E) is Outside the Scope. The author makes a recommendation based on a general rule. That some tourists don't have the same goals would, if anything, weaken the argument.

4. (B) Paradox (EXCEPT)

Step 1: Identify the Question Type

The phrase "helps to account for" indicates that this is a Paradox question. Summarize the seemingly inconsistent facts in the argument. The EXCEPT indicates that four of the answers will explain why the facts are not actually inconsistent, while the correct answer will not resolve the paradox.

Step 2: Untangle the Stimulus

The first part of the stimulus sets the scene, while the paradox comes in the last two sentences. In this argument, a three-piece modular sofa costs almost twice as much as a standard sofa, even though the modular sofa and the standard sofa are of similar size and quality.

Step 3: Make a Prediction

Four of the answer choices will help explain why the modular sofa is twice as expensive as the standard sofa, while the correct answer will not help to resolve this issue.

Step 4: Evaluate the Answer Choices

(B) is correct. The level of demand for sofas in general does not explain why certain sofas of similar size and quality are priced differently.

(A) resolves the paradox by stating that modular sofas are not mass-produced. This would increase their manufacturing cost relative to that of standard sofas, which can be mass-produced. This in turn would explain why a modular sofa is more expensive.

(C) resolves the paradox. Because the most fashionable designers use modular furniture designs, the status of modular sofas would increase, leading to higher prices for consumers.

(D) resolves the paradox by demonstrating that the average price difference is due to modular sofas being custom-made and never going on sale.

(E) accounts for the paradox because the increased upholstered surface area on modular sofas would increase the amount of fabric needed as well as production time and care. That would increase the cost of manufacturing and thus the cost to consumers.

5. (E) Inference

Step 1: Identify the Question Type

The phrase "most logically completes" indicates you are dealing with an Inference question. The correct answer must be true based on the statements in the stimulus.

Step 2: Untangle the Stimulus

Paraphrase the statements in the stimulus. Testosterone protects brain cells from damage and can lower levels of beta-amyloid in the brain. Beta-amyloid helps cause Alzheimer's disease, and people whose brain cells are susceptible to injury are probably more likely to get Alzheimer's disease.

Step 3: Make a Prediction

The answer choice must be a conclusion supported by the stimulus. Some Inference stimuli with duplicated terms yield themselves nicely to predictions. Use that strategy whenever possible. Testosterone can likely help prevent Alzheimer's disease because it reduces the level of beta-amyloid and protects brain cells from injury. We can write this succinctly in Formal Logic terms:

| If | testosterone | → | decrease in beta-amyloid |
| If | beta-amyloid | → | Alzheimer's |

Step 4: Evaluate the Answer Choices

(E) is correct. If testosterone reduces levels of beta-amyloid, which in turn provides some protection from Alzheimer's disease, then it follows that a decline in testosterone will increase the risk of Alzheimer's disease.

(A) is Extreme. According to the stimulus, people whose brain cells are susceptible to injury are "probably more susceptible" to Alzheimer's. Both *probably* and *susceptible* are tentative words. It is extreme to say that everyone who is susceptible will eventually develop Alzheimer's disease.

(B) is Extreme. Beta-amyloid levels contribute "causally" to Alzheimer's disease, but saying the disease is entirely dependent on beta-amyloid levels goes beyond the facts provided in the stimulus.

(C) is a Distortion. This answer choice incorrectly reverses the causality. People whose brain cells are susceptible to injury (something testosterone protects against) are susceptible to Alzheimer's disease, but the stimulus never says it works the other way around.

(D) is also a Distortion. The argument states that susceptibility to brain cell injury can contribute to developing Alzheimer's disease. Limiting the risk of brain cell injury only to people with Alzheimer's disease distorts the relationship presented in the stimulus.

6. (A) Assumption (Necessary)

Step 1: Identify the Question Type

The word *assumption* identifies this as an Assumption question. In addition, the word *depends* indicates you're looking for an assumption necessary for the author's conclusion to follow from her evidence. You can use the Denial Test to check or eliminate answers.

Step 2: Untangle the Stimulus

The author concludes that paying senior staff with stock options "is not a wise policy." The author provides two reasons to support this position: (1) stock options greatly increase the difference in income between senior staff and other employees, and (2) anything that undermines morale reduces the profitability of a business.

Step 3: Make a Prediction

Based on the evidence, anything that lowers morale reduces profitability. Plus, the author does not want to see large differences in income between senior staff and employees. The author is assuming that morale and a large difference in income are related. The correct answer will bring together these two pieces of evidence to fully support the conclusion.

Step 4: Evaluate the Answer Choices

(A) correctly connects large differences between fixed-salary employees and senior staff to lower employee morale.

(B) simply restates evidence already provided in the stimulus. The author has already stated that the profitability of a business is impacted by low employee morale.

(C) describes an Irrelevant Comparison. The focus of the argument is to convince a company not to offer stock options because doing so will lower morale and, by extension, profitability. However, for other reasons, those companies may still be more profitable than firms that don't offer stock options. The author does not need companies that offer stock options to be less profitable than others for her conclusion (don't offer stock options) to follow.

(D) incorrectly negates the argument's logic. The stimulus says that undermined morale results in reduced profitability. But the author doesn't provide any evidence about what would increase profitability. Also, the word *invariably* is Extreme and not supported by the stimulus.

(E) is an Irrelevant Comparison. A comparison of the productivity level of two groups of employees is beyond the Scope of the argument. The correct answer needs to be centered on employee morale and, by extension, profitability.

7. (E) Inference

Step 1: Identify the Question Type

The phrase "most strongly supported by the information above" identifies this as an Inference question. Work through the stimulus to paraphrase the statements and make any logical connections between them.

Step 2: Untangle the Stimulus

Paraphrase the stimulus. Antibiotics are fed to animals because the drugs keep animals healthy and increase meat yields. Scientists recommend ending the use of antibiotics because feeding these drugs to animals makes them less effective in humans. But, if animals yield less meat, some farmers will go out of business.

Step 3: Make a Prediction

The correct answer choice must be supported by the stimulus. Some Inference stimuli with duplicated terms yield themselves nicely to predictions. Use that strategy whenever possible. Based on the statements in the stimulus, it must be true that if antibiotics are phased out and no other way is found to maintain meat yields, some farmers will go out of business.

Step 4: Evaluate the Answer Choices

(E) correctly connects phasing out antibiotics to some farmers going out of business.

(A) is incorrect. The accuracy of scientists' claims is irrelevant. While it is true that if the scientists' recommendation is followed, some farmers will go out of business, it's possible that the recommendation may be followed even if the scientists' belief is incorrect.

(B) is Extreme. Scientists believe that including antibiotics in animal feed "may" make the drugs "less effective" in humans. That language is a lot more tentative than this answer choice, which states that the result "will" happen and that the antibiotics will become completely "ineffective."

(C) incorrectly reverses the logic of the stimulus. You can conclude that if the scientists' recommendation is heeded, some farmers will go out of business. But if the scientists' recommendation is not heeded, there is no guarantee that "no farmers" will go out of business. A farmer may go out of business for other reasons.

(D) is Outside the Scope. The stimulus doesn't say what would happen if animals became less healthy, only what would occur if meat yields were reduced. In any case, saying that "most" farmers will go out of business is also Extreme.

8. (E) Principle (Identify/Strengthen)

Step 1: Identify the Question Type

The words *principles* and *justifying* are common signals of a Principle question. Also, you're asked to determine which of the principles in the answer choices justifies the application of the guideline in the stimulus, so this mimics a Strengthen question.

Step 2: Untangle the Stimulus

The guideline states that public officials should not influence contracts or perform acts that benefit themselves. They should even avoid the appearance of such impropriety. The application states that the mayor of Greenville acted improperly by awarding a contract to a relative's company.

Step 3: Make a Prediction

The guideline does not mention relatives of public officials. The correct answer will treat actions that benefit the mayor's relatives as similar to actions that would benefit the mayor, thereby supporting the application of the guideline to the mayor.

Step 4: Evaluate the Answer Choices

(E) correctly states that benefits to the mayor's relatives essentially benefit the mayor directly. In that case, the Greenville mayor did act inappropriately by urging the contract be awarded to one of his relatives.

(A) is an Irrelevant Comparison. While it might be true that public officials should be held to a higher standard than private individuals, this does not justify the application of the guideline to the mayor in this situation.

(B) is Outside the Scope. The mayor may have supported the awarding of the contract to the relative's company because the company was the lowest-cost and most reliable option. However, cost and reliability are not mentioned in the guideline being applied, whereas the appearance of impropriety is.

(C) is another Irrelevant Comparison. Based on the guideline, the appearance of impropriety should be avoided just as much as Improper actions. This answer does not provide any additional justification for why the guideline should apply to the mayor.

(D) is Outside the Scope. The guideline only discusses actions that would be considered improper, not actions that would be considered risky. Considering the riskiness of the mayor's decision would not justify the application.

9. (B) Flaw

Step 1: Identify the Question Type

The word *flawed* identifies this is a Flaw question. You'll need to break down the author's argument, identifying the conclusion and evidence and determining the assumption. Then, you must evaluate how the author's reasoning goes wrong. Remember to keep an eye out for common flaw types.

Step 2: Untangle the Stimulus

The conclusion is signaled by the Keyword *therefore*: Sarah must sometimes use the pool at City Gym. To support this conclusion, the author provides a conditional statement: if a person uses the City Gym pool, then that person must have a membership. Additionally, you know that Sarah has such a membership.

Step 3: Make a Prediction

This is the classic flaw of confusing the necessary term in a conditional statement for the sufficient term. Having a gym membership is necessary to use the pool, but having a membership does not guarantee Sarah will use the pool.

Step 4: Evaluate the Answer Choices

(B) is correct. The answer choice is convoluted but matches our prediction. The statement required for the conclusion to be true is the necessary term (Sarah having a membership at the gym), and the author is treating this necessary term as though it is sufficient (i.e., guarantees the conclusion that Sarah uses the pool).

(A) is Outside the Scope. Nothing in the argument indicates that exceptions are ever made to this policy.

(C) is also Outside the Scope. The argument provides only one result: Sarah must use the pool. There is no discussion of a second alternative.

(D) is the classic pieces-of-a-whole flaw. The stimulus does not say how many people with gym memberships use the pool, let alone that "most" do. This answer choice says the stimulus tries to attribute what most people do with gym memberships to what Sarah does with her gym membership, but that is not the flaw in play here.

(E) is incorrect. This is the classic circular reasoning flaw. The author incorrectly applies the conditional statement in the stimulus, but that is different from merely restating the evidence in the conclusion.

10. (D) Point at Issue

Step 1: Identify the Question Type

The dialogue-response stimulus and the task of identifying what the two speakers "disagree about" make this a Point at Issue question. Characterize both arguments and use the Decision Tree to evaluate the answer choices.

Step 2: Untangle the Stimulus

The two individuals are discussing the poor condition of the university libraries. Annie believes the university should remedy the situation by charging students a fee to use the libraries and then using those funds to improve the libraries. Matilda believes the condition of the libraries is the fault of the administrators and the students should not have to pay for a fee for library improvement.

Step 3: Make a Prediction

For an answer choice to be correct, both Annie and Matilda must have opinions about the answer choice. When reviewing the answers, consider whether Annie and Matilda have an opinion and then consider whether their opinions disagree.

Step 4: Evaluate the Answer Choices

(D) is correct. Matilda believes that the students are not responsible for the condition of the libraries and should not bear the cost to remedy the situation. On the other hand,

Annie believes the students should pay the cost even though they are not responsible.

(A) is incorrect. Both Annie and Matilda agree that the administrators are to blame for the poor condition of the libraries.

(B) is incorrect. Only Annie expresses an opinion concerning the speed of the project to remedy the libraries.

(C) is Outside the Scope. Neither Matilda nor Annie expresses an opinion concerning who will benefit from the library improvements.

(E) is also Outside the Scope. Neither Matilda nor Annie expresses an opinion about whether it is possible to raise enough funds for the libraries without charging additional student fees.

11. (C) Inference

Step 1: Identify the Question Type

The question stem asks which answer choice the stimulus "most strongly supports." This is a straightforward Inference question. The right answer must be true based on the stimulus.

Step 2: Untangle the Stimulus

Paraphrase the stimulus. Diamonds from 2.9 billion years ago had higher-than-normal concentrations of sulfer-33. This is attributable only to chemical reactions sparked by ultraviolet light. More than a trace of oxygen in the atmosphere would have prevented those reactions, because in that case, not enough ultraviolet light would have reached Earth's surface.

Step 3: Make a Prediction

The correct answer choice must be supported by the stimulus. Based on the statements in the stimulus, it must be true that 2.9 billion years ago, Earth's atmosphere contained so little oxygen that enough ultraviolet light reached the surface to stimulate the reactions needed to create diamonds with high concentrations of sulfer-33.

Step 4: Evaluate the Answer Choices

(C) correctly states that Earth's atmosphere contained very little oxygen 2.9 billion years ago. This must be true since the specific chemical reactions are the "only" way to explain the concentration of sulfur-33.

(A) is Extreme. The scientists happened to examine diamonds from 2.9 billion years ago, but the stimulus never says that "most" diamonds with high concentrations of sulfur-33 were formed at least 2.9 billion years ago.

(B) is a Distortion. Oxygen prevents ultraviolet light from reaching the surface, but that light is necessary for the chemical reactions that produce sulfur-33. However, according to the stimulus, ultraviolet light doesn't cause oxygen to do anything; rather, oxygen hinders ultraviolet light. Additionally, the stimulus doesn't discuss oxygen itself reacting with sulfur-33; sulfur-33 is the by-product of other reactions.

(D) is Extreme. The diamonds from 2.9 billion years ago had higher-than-normal concentrations of sulfur-33. But that doesn't mean diamonds formed later rarely contain any sulfur-33; they might just contain less. Additionally, you don't know when oxygen levels became high enough to start blocking ultraviolet light, so you don't know when reactions that resulted in the high concentration of sulfur-33 stopped occurring.

(E) is Extreme. The stimulus states that diamonds with high concentrations of sulfer-33 need ultraviolet light. However, nothing says that all diamonds need ultraviolet light to form.

12. (D) Method of Argument

Step 1: Identify the Question Type

The phrase "describes the manner" identifies this as a Method of Argument question. The correct answer will reflect, likely in abstract terms, the way in which the doctor's second set of recommendations and the results of those recommendations support the doctor's initial hypothesis.

Step 2: Untangle the Stimulus

The doctor initially hypothesized the dosage was insufficient. First, the doctor doubled the dosage with no result. After learning the patient was drinking an herbal beverage that inhibits the medication, the doctor instructed the patient to stop drinking the herbal beverage and resume the initial dosage. This did not alleviate the patient's symptoms. Finally, the doctor recommended doubling the dosage of medication and still avoiding the herbal beverage. This caused the patient's symptoms to disappear.

Step 3: Make a Prediction

The correct answer will explain how the doctor's second set of recommendations show that the initial hypothesis—the dosage was insufficient—was correct. The doctor's second set of recommendations was to take the original dosage and stop drinking the herbal beverage and then to double the dosage and continue not to drink the beverage. The fact that the doctor had to increase the dosage even after the herbal beverage was cut out shows that his initial hypothesis was correct.

Step 4: Evaluate the Answer Choices

(D) correctly explains that once the herbal beverage was removed, the ineffectiveness of the initial amount of medication still needed to be resolved. In other words, while the beverage was partially responsible for the medication not working, the insufficient dosage was the other reason.

(A) is Outside the Scope. The doctor never indicates any concern about the beverage's healthfulness, only about its inhibiting quality.

(B) is a 180. The fact that the double dosage was only effective after the beverage was removed from the patient's diet proves that the beverage was at least partly responsible for the ineffectiveness of the medication.

(C) is Half-Right/Half-Wrong. While the beverage was responsible for the ineffectiveness of the medication, it was only partly to blame. The second set of recommendations shows that dosage amount was also a factor.

(E) is a 180. The doctor did not change the type of medication, yet the patient's symptoms disappeared. Therefore, it must be that the prescribed medication was correct.

13. (E) Flaw

Step 1: Identify the Question Type

The phrase "vulnerable to criticism" identifies this as a Flaw question. You'll need to break down the author's argument, identifying the conclusion and evidence and determining the assumption. Then, evaluate how the author's reasoning goes wrong. Remember to keep an eye out for common flaw types.

Step 2: Untangle the Stimulus

Currently, papercrete is not commonly used in large-scale projects. However, the author concludes that papercrete is promising for large-scale construction because those who regularly use papercrete on small-scale projects are familiar with the material's properties and believe it can be used in large-scale projects.

Step 3: Make a Prediction

The author indicates that the authority of those who regularly use papercrete comes from their familiarity with the material. For this evidence to be valid, the author must be assuming that only those who regularly use papercrete are familiar with the material's properties. However, it may be that most builders are familiar with the properties of papercrete and still choose not to use papercrete on large-scale projects. The correct answer will identify this mistake in the author's reasoning.

Step 4: Evaluate the Answer Choices

(E) correctly states the author fails to consider whether the builders who do not use papercrete are familiar with its properties yet still choose not to use it.

(A) is a Distortion. While papercrete is typically used on small-scale projects, those who regularly work with the material—the author's primary sources—do not assume that what is good for small-scale projects will automatically be good for large-scale projects. Instead, given their familiarity with the material's properties, they think it is also good for large-scale projects. The author commits a flaw by believing most builders are not also aware of papercrete's properties.

(B) is another Distortion. The author does not assume that what most builders think must be fact. Instead, the author actually takes the side of the minority.

(C) represents the classic equivocation flaw. However, this flaw is not at play here. The author does not change the meaning of the word *promising* in the argument. The meaning stays consistent.

(D) is a 180. The views of those who regularly use papercrete are the author's main evidence, so the author definitely considers their views.

14. (A) Assumption (Necessary)

Step 1: Identify the Question Type

The word *assuming* identifies this as an Assumption question. Additionally, the word *relies* indicates you are looking for a necessary assumption, one without which the conclusion cannot be logically drawn from the evidence. You can use the Denial Test to check or eliminate answer choices.

Step 2: Untangle the Stimulus

The drama critic claims that none of the plays written last year will be popular several centuries from now. To support this position, the critic states the only plays that continue to be performed regularly over many decades and centuries are those that explore human nature skillfully. Furthermore, none of the plays written last year explore human nature skillfully.

Step 3: Make a Prediction

While the evidence discusses plays that are performed regularly over long periods of time, the conclusion is about popularity. The drama critic is assuming that the two are one and the same. Yet, arguably, a play could be popular in several centuries without being performed continually. The critic must be assuming this is not the case.

Step 4: Evaluate the Answer Choices

(A) correctly states that no play will be popular several centuries from now unless it is continually performed.

(B) is Outside the Scope. Though the critic mentions some recent plays will receive high critical acclaim, this is not part of the main argument. The critic provides no information on the requirements for achieving high acclaim.

(C) is also Outside the Scope. The drama critic does need to see or read every play to know that the plays don't skillfully explore human nature. This is not necessary to the argument.

(D) is a Distortion. The critic said some plays written last year would receive critical acclaim despite the fact that no play written last year skillfully explored human nature.

(E) incorrectly confuses what is needed for a play to be performed for centuries with what is sufficient.

15. (C) Principle (Identify/Strengthen)

Step 1: Identify the Question Type

The word *principles* is a clear tip-off that this is a Principle question. Because the principle is found in the answer choices, this is an Identify the Principle question. In addition, this Principle question mimics the Strengthen question type, as evidenced by the phrase "most helps to justify the … argument," so attack it the same way you would a Strengthen question. Look for an answer that would make the doctor's conclusion more likely to follow from the evidence. Just be sure the correct answer can support a broader application than the specific example cited in the argument.

Step 2: Untangle the Stimulus

The doctor believes that all medical research should be public because not sharing results may delay effective medical treatments, thereby possibly causing humans to suffer.

Step 3: Make a Prediction

The correct answer will support the doctor's belief that research should be released for the sake of humanity, but it may be couched in more general terms.

Step 4: Evaluate the Answer Choices

(C) correctly supports the doctor's position that medical research should be made public if the research might prevent human suffering.

(A) is a Distortion. The doctor wants research released in order to prevent human suffering. He does not argue, however, that medical researchers' secrecy "cause[s]" suffering.

(B) is Extreme. In fact, it actually restricts the argument. It adds a conditional statement that must be satisfied for the doctor's argument—medical research should not be kept confidential—to stand. Yet nothing in the argument indicates that preventing human suffering is the "most" moral principle.

(D) is a Distortion and Extreme. This answer choice fails to explain why medical research should be made public. The correct answer needs to connect making medical research public and reducing human suffering. Additionally, the doctor focuses on not delaying research, which is not the same as "always" developing treatments "as rapidly as they can."

(E) is Outside the Scope. This answer choice focuses on what companies should request, whereas the doctor's argument is about what medical researchers should do regardless of what their companies want.

16. (C) Point at Issue

Step 1: Identify the Question Type

The dialogue-style stimulus and the task of identifying what the two speakers "disagree about" make this a Point at Issue question. Characterize both arguments and use the Decision Tree to evaluate the answer choices.

Step 2: Untangle the Stimulus

Marife believes the movie was bad because a requirement of murder mysteries is to provide enough information to solve the murder yet this film did not do so. Nguyen believes the primary focus of the movie was the relationship between the chief detective and her assistant and the murder was not central to the movie.

Step 3: Make a Prediction

The correct answer is the one on which the two speakers have differing opinions. Wrong answers may be something on which neither speaker expresses an opinion, something on which only one of the two speakers expresses an opinion, or something on which the two speakers agree. Here, Marife and Nguyen disagree about the central theme of the movie.

Step 4: Evaluate the Answer Choices

(C) correctly states a position that Marife supports and Nguyen does not. Nguyen believes the murder was not an important characteristic of the movie, whereas Marife's criticism revolves around the murder.

(A) is incorrect. Only Marife expresses this opinion. It's possible that Nguyen also thinks the movie is bad, just not for the same reasons as Marife.

(B) is incorrect. Nguyen agrees with this position. However, Marife does not express an opinion on whether the relationship between the chief detective and her assistant was important to the movie.

(D) is incorrect. Marife arguably has a positive opinion on this, since her criticism is based on such a criterion. Nguyen, however, doesn't say that such a criterion is inappropriate, just that it is irrelevant since this movie was not a murder mystery.

(E) is Outside the Scope. Neither Marife nor Nguyen discusses whether the filmmaker wanted viewers to be able to solve the murder. Nguyen mentions that the filmmaker wanted viewers to focus on the relationship, which is different from solving the murder.

17. (B) Weaken

Step 1: Identify the Question Type

The phrase "most weakens" indicates that you are dealing with a Weaken question. Identify the educator's conclusion,

paraphrase the evidence, determine the central assumption, and then look for a fact that attacks that assumption.

Step 2: Untangle the Stimulus

The educator concludes that some programs based on the idea that "children's first education should take place at home ... are successful and should be expanded." This conclusion is supported by the fact children in such programs perform better than average in school.

Step 3: Make a Prediction

The author's causal argument assumes that these programs are solely responsible for the better-than-average results. The correct answer will challenge this assumption and make it less likely to be true. Probably, it will show that another cause is responsible for the high performance.

Step 4: Evaluate the Answer Choices

(B) correctly weakens the assumption. If most parents participating in the programs have prior experience as educators, it is less likely that the programs are the cause of the better-than-average results. Instead the parents' experience as educators could have caused the high performance.

(A) is Outside the Scope. Whether small children enjoy being taught by their parents is not relevant to the argument that the programs are effective.

(C) could strengthen part of the argument. If most parents are likely to support the programs, then participation would be high, and expansion would be possible. However, the educator's argument is also to show that the program caused the improved results. Survey results of parents wanting the program to expand do not impact that aspect of the educator's argument.

(D) is Outside the Scope. The educator's focus is to demonstrate the programs are successful and should be expanded. If costs were astronomically high, that would weaken the argument, but this answer choice simply says costs are unknown.

(E) is Outside the Scope. The fact that some children were successful without the programs does not hamper the educator's argument that the programs improved results for others and should be expanded. The argument stated that the "school performance of the children in these programs is better than average." Exceptions do not diminish that generalization.

18. (D) Principle (Identify/Strengthen)

Step 1: Identify the Question Type

The word *principles* is a clear signal that this is a Principle question. In addition, this Principle question mimics the Strengthen question type, as evidenced by the phrase "most helps to justify," so attack it the same way you would a Strengthen question. Look for an answer that would make the censor's conclusion more likely to follow from her evidence. Just be sure the correct answer can support a broader application than the specific example cited in the argument.

Step 2: Untangle the Stimulus

This argument contains Formal Logic. The censor's conclusion states it is permissible to ban any anarchist novel that would do more harm than good to society. So, if an anarchist novel does more harm than good to society, then it can be banned. According to the evidence, if a book is an anarchist novel, then it includes both a subversive outlook and the depiction of violence.

Step 3: Make a Prediction

The correct principle will link the evidence to the conclusion. Evidence: anarchist novels have two objectionable characteristics. Conclusion: if an anarchist novel does more harm than good, it can be banned. The missing link will connect two objectionable characteristics to a novel that would cause society more harm than good.

Step 4: Evaluate the Answer Choices

(D) correctly links the permissibility of banning a novel that does more harm than good to a novel with two or more objectionable characteristics.

(A) is incorrect. The stimulus only focuses on anarchist novels, which have two objectionable characteristics. Books with only one objectionable characteristic are not anarchist novels and are therefore Outside the Scope. Additionally, the argument gives sufficient characteristics to ban a novel, but it does not give sufficient characteristics not to ban a novel. So that is also Outside the Scope.

(B) is a Distortion. The correct principle needs both objectionable characteristics, not just one. Additionally, the stimulus's conclusion applies the qualification that novels do "more harm than good" to be banned, whereas this answer choice applies the opposite qualification of doing "more good than harm."

(C) distorts the logic in the stimulus by reversing the terms. This answer choice states that if a book can be banned, then it is subversive and would do more harm than good to society. Also, violence isn't mentioned.

(E) is incorrect. This answer choice fails to include the qualification of causing more harm than good to society, which is necessary for the correct answer. Additionally, this choice reverses the logic. The stimulus presents the characteristics that are sufficient to result in banning being permissible, whereas this choice discusses what is necessary of novels that are banned.

19. (B) Parallel Reasoning

Step 1: Identify the Question Type

The phrase "most similar in its reasoning to" is standard to Parallel Reasoning questions.

Step 2: Untangle the Stimulus

In 1996, either the government or private corporations funded all ResearchTech projects. One ResearchTech project, the Gilman Survey, was not funded by the government but was conducted in 1996. Therefore, private corporations must have funded the project.

Step 3: Make a Prediction

The correct answer will be similar in its logic. Two possibilities will be provided. The answer choice will then remove one of the two options and conclude that the remaining option must be the case.

Step 4: Evaluate the Answer Choices

(B) is correct. It provides two characteristics of legal restrictions on consumer purchases, such as Ordinance 304: they are either paternalistic or protect civil liberties. Ordinance 304 is not paternalistic (one option is removed), so it must protect civil liberties (the remaining option must be the case). Perfect match.

(A) is incorrect. By saying legal restrictions have a "variety of aims," this answer choice provides more than two possibilities for the legal restriction. Also, the two possibilities discussed are not mutually exclusive, as those in the stimulus are.

(C) is a 180. For the logic to follow that of stimulus, this answer choice would have to conclude that Ordinance 304 is designed to protect the environment, but this choice says it is not. Also, to be parallel, the conclusion should be a positive assertion of fact, not a negative one.

(D) has too many terms, and this answer choice fails to reject one of two options and conclude that the other option is the case. Instead this answer choices states that ordinances passed in 1993, of which Ordinance 304 was one, were paternalistic. Thus, Ordinance 304 is paternalistic. The answer choice also states that legal restrictions on consumer purchases are either paternalistic or designed to protect civil liberties. But just because Ordinance 304 is paternalistic doesn't mean it is a legal restriction on consumer purchases, as this answer choice concludes.

(E) is too weak. It fails to limit the uses of Ordinance 304 to only two possibilities, instead discussing what should be done. Just because there are only two ways Ordinance 304 should be exercised doesn't mean people—in this case, the mayor—will abide by that. If the mayor properly exercises Ordinance 304, then the answer is correct, but we cannot be sure that she does properly exercise it.

20. (C) Role of a Statement

Step 1: Identify the Question Type

The phrase "role played ... by the statement" identifies this as a Role of a Statement question. The correct answer will reflect, likely in abstract terms, the way in which the claim quoted in the question stem functions in the argument. Decide whether the statement in question is evidence or conclusion and then go back to refine your prediction as necessary.

Step 2: Untangle the Stimulus

The beginning of the argument states that early in its history, Earth was bombarded with comets and asteroids, which would have prevented life from originating. Mars was not bombarded with comets. This information is used to support the claim that there could have been life on Mars prior to life on Earth. Additionally, many meteorites originating from Mars landed on Earth. This, linked with the earlier evidence, leads to the astronomer's main conclusion: life on Earth could have started when microbes from Mars traveled on a meteorite to Earth.

Step 3: Make a Prediction

The task is to identify the role of the claim that appears in the second half of the third sentence: there could have been life on Mars before there was life on Earth. The Keyword *so* indicates this statement is a conclusion, and, in fact, the first two sentences of the argument support it. However, the position that life existed on Mars before it appeared on Earth is also necessary for the astronomer's conclusion that life on Earth may have originated from life on Mars. Therefore, the role of the sentence in question is twofold: (1) this statement is supported by the first two sentences in the argument, and (2) this statement is necessary for the main conclusion to be true. In other words, the statement is a subsidiary conclusion. The correct answer will highlight its roles as both conclusion and evidence.

Step 4: Evaluate the Answer Choices

(C) correctly identifies both roles of the claim in the question stem. The claim is both supported by the first two sentences and is required for the main conclusion to be true.

(A) is Half-Right/Half-Wrong. The claim is needed for the conclusion, but it's false that no justification is provided for it; the claim is supported by the first two sentences in the argument.

(B) is Extreme. The claim does not guarantee the conclusion. Instead, the claim is necessary to the conclusion. Additionally, it is supported by the first two sentences in the argument.

(D) is also Half-Right/Half-Wrong. The astronomer did provide justification. However, the claim that there was life on Mars before there was life on Earth is needed for the conclusion but does not guarantee that life on Earth did in fact originate from life on Mars. To say that it "establishes the truth" that life originated on Mars is Extreme.

(E) is a 180. The claim is required for the astronomer's conclusion to be true. For life on Earth to originate from life on Mars, there had to be life on Mars first.

21. (D) Flaw

Step 1: Identify the Question Type

The phrase "most accurately describes a flaw" identifies this as a Flaw question. Break down the author's argument, identifying the conclusion and evidence and determining the assumption. Then, evaluate how the author's reasoning goes wrong. Remember to keep an eye out for common flaw types.

Step 2: Untangle the Stimulus

The author concludes that gardeners who have no use for homegrown honey will not have beehives, so their gardens will fail to have excellent pollination. This is because establishing a beehive ensures the presence of bees, which are necessary for pollination.

Step 3: Make a Prediction

The author assumes there is no way to have the presence of bees without a beehive. Having a beehive guarantees the presence of bees, but the author has overlooked the possibility that bees may still be present without a beehive. The correct answer will target this overlooked possibility.

Step 4: Evaluate the Answer Choices

(D) correctly points out the possibility the author overlooked: bees may be present even in the absence of a condition (beehives) that would ensure their presence.

(A) is incorrect. The author does consider more than one benefit of bees: pollination and homegrown honey. The author only considers one advantage of keeping bees, but that is not why the argument is flawed.

(B) is incorrect. This answer choice discusses the classic flaw of confusing the necessary term with the sufficient term. The author does believe the presence of bees is necessary for pollination; however, the author does not argue that the presence of bees is sufficient to ensure pollination will result. This is the type of flaw you're looking for, but it's applied to the wrong terms.

(C) is incorrect. This answer choice also targets the flaw of confusing the necessary term with the sufficient term. However, the author stated that excellent pollination usually results in an abundance of fruits and vegetables. There was no switching of a necessary term to a sufficient position. Also, the author's flawed argument did not ultimately rely at all on the statement concerning fruits and vegetables.

(E) is incorrect. This answer choice describes the classic correlation versus causation flaw. The author does not assume causation on the basis of a correlation, so this flaw type does not apply to this argument.

22. (B) Role of a Statement

Step 1: Identify the Question Type

The phrase "role played in the argument" identifies this as a Role of a Statement question. The correct answer will reflect, likely in abstract terms, the way in which the claim quoted in the question stem functions in the argument. Decide whether the statement in question is evidence or conclusion and then go back to refine your prediction as necessary.

Step 2: Untangle the Stimulus

The first statement is a common occurrence: people often praise poems' truth. The second sentence, which starts with the contrast Keyword [*b*]*ut*, is the conclusion and counters the validity of the occurrence in the first sentence. The last two sentences function as evidence to support the conclusion. Combined, they essentially say that since most of what most people believe is true, then something other than truth (which is "common") must be the basis of poetic excellence.

Step 3: Make a Prediction

The claim in the question stem is the last sentence in the stimulus. The correct answer will say that the statement in question, along with the third sentence in the argument, supports the argument's conclusion. In other words, the statement in question is evidence.

Step 4: Evaluate the Answer Choices

(B) correctly identifies the statement as a premise, which means evidence, that supports the argument's conclusion. Also, the answer choice notes this piece of evidence is used in conjunction with the third sentence, another premise used to support the conclusion.

(A) is incorrect. The second sentence of the argument is the conclusion.

(C) is Extreme. There are two premises that both support the conclusion, so the statement in question is not the sole support for the conclusion.

(D) is incorrect. This is the role of the first sentence in the argument, which provides the statement the author intends to disagree with.

(E) is incorrect. The statement in the question stem is not a proposition (or principle) that the argument is trying to explain. Instead, it is evidence offered to support the conclusion. If anything, the conclusion of the argument would play the role stated in **(E)**.

23. (B) Parallel Flaw

Step 1: Identify the Question Type

The question uses the phrase "parallel reasoning"—and this is a Parallel Reasoning question. Moreover, in this question, the correct answer will mirror the "flawed nature" of the stimulus. Characterize the flaw in the argument before evaluating the answer choices.

Step 2: Untangle the Stimulus

The author concludes that some members of the mayor's staff are suspects. To support this position, the author states that all of the suspects are former employees of the City Treasurer's Office and the mayor's staff includes some former employees of that office.

Step 3: Make a Prediction

The author discusses two groups: 1) suspects, who all formerly worked at the City Treasurer's Office, and 2) members of the mayor's staff, some of whom formerly worked at the City Treasurer's Office. The author, by saying that some of the mayor's staff must then be suspects, assumes that the two groups overlap. Yet the former City Treasurer's Office employees on the mayor's staff might be wholly separate from the former City Treasurer's Office employees who are suspects.

Evaluating the Formal Logic of this argument can be helpful.

$$\textit{If} \quad \textbf{suspect} \quad \rightarrow \quad \textbf{former employee}$$

Some members of the mayor's staff are former employees.

Therefore, some members of the mayor's staff are suspects.

The flawed reasoning attempts to go against the flow of the logic of the first statement. While all suspects are former employees, not all former employees are necessarily suspects. So the author is wrong to conclude that members of the mayor's staff are suspects.

The correct answer will include a strict Formal Logic statement about two groups (all suspects are former employees). The other piece of evidence will be a statement linking "some" of the members of the necessary group to "some" of the members of a third group (mayor's employees). The conclusion will state that "some" of the members in the third group must therefore be linked to the sufficient condition (suspects).

Step 4: Evaluate the Answer Choices

(B) correctly parallels the flawed argument structure in the stimulus. All skyscrapers are buildings. In addition, some buildings (necessary condition) are cabins (third group). But, this does not mean that some cabins (third group) are skyscrapers (sufficient condition). While it is possible there is a skyscraper that is also a cabin, this does not have to be the case.

(A) is incorrect. This answer choice is not parallel in structure. The stimulus has a strict sufficient-and-necessary relationship (between suspects and former employees), but every statement in this answer choice begins with *some*.

(C) is incorrect. This answer choice is not parallel in structure because, while the stimulus has one strict sufficient-and-necessary relationship (between suspects and former employees), this answer choice has two.

(D) is incorrect. This answer choice includes two strict sufficient-and-necessary relationships: one in the evidence and one in the conclusion.

(E) is incorrect. This answer choice is not parallel in structure because, while like the stimulus it has one strict sufficient-and-necessary relationship, that relationship appears in the conclusion and not in the evidence.

24. (D) Inference

Step 1: Identify the Question Type

The phrase "most logically completes" indicates you are dealing with an Inference question. The correct answer must be true based on the stimulus.

Step 2: Untangle the Stimulus

Paraphrase the statements in the stimulus. The author questions why violins made by Stradivarius are superior to most other violins. During the time when Stradivarius made violins, the region he lived in experienced weather patterns that caused trees to grow in such a way that their wood has special acoustic properties.

Step 3: Make a Prediction

The answer choice must be a conclusion supported by the stimulus. Based on the statements in the stimulus, "it is likely that" the wood available to Stradivarius contributed to the superior quality of the violins he made.

Step 4: Evaluate the Answer Choices

(D) correctly states that the wood used by Stradivarius plays a part in the special qualities of his violins. Note the tentative language: this answer does not say the wood is the only reason his violins are special.

(A) is Outside the Scope. Other violin makers are not mentioned in the stimulus, and therefore this answer choice is possible, but it is not supported.

(B) is Extreme. The stimulus does not state that Stradivarius was the "only" one to use wood from that part of Italy. Other violin makers might have used the same type of wood.

(C) is also Extreme. The author says that Stradivarius's violins are superior to "most" other violins. But that doesn't mean "no" recently made violin could equal one of his.

(E) is unsupported. Stradivarius still could have used secret techniques (perhaps even those varnishes) in constructing his violins. The wood was likely a contributing factor to the special acoustic properties, but it may not have been the only factor.

25. (C) Strengthen

Step 1: Identify the Question Type

The combination of a Principle/Application stimulus and a stem calling for the answer that "justifies the application of the principle" makes this a variant of the Strengthen question type. Treat the application as a conclusion and the stated principle as evidence. The correct answer will strengthen the assumption that ties the two together. Note that the stem here is very strong—the correct answer "justifies" the application of the principle.

Step 2: Untangle the Stimulus

The principle states that for a professor to make an official determination that a student has committed plagiarism, the professor must believe the student knowingly presented someone else's idea without giving credit to that person. The application states that Professor Serfin should not make an official determination.

Step 3: Make a Prediction

Since Professor Serfin should not make an official determination that Walters plagiarized, it must be the case that all of the requirements necessary to make an official determination were not met. The correct answer will demonstrate that a requirement of the principle (believing the student was aware) was not met to make the official determination.

It is helpful to summarize the argument in terms of Formal Logic:

$$\text{If} \quad \text{plagiarism} \quad \rightarrow \quad \text{\textit{knowingly presented ideas without attribution}}$$

If plagiarism → knowingly presented ideas without attribution

$$\text{If} \quad \text{\textit{\textasciitilde presented ideas without attribution}} \quad \rightarrow \quad \text{\textit{\textasciitilde plagiarism}}$$

Step 4: Evaluate the Answer Choices

(C) correctly demonstrates that the professor does not believe Walters knowingly tried to pass anyone else's ideas off as his own. Without this element, the professor is justified in not making the official declaration of plagiarism.

(A) is Outside the Scope. This answer choice provides a new requirement to make an official declaration. According to the principle, the professor does not need compelling evidence to make the declaration. Instead, the professor only needs a belief that the student intended to plagiarize.

(B) is Outside the Scope. The principle does not take into account what the student believes or does. The determination depends solely on what the professor believes the student was attempting to do.

(D) is Outside the Scope. The principle does not mention what the student thinks the professor should do.

(E) is incorrect. The professor's intention not to make the declaration does not impact whether the principle was properly applied to Walters. The focus must remain on what would strengthen the principle's application.

Section III: Logic Games

Game 1: Student Speeches on Friendship and Liberty

Q#	Question Type	Correct	Difficulty
1	Partial Acceptability	C	★
2	"If" / Could Be True	D	★★
3	"If" / Must Be True	A	★
4	"If" / Must Be False	A	★★
5	Supply the If	C	★★★

Game 2: Literary Theory Lectures

Q#	Question Type	Correct	Difficulty
6	Acceptability	B	★
7	Could Be True	B	★
8	Must Be False (CANNOT Be True)	E	★
9	"If" / Could Be True	A	★
10	Must Be False (CANNOT Be True)	E	★
11	"If" / Must Be True	C	★
12	"If" / Could Be True	E	★

Game 3: Toy Store Aisles

Q#	Question Type	Correct	Difficulty
13	"If" / Could Be True	D	★
14	"If" / Must Be True	A	★★
15	"If" / Must Be True	B	★★
16	Must Be False (CANNOT Be True)	A	★★★
17	"If" / Must Be True EXCEPT	E	★★

Game 4: Millville's Development Zones

Q#	Question Type	Correct	Difficulty
18	Acceptability	E	★★
19	Must Be False (CANNOT Be True)	D	★★
20	Maximum	D	★★★★
21	"If" / Could Be True	B	★★★★
22	"If" / Could Be True	A	★★★★
23	"If" / Could Be True	A	★★★★

Game 1: Student Speeches on Friendship and Liberty

Step 1: Overview

Situation: Students delivering speeches

Entities: Five students (Manolo, Nadia, Owen, Peng, Rana), two speech topics (friendship, liberty), and three majors (geology, history, journalism)

Action: Matching. Your task is to determine both the speech topic and major for each of the five students. Therefore, this Matching game includes two layers of matching.

Limitations: Each student gives a speech on exactly one of two topics and has only one of three majors. The numbers for the majors are predetermined: two geology, two history, and one journalism. The first rule will provide the numbers for the speech topics.

Step 2: Sketch

Since you must determine two pieces of information for each student, simply list the students by initial at the top of a table. Under each student, place two slots. The speech topic will be placed on the top slot, and the major will be placed on the bottom. List the entities to be matched, by initial, next to each row. For the majors, be sure to list two g's, two h's, and one j to represent the numbers given.

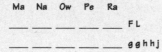

Step 3: Rules

Rule 1 sets the numbers for the speech topics. There will be exactly two speeches on friendship, which means the remaining three speeches will be on liberty. Adjust the entity list to show two F's and three L's.

Rule 2 provides much more information than what it directly states. The two friendship speeches will be assigned to a geology major and a history major. And, according to the previous rule, those are the only two friendship speeches. So not only can those Blocks of Entities be set up, but so can those for the liberty speeches, which must be assigned to the remaining three majors: one to geology, one to history, and one to journalism.

Rule 3 can be added directly to the sketch, assigning friendship as Manolo's speech topic.

Rule 4 can also be added directly to the sketch, assigning liberty as Rana's speech topic.

Rule 5 limits the majors for both Peng and Rana. Since neither can be a geology major, that leaves only history or journalism as a major for each.

Rule 6 can be added directly to the sketch, assigning geology as Nadia's major.

Before making deductions, take note that Owen is never mentioned in any of the rules. Owen is the game's Floater and is not directly restricted from any speech topic or major.

Step 4: Deductions

With so many concrete rules and Established Entities, the game already provides a wealth of information. The best thing to do is consider the established information. With an assigned speech topic of friendship, Manolo can only be a geology or history major (by Rule 2). As a geology major, Nadia can still give a speech on either friendship or liberty. And without knowing Peng's major for sure, you cannot limit Peng to either speech topic.

Your final Master Sketch should look similar to this:

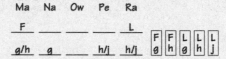

As a final note, there are a couple of opportunities to set up Limited Options for this game. While a couple of them are potentially helpful, the question set (which consists of mostly "If" questions and an Acceptability question) indicates that Limited Options are hardly necessary for this game. The rules have already established substantial information to tackle the questions.

Step 5: Questions

1. (C) Partial Acceptability

Since this question doesn't mention the speech topics, it's only a Partial Acceptability question. Still, the first step is to go through the rules one at a time, eliminating answers that violate those rules. Because the question focuses on the students' majors, pay attention to those rules that affect the assignments of majors, rather than the rules that address the speech topics. And don't forget unlisted rules presented as limitations in the Overview.

According to the Overview, there must be two geology majors, two history majors, and one journalism major. That eliminates **(A)**, **(B)**, and **(E)**, all of which get the numbers wrong. The first four rules all deal with the speech topics. Rule 5 states that neither Peng nor Rana can be a geology major, which eliminates **(D)**. That leaves **(C)** as the correct answer.

2. (D) "If" / Could Be True

If Peng speaks on friendship, then Peng and Manolo will give the two speeches on friendship. Since the friendship speeches are given by a geology major and a history major (Rule 2), and Peng can't be a geology major (Rule 5), Peng must be the history major and Manolo the geology major. The remaining students (Nadia, Owen, and Rana) will all speak on leadership (Rule 1). Nadia is a geology major (Rule 6), so Owen and Rana will be a history major and a journalism major, in either order.

Ma	Na	Ow	Pe	Ra
F	L	L	F	L
g	g	h/j	h	j/h

With all that determined, only **(D)** is possible. **(A)**, **(B)**, **(C)**, and **(E)** all must be false.

3. (A) "If" / Must Be True

This question provides both pieces of information for Owen: Owen will be assigned a friendship speech and be a geology major. As the remaining speaker on friendship, Manolo must be a history major (Rule 2).

Ma	Na	Ow	Pe	Ra
F	L	F	L	L
h	g	g	h/j	j/h

That makes **(A)** the correct answer. **(B)** and **(C)** both must be false, because Manolo and Owen have taken the two friendship spots so each of the other students must speak on liberty. **(D)** and **(E)** could be true because both Peng and Rana could major in either history or journalism; neither can major in geology (Rule 5). That still leaves one geology major open though, which must go to Nadia. However, you would not have needed to take the deductions that far to get to correct answer **(A)**.

4. (A) "If" / Must Be False

If Nadia speaks on friendship, then Nadia and Manolo will give the two speeches on friendship. Since Nadia is a geology major (Rule 6), Manolo must be the history major (Rule 2).

Ma	Na	Ow	Pe	Ra
F	F	L	L	L
h	g	g	h/j	j/h

That means Manolo can't be a geology major, making **(A)** the correct answer. **(B)** must be true, as discussed above. **(C)** also must be true, because since neither Peng nor Rana can be a geology major (Rule 5), then Owen must be the second geology major. That leaves Peng and Rana as the journalism major and the second history major, which makes **(D)** and **(E)** both possibly true.

5. (C) Supply the If

The correct answer will be a "new rule" that guarantees Rana is a journalism major, with no uncertainty. When faced with approaching answers by trial and error, do so strategically and be sure to use previous work to quickly eliminate answers.

In this case, astute test takers will realize that **(A)**, **(B)**, **(D)**, and **(E)** have all occurred in previous questions. The rules in **(A)** and **(E)** appeared in the sketch for the second question of the set. The rule in **(B)** occurred in the sketch for the third question of the set. And the rule of **(D)** occurred in the sketch for the fourth question of the set. While Rana could have been a journalism major in any of those scenarios, it was never determined with certainty.

That leaves **(C)**. Sure enough, if Owen is a geology major and Peng is a history major, that leaves Rana as the only student who could be a journalism major. After all, Nadia is always a geology major (Rule 6), and Manolo can't be a journalism major since Manolo gives a speech on friendship (Rule 3), which can only be given by a geology or history major (Rule 2). With all the other majors taken, Rana must be the journalism major, and that makes **(C)** the correct answer.

Game 2: Literary Theory Lectures

Step 1: Overview

Situation: Professors giving guest lectures in a literary theory course

Entities: Seven professors: Powell, Shihab, Taylor, Vaughan, Wood, Young, Zabel

Action: Strict Sequencing. Your task is to determine the order in which the professors give lectures—a typical Sequencing game.

Limitations: Each professor gives exactly one lecture, and the lectures are ordered first through seventh. That's a basic one-to-one setup.

Step 2: Sketch

A quick glance at the rules shows three loose rules followed by three rules that indicate specific positions. Those last rules indicate that a Strict Sequencing sketch is needed. Simply list the entities by initial and draw seven slots underneath numbered 1 through 7.

$$P \ S \ T \ V \ W \ Y \ Z$$
$$\overline{1} \ \overline{2} \ \overline{3} \ \overline{4} \ \overline{5} \ \overline{6} \ \overline{7}$$

Step 3: Rules

Rules 1, 2, and 3 provide three simple, loose relationships: Powell before Wood, Taylor before Shihab, and Vaughan before Zabel. Notice that there are no duplicates in these rules, so they cannot be combined. Instead, simply draw out these three relationships separately.

$$P \ldots W$$
$$T \ldots S$$
$$V \ldots Z$$

In addition, note where each of these entities are limited in the sketch. Since Powell, Taylor, and Vaughan each have to lecture before another professor, none of them can be last. Similarly, since Wood, Shihab, and Zabel each have to lecture after another professor, none of them can be first.

Rule 4 limits the placement of Shihab, who can only be one of the first three lecturers. In addition, since Rule 2 says Taylor speaks before Shihab, Shihab cannot be in the first slot. You can draw an S with two arrows pointing to slots 2 and 3 in the sketch, or you can make a note to the side.

Rule 5 simply prohibits Young from being the last lecturer. Note this under the seventh slot.

Rule 6 provides some complex Formal Logic. The phrase "if, but only if" indicates a condition that is both sufficient and necessary, essentially creating two Formal Logic statements. Therefore, this rule translates into both "Powell lectures first if Young lectures before Vaughan," and "Powell lectures first only if Young lectures before Vaughan." In other words, Young

lecturing before Vaughan is sufficient to guarantee that Powell lectures first:

$$Y \ldots V \rightarrow \frac{P}{1}$$

Furthermore, Young lecturing before Vaughan is also necessary for Powell to lecture first:

$$\frac{P}{1} \rightarrow Y \ldots V$$

Be sure to form a contrapositive for both statements. In both cases, negating the condition of Young lecturing before Vaughan means Vaughan lectures before Young:

$$Y \ldots V \rightarrow \frac{P}{1} \qquad\qquad \frac{P}{1} \rightarrow Y \ldots V$$
$$\sim\frac{P}{1} \rightarrow V \ldots Y \qquad V \ldots Y \rightarrow \sim\frac{P}{1}$$

Before moving on, think a little about what those statements mean. "If, but only if" Formal Logic statements essentially boil down to "both or neither." Either both conditions will occur (in this case, Y … V and P in the first lecture), or neither will. With "if, but only if" statements, it is impossible for one condition to occur without the other.

Step 4: Deductions

The nature of an "if, but only if" rule lends itself to setting up Limited Options. Coupled with the limited placement of Shihab by Rules 2 and 4, Limited Options can be tremendously helpful. In this case, there are two possible outcomes based on whether or not Powell is first. (Note: Limited Options are also possible based on when Shihab lectures, but those options leave more uncertainty due to the complications of the last rule.)

For Option I, if Powell is first, then Young must lecture before Vaughan. This can be combined with Rule 3 to create a longer string in which Young lectures before Vaughan, who lectures before Zabel. Furthermore, Shihab must be the third lecturer, since Shihab cannot lecture any later (Rule 4) and must lecture after Taylor (Rule 2). That means Taylor must lecture second. That leaves the loose sequence of Young, Vaughan, and Zabel, with Wood floating in any of the remaining open positions.

Option I

P	T	S	Y/W			W/Z
1	2	3	4	5	6	7

$$Y \ldots V \ldots Z \qquad W?$$

Option II

T/V						W/Z
1	2	3	4	5	6	7

~V (under slot 6), S (between slots 2 and 3)

$$P \ldots W \qquad V \overset{\cdots Y}{\underset{\cdots Z}{}}$$
$$T \ldots S$$

For Option II, Powell is not first. That means Vaughan must lecture before Young (Rule 6). This means Vaughan cannot be last and Young cannot be first. While no entities can be established, numerous limitations affect the first and last lectures. In addition to Powell and Young, other professors who can't be first include Wood (Rule 1), Shihab (Rule 2), and Zabel (Rule 3). That leaves just two professors: Taylor or Vaughan. As for the last lecture, in addition to Vaughan, none of Powell (Rule 1), Taylor (Rule 2), Shihab (Rule 4), or Young (Rule 5) can give it. Again, that leaves just two professors: Wood or Zabel. It's also worth noting that, since Vaughan now has to precede both Young and Zabel, Vaughan cannot lecture sixth.

Option I

P	T	S	Y/W			W/Z
1	2	3	4	5	6	7

Y...V...Z   W?

Option II

T/V						W/Z
1	2	3	4	5	6	7

S↗   ~V

P ... W   V⋰Y
T ... S   V⋱Z

Step 5: Questions

6. (B) Acceptability

As always, running through the rules one at a time helps eliminate all the incorrect answers. Rule 1 states Powell must lecture before Wood, so that eliminates **(C)**. Rules 2 and 3 order Taylor and Shihab as well as Vaughan and Zabel, but none of the answers violate those two rules. Rule 4 states that Shihab cannot lecture later than third. That eliminates **(A)**, which places Shihab fourth. Rule 5 indicates that Young cannot lecture last, which eliminates **(D)**.

That leaves the complex final rule. Powell is not first in either of the remaining answers. Based on the Formal Logic of Rule 6, that means Vaughan must lecture before Young, which eliminates **(E)**. **(B)** remains as the correct answer.

7. (B) Could Be True

This is an example of where paying attention to heavily limited positions pays off. The correct answer will be the one person in the choices who could possibly be the first lecturer. According to the first option, it could be Powell. According to the second option, it could be either Taylor or Vaughan. Only **(B)** lists one of those three possibilities.

If you didn't set up Limited Options, a strong grasp of the rules can also make quick work of this question. Based on the first three rules, the first lecturer can't be Wood, Shihab, or Zabel, eliminating **(A)**, **(C)**, and **(E)**. Then, if Young were first, Vaughan would have to lecture later. However, according to

Rule 6, Powell would have to be first in that case, not Young. That contradictory, and thus impossible, outcome eliminates **(D)**.

8. (E) Must Be False (CANNOT Be True)

The correct answer to this question will be a professor who cannot be the second lecturer. That means you should eliminate any professor who could be second.

In Option I, Taylor is second. That eliminates **(C)**. The second option has no such established possibilities. So, work strategically rather than drawing out sketches for each remaining answer. In the second option, the first professor is either Taylor or Vaughan, which means the second entity cannot be any professor who must follow someone other than Taylor or Vaughan. According to the first rule, Wood has to follow Powell, but the earliest Powell could lecture in Option II is second. That means Wood can't lecture earlier than third, which means Wood cannot lecture second. That makes **(E)** the correct answer.

Another successful strategy for this question would be to skip it temporarily in favor of drawing sketches for the upcoming "If" questions. Those sketches may be helpful in eliminating other answers that list professors who could be second. In this case, the correct answer to the Acceptability question lists Powell as second, which eliminates **(A)**. The new "If" for the question after this one says, "If Shihab lectures second," which would eliminate **(B)**. The sketch for the second-to-last question of the set indicates that either Shihab or Vaughan could be second, which eliminates **(D)** and, incidentally, **(B)** once again.

9. (A) "If" / Could Be True

This question provides two pieces of information: Shihab lectures second, and Zabel lectures fourth. This scenario is only possible in Option II. With Shihab lecturing second, Taylor will lecture first (Rule 2). That means Vaughan must lecture third (Rule 3). For the remaining three lectures, Powell can't be last (Rule 1), and Young can't be last (Rule 5). Therefore, the last professor to lecture must be Wood. Powell and Young will be the fifth and sixth professors in either order.

T	S	V	Z	P/Y	Y/P	W
1	2	3	4	5	6	7

That makes **(A)** the only possible answer. **(B)**, **(C)**, **(D)**, and **(E)** all must be false based on the sketch.

10. (E) Must Be False (CANNOT Be True)

The correct answer for this question will be a position in which Vaughan cannot give a lecture. Based on Rule 3, Vaughan must lecture before Zabel, which means Vaughan cannot be the last lecturer. That immediately makes **(E)** the correct answer.

For the record, **(A)** is possible in the sketch for the second-to-last question of the set, and **(B)** is possible in the sketch for the fourth question of the set. In Option II, if Vaughan is fourth, Taylor is first, with Shihab and Powell second and third in either order. Young, Zabel, and Wood will fill spots five, six, and seven in almost any order (Young can't be last). This is an acceptable sketch, and therefore **(C)** is incorrect. Finally, in Option I, Powell, Taylor, and Shihab take the first three spots, and Young and Wood can lecture in spots four and five in either order. This lets Vaughan lecture sixth and Zabel seventh. So **(D)** is also possible and thus incorrect.

11. (C) "If" / Must Be True

This is another question that provides two pieces of information: Young lectures fourth, and Taylor lectures first. This could only happen in the second option. Even without Limited Options, this information still triggers the Formal Logic of Rule 6: with Taylor first, Powell can't be, which means Young can't lecture before Vaughan. Therefore, Vaughan must lecture before Young, which in this case would be either second or third. Furthermore, Shihab can only be second or third (Rule 3), so the second and third lectures will be Vaughan and Shihab in some order.

$$\frac{T}{1} \quad \frac{S/V}{2} \quad \frac{V/S}{3} \quad \frac{Y}{4} \quad \frac{}{5} \quad \frac{}{6} \quad \frac{}{7}$$

With that, **(C)** must be true, making it the correct answer. For the record, Shihab could lecture second, eliminating **(B)**. Powell merely has to lecture before Wood, so Powell could be the fifth or sixth professor; that eliminates **(A)**. Wood, then, could be sixth or seventh, which eliminates **(D)**. Zabel, who must merely follow Shihab, could fill the fifth, sixth, or seventh positions, eliminating **(E)**.

12. (E) "If" / Could Be True

There are two ways to handle this question. The first, and most efficient, is to use previous work. The fourth question of the set also placed Zabel fourth, as this question dictates. Based on that mini-sketch, **(E)** could be true and is thus the correct answer.

The second way is to build a new sketch. If Zabel is fourth, Vaughan must be one of the first three lecturers (Rule 3). Shihab also has to be one of the first three lecturers (Rule 4), which means Taylor has to be one of the first two lecturers (Rule 2). Since Vaughan, Shihab, and Taylor will be the first three lecturers, the remaining professors (Powell, Wood, and Young) will be the last three lecturers.

$$\frac{}{1} \quad \frac{}{2} \quad \frac{}{3} \quad \frac{Z}{4} \quad \frac{}{5} \quad \frac{}{6} \quad \frac{}{7}$$

T...S; V   P...W; Y

That eliminates **(A)**, **(C)**, and **(D)**. Furthermore, Powell can't be the last lecturer (Rule 1), so that eliminates **(B)**. That leaves **(E)** as the only possible answer.

Game 3: Toy Store Aisles

Step 1: Overview

Situation: A toy retailer designing the aisle layout at a new store

Entities: Three aisles, numbered 1 through 3, and six sections: Fantasy, Hobbies, Music, Puzzles, Reading, Science

Action: Strict Sequencing. Your task is to arrange the six sections in order, from the lowest aisle (1) to the highest (3). This, along with the rules, indicates a Sequencing game. However, with six sections and only three aisles, there will be duplication among the aisles. While there's a Distribution feel to this game, the "highest" and "lowest" designation of the aisles gives it a definitive Sequencing component. Whether you pegged this game as Sequencing, Distribution, or a Sequencing/Distribution Hybrid, the important thing is that the sketch will look pretty much the same: a table with the three aisles (either horizontally or vertically). The reason this game is single action rather than a Hybrid is that if you Sequence all the entities into their aisles, you do not need to also distribute them; alternatively, if you distribute them into each of the aisles, you do not need to also sequence them within the aisles.

Limitations: While each section will be assigned to exactly one aisle, the number of sections in each aisle is not explicitly defined. Each aisle must have at least one section. However, just because there are six sections and three aisles, that doesn't mean each aisle must get two sections. It's possible but not definitely true.

Step 2: Sketch

With the aisles labeled "highest" and "lowest," it makes sense to draw the sketch vertically, with the highest aisle (aisle 3) on top and the lowest aisle (aisle 1) on the bottom. Since each aisle needs at least one section, draw one slot in each row, leaving room to add more.

```
        F H M P R S

     3: ___
     2: ___
     1: ___
```

Step 3: Rules

Rule 1 creates a Block of Entities for one of the aisles: Reading must be together with either Fantasy or Music.

$$\boxed{\text{R F/M}}$$

There are two things to note. First, this rule doesn't explicitly prevent Reading from being placed in the same aisle as both Fantasy and Music. However, the next rule (which forces Fantasy and Music into different aisles) does set up that limitation. Second, this rule doesn't prevent other sections from being placed in the same aisle. So, for example, an aisle can have Reading and Fantasy together and also have Hobbies.

Rule 2 sets up sequencing for three sections. Fantasy will be placed lower than both Music and Puzzles. However, the rule does not define the order of Music and Puzzles. Therefore, Music and Puzzles can be in the same aisle or in different aisles.

```
      P   M
       \ /
        F
```

While none of these entities can be established with certainty, it can be noted in the sketch that Fantasy cannot be in the highest aisle, while Music and Puzzles cannot be in the lowest aisle.

Rule 3 is pretty straightforward, placing Science lower than Puzzles, which can be combined with Rule 2.

```
      P   M
     / \ /
    S   F
```

Again, it's helpful to note in the sketch that Science cannot be in the highest aisle. It's already been noted that Puzzles cannot be in the lowest aisle.

Rule 4 says Science cannot be placed lower than Hobbies. However, this does not mean Science must be placed higher than Hobbies; they can also be placed in the same aisle. You can either shorthand both possible outcomes or make one note that H is never above S.

$$\boxed{\text{H S}} \text{ or } \begin{array}{c} \text{S} \\ | \\ \text{H} \end{array}$$

Step 4: Deductions

The biggest deduction to make in this game is to combine the information about Science from Rules 3 and 4. Because Rule 3 prevents Science from being in the highest aisle, Hobbies is also restricted from that aisle (by Rule 4). This places a lot of restrictions on aisle 3. The only sections that can go there are Music, Puzzles, and Reading. However, this is not enough information to warrant Limited Options. Similarly, except for Reading, every section is limited to only two aisles. However, facing a set of mostly "If" questions, it's not worth the time to decide which section, if any, might set up substantial Limited Options. Instead, know the restrictions and pay attention to the Numbers.

```
     3: ___   ~F; ~S; ~H
     2: ___
     1: ___   ~M; ~P
```

```
    P   M     ┌─────┐        ┌───────┐
   / \ /      │ H S │ or  S  │ R F/M │
  S   F       └─────┘      | │       │
                           H └───────┘
```

Step 5: Questions

13. (D) "If" / Could Be True

The word *only* is important in setting up the information for this question. Hobbies will placed in aisle 1, and that's it. With only aisles 2 and 3 open, Fantasy will have to be located in aisle 2 with Music and Puzzles in aisle 3 (Rule 2). And that places Science in aisle 2 (Rule 3). With Fantasy and Music in aisles 2 and 3, respectively, Reading can go into either of those aisles to satisfy Rule 1.

```
3:  M   P
2:  F   S
1:  H   ||
```

That makes **(D)** the only possible answer. **(A)**, **(B)**, **(C)**,and **(E)** all must be false based on the sketch.

14. (A) "If" / Must Be True

Again, it's important to note the word *only* in the question stem. Here, Puzzles will be placed in aisle 3, and that's it. With only aisles 1 and 2 open, Fantasy will have to be located in aisle 1 with Music in aisle 2 (Rule 2).

```
3:  P   ||
2:  M
1:  F
```

That immediately makes **(A)** true and thus the correct answer. For the record, **(C)** can be eliminated immediately once Music is placed in aisle 2. With Puzzles in the highest aisle, Science is free to be in either aisle 1 or aisle 2, and Hobbies can be in either of those aisles with Science. That means both **(B)** and **(E)** could be true but don't have to be and so must be eliminated. And with Fantasy in aisle 1 and Music in aisle 2, Reading could be in either of those aisles to satisfy Rule 1. That leeway eliminates **(D)**.

15. (B) "If" / Must Be True

For this question, each aisle will have exactly two sections. Since the question asks about Science, that's the most strategic section to tackle first. Science cannot be in aisle 3 (Rule 3), so that leaves two possibilities. If it were in aisle 1, it would have to be with Hobbies (Rule 4). This is a good sign that **(B)** is the correct answer. To confirm that this must be true, consider what would happen if Science were in aisle 2.

In that case, Puzzles would have to be in aisle 3 (Rule 3). Reading, which must be with either Fantasy or Music (Rule 1), would have to be in aisle 1, since there aren't enough spots left in aisles 2 or 3. Since Fantasy has to be in a lower aisle than Music, Fantasy will have to be the section with Reading in aisle 1. With only Music and Hobbies left, Hobbies will have to be in aisle 2 (Rule 4), leaving Music for aisle 3.

```
3:  P   M
2:  S   H
1:  R   F
```

No matter what, with two sections in each aisle, Science will always be with Hobbies, making **(B)** the correct answer. **(A)**, **(C)**, **(D)**,and **(E)** must be false based on both sketches.

16. (A) Must Be False (CANNOT Be True)

This question works similarly to a Partial Acceptability question, with the correct answer being the outcome that cannot happen. While it might seem like these answers would have to be tested one at a time, a quick glance shows that every answer choice includes Music. Therefore, the most strategic approach would be to set up a sketch with Music in aisle 2 and find out which of the five answer choices cannot happen.

If Music is in aisle 2, then Fantasy must be in aisle 1 (Rule 2). Reading must then be in either of those two aisles (Rule 1). Furthermore, since Science cannot be in aisle 3 (Rule 3), Hobbies cannot be in aisle 3 (Rule 4). That leaves Puzzles as the only section in aisle 3. Science is the most limited section left, so check out both possible outcomes.

```
3:  P   ~S; ~H
2:  M  ↙
1:  R  ↙R
```

If Science were in aisle 1, then Hobbies would be in aisle 1 (Rule 4). So, for aisle 2, Music can be left alone or can be paired up with Reading, which eliminates **(B)**.

```
3:  P
2:  M        ←R
1:  F   S   H  ↙
```

If Science were in aisle 2, then Hobbies could be in either aisle 1 or aisle 2 (Rule 4). That means Music and Science can be left by themselves in aisle 2, which eliminates **(C)**. Alternately, Hobbies or Reading could be added alongside, eliminating **(D)** and **(E)**.

```
3:  P
2:  M   S  ←R; H
1:  F      ↙
```

That leaves **(A)**, which must be the correct answer. To confirm, if Music and Hobbies were the only sections in aisle 2, then Science would have to be in aisle 3 (Rule 4), but that would violate Rule 3. Therefore, **(A)** must be false and is the correct answer.

17. (E) "If" / Must Be True EXCEPT

Once the sketch is set up for this question, the correct answer will be the one that doesn't have to be true. In other words, if there's any chance the answer choice could be false, that will be the correct answer.

For this question, Science will be the only section in aisle 2. That leaves only aisles 1 and 3 for the remaining sections. In that case, Fantasy will have to be aisle 1 with Puzzles and Music in aisle 3 (Rule 2), and Hobbies will have to be in aisle 1

(Rule 4). That leaves Reading, which could be in either aisle 1 with Fantasy or in aisle 3 with Music.

3: P M
2: S ‖ ⟩R
1: H F

Since Reading's placement is undetermined, **(E)** is the correct answer. **(A)**, **(B)**, **(C)**,and **(D)** are all definitely true.

Game 4: Millville's Development Zones

Step 1: Overview

Situation: A city designating subzone usage within three new development zones

Entities: Three development zones (Z1, Z2, Z3) and three possible uses for subzones (housing, industrial, retail)

Action: Matching. Your task is to determine the number and types of subzones in each development zone. Essentially, you'll be matching types of subzones to the three development zones.

Limitations: This game is highly unorthodox. First, each development zone can have subzones, but that doesn't mean there must be subzones in any given development zone. Furthermore, although each subzone is limited to one use, two subzones with the same use can be in the same development zone. For example, in any given development zone, there may be two subzones that are both designated for housing use.

However, there is one limitation: each use is limited to three subzones. Or in other words, there is a maximum of three for each subzone type. However, because that's a maximum, there's a chance that a given use (e.g., retail) will be designated to only one or two subzones—or even zero. Clearly, Numbers will be crucial to managing this game efficiently. Make a note that each use can be used a maximum of three times and be careful not to make any false assumptions.

Step 2: Sketch

You'll deal with this game best by setting up a chart. Sketch a table with three columns, one for each of the development zones (Z1, Z2, and Z3). In these columns, you'll place subzones. However, because no zone is required to have subzones, the columns will be left empty until the rules or questions dictate otherwise. For now, simply list the maximum possible subzones to the side: "H H H I I I R R R." Remember, not all of these have to be used.

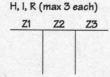

Step 3: Rules

Rule 1 is fairly straightforward rule. Simply designate "No R" under the column for Z1. However, remember this doesn't mean there must be retail subzones in either of the other two development zones.

Rule 2 places a numeric restriction on housing subzones. There cannot be more than two in any given development zone. Since there can only be three housing subzones overall,

a simpler way of expressing this rule is that you can never have all three housing subzones together.

Rule 3 restricts retail subzones if there are housing subzones in the same development zone. In that case, there cannot be more than one retail subzone. Jot this down in Formal Logic and consider its contrapositive: if a development zone does have more than one retail subzone, then it cannot contain any housing subzones.

$$H \rightarrow Max\ 1\ R$$
$$2+R \rightarrow \sim H$$

Rule 4 presents two conditions that prevent the designation of industrial subzones. First, they can't be placed in any development zone that already has housing subzones. In short, this means that no development zone can contain both housing and industrial subzones.

Second, industrial subzones can't be placed in any development zone that contains three retail subzones. So, in short, this means that no development zone can have three retail zones with any industrial zones.

Step 4: Deductions

As far as development zones go, only Z1 has any restriction: it can't have retail subzones. And, since no development zone can have both housing and industrial subzones, Z1 is limited to one type of subzone, either housing or industrial. But again, that doesn't mean Z1 must have one of those types of subzones—it could have none.

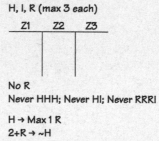

Z2 and Z3 are unrestricted. Furthermore, since no development zone and no subzones have to be used, there's no way to determine anything for certain. This game will merely require a solid application of the rules and consistent attention to the numeric limitations.

Step 5: Questions

18. (E) Acceptability

Even for such a complex game, the Acceptability question can be deftly handled by running through the rules one at a time, eliminating any answer that violates those rules.

Rule 1 states that Retail subzones are not allowed in Z1, so that eliminates **(C)**. Rule 2 limits the number of housing subzones in any one development zone to two. That eliminates **(D)**. Rule 3 states that any development zone with a housing subzone cannot have more than one retail subzone. That eliminates **(A)**, which puts two retail subzones with a housing subzone in Z2. Finally, Rule 4 dictates that industrial subzones cannot be in any development zone that has a housing subzone. That eliminates **(B)**, leaving **(E)** as the only acceptable answer.

19. (D) Must Be False (CANNOT Be True)

Four of the answers will be possible based on the limitations and the rules. The correct answer will be the one that is impossible for any given development zone. With no major deductions in this game, the answer choices will need to be tested one at a time. Try to consider the Numbers without drawing an entire sketch for each answer choice.

According to Rule 3, housing and retail subzones can be together, as long as there's only one retail subzone. Therefore, **(A)** is acceptable and can be eliminated.

According to Rule 4, industrial subzones cannot be in any development zone with three retail subzones. However, there's nothing against industrial subzones being together with just one retail subzone. Therefore, **(B)** is acceptable and can be eliminated.

Housing is the only subzone type that can't be used three times in one development zone. And since retail subzones are only restricted from Z1, there's no reason there can't be three retail subzones in one of the other two development zones. That eliminates **(C)**.

If a development zone has no industrial subzones, then only housing and retail subzones are left. No development subzone can have three housing subzones (Rule 2), so only two subzones could be housing. However, with any housing subzones, there can only be one retail zone (Rule 3). That would only create three subzones, not four. And even if you tried to maximize retail subzones, putting three together, you couldn't have any housing subzones (Rule 3). That means there's no way to get four subzones in this case, making **(D)** the correct answer.

For the record, an industrial subzone can't accompany three retail subzones (Rule 4), but with only two retail subzones, it's acceptable to have two industrial subzones as well. That eliminates **(E)**.

20. (D) Maximum

When testing numbers, be systematic. Don't just test random scenarios.

By itself, Z3 doesn't have any numeric restrictions. The biggest restriction for any development zone is that it cannot have both housing and industrial subzones. It would be strategic to test which type of subzone (housing or industrial) allows for the greatest number of retail subzones.

Setting up housing subzones restricts the Numbers in three ways. First, there can't be more than two housing subzones in any development zone (Rule 2). Furthermore, with housing subzones, there can be only one retail subzone (Rule 3). Finally, with housing subzones, there cannot be any industrial subzones (Rule 4). So, by having a housing subzone, that would be three subzones at most.

Industrial subzones aren't as restricted. It's acceptable to have all three industrial subzones in Z3. The only restriction is that the development zone cannot then have three retail subzones (Rule 4). However, there's no reason there cannot be two retail zones. That would set up a maximum of five subzones.

If there were no housing or industrial subzones, then there could only be three retail subzones max. That means the group of five subzones, created by three industrial subzones and two retail subzones, is the maximum possible. That makes **(D)** the correct answer.

21. (B) "If" / Could Be True

For this question, three subzones will be designated for each use. Unfortunately, there's no indication of where these subzones will be placed. Once again, think strategically before testing out every answer individually.

The three housing subzones can't all be placed in one development zone (Rule 2). Also, they can't be split up into all three development zones, because that would prevent any industrial subzones from being designated (Rule 4). So, the housing subzones will be divided between two development zones—one zone with two housing subzones and the other zone with one. That means all three industrial subzones will be placed together into the remaining development zone. So far, the three development zones will be broken down as such:

$$III \quad HH \quad H$$

That leaves the retail subzones. They can't be all together with housing subzones (Rule 3) or with industrial zones (Rule 4). They also can't be split among all three development zones, since they're not allowed in Z1 (Rule 1). That means they will be split into two development zones—one zone with two retail subzones and the other with one. Since housing subzones can never be with two retail subzones (Rule 3), the group of two retail subzones must accompany the three industrial subzones. The last retail subzone could be placed in either one of the development zones with housing subzones.

$$IIIRR \quad HH \quad H$$
$$\quad\quad \nwarrow \quad \nearrow$$
$$\quad\quad\quad R$$

Since Z1 can't have retail subzones, it must have the group of only housing subzones. Z2 and Z3 will be, in either order, the development zone with housing subzone(s) and one retail subzone, and the development zone with all three industrial subzones and two retail subzones.

From that, only **(B)** is possible. **(A)**, **(C)**, **(D)**, and **(E)** all must be false based on the groupings.

22. (A) "If" / Could Be True

For this question, all three development zones will have one industrial subzone. That means no development zone can have housing subzones (Rule 4). That eliminates **(B)**.

Since Z1 cannot have retail subzones either (Rule 1), Z1 will include one industrial subzone only. That eliminates **(C)**.

```
    Z1    Z2    Z3
     I  |  I  |  I
     
    ~H    ~H    ~H
    ~R
```

Any remaining spaces in Z2 and Z3 can only be filled by retail subzones, but no development zone can have three retail subzones (Rule 4). That eliminates **(E)**.

However, if Z2 had two retail subzones and Z3 had one, then Z2 could have more retail subzones than Z3. That means **(A)** is possible, making it the correct answer. For the record, since there can only be three retail subzones (opening paragraph limitation) and no housing subzones are allowed, it's impossible to fill up both Z2 and Z3 with three subzones. That eliminates **(D)**.

23. (A) "If" / Could Be True

This question provides two pieces of information. First, three retail subzones will be designated. Furthermore, Z2 will get a housing subzone. That means there can be no industrial subzones in Z2 (Rule 4). As for the three retail subzones, none of them can be in Z1 (Rule 1). Because Z2 already has a housing subzone, Rule 3 dictates two options: either one retail subzone will go in Z2 and two will go in Z3, or all three retail subzones will go in Z3. In either scenario, Z3 will have at least two retail subzones, so no housing subzones can be placed in Z3 (Rule 3). Z1, however, has no restrictions other than Rule 1: no retail subzones. That means **(A)** is possible and thus correct.

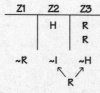

For the record, since there can't be any industrial subzones in Z2, **(B)** can be eliminated. Since Z2 can only have one retail subzone while Z3 has at least two, **(C)** and **(D)** can be eliminated. And since Z3 can no longer have housing subzones, **(E)** can be eliminated.

Section IV: Logical Reasoning

Q#	Question Type	Correct	Difficulty
1	Main Point	B	★
2	Assumption (Necessary)	A	★
3	Paradox	C	★
4	Strengthen	C	★★
5	Inference	A	★
6	Weaken	A	★★
7	Principle (Identify/Strengthen)	E	★
8	Strengthen	D	★
9	Flaw	C	★
10	Weaken	B	★
11	Assumption (Necessary)	A	★★★
12	Method of Argument	D	★★
13	Assumption (Sufficient)	B	★
14	Flaw	B	★★
15	Inference	E	★★★
16	Assumption (Necessary)	D	★★★★
17	Inference	B	★★★
18	Assumption (Necessary)	A	★★★
19	Parallel Reasoning	B	★
20	Inference	E	★★
21	Flaw	C	★★
22	Role of a Statement	E	★★★
23	Paradox	B	★★
24	Weaken	C	★
25	Parallel Flaw	D	★★

1. (B) Main Point

Step 1: Identify the Question Type

The phrase "states the overall conclusion" identifies this as a Main Point question. Focus on Keywords, look out for subsidiary conclusions, and expect to combine statements in the argument to paraphrase the author's main point. Also consider using the One-Sentence Test.

Step 2: Untangle the Stimulus

Evaluate the stimulus sentence by sentence and think about the relationships between each. The first sentence states that prosperity is a large reason for increases in carbon dioxide, which is the main cause of global warming. The second sentence states that people buy energy-consuming devices, such as cars (which produce carbon dioxide), when their incomes rise. Notice that the second sentence helps to explain why more money increases the release of carbon dioxide, strongly suggesting that sentence 1 is the economist's overall point. The continuation Keyword [a]lso indicates that sentence 3 provides additional evidence: large drops in carbon dioxide emissions occurred in countries that experienced large economic recessions.

Step 3: Make a Prediction

Both the second and third sentences support the economist's overall conclusion in the first sentence: prosperity is a driving force behind increases in the release of carbon dioxide. Find an answer choice that paraphrases this main point.

Step 4: Evaluate the Answer Choices

(B) is correct and nicely summarizes the economist's overall conclusion in the first sentence.

(A) is a Faulty Use of Detail. While the argument does state that the main cause of global warming is the increased release of carbon dioxide, the author provides no evidence for this. The evidence supports the first part of the first sentence: that prosperity results in more carbon dioxide in the atmosphere.

(C) references evidence from sentence 2, which supports the economist's overall conclusion that prosperity is a driving force behind increased levels of carbon dioxide.

(D) is another Faulty Use of Detail. It incorrectly identifies a piece of evidence from sentence 3 as the author's main point. The continuation Keyword [a]lso should have indicated this sentence (and by extension, the one before it) is evidence.

(E), like **(C)**, also provides evidence from sentence 2 but does not state the economist's overall point. If the author could only keep one sentence, this wouldn't be it.

2. (A) Assumption (Necessary)

Step 1: Identify the Question Type

The word *assumption* identifies this as an Assumption question. Additionally, the word *required* indicates that you are looking for a necessary assumption, one without which the conclusion cannot be logically drawn from the evidence. You can use the Denial Test to check or eliminate answer choices.

Step 2: Untangle the Stimulus

The spokesperson concludes that the "Clean City" campaign has been a success. The Keywords "[a]fter all" indicate his evidence: there is less trash on the city's streets now than before the campaign began.

Step 3: Make a Prediction

The spokesperson is making an argument of causation. For that to work, he must assume that the "Clean City" campaign is responsible for the lower amount of trash on the city streets. In other words, the spokesperson assumes that there is no other reason or cause. Find an answer choice that states this assumption.

Step 4: Evaluate the Answer Choices

(A) is correct and matches your prediction. Using the Denial Test confirms this choice: if the amount of trash on the city's streets was declining at the same rate or faster prior to the campaign, then there is reason to believe that something other than the campaign was responsible for lowering the amount of trash. Since the spokesperson assumes this is not the case, **(A)** must be correct.

(B) is Outside the Scope. Whether critics are aware of the degree to which the amount of trash has declined since the campaign began has nothing to do with whether the campaign itself is responsible for that decline.

(C) is an Irrelevant Comparison. Whether or not the "Clean City" campaign has been more successful at removing trash from city streets than any other campaign is irrelevant to whether the "Clean City" campaign is a success. Even if "Clean City" were not as effective as previous campaigns, it's possible for the spokesperson's assertion still to be valid.

(D) is Outside the Scope. Funding for the "Clean City" campaign has nothing to do with whether the campaign was a success.

(E) is Outside the Scope. Whether or not the amount of trash declined steadily or all at once throughout the course of the "Clean City" campaign does not affect the spokesperson's argument. He doesn't need to assume this is true in order to claim the campaign was successful.

3. (C) Paradox

Step 1: Identify the Question Type

The phrase "resolve the apparent paradox" identifies this as a Paradox question. Read the stimulus to identify the seemingly contradictory statements. Then evaluate the answers to find the one choice that explains how the two statements may reasonably coexist.

Step 2: Untangle the Stimulus

The first sentence states that consuming sugar raises the level of unmetabolized sugar in the blood. The contrast Keyword [*yet*] introduces the discrepancy: people who consume lots of sugar tend to have lower levels of unmetabolized sugar in their blood.

Step 3: Make a Prediction

Begin by stating the paradox: How can people who consume large amounts of sugar tend to have below-average levels of unmetabolized sugars when eating sugar raises the level of unmetabolized sugar in the blood? You do not need to predict the exact way that this happens, but you should specifically look for an answer choice that explains how both these things are possible.

Step 4: Evaluate the Answer Choices

(C) explains the discrepancy and is correct. If eating lots of sugar causes one to secrete abnormally high amounts of insulin, "a sugar-metabolizing enzyme," then the excess sugar would not likely be measured in the blood. This explains why people who consume large amounts of sugar tend to have below-average levels of unmetabolized sugars.

(A) is Outside the Scope. What is true of people who are overweight has nothing to do with why, in general, people who consume large amounts of sugar tend to have below-average levels of unmetabolized sugar in their blood.

(B) is Outside the Scope. Knowing what foods contain sugar doesn't address how the body reacts to it.

(D) is a 180. That consuming sugar hinders the production of insulin, and thus the ability to metabolize sugar, makes it even more surprising that people who eat a lot of sugar have lower levels of unmetabolized sugar in their blood.

(E) is Outside the Scope. A process that occurs uniformly in everyone doesn't explain the difference between the two groups—those who consume a lot of sugar and those who don't.

4. (C) Strengthen

Step 1: Identify the Question Type

The phrase "most strengthens the economist's argument" identifies this as a Strengthen question. Break down the argument into conclusion and evidence, predict the central

assumption, and find an answer choice that validates the economist's assumption.

Step 2: Untangle the Stimulus

The economist provides her conclusion in the first sentence: "consumers often benefit when government permits a corporation to obtain a monopoly." Why? She states that, without competition, a corporation can raise prices without spending much on advertising. Moreover, the corporation can invest this money into research or infrastructure and pass along those benefits to consumers.

Step 3: Make a Prediction

The only reason the economist claims consumers will benefit from government allowing monopolies is that companies can pass along to consumers the fruits of investing in expensive research or industrial infrastructure. Remember, however, that she also states that these companies can raise prices. For these monopolies to benefit consumers, she must assume that the negatives of price increases will not surpass the benefits from investments in research or infrastructure. Find an answer choice that validates this assumption.

Step 4: Evaluate the Answer Choices

(C) is correct. If the disadvantage to consumers of higher prices will be outweighed by advantages from investing more in research or infrastructure, then the economist's conclusion—that monopolies are to consumers' advantage—is more likely to be true.

(A) is an Irrelevant Comparison. The benefits to consumers may be greater if a corporation invests in research or infrastructure than if that corporation invests in something else, but that doesn't mean the benefits are great enough to outweigh other disadvantages to consumers. You need to strengthen the fact that investing in research and infrastructure ultimately benefits consumers despite the increased prices corporations can charge.

(B) is a Distortion. It states that the only time a corporation's monopoly is advantageous to consumers is when that corporation passes along the fruits of some of its investments to consumers. To strengthen the argument, the "fruits of these investments" need to exceed the detriment of the price hikes. Whether or not the benefit mentioned is the sole way to benefit consumers is immaterial without knowing its value in comparison to price hikes.

(D) would weaken the argument and is a 180. The author relies on the benefits of monopolies outweighing their negatives, but if the benefits are achievable without monopolization, then the threat of monopolies' disadvantages is increased.

(E) also weakens the author's argument. This answer choice says the disadvantages to consumers (higher prices) will almost always occur, but it doesn't mention the advantages at all. How likely are they? Without stating that they are at least as lIkely as higher prices, this answer choice can't help the argument.

5. (A) Inference

Step 1: Identify the Question Type

The phrase "statements above ... support which one of the following" identifies this as an Inference question. Accept each sentence in the stimulus as true and find an answer choice that must be true on the basis of one or more of those sentences.

Step 2: Untangle the Stimulus

The first two sentences state that a natural history museum contains taxidermy displays. Next, you're told that the animals' skins in some older displays have started to deteriorate because of low humidity and heat from lights. The fourth sentence states that newer, compact fluorescent lamps designed for use in museums illuminate newer displays and that older displays are lit by tungsten lamps. Finally, the stimulus states that fluorescent lamps give off less heat but as much light as tungsten lamps.

Step 3: Make a Prediction

The stimulus suggests that the fluorescent lamps used to illuminate newer displays are better than the tungsten lamps used to illuminate older displays, because fluorescent lamps give off less heat than do tungsten lamps and heat is one cause of the animals' skins deterioration.

Step 4: Evaluate the Answer Choices

(A) is correct and matches your prediction. Older displays will last longer if the tungsten lamps are replaced by fluorescent lamps, because the latter give off less heat.

(B) is an Irrelevant Comparison. Nothing in the stimulus provides enough information to exactly compare how many of each type of lamp is needed before one causes more deterioration than the other. Numbers are not discussed.

(C) is another Irrelevant Comparison. The stimulus simply states that the museum contains both older displays and newer displays. Nothing in the stimulus provides information about the actual number of older and newer displays and how many of each is lit by each type of lamp.

(D) is unsupported. The stimulus indicates the fluorescent lamps used on the newer displays address the heat problem, but it does not discuss any changes between the old and new displays that would address the low humidity issue.

(E) is yet another Irrelevant Comparison. The stimulus does not compare the current level of humidity in the museum to the level of humidity in the museum when the older displays were first put in place.

6. (A) Weaken

Step 1: Identify the Question Type

The phrase "most weakens" identifies this as a Weaken question. Break down the argument into evidence and conclusion, determine the central assumption, and then look for an answer choice that attacks that assumption.

Step 2: Untangle the Stimulus

The columnist concludes in the first sentence that the number of species on Earth is probably not decreasing. His evidence states that extinction is natural and as many species are likely to go extinct this year as went extinct in 1970. However, new species emerge naturally as well, and new species are likely emerging at about the same rate as they have been for the last few centuries.

Step 3: Make a Prediction

The columnist equates current extinction rates with those of 1970 to prove that the total number of species is not dwindling. But what if the overall species number was dwindling in the 1970s? For the columnist's conclusion to work, he must assume that the rate at which new species emerge is at least as great as the rate of extinction for current species. Find an answer choice that calls into question this central assumption by suggesting that the rate of extinction is greater than the rate at which new species emerge.

Step 4: Evaluate the Answer Choices

(A) is correct and matches your prediction. If fewer new species emerged than went extinct in 1970, and the columnist expects about the same number of species to go extinct now as did in 1970, then there is reason to believe that the number of extinct species will be greater than the number of new species.

(B) is Outside the Scope. Knowing where in the world species emerge and go extinct at the highest rates has no impact on whether there is an overall decline in the number of species on Earth.

(C) is Outside the Scope. Whether or not most species that ever existed are now extinct has nothing to do with whether the overall number of currently existing species on Earth is dwindling.

(D) is an Irrelevant Comparison. The level of concern about extinction that exists now versus in 1970 has no bearing on whether, in reality, the number of species currently on Earth is decreasing.

(E) is another Irrelevant Comparison. Scientists' ability to better identify species facing serious risk of extinction would not invalidate the author's evidence that extinction and emergence rates have not changed. Therefore, his conclusion would remain unchanged.

7. (E) Principle (Identify/Strengthen)

Step 1: Identify the Question Type

The word *principles* clearly identifies this as a Principle question. Because the principles show up in the answer choices, this is an Identify the Principle question. In addition, the phrase "most helps to justify" indicates a task identical to that in Strengthen questions. So, approach this question the same way you would a Strengthen question: look for a generalized answer that would make the conclusion more likely to follow from the evidence. The correct answer will be a principle that supports the argument's assumption.

Step 2: Untangle the Stimulus

The author concludes in the first sentence that MacArthur should not have published his diet book, despite it helping people lose weight. Why? Because the book recommended such small portions of fruits and vegetables that following the diet would be unhealthy. Additionally, MacArthur, as a physician, "either knew or should have known" that the book contained unhealthy advice.

Step 3: Make a Prediction

Remember that when you must identify the principle in an argument, the correct answer represents the broad rule that underlies the specific situation in the stimulus. Here, the author claims that MacArthur should not have published his book because it recommended something that he knew or should have known to be unhealthful. Thus, the author believes that one should not recommend something that one knows, or should know, to be unhealthful.

Step 4: Evaluate the Answer Choices

(E) is correct and matches your prediction perfectly.

(A) is Extreme. MacArthur knew or should have known that if people followed his diet recommendation, it would be unhealthful, but nothing in the argument suggests that he knew people would definitely follow the advice or that, if they did, it would "seriously" damage the health of "many" people.

(B) is Outside the Scope. The argument critiques not those who followed the diet but rather MacArthur for publishing it in the first place.

(C) is Outside the Scope. The author only says what should not be published, not what should be.

(D) is a Distortion. The issue is not whether publishing MacArthur's diet book will actually lead people to attaining a goal (losing weight). The author even concedes MacArthur's book helped people accomplish the intended result.

8. (D) Strengthen

Step 1: Identify the Question Type

The combination of a Principle/Application stimulus and the question stem calling for an answer choice that "most justifies" the specific application of the principle makes this a variant on a Strengthen question. Treat the application as a conclusion and the stated principle as evidence. The correct answer will strengthen the assumption that ties the two together.

Step 2: Untangle the Stimulus

The principle states that a policy change should not be made if doing so would disproportionately hurt people with low incomes. The application makes the rule relevant to the city of Centerburgh's proposed plans to return to using rock salt as a de-icing agent. In this case, the application states that the city's plan should be halted.

Step 3: Make a Prediction

As with any Assumption-family question, take note of how the conclusion differs from the evidence. Here, the conclusion (application) states that the city's proposed plan should be halted because salt speeds up the corrosion of cars. The evidence (principle) states that a policy change should not be made if the burden of that proposed change would fall unevenly on people with low incomes. Notice the disconnect: nothing in the application states that reintroducing rock salt as a de-icing agent would disproportionately trouble people with low incomes. The application must assume this to be true. Thus, the correct answer must strengthen this assumption by stating that the threat to cars somehow affects low-income people more than others.

Step 4: Evaluate the Answer Choices

(D) is correct. If people with low incomes are more likely to have older vehicles, and those older vehicles are not as protected against salt's corrosive properties as are newer vehicles, then adopting this policy would disproportionately burden people with low incomes.

(A) is a 180. If individuals with low incomes are more likely to use public transportation, then any ill effects of using rock salt as a de-icing agent would more negatively impact individuals with higher incomes who travel in their own cars.

(B) is Outside the Scope. The principle says policy changes should not be made if they would hurt low-income people. It says nothing about policy that is already in effect. So, if low-income people are already disproportionately paying for road maintenance, a change to how that road maintenance is conducted may not affect them further. No mention is made that the de-icing would be a more expensive practice thereby creating more sales taxes and thereby more strain on low-income people.

(C) is an Irrelevant Comparison. The price of automobiles now versus several years ago doesn't pinpoint how low-income people specifically would be negatively affected. It's possible that incomes have also doubled.

(E) is another 180. If low-income drivers are less likely to use de-iced roads, then rock salt would endanger their cars less than it would high-income drivers' cars.

9. (C) Flaw

Step 1: Identify the Question Type

The phrase "reasoning ... is most vulnerable to criticism" identifies this as a Flaw question. Break down the argument into conclusion and evidence and think about why the evidence does not allow the conclusion to be properly drawn.

Step 2: Untangle the Stimulus

The Keyword [o]bviously identifies the conclusion: many Groverhill residents who consulted physicians for severe headaches do not remember doing so. The author claims this is true because physician records indicate that 105 consultations occurred last year but only 35 people reported going to the doctor.

Step 3: Make a Prediction

The author assumes each resident consulted his or her physician for severe headaches only once last year. This is not necessarily the case, as it is likely that some residents consulted their physicians more than once over the course of last year. This reflects a scope shift between reports of headaches and actual consultations. It can also be viewed as a failure to consider the possibility that each report of a headache led to more than one consultation.

Step 4: Evaluate the Answer Choices

(C) is correct and matches your prediction.

(A) is incorrect because representativeness is not at issue. The study in question surveyed "all of the residents of Groverhill" and made a conclusion about residents of Groverhill, so the sample certainly is representative.

(B) is Outside the Scope. The author says the medical study of all the people in Groverhill revealed 35 reports of people consulting their physician about headaches—it does not indicate where those physicians are located. It then says, "Those same physicians' records ... ," which means that every doctor who was consulted about the headaches also had his or her records consulted. This does not leave open the possibility that there were physicians, in or out of Groverhill, whose records were not consulted.

(D) is Outside the Scope because the number of occurrences, high or low, is irrelevant.

(E) is incorrect because the evidence only discusses the reported number of consultations. The argument is unconcerned with headaches that went unaddressed.

10. (B) Weaken

Step 1: Identify the Question Type

The phrase "most weakens" identifies this as a Weaken question. Identify the conclusion, paraphrase the evidence, determine the central assumption, and then look for a fact that attacks that assumption.

Step 2: Untangle the Stimulus

The economist concludes in the last sentence that "business executives have become public officials." Why? In the first sentence, the economist says that the primary responsibility of executives is to guide a nation's industry. In the second sentence, the author states that executives also make decisions about what is to be produced and in what quantity. In essence, business executives make a lot of decisions concerning a nation.

Step 3: Make a Prediction

The economist lists the roles and responsibilities held by corporate executives and then equates executives to public officials. She must be assuming their responsibilities are similar. Find an answer choice that attacks this assumption.

Step 4: Evaluate the Answer Choices

(B) is correct and matches your prediction. If making these types of decisions is not the core of a public official's job, but is the primary responsibility of corporate executives, then it is less likely that these executives are themselves public officials. This answer choice widens the gap between the two jobs.

(A) is Outside the Scope. The argument never discusses countries with centrally planned economies, and this choice fails to invalidate the economist's assumption.

(C) is an Irrelevant Comparison. The salaries of business executives and high-ranking public officials do not have any effect on the author's argument that the two jobs are essentially the same. The author's argument centers on their job duties, not their compensation.

(D) is Outside the Scope. Whether corporate executives completely control what a country produces and in what quantities—or only mainly control it—is irrelevant to whether or not those executives have become public officials by making such decisions.

(E) is a 180. If business executives and public officials often cooperate in making decisions that affect the entire nation, the economist's central assumption is validated, and it is more likely to be true that these two groups have similar duties. Therefore, the executives might actually have become public officials.

11. (A) Assumption (Necessary)

Step 1: Identify the Question Type

The word *assumption* identifies this as an Assumption question. Additionally, the word *requires* indicates that you are looking for a necessary assumption, one without which the conclusion cannot be logically drawn from the evidence. You can use the Denial Test to check or eliminate answer choices.

Step 2: Untangle the Stimulus

The author's conclusion ends the stimulus: science fiction has created an unproductive dissatisfaction with the way the world actually is. Why? His main piece of evidence, signaled by the Keyword [s]*ince*, is that "gaps between expectations and reality" cause people to feel discontented.

Step 3: Make a Prediction

The author makes two troublesome scope shifts here. First is the disparity between the terminology in the conclusion and evidence. The evidence says unfulfilled expectations create discontent, but the conclusion is that unproductive dissatisfaction with the world arises. The author must be assuming those two emotions are synonymous. It's possible your original prediction looked like that and you were disappointed when you went to the answer choices. So, go back and look for a gap within the evidence itself: specifically, how the author defines "reality" and "expectations." The reality is that humanity is nowhere near achieving interstellar space travel. Yet, for the conclusion to make sense, people must be expecting such travel. However, the author never explicitly states this is so; instead, he says that science fiction "creates an appetite." The author assumes that wanting something is the same as expecting it.

Step 4: Evaluate the Answer Choices

(A) explicitly links appetite with expectations and is correct. The desire for space exploration has led some people to have an unhealthy gap between their expectations and reality. If you were to use the Denial Test, this choice would say, essentially: "That humanity can't travel across space has not created a gap between reality and expectations." If no gap exists, then the author can no longer conclude that discontent and, by extension, unproductive dissatisfaction will arise.

(B) is Extreme. The argument says creating an appetite for space travel is one way in which science fiction has created an unproductive dissatisfaction with the world, but the author does not say—or need to say—that this is the only way science fiction has spurred dissatisfaction.

(C) is Outside the Scope. Whether or not few of the desires science fiction sparks in people can be satisfied with any human technology is irrelevant. This argument is concerned with only one particular desire.

(D) is Extreme. The argument discusses some people who have a gap between their expectations and reality. This answer choice says most people. Furthermore, even if most people do believe, unrealistically or not, that humanity will soon have the technology for space exploration, then, if anything, the author's argument would be weakened because no gap would exist for those people.

(E) is Outside the Scope. The argument does not discuss any situation in which the desires that science fiction creates in people could be satisfied with technology that humanity will soon possess. In any event, this choice fails to show that an appetite is the same as an expectation.

12. (D) Method of Argument

Step 1: Identify the Question Type

The phrase "proceeds by" may be short, but it indicates that the question is asking for how Tamika makes her argument and thus identifies this as a Method of Argument question. The correct answer will reflect, likely in abstract terms, the way in which Tamika advances her main point. Note the Keywords and paraphrase how Tamika attempts to convince her readers.

Step 2: Untangle the Stimulus

The first sentence states that many people have been fooled by those who market certain questionable medical products. The second sentence explains why this happens: people desire easy solutions to complex medical problems but do not know enough to see through the marketers' false claims. The Keyword [h]*owever* in sentence 3 introduces a contrast: Tamika states that this same explanation does not explain a recent trend among medical professionals toward susceptibility to fraudulent claims, because these professionals do not lack medical knowledge.

Step 3: Make a Prediction

To prepare yourself to evaluate the answer choices, paraphrase Tamika's argumentative strategy in broad terms. Tamika states that two different groups (many people and medical professionals) have the same response to something (they are both susceptible to fraudulent medical claims). She also states that the explanation for why one group (many people) acts that way does not explain why the other group (medical professionals) acts that way. Her reason is that the two groups are dissimilar: medical professionals have the medical knowledge many people do not.

Step 4: Evaluate the Answer Choices

(D) is correct. Tamika argues that since many people and medical professionals are not analogous in an important respect (the level of medical knowledge), there must be different explanations for their similar behavior.

(A) is a Distortion. Tamika does not attempt to show that medical professionals should not be susceptible to fraudulent claims altogether but rather that their susceptibility cannot be explained in the same way as other people's susceptibility.

(B) is a Distortion. While Tamika does argue that an explanation for some people's behavior does not explain other people's behavior (medical professionals), she doesn't proceed by entirely rejecting the hypothesis about why some people (non-medical professionals) are susceptible.

(C) is a 180. Tamika never casts doubt on the expertise of the medical professionals. Rather, she claims medical professionals have "no lack of" medical knowledge. That existence of expertise is precisely why she concludes there must be some other explanation as to why these professionals are susceptible to the fraudulent claims.

(E) is incorrect because Tamika argues that the evidence proves a different explanation must exist. She does not recommend accepting an explanation in the face of conflicting evidence.

13. (B) Assumption (Sufficient)

Step 1: Identify the Question Type

The word *assumed* identifies this as an Assumption question. Additionally, the question stem tells you that the argument will be complete "If" the assumption is added, so you are looking for an assumption sufficient to establish the conclusion from the evidence. Only one answer choice will provide an assumption that makes the conclusion follow inevitably from the evidence.

Step 2: Untangle the Stimulus

The Keyword [t]*herefore* signals the ethicist's conclusion: corporate managers must act "in the shareholders' best interest." The sole piece of evidence to support this conclusion is that corporate managers must serve shareholders the way shareholders "would want to be served."

Step 3: Make a Prediction

Notice the disconnect between the conclusion and evidence: the former discusses acting in shareholders' best interest, while the latter discusses serving shareholders as they would want to be served. The ethicist must assume shareholders want to be served in ways that are in their best interest. Find an answer choice that states this assumption.

Step 4: Evaluate the Answer Choices

(B) is correct and matches your prediction perfectly.

(A) is a Distortion. Whether corporate managers are always able to discern what is in the best interest of shareholders does not change their obligation.

(C) is Outside the Scope. The argument doesn't address corporate managers' other obligations.

(D) is Outside the Scope. Whether corporate managers or others can best serve the shareholders' interests is irrelevant. As far as they can, corporate managers must act in shareholders' best interest.

(E) is Outside the Scope. All shareholders may or may not want to be served in the same way. Regardless, corporate managers must serve their best interests.

14. (B) Flaw

Step 1: Identify the Question Type

The phrase "describes a flaw in the reasoning" identifies this as a Flaw question. Break down the author's argument, identifying her conclusion and evidence and determining her assumption. Then, evaluate how the author's reasoning goes wrong. Remember to keep an eye out for common flaw types.

Step 2: Untangle the Stimulus

The Keyword [h]*owever* signals the astronomer's conclusion: Tagar's view is not right. In other words, the bacteria-like structures found in the Martian meteorite can be fossilized bacteria, even though they are one-tenth of 1 percent the volume of the smallest earthly bacteria. The astronomer believes Tagar's view is incorrect simply because Tagar does not accept the views of two other biologists, Swiderski and Terrada, who state that Martian bacteria would shrink to one-tenth of 1 percent of their normal volume when water or other nutrients were in short supply.

Step 3: Make a Prediction

The sole basis for the astronomer's claim that Tagar is wrong is simply that Tagar does not accept the views of two other biologists. Herein lies the issue. The astronomer provides no information as to why the views of Swiderski and Terrada take precedence over Tagar's view. Find an answer choice that states this flaw more broadly.

Step 4: Evaluate the Answer Choices

(B) is correct and describes the flaw in general terms that match your prediction. The argument does not justify giving preference to the views of Swiderski and Terrada rather than those of Tagar.

(A) is Outside the Scope. Whether the authorities cited have always held the views discussed is not the issue. Rather, the issue is favoring some authorities over another without any justification for doing so.

(C) is a Distortion. The astronomer does not claim that Swiderski and Terrada are correct because there are two of them whereas Tagar is only one scientist. Instead, the astronomer gives no reason for preferring Swiderski and Terrada over Tagar.

(D) is a Distortion. The argument does give two opposing views (Tagar versus Swiderski and Terrada), but the astronomer does not try to use the conflicting arguments to prove a unified point. The flaw is not in citing opposing views but in arbitrarily accepting one view over the other.

(E) is a 180. The astronomer does not assume that the opinions of all experts are equally justified but rather that these opinions are not equal. She gives preference to Swiderski and Terrada's opinion.

15. (E) Inference

Step 1: Identify the Question Type

The phrase "is most strongly supported by the information above" identifies this as an Inference question. Accept each sentence as true and find an answer choice that must be true on the basis of one or more of those sentences.

Step 2: Untangle the Stimulus

The first two sentences state that all good garden compost can be used for soil drainage and fertility, and they assert that the best compost is dark brown in color and between 40 and 60 percent organic matter. But, for drainage and fertility purposes, one should not use compost that emits a strong ammonia smell, because the organic matter in such compost has not sufficiently decomposed.

Step 3: Make a Prediction

The stimulus states that any good garden compost can be used for soil drainage and fertility. Note that this also means that if the compost cannot be used for drainage or cannot be used for fertility, then it is not good garden compost. Additionally, since compost that emits a strong odor of ammonia should not be used for drainage and fertility, it is therefore not good garden compost. Find an answer choice that makes this connection.

Step 4: Evaluate the Answer Choices

(E) is correct and matches your prediction. No matter what color the compost, the last sentence in the stimulus states that compost emitting a strong ammonia odor should not be used for drainage and fertility. Since the compost in this choice emits a strong smell of ammonia, it should not be used for drainage and fertility, and it is therefore—based on the Formal Logic—not good garden compost.

(A) is Outside the Scope. The stimulus provides no information about compost that is 80 percent organic matter, nor does it link organic matter percentage and

decomposition. This choice cannot be supported by information in the stimulus.

(B) is Outside the Scope. The stimulus does not provide information about compost that is less than 40 percent organic matter and is not dark brown in color. Moreover, the stimulus does not provide information about what will make soil less fertile or worsen soil drainage.

(C) mixes up the Formal Logic. The stimulus says the best compost is between 40 and 60 percent organic matter and dark brown. That could be translated as "If the compost is the best, then It's between 40 and 60 percent organic matter AND dark brown." It doesn't logically follow that if the compost is 50 percent organic matter AND dark brown, then it is good. This reverses the Formal Logic without negating. For example, you know that if the compost has a strong ammonia smell (i.e., has not sufficiently decomposed), then it can't be used for drainage and fertility and thus it isn't good. So, there could be compost that is between 40 to 60 percent organic matter and dark brown but is still not serviceable because it is not sufficiently decomposed.

(D) is Extreme. The stimulus's logic train says that if organic matter is not sufficiently decomposed, then the compost is not good. The contrapositive would be if the compost is good, then the organic matter is sufficiently decomposed. But "good" is different from "best," and "sufficiently decomposed" is different from "completely decomposed."

16. (D) Assumption (Necessary)

Step 1: Identify the Question Type

The word *assumption* identifies this as an Assumption question. Additionally, the word *relies* indicates you are looking for a necessary assumption, one without which the professor's conclusion cannot be logically drawn from the evidence. You can use the Denial Test to check or eliminate answer choices.

Step 2: Untangle the Stimulus

The Keyword [*t*]*hus* identifies the professor's conclusion: if the chemistry department does not receive more money from sources other than for-profit institutions, then it is unlikely to gain the prestige that comes only from achievements in basic science research. The professor's support is in the first two sentences. First, he states that profit-driven companies "provide nearly all the funding for the chemistry department's research." Then he states that it is highly unlikely the department will generate any major advances in basic research unless more funding for basic research is secured. Said another way, if the department does not secure more funding for basic research, then it is unlikely to produce any major advances in basic research.

Step 3: Make a Prediction

Though nearly all funding for the department's research comes from profit-driven institutions, the professor states that without increased funding from sources other than profit-driven institutions, the department likely won't gain the prestige that only achievements in basic science research confer. In short, the department needs funds from sources other than profit-driven institutions. Notice that the professor provides no information as to why the department must secure funding from those particular sources. It may be possible that profit-driven institutions could provide the additional funding that is needed. Thus, for his conclusion to work, the professor must assume there is no way to increase funding for basic science research apart from getting money from sources other than profit-driven institutions.

Step 4: Evaluate the Answer Choices

(D) is correct and matches your prediction. Use the Denial Test to confirm the answer: if funding for basic science research is likely to increase even if funding from sources other than profit-driven institutions does not increase, then the professor's conclusion holds little weight.

(A) twists the logic of sentence 2. Securing more funding is necessary to making advances in science, but it does not guarantee that advances will be made. More importantly, it does not bridge the evidence-conclusion gap in the professor's argument that the department must secure funding from institutions that are not profit driven.

(B) distorts the conclusion. According to the argument, if the department's prestige increases substantially, then it did receive increased funding from sources other than profit-driven institutions. The professor's argument is about what must happen to gain prestige, not what will happen after prestige is gained.

(C) is Outside the Scope. Nothing in the argument suggests that the chemistry department would or should no longer accept the funding it currently receives from profit-driven institutions, and thus the effects that would result from doing so are irrelevant.

(E) is Outside the Scope. The likelihood that profit-driven institutions will benefit from the basic scientific research they fund is irrelevant to whether the chemistry department is unlikely to gain prestige from basic scientific research without increased funding from non-profit-driven institutions.

17. (B) Inference

Step 1: Identify the Question Type

The word *inferred* identifies this as an Inference question. Accept each sentence in the stimulus as true and find an answer choice that must be true on the basis of one or more of those sentences.

Step 2: Untangle the Stimulus

The stimulus begins by stating that, to save money, many consumers use coupons distributed by retailers. The next sentence states that, in general, retail stores with coupon programs "charge more for their products, on average, than other retail stores charge for the same products," even considering the coupon savings. According to the stimulus, this happens because it costs a lot of money to produce and distribute coupons, and retail stores compensate for this expense by passing it on to consumers.

Step 3: Make a Prediction

Paraphrase the stimulus: consumers do not necessarily save money when using coupons, and retail stores that use coupons charge more on average to make up for the cost of producing and distributing those coupons. Once you have paraphrased the stimulus, move into the answer choices and find one that must be true on the basis of one or more of the statements.

Step 4: Evaluate the Answer Choices

(B) is correct and nicely summarizes the statements in the stimulus.

(A) is Extreme. In the stimulus, you learned that stores cover the price of producing coupons by charging higher prices on some products, maybe those covered by the coupons and maybe other products as well. The stimulus doesn't tell you whether customers who redeem coupons buy the other, higher priced items, so you cannot infer that this specific group of consumers winds up with little savings.

(C) is unsupported. The stimulus says retail stores that use coupons pass the costs on to protect their profits, but it provides no information about the profits of those stores as compared to profits of retail stores that do not use coupons. Thus, comparing the profits of these two types of retail stores is impossible.

(D) is Outside the Scope. While the stimulus says stores that use coupons pass on those costs, that doesn't mean stores without coupon programs don't transfer other expenses to consumers. There is no support for the claim that at least one of these retail stores does not pass on expenses to consumers.

(E) is a Distortion. The second sentence states that, even after factoring in the discounted price, retail stores that use coupons charge more for their products, on average, than other retail stores charge for the same products. Thus, it is possible for the undiscounted price of a particular item for which a retail store offers a coupon to be lower than the price of the same item at a retail store that does not offer a coupon for it. This choice does not need to be true based on the statements and can be eliminated.

18. (A) Assumption (Necessary)

Step 1: Identify the Question Type

The word *assumption* identifies this as an Assumption question. Additionally, the word *required* indicates you are looking for a necessary assumption, one without which the psychologist's conclusion cannot be logically drawn from the evidence. You can use the Denial Test to check or eliminate answer choices.

Step 2: Untangle the Stimulus

The phrase "show that" signals the conclusion: taken together, the birth-order studies indicate that birth order affects how a sibling's behavior is perceived but does not have a lasting effect on personality. The first sentence states that standard personality tests have not detected birth-order effects in studies of adults. Signaled by the Keyword [*h*]*owever*, the second sentence introduces a contrast: birth-order effects have been seen in studies based on parents' and siblings' reports of the subjects' personalities.

Step 3: Make a Prediction

For the psychologist to properly conclude that birth order does not have a lasting effect on personality, she must assume that the standard personality tests used in the studies of adults are valid and capable of identifying any existing birth-order effects. If these tests are not adequate, then there is no way to be sure that birth order does not have a lasting effect on personality. Find an answer choice that states this necessary assumption.

Step 4: Evaluate the Answer Choices

(A) is correct and matches your prediction perfectly. Use the Denial Test to confirm your response. If standard personality tests do not detect at least some birth-order effects on personality if those effects are present, then the tests are inadequate, and the psychologist's conclusion is not valid.

(B) is Outside the Scope. How people behave when they are with family versus when they are not with family is irrelevant to whether standard personality tests are capable of identifying birth-order effects in studies of adult personalities.

(C) is Outside the Scope. Whether or not family perceptions of a person's personality change over time is irrelevant. Perceptions don't need to be consistent for the psychologist's conclusion that birth order has no lasting effect to hold.

(D) is also Outside the Scope. Whether standard personality tests have detected birth-order effects in young children's personalities is irrelevant. The psychologist's conclusion is that birth order has no lasting effect; whether or not it had an effect at one point doesn't affect her argument.

(E) also does not need to be true for the psychologist's argument to follow. The argument requires that standard personality tests be able to detect birth-order effects on personality, not that parents and siblings have accurate perceptions of each other's behavior patterns. Because the psychologist concludes that birth-order effects are merely perception and not reality, those perceptions don't have to be accurate at all.

19. (B) Parallel Reasoning

Step 1: Identify the Question Type

The phrase "pattern of reasoning … most similar to" identifies this as a Parallel Reasoning question. Analyze the argument and find an answer choice that matches the reasoning piece by piece. Alternatively, characterize the conclusion in the argument and eliminate any answer choice with a different type of conclusion.

Step 2: Untangle the Stimulus

The Keyword *so* signals the conclusion: the jury must have returned a verdict. Why? The rest of the stimulus provides the evidence. Sentence 1 in the argument is written in Formal Logic terms, so begin by translating the statement:

| If | ~ jury returned verdict | → | media trucks still outside courthouse |

Now, sentence 2 states that there are no media trucks outside, leading to the logical conclusion that the jury returned a verdict. This sentence is the contrapositive of the first.

| If | ~ media trucks outside courthouse | → | jury returned verdict |

Step 3: Make a Prediction

Break down the argument using simple letters to better understand how the pieces fit together. Remember that the correct answer will parallel the reasoning of the argument and will probably discuss content unrelated to the content of the stimulus. For this reason, do not get bogged down by the specifics of the argument. In simple terms, the reasoning of the argument is as follows: if not X (no jury verdict), then Y (media trucks outside courthouse). The second sentence is the contrapositive: if not Y (media trucks not outside the courthouse), then X (jury verdict). Find an answer choice that parallels this line of Formal Logic reasoning. Note also that the conclusion is an assertion of fact with a very high degree of certainty. You can use this conclusion type to eliminate any answer choices that do not have the same type of conclusion.

Step 4: Evaluate the Answer Choices

(B) is correct and perfectly parallels the reasoning in the stimulus. If not X (did not buy house), then Y (rented apartment); if not Y (did not rent an apartment), then X (bought a house).

(A) can be quickly eliminated because its conclusion is a comparison (there will be no less tourism than usual) and not an assertion of fact. Also, the reasoning is not parallel. This choice states: if X (hurricane), then Y (less tourism); not X (no hurricane), then not Y (not less tourism). The second sentences negates without reversing.

(C) is incorrect because it does not parallel the reasoning in the stimulus. Here, the logic breaks down as follows: if not X (Linus's car not working), then Y (Renate will drive him to work); not X (Linus's car not working), then Y (Renate will drive him to work). The second sentence is simply a restatement of the first.

(D) is incorrect because terms don't match up between the two statements. "Not working last night" and "not working for the past week" are two different things. Even if one assumes that if the television was out for the past week, then it must have been out last night, the reasoning does not match the reasoning in the stimulus. The reasoning here is as follows: if not X (Kay's television did not work last night), then Y (Kay would have gone to a movie); not X (Kay's television has not worked in a week), then Y (Kay must have gone to a movie). The second sentence is a restatement of the first.

(E) is incorrect because its reasoning is not parallel. This choice states: if X (Ralph told Manuela the problem), then Y (Manuela solved it); not X (Ralph did not tell Manuela the problem), then not Y (Manuela did not solve it). As does **(A)**, this choice negates without reversing.

20. (E) Inference

Step 1: Identify the Question Type

The phrase "most logically completes the argument" identifies this as an Inference question. Look for what the author would say based on the statements already provided. Work through the stimulus and paraphrase the statements. The correct answer choice will be the logical "fill-in-the-blank" conclusion.

Step 2: Untangle the Stimulus

The stimulus begins by stating that salespeople who make sales do not change customers' desires but rather find out what those desires are and then convince customers "that a particular product will satisfy them." The next sentence states that people persuade others to vote for a particular politician in a similar way. Lastly, the stimulus wants you to determine what one tries to do after discovering what policies the voter would like to see enacted.

Step 3: Make a Prediction

The argument draws a parallel between how salespeople persuade customers to buy goods and how people persuade

voters to vote for a politician. If persuading people to vote for a particular politician is not significantly different from persuading people to purchase a particular item, then once one knows what policies the prospective voter would like to see in place, one should try to convince the voter that the politician will put into place those policies, thus satisfying the voter's desires.

Step 4: Evaluate the Answer Choices

(E) is correct and matches your prediction. Voters need to be persuaded that their desires will be satisfied if they vote for the politician in question.

(A) is Outside the Scope. According to the stimulus, salespeople simply need to convince customers one particular product fits their desires; salespeople don't need to discount other products. Similarly unnecessary is discounting the politician's opponents.

(B) is Outside the Scope. The point is to "sell" the politician. Disguising differences between the politicians would make it much more difficult to sell a particular one. The argument does not suggest that one need disguise the differences between policies that the politician supports and policies that other candidates support. In fact, other candidates are irrelevant. Instead, one should convince the voter that the politician will put into place the policies about which that particular voter cares.

(C) is a 180. Essentially, this would be trying to change the desires of the customer, something a salesperson does not do. Rather than trying to convince the voter that the policies favored by the politician are preferable to the voter's, one should convince the voter that the politician will put into place the policies the voter prefers.

(D) is Outside the Scope. The character of the politician and the politician's interest in some of the same issues as the voter are irrelevant to persuading the voter that the politician will adopt the policies that the voter would like to see in place. This choice introduces two new ideas (personality and issues), whereas the stimulus is only concerned with one: "desires" for customers and "policies" for voters.

21. (C) Flaw

Step 1: Identify the Question Type

The phrase "most accurately describes a reasoning flaw" identifies this as a Flaw question. Break down the author's argument, identifying his conclusion and evidence and determining his assumption. Then, evaluate how the author's reasoning goes wrong. Remember to keep an eye out for common flaw types.

Step 2: Untangle the Stimulus

The word *but* signals the farmer's conclusion: his pesticides are not spreading to his neighbor's farm in runoff water. He supports this contention by stating three things: 1) he uses only organic pesticides; 2) nothing suggests these pesticides harm domestic animals or people; and 3) he is careful to avoid spraying on his neighbor's land.

Step 3: Make a Prediction

Notice that the farmer's evidence does not address the actual issue of whether the pesticides might be spreading to a neighbor's farm in runoff water. Instead, the farmer provides irrelevant information about the pesticides and the use of them. Find an answer choice that identifies this reasoning error.

Step 4: Evaluate the Answer Choices

(C) is correct and matches your prediction. The farmer fails to provide any relevant information to support his claim that pesticides are not spreading to his neighbor's farm in runoff water.

(A) is a Distortion. The farmer does claim there is no evidence that organic pesticides cause harm to domestic animals or people, but he uses this (questionably) to support his point that pesticides are not ending up on his neighbor's farm. He does not use this information to conclude pesticides cannot cause harm.

(B) is a Distortion. The farmer states he is careful to avoid spraying on his neighbor's land, but he does not incorrectly assume that being careful usually means he avoids doing so. In fact, the farmer's error is using this point as evidence to support a conclusion about transfer via runoff water.

(D) is Outside the Scope. The farmer's argument is not flawed because it fails to provide an explanation for the presence of pesticides on his neighbor's land but rather because the farmer fails to provide any relevant evidence to support his claim that runoff water from his land is not responsible for spreading pesticides.

(E) is Outside the Scope. While it's true that he does this, failing to consider other possible dangerous effects of pesticides is irrelevant to why the farmer's conclusion is faulty. This doesn't address the gap between the evidence and conclusion.

22. (E) Role of a Statement

Step 1: Identify the Question Type

The phrase "plays which of the following roles" identifies this as a Role of a Statement question. Using Keywords, determine whether the statement in question is evidence or conclusion. Then go back and refine your categorization as necessary.

Step 2: Untangle the Stimulus

The statement in question is part of the third sentence. The Keyword *since* precedes the statement and identifies it as evidence for the overall conclusion that ends sentence 3.

Step 3: Make a Prediction

As noted, the statement in question is used as a piece of evidence to support the argument's main point. Specifically, the statement is a fact both groups of critics accept as being true. The linguist uses it to conclude that the two groups' disagreement is not over the word *art*.

Step 4: Evaluate the Answer Choices

(E) correctly identifies the statement in question both as a claim with which both disputing parties agree and also as a piece of evidence used to support a conclusion about the parties' disagreement.

(A) is a 180 because it incorrectly identifies the statement as the main point of disagreement between the two groups of critics. In fact, both groups agree with the statement.

(B) is incorrect. If anything, the linguist's hypothesis is her conclusion: these two groups are not disagreeing over the meaning of "art." And while the statement in question does support the conclusion, it would be the linguist's independent evidence; it is not a commonly accepted reason to accept the conclusion.

(C) is a Distortion. While the statement in question is accepted by both groups of critics, the linguist does not use this agreement between the groups to prove the statement's truth.

(D) is incorrect. The statement in question is not a claim that the linguist uses to account for disputes of any kind. In fact, the statement is a point of agreement among the two groups of art critics.

23. (B) Paradox

Step 1: Identify the Question Type

The phrase "most helps to explain" identifies this as a Paradox question. Read the stimulus to identify the seemingly contradictory statements. Then evaluate the answers to find the one choice that helps explain how those statements may reasonably coexist.

Step 2: Untangle the Stimulus

The argument states that the population of P-plankton in a certain region has recently dropped. Additionally, "extraordinarily high death rates" of fish species X, Y, and Z have been noted in the area. Biologists think there is a connection between these two events, since these three fish species sometimes eat P-plankton, but the biologists cannot determine the exact connection. Lastly, the argument states that "[n]o other species in the ecosystem appear to be affected."

Step 3: Make a Prediction

Scientists believe a connection exists between the decrease in P-plankton and the very high death rates of fish species X, Y, and Z, but the biologists are unable to identify the exact nature of the connection. No other species in the ecosystem is being negatively affected, so why are these specific species declining? Find an answer choice that explains why these particular species are experiencing difficulties while no other species in the ecosystem are.

Step 4: Evaluate the Answer Choices

(B) is correct. If a new strain of bacteria attacks P-plankton and fish species X, Y, and Z, then this explains why these particular species in the region are experiencing decreases in population size while no other species appear affected.

(A) fails to explain why P-plankton and fish species X, Y, and Z are experiencing high death rates but no other species are. The large amounts of waste that pharmaceutical companies dump in the ocean should impact all the species in the ecosystem.

(C) may explain why the population of P-plankton has decreased by 10 percent, but it does not explain why fish species X, Y, and Z are also experiencing high death rates while other species in the ecosystem are not.

(D) may help explain why the decreased population of P-plankton is causing fish species X, Y, and Z to experience extraordinarily high death rates, but it fails to explain why the P-plankton population is decreasing in the first place.

(E) fails to explain exactly why these species, and no others, would be negatively impacted by changes in climatic conditions in the region brought on by global warming.

24. (C) Weaken

Step 1: Identify the Question Type

The phrase "most weakens" identifies this as a Weaken question. Break down the argument into evidence and conclusion, determine the central assumption, and then look for an answer choice that attacks that assumption.

Step 2: Untangle the Stimulus

The Keyword [*t*]*herefore* signals the conclusion of the argument: Nightbird must have been painted by one of Larocque's students. The evidence states that experts agree either Larocque or one of his students painted Nightbird. Moreover, a recent analysis of the painting showed a pigment that has never yet been found in a work attributed to Larocque.

Step 3: Make a Prediction

The argument assumes that any painting containing the pigment orpiment cannot be one painted by Larocque simply because no painting that contains orpiment has been attributed to him. Thus, according to the argument, one of Larocque's students must have painted it. Find an answer choice that weakens the conclusion that one of Larocque's students painted Nightbird. Remember, the correct answer does not need to prove Larocque painted the piece; rather, it needs to support the idea that he could have painted it or that the piece was not necessarily painted by one of his students.

Step 4: Evaluate the Answer Choices

(C) is correct. If no work currently attributed to one of Larocque's students contains the pigment orpiment either, that invalidates the one reason why the author attributes Nightbird to one of Larocque's students and not Larocque himself.

(A) is Outside the Scope. Whether or not Larocque's students ever used painting techniques that differed from his does not make it less likely that one of Larocque's students painted Nightbird.

(B) is Outside the Scope. That Larocque never signed his paintings has nothing to do with whether Nightbird was painted by one of Larocque's students.

(D) is Outside the Scope. The level of importance granted to Larocque's students has no effect on whether or not one of his students painted Nightbird.

(E) is a 180. If only after Larocque's death did use of orpiment become popular, then it is more likely that one of Larocque's students painted Nightbird.

25. (D) Parallel Flaw

Step 1: Identify the Question Type

The phrase "most similar to the flawed reasoning" identifies this as a Parallel Flaw question. Approach the argument as you would a standard Flaw question. Identify the evidence and conclusion and pinpoint the relevant gap between the two, keeping in mind common flaw types. The correct answer choice will exhibit the same pattern of reasoning and the same flaw as the stimulus.

Step 2: Untangle the Stimulus

The advertisement concludes in the first sentence that the dental profession knows that the best way to fight cavities is to brush with Blizzard toothpaste. Why? Five dentists were surveyed, each of whom agreed that the tartar control formula in Blizzard is the most effective cavity-fighting formula available in a toothpaste.

Step 3: Make a Prediction

The argument assumes that because Blizzard contains the best cavity-fighting formula of all toothpastes, using the toothpaste is the best way to fight cavities. Note the disconnect: there might be other ways to fight cavities that are better, but this argument assumes there are not. Just because Blizzard is the best of its narrow group (toothpastes) doesn't mean its group is the most effective means of cavity combat. Additionally, note that the sample size of the survey used as evidence (five dentists) is not representative of the group in the conclusion (the dental profession). Find an answer choice that parallels this reasoning and makes a conclusion based on an unrepresentative sample.

Step 4: Evaluate the Answer Choices

(D) is correct. This choice uses an unrepresentative sample (10 voters) to claim that electing Gomez is the best way to help the nation because polled voters agree that his policies are the best of all policies. Notice also that this choice incorrectly assumes there is no better way to help the nation other than by enacting Gomez's policies.

(A) is not parallel in its reasoning to the stimulus. The evidence and conclusion are disconnected; nothing suggests that popularity has anything to do with Gomez's policies being the best for the nation.

(B) is close because its reasoning parallels the reasoning in the stimulus, but the conclusion is not based on an unrepresentative sample. Here, the conclusion is about only some of the nation's voters, as is the cited survey.

(C) can be quickly eliminated because the size of the sample used as evidence (thousands of voters) is representative of the population in the conclusion (the nation's voters generally).

(E) states that electing Gomez is the best course of action because surveyed voters agreed that electing him would help the nation. However, to be parallel to the stimulus, the polled voters would need to believe Gomez is the best of a narrow group. Additionally, this choice introduces "we" rather than "the nation's voters." In the stimulus, "we" only shows up in the evidence, not the conclusion. Instead, the conclusion discusses the polled dentists, so to be correct, this choice should have discussed the polled voters.

PrepTest 68

The Inside Story

PrepTest 68 was administered in December 2012. It challenged 30,226 test takers. What made this test so hard? Here's a breakdown of what Kaplan students who were surveyed after taking the official exam considered PrepTest 68's most difficult section.

Hardest PrepTest 68 Section as Reported by Test Takers

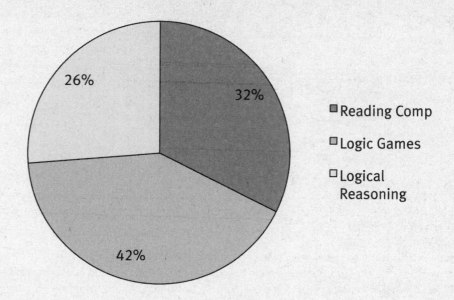

- Reading Comp
- Logic Games
- Logical Reasoning

Based on these results, you might think that studying Logic Games is the key to LSAT success. Well, Logic Games is important, but test takers' perceptions don't tell the whole story. For that, you need to consider students' actual performance. The following chart shows the average number of students to miss each question in each of PrepTest 68's different sections.

Percentage Incorrect by PrepTest 68 Section Type

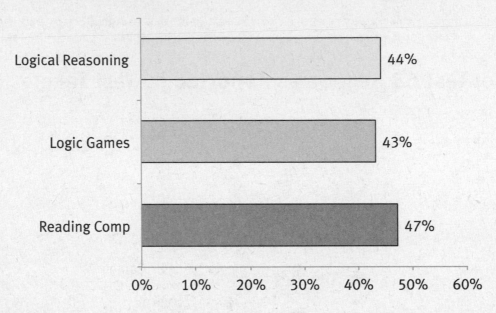

Actual student performance tells quite a different story. On average, students were almost equally likely to miss questions in all three of the different section types, and on PrepTest 68, Logical Reasoning and Reading Comprehension were somewhat harder, on average, than Logic Games in actual difficulty.

Maybe students overestimate the difficulty of the Logic Games section because it's so unusual, or maybe it's because a really hard Logic Game is so easy to remember after the test. But the truth is that the testmaker places hard questions throughout the test. It's striking, perhaps, that only two of the ten hardest questions were in the Logic Games section, while six were in Logical Reasoning. Here were the locations of the 10 hardest (most missed) questions in the exam.

Location of 10 Most Difficult Questions in PrepTest 68

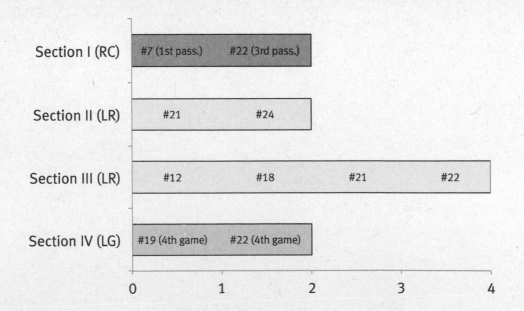

The takeaway from this data is that, to maximize your potential on the LSAT, you need to take a comprehensive approach. Test yourself rigorously, and review your performance on every section of the test. Kaplan's LSAT explanations provide the expertise and insight you need to fully understand your results. The explanations are written and edited by a team of LSAT experts, who have helped thousands of students improve their scores. Kaplan always provides data-driven analysis of the test, ranking the difficulty of every question based on actual student performance. The 10 hardest questions on every test are highlighted with a 4-star difficulty rating, the highest we give. The analysis breaks down the remaining questions into 1-, 2-, and 3-star ratings so that you can compare your performance to that of thousands of other test takers on all LSAC material.

Don't settle for wondering whether a question was really as hard as it seemed to you. Analyze the test with real data, and learn the secrets and strategies that help top scorers master the LSAT.

7 Can't–Miss Features of PrepTest 68

- PrepTest 68's Logical Reasoning section stands out for two reasons: first, and for only the fourth time in LSAT history, this test featured just five Assumption questions, something that had not happened since PrepTest 30 (December 1999), and …
- Second, and for only the fifth time in LSAT history, PrepTest 68 featured *four* Main Point questions. The most recent prior administration in which that happened was just two administrations prior; the time before that was all the way back to PrepTest 45 (December 2004).
- In its Logic Games section, PrepTest 68 featured a Matching *and* a Distribution game for the first time since PrepTest 44 (October 2004). It's not uncommon to see one or the other, but both Matching and Distribution in a single section is quite rare.
- PrepTest 68 was the second test in a row to contain no Rule Substitution questions in Logic Games, even though all but three tests have featured at least one since this question type debuted on PrepTest 57 (June 2009).
- As of its release date, this was only the fourth time in LSAT history that a Reading Comprehension section featured just three Global questions. PrepTests 62, 43, and 14 were the others.
- As a favor to all (C) guessers, 10 more questions had correct answer (C) than had correct answer (A) (25 to 15) over the course of the test. Two sections both started and ended with questions on which the correct answer was (C).
- The #1 song on the day of PrepTest 68 was Bruno Mars's "Locked Out of Heaven," but students who aced this LSAT administration were not locked out of their top law school choices at least.

PrepTest 68 in Context

As much fun as it is to find out what makes a PrepTest unique or noteworthy, it's even more important to know just how representative it is of other LSAT administrations (and, thus, how likely it is to be representative of the exam you will face on Test Day). The following charts compare the numbers of each kind of question and game on PrepTest 68 to the average numbers seen on all officially released LSATs administered over the past five years (from 2012 through 2016).

Number of LR Questions by Type: PrepTest 68 vs. 2012–2016 Average

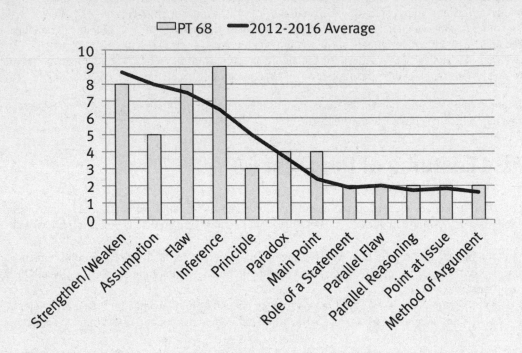

Number of LG Games by Type: PrepTest 68 vs. 2012–2016 Average

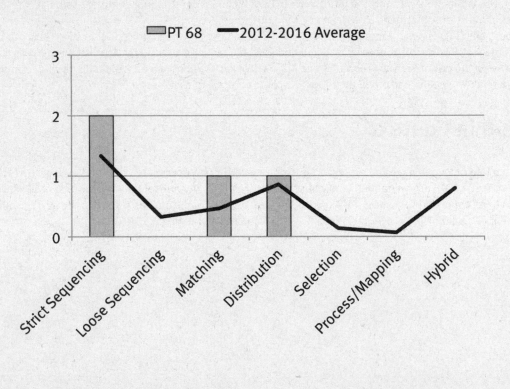

KAPLAN

Number of RC Questions by Type: PrepTest 68 vs. 2012–2016 Average

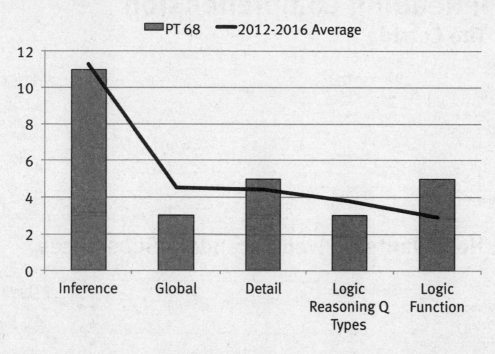

There isn't usually a huge difference in the distribution of questions from LSAT to LSAT, but if this test seems harder (or easier) to you than another you've taken, compare the number of questions of the types on which you, personally, are strongest and weakest. And then, explore within each section to see if your best or worst question types came earlier or later.

Students in Kaplan's comprehensive LSAT courses have access to every released LSAT, and to an online Q-Bank with thousands of officially released questions, games, and passages. If you are studying on your own, you have to do a bit more work to identify your strengths and your areas of opportunity. Quantitative analysis (like that in the charts shown) is an important tool for understanding how the test is constructed, and how you are performing on it.

Section I: Reading Comprehension
Passage 1: The Corrido

Q#	Question Type	Correct	Difficulty
1	Global	E	★
2	Detail	C	★
3	Inference	E	★★
4	Detail	B	★★
5	Logic Function	A	★
6	Inference	C	★★
7	Inference	E	★★★★

Passage 2: How Plants Evolved Secondary Substances

Q#	Question Type	Correct	Difficulty
8	Global	C	★★
9	Detail	A	★
10	Logic Function	B	★
11	Inference	A	★★
12	Logic Reasoning (Parallel Reasoning)	B	★★
13	Inference	A	★
14	Inference	D	★★★

Passage 3: Modeling Smith's Pin Factory

Q#	Question Type	Correct	Difficulty
15	Global	E	★★
16	Inference	E	★★
17	Logic Function	B	★★
18	Inference	C	★
19	Logic Function	D	★★★
20	Logic Reasoning (Principle)	B	★★
21	Detail	C	★★
22	Logic Reasoning (Weaken)	E	★★★★

Passage 4: Selective Enforcement of Laws

Q#	Question Type	Correct	Difficulty
23	Detail	C	★
24	Inference	D	★★★
25	Logic Function	D	★★
26	Inference	B	★★★
27	Inference	E	★★★

Passage 1: The Corrido

Step 1: Read the Passage Strategically

Sample Roadmap

line #	Keyword/phrase	¶ Margin notes
1		*corridos*:
5	long-standing ... tradition	origin
6	roots	
8	but	subject matter
10	For example	example
13	important	
14	yet	
15	all	
16	served to	
17	significant ... but more ...	
18	importantly ...heavy reliance	function: community cohesion
19	served to affirm	
20		origin of *corrido* name
24	generally rare	
27		metaphors use familiar images
28	for example	
30		example: storm
35	Such	
37	reflects and strengthens	effect of imagery
39	not only	another element: stock lines
40	but also	
41	most evident	
43		closing verse
45		example of *despedida* structure
51	clearest marker ... both	*despedida* function
54	accomplished	

Discussion

The first line of the passage Introduces and defines the Topic (the *corrido*). The author goes on to locate the corrido in a specific time and place. Steeped in the Spanish ballad tradition, the corrido is a mishmash of formal folk song features that has as its subject matter events and figures specific to the Border region—the Kiansis corrido is given as an example of such a song. Paragraph 1 ends by giving the chief effect of the corrido (note the emphasis Keywords *more importantly* in lines 17–18), which is to affirm community cohesion through familiar language and themes.

By the time you get to paragraph 2, where the author discusses the stylistic features of the corrido, you can conclude that the Scope is the features and conventions of the corrido. The majority of paragraph 2 discusses the corrido's use of metaphor: figurative language isn't used often, but when it is, it sticks to images that are familiar to listeners.

Paragraph 3 gives another feature common to corridos: stock lines that can move from one ballad to another. These stock lines are most clearly seen in the *despedida*, the formal closing verse that every corrido contains. The author introduces and breaks down an example of such a verse and then ends the passage by discussing how the despedida shows both the corrido's uniqueness and its recognizability.

The Purpose of the passage is clear now: the author sets out to describe the conventions and effects of the corrido. Therefore, the Main Idea is that the corrido's use of linguistic, narrative, and thematic conventions has served to strengthen the social bonds of the Border region.

1. (E) Global

Step 2: Identify the Question Type

Any question that asks for the main point of the passage is a Global question. Use your understanding of the Main Idea to predict the answer.

Step 3: Research the Relevant Text

For a Global question, particularly one seeking the passage's Main Idea. you do not need to research the actual text, given your work in Step 1. Instead, consult your Roadmap and your broader assessment of Topic, Scope, Purpose, and Main Idea.

Step 4: Make a Prediction

During Step 1 of the Kaplan Method, you noted that the author's Main Idea was that the corrido's consistent use of familiar conventions concerning language, imagery, and theme helped crystallize community cohesion among the people of the Border region.

Step 5: Evaluate the Answer Choices

(E) is the best match.

(A) is both a Distortion and Extreme. The passage says figures of speech occurred only rarely in corridos and that the cohesiveness of Border communities was affirmed, not by imagery, but by familiar linguistic and thematic conventions. Additionally, while corridos may be one indicator of cohesiveness among Border communities, the passage never goes so far as to say they are the clearest.

(B), even if it were stated in the passage (which it isn't), would be far too narrow. The Spanish ballad tradition is mentioned early in the passage during the discussion of the corrido's origin and is never mentioned again.

(C) is Extreme and misrepresents the passage's use of the "Gregorio Cortez" corrido. The author never holds the folk song up as an ideal example of the form, nor is it the focus of the passage. The author introduces the popular folk song merely as an example to support a broader point about the language in corridos.

(D) is Half-Right/Half-Wrong. While lines 16–17 do show that corridos commemorated local events, the author specifically says in lines 24–25 that imagery is rare and, when it does appear, conventional. Vivid imagery, therefore, can't be a defining characteristic of corridos.

2. (C) Detail

Step 2: Identify the Question Type

The key phrase "[a]ccording to the passage" indicates a Detail question.

Step 3: Research the Relevant Text

The answer here is tough to predict, since the passage mentions the features of corridos in multiple places. But the word "characteristic" provides some guidance. You're looking for features that define the corrido.

Step 4: Make a Prediction

According to the passage, the features that define corridos are subject matter concerning the Border region; simple, swift narratives; familiar language and images; ready-made lines; and a conventional closing verse. Look for one of these in the answer choices.

Step 5: Evaluate the Answer Choices

(C) is directly stated in lines 39–42 and is therefore the correct answer.

(A) contradicts lines 21–23, which say corridos tell their stories simply, without embellishments.

(B) contradicts line 24, which says figures of speech are rarely used in corridos. That hardly suggests they're characteristic.

(D) isn't supported by the passage. While the third paragraph briefly mentions rhyming, the pattern referenced (lines two and four rhyme) is hardly "complex."

(E) contradicts line 6, which says corridos are sung in Spanish.

3. (E) Inference

Step 2: Identify the Question Type

The phrases "most likely" and "[g]iven its tone and content" mean you'll need to make an Inference, since the correct answer won't be stated directly. The focus on overall tone gives this question a Global aspect as well.

Step 3: Research the Relevant Text

The entire text is relevant in this case because the question stem asks what kind of work might include this passage.

Step 4: Make a Prediction

Even if you can't predict the answer here, you know that the right answer has to be in line with the author's tone (neutral, informative) and content (a description of the features and conventions that define the corrido).

Step 5: Evaluate the Answer Choices

(E) is the correct answer because the entire passage does exactly what (E) says: it describes a particular folk song form that's native to North America. So it makes perfect sense that the passage would be excerpted from a larger work about various folk song forms.

(A) is Out of Scope. The passage contains no information on tourist attractions, and the scope of the first paragraph is anything but contemporary. While the passage could arguably come from a travel book focusing on culture, it would be out of place in a condensed brochure.

(B) is a 180. The passage says the music of 18th-century Spain influenced the corrido, not the other way around.

(C) doesn't comport with the author's neutral tone. The author is not nearly argumentative enough for this to be part of an editorial.

(D) is a Distortion that misrepresents the Topic and Scope of the passage. Cortez is the only famous person mentioned in the passage, and he is only discussed in relation to the corridos written about him.

4. (B) Detail

Step 2: Identify the Question Type

This is a Detail question since it asks about what is "mentioned in the passage."

Step 3: Research the Relevant Text

The phrase "example of the use of metaphor in corridos" leads you directly to paragraph 2, lines 27–32.

Step 4: Make a Prediction

The lines from "El Corrido de Gregorio Cortez" contain the answer: the correct choice will have something to do with either a thunderstorm or mist.

Step 5: Evaluate the Answer Choices

(B) is a direct match. The more frequently mentioned "thunderstorm" metaphor is not present in the answers, but a careful reading of line 32 turns up "mist."

(A) is not a metaphor but rather the subject matter of the Kiansis corrido. The imagery mentioned has to do with the storm, not its effects.

(C) is mentioned in line 45 as part of the Gregorio Cortez despedida, but it isn't mentioned as an example of a metaphor. It's possible the song's writer was being literal here, not figurative.

(D) is a Distortion. In the Cortez example, the thunderstorm is used as a metaphor for a fight, not the other way around.

(E) is too similar to (A), which should ring a warning bell. This answer choice also involves the subject matter of the Kiansis corrido but not a metaphor.

5. (A) Logic Function

Step 2: Identify the Question Type

The phrase "primarily in order to" indicates a Logic Function question. What the author says about metaphor isn't important; rather, the question is concerned with why the author mentions it at all.

Step 3: Research the Relevant Text

The question stem directs you to paragraph 2, where the author discusses metaphor. Lines 24–27 mention that metaphors are rarely used and incorporate everyday images that are already familiar to the corrido's listeners.

Step 4: Make a Prediction

The key to predicting the answer to any Logic Function question is understanding context. The claim about metaphors comes on the heels of the previous sentence (lines 21–23), in which the author says corridos' stories are told simply and quickly, without embellishments. The author is therefore discussing metaphors (or rather the general lack thereof) in order to support that idea.

Step 5: Evaluate the Answer Choices

(A) matches perfectly.

(B) is Extreme because nothing in the passage indicates that narrative is the *main* object of corridos. Furthermore, you could have stopped reading at the argumentative word *counter*, which is not in line with the author's overall purpose to merely describe the corrido.

(C) is a 180. The author says in line 24 that figures of speech are rare in corridos.

(D) is a Distortion. The author does mention at the end of paragraph 2 that the conventional and recognizable aspect of corridos' imagery in general "reflects and strengthens the continuity of the corrido tradition," but *continuity* is used here to mean sameness, not longevity.

(E), like choice **(C)**, suggests that the author says metaphor is pervasive in corridos, an idea the passage contradicts.

6. (C) Inference

Step 2: Identify the Question Type

The language of the question stem is clear: the right answer will be inferable from (or, in other words, supported by) the passage.

Step 3: Research the Relevant Text

The stem provides no clues to help you research the passage's relevant lines. This makes prediction difficult.

Step 4: Make a Prediction

Because prediction is difficult here, keep in mind that you're looking for the answer choice that must be true based on the passage. Look to eliminate choices that are extreme, distorted, or outside the scope of the passage.

Step 5: Evaluate the Answer Choices

(C) is directly supported by paragraph 3, which says that each corrido contains ready-made lines. The paragraph goes on to give two lines from a despedida that are "a set convention." This is the correct answer.

(A) is a 180. The author says in line 16 that corridos were sung at social gatherings and goes on to call this particular corrido "popular" in line 27. Most likely, it was often sung at gatherings.

(B) is unsupported. Paragraph 1 says "El Corrido de Kiansis" is the oldest surviving corrido in complete form, but that doesn't mean that most corridos since then haven't also survived in complete form.

(D) is Extreme. All corridos have a despedida, but that isn't to say *most* corrido variants have the exact same one.

(E) is Out of Scope. The author of "El Corrido de Kiansis" is never mentioned.

7. (E) Inference

Step 2: Identify the Question Type

Two clues indicate an Inference question here: the phrase "most strongly suggests" and the phrase "author would agree with."

Step 3: Research the Relevant Text

Just as in the previous question, there's no specific research you can do to help predict the answer here.

Step 4: Make a Prediction

This is a difficult one, since the author is neutral throughout the passage and doesn't put forth any easily identifiable viewpoints. As you proceed to the answer choices, keep in mind that you're seeking the choice that must be true based on the passage, not one that just sounds reasonable. Keep an eye out for Extreme or Out of Scope wrong answers.

Step 5: Evaluate the Answer Choices

(E) must be true (and is therefore correct) because the author details many characteristic features of the corrido, such as Border-specific subject matter, the use of unadorned stories, and "familiar linguistic and thematic conventions" (lines 18–19).

(A) is Out of Scope. It can't be inferred because the author states that the use of metaphor was rare and thus wasn't a major goal of corrido makers. There is no discussion of what *hindered* the corrido makers.

(B) is Extreme because, while the author does say that the corrido's language was familiar to local audiences, the author never claims the corridor was *unique* in this respect among song forms.

(C) is a Distortion. The corrido is mentioned as part of a ballad tradition that started in Spain, but you can't infer that the use of similar imagery is shared by both Spanish ballads and corridos. In fact, since corridos focused specifically on the Border region, shared imagery arguably would be unlikely.

(D) is Out of Scope. Line 5 says corridos are part of a long-standing ballad tradition, and lines 47–50 discuss the rhyming of the despedida. The scope of corridos' reportorial capability is never discussed.

Passage 2: How Plants Evolved Secondary Substances

Step 1: Read the Passage Strategically

Sample Roadmap

line #	Keyword/phrase	¶ Margin notes
1		chem determine taste/smell of plants
2	depends on	
3	two	2 types: primary defined
4	":"	
5	such as	
8		secondary defined
11	Only a few	secondary → taste/smell
12	but	
13	such as	
17		insects played role in secondary subst.
19	undoubtedly	secondary subst. from mutations
20	as a result of	
21	But	
23	that is	
25		reasons why natural selection favored secondary subst.
26	because	
31	because	
36	not in themselves harmful	
37	but ... dissuade	
40		plants/insects compete
44	must ... or	how insects get around plant defenses
45	may	
48	quickly come to prefer	
52		competition leads to narrowing of insect diets
54	thus	

Discussion

From the first sentence, you can derive the Topic—chemical composition of plants. Paragraph 1 goes on to break up plants' chemicals into two broad categories: primary and secondary substances. Primary substances are briefly discussed, but the majority of the paragraph is devoted to secondary substances, which, as it turns out, are the ones that determine a plant's unique taste and smell.

By the beginning of paragraph 2, when the author is still discussing secondary substances, you know that secondary substances are the Scope of the passage. Now you learn how secondary substances evolved from plants' interactions with insects over time. Any evolutionary mechanism that produced secondary substances had to be favored by natural selection, and lines 25–39 detail the advantages secondary substances confer on plants as they relate to insects.

Paragraph 3 examines the relationship from the other side, describing how insects have responded to the defenses created by plants. The author ends by explaining that insects develop a preference for the plants whose defenses they can get around and, once they can identify said plants, their diets narrow considerably as a result. The Purpose of the passage is to explain how secondary substances evolved in plants, and the Main Idea is that those substances evolved from interactions between plants and insects over evolutionary time.

8. (C) Global

Step 2: Identify the Question Type

The phrase "main point of the passage" indicates a Global question.

Step 3: Research the Relevant Text

In the case of a Global question, the relevant text is the entire passage. But instead of rereading the whole passage, use your Roadmap and the big picture to form your prediction.

Step 4: Make a Prediction

From Step 1 of the Kaplan Method, you know that the main point is that the secondary substances that determine the tastes and smells of plants evolved because natural selection favored them for the function they served in regulating plants' interactions with insects.

Step 5: Evaluate the Answer Choices

That makes choice **(C)** the correct answer.

(A) is too narrow. Only some of the secondary substances discussed in the passage evolved as defenses against insects. The relationship between plants and insects, as described by the author, is much broader.

(B) is a Distortion of the last paragraph of the passage. The range of food sources for any one insect species has narrowed thanks to secondary substances, but that's a far cry from saying that there's a narrower range of secondary substances present in plants.

(D) ignores the entire second and third paragraphs. It's also not true that the *diversity* of secondary substances is due to evolutionary pressure from insects.

(E) is a Distortion. It overemphasizes the plant-insect competition. Furthermore, it's not the secondary substances that led to the competitive relationship between plants and insects; the passage suggests that it's the other way around.

9. (A) Detail

Step 2: Identify the Question Type

This is a Detail question because the stem seeks a statement that was "mentioned in the passage."

Step 3: Research the Relevant Text

Your Roadmap should tell you that insect adaptations to plant defenses are discussed in paragraph 3, lines 42–48.

Step 4: Make a Prediction

These lines say that in order to adapt to plants' defenses, insects have to switch to other food sources or evolve ways to get around those defenses, such as a detoxification method or a method of storage that prevents secondary substances from inflicting harm.

Step 5: Evaluate the Answer Choices

(A) is a perfect match.

(B) is Out of Scope. Nothing in the passage says that the leaf or flower structures help an insect avoid harmful substances. The taste and smell of a plant give those substances away.

(C) is Out of Scope. Nothing is discussed regarding the rate of reproduction.

(D) is a Distortion/Out of Scope. There are natural selection advantages to attracting pollinating insects. The passage does not discuss plants that develop defenses against pollinating insects, only against plant-eating insects.

(E) is a Distortion/Out of Scope. Insects may be able to tell from taste and smell which plants might be dangerous, but nothing in the passage indicates that they're able to distinguish between harmful and innocuous parts of an individual plant.

10. (B) Logic Function

Step 2: Identify the Question Type

The phrase "in order to" indicates that this is a Logic Function question. Your task is to determine why the author discusses primary substances.

Step 3: Research the Relevant Text

Primary substances are discussed only in paragraph 1, in lines 5–8.

Step 4: Make a Prediction

The passage is almost exclusively devoted to discussing secondary substances. So the author only mentions primary substances in order to distinguish them from secondary substances.

Step 5: Evaluate the Answer Choices

(B) is the match for this prediction.

(A) is Out of Scope. The author never actually provides information about *how* plants grow and metabolize nutrients.

(C) is a Distortion. Primary and secondary substances are not two different ways in which insects have affected plant evolution. Nothing in the passage indicates that insects have influenced primary substances.

(D) is a 180. The passage says that *secondary* substances are diverse; primary substances are common to all plants.

(E) is also a 180. The passage doesn't say that plants adapted to insects by making primary substances. Some secondary substances, on the other hand, have been favored by natural selection.

11. (A) Inference

Step 2: Identify the Question Type

This is an Inference question because of the phrase "most support for inferring." The correct answer will be implied rather than directly stated.

Step 3: Research the Relevant Text

The question stem is too vague to lead to specific, focused research. So you'll have to rely on your understanding of the big picture from Step 1.

Step 4: Make a Prediction

As with other broadly worded Inference questions, this question's answer is next to impossible to predict. So before you select the correct answer, find support for it in the passage.

Step 5: Evaluate the Answer Choices

(A) is inferable from a combination of lines 8–11 and lines 29–33. Lines 8–11 establish that secondary substances have no known role in the growth or metabolism of plants, and lines 29–33 establish that some secondary substances stuck around because they formed defenses against plants' natural enemies. This could definitely be considered a "vital role."

(B) is Extreme. Paragraph 3 does establish that some insects have found ways to circumvent certain plants' defenses, but

that doesn't mean that *most* plants' defenses have been overcome by the insects that use them as food.

(C) is Out of Scope and Extreme. The passage says in lines 49–51 that insects have come to identify their preferred plants by taste or smell or both. Other means of identification beyond those are not discussed, so it is certainly not inferable that *most* insects identify plants by something other than taste or smell.

(D) is Out of Scope. There's no evidence in the passage that the toxic secondary substances had the evolutionary history described here.

(E) is Out of Scope. The passage never addresses toxic substances in plants other than secondary substances.

12. (B) Logic Reasoning (Parallel Reasoning)

Step 2: Identify the Question Type

The question stem resembles a Parallel Reasoning question from the Logical Reasoning section, because it asks you to take a relationship in the passage and find the answer choice "most closely analogous" to it.

Step 3: Research the Relevant Text

The relationship between plants and their primary and secondary substances is discussed in paragraph 1.

Step 4: Make a Prediction

In paragraph 1, the passage says that primary substances are consistent and ubiquitous in plants and are required for proper growth and functioning. Secondary substances, in contrast, vary widely in type and don't play a role in proper functioning. So regardless of its content, the correct answer will reflect that relationship.

Step 5: Evaluate the Answer Choices

(B) is correct. The mechanical components are similar to primary substances. Paint and taillights are analogous to secondary substances; they serve important but not absolutely essential functions and help make the cars distinctive, much as secondary substances function for plants.

(A) is incorrect because secondary substances in plants are not intended to stand in for primary substances in the event that primary substances are unavailable.

(C) is incorrect because unlike the electrical components, which supply necessary power to the mechanical components, secondary substances in plants aren't a power source for primary substances.

(D) is incorrect because primary and secondary substances don't work together to perform necessary functions in the same way that the friction and pneumatic components do in the braking system.

(E) is Half-Right/Half-Wrong. The specially designed word processing programs are analogous to primary substances. However, nothing in (E) parallels the function of secondary substances in plants, and that was what was asked for by the question stem.

13. (A) Inference

Step 2: Identify the Question Type

The phrase "most strongly suggests" indicates an Inference question. You need to find the answer that must be true concerning secondary substances.

Step 3: Research the Relevant Text

Secondary substances are discussed from line 8 all the way down to line 39.

Step 4: Make a Prediction

The passage says far too many things about secondary substances for you to make a targeted prediction here. But the correct answer will be completely supported by a statement made by the author between lines 8 and 39.

Step 5: Evaluate the Answer Choices

(A) is directly supported by lines 20–21, in which the passage says that new secondary substances continue to appear as the result of genetic mutations. This is the correct answer.

(B) is unsupported. Nothing in the passage suggests that a secondary substance can't contribute to both the smell and taste of a plant.

(C) is Out of Scope. The passage never discusses substances produced by insects, much less interactions between those substances and the ones made by plants.

(D) is contradicted by lines 11–12, which say that any one species of plant will contain *only a few* secondary substances, which suggests more than just one substance.

(E) is a 180. Lines 9–11 say that secondary substances have no role in the growth or functioning of plants. Therefore, secondary substances wouldn't regulate the production of primary substances, which are necessary for the growth and functioning of plants.

14. (D) Inference

Step 2: Identify the Question Type

The phrase "most likely to agree with" indicates an Inference question.

Step 3: Research the Relevant Text

The relationship between plants and insects is discussed throughout paragraphs 2 and 3, so there's a lot of relevant text here.

Step 4: Make a Prediction

From your Roadmap, you already know some of the broad strokes about the plant-insect relationship, especially as it relates to the development of secondary substances. But from what's stated in the passage, there are several things to infer; instead, read each of the answer choices first and then look for support in the text for the correct answer.

Step 5: Evaluate the Answer Choices

(D), the correct answer, is supported largely by paragraph 2, which says that secondary substances appeared "as the result of genetic mutations" and that "[i]nsects appear to have played a major role" in the development of many of these substances.

(A) is a Distortion. The passage says that insects have played a role in the appearance of secondary substances in plant populations, but the passage doesn't suggest that more insect interactions translate to more secondary substances.

(B) is Out of Scope. The passage does not imply that only a few species of plants have benefited from their interactions with insects. Furthermore, because the passage says that some secondary substances benefit plants by attracting insects to them for pollination, there's evidence to suggest that at least some insects actually do increase plants' chances of survival.

(C) is Out of Scope. The passage never provides enough information to draw conclusions about the number of plant species in any given family or, for that matter, the number of families.

(E) is Out of Scope and Extreme. Lines 45–46 suggest that some insects are capable of circumventing plants' defenses. It is possible that immunity is one such way. Not enough information is provided to categorically say that no species of insect has developed outright immunity.

Passage 3: Modeling Smith's Pin Factory

Step 1: Read the Passage Strategically

Sample Roadmap

line #	Keyword/phrase	¶ Margin notes
1	great	W's book: econ. contradiction
2	contradiction	
7	huge	Smith pin factory: more size → more efficiency
11	Also … first	
12		Smith invisible hand: self-interest → common good
15	For example,	example
16	not because	
17	but …	
18	because	
20	however … opposed	PF/IH discrepancy
24	therefore	
25	But	PF emphasizes increased returns to scale, which leads to monopoly
26	because	
27	hence	
28	So	IH only works w/o monopoly (dimin. returns)
30	But	
31	must	
33	Therefore	
34	depends on	
37	dominated	dimin. returns assump dominant
38	Why?	
39	it wasn't … it was	
41	always	reason: easier to express w/ math than incr. returns (PF)
42	always	
45	lend themselves readily	
46	while	
47	notoriously hard	
48	tried	Econs tried to get acceptance for PF
50	obviously	
51	such as	why they failed
52	Yet … failed because	
53	Only since	
57	By then … finally	late 70s: PF finally expressed with rigor, accepted
58	needed	
59	respectable	

Discussion

In the first line, the author introduces a book written by David Warsh. But that book isn't the Topic; it's more helpful to think of the Topic as the book's subject matter: Adam Smith's two economic concepts—the Pin Factory and the Invisible Hand. And the Scope, or the aspect of the Topic that the author wishes to explore, is the contradiction between these two concepts, which you can be confident that the author will describe in much greater detail throughout the passage.

But before the author can discuss the contradiction, you first need to know more about the concepts themselves. Enter paragraph 2. The Pin Factory model says that increased size can help a business boost its efficiency through specialization of labor. The Invisible Hand model says that a free market economy can actually lead someone to act in service of the common good by following his or her self-interest.

Paragraph 3 describes how these two models are at odds. The Pin Factory model promotes increased size and efficiency, which in turn promote monopolies in an industry. However, the Invisible Hand model only works if no one is allowed to form a monopoly. In short, the Invisible Hand promotes diminished size.

The author goes on to point out that the assumptions underlying the Invisible Hand have been dominant. This is due not to some rigid adherence to belief but to the nature of economists' preference for theories that can be explained with mathematical rigor. The Invisible Hand was such a theory; the Pin Factory wasn't.

The final paragraph outlines some economists' attempts to achieve that rigor in their description of the Pin Factory model—attempts that were finally successful by the late 1970s. The Purpose is a little clearer now: to describe the difficulties economists have had in bringing the Pin Factory model as far into the mainstream as the Invisible Hand. The Main Idea is that the Pin Factory and Invisible Hand models were based on contradictory assumptions and that, until the late 1970s, economists were unable to sufficiently validate the assumptions on which the Pin Factory model was based.

15. (E) Global

Step 2: Identify the Question Type

The phrase "main point of the passage" indicates a Global question.

Step 3: Research the Relevant Text

The entire passage is relevant in a Global question. But instead of rereading the whole text, use your Roadmap and your grasp of the Big Picture (Topic, Scope, Purpose, Main Idea) to make your prediction.

Step 4: Make a Prediction

By completing Step 1, you're already predicting the answer to a Global question like this one. The Main Idea of the passage is that economists' success in rigorously modeling one of two contradictory economic assumptions is a recent development.

Step 5: Evaluate the Answer Choices

(E) is a match and is therefore correct.

(A) is a 180. The author makes the point that mainstream economists had for decades sidelined the idea of increasing returns to scale (the Pin Factory) in favor of the idea of decreasing returns (the Invisible Hand).

(B) would be correct if paragraph 4 were the central piece of the passage. But this choice ignores, among other things, paragraph 5, in which the author describes the attempts and eventual success of economists to garner acceptance for the theories underlying the Pin Factory model.

(C) is Extreme. The author concludes by saying that the Pin Factory had finally been modeled with the rigor necessary for acceptance in the wider economic community, but that doesn't mean that it was modeled *more* rigorously than the Invisible Hand.

(D) is a Faulty Use of Detail. It is mentioned in paragraph 2; however, this is far from the author's main point, especially because it doesn't include any mention of more contemporary economists' struggles to reconcile the contradiction in Smith's theories.

16. (E) Inference

Step 2: Identify the Question Type

Any question that asks for the author's attitude toward a particular part of the passage is a variation on an Inference question.

Step 3: Research the Relevant Text

The idea that the Pin Factory model should be part of the economic mainstream is discussed in paragraphs 4 and 5.

Step 4: Make a Prediction

The author says that the assumption of increasing returns, an assumption central to the Pin Factory model, "obviously characterized many enterprises" (lines 50–51), so it stands to reason that the author would feel positively about the Pin Factory model moving more into the mainstream of economic thought to reflect this reality.

Step 5: Evaluate the Answer Choices

(E) is the only choice that accurately reflects the author's positive tone.

(A) is a 180. The author says nothing to indicate that the Pin Factory model should remain on the back burner.

(B) is wrong because there's no language in the passage suggesting that the author is hesitant or unsure about the recent developments moving the Pin Factory into the mainstream.

(C) flies in the face of the author's use of words such as *obviously* in line 50. Such words make it clear that the author isn't curious about whether the Pin Factory should be more widely used.

(D) implies neutrality. But the author appears sympathetic to the challenge that faced economists who were trying to increase the rigor with which they described the Pin Factory model.

17. (B) Logic Function

Step 2: Identify the Question Type

Because this question stem asks for the purpose of a particular paragraph, it's a Logic Function question.

Step 3: Research the Relevant Text

It's clear that the relevant text is the fourth paragraph. But in addition to revisiting the paragraph itself, be sure to look at your Roadmap to form the basis of your prediction.

Step 4: Make a Prediction

The author uses paragraph 4 to demonstrate that the assumptions underlying the Invisible Hand have been dominant, to the detriment of those underlying the Pin Factory. Then the author goes on to describe the reason: the Pin Factory is harder to represent with the rigor and clarity that often accompany more math-friendly theories.

Step 5: Evaluate the Answer Choices

(B) matches perfectly.

(A) is wrong because the author never introduces, much less critiques, any theory that tries to resolve the paradox between the Pin Factory and the Invisible Hand.

(C) is a Distortion. The author spends paragraph 4 outlining the inherent obstacles to the Pin Factory model's wider use in the mainstream economic community. The author doesn't say that either model is more intuitively supported than the other.

(D) is much closer to the author's intention in paragraph 3, where the paradoxical assumptions underlying the two models are discussed. But even in that paragraph, the author never mentions that any tension came out of attempts to create the models themselves.

(E) is Extreme. The author never attempts to *refute* any of the economic assumptions in the passage. On the contrary, the author discusses attempts to eliminate the contradiction between the two assumptions.

18. (C) Inference

Step 2: Identify the Question Type

The phrase "can be inferred" is a clear indication of an Inference question.

Step 3: Research the Relevant Text

Fortunately, this question stem is very specific and leads you directly to paragraph 5 for research.

Step 4: Make a Prediction

Lines 53–57 state that the "underground river" of the Pin Factory model has only been accepted in the mainstream since the 1970s. But as always, context is key. The sentence before states that economists failed to gain this acceptance for the Pin Factory because they "could not state their ideas rigorously enough." Therefore, you can infer that if they could state those ideas with enough rigor, their ideas would have been accepted more readily.

Step 5: Evaluate the Answer Choices

(C) matches the prediction.

(A) is a 180. It isn't economists' desire to make their discipline more scientific that gained greater acceptance for the Pin Factory model. It's precisely because of this desire that the Pin Factory was relegated to the background for so long.

(B) is unsupported because the passage never credits David Warsh's book with elevating the status of the Pin Factory model.

(D) is Out of Scope. No outside events helped the Pin Factory gain credence; the work was all done in the theoretical sphere by economists.

(E) is a 180. The passage never mentions a lowering of the economists' standards. Rather, the Pin Factory's advocates finally raised the level of mathematical rigor in their model so that it could meet those standards (lines 57–59).

19. (D) Logic Function

Step 2: Identify the Question Type

This is a Logic Function question because it asks why the author refers to railroads. Use the Keywords surrounding the reference to make your prediction.

Step 3: Research the Relevant Text

The sentence in which the author mentions railroads stretches from line 48 to line 51. Reading all these lines will give you the proper context on which to base your prediction.

Step 4: Make a Prediction

The Keywords *such as* before *railroads* in line 51 indicate that railroads are being used as an example. The previous lines tell you that they're being used as an example of industries for which increasing returns, like those modeled by the Pin Factory, ruled the day. Economists wanted to make room for the Pin Factory precisely to account for these industries.

Step 5: Evaluate the Answer Choices

(D) is a match. The shortcoming of emphasizing is the Invisible Hand its failure to account for the Pin Factory model.

(A) brings in the Invisible Hand, which this part of the passage doesn't touch. Moreover, the author never indicates any ambiguity in the Invisible Hand model.

(B) is a Faulty Use of Detail. Railroads are introduced to show why the Invisible Hand model didn't explain business operations across all industries. The failure to state the theory with mathematical rigor is discussed in the fourth and fifth paragraphs, but the example of the railroads does not illustrate the difficulty of that rigor.

(C) is a Distortion. Nothing in paragraph 5 indicates that industries for which the Pin Factory is relevant are becoming more common as time goes on.

(E) is Out of Scope because the author never discusses the level of competition in any industry, much less transportation.

20. (B) Logic Reasoning (Principle)

Step 2: Identify the Question Type

The question stem tells you that a concept is outlined in paragraph 2 and then asks for the answer choice that best illustrates, or applies, that concept. So you can think of this as an Apply the Principle question.

Step 3: Research the Relevant Text

Lines 22–25 are the heart of the author's discussion of increasing returns to scale.

Step 4: Make a Prediction

You can't predict exactly what content the correct answer will contain. You do know, however, from your research during Step 3, that the Pin Factory example says increased size leads to increased specialization, which in turns leads to increased productivity. The correct answer will follow the same chain of logic.

Step 5: Evaluate the Answer Choices

(B) is the correct answer. The guard bees have a specialized task, which leads directly to the colony being able to collect more nectar and process it more efficiently. This is a clear example of the Pin Factory model from lines 22–25.

(A) doesn't discuss the editors at the publishing house being more specialized in their duties. It instead has the publishing house relaxing its standards. Furthermore, unlike **(A)**, the passage doesn't have a smaller workforce as the goal of businesses.

(C) would be a better match if paragraph 2 discussed businesses increasing productivity by having more rotating shifts of workers. But because paragraph 2 instead discusses specialization, this isn't a match.

(D) says increases in productivity come out of advances in technology, which isn't the same as a higher degree of specialization in the lobster industry's workers.

(E) is a 180. It does discuss higher "productivity"—if it makes sense to speak of more ants as equivalent to higher productivity. However, this isn't a match because the author discusses efficiency improvements from increased size and specialization. Here, the colonies are broken into separate colonies, where each presumably perform the same tasks rather than specialized tasks.

21. (C) Detail

Step 2: Identify the Question Type

This is a Detail question because it asks for what the passage states.

Step 3: Research the Relevant Text

The question stem doesn't have any clues to help focus your research. Any part of the passage is fair game.

Step 4: Make a Prediction

Of course, the passage states a wide variety of things, so this answer is impossible to predict. You'll have to go directly into the answer choices. However, be prepared to research the passage to verify that your correct answer is actually stated.

Step 5: Evaluate the Answer Choices

(C) is mentioned in lines 36–40. In these lines, the author says that Warsh points out that the failure of the Pin Factory's adherents to get their model more widely accepted was due to a lack of mathematical rigor and clarity, not due to ideology. Check the emphasis Keywords of *it wasn't* and *it was* in line 39. This is the correct answer.

(A) is Extreme. The author says in lines 21–25 that increased specialization can lead to increasing returns to scale under the Pin Factory model, but that's not the same as saying that increasing returns to scale can't come about some other way.

(B) is a Distortion. The author does say in lines 41–44 that economists have sought mathematical rigor for their models, but it doesn't say that they have generally failed in that pursuit.

(D), if anything, is a 180. According to the passage, the Pin Factory model, which emphasizes increasing returns to scale, makes it possible for certain businesses to achieve monopolies in their industries (lines 25–30).

(E) is Out of Scope. It's impossible to know from the passage whether or not Smith was aware of the discrepancy between the two economic models.

22. (E) Logic Reasoning (Weaken)

Step 2: Identify the Question Type

The word *undermine* tells you that the correct answer will weaken an assertion the author makes in the passage. Therefore, this is a Logic Reasoning Weaken question.

Step 3: Research the Relevant Text

The author draws a connection between increased size and monopoly power in paragraph 3—specifically, lines 21–33.

Step 4: Make a Prediction

In these lines, the author argues that the bigger businesses get, the more likely they are to squeeze out smaller competitors and create monopolies. The Keyword *because* in line 26 signals the author's evidence for this belief: bigger businesses can "achieve larger scale and hence lower costs" than smaller businesses can. So the correct answer will undermine the logical link between lower costs and a higher tendency toward monopoly.

Step 5: Evaluate the Answer Choices

(E) fits the prediction. Increased size creates greater specialization among workers. But if, as choice **(E)** says, that specialization leads to higher costs that offset productivity, then bigger isn't necessarily better, and the author's contention is weakened.

(A) doesn't weaken the author's argument because that argument doesn't depend on monopoly power being spread throughout various geographical regions.

(B) is a 180. It actually strengthens the argument by indicating that more specialized workers earn less, thus driving down a business's costs—a central point in the author's argument.

(C) shows how businesses can make more money once they move closer to monopoly, but it does nothing to affect the author's argument that increased size and specialization of tasks can spur that movement toward monopoly.

(D) is Out of Scope. It does nothing to either confirm or undermine the link between increased size and monopoly. The author's argument doesn't depend on consistency among industries in terms of the size necessary for increasing returns to scale.

Passage 4: Selective Enforcement of Laws

Step 1: Read the Passage Strategically

Sample Roadmap

line #	Keyword/phrase	¶ Margin notes
Passage A		
1	effectively	Law enf. freq. declines prosecution
4	frequently ... I attempt	
6	almost always ... ":"	laws are overinclusive
10	prohibitive	reason why
15	very ...	
16	heavy	cost of enforcing overinclusive law
18	Of course ... danger	
19	not a decisive blow	
21	danger ... must be traded off against	
22	But	way to reduce cost without increasing loopholes
23	"—"	
26	Of course	unclear how agencies will select cases
28	Conceivably	
31	But ... unlikely	
33	but ... since	even w/nonenforc, agencies stick to intent of law
34	assures	
Passage B		
37		customers delinquent paying water bills
41	So	
43		city response: shut off water
48	But	auth: why not attach lien?
49	So	
51	?	
54	powerful	
56	here's an answer	answer: can't put lien on water bill (not tax)
58	But	
59	?	auth recommends changing law
60	easier ... smarter	
61	?	

Discussion

Passage A begins with a short, clear paragraph that establishes the Topic (law enforcement) and the Scope (the frequently erratic nature of prosecution). What's more, the key phrase that ends paragraph 1—"I attempt here to explain why"—hints at the Purpose.

Paragraph 2 takes a step back and explains that laws necessarily prohibit more behavior than they intend to. Laws have to be enforced, of course, but it would be too socially costly to enforce an overinclusive law to the letter—people would be punished whose conduct was never even meant to be forbidden. The problem can be solved, says the author, through "discretionary nonenforcement."

The last paragraph of passage A discusses the challenge that accompanies discretionary nonenforcement: law enforcers don't always have a set rule for selecting the cases they will and won't prosecute. More often than not, though, oversight ensures that enforcers stick to the intent of the law as much as possible. The Purpose of this passage is to explain why certain laws are not always strictly enforced. And the Main Idea is that the overinclusive nature of laws keeps them from being enforced to the letter, leaving discretionary nonenforcement as a workable strategy.

Passage B is a bit less abstract than passage A. It even has a different Topic (the city's delinquent water customers). Most of the first paragraph is spent discussing what the city's officials want to do about all the outstanding bills. They want to shut off water to only some high-income households in order to make examples of people who are most in a position to weather the effects of the shutoff.

Then in the next paragraph, the author weighs in with an alternative, establishing the Scope as possible responses to these overdue bills. The author asks a simple question: Why not just attach a lien to the properties of those who won't pay? That would incentivize the offending customers to keep current with their water bills. It turns out the author intends to answer the question in the next paragraph. The city can only attach liens on taxes, and water bills aren't considered taxes. So the author's final suggestion is to change the law so that the city would be empowered to attach liens to other debts, including water bills. This last paragraph establishes the Purpose (to advocate for an alternative to the city's enforcement plan) and the Main Idea—changing the city's law prohibiting liens on non-tax debts would be smarter and easier than the current plan of shutting off the debtors' water.

With all Comparative Reading passages, it's wise to take a moment to determine the relationship between the passages. Here, passage A is a general discussion of how broad laws may be overinclusive and how to circumvent the challenge by using selective prosecution. Passage B is a specific example of a broad law and a proposed solution to narrow the scope of the law.

23. (C) Detail

Step 2: Identify the Question Type

This is a Detail question because it asks for the answer choice that was explicitly mentioned in the passages.

Step 3: Research the Relevant Text

Since this question asks for something mentioned in both passages, the entire text is relevant to your research.

Step 4: Make a Prediction

You could take some time to list the subjects and concepts common to both passages, but that may take longer than just going through the choices and eliminating those answers that are mentioned in only one passage and not the other.

Step 5: Evaluate the Answer Choices

(C) is the only choice mentioned in both passages. Passage A discusses loopholes in line 25, and passage B discusses them in lines 56–58.

(A)—legal technicalities—aren't mentioned in either passage.

(B)—incentives—are mentioned in paragraph 2 of passage B but nowhere in passage A.

(D)—language—is mentioned in line 12 of passage A but nowhere in passage B.

(E)—overinclusive laws—is mentioned throughout paragraph 2 of passage A but nowhere in passage B.

24. (D) Inference

Step 2: Identify the Question Type

This question stem couldn't be clearer: it asks what "can be inferred," so it's an Inference question.

Step 3: Research the Relevant Text

Here, the relevant text is everything in passage B. Beyond that, the question stem offers no clues for more specific research.

Step 4: Make a Prediction

Many things are inferable from the 26 lines of passage B. So instead of predicting, you'll have to go directly to the answer choices. But before selecting the answer you believe is correct, find the information in the passage that supports it.

Step 5: Evaluate the Answer Choices

(D) is supported by lines 41–47. If officials are planning to shut off delinquent customers' water "to show that they are serious about collecting ... debts" and "to make examples" of certain residents, then this must be a course of action the city doesn't habitually adopt. **(D)** is therefore the correct answer.

(A) is Extreme. Lines 37–38 tell you that 231,000 customers are late paying their water bills, but without knowing the total number of water customers in the city, you can't conclude that that's *most* water customers.

(B) is also Extreme. Just because the high-income neighborhoods are being exclusively targeted for shutoff doesn't mean that these neighborhoods account for *most* of the delinquent water customers.

(C) is, if anything, a 180. If the author of passage B can be said to be expressing an opinion on the city's plan to shut off late-paying customers' water, that opinion would probably be disapproval, because the author ends passage B by proposing an "easier, and politically smarter," alternative plan. So the author would not recommend shutting of the water of residents who were only *a few days late*.

(E) is Extreme. The author does suggest changing the city's law to classify water bills as taxes, but in no way is this put forward as the *only* reasonable solution to the problem.

25. (D) Logic Function

Step 2: Identify the Question Type

This is a Logic Function question because it focuses on the *role* of a word as it's used in the passage; in other words, the question asks about the function of a word and asks you to find a word in passage A that serves a similar function.

Step 3: Research the Relevant Text

The relevant text is the sentence containing line 42. You'll need to read for context so you can determine how the author is using *selectively*.

Step 4: Make a Prediction

The author is using the word *selectively* to mean that the city is deliberately shutting off water to some customers but not to others. You'll need the answer choice that is used similarly in passage A to describe the action of targeting some people, but not others, for enforcement of a statute.

Step 5: Evaluate the Answer Choices

(D) is a perfect match. Passage A's discussion of *discretionary* nonenforcement refers to law enforcement agencies being selective about which cases they do and do not prosecute.

(A) is tempting if you're not reading for context. "Particularly" in line 12 has nothing to do with anyone being *particular* in the picky or selective sense; rather, the word means "specifically" in its context in passage A.

(B) just means "likelihood," which has nothing to do with being selective or discretionary.

(C) is used to refer to different methods of law enforcement; no aspect of selectivity is discussed here.

(E) is close, but *capricious* means "fickle" or "erratic," which is different from "selective." Passage B's use of *selectively* implies more deliberate thought.

26. (B) Inference

Step 2: Identify the Question Type

Any question asking you what an author "would be most likely to agree with" is an Inference question. Here, you have to determine what passage A's author would say about a certain part of passage B (a common task in Comparative Reading).

Step 3: Research the Relevant Text

The question stem directs you to lines 41–47 in passage B. The plan cited in the question stem is to cut off water to residents in high-income neighborhoods who haven't been paying their water bills. They are being selectively targeted for shutoff so that the city can send a message by making examples of just a few affluent residents.

Step 4: Make a Prediction

The author of passage A would consider this plan an example of discretionary nonenforcement (line 23), since the city is exercising its shutoff authority against some people but not against others. Passage A's author says that this type of enforcement is a strategy to contain the social costs of overinclusion without making the law so specific that loopholes skyrocket.

Step 5: Evaluate the Answer Choices

(B) is a good summary of the attitude of passage A's author toward the city's plan.

(A) is Out of Scope. It implies that budgetary constraints have an impact on the feasibility of the city's shutoff plan. However, passage A's author doesn't say that enforcement should be dictated by financial concerns.

(C) is a Distortion. The author of passage A does seem to be against enforcing overinclusive rules to the letter. However, passage B indicates neither that the water department's rules regarding payment are overinclusive nor that the water department has been enforcing them to the letter.

(D) is not necessarily in line with the strategy of discretionary nonenforcement advocated by passage A's author. Presumably, attaching liens to the delinquent property owners would involve all of the rule breakers, and according to author B, the law currently prohibits such liens.

(E) implies that passage A's author is in favor of making laws more specific, but there's no evidence to suggest this. Passage A's author is only concerned with discussing strategies for discretionary enforcement of existing laws.

27. (E) Inference

Step 2: Identify the Question Type

The phrase "Passage A suggests" indicates that this is an Inference question, since the focus is on what is implicit rather than explicit.

Step 3: Research the Relevant Text

Lines 32–36 contain the author's discussion of capricious enforcement of laws.

Step 4: Make a Prediction

The passage says that capricious enforcement doesn't happen too often because there are mechanisms to ensure that the agency doesn't stray from the intent of the legislation being enforced. It follows from this that capricious enforcement would involve straying from legislators' intent.

Step 5: Evaluate the Answer Choices

(E) follows straight from the prediction.

(A) is Out of Scope. Nothing in passage A indicates that capricious enforcement is bound by the resources that a municipality can devote to enforcement.

(B) is a 180. If choice **(B)** were true, then capricious enforcement would be the rule rather than the exception.

(C) is Out of Scope. The author says that the principle on which enforcement is decided is undetermined, so it's unknown whether the amount of damage caused by the crime has any effect on the likelihood of enforcement.

(D) is a Distortion. Even in cases of capricious enforcement, when law enforcement agencies stray from the intent of the law, there's no indication that they stray because of a failure to distinguish between the intent of the law and its letter.

Section II: Logical Reasoning

Q#	Question Type	Correct	Difficulty
1	Inference	C	★
2	Strengthen/Weaken (Evaluate the Argument)	A	★
3	Paradox	B	★
4	Weaken	B	★
5	Strengthen	A	★
6	Paradox	D	★
7	Flaw	B	★
8	Inference	C	★
9	Parallel Reasoning	C	★
10	Inference	C	★★★
11	Role of a Statement	C	★★
12	Flaw	D	★★
13	Strengthen	B	★★
14	Strengthen/Weaken (Evaluate the Argument)	E	★★
15	Assumption (Necessary)	D	★★
16	Principle (Identify/Strengthen)	C	★★
17	Main Point	A	★★
18	Inference	C	★★★
19	Main Point	B	★
20	Flaw	D	★★
21	Point at Issue	E	★★★★
22	Role of a Statement	B	★★★
23	Assumption (Sufficient)	C	★★★
24	Flaw	E	★★★★
25	Parallel Flaw	B	★★
26	Method of Argument	D	★

1. (C) Inference

Step 1: Identify the Question Type

The question stem directs you to use the statements above to infer the correct answer below, so this is an Inference question. A valid inference must be true based on the information provided; avoid speculating beyond that information. Paraphrase the statements and chain together any facts and logic to make relevant logical deductions.

Step 2: Untangle the Stimulus

The first two sentences indicate that animals used in human-health research are usually kept under non-normal conditions. The final sentence, which begins with the continuation Keyword [*m*]*oreover*, introduces Formal Logic: If animals are kept in non-normal conditions → research reliability is diminished.

Step 3: Make a Prediction

By combining the Formal Logic statement with the beginning of the argument, you can deduce that keeping lab mice in cages actually compromises human-health research.

Step 4: Evaluate the Answer Choices

(C) matches the prediction.

(A) improperly predicts the future. While it is possible to speculate that the status quo will be maintained, despite these problems, it is also perfectly reasonable to think scientists will change lab conditions in order to get more reliable research. However, the stimulus discusses only the present, so based on it alone, you cannot deduce that anything in the future must be true.

(B) is Out of Scope. It sets up a conditional statement that doesn't have to be true based on the stimulus. First, the stimulus discusses reliability, whereas this answer choice introduces appropriateness. Those aren't the same. Additionally, while the stimulus indicates that current conditions are not ideal for research, you can't actually infer that better conditions would solve the problem.

(D) might make sense, since current conditions affect research reliability. But it is possible the benefits of keeping mice in small cages outweigh the negatives. You can't infer for sure that researchers will change. Additionally, environmental conditions (in the stimulus) are not necessarily the same as research techniques (in the answer).

(E) is another Out of Scope answer. This stimulus provides information only regarding animals used in human-health research, so nothing can be inferred about how any other laboratory animals are kept.

2. (A) Strengthen/Weaken (Evaluate the Argument)

Step 1: Identify the Question Type

A question that asks you to "evaluate" an argument is a twist on Strengthen and Weaken questions. Evaluate the Argument questions are essentially a relevance test: the correct answer could be used either to strengthen or weaken the author's conclusion. Wrong answers are irrelevant to the argument. For each answer choice, ask yourself, "Assuming this is true, does it weaken the argument? Strengthen it? Or have no effect?" Also, notice this particular Evaluate question has a bit of a twist, asking what is "necessary" to evaluate the argument, not just helpful.

Step 2: Untangle the Stimulus

The author first defines *dumping*: selling a product in another country below production costs. Based on this, the author concludes that shrimpers in Country F are dumping their shrimp in Country G because they are selling below the cost of producing shrimp in Country G.

Step 3: Make a Prediction

First, evaluate the definition of *dumping*. The author states that dumping occurs when the sales price in another country is less than the production cost. But the author doesn't distinguish whether "production cost" means that of Country F or G. Based on the stimulus, you know only that prices are less than production in Country G. You know nothing about how sales prices relate to production costs in Country F. Therefore, the key question becomes: Which production cost (the cost in Country F or the cost in Country G) is relevant?

Step 4: Evaluate the Answer Choices

(A) is a convoluted way of asking that question. For broadly worded answers, substitute the concrete terms in the stimulus for the abstract terms in the answer. **(A)** then becomes: "In the definition of dumping, does production cost refer to the cost in Country F or in Country G?" Correct.

(B) is Out of Scope. It discusses whether dumping is harmful to a country's economy, which is irrelevant to the question of whether dumping is occurring.

(C) is an Irrelevant Comparison. The definition of dumping depends solely on production costs and the price charged in *another* country. Therefore, it is not necessary to know what shrimpers charge in their country. You could speculate that higher sales prices in the shrimpers' own country indicates higher production costs, but there might be other reasons for the higher price (e.g., higher demand or relative wealth). Thus, this information is neither necessary nor even sufficient to evaluate the conclusion.

(D) is Out of Scope. It is problematic because it speculates about the future. That doesn't help you evaluate an argument about what is currently occurring.

(E) is Out of Scope. The author's definition of dumping doesn't mention the *degree* of difference between price and production costs. The critical concern is whether dumping is occurring or not based on the definition, not the flagrancy of the infraction.

3. (B) Paradox

Step 1: Identify the Question Type

The question asks you to *resolve* the discrepancy, which requires making sense of apparently contradictory information. The correct answer to a Paradox question will provide an explanation or reason that allows the surprising occurrence in the stimulus to reasonably exist.

Step 2: Untangle the Stimulus

The stimulus says both Earth and Venus contain a hot, molten core and must expel the excess heat generated by the core. However, Venus does not do this through active volcanos and fissures as Earth does.

Step 3: Make a Prediction

The correct answer must provide an alternative way Venus expels heat from its core. Don't try to predict more specifically what the mechanism will be; instead, be open to whichever answer provides a reasonable way for Venus to get rid of its excess heat.

Step 4: Evaluate the Answer Choices

(B) indicates that Venus's heat is simply released into space through its thin crust. Even without being a scientist, you can recognize that this is a plausible way to get rid of heat. Correct.

(A) is a 180. One possible way Venus could expel heat is if the rocks on the surface liquefied and let heat out. The fact that they stay solid at higher temperatures than Earth's rocks removes a possible explanation and thus makes the paradox even stronger.

(C) doesn't provide an alternative way for Venus to release its heat. That the core fluctuates doesn't remove the need for Venus to expel the heat. In fact, if the core gets hotter than Earth's core due to the fluctuations, that would increase the need for Venus to dissipate the excess heat.

(D) provides a way that Venus and Earth are similar (i.e., similar surface movement). But since the stimulus specifies that Earth dissipates heat entirely through volcanos and fissures, there is no indication that such surface movement is a means of expelling heat. Thus, this answer does not resolve the discrepancy.

(E) does not provide an explanation of how Venus expels its core's heat. The fact that the atmosphere is hotter than Earth's might indicate that the heat has been expelled somehow, but the answer choice doesn't lay out how.

4. (B) Weaken

Step 1: Identify the Question Type

This question asks you to weaken the argument. Additionally, the stem directs you to the argument's flaw: its analogy. Focus on that as you read the stimulus and think about what might make the analogy unrepresentative of the situation.

Step 2: Untangle the Stimulus

The columnist's conclusion is that donating company profits to charity is unjustified. The columnist uses the analogy of Robin Hood (a celebrated thief, but a thief nonetheless) as evidence. The columnist believes this is a valid analogy because the profits donated belong to the company owners, not the managers, and thus the managers' practice constitutes stealing.

Step 3: Make a Prediction

To weaken an analogy, find an answer that suggests a difference between the two items being compared. The columnist's evidence, highlighted by the evidence Keywords *after all*, plus the analogy suggest that both company owners and Robin Hood's rich are being robbed. Look for an answer choice that shows how the rich and company owners differ.

Step 4: Evaluate the Answer Choices

(B) attacks the assumption that the corporation owners, just like Robin Hood's rich victims, don't want their money redistributed. In actuality, owners are consenting to the donations and therefore can't be considered victims of theft.

(A) is essentially a 180 answer. It indicates that the profits are *in part* returned to the owners. That would still leave open the possibility that a portion of the profits were indeed stolen, as the analogy suggests, which is in keeping with the columnist's rationale.

(C) is Out of Scope. Based on the columnist's analogy, managers are equivalent to Robin Hood. Suppose Robin Hood donated some of his own funds to Nottingham's poor; that wouldn't affect the argument that he was also stealing from the rich. Likewise, regardless of the managers' good acts (donating their own money), the columnist could still be correct in asserting that managers' practice of donating *company* money is unjustified and not admirable.

(D) is also Out of Scope. Its requirement that charities track spending does not affect the claim of theft. Additionally, this answer choice focuses on the charity, whereas the stimulus centers on the business owners and managers, as well as the analogy to the rich and Robin Hood.

(E) is also Out of Scope. The argument centers around whether corporate managers are stealing or not, not whether the charities are soliciting the managers to do so.

5. (A) Strengthen

Step 1: Identify the Question Type

This is a variation on a Strengthen question. Its stimulus has a combination of a principle/application, and its stem calls for the answer that justifies the specific application of the principle. Treat the Application as a conclusion and the stated Principle as evidence. The correct answer will strengthen the assumption that ties the two together.

Step 2: Untangle the Stimulus

The evidence sets out the general rule: if a law's goal is to protect wild animal populations and a group does not threaten those populations, then the law should not be used against that group. The conclusion, specific to protecting wild snakes, indicates that snake charmers should not be prosecuted for capturing snakes.

Step 3: Make a Prediction

For the application to be strengthened, it must meet the logic set out by the principle. Therefore, to maintain the intent of the general rule (principle) in moving to the specific application to snake charmers, it should be the case that snake charmers meet the sufficient condition of not threatening snake populations. Find an answer choice that shows snake charmers are not a threat.

Step 4: Evaluate the Answer Choices

(A) matches that prediction.

(B) is Out of Scope. The principle excuses prosecution if someone is not threatening an animal population. The principle is not concerned with the difficulties of prosecution.

(C) is Out of Scope. It brings in the irrelevant issue of the violator's awareness of the prohibition, which is not addressed in the principle.

(D) makes an Irrelevant Comparison between the general level of threat to snake populations versus other species of wildlife. But this does not address whether or not specific acts of snake charmers (capturing snakes) threaten the snake population. Just because capture isn't a threat to these other species' populations (perhaps it's for their own good) doesn't mean capture isn't a threat to snakes. The answer choice needs to spell out that it isn't.

(E) is yet another Out of Scope answer. The principle addresses solely the threat to wild animal populations. The principle is not concerned with any threat, financial or otherwise, to the snake charmers.

6. (D) Paradox

Step 1: Identify the Question Type

When you're asked to "resolve" or "explain" a situation, you're dealing with a Paradox question. Read the two seemingly contradictory statements and then seek an alternative explanation or factor that lets the two reasonably coexist.

Step 2: Untangle the Stimulus

The stimulus sets up a contrast: while movie executives seek to maximize the number of a movie's viewers, television executives do not primarily seek to maximize the number of television viewers. Also, the stimulus further indicates that the revenue from ticket sales is the source of a film's profit.

Step 3: Make a Prediction

If movie executives primarily want to increase audiences, yet television executives don't, television shows must differ in some way from movies. Since the stimulus introduces profits, it's likely the difference centers on that. Thus, look for an answer choice that shows television shows have an alternative source of profit that requires a primary goal other than maximum viewership.

Step 4: Evaluate the Answer Choices

(D) introduces an alternative source of profits for television shows. Sponsors aren't necessarily interested in the largest audience but rather in the audience that will buy the most.

(A) helps explain how movies make money off ticket sales, but it doesn't explain why television executives would not have the primary goal of maximizing viewers. Nor does this answer explain how television shows make their profits.

(B) is Out of Scope. It discusses the profits of movie theater owners, while the stimulus addresses only movie and television executives.

(C) indicates that television executives may need less revenue than movie executives to turn a profit, but again it provides no explanation of how they make that profit, if not by maximizing show viewers.

(E) does not absolutely explain the difference. It does lessen the direct connection between television viewers and revenue. However, for the less than half (potentially as many as 49 percent) of shows that viewers do pay to watch, this answer provides no explanation as to why maximizing viewers would not be the primary goal of television executives. Moreover, for the shows that viewers don't pay to watch, this answer doesn't explain why revenue—however it is generated from those shows—would not be maximized by maximizing viewers. Predicting in advance that the resolution demands an alternative way for television executives to earn profits is more efficient than balancing the relative merits of (D) and (E).

7. (B) Flaw

Step 1: Identify the Question Type

The word *flawed* clearly indicates this is a Flaw question. To identify the flaw in the reasoning, look at how the conclusion goes beyond or deviates from the evidence. Keep common flaw types in mind.

Step 2: Untangle the Stimulus

The author concludes that "these marketing campaigns make false claims." Since the claims are that "ginseng counteracts the effects of stress," the author essentially concludes the opposite: ginseng does not relieve stress. The most important piece of evidence is highlighted by the contrast Keyword [*y*]*et* and says "no definitive study links ginseng with the relief of stress."

Step 3: Make a Prediction

The author assumes that the absence of a clear scientific link means ginseng does not in fact relieve stress. The author commits a classic logical flaw by assuming that the absence of evidence for an assertion thereby disproves the assertion.

Step 4: Evaluate the Answer Choices

(B) describes this classic flaw.

(A) involves an ad hominem attack, another classic flaw. This answer would work if the author's evidence stated: "Yet, the studies indicating the benefits of ginseng were funded by the ginseng industry." While the author does mention that tea companies are the ones promoting ginseng's benefits, that isn't the evidence the author uses to back up her conclusion.

(C) describes the classic flaw of representativeness. Oftentimes, when a study is mentioned in a Flaw question, this will be the correct answer. However, here there is simply no "sample" included in the evidence, whether representative or not.

(D) can be easily eliminated if the conclusion's focus is kept at the forefront. The author concludes ginseng does not relieve stress. People's reasons for buying herbal teas don't affect that conclusion. This answer would be correct had the author concluded people should not buy herbal tea since ginseng has not been shown to relieve stress. In that case, alternative reasons for drinking tea would be relevant.

(E) can also be eliminated if the conclusion is paraphrased correctly. Again, the conclusion asserts that ginseng does not relieve stress, not that herbal teas in general don't. Only if the conclusion were that herbal teas do not relieve stress would it be necessary to consider whether other ingredients relieve stress.

8. (C) Inference

Step 1: Identify the Question Type

Distinguish Inference question stems containing the word *support* from Strengthen questions by noticing the direction of support. If the stimulus is used to support "one of the following" answers (i.e., if the direction of support is down), then it is an Inference question. Look to combine information in the stimulus to make a deduction.

Step 2: Untangle the Stimulus

The second and third sentences of the stimulus can be linked through warming temperatures. According to the second sentence, the action of microbes generating carbon dioxide promotes global warming. The third sentence indicates that warmer temperatures promote an increase in the number of microbes.

Step 3: Make a Prediction

So microbes lead to warming, which leads to more microbes, which leads to more warming. In science, this self-reinforcing process is known as a feedback loop.

Step 4: Evaluate the Answer Choices

(C) makes the link between global warming and the resultant increased microbe activity, which will exacerbate that warming.

(A) is wholly speculative. Nothing in the stimulus indicates the time frame ("soon") for the depletion of the organic molecules that microbes consume. Nor does the stimulus give any reason to assume that the organic molecules will not continue to be generated by whatever process produced them in the first place.

(B) is Extreme. The word *every* is a red flag. The stimulus does not discuss any organisms besides the microbes, so it cannot be inferred that *any* other organism reacts the same way to higher temperatures, let alone *every* carbon dioxide–generating organism.

(D) is also Extreme. Simply because the stimulus mentions only the removal of oxygen, it cannot be inferred that the microbes don't remove any other elements from the atmosphere.

(E) is Out of Scope. Be wary of subjective qualifying words such as *significant* in Inference answers. The stimulus does not indicate what percentage of carbon dioxide in the atmosphere the microbes produced or whether that qualifies as *significant*.

9. (C) Parallel Reasoning

Step 1: Identify the Question Type

A Parallel Reasoning question asks which answer contains an argument with reasoning that is "similar to" or "resembles" the reasoning in the stimulus. Many answers to Parallel Reasoning questions can be eliminated solely by comparing the stimulus's conclusion with the conclusions in the answer choices. When doing this, however, make sure you read the conclusions of all five answer choices.

Step 2: Untangle the Stimulus

The argument concludes that a particular course of action (everyone eating fish instead of red meat) should not be recommended. The evidence, if needed, says that although eating fish is healthier than eating red meat, if everyone did so, marine species would die, making the diet impossible.

Step 3: Make a Prediction

The correct answer must also have a conclusion that recommends against a course of action. If more than one answer has the proper conclusion type, then the evidence in the remaining answers should be compared with the evidence in the stimulus.

Step 4: Evaluate the Answer Choices

(C) has that type of conclusion. It actually contains the exact phrase "we should not recommend," though that is not necessary as long as the conclusion counsels against making a proposal or suggestion. Additionally, the evidence in **(C)** shows that universal adoption of a course of action (limiting spending) would actually make that action impossible. This matches the evidence in the stimulus.

(A) also has a conclusion that matches the stimulus. It says we shouldn't recommend that everyone take daily vitamin E supplements. For this answer choice to match the stimulus, the evidence would have to show that if everyone took vitamin E supplements, then taking those supplements would become impossible. However, **(A)** says that vitamin E supplements are not conclusively proven to be safe for everyone. This doesn't match.

(B) can be eliminated because its conclusion does not relate to whether a course of action should be recommended but instead indicates that an action *might* have to be taken. The level of certainty does not match the stimulus's conclusion.

(D) can be eliminated because its conclusion involves whether an action is *surprising*, not whether it should or should not be recommended.

(E)'s conclusion does not definitely indicate that an action should not be recommended. Instead, it says (less definitively) that "it is not always clear" what should be recommended.

10. (C) Inference

Step 1: Identify the Question Type

This question directs you to use the information above to support one the following answers, which makes it an

Inference question. Look for the most modestly phrased answer that is neither too extreme nor speculative. In Inference stimuli, just as in Reading Comprehension passages, contrast Keywords often emphasize the most important pieces of information.

Step 2: Untangle the Stimulus

The contrast words *however* and *although* highlight two pieces of information: 1) the proteins from cats that trigger allergic reactions can vary from person to person, and 2) often an individual cat will trigger an allergic reaction in some but not all cat-allergy sufferers.

Step 3: Make a Prediction

It can be inferred that cats can have varying mixtures of proteins, which results in a given cat affecting some cat-allergy sufferers but not other cat-allergy sufferers.

Step 4: Evaluate the Answer Choices

(C), which simply indicates there are differences in cats' proteins, must be true. Otherwise, all cat-allergy suffers would have the same reaction to all cats.

(A) is Extreme. The stimulus is limited to people who are allergic to cats. That means there could be people who aren't allergic to any cat. Additionally, it is entirely possible that at least one cat allergy sufferer will be allergic to all breeds of cats (i.e., allergic to all the different proteins found in cats). Also, there is no reference to *breeds* of cats in the stimulus, just individual cats.

(B) is similarly Extreme. Again it is possible that at least one cat is capable of causing a reaction in all types of allergy sufferers despite it being, as the stimulus says, common (but not necessarily universal) for individual cats to affect some but not all allergy sufferers.

(D) is an Irrelevant Comparison. It may be true, but the *intensity* of reactions is found nowhere in the stimulus. Further, other types of allergy sufferers aren't mentioned either.

(E) is Extreme. If there are variations in both cat proteins and people's reactions, then it might be difficult to predict how a given allergy sufferer will react to an individual cat. But maybe there's a foolproof test. Who knows? Nothing in the stimulus supports the extreme assertion that there is *no way* to predict an allergic reaction.

11. (C) Role of a Statement

Step 1: Identify the Question Type

When asked to describe the role or function of a specific statement in the argument, you are dealing with a Role of a Statement question. Focus on the structure of the argument (splitting it into evidence and conclusion) and identify how the statement fits in that structure. Understanding the conclusion is usually also important in Role of a Statement questions.

Step 2: Untangle the Stimulus

The argument initially compares maps to language in one respect (they can be manipulated in order to mislead). The conclusion, indicated by the contrast Keyword *however*, argues that language and maps are *different* in their ability to mislead (that people aren't generally misled by language doesn't mean that they aren't generally misled by maps). Thus, the evidence must provide a reason for this distinction, and it does: people are taught to cautiously interpret language but not maps.

Step 3: Make a Prediction

The statement at issue appears in the evidence following the cartographer's conclusion. It identifies a characteristic of language that the cartographer says does not apply to maps. Thus, the role of the statement is to support the conclusion's distinction between maps and language.

Step 4: Evaluate the Answer Choices

(C) matches the prediction.

(A) is a 180. The point of this part of the argument is to draw a distinction between maps and language (as indicated by the contrast Keyword *but*), not to make an analogy, despite the initial comparison in the first sentence.

(B) is wrong since the statement is not a conclusion. The second sentence is the conclusion because it is the author's subjective recommendation, indicated by *should*. The final sentence supports that conclusion by providing a basis for the distinction between maps and language.

(D), like (A), is a 180. The sentence in question points out a difference between maps and language, not a similarity.

(E) is incorrect because the statement is not the conclusion. Ask yourself which statement supports what. Here, the last sentence would make sense supporting the second sentence, but not the other way around.

12. (D) Flaw

Step 1: Identify the Question Type

The phrase "vulnerable to criticism" means your task is to identify the logical flaw in the argument. Break the argument into conclusion and evidence and try to recognize the common logical flaw before looking at the answers, which often consist of convoluted descriptions of the argument.

Step 2: Untangle the Stimulus

Based on an assertion of bias and self-interest of the reviewer of a book, the journalist concludes that the physician's critique does not provide legitimate grounds for denying the book's claims of a drug's dangerous side effects.

Step 3: Make a Prediction

This is an ad hominem attack, a classic flaw. An ad hominem attack tackles the proponent of an argument rather than the argument itself. In other words, the journalist assumes that anyone with self-interest in the argument cannot have legitimate grounds for her assertion as well.

Step 4: Evaluate the Answer Choices

(D) paraphrases this assumption. The journalist overlooks the possibility that someone with personal interest in the argument may nonetheless have the facts on her side.

(A) is Out of Scope. Because the scope of the journalist's conclusion is limited to the book's claims about the drug's side effects, there is no need to address the potential existence of other claims in the book.

(B) is Extreme. Treat a Flaw answer as an accusation to which the author should not have an easy retort. If the journalist were accused of assuming that "anyone even remotely associated" with a company is unable to fairly weigh the evidence, the journalist could easily object that a physician directly employed by the company is anything but "remotely associated."

(C) is Out of Scope because it brings the book itself into question. The journalist dismisses the physician's critique of the book because of where the physician works. While the book's author may or may not have his own biases, the journalist isn't commenting on that, and therefore lack of consideration of the author's biases is not a flaw in the argument.

(E) turns the logic, such that it is, on its head. The journalist takes evidence of personal bias to conclude that there must be a lack of legitimate grounds. This answer indicates that the journalist assumes that a lack of legitimate grounds dictates that there must be personal bias involved.

13. (B) Strengthen

Step 1: Identify the Question Type

The question says the task is to "justify" the publisher's prediction so that prediction will function as the conclusion. Make a general prediction of how to bolster the assumption and be open to an answer's specific way of doing so.

Step 2: Untangle the Stimulus

The argument concludes that sales, which currently meet expectations, will soon exceed expectations for two reasons: 1) rentals are exceeding expectations, and 2) renters are given a discount to go on and purchase the game. The argument assumes that the large number of renters will translate to increasing sales.

Step 3: Make a Prediction

The publisher's prediction would be strengthened by an answer choice that shows rentals are converting into purchases or will soon do so. A correct answer may present another reason for renters to want to buy the game, in addition to the sales incentive.

Step 4: Evaluate the Answer Choices

(B) provides the incentive for renters to purchase the game. If the game takes several weeks to complete, far longer than the two-day rental periods, then renters who wish to finish their game would have to either re-rent the game many times or purchase it. This specific reason is unlikely to be predicted from the stimulus, but it fits within a general prediction of some reason for renters to go buy the game. Additionally, the evidence indicates that the game "induce(s) even casual players to ... complete it." When the evidence is accepted as true, the length of time needed to complete the game unambiguously supports the prediction that renters will turn into buyers.

(A) indicates there are multiple outlets for purchasing the game, but that doesn't explain why the author thinks sales will soon exceed expectations. Also, this factor wouldn't lead to an increase in future sales, since it is not presented as a newly added convenience.

(C) is an ambiguous answer that arguably could either strengthen or weaken the conclusion. The game's high popularity might be indicative of growing sales or could just as easily be indicative of a product that has reached its peak and is on its way to becoming yesterday's fad. A Strengthen or Weaken answer need only make the conclusion more or less likely, but it should unambiguously take the argument in one of the two directions.

(D) is a 180. It weakens the argument by indicating that a renter who completes the game would be less likely to go on to purchase it.

(E) is another 180. It weakens the argument by reducing the potential customer base, since some people will receive the game for free from friends.

14. (E) Strengthen/Weaken (Evaluate the Argument)

Step 1: Identify the Question Type

This Evaluate the Argument question, indicated by the phrase "evaluate the argument," asks what would be useful in evaluating the argument. This question type is essentially a relevance test, and the correct answer will usually address the author's assumption.

Step 2: Untangle the Stimulus

The author concludes that a lost cocker spaniel found near Flynn Heights is likely to be from that neighborhood because

there are more registered cocker spaniels in Flynn Heights than in all other neighborhoods combined.

Step 3: Make a Prediction

The conclusion's math assumes two things: 1) that stray cocker spaniels are sufficiently likely to wander from their home neighborhood; and 2) that registration records adequately reflect the actual numbers of cocker spaniels. In other words, cocker spaniel owners in Flynn Heights must be as likely as cocker spaniel owners in other neighborhoods to register their dogs. This argument plays off a common LSAT pattern of authors confusing the number of occurrences of an event and the relative likelihood of that event. For example, an author might take the smaller number of deaths from sky diving to conclude that skydiving is safer than riding a bike, failing to consider the far greater numbers of bike riders than skydivers.

Step 4: Evaluate the Answer Choices

(E) reflects that scope shift (i.e., the relevant comparison). If residents of Flynn Heights are as likely as other residents to license their dogs, then the author's conclusion is strengthened. If they are not (i.e., if they are more likely to register their dogs), then the author's conclusion is weakened because the registrations don't match the actual number of dogs.

(A) is a classic Irrelevant Comparison. Since the author's conclusion is limited to cocker spaniels, it does not matter if cocker spaniels are more or less likely to stray than other breeds. If the author had concluded that an unidentified stray dog was likely a cocker spaniel based on the large number of cocker spaniels, only then would the relative frequency at which cocker spaniels and other dogs stray be relevant.

(B) is another Irrelevant Comparison. The conclusion discusses only cocker spaniels and not other breeds of dog. Whether cocker spaniels outnumber other breeds or other breeds outnumber cocker spaniels, the author's conclusion about stray cocker spaniels is not affected.

(C) is another Irrelevant Comparison. The stimulus is concerned solely with stray cocker spaniels, not stray dogs in general. Whether Flynn Heights has more or fewer stray dogs than any other part of the city doesn't affect the likelihood that a lost cocker spaniel belongs in Flynn Heights.

(D) is not helpful because the stimulus already provides the relative actual numbers of cocker spaniels in the different neighborhoods (assuming again that registrations reflect actual numbers), and that is the correct data for determining the likelihood that a cocker spaniel is from Flynn Heights. Also, **(D)** is far too broad in scope, going not just beyond cocker spaniels but beyond dogs. It is irrelevant to the conclusion if there are large numbers of pet ferrets per capita in Flynn Heights.

15. (D) Assumption (Necessary)

Step 1: Identify the Question Type

The word *depends* indicates that this is a Necessary Assumption question. Break down the argument into conclusion and evidence and find the gap between the two. Keep in mind that you can use the Denial Test to check answers.

Step 2: Untangle the Stimulus

The phrase at the beginning of the final sentence dictates what the evidence is and what the conclusion is: "this (preceding evidence) shows that (subsequent conclusion)." The argument concludes that associating facial expressions with basic emotions is genetically inherent. The author bases her conclusion on a study in which all subjects, despite being from disparate cultures, agreed on what emotions were expressed in five photographs of faces.

Step 3: Make a Prediction

The author assumes that universal agreement among people from different cultures indicates that genetics is at play. This ignores the possibility of some nongenetic basis for the agreement among the subjects. The correct answer here could be expressed either as linking cross-cultural agreement to genetic predisposition or by eliminating some other explanation the author is *not* considering (i.e., globalized interaction among all cultures involved).

Step 4: Evaluate the Answer Choices

(D) explicitly states the assumed connection between universal agreement and genetics. The author's conclusion would fall apart if you were to deny this and say, "If there is a behavior common to people from widely disparate cultures, then there is probably NOT a genetic predisposition to that behavior."

(A) is Out of Scope. The author is not concerned with the correctness of people's identification of facial expressions. Rather the author is interested in the cause of the agreement across cultures, whether accurate or not.

(B) is similarly Out of Scope. The point of the author's argument is not the *source* of emotional dispositions but how the expression of those emotions is interpreted. If you are tempted by this choice, the Denial Test is helpful here; the correct necessary assumption answer when denied should cause the logic of the argument to fall apart. Denying this answer yields: "One's emotional disposition can be influenced by one's culture." Even if culture influences whether somebody is happy or sad, that does not preclude the author's contention that there is a genetic predisposition to interpret that smile as a sign of happiness or that frown as a sign of sadness. Since the denied version of the answer does not cause the logic of the argument to fall apart, then

the original version of the answer was not necessary to the argument.

(C) weakens the argument by indicating that cultural influences *are* at play in universal reactions. The author assumes that any nongenetic factors are *not* significant.

(E) is also a good candidate for elimination using the Denial Test. Denying this answer yields: "The photographs were all of people from a single culture." That in no way decreases the likelihood that genetic predisposition explains why the people from widely disparate cultures all interpreted the expressions of people from a single culture the same way.

16. (C) Principle (Identify/Strengthen)

Step 1: Identify the Question Type

The question stem directs you to strengthen the argument using one of the principles, or general rules, found in the answers. This is an Identify the Principle question that mimics a Strengthen question. Approach it the way you would a Strengthen question. Look for the answer choice (usually phrased in more general terms) that makes the judge's conclusion more likely to be true.

Step 2: Untangle the Stimulus

The judge concludes that confusion as to whether local or national building codes apply to an area is not an acceptable excuse because the defendant is charged with noncompliance with national codes. The judge indicates that noncompliance with local codes due to confusion might have been excusable.

Step 3: Make a Prediction

Thus, at the most basic level, the judge assumes violations of local codes are more readily excusable than violations of national codes. Be open to an answer that supports this distinction.

Step 4: Evaluate the Answer Choices

(C) indicates that local codes could have additional restrictions beyond those of national codes. Therefore, while the defendant might understandably be confused about some of the extras in the local codes, he should still be covering the basics (i.e., the national codes). After all, anything in the national code is also in the local code, so no matter what, the defendant should have known to follow the provisions of the national code. Thus, this answer supports the judge's reasoning that the defendant's failure to follow the national code was unacceptable.

(A) misses the mark because mutually exclusive national and local codes would not guide the judge to favor one code over the other.

(B) is a 180. If local codes are as strict or less than national codes, then it would make sense that a builder should at least have to comply with the less strict local codes and could arguably be confused about whether the national codes apply.

(D) is a Distortion. Even if the defendant's confusion is akin to ignorance, the judge indicated such ignorance of local codes may be acceptable. So this answer does not strengthen the judge's categorical finding that just the failure to follow national codes is unacceptable.

(E) may be true, but it doesn't give the judge a reason to stress national codes over local codes.

17. (A) Main Point

Step 1: Identify the Question Type

The question tasks you with identifying the argument's "overall conclusion." The correct answer to a Main Point question should match the sentence or statement in the argument that would be bracketed as the conclusion. Be wary of conclusion Keywords and keep in mind the One Sentence Test.

Step 2: Untangle the Stimulus

The first sentence of the argument is the conclusion. It is Brianna's comparative value judgment that one course of action would have been better than another. The remainder of the argument provides supporting reasons for why it would have been better to buy the tree a year earlier.

Step 3: Make a Prediction

Select the answer matching the first sentence.

Step 4: Evaluate the Answer Choices

(A) is a verbatim quotation of the first sentence and thus is correct.

(B) repeats a piece of evidence. That the tree is struggling is *why* they should have bought a tree last year.

(C) is a subsidiary conclusion. The information about roots supports it (indicated by the evidence Keyword *because*), but it is used to further the main argument, which is that a tree should have been bought last summer.

(D) is the argument's assumption. Brianna points out that last summer's normal rainfall would have *enabled* a tree to develop roots; she assumes, then, that the tree would have actually done so.

(E) is a Faulty Use of Detail. It just repeats the last sentence, which is evidence. Nothing in the argument supports the idea that trees with established roots can better withstand droughts, but that statement does support the first sentence—that a tree should have been purchased last year.

18. (C) Inference

Step 1: Identify the Question Type

This question asks you to use the statements above to determine which answer must be true, making this an Inference question. Look to link together statements in the stimulus that contain a common term, especially if at least one of the statements is absolute.

Step 2: Untangle the Stimulus

The stimulus gives two absolute statements. The first can be translated as follows:

If	*delegate to convention*	→	*party member*

The second translates as follows:

If	*government official at convention*	→	*speaker*

Additionally, you know that *some* delegates to the convention are government officials.

Step 3: Make a Prediction

You can link the statements through the "government officials." If some delegates to the convention are government officials, then you know that those particular people who overlap are also both party members and speakers. In other words, some people fulfill all four roles: delegates to the convention, government officials, party members, and speakers.

Step 4: Evaluate the Answer Choices

(C) matches the prediction.

(A) incorrectly reverses the logic of the first statement in the stimulus. Any LSAT question dependent on Formal Logic will likely have at least one answer that involves an incorrect contrapositive of the Formal Logic in the stimulus.

(B) could be true but does not have to be. It's possible no speakers at the convention aren't diplomats and aren't party members. Or, in other words, eliminating the double negative, it's possible that all the speakers at the convention are delegates or party members or both.

(D) incorrectly reverses the Formal Logic of the last statement in the stimulus without negating it.

(E) isn't supported by the stimulus. This translates to: If government official → party member. But you know only that *some* government officials (those who are also delegates to the convention) are party members. There may be government officials at the convention who are not delegates. You don't know if they are party members or not.

19. (B) Main Point

Step 1: Identify the Question Type

This question calls for the main conclusion of the argument, making it a Main Point question. Pinpoint the argument's conclusion, usually the most opinionated statement in the stimulus.

Step 2: Untangle the Stimulus

The first sentence is the author's subjective prediction and, thus, the conclusion of the argument. If an author predicts that something "will" happen, there needs to be evidence to explain why the author believes so. The rest of the argument supports the idea that truly intelligent machines won't be created unless the discipline changes focus. The beginning of the second sentence makes a concession to progress, and then the contrast word "but" points out that the current concentration on computation will limit future devices' ability to achieve "true intelligence."

Step 3: Make a Prediction

Select the answer matching the first sentence of the argument. Notice that the conclusion, because it includes the word *unless*, is really an "If"/then statement. The answer choice will need to include both parts.

Step 4: Evaluate the Answer Choices

(B) correctly restates the first sentence.

(A) is a paraphrase of the second sentence, the evidence.

(C) is a Distortion of the evidence in the second sentence and contains an Out of Scope reference to fulfilling the *objectives* of artificial intelligence. Additionally, the stimulus's conclusion is a prediction of what *will* happen if the status quo doesn't change, whereas this answer choice looks backward and says research into artificial intelligence "has failed."

(D) is an Irrelevant Comparison not made in the stimulus. The argument does not balance the relative importance of computational ability versus noncognitive responses. The argument merely indicates that the complete absence of emotional and other noncognitive responses precludes true intelligence.

(E) is an assumption of the argument, linking the evidence to the conclusion.

20. (D) Flaw

Step 1: Identify the Question Type

The phrase "vulnerable to criticism" indicates a Flaw question. Break the stimulus into conclusion and evidence and identify where the author's reasoning goes wrong. Keep in mind that one of the most common flaws incorporated into stimuli by the testmakers is the failure to consider alternative possibilities.

Step 2: Untangle the Stimulus

According to a study, parents mainly consider their own entertainment and rarely take into account the views of educational psychologists when rating the educational value of children's television shows. The author concludes that if the psychologists are accurate in rating shows, then parents must not be.

Step 3: Make a Prediction

The author assumes that since the psychologists are experts, parents must not be as accurate at rating shows for educational value. But couldn't *both* the psychologists and the parents be good at rating shows and come to similar judgments? Sure!

Upon reading the author's conclusion, it is tempting to improperly infer that the parents' ratings disagreed with those of the psychologists. That would make sense of the argument. But remember the argument is flawed (as the question stem dictates) and never explicitly states that the ratings differed.

Step 4: Evaluate the Answer Choices

(D) matches the prediction that parents might be rating shows similarly to the experts.

(A) is a common flaw but isn't at play here. Any time a study is mentioned, look for indications that the study group may have been unrepresentative or otherwise inadequate. Here, however, the groups are relevant and of an undetermined size, so the author cannot be accused of relying on an unrepresentative sample.

(B) goes Out of Scope by referencing the children's enjoyment. The stimulus is concerned only with how focusing on their own enjoyment affects parents' rating of the educational value of shows.

(C) is Extreme because the argument is limited to whether parents are good judges of a show's educational value. The author does not indicate that parents should use educational worth as the *only* consideration of what programs their children should watch. Other reasons for viewing are immaterial to this argument.

(E) is Extreme. While the author does assume that educational psychologists are better than parents at ranking shows, the author does not necessarily assume that no other groups of people exist who could accurately judge shows' educational value.

21. (E) Point at Issue

Step 1: Identify the Question Type

This question has a dialogue stimulus, and the question stem asks for the point of disagreement between the two speakers. Your test for Point at Issue answer choices is that both speakers must address the topic of the answer and disagree with each other about that issue.

Step 2: Untangle the Stimulus

According to Justine, the company's agreeing to a large settlement indicated an expectation to lose in court.

Simon indicates that he doesn't know whether the company expected to win or lose but does believe that the company expected to pay more in legal fees whether it won or lost, so settling was cost-effective regardless.

Step 3: Make a Prediction

The important point to glean from the stimulus is that both speakers are focused on the company's expectations and thought process in deciding whether or not to settle.

Step 4: Evaluate the Answer Choices

(E) What would Justine say to the idea that if the company expected to win, it would not have settled? A resounding "Yes!" That is Justine's big idea. What would Simon say? "No!" According to Simon, whether expecting to win or lose, the company was going to settle. If one speaker would say "yes" to an answer choice and the other would say "no," then that is the point of disagreement.

(A) is Out of Scope. Does either author address the actual likelihood the company would lose in court? No. Both authors focus on the company's expectations, not the actual objective likelihood of a loss or even their own estimations of the likelihood of a loss.

(B) is more on track in focusing on the company's expectations or estimations, but does either author present a view on the accuracy of those estimations? No.

(C) similarly is focused on whether settling would factually be the most cost-effective solution rather than on prognostications regarding the company's thought process and expectations. So again, neither author addresses the issue in this answer.

(D) may be a tempting answer. What would Justine say to the idea that the company would have taken the case to trial if the legal fees were less than the $1 million settlement? Justine essentially says that settling is an indication that Pellman's leaders expected to lose. She does not weigh in on cost-effectiveness, so she would not have an opinion on **(D)**. What would Simon say? It is actually not clear what Simon, would say to this idea either. Simon indicates he believes that if Pellman's leaders think it's more cost-effective to settle, then they will settle. However, that does

not also mean that he believes Pellman's leaders think if it's more cost-effective to go to trial, then they will go to trial. Perhaps there are other reasons why they would not want to go to trial.

22. (B) Role of a Statement

Step 1: Identify the Question Type

You are asked to describe the role a particular statement plays in the argument. This is a Role of a Statement question.

Step 2: Untangle the Stimulus

Any time the author identifies a claim of others and states that that claim is wrong, then that is the author's conclusion. Here the author states that some scientists claim there is no correlation between astrological signs and personality types, then indicates that this claim is scientifically unjustified.

Thus, the author's ultimate conclusion is that it is scientifically unjustifiable for scientists to make their claim regarding astrology. However, the next sentence starts with the word [*s*]*ince*. Any time a sentence starts with *since* or *because*, the structure of that sentence will be "Since, [evidence], [conclusion]."

The statement, the role of which must be identified, is the conclusion of that final sentence, supported by the evidence preceding the comma. Therefore, it must be a subsidiary conclusion, which has its own supporting evidence and in turn supports the ultimate conclusion.

Argument Structure: "Although [claim of other scientists], [author's conclusion that other scientists' claim unjustified]. Since [evidentiary premise], [subsidiary conclusion]."

Step 3: Make a Prediction

Select the answer that describes the statement as a subsidiary conclusion.

Step 4: Evaluate the Answer Choices

(B) correctly describes the statement's role as a subsidiary conclusion that both is supported by evidence and in turn supports the ultimate conclusion of the argument.

(A) describes the role of the first half of the last sentence rather than the portion after the comma, which the question asks about.

(C) describes the role of the second half of the first sentence—"this claim is scientifically unjustified."

(D) describes the role of the first half of the first sentence—the scientists' claim.

(E) is a Distortion. The argument is not seeking to establish a general principle but rather to assert that the claim of the other scientists is unjustified.

23. (C) Assumption (Sufficient)

Step 1: Identify the Question Type

This question asks for a statement that, "if assumed," allows the conclusion to be properly drawn. Therefore, it is a Sufficient Assumption question. Sufficient Assumptions typically follow the format of "If assumed ... conclusion follows logically/is properly drawn/is properly inferred." Sufficient Assumption questions frequently have Formal Logic that should be mapped out to make apparent the link between the evidence and conclusion.

Step 2: Untangle the Stimulus

Evidence:

If	justified in praising or blaming	→	know a lot about events leading to action

Conclusion: *Reject Tolstoy's claim that:*

If	know a lot about events leading to action	→	not regard as freely performed

Step 3: Make a Prediction

This is a very high-level question and difficult to map out because the conclusion argues for rejecting a conditional claim. Still, looking at the mapped-out Formal Logic, the common term between the evidence and conclusion is "know a lot about events leading to an action." That common denominator cannot be part of the scope shift between the evidence and conclusion. Instead, you need to link the other mismatched terms from the evidence ("justified in praising or blaming") and conclusion ("not regard as freely performed"). Since the author is rejecting the conclusion, make the conclusion term "regard as freely performed."

Thus, the link is this: If "justified in praising or blaming" → "regard as freely performed."

Step 4: Evaluate the Answer Choices

(C) matches the prediction.

(A) is Out of Scope. The stimulus has nothing to do with whether or not conditions are beyond control.

(B) is a Distortion. It ties together two concepts from the conclusion, but it does not bridge the conclusion back to the concept in the evidence of whether or not praise is justified.

(D) is Out of Scope. The argument is not concerned with one's inclination (desire) to praise or blame another but instead whether one is justified in doing so.

(E), like (B), does not link evidence and conclusion but merely makes a Distortion of the author's conclusion. The author's rejection of Tolstoy's claim really means that the author's conclusion could be paraphrased as "If know a lot about

events leading to any action, then might still regard that action as freely performed." Rejecting another's conditional (if-then) claim means asserting that the trigger in the initial claim will not necessarily lead to the claimed result. The author's rejection of Tolstoy's claim should not be interpreted by simply negating both sides of Tolstoy's Formal Logic.

24. (E) Flaw

Step 1: Identify the Question Type

Again, the commonly used phrase "vulnerable to criticism" indicates a Flaw question. Be on the lookout for common LSAT flaws such as, in this case, confusing correlation with causation.

Step 2: Untangle the Stimulus

The author concludes that crying causes reduced emotional stress. The author's evidence is that tears contain significant amounts of hormones produced in times of stress. The author assumes that these hormones cause stress and that removing them will reduce the levels of stress induced by the hormones.

Step 3: Make a Prediction

The key is recognizing this as a causal argument and applying the common alternatives to claims of causation, such as another cause or reverse causation. Just because these hormones are produced in times of stress does not mean that the hormones are causing the stress rather than the stress causing the production of hormones (or some other alternative factor could be responsible for causing both the stress and the production of these hormones). Keeping the common alternatives to causation in mind, scan for the answer addressing that flaw. Keep in mind that Flaw answer choices are often worded in convoluted and abstract ways. If you have trouble assessing a Flaw answer choice, translate it by substituting concrete terms from the stimulus for vague language in the answers.

Step 4: Evaluate the Answer Choices

(E) matches the prediction. When substituting in concrete terms, it looks like this: "takes for granted that because [hormones] are present whenever [stressed], [hormones] cause [stress]." Wow! It is a lot easier to see that (E) is correct once you use the specific language of the stimulus. That is exactly what the author is assuming.

(A) sounds like an alternative cause, but the real issue is whether the author commits a flaw in concluding that crying does reduce stress. This answer starts with the premise that crying does reduce stress (in the trigger of the answer's Formal Logic), so it cannot identify a flaw in concluding that very thing.

(B) misses the mark because the issue in the argument is whether the hormones are a cause of stress, not whether they are the only cause of stress, which is what it means to say something is required to produce that phenomenon.

(C) essentially indicates that the author failed to consider the possibility that while hormones cause stress, stress could cause the production of hormones as well. This answer does not deal with reverse causation as it applies to the author's assumed causal relationship between crying and stress. Rather, one premise of this answer is that hormones are a cause of stress, just as the author assumes. The author's conclusion could still logically follow even if stress also causes hormone production, so long as hormones cause stress as well.

(D) does not match the stimulus. "Stress" fits for the answer's reference to a "given phenomenon." But there are not "two distinct factors" in the stimulus responsible for stress that the author fails to distinguish between, only hormones. Alternatively, if "reducing stress" is used as the "phenomenon," then only "crying" is available as a factor causing a reduction in stress (the hormones cause stress). So while the author may be accused of failing to consider an alternative cause of the stress, the author cannot be accused of failing to distinguish between two identified factors.

25. (B) Parallel Flaw

Step 1: Identify the Question Type

The question asks you to find the answer that has similar flawed reasoning as the stimulus. If the stimulus for a Parallel Reasoning or Parallel Flaw question has multiple Formal Logic statements, it is less likely that you will be able to eliminate multiple answers just based on the conclusion type. More commonly, you will need to map out the logic of the stimulus and find an answer that maps out the same way. For Parallel Flaw questions, try to recognize the flaw involved in the stimulus before moving on to the choices.

Step 2: Untangle the Stimulus

Evidence:

If	squirrels eat from feeder (X)	→	not attract birds (Y)
If	squirrels eat from feeder (X)	→	no protective cover (Z)

Conclusion:

If	no protective cover (Z)	→	not attract birds (Y)

The logic is flawed because, although squirrels eating from a feeder is sufficient to trigger that the feeder both lacks a cover and will not attract birds, it does not have to be true that the lack of a cover guarantees that birds will not be attracted. The lack of a cover is not a sufficient condition to trigger that squirrels will feed from the feeder. For example, a feeder that

lacks a cover in an area that does not have squirrels could very well attract birds.

Step 3: Make a Prediction

Parallel Reasoning questions are not about the details of a particular situation, since none of the answers will be about bird feeders. The correct answer will have evidence of a sufficient condition that triggers two different results and a conclusion that indicates one of those results is sufficient to trigger the other result.

Step 4: Evaluate the Answer Choices

(B) is a match.

Evidence:

If	tire pressure too low (X)	→	tire wear prematurely (Y)
If	tire pressure too low (X)	→	owner neglects to check (Z)

Conclusion:

If	owner neglects to check (Z)	→	tire wear prematurely (Y)

A single sufficient condition (tire pressure too low) triggers two independent results (tire wear prematurely and owner neglects to check) in the evidence. But in the conclusion, one result (owner neglects to check) triggers the other result (tire wear prematurely). That is precisely what the argument in the stimulus does, even though the subject matter has shifted from bird feeders to tires.

(A) is not a match. The logic of **(A)** is this:

Evidence:

If	tire pressure too low (X)	→	tire wear prematurely (Y)	→	likely cause is low pressure

Eliminate **(A)** at this point. It is now apparent that it is not following the pattern of the stimulus and is not setting up a sufficient condition that has two independent results. Also, the qualifier *likely* is unacceptable since all the statements in the stimulus are certain.

(C) is also not a match.

Evidence:

If	owner neglects to check (X)	→	tire wear prematurely (Y)
If	owner neglects to check (X)	→	owner unaware (Z)

The evidence is lining up as a match, but for **(C)** to be correct, the conclusion would have to progress to this:

| If | owner unaware (Z) | → | *tire wear prematurely (Y)* |

Instead, **(C)**'s conclusion contains a recommendation to make owners aware. Thus, **(C)** could be eliminated solely by comparing it to the conclusion type in the stimulus.

(D) is not a match.

Evidence:

| If | tire pressure low (X) | → | *tire wear prematurely (Y)* |

| If | *owner neglects check (Z)* | → | tire pressure low (X) |

Conclusion:

| If | *owner neglects check (Z)* | → | *tire wear prematurely (Y)* |

This answer contains valid logic. The evidence sets up a chain of Formal Logic statements that can be linked to properly to reach the conclusion. A flawed Parallel Reasoning question will often contain at least one wrong answer that in fact has correct logic.

(E) is not a match.

Evidence:

| If | tire pressure low (X) → | | *tire wear prematurely (Y)* |

| If | *driven gravel roads (Z)* | → | *tire wear prematurely (Y)* |

This answer can be eliminated at this point of mapping out the argument. Rather than containing a single sufficient condition that triggers two independent results, this answer has two different conditions that are sufficient to trigger the same result.

26. (D) Method of Argument

Step 1: Identify the Question Type

A question asking you to identify the technique or strategy employed by the author is a Method of Argument question. Method of Argument questions have answer choices that, similar to many Flaw answer choices, are abstract descriptions of what the author does in presenting her argument. For each answer, ask, "Does the author do this?" Look at the stimulus to determine if the author does what the answer indicates.

Step 2: Untangle the Stimulus

Sarah argues that fishers should be able to keep fish caught accidentally, even if they don't have a permit for that species of fish, since the fish often die anyway if thrown back.

Amar says that this would lead to more "accidents."

Step 3: Make a Prediction

Placing "accidents" in quotes is a big hint that Amar is being facetious and is asserting that Sarah is creating an incentive for fishers to improperly catch more fish of species that are not permitted. So Amar's technique is to indicate a possible negative consequence of Sarah's plan. Though most commonly on the Reading Comprehension section, the LSAT in Logical Reasoning occasionally rewards the test taker for picking up on author attitudes, such as appreciation or sarcasm, in addition to meaning and logic.

Step 4: Evaluate the Answer Choices

(D) Does Amar allude to a potential negative consequence? Yes! Amar asserts that there will be more "accidents."

(A) is Out of Scope. Does Amar do this? No. Amar questions whether a rule should be put into practice due to the undesirable potential consequence of doing so, but he does not weigh in on whether it is feasible to implement.

(B) Despite putting "accidents" in quotes, Amar is not accusing Sarah of using that term in two ways. Indeed, Amar himself is adding the facetious alternative sense of the word.

(C) is a 180. Amar is attacking Sarah's argument, not strengthening it.

(E) is Out of Scope. Does Amar make any references to past policies? No.

Section III: Logical Reasoning

Q#	Question Type	Correct	Difficulty
1	Principle (Identify/Strengthen)	C	★
2	Inference	D	★
3	Flaw	B	★
4	Inference	E	★★
5	Flaw	A	★
6	Paradox	A	★
7	Strengthen	E	★
8	Main Point	B	★★
9	Weaken	A	★
10	Inference	C	★★
11	Main Point	D	★
12	Principle (Identify/Strengthen)	B	★★★★
13	Inference	E	★
14	Paradox	B	★★
15	Assumption (Sufficient)	E	★★
16	Flaw	A	★
17	Strengthen	D	★★★
18	Assumption (Necessary)	E	★★★★
19	Inference	E	★★
20	Method of Argument	D	★★★
21	Flaw	A	★★★★
22	Parallel Reasoning	B	★★★★
23	Assumption (Necessary)	B	★
24	Parallel Flaw	C	★★★
25	Point at Issue	C	★★

1. (C) Principle (Identify/Strengthen)

Step 1: Identify the Question Type

The word *principle*, added to the phrase "most helps to justify the curator's reasoning" indicates that the correct answer will identify a principle that strengthens the curator's argument. Attack the stimulus as you would a Strengthen question. Break it down into conclusion and evidence and find the answer choice that makes the conclusion more likely to be true. Remember that the correct answer will likely be broader than the specific situation discussed in the stimulus.

Step 2: Untangle the Stimulus

The curator's argument is in the last sentence of the stimulus. The curator concludes that the restoration should continue even though that will expose the frescoes to acids. The curator's evidence, indicated by the Keyword *for,* is that the frescoes' present condition makes it impossible to see them as they were when Michelangelo painted them.

Step 3: Make a Prediction

Start by identifying the assumption. In the conclusion, the author recommends a course of action—continuing the restoration—despite critics' concerns. So the author thinks the value of the restoration outweighs any negative side effects of exposing the frescoes to acids. Look to the evidence for why the author thinks the restoration is so valuable: without the restoration, viewers cannot see the frescoes as they were originally intended. Therefore, the author assumes that seeing the frescoes in their original state outweighs the possible risk of exposing them to acids. The correct answer will reinforce this assumption, likely in more general terms.

Step 4: Evaluate the Answer Choices

(C) matches the prediction by suggesting that it is worth potentially damaging an artwork in order to see it as it was originally seen.

(A) is Out of Scope. While the argument is about whether or not artwork should be restored, the evidence does not propose a criterion for restoration based on aesthetic standards. Based on the argument alone, art should be restored regardless of "greatness."

(B) fails to link the evidence to the argument's conclusion about restoration. The argument is about whether or not a restoration should be continued, not about whether or not an artwork has aesthetic value.

(D) goes Out of Scope by introducing both cost and accessibility. The stimulus includes neither of these ideas.

(E) is a Distortion. The curator obviously wants frescoes to be seen in their original form but never goes so far as to say that in their current state, they can't be regarded as Michelangelo's work. Even more importantly, **(E)** fails to

support the conclusion because it gives no reason why the restoration should continue.

2. (D) Inference

Step 1: Identify the Question Type

Because the correct answer is "strongly supported" by the information in the stimulus, it is a statement that must be true based on the stimulus. This is an Inference question. Work through the stimulus to paraphrase the statements and make any logical connections between them.

Step 2: Untangle the Stimulus

Forest fragmentation is when development breaks a big area of forest into smaller areas. When forest fragmentation happens, the population density of some animals grows in the new smaller forest fragments. One such animal is the white-footed mouse. The white-footed mouse carries Lyme disease. Lyme disease is serious, and humans get it from white-footed mice via deer ticks.

Step 3: Make a Prediction

Predict by linking the ideas together like a chain. Forest fragmentation leads to more mice. Mice lead to people getting sick. Therefore, forest fragmentation leads to people getting sick.

Step 4: Evaluate the Answer Choices

(D) matches the prediction. Stopping forest fragmentation *could* prevent the mouse population from skyrocketing, which *could* help people avoid Lyme disease. Notice the tentative language, which is easier to support.

(A) is Extreme. While the stimulus says the population of white-footed mice is at its most dense in fragmented forests, that doesn't prove the mice are "very rarely" found in unfragmented forests.

(B) is also Extreme. The stimulus only provides information about some animals, regardless of size. Based on this, you cannot infer what happens to most small animals. *Some* animals could be as few as one species, whereas *most* means more than half of the small species.

(C) goes Out of Scope. The stimulus provides no information about the number or variety of species that can live in the smaller forest fragments. All the stimulus says is that some species really thrive in the fragments. You can't infer what happens to other species based on this.

(E) goes Out of Scope by discussing the population density of deer ticks. The stimulus provides information about the population density of white-footed mice but not of deer ticks.

3. (B) Flaw

Step 1: Identify the Question Type

The phrase "most vulnerable to criticism" indicates this is a Flaw question. Break down the author's argument, identifying the conclusion and evidence and determining the assumption. Then evaluate how the author's reasoning goes wrong. Remember to keep an eye out for common flaw types.

Step 2: Untangle the Stimulus

The author concludes that adding designated bicycle lanes to roads won't make bikers safer. The evidence is that on the roads with designated lanes, there are more crashes between bikes and cars than on roads without bike lanes.

Step 3: Make a Prediction

The author assumes that because there are more collisions on roads with designated lanes, the lanes do nothing to increase safety for bicyclists. In other words, the author overlooks the alternative that if the designated lanes weren't there, the bikers would be much less safe (i.e., there would be even more crashes). The author also ignores that the designated lanes may have been added to the most dangerous roads or that bikers are more likely to keep to roads with bike lanes.

Step 4: Evaluate the Answer Choices

(B) matches the prediction. If there are more bicyclists on the roads with designated lanes, it would explain why more accidents happen on those roads, even with the bike lanes.

(A) is an Irrelevant Comparison. It is true that the author never explicitly mentions that the injuries to bikers on roads with the designated lanes are as bad as the injuries to bikers on other roads. However, this is not a flaw in the argument. If injuries on the roads with bike lanes are as bad, this supports the author's conclusion that the lanes fail to make bikers safer.

(C) goes Out of Scope by focusing on the safety of motorists, which the stimulus never mentions.

(D) matches the author's conclusion, but it gets the evidence wrong. The stimulus never differentiates between the safety of various roads with designated bike lanes. Rather, it compares roads with designated lanes to roads without them.

(E) is a Distortion. While it is true that the provided evidence is insufficient to fully prove the argument's conclusion, the author never attempts to use it to prove the opposite conclusion (that adding bike lanes is likely to enhance bicyclists' safety).

4. (E) Inference

Step 1: Identify the Question Type

Because the correct answer "can be properly inferred" from the stimulus, it is an Inference, a statement that must be true based on the information in the stimulus. Paraphrase the statements provided and make any logical connections between them.

Step 2: Untangle the Stimulus

People complained about air pollution, and their complaints led to stricter emission regulations. Cities that were the most polluted 30 years ago are less polluted now. The regulations caused this improvement.

Step 3: Make a Prediction

Connect the statements. Public complaints led to regulations. Regulations led to improved air quality in certain cities. Therefore, public complaints led to improved air quality in those cities.

Step 4: Evaluate the Answer Choices

(E) matches the prediction.

(A) is Out of Scope. The stimulus discusses only the cities with the worst air pollution 30 years ago. It says nothing about the city with the highest current pollution. That city's air may have remained the same over time or even gotten worse.

(B) is Extreme. The stimulus supports the inference that some cities (those that had the worst air quality 30 years ago) have less air pollution than previously. Other cities (those that weren't originally among the worst polluted) may not have changed their emission regulations and could conceivably have worse air pollution today than they did previously.

(C) is Out of Scope. It might seem reasonable, but it isn't supported by the stimulus. The author gives no information about what percentage of the people who complained about air pollution lived in the most polluted cities.

(D) may be true, but it doesn't have to be. The most polluted cities of 30 years ago are less polluted now than they were then, but the stimulus never compares the present-day level of pollution of those cities against the present-day level of pollution in other cities. It is possible that the most polluted cities 30 years ago were so bad that despite improvements, they are still among the worst in air quality.

5. (A) Flaw

Step 1: Identify the Question Type

The phrase "most vulnerable to criticism" indicates this is a Flaw question. Break down the author's argument, identify the conclusion and evidence, and determine the assumption.

Then evaluate how the author's reasoning goes wrong. Remember to keep an eye out for common flaw types.

Step 2: Untangle the Stimulus

The author concludes that music-sharing services aren't at fault for depriving musicians of their deserved royalties. The author's evidence is that record companies, publishers, managers, and others take a big chunk of the revenue from music sales.

Step 3: Make a Prediction

Start by finding the assumption. The author argues that one group is not to blame simply because other groups do the same thing (take musicians' money). The author overlooks the possibility that all groups involved are at fault.

Step 4: Evaluate the Answer Choices

(A) matches the prediction.

(B) is Out of Scope. While the author does try to prove his conclusion by showing that many people engage in the same behavior, his goal is simply to deny blame, not promote a behavior.

(C) describes an ad hominem attack, which is not what happens here. The only position presented is that of the musicians, but the editorialist never attacks the character of anyone. Additionally, even if the musicians' claim that music-sharing services "rob musicians," that is based on musicians being deprived on royalties, not on the character of the music-sharing services.

(D) goes Out of Scope. The editorialist never shows that the musicians' position has any consequences at all, let alone undesirable ones.

(E) describes a sufficient versus necessary flaw. However, the stimulus doesn't use Formal Logic or introduce any sufficient or necessary clauses. In other words, it doesn't take a result of blameworthiness and say it is a cause.

6. (A) Paradox

Step 1: Identify the Question Type

The phrase "most helps to explain" indicates that this is a Paradox question. Read the stimulus and then evaluate the answers with an eye to finding a reason why doctors would want to give cancer patients and the general public differing advice regarding vitamin C.

Step 2: Untangle the Stimulus

The first half of the stimulus describes the benefits of taking vitamin C, an antioxidant. Yet after the contrast Keyword [h]owever, the medical columnist says cancer patients are not supposed to take vitamin C.

Step 3: Make a Prediction

To resolve the paradox, you must find a reason why cancer patients shouldn't take vitamin C, even though it is usually beneficial. There must be something distinctive about cancer patients that makes it harmful (or, at the very least, not beneficial) for them to take vitamin C.

Step 4: Evaluate the Answer Choices

(A) matches the prediction. The antioxidant properties of vitamin C might, by interfering with oxygen-based treatments, actually help cancer cells survive. Given this, it makes sense that cancer patients shouldn't take vitamin C.

(B) is Out of Scope. It focuses on vitamin C's role in the prevention of *developing* cancer, rather than on how it affects those who already have cancer.

(C) is a 180 because it deepens the paradox rather than resolving it. If cancer cells aren't affected (for good or bad) by vitamin C, then it would seem perfectly reasonable for cancer patients to take vitamin C in order to receive its other health benefits.

(D) is another 180. This answer choice increases the paradox because if vitamin C protects the body, then it would arguably improve health, which would be helpful to cancer patients.

(E), like **(C)** and **(D)**, deepens the paradox. This answer choice suggests that vitamin C does not affect (for good or bad) the side effects of cancer treatments. Yet the vitamin could still be beneficial to patients' health in other ways, so there is no reason for doctors to discourage people from taking it.

7. (E) Strengthen

Step 1: Identify the Question Type

This is a Strengthen question. The one correct answer will "strengthen" the researcher's argument. Break down the argument into conclusion and evidence, predict the central assumption, and find an answer choice that supports the author's assumption.

Step 2: Untangle the Stimulus

The researcher concludes in the last sentence that lichens can be used to monitor pollution just as well as expensive mechanical devices can. The evidence is more complicated. Starting with the words "[t]o investigate this," the researcher describes a study. The researcher visited polluted areas and measured the amount of copper concentrated in lichens found there. The researcher compared those results to data gathered by mechanical devices and found that the lichens and the mechanical devices were equally accurate in their measurements.

Step 3: Make a Prediction

Whenever an author introduces a study as evidence, you should ask yourself if the study is representative. Here, the conclusion is about replacing pollution-monitoring mechanical devices with lichens. Yet the evidence is more specific: it addresses copper pollution only. For the study to be relevant, the researcher must assume the results found with copper could be replicated for other pollutants. The correct strengthener will support this assumption.

Step 4: Evaluate the Answer Choices

(E) matches. By saying lichens absorb other pollutants as well as they do copper, this answer choice shows that the study described is relevant to the more general conclusion.

(A) is Out of Scope. Whether or not mechanical pollution-monitoring devices have already been installed in problem areas doesn't affect the author's conclusion that lichens could effectively replace them. Additionally, the researcher discusses monitoring air quality in general, not just at the problem areas, so this answer choice is too specific.

(B) gives more information about copper, but it fails to link copper to pollutants in general. Additionally, *several* on the LSAT is too vague: it could mean as few as two. If copper is in as few as two locales, then (since the researcher's evidence only addresses lichens' interactions with copper) the proven effectiveness of lichen to *effectively replace* the devices is not strengthened since the lichens could provide less information than the devices do.

(C) is Out of Scope. Though lichens may thrive in cleaner areas, the researcher's study shows they also exist (though possibly in smaller quantities) at polluted sites. This doesn't address lichens' effectiveness at monitoring air quality.

(D) is also Out of Scope. This may be helpful, but it doesn't show that lichens would be equally as *effective* as mechanical pollution-monitoring devices. This choice simply strengthens the idea that lichens are readily accessible.

8. (B) Main Point

Step 1: Identify the Question Type

Because the correct answer "expresses the main conclusion," this is a Main Point question. Focus on Keywords, look out for subsidiary conclusions, and expect to combine statements in the argument to paraphrase the author's main point. Also consider using the One-Sentence Test.

Step 2: Untangle the Stimulus

The stimulus opens with a claim made by "[s]ome" about migratory birds having an innate homing sense. The next sentence contrasts with the opening claim, suggesting there's no reason to believe birds have this ability because studies testing it have been inconclusive. After the evidence Keywords "[a]fter all," the author provides another way that migratory birds could navigate, drawing an analogy between birds and humans.

Step 3: Make a Prediction

In Main Point questions, contrasting points of view frequently lead to the main conclusion, and this question is no exception. The contrast Keyword [*h*]*owever* signals the author's main conclusion: the opinion held by "some" people (that migratory birds use an innate homing sense) is not supported by evidence. The information following the evidence Keyword *since* and the final sentence (beginning with "[a]fter all") are both pieces of evidence supporting the author's main point.

Step 4: Evaluate the Answer Choices

(B) matches the prediction.

(A) is Extreme. The author does use humans (who don't have a homing ability) as evidence, but he does so only to posit that birds "may" navigate using landmarks. This answer choice goes too far by asserting that the birds absolutely do not have an innate homing sense.

(C) is a Faulty Use of Detail. It matches the author's main evidence, but not his main conclusion. It repeats the information following the evidence Keyword *since*.

(D) is a Distortion. It is neither the author's main conclusion nor main evidence. This answer refers to the author's alternate explanation for how birds might find their way home. However, the author does not posit that using landmarks is not an innate ability of birds; the author indicates that it is a possibility.

(E) is Extreme. The author does not claim that it is false that birds have an innate homing sense, merely that there is little evidence to support it. The comparison about whether humans have an innate sense of direction is immaterial to the main dispute between the author and the claim by "some."

9. (A) Weaken

Step 1: Identify the Question Type

This is a Weaken question because the correct answer "weakens the argument."

Step 2: Untangle the Stimulus

The author concludes that there is no evidence to suggest that laundry detergent labeled as ecologically friendly actually is ecologically friendly. It could be just as bad as other laundry detergents. The author's evidence comes in two pieces. First, every detergent has surfactants, which are bad for aquatic life. Second, the ecological effects of other ingredients in laundry detergents are not known.

Step 3: Make a Prediction

Start by finding the assumption. The conclusion is about how detergents labeled as ecologically friendly probably aren't any better than the other detergents. The evidence is about the ingredients in detergents—surfactants as well as the other ones. The assumption must suggest that whatever is bad in all the other detergents is just as bad in the detergents labeled as ecologically friendly. So the weakener will attack this assumption in order to show that the detergents labeled ecologically friendly are actually better for the environment.

Step 4: Evaluate the Answer Choices

(A) matches the prediction because it shows that the ecologically friendly detergents have much less surfactants, which we know are harmful to wildlife.

(B) goes Out of Scope by focusing on how significantly laundry detergents damage the environment. Even if those detergents that are not labeled ecologically friendly don't significantly damage the environment, they may still damage the environment more than those labeled ecologically friendly.

(C) is too vague because it doesn't tell us which type of detergents has which kinds of surfactants. If the ecologically friendly ones have the more damaging surfactants, they may actually be more damaging, which would strengthen the author's argument.

(D) makes an Irrelevant Comparison between surfactants and other chemicals. The conclusion compares one laundry detergent to another rather than one set of ingredients in detergents to another set of ingredients.

(E) is a 180 because it actually strengthens the argument. If consumers need to use more of the detergents labeled as environmentally friendly, then they would be putting more surfactants into the environment and aquatic life would potentially be harmed even more than if consumers had used the non-ecologically friendly ones.

10. (C) Inference

Step 1: Identify the Question Type

Because the correct answer is "supported by the information above," it is a statement that must be true based on the stimulus. This is an Inference question.

Step 2: Untangle the Stimulus

Take an inventory of the statements. At Lake Davis, officials are thinking about doing something to get rid of the razor-toothed northern pike. These fish might cause problems for salmon and trout if they go from the lake into the rivers that flow into the lake. Officials are no longer thinking about using diseases or draining to get rid of the pike. In the past, the officials tried poison, but it made the water dangerous for a long time and was bad for tourism. Locals got angry.

Step 3: Make a Prediction

Connect the statements to figure out what must be true. First of all, the whole stimulus is about these nasty pike. Officials

tried to get rid of them with poison four years ago, and they're still trying to get rid of the pike today.

Step 4: Evaluate the Answer Choices

(C) must be true based on the stimulus. If the officials are still trying to get rid of the pike today, it must be that the poison four years ago failed to get rid of them.

(A) is Out of Scope. We know that the officials have rejected draining the lake as an option, but the stimulus does not tell us why. Just because poisoning the lake hurt the tourist economy does not prove that draining the lake also would.

(B) is Extreme. Poison was used four years ago, but the stimulus does not specify whether that was the only time it had been used or not. It could be true that poison was used previously as well.

(D) is Out of Scope because the stimulus does not tell us what happened four years ago besides the fact that officials did use poison and the consequences that followed. No information is given about whether or not officials considered other options as well.

(E) is Extreme. The stimulus does show that one of the reasons officials want to get rid of the pike is that the pike could hurt salmon and trout. But we do not know if the officials are trying to protect salmon and trout because of their economic value or for some other reason. *Essential* is extreme language that does not match the tone of this stimulus.

11. (D) Main Point

Step 1: Identify the Question Type

Because the correct answer "accurately expresses the main conclusion," this is a Main Point question.

Step 2: Untangle the Stimulus

Read the stimulus with an eye toward its overall structure, paying special attention to Keywords. The counselor starts by telling us what many people assume. Then, after "but," the counselor tells us this commonly held assumption is wrong. Next, the author tells us what is really the case—irrational behavior is what really leads to personal conflicts. The counselor then provides an extended example of this.

Step 3: Make a Prediction

Remember that contrasting points of view are often the key to predicting the right answer in Main Point questions. Here, the counselor disagrees with the assumption held by many people. Therefore, the counselor's conclusion is that personal conflicts are not inevitable. Rather, they are caused by people's irrationality.

Step 4: Predict

(D) matches the first part of the prediction. This question is true to form—Main Point questions typically evaluate your ability to sort out contrasting points of view.

(A) is a 180. It is the statement that the counselor disagrees with, not the counselor's main point.

(B) is part of the example the counselor uses as evidence rather than the main point itself.

(C) is the assumption of the counselor's example. For the example to demonstrate the counselor's point, **(C)** must be true. But it is not the counselor's main conclusion.

(E) also matches the example used as evidence rather than the conclusion the example illustrates.

12. (B) Principle (Identify/Strengthen)

Step 1: Identify the Question Type

The phrase "most clearly helps to Justify" indicates that the correct answer is the principle that will strengthen the argument. This is a Principle question.

Step 2: Untangle the Stimulus

The evidentiary Keyword *for* in the middle of the sentence makes it clear that the first half is the conclusion and the second half is the evidence. So the author concludes that you should never cook with dried parsley because it doesn't compare well with fresh parsley for either taste or health.

Step 3: Make a Prediction

First, find the assumption. The conclusion is a strong recommendation against using dried parsley, so it must be true that the author thinks there is something undesirable about it. In the evidence, the author suggests that dried parsley is deficient in terms of taste and nutrition. The assumption will connect less taste and nutrition with not using an ingredient in cooking. Therefore, the author is assuming that if something has little taste and nutritional value, it shouldn't be used in cooking. The correct answer will suggest a general principle that supports this assumption.

Step 4: Evaluate the Answer Choices

(B) matches the prediction by giving us a variation on its contrapositive. **(B)** can be translated into Formal Logic as follows: If used in cooking → tastiest. If this is true, then there's no way dried parsley should be used in cooking, because we know it is not as tasty as fresh parsley. **(B)** is an extreme statement because it talks about "[o]nly the tastiest ingredients," but an extreme principle is frequently used to strengthen an argument.

(A) is a Distortion. The stimulus indicates that cooks should never use dried parsley. This answer says to use fresh ingredients whenever *possible*. That could mean that sometimes it is still acceptable to use dried parsley if fresh is

not available. Therefore, this answer fails to strengthen the author's recommendation against ever using dried parsley.

(C) reverses the Formal Logic. The evidence indicates the following:

$$\text{If} \quad \textit{less tasty and less healthful} \quad \rightarrow \quad \sim \textit{use}$$

This answer reverses the arrow and says if an ingredient is not used, it is neither tasty nor healthful. That conditional statement does not strengthen the criteria to determine what sufficient information would guarantee what should not be used in cooking.

(D) is a Distortion. It suggests that some fresh parsley should not be used in cooking. The conclusion in the stimulus is just about why dried parsley should not be used.

(E) goes Out of Scope by introducing the idea of what is inferior. The stimulus is about what should be used in cooking, not about what is inferior or superior. There could be reasons for using something In cooking even though it is inferior. You cannot add to the argument the assumption that just because something is inferior, it should never be used in cooking. While this assumption might be plausible in the real world, it is not part of the stimulus.

13. (E) Inference

Step 1: Identify the Question Type

Because the statements in the stimulus "provide the most support" for the one correct answer, this is an Inference question.

Step 2: Untangle the Stimulus

Take an inventory of the statements in the stimulus. The opening sentence gives us the relationship between average seal body size and seal population. When seal bodies are smaller, the seal population is greater. When seal bodies are larger, the population is smaller. Archeologists have studied seal fossils from an 800-year period, and they have found that the average body size did not vary. During this 800-year period, seals were hunted by Native peoples.

Step 3: Make a Prediction

Connect the statements to figure out what must be true. During the 800-year period that archeologists studied, the average body size of the seals stayed constant. Average body size of seals relates to size of seal population. Therefore, during the 800-year period, the size of the seal population must also have remained constant. Additionally, we know that during those 800 years, Native peoples hunted the seals.

Step 4: Evaluate the Answer Choices

(E) matches the prediction by connecting the constant seal population to Native hunting. Even though Natives hunted the seals for many years, that did not lead to a decrease in the overall size of the seal population.

(A) is Out of Scope. The stimulus informs us that seal hunting did occur, but it provides no information about the specific practices involved.

(B) is also Out of Scope because it introduces the idea of overall seal health. The stimulus informs us about body size, but we cannot assume that there is any particular connection between body size and overall health.

(C) is Outside of Scope as well. The stimulus tells us about the 800-year period that archaeologists studied but not about what happened prior to it.

(D) is yet another Out of Scope choice. While we know that Native peoples hunted seals and that the seal population remained constant, the stimulus does not provide any explanation for how this occurred or what efforts the Native peoples made.

14. (B) Paradox

Step 1: Identify the Question Type

Because the correct answer will "help to resolve the apparent inconsistency," this is a Paradox question.

Step 2: Untangle the Stimulus

First, read for the paradox. In other words, what is apparently inconsistent about the mayor's claims regarding the new recycling projects? On the one hand, the mayor suggests that the new recycling projects would greatly reduce the amount of trash. That would seem to help the city's environmental problem of too much trash. Yet the mayor also suggests that the recycling projects could actually increase environmental damage in the city.

Step 3: Make a Prediction

There must be something about the recycling projects that is actually bad for the environment and that would outweigh the good benefits they create.

Step 4: Evaluate the Answer Choices

(B) matches the prediction by suggesting that the cost of new recycling projects would stop the city from undertaking other environmental protection efforts.

(A) is a 180. The paradox would deepen if recycling is less damaging than an alternative. If this is the case, then the mayor's final comment about the recycling projects being counterproductive doesn't make sense. It could also be argued that **(A)** goes Out of Scope because it talks about recycling in general rather than about the specific new projects that the mayor discusses.

(C) is Out of Scope because it fails to discuss the recycling projects at all. No explanation is given as to why the recycling projects should not be implemented.

(D) is a 180. Like **(A)**, it suggests that the effects of more recycling are all good for the environment. The answer that resolves the paradox must show that there is something environmentally bad about the new recycling projects.

(E) is yet another 180. It suggests something environmentally good about recycling. The most efficient way to eliminate it, though, is to see that it goes Out of Scope by focusing on the feelings of people who recycle rather than on the actual new recycling projects.

15. (E) Assumption (Sufficient)

Step 1: Identify the Question Type

The correct answer is the assumption that allows the conclusion to logically follow. Therefore, this is a Sufficient Assumption question.

Step 2: Untangle the Stimulus

The conclusion is in the second sentence, marked by the conclusion Keyword [s]o. It is a Formal Logic statement, so translate it:

| If | you know Ellsworth → | ~ surprised that Ellsworth is offended |

The contrapositive is this:

| If | surprised that Ellsworth is offended | → | ~ know Ellsworth |

The evidence, here the first sentence of the stimulus, is also Formal Logic, marked by the sufficiency Keyword *anyone*. The translation is as follows:

| If | you know Ellsworth → | you know Ellsworth is self-righteous |

The contrapositive is this:

| If | ~ know that Ellsworth is self-righteous | → | ~ know Ellsworth |

Step 3: Make a Prediction

Find the assumption by connecting the mismatched terms. In this argument, the idea of knowing Ellsworth comes up in both the evidence and the conclusion, so it is a matched term and does not need to be included in the assumption. In the conclusion, the idea of not being surprised at Ellsworth's offense is left over and thus mismatched. In the evidence, the idea that you know Ellsworth is self-righteous is left over and thus mismatched. Therefore, the assumption will create some connection between knowing that Ellsworth is self-righteous and not being surprised that Ellsworth is offended. The assumption is that if you know someone is self-righteous, then you shouldn't be surprised when that person gets offended.

Step 4: Evaluate the Answer Choices

(E) matches the prediction by substituting the idea of what everyone expects for the idea that you shouldn't be surprised. While this answer may be phrased differently than your prediction, the underlying idea is the same.

(A) is Out of Scope. It focuses on the suggestions that offend Ellsworth rather than on the fact that no one should be surprised at Ellsworth's taking offense.

(B) is also Out of Scope. The stimulus is written about the present rather than the past, so the assumption will also be about the present.

(C) introduces the idea of hypocrites, which are Out of Scope. The stimulus never informs us whether or not Ellsworth is actually a hypocrite.

(D) brings up Ellsworth's innocence, which is Out of Scope. This one is similar to **(A)** in that it fails to capture what the conclusion is really about—the fact that we shouldn't be surprised at Ellsworth's taking offense.

16. (A) Flaw

Step 1: Identify the Question Type

The phrase "most vulnerable to criticism" indicates that this is a Flaw question.

Step 2: Untangle the Stimulus

The political scientist's conclusion is that people don't vote because they believe that politicians can't fix the most serious problems. The evidence is that when people think that the most serious problems can only be addressed by big attitude changes in large numbers of people rather than government action, then people aren't very excited about voting.

Step 3: Make a Prediction

Start by finding the assumption. The conclusion purports to give the only reason why people don't vote. The evidence gives one reason why people become unenthusiastic about voting. The assumption, therefore, must be that the thing that makes people unenthusiastic about voting is the only thing that stops them from voting. So the political scientist is assuming that the belief that the important problems can only be changed by big attitude changes and not by government action is the only thing that stops people from voting. The political scientist is overlooking the possibility that there could be many other things that would lower voter turnout.

Step 4: Evaluate the Answer Choices

(A) matches the prediction by pointing out that the political scientist's assumption is unjustifiably extreme. The political

scientist suggests there is only one cause, when there could actually be many causes.

(B) fails to match the political scientist's assumption by focusing only on the conclusion. Remember, flaws come from assumptions, and the assumption is the missing link between the evidence and the conclusion. Further, **(B)** misses the fact that it is the people in general (i.e., "a growing conviction") rather than the political scientist who believe that there are no political solutions.

(C) fails to match the political scientist's conclusion. Nowhere in the stimulus does the political scientist imply that important problems can actually be addressed. Rather, the conclusion is about how the political scientist explains decreasing voter turnout. Similarly, **(C)** mischaracterizes the evidence. As in **(B)**, it is not the political scientist who suggests that the problems cannot change if people's attitudes do not change. That belief is one that the political scientist attributes to other people as part of the evidence about what makes them unenthusiastic about voting.

(D) goes Out of Scope. The stimulus never includes the idea that people are dissatisfied with politicians—that is one step farther than indicating "that politicians cannot solve the most important problems."

(E) reverses the logic. It indicates that the political scientist presumes voter apathy prevents something, whereas the stimulus actually gives a cause for voter apathy.

17. (D) Strengthen

Step 1: Identify the Question Type

This is a Strengthen question because the correct answer will "most help to support" the argument made by the iconoclastic geophysicist.

Step 2: Untangle the Stimulus

First, identify where the iconoclastic geophysicist's point of view is put forward. The second sentence starts with "[o]ne iconoclastic geophysicist claims instead that," so the conclusion to strengthen will follow that phrase. The conclusion is that asteroids hit the earth in a highly organized way. The evidence for this view is the pattern of impact craters.

Step 3: Make a Prediction

Start by finding the assumption. The conclusion is about the highly organized natural process. The evidence is about the pattern of craters. Thus, the assumption is that the pattern of craters is determined by the natural process. The correct answer will support this assumption by providing an additional piece of evidence showing that the pattern is created by something natural and highly organized.

Step 4: Evaluate the Answer Choices

(D) matches the prediction by introducing a natural phenomenon, lumpy masses within the earth, which resulted in the highly organized pattern of impact craters.

(A) is a Distortion. Although mass extinctions are mentioned in the stimulus, they do not directly relate to whether the pattern of craters was formed by a natural organized process. The cause of the asteroid craters , not their results, is the focus.

(B) is Out of Scope. The argument is about how asteroids seem to strike the earth in an organized way, not about the potential effect such organized strikes might have on continental drift.

(C) is a 180. It weakens the argument by suggesting that the unusual pattern that the geophysicist cites as evidence was created by a single event. If the pattern was created by a single event, then it is less likely that the asteroid strikes happened through a highly organized natural process. After all, one event is just as likely to have been random as it is to have been highly organized.

(E) is Out of Scope. In the stimulus, the details about the time period are provided to give context for the evidence, but they do not really contribute to the evidence.

18. (E) Assumption (Necessary)

Step 1: Identify the Question Type

This is a Necessary Assumption question, because the correct answer is the assumption that the argument "requires."

Step 2: Untangle the Stimulus

The conclusion is that after the company moves, most of its employees will commute more than 30 minutes to get there. The evidence is that most of the employees cannot afford housing within 30 minutes of the new office location.

Step 3: Make a Prediction

Use the mismatched terms to find the assumption. In this argument, both the evidence and conclusion discuss most of the Acme employees, so that term is matched and does not need to be included in the assumption. The conclusion also discusses the over 30-minute commute. The evidence also talks about the expense of housing that is close to the new office. The assumption will create some connection between the idea of the expense of housing and employees being forced to commute more than 30 minutes. Because we're looking for the necessary assumption, the assumption could also rule out some possibility that the author is overlooking. For example, the assumption could rule out the possibility that after the company moves, Acme's employees will be telecommuting from home rather than commuting to the new location.

Step 4: Evaluate the Answer Choices

(E) matches the prediction by ruling out the possibility that the employees will get a pay raise. Some test takers may eliminate this as Out of Scope because a pay raise was never discussed, but any change to the current conditions could affect the viability of the author's conclusion. Because this is a Necessary Assumption question, check the answer using the Denial Test. The denied version would say that Acme's employees will get a significant raise when the company moves to Ocean View. If that is true, then there's no longer a reason to think that the employees would be unable to afford housing within 30 minutes of the new location. Because the denied version of the answer directly attacks the argument, the Denial Test proves that **(E)** is the correct answer.

(A) is Out of Scope. Although Milltown, the company's old location, is discussed in the stimulus, both the evidence and the conclusion are about Ocean View, the company's new location. So facts about Milltown are immaterial.

(B) is also Out of Scope. The reasoning behind the chairperson's decision to move does not affect the argument. The effect the move will have on the employees' commute time is what is central to the argument.

(C) is Out of Scope and Extreme. Who within the company is in favor of and who is against the move does not affect commute times. Also, the Extreme word [*n*]*one* is a red flag, because even if there is one other person beyond the chairperson that is in favor of the move, the argument is not dismantled.

(D) is like **(A)** in that it focuses on how things are now. The argument, however, is about how things will be in the future, after the company has moved.

19. (E) Inference

Step 1: Identify the Question Type

Because the correct answer is a statement that "logically completes" the argument in the stimulus, it is a statement that must be true based on the stimulus. Therefore, this is an Inference question.

Step 2: Untangle the Stimulus

The stimulus creates an analogy between painting and education. To do either, you need many layers, and later layers require proper application of earlier layers. In painting, the most important layers are the first ones, the preparation of the surface and the application of the primer coat.

Step 3: Make a Prediction

To continue the analogy between painting and education, the correct answer will complete the stimulus by suggesting that, as in painting, the most important layers of education are the first ones.

Step 4: Evaluate the Answer Choices

(E) matches the prediction by suggesting that the initial educational experiences are the most important in a student's overall education.

(A) is Out of Scope because it addresses the way the educator should act. The painting analogy includes no information about how the painter should act.

(B) is a Distortion. Although the foundation or fundamentals are important in painting and education, the discussion of a specific subject strays from the analogy. The painting analogy is about which layer is the most important, not about anticipating which specific aspects of a painting are likely to make progress.

(C) is Out of Scope in the same way as **(A)** in that it focuses on how educators should act rather than on which step in the educational process is ultimately the most important one for the student.

(D) goes Out of Scope by discussing how teaching students is rewarding for teachers. The painting analogy has no information about which layer is most rewarding for the painter to paint.

20. (D) Method of Argument

Step 1: Identify the Question Type

Because the correct answer will describe how the argument proceeds, this is a Method of Argument question.

Step 2: Untangle the Stimulus

Pay special attention to Keywords as you read the stimulus for the argument's overall structure, rather than its specific content. The first sentence gives information about what some people believe will happen in the future. Following "if so," the second sentence explains a consequence of that belief. In the third sentence, the author introduces two new premises and uses them to draw a further consequence of the belief introduced in the first sentence. Finally, in the last sentence, the author suggests that because the further consequence has not occurred, the belief held by some people is unlikely to be true.

Step 3: Make a Prediction

The author argues against a particular belief by showing that consequences that would follow from the belief have not occurred.

Step 4: Evaluate the Answer Choices

(D) uses different words but expresses the same idea as the prediction. For example, the answer describes the belief introduced in the first sentence as a "hypothesis." The "event that is taken to be likely on a given hypothesis" would be that we are alive during the period of galactic colonization by humans. Because that has not occurred, the author thinks the hypothesis is wrong.

(A) is a Distortion of the scientist's conclusion. While it is true that the evidence describes an event that has not occurred (that we're alive during the galactic colonization), the conclusion of the stimulus is not that the same event is unlikely to occur. Rather, the conclusion in the stimulus is that the prediction of some people that humans will eventually colonize the galaxy is probably wrong.

(B) is another Distortion. It describes the flawed method of reasoning that the scientist is trying to demonstrate that "some people" have used in making their prediction about human colonization of the galaxy. The scientist's conclusion, however, does not contradict any of his own premises.

(C) is Extreme because the author is arguing against a specific prediction but does not reach a more general conclusion that dependable predictions are impossible to make.

(E) mischaracterizes the scientist's evidence. It suggests that the scientist's evidence is just about established human tendencies, but in fact the scientist's evidence is more complicated—it is based on the fact that consequences of the other belief have not yet occurred. **(E)** leaves out altogether the crucial fact that the scientist is arguing against another point of view.

21. (A) Flaw

Step 1: Identify the Question Type

The stem indicates that the argument is "flawed," so this is a Flaw question.

Step 2: Untangle the Stimulus

The conclusion comes at the end, after "[t]herefore." While the conclusion can be translated into Formal Logic, the evidence is not also Formal Logic, so it would be simpler to paraphrase the conclusion. Basically, the author concludes that the president's speech wasn't necessarily inappropriate. The evidence comprises the first two sentences. Professor Riley describes the speech as inflammatory, but because of the feud between Riley and the president, the author suggests we shouldn't trust Riley's description. Adding those pieces together, the evidence is that the speech wasn't necessarily inflammatory.

Step 3: Make a Prediction

The author is assuming that if the speech wasn't necessarily inflammatory, then it wasn't necessarily inappropriate. Thus, the author overlooks the possibility that other things could have made the speech inappropriate, whether or not it was inflammatory.

Step 4: Evaluate the Answer Choices

(A) matches the prediction by suggesting that the author has unjustifiably assumed that the speech could be inappropriate only if it is inflammatory.

(B) is a Distortion. The point of the author's evidence is that there is not sufficient reason to believe that the speech was inflammatory, yet this answer gives information about inflammatory speeches—ones that may be appropriate. Because the author did not classify the speech as inflammatory, this answer does not capture the author's flaw.

(C) is Out of Scope. The author's conclusion is not based on the president's position. Instead, the author introduces a separate piece of evidence about the feud between the president and Riley as support for the conclusion.

(D) is Extreme. While the author's main reason for rejecting Riley's characterization is the feud between Riley and the president, the author still leaves open the possibility that the speech is inappropriate. The conditional nature of the conclusion ("unless there are independent reasons") indicates that the author does not view Riley's claim as absolutely false based *merely* on one piece of evidence.

(E) is Out of Scope. The author does indeed fail to address whether Riley's views on the president have merit. However, the author's conditional conclusion that the speech was appropriate is not flawed in this respect. This answer focuses on the author's evidence about the feud but fails to refer to the author's conclusion.

22. (B) Parallel Reasoning

Step 1: Identify the Question Type

Because the correct answer is "most similar in its pattern of reasoning" to the argument in the stimulus, this is a Parallel Reasoning question.

Step 2: Untangle the Stimulus

The conclusion is that the station should not risk sticking with just classical music but should devote some airtime to less risky genres of music. The evidence is that the risk of going out of business is just too great to stick with exclusively classical music.

Step 3: Make a Prediction

While you typically want to begin by testing the conclusions on a Parallel Reasoning question, a quick scan of the answer choices shows that the conclusion of each one of them is a recommendation and thus matches (at least superficially) the conclusion of the stimulus. So take the evidence into account as well. In general terms, the conclusion is that the less risky course of action should be taken. The evidence is about the seriousness of the risk involved. The correct answer will have a matching argument about risk.

Step 4: Evaluate the Answer Choices

(B) matches the prediction because the conclusion is to take the less risky option (making curtains) and the evidence is about the impending seriousness of the risk (there's just no time to wait for blinds). Likewise, the radio producer uses the need for revenue to pay bills as an impending serious risk in order to make the decision to devote airtime to other styles of music.

(A) gets the evidence wrong by introducing the idea of which option is more expensive. The radio producer opts for a choice based on risk rather than on cost savings.

(C) goes Out of Scope by introducing the idea of privacy.

(D) also goes Out of Scope by introducing the idea of what is difficult to buy and match.

(E) gets the conclusion wrong. In the stimulus, the conclusion is a definite recommendation of one specific course of action. In this answer, the conclusion is a conditional recommendation of what we should do *if* something else doesn't happen. The conclusion in the stimulus has no parallel condition.

23. (B) Assumption (Necessary)

Step 1: Identify the Question Type

Because the correct answer is the assumption that the art historian's argument "depends on," this is a Necessary Assumption question. Use the Denial Test to double-check your work. If an answer is correct, inserting its denial into the stimulus will destroy an argument for a Necessary Assumption question.

Step 2: Untangle the Stimulus

The conclusion is that the painting was definitely not painted by Cassatt. The evidence is that the work displays a brush style not known from any other works by Cassatt.

Step 3: Make a Prediction

Use the mismatched concepts to find the assumption. The mismatched idea in the conclusion is that the painting is definitely a forgery. The mismatched idea in the evidence is that the painting has a brush style that does not appear in any of Cassatt's other paintings. Therefore, the assumption will connect this unique brush style to the fact that the painting absolutely could not have been done by Cassatt. The assumption, then, is that if a painting has a brush style not found in other works by Cassatt, then Cassatt did not paint it.

Step 4: Evaluate the Answer Choices

(B) matches the prediction by showing that all of the works done by Cassatt have a brush style that can be seen in at least one other work by her. We can check this answer using the Denial Test. The denied version of **(B)** would say that Cassatt does have other works with one-of-a-kind brush styles. If that is the case, it directly attacks the author's argument, because the author uses the unique brush style as the only reason for thinking the painting is not by Cassatt. Because the denied version of **(B)** directly attacks the argument, **(B)** is the necessary assumption.

(A) is Out of Scope. The author's evidence hinges on brush style and genuineness, not on the availability of canvas and materials as mentioned in **(A)**.

(C) is also Out of Scope. Other painters of Cassatt's era are irrelevant to whether or not the painting in question is or is not by Cassatt. Also, even if Cassatt's work *generally* had a certain subject matter, the painting in question could just be an exception to that generality.

(D) is Extreme. Cassatt's brush style is certainly relevant to the argument, but it needs to be connected to whether or not the painting is by Cassatt. If **(D)** is subjected to the Denial Test (i.e., even if Cassatt's work has a feature *more* characteristic than her brush style), it could still be that the work in question, with its unique brush style, wasn't painted by her.

(E) is Extreme and Out of Scope. The argument's main point is to show that Cassatt didn't make the painting. The author does not need it to be true that Cassatt was the *only* painter to be able to paint in the manner she does. What other painters are capable of may strengthen or weaken an argument about whether a forgery is possible, but the author need not have that information to bridge the gap between evidence and conclusion in this argument.

24. (C) Parallel Flaw

Step 1: Identify the Question Stem

The phrase "parallel reasoning" shows that this is a Parallel Reasoning question. Moreover, this is specifically a Parallel Flaw question, because the correct answer has the same "flawed nature" as the argument in the stimulus.

Step 2: Untangle the Stimulus

Because the stimulus is short and each of its sentences includes a Formal Logic word, the best method of attack is to reduce the statements to Formal Logic algebra. Start with the conclusion, which is in the last sentence after "[s]o." Here, the Formal Logic Keyword is *none*, so the translation into Formal Logic is as follows:

If   one bedroom   →   ~ fireplace

Now substitute variables for the content to reduce the statement into algebra, thus:

If $X \rightarrow \sim Y$. X stands for "one bedroom," and Y stands for "fireplace:"

If   one bedroom (X)   →   ~ fireplace (~ Y)

The first sentence of the stimulus translates to: If balcony → fireplace. The algebraic version is If Z → Y. Z stands for "balcony," and we've already assigned "fireplace" to Y:

If   balcony (Z)   →   fireplace (Y)

The second sentence translates to: If balcony → ~ one bedroom. We've assigned variables to both of those terms already, so the algebra is If Z → ~ X:

If   balcony (Z)   →   ~ one bedroom (~ X)

Step 3: Make a Prediction

The author reasons backward on the first Formal Logic statement (going from Y → Z) to chain the evidence as Y → Z → ~ X, thereby concluding Y → ~ X—or its contrapositive, X → ~ Y.

You can look for the argument that makes the same Necessity vs. Sufficiency mistake in drawing its conclusion, or you can use the Formal Logic algebra to chart out the entire argument and find a match, The author concludes, "If X → ~ Y", on the basis of "If Z → Y," and "If Z → ~ X." The correct answer will be built using the same flawed structure.

Step 4: Evaluate the Answer Choices

(C) matches the prediction. "No dog has fur," becomes "If X → ~ Y." "Every cat has fur," becomes "If Z → Y." "No cat is a dog," becomes "If Z → ~ X."

(A) has the wrong kind of conclusion. "Every fish has fur," would become "If X → Y."

(B) has a conclusion that is too weak—"some" fails to match "none" from the stimulus.

(D), like **(A)**, has a conclusion ("every cat is a fish") that would become "If X → Y."

(E) has the correct kind of conclusion, because "no fish is a dog," becomes "If X → ~ Y." The evidence, however, fails to match. "Every dog is a mammal," becomes "If Y → Z," and the stimulus includes no such statement. In fact, **(E)** is not flawed because its premises do logically establish its conclusion.

25. (C) Point at Issue

Step 1: Identify the Question Stem

Because the stem indicates that the correct answer is the point that two speakers disagree on, this is a Point at Issue question.

Step 2: Untangle the Stimulus

Read each speaker's statement and summarize the arguments. Alissa argues that the city should fund the museum rather than the TV programming because the museum is interactive. Greta argues that the city should fund the TV programming rather than the museum because TV reaches a larger audience.

Step 3: Make a Prediction

Because the speakers appear to disagree over their conclusions on which thing the mayor should fund, a prediction may be able to neatly match the correct answer. Also, remember that the Point at Issue Decision Tree will help to eliminate any wrong answers.

Step 4: Evaluate the Answer Choices

(C) matches the prediction because Alissa argues the city should stop funding the TV programming but Greta argues that the city should keep funding the TV programming.

(A) is a statement that both Alissa and Greta agree on. They both refer to the mayor, who suggests that the city needs to choose between the TV programming and the museum.

(B) is Out of Scope. Neither Alissa nor Greta explicitly addresses the truthfulness of the mayor's claim.

(D) is Out of Scope because Alissa states no opinion about whether or not the museum reaches a greater number of children and Greta states no opinion about whether or not the TV programming provides a better educational experience.

(E) is Out of Scope. Alissa certainly agrees with this statement, but Greta states no opinion about whether or not the museum provides a rich educational experience for children.

Section IV: Logic Games

Game 1: Realtor Showings

Q#	Question Type	Correct	Difficulty
1	Acceptability	C	★
2	Must Be False (CANNOT Be True)	A	★
3	Must Be True	B	★
4	Could Be True	C	★
5	"If" / Must Be True	E	★

Game 2: Three Days of Witness Testimony

Q#	Question Type	Correct	Difficulty
6	Acceptability	D	★
7	Must Be False (CANNOT Be True)	E	★
8	"If" / Must Be True	C	★
9	"If" / Must Be True	B	★
10	"If" / Must Be True	D	★

Game 3: Maintenance Service Targets

Q#	Question Type	Correct	Difficulty
11	"If" / Must Be True EXCEPT	B	★★
12	"If" / Must Be True	E	★★★
13	"If" / Must Be True	A	★★★
14	"If" / Could Be True	C	★★
15	Must Be False (CANNOT Be True)	E	★★★
16	"If" / Could Be True	C	★★★

Game 4: Article Editing

Q#	Question Type	Correct	Difficulty
17	Acceptability	C	★
18	"If" / Must Be True	A	★★
19	"If" / Could Be True	E	★★★★
20	Could Be True	B	★★★
21	"If" / Could Be True	E	★★★
22	Could Be True EXCEPT	D	★★★★
23	Completely Determine	C	★★★

Game 1: Realtor Showings

Step 1: Overview

Situation: Realtor showing houses

Entities: Seven houses—J, K, L, M, N, O, P

Action: Strict Sequencing. Your task is to determine the order in which the realtor shows the houses. This is a Strict Sequencing game.

Limitations: The day is split up so that the first two houses are shown in the morning, the next three are shown in the afternoon, and the last two are shown in the evening. Otherwise, it's a typical one-to-one Strict Sequencing game, with seven houses being shown one at a time.

Step 2: Sketch

As with any Strict Sequencing game, simply list the entities and set up seven numbered slots. In addition, draw lines to separate the different times of day and label the areas appropriately:

Step 3: Rules

Rule 1 limits J to the evening, which will be one of the last two showings. Simply add J to the sketch under the evening slots, noting that it could go in either space.

Rule 2 restricts K from being shown in the morning. So write "No K" under each of the first two slots.

Rule 3 provides a loose relation among L, K, and M. In order, K will be followed sometime later by L, which in turn will be followed sometime later by M:

$$K \ldots L \ldots M$$

Before making deductions, it's helpful to note that this game has three Floaters: N, O, and P. That means they can be interchanged with one another without directly affecting any of the rules.

Step 4: Deductions

The duplication of K as well as the loose sequencing in the last rule provides a surprisingly substantial number of deductions. Because K must be followed by both L and M, that means K cannot be shown sixth or seventh. Thus, K will not be shown in the evening. Combined with the fact that K is not shown in the morning (Rule 2), K must be shown in the afternoon. This also means that L and M, both of which come after K, must also not be shown in the morning.

While K must be in the afternoon, neither L nor M appear similarly restricted. However, because J has to be shown in

the evening (Rule 1), there isn't room for both L *and* M to be shown in the evening. So, because L has to be shown before M, L can only be shown in the afternoon, which in turn means that K must be either third or fourth. L can only be shown fourth or fifth. M, on the other hand, could be shown in either the afternoon (fifth—making the entire afternoon K L M) or in the evening along with J (one in sixth and one in seventh).

Finally, the morning is severely restricted. With J, K, L, and M all being shown in either the afternoon or evening, that leaves only three houses that can be shown in the two morning slots: N, O, and P—the Floaters. Due to their nature as Floaters, the morning houses can be any two. The third Floater will be shown in whatever space is left in the afternoon or evening after everything else is set:

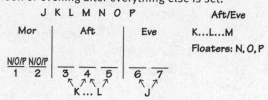

Step 5: Questions

1. (C) Acceptability

As with any Acceptability question, this will be most efficiently managed by going through the rules one at a time, eliminating any answer that violates a rule.

Rule 1 dictates that J be shown in the evening, which means in the last two spots. That eliminates **(E)**, which places it fifth (in the afternoon). Rule 2 doesn't allow K to be in the morning, which means the first two spots. That eliminates **(A)**, which places it first. Finally, Rule 3 sets up the relative order of K followed by L followed by M. That eliminates **(B)**, which places L before K, and **(D)**, which places M before both K and L. That leaves **(C)** as the correct answer.

2. (A) Must Be False (CANNOT Be True)

The correct answer to this question will list two houses that are not allowed to be next to one another. The remaining four answers will feature pairs that *can* be next to one another.

The only entities that are definitely placed at some period of the day are J, K, and L. While the afternoon and evening are next to one another, K still needs to be followed by L in the afternoon before J can be shown in the evening. Thus, there's no way for K and J to be consecutive, making **(A)** the correct answer.

For the record, if M is shown in the evening, it would be consecutive with J. And if K and L are third and fourth, then M can be shown immediately after any of the Floaters. For example:

Mor		Aft			Eve	
N	O	K	L	P	M	J
1	2	3	4	5	6	7

This eliminates **(B)** and **(E)**. Furthermore, if K, L, and M were all in the afternoon, then any of the Floaters (including O or P) could be shown in the evening along with J, which eliminates **(C)** and **(D)**.

3. (B) Must Be True

The correct answer to this question will definitely be true. The remaining answers will all be false or even possibly false.

By the deductions, L must be shown in the afternoon, making **(B)** the correct answer. Again, L can't be shown in the morning because it has to be shown after K (Rule 3), which can't be shown in the morning (Rule 2). And L can't be shown in the evening because then M would have to follow it in the evening (Rule 3) and there wouldn't be room with J already in the evening (Rule 1). So L can only be in the afternoon.

For the record, both K and L must be shown in the afternoon, which eliminates **(A)** and **(C)**. M has to come after K and L, so it can't be shown in the morning, which eliminates **(D)**. And, while M could be shown in the afternoon, it could also be shown in the evening, which eliminates **(E)**.

4. (C) Could Be True

The correct answer to this question will be the only one that could possibly be true (or even definitely be true). The remaining answers will all be impossible.

Because K and L must be shown in the afternoon and J must be shown in the evening, it's impossible for K or L to be shown after J. That eliminates **(A)** and **(B)**. As a Floater, P can certainly be shown after J. This would mean J is the sixth house shown, with K, L, and M making up the entire afternoon:

Mor		Aft			Eve	
N/O	O/N	K	L	M	J	P
1	2	3	4	5	6	7

Therefore, **(C)** is possible, making it the correct answer. For the record:

Because N, O, and P are the only three houses that can be shown in the morning, two of them must be shown then. That means only one of those houses can be shown in the afternoon or evening. With K and M being shown in the afternoon or evening, neither one can have *two* Floaters shown after it. That eliminates **(D)** and **(E)**.

5. (E) "If" / Must Be True

By placing one of the Floaters in the afternoon, it can be determined at what time of day all seven houses are shown. The afternoon will consist of P along with K and L. That leaves M to be shown in the evening along with J. And that leaves the remaining two Floaters (N and O) as the two houses shown in the morning. And that makes **(E)** the correct answer.

Mor		Aft			Eve	
N/O	O/N				M/J	J/M
1	2	3	4	5	6	7
		K … L				
		P				

For the record, the order of J and M cannot be determined, so J could be sixth with M seventh. That eliminates **(A)**. P could be third, with K and L fourth and fifth, so that eliminates **(B)**. The order of N and O cannot be determined in the morning, so O could be first, which eliminates **(C)**. And M is shown in the evening, not the afternoon, which eliminates **(D)**.

Game 2: Three Days of Witness Testimony

Step 1: Overview

Situation: Witnesses testifying at a hearing

Entities: Five witnesses (Franco, García, Hong, Iturbe, Jackson) and three days (Monday, Tuesday, Wednesday)

Action: Distribution. You'll need to determine which day each of the five witnesses will testify. Because the witnesses will be divvied up among the three days and each witness will be placed only once, this is a Distribution game.

Limitations: Each witness will testify on only one day, but there is no limitation as to how many witnesses testify on any given day. Don't assume each day will contain witnesses until stated or suggested otherwise.

Step 2: Sketch

Because there are no restrictions on the number of witnesses for each day, simply list the five witnesses by initial and set up a chart with three empty columns for the three days:

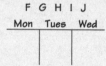

Step 3: Rules

Rule 1 prevents Franco and García from testifying on the same day. Make a shorthand note of this rule:

NEVER | F
      | G

Rule 2 can be inserted directly into the sketch, placing an "I" under Wednesday. Note that this rule does not say Iturbe is the *only* person to testify on Wednesday, so leave the column open in case others testify that day.

Rule 3 sets up concrete numbers for Tuesday, which again can be drawn directly into the sketch. Draw two slots under Tuesday and close the column off.

Rule 4 limits the placement of Hong, who cannot testify on Monday. Simply write "No H" under the Monday column. Alternatively, because H must go somewhere, you can draw "H" with an arrow to Tuesday or Wednesday.

Rule 5 is a little open-ended, but it can still be drawn directly into the sketch. Draw one slot under Monday. However, because the rule indicates that there is *at least* one witness on Monday, leave the column open in case others testify that day.

Before making deductions, it's worth noting that Jackson is a Floater, which means Jackson can testify on any day without directly affecting the rules.

Step 4: Deductions

As with many Distribution games, this game hinges on its numeric limitations. At this point, there are four slots set in the sketch: one on Monday, two on Tuesday, and one (Iturbe) on Wednesday. With five witnesses, there's one more slot needed, which can only be in Monday or Wednesday (because Tuesday is capped off at two by Rule 3).

However, with no entities duplicated in the rules, it's difficult to combine the rules to come up with any substantial deductions. There are two potential ways to set up Limited Options: placing Hong on Tuesday or Wednesday or finalizing the numbers by placing the last slot in either Monday or Wednesday. Both ways set up one fairly complete sketch and one relatively empty sketch. Either set of Options can certainly be valuable. However, with only five questions to the set, three of which are "If" questions, this game can be managed just as efficiently with or without Limited Options. Just be sure to keep track of the numbers:

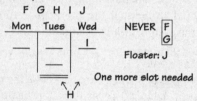

Step 5: Questions

6. (D) Acceptability

As always, running through the rules one at a time helps eliminate all of the incorrect answers. Rule 1 states that Franco and García must testify on different days. However, no answer choice violates that rule. Rule 2 dictates that Iturbe testify on Wednesday. That eliminates **(A)**,**(B)**, and **(C)**—all of which place Iturbe on Tuesday. Rule 3 states that there must be two witnesses on Tuesday. That eliminates **(E)**, which only has one witness on Tuesday. That leaves **(D)** as the correct answer. For the record, Rule 4 indicates Hong cannot testify on Monday, so that would also eliminate **(B)**.

7. (E) Must Be False (CANNOT Be True)

The correct answer to this question will be the one that must be false no matter what. The remaining four answers will all be possibly, if not definitely, true. Without any major deductions, this question can be handled in one of two ways. You can either test each answer one at a time. Or you can temporarily skip this question in favor of drawing sketches for the remaining questions. If you strategically skipped questions, you would find **(A)** possible in the sketch for the next question and **(B)** and **(C)** possible in the sketch for the fourth question of the set. That would leave you only two answers to test for this question rather than having to slog through all five individually.

Without sketches from the other questions, test the answers one at a time. Monday has to have at least one witness, and it could be just one as long as there's a second witness on Friday. In that case, Franco can certainly be that one witness on Monday, which eliminates **(A)**.

There's no restriction that prevents Franco from testifying on Wednesday with Iturbe, so that eliminates **(B)**.

If García and Hong were the two witnesses testifying on Tuesday, then either Franco or Jackson could testify on Monday, leaving the other to also testify on Monday or testify on Wednesday with Iturbe. That eliminates **(C)**.

If Garcia testified on Monday and Hong testified on Wednesday, that would leave Franco and Jackson to be the two witnesses on Tuesday. Because that's acceptable, that eliminates **(D)**.

If Jackson testified on Tuesday and there were two witnesses on Monday, there would be a problem. After all, neither Hong (Rule 4) nor Iturbe (Rule 2) can testify on Monday. With Jackson on Tuesday, that would leave Franco and García to testify together on Monday—but that would violate Rule 1. That makes **(E)** impossible and thus the correct answer.

8. (C) "If" / Must Be True

If Jackson testifies on Wednesday, that sets up the numbers of the game. That means there will be one witness on Monday and two witnesses each on Tuesday and Wednesday. With Wednesday finished up, Hong can only testify on Tuesday (Rule 4). That leaves Franco and García to be split up—one on Monday and the other on Tuesday:

Mon	Tues	Wed
F/G	H	I
	G/F	J

With only one witness on Monday, that makes **(C)** the correct answer.

For the record, Franco and García each could testify on Tuesday, which eliminates **(A)** and **(B)**. Monday only has one witness, which eliminates **(D)**. And García could testify alone on Monday, which eliminates **(E)**.

9. (B) "If" / Must Be True

If Jackson was the *only* witness on Monday, that would again set up the numbers of the game. There would be just one witness (Jackson) on Monday, two on Tuesday, and two on Wednesday. Because Franco and Garcia cannot be together (Rule 1), they will be split up—one on Tuesday and one on Wednesday. That leaves Hong to be the second witness on Tuesday:

Mon	Tues	Wed
J	H	I
	F/G	G/F

That makes **(B)** the correct answer.

10. (D) "If" / Must Be True

If Franco and Hong testify on the same day, it must be on Tuesday. Hong can't testify on Monday (Rule 4), and if they testified on Wednesday with Iturbe, that would leave two people on Tuesday and nobody on Monday, which would violate Rule 5:

Mon	Tues	Wed
G/J	F	I
	H	

↖ J/G ↗

That leaves García and Jackson. Either one can testify on Monday, with the other witness also testifying on Monday or testifying on Wednesday with Iturbe.

In any case, **(D)** must be true, making it the correct answer.

For the record, Franco is on Tuesday, not on Wednesday, which eliminates **(A)**. And García can testify on either Wednesday with Iturbe, which eliminates **(B)** and **(E)**, or on Monday, which eliminates **(C)**.

Mon	Tues	Wed
J	H	I
	F/G	G/F

That makes **(B)** the correct answer.

Game 3: Maintenance Service Targets

Step 1: Overview

Situation: A maintenance company determining target times for responding to service requests from three clients

Entities: Three clients (Image, Solide, Truvest), three service targets (1, 2, 3 minutes), and two sources of requests (website and voicemail)

Action: Matching. Determine the service target (i.e., target number of days to respond to service requests) for each of three clients—setting one target for website requests and one target for voicemail requests. This is a Matching game that requires matching two distinct service targets for each client.

Limitations: There are no clear limitations in the overview. Each client must be assigned two service targets: one for website requests and one for voicemail requests. However there's no indication whether voicemail and website targets have to be different, nor is there any indication whether each client has to have a different set of targets. In fact, with two targets each for three clients, there will be six targets set—but there are only three possible targets (one, two, or three days). So some targets will be repeated.

Step 2: Sketch

There will be two service targets assigned to each of the three clients. So draw a simple chart with the clients listed at the top and two spaces listed in each column. (Note: You could also set up the chart vertically, with each row assigned to a client and two spaces listed in each row.) Be sure to label one set of spaces "web" and one set of spaces "voice" in order to differentiate the targets.

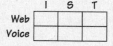

Step 3: Rules

Rule 1 sets a relationship between the website target and voicemail target for each client. The website target cannot be longer than the voicemail target. This means that the website target has to be shorter *or the same* as the voicemail target. Remember, there is no limitation that suggests the two targets must be different for each client.

$$web \leq voice$$

Rule 2 states that Image's voicemail target has to be shorter than that of the other two clients' voicemail targets. Be sure to note that this rule only applies to voicemail targets, not the website targets:

$$I\ voice < S\ voice$$
$$I\ voice < T\ voice$$

Rule 3 states that Solide's website target has to be shorter than Truvest's. Again, note that this only applies to the website targets, not the voicemail targets:

$$S\ web < T\ web$$

Step 4: Deductions

Because the rules are all numerically based, just about every deduction will come from working with the numbers. According to Rule 2, Image's voicemail target has to be lower than the other two clients' voicemail targets. That means that Image cannot have a voicemail target of three days (the highest target allowed in this game), and neither Solide nor Truvest can have a voicemail target of one day. So Image's voicemail target will be either one or two days, and Solide's and Truvest's voicemail target will be either two or three days.

Similarly, by Rule 3, Solide's website target has to be shorter than Truvest's. So Solide's website target cannot be three days (i.e., it can only be one or two days), while Truvest's website target cannot be one day (i.e., it can only be two or three days).

The last piece of the puzzle is Image's website target, which has to be lower or equal to its voicemail target (Rule 1). Because its voicemail target can never be three days, its website target can never be three days. So Image's website target will also be one day or two days:

	I	S	T	
Web	1/2	1/2	2/3	$web \leq voice$
Voice	1/2	2/3	2/3	$I_{voice} < S_{voice}$
				$I_{voice} < T_{voice}$
				$S_{web} < T_{web}$

There are numerous ways to consider Limited Options. However, every space in the sketch is already limited to two possible outcomes. Almost every question is an "If" question—so you'll already be drawing extra sketches anyway. And there's no way to determine for sure which way Limited Options would work best. While there's no disadvantage to Limited Options (i.e., there's nothing wrong if you set them up), it's ultimately not necessary for this game.

Step 5: Questions

11. (B) "If" / Must Be True EXCEPT

If none of the clients has a voicemail target of three days, that immediately affects Solide and Truvest, neither of which can have a voicemail target of one day (Rule 2). So they must have voicemail targets of two days, leaving Image to have a voicemail target of one day (Rule 2). That means Image can only have a website target of one day (Rule 1). Additionally, neither Solide nor Truvest can have a website target of three days (Rule 1). And, because Solide's website target has to be shorter than Truvest's (Rule 3), Solide must have a target of one day while Truvest has a target of two days:

	I	S	T
Web	1	1	2
Voice	1	2	2

This questions is asking for the one answer that doesn't have to be true, and that would be **(B),** because Solide's website target is one day, not two days. **(A), (C), (D),** and **(E)** all must be true.

12. (E) "If" / Must Be True
Per the Master Sketch, Truvest's website target and voicemail targets are each two or three days. If Truvest's website target is shorter than its voicemail target, then its website target must be two days and its voicemail target must be three days. And, because Solide's website target must be shorter than Truvest's website target (Rule 3), that makes Solide's website target one day:

	I	S	T
Web	1/2	1	2
Voice	1/2	2/3	3

Because this question is asking for something that must be true, that makes **(E)** the correct answer.

For the record, nothing additional can be deduced about Image's website or voicemail targets, so neither of them are definitively set, and that makes **(A), (B),** and **(C)** all possibly false. Also, **(D)** must be false because if Solide's website target was two days, Truvest's website target would have to be three days (Rule 3), and then it would be impossible for Truvest's website target to be shorter than its voicemail target, as the question stem calls for.

13. (A) "If" / Must Be True
If Image's website target is two days, then its voicemail target cannot be one day (Rule 1). And, because its voicemail target has to be shorter than Solide's and Truvest's (Rule 2), its voicemail target cannot be three days. So it must have a voicemail target of two days, meaning Solide's and Truvest's voicemail targets must be three days:

	I	S	T
Web	2	1/2	2/3
Voice	2	3	3

Because this question is asking for a target that must be two days, that makes **(A)** the correct answer.

For the record, **(B)** and **(D)** could be true, but they do not need to be. **(C)** and **(E)** must be false because Solide's and Truvest's voicemail targets must be more than Image's voicemail target, which was already determined to be two days.

14. (C) "If" / Could Be True
Solide's voicemail target cannot be one day (Rule 2), nor could Truvest's website target (Rule 3). Each one must be two or three days. If Solide's voicemail target is the shorter of the two, then Solide's voicemail target must be two days and Truvest's website target must be three days. With Truvest's website target at three days, its voicemail target must also be three days (Rule 1). Furthermore, with Solide's voicemail target at two days, Image's voicemail target must be one day (Rule 2), which means Image's website target must also be one day (Rule 1). Solide's website target can still be either one or two days:

	I	S	T
Web	1	1/2	3
Voice	1	2	3

Because the question is looking for a target that could be two days, only **(C)** fits the bill.

For the record, **(A)** and **(B)** both must be false because Image has a one-day target for both website and voicemail. **(D)** and **(E)** also both must be false because Truvest has a three-day target for both website and voicemail.

15. (E) Must Be False (CANNOT Be True)
For this question, the correct answer will be the target that cannot be set more than once in the sketch. The remaining four answers will all be targets that could be set at least twice in the sketch.

Both Image and Solide can have one-day or two-day website targets, so that eliminates **(A)** and **(C)**. Both Solide and Truvest can have two-day or three-day voicemail targets, so that eliminates **(B)** and **(D)**. However, Truvest is the only client that can have a three-day website target, making **(E)** the correct answer.

You could also answer this question using previous work. **(A)** and **(B)** were drawn in the sketch for the first question of the set. **(D)** is drawn in the sketch for the third question of the set. And **(C)** is also possible in the sketch for the third question of the set if either Solide or Truvest gets a two-day voicemail target (along with Image).

16. (C) "If" / Could Be True
If none of the clients has a website target of two days, this immediately affects all of the clients. Per the Master Sketch, if a two-day target is not possible for any website target, then Image and Solide must have a website target of one day with Truvest getting a website target of three days. Finally, with a website target of three days, Truvest must also have a voicemail target of three days (Rule 1):

	I	S	T
Web	1	1	3
Voice	1/2	2/3	3

Note that either Image or Solide can have a two-day *voicemail* target without violating this question's "If" rule. Because the question is looking for something that could be true, only **(C)** is possible.

For the record, Image and Solide have the same website target, eliminating **(A)** and **(B).** And with both targets set at three days, Truvest has no target shorter than any other client's target, which eliminates **(D)** and **(E).**

Game 4: Article Editing

Step 1: Overview

Situation: An editor reviewing articles

Entities: Seven articles—three on finance (G, H, J); three on nutrition (q, r, s); one on wildlife (y)

Action: Strict Sequencing. You'll need to determine the order in which the articles are edited. This is a Strict Sequencing game.

Limitations: Other than the fact that the articles are broken up into topics (three are finance, three are nutrition, and one is wildlife), it's a standard one-to-one Sequencing game with the articles being edited one at a time.

Step 2: Sketch

Because the first two rules use concrete words such as *consecutive* and *third*, this is a Strict Sequencing game. So simply list the entities—being sure to use different styles for the different topics—and set up seven spaces to determine the order:

```
        Fin:     Nut:     Wild:
        G H J    q r s      y

        ___ ___ ___ ___ ___ ___ ___
         1   2   3   4   5   6   7
```

Step 3: Rules

Rule 1 prevents articles of the same topic from being next to one another. It would be a little time-consuming to list every possible pair, so make a general note next to the sketch for reference:

Never same topic consec.

Rule 2 provides some Formal Logic. In order for s to be edited before q, q would have to be third:

$$s...q \rightarrow \dfrac{q}{3}$$

As with any Formal Logic, be sure to include the contrapositive:

$$\sim\dfrac{q}{3} \rightarrow q...s$$

Rule 3 is a standard Sequencing rule: s will be edited sometime before y:

$$s ... y$$

Based on this, note in your sketch that s cannot be the last article and that y cannot be the first (writing "No s" or "No y" under the appropriate space).

Rule 4 provides more loose sequencing. In order, J must be sometime before G, which will be sometime before R:

$$J ... G ... r$$

Again, note in your sketch where these entities can no longer be placed. With two articles after it, J cannot be edited seventh or sixth. G, which has to be in between two articles,

cannot be first or last. And r, which must follow two articles, cannot be first or second.

It also helps to note that H is a Floater, so its placement does not directly impact any of the rules.

Step 4: Deductions

The only entity duplicated in the rules is s, but there's no absolute deduction to be made from combining those two rules. The best that can be said is that if q is not third, then q will come before S, which in turn will come before y. However, that's conditional and cannot be determined for certain.

However, there are two things to note that can help with this game. First is that there's only one way for s to be edited before q. In that case (by Rule 2), q would have to be edited third. If s is edited before that, it would have to be edited first, because q and s are both nutrition articles and they cannot be edited consecutively (Rule 1). So s could be edited first. Otherwise, s would have to be edited after q.

Second is that J and G are both finance articles. So they cannot be consecutive (Rule 1). This affects the sequencing in the last rule. When J is edited before G, there must be at least one other article in between (J ... __ ... G ... r). This further limits the placement of J, G, and r. Thus, J cannot be fifth, G cannot be second, and r cannot be third.

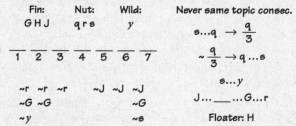

Step 5: Questions

17. (C) Acceptability

As usual, the best way to handle Acceptability questions is to go through the rules one at a time, eliminating answers that violate the rules. Because the first rule can be time-consuming to test, this is a situation in which it's more efficient to start with the last rule and work your way up.

Rule 4 states that J must be edited before G, which must be edited before r. That eliminates **(E)**, which has G edited before J. Rule 3 states that s must be edited before y. That eliminates **(D)**, which gets the order backward. According to Rule 2, s can be before q only when q is third. However, **(A)** has s before q with q fourth, so that can be eliminated. Finally, Rule 1 states that articles of the same topic cannot be consecutive. That eliminates **(B)**, which has two finance articles, G and H, next to one another. That leaves **(C)** as the correct answer.

18. (A) "If" / Must Be True

If y is fourth, that places the only wildlife article. That leaves the three finance articles and the three nutrition articles. s, one of the nutrition articles, must be before y (Rule 3). If s is before q (also nutrition), q would have to be third (Rule 2), and s would have to be first because s and q cannot be consecutive (Rule 1). If q is before s, q would have to be first and s would have to be third. That means s and q will be the first and third article, in either order.

That leaves four spaces for the ordering of J, G, and r presented in Rule 4. Because J and G are both finance articles, they cannot be consecutive. So J, G, and r cannot be the fifth, sixth, and seventh, respectively. So J must be edited second. That leaves G, H, and r for the last three positions. G and H are both finance articles, so they cannot be consecutive. And, because G has to come before r, the only possible order for the last three articles is G, r, H:

s/q	J	q/s	y	G	r	H
1	2	3	4	5	6	7

In this case, J must be second, making **(A)** the correct answer.

For the record, based on the sketch for this question, **(B)** and **(E)** must be false. **(C)** and **(D)** could be true but need not be true.

19. (E) "If" / Could Be True

If G is fourth, J must be one of the first three articles, and r must be one of the last three (Rule 4). More specifically, because J and G are both finance articles, J cannot be third (Rule 1), so it must be first or second. That would leave nowhere to place the remaining finance article, H, in the first three positions without violating Rule 1. So H must be placed at some point after G, although not fifth (Rule 1).

That leaves q, s, and y. There are two positions left before G and one position after. q and s are both nutrition articles, so they cannot be next to one another. If s is before q, they would have to be first and third, respectively (Rule 2). If s is before s, s also has to be before y, so q and s would again be first and third, respectively. In either case, y will always be the article that comes *after* G. Also, J, which has to come before G, will have to be edited second, in between q and s:

s/q	J	q/s	G	r/y		
1	2	3	4	5	6	7

H, r, y

With that, **(E)** is the only possible answer. For this question, G is fourth so H can't be edited fifth (Rule 1), which eliminates **(A)**. J is edited second, which eliminates **(B)** and **(C)**. And s is edited before G, which eliminates **(D)**.

20. (B) Could Be True

The correct answer to this question will be the one answer that is possibly or definitely true. The remaining four answers will all be impossible.

G must come after J (Rule 4), but because they're both finance articles, G cannot be immediately after J (Rule 1). So the earliest G can be edited is third, which eliminates **(A)**.

H is the Floater of the game, which makes it seem likely that **(B)** is the correct answer. Instead of spending time testing it out, it's typically more efficient to see why the other answers are all definitely false.

If s were second, q couldn't be first because they're both nutrition articles (Rule 1). However, in order for s to be edited before q, q would have to be third, which would again violate Rule 1. Therefore, it's impossible for s to be second, eliminating **(C)**. Note: This was not part of the original deductions. It's not difficult to test why it must be false, but it's not an immediately apparent deduction. If you figured this out ahead of time, it's a fantastic deduction. If you didn't, then this question is a great opportunity to carry that new information forward. Because there is no "If" for this question, you can confidently add "no s" to the Master Sketch and use that information on later questions.

r has to come after both J and G (Rule 4), but because J and G are finance articles that cannot be next to one another (Rule 1), r cannot be edited earlier than fourth. That eliminates **(D)**.

If y were third, s would have to be first or second (Rule 3). y being third prevents q from being third, so q would have to be edited before s (Rule 2). However, that would place q and s first and second, making them consecutive. Because they're both nutrition articles, that would violate Rule 1, making this impossible. That eliminates **(E)**.

For the record, here is a possible sequence that confirms **(B)** could be true:

s	H	q	J	y	G	r
1	2	3	4	5	6	7

21. (E) "If" / Could Be True

If J is third, G will have to be edited no earlier than fifth, because it has to be edited after J (Rule 4), but not immediately after (Rule 1). That places r either sixth or seventh (Rule 4). Also, if J is third, then q cannot be third, which means s must be edited after q (Rule 2). And because y has to be edited after s, that creates a loose sequence:

$$q \ldots s \ldots y$$

With G and r after J, there isn't enough room after J for q, s, *and* y. However, with only two spaces before J, q and s cannot both be before J—otherwise they would be next to each other, violating Rule 1. So q must be edited before J, with s and y edited after. That means G, r, s, and y are all edited after J, leaving H to be edited before J. However, H and J cannot be consecutive (Rule 1), so H must be first, leaving q to be second. Finally, only G or s could be fourth, but G cannot be next to J (Rule 1), so s must be fourth:

$$\frac{H}{1} \quad \frac{q}{2} \quad \frac{J}{3} \quad \frac{s}{4} \quad \frac{}{5} \quad \frac{}{6} \quad \frac{}{7}$$
$$\underset{\underset{y}{G...r}}{}$$

With that, only **(E)** is possible.

For the record, G can't be fourth because then it would be consecutive with J in third (Rule 1), and that eliminates **(A)**. Per the sketch for this question, H must come before J, but not immediately before, which eliminates **(B)** and **(C)**. s can't be second because that would force q to be first, and those two nutrition articles can't be consecutive, thereby eliminating **(D)**.

22. (D) Could Be True EXCEPT

The correct answer to this question will be a position that s cannot occupy. The remaining answers will all be possible positions for s.

Because s has to be edited before y, it cannot be seventh—but that's not a choice. Based on the work from the fourth question of the set, s cannot be second—but that's not a choice either. Without previous work, this question would require testing each answer choice one at a time. However, the sketches from the second and third questions of the set both show that s could be first or third. That eliminates **(A)** and **(B)**. The sketch from the fifth question of the set shows that s could be fourth, so that eliminates **(C)**. That leaves only two answers to be tested.

If s were fifth, y would have to be sixth or seventh. r, which has to come after J and G, cannot be first or second. And because J and G are both finance articles, they cannot be next to each other, so r cannot be third either. r and s are both nutrition articles, so r couldn't be fourth or sixth (Rule 1). So r would have to be seventh, placing y sixth. However, that leaves all three finance articles (G, H, and J) to be edited in the first four positions. There's no way to place those articles in those slots without violating Rule 1. So, because this situation is impossible, **(D)** is the correct answer.

For the record, **(E)** could be true. If s were sixth, y would have to be seventh (Rule 3). The rest of the sketch could then be filled in like so:

$$\frac{J}{1} \quad \frac{q}{2} \quad \frac{G}{3} \quad \frac{r}{4} \quad \frac{H}{5} \quad \frac{s}{6} \quad \frac{y}{7}$$

23. (C) Completely Determine

The correct answer to this question will contain a piece of information that will allow the entire sequence to be determined, with no uncertainty. There are several approaches to a question like this: look to slot a duplicated entity, nail down the Floater, or check each answer individually. In this case, some time can be saved by using previous work and your knowledge of the entities.

Taking a look at the sketch for the third question of the set, it's possible for H, r, and y to fill out the remainder of the sketch with y fifth, H sixth, and r seventh:

$$\frac{s/q}{1} \quad \frac{J}{2} \quad \frac{q/s}{3} \quad \frac{G}{4} \quad \frac{y}{5} \quad \frac{H}{6} \quad \frac{r}{7}$$

In that case, the order still couldn't be completely determined because it isn't certain whether q is first and s is third or vice versa. Because of that, none of **(B)**, **(D)**, and **(E)** would be enough to create a fully determined sketch.

Of the remaining two answers, **(A)** mentions H, which is a Floater. **(C)** mentions r, which affects both J and G by Rule 4. So either of the choices could work well for testing.

In **(C)**, if r was fourth, J and G would have to be edited, in that order, before r (Rule 4). However, J and G are both finance articles, so they cannot be consecutive (Rule 1). So J will be first and G will be third. Because q now cannot be third, it must be edited before s (Rule 2), which must be edited before y (Rule 3). q couldn't be fifth, because that would place s sixth and y seventh, putting q and s next to one another (violating Rule 1). So q must be second. s cannot be next to r (Rule 1), so it must be sixth, putting y seventh. That leaves H for the fifth position, resulting in a completely determined outcome:

$$\frac{J}{1} \quad \frac{q}{2} \quad \frac{G}{3} \quad \frac{r}{4} \quad \frac{H}{5} \quad \frac{s}{6} \quad \frac{y}{7}$$

With a fully determined sketch, this makes **(C)** the correct answer.

Although definitively placing the Floater is often a solution for this type of question, in the instance of **(A)**, it does not complete the sketch. If H was fourth, there wouldn't be room before H for both remaining finance articles (G and J) without violating Rule 1. There also wouldn't be room after H for both finance articles, so G and J would have to be split, with J before H and G after H (to satisfy Rule 4). Because G cannot be next to H (Rule 1) and G has to be edited before r (Rule 4), G would have to be sixth and r would be seventh.

y cannot be first (Rule 3). y also cannot be second because that would force s to first (Rule 3), leaving only space 3 for J, which cannot be next to H (Rule 1). Additionally, y cannot be third because that would trigger the contrapositive, or Rule 2, which would make q go before s, meaning the first three spots would be q, s, y, forcing J and H to be next to one another in violation of Rule 1. So the only remaining place for y is fifth.

In order to keep q and s apart (Rule 1), they would have to be placed in the first and third slots, with J in between them in the second slot. However, s could be first with q third or vice versa:

$$\frac{s/q}{1} \quad \frac{J}{2} \quad \frac{q/s}{3} \quad \frac{H}{4} \quad \frac{y}{5} \quad \frac{G}{6} \quad \frac{r}{7}$$

Note that this is similar to the sketch from the third question of the set, with G and H swapped. In either case, the order of q and s cannot be determined with certainty, which eliminates **(A)**.

PrepTest 69

The Inside Story

PrepTest 69 was administered in June 2013. It challenged 23,997 test takers. What made this test so hard? Here's a breakdown of what Kaplan students who were surveyed after taking the official exam considered PrepTest 69's most difficult section.

Hardest PrepTest 69 Section as Reported by Test Takers

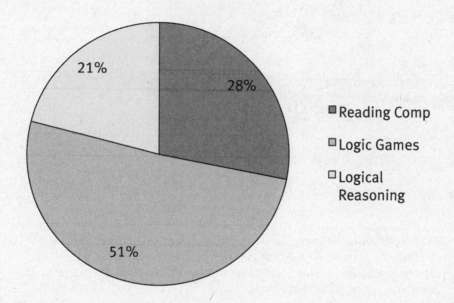

Based on these results, you might think that studying Logic Games is the key to LSAT success. Well, Logic Games is important, but test takers' perceptions don't tell the whole story. For that, you need to consider students' actual performance. The following chart shows the average number of students to miss each question in each of PrepTest 69's different sections.

Percentage Incorrect by PrepTest 69 Section Type

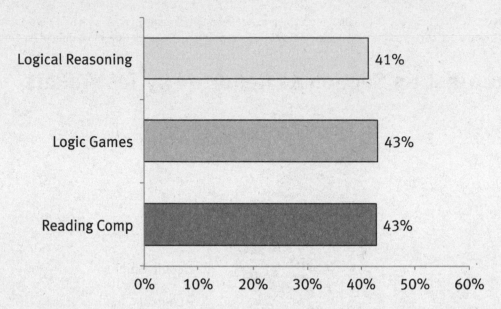

Actual student performance tells quite a different story. On average, students were almost equally likely to miss questions in all three of the different section types.

Maybe students overestimate the difficulty of the Logic Games section because it's so unusual, or maybe it's because a really hard Logic Game is so easy to remember after the test. But the truth is that the testmaker places hard questions throughout the test. For example, eight of the ten hardest questions were in the Logical Reasoning sections of this LSAT administration. Here were the locations of the 10 hardest (most missed) questions in the exam.

Location of 10 Most Difficult Questions in PrepTest 69

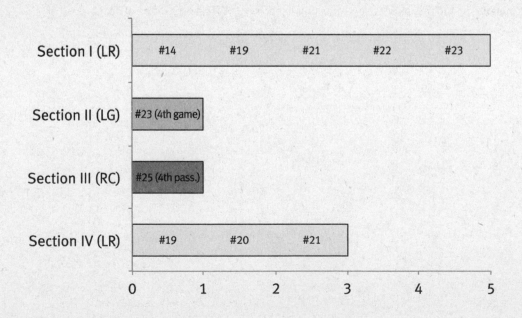

The takeaway from this data is that, to maximize your potential on the LSAT, you need to take a comprehensive approach. Test yourself rigorously, and review your performance on every section of the test. Kaplan's LSAT explanations provide the expertise and insight you need to fully understand your results. The explanations are written and edited by a team of LSAT experts, who have helped thousands of students improve their scores. Kaplan always provides data-driven analysis of the test, ranking the difficulty of every question based on actual student performance. The 10 hardest questions on every test are highlighted with a 4-star difficulty rating, the highest we give. The analysis breaks down the remaining questions into 1-, 2-, and 3-star ratings so that you can compare your performance to that of thousands of other test takers on all LSAC material.

Don't settle for wondering whether a question was really as hard as it seemed to you. Analyze the test with real data, and learn the secrets and strategies that help top scorers master the LSAT.

7 Can't–Miss Features of PrepTest 69

- In Logical Reasoning, PrepTest 69 was exceptional for featuring *two* Point at Issue (Agree) questions; prior to this test, Point at Issue (Agree) had only appeared five times ever, and not at all since PrepTest 56 (December 2008).
- At the same time, PrepTest 69 contained only two Paradox questions, the lowest Paradox question total since PrepTest 55 (October 2008).
- On the other hand, PrepTest 69 matched a historical high-water mark, with three Strict Sequencing games in its Logic Games section.
- Of those three Strict Sequencing games, one was of the standard seven-entities-in-seven-slots variety, but the other two had big twists: vertical sequencing (six items on three shelves) in one, and multiple sequencing (four delivery destinations in two different orders) in the other.
- PrepTest 69 was the first test since PrepTest 61 (October 2010) with no eight-question passage in Reading Comprehension.
- This was the fourth time in five consecutive tests that the Comparative Reading passage was the Law passage.
- Despite being administered during the same month as Father's Day, PrepTest 69 never featured the correct answer sequence (D)-(A)-(D) on three consecutive questions, but it managed to get (B)-(A)-(D) in there *twice*!

PrepTest 69 in Context

As much fun as it is to find out what makes a PrepTest unique or noteworthy, it's even more important to know just how representative it is of other LSAT administrations (and, thus, how likely it is to be representative of the exam you will face on Test Day). The following charts compare the numbers of each kind of question and game on PrepTest 69 to the average numbers seen on all officially released LSATs administered over the past five years (from 2012 through 2016).

Number of LR Questions by Type: PrepTest 69 vs. 2012-2016 Average

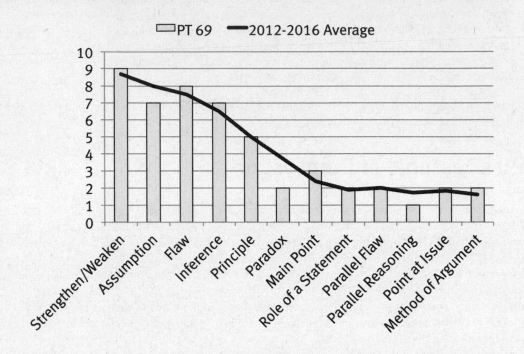

Number of LG Games by Type: PrepTest 69 vs. 2012-2016 Average

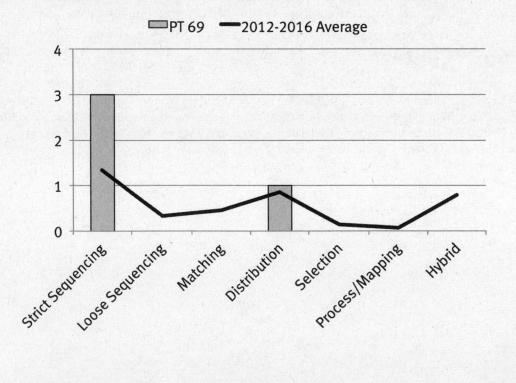

Number of RC Questions by Type: PrepTest 69 vs. 2012-2016 Average

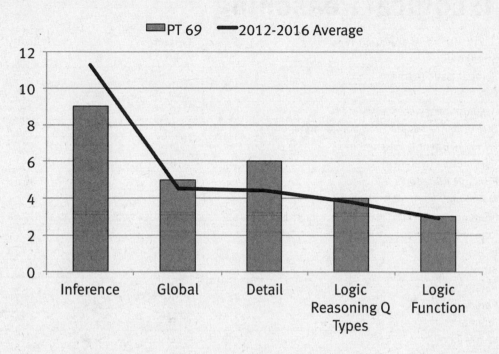

There isn't usually a huge difference in the distribution of questions from LSAT to LSAT, but if this test seems harder (or easier) to you than another you've taken, compare the number of questions of the types on which you, personally, are strongest and weakest. And then, explore within each section to see if your best or worst question types came earlier or later.

Students in Kaplan's comprehensive LSAT courses have access to every released LSAT, and to an online Q-Bank with thousands of officially released questions, games, and passages. If you are studying on your own, you have to do a bit more work to identify your strengths and your areas of opportunity. Quantitative analysis (like that in the charts shown here) is an important tool for understanding how the test is constructed, and how you are performing on it.

Section I: Logical Reasoning

Q#	Question Type	Correct	Difficulty
1	Strengthen	B	★
2	Point at Issue (Agree)	A	★
3	Flaw	D	★★
4	Assumption (Necessary)	D	★
5	Strengthen/Weaken (Evaluate the Argument)	C	★
6	Principle (Identify/Strengthen)	A	★
7	Assumption (Necessary)	B	★
8	Principle (Parallel)	C	★
9	Main Point	A	★
10	Inference	D	★
11	Role of a Statement	E	★
12	Inference	E	★★
13	Strengthen	B	★
14	Parallel Flaw	A	★
15	Paradox	C	★★
16	Inference	D	★
17	Weaken	C	★★
18	Principle (Apply/Inference)	E	★★★★
19	Assumption (Necessary)	E	★★★★
20	Flaw	B	★★★
21	Inference	C	★★★★
22	Weaken	B	★★★★
23	Method of Argument	A	★★★★
24	Flaw	C	★
25	Assumption (Sufficient)	B	★★

1. (B) Strengthen

Step 1: Identify the Question Type

The question stem directs you to "justify" the police chief's argument, so this is a Strengthen question. Additionally, the question stem identifies what you should use as the conclusion: "the exception to the police department's rule." Many LSAT question stems will provide important information or direction beyond just the question type. Strengthen and Weaken questions in particular will often indicate what part of the argument to support or attack, respectively.

If you identified this as a Paradox question, you would be just as likely to choose the correct answer because the question asks you to strengthen—or make sense of—an "exception" or contradiction to the general rule.

Step 2: Untangle the Stimulus

Occasionally, a Strengthen or Weaken stimulus will assert a conclusion without any evidentiary support. In such a case, your task is greatly simplified. You don't need to ascertain the author's assumption. Simply find the answer choice that, if added to the stimulus, could function as pertinent evidence.

Step 3: Make a Prediction

Don't get too specific. A great prediction here is "some reason officers should be allowed to drink while working undercover in a nightclub."

Step 4: Evaluate the Answer Choices

(B) matches the prediction by providing a relevant reason for allowing undercover officers to drink in nightclubs. According to this answer, the failure to drink would blow their cover.

(A) is tempting and is the type of answer a test taker might attempt to build a case for: "If only very experienced officers are allowed to work undercover in nightclubs then their experience would better allow them to function professionally while drinking in moderation." However, while that might explain why officers working in nightclubs *could* drink, it doesn't explain why they *should*, and thus, doesn't provide sufficient justification for the exception.

In general, when stuck choosing between an answer that directly relates to the conclusion and an answer for which you find yourself constructing a chain of logical support, select the former.

(C) is a 180 because it indicates a growing number of officers qualify for the exception. Arguably, deviations from the general rule would, thus, require even greater justification, which this answer choice doesn't provide.

(D) is similar to an opinion-versus-fact flaw. Though most officers "believe" drinking during undercover work doesn't cause significant problems, their belief is not necessarily true. Also, even if drinking on the job doesn't cause

"significant" problems, it may cause smaller ones. The police chief has set a general rule restricting officers from drinking on the job. What the majority of those officers that fall under the rule and exception believe is immaterial as a justification.

(E) is Out of Scope. The public's awareness of the exception does not provide any justification for the creation of the exception itself.

2. (A) Point at Issue (Agree)

Step 1: Identify the Question Type

While most Point at Issue questions will ask what two speakers *disagree* about, this question stem asks you to identify the point of *agreement* between the two speakers.

Step 2: Untangle the Stimulus

Jake recommends that people who want to kill bacteria in their homes should use cleaning products with antibacterial agents.

Karolinka's argument starts with the contrast Keyword *but*. Because the question asks for a point of agreement, it is vital to notice that she actually disagrees with Jake's recommendation.

Step 3: Make a Prediction

Because the contrast Keyword indicates the two speakers disagree about whether people should use household cleaners with antibacterial agents, you can predict that they must agree either on a piece of evidence or an unstated assumption. If you don't quickly spot a point of agreement for a prediction, use the Kaplan Decision Tree for Point at Issue questions while you go through the answer choices. Ask yourself: *Does Speaker 1 have an opinion on this issue? Does Speaker 2 have an opinion on this issue? Do those opinions differ?* For regular Point at Issue questions, you want the answer to the last question to be yes. Here, you want the answer to be no.

Step 4: Evaluate the Answer Choices

(A) is correct. Jake would agree that antibacterial cleaners kill some common bacteria—that's why he recommends them. Karolinka recommends against using the cleaners, but not because she thinks the cleaners are ineffective at killing bacteria. Karolinka is concerned that surviving bacteria will eventually produce strains of antibiotic-resistant bacteria. The fact that she discusses "survivors" indicates that she would agree the cleaners do kill some bacteria.

(B) is an Irrelevant Comparison because neither speaker talks about removing dirt.

(C) doesn't work because Jake never addresses antibacterial strains of bacteria. Because Jake does not address the issue, this choice cannot be correct. Both speakers must have an opinion on the statement for it to be a point of agreement.

(D) is Out of Scope. While Jake recommends that those wishing to minimize the amount of bacteria in their homes should use these products, he does not indicate whether he considers the bacteria to be a serious health concern. Because Jake does not address the issue, this choice cannot be correct; there's no need to research Karolinka's view.

(E) is a 180. The two speakers clearly disagree as to whether these products should be used to clean homes. This answer highlights the importance of reading the question stem carefully. Usually, the LSAT will ask what two speakers *disagree* about, in which case this would be the correct answer.

3. (D) Flaw

Step 1: Identify the Question Type

This question stem asks you to find an objection to the argument's reasoning, so you are dealing with a Flaw question. If you weren't sure whether this was a Weaken or Flaw question, you could have glanced at the answer choices. A Flaw question's answer choices will describe what is already wrong with the argument, while the answer choices for a Weaken question will introduce new facts to undermine the conclusion.

Step 2: Untangle the Stimulus

The author concludes that excess galactose—beyond the body's ability to process it—is carcinogenic.

The author's evidence is a study of two groups: those with cancer did not have enough of the enzyme needed to process galactose, while those without cancer did.

Step 3: Make a Prediction

The critical LSAT pattern to recognize is that the argument sets up a causal relationship between the inability to process galactose and the development of cancer. Thus, your prediction should be that the author fails to consider: 1) alternative cause; 2) reverse causation; or 3) coincidence.

Step 4: Evaluate the Answer Choices

(D) introduces reverse causation. By assuming that ingesting more galactose than the body can process causes cancer, the author ignores the possibility that the subjects in the study may have developed cancer first, which in turn caused the low enzyme levels.

(A) is a tempting answer because it appears to suggest the possibility of an alternative cause. However, the argument doesn't suggest that the study failed to consider other dietary factors, rather the opposite. Additionally, even if the researchers didn't consider all other factors, the conclusion might still be valid. Conversely, with the correct answer, if it were true that the cancer caused the low levels of the enzyme, then the author's argument would fall apart.

(B) is Out of Scope. That the stimulus doesn't make any recommendations is not a flaw in the argument. What people should do doesn't affect the logic the author used to conclude that excess galactose causes cancer.

(C) also goes beyond the scope of the argument. While it's true there may be many substances that cause cancer, this argument is limited to one. That makes this argument narrow, but not necessarily flawed.

(E) is Extreme. Lacking the enzyme entirely would qualify as "low levels," so the argument could still follow. The researchers don't need to confirm whether any member had no galactose whatsoever for the argument to logically follow.

4. (D) Assumption (Necessary)

Step 1: Identify the Question Type

Because the question stem asks for the assumption "required" by the argument, this is a Necessary Assumption question. That means you can use the Denial Test to evaluate answers, if needed.

Step 2: Untangle the Stimulus

The employee concludes that the company releases more pollutants than most similarly sized chemical companies. The evidence is that the company, in combination with just four other companies, accounts for 60% of the pollutants released by 30 small chemical companies included in a study.

Step 3: Make a Prediction

A classic LSAT flaw is the jump from a percentage or proportion in the evidence to an actual amount in the conclusion. By doing so, the author ignores ways that percentages can distort or mask actual amounts. Here, notice that the employee groups his company with four others in the evidence. While it is true that the five collectively release the majority of pollutants, there is no indication that each of the five release similar amounts. Quite possibly, the company in question releases significantly fewer pollutants than some or all of the other four companies with which it is grouped. However, for the employee's assertion to follow, it must be true that such is not the case. Use this as your prediction. If needed, negate the answer choices to see if doing so would destroy the conclusion. For an Assumption question, such an ignored possibility answer will generally be phrased negatively with the word *not* in it. Such answers are easy to test using your Kaplan Denial Test by removing the word *not* and seeing if the newly phrased answer destroys the conclusion.

Step 4: Evaluate the Answer Choices

(D) is complexly and negatively phrased, but use the Denial Test. Removing the word *not* produces this statement: "The four other companies mentioned by the employee *do* together account for very close to 60% of the total pollution by the 30 companies." If that is the case, then the employee's company accounts for only a very small percentage of the pollution, which results in the employee's conclusion no longer making sense. Therefore, the original version of the answer choice is necessary to the argument and, thus, the correct answer.

(A) does not necessarily need to be true. The conservation group's hostility, or lack thereof, doesn't affect the employee's conclusion about the amount of pollutants that his company releases in comparison to others.

(B) is a convoluted sentence, and employing the Denial Test can really help here. Removing the word *not* from the answer leaves the implication that the company *does* produce a lot of pollutants, which concurs with the argument's conclusion. Thus, the original version of the answer weakened the argument and is not a necessary assumption.

(C) is an Irrelevant Comparison. The study discusses only small companies. The amount of pollutants they release as compared to large companies is immaterial.

(E) is also incorrect. Use the Denial Test again here. If there *were* significant variation among the other 25 small chemical companies (say 24 companies each account for 1% of the total pollution and one company accounts for the remaining 16%) it could still be possible that the employee's company accounts for merely "more" pollutants than most similarly sized chemical companies. Therefore, this answer is not a necessary assumption.

5. (C) Strengthen/Weaken (Evaluate the Argument)

Step 1: Identify the Question Type

Questions that ask you to identify information useful to "evaluate" an argument are akin to Strengthen and Weaken questions. The difference is that they do not ask you to take the argument in either direction, pro or con. Instead, you should select that answer that hits on a relevant topic that could affect the conclusion's likelihood.

Step 2: Untangle the Stimulus

The journalist concludes that something in decaffeinated coffee, not present in regular coffee, causes damage to connective tissue. The evidence is a study that shows higher rates of inflammation among those who consume three cups of decaffeinated coffee daily than those who consume the same amount of regular caffeinated coffee.

Step 3: Make a Prediction

For any causal argument there are three important considerations: 1) alternative cause; 2) reverse causation; and 3) coincidence. Scan the answers for a choice that suggests one of the three.

Step 4: Evaluate the Answer Choices

(C) suggests an alternative potential cause. Rather than something additional in decaffeinated coffee causing inflammation, something in caffeinated coffee might protect against inflammation. If caffeine is a benefit, it weakens the conclusion that decaffeinated coffee is a detriment. If caffeine turns out not to protect against inflammation, then the removal of an alternative reason strengthens the argument. An answer choice that introduces an issue that could either strengthen or weaken an argument is the correct answer to an "evaluation" question.

(A) is incorrect even though exercise rates may be relevant to the development of arthritis, and might seem to provide an alternative explanation for why drinkers of decaffeinated coffee were more likely to develop arthritis. However, this answer discusses decaffeinated beverages generally, not decaffeinated coffee, which is the journalist's purported culprit. Also, the LSAT wants you to recognize that even if those who exercise regularly are more likely to drink decaffeinated beverages, those who drink decaffeinated beverages are not necessarily more likely to exercise. This initially seems like a tough distinction to make. However, consider an extreme hypothetical dealing with skydivers and soda drinkers. Assume that there are 100 skydivers in the world and 1 million soda drinkers. Just because most skydivers (say 90) drink soda doesn't mean most soda drinkers skydive. In fact, given the numbers, it is impossible for the majority of soda drinkers to skydive because there are a million of them and only 100 skydivers. Therefore, to be relevant, this answer choice would need to refer instead to the amount of decaffeinated-beverage drinkers who exercise.

(B) is incorrect because neither answer would affect the conclusion. The study controlled for this by including only those drinking three cups a day.

(D) is Out of Scope. Knowing how much coffee drinkers *in general* drink would not reveal any differences between decaffeinated and caffeinated coffee.

(E), like **(D)**, only addresses coffee in general, when the argument is concerned with the differences between caffeinated and decaffeinated coffee. Additionally, this answer could have indicated a reverse causation if it had focused on whether arthritis suffers were likely to pick one type of coffee over the other, but it only focused on whether they drink coffee at all.

6. (A) Principle (Identify/Strengthen)

Step 1: Identify the Question Type

This question stem asks you to use a principle (found in the answers) to justify the decision in the stimulus. So this is a Principle/Strengthen hybrid that you should approach as a Strengthen question. Keep in mind that because the answer is in the form of a principle it will likely be more generally worded than a typical Strengthen answer.

Step 2: Untangle the Stimulus

The question stem directs you to use the "government agency's decision" as the conclusion. That decision was to reject the company's request. If the conclusion has a vague term, such as the "request," make sure to swap out the vague term with its definition. Here, the government rejected the company's attempt to classify collectible figurines as toys. The reason for the government's decision was that the company markets its figurines as collectibles and not toys.

Step 3: Make a Prediction

For any Strengthen question, try to identify the assumption. This argument contains a scope shift from evidence about how the figurines are marketed to a conclusion regarding how the figurines should be classified for tariff assessment. Thus, the assumption is that marketing should indicate tariff classification to some degree.

Step 4: Evaluate the Answer Choices

(A) matches your prediction. If you considered **(A)** to be too broad—referring to any item, not just figurines and toys—you need to refine how you apply wrong answer traps to different question types. If this were an Inference question, the example about figurines could not support an inference about all items. In general, it is acceptable for a Strengthen answer choice to be "bigger" than necessary, and should be expected in Principle questions.

(B) is irrelevant because it pertains to what classification the *company* should seek rather than what the *government* should allow.

(C) strays from the argument by discussing how a toy is used, rather than how it is marketed. Additionally, the stimulus is about collectibles being classified as toys, not toys as collectibles.

(D) would support the evidence (that toys have lower tariffs), not the conclusion. This answer choice doesn't touch on marketing, but rather focuses on purpose. Additionally, this answer discusses the comparative levels of tariffs, not classification requirements.

(E) leaves out tariff classification, merely discussing marketing strategy. The answer choice needs to support the government's decision, not the company's marketing choices.

7. (B) Assumption (Necessary)

Step 1: Identify the Question Type

This question asks for the assumption on which the argument "relies" and thus is a Necessary Assumption question.

Step 2: Untangle the Stimulus

The argument puts forth the premise that if a store does not process pictures properly then the customer is owed a refund. Given that neither the film nor the camera was defective, the author then concludes that if the customer is correct in her claim that she did not mishandle the film, the customer is owed a refund.

Step 3: Make a Prediction

Arguments on the LSAT often overlook alternative possibilities. Here, the author, accepting that customer and product error are absent, assumes the only remaining possibility is that the store improperly processed the film.

The Formal Logic can be mapped out as follows:

Evidence:

If	*store did not process the film properly*	→	*customer owed refund*

Conclusion:

If	*no customer mishandling AND film/camera not defective*	→	*customer owed refund*

Note that the idea of being owed a refund is common to both the evidence and the conclusion and, thus, is *not* part of the assumption. The assumption should link the mismatched terms that are unique to the evidence and conclusion, not the common denominator that shows up in both.

Step 4: Evaluate the Answer Choices

(B) properly links the mismatched terms from the evidence (improper processing) and the conclusion (no customer mishandling and no defective products). Because this is a Necessary Assumption question, you can confirm this with the Denial Test. The answer is in the form of a Formal Logic statement, therefore, it is important to remember that the Denial Test is about negating an answer, not taking the contrapositive (which is both reversing and negating both the necessary and sufficient clauses). The denied version of **(B)** is: "If neither the film nor the camera was defective, and the customer handled the film correctly, then the store processed it *properly*." It no longer makes sense to assert the store owes a refund. Denying this answer causes the conclusion to fall apart and, thus, the original version was necessary to the argument.

(A) is incorrect because it mentions the refund, which is common to both the evidence and the conclusion. This answer choice ignores both the store's processing and the customer's handling of film and, therefore, does not link up the mismatched terms. Additionally, the Formal Logic in the stimulus only mentions what *results* in a store owing a refund. It doesn't give any information about what must be true *if* a store owes a refund.

(C) is Out of Scope. The stimulus concerns only pictures taken with a nondefective camera. Whether a store can or cannot process pictures from a defective camera is irrelevant. Also, denying **(C)** yields, "If pictures are taken with a defective camera, then it is possible for the store to develop those pictures improperly." A statement that allows for the possibility of improperly developed pictures would certainly not destroy the conclusion that the customer is owed a refund.

(D) is a 180 because it supports the claim that the store does not owe the customer a refund.

(E) is the incorrect contrapositive of the argument's conclusion. It negates both sides of the Formal Logic without denying either. Additionally, it doesn't link the conclusion to the evidence about the store's processing.

8. (C) Principle (Parallel)

Step 1: Identify the Question Type

This is clearly a Principle question. Notice with "underlying," the question stem indicates that the principle will never be directly stated in either the stimulus or the answer choices. Instead, both will contain specific arguments that revolve around the same broad assumption.

Step 2: Untangle the Stimulus

Not all Principle questions are argument-based. In some cases the stimulus will contain just information or a general rule. However, if the question stem specifically refers to an "argument above," then the stimulus needs to be broken down into the evidence and conclusion. Here, the author concludes that gardeners shouldn't try to pull every weed from their vegetable gardens. The evidence for this is that the effort saved by not trying to find and pull every weed outweighs the loss in the garden's productivity resulting from having a few weeds in the garden.

Step 3: Make a Prediction

Because this is an Identify and Apply Principle question, the correct answer will not refer to weeds or garden productivity. Therefore, paraphrase the argument in very general terms: "If the effort saved by shooting for a little less than perfection outweighs the downside of not achieving perfection, then don't shoot for perfection." Watch out for answer choices that deviate from the general components of the stimulus.

Step 4: Evaluate the Answer Choices

(C) matches the prediction. Not all personality imperfections should be removed, because the effort saved outweighs the damage to one's personality.

(A) deviates by suggesting that imperfections are necessary and beneficial rather than something that is too much trouble to eliminate entirely.

(B) deviates by focusing on "change" generally rather than efforts to eliminate problems or imperfections. Also, this answer choice is too negative; it says complete change would "make one worse off," whereas the stimulus merely says complete elimination is insufficiently worthwhile.

(D) begins well, but then becomes Extreme. It says removing all imperfections is "never possible," not just that the cons outweigh the pros.

(E) deviates in two regards. First, it distinguishes between the severity of various imperfections (the stimulus does not suggest that some weeds are worse than others). Second, it suggests that removing some imperfections will lead to other imperfections (the stimulus does not suggest that pulling some weeds will cause worse weeds to grow in their place).

9. (A) Main Point

Step 1: Identify the Question Type

The question stem directs you to identify the conclusion—or main point—of the argument.

Step 2: Untangle the Stimulus

For a Main Point question, find the claim or part of the stimulus that you will bracket as the conclusion and find the answer that matches. Here, there are no Keywords to assist in breaking down this argument to its components. However, the first sentence is the most subjective or opinionated statement, while the other two sentences provide support for why the public would benefit from the taxing of junk food.

Step 3: Make a Prediction

Look for the closest match to the first sentence: "It would benefit public health if junk food were taxed."

Step 4: Evaluate the Answer Choices

(A) even uses most of the same words as the first sentence of the stimulus. Pick it and move on.

(B) is the first piece of evidence supporting the idea of taxing junk food.

(C) is the second piece of evidence supporting the benefits of taxing junk food.

(D) is the doctor's assumption, not her main point. This answer choice links the evidence to the conclusion, but is not, in and of itself, the conclusion.

(E) is an incorrect contrapositive of the doctor's conclusion, reversing her logic but not negating it. The doctor says, if junk food were taxed, public health would benefit. However, this answer choice says, if public health would benefit, junk food should be taxed. The doctor takes for granted that public health would benefit, while this answer choice introduces that idea as a condition for implementation.

10. (D) Inference

Step 1: Identify the Question Type

The question stems asks you to use information from the stimulus to support an answer choice, so this is an Inference question. The support flows from the passage downward to the choices. The support in a Strengthen question would flow in the opposite direction; the correct answer would support the stimulus.

Step 2: Untangle the Stimulus

Most Inference questions are not argument based. Do not break the stimulus down into evidence and conclusion to ascertain the assumption. Instead, treat all facts in the stimulus as true. Focus first on the most concrete facts and try to combine statements to make a deduction. If you recognize Formal Logic in the stimulus, start there. The second sentence has the Formal Logic key phrase "only when," which is the same as "only if" and can be translated to:

If	*nahcolite forms*	→	*atmosphere contains at least 1,125 ppm carbon dioxide*

The first sentence indicates that during the Eocene epoch, nahcolite formed.

Step 3: Make a Prediction

A classic and predictable Inference answer links the two sentences. Nahcolite formation is the common link here. The Eocene saw the formation of nahcolite, which requires at least 1,125 ppm carbon dioxide in the atmosphere. Thus, it can be inferred during some part of the Eocene, the atmosphere contained carbon dioxide concentrations of at least 1,125 ppm. While the correct Inference answer can come from anywhere in the stimulus and thus may be less predictable than argument-based questions, making a deduction by combining statements can be helpful. Scan the choices for that deduction.

Step 4: Evaluate the Answer Choices

(D) is an exact match to the prediction. Notice how vague the wording is: "at least 1,125 parts … during at least some part of the Eocene epoch." Correct answers on Inference questions will often be tentative, so that they aren't more extreme than the facts in the stimulus.

(A) is Outside the Scope. The stimulus discusses only 50 million to 52 million years ago. You are told nothing about what has occurred since the Eocene epoch.

(B) is an Extreme statement unsupported by the evidence. The stimulus provides the minimum carbon dioxide levels

needed for nahcolite production, and you can deduce that they were present for at least some of the Eocene epoch. However, you have no way of knowing how much levels fluctuated, whether greatly or at all.

(C) goes well beyond the scope of the stimulus. The stimulus contains no information on what causes lakes to be salty. Nahcolite formed in salty lakes 50–52 million years ago, but it cannot be inferred whether that saltiness was at all related to the carbon dioxide level.

(E) has the same problem as **(A)**. The stimulus does not discuss post-Eocene events. Just because the stimulus happens to discuss significant nahcolite deposits during this time period, you cannot infer that they did not occur during other time periods as well.

11. (E) Role of a Statement

Step 1: Identify the Question Type

The question stem asks you to identify the function of a particular statement from the argument, which is a Role of a Statement question. Underline the statement in the stimulus. (A near verbatim match is the second half of the first sentence, " … 60% of high school students picked a twentieth-century poet.")

Step 2: Untangle the Stimulus

Next, break down the stimulus to conclusion and evidence and note where the underlined statement falls. The conclusion is the opinionated last sentence, indicated by the contrast Keyword *however*. Thus, the relevant statement must be part of the evidence.

Step 3: Make a Prediction

If the relevant statement is part of the evidence, you will usually need to further refine its role. Glance at the choices and see how many indicate that the relevant statement is evidence. Notice that all five choices—including **(C)**, which uses the verb *illustrate*—indicate that the statement is evidence. Each choice then goes on to describe what claim that evidence is supporting. This variant of the Role of a Statement question actually becomes akin to a Main Point question. Which answer choice accurately describes the conclusion?

Step 4: Evaluate the Answer Choices

(E) correctly indicates that the statement in question is evidence supporting the conclusion that "there is clearly something deeply wrong with the educational system."

(A) incorrectly identifies the conclusion. The editor insinuates it's possible that the students are ignorant of the history of poetry, but he also says they simply might not know the word *contemporaneous*.

(B) is a Distortion. It incorrectly focuses on the question and not the answers. There is nothing ambiguous about "What is the name of a poet contemporaneous with Shakespeare?" The ambiguity lies in interpreting the students' answers.

(C) incorrectly says the statement is evidence of a concession the author makes, not the conclusion.

(D) improperly says the statement supports an assumption of the editor. The editor *does* draw a conclusion from ambiguous data, so clearly he must think doing so is appropriate, but that's not his main point. The statement from the question stem supports the final sentence of the stimulus, not an assumption.

12. (E) Inference

Step 1: Identify the Question Type

This question stem directs you to use information in the stimulus to support the correct answer choice, making this an Inference question. Keep an eye out for words that indicate Formal Logic, which will often show up in Inference questions.

Step 2: Untangle the Stimulus

The stimulus contains multiple Formal Logic statements that can be diagrammed.

Sentence 1:

If	apologize	→	must be to person wronged AND for having wronged that person

Sentence 2 and 3:

If	apologize sincerely	→	acknowledge acted wrongly AND intend to not do it again

Sentence 4:

If	accept apology sincerely	→	acknowledge a wrong AND not hold grudge

Step 3: Make a Prediction

For an Inference question with Formal Logic in the stimulus, seek to combine statements and then scan the choices for that deduction. Here, sentences 2 and 3 can be combined to show that the trigger of apologizing sincerely has two results: acknowledging a wrongful action and intending to not repeat the wrongful act. Also, notice that a necessary condition of both a sincere apology and a sincere acceptance of an apology is the acknowledgement of a wrong. Therefore, employing the contrapositive, without an acknowledgement of a wrong, there can be neither a sincere apology nor a sincere acceptance of an apology.

While not really contradictory, it is curious that both the apology and the acceptance of that apology have the same necessary condition. Scan the choices for an answer that must be true based on that curious coincidence.

Step 4: Evaluate the Answer Choices

(E) matches the prediction. Both the sincere offering and sincere accepting of an apology require the acknowledgement of a wrongful act. This answer could be translated as:

If	sincere apology and accept apology sincerely	→	acknowledge wrongful act

This follows the logic of sentences 2 and 4.

(A) is a Distortion of the contrapositive of sentence 3. The answer focuses on action rather than intent. When translating Formal Logic statements in the Logical Reasoning section, while it is important to make the diagrammed statement as concise as possible, it is also vital to retain important qualifiers and/or go back to the stimulus to double check an answer before selecting it.

(B) is not supported by the statements. The conditions for a sincere acceptance in the last sentence do not require that the apology was sincere. This is an example of an answer that could well make sense to a test taker in the real world, but is not supported by the stimulus itself.

(C) is an incomplete contrapositive of the logic of the first sentence (a common wrong answer trap in any question with Formal Logic). The first sentence indicates that a sincere apology requires a wrongful act against a person. This answer flips that (without negating it) to indicate that a wrongful act requires an apology.

(D), like **(B)**, improperly connects sincere apologies and sincere acceptances, which is not deducible from the statements; the only connection is the similarity that both require the acknowledgement of a wrong. For example, if the apology cannot be accepted because the person wronged still wants to hold a grudge then that would not impact whether or not the apology was sincerely offered.

13. (B) Strengthen

Step 1: Identify the Question Type

The question stems very concisely directs you to strengthen the argument. Look for the answer choice that makes the assumption more likely to be true.

Step 2: Untangle the Stimulus

The conclusion is that a collection of kitchen implements was dropped into a well in 375 ad or later. The author supports this with evidence that coins found beneath the implements dated back to 375 ad. The argument assumes that items at the bottom of the well were dropped first and the subsequent implements neatly piled on top. That way, the age of the coins limits when the implements could have been dropped.

Step 3: Make a Prediction

Strengthen and Weaken questions often suggest an alternative that the author seems to ignore or discount. The correct weaken answer choice will raise that ignored possibility, while the correct strengthener will discredit the alternative possibility, thus supporting the author's original explanation.

In this case, a general prediction for a weakener would be anything that could disrupt the orderly chronological layering of stuff tossed into the well. Predict that a strengthener will eliminate a possible disruption of the order.

Step 4: Evaluate the Answer Choices

(B) strengthens by eliminating the weakening possibility that the kitchen implements were dropped first and the coins were dropped later and just filtered through and ended up underneath the implements.

(A) insinuates that the coins may have been dropped into the well long after 375 ad, which means the kitchen implements might have been dropped even later, which would agree with the conclusion. However, this answer choice does not actually *strengthen* the argument, because it doesn't shore up the assumption that the dates of the coins are valid evidence for when the kitchen implements were dropped. It's still possible those coins slipped through the mass of kitchen implements, which would break the author's conclusion.

(C) is Out of Scope because *value* is wholly irrelevant to the time-frame issue.

(D) provides an answer to *why* the items were dropped into the well, but not *when*. This answer gives no indication as to the actual date the items were dropped into the well or how that date compares to the date the coins were dropped in. Therefore, it does not address the author's conclusion.

(E) seems at first to add to the ordered chronology of the items in the well, but is too vague to be a valid strengthener. First, jewelry which was "*probably* made around 300 ad." could very well have been made after 375 ad. Second, coins are arguably far more likely to be tossed into a well sooner after production than jewelry, which would not normally be tossed into a well until considered junk. Third, jewelry is small and could possibly slip through the other items in the well, down to a lower level.

While the correct strengthener or weakener need not prove or disprove an argument, it should unambiguously take the argument in one direction. Granted, eliminating this answer could be tough if you hadn't predicted that this question would follow a common pattern found in Strengthen/Weaken questions on the LSAT: the evidence identifies a

phenomenon, the conclusion provides a cause, the assumption says there is no other explanation, a weakener provides an alternative explanation, and a strengthener eliminates an alternative explanation.

14. (A) Parallel Flaw

Step 1: Identify the Question Type

A question stem asking for the similar reasoning or, as here, the reasoning that most closely "resembles" the reasoning in the stimulus, is a Parallel Reasoning question. Notice in addition that the stem specifies that the reasoning is flawed. Your knowledge of common flaw types can come in handy here.

Step 2: Untangle the Stimulus

The author concludes (indicated by the conclusion Keyword *so*) that investigators have not proven a blaze was caused by campers or lightning. The evidence provided is that investigators: 1) have not proven the blaze was caused by campers; and 2) have not proven the blaze was caused by lightning.

Step 3: Make a Prediction

Often, on the LSAT, authors assume that there is no other alternative. This question, however, is a reversal of that. Here, the author assumes that there *are* other potential causes of this type or magnitude of forest fire. However, it potentially could be true that *only* campers or lightning could have caused the fire even if investigators cannot prove which of the two is at work.

Start by eliminating answers that don't have the right type of conclusion. Here, the conclusion should relate to two things both not having been proved.

For Parallel Flaw questions, if eliminating answers based on conclusions does not get you all the way to the correct answer, paraphrase the flaw type and look for an answer that commits a similar flaw. Here, the failure to prove individually that one thing or another happened doesn't mean it can't be narrowed down to those two potential results.

Step 4: Evaluate the Answer Choices

(A) concludes that Kim has no reason to believe either Sada or Brown will win the election. This conclusion is in the ballpark of investigators not having proved either of two things happened. If you are simply going through conclusions, keep this choice. If you look at the answer choice as a whole, however, you'll notice the evidence matches the evidence in the stimulus nicely: 1) no reason to believe Sada will win and 2) no reason to believe Brown will win. In concluding that Kim has no reason to believe either Sada or Brown will win, the author ignores the possibility that only those two are in the election and, thus, one of them *must* win. This choice matches and is correct.

(B) concludes "one theory is as plausible as the other," which doesn't match the conclusion in the stimulus. This conclusion indicates either of two choices are possible, whereas the original combines both choices, saying neither have been proved.

(C) can be eliminated by the qualifier *most*. Such quantity qualifiers and level of certainty qualifiers (e.g., probably) are often more handy than conclusion type in eliminating answer choices. Also, the stimulus's conclusion indicates two things cannot be proven, while this answer clearly states that the engineers *are* from out of town.

(D), as with **(C)**, can be eliminated because it clearly states what *is* the case, rather than that two things cannot be known or proven. Likewise, it focuses on quantities of "some," which were not present in the stimulus.

(E) talks about evidence that could show two things, whereas the stimulus indicated lack of evidence. Additionally, this answer choice adds the possibilities together to say *both* could have been driving, which is a different flaw than assuming there are other possibilities, when there might not actually be.

15. (C) Paradox

Step 1: Identify the Question Type

The question stem explicitly refers to a paradox, though any question that asks you to *explain* or *resolve* a result is a Paradox question.

Step 2: Untangle the Stimulus

Paradox questions, along with Inference questions, are not argument based. Don't spend your time looking for a conclusion, because it won't be there. Instead, identify the two seemingly contradictory facts. Here, more birds are eating many mosquitoes, but the mosquito population has grown.

Step 3: Make a Prediction

The resolution to a paradox will often involve some alternative factor that the author did not consider or mention. In this case, look for a reason why the increased bird population indirectly led to an increase in mosquitoes despite all the mosquitoes eaten by those birds. Nevertheless, because there are so many possible answers, do not try to predict specifically what happened.

Step 4: Evaluate the Answer Choices

(C) matches the prediction by indicating that the birds ate more predators of mosquito than they ate mosquitoes, thus actually decreasing the overall amount of mosquitoes eaten.

(A) would explain why the birds would not greatly decrease the mosquito population, but does not explain why the mosquitoes would actually increase in number.

(B) is nearly identical to **(A)**. Be wary when two choices are so similar—it probably means both are wrong. Again, this answer choice would explain why the birds would not have a huge effect in decreasing the mosquito population, but it does not explain why the mosquitoes would actually increase in number.

(D) is a 180. It provides another reason why the mosquito population should have decreased, so it only deepens the mystery rather than resolving it.

(E) is a tempting choice, but actually could either resolve or complicate the paradox depending on whether the time period at issue coincides with a cyclical decrease (deepening the mystery) or a cyclical increase (resolving the paradox).

16. (D) Inference

Step 1: Identify the Question Type

Question stems that ask you to complete the argument should be treated as an Inference question. The testmakers do not want you to creatively extrapolate to a conclusion that *could* follow; they want you to select the answer that must be true based on the earlier statements.

Step 2: Untangle the Stimulus

The author sets up an analogy between Roxanne's promise to Luke to finish their report with a hypothetical lunch date in which one planned participant fell ill. The author asserts that the other would not expect the ill friend to attend, and so it would not be wrong for the ill friend to miss the lunch.

Step 3: Make a Prediction

Apply the terms of the hypothetical as closely as possible to Roxanne and Luke. In the hypothetical, the conclusion is that because the friend did not expect attendance due to a change in circumstances, then it would not be wrong to be absent. Therefore, you want the choice that concludes Roxanne would not be wrong in failing to finish the report due to a change in circumstances, if Luke did not expect her to finish.

Step 4: Evaluate the Answer Choices

(D) matches the prediction with the components "not expect" then it would "not be wrong" to "fail to finish."

(A) deviates from the hypothetical by focusing on what Roxanne believes (not Luke) and also by concluding that Roxanne would be wrong for finishing the report (when the correct answer needs to say she would *not* be wrong for *not* finishing it).

(B) deviates from the hypothetical because it involves Roxanne actually finishing the report, while the hypothetical involves *not* keeping the promise or appointment. Additionally, this choice mentions Luke did not expect the *deadline* to be postponed, whereas to match, it would need to say that he would not expect Roxanne to keep her promise.

(C) gives an incorrect contrapositive of the correct answer. The hypothetical (and, thus, the correct answer) could be phrased as, if not expected to keep promise → not wrong. However, this answer choice says: if expected to keep promise → wrong. It negates without reversing.

(E), like (A), incorrectly concludes that Roxanne would be wrong to finish the report, when the correct answer would need to say that she's *not* wrong for *not* finishing.

17. (C) Weaken

Step 1: Identify the Question Type

The question stem concisely directs you to weaken the politician's argument.

Step 2: Untangle the Stimulus

Identifying the politician's conclusion is a bit difficult. The first sentence sounds like an opinion that could be the conclusion of the argument. However, none of the remaining sentences provide any evidence that children hurting other children is a major social problem. The second sentence makes a causal claim: based on a recent experiment, "watching violent films is at least partly responsible for this aggressive behavior." The remainder of the stimulus outlines the result of the experiment that supports the causal claim. Thus, the conclusion is that violent films induce aggressive behavior in children toward other children. The evidence is a correlation between children who watched a film of people punching a clown doll subsequently hitting a clown doll more frequently than children who did not watch the video.

Step 3: Make a Prediction

This is a causal argument with a scope shift twist. Generally, in causal arguments the question is whether assumed causation (watching a violent film and then being violent) is actually just correlation. However, here the conclusion goes beyond blaming violent films for violence against Bobo dolls and actually blames violent films for child aggression toward other children—quite a leap! To weaken this argument, find an answer that suggests that punching Bobo does not mean a kid is more likely to smack his human pals.

Step 4: Evaluate the Answer Choices

(C) works. The conclusion that a violent film causes aggressive behavior in children is weakened if there is no difference shown between kids who watched the video and kids who did not in regard to their aggression toward other children. This is an example of a Weaken question that is answerable by merely focusing on damaging the conclusion, without even considering the assumption.

(A) shows some kids are willing to stand up to their peers, but the argument doesn't address that. Those kids may be the outliers. It's still possible that the video caused the violence against the doll and subsequently against other children.

(B) is incorrect because a single contradictory example will not weaken a causal argument that already acknowledges exceptions (because the stimulus says *most*).

(D) is a 180, suggesting that violent films do induce aggression in children, not only directly in those that watch them, but also indirectly in those that pick up the behavior from those that had watched the film.

(E) is irrelevant to whether the violent films cause aggression. Additionally, this answer choice doesn't distinguish between the two groups of children.

18. (E) Principle (Apply/Inference)

Step 1: Identify the Question Type

The question stem informs you that the stimulus contains a principle or general rule and directs you to select an answer that is inconsistent with that principle. Because the principle is in the stimulus, that makes this an Apply the Principle question. Additionally, rather than looking for the specific situation where the principle is valid, you are looking for the one answer choice where it is not. That makes this akin to an EXCEPT question, even though the stem doesn't specifically state so. This example should remind you to read all question stems carefully for every hint they provide.

Step 2: Untangle the Stimulus

While some Principle questions contain an argument in the stimulus, Apply questions rarely do. Here, the question stem indicates you need only identify the general rule in the stimulus. That general rule is to not restrict the actions of adults or interfere in the results of those actions, with the exception of preventing negative effects on others.

Step 3: Make a Prediction

To contradict the rule, the correct answer should contain a restriction on the actions of an adult or interference in the results of those actions without the goal of preventing negative effects on others.

Step 4: Evaluate the Answer Choices

(E) matches the prediction because it involves a restriction on adults consuming products that only harm themselves, not others.

(A) is consistent with the rule because it involves restricting only actions that are disruptive to others.

(B) is consistent with the rule because it promotes a lack of restrictions (everyone should be allowed to profit).

(C) is consistent with the rule because it finds a way around harming others while allowing the greatest freedom.

(D) is consistent with the rule because it involves restricting speeders based on the negative effects on others that speeding often has.

19. (E) Assumption (Necessary)

Step 1: Identify the Question Type

The question asks you to identify the assumption on which the argument *depends*, making this a Necessary Assumption question. You can use the Denial Test, if needed.

Step 2: Untangle the Stimulus

The author concludes that the earthworm (*L. rubellus*) likely caused the fern's disappearance and a thinning of the leaf litter. The author bases this on a correlation of many such worms in areas in which the fern has vanished.

Step 3: Make a Prediction

Again, you see the classic LSAT pattern of causality. If an author jumps to causation, the author assumes that: 1) there is not an alternative cause; 2) it is not reverse causation; and 3) it is not coincidence. Seek a choice indicating one of those three, but also notice that there is a built-in alternative cause mentioned in the stimulus (the unusually thin leaf litter).

Step 4: Evaluate the Answer Choices

(E) matches the prediction by removing the possibility that reverse causality (that the disappearance of the ferns caused the thriving of the worms) is at play. Use the Denial Test to check your answer. If the worms *do* favor thin leaf litter layers, then it's unlikely they would have moved into the fern's territory while the fern was still thriving. That would hurt the conclusion that the worms caused the fern's disappearance, and the original statement, therefore, must be necessary to the argument.

(A) is Extreme and doesn't need to be true for the conclusion to follow. Even if goblin ferns aren't everywhere, there is a thick layer of leaf litter, and it still could be true that the worm is responsible for their disappearance.

(B) seems to work at first because it indicates native worms are not an alternative cause, but it's actually too extreme to be necessary. Employ the Denial Test: Even if some native worms ate leaf litter, it would not destroy the conclusion that *L. rubellus* is the real perpetrator.

(C) has nothing to do with whether or not *L. rubellus* is responsible for the dead ferns.

(D) is a strengthener and Extreme. Employ the Denial Test: even if there were at least a spot or two where the ferns and worms are both found, that would not destroy the conclusion. Maybe the ferns are on their way out.

20. (B) Flaw

Step 1: Identify the Question Type

The phrase "vulnerable to criticism" indicates a flaw question. Keep common flaw types in mind as you read the stimulus.

Step 2: Untangle the Stimulus

The author concludes that, for most people in industrialized nations, taking aspirin would cause improved health. The medical reporter concludes this based on the fact that aspirin lessens the risk and severity of heart disease, which is one of the most common types of health problems in these countries.

Step 3: Make a Prediction

To answer a Flaw question efficiently you should be fluent in and consider the common LSAT flaws. This stimulus implicates a few. First, the argument assumes that the benefits of aspirin for heart health outweigh any potential unmentioned negative effects on overall health. Relatedly, there is a scope shift from heart health to better overall health. Thirdly, there is a subtle proportion versus actual number problem. The evidence suggests only that heart disease is one of the "most common" diseases, but that does not mean it will affect "most people." In which case, taking aspirin might not necessarily help "most people," as the conclusion suggests. For instance, it's quite possible that the "most common" disease, only strikes a quarter of the population.

Step 4: Evaluate the Answer Choices

(B) implicates the classic proportion versus actual number flaw and is the correct response. The author ignores that possibility that most people might not be affected by the most common disease. While you might think, "But everybody would potentially be at risk and would be better off if they lowered their risk," the conclusion is not whether it makes sense for most people to lower their risk, but rather—more forcefully—argues that most people will actually have better health.

(A) describes a piece of evidence (which could be accepted as true) as an assumption. The "be in better health" mentioned in the conclusion need not be the actual prevention of some cases of heart disease; the argument could still work even if taking the aspirin merely caused a lowering of the severity of heart disease and, thereby, those people would still "be in better health."

(C) is not a flaw in the argument. Even if the author ignores that tackling heart disease will have little effect on other diseases, the conclusion that lessening heart disease has some benefit for overall health could still be true. Not all possibilities necessarily need to be considered.

(D) is Extreme. It presents another example of a possibility that the author does not need to consider. This choice would correctly describe a flaw had the author concluded aspirin is the best way to improve heart health. However, the author merely asserts that taking aspirin is one way to improve health.

(E) describes a representativeness flaw, and is therefore not correct. The author's conclusion is only about people in industrialized nations, and therefore, even if the studies were only conducted in industrialized nations, they would still be relevant evidence and, thus, the conclusion could still be accurate. If a Flaw answer choice is phrased as an ignored possibility, to be correct that possibility, if true, would have to weaken the argument. This one wouldn't.

21. (C) Inference

Step 1: Identify the Question Type

A question stem that asks you to determine which answer *must be true* based on the statements in the stimulus is an Inference question. While the correct answer does not have to take the entire stimulus into account, it cannot go beyond the information in the stimulus.

Step 2: Untangle the Stimulus

Inventory your facts from the Inference stimulus, but also pay extra attention to statements that are emphasized or can be combined. Contrast Keywords are your best friends on the test, as they will usually highlight something important. Here, the *but* shines the spotlight on amateur scientists and their significant contributions. The last phrase in the paragraph tells you these amateur scientists are motivated by the love of discovery.

Step 3: Make a Prediction

Linking these statements about amateur scientists together yields the deduction that the significant contributions of amateur scientists were motivated by the love of discovery.

For an Inference question, if you can link two statements together to make a deduction, scan the answers for that deduction before considering other choices. If you do not see that deduction then assess all the choices, keeping in mind that Extreme and Out of Scope answers are common Inference red flags.

Step 4: Evaluate the Answer Choices

(C) matches the prediction and is correct. It is not a concern that the answer does not mention amateur scientists; the common term used to link two statements will typically not show up in the answer. If A → B and B → C, the deduction that will show up in the answer will be A → C, with the middle, common term, B, dropping out.

(A) very well could be true, but certainly does not have to be. The "many" significant contributions made by amateur scientists only necessarily implies (on the LSAT) at least one. Additionally, all of those contributions could have been made by a single or a very small number of amateur scientists, each of whom could have won a Nobel prize because professional scientists only "typically," not always, win the prize.

Therefore, it is possible that every single amateur scientist who made a significant contribution also won the Nobel prize.

(B) is Extreme. While the stimulus says professional scientists (who usually win the Nobel prize) *are often* motivated by money or fame, that does not mean "mostly." Additionally, those winners might *also* be motivated by the love of discovery; motivations are not necessarily mutually exclusive.

(D) makes an Irrelevant Comparison. It is very possible, based on the information provided, but nothing concrete indicates that it *must* be true. Which group has made more significant contributions is not discussed, and a discussion of what group made the "greater overall contribution to science" would be highly subjective even with far more information.

(E) may be true, but isn't supported. The stimulus says amateurs are motivated by love of discovery and have gone on to make significant contributions, but it does not say how the love of discovery may affect professionals.

22. (B) Weaken

Step 1: Identify the Question Type

The question stem clearly directs you to weaken the company president's argument.

Step 2: Untangle the Stimulus

The company president concludes that they should favor sales candidates with engineering degrees rather than sales experience because most of their best sales representatives had engineering degrees, but not much sales experience.

Step 3: Make a Prediction

This is another classic LSAT causal argument. The company president assumes that the engineering degree is the cause of the success of the sales representatives. Generally, predict that the correct answer will give some other reason for the relative success of the existing sales representatives besides their engineering degrees.

Step 4: Evaluate the Answer Choices

(B) is somewhat subtle, but it does match the prediction of an alternative explanation for the success of sales representatives with engineering degrees. If the majority of sales reps at the company (regardless of success) have engineering degrees, then that increases the odds that the most successful reps will be ones with engineering degrees. This means the results the company president cites are really due to a numbers game, rather than a genuine advantage of engineering degrees.

(A) is Out of Scope. The company president bases his conclusion on the fact that *most* (more than 50%) of the best sales reps came to the job already with an engineering degree. That *some* (at least one) sales reps got a degree after being hired doesn't affect the president's conclusion. The conclusion only modestly recommends that candidates with engineering degrees should be favored rather than absolutely dictating that only candidates with engineering degrees be selected.

(C) is arguably a 180 strengthener because it provides a potential reason to hire reps with engineering degrees, as they will be able to better relate to their customers. However, customers, in general, are likely Out of Scope for this argument.

(D) is also incorrect. While it provides a reason why it may be difficult to fill many of the positions with candidates with engineering degrees, it in no way provides a reason against favoring those who do have those degrees.

(E) is problematic because it provides only some counterexamples. Because the author's conclusion is not absolute, the existence of one or two counterexamples will not weaken it. Perhaps those people who were not good at their job and were hired without sales experience were also without an engineering degree.

23. (A) Method of Argument

Step 1: Identify the Question Type

This question stem doesn't give you much to go by. Nevertheless, if you read the stem *and* the verbs starting each answer choice, you can see the question is *how* the anthropologist makes her argument. Thus, this is a Method of Argument question.

Step 2: Untangle the Stimulus

For Method of Argument questions, focus on the mechanical structure of the argument (points of view, examples, counterexamples, types of evidence, etc.) rather than the topic. Here, the first sentence is a generalization about a phenomenon found in all cultures. The second sentence says some researchers explain that phenomenon and gives a supporting example. The third sentence, which starts with the contrast Keyword *but*, introduces the author's conclusion: those researchers' explanation is unwarranted. It also presents the author's potential alternative explanation, based on the same example cited earlier.

Step 3: Make a Prediction

The correct answer will describe how the author presents someone else's explanation, claim that explanation is unwarranted, and then provide an alternative explanation.

Step 4: Evaluate the Answer Choices

(A) matches the prediction. Notice the modest language in the stimulus ("might instead") matches the modest tone of this answer choice ("also compatible with an alternative explanation").

(B) is both Extreme and a Distortion. The anthropologist does not *prove* the researchers' explanation is false. This choice also improperly asserts that the other researchers' evidence was inadequate, even though the anthropologist points to the same example. Finally, this answer choice fails to include the vital component of providing an alternative explanation.

(C) also is Extreme. The author simply says that there "might instead" be another explanation, but does not state that the alternative explanation is "more plausible."

(D) is incorrect because the author cites the same example as the researchers. The anthropologist does not assert the example is *incompatible* with the rival explanation, just that the example could also be compatible with another explanation. Therefore, the anthropologist does not argue "in support of one explanation," just that more than one explanation exists.

(E) is tempting because the anthropologist does argue that reverse causality might be at play: instead of practicality causing taboos, taboos caused practical workarounds. However, this answer choice is also Extreme. The anthropologist does not argue that the events occurred in a different sequence, but that they *might* have. Always pay attention to the strength of language in the stimulus.

24. (C) Flaw

Step 1: Identify the Question Type

The phrase "vulnerable to criticism" indicates a Flaw question.

Step 2: Untangle the Stimulus

The conclusion is that "this seems to be successful." Any time the conclusion includes a vague term such as *this*, make sure your paraphrase of the conclusion incorporates a definition of that vague term. Therefore, paraphrase the conclusion as: the adolescent anti-drinking pledge seems to be successful. The evidence is a survey showing almost all 17-year-old drinkers did not take the pledge, while "many" 17-year-old non-drinkers did. Thus, the author assumes the pledge itself causes teens to refrain from drinking.

Step 3: Make a Prediction

This stimulus includes yet another classic correlation-to-causation argument. Look for an answer choice that says the author ignores a possible alternative cause, reverse causality, or coincidence.

Step 4: Evaluate the Answer Choices

(C) matches the prediction (*association* is synonymous with *correlation*).

(A) goes astray by raising morality, which is Out of Scope.

(B) is incorrect because the author limits his scope to merely concluding that the pledge is successful, not that it is the best or recommended method. While the author does not consider alternative methods, choosing not to do so isn't a flaw.

(D) is incorrect. While confusing necessary and sufficient conditions is a classic LSAT flaw, this flaw typically only occurs if there is Formal Logic in the stimulus. Nothing in this stimulus suggests this pledge is necessary. The vague language ("many" and "almost all") shows that it is not.

(E) indicates a confusion of proportions, but is irrelevant to the success of the pledge (i.e., whether taking the pledge causes teens to refrain from drinking). This is an example of an LSAT answer that, although it may sound profound, is off base. Never pick an answer for the sole reason that you do not really understand what it means. The more you predict, the less chance you will fall for such answers.

25. (B) Assumption (Sufficient)

Step 1: Identify the Question Type

Do not be thrown by the words *main conclusion* or *inferred*. The question is not asking for the main conclusion, or for an inference. Make sure you read the entire question stem. This question really wants to know what assumption allows the conclusion to logically follow/be properly drawn/be properly inferred. This is a Sufficient Assumption question. Keep an eye out for Formal Logic, which is often found in Sufficient Assumption questions.

Step 2: Untangle the Stimulus

The conclusion is indicated by the contrast Keyword *but*. The literary critic says "this is not the case." Make sure you fill in what *this* is. In other words, the author concludes folktales do not lack deeper meaning. The evidence is that due to the process of each generation's storytellers adding something to the story, folktales provide great insight into the wisdom of the culture.

Step 3: Make a Prediction

There is a scope shift from the evidence—"providing insight into the wisdom of the culture"—to the conclusion—"deep[er] meaning." One common assumption is that the evidence is relevant to the conclusion, or that: if I have this evidence then I can reasonably reach this conclusion. Because three of the answers **(A)**, **(B)**, and **(D)** are in "If"/Then form (*any* means *if* in Formal Logic), test them to see if one of them indicates that: if something provides insight into a culture (evidence) then it has a deeper meaning (conclusion).

Step 4: Evaluate the Answer Choices

(B) matches that prediction.

(A) restates the evidence and does not bridge the gap to the conclusion's new term (deeper meaning).

(C) goes Out of Scope by introducing the term *beauty*. Additionally, this answer choice goes backward, saying not every tale without deep meaning is told for entertainment, while the literary critic argues not every tale told for entertainment lacks deep meaning.

(D) reverses without negating, indicating that if a tale has deep meaning (conclusion) then it provides great insight into the wisdom of the culture (evidence). However, you need to prove that the evidence leads to the conclusion, not the other way around.

(E) is too modest to be the correct sufficient assumption. The task of a sufficient assumption is to prove or guarantee that the conclusion is true and, thus, is a rare LSAT question type that usually requires an absolute, forceful answer. Indicating that a story does not necessarily lack deeper meaning does not prove that they do have deeper meaning. Additionally, the stimulus does not indicate that folktales are told "primarily" for entertainment, just that they are told in an entertaining way.

Section II: Logic Games

Game 1: Manuscript Ages

Q#	Question Type	Correct	Difficulty
1	Acceptability	E	★
2	Must Be False (CANNOT Be True)	A	★
3	"If" / Could Be True	E	★★
4	Must Be False (CANNOT Be True)	C	★★
5	"If" / Could Be True EXCEPT	D	★★★

Game 2: Storing Petri Dishes

Q#	Question Type	Correct	Difficulty
6	Acceptability	B	★
7	"If" / Could Be True	E	★
8	"If" / Could Be True	C	★
9	"If" / Must Be True	B	★★
10	"If" / Must Be True	C	★★
11	"If" / Could Be True	A	★★

Game 3: Juice and Snack Deliveries

Q#	Question Type	Correct	Difficulty
12	Acceptability	A	★
13	"If" / Must Be True	D	★★
14	"If" / Could Be True	C	★★
15	"If" / Could Be True	A	★★
16	Could Be True	D	★★★
17	Rule Substitution	B	★★★

Game 4: Cases for Paralegals

Q#	Question Type	Correct	Difficulty
18	Acceptability	D	★
19	Partial Acceptability (CANNOT)	E	★★★
20	"If" / Could Be True	A	★★★
21	"If" / Must Be False EXCEPT	C	★★★
22	Partial Acceptability (CANNOT)	D	★★★
23	"If" / Complete and Accurate List	B	★★★★

Game 1: Manuscript Ages

Step 1: Overview

Situation: Researcher determining the age of manuscripts

Entities: Seven manuscripts (F, G, H, L, M, P, S)

Action: Strict Sequencing. Your task is to determine the order in which the manuscripts were written. This is a Strict Sequencing game.

Limitations: No two manuscripts were written at the same time, so this is standard one-to-one Strict Sequencing.

Step 2: Sketch

This is as typical as sketching gets. Simply list the seven entities and set up a series of seven spaces to determine the order. To avoid any confusion, you can also label the left side "early" and the right side "late."

Step 3: Rules

Rule 1 sets up a loose relationship between three entities. In order, F will be the earliest, with H sometime later, which will be some time earlier than S:

$$F...H...S$$

Because there must be two manuscripts written after F, F cannot be sixth or seventh. Similarly, S cannot be first or second because there must be two manuscripts written before it. H must have at least one manuscript before and after it, so it cannot be first or last.

Rule 2 sets up an absolute block, with G immediately followed by P:

$$\boxed{GP}$$

Because G was written before P, G cannot be last and P cannot be first.

Rules 3 and 4 limit the placement of L and M. L cannot be any of the first four manuscripts (because it has to be predated by at least four others) and M cannot be any of the last four (because it was written before at least four others). That means L has to be one of the last three and M has to be one of the first three.

You can simply mark "No L" under spots 1–4 and "No M" under spots 4–7. Alternatively, or in addition, you can draw an L over the last three spots with arrows and do the same for M over the first three spots.

Rule 5 simply precludes H from being fifth, so simply mark "No H" under the fifth spot.

Step 4: Deductions

This game has a lot of restrictions. In fact, every space is limited somehow. The most limited spaces are at the ends.

The earliest manuscript can't be H, L, S, or P, so that leaves only G, M, and S. Similarly, the latest manuscript can't be F, G, H, or M, so that leaves only L, P, and S.

Unfortunately, further deductions are almost impossible to come by. After all, only one entity, H, is duplicated in the rules. Furthermore, keeping H out of the fifth space doesn't have any noticeable effect on where F and S can go. The block of G and P, meanwhile, seems to be acceptable in any pair of consecutive slots.

Therefore, the final sketch consists of two sequencing rules and a sketch with lots of restrictions under the spaces. Not all test takers prefer to write out each of the negative deductions underneath the rules. Certainly with Rule 5, "No H" should be under the fifth slot, but, seeing the GP block written to the side, for example, may be sufficient for you to spot that G can't be last and P can't be first, without writing those negative deductions under the first and seventh spots. It's personal preference and continual practice that will inform you as to whether or not writing all the negative deductions is helpful for you or whether it unnecessarily muddles the sketch.

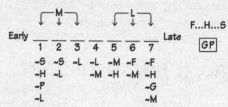

Step 5: Questions

1. (E) Acceptability

As with any Acceptability question, simply go through the rules one at a time, eliminating any answer choice that violates those rules.

Rule 1 indicates that F must be earlier than H, which must be earlier than S. That eliminates **(C)**, which has H earlier than F. Rule 2 states that G comes immediately before P. That eliminates **(A)**, which places H in between them. Rule 3 states that there must be at least four manuscripts before L, which eliminates **(D)**. No answer violates Rule 4. However, H is fifth in **(B)**, which violates Rule 5. That leaves **(E)** as the correct answer.

2. (A) Must Be False (CANNOT Be True)

The correct answer here will be a manuscript that cannot be written third. The only manuscript that's clearly not written third is L (by Rule 3), but that's not a choice. The best strategy would be to skip this question and draw sketches for the set's "New-If" questions first. Then, you could use those sketches, along with the correct answer for the Acceptability question, to eliminate manuscripts that could be written third.

Otherwise, the answers must be tested one at a time. Starting with **(A)**, if S was written third, then F and H would be the first two manuscripts. However, that prevents M from being one of the first three manuscripts. That violates Rule 4, so S cannot be written third. That makes this the correct answer.

If you had skipped this question temporarily, here's what you would find after all sketches were drawn: H is third in the Acceptability question and in the sketch for the third question of the set, so that would eliminate **(D)**. P, M, and G could all be third in the sketch for the fifth question of the set, as so:

M G P F L H S
‾‾ ‾‾ ‾‾ ‾‾ ‾‾ ‾‾ ‾‾

G P M F L H S
‾‾ ‾‾ ‾‾ ‾‾ ‾‾ ‾‾ ‾‾

F/M M/F G P L H S
‾‾‾ ‾‾‾ ‾‾ ‾‾ ‾‾ ‾‾ ‾‾
 1   2   3 4 5 6 7

That would eliminate **(B)**, **(C)**, and **(E)**.

3. (E) "If" / Could Be True

This question creates a block of MH. Combining this information with Rule 1, this sets up a loose string of:

F...MH...S

However, by Rule 4, M can only be one of the first three manuscripts. With F before M and H, M can only be second or third. Therefore, test out both possibilities.

If M was second, F would be first and H would be second. That leaves the block of GP, which could be in any remaining pair of spaces, L, which can be in any of the last three spaces, and S, which can be anywhere:

F M H
‾‾ ‾‾ ‾‾ ‾‾ ‾‾ ‾‾ ‾‾
1 2 3 4 5 6 7

If M was third, H would be fourth. F would be one of the first two manuscripts. However, that creates a problem. There'd be no other manuscripts to take up the last spot before M and H. G and P must be together. L can't be in the first two spaces, and S has to come after H. That means the previous sketch, with F, M, and H in spaces 1, 2, and 3, respectively, is the only possible outcome.

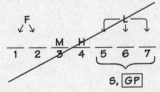

With that, F must first, so that eliminates **(A)**. H has to be third, which eliminates **(B)**, **(C)**, and **(D)**. That leaves **(E)** as the only possible answer.

4. (C) Must Be False (CANNOT Be True)

The correct answer to this question will be a manuscript that cannot be written fourth. From the master sketch, L and M cannot be fourth (by Rules 3 and 4), but neither of those are

listed. Again, this question is worth skipping temporarily. Once the sketch for the fifth question is drawn, the sketch for that question, as well as the ones for the first and third questions, can be used to eliminate manuscripts that could be fourth. Otherwise, the answers must be tested one at a time. For **(A)**, if F is fourth, then H and S will be in two of the last three spaces (Rule 1). L will also be in one of the last three spaces. That leaves M, G and P for the first three spaces. This is acceptable; therefore, this choice can be eliminated.

                 F
‾‾ ‾‾ ‾‾ ‾‾ ‾‾ ‾‾ ‾‾
1 2 3 4 5 6 7
  M, |GP| H...S, L

For **(B)**, if G is fourth, then P would be fifth (Rule 2). With that block placed, M can be any of the first three spaces, L can be in either of the last two spaces, and F, H, and S can fill in the remaining spaces in that order, with S definitely either sixth or seventh. This is acceptable, so this choice can be eliminated.

      ┌─ M ─┐
      ↓ ↓ ↓
‾‾ ‾‾ ‾‾ G P L/S S/L
1 2 3 4 5 6   7
└───┘
 F...H

For **(C)**, if H is fourth, then F will be one of the first three spaces and S will be one of the last three spaces (Rule 1). M is also in one of the first three spaces (Rule 4) and L is in one of the last three spaces (Rule 3). That leaves one more space before H and one more space after H. However, the remaining two entities are G and P, which must be consecutive. This cannot happen, making this the correct answer.

      ┌─ M ─┐   ┌─ L ─┐
      ↓ ↓ ↓   ↓ ↓ ↓
‾‾ ‾‾ ‾‾ H ‾‾ ‾‾ ‾‾
1 2 3 4 5 6 7
      F |GP|?   S

For the record, if you had used sketches from other questions, S was fourth in the answer to the Acceptability question, eliminating **(E)**. In the third question, G could be fourth:

F M H G P L/S S/L
‾‾ ‾‾ ‾‾ ‾‾ ‾‾ ‾‾ ‾‾
1 2 3 4 5 6   7

That eliminates **(B)**, and in the fifth question, either F or P could be fourth:

M, |GP|
‾‾ ‾‾ ‾‾ F L H S
1 2 3 4 5 6 7

F/M M/F G P L H S
‾‾‾ ‾‾‾ ‾‾ ‾‾ ‾‾ ‾‾ ‾‾
 1   2   3 4 5 6 7

That would eliminate **(A)** and **(D)**.

5. (D) "If" / Could Be True EXCEPT

For this question, P will be written earlier than H. Because P was written immediately after G (Rule 2), that means the entire GP block must be before H. Because F also has to be written before H (Rule 1), H cannot be earlier than fourth. H can't be fifth (Rule 5) and it can't be last, because it has to be before S (Rule 1). Therefore, it must be either fourth or sixth.

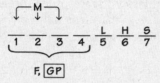

If H is fourth, F, G and P will take up the first three spots. However, that leaves no room for M, which must be one of the first three manuscripts (Rule 4). Therefore, H can't be fourth, it must be sixth.

With H sixth, S must be last (Rule 5). Because L has to be one of the last three manuscripts (Rule 3), L must be fifth.

$$\overbrace{\underline{}\ \underline{}\ \underline{}\ \underline{}}_{F,\ \boxed{GP}}\underset{1\ \ 2\ \ 3\ \ 4}{\quad}\ \underset{5}{\underline{L}}\ \underset{6}{\underline{H}}\ \underset{7}{\underline{S}}$$

F and the block of GP can take up any remaining spaces. M can be any of the first three spaces. With that, all of the answer choices are possible except for **(D)**, because L has to be fifth. That makes it the correct answer.

Game 2: Storing Petri Dishes

Step 1: Overview

Situation: Storing petri dishes in an empty refrigerator

Entities: Six petri dishes (1, 2, 3, 4, 5, 6)

Action: Strict Sequencing. Because the rules call for the six petri dishes to be "above" and "below" one another, the order matters, and that's why this game is classified as Sequencing. However, if you perceived the game as Distribution, it is likely your sketch would look exactly the same—you would just need to be mindful of the twist of spatially organizing the groups. Either characterization of the game would work; the important part will be building the rules into the sketch and making accurate deductions.

Limitations: The overview provides no limitation on shelf space. However, because every petri dish goes on a shelf, and there are more petri dishes than shelves, you know some shelves will have more than one petri dish. Don't assume even placement (i.e., each shelf gets two petri dishes). In fact, it's possible that one or more shelves go unused. As always, the rules will limit the possibilities.

Step 2: Sketch

Because you have to assign the petri dishes to shelves, list the numbers 1–6 (representing the petri dishes) and set up a chart with three rows labeled top, middle, and bottom (drawn vertically as they would appear in the refrigerator):

```
        1 2 3 4 5 6

Top:

Mid:

Bot:
```

Because the number of dishes per shelf isn't defined, leave the shelves empty for now until the rules provide more information.

Step 3: Rules

Rule 1 sets a maximum of three petri dishes for each shelf. While this means the petri dishes can't all be on the same shelf, it still doesn't mean that every shelf has to be used (because there could still be two shelves of three dishes each). Therefore, make a shorthand note of the maximum and move along.

Rule 2 provides some loose sequencing, with dish 2 being placed higher than dish 6:

```
2
|
6
```

This means that dish 2 can't be on the bottom shelf and dish 6 can't be on the top shelf.

Rule 3 sets up a sequencing block. Dishes 5 and 6 must be placed on consecutive shelves, in either order:

```
5  or  6
6      5
```

Rule 4 prevents dishes 1 and 4 from being on the same shelf. Since they can be on any pair of shelves, simply shorthand the rule:

```
Never  1 4
```

Step 4: Deductions

Because 5 and 6 must be on consecutive shelves, they must be on either the top and middle shelves, or the bottom and middle shelves. Either way, one of them must be on the middle shelf. It's also worth noting that dish 3 is a Floater because it is never mentioned in any rule, so we've marked it with an asterisk.

```
        1 2 3 4 5 6

Top:                ~6

Mid:    5/6

Bot:                ~2
```

There are a couple of possibilities for Limited Options, both of which can be very helpful. Because dish 6 is a key player (it is the only entity duplicated in the rules), you can set up one sketch with dish 6 in the middle (allowing you to place dish 2 on the top) and one with dish 6 on the bottom (allowing you to place dish 5 in the middle). You could also set up Limited Options depending on which dish, 5 or 6, is in the middle. Dish 6 in the middle would put dish 2 on top, and Dish 5 in the middle would put dish 6 on the bottom. Either of those approaches would yield this sketch:

```
Opt. I   Top:  2  ←    Opt. II  Top:       ←
                                            2
         Mid:  6   5            Mid:  5  ←

         Bot:      ←            Bot:  6
```

Either setup can save time on certain questions, and it's certainly worth setting up Limited Options if you recognized them. However, the game can still be handled efficiently without Limited Options.

Step 5: Questions

6. (B) Acceptability

This is a typical Acceptability question that is best handled by going through the rules and eliminating unacceptable answers. Be very careful, though. The LSAT has unintuitively put the bottom shelf at the top of each answer and the top shelf on the bottom of each answer.

Rule 1 sets a maximum of three dishes per shelf. That eliminates **(A)**, which has four dishes on the top shelf. Rule 2 states that dish 2 has to be above dish 6. That eliminates **(C)**, which puts dish 2 on the bottom shelf, which would be below dish 6 on the middle shelf. Rule 3 states that dishes 5 and 6 must be on consecutive shelves. That eliminates **(E)**, which puts one shelf in between them. Finally, Rule 4 states that dishes 1 and 4 must be on different shelves, which eliminates **(D)**. That leaves **(B)** as the correct answer.

7. (E) "If" / Could Be True

For this question, dish 6 will be on the bottom shelf by itself. Dish 5 must then by on the middle shelf (Rule 3). This alone eliminates **(A)**, **(B)**, and **(C)**. Because the bottom shelf is finished, dishes 1 and 4 must be placed on the top and middle shelves, in either order (Rule 4).

> Top: 1/4
>
> Mid: 5   4/1
>
> Bot: 6 ||

The middle shelf has to have dish 5 and either dish 1 or 4. Only **(E)** is possible in this case, making it the correct answer.

8. (C) "If" / Could Be True

If dishes 1, 2 and 3 are together, there will be no other dishes on that shelf (Rule 1). They cannot be on the bottom shelf, because dish 2 has to be above dish 6 (Rule 2). They also cannot be on the middle shelf, or dishes 5 and 6 will be separated, violating Rule 3. Therefore, they must be on the top shelf. That eliminates **(A)** and **(B)**.

With the top shelf closed, dishes 5 and 6 must be on the middle and bottom shelf, in either order (Rule 3). Dish 4 could be on either the middle or the bottom shelf. The shelf that gets dish 4 will have two dishes; the other shelf will have just one.

> Top: 1   2   3 ||
>
> Mid: 5/6 ↖
>   ↘ 4
> Bot: 6/5 ↙

That makes **(C)** the only possible answer.

9. (B) "If" / Must Be True

If one shelf has no dishes, it can't be the middle shelf. That would force dishes 5 and 6 to be separated, violating Rule 3. Furthermore, each shelf can only hold three dishes (Rule 1). If one shelf is empty, the remaining two shelves must have three dishes each. By deduction, the middle shelf—which cannot be empty—must have three dishes, making **(B)** the correct answer.

> Top: || Top: 2   5   1/4
>
> Mid: 2   5   1/4   or   Mid: 6   4/1   3
>
> Bot: 6   4/1   3   Bot: ||

10. (C) "If" / Must Be True

For this question, dish 5 and nothing else will be on the bottom. There will also be two dishes on the middle shelf, which leaves three dishes for the top shelf. Dish 6 will have to

be on the middle shelf (Rule 3), and dish 2 will have to be on the top shelf (Rule 2). Dishes 1 and 4 will be split among the top and middle shelves (Rule 4). That fills the middle shelf, leaving the remaining space on the top shelf for dish 3:

> Top: 2   1/4   3
>
> Mid: 6   4/1 ||
>
> Bot: 5 ||

While either dish 1 or 4 could be on the top shelf, dishes 2 and 3 must be, making **(C)** the correct answer. Note that **(A)** and **(B)** both contain dish 1 and **(D)** and **(E)** both contain dish 4. Although dishes 1 and 4 are not true Floaters in the sense that they were mentioned in the rules, their ability to interchange means that they will not be the answer to a must be true question unless the other one of them is definitively placed.

11. (A) "If" / Could Be True

If there's only one dish on the middle shelf, it must be 5 or 6; otherwise, those two dishes would be split on the top and bottom shelves, violating Rule 3. This sets up two options.

If dish 6 was alone on the middle shelf, dish 2 would have to be on the top shelf (Rule 2). Dishes 1 and 4 would be split on the top and bottom shelves, in either order (Rule 4). Dishes 3 and 5 could be on either the top or bottom shelf.

If dish 5 was alone on the middle shelf, dish 2 would have to be on the top shelf and dish 6 would have to be on the bottom (Rule 2). Dishes 1 and 4 would be split on the top and bottom shelves, in either order (Rule 4). Dish 3 would fill in a third space on either the top or bottom shelf.

> Top: 2   1/4   Top: 2   1/4
>
> Mid: 6 || or   Mid: 5 ||
>
> Bot: 4/1   Bot: 6   4/1

In either option, the top shelf must contain dish 2 and either dish 1 or dish 4. That makes **(A)** the only answer that could be true.

Game 3: Juice and Snack Deliveries

Step 1: Overview

Situation: A vending machine company delivering juice and snacks to schools

Entities: Four schools (Ferndale, Gladstone, Hafford, Isley)

Action: Strict Sequencing. Determine the order in which both juice and snacks are delivered to the four schools. This is a Double Strict Sequencing game; you'll need to sequence the four schools for the order of both snack and juice deliveries.

Limitations: Juice will be delivered to each school exactly once, as will snacks. That means each sequence (one for juice and one for snacks) will be one-to-one.

Step 2: Sketch

List the schools by initial. Then, set up a row for each truck (one for juice and one for snacks). In each row, draw four spaces to determine the order in which the schools are visited:

```
          F G H I
Jui:  ___ ___ ___ ___

Sna:  ___ ___ ___ ___
       1   2   3   4
```

Step 3: Rules

Rule 1 applies only to the snacks. Ferndale must be before Hafford (F...H). This means F cannot be the last school to get snacks, and H cannot be the first. Note that this rule has no effect on the order of juice deliveries.

Rule 2 states that Gladstone can't be the last school to get juice. Simply notate that by the fourth space in the juice row.

Rule 3 is as direct as it gets. Just put a G in the third space in the snack row.

Rule 4 dictates that the first school to get juice will be the same as the last school to get snacks. Make a note to the side, but be ready to consider what school that could be.

Step 4: Deductions

Sure enough, Rule 4 is the most important piece of information in this game. The last school to get snacks cannot be Ferndale (Rule 1) and it cannot be Gladstone (Rule 3). Therefore, it can only be Hafford or Isley. By Rule 4, that means the first school to get juice can only be Hafford or Isley.

```
          F G H I
Jui:  H/I ___ ___ ___
                  ~G
Sna:  ___ ___  G  H/I    F...H
       1   2   3   4
      ~H
```

This seems to be a potential for Limited Options. However, whether the school that gets juice first and snacks last is Hafford or Isley doesn't make much of a difference. If it was

Isley, then Ferndale and Hafford would be the first and second schools to get snacks, in that order (Rule 1). Otherwise, the sketches would look pretty much the same either way.

Stay focused on the school that gets juice first and snacks last, and you'll be prepared for just about anything.

Step 5: Questions

12. (A) Acceptability

As with any standard acceptability question, go through the rules one at a time, eliminating answers that violate the rules. According to Rule 1, snacks must go to Ferndale before Hafford. That eliminates **(C)**. Rule 2 states that Gladstone can't be the fourth school to get juice, which eliminates **(B)**. Rule 3 states that Gladstone must be the third school to get snacks, which eliminates **(D)**. Rule 4 states that the first school to get juice must be the same as the last school to get snacks, which eliminates **(E)**. That leaves **(A)** as the correct answer.

13. (D) "If" / Must Be True

If Hafford is the fourth school to get juice, it means Isley is the only school that could get juice first and snacks fourth. From there, the second and third school to get juice will be Ferndale and Gladstone, in either order. The first two schools to get snacks will be Ferndale and Hafford, in that order (by Rule 1):

```
Jui:   I  F/G  G/F   H

Sna:   F   H   G   I
       1   2   3   4
```

In that case, **(D)** is the only answer that must be true. **(A)** and **(B)** are merely possible and **(C)** and **(D)** must be false.

14. (C) "If" / Could Be True

If Isley is the third school to get juice, that leaves Hafford as the only school that can get juice first and snacks fourth. For the juice delivery, Gladstone cannot be fourth (Rule 2), so it must be second, leaving Ferndale fourth. For the snacks, the first two deliveries will be Ferndale and Isley, in either order.

```
Jui:   H   G   I   F

Sna:  F/I  I/F  G   H
       1   2   3   4
```

That leaves **(C)** as the only possible answer. The rest all must be false.

15. (A) "If" / Could Be True

If Isley is the first school to get snacks, then Hafford must be the school that gets juice first and snacks fourth. That leaves Ferndale as the school that gets snacks second. Because Gladstone can't be the fourth school to get juice (Rule 2), either Ferndale or Isley will get juice fourth. The second and third schools to get juice could be any of Ferndale, Gladstone, and Isley.

Jui: H ___ ___ F/I

Sna: I   F   G   H
       1   2   3   4

With that, **(A)** is the only answer that could be true. The rest all must be false.

16. (D) Could Be True
The correct answer merely has to be possible. The four incorrect answers will all be false no matter what.

If snacks were delivered to Gladstone before Ferndale, then Ferndale would be the last school to get snacks. However, that would violate Rule 1, so **(A)** can be eliminated.

If snacks were delivered to Gladstone before Isley, then Isley would be the fourth school to get snacks. That would make Isley the first school to get juice (Rule 4), making it impossible for Gladstone to also deliver juice before Isley. That eliminates **(B)**.

If Hafford gets juice before Isley, Hafford would have to be the school to get juice first and snacks fourth, but then it would get snacks after Isley, which eliminates **(C)**. Similarly, if Isley gets juice before Hafford, Isley would be the school to get juice first and snacks fourth, but then it would get snacks after Hafford, which eliminates **(E)**.

That leaves **(D)** as the only possible answer. In fact, strategic test takers will notice that this scenario is potentially laid out in the sketch for the fourth question of the set. In that "New-If" sketch, Isley could get juice before Ferndale, and the first two schools to get snacks are Isley and Ferndale, in that order, verifying this as the correct answer.

17. (B) Rule Substitution
For this question, the rule that prevents Gladstone from getting juice fourth is removed. The correct answer to this question will be a new rule that would once again prevent Gladstone from getting juice fourth without creating any new limitations.

(A) places a new limitation on Ferndale. This fails on two accounts. First, this doesn't stop Gladstone from being fourth. Second, it sets a limit on Ferndale (being the third school for juices) that wasn't originally there.

(B) limits Gladstone to the second and third juice delivery. This does revive the original limitation that prevents Gladstone from being fourth. It seems to be more restrictive, because it doesn't allow Gladstone to get juice first. However, Gladstone never could get juice first. Otherwise, it would get snacks fourth (Rule 4), and that would violate Rule 3. Therefore, this restores all of the original restrictions without adding any new ones, making this the correct answer.

For the record, **(C)** and **(D)** fail to prevent Gladstone from getting juice fourth, and they both add restrictions that were never set by the original rules (limiting the placement of Hafford and preventing Hafford from getting juice first, respectively). **(E)** doesn't work because, while it does prevent Gladstone from getting juice fourth, it adds the restriction that Ferndale can't get juice fourth—which was acceptable under the original rules.

Game 4: Cases for Paralegals

Step 1: Overview

Situation: Paralegals being assigned to cases

Entities: Five paralegals (Frank, Gina, Hiro, Kevin, Laurie) and three cases (Raimes, Sicoli, Thompson)

Action: Distribution. Distribute the paralegals to the three cases.

Limitations: Each paralegal is assigned to exactly one case, and each case must have at least one paralegal.

Step 2: Sketch

Because the paralegals will be assigned to the cases, set up three columns for the three cases. Each case gets one slot to start. List the paralegals by initial, and begin.

FGHKL

Rai	Sic	Tho
—	—	—

Step 3: Rules

Rule 1 sets up two possible outcomes, which immediately suggests setting up Limited Options. In the first option, Frank will be assigned to Raimes and Kevin will be assigned to Thompson. In the second option, note that Frank can't be assigned to Raimes and Kevin can't be assigned to Thompson.

Rule 2 states that either Frank or Gina is alone on one case. However, only one of them can be alone. This can't be built into the sketch, so make a note to the side in shorthand.

Rule 3 places Hiro. Add an H under Sicoli in both sketches created by the first rule.

Step 4: Deductions

In the first option, each case now has one paralegal assigned to it. That leaves Gina and Laurie (the Floater of this game). Gina will have to be paired with somebody, so that means Frank must be assigned the Raimes case by himself (Rule 2). Gina and Laurie will each be assigned to either of the remaining cases, either together or separately.

In the second option, there are too many possibilities to make any definite deductions. Anybody could be on the Sicoli case with Hiro, and the other cases are minimally limited. In addition, there's no way to determine with Frank or Gina will be assigned to a case alone. Therefore, this sketch remains empty except for Hiro.

Opt. I

FGHKL

Rai	Sic	Tho
F	H	K

Opt. II

FGHKL

Rai	Sic	Tho	
	H		F or G
~F		~K	not both

There's not a lot to keep track of in this game. In fact, the only rule not already incorporated into the sketch is Rule 2. Therefore, when you're stuck, consider which paralegal—Frank or Gina—has to be assigned a case alone.

Step 5: Questions

18. (D) Acceptability

This is a typical question to open up a game. Just go through the rules one at a time and knock off choices as they violate the rules.

Rule 1 sets up only two possibilities: Frank and Kevin assigned to Raimes and Thompson, respectively, or both Frank and Kevin assigned to other cases. That eliminates (A) and (E), both of which only assign Frank to Raimes without assigning Kevin to Thompson. Rule 2 states that Frank or Gina, and not both, must be on a case alone. That eliminates (C), which puts them both on cases with other paralegals. Rule 3 states that Hiro must be assigned to Sicoli, which eliminates (B) and leaves (D) as the only acceptable answer.

19. (E) Partial Acceptability (CANNOT)

Four of the answers will be an acceptable assignment of paralegals to Sicoli. The correct answer will be an assignment that cannot happen.

Every answer choice lists three paralegals. If that were true, then Raimes and Thompson would each get just one paralegal. In the first option of Rule 1, Raimes and Thompson would get Frank and Kevin. That would leave Gina, Hiro, and Laurie for Sicoli. That means (D) is acceptable. Eliminate it.

For the rest, think strategically instead of testing every answer. Per Rule 2 either Frank or Gina—but not both—must be one of the single paralegals for Raimes and Thompson. However, if Hiro, Kevin, and Laurie were assigned to Sicoli, that would put both Frank and Gina on cases alone. That's unacceptable, making (E) the correct answer.

20. (A) "If" / Could Be True

If Thompson is assigned two paralegals, then either option from Rule 1 is acceptable. Therefore, Frank could be assigned to Raimes, but that's not an answer choice, so you have to consider the second option.

In the second option, Kevin is not assigned to the Thompson case and Hiro is assigned to the Sicoli case. That leaves Frank, Gina, and Laurie for the Thompson case. Frank and Gina cannot be together, or else neither one would be assigned a solo case. Therefore, the two paralegals for the Thompson case must be Laurie with either Frank or Gina. Whoever isn't with Laurie must be assigned another case alone. Because Sicoli has already been assigned Hiro, the solo case must Raimes. However, Frank can't be assigned to Raimes in this option, so Gina gets assigned to Raimes alone, leaving Frank with Thompson. Kevin must then be assigned to Sicoli with Hiro.

Rai	Sic	Tho
G	H	L
	K	F

That means **(A)** is a possible assignment for the Raimes case.

21. (C) "If" / Must Be False EXCEPT

For this question, once the sketch is set up, four of the answer choices will be false. The correct choice will be the only answer that is possible, if not definitely true.

If one case has Gina and Laurie together, then Frank must be assigned a case alone (Rule 2). The first option from Rule 1 doesn't allow a case to have just Gina and Laurie. Therefore, this can only happen in the second option. If Frank is assigned a case alone, it must be Thompson (because he can't be assigned to Raimes in this option). With Hiro on the Sicoli case, that leaves Raimes as the only case that can be assigned to Gina and Laurie. Kevin must then be assigned to the Sicoli case with Hiro:

G		
L	F	

Rai	Sic	Tho
G	H	F
L	K	

In that case, **(C)** is true, and is the only answer that isn't false. Thus, it's the correct answer.

22. (D) Partial Acceptability (CANNOT)

Four answers to this question will be acceptable assignments for the Thompson case. The correct answer will be the one assignment that isn't possible without violating the rules.

The fastest way to answer this question is to consider the fourth question of the set. That question demonstrated that If Gina and Laurie are together with no one else, they must be

on the Raimes case, not the Thompson case. That immediately makes **(D)** the correct answer.

Otherwise, you would consider both options created by Rule 1. In the first option, Thompson is assigned Kevin. Either Gina or Laurie could be assigned with Kevin without violating another rule, so **(C)** and **(E)** are possible and, therefore, incorrect. In the second option, either Gina or Laurie could be assigned to Thompson. Gina could be there alone, forcing Frank to Sicoli (he can't be assigned to Raimes in this option) and Kevin and Laurie to Raimes or Sicoli.

Rai	Sic	Tho
K/L	H	G
	F	

That eliminates **(A)**.

Laurie could also be at Thompson alone, which would force Gina to be alone at Raimes (Rule 2) because Frank can't be at Raimes in this option. Then, Frank and Kevin would go to Sicoli.

Rai	Sic	Tho
G	H	L
	F	
	K	

That eliminates **(B)**. However, if Gina and Laurie are both assigned to Thompson, then Frank would have to be on a case alone (Rule 2). That's a problem because Frank can't be on Raimes in this option, and all other cases are now assigned other paralegals. Therefore, Gina and Laurie cannot be together on the Thompson case, confirming **(D)** as the correct answer.

23. (B) "If" / Complete and Accurate List

The correct answer to this question will list every paralegal that could be assigned to Raimes if Kevin is assigned to a case by himself.

Consider both options presented by Rule 1. In the first option, Kevin would be assigned to the Thompson case. In that option, Frank is assigned to the Raimes case alone. In the second option, for Kevin to be alone, he would have to be assigned to the Raimes case, leaving Frank or Gina to be assigned alone to the Thompson case. The other paralegals would all go to the Sicoli case.

	I.	Rai	Sic	Tho
		F	H	K
			G	
			L	

	II.	Rai	Sic	Tho
		K	H	F/G
			G/F	
			L	

That means, for this question, the only two paralegals who can be assigned to the Thompson case are Frank and Kevin. That makes **(B)** the correct answer.

Section III: Reading Comprehension
Passage 1: Keeping Small Farms Profitable

Q#	Question Type	Correct	Difficulty
1	Global	A	★
2	Inference	B	★
3	Detail	C	★
4	Global	A	★
5	Inference	D	★★★
6	Detail	D	★
7	Inference	B	★★★

Passage 2: Forward Into Photography's Past

Q#	Question Type	Correct	Difficulty
8	Logic Function	A	★
9	Inference	B	★
10	Detail	E	★
11	Global	C	★★★
12	Logic Reasoning (Parallel Reasoning)	D	★★
13	Inference	B	★★
14	Logic Reasoning (Strengthen)	A	★★★

Passage 3: Patents—The Tech Company's Best Defense

Q#	Question Type	Correct	Difficulty
15	Global	C	★★
16	Detail	B	★★
17	Inference	E	★
18	Logic Reasoning (Method of Argument)	B	★
19	Inference	A	★★
20	Logic Function	D	★
21	Logic Reasoning (Weaken)	D	★★★

Passage 4: *Calvaria major* and the Dodo Bird

Q#	Question Type	Correct	Difficulty
22	Global	B	★★
23	Detail	A	★★★
24	Logic Function	D	★★
25	Detail	A	★★★★
26	Inference	E	★★★
27	Inference (EXCEPT)	C	★★★

Passage 1: Keeping Small Farms Profitable

Step 1: Read the Passage Strategically

Sample Roadmap

line #	Keyword/phrase	¶ Margin notes
1	prevailing trend	Mass prod. in agriculture → Bankruptcy on small farms
3	heavy dependence	
4	linked to … growing problem	
6	proposed	
8	runs counter …maintains	Whatley: small farms can succeed w/ his approach
9	despite	
10	obstacles	
11	believes	
12	emphasizes	Whatley's recs:
15	recommends	1. Grow 10 crops
19	should	2. Develop CMC
23	encourages	3. Honor client requests on crops/chem
26	stresses	Link between "pick-your-own" and profits
27	crucial … because	
33	thus	
34	for example … suggests	CMC–no dist. costs
35	is needed	
38	cautions	Additional req. for success
39	depends in large part … ":"	
40	should	
44	reverses the traditional view	Locate farms near hard roads
46	should also	
47		Soil, water
49	Lastly	
50	recommends	Insurance
52	contends	

Discussion

In the first few lines, the author introduces the Topic, which is the problem affecting small farms: trends in agriculture have left small farms struggling under the weight of bankruptcy. Then we meet Booker T. Whatley, who has devised a solution. As soon as the author ends paragraph 1 by alluding to Whatley's "guidelines," you can bet that the rest of the passage will elaborate on those guidelines and perhaps evaluate them. Thus, the Scope is Whatley's solution to the economic problems facing small farms.

Paragraph 2 discusses three objectives of small farms and three recommendations Whatley proposes to achieve those objectives. To keep cash coming in, small farms should diversify their crops. To lessen reliance on borrowed money, small farms should develop clubs called CMCs. Finally, to assure a market for their crops, small farms should adhere to their club members' requests with regard to which crops they grow and which chemicals they use.

Paragraph 3 discusses the advantages of Whatley's plan. By adopting one key feature of the CMC (having customers come to the farm and harvest their own produce), farmers can turn a profit even by charging less than what supermarkets do. Selling directly to consumers also helps farms cut down on distribution costs to their customers, who are primarily urban dwellers willing to travel for their produce.

Paragraph 4 concludes the passage with a set of additional conditions that Whatley says are crucial for the success of his plan. These include strategic location on a hard-surfaced road, well-drained soil, water for irrigation, and liability insurance for customers coming onto the farm.

The author never gives an opinion on Whatley's plan, so the Purpose is neutral—to describe key aspects of a plan designed to help small farms combat bankruptcy. The Main Idea is that Whatley's plan carries a set of specific recommendations he says will help small farms thrive in the wake of the trend toward mass agricultural production.

1. (A) Global

Step 2: Identify the Question Type

The phrase "main point of the passage" indicates a Global question.

Step 3: Research the Relevant Text

The scope of a Global question is the passage as a whole. Instead of researching a specific set of lines, consult your Purpose and Main Idea that you determined during Step 1.

Step 4: Make a Prediction

The main point of the passage is that in the face of the growing bankruptcy problem among small farms, Whatley has come up with specific plans for those farms to stay profitable.

Step 5: Evaluate the Answer Choices

(A) is a clear match for this prediction and is, therefore, correct.

(B) misrepresents the passage's purpose. The author doesn't set out to contrast Whatley's approach to farming with the "dominant approach." Furthermore, nothing in the passage suggests that large farms are insensitive to consumer demands.

(C) is a Distortion. Whatley doesn't try to determine whether small farms can compete with large farms. He tries to devise ways to help small farms stay economically viable independent of how their larger counterparts are doing.

(D) is too narrow. According to Whatley, CMCs are indeed "crucial" for profitability. However, the main point of passage encompasses the entire series of recommendations, not just one important one.

(E) is an Extreme prediction. It suggests that the author is trying to make a prediction about the effect of Whatley's plan on large corporate farms. No such prediction occurs.

2. (B) Inference

Step 2: Identify the Question Type

The question stem asks for the answer choice most consistent with Whatley's views. That makes this an Inference question.

Step 3: Research the Relevant Text

Whatley's plan for small farm operation is discussed in the last three paragraphs of the passage.

Step 4: Make a Prediction

Whatley's plan has a lot of aspects that are discussed throughout paragraphs 2, 3, and 4. Instead of trying to list them and predict which will show up in the answer, find the answer choice that matches one of the aspects.

Step 5: Evaluate the Answer Choices

(B), if implemented, would facilitate the movement of a farm's customers to collect their own produce, which is a key provision in Whatley's plan (lines 20–21).

(A) goes against Whatley's recommendation that small farms grow only those crops that customers request (lines 23–24).

(C) goes against Whatley's recommendation for the creation of a CMC. In Whatley's plan, customers travel to the farms to harvest their own produce (lines 44–46).

(D) is unsupported because Whatley never says that blindly trusting customers to pay for their produce will somehow help a small farm stay afloat economically.

(E) is a Distortion because Whatley recommends that farmers tailor their chemical use to the requests of their customers, not to the needs of the environment (lines 24–25).

3. (C) Detail

Step 2: Identify the Question Type

The phrase "according to the passage" indicates a Detail question.

Step 3: Research the Relevant Text

The question stem directs you to the beginning of paragraph 3, since that's the part of the passage concerned with "pick-your-own" farming.

Step 4: Make a Prediction

Lines 26–31 say that "pick-your-own" farming is "crucial for profitability" because the CMC farmer can turn a profit despite only charging 60 percent of supermarket prices. The correct answer will restate or paraphrase this idea.

Step 5: Evaluate the Answer Choices

(C) matches this prediction exactly.

(A) might describe a fringe benefit, but giving customers a firsthand experience is never mentioned as integral to a small farm's profitability.

(B) is a Distortion. According to lines 13–17, a substantial year-round cash flow comes from growing at least 10 different crops. No such claim is made about "pick-your-own" farming.

(D) is a Faulty Use of Detail. While only growing selected crops is "encouraged" as part of Whatley's proposal (lines 23–25), it's never mentioned as a reason why pick-your-own farming is "necessary" to small farms' success.

(E) might explain why farmers would do well to start a CMC, but it doesn't explain why their profits rely on the customers literally harvesting their own crops.

4. (A) Global

Step 2: Identify the Question Type

This is a Global question because it asks what the author is "primarily concerned" with. In other words, you're being asked to identify the author's primary purpose.

Step 3: Research the Relevant Text

There are no specific lines to research when answering a Global question. The answer instead will come from your understanding of the passage's big picture from Step 1.

Step 4: Make a Prediction

The author's neutral purpose was simply to describe aspects of Whatley's plan for small farms to circumvent bankruptcy and operate profitably.

Step 5: Evaluate the Answer Choices

(A) matches the prediction.

(B) is too broad. While the author does open the passage by discussing a contemporary trend in agriculture, there's no

evaluation of the trend anywhere in the passage. The author moves quickly to Whatley's response to the trend.

(C) is wrong on two counts. First, the author's tone is neutral; there's no element of criticism. Second, Whatley's CMC recommendations aren't characterized as "widely accepted practices."

(D) is incorrect because the author doesn't demonstrate any disadvantages to Whatley's approach to farming.

(E) is wrong because nothing in the passage indicates that small farming is tradition-driven. Furthermore, the author doesn't discuss the effect of Whatley's ideas on the industry.

5. (D) Inference

Step 2: Identify the Question Type

The question stem's indirect wording ("most support for inferring") indicates an Inference question.

Step 3: Research the Relevant Text

The question stem doesn't have any research clues, so you'll need to use your big-picture understanding of the passage to form your prediction.

Step 4: Make a Prediction

The correct answer to a broadly worded Inference question is tough to predict. Instead, go straight to the answer choices and select the one that *must* be true based on the information in the passage.

Step 5: Evaluate the Answer Choices

(D) must be true because one of Whatley's recommendations is for small farms to grow at least 10 different crops (lines 14–17). Therefore, if a small farm fails to do this, then it fails to follow that recommendation.

(A) is Out of Scope. It can't be inferred because the passage never compares corporate farms to small farms.

(B) is a Distortion of lines 29–31. The passage does say that cutting harvesting costs allows a small farm to be profitable even if they charge 60 percent of supermarket prices, but that doesn't mean that charging an even higher price would *guarantee* higher long-term profits.

(C) is a Distortion. A hypothetically profitable CMC "would consist primarily of people from metropolitan areas," but that doesn't mean that, in general, CMCs would attract more rural dwellers than urban dwellers.

(E) is another Distortion. Paragraph 3 says that distribution costs are actually eliminated in a CMC because the farm would sell directly to the produce's consumers.

6. (D) Detail

Step 2: Identify the Question Type

Any question beginning with the phrase "according to the passage" is a Detail question.

Step 3: Research the Relevant Text

The question stem gives you the research clue "guarantee that small farms have buyers for all of their produce." This leads you to paragraph 2, where Whatley's main recommendations are laid out.

Step 4: Make a Prediction

Lines 21–25 contain the answer. For farmers to guarantee a market for their crops, they should grow only those crops that clients request, and they should also comply with customers' chemical use requests. The correct answer will paraphrase this information.

Step 5: Evaluate the Answer Choices

(D) is a perfect match and is, therefore, correct.

(A) is mentioned as a recommendation in line 15, but growing a variety of crops ensures that farmers will have year-round cash flow, not a guaranteed market for their crops.

(B) is mentioned in paragraph 3 as an additional advantage of customers picking their own produce from CMC farms.

(C) is a Distortion. Line 37 mentions that CMCs would mainly consist of city dwellers who value fresh produce, but nowhere does Whatley recommend that farmers use a preference for fresh produce as a recruitment criterion.

(E) is mentioned in paragraph 4 as a necessary step given that many preferred crops will not be drought-resistant. This has nothing to do with guaranteeing a market for those crops, however.

7. (B) Inference

Step 2: Identify the Question Type

The question stem gives you two clues as to its type: the word *inferences* and the phrase "most supported by ... the passage."

Step 3: Research the Relevant Text

Without a clear reference to a specific line or group of lines, the entire passage is fair game.

Step 4: Make a Prediction

On Inference questions without clear research clues, it's difficult, if not impossible, to predict the correct answer. So instead, take each choice in turn and ask if that choice *must* be true based on the passage. If you can't find definitive support in the passage for an answer choice, suspect that answer choice is incorrect.

Step 5: Evaluate the Answer Choices

(B) is directly supported by lines 44–45, in which the author says that the traditional view of hard-surfaced roads is that they are "farm-to-market," meaning that farmers use these roads to bring their crops to customers.

(A) is Extreme. Whatley does encourage CMC farmers to grow only what clients ask for, and CMC clients do pay in advance, but that doesn't mean that advance payments "guarantee" that members get what they want.

(C) is a Distortion. For it to be correct, it would have to be true that every single person in the typical 50,000-person city participates in a CMC. This idea isn't supported by the passage.

(D) is unsupported because nothing in the passage mentions any type of road other than hard-surfaced roads.

(E) is Out of Scope. The passage doesn't discuss why hard-surfaced roads were paved in the first place.

Passage 2: Forward Into Photography's Past

Step 1: Read the Passage Strategically

Sample Roadmap

line #	Keyword/phrase	¶ Margin notes
2	so struck	Bidaut's reaction to tintype
3	could hardly believe	
4	abandoned … set out to review	
6	but	
8		What tintype provided
13	inspired … imagines	Estabrook inspired by old prints/tintypes
17	On the verge	Photog. moving forward into past
18	moving forward … In addition to	
20		Old processes being revised
24	So diverse	
25	more like a groundswell	
27	source of their appeal	Old techniques
28	prime	How/why they became obsolete
31	Only	
33	exploit … court	Appeal of old tech to newer artists
34	sought to banish	
35	attracted … embraces	Estabrook's views
37	In his view	
40	So	
43	heighten	
45	preoccupation … offers a clue	Deeper motivations of artists
46	deeper motivations	
48	virtually guarantees	Uniqueness
50		Mark of encounter
51	At the same time	Regain intimacy
52	offer the possibility	
54	all but overwhelmed	

Discussion

Paragraph 1 introduces Jayne Hinds Bidaut, a photographer who used the bygone tintype process to produce in her insect photographs the effects she so admired in the tintypes of the past. The author ends the paragraph with more detail on the features and effects of the tintype.

Paragraph 2 introduces another photographer, Dan Estabrook, whose use of albumen prints and tintypes feeds his fantasy of creating an antique look in contemporary images.

You might not have zeroed in on the passage's Topic (photographic techniques) and Scope (the recent trend of contemporary photographers using antique processes in their work) until paragraph 3, which locates Bidaut and Estabrook in a movement. The paragraph also lists other old-fashioned techniques that photographers are using to produce expressive effects in their photographs.

The first part of paragraph 4 mentions that the idiosyncrasy of the old techniques that appeals to so many photographers these days is the same idiosyncrasy that led to their elimination. Contemporary artists actually embrace this contingency. Estabrook, in particular, preserves imperfections in his photos because they evoke a sense of nostalgia in the viewer.

Paragraph 5 gets into why these contemporary photographers prefer the idiosyncrasy that old-fashioned techniques afford. By using these techniques, these photographers can simultaneously ensure the uniqueness of each print and recover the intimacy of photographic communication. The author's Purpose is therefore to discuss the trend toward reviving old-fashioned photographic techniques, and the Main Idea is that the revival of these techniques is part of an attempt by these artists to recapture the uniqueness, intimacy, and idiosyncrasy that has been all but lost in modern mass media.

8. (A) Logic Function

Step 2: Identify the Question Type

This is a Logic Function question, because it asks you to determine the function of a phrase as the author uses it in the passage.

Step 3: Research the Relevant Text

The question stem directs you to line 17, but read the lines before and after it for context to help make your prediction.

Step 4: Make a Prediction

The sentence beginning in line 17 ends by saying that photography is moving forward into its past. So by using the phrase in question, the author is locating this nostalgic trend in a context that runs counter to that trend.

Step 5: Evaluate the Answer Choices

(A) matches perfectly.

(B) is a 180. If the trend is toward digital, filmless photography, then it's clear that the author is indicating that most photographers are embracing advanced techniques.

(C) is unsupported because nothing the author says indicates skepticism. In fact, as the passage goes on, the author gives legitimacy to the trend toward old-fashioned photographic techniques.

(D) is Extreme. You can't infer that the majority of artistic photographers are turning away from modern technology. Nevertheless, even if they were, that's not indicated by the phrase in line 17.

(E) is unsupported because the author doesn't make any predictions regarding the longevity of this current nostalgia among photographers.

9. (B) Inference

Step 2: Identify the Question Type

If a question stem asks about the author's attitude toward some aspect of the passage, it's an Inference question.

Step 3: Research the Relevant Text

The author discusses artists' uses of old photographic techniques, but clues to the author's attitude about those uses can be found mainly in paragraph 5.

Step 4: Make a Prediction

The author says in paragraph 5, among other things, that "old methods offer the possibility of recovering an intimacy with photographic communication that mass media have all but overwhelmed" (lines 53–55). This suggests that the author supports the artists' goals and understands their motivations.

Step 5: Evaluate the Answer Choices

(B) is a match.

(A) is a 180; it is contradicted by most of the statements made in paragraph 5, including the lines cited here (lines 53–55).

(C) is unsupported because the author doesn't seem ironically amused. The passage's tone is much more positive and sincere than that.

(D), to be correct, would require the author to spend more time criticizing modern photographic technology. But the author doesn't offer his/her own opinion on this technology.

(E) isn't supported because nothing in the passage indicates a whimsical curiosity. If anything, the author appears well-informed about the old techniques used by modern photographers.

10. (E) Detail

Step 2: Identify the Question Type

The correct answer will be a question that is directly answered by information in the passage, so this is a Detail question.

Step 3: Research the Relevant Text

The question stem doesn't have any research clues. Instead of researching before you evaluate the answer choices, research during Step 5.

Step 4: Make a Prediction

The 55 lines of the passage provide enough information to answer a whole slew of questions. Therefore, instead of predicting which question will be contained in the correct answer, review the answer choices and be sure to locate the part of the passage that supports the correct answer.

Step 5: Evaluate the Answer Choices

(E) is answered in lines 29–32. Early photographic techniques went obsolete in favor of "simpler, cheaper, faster, and more consistent" ones. That's four perceived advantages right there.

(A) is never answered. The passage is concerned only with those techniques that *have* been revived by contemporary photographers.

(B) is never answered. The end of paragraph 1 discusses the effect of the iron emulsion on the tintype, but the author never describes the emulsion's chemical composition.

(C) is never answered. The only two photographers mentioned by name are Jayne Hinds Bidaut and Dan Estabrook, and neither is mentioned as having used pinhole cameras.

(D) is never answered. Lines 20–21 cite coating with egg whites as an example of the antiquated techniques being revived by photographers. However, the passage never says what effect this technique has on photographs.

11. (C) Global

Step 2: Identify the Question Type

Any question asking for the "primary purpose" of a passage is a Global question.

Step 3: Research the Relevant Text

As with any Global question, the entire passage is relevant. Use the Purpose you determined during Step 1.

Step 4: Make a Prediction

The author's Purpose is to describe the recent trend among contemporary photographers of using old-fashioned techniques to produce antique-seeming photographs.

Step 5: Evaluate the Answer Choices

(C) is a match.

(A) is too slanted. The author doesn't advocate for any of the techniques used by this group of contemporary photographers.

(B) is too narrow. The author doesn't go into detail about the steps involved in the old-fashioned photographic methods.

(D) is wrong because the author stops short of discussing how the work of these contemporary photographers has been received by crltics or the public.

(E) is incorrect because the author doesn't contrast the approaches used by Bidaut and Estabrook. If anything, they're both used as examples of photographers who are using the same kind of old-fashioned approaches.

12. (D) Logic Reasoning (Parallel Reasoning)

Step 2: Identify the Question Type

The phrase "most analogous to" makes this a Logic Reasoning (Parallel) question.

Step 3: Research the Relevant Text

Paragraphs 3 and 4 provide the rationale behind the processes used by contemporary photographers. Estabrook, for example, "embraces accident and idiosyncrasy in order to foster the illusion of antiquity" (lines 36–38).

Step 4: Make a Prediction

It's impossible to know for sure what the correct answer will specifically say. However, you know the elements you're looking for: intentionally using old-fashioned techniques to produce the uniqueness and idiosyncrasy present in older artworks.

Step 5: Evaluate the Answer Choices

(D) is a perfect match. The designer is using old-fashioned equipment to intentionally produce vintage irregularities, just like the photographers in the passage are using old-fashioned techniques for the same effect.

(A) doesn't match because the researcher isn't deliberately using antiquated remedies to produce a certain idiosyncratic effect.

(B) is Half-Right/Half-Wrong, because the architect is examining ancient building styles. It's just for inspiration, however; the architect isn't trying to produce the look and feel of an ancient building.

(C) is also Half-Right/Half-Wrong. The engineer is using an older design, but he doesn't prefer the earlier design so that the turbocharger can inspire some kind of nostalgia in its user through its imperfections and idiosyncrasies.

(E) is almost a 180 because the artist is using a contemporary technique to reproduce old figures.

13. (B) Inference

Step 2: Identify the Question Type

The phrase "it can be inferred" indicates an Inference question.

Step 3: Research the Relevant Text

The question stem asks not what the author believes, but what Estabrook believes. Therefore, lines 12–16 and 35–45 will be most relevant.

Step 4: Make a Prediction

Estabrook's view is that the "illusion of antiquity" and the imperfections that accompany it tend to "heighten the sense of nostalgia" thereby enhancing the viewer's emotional response to the photo.

Step 5: Evaluate the Answer Choices

(B) would have to be something Estabrook believes, because he intends to "heighten the sense of nostalgia" by retaining stains and imperfections and embracing the "accident and idiosyncrasy" of old-fashioned techniques, despite the availability of techniques that could avoid such contingency.

(A) is unsupported. Estabrook is interested in the techniques used to create 19th-century photographs, not in the subjects of those photographs.

(C) requires Estabrook to believe that the old-fashioned techniques were used for intentional effect. None of Estabrook's statements suggest this.

(D) is a 180 from Estabrook's view, which attempts to "foster the illusion of antiquity" (lines 37–38).

(E) is another 180. Estabrook believes that a photograph's aesthetic significance depends on the viewer's perception and how the photograph is taken (allowing for uncertainty). If the photograph is manipulated after it is taken, that would run counter to lines 35–36 which state the "unpredictability attracted Estabrook to old processes."

14. (A) Logic Reasoning (Strengthen)

Step 2: Identify the Question Type

This question stem asks you to find the answer that strengthens Estabrook's reasoning, so this is a Logic Reasoning (Strengthen) question.

Step 3: Research the Relevant Text

Estabrook is first mentioned in paragraph 2, but the reasoning behind his photographic techniques is found in paragraph 4, specifically lines 35–45.

Step 4: Make a Prediction

Estabrook's view is that accident, unpredictability, and idiosyncrasy contribute to the viewer's experience of a photograph. That's why he deliberately embraces them by using old-fashioned techniques that all but guarantee them.

Step 5: Evaluate the Answer Choices

(A), if true, suggests that modern techniques aren't sufficient to produce the effects that Estabrook seeks. Therefore, if one wants to use 19th-century imperfections to produce those effects, one needs to use 19th-century techniques.

(B) suggests that Estabrook wouldn't need to go to such lengths to produce the desired effects in his viewers.

(C) doesn't support Estabrook's choice of techniques because using old-fashioned photographic processes has nothing to do with the photographs' ability to record subjects accurately. If anything, the imperfections of antiquated techniques could interfere with that ability.

(D) actually weakens Estabrook's position because his photographs do appear antique despite being new. If people don't engage artistically with such photos, then Estabrook's work has no impact.

(E) doesn't strengthen Estabrook's position because he places little value in blemish-free photographs. Such photographs would likely not have the personality Estabrook seeks.

Passage 3: Patents—The Tech Company's Best Defense

Step 1: Read the Passage Strategically

Sample Roadmap

line #	Keyword/phrase	¶ Margin notes
Passage A		
1	Theoretically … only supposed	Patents supposed to be "nonobvious"
4	certainly seems … Still	
5	recently held	Court: patents legit for "obvious" invention
6	infringed	
8	In an ideal world	Ideal: narrow patents
10	Unfortunately	
12	In recent decades … dramatically lowered	Reality: patents grown very broad
13	the bar … As a result	
14	so broad	
15	practically impossible	
17	proliferation … bad	Response: stockpile patents
20	credible deterrent … ":"	Protects against suits
23	Often, however … fundamental mistake :	w/o patents, company defenseless
24	As a result	
26	particularly ripe for abuse …	Difficulty w/software patents
27	because	
29	almost impossible	
31	Moreover, because of	Tough to find and license all patents
32	often prohibitively	
34	So even	
36	unlikely	

line #	Keyword/phrase	¶ Margin notes
Passage B		
37	consistently taken ...	Software maker: patents hurt innov
38	the position that ... generally impede	
39	inconsistent with	
41	pleased	
45	At the same time ... forced	Patents hoarded by
46	currently permits	large companies
48	We believe	Why patents get misused
49	ripe for ...	
50	misuse because ... questionable	
51	because	
53	One defense against such misuse	Defense: build our own patent portfolio
57	In the interests of	
59	elected to adopt	
60	reluctantly because of ... perceived inconsistency	Conflict w/above position
61	however	
62	dictates	

Discussion

Passage A begins by describing an ostensible requirement for patents: the invention being patented should be "nonobvious." There's a problem, however: fewer and fewer inventions are being classified by courts as "obvious." As a result, it's become nearly impossible for companies to innovate around these constraints.

By paragraph 3, the author provides a response from some large tech companies. In a nuclear arms race of sorts, companies scramble to stockpile patents as deterrents against patent lawsuits. Some companies can, however, find themselves left out if they don't amass enough patents.

Passage A ends by saying that the phenomenon of patent abuse is especially problematic for software companies because software is by nature assembled from individually patentable components. Also, because software is so complex, it's nearly impossible to find and license all relevant patents for a particular software product.

From the first lines of passage B, you can tell it was written by an employee of a software company, who lays out the company's position right away: patents are bad for innovation.

However, in paragraph 2, the company rep admits that software patents are not only allowed, but are being amassed by a small number of large companies. These companies, say the rep, can easily misuse those patents.

Therefore, the solution, according to the company, is to develop the company's own software patent portfolio to defend itself from costly litigation. While the company is clearly reluctant to make this move, it sees this defensive patent gathering as the only wise move.

While both passages share the same Topic (patents), they diverge slightly in terms of Scope: passage A concerns the problem of how to patent in an environment when nearly everything has become patentable, while passage B is more specific, dealing with the problem from the perspective of one software firm.

The Purpose of passage A is to describe a problem with the current patent climate, and to introduce a solution that some companies have used to confront that problem. Passage B's author sets out to give the position of a company that is trying to combat that problem. Passage A's Main Idea is that as fewer inventions are classified as *obvious*, companies are facing the problem of how to innovate while still avoiding patent lawsuits from competitors. Passage B's Main Idea is that as much as it may conflict with the company's stated position on patents, the company has no choice but to amass a defensive portfolio of patents.

15. (C) Global

Step 2: Identify the Question Type

Any question asking you for an appropriate title for a passage is a Global question.

Step 3: Research the Relevant Text

The entire passage is relevant in a Global question, but instead of rereading the whole text, use your Roadmap and your grasp of the Big Picture (Topic, Scope, Purpose, Main Idea) to make your prediction.

Step 4: Make a Prediction

Use Topic and Scope for each passage to predict the broad subject matter for each. Passage A is about the problem of creating patents when nearly everything is patentable, and passage B is about one company that, despite its opposition to patents, has to begin collecting them for defensive purposes.

Step 5: Evaluate the Answer Choices

(C) is the only choice that matches the subject matter of both passages.

(A) is wrong primarily because passage B does not advocate eliminating software patents. Although the author cites "our stance against software patents" in line 62, no plan is discussed to eliminate patents. In fact, passage B concludes that patents are unavoidable to maintain a defense against litigation.

(B) fails because passage A doesn't discuss any attempt to reform the laws that allow patents to get out of control. Additionally, it does not encompass passage B's reluctant acceptance of patents.

(D) is a Distortion. Passage A discusses not the misunderstanding of patent policies by software companies, but rather the response of those companies to palpable shifts in patent policy.

(E) is wrong because there's no evidence that passage B is a letter written to the company's customers. Even if it was, the reluctant acceptance of developing a patent portfolio is not necessarily indicative of an apology. Also, the idea of the "credible deterrent" from paragraph 3 of passage A is too narrow to serve as the title of the entire passage.

16. (B) Detail

Step 2: Identify the Question Type

This is a Detail question because it asks about what is directly stated in the passage.

Step 3: Research the Relevant Text

Without research clues in the question stem, you'll have to conduct your research as you evaluate the answer choices.

Step 4: Make a Prediction

You could list every single thing that's mentioned in passage A and then cross off the ones that are also in passage B, but that would be too time-consuming. Instead, read through each answer choice. If one pops out as correct, pick it, otherwise, research the ones you are unsure about in the passages.

Step 5: Evaluate the Answer Choices

(B) is mentioned in lines 31–34 of passage A. However, it doesn't appear in passage B.

(A) is mentioned throughout both passages.

(C) is mentioned in lines 26–37 of passage A and is central to the discussion in passage B.

(D) is mentioned in passage B in line 53.

(E) is mentioned in lines 51–52 of passage B, noted by the Keyword q*uestionable*.

17. (E) Inference

Step 2: Identify the Question Type

This is an Inference question because it asks for the intended meaning of a vocabulary term in context.

Step 3: Research the Relevant Text

The term "invent around" is in line 9, but to know its meaning, the entire context is key (at least lines 8–12).

Step 4: Make a Prediction

From context, you can determine that by "invent around," the author means that ideally, companies would be able to avoid violating the patent for an invention by inventing a product similar enough in function but not so similar that it gets the company in trouble legally.

Step 5: Evaluate the Answer Choices

(E) matches this prediction.

(A) is a Distortion. To "invent around" doesn't mean to invent *around* the concept of patents entirely; it just means inventing a product so that you sidestep violating the particular patents that could affect your invention.

(B) implies that companies in an ideal world would willfully hide their patent infringements, which the author never suggests.

(C) involves co-opting an already patented idea for a different purpose, when the author is suggesting that companies would ideally keep the purpose the same but tweak the product in a way that didn't violate the patent.

(D) is also a Distortion. The author doesn't intend to say that companies can ideally invent *around* the principles that governed the invention of similar products. Those principles don't enter into the discussion at all.

18. (B) Logic Reasoning (Method of Argument)

Step 2: Identify the Question Type

This question does have a broad, almost Global focus, but because it asks how the passages function in relation to each other, it resembles a Method of Argument question from Logical Reasoning.

Step 3: Research the Relevant Text

Because of the broad focus of the question stem, there are no specific lines to research. Instead, use your Scope and Purpose from Step 1.

Step 4: Make a Prediction

The relationship between the passages is that while passage A deals generally with an issue facing patent holders, passage B deals specifically with how one particular software company is handling that issue.

Step 5: Evaluate the Answer Choices

(B) matches this prediction.

(A) misrepresents the scope of both passages. The problem of patent hoarding isn't a set of events, but rather a worsening phenomenon. The passages agree that it's occurring, so passage B doesn't take issue with anything reported in passage A.

(C) imputes a stronger tone to passage A than is actually present—the author doesn't criticize companies for gathering patents defensively.

(D) is wrong because passage A doesn't describe a deadlock or stalemate, which is what an impasse is. Also, passage B doesn't try to avoid the problem set forth in passage A. It offers one imperfect way of defending against the effects of the problem.

(E) is wrong because there's no dispute between competing viewpoints in passage A. The author of passage A doesn't introduce anyone who believes that the proliferation of broad patents is a good thing.

19. (A) Inference

Step 2: Identify the Question Type

The phrase "most likely to agree" indicates an Inference question. In Comparative Reading, expect one or more questions that focus on points of agreement or disagreement between the authors.

Step 3: Research the Relevant Text

The phrase "software companies would be well advised" leads you to paragraph 3 of passage A and paragraph 3 of passage B, where these passages discuss steps taken by companies to combat the patent problems they face.

Step 4: Make a Prediction

To determine what the authors would agree on, look for overlaps between the Main Ideas of each passage. The fourth and sixth questions of the set both hint at the answer: Both passages agree that there is a serious problem with patents getting issued for *obvious* concepts and inventions, and that companies are amassing competing stockpiles of patents to avoid being sued by each other.

Step 5: Evaluate the Answer Choices

(A) is a solid match.

(B) isn't discussed in passage B, and in passage A the author says that licensing software patented by other companies isn't always a workable solution (lines 34–37).

(C) seems to be something both authors would advise against. Line 25 in passage A discusses companies avoiding lawsuits that could result from patent exploitation, and line 53 in passage B alludes to "the high cost of patent litigation."

(D) seems to be infeasible to the author of passage A (lines 29–37).

(E) is unlikely to be recommended by the author of passage A, who calls such research "prohibitively expensive" (lines 32–33) and "unlikely to be [done]" (line 36–37).

20. (D) Logic Function

Step 2: Identify the Question Type

This is a Logic Function question because it asks you to find a phrase in passage A that functions in the same way as a phrase from passage B.

Step 3: Research the Relevant Text

Line 60 contains the phrase in question, but you'll have to look earlier in passage B to know what *stance* the phrase refers to.

Step 4: Make a Prediction

The stance referred to in line 60 is elaborated in lines 54–56, which say that developing a defensive portfolio of patents can help safeguard against the misuse of the massive portfolios amassed by "a small number of large companies" (lines 48–49). Your Roadmap tells you that this same idea is discussed in lines 18–23.

Step 5: Evaluate the Answer Choices

(D), "credible deterrent," is a phrase that passage A uses to describe the practice being adopted by the software company in passage B.

(A), "nonobvious," refers to the standard used to determine whether or not an invention is patentable.

(B), "invent around," refers to the idea that a software company could still produce a product that has a desired

effect without risking a violation of a patent held by a competing firm.

(C), "lowered the bar," refers to the idea that courts are finding fewer and fewer inventions to be too obvious to patent.

(E), "modular components," refers to the idea that software is assembled from individually patentable pieces, which makes it nearly impossible for a company to invent software without violating one or more existing patents.

21. (D) Logic Reasoning (Weaken)

Step 2: Identify the Question Type

The phrase "cast doubt on the position" should remind you of a Weaken question in the Logical Reasoning section. That makes this a Reading Comp Weaken question.

Step 3: Research the Relevant Text

Lines 39–41 outline the position in question, which is that patents hamper innovation and don't comport with the idea of free software.

Step 4: Make a Prediction

You may not be able to predict the correct weakener verbatim, but know that the right answer will suggest that patents either don't get in the way of innovation or actually work to encourage it.

Step 5: Evaluate the Answer Choices

(D) is a valid weakener, if true, because it means that without patents, software innovation would suffer in some way.

(A) doesn't weaken the author's position because it isn't clear how the duration of a software patent affects the ability of developers to innovate.

(B) is Outside the Scope. Whether or not patents affect the reliability of software products has no bearing on whether or not they affect innovation.

(C) doesn't weaken the position in lines 39–41. It doesn't matter why proprietary vendors oppose software patents; if that opposition hampers their ability to innovate, then the author's position remains valid.

(E) has no effect on the position in lines 39–41 because it doesn't discuss the effect of patents.

Passage 4: *Calvaria major* and the Dodo Bird

Step 1: Read the Passage Strategically

Sample Roadmap

line #	Keyword/phrase	¶ Margin notes
1	rare but once-abundant	C. major found in same place as dodo
7	proposed	Temple: tree decline tied to dodo extinct
9	hypothesis ... subsequently gained considerable ...	
10	currency	Temple's observ.
14	assumed	
16		Coincidence → causation
19	led him to posit	
20	he hypothesized	C. major pit walls: relationship to dodo
26	though, ultimately prevented	w/ dodo gone, pit walls too thick for seeds to germ.
29	maintained ... lethal	
31	Although ... proof was unattainable	Add'l findings in support of Temple
33	semblance of ...	
34	rigor	Concl. from tests/observ.
38	concluded	
41		Experim. results from turkeys
43	he saw as vindicating his hypothesis	
44	Though ... dramatic	Response to theory from sci.
45	intriguing ... plausible	
46	strongly challenged	Challenges for Temple
51	So	Strohm: C. major has germ. since dodo
53	thus ... since	
54	Additional counterevidence	Speke: C. major unlikely to become extinct
55	shows that	
57	probably sufficient	Other causes for C. major's decline
59	could easily	

Discussion

Paragraph 1 introduces the Topic (the scarce *Calvaria major* tree) and moves quickly into the Scope (Temple's explanation for its scarcity). While Temple was researching birds, he offered a theory that linked the decline of the tree to the extinction of the dodo bird. He observed only 13 overmature *Calvaria major* trees that allegedly produced fruit that could no longer germinate. Note the phrase "Temple assumed" in line 14—just because Temple found no younger trees, he assumed there were none. It's as if the author is already pointing out the classic flaw of an absence of evidence being mistaken for evidence of absence.

The beginning of paragraph 2 alludes to another LSAT flaw—correlation versus causation—and then gets into the specifics of Temple's argument. According to him, the dodo's extinction was the death knell for *Calvaria major* because the tree had come to depend on the dodo to thin the walls of its pit enough for the seed inside to germinate.

Paragraph 3 describes additional research conducted by Temple to bolster his hypothesis. He estimated the abrasive force exerted by the dodo's gizzard and then determined that *Calvaria major* pits could likely have withstood that force. Then he fed pits to turkeys, and several of those pits were abraded enough to germinate.

LSAT authors rarely describe scientific theories without either evaluating them or discussing others' evaluations of them, and you have subtle clues throughout that the author is skeptical about Temple's theory. True to form, the passage ends by introducing evidence challenging Temple's theory. As it turns out, the tree is not as scarce as Temple thought, and not as endangered. The final lines of the passage give alternative causes for *Calvaria major*'s population decline. From these lines, you can determine that the Purpose of the passage is to describe and evaluate Temple's hypothesis, and the Main Idea is that while Temple's hypothesis is intriguing and ostensibly supported by experimental evidence, there are other more likely explanations for *Calvaria major*'s decline.

22. (B) Global

Step 2: Identify the Question Type

Because this question asks you to identify the "main point of the passage," it's a Global question.

Step 3: Research the Relevant Text

For a Global question, the entire passage is relevant. Instead of researching a specific portion, use your assessment of the big picture from Step 1 to form your prediction.

Step 4: Make a Prediction

The main idea of the passage is that Temple developed a theory (the dodo's extinction caused the scarcity of the *Calvaria major* tree) that he supported with experimental evidence but that ultimately has been called into question by experts in the field.

Step 5: Evaluate the Answer Choices

(B) is a solid match and is, therefore, correct.

(A) doesn't even mention Temple or his theory on the tree's scarcity.

(C) is a Distortion. The author doesn't call Temple's methodology into question, but rather the validity of his hypothesis. Furthermore, because the author introduces evidence challenging Temple's hypothesis, it could hardly be characterized as a "probable solution."

(D) ignores paragraph 3, which is devoted exclusively to a discussion of Temple's supporting research. It also characterizes the author's attitude toward Temple's hypothesis too positively.

(E), like **(A)**, ignores the scope and purpose of the passage. Furthermore, the author never makes a counterfactual claim about what would happen to *Calvaria major* had the dodo stuck around.

23. (A) Detail

Step 2: Identify the Question Type

The key phrase "the author indicates" means that the answer will be stated in the passage. Thus, this is a Detail question.

Step 3: Research the Relevant Text

Temple's research on the birds of Mauritius is primarily discussed in lines 4–10.

Step 4: Make a Prediction

In lines 4–10, the author states that Temple was researching the endangered birds of Mauritius when he began investigating the population decline of *Calvaria major*.

Step 5: Evaluate the Answer Choices

(A) is a perfect paraphrase of "endangered" and is, therefore, correct.

(B) distorts a detail from paragraph 3. Temple's estimates of the crush resistance of *Calvaria major* pits came from "test results," not from his studies of birds. Also, nothing in the passage says his estimates were "highly accurate."

(C) is also a Distortion. Lines 34–35 say that Temple estimated the abrasive force inside a dodo's gizzard by studying "other birds," not necessarily the birds of Mauritius.

(D) isn't mentioned. The author doesn't discuss the scope and precision of Temple's studies on birds.

(E) gets it backward. Temple's studies of *Calvaria major* trees were inspired by work he was doing on the birds of Mauritius, not the other way around.

24. (D) Logic Function

Step 2: Identify the Question Type

This is a Logic Function question because it asks how an author uses a particular phrase in context.

Step 3: Research the Relevant Text

The first sentence of paragraph 3 contains the lines cited in the question stem. Read these lines in context so you'll grasp the author's intended meaning.

Step 4: Make a Prediction

The "semblance of rigor" that the author refers to in these lines is the appearance of intellectual credibility that Temple conferred on his hypothesis by going through the trouble of studying other birds, performing crush tests on *Calvaria major* pits, and planting the pits he fed to turkeys.

Step 5: Evaluate the Answer Choices

(D) matches this prediction.

(A) is unsupported. Nothing in paragraph 3 suggests that Temple conducted his experiments carelessly.

(B) is a Distortion. Line 31 says that direct proof was unattainable for Temple, but that doesn't mean that such proof is always impossible to attain.

(C) is wrong because the author never weighs in on the accuracy of Temple's research. If anything though, Temple's rudimentary experiment attempting to compare the digestive prowess of turkeys and dodos would likely not be considered "careful and accurate."

(E) goes too far. Lines 44–45 establish that there is not a consensus that Temple is wrong. Also, the author never suggests that Temple's findings were at all precise.

25. (A) Detail

Step 2: Identify the Question Type

The phrase "the passage indicates" is a sign of a Detail question, because the focus is on what the passage states rather than on what it implies.

Step 3: Research the Relevant Text

"The abrasion of *Calvaria major* pit walls" is a research clue leading you primarily to paragraphs 3 and 4.

Step 4: Make a Prediction

The passage says a number of things about the abrasion of *Calvaria major* pit walls. Such abrasion can occur within the digestive tract of a bird that consumes the pit. This abrasion has also been posited as necessary for the seed to germinate, a claim that Temple thought was supported by his experiments but was ultimately challenged by experts.

Step 5: Evaluate the Answer Choices

(A) is mentioned in lines 56–57, which say that a minority of unabraded *Calvaria major* seeds germinate. This means that abrasion is not necessary for germination.

(B) is not only Extreme ("always released … seeds undamaged"), but contradicted by lines 40–41, which say that many of the seeds were destroyed by the turkeys' digestive tracts.

(C) is a Distortion. The passage doesn't say that Temple was wrong about the dodo's ability to abrade the tree's pit walls. It suggests that Temple may have been wrong to assume that abrasion is necessary for germination.

(D) makes an Irrelevant Comparison that isn't warranted by the information in the passage, especially because Temple found that *Calvaria major* pit walls were abraded, if not destroyed, by the turkeys in his experiments.

(E) is Outside the Scope. No other natural abrasive forces were discussed in the passage.

26. (E) Inference

Step 2: Identify the Question Type

The phrase "can be most logically inferred from the passage" is a sure sign of an Inference question.

Step 3: Research the Relevant Text

Because this question asks about the author's point of view, the bulk of your research will be done in paragraph 4, where that point of view is clearest.

Step 4: Make a Prediction

You can think of this like an Author's Attitude question. In addition to lines 58–62, which cast doubt on Temple's cause-effect hypothesis, Keywords such as "semblance of rigor" (line 33–34) and "which *he saw* as vindicating his hypothesis" (lines 42–43) suggest that the author is not enthusiastically supportive of Temple's theory.

Step 5: Evaluate the Answer Choices

(E) is a direct match. The author concludes the passage by pointing out that the tree has not lost its ability to germinate, despite the dodo's disappearance. Therefore, Temple has been trying to find a cause for a nonexistent effect.

(A) is contradicted by the last few lines of the passage, in which the author says that the tree's population decline could be due to many factors other than the dodo's disappearance.

(B) suggests that the author finally comes down on Temple's side, which goes against paragraph 4.

(C) is unsupported. The words "valuable scientific achievement" connote a positive attitude that doesn't exist in the passage.

(D) gets the author's tone wrong. The author doesn't praise Temple's precision. In fact, the entirety of paragraph 4 is devoted to introducing evidence calling Temple's work into question.

27. (C) Inference (EXCEPT)

Step 2: Identify the Question Type

Two clues tell you this is an Inference question: the word *inferred* and the phrase "author would be likely to agree with." Note the EXCEPT; here you'll have to find the one answer NOT supported by the passage.

Step 3: Research the Relevant Text

In the absence of strong research clues, the entire passage is relevant. In this case, it's best to evaluate the answer choices, and then do your research on those you still have remaining after eliminating those you already know the author would definitely agree with.

Step 4: Make a Prediction

It's tough to predict something that isn't supported by the passage. As with most EXCEPT questions, you're better off eliminating answer choices that are supported by the author's statements.

Step 5: Evaluate the Answer Choices

(C) is challenged by lines 54–59. It's clear from the research cited in these lines that more often than not, *Calvaria major* seeds do not germinate. Under these circumstances, it would *not* be surprising that the tree is less abundant.

(A) is supported. Paragraph 4 introduces evidence that challenges Temple's theory, but the research of Temple's critics isn't totally conclusive regarding either Temple's claims or the causes of the tree pit's durability.

(B) is similarly supported by the same part of the passage. The author says that many scientists find Temple's theory plausible, suggesting that it hasn't yet been completely invalidated.

(D) is supported by lines 57–58, in which the author says that there are enough germinating seeds to keep the tree from becoming extinct.

(E) is supported by lines 56–57. If some unabraded seeds germinate, then that means it's possible for a seed to germinate without passing through the digestive tract of a bird like the dodo.

Section IV: Logical Reasoning

Q#	Question Type	Correct	Difficulty
1	Main Point	E	★
2	Inference	D	★
3	Flaw	B	★
4	Method of Argument	B	★
5	Paradox	E	★
6	Principle (Apply/Inference)	D	★★
7	Weaken	E	★★
8	Assumption (Necessary)	C	★★
9	Inference	B	★★★
10	Parallel Reasoning	B	★
11	Flaw	E	★★★
12	Role of a Statement	A	★★
13	Assumption (Sufficient)	C	★
14	Parallel Flaw	C	★★
15	Weaken	D	★
16	Flaw	B	★★
17	Principle (Identify/Strengthen)	D	★★★
18	Flaw	A	★★
19	Weaken	E	★★★★
20	Inference	E	★★★★
21	Assumption (Sufficient)	A	★★★★
22	Flaw	E	★★
23	Strengthen	E	★★★
24	Main Point	D	★★
25	Point at Issue (Agree)	B	★★

1. (E) Main Point

Step 1: Identify the Question Type

Because the correct answer will accurately express the argument's conclusion, this is a Main Point question. Beware of conclusion Keywords, which will often lead to subsidiary conclusions, and keep an eye out for contrast Keywords, which often indicate the author's opinion.

Step 2: Untangle the Stimulus

The stimulus opens with the point of view generally held by scientists. They think that deep-sea creatures cannot see red light. Next, the author uses the contrast Keyword *but* to shift away to the opinion that the scientists may be mistaken. Finally, the second and third sentences of the stimulus give a detailed example of a deep-sea creature that has red lights on its body, which it probably uses as bait.

Step 3: Make a Prediction

Follow the points of view to predict the answer to a Main Point question. The stimulus presents two points of view: scientists and, in contrast, the author. The correct answer will match the author's opinion that scientists need to reassess their belief that deep-sea creatures cannot detect red light. Notice that the stimulus ends with a subsidiary conclusion about the deep-sea creature (beginning with *probably*). Expect this to show up as a wrong answer choice, especially because it is stated last.

Step 4: Evaluate the Answer Choices

(E) directly matches the prediction.

(A) mentions the subsidiary conclusion in the author's evidence—the example of the newly discovered deep-sea creature—rather than the conclusion.

(B) also focuses on the author's evidence rather than on the conclusion. If the author could only keep one sentence, this wouldn't be it.

(C), like **(A)** and **(B)**, references evidence the author uses to support the main point.

(D) is the opinion the author argues against, rather than the author's conclusion.

2. (D) Inference

Step 1: Identify the Question Type

Because the correct answer is the one "supported by the statements above," this is an Inference question. The correct answer must be true based on the information given in the stimulus.

Step 2: Untangle the Stimulus

Inventory the statements. First, acrylic paints are good for house painting. Second, acrylic paints have many good features. In fact, they "provide everything that a good paint

should." Third, acrylics can't fix everything. Finally, when there's a situation acrylics can't fix, there's a deeper problem that needs repair.

Step 3: Make a Prediction

Follow the Keywords to make a prediction. In the second statement, *everything*, is a very strong assessment of value. The third statement contains *however*, which is a contrast Keyword. How can it be that acrylics do "everything that a good paint should" and yet they can't fix surface defects? It must be true that a good paint shouldn't have to fix surface defects.

Step 4: Evaluate the Answer Choices

(D) matches the prediction by stating that good paints do not have to correct surface defects.

(A) is Out of Scope. The stimulus says badly cracked paint would indicate some underlying problem, which may or may not be caused by harsh weather conditions.

(B) is Extreme. Even though the stimulus says acrylics provide everything a good paint should, that does not mean that acrylics are the *only* paints that do so. It could be true that other types of paints not mentioned in the stimulus also provide everything homeowners need.

(C) goes Out of Scope because the stimulus never recommends against using acrylics for painting over other house paints. Additionally, **(C)** is Extreme. Just because acrylics can't fix badly cracked paint does not mean homeowners should not use acrylics over other (perhaps noncracked) paint.

(E) makes an Irrelevant Comparison. The stimulus does not provide information to make a comparison about color ranges in different types of paint.

3. (B) Flaw

Step 1: Identify the Question Type

Because the stimulus contains an argument that is "vulnerable to criticism," this is a Flaw question. The correct answer will describe the argument's logical flaw.

Step 2: Untangle the Stimulus

The Keywords "of course" suggest that the author's opinion is in the second sentence. Thus, the conclusion is that philanthropists do not want to make the nonprofit sector as efficient as private business. The evidence comes in the final sentence of the stimulus, where the author points to the example of Byworks Corporation, a very inefficient business.

Step 3: Make a Prediction

The author's conclusion is very broad, because it is about the entire nonprofit sector and private business in general. However, the evidence is very narrow: it introduces one specific business. Thus, the argument relies on a scope shift from this one specific business to private business in general. The argument overlooks the fact that private business in general might not be similar to Byworks Corporation. Look for an answer choice that describes a representativeness flaw.

Step 4: Evaluate the Answer Choices

(B) matches the prediction by pointing out the scope shift in the argument. The author treats Byworks Corporation as if it was representative of all private business, when in fact there is no reason to believe that the private sector in general is as inefficient as Byworks.

(A) mischaracterizes the author's conclusion. The author is not arguing that something "ought to be the case," but rather that something is not the case.

(C) describes an ad hominem attack, which is not at play here. While it is true the author rejects the editor's claim, the author never attacks the editor personally to do so.

(D) mischaracterizes the author's evidence. The author introduces the example of the Byworks Corporation to suggest that the editor's claim is false. In other words, the author uses a counterexample, rather than suggesting the editor had no proof.

(E) goes Out of Scope by introducing causation. This argument does not discuss a cause and effect situation, but rather it discusses what a certain group wants.

4. (B) Method of Argument

Step 1: Identify the Question Type

Because the correct answer describes *how* the "argument proceeds," this is a Method of Argument question. Break down the structure of the argument, not the content.

Step 2: Untangle the Stimulus

The stimulus opens with the author's conclusion. The Keyword *probably* shows that this statement contains an opinion. Basically, crime stats are as much about those who record and report the stats as they are about actual crime. In the next three sentences, the author gives examples of different people who would use crime stats—police, politicians, and newspapers—and describes their potential motives.

Step 3: Make a Prediction

The author uses three specific examples to support a general claim.

Step 4: Evaluate the Answer Choices

(B) matches the prediction by focusing on how the author's evidence comes in the form of examples.

(A) goes Out of Scope because the author never evaluates evidence that might go against the conclusion.

(C) is a Distortion of the argument's logic. While it is true the conclusion is a generalization, the author does not assume it to be true. Rather, the conclusion is supported by the specific examples given as evidence. In other words, the conclusion is derived from the evidence, not the other way around as **(C)** suggests.

(D) mischaracterizes the conclusion because the conclusion suggests a problem (or at least a problematic situation) rather than a solution.

(E) mischaracterizes the author's evidence. The examples of people who might use crime stats in their favor do not contradict the author's conclusion.

5. (E) Paradox

Step 1: Identify the Question Type

Because the correct answer resolves an "apparent" discrepancy, this is a Paradox question. Paradox questions usually include *resolve* or *explain* in the question stem.

Step 2: Untangle the Stimulus

Read to find the paradox. In other words, what does the physiologist say that does not seem to fit together? Calcium deficiency increases the chance of getting osteoporosis. Dairy usually has more calcium per serving than fruits and vegetables. However, there is less osteoporosis in countries where people get their calcium from fruits and vegetables rather than from dairy. How can this be?

Step 3: Make a Prediction

While you would expect countries where people get a large amount of calcium from dairy products would have lower rates of osteoporosis, this is not the case. To resolve the paradox, the correct answer will suggest something about dairy products that leads to higher rates of osteoporosis despite the higher amount of calcium, or something about fruits and vegetables (besides calcium) that protects against osteoporosis.

Step 4: Evaluate the Answer Choices

(E) matches the prediction by suggesting something negative about dairy products. If dairy fats stop the body from absorbing calcium, then people who eat lots of dairy might actually be missing out on the calcium they need to protect them from osteoporosis.

(A) goes Out of Scope by focusing on how healthy bodies deal with excess calcium. By leaving out dairy and fruits and vegetables, this answer choice fails to affect the paradox. Additionally, excess calcium is not at issue here—insufficient calcium is.

(B) fails to resolve the paradox because it combines fruits and vegetables with dairy, rather than showing a difference between them. The stimulus is about the difference between those countries whose residents get their calcium from fruits and vegetable products but very little dairy versus those countries where people get a lot of calcium from dairy. **(B)** could be about the people in either or both of these countries, and therefore doesn't explain why the amount of osteoporosis in those countries is different.

(C) makes an Irrelevant Comparison about the number of people with calcium deficiencies versus people with osteoporosis. That comparison does not explain why different diets may account for those conditions. **(C)**, like **(A)**, never mentions dairy or fruits and vegetables.

(D) is Out of Scope. Deficiencies in other minerals do not explain why those with the higher consumption of dairy have a higher likelihood of developing osteoporosis. **(D)**, like **(A)** and **(C)**, fails to mention dairy or fruits and vegetables.

6. (D) Principle (Apply/Inference)

Step 1: Identify the Question Type

Because the correct answer "conforms to the principle stated above," this is a Principle question. This Apply the Principle question resembles an Inference question because the correct answer will be the specific scenario that must be true based on the principle in the stimulus.

Step 2: Untangle the Stimulus

Don't expect to see an argument-based stimulus in Principle (Apply) questions, but do keep an eye out for Formal Logic statements, which are often found instead. Here, the phrase, "not … unless" indicates Formal Logic. Translated, this statement reads:

If	*first-term board member who should be on the finance committee*	→	*accountant OR all board members support membership*

Contraposed, the statement reads:

If	*~ accountant AND ~ all board members support membership*	→	*~ first-term board member who should be on the finance committee*

Step 3: Make a Prediction

The correct answer must follow the Formal Logic statement or its contrapositive.

Step 4: Evaluate the Answer Choices

(D) matches the Formal Logic. Because Klein is a first-term board member who isn't an accountant, look to the contrapositive, which includes *not accountant* as a sufficient term. If, as **(D)** states, Klein also isn't supported unanimously, then it must be true he should not be on the finance committee.

(A) is Extreme. Just because Simkins is not an accountant does not mean that he should not be on the finance committee. To accurately conclude that Simkins should not be on the committee, then the answer choice would also need to say that not all board members support him.

(B) goes Out of Scope because Timmons is a third-year board member. The principle in the stimulus covers only first-year board members. Additionally, the Formal Logic doesn't work. Neither the original statement nor the contrapositive has "should be on the committee" as the necessary result. The stimulus says only what restricts membership, not what guarantees it.

(C) goes Out of Scope, like **(B)**, by not specifying if Ruiz is a first-year board member or not. The principle in the stimulus covers only first-year board members.

(E) is like **(B)** and **(C)** in that it fails to specify whether or not Mabry is a first-year board member.

7. (E) Weaken

Step 1: Identify the Question Type

Because the correct answer weakens the argument in the stimulus, this is a Weaken question.

Step 2: Untangle the Stimulus

Start by analyzing the argument into evidence and conclusion. The phrase "these survey results support the contention that" suggests that the conclusion follows, while the evidence is the survey. Thus, the conclusion is that people who listen to a novel on tape will enjoy it more than people who read the novel to themselves. The evidence is a survey taken by the magazine. Apparently most respondents who listened to a specific novel enjoyed it but most of those who read it did not.

Step 3: Make a Prediction

Start by finding the author's assumption. Here the conclusion is very general—it covers all novels—but, the evidence is quite specific, it covers one survey about one specific novel. Thus, the author must be assuming that the survey results are applicable to all other novels. If this were a Flaw question, you would be looking for a representativeness flaw. The correct weakener will demonstrate this survey is not actually representative. It may introduce an alternative that the author overlooks, for example that this particular novel had some aspect that made listening to it more enjoyable than reading it.

Step 4: Evaluate the Answer Choices

(E) matches the prediction because the novel in the survey is special in that it includes dialects that are easier to understand when heard. If this is the case, then no wonder survey respondents who listened to the novel enjoyed it more than those who read it. Therefore, the survey results cannot be expanded to cover all novels, and thus the author's broad argument falls apart.

(A) eliminates the possibility that the survey results were skewed by some people who had both read and listened to the novel. If anything, this strengthens the argument. It certainly doesn't weaken it, because it doesn't provide any new information that would hurt the conclusion that people like to listen to books more than read them.

(B) goes Out of Scope by introducing speed. This fails to affect the argument because finishing a novel more quickly could be more enjoyable or less enjoyable, and thus could possibly both support or weaken the argument.

(C) is Out of Scope. It fails to affect the argument because it does not distinguish between those who read novels and those who listen to them. All **(C)** shows is a commonality among everyone who is likely to enjoy novels.

(D) goes Out of Scope, like **(C)**, by not discussing the specific novel mentioned in the stimulus. Additionally, **(D)** introduces the new (and irrelevant) idea of availability.

8. (C) Assumption (Necessary)

Step 1: Identify the Question Type

Because the correct answer is "an assumption on which the argument depends," this is a Necessary Assumption question. You can use the Denial Test to check your answers, if necessary.

Step 2: Untangle the Stimulus

Break down the argument into evidence and conclusion. The Keyword, *therefore*, in the last sentence signals the conclusion. The author concludes that doctors who have qualified as recognized medical specialists must be competent to practice in their specialty. The evidence is the rest of the stimulus: basically, a list of the qualifications that one must fulfill to become a recognized medical specialist.

Step 3: Make a Prediction

Identify the mismatched concepts, starting with the conclusion. The conclusion introduces the idea of competency. The evidence, on the other hand, describes all the qualifications that a recognized medical specialist must have. Thus, the author assumes that the qualifications guarantee competency.

Step 4: Evaluate the Answer Choices

(C) matches the prediction. Basically, **(C)** says that if you have completed the evaluation program, then you are not incompetent. In other words, the only people who have completed the evaluation programs are competent people.

(A) goes Out of Scope by introducing motivation, rather than focusing on competency.

(B) goes Out of Scope by introducing talent, rather than focusing on competency.

(D) is not needed by the author. The conclusion is an extreme statement, phrased in categorical Formal Logic terms. The author concludes that anyone who has qualified as a recognized medical professional is competent. **(D)**, on the other hand, is less certain because of the qualifier, *usually*. The six to ten years of medical school plus residency may not *usually* be enough to achieve that competence. Perhaps less than half of those who attempt to complete the final step of the evaluation program actually get qualified.

(E) is also not needed by the author. **(E)** gets the logical order wrong by describing medical training as necessary for competence, while the stimulus suggests that qualifying as a medical specialist (which includes medical training) is sufficient to establish competence.

9. (B) Inference

Step 1: Identify the Question Type

Because the stimulus "most strongly support[s]" the correct answer, this is an Inference question. The correct answer must be true based on the information in the stimulus.

Step 2: Untangle the Stimulus

Make an inventory of the statements. First, archaeologists are examining plant remains from an ancient site. Next, there is some Formal Logic. If the plants were cultivated, then the site occupants had agriculture earlier than anyone else known. However, if the plants were not cultivated, then the site occupants ate a greater range of wild plants than anyone else known.

Step 3: Make a Prediction

The entire stimulus is about the plant remains at the archaeological site and the people who once ate them. Those people, whether or not they cultivated the plants, were doing something exceptional: either discovering agriculture very early or eating an unprecedented variety of wild plants. The correct answer will likely state that the people who once lived at the agricultural site did something exceptional.

Step 4: Evaluate the Answer Choices

(B) matches the prediction because, whether due to early agriculture or a diet of a wide variety of wild plants, the site occupants were different than their contemporaries.

(A) is Extreme. The stimulus offers two options but does not guarantee that the archaeologists *will* be able to determine whether or not the plants were cultivated. All we know is that *if* the archaeologists can figure this out, then they will be able to make some inferences about the site occupants.

(C) incorrectly reverses (and does not negate) the Formal Logic of the last sentence of the stimulus.

(D) incorrectly reverses (and does not negate) the Formal Logic of the second sentence of the stimulus.

(E) goes Out of Scope by suggesting that one possibility is more likely than the other. The stimulus describes what archaeologists can infer based on the results of the plant analysis, but nothing suggests that one outcome is more likely than the other.

10. (B) Parallel Reasoning

Step 1: Identify the Question Type

Because the correct answer is the argument that is "most similar in reasoning" to the argument in the stimulus, this is a Parallel Reasoning question.

Step 2: Untangle the Stimulus

Focus on characterizing the argument's conclusion so that you can knock out wrong answers. Signaled by the Keyword *thus*, the conclusion is the last sentence. Noting the word *than* the conclusion is a comparison of the fuel efficiency of two cars. If knocking out mismatched conclusions is not enough to get you to the right answer, go back and look at the evidence. Here, despite different conditions (fuel-efficient versus less fuel-efficient driving), the results (gas mileage) of the two cars were the same.

Step 3: Make a Prediction

The correct answer must have a conclusion that is a comparison between two things. The evidence in the correct answer will include a single test or event in which the results were identical but achieved under different conditions.

Step 4: Evaluate the Answer Choices

(B) matches the prediction because its conclusion compares calories burned by two hamsters. Both hamsters burned the same number of calories, but did so under different conditions.

(A) fails to match the prediction because its conclusion is not a comparison but a contrast. The answer choice doesn't say that X experiences less pain than Y, just that their experiences are different.

(C) fails to match the prediction because its conclusion includes Formal Logic. Also the coasting and pedaling did not provide identical results.

(D) fails to match the prediction because its conclusion fails to compare two things. Although it jumps out less than in **(C)**, **(D)**'s conclusion also includes Formal Logic. It can be translated to: If we both gave the same estimate → I must have overestimated the value. Additionally, the two judges did not have identical results. Finally, **(D)** isn't based on a single event or test.

(E) is like **(C)** and **(D)** in that its conclusion includes Formal Logic. Here, the conclusion translates to: If ~ prescription glasses → lower visual acuity. Additionally, this choice does not compare two separate objects.

11. (E) Flaw

Step 1: Identify the Question Type

Because the correct answer will describe the flaw in the stimulus, this is a Flaw question.

Step 2: Untangle the Stimulus

Break down the argument into the evidence and conclusion. The conclusion, signaled by the Keywords *but clearly*, is that the certification process can't be that challenging. The evidence, signaled by *because*, is that there is a high pass rate on the exam's written portion.

Step 3: Make a Prediction

Start by finding the author's assumption. The evidence introduces the exam's written portion, but the conclusion focuses on the entire exam. Thus, the author shifts scope from a part of the exam to the whole exam. The author must be assuming that what is true of the written portion is true of the whole exam. This overlooks the possibility that the written portion could be very easy, while some other portion of the exam is very challenging. This is a part-versus-whole flaw.

Step 4: Evaluate the Answer Choices

(E) matches the prediction because the author assumes that just because the written portion is easy (in other words, lacks difficulty), the whole exam must lack difficulty.

(A) goes Out of Scope by introducing necessity versus sufficiency, a common flaw that often appears in stimuli with Formal Logic, but is not at play here. If the author's argument were written in Formal Logic, it would say: If nearly everyone passes written portion → ~ difficult exam. The contrapositive would be: If difficult exam → ~ nearly everyone passes written portion. However, the author *doesn't* take something necessary for difficulty (~ nearly everyone passes written portion) and say it's sufficient. That would be: ~ nearly everyone passes written portion → difficult. The author never puts this forth.

(B) goes Out of Scope by focusing on whether or not plumbers are qualified. Additionally, this answer choice goes against the evidence. The author doesn't assume plumbers have to complete a certification process to be qualified: He even says that Plumb-Ace plumbers, who must become certified, "may or may not" be more qualified than other plumbers.

(C) goes Out of Scope by introducing other certification processes not mentioned in the stimulus. The author's conclusion that the Plumb-Ace process is easy could be valid regardless of other companies' processes. Not considering those other certifications doesn't make this argument flawed.

(D) mischaracterizes the conclusion. Rather than concluding that the claim made by Plumb-Ace that their plumbers are more qualified is false (as this answer choice suggests), the author refrains from passing judgment on the claim, saying that they "may or may not be more qualified." The argument is really about the difficulty of the exam, rather than about the claim made by Plumb-Ace.

12. (A) Role of a Statement

Step 1: Identify the Question Type

Because the correct answer will describe the role a claim from the stimulus plays in the argument, this is a Role of a Statement question.

Step 2: Untangle the Stimulus

First, identify the statement in question. Here, the statement comes in the second sentence, right before the important Keyword phrase, *however, for*. Next, read the stimulus from the beginning and separate the argument into evidence and conclusion. The first sentence gives background information about the spending of pharaohs. The next statement—the one in question—is the author's conclusion. The emphasis Keyword *mere* and the contrast Keyword *however* both show that this statement is opinionated. The evidence, which is the rest of the stimulus, is introduced by for, one of the LSAT's most frequently used evidentiary Keywords.

Step 3: Make a Prediction

The statement in question is the author's conclusion.

Step 4: Evaluate the Answer Choices

(A) matches the prediction.

(B) wrongly says the statement is offered as support, or evidence.

(C) wrongly says the claim is a "premise given in support," again suggesting that the statement is evidence, whereas it is the conclusion.

(D) wrongly suggests that the claim is an illustration, or example. An illustration would be evidence.

(E) wrongly suggests that the claim is a premise used as support, which, again, would make it evidence. Additionally, the phrase "only military" is a Distortion that the pharaohs' architecture served a purpose that prevented the need for military coercion.

13. (C) Assumption (Sufficient)

Step 1: Identify the Question Type

Because the correct answer is an assumption that makes the conclusion in the stimulus follow logically, this is a Sufficient Assumption question.

Step 2: Untangle the Stimulus

Break down the argument into evidence and conclusion. The very certain prediction that the change in the patent system would discourage research is the conclusion. This is the most opinionated piece of the argument, and is supported by the last sentence, in which the author describes the effect of the proposed change. Note that in between the first and last sentence, the author gives some background information, describing the present system. You won't need to focus on this in your prediction because information about the present system is irrelevant to determining the effects of the future system.

Step 3: Make a Prediction

Both the evidence and the conclusion describe effects of the change in the patent system. In the conclusion, the author argues the change would hurt scientific research. In the evidence, the author says the change would delay the communication of discoveries. Thus, the author assumes that the delayed communication of discoveries would harm scientific research.

Step 4: Evaluate the Answer Choices

(C) matches the prediction. When an author makes a scope shift (assumes, in other words, that the evidence is relevant to the conclusion), the correct answer can simply link up the two pieces of the argument into one sentence, as **(C)** does.

(A) goes Out of Scope by failing to include the key idea from the conclusion, that the change would discourage scientific research. It's unclear if more patents would help or hinder scientific research, therefore, this isn't the assumption. The author isn't concerned with the *number* of patents filed, just the *time line* in which they're filed.

(B) goes Out of Scope by focusing on the effect of the current rules rather than on what would happen in the future with the proposed change. Knowing that dramatic advances have occurred under the current system is not enough to guarantee the conclusion.

(D) goes Out of Scope by introducing the opinion of most researchers. Other people's opinions are irrelevant to whether what the author predicts will happen or not.

(E) goes Out of Scope by focusing on the current rules, just as **(B)** did. This assumption isn't enough to get the author to the conclusion that the future system will be harmful.

14. (C) Parallel Flaw

Step 1: Identify the Question Type

Because the correct answer uses "questionable reasoning most similar" to the questionable reasoning in the stimulus, this is a Parallel Flaw question. Keep common flaws in mind as you approach the stimulus.

Step 2: Untangle the Stimulus

Look at the argument's evidence and conclusion. The conclusion is that the *only* thing people really want is pleasure. The evidence is that when people get what they want, they always feel pleasure.

Step 3: Make a Prediction

Find the flaw in the stimulus. Here, the author assumes that just because getting what you want gives you pleasure, that pleasure is the only thing that people want. In other words, the author assumes that a consistent result is an exclusive reason for an action. The correct answer will use that same structure, but will introduce new details.

Step 4: Evaluate the Answer Choices

(C) matches the prediction because the author suggests that one result that always comes from eating pizza is the only reason for eating pizza.

(A) goes Out of Scope because it fails to introduce a consistent result that always comes from doing something.

(B) goes Out of Scope because it fails to introduce a consistent result that always comes from doing something. Arguably, thinking of skiing always results in being terrified, but then to be correct, the rest of the argument needs to say that seeking terror is the only reason to think about skiing.

(D) introduces an action (going to parties) causing a consistent result (enjoyment), but then merely says the same result will probably happen again. To be correct, **(D)** would have to assert that enjoyment is the only reason for going to a party.

(E) goes Out of Scope in two ways. First, the stimulus says an action causes a consistent result, whereas **(E)** reverses the logic, saying the result (enjoying a soccer game) means that the action (eating hot dogs) happened. Additionally, this answer choice introduces an extra term. In the stimulus, the terms are getting what you want and feeling pleasure. In **(E)**, the terms are eating hot dogs, enjoying soccer, and enjoying basketball.

15. (D) Weaken

Step 1: Identify the Question Type

Because the correct answer is a "logical counter" the linguist can make to the philosopher, this is a Weaken question. The correct answer will allow the linguist to make the philosopher's argument less likely to be true. Likely, in a dialog stimulus like this, rather than introducing new information, the linguist will point out a flaw in the philosopher's argument.

Step 2: Untangle the Stimulus

The philosopher attempts to provide evidence for why linguists do not have a deep understanding of language,

citing the example of two sentences with a different word order. The philosopher's conclusion is that the two sentences cannot have the same meaning. The philosopher's evidence is that the two sentences are structurally different and, thus, not completely identical.

Step 3: Make a Prediction

Start by finding the philosopher's assumption. The philosopher's conclusion is about two sentences not having the same meaning, but the philosopher's evidence is about two sentences not being completely identical. Thus, the philosopher must be assuming that sentences must be identical to have the same meaning. The correct answer will likely suggest that being identical is different from having the same meaning.

Step 4: Evaluate the Answer Choices

(D) matches the prediction. The philosopher says the linguist believed the sentences were "identical in meaning." Thus, the linguist can counter the philosopher by saying that whether the sentences are identical in structure is immaterial. The linguist's belief only rests on the meaning of the sentences, and the philosopher has given no evidence the sentences don't have identical meanings.

(A) doesn't go far enough. It only says that the philosopher may be wrong about what makes things identical, but it doesn't attack the biggest jump in logic. Even if the philosopher is confused about what makes things identical, he still might be right that things need to be structurally identical to have the same *meaning*.

(B) is backward. The linguist wants to show two sentences that are not structurally identical can be identical in meaning, not the other way around.

(C) may be true, but doesn't address the connection (or lack thereof) between identical structure and identical meaning.

(E) makes an Irrelevant Comparison by looking at the relative experience of each speaker, rather than the logical merits of their arguments. This answer choice is an example of an ad hominem attack, a logical flaw in which a speaker's personal characteristics are cited as evidence for or against his views. If the linguist were to make this argument, he would be committing a flaw, not pointing out one in the philosopher's argument.

16. (B) Flaw

Step 1: Identify the Question Type

Because the correct answer describes the flaw in the argument given in the stimulus, this is a Flaw question.

Step 2: Untangle the Stimulus

Analyze the argument's evidence and conclusion. Signaled by *hence*, the conclusion is that salespeople in major health stores always make inaccurate claims about the vitamins they sell. The evidence is that salespeople working on commission always steer people toward expensive products.

Step 3: Make a Prediction

Start by finding the assumption. The conclusion is about inaccurate claims. The evidence is about getting bigger commissions by selling more expensive products. Thus, the author must be assuming that just because salespeople want bigger commissions, they never give accurate claims. This is an example of an ad hominem attack, a common logical flaw in which a speaker's statements are judged on the basis of the speaker's personal characteristics. This argument also overlooks the possibility that salespeople might still make accurate claims (perhaps the quality of the vitamins *is* that good), regardless of whether their commissions are affected or not. The correct answer could be phrased either way.

Step 4: Evaluate the Choices

(B) matches the prediction by suggesting that the author makes an ad hominem attack on the salespeople.

(A) incorrectly characterizes the evidence. In the stimulus, the evidence does significantly more than restate the conclusion. For example, it offers details about how salespeople are paid that are not mentioned in the conclusion.

(C) describes a parts-versus-whole flaw. It suggests a scope shift from the general to the specific, which is different from discounting claims simply because of who the claimant is. To be correct, **(C)** would have to say, "infers that just because a group of people has a certain property, each member of the group *also has another* property." In the rewritten version, the first property would be— gets paid on commission; the second property would be—always makes inaccurate claims.

(D) is Out of Scope. It describes a necessity-versus-sufficiency flaw, which is not at play here. The author's evidence could be translated into Formal Logic:

If	salesperson	→	*steer customers to highest commissions*

and

If	salesperson in health store	→	*work on commission*

For this answer choice to be correct, the author would have to give an incorrect contrapositive of either of those statements. Instead he introduces two new concepts in the conclusion:

If	buy vitamins at a health store	→	*salespeople's claims are inaccurate*

(E) goes Out of Scope by introducing the concept of authority. The stimulus never describes an authority on a topic or that authority's area of expertise.

17. (D) Principle (Identify/Strengthen)

Step 1: Identify the Question Type

Because the correct answer is a principle, this is an Identify the Principle question. Additionally, because the correct principle will "justify the argument," this Principle question resembles a Strengthen question. The answer will be a broad rule that supports the specific situation described in the stimulus.

Step 2: Untangle the Stimulus

Break down the argument into evidence and conclusion, just as you would a Strengthen question. Signaled by *therefore*, the conclusion is that the veracity of Einstein's theory is not buoyed by the fact that the theory accurately predicts the perihelion advance. The evidence comes after *however*, and is that Einstein knew of the perihelion advance and likely made sure the theory he was developing would account for it.

Step 3: Make a Prediction

Start by finding the assumption. Here, the conclusion is that predicting the perihelion advance doesn't count as evidence that Einstein's theory is correct. The evidence is that Einstein knew about the perihelion advance and accounted for it in his theory. Thus, the author assumes that if you know about some phenomenon and account for it when making a theory, then the fact that the theory accurately predicts the phenomenon does not count as support for your theory. The correct answer will make that more likely to be true.

Step 4: Evaluate the Answers

(D) matches the prediction. Einstein adjusted his theory to account for the perihelion advance and that is the reason why the author thinks that the theory's explaining the advance does not count as support for the theory. This answer choice essentially states the assumption, which is a perfectly good answer for a Strengthen question. If the assumption is true, then the conclusion automatically becomes more likely.

(A) goes Out of Scope by introducing the idea of discovering a phenomenon, which does not appear in the stimulus. The stimulus is only concerned with known phenomena, whereas this answer choice discusses unknown phenomena.

(B) is a Distortion of the argument's logic. Because **(B)** uses "not … unless," translate it into Formal Logic and it reads:

If	*predicting a phenomenon counts as evidence in favor of a theory*	→	*the theory was developed with that phenomenon in mind*

The stimulus reads:

If	theory developed with phenomenon in mind	→	predicting the phenomenon does not count as evidence in favor of the theory

This answer choice reverses the logic, but then only negates one side.

(C) is Extreme in the way it characterizes both the evidence and conclusion. The conclusion is not whether or not Einstein's theory is well supported, but rather whether or not this one piece of evidence supports the theory. Similarly, the evidence is not about accounting for all relevant phenomena, but rather about how Einstein's theory accounts for one specific phenomenon.

(E) incorrectly characterizes the conclusion. The conclusion says predicting the phenomena doesn't count as support for the theory. The conclusion is not, as **(E)** suggests, about whether Einstein's theory actually predicts the phenomena. The background information at the opening of the stimulus explicitly says Einstein's theory predicts the perihelion advance. Thus, this answer choice would actually go against the evidence.

18. (A) Flaw

Step 1: Identify the Question Type

Because the correct answer describes how the "manager's argument is vulnerable to criticism," this is a Flaw question.

Step 2: Untangle the Stimulus

Here, the manager's main conclusion is that the store should sell only low-end computer models. The evidence is the subsidiary conclusion that this plan would maximize profits because the store would likely sell the same total amount of computers, and the low-end models each have a greater profit percentage than the high-end models.

Step 3: Make a Prediction

Start by finding the assumption. Here, the conclusion is about total profit, i.e., total dollars. The evidence is about the percentage of return that comes from selling different models. To achieve maximum profits just by selling low-end computers, the computer store manager must be assuming that the profit on a low-end computer is a greater amount of money than the profit on a high-end computer. This is the classic flaw of confusing numbers and percentages. The store manager overlooks the possibility that even though the percentage of profit on a high-end computer is low, the total price charged for a high-end computer could be very high, and, thus, the total amount of dollars it brings in might be greater than that coming from a low-end computer. For example, if a high-end computer sells for $5,000, the profit

on it would be $650, based on the average rate of 13%. By contrast, the profit for a low-end computer costing $1,000 would likely be $250 based on the average rate of 25 percent.

Step 4: Evaluate the Answer Choices

(A) matches the prediction.

(B) goes Out of Scope by focusing on the number of high-end models the store sold last year. The argument is about what would happen in the future if the store adopted the new sales strategy, not about what has already happened. Additionally, the store manager does address the anticipated number of sales, saying the store could probably sell as many low-end models as they sold both low- and high-end models last year.

(C) says the manager ignores the possibility of an upsell, but this isn't a flaw in the argument. According to the manager's logic, they don't want to encourage upsells anyway.

(D) is Extreme. While the manager does suggest the new strategy would maximize profits, the manager never says maximizing profits is the *only* objective for the store.

(E) mischaracterizes the evidence because the computer store manager explicitly suggests that future sales of low-end computers may not be the same as past sales. The manager thinks that future sales of low-end computers will likely be much greater than past sales.

19. (E) Weaken

Step 1: Identify the Question Type

Because the correct answer "weakens" the argument in the stimulus, this is a Weaken question.

Step 2: Untangle the Stimulus

The professor's conclusion is that economists are wrong; it is faulty to think that just because people spend more money on average than they win by buying a lottery ticket, that to do so is unwise. The author's evidence is based on the counterexample of insurance. There too, on average, individuals spend more money than they get in return, but no one argues that insurance is an unwise expense.

Step 3: Make a Prediction

Start by finding the assumption. Here, the conclusion is about lottery tickets while the evidence is about insurance policies. Thus, the author assumes lottery tickets are comparable to insurance policies. The weakener will likely point out the overlooked alternative: insurance policies are different from lottery tickets in important ways. For example, insurance policies pay you when something bad happens, while lottery tickets pay you when you get lucky.

Step 4: Evaluate the Answer Choices

(E) matches the prediction by suggesting that the value of an insurance policy in protecting against loss outweighs the (remote) possibility of winning big in the lottery.

(A) arguably strengthens the argument, because if people spend more on insurance, and that is acceptable, then buying lottery tickets at much lower prices seems less unwise.

(B) goes Out of Scope by focusing on the insurance companies and lottery organizations, rather than on those who purchase insurance and lottery tickets. Again, if anything, it strengthens the argument by indicating a positive of lotteries: They distribute a larger proportion of revenue than do insurance companies.

(C) goes Out of Scope by failing to mention either lottery tickets or insurance. This answer choice provides a general principle that arguably shows purchasing lottery tickets is not so foolish, which would, if anything, strengthen the professor's argument.

(D) goes wrong in two ways. First, it focuses on the *odds* of getting a payout from the lottery and from insurance, rather than on the average *amount* of the payout compared to the average amount spent on purchases. Second, while this answer choice indicates that the odds in the lottery are worse than in insurance (which might at first seem to weaken the professor's analogy), it is actually worded too narrowly. **(D)** is limited only to the lottery's grand prize, not to all payouts, which the professor's argument encompasses.

20. (E) Inference

Step 1: Identify the Question Type

Because the correct answer "can be properly inferred" from the stimulus, this is an Inference question. The correct answer must be true based on the information in the stimulus.

Step 2: Untangle the Stimulus

Make an inventory of the statements. This stimulus contains a list of effects and causes. There were exceptionally strong forest fires in the tropics in 1997. The tropics were prone to fires then because of the El Niño-caused drought. Some scientists think global warming, caused by air pollution, made El Niño stronger.

Step 3: Make a Prediction

Connect the chain of ideas in the stimulus. Many scientists think air pollution led to global warming, which led to a stronger El Niño, which led to drought. Therefore, it could be said that air pollution led to drought. Drought led to the forest fires of 1997, so you could also say air pollution led to the forest fires of 1997. Notice, however, the tentative clause, "many scientists believe." The correct answer will also be tentative; it may point out this chain of events is possible, but

will not say the links are certain. The correct answer to an Inference question can't be stronger than the language in the stimulus.

Step 4: Evaluate the Answer Choices

(E) matches the prediction by tying together air pollution with the widespread drought of 1997. Note that **(E)** is phrased cautiously, using *if*. Based on the stimulus, we know that some scientists suspect air pollution enhanced the strength of El Niño, but we can't be sure if those scientists are correct or not. The conditional language takes care of that potential problem with **(E)**. Additionally, the weak verb *contributed* keeps this answer choice within scope, whereas *caused* would be too strong.

(A) is Extreme by suggesting that air pollution was "largely responsible" for the fires of 1997. Some scientists think air pollution played a role in those fires, but, even if those scientists are correct, we cannot say with certainty how great a role the air pollution played.

(B) goes Out of Scope by introducing a hypothetical situation. There is no way to know what would have occurred had El Niño been weaker. Even had there not been an unusually strong El Niño at that time, some other factor might have led to large and intense forest fires in the tropics.

(C) is Extreme and an Irrelevant Comparison. The stimulus provides one example of the effects of a strong El Niño. That is not sufficient date to conclude that fires are *generally* larger and more intense during a strong El Niño.

(D) is tempting, but also Extreme. While the stimulus says many scientists think air pollution caused global warming, which *enhanced* the strength of El Niño, we do not know if these same scientists believe that air pollution is *responsible* for (rather than just a contributing factor to) the size and intensity of the 1997 forest fires.

21. (A) Assumption (Sufficient)

Step 1: Identify the Question Type

Because the correct answer is the assumption that makes the conclusion properly inferred (or drawn), this is a Sufficient Assumption question. Don't let the word *inferred* mislead you. Keep an eye out for Formal Logic, which is often found in Sufficient Assumption questions.

Step 2: Untangle the Stimulus

This stimulus contains a large amount of "If"-Then statements. Begin with the conclusion, signaled by the Keyword *thus*. Translated, the conclusion is:

If	*Skiff's book is as important and well written as Skiff claims*	→	*Skiff will be promoted*

The rest of the stimulus provides a chain of evidence (signaled by the Keyword "for"). Translated, it becomes:

If	Skiff's book is published	→	Nguyen will recommend that the dean promote Skiff	→	the dean will promote Skiff

Step 3: Make a Prediction

Both the evidence and conclusion say Skiff will be promoted by the dean as their necessary term. The evidence says the sufficient condition is publishing, while the conclusion says it's being important and well written. The conclusion never says that Skiff's book will be published. Thus, the assumption must connect the mismatched concepts: being important and well written and being published. Therefore, the assumption is:

If	Skiff's book is as important and well written as Skiff claims	→	Skiff's book is published

If this is true, then the conclusion logically follows. This is similar to the pattern:

Ev: X → Y → Z ; Conc: W → Z ; Suff Assm: W → X

For example:

Evidence: Dog → Mammal → Animal

Conclusion: Terrier → Animal

Sufficient Assumption: Terrier → Dog

Step 4: Evaluate the Answer Choices

(A) matches the prediction. You can test it by adding the answer choice to the chain of evidence:

If	Skiff's book is as important as he claims	→	it will be published	→	Nguyen will recommend that the dean promote Skiff	→	the dean will promote Skiff

Notice that the first term and the last term make up the conclusion. That means this answer choice allows the logic chain to progress correctly.

(B) fails to include the mismatched concept from the conclusion, that Skiff's book is as important and well written as Skiff claims. *Needs* is too strong as well; there could be other sufficient ways for Skiff to be promoted. Finally, *a book*, is too vague. The evidence is only about one particular book.

(C) goes Out of Scope by introducing Nguyen's opinion. The question is not whether Professor Nguyen *believes* the book

is as important and well written as Skiff claims, but whether it actually is.

(D) improperly connects the mismatched concepts. It reverses the order of the terms from the prediction, without negating them. Translated, **(D)** reads:

If	Skiff's book is published	→	it is as important and well written as he claims it is

Remember that "not...unless" phrasing is one of the most common forms of Formal Logic on the LSAT. In the example from Step 3, this reversed answer would be akin to stating improperly that the assumption was all dogs are terriers: If Dog → Terrier.

(E) translates to:

If	promoted	→	Nguyen urges dean

This reverses the logic in the evidence, which says Nguyen will recommend that the dean promote Skiff → the dean will promote Skiff. This answer choice takes something that is sufficient (Nguyen urging the dean) and says it is necessary for promotion. Nevertheless, the dean may promote Skiff anyway, or Skiff may find outside promotion. Additionally, this doesn't link up to the mismatched concept in the conclusion.

22. (E) Flaw

Step 1: Identify the Question Type

Because the correct answer describes the flaw in the stimulus, this is a Flaw question.

Step 2: Untangle the Stimulus

Break down the argument into evidence and conclusion. The conclusion is the last sentence, that in 10 years the magazine will not have the biggest sales. The main piece of evidence follows *unfortunately*, where the stimulus says the managing editor will not be allowed to make changes and that without those changes the magazine's sales cannot continue to rise as quickly as they have.

Step 3: Make a Prediction

Start by finding the assumption. The conclusion is that the magazine will not be the largest-selling in 10 years. The evidence is that the rate of increased circulation in the next 10 years will not be as great as it has been for the past 10 years. The author must be assuming that the only way the magazine could become the largest-selling is if its circulation continues to rise at the same rate. This overlooks the possibility that there are other ways the magazine could still be the largest-selling in 10 years even if the rate of increase in circulation diminishes. The Formal Logic of the stimulus looks like this:

Evidence:

> **If   rise continues   →   top seller**

The conclusion then improperly makes deductions based on a trigger of *no changes*.

Step 4: Evaluate the Answer Choices

(E) matches the prediction. The occurrence that will ensure that the magazine becomes the largest-selling is the magazine's circulation rising as it has been over the past 10 years. However, it is not necessarily true that is the *only* occurrence that would ensure that outcome. For example, if all the other martial arts magazines closed down, then this magazine would be the largest-selling no matter what happened to its circulation rate. This is essentially a necessity-versus-sufficiency flaw.

(A) mischaracterizes the argument's conclusion, which is that the magazine will not become the largest-selling. "[O]ther changes" are Out of Scope.

(B) mischaracterizes the argument's conclusion. While the author does cite a reduction in the rate at which circulation is increasing as evidence, the conclusion is not that the magazine's circulation will actually decline.

(C) describes a circular reasoning flaw, which is not at play here. That the magazine will *not* be the largest-selling in 10 years (the conclusion) is never mentioned in the evidence. Therefore, the conclusion cannot simply restate the evidence.

(D) mischaracterizes both the evidence and conclusion. First, the conclusion does not demonstrate that a claim previously made in the stimulus is false. Second, the evidence is not incompatible with any general claim made in the stimulus. Incompatible claims are those that cannot be true at the same time. No such inconsistency exists here.

23. (E) Strengthen

Step 1: Identify the Question Type

Because the correct answer "most strengthens" the argument in the stimulus, this is a Strengthen question.

Step 2: Untangle the Stimulus

Look at the argument's evidence and conclusion. Following the phrase "this suggests that," comes the conclusion. Basically, the botanist believes that domesticated crops would pass pesticide resistance to their wild relatives. The evidence is that domesticated radishes passed flower color to wild radishes, when planted in the same field.

Step 3: Make a Prediction

Start by finding the assumption. Here, the conclusion is about plants in general passing on resistance to pesticides, but the evidence is about radishes, in particular, passing on flower color. There are two different scope shifts at play here. Thus,

the author must be assuming both that what is true of radishes is true of all plants, and that resistance to pesticides is a trait that can be passed along similarly to flower color. The correct answer will introduce some idea that makes it more likely that radishes are representative of plants in general and/or that flower color and resistance to pesticides can both be passed from domesticated to wild plants.

Step 4: Evaluate the Answer Choices

(E) matches the prediction. If flower color is more difficult to pass along between domesticated and wild radishes than other traits (such as resistance to pesticides) are to pass along between plant species in general, then the fact that the more difficult event took place makes it more likely that the easier event could as well.

(A) introduces an Irrelevant Comparison. The author is only concerned with the transfer of traits from domesticated plants to wild plants, not the other way around. If anything, this weakens the argument because it indicates that trait transfer may not be as easy as the botanist thinks.

(B) goes Out of Scope by focusing on the speed at which traits passed. The botanist is concerned only with whether or not resistance to pesticides could be passed on, not with how fast the transference could be.

(C) is a 180. If radishes are not representative of crop plants in general, then they wouldn't be relevant evidence and the botanist's conclusion falls apart.

(D) goes Out of Scope by focusing on how the domesticated radishes got their color in the first place. The botanist's focus is not how traits originated, but whether or not they can be passed on from domestic to wild species. If the color, which passed to the wild radishes, was not introduced to the domesticated radishes via genetic engineering, then it is not relevant to whether a genetically engineered trait (pesticide resistance) can pass.

24. (D) Main Point

Step 1: Identify the Question Type

Because the correct answer "accurately expresses the overall conclusion," this is a Main Point question.

Step 2: Untangle the Stimulus

Read the entire stimulus from the top down, paraphrasing each statement as you go. The stimulus begins by suggesting that parents hurt their child's self-esteem when they praise the child regardless of the child's success. Next, it says that children need acknowledgement of their accomplishments, but that children come to disregard praise if it's given indiscriminately.

Step 3: Make a Prediction

The second and third sentences support the first sentence, making it the conclusion. The fact that children who are always praised discount that praise is *why* parents who always praise their children are hurting their children's self-esteem. In a stimulus such as this, when Keywords don't map out the structure, always looks for what supports what and add in your own evidence and conclusion Keywords, if helpful. Here, if you were to turn the argument around and try to make the first sentence support the second, the argument wouldn't make sense.

Step 4: Evaluate the Answer Choices

(D) restates the first sentence and, therefore, matches the prediction.

(A) goes Out of Scope because the author never actually recommends any specific course of action.

(B) describes the evidence, rather than the conclusion. The fact that children who are praised undeservedly discount that praise is evidence for the conclusion that parents who always praise their children hurt their children's self-esteem.

(C) goes Out of Scope by introducing parents' expectations The stimulus only tells the effect of one thing parents might do (i.e., always praising hurts self-esteem). Additionally, this answer choice indicates that parents are praising their children too little (their expectations don't match their children's ability) rather than too much, which is what this stimulus addresses.

(E) goes Out of Scope because the stimulus never describes the effects of *not* praising children when they succeed. Rather, the stimulus describes the effects of praising children both when they do and do not succeed. Additionally, the phrase "will develop low self-esteem" is Extreme. The stimulus said the children's self-esteem would erode, but that does not guarantee that it will be *low*; it could erode, for example, from very high to average.

25. (B) Point at Issue (Agree)

Step 1: Identify the Question Type

Because the correct answer is the statement that Pauline and Roger agree on, this is a twist on the Point at Issue question. Instead of looking for the point of disagreement, as in the typical Point at Issue question, look for the agreement. Make sure you characterize what you are looking for, because the stimulus will likely present a disagreement as well.

Step 2: Untangle the Stimulus

Paraphrase both Pauline's and Roger's statements. Pauline suggests that if the dams are breached to save the salmon, then the cost of electricity will increase. Roger suggests that because the dams are already at optimal capacity, new

sources of electricity will need to be found whether the dams are breached or not.

Step 3: Make a Prediction

Both Pauline and Roger look toward the future of energy in the region. Pauline thinks that costs will go up if the dams are breached. In other words, due to the rules of supply and demand, she thinks the demand for electricity will at least stay the same. Roger thinks new sources of energy must be found. Both must agree that the fulfillment of energy demands will be an issue.

Step 4: Evaluate the Answer Choices

(B) matches the prediction. Both of them see a problem in the future with energy: Pauline with costs if the dams are breached, Roger with demand regardless. Therefore, both of them must think that the current energy sources will not be sufficient to fulfill the need.

(A) is Out of Scope because Pauline makes no mention of finding other energy sources, although arguably she assumes they would not be and that's why electricity costs would go up. Roger, however, seems to think finding alternative energy is a possible goal.

(C) goes Out of Scope because Roger makes no mention of electrical costs rising. Additionally, Pauline's only says costs will rise *if* the dams are breached. The stimulus doesn't say that she thinks costs will also rise if the dams *aren't* breached.

(D) goes Out of Scope because neither of the speakers weighs in on what the environmentalists think.

(E) goes Out of Scope because neither Pauline nor Roger mentions what would happen to energy prices after additional sources are found.

PrepTest 70

The Inside Story

PrepTest 70 was administered in October 2013. It challenged 33,673 test takers. What made this test so hard? Here's a breakdown of what Kaplan students who were surveyed after taking the official exam considered PrepTest 70's most difficult section.

Hardest PrepTest 70 Section as Reported by Test Takers

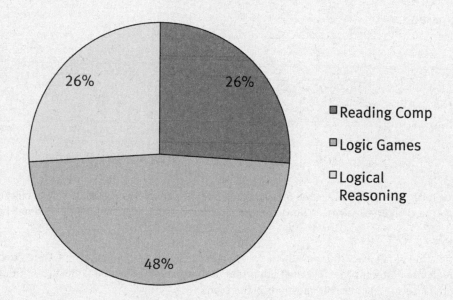

26%   26%

■ Reading Comp

□ Logic Games

□ Logical
  Reasoning

48%

Based on these results, you might think that studying Logic Games is the key to LSAT success. Well, Logic Games is important, but test takers' perceptions don't tell the whole story. For that, you need to consider students' actual performance. The following chart shows the average number of students to miss each question in each of PrepTest 70's different sections.

Percentage Incorrect by PrepTest 70 Section Type

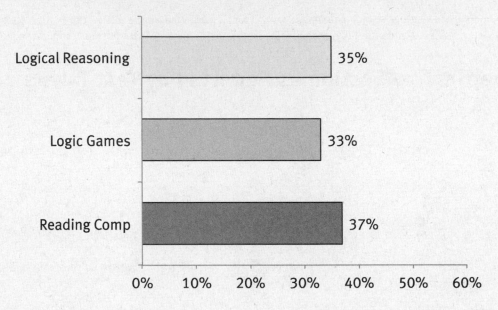

Actual student performance tells quite a different story. On average, students were almost equally likely to miss questions in all three of the different section types, and on PrepTest 70, Reading Comprehension and Logical Reasoning were somewhat higher than Logic Games in actual difficulty.

Maybe students overestimate the difficulty of the Logic Games section because it's so unusual, or maybe it's because a really hard Logic Game is so easy to remember after the test. But the truth is that the testmaker places hard questions throughout the test. Here were the locations of the 10 hardest (most missed) questions in the exam.

Location of 10 Most Difficult Questions in PrepTest 70

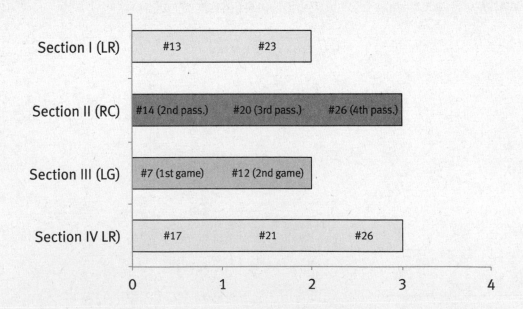

The takeaway from this data is that, to maximize your potential on the LSAT, you need to take a comprehensive approach. Test yourself rigorously, and review your performance on every section of the test. Kaplan's LSAT explanations provide the expertise and insight you need to fully understand your results. The explanations are written and edited by a team of LSAT experts, who have helped thousands of students improve their scores. Kaplan always provides data-driven analysis of the test, ranking the difficulty of every question based on actual student performance. The 10 hardest questions on every test are highlighted with a 4-star difficulty rating, the highest we give. The analysis breaks down the remaining questions into 1-, 2-, and 3-star ratings so that you can compare your performance to that of thousands of other test takers on all LSAC material.

Don't settle for wondering whether a question was really as hard as it seemed to you. Analyze the test with real data, and learn the secrets and strategies that help top scorers master the LSAT.

7 Can't-Miss Features of PrepTest 70

- PrepTest 70 had some real rarities in Logical Reasoning. For example, this was the first LSAT since PrepTest 55 (October, 2008) that had a fill-in-the-blank Sufficient Assumption question that ended in ", since _____." And it's the first question of the test!
- This test was also just the fourth time ever in LSAT history that the test asked the very rare Logical Reasoning question that calls for the statement that LEAST helps you to evaluate the argument.
- As if that weren't enough, PrepTest 70 was also just the eighth LSAT in history to feature the very rare Point at Issue (Agree) LR question type.
- The rarities on PrepTest 70 continue in the Logic Games section where it was the first LSAT in five years to contain *two* Hybrid games and …
- … was only the second LSAT since June 2010 to have a Selection game. Viva Formal Logic!
- In Reading Comprehension, PrepTest 70 was just the second LSAT since June 2010 on which the Comparative Reading passages came from social science (they come far more often from topics in law).
- On the day PrepTest 70 was administered, the #1 song in the country was "Royals" by Lorde. Hum that one to yourself while tackling the Reading Comprehension passage that questions the relationship between wealth and happiness.

PrepTest 70 in Context

As much fun as it is to find out what makes a PrepTest unique or noteworthy, it's even more important to know just how representative it is of other LSAT administrations (and, thus, how likely it is to be representative of the exam you will face on Test Day). The following charts compare the numbers of each kind of question and game on PrepTest 70 to the average numbers seen on all officially released LSATs administered over the past five years (from 2012 through 2016).

Number of LR Questions by Type: PrepTest 70 vs. 2012-2016 Average

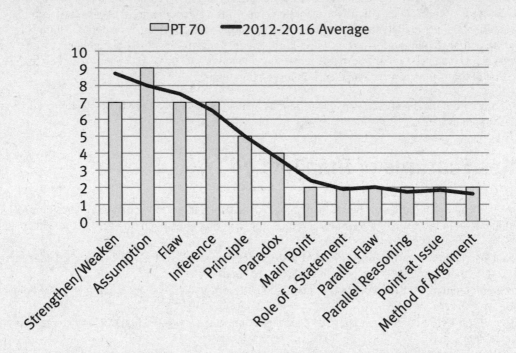

Number of LG Games by Type: PrepTest 70 vs. 2012-2016 Average

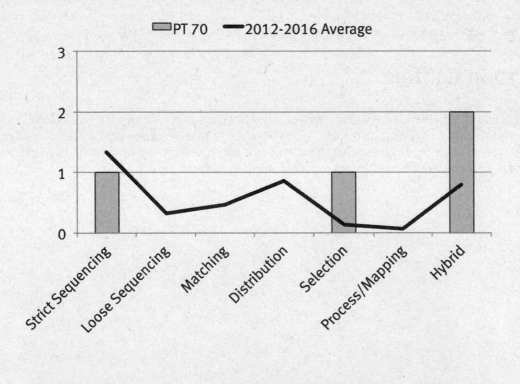

Number of RC Questions by Type: PrepTest 70 vs. 2012-2016 Average

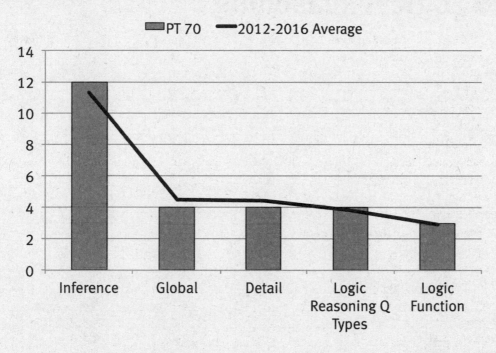

There isn't usually a huge difference in the distribution of questions from LSAT to LSAT, but if this test seems harder (or easier) to you than another you've taken, compare the number of questions of the types on which you, personally, are strongest and weakest. And then, explore within each section to see if your best or worst question types came earlier or later.

Students in Kaplan's comprehensive LSAT courses have access to every released LSAT, and to an online Q-Bank with thousands of officially released questions, games, and passages. If you are studying on your own, you have to do a bit more work to identify your strengths and your areas of opportunity. Quantitative analysis (like that in the charts shown here) is an important tool for understanding how the test is constructed, and how you are performing on it.

Section I: Logical Reasoning

Q#	Question Type	Correct	Difficulty
1	Assumption (Sufficient)	A	★
2	Flaw	D	★
3	Strengthen	D	★
4	Point at Issue	A	★
5	Paradox	E	★★
6	Principle (Apply/Inference)	C	★
7	Assumption (Sufficient)	E	★
8	Inference	B	★★
9	Flaw	A	★
10	Parallel Flaw	A	★
11	Strengthen/Weaken (Evaluate the Argument)	B	★★
12	Paradox	E	★
13	Assumption (Necessary)	B	★★★★
14	Principle (Identify/Inference)	D	★
15	Flaw	A	★★
16	Weaken	E	★★★
17	Role of a Statement	D	★★★
18	Main Point	A	★★
19	Parallel Reasoning	C	★★★
20	Flaw	E	★★★
21	Assumption (Necessary)	D	★
22	Inference	C	★
23	Principle (Identify/Strengthen)	E	★★★★
24	Inference	C	★★
25	Strengthen	B	★★

1. (A) Assumption (Sufficient)

Step 1: Identify the Question Type

This question is a unique twist on two common question types: Inference and Assumption. The LSAT Logical Reasoning section has long had questions asking you to fill in the blank at the end of the stimulus, but typically with a conclusion that must be inferred. This question asks you to fill in a new piece of evidence that would allow the conclusion to be properly drawn. In other words, the question wants an assumption. The phrasing "the conclusion … is properly drawn" makes it a Sufficient Assumption. The correct answer will be one way to prove the conclusion true.

Step 2: Untangle the Stimulus

The author concludes that the *Messenger* will not interview Hermann. The evidence is that the *Messenger* will not do anything to compromise editorial integrity. Also, Hermann requires the right to approve the article before publication.

Step 3: Make a Prediction

A Sufficient Assumption question asks you to find the new piece of evidence that, if combined with existing evidence, guarantees the conclusion is true. Here, you must prove the *Messenger* will not interview Hermann.

Hermann won't interview without the right to approve articles and the *Messenger* won't interview him if it believes doing so will compromise its editorial integrity. So, a belief that granting an interview subject the right to approve articles compromises its editorial integrity would guarantee that the *Messenger* will not interview Hermann.

Step 4: Evaluate the Answer Choices

(A) matches the prediction. If the editors believe giving an interview subject the right to approve an article compromises their editorial integrity, they will not grant it. And, since Hermann requires such a right of approval, the interview will not happen. This answer guarantees the conclusion.

(B) certainly strengthens the argument, but just because the *Messenger* has never before given an interviewee the right of approval is not enough to guarantee that it will not do so for Hermann.

(C) is Out of Scope because you know Hermann refuses to give interviews without a right to approve the article; it does not matter what other stars are willing to do.

(D), like **(B)**, strengthens the argument by providing a reason for the *Messenger* to not accede to Hermann's demand for approval rights. Still, as with **(B)**, that is not enough to guarantee the *Messenger* will not give Hermann an interview.

(E) does not add anything to the argument. This choice provides a reason for Hermann to insist on approval rights for an interview with the *Messenger*, but based on the evidence,

he would do so regardless. So this added incentive is superfluous.

2. (D) Flaw

Step 1: Identify the Question Type

The phrase "vulnerable to criticism" is common Flaw question wording. Look for the disconnect between the conclusion and the evidence, keeping common LSAT flaws in mind.

Step 2: Untangle the Stimulus

The columnist's conclusion comes after the contrast Keyword [*b*]*ut*, which is a common pattern on the LSAT. The columnist says "that is absurd," but what is *absurd*? Do not leave vague terms in your paraphrase of the conclusion. Here, the conclusion would be: it is absurd to say GIAPS leads people to develop ineffective presentations. The columnist backs up the conclusion with two pieces of evidence, including a subsidiary conclusion: GIAPS is just a tool, so it can't be responsible. Additionally, those who use the tool poorly are responsible. While it's arguable that the last sentence in the stimulus is the conclusion, the thrust of the columnist's argument is to discount claims against GIAPS, not to assign responsibility. Using the One Sentence Test and keeping an eye out for contrast Keywords can help you determine the author's main point.

Step 3: Make a Prediction

The columnist seems to believe that a tool cannot be responsible for the poor product the tool is used to create. The correct answer choice will present that as an unwarranted assumption or indicate that the author ignores the possibility that a tool can in some way be responsible for poor results.

Step 4: Evaluate the Answer Choices

(D) is correct. In order to be correct, a Flaw answer choice presented as an ignored possibility must, if true, weaken the argument. This one does. If it is true that a tool might not effectively perform its intended function, then the tool might bear responsibility.

(A) cannot be correct because the columnist does not use inconsistent claims as evidence. The author does present a claim she disagrees with, so there are inconsistent claims in the stimulus, but the LSAT wants you to recognize who says what. The columnist is refuting one claim, not using both to support her argument.

(B) is a Distortion. There is a scope shift from "ineffective" presentations to "bad" presentations, meaning the author assumes that if a presentation is ineffective then it is bad. But that does not imply that the author thinks *not* ineffective presentations are good presentations. More importantly, the crux of the conclusion is whether GIAPS can be blamed for bad (ineffective) presentations. The flaw will revolve around that determination of responsibility.

(C) is also a Distortion. While the columnist lets a popular product off the hook for producing bad presentations, this is not the same as endorsing the product. Additionally, while the columnist mentions the product's popularity when giving background, she in no way refers to that popularity when giving her reasons why GIAPS does not bear responsibility.

(E) describes an ad hominem attack, which is not at play here. The author does not criticize or comment on the information design expert that she contradicts.

3. (D) Strengthen

Step 1: Identify the Question Type

The question stem explicitly asks you to strengthen the argument. Find additional support for the author's conclusion, possibly by stating (and thus firming up) the assumption.

Step 2: Untangle the Stimulus

The conclusion is "that claim is easily disproven." However, that phrase is uninformative and ineffective to use in assessing the argument. Many LSAT arguments present the claim of another followed by the author's conclusion that such a claim is wrong. To translate the author's conclusion, reverse the other party's claim. In this case, supporters claim that allowing oil drilling in the preserve will not damage the environment. So, the author's conclusion must be: oil drilling in the preserve *will* damage the environment. The author discounts the argument that modern drilling methods will not cause damage by pointing to a nearby bay, where oil drilling beginning five years ago has spoiled the landscape with industrial sprawl, drilling platforms, and roads and pipelines.

Step 3: Make a Prediction

The author commits a subtle scope shift, arguing against a current plan by using an older site as evidence. In predicting similar environmental damage at the two locations, the author assumes the drilling methods will be similar, which ignores the possibility that changes have been made in drilling methods. Strengthen this argument by firming up the analogy between the two situations. The correct answer may minimize or eliminate a potential difference.

Step 4: Evaluate the Answer Choices

(D) strengthens the argument by eliminating the possibility that the drilling in the preserve would utilize less damaging - methods than those used in the nearby site. If you noticed that the author points to a five-year-old example while the proponents assert that "modern" drilling methods would be used, you likely would have been led straight to this answer. However, a general recognition that the two drilling situations might not be sufficiently similar could have led you to this choice as well.

(A) is Out of Scope. It may be a reason to leave the preserve alone, but it does not affect the editorial's actual argument. The editorial discusses whether the drilling will cause environmental damage, not whether it should or should not occur. This answer highlights the importance of being clear on the author's conclusion. Even though the first sentence mentions that the legislature is considering allowing oil drilling, that is not the claim against which the author argues. The structure of the paragraph makes clear that the author is rebutting the claim that "there will be no damage to the environment."

(B) is Out of Scope. Whether the companies drilling at Alphin Bay claimed there would be environmental damage or not is irrelevant. The fact is there was environmental damage based on the methods they used over the last five years. Whether they acknowledged that or not doesn't affect whether any drilling at Cape Simmons will also lead to environmental damage.

(C) is Extreme. Similar to the problem with **(A)**, the author's conclusion is limited to whether there will be damage to the environment and does not extend to whether or not drilling should be allowed. So, to give a necessary condition to allow drilling would be Extreme.

(E) is, if anything, a 180. It weakens the argument by indicating other industries may be responsible for the environmental damage at Alphin Bay. Thus, the author may not be correct that oil drilling will certainly lead to damage at Cape Simmons.

4. (A) Point at Issue

Step 1: Identify the Question Type

A question stem asking what two people disagree about is a Point at Issue question. Find the answer that both people have an opinion on and about which they disagree.

Step 2: Untangle the Stimulus

James asserts that community colleges work to meet the educational needs of their communities, while universities have different goals and do not.

Margaret asserts that the primary goal of any university is to serve the needs of its community. Also, she asserts that preparing for a career is the main goal of anyone attending either a community college or a university.

Step 3: Make a Prediction

If you recognize a clear difference between the two, look for that in the answers. The explicit point of disagreement is that James asserts that universities do not work to meet the needs of their community while Margaret asserts that it is their primary goal.

You should also note that there are issues that only one of the two addresses. Such issues thus cannot be the focus of the correct answer. James asserts that community colleges work to meet the needs of their community while Margaret is silent on that. Also, Margaret asserts that the main reason people attend either a community college or a university is to prepare for a career. James does not proffer an opinion on this.

Step 4: Evaluate the Answer Choices

(A) is correct. Both address whether a primary goal of any university is to serve the education needs of its community. James asserts it is not a goal of universities to meet the educational needs of the community, while Margaret very explicitly asserts it is a primary goal.

(B) is Out of Scope because neither addresses how adequately universities actually meet the needs of the community, only whether it is their goal to do so.

(C) is incorrect because only Margaret addresses the attendees' reasons for attending school.

(D) is Out of Scope because neither defines the needs of the community, only whether it is a goal of the educational institutions to serve those needs. Margaret does assert that the primary reason why individuals attend either type of institution is to prepare for a career, but this goal could be different from the needs of the community. Additionally, James does not mention this at all.

(E) is incorrect because only Margaret discusses students' reasons for attending school. James discusses only institutions.

5. (E) Paradox

Step 1: Identify the Question Type

A question stem that asks you to "resolve" or "explain" a conflict, discrepancy, dispute, or paradox is a Paradox question. Focus on the two apparently contradictory facts, and identify the potential explanation for how both can be true.

Step 2: Untangle the Stimulus

According to the stimulus, most people who have taken an organizational-skills seminar became more organized, but few became more efficient.

Step 3: Make a Prediction

You might expect that becoming more organized would cause people to become more efficient. So the correct answer needs to identify some explanation for why organization does not result in greater efficiency. The correct answer will likely address both qualities, either directly or indirectly. That general understanding serves as a sufficient prediction. If you make a specific prediction on a Paradox question, be open to other explanations that could also explain the mystery.

Step 4: Evaluate the Answer Choices

(E) matches the general prediction. It indicates that the effort spent organizing costs about as much time as it saves.

(A) is consistent with the situation in the stimulus, indicating that efficiency and organization aren't connected. However it does nothing to explain *why* that would be the case.

(B) is Out of Scope. The mystery concerns people who *have* taken the organizational-skills seminar. More importantly, this answer provides no explanation for why organizational skills, whether innate or learned in the seminar, do not translate to greater efficiency.

(C) is also Out of Scope. It introduces a new characteristic about who the seminars target, but that doesn't explain why the result of the seminars is increased organization but not increased efficiency.

(D) explains why people took the seminar but fails to explain why the improvements in organizational skills did not translate to greater efficiency.

6. (C) Principle (Apply/Inference)

Step 1: Identify the Question Type

The stem introduces a twist on common Principle questions. Typically, the word *justify* is used in Principle/Strengthen hybrid questions, which ask you to find the principle in the answer choices that supports the conclusion above. However, this time the principle is in the stimulus, so it's an Apply the Principle question, and notice that this question asks you to justify or support an answer choice. If the support (or justification) flows downward from the stimulus to an answer choice, you are dealing with an Inference question. Find the answer that must be true based on the information in the stimulus.

Step 2: Untangle the Stimulus

The stimulus describes a problem with rebate coupons, some of which bore an inaccurate expiration date. This mistake created an unfair situation in which some customers incorrectly believed the rebate offer had already expired.

The stimulus also articulates a Formal Logic principle, which holds that if someone creates an unfair situation, then that person has an obligation to correct any unfair result of that situation.

Step 3: Make a Prediction

Under the principle, because the corporation created the unfair situation, it has an obligation to rectify any unfair result. So, if customers did not get their rebates because of the wrong expiration date, the corporation, under the principle, should make an effort to rectify the situation.

It is important to notice that the *result* of the Formal Logic principle is that there is an obligation to rectify. Thus, any answer choice that concludes that Thimble Corporation does *not* have an obligation cannot be correct. For that reason alone, **(A)** and **(E)** can be eliminated.

Step 4: Evaluate the Answer Choices

(C) matches the prediction, basically inserting the facts of the specific situation with the Thimble Corporation into the Formal Logic rule of the principle in the stimulus.

(A) is a 180 because, as explained previously, the principle identifies circumstances resulting in an obligation, while this answer indicates that Thimble Corporation would not be obligated to give a rebate. The stimulus doesn't provide any information about what circumstances would lead to Thimble Corporation not having an obligation.

(B) does not follow from the stimulus. While this certainly could be true, the information and principle in the stimulus do not cover this type of situation: customers freely deciding not to apply for a rebate. In other words, this choice does not have to be true based on the stimulus. This choice illustrates the importance of recognizing this question as an Inference question despite the question stem's phrasing.

(D) is incorrect because it arguably creates a greater unfairness (none of the customers getting their deserved rebate and Thimble Corporation keeping all the money). Based on the principle in the stimulus, Thimble Corporation would then be obligated to rectify an even worse situation.

(E) is similar to **(A)** in that it offers an Out of Scope situation that leads to Thimble Corporation not having any obligation. The stimulus doesn't provide any information about such a situation (denials for reasons *other* than wrong expiration dates) or such a result (lack of obligation). Based on the lack of support in the stimulus, this answer choice could be true but does not have to be.

7. (E) Assumption (Sufficient)

Step 1: Identify the Question Type

The phrasing "conclusion … can be properly drawn if … assumed" indicates a Sufficient Assumption question, requiring you to identify the additional evidence that proves the conclusion true.

Step 2: Untangle the Stimulus

The critic concludes that a recent biography does not explain what is of most interest about Shakespeare because, while it shows what life would have been like for Shakespeare, it does not explain what made Shakespeare different from his contemporaries.

Step 3: Make a Prediction

To make an assumption in an argument, the author must believe the following: if I have this evidence, then I can reasonably reach this conclusion. So, a good way to

paraphrase the assumption is to identify the key reason in both the evidence and the conclusion, and then put them into "if evidence, then conclusion" form.

Thus, the assumption is that if you do not explain what makes Shakespeare different from his contemporaries (evidence), then you have not explained what is of most interest about him (conclusion). The contrapositive of that assumption is that explaining what is of most interest about Shakespeare requires explaining what makes Shakespeare different from his contemporaries.

Step 4: Evaluate the Answer Choices

(E) matches the prediction and proves the conclusion true. If what is *most* interesting about Shakespeare is what made him different from his contemporaries, and this biography does not explain that, then it must follow that this biography does not explain what is of most interest about Shakespeare. Notice that this is the only choice that references "what is of most interest" about Shakespeare, and thus almost certainly has to be the right answer, because that is the unique concept in the conclusion.

(A) does not bridge the gap to the conclusion about what is most interesting about Shakespeare. Additionally, it would be Extreme for the critic to believe that explaining Shakespeare's distinctiveness is impossible, because not doing so is the critic's specific criticism of the book.

(B) is a Distortion. The critic says the biography doesn't explain what is most interesting about Shakespeare, but that doesn't mean he thinks life in Elizabethan England is therefore uninteresting. Additionally, this choice does not prove anything about Shakespeare, let alone the conclusion that the recent biography failed to explain what is most interesting about Shakespeare.

(C) is incorrect, even though the argument does necessarily assume that Shakespeare was different from his contemporaries. However, the argument does not assume that Shakespeare was *very* different from his contemporaries. More importantly, this choice does not prove that this difference is what was most interesting about Shakespeare.

(D) is also Extreme. It may be something the critic believes, but this choice does not make the connection to what is most interesting about Shakespeare, which is the focus of the conclusion. A rule that a biography should *always* focus on a subject's distinctiveness does not imply that a subject's distinctiveness is what is of most interest about him.

8. (B) Inference

Step 1: Identify the Question Type

This question stem provides the basic test for an Inference answer: it asks what must be true based on the information above.

Step 2: Untangle the Stimulus

The stimulus describes the inadequacies of using a blender to make whipped cream due to the container's poor air intake.

Step 3: Make a Prediction

The stimulus does not contain any Formal Logic, readily combinable statements, or emphasized statements. Thus, like many Inference questions, there is no clear prediction. Assess each answer by comparing it to the stimulus and asking "Does this have to be true?" Prioritize modestly phrased answers, and watch out for Inference red flags, e.g., Out of Scope and Too Extreme answers.

Step 4: Evaluate the Answer Choices

(B) is a nice, modestly phrased answer that basically matches the information in the final sentence: that a special attachment can help but it does not fully compensate for a blender's poor air intake.

(A) goes beyond the information provided. While using a blender results in a thick velvety substance, it cannot be inferred that other ineffective methods produce the same type of flawed result.

(C) is Extreme. The last sentence indicates only that a special attachment "*can* help somewhat," so it cannot be inferred that the special attachment "*always* produces a fluffier result" than a blender without the attachment.

(D) is unsupported. The stimulus does not explain how the special attachment works. It is just as likely that the attachment functions by increasing the blender's air intake.

(E) is Out of Scope. The stimulus discusses the *effectiveness* of using a blender but does not mention how *common* any methods are.

9. (A) Flaw

Step 1: Identify the Question Type

This question stem explicitly asks you to identify the flaw. Notice how the conclusion goes beyond the evidence, and keep common LSAT flaws in mind.

Step 2: Untangle the Stimulus

The stimulus contains a substantial amount of important-sounding background information regarding the chronology of a meteorite bombardment that would have destroyed any life on Earth and subsequent development of life on Earth. However, the astronomer's logic really is contained in the last third of the stimulus. The astronomer's conclusion is that the extraterrestrial origin of life hypothesis is *false*. In doing so, the astronomer claims proponents of the extraterrestrial origin hypothesis have only provided evidence for why life could not have arisen on Earth. They have not provided evidence that life came from extraterrestrial spores.

Step 3: Make a Prediction

This argument implicates an uncommon, yet still classic LSAT flaw: assuming that absence of evidence in favor of a claim constitutes evidence against that claim. In other words, assuming lack of support is support for the opposite. For example, if I conclude that Ray's Pizza on Broadway is awesome based on a review I read, subsequently being told that the review was really for the Ray's Pizza on Fifth Avenue is not evidence that the Ray's Pizza on Broadway stinks. I am simply left with no evidence to make any judgment about that particular pizza joint. Similarly, asserting that no one has provided evidence for the extraterrestrial origin hypothesis does not support a claim that the hypothesis is false, merely that the hypothesis is *unsupported*.

If you did not recognize this flaw, then you should have assessed each answer with these basic questions: "Does the author do this?" "Does it accurately describe the argument?"

Step 4: Evaluate the Answer Choices

(A) matches the prediction and is correct because it accurately describes the argument. Many Flaw answer choices are simply descriptive of the evidence and conclusion in the stimulus. Such an answer will be correct if it is accurate and if it shows a hole in the reasoning.

(B) is incorrect because it mischaracterizes the author's conclusion. The astronomer does not claim that the extraterrestrial hypothesis is inherently *implausible*, just that it is not actually true. There is a difference between stating something did not happen versus stating that it could not have happened.

(C) also does not accurately describe what the author does. The astronomer never offers a competing hypothesis, and thus does not compare the likelihood that different hypotheses are true. Even if it is presumed that the astronomers alternate hypothesis is that life originated on Earth, the astronomer would not view that hypothesis as *equally* true.

(D) does not describe the logic of the argument. The author's only premise supporting his conclusion is that the other side does not have any real evidence. That assertion does not contradict the conclusion. It is insufficient to support the conclusion, but does not contradict it.

(E) is wrong because the astronomer does not actually grant the truth of the proponents' claims; he merely says what type of evidence they offer. Additionally, even if the astronomer had done so, it is not a flaw to acknowledge the truth of claims that do not support one's argument *as long as* one then presents additional reasoning. The flaw is the inadequacy of the astronomer's reasons for dismissing the extraterrestrial theory.

10. (A) Parallel Flaw

Step 1: Identify the Question Type

Though phrased a little differently than normal, the question stem asks you to identify the parallel reasoning to a flawed argument. Recognize the flaw in the stimulus before seeking the answer that contains an argument with the same flaw. The answer choices all start with "Similarly, you could conclude that … " The correct answer will introduce an analogous situation that points out the flaw of the argument in the stimulus.

Step 2: Untangle the Stimulus

The argument in the stimulus jumps from evidence of a few successful users of the VIVVY language course to a conclusion that any child who uses it can expect to become successful.

Step 3: Make a Prediction

The argument commits the classic flaw of assuming that correlation indicates causation. In other words, the ad suggests that VIVVY caused the three students to become successful university students and would do the same for other children. You could also categorize this flaw as one of representativeness. The three students discussed may not be representative of all the children who studied with VIVVY. Look for an answer containing evidence that a few people were successful using something to support a claim that others who use it will be successful.

Step 4: Evaluate the Answer Choices

(A) is correct because it similarly assumes that correlation indicates causation. It argues that just because three lottery winners happened to carry good-luck charms that good-luck charms will cause others to win as well.

(B) is not a match. The stimulus involves three examples that the ad presents as representative. This choice, however, shows one of the three (Christine) is different from the other two. Additionally, this choice does not then expand its findings (unlikeliness to get food poisoning) to a larger group.

(C)'s flaw is confusing necessary and sufficient conditions. The evidence indicates that being hired within the last year is sufficient to result in someone's being laid off, but the conclusion assumes that it is necessary, claiming that *only* those hired in the last year will be laid off.

(D) is not a match. Like **(C)**, this answer choice confuses the Formal Logic; just because routinely exceeding the speed limit will yield speeding tickets does not mean that everybody who has speeding tickets routinely exceeds the speed limit. Additionally, this choice does not follow the pattern of predicting that anyone can follow in the footsteps of the three examples. Rather, the conclusion is limited to the three people mentioned.

(E) is a 180. The stimulus uses evidence of the good fortune of three specific examples to extrapolate to a broader claim that anybody can achieve the same results the same way. In an opposite manner, this choice uses evidence of a broader trend to reach a conclusion about specific individuals.

11. (B) Strengthen/Weaken (Evaluate the Argument LEAST)

Step 1: Identify the Question Type

A question stem that asks you to *evaluate* an argument is a spin-off from a Strengthen/Weaken question—an Evaluate the Argument question. It requires you to identify the relevant type of information that could affect the likelihood that the conclusion is true. The "LEAST" in the question stem means you must identify the answer choice that is *irrelevant* to the argument.

Step 2: Untangle the Stimulus

Notice that the phrase "Recently, however" signals the transition from the background information to the heart of the activist's argument. The activist concludes with the hope that we can eventually replace nuclear power with a more environmentally safe source of energy. The evidence is that the technology to derive power from sewage sludge has been developed.

Step 3: Make a Prediction

When an author concludes that one option is better than another, the author assumes that on balance the pros and cons of each option favor the author's choice. You would strengthen or weaken such an argument with additional factors (other pros and cons) that tip that balance one way or the other. Here, you should anticipate answer choices introducing potential harm to the environment from using sewage sludge as an energy source. Other choices may discuss the practicality of meeting energy needs this way. The exception will be the answer choice that is irrelevant to the practicality or safety of using sewage sludge for energy.

Step 4: Evaluate the Answer Choices

(B) is correct. Whether the process for creating sewage sludge has improved in some unspecified way in recent decades does not affect the conclusion, because the current quality of sewage sludge can be used to create energy. This answer does not address the practicality or environmental harms of doing so. Whether sewage can also be turned into clean water is immaterial to those environmental harms.

(A) is potentially relevant because if current methods of disposing of sludge damage the environment, then using the sludge for energy would help protect the environment.

(C) is relevant because whether or not energy from sewage sludge is economically sustainable will factor highly in whether it can contribute to meeting our energy needs and replacing nuclear energy.

(D) is relevant because potential environmental harms caused by sewage sludge energy production would directly affect the claim that this energy source will be less environmentally damaging than nuclear energy.

(E), like **(D)**, is relevant because potential dangers from using sewage sludge as energy would directly affect the claim that this energy is a viable and less environmentally damaging source than nuclear energy.

12. (E) Paradox

Step 1: Identify the Question Type

A question stem that asks you to "explain" a set of circumstances is a Paradox question. This stem actually points out the two apparently contradictory facts.

Step 2: Untangle the Stimulus

According to the stimulus, the most common trees in any tropical forest reproduce the most, but the rarest species tend to survive longer.

Step 3: Make a Prediction

This might not seem paradoxical to you at all, but don't worry; there is no need for a specific prediction to a Paradox question. Look for some factor that results in common trees having shorter life spans than rare trees, or in rare trees having longer life spans.

Step 4: Evaluate the Answer Choices

(E) is correct. The additional factor, which explains the mystery, is competition for resources. Because the paradox involves a comparison between two things (i.e., common and rare trees), the correct answer is likely a comparative choice that identifies a factor that differs for both types of tree. This is the only choice in the set that does so.

(A) only explains why some trees are more common, but it does not explain why they have shorter life spans. Additionally, the stimulus says that the pattern holds regardless of the species that is most common.

(B) doesn't distinguish between species. Older trees in both species probably reproduce the least. This does not explain the central mystery of why rare trees live longer than common trees.

(C) is Out of Scope. Even though the correct answer to a Paradox question will often bring in a new factor that explains the discrepancy, introducing a new distinction of pre-existing species versus new species is irrelevant to explaining the difference between common and rare species. The mystery still holds, regardless of whether the study introduced new types of trees or not.

(D) provides a benefit from the long lives of rare species, but it does not explain what causes them to survive better in the first place.

13. (B) Assumption (Necessary)

Step 1: Identify the Question Type

Because the question asks for the assumption on which an argument *relies* that means this is a Necessary Assumption question, which asks you to bridge the gap between the evidence and conclusion. The assumption must be true if the conclusion is true. You can use the Denial Test to check your answer.

Step 2: Untangle the Stimulus

The author concludes that the network's advertisement will not be as effective as the advertisement favored by the show's producers in attracting repeat viewers. The reasons are that the network's ad grossly misrepresents the program and false expectations could turn off initial viewers.

Step 3: Make a Prediction

The primary scope shift is from misleading ads potentially turning off initial viewers to the claim that these ads will not be effective in attracting continuing viewers. This ignores the possibility that once a large number of viewers are lured in by the misleading ad, a sufficient percentage will be hooked by the show anyway.

However, also note that the conclusion is not simply that the network's ad won't be effective, but that it won't be *as effective* as the ad favored by the producers. The conclusion really is a comparison of potential effectiveness. So, the argument also assumes that the producers' ad would have been different and better in some way.

Step 4: Evaluate the Answer Choices

(B) is correct because this must be true for the argument to make any sense. If you are not sure, use the Denial Test. The denied version of this answer would indicate that the ad favored by the producers would have grossly misrepresented the program as well. Thus, according to the evidence, the ad would have created similarly false expectations. So, it would not make sense to conclude that the ad favored by the producers would be more effective than the network's ad. The original version of this choice, therefore, is necessary to the argument.

(A) strengthens the argument but is not necessary to it. Even if only a minority of viewers tuned in because of the ad and had false expectations, the author could still claim that alienating those viewers made the misleading ad less effective than the alternative ad would have been.

(C) is incorrect. It points out that most initial viewers will not have been drawn by the ad, so this lessens the damage done by the misleading ad. Therefore, this answer choice cannot be what the author necessarily relies on to claim that the ad is less effective.

(D) is a Distortion and Extreme. Although it is powerful support for the argument, it neither guarantees that the conclusion is true nor, more importantly, is it necessary for the conclusion to be true. Even if the ad favored by the producers did attract loyal viewers, it might have attracted fewer total initial viewers than the misleading ad would have. It is also Extreme, because only a *greater* number of loyal viewers is necessary to the argument, not that *almost all* viewers will stick with the show.

(E) is not necessary to the argument. If anything, it is a 180 because it highlights the importance of getting people to tune in for the first episode. So a misleading ad that attracts multitudes of initial viewers might be more effective than an accurate ad that attracts a smaller number of initial viewers.

14. (D) Principle (Identify/Inference)

Step 1: Identify the Question Type

Both the term *principles* and the phrase "conforms ... to" indicate a Principle question, which requires you to match the specific situation in the stimulus with the general rule in the answers. That makes this an Identify the Principle question.

Step 2: Untangle the Stimulus

The stimulus describes a situation in which Sharon maintained a high opinion of a political candidate she supports and lowered her opinion of her favorite novelist after the novelist criticized the politician.

Step 3: Make a Prediction

Your task is to identify the issue that drove Sharon's reaction. Potentially, you might predict that the factor is favoring politicians over artists. However, other than noting that the two people involved were a novelist and a politician, the stimulus does not emphasize those roles in any way. However, the stimulus does indicate that Sharon has supported the politician for years without specifying how long she has favored the novelist. So, that is likely the focus of the correct answer.

Step 4: Evaluate the Answer Choices

(D) is correct, describing the situation in general terms. Sharon has been a long-standing supporter of the politician and upon hearing criticisms of the politician, she had doubts about the source (the novelist).

(A) may not be relevant because it's unclear if Sharon was one of the "most dedicated" fans of the novelist. Additionally, if anything, this is a 180, because the novelist was unable to influence Sharon, despite being Sharon's *favorite*.

(B) is Out of Scope. The only factor the stimulus mentions, besides the fact that the two people involved were a novelist and a politician, is the length of time Sharon had supported the politician. Nothing in the stimulus matches up with this

answer's reference to an artist having a reputation for being honest and knowledgeable about politics.

(C) is also Out of Scope. It is possible Sharon would have been fine with the novelist speaking out in favor of the political candidate she supports. The issue is not a general aversion to artists speaking out on political issues. The author makes no recommendation on what artists should speak about.

(E) recognizes that length of support is central to the situation in the stimulus. However, this answer is Extreme because Sharon does not "renounce" any allegiances. Additionally, it is unclear how long the novelist has had Sharon's "allegiance" and whether that relationship was new or not. Perhaps she has followed the novelist for as long as or longer than she has followed the politician.

15. (A) Flaw

Step 1: Identify the Question Type

The phrase "vulnerable to criticism" indicates a Flaw question. Note how the conclusion goes beyond the evidence, and keep common LSAT flaws in mind.

Step 2: Untangle the Stimulus

The advertisement concludes that Sparkle Cola gets a more favorable response in taste tests than any of the five competing colas tested. In the test, most of the participants said they preferred Sparkle Cola to the single competing cola they tasted.

Step 3: Make a Prediction

While the numbers look good for Sparkle, this is a Flaw question so there must be something about the study that allows Sparkle to *not* be the most preferred cola. For a Flaw question, treat the conclusion as wrong to help you understand how it could be false. Now you might have noticed that the testers were divided into groups, and in each group Sparkle was paired against a different competitor. So, it is possible that in four groups, Sparkle edged out the competition but in the fifth group the competitor won unanimously. That competitor could rightly claim to be the most preferred, because it competed in only one group, even though overall Sparkle got the most votes, given that it was involved in all five matches.

It is likely that many test takers did not catch that play on numbers. In that case, for each answer, ask yourself if this is the issue that allows Sparkle to *not* be the favorite. Watch out for answers that go beyond the scope of this specific conclusion, and try to bring in something besides taste.

Step 4: Evaluate the Answer Choices

(A) is correct, as this possibility allows this superficially solid conclusion to be false. This choice points to the subgroups.

As described previously, these subgroups could result in another cola being able to claim it was most popular, due to its performance in its subgroup, despite Sparkle getting the most votes overall.

(B) is Out of Scope. The conclusion is limited to whether Sparkle was the most preferred on *taste*. The argument does not assume anything about whether those testers would actually buy Sparkle, or what role cost would play.

(C) is Out of Scope because while the advertisement does ostensibly overlook this possibility, doing so is not a flaw. If the possibility were true, it would not actually weaken the conclusion, which is limited to whether Sparkle was the favorite among competitors *in this test*.

(D) is Out of Scope because the sole issue in the stimulus is whether Sparkle was the most preferred cola for *taste*. The evidence is clearly only about taste, and while the conclusion doesn't mention specifically that Sparkle Cola's more favorable response is limited to taste, that favorable response in this study did not involve the other considerations such as packaging or price. So, while it may be true that people in the marketplace prefer Sparkle for other reasons, overlooking that possibility is not a flaw because in this study those other considerations were not at play—the volunteers were blindfolded.

(E) is true, but so what? There is no reason why cola taste tests cannot be limited to colas. Again, the conclusion is specifically limited to the issue of whether Sparkle was the preferred cola based on taste in this particular taste test. Any failure to consider other beverages is not a flaw.

16. (E) Weaken

Step 1: Identify the Question Type

The question stem explicitly asks you to weaken the reasoning above. Identify the assumption and attack it.

Step 2: Untangle the Stimulus

The author concludes that too much television viewing causes people to overestimate the risks the world poses. The evidence is a study showing a correlation between a person's above-average amount of television viewing and how likely the person is to believe a natural disaster will strike her.

Step 3: Make a Prediction

This is a classic correlation-to-causation pattern. The built-in way to weaken such an argument is to suggest one of the following three: an alternative cause, reverse causation, or coincidence.

Step 4: Evaluate the Answer Choices

(E) is correct. It suggests reverse causation. Rather than television viewing causing an unfounded fear of natural disasters, a well-founded fear of natural disasters due to geography correlates with above-average television viewing.

(A) is an important type of wrong answer to a Weaken question. It introduces a counterexample. However, the word *many* on the LSAT should only be interpreted as "at least one"; a small number of counterexamples does not weaken a non-absolute relationship. The argument only asserts that people are more likely to inflate the risk of being the victim of a disaster if they watch an above-average amount of TV. Because the argument already allows for exceptions, pointing out those exceptions does not weaken the argument.

(B) is a 180 because it strengthens the argument. It is very consistent with the claim that watching television causes people to inflate the risk of being a victim of a natural disaster, especially since those people are less likely to live in an area prone to natural disasters.

(C) has only a tenuous relationship to the argument, which concerns the causal relationship between high television viewing and an inflated concern of the risk of natural disasters. Knowing that a low amount of television viewing is correlated with accurate assessments of risk doesn't necessarily mean a high amount of television viewing causes exaggerated assessments of risk. However, to whatever extent this answer is relevant, it is a 180 because it is consistent with the relationship espoused by the author. Thus, it cannot weaken the argument.

(D) says that accurate assessments of risk result from information sources other than television. Like the prior choice, this answer is wholly consistent with the relationship espoused by the author, i.e., that television causes a distorted view of the risks posed by natural disasters. Thus, it does not weaken the argument.

17. (D) Role of a Statement

Step 1: Identify the Question Type

The question stem restates a claim from the stimulus and asks you what role it plays in the argument. Thus, this is a Role of a Statement question, which requires you to follow the structure of *how* the argument proceeds and to identify the relevant statement's purpose within that structure.

Step 2: Untangle the Stimulus

The question stem reiterates the claim from the stimulus that "in general, as water vapor in larger clouds condenses, heavier downpours are more likely to result." Underline this statement in the stimulus. It is the final sentence in the stimulus. Next, break down the argument, identifying the conclusion and evidence.

The conclusion is the prediction in the first sentence. Even though there are no evidence or conclusion Keywords, the rest of the stimulus provides a chain of causation supporting the prediction of more frequent downpours as the atmosphere warms. So, the statement in question is the last piece in the evidentiary chain supporting the conclusion.

Step 3: Make a Prediction

The correct answer must at least describe the referenced statement as a piece of evidence.

Step 4: Evaluate the Answer Choices

(D) correctly describes the statement as evidence in the argument.

(A) misidentifies the statement as the conclusion of the argument.

(B) both misidentifies the statement as the conclusion of the argument and incorrectly introduces the existence of a second conclusion.

(C) describes the statement as a subsidiary conclusion. In other words, some of the argument supports the subsidiary - conclusion, which then supports the conclusion of the argument as a whole. However, this statement *adds* additional evidence to the rest of the evidence presented; it is not *supported* by the previous evidence and therefore is not a subsidiary conclusion.

(E) is Half-Right/Half-Wrong. The statement *is* part of a causal evidence chain. However, this choice cannot be correct because it incorrectly indicates that the statement is not intended to support the conclusion.

18. (A) Main Point

Step 1: Identify the Question Type

The question asks you to identify the conclusion of the argument, which means to identify the Main Point. Do not concern yourself with the entire argument, and be wary of conclusion Keywords.

Step 2: Untangle the Stimulus

The contrast Keyword [*h*]*owever* indicates the transition from the background information to the author's judgment regarding the usefulness of field studies.

Step 3: Make a Prediction

The correct answer should match the argument that anthropologists tend to overrate the usefulness of field studies. Watch out for answers that drift into the evidence, summarize the entire argument, or speculate beyond the argument.

Step 4: Evaluate the Answer Choices

(A) is correct as it is a precise match for the conclusion, which is in the sentence beginning with [*h*]*owever*.

(B) is background information. It is a definition found in the introduction to the argument.

(C) is also background information. It is detail mentioned in the introduction to the argument.

(D) is mentioned as a preface to the author's supporting premise. It is a concession that anthropologists make to indicate that field studies are not ideal, yet they still overrate the usefulness of field studies.

(E) is the author's primary piece of evidence.

19. (C) Parallel Reasoning

Step 1: Identify the Question Type

A question that asks you to identify *similar reasoning* is a Parallel Reasoning question. These questions require you to find the answer choice that uses the same type of evidence to reach the same type of conclusion as in the stimulus.

Step 2: Untangle the Stimulus

The argument concludes that the proposal will probably be rejected. The evidence is that the proposal will not be rewritten; according to a reliable source, if the proposal is not rewritten then it will be rejected.

Step 3: Make a Prediction

The correct answer must have the same basic pieces: 1) a piece of factual evidence (the proposal will not be rewritten); 2) a reliable opinion (Juarez is very reliable) that if such a fact is true, it will indicate a certain result (if not rewritten, then rejected); and 3) a conclusion that the result is thus probable (probably rejected).

Step 4: Evaluate the Answer Choices

(C) is correct because it has all the right pieces: a piece of factual evidence (that the company's data are accurate); a reliable opinion (the science journal is rarely wrong) that if such a fact is true, it will indicate a certain result (if the data are accurate a new medication is safe); and a conclusion that the result is probable (the medication is probably safe).

(A) has the right pieces but they are jumbled up. The conditional statement should come from the reliable source, but here it is presented as the evidence (if accurate then safe). The reliable source, on the other hand, simply expresses a piece of factual evidence (data is accurate). These pieces are transposed.

(B) is incorrect. This is most clear from the conclusion, which is expressed as a certainty (*prove* that the medication is safe) rather than as a probability.

(D) does not match. First, this argument does not have a concrete fact—the journal gives a conditional statement and a statement that the data is *probably* accurate. That means there are too many "probably" statements. In the stimulus, only the conclusion is stated as a probability.

(E) does not match. Again, this choice does not have a concrete fact from which the evidence proceeds to the conclusion. Also, as with the prior choice, there are too many "probably" statements to match the single probability in the conclusion of the stimulus. And finally, there is no conditional statement from a reliable expert.

20. (E) Flaw

Step 1: Identify the Question Type

The phrase "vulnerable to criticism" indicates a Flaw question. Notice how the conclusion goes beyond the evidence, and keep common LSAT flaws in mind.

Step 2: Untangle the Stimulus

The advertisement concludes that switching to Popelka could save people hundreds of dollars on car insurance. The evidence is that in a recent survey, a sample representative of all new Popelka insurance policyholders reported saving $250 on average.

Step 3: Make a Prediction

Any time a Flaw question introduces a statistic, study, or survey, you should immediately be questioning whether the subjects studied are representative. While the evidence states that the people surveyed are a representative sample of *new* Popelka insurance policyholders, it does not follow that they are representative of *all* car drivers. Indeed, it is likely that those who could save the most by switching to Popelka insurance would be among the first to do so and might therefore not be representative of the population in general.

Step 4: Evaluate the Answer Choices

(E) is correct, raising the possibility that those most capable of saving money with Popelka are those who recently switched. Therefore, new Popelka policyholders are not representative of the broader population.

(A) is not a flaw. An argument based on averages allows that a portion will be below the average. It does not weaken such an argument to point out that a few counterexamples are below, even far below, the average.

(B) is an Irrelevant Comparison. The argument does not necessarily assume any particular comparison between new and longtime Popelka policyholders. The relevant comparison is between Popelka and other companies, not old and new Popelka customers.

(C) may be true, but it is irrelevant. The argument does not claim that switching to Popelka will save customers more than switching to other companies. There may be one insurance company that's consistently cheaper than Popelka, but that doesn't hurt the argument that *most* people could save by switching to Popelka. It is vital to understand the conclusion and stay within its scope.

(D) is a 180. The argument actually assumes that a significant number of survey respondents did not *overestimate* how much they saved.

21. (D) Assumption (Necessary)

Step 1: Identify the Question Type

A question that asks for the assumption *required* by the argument is a Necessary Assumption question. Identify the core missing link between the evidence and conclusion.

Step 2: Untangle the Stimulus

The magazine concludes that specially formulated detergent is necessary to properly clean clothes in a front-loading washer. The evidence is that since front-loaders use less water, ordinary powder detergents do not dissolve readily.

Step 3: Make a Prediction

There are two core assumptions in this argument. First, the argument assumes that there is no other option besides ordinary powder detergent and specially formulated detergents for front-loading washers, such as ordinary liquid detergent. Second, the magazine's argument contains mismatched concepts. The evidence is that the powder does not *dissolve readily*, and the conclusion is that an alternative is needed to really *clean* the clothes. This assumes that really cleaning clothes requires a detergent that dissolves readily.

Step 4: Evaluate the Answer Choices

(D) matches the prediction that a detergent that dissolves readily is required in order to really clean clothes.

(A) is both Extreme and Out of Scope. The evidence states that top-loaders use more water than front-loaders, but this does not imply that they *all* use the same amount of water. Moreover, the conclusion is about the detergent type needed in a front-loader, not a top-loader.

(B) is an Irrelevant Comparison. The author necessarily assumes that a detergent specially formulated for front-loaders will dissolve more readily than ordinary detergent. But it is not necessary to the argument that such detergents dissolve less readily in top-loaders.

(C) is Extreme. The author only asserts that *front-loaders* require a specially formulated detergent. That requirement for a specially formulated detergent does not extend to other washers generally.

(E) is not necessary to the argument. It is quite possible that the magazine believes that a front-loader will get clothes as clean or cleaner with the right detergent. More importantly, the focus of the argument is on what type of detergent to use in a front-loader to get clothes clean, not on what type of washer gets clothes the cleanest.

22. (C) Inference

Step 1: Identify the Question Type

This question articulates the basic test for an Inference question: what "must be true" based on the information in the stimulus.

Step 2: Untangle the Stimulus

On the one hand, most physicians believe that they personally are not influenced in their prescription decisions by gifts from drug companies. On the other hand, most physicians believe that most other doctors are influenced by such gifts.

Step 3: Make a Prediction

The information in this Inference question stimulus creates a paradox. Whenever paradoxical information is found in an Inference question stimulus, it is highly likely, if not certain, that the correct answer will focus on that paradox. Since *most* means "more than half" on the LSAT, it is numerically impossible that *most* doctors are not influenced by gifts (doctors' opinions about themselves) and that *most* doctors are influenced by gifts (doctors' opinions about others). *Some* of those doctors must be mistaken either about themselves or about other doctors.

Step 4: Evaluate the Answer Choices

(C) matches the prediction. It matches what must be true due to the inconsistent beliefs of the physicians.

(A) is consistent with the information in the stimulus and certainly could be true, but does not *have* to be true. All the stimulus provides is information about physicians' beliefs. It doesn't give any concrete facts about those who actually do or do not accept gifts.

(B) is Out of Scope. While it is certainly plausible that physicians who believe other doctors are being influenced by drug companies' gifts would believe regulations are in order, it is just speculation because there is no mention of this in the stimulus. You cannot know this to be true.

(D) cannot be inferred from the information in the stimulus. There is no comparison of *degrees* of influence.

(E) is Extreme. There is no such breakdown of the correlation between physicians who admit they are influenced by the gifts and what they believe about other physicians. Without that breakdown, it can't be known if *all* physicians who admit to being influenced feel this way.

23. (E) Principle (Identify/Strengthen)

Step 1: Identify the Question Type

A question stem that asks you to select a principle to justify an argument is an Identify the Principle question that should be treated initially as a Strengthen question. Keep in mind that the answer will likely be stated more generally than a standard Strengthen question answer would be.

Step 2: Untangle the Stimulus

The phrase "this shows that" explicitly directs that the evidence precedes it and the conclusion follows it. Thus, the columnist's conclusion is that the country is either not a democracy or not a well-functioning democracy. The evidence is that a bill adverse to the very influential will not be passed for many years, even though it does not violate anyone's basic human rights and is favored by most people.

Step 3: Make a Prediction

The correct answer to an Identify the Principle question that mimics a Strengthen question will often restate the evidence and conclusion in somewhat more generalized terms. This sounds like a paraphrase of the argument. Here, the paraphrase may be: if a bill is favored by most and doesn't violate human right but will not be passed into law, then the government is not a well-functioning democracy.

Step 4: Evaluate the Answer Choices

(E) is correct. This choice is a nice paraphrase of the argument. That a well-functioning democracy would promptly pass such a bill would support the claim that a country that *fails* to promptly pass such a bill is *not* a well-functioning democracy. Keep in mind that you are aiming to strengthen the conclusion, not necessarily prove it. While the principle articulated in this choice is not a proper contrapositive of the argument in the stimulus and thus does not have to be true, it does lend support to the argument.

(A) contains a Distortion, substituting a reference to a bill that would *benefit* most people rather than a bill *favored by* most people.

(B) contains a couple Distortions because it fails to include the caveat that the bill does not violate anyone's basic human rights and, more importantly, improperly indicates that in a well-functioning democracy such a bill will eventually pass. The columnist acknowledges that the bill might eventually pass ("it will not be passed for many years") but still says the country does not have a well-functioning democracy. Thus, this choice is also a 180.

(C) doesn't strengthen the columnist's argument. Based on this principle, the columnist's country might very well be a well-functioning democracy. Because the bill in the stimulus is opposed by the very influential, this principle is Out of Scope. It doesn't provide any information about what happens when those who oppose a bill are influential, which is what occurs in the stimulus.

(D) can be translated into the following:

	passed into law in		favored by most
If	well-functioning	→	AND consistent
	democracy		with human rights

The contrapositive would be:

	~ favored by most		~ passed into law in
If	OR ~ consistent	→	a well-functioning
	with human rights		democracy

In both translations, the principle doesn't explain what would make a poorly functioning democracy, which is what is needed to support the columnist's argument. Alternatively, the principle would need to indicate that in a well-functioning democracy any bill favored by most people will become law. This choice flips that around, indicating that any bill that becomes law will be favored by most people. This allows for the possibility that lots of bills favored by most people do not become law.

24. (C) Inference

Step 1: Identify the Question Type

The question stem directly asks you what can be inferred from the information in the stimulus. Look to combine Formal Logic statements to make a concrete deduction.

Step 2: Untangle the Stimulus

There are three pieces of information on which to focus. First, commercial fertilizers contain *only* macronutrients, meaning they contain macronutrients and nothing else. Second, there is a Formal Logic statement indicating that there are two necessary conditions for maintaining healthy soil to support a lawn: macronutrients and trace amounts of micronutrients. Third, micronutrients are depleted from the soil when grass clippings are collected instead of left to decay.

Step 3: Make a Prediction

Combining the two pieces of concrete information indicates that commercial fertilizers lack one of the two necessary ingredients to maintain healthy soil for lawns. Thus, you can deduce that using commercial fertilizers is not sufficient to maintain healthy soil for lawns *if* clippings are raked up.

Step 4: Evaluate the Answer Choices

(C) is correct as it is the deduction produced by combining the information in the stimulus. These lawns would lack the requisite micronutrients.

(A) does not have to be true. Because the information in the stimulus pertains only to "widely available commercial fertilizers," it is possible that other fertilizers provide both the macronutrients and micronutrients necessary for healthy soil.

(B) could be true, but does not have to be. As with **(A)**, the stimulus does not provide information about any other fertilizers that might be available to homeowners. While the

stimulus does say commercial fertilizers contain *only* macronutrients, that's not the same as saying *only* commercial fertilizers contain macronutrients, as this answer choice does.

(D) is an attractive answer but has some subtle Distortions. First, the stimulus is limited to soil for lawns, while this choice addresses the needs of soil in general. It is possible, for example, that soils for forests or some other area do not require regular additions of fertilizer. Second, commercial fertilizers are not *required*, just the macronutrients they contain. So, if there is another source of macronutrients, the commercial fertilizers are not needed.

(E) is Extreme. Just because commercial fertilizers are insufficient to compensate for the micronutrients lost from removed lawn clippings does not mean they are *unable* to maintain healthy soil for lawns and gardens. Perhaps there is another other way for homeowners to acquire those micronutrients from somewhere else.

25. (B) Strengthen

Step 1: Identify the Question Type

Be sure to read this question stem carefully as it indicates both the question type and what to use as the conclusion. Your task is to strengthen a recommendation for the inclusion of the antidilution provision of the law.

Step 2: Untangle the Stimulus

The stimulus actually reads like an Inference question stimulus, with only factual information. The last sentence also just reads as a piece of factual information. However, the question stem directs you to use that as the conclusion, with the task of justifying the inclusion of the antidilution provision.

So, consider the conclusion to be that the law should prohibit manufacturers from diluting XTX-containing waste products to bring their concentration down to a permissible level for dumping. The reason is that XTX disposal is harmful to the environment. The law favors incineration of XTX waste, only allowing dumping of the waste in landfills if the concentration is below 500 parts per million.

Step 3: Make a Prediction

The argument assumes that incineration is preferable for the disposal of XTX-contaminated waste and that it is not desirable for companies to increase the total amount of XTX going to landfills by diluting their waste. To strengthen this argument, you need a reason why incineration of XTX is preferable to dumping or why, even when diluted, the accumulation of XTX waste in landfills is worse than incineration of those wastes.

However, if you did not fully grasp that assumption, focus on the conclusion. The conclusion is that the law should not allow the dilution of waste containing XTX. Strengthen that with an answer that shows a negative consequence that can result from diluting waste containing XTX.

Step 4: Evaluate the Answer Choices

(B) is correct. It indicates that, even though the law allows the dumping of some waste containing XTX, XTX is harmful to the environment when it accumulates. Therefore, the law should not allow manufacturers to avoid incinerating waste with high concentrations of XTX by instead diluting and dumping. But, at a more basic level, it is the only answer choice that says something bad about the environmental effects of allowing dilution.

(A) is a 180. It provides a reason why incinerating waste containing XTX is dangerous. That, in turn, is a reason to potentially allow companies to dilute their waste and dump it in a landfill instead.

(C) is largely irrelevant to whether to allow manufacturers to dilute waste containing XTX for disposal in a dump. The evidence has already said that XTX can result in harm when introduced into the environment, and you must accept the evidence as true. The fact that XTX eventually becomes less dangerous (answer choice) doesn't negate the fact that it can cause harm initially (evidence). However, if anything, this choice would weaken the case against the further restrictions on dumping by lessening the length of time the chemical can harm the environment.

(D) does not provide a reason for banning dilution. It shows that the restriction to 500 parts per million is not unduly - excessive, because dumps won't accept much higher anyway, but it doesn't show any sort of danger from the accumulation of XTX in dumps.

(E) explains why it wouldn't be a problem for manufacturers to incinerate waste containing XTX rather than dilute it, because costs are roughly equivalent. However, it doesn't provide any evidence for why the law should favor incineration over dumping. It doesn't weaken the argument, but it doesn't strengthen it either. If it had said that dilution was substantially cheaper than incineration, but incineration was preferable environmentally, then that would be a reason to include the antidilution provision.

Section II: Reading Comprehension
Passage 1: The Discovery of Prions

Q#	Question Type	Correct	Difficulty
1	Global	B	★
2	Inference	A	★
3	Logic Reasoning (Evaluate the Argument)	E	★
4	Inference	C	★★
5	Inference (LEAST)	B	★
6	Inference	A	★★
7	Logic Reasoning (Weaken)	E	★★★

Passage 2: Katherine Dunham's Contribution to Modern Dance

Q#	Question Type	Correct	Difficulty
8	Global	E	★
9	Detail	C	★
10	Inference	C	★★
11	Logic Function	D	★
12	Detail	E	★★
13	Logic Reasoning (Parallel Reasoning)	D	★★
14	Inference	D	★★★★

Passage 3: Happiness and Wealth

Q#	Question Type	Correct	Difficulty
15	Global	B	★
16	Inference	C	★★
17	Inference	A	★★★
18	Logic Function	D	★★★
19	Inference	D	★★★
20	Logic Reasoning (Method of Argument)	E	★★★★

Passage 4: Factors in Risk-Reduction Policy-Making

Q#	Question Type	Correct	Difficulty
21	Global	B	★★
22	Detail	C	★
23	Detail	D	★
24	Inference	B	★★★
25	Logic Function	E	★★★
26	Inference	B	★★★★
27	Inference	C	★★★

Passage 1: The Discovery of Prions

Step 1: Read the Passage Strategically

Sample Roadmap

line #	Keyword/phrase	¶ Margin notes
4	only if	Pathogens cause infection thru reproduction
5	only ... believed	
6	until recently	genet. material
9	thus	Assm: all path have genet material
10	widely assumed	
12	has been challenged, however	Assm challenged
13		CJD
15		Symptoms
17		Discovery of prion-cause of CJD
21	surprisingly	
25	Upon further study ... discovered	How prions become deadly
28	however	
30	dangerous ... abnormal	change shape
32		reproduce
38		form a plague
39	Because	kills cells
42	And	
45	inevitably fatal ... though	
48	Although	scientists skeptical
49	initially ... great skepticism	
50	subsequent	
51	supported	more research supports prion theory
52	Furthermore	
53	now believed	
57	yet to be fully explored ... however	
59	yet to	Questions remain
60	be completely understood	

Discussion

The **Topic**, pathogens, hopefully became clear right away. Paragraph 1 describes what pathogens are and how they create disease in organisms through reproduction. All the known pathogens use genetic material to reproduce, so the wide assumption was that all pathogens contained such material.

Whenever an LSAT author tells you something was "widely assumed," expect the next part of the passage to describe a challenge to that assumption. And that's exactly what paragraph 2 does. The search for the pathogen that causes CJD led scientists to discover a disease agent that doesn't contain genetic material. The researchers gave this pathogen the name *prions*. So the **Scope** of the passage is the discovery of this particular type of pathogen and how it works.

Paragraph 3 describes how prions work to create the tissue damage associated with CJD. Prions, like other pathogens, have the ability to reproduce, turning normally shaped proteins into abnormal plaque-forming ones. And because prions occur naturally in the body, there's no immune response to stave off their destructive tendencies.

Paragraph 4 provides more support for the prion theory of infection and suggests that similar mechanisms may underlie other degenerative conditions. By now, the author's **Purpose** should become clear: to describe prions and detail how their discovery caused scientists to rethink their ideas on pathogens. The **Main Idea** is that prions are a new type of protein pathogen whose unique reproductive capability forced scientists to question long-held assumptions.

1. (B) Global

Step 2: Identify the Question Type

The phrase "main point of the passage" indicates a Global question.

Step 3: Research the Relevant Text

The scope of the question is the passage as a whole; instead of researching specific lines, consult the Big Picture understanding that you gained during Step 1 of the Kaplan Method.

Step 4: Make a Prediction

During Step 1, you already predicted the Main Idea of the passage: that the discovery of prions has challenged scientists' assumption that pathogens need genetic material to reproduce.

Step 5: Evaluate the Answer Choices

(B) matches this prediction.

(A) is a Faulty Use of Detail. It is mentioned in the last sentence of the passage, but it's the existence of prions, not their mechanism of reproduction, that the author is primarily concerned with. Don't fall into the trap of selecting the answer that reiterates the end of the passage; that doesn't necessarily make it the Main Idea.

(C) is Extreme. It blows up a detail from the last paragraph, but that detail is only given to help substantiate prions as real pathogens. There are *other* conditions that may be caused by a similar process to how prions are formed, but that is not to say *most* conditions have that cause.

(D) is incorrect because although the scientific community initially was skeptical, lines 50–52 indicate that "subsequent research has supported the conclusion." So, this answer omits what has changed about the scientific view of prions.

(E) is another Faulty Use of Detail. It doesn't include the role of prions in causing diseases like CJD, which was the way scientists discovered prions in the first place.

2. (A) Inference

Step 2: Identify the Question Type

The phrase "most strongly supported by the passage" indicates an Inference question.

Step 3: Research the Relevant Text

The question stem doesn't give you any content clues to guide your research. When this happens, be prepared to save your research for the answer choices, remembering that the correct answer is the one that *must* be true based on the passage.

Step 4: Make a Prediction

It's difficult to make a prediction here because the passage supports countless valid Inferences. So, consider each answer choice one by one, and find textual support for an answer before you select it.

Step 5: Evaluate the Answer Choices

(A) can be inferred because the discovery of prions (the cause of CJD) did make scientists change their belief that all pathogens have genetic material (lines 9–15).

(B) is unsupported. Prions originate within the human body, so no evidence is given that CJD is contagious.

(C) is Outside the Scope. Effective prevention of CJD isn't discussed; furthermore, CJD is cause by prions, which don't have genetic material and which originate in the body's tissues as normal proteins.

(D) is a 180. It contradicts lines 45–47, which say that the aggressiveness of CJD's progression varies widely.

(E) is another 180. It was initially true (lines 48–50), but the author goes on to say that subsequent research has helped bolster the prion theory of infection.

3. (E) Logic Reasoning (Evaluate the Argument)

Step 2: Identify the Question Type

The question stem asks you to take the information in the passage and go one step further to infer what question would help a physician diagnose CJD. That means that depending on whether the answer is yes or no, the physician will have a better indication of the presence of CJD. Thus, this is an Evaluate the Argument question.

Step 3: Research the Relevant Text

Paragraph 3 talks about how prions cause CJD, so the right answer will be based on something stated there.

Step 4: Make a Prediction

Lines 36–39 say that the cascade of transformations undergone by prions produces a plaque of thread-like structures that accumulates in the brain and destroys neurons. This is something a physician could observe in his or her diagnosis.

Step 5: Evaluate the Answer Choices

(E) matches this prediction.

(A) wouldn't help because nothing in the passage indicates that CJD or prion formation is brought on by blunt trauma to the head.

(B) is a Distortion. Insomnia is mentioned in line 19 as a symptom of CJD, but not everyone with insomnia has the disease, of course. Furthermore, the insomnia experience by CJD sufferers is characterized as chronic, not occasional.

(C) is another Distortion. It wouldn't help because the author doesn't say that prions undergo their abnormal transformations due to genetic damage. Prions don't have genetic material at all.

(D) is Out of Scope. It wouldn't help because a family history of brain disease isn't cited as a risk factor for CJD.

4. (C) Inference

Step 2: Identify the Question Type

The phrase "most strongly supported by the passage" makes this an Inference question.

Step 3: Research the Relevant Text

Like the second question of the set, this question doesn't give you any content clues to help you research. So save your research for the answer choices.

Step 4: Make a Prediction

The correct answer here is nearly impossible to predict. Instead, evaluate the answer choices carefully, finding direct textual evidence to justify your answer. Remember, a valid LSAT Inference *must* be true.

Step 5: Evaluate the Answer Choices

(C) is a valid Inference because paragraph 3 says that CJD manifests itself once an abnormal prion incites a chain reaction of reproduction to turn other prions into plaques that destroy brain cells.

(A) is Outside the Scope and Extreme. Mechanisms of transmission of CJD aren't discussed at all, so it is not known if there is *only* one way transmission can occur.

(B) is Extreme. The prion theory of infection hasn't been extended to most infectious diseases. Lines 52–56 are much more cautiously worded than that.

(D) is a Distortion of lines 52–56. The mechanisms behind Alzheimer's and Parkinson's may be similar to those behind CJD, but to say that those other diseases are also caused by the *same* prion pathogen is a stretch and isn't supported by the passage.

(E) is Outside the Scope. The disease progression of other pathogens isn't discussed.

5. (B) Inference (LEAST)

Step 2: Identify the Question Type

This is an Inference question because it asks about what the author would agree with—or, in this case, what the author would disagree with. Pay close attention to question stems!

Step 3: Research the Relevant Text

The question stem doesn't have any content clues, so you'll need to evaluate the choices one by one and do your research then.

Step 4: Make a Prediction

The correct answer to a broadly worded Inference question is tough to predict. Instead, go straight to the answer choices and select the one that is contradicted by the passage. All four incorrect answers will be supported by the passage.

Step 5: Evaluate the Answer Choices

(B) is contradicted by line 45, which says that CJD is "inevitably fatal."

(A) is supported by paragraph 3, which identifies abnormal prion formations as a catalyst for the onset of CJD.

(C) is supported by lines 19–24, which say the prions generate themselves without nucleic acid.

(D) is supported by lines 39–42, which say that the body doesn't produce an immune response to prions because they occur naturally.

(E) is supported by lines 58–60, which say that scientists don't yet fully understand how prions reproduce and cause cell death.

6. (A) Inference

Step 2: Identify the Question Type

This is an Inference question because it asks you to accept the passage as true and determine which answer choice must be false. The testmaker didn't capitalize *false*, though, so reading carefully is an absolute must.

Step 3: Research the Relevant Text

This question stem gives you a content clue about the term *pathogen*. Paragraph 1 is where the term is defined.

Step 4: Make a Prediction

The correct answer will contradict one of the facts the author lays out about pathogens in paragraph 1. You could try to predict them all, but going straight to the answers will be more efficient.

Step 5: Evaluate the Answer Choices

(A) must be false because the author says prions are pathogenic in patients with CJD, and prions do indeed lack nucleic acid.

(B) is supported by line 24, which calls prions a "new type of protein pathogen."

(C) is supported by lines 1–3, which say that the presence of pathogens is a defining characteristic of an infection.

(D) is supported by paragraph 2, which is all about the search for "the pathogen that causes CJD" (lines 13–14).

(E) is supported by the entire passage, which concerns the discovery of a pathogen (prions) that isn't a foreign agent that reproduces through genetic material.

7. (E) Logic Reasoning (Weaken)

Step 2: Identify the Question Type

This is a Weaken question because it asks you for an answer choice that "undermine(s)" a claim in the passage.

Step 3: Research the Relevant Text

The claim that prions cause CJD is introduced in paragraph 2 and elaborated on in paragraph 3.

Step 4: Make a Prediction

There's a lot of information about how exactly prions contribute to CJD. That makes predicting the exact weakener difficult. But you know from the Logical Reasoning section (and causal arguments, specifically) that a valid weakener will be a new fact that suggests that CJD is caused by something other than prions.

Step 5: Evaluate the Answer Choices

(E) weakens the claim that prions cause CJD because it suggests that bacteria also play a role.

(A) may be tempting, but the patients that have a viral infection could be suffering from an entirely different disease. Just because the symptoms resemble those of CJD doesn't mean that the infected patients have to be suffering from CJD.

(B) is a Distortion. Just because none of the therapies available is designed to tackle a purported cause of CJD doesn't mean that the purported cause is invalid.

(C) doesn't affect the prion-CJD link. Prions can cause other degenerative conditions *as well as* CJD.

(D) is Outside the Scope. Nothing in the passage suggests that prions cause CJD through inherited means. On the contrary—prions cause CJD without the help of genetic material at all.

Passage 2: Katherine Dunham's Contribution to Modern Dance

Step 1: Read the Passage Strategically

Sample Roadmap

line #	Keyword/phrase	¶ Margin notes
1	more striking	
4		Dunham important for dance-isolation
8	relatively recent	
9	although … long	
10	been essential	
14	due …	Success due to training in 1) anthro 2) dance
15	in no small part	
19	Previously …neglected	Dunham—pioneer
20	primarily because	
23	therefore legitimate … Moreover	Why dance neglected
26	while	
31	Especially critical	Dunham's research
32	diverged radically	novel approach
35	both	colleague's view
36	because	
37	because	
38	fortunately recognized	Auth—colleagues wrong
39	must be	
40	But … because	
42	eschewed such caution	
44	not only	Dunham's participation
45	but also	
49		Use of research in performance
53	among the first … to rectify …	
54	the exclusion	
55	thus crucial	Impact on dance
57	making possible	

Discussion

It's clear from the first sentence (and the Keyword *striking* in line 1) that the author is a fan of Katherine Dunham and appreciative of her contributions to modern North American dance. In fact, modern North American dance is the **Topic** of the passage, and Dunham's unique contributions are the **Scope**. Paragraph 1 details one of those contributions—the introduction of dance-isolation, which is derived from techniques traditionally found in African, Caribbean, and Pacific-Island cultures. The author ends the paragraph by attributing Dunham's success to her dual status as social scientist and trained choreographer.

Paragraph 2 examines Dunham the anthropologist and provides some context for her pioneering. The author explains why dance hadn't been studied by social scientists. Prevailing attitudes didn't consider dance scientifically rigorous enough. Also, scientists didn't understand dance, and dancers weren't trained as researchers.

Paragraph 3 gives details on Dunham's research projects. The author explains how her immersive approach differed from the more clinical, objective approach of her colleagues (and you get a hint of the author's attitude toward those colleagues with the opinion Keyword *fortunately* in line 38). Dunham's immersive technique enabled her both to understand the dances as a social researcher and to teach and choreograph using what she had learned abroad.

Paragraph 4 discusses how Dunham used her research results back home. She created groundbreaking ballets that helped establish African American dance as its own art form. This further appreciation from the author sets the **Purpose** (to describe how Dunham used her anthropological and choreographic expertise to influence North American modern dance) and the **Main Idea** (Dunham pioneered new forms of modern dance in North America by utilizing her unique skill set as a choreographer-researcher).

8. (E) Global

Step 2: Identify the Question Type

The words "main point of the passage" indicate a Global question.

Step 3: Research the Relevant Text

The entire passage is relevant in a Global question. Instead of targeted research, use your Roadmap and your understanding of Topic, Scope, Purpose, and Main Idea to form your prediction.

Step 4: Make a Prediction

The Main Idea is that Katherine Dunham changed the landscape of modern North American dance with the work she did combining her anthropological training and her skills as a choreographer.

Step 5: Evaluate the Answer Choices

(E) matches this prediction.

(A) is a Distortion. The passage is about how Dunham transformed modern dance, not how she changed the field of anthropology.

(B) is too narrow and also distorts the passage. The author's intent in the passage is not to compare and contrast Dunham's ballets with other ballets in North America. Also, nothing in the passage indicates that other ballets didn't use traditional cultures' dance techniques.

(C) is Outside the Scope. The content of Dunham's dances and any political messages they may have contained are never discussed.

(D) is a Distortion. The passage doesn't suggest that Dunham was the first to note that Caribbean dance forms were derived from African traditions.

9. (C) Detail

Step 2: Identify the Question Type

This is a Detail question because it begins with the phrase "[a]ccording to the passage."

Step 3: Research the Relevant Text

The author differentiates Dunham's anthropological approach from that of other researchers in lines 31–43.

Step 4: Make a Prediction

According to the passage, Dunham differed from her colleagues by involving herself in the dances she was researching instead of remaining detached while gathering data.

Step 5: Evaluate the Answer Choices

(C) matches this prediction.

(A) is a Distortion. The passage doesn't state or suggest that Dunham's colleagues only performed fieldwork for a short time period.

(B) is Out of Scope. The passage doesn't mention a relation between Dunham's culture and her studies. For all we know, all anthropologists worked to relate the traditions they studied to those of their own cultures.

(D) is also Out of Scope. The idea of political significance is not present in the passage.

(E) is also Out of Scope. The passage doesn't say that Dunham had such familiarity, nor does it say that anthropologists of the time weren't familiar with the cultural practices of those they studied.

10. (C) Inference

Step 2: Identify the Question Type

Two clues indicate an Inference question: the word *suggests* and the phrase "most likely to agree."

Step 3: Research the Relevant Text

The question stem asks about the "peers" mentioned in line 22. You'll have to read the lines surrounding line 22 to fully grasp the peers' point of view.

Step 4: Make a Prediction

Social scientists of Dunham's time liked to do work in areas that their peers would see as legitimate and scientifically rigorous. This is given as the reason why dance wasn't researched much by social scientists. The correct answer will be consistent with this view.

Step 5: Evaluate the Answer Choices

(C) is therefore a valid inference.

(A) is unsupported because the peers mentioned in line 22 wouldn't have studied dance in the first place, so they wouldn't be able to determine whether other social scientists had misinterpreted it.

(B) is also unsupported because the peers don't believe that reliable data can be gathered about dance traditions at all due to the lack of scientific rigor involved.

(D) is a 180. It contradicts paragraph 2, which says that experts in dance didn't conduct studies in the field of dance ethnology because they lacked the proper training, not because they were preoccupied.

(E) is Out of Scope because nothing in the passage suggests that dance traditions aren't regarded as rigorous for study due to their variability.

11. (D) Logic Function

Step 2: Identify the Question Type

The phrase "in order to" makes this a Logic Function question because it asks why the author made a certain mention, as opposed to what the author says.

Step 3: Research the Relevant Text

The last sentence of paragraph 2 is clearly relevant, as are the preceding lines. You need to understand how the lines in question fit into the thrust of the paragraph as a whole.

Step 4: Make a Prediction

The Keyword [*m*]*oreover*, which begins the last sentence of paragraph 2, suggests that this sentence is adding support to the main idea of the paragraph in lines 17–18. The author mentions experts in dance, as well as social scientists of Dunham's day, in order to support the contention that Dunham was unique in her pioneering of dance ethnology.

Step 5: Evaluate the Answer Choices

(D) says this a different way, but the idea is the same: the author is trying to explain why no one had done any rigorous dance ethnology before Dunham.

(A) is a Faulty Use of Detail. It is something the author does earlier in the paragraph, but the author doesn't mention "experts in dance" to make a point about social scientists.

(B) is wrong because the author doesn't compare the qualifications of different groups of researchers when it comes to studying dance forms.

(C) suggests that Katherine Dunham was motivated to conduct her studies of dance forms because other dance experts weren't trained in social research. But the author never makes this claim.

(E) is a Distortion because the author never cites any tension between dance experts and social scientists.

12. (E) Detail

Step 2: Identify the Question Type

The phrase "[a]ccording to the passage" indicates a Detail question.

Step 3: Research the Relevant Text

The content clue "1935" directs you to the beginning of paragraph 3.

Step 4: Make a Prediction

Lines 28–31 say that the traditional Caribbean dance forms Dunham studied had "origins in African culture."

Step 5: Evaluate the Answer Choices

(E) matches this prediction.

(A) is an Irrelevant Comparison. The passage doesn't compare Caribbean dance forms to Pacific-island dance forms, or any others for that matter.

(B) is Extreme. Katherine Dunham learned dance-isolation by studying Caribbean dance forms, but nothing indicates that these cultures were the *first* ones to use the technique.

(C) is a 180. It is contradicted by the first paragraph, which says that the use of Caribbean techniques in North American choreography is relatively recent.

(D) goes against the main thrust of the passage, which is all about how Katherine Dunham introduced the Caribbean techniques to North America.

13. (D) Logic Reasoning (Parallel Reasoning)

Step 2: Identify the Question Type

This is a Parallel Reasoning question because it asks for the answer choice that is "most analogous to" something discussed in the passage.

Step 3: Research the Relevant Text

Dunham's work in anthropology and choreography is discussed throughout the passage, but paragraphs 3 and 4 get into the nitty-gritty of her methodology.

Step 4: Make a Prediction

The hallmarks of Dunham's approach are the following: a blending of her skill as an artist with her skill as a scientific researcher, an active participation and engagement with her subjects, and the use of her cultural discoveries in her future work. The correct answer will have all of those elements.

Step 5: Evaluate the Answer Choices

(D) is a piece-by-piece match.

(A) doesn't match because Dunham's discoveries weren't used by someone in another country to develop innovations. Also, the archaeologist in **(A)** researched instruments in her own country, but Dunham studied cultural traditions of other countries.

(B) doesn't match because Dunham didn't analyze the work of other researchers; she went to the Caribbean and did her own data gathering.

(C) doesn't match because Dunham didn't collaborate with another dancer or social scientist to develop her innovative dances that were inspired by her work in other cultures.

(E) doesn't match because the fashion designer isn't blending two areas of expertise in his work the way that Dunham did.

14. (D) Inference

Step 2: Identify the Question Type

The phrase "author would be most likely to agree with" indicates an Inference question.

Step 3: Research the Relevant Text

The question stem directs you to line 33, but you'll also need to read the surrounding lines for context.

Step 4: Make a Prediction

The opinion Keyword *fortunately* in line 38 means that the author thinks it's good that the colleagues' view (that a researcher can only effectively gather data from a detached stance) has come to be regarded as unrealistic.

Step 5: Evaluate the Answer Choices

(D) is therefore a valid inference.

(A) is Out of Scope because the author doesn't lend credence to the idea that Dunham risked injury by participating in the dances she studied.

(B) is also Out of Scope. Nothing in the passage suggests that Dunham's participation in the dances helped improve her skill as a performer.

(C) is a Distortion. The author does seem to approve of Dunham's personal investment in her fieldwork, but there's no support for the idea that such investment lent scientific rigor to her studies.

(E) is another Distortion and a 180. It was the social scientists discussed in lines 20–23 that did not believe studying dance warranted a scientific mode of inquiry. The question stem, however, asks about the colleagues in line 33, and they did not take issue with Dunham researching dance, just her methodology of doing so. So, the author and the colleagues would not be *incorrect* for assuming dance *could* be studied with scientific rigor; they would both be accepting of that notion.

Passage 3: Happiness and Wealth

Step 1: Read the Passage Strategically

Sample Roadmap

line #	Keyword/phrase	¶ Margin notes
Passage A		
2	paradox:	Paradox
4	and yet	
6	Apparently	People compare selves to norm
7	must be	
8	Two phenomena	Norm ↑
10	love it	1. Habituation
11	initially ... but ... makes little difference	
12	For example	
14	correlates strongly	People get used to income level
17	depends little	
18	but	
20	do not	Unique
21	do not	
22	so	Consequences
24	Now consider	2. Rivalry
28		S and H study
32	happy	Relative wealth › Absolute wealth
33	provided	
35	crucial	Happiness is based on comparison
36	for example	
37	but	Ex. E Germ
38	plummeted because	
39	rather than	

line #	Keyword/phrase	¶ Margin notes
Passage B		
42	? ... Perhaps	Exp. for S and S study
46	unexplainable	Mating prospects?
48	may sound good	Not valid
49	but ... not the explanation best supported	
50	Rather	
51	because	More $ = Happy b/c create value
56	Of course	Success, not $, gives happiness
57	But	
59	not just	
60	but	Value is key
62	ignoble	
64	is really evidence of	Wanting more = wanting to add value
65		Auth—good for society

Discussion

Passage A introduces a paradox: people with more relative wealth are relatively happier, but as the total wealth of a society increases, there's no corresponding rise in total happiness. This is because people weigh their wealth against a norm that is steadily rising due to two factors—habituation and rivalry. You can expect this author to discuss those phenomena in greater detail. The **Topic** of the passage is the effect of wealth on happiness, and the **Scope** is the phenomena explaining the relationship between increased wealth and increased happiness.

In paragraph 2, the author of passage A explains habituation. As one's standard of living increases, so does the amount of money one believes is required for satisfaction. The author weighs in on this phenomenon in paragraph 3: it produces people who will sacrifice leisure for the continual acquisition of material possessions.

Then, in paragraph 4, the author turns to rivalry, and explains this phenomenon by way of a study in which survey respondents preferred having greater relative wealth and lower absolute wealth to the reverse. The author uses this data to show that people's happiness is based on their position relative to others in their reference group, and the author gives East Germany as an example of this.

So the **Purpose** of passage A is to describe the phenomena affecting the relationship between wealth and happiness. The **Main Idea** is that people are happier when their relative wealth is greater because of the phenomena of habituation and especially rivalry.

Passage B begins by introducing the study cited in passage A. This author then gives a possible explanation for people's desire for greater relative wealth: primeval competition instincts. However, the author disagrees with this explanation, saying instead that the happiness that comes from greater relative wealth is about the desire to feel successful and create value.

The next paragraph elaborates on this position. The real driver of the happiness is not the money, but the success that the money represents. According to the author, we're not after prosperity for its own sake, but for the sake of creating value.

And the last paragraph extends the author's point of view. Unlike the author of passage A, the author of passage B considers those who want more wealth to be motivated by a genuine and beneficial desire to create value.

The **Topic** of passage B is the same as that of passage A: the wealth-happiness correlation. The **Scope** is also similar: explanations for why earning more makes people happier. However, the **Purpose** of passage B is to argue for an alternate explanation to the one discussed in passage A. The **Main Idea** of passage B is that people are happier when they

earn more not because of some innate competitive drive, but because of their desire to feel successful and create value.

As for the relationship between the passages, it's that they both use some of the same data to draw different conclusions. Never forget to characterize the relationship between the passages on Test Day. You're almost guaranteed to see questions about it.

15. (B) Global

Step 2: Identify the Question Type

The phrase "primarily concerned" indicates a Global question.

Step 3: Research the Relevant Text

Both passages are relevant in this Global question. But instead of re-reading the whole text, use your Roadmap and your grasp of the Big Picture (Topic, Scope, Purpose, Main Idea) to make your prediction.

Step 4: Make a Prediction

Both passages attempt to explain how income relates to happiness. Passage A explains why increases in relative income, but not absolute income, correlate with more happiness. Passage B explains why earning more makes people feel happier.

Step 5: Evaluate the Answer Choices

(B) matches this prediction.

(A) is only discussed in passage B. Passage A doesn't examine the desire to create value.

(C) is also touched on in passage B only, specifically in the first paragraph.

(D) is only discussed in the second paragraph of passage A.

(E) is only discussed in the second paragraph of passage A.

16. (C) Inference

Step 2: Identify the Question Type

Any question asking you to determine what the author of a passage "would be most likely to agree with" is an Inference question.

Step 3: Research the Relevant Text

Without content clues in the question stem, you'll have to conduct your research as you evaluate the answer choices.

Step 4: Make a Prediction

The author of passage B makes many statements from which you could draw inferences. Instead of listing each possible one, go to the answer choices and select the choice that *must* be true based on the information given.

Step 5: Evaluate the Answer Choices

(C) is inferable from paragraphs 2 and 3 of passage B. Specifically, lines 57–58 say that the happiness of wealthier people comes not from the money, but from the success—the feeling of having created value. If it were all a fluke, that feeling would no longer exist, and neither would the happiness.

(A) is a 180. It's something the author would disagree with. It's offered as an explanation for the Solnick-Hemenway study, but it's an explanation the author discounts in paragraph 2.

(B) is Outside the Scope of passage B. Trading away a higher standard of living for greater relative wealth is something the author of passage A discusses.

(D) is also within the scope of passage A, but not of passage B. Job satisfaction isn't something passage B offers an opinion on.

(E) is contradicted by the beginning of passage A and is not even discussed In passage B.

17. (A) Inference

Step 2: Identify the Question Type

This is an Inference question because it asks for the author's opinion or attitude toward something mentioned in the other passage.

Step 3: Research the Relevant Text

Line 24 is relevant, of course, but because you're asked about the opinion of passage B's author, look for where that author touches on the same idea. The Solnick-Hemenway study is common ground here.

Step 4: Make a Prediction

The author of passage A uses the Solnick-Hemenway study to show that people care more about relative wealth than absolute wealth. In lines 48–53, the author of passage B challenges this competitive interpretation, saying instead that the happiness associated with greater relative wealth comes from a feeling of having created value.

Step 5: Evaluate the Answer Choices

(A) is therefore the correct answer for the attitude in passage B.

(B) is a 180. Passage B sees the phenomenon of rivalry as unflattering (and even uses the term *ignoble* in line 62).

(C) characterizes the phenomenon of rivalry too generously. Also, nothing in passage B suggests that the evidence (namely, the Solnick-Hemenway study) is ambiguous.

(D) is Half-Right/Half-Wrong. The author of passage B might think the phenomenon of rivalry is unflattering, but he also

thinks it's not a valid interpretation of the evidence (lines 49–50).

(E) is a 180. The author of passage B clearly says that the idea of people being competitive and demonstrating superiority is *not* the explanation best supported by the evidence.

18. (D) Logic Function

Step 2: Identify the Question Type

This is a Logic Function question because it asks why an author made a particular mention. In this case, it asks why each author mentioned the same study.

Step 3: Research the Relevant Text

The Solnick-Hemenway study is discussed in lines 24–33 in passage A and in lines 41–47 in passage B.

Step 4: Make a Prediction

In passage A, the study is introduced to support the theory of rivalry as an explanation for why society-wide increases in absolute income don't increase happiness. In passage B, the study is used to introduce the phenomenon the author wishes to explain (i.e., relative prosperity is desired to reflect relative value).

Step 5: Evaluate the Answer Choices

(D) matches this prediction.

(A) contradicts passage A, which uses the study to help argue *for* the phenomenon of rivalry. It also contradicts passage B, which uses the study not to present a view, but just to introduce the passage.

(B) is another 180 because it also says that passage A seeks to argue against the view in the study. Likewise, it mischaracterizes passage B, which does not use the study as evidence.

(C) is Half-Right/Half-Wrong. It gives an accurate assessment of passage A, but it mischaracterizes passage B. The study isn't brought up to present a view that the passage supports. It introduces the topic and an interpretation of the data that the passage challenges.

(E) mischaracterizes passage A in particular. The study isn't even mentioned until the fourth paragraph of that passage, so it can't be used to introduce the passage's *main* topic. Furthermore, the author of passage B doesn't argue *against* the study; she attempts to explain the results of the study.

19. (D) Inference

Step 2: Identify the Question Type

This is an Inference question because it asks you to characterize the author's attitude toward something discussed in the passage.

Step 3: Research the Relevant Text

Emphasis and opinion Keywords are important to identify during Step 1 because LSAT questions often focus on author point of view. Paragraph 3 of passage A and paragraphs 3 and 4 of passage B are where author point of view is strongest.

Step 4: Make a Prediction

The author of passage A says that people who are concerned with gaining material wealth "overinvest in acquiring" possessions (line 22). The author of passage B says that this desire is tied to the desire to create value, which "benefits society" (line 65). So, the first term should be somewhat negative and the second term should be positive.

Step 5: Evaluate the Answer Choices

(D) is therefore correct.

(A) uses terms that are Outside the Scope. Passage A doesn't suggest that people are somehow small-minded or provincial, and passage B doesn't portray a desire for wealth as sophisticated.

(B) is a 180. It reverses the tone of each passage.

(C) is too reductive and is also a 180. Passage A's author wouldn't just classify the person as happy, but would explain *why* more money would make someone happy. Passage B speaks highly of people's desire to acquire more wealth and create value, so *miserable* would be the opposite of the author's view.

(E) is a Distortion. Passage B alludes to the idea of primitive natures, but only to describe the explanation that the passage ultimately refutes. And nothing in passage A suggests that people who want more wealth are inherently luckier.

20. (E) Logic Reasoning (Method of Argument)

Step 2: Identify the Question Type

This is a Method of Argument question because it asks what each author does to structure his or her argument.

Step 3: Research the Relevant Text

This question is more global in its scope, so use your Roadmaps to find techniques that the authors have in common.

Step 4: Make a Prediction

Both authors attempt to explain how happiness relates to wealth. And both authors support their explanations with data—in fact, the Solnick-Hemenway study is cited by both authors in their analysis.

Step 5: Evaluate the Answer Choices

(E) is the correct match.

(A) isn't something done by the author of passage A. And even when the author of passage B brings up biology, it's in the context of an explanation that the passage goes on to challenge.

(B) is contradicted by passage B, which disagrees with a "commonly heard" theory (lines 48–49).

(C) is not something done by passage A. In Passage B, line 56, the author acknowledges many people perceive high incomes as an indication of success. The author of passage A makes no similar concessions.

(D) isn't done by the author of passage B. Only passage A deals with "a paradox" (line 2).

Passage 4: Factors in Risk-Reduction Policy-Making

Step 1: Read the Passage Strategically

Sample Roadmap

line #	Keyword/phrase	¶ Margin notes
1	generally believed	
2	should	
3	for example	Gov't or individual protection from risk
4	such as … onus …	
5	should be on	
6	eyes of the public	
7	mainly	
10	chief difference	vol vs. invol
14	However	experts vs. laypeople
16	real reason	
18	thus … little utility	Auth—vol v. invol judgments not useful
20	First	
21	Although	Not easy to determine level of vol
24	not	
25	but rather	Not binary—of degree
26	typically	
27	since	
28	but	Ex. air travel
31	focus on a small part … not	
32	but	People's focus too narrow
33	Second	
35	unlikely	Risks called "vol" when people disapprove
36	want	
38	even if	
39	By contrast	Ex. skydiving
40	probably not object	
41	even though	vs. Ex. firefighting
42	In …	
43	short … no special magic	
44	Therefore	
45	should be	
47	In general … should	Auth—gov't should decide based on saving lives
50	should be … not …	
51	by	
52	but rather by	If need to dig deeper—do so other than vol vs. invol discussion

Discussion

LSAT authors often like to begin passages with a discussion of what is "generally believed." To most people, the government should protect people from risk in some cases and not in others. They (laypeople) classify these cases on the basis of whether the risk is incurred voluntarily. But experts, the author says, focus on the number of lives at stake. The contrast Keyword *however* in line 14 and the quotation marks around "involuntary" in line 15 introduce the author's point of view: Judging whether a risk is voluntary or not isn't a reliable or useful metric for policy decisions. When the author ends a paragraph with such a strong statement of opinion, expect the rest of the passage to give support for that opinion.

The beginning of paragraph 2 confirms the **Topic** (government risk-reduction policies) and the **Scope** (what factors should guide decisions on those policies). The author defends his argument by pointing out that determining voluntariness isn't as simple or as binary as laypeople often think. The example of air travel is given—it's often seen as involuntary risk, but if one broadens the context, people can voluntarily elect to fly with safer airlines or not to fly at all.

In paragraph 3, the author provides a second supporting point: people rely on judgments of the purpose of a risk in order to decide whether or not it's voluntary. More examples are given to show how problematic such judgments are, and the author clearly doesn't think these judgments should guide policy decisions.

The author concludes by coming down on the side of the experts. The government should generally attempt to save as many lives as possible. And if the government departs from this standard, it should consult deeper considerations than the gray area of voluntariness. Since most of the passage is spent refuting the standard of voluntariness, the author's **Purpose** is to challenge voluntariness as a standard for making risk-reduction policy decisions. The **Main Idea** is that the number of lives saved, and not whether or not a risk is voluntary, is a useful standard for those policy decisions.

21. (B) Global

Step 2: Identify the Question Type

Since this question asks you to identify the "main point of the passage," it's a Global question.

Step 3: Research the Relevant Text

For a Global question, the entire passage is relevant. Instead of researching a specific portion, use your understanding of the Big Picture from Step 1 to form your prediction.

Step 4: Make a Prediction

The Main Idea of the passage is that the government should intervene to protect people from risks based on how many

lives can be saved, and not on a misguided attempt to determine the voluntariness of the risks.

Step 5: Evaluate the Answer Choices

(B) is therefore correct.

(A) blows up a minor point from paragraph 3. But the author didn't write the entire passage just to give criteria for determining voluntariness. The author thinks people shouldn't waste their time with voluntariness in the first place.

(C) also suggests that the author places value in determining whether an action carries a voluntary or involuntary risk. But the author says that such judgments are "of little utility" (line 18).

(D) ignores the last paragraph of the passage, in which the author spells out just how the government should make its determinations about policies protecting people from risk.

(E) summarizes paragraph 2, except it is Extreme based on the word *usually*. Ultimately, **(E)** can be eliminated because it ignores why the author is discussing voluntariness of risk in the first place—to dismiss it as a criterion for public-policy decisions.

22. (C) Detail

Step 2: Identify the Question Type

The phrase "the passage indicates" is a sign of a Detail question. The answer will be stated directly in the passage.

Step 3: Research the Relevant Text

Laypeople and the criteria important to them are discussed in paragraph 1, specifically in lines 12–13.

Step 4: Make a Prediction

Lines 12–13 say that laypeople are concerned with whether a risk was undertaken voluntarily or involuntarily and that the answer to that question determines their public-policy judgments.

Step 5: Evaluate the Answer Choices

(C) is the match for this prediction.

(A) is mentioned in lines 38–39, but it's mentioned as a factor that wouldn't affect people's judgment about whether the government should attempt to lower a certain group of risks.

(B) isn't mentioned in the passage. Nothing indicates that laypeople consult expert judgments when deciding whether to support certain risk-reduction measures.

(D) is a 180. Lines 11–12 say that policy experts are the ones who care most about the number of lives at stake.

(E) is given as a factor that the author thinks should guide government decisions about risk reduction, but this isn't mentioned in connection with laypeople.

23. (D) Detail

Step 2: Identify the Question Type

This is a Detail question because it begins with the telltale phrase "[a]ccording to the passage."

Step 3: Research the Relevant Text

"Risk that is not freely assumed" is a content clue that means the same thing as *involuntary*. Use your Roadmap to locate an example of an activity that is agreed upon as carrying involuntary risks. This should guide you mainly to paragraph 2.

Step 4: Make a Prediction

Lines 25–27 say that risks incurred by airline passengers are seen as involuntary.

Step 5: Evaluate the Answer Choices

(D) is therefore correct.

(A) isn't mentioned anywhere in the passage.

(B) is mentioned as an activity that would generally be seen by people as involving voluntary risk (lines 33–38).

(C) is a Distortion. While the author says that most people would approve of spending resources to ensure firefighter safety, the consensus is still that firefighters risk themselves voluntarily.

(E) is mentioned in paragraph 1 as an activity for which the individual is widely thought to be responsible for his or her own risk reduction (lines 4–6).

24. (B) Inference

Step 2: Identify the Question Type

This is an Inference question because it asks what "the author would be most likely to agree with."

Step 3: Research the Relevant Text

This question stem doesn't provide any content clues to help you research. So you'll have to research as you evaluate the answer choices.

Step 4: Make a Prediction

You may not be able to predict the correct answer verbatim, but you do know that it will be in line with the author's general position concerning the idea of voluntary versus involuntary risks. Also, because the passage discusses multiple viewpoints, count on one or more wrong answers to reflect a view in the passage held by someone other than the author.

Step 5: Evaluate the Answer Choices

(B) is a valid inference. The author says that policy experts care about the number of lives at stake (lines 11–12), not about whether a risk was undertaken voluntarily.

(A) sounds like a position taken by one of the people mentioned in lines 33–35, but the author doesn't weigh in on whether skydivers deserve government intervention to reduce their risks.

(C) is an Irrelevant Comparison and is Outside the Scope. The author never discusses risks faced by airline passengers other than crashes.

(D) might be something a layperson would agree with, but the author never sets forth a criterion for determining voluntariness.

(E) is unsupported because the author is reluctant to decide definitively whether a given risk is voluntary or involuntary. The point of the passage is that such decision-making is inconsistent and leads to confusion.

25. (E) Logic Function

Step 2: Identify the Question Type

This is a Logic Function question because it asks about why an author used a particular phrase in context.

Step 3: Research the Relevant Text

Line 43 is relevant, but it's also necessary to read around that line for context.

Step 4: Make a Prediction

Line 43 is in paragraph 3, which is all about the idea that people use notions like *voluntary* and *involuntary* as substitutes for other judgments about the purposes of certain risks. To say that these notions carry "no special magic" is to say that they don't provide immediate answers for policy decisions.

Step 5: Evaluate the Answer Choices

(E) is therefore correct.

(A) is Outside the Scope. The author is never concerned with making sure we catalog all the risks people commonly face.

(B) is a Distortion. The author does say that notions like *voluntary* and *involuntary* are often based on other factors and judgments, but that doesn't mean that people are *intentionally* hiding behind these notions.

(C) is also a Distortion. The author allows that the terms *voluntary* and *involuntary* have meaning in policy discussions. The author just takes issue with the judgments people use when they apply one term over another.

(D) is a 180. According to the author, notions like *voluntary* and *involuntary are* characteristics that inform public understanding about risk. And that's precisely what the author doesn't like.

26. (B) Inference

Step 2: Identify the Question Type

Two clues identify this as an Inference question: the phrase "the passage most strongly supports" and the word *inference*.

Step 3: Research the Relevant Text

This is similar to the fourth question of the set in that there are no content clues to help you research. Save your research for the answer choices, being sure to find direct support in the passage for your selected answer.

Step 4: Make a Prediction

Making a prediction here will be difficult. The correct answer can be as broad or narrow as the passage allows. Just keep two things in mind: the right answer will have direct textual support, and it will be consistent with the author's view, not the views of others with whom the author differs.

Step 5: Evaluate the Answer Choices

(B) is a valid Inference. Lines 23–25 confirm that when it comes to assessing the voluntariness of "most environmental, occupational, and other social risks," it's a matter of degree.

(A) is Extreme. The author says in lines 47–49 that the government should intervene to reduce risk and save lives, but that mandate is subject to resources. That's different from saying that government should intervene in *all* cases, as **(A)** says.

(C) is a Distortion. According to the author, policy experts don't even engage in judgments about the voluntariness or involuntariness of activities—that's the province of laypeople only.

(D) is another Distortion. The author does say that resources devoted to risk reduction are limited (line 48), but the author makes no recommendation that such resources should be increased.

(E) is a 180 because the author recommends that the government use a different yardstick to determine its risk-reduction policies than the one most people use (that of voluntariness).

27. (C) Inference

Step 2: Identify the Question Type

Any question asking you for the author's attitude is an Inference question.

Step 3: Research the Relevant Text

Instead of determining the author's attitude toward a particular part of the passage, you're asked to determine the general attitude. Use any emphasis or opinion Keywords you circled in the passage to help you form your prediction.

Step 4: Make a Prediction

The author seems to be unconvinced that laypeople's focus on the voluntariness of a risk has any bearing on whether the government should spend resources protecting people from that risk (lines 14–19). The author also seems supportive of the idea that government should focus on saving as many lives as possible (lines 47–49).

Step 5: Evaluate the Answer Choices

(C) is the correct match. The term *skepticism* matches the tone of the last few lines of paragraph 1.

(A) is a Distortion. The author doesn't fault laypeople for misunderstanding the relative riskiness of specific activities. However, the author does deem that it is irrelevant whether those activities were voluntary or involuntary risks.

(B) is a Distortion. The author doesn't put faith in laypeople's emphasis on the voluntariness of risk because such an emphasis is founded on shaky ground (lines 14–18)—*not* because of the potential for government overreach.

(D) is Extreme. Lines 50–54 describe circumstances under which the government is justified in straying from the criterion of the saving of human lives.

(E) is a 180. The author seems to endorse policy experts' focus on the number of lives that would be saved by a particular risk-reduction measure (lines 11–12, 47–49).

KAPLAN

Section III: Logic Games

Game 1: Benefit Concert

Q#	Question Type	Correct	Difficulty
1	Must Be False (CANNOT Be True)	B	★
2	"If" / Earliest	C	★
3	"If" / Must Be True	B	★
4	"If" / Must Be True	E	★
5	Complete and Accurate List	D	★
6	"If" / Could Be True	D	★
7	Rule Substitution	A	★★★★

Game 2: Corporate Research Team

Q#	Question Type	Correct	Difficulty
8	Acceptability	B	★
9	Must Be False (CANNOT Be True)	D	★★
10	"If" / Could Be True EXCEPT	E	★★
11	"If" / Could Be True	D	★★
12	Must Be True	D	★★★★

Game 3: Repertory Theater Screenings

Q#	Question Type	Correct	Difficulty
13	Acceptability	A	★
14	Must Be False (CANNOT Be True)	C	★★
15	"If" / Could Be True	B	★★
16	"If" / Must Be True	E	★★★
17	Must Be False (CANNOT Be True)	E	★★★
18	"If" / Must Be True	A	★★

Game 4: Bird Lectures

Q#	Question Type	Correct	Difficulty
19	Partial Acceptability	E	★
20	Must Be False	B	★★
21	"If" / Could Be True	A	★★★
22	Could Be True	A	★★
23	"If" / Could Be True	D	★★

Game 1: Benefit Concert

Step 1: Overview

Situation: A promoter scheduling bands at a benefit concert

Entities: Six bands (Uneasy, Vegemite, Wellspring, Xpert, Yardsign, Zircon)

Action: Strict Sequencing. Determine the order in which the bands will perform. A quick glance at the final two rules tells you that there are rules about specific slots, so this is Strict Sequencing.

Limitations: There are six slots, and each band performs just once, so this is standard one-to-one Sequencing.

Step 2: Sketch

Nothing out of the ordinary here. Simply list the six bands by initial and set up a series of six numbered spaces to determine the order.

U V W X Y Z

$$\overline{1} \quad \overline{2} \quad \overline{3} \quad \overline{4} \quad \overline{5} \quad \overline{6}$$

Step 3: Rules

Rule 1 sets up a loose relationship: Vegemite will perform at some time before Zircon.

V ... Z

That means Vegemite cannot perform last, and Zircon cannot perform first. Note these restrictions under the appropriate slots in the sketch.

Rule 2 sets up more loose relationships: Wellspring and Zircon each perform at some time before Xpert. The order of Wellspring and Zircon cannot be determined, so keep them separate.

Z ···
　　　X
W ···

This means that neither Wellspring nor Zircon can be the last band to perform. Furthermore, because there are *two* bands that must perform before Xpert, Xpert cannot be one of the first two performers. If you notice that this rule can be combined with Rule 1, go ahead and chain them together right away.

Rule 3 limits Uneasy to one of the last three slots. Either make a note in shorthand where Uneasy *cannot* go: draw "No U" under the first three slots or—perhaps more helpful—note directly in the sketch where Uneasy can go (e.g., U = 4, 5, or 6).

Rule 4 is similar to the previous rule, except it limits Yardsign to one of the *first* three slots. Again, either make a note in shorthand (e.g., Y = 1, 2, or 3), or draw "No Y" under the last three slots.

Step 4: Deductions

Any deduction made in this game comes more from where bands *cannot* perform, rather than exactly where they *must* perform. For starters, the first two rules should be combined using Duplication to form a mini Loose Sequencing sketch. Vegemite comes before Zircon (Rule 1), which comes before Xpert (Rule 2). Wellspring also comes before Xpert (Rule 2), branched off unconnected to Vegemite and Zircon.

V ... Z ... X
　　　W ···

Based on that, Vegemite must perform before at least *two* bands (Zircon and Xpert), so Vegemite cannot perform fifth or sixth. On the other end of the spectrum, Xpert has to perform after at least *three* bands (Vegemite, Zircon, and Wellspring). That means Xpert cannot be in any of the first three slots. (Strong test takers will note that Xpert also cannot be fourth. If it were, then Vegemite, Zircon, and Wellspring would be the first three bands to perform, leaving no room for Yardsign, which is required to be in one of the first three slots per Rule 4. This is a nifty deduction to make, but not vital to one's success on this game).

There are no additional limitations to Zircon and Wellspring beyond what was determined through the rules. And because Uneasy and Yardsign are not directly affected by the other bands, neither one is restricted further than Rules 3 and 4 indicate.

U V W X Y Z

$$\overline{1} \quad \overline{2} \quad \overline{3} \quad \overline{4} \quad \overline{5} \quad \overline{6}$$

~U	~U	~U	~Y	~Y	~Y
~X	~X	~X	~X	~V	~V
~Z					~Z
					~W

It's personal preference and continual practice that will inform you as to whether or not writing all the negative deductions is helpful for you or whether it unnecessarily muddles the sketch. Some test takers will not want the negative deductions present because the mini Loose Sequencing sketch will be sufficient. Additionally, there is room to turn some of the negatives to positives. At this point, no entity is above the slot; there are just negative deductions below. However, in an instance like the sixth slot where there are four entities ruled out (Vegemite, Wellspring, Yardsign, and Zircon), some test takers find it helpful to build that into a positive, noting that slot 6 must be Uneasy or Xpert. Likewise, after noting that Xpert can't go to slots 1 to 4, you could put an X above the sketch with arrows to 5 and 6. There is not enough additional information to warrant drawing Limited Options with either of those, but they are worth noting.

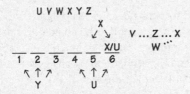

Step 5: Questions

1. (B) Must Be False (CANNOT Be True)

The correct answer will be a band that cannot perform fifth. The remaining four answers will list bands that *could*. Yardsign certainly cannot be fifth (Rule 4), but Yardsign is not listed in the answers. However, Vegemite has to perform before Zircon (Rule 1), which must perform before Xpert (Rule 2). So, Vegemite cannot be one of the last two bands to perform. That means it cannot be fifth, making **(B)** the correct answer.

All of the remaining bands listed could be fifth, and that will also be seen in the various sketches drawn for later "If" questions.

2. (C) "If" / Earliest

For this question, Zircon has to perform before Yardsign. Yardsign has to be one of the first three bands to perform (Rule 4), so Zircon must be one of the first two. However, Zircon has to perform after Vegemite (Rule 1). To satisfy all these conditions, the first three bands must be Vegemite, Zircon, and Yardsign—in that order.

$$\frac{V}{1} \quad \frac{Z}{2} \quad \frac{Y}{3} \quad \frac{}{4} \quad \frac{}{5} \quad \frac{}{6}$$

That leaves Uneasy, Wellspring, and Xpert to fill the last three slots. Uneasy can perform in any of the last three slots, while Wellspring just has to perform before Xpert. That means Wellspring could perform fourth or fifth, but the question asks for the *earliest* slot in which Wellspring could perform. If Wellspring performs fourth, Uneasy and Xpert would perform fifth and sixth in either order.

$$\frac{V}{1} \quad \frac{Z}{2} \quad \frac{Y}{3} \quad \frac{W}{4} \quad \frac{X/U}{5} \quad \frac{U/X}{6}$$

That confirms that Wellspring could perform fourth. With other bands taking up the first three slots, that makes **(C)** the correct answer.

3. (B) "If" / Must Be True

This question establishes Vegemite as the third band to perform. Zircon has to perform after Vegemite (Rule 1), and Xpert has to perform after Zircon (Rule 2). So, Zircon and Xpert will perform in two of the last three slots. By Rule 3, Uneasy will take up the remaining slot among those last three. That leaves Wellspring and Yardsign, in either order, to fill the first two slots.

While no other entities can be established for certain, it can be determined that Wellspring must perform before Zircon, because Wellspring has to perform *before* Vegemite here while Zircon has to perform *after* Vegemite. That makes **(B)** the correct answer. For the record:

If Zircon performs fourth, Uneasy and Xpert could perform in either order, so neither **(A)** nor **(C)** has to be true. Uneasy could perform fourth, before both Zircon and Xpert, so **(E)** does not have to be true. And Wellspring and Yardsign perform first and second in either order, so **(D)** does not have to be true.

4. (E) "If" / Must Be True

This question sets up a Block of Entities, with Zircon performing *immediately* before Wellspring. As a block, these bands must perform at some point after Vegemite (Rule 1) and before Xpert (Rule 2):

$$V \dots \underline{Z} \quad \underline{W} \dots X$$

So, Zircon and Wellspring cannot be the first two bands or the last two bands. If they performed second and third, that would mean Vegemite performs first—but that would leave no room in the first three slots for Yardsign, violating Rule 4. Similarly, if they performed fourth and fifth, that would mean Xpert performs sixth—but that would leave no room in the last three slots for Uneasy, violating Rule 3. That means the only acceptable schedule for Zircon and Wellspring is third and fourth.

$$\frac{V/Y}{1} \quad \frac{Y/V}{2} \quad \frac{Z}{3} \quad \frac{W}{4} \quad \frac{U/X}{5} \quad \frac{X/U}{6}$$

Because Zircon has to perform third, that makes **(E)** the correct answer. For the record, Uneasy and Xpert will be the last two bands to perform, but in either order. So either one could be fifth *or* sixth, which eliminates **(A)** and **(C)**. Similarly, Vegemite and Yardsign will be the first two bands to perform, but in either order. So neither **(B)** nor **(D)** has to be true.

5. (D) Complete and Accurate List

The correct answer to this question will list every band that could possibly be the first band to perform, and only those bands. Zircon has to perform later than Vegemite, so Zircon cannot be first. That eliminates **(E)**. Xpert and Uneasy also cannot be first by Rules 2 and 3, respectively. However, they're not listed in any answer choices anyway.

That leaves Vegemite, Wellspring, and Yardsign. None of the rules require bands to perform before any of those three, so any of them could perform first. That makes **(D)** the correct answer.

For the record, the sketches for the second and third questions of the set confirm that those three bands could all perform first. That previous work, combined with the knowledge that Zircon could never be first by Rule 1, makes work on this question remarkably efficient.

6. (D) "If" / Could Be True

This question creates a Block of Entities, with Wellspring performing *immediately* before Xpert.

$$V \dots Z \dots \underline{W \quad X}$$

Because Xpert has to perform after Zircon (Rule 2), which has to perform after Vegemite (Rule 1), at least two bands must perform before the Wellspring/Xpert block. However, if Wellspring and Xpert performed third and fourth, that would make Vegemite and Zircon the first two bands to perform, leaving no room for Yardsign in the first three slots (violating Rule 4). So, that leaves two locations for Wellspring and Xpert: they can be fourth and fifth, or fifth and sixth. In either case, they take up two of the last three slots. The remaining slot must be taken up by Uneasy (Rule 3).

$$\frac{\quad}{1} \frac{\quad}{2} \frac{\quad}{3} \frac{U}{4} \frac{W}{5} \frac{X}{6}$$

$$\frac{\quad}{1} \frac{\quad}{2} \frac{\quad}{3} \frac{W}{4} \frac{X}{5} \frac{U}{6}$$

$$\underbrace{\qquad\qquad}$$

$$V \dots Z ; Y$$

In both options, Vegemite and Zircon—in that order—will take up two of the first three slots, with Yardsign taking up whatever slot remains. In that case, only **(D)** is possible, making that the correct answer. For the record:

Uneasy cannot be fifth without splitting up Wellspring and Xpert, which eliminates **(A)**. Vegemite cannot be third, because that would leave no slot after it for Zircon (Rule 1). That eliminates **(B)**. Wellspring has to be fourth or fifth, which eliminates **(C)**. And the fourth band is either Wellspring or Uneasy, not Zircon. That eliminates **(E)**.

7. (A) Rule Substitution

This question removes Rule 2 from the game. That means Wellspring and Zircon no longer have to perform before Xpert. The question is looking for a new limitation that would reestablish the relationship among Wellspring, Zircon, and Xpert, without adding any further restrictions. The only way to find the correct answer is to test each one individually until you find one that accurately replaces the relationship.

(A) states that Uneasy is the only band that can perform later than Xpert. If that were true, Wellspring and Zircon would have to perform *before* Xpert, which does reset the limitation set up by the original Rule 2. It's important, though, to make sure there are no additional restrictions here. Letting Uneasy be the only band that could perform after Xpert prevents Vegemite and Yardsign from performing after Xpert. However, Vegemite always had to be before Xpert because it had to perform before Zircon (Rule 1). And Yardsign always had to

perform before Xpert because Yardsign could only be one of the first three bands, and Xpert could never perform earlier than that. Therefore, because this rule reestablishes the original scenario without adding any new restrictions, **(A)** is the correct answer. For the record:

(B) sets Vegemite to perform before Wellspring, a restriction that was not in place with the original rules.

(C) is only partially helpful by having Wellspring perform before Xpert. However, even though Vegemite has to perform before Zircon, this rule does not reestablish the condition that Zircon must perform before Xpert.

(D) creates a block of Uneasy and Xpert that was not part of the original restrictions. In fact, the second sketch for the sixth question of the set shows that Uneasy and Xpert could be separated.

(E) accurately resets the limit that Xpert could only be one of the last two bands to perform. However, that does not force Wellspring and Zircon to perform before it. With Xpert fifth, this rule would still allow either Wellspring or Zircon to perform last, which would have been unacceptable by the original rules.

Game 2: Corporate Research Team

Step 1: Overview

Situation: A corporate manager putting together a research team

Entities: Eight employees (Myers, Ortega, Paine, Schmidt, Thomson, Wong, Yoder, Zayre)

Action: Selection. Determine which employees will be selected for the team.

Limitations: At least four employees will be selected, but there's no maximum.

Step 2: Sketch

This is a standard Selection game, which requires little more than a list of the entities and a note about the minimum. As the game proceeds, selected employees will be circled, and non-selected employees will be crossed out.

4+ selected
M O P S T W Y Z

Step 3: Rules

Rule 1 is Formal Logic, as can be expected in a Selection game. If Myers is selected, then neither Ortega nor Paine will be. By the contrapositive, if either Ortega or Paine *is* selected, then Myers will *not* be. While this Formal Logic can be written out, there's an easier way to interpret this: Neither Ortega nor Paine can be selected with Myers. This can be expressed as so:

Never MO ; Never MP

Note that Ortega and Paine do not affect one another. They can both be selected or not selected, or either one can be selected alone. However, selecting either one will automatically kick Myers off the team.

Rule 2 is more Formal Logic. In this case, if Schmidt is selected, then Paine and Thomson will also be selected. By contrapositive, if either Paine or Thomson is *not* selected, then Schmidt will not be selected.

S → P and T
~P or ~T → ~S

This rule is not susceptible to a simpler interpretation, as Rule 1 was.

Rule 3 is similar to the previous rule, only with Wong's selection dictating that Myers and Yoder also be selected. By contrapositive, if either Myers or Yoder are *not* selected, then Wong will not be selected:

W → M and Y
~M or ~Y → ~W

Step 4: Deductions

Because all three rules are conditional, there will be no way of establishing any employee as certainly selected or certainly left out. With games that rely entirely on conditional rules, it's often not worth trying to combine the rules based on Duplications. Questions will typically provide information that will trigger the Formal Logic, and each deduction can trigger something else.

However, in this case, there are only three rules and only five questions, so it doesn't hurt to spend a little extra time seeing how these rules impact one another.

If Myers is selected, then Paine and Ortega will not be selected (Rule 1). Eliminating Paine would also eliminate Schmidt (Rule 2). So, it can be further determined that Myers cannot be selected with Schmidt (No MS).

If Schmidt is selected, then Paine and Thomson would be selected. Paine cannot be selected with Myers, which means Schmidt cannot be selected with Myers (as determined earlier). However, without Myers, Wong is also unable to be selected (Rule 3). So, Schmidt cannot be selected with Wong (No SW).

Finally, if Wong is selected, Myers and Yoder will be selected. With Myers selected, that would prevent Ortega and Paine from being selected (Rule 1). So, Wong cannot be selected with either of those two (No WO and No WP). Furthermore, without Paine, Schmidt would also be left out (Rule 2). So, Wong cannot be selected with Schmidt, which was already determined earlier.

All told, the following restrictions could all be figured out by translating and combining the rules:

No MO
No MP
No MS
No WO
No WP
No WS

Note that Wong and Myers are the most prominent employees here. Their selection will have a major impact on any Numbers deductions. Because the selection must include at least four employees, this is significant. Also, it's good to note that Zayre is a Floater. Never mentioned in the rules, Zayre could be selected or not as needed without affecting anyone else.

Step 5: Questions

8. (B) Acceptability

Use the logic of the rules to eliminate any answer that violates those rules. By Rule 1, any team with Myers cannot have Ortega or Paine. However, **(A)** has Myers with Paine, so that can be eliminated. By Rule 2, any team with Schmidt must also include Paine and Thomson. **(C)** includes Schmidt, but does not have Thomson, while **(D)** includes Schmidt, but does not have Paine. Those answers can be eliminated. Finally, by Rule 3, any team with Wong also has to have Myers and Yoder. **(E)** has Wong, but does not include Myers, so that can be eliminated. That leaves **(B)** as the only answer that does not violate the rules, making that the correct answer.

9. (D) Must Be False (CANNOT Be True)

The question asks for two employees that cannot be selected together. If you spent time considering the outcomes, **(D)** stands out as the correct answer immediately. After all, if Schmidt is selected, then Paine must be selected (Rule 2). This means Myers cannot be selected (Rule 1), which means Wong cannot be selected (Rule 3).

For the record, the remaining answers all include either Thomson, Yoder, or Zayre. There are no deductions that can be made by selecting any of those employees, because their selection does not trigger any of the Formal Logic. So, any one of them can be selected with any other employee without violating the rules.

10. (E) "If" / Could Be True EXCEPT

For this question, Yoder is not selected. By Rule 3, that means Wong is also not selected.

M O P S T W̶ X̶ Z

That leaves six employees, at least four of whom must be selected. The most restricted entity remaining is Myers. Selecting Myers would automatically eliminate Ortega and Paine (Rule 1). Without Paine, Schmidt would not be selected (Rule 2). That would leave only two other people: Thomson and Zayre. That would mean only three employees could be selected, which is not enough. Selecting Myers would eliminate too many employees, so Myers must be left off the team. That makes **(E)** the correct answer.

For the record, the correct answer to the Acceptability question shows that Ortega, Paine, Thomson, and Zaire would make an acceptable team. That proves that all of those employees could be on a team without Yoder, effectively eliminating all four wrong answers.

11. (D) "If" / Could Be True

For this question, Paine will not be selected. By Rule 2, that means Schmidt will also not be selected.

M O P̶ S̶ T W Y Z

That leaves six employees, at least four of whom must be selected. There are too many possible outcomes at this point, so it's best to check the answers. However, instead of testing one answer at a time, use duplicated entities to test multiple answers all at once.

The first three answers all suggest that Myers is not selected. If that were the case, then Wong could not be selected (Rule 3). That would leave four employees—Ortega, Thomson,

Yoder, and Zayre—all of whom would have to be selected to satisfy the minimum requirement.

M̶ O̶ P̶ S̶ T W Y Z

So, if Myers if off the team, it would be impossible to take Ortega, Thomson, or Zayre off the team without violating the game's restrictions. So, **(A)**, **(B)**, and **(C)** can all be eliminated as impossible.

The remaining answers state that Ortega is off the team. Without Ortega, five employees are left: Myers, Thomson, Wong, Yoder, and Zayre.

M O̶ P̶ S̶ T W Y Z

Without Schmidt, Thomson does not have to be selected. If Thomson was not on the team, along with Ortega, that would leave Myers, Wong, Yoder, and Zayre—a perfectly acceptable team.

M̶ O̶ P̶ S̶ T̶ W Y Z

That makes **(D)** the correct answer. For the record:

If Yoder was also off this team, that would mean Wong could not be selected. That would leave only three employees: Myers, Thomson, and Zayre—not enough to satisfy the minimum requirement. That eliminates **(E)**.

M̶ O̶ P̶ S̶ T W̶ X̶ Z

12. (D) Must Be True

This question asks for two people, at least one of whom must be selected. In other words, the correct answer must list two people such that if one of them is not selected for the team, the other one *must* be. That means that the two people listed cannot *both* go unselected.

The first answer to eliminate is **(E)**, which includes Zayre. Because Zayre is not listed in the rules, selecting or not-selecting Zayre has no direct impact on the rest of the selection. So, if Zayre is not selected, then there is no need for Yoder to be selected. The team does not have to include one of those two employees.

From there, the first two answers can be tested by considering Ortega. If Ortega is *not* selected, that does not trigger any of the rules. In that case, Schmidt and Wong could both be not selected as well. So, because acceptable teams could be made without any of those three employees, **(A)** and **(B)** can be eliminated.

This same logic applies to Schmidt. If Schmidt is not selected, that does not trigger any of the rules. In that case, Paine could also be not selected. So, an acceptable team could be made without Paine and Schmidt, which eliminates **(C)**. In the previous question, the question stem gave the condition that Paine was not on the team, which automatically meant Schmidt was not on the team, so you've already worked with a scenario where neither Schmidt nor Paine were on the team.

For the record, a team consisting of Myers, Thomson, Yoder, and Zayre would be acceptable, showing that none of the employees listed in the first three answers need to be selected.

That leaves **(D)** as the correct answer. After all, if Thomson and Yoder were both left off the team, then Schmidt could not be selected (Rule 2), nor could Wong (Rule 3). That would leave a team of Myers, Ortega, Paine, and Zayre. However, such a team would violate Rule 1. Therefore, it's impossible to have a team without Thomson *and* Yoder. At least one of those two employees must be selected in order to avoid violating the rules.

Game 3: Repertory Theater Screenings

Step 1: Overview

Situation: A movie theater showing films

Entities: Five films (horror, mystery, romance, sci-fi, western)

Action: Distribution/Sequencing Hybrid. Determine which screen each film is shown on and what time the film is shown. Assigning the films to screens is Distribution. However, determining the times adds a Sequencing component (as further evidenced by the use of the word *before* in Rule 1).

Limitations: Each film is shown once, on just one screen. Two movies each are shown on screens 1 and 2 (one at 7 pm and one at 9 pm), and one movie is shown on screen 3 at 8 pm.

Step 2: Sketch

A standard Distribution chart is a good start, with a row or column for each screen and slots to assign the films. There should be two slots under screens 1 and 2 and one slot under screen 3. However, due to the temporal aspect of this game, the slots need to be organized and labeled to reflect the order in which the movies are shown.

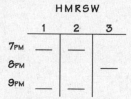

Note: This chart could also be arranged with the times at the top, left to right, and a separate row for each screen. It's a simple rotation, and the rules will be applied the same way.

Step 3: Rules

Rule 1 sets some relative ordering: The western film must start before the horror film.

That means the western cannot begin at 9 pm and the horror film cannot begin at 7 pm. Note these restrictions next to the appropriate row in the sketch.

Rules 2 and 3 state that the sci-fi film cannot be shown on screen 3, and the romance film cannot be shown on screen 2. Simply add "~ S" and "~ R" under the appropriate columns in the sketch.

Rule 4 prevents the horror film and the mystery film from being on the same screen.

Step 4: Deductions

The rules don't provide a lot to work with. The horror film is the only Duplication in the rules, but those two rules cannot

be combined. The horror film must be shown on a different screen from the mystery (Rule 4), but Rule 1 simply limits the horror film to either an 8 pm or 9 pm. showing. It could still be shown on any of the three screens, so there is no way to limit the placement of the mystery.

All of the other films are mentioned just once in the rules. Each rule limits films to two possible outcomes (e.g., by Rule 2, the sci-fi film can only be shown on screen 1 or screen 2), but none of those outcomes leads to substantial concrete deductions. Therefore, Limited Options do not add any value here.

Instead, success on this game will rely on applying the rules carefully and making deductions as the game proceeds.

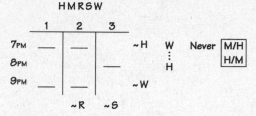

Step 5: Questions

13. (A) Acceptability

As with any Acceptability question, go through the rules one at a time, knocking out answers as they violate those rules. Rule 1 requires that the western start before the horror film. That eliminates **(B)**, which has the horror film start at 7 pm and the western start at 8 pm. By Rule 2, the sci-fi film cannot be on screen 3, which eliminates **(D)**. By Rule 3, the romance film cannot be on screen 2, which eliminates **(E)**. And Rule 4 requires the horror film and the mystery to be on different screens. That eliminates **(C)**, which puts them both on screen 2. That leaves **(A)** as the correct answer.

14. (C) Must Be False (CANNOT Be True)

The correct answer will be two films that cannot be shown together on screen 2—in the order provided. The times for screen 2 are 7 pm and 9 pm. The only film that cannot be on screen 2 is the romance, but that's not listed in any of the answers. However, because the western has to start before the horror film (Rule 1), the western cannot be shown at 9 pm. That means **(C)** is an unacceptable schedule, making that the correct answer.

15. (B) "If" / Could Be True

For this question, the western and the sci-fi film will be shown on the same screen. That means they will be on either screen 1 or screen 2, one beginning at 7 pm and one at 9 pm. However, the western cannot be shown at 9 pm because It has to start earlier than the horror film (Rule 1). So, the western will start at 7 pm and the sci-fi film will start at 9 pm.

That leaves the horror, the mystery, and the romance. The romance film cannot be on screen 2 (Rule 3). If the romance film were on screen 3, then the horror film and the mystery would be shown together on whatever screen does not show the western and sci-fi film. But that would violate Rule 4. So, the romance can only be shown on screen 1—at either time.

With the romance on screen 1, that puts the western and sci-fi on screen 2.

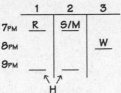

R; M/H

With that, only **(B)** is possible, if the mystery is shown on screen 1 with the romance at 7 p.m.

16. (E) "If" / Must Be True

This question requires that the romance start before the western. By Rule 1, the western has to begin before the horror film. That means, in order, the romance, western, and horror film must begin at 7 pm, 8 pm, and 9 pm, respectively. Because the western begins at 8, it must be shown on screen 3 (the only screen with an 8 pm showing). The romance film cannot be shown on screen 2 (Rule 3), so it must be shown on screen 1—the only remaining screen with a 7 pm showing. The horror film could still be shown on either screen 1 or screen 2, but it has to be at 9 pm. That leaves either the sci-fi or mystery film to be the 7 pm show on screen 2.

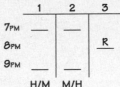

Expert test takers will also notice that the sci-film cannot be on screen 1, because that would put the horror film and the mystery on the same screen, violating Rule 4. So, the sci-fi film has to be on screen 2, making **(E)** the correct answer.

If that was not immediately clear, do not hesitate to draw two sketches: one if the horror film was on screen 1, and one if it was on screen 2. If the horror film was on screen 1, then screen 2 would show the mystery and sci-fi film, in either order. If the horror film was on screen 2, the mystery would have to be on screen 1 (Rule 4), leaving the sci-fi film as the 7 pm film on screen 2.

In either case, the sci-fi film must be shown on screen 2.

17. (E) Must Be False (CANNOT Be True)

This question is asking for a pair of films that cannot be shown together on screen 1—in the order given. The screen 1 showings are at 7 pm and 9 pm. There are no rules restricting a film from being shown on screen 1. The horror film and the western cannot be shown at 7 pm and 9 pm, respectively (Rule 1), but no answer violates that.

The pairs listed allow for testing multiple answers simultaneously (e.g., **(C)**, **(D)**, and **(E)** can all be tested at the same time by placing the western film on screen 1 at 7 pm). However, it's even more helpful to note that none of the answers list the romance, which means it will not be shown on screen 1. Because the romance cannot be on screen 2 (Rule 3), the romance will be on screen 3 for this question. Because screen 3 only shows one movie, the horror film and the mystery will be have to be split between the remaining two screens (Rule 4). That means one of those films must be shown on screen 1, and the other will be shown on screen 2.

	1	2	3
7PM	—	—	
8PM			R
9PM			
	H/M	M/H	

Because one of those films must be shown on screen 1, **(E)** is an unacceptable schedule for screen 1, making that the correct answer. After all, if screen 1 showed the western and the sci-fi film, that would leave the horror film and the mystery together on screen 2, violating Rule 4.

18. (A) "If" / Must Be True

This question puts the sci-fi film and the romance on the same screen. Screen 3 only shows one film, and the romance cannot be shown on screen 2 (Rule 3), so these films will have to be shown on screen 1, in either order.

That leaves the horror film, the mystery, and the western for screens 2 and 3. The horror film and the mystery cannot be shown on the same screen (Rule 4), so one of them will be shown on screen 2 and the other will be on screen 3. That leaves one time on screen 2 for the western. Because the western has to be shown before the horror film, it cannot be shown at 9 pm, so it must be shown at 7 pm.

	1	2	3
7PM	S/R	W	
8PM			H/M
9PM	R/S	M/H	

With that, **(A)** must be true, making it the correct answer. The remaining answers are all possible, but none of them *have* to be true.

Game 4: Bird Lectures

Step 1: Overview

Situation: A naturalist lecturing on birds

Entities: Five lectures on birds (oystercatchers, petrels, rails, sandpipers, terns); two locations (Gladwyn and Howard)

Action: Sequencing/Matching Hybrid. Determine the order in which the lectures are given, and then match each lecture to its location.

Limitations: The lecture topics cannot be repeated, and each one will be given at one of the two locations. There's no indication in the overview of how many lectures will be given at each location.

Step 2: Sketch

The primary action is to determine the order of the lectures. Once the order is determined, each lecture can be matched to one of the two halls. So, draw five slots in order. The lecture topics will be entered in order on top, with the location entered below—or if you'd prefer, make two rows of five slots.

```
lect oprst  ___ ___ ___ ___ ___
             1   2   3   4   5
Loc  GH
```

The game's second element, after Sequencing, is considered Matching rather than Distribution because Sequencing is the predominant action. The lectures are all given at different times, so the sketch is most easily set up as a sequence with the locations matched below. The game could also, in theory, be set up as a Distribution-Sequencing Hybrid, where there is a column for Gladwyn Hall and a column for Howard Auditorium, and then the lectures are distributed sequentially underneath. However, because four of the five rules deal with Sequencing and each lecture gets a unique time, it's preferable to set the game up as shown here.

Step 3: Rules

Rules 1 and 2 establish the first and fourth lectures at Gladwyn Hall and Howard Auditorium, respectively. Add a G and H under the appropriate slots in the sketch.

Rule 3 provides some important numerical information. There will be three lectures in Gladwyn Hall, which means the remaining two lectures must be in Howard Auditorium. Adjust the entity list to include 3 Gs and 2 Hs.

Rule 4 provides two pieces of information. First, the lecture on sandpipers is given in Howard Auditorium. Second is that the lecture on sandpipers is given at some time before the lecture on oystercatchers. Draw out the block, adding the sequencing component.

```
s ... o
─
H
```

Even though the fourth lecture is in Howard Auditorium, it is not necessarily the lecture on sandpipers. By Rule 3, there will

be two lectures in Howard Auditorium, so the fourth lecture can still be on another bird. However, because the lecture on sandpipers is given before the lecture on oystercatchers, the sandpiper lecture cannot be last, and the oystercatcher lecture cannot be first.

Rule 5 also provides two pieces of information. First, the lecture on terns is given before the lecture on petrels. Second, the lecture on petrels is given in Gladwyn Hall. Again, draw out the block, adding the sequencing component.

```
t ... p
      ─
      G
```

Because the lecture on terns is given before the lecture on petrels, the tern lecture cannot be last, and the petrel lecture cannot be first. Putting these negative deductions directly into the sketch may be helpful for you. If you find these small deductions crowd your sketch, you can omit them, provided your continual practice indicates that you don't miss them when doing the questions.

Step 4: Deductions

Of the five lectures, one of them (rails) is a Floater—not directly restricted by any rule—so mark it with an asterisk. The other four lectures are mentioned only once each, so deductions will be minimal. However, because the first two rules establish the location for two lectures, there are two minor deductions. The first lecture is in Gladwyn Hall (Rule 1), so it cannot be on sandpipers, which must be given in Howard Auditorium (Rule 4). Similarly, the fourth lecture is in Howard Auditorium (Rule 2), so it cannot be on petrels, which must be given in Gladwyn Hall (Rule 5).

There are too many possible outcomes to make any further concrete deductions. It's good to note, given the three negatives, that the first lecture must be on either rails or terns, but there is not enough additional information in either case to warrant drawing Limited Options. Just keep that in mind and be sure to keep track of the Numbers, knowing that there can only be one additional lecture in Howard Auditorium and two more in Gladwyn Hall.

```
              ~s
              ~p              ~t
              ~o         ~p   ~s
oprst*   r/t  ___ ___ ___ ___ ___
              1   2   3   4   5
GGGHH    G                H
```

Step 5: Questions

19. (E) Partial Acceptability

As with any Acceptability question, the four wrong answers will all violate at least one rule. However, because the answers only list the lectures, it's important to consider the location as you test the rules.

Without knowing the locations, Rules 1–3 cannot be used to immediately rule out answers. However, the information in these rules will be helpful in testing the last two rules. Rule 4 requires the sandpiper lecture to be given before the oystercatcher lecture. That eliminates **(A)**. Rule 4 also requires the sandpiper lecture to be given in Howard Auditorium. Therefore, the sandpiper lecture cannot be first, because that lecture is in Gladwyn Hall (Rule 1). That eliminates **(D)**.

Rule 5 requires the tern lecture to be given before the petrel lecture. That eliminates **(B)**. Rule 5 also requires the petrel lecture to be given in Gladwyn Hall. Therefore, the petrel lecture cannot be fourth, because that lecture is in Howard Auditorium (Rule 2). That eliminates **(C)**, which leaves **(E)** as the correct answer.

20. (B) Must Be False

The correct answer to this question must be false no matter what. The four incorrect answers will all be possible.

The first and fourth lectures must be in Gladwyn Hall and Howard Auditorium, respectively. However, there is no restriction to the location of the remaining lectures, individually. Instead, consider the numbers: three lectures will be Gladwyn Hall, with the other two in Howard Auditorium (Rule 3). Since the fourth lecture is already in Howard Auditorium, there can only be one more lecture there. That means **(B)** is impossible, because putting the second and third lecture in Howard Auditorium would leave only two lectures (first and fifth) to be in Gladwyn. That makes it the correct answer.

21. (A) "If" / Could Be True

This question puts the tern lecture in Howard Auditorium. With the sandpiper lecture also in Howard Auditorium (Rule 4), there can be no other lectures in Howard Auditorium. By Rule 3, the remaining three lectures (oystercatchers, petrels, and rails) have to be in Gladwyn Hall. The fourth lecture must be given in Howard Auditorium, so it must be either sandpipers or terns. Test out both options.

If the fourth lecture is on sandpipers, the fifth lecture must be on oystercatchers (Rule 4) in Gladwyn Hall. Because the first lecture must be in Gladwyn Hall, the tern lecture can only be given second or third. However, it also has to be given before the petrel lecture (Rule 5). That means the tern lecture will be second, with the petrel lecture (in Gladwyn Hall) third. That leaves the rail lecture to be first.

If the fourth lecture is on terns, the fifth lecture must be on petrels (Rule 4) in Gladwyn Hall. Because the first lecture must be in Gladwyn Hall, the sandpiper lecture can only be given second or third. However, it also has to be given before the oystercatcher lecture (Rule 4). That means the sandpiper lecture will be second, with the oystercatcher lecture (in Gladwyn Hall) third. That leaves the rail lecture to be first.

Opt. 1

r	t	p	s	o
1	2	3	4	5
G	H	G	H	G

Opt. 2

r	s	o	t	p
1	2	3	4	5
G	H	G	H	G

In either case, the third lecture is given in Gladwyn. It could be on either oystercatchers or petrels, making **(A)** the only possible answer.

22. (A) Could Be True

The correct answer will present a possible outcome for the fifth lecture. The four incorrect answers will list something that cannot happen at the fifth lecture.

The sandpiper lecture and the tern lecture are both given before other lectures (Rules 4 and 5), so neither one of them can be given fifth. That eliminates **(D)** and **(E)**. Furthermore, by Rule 5, the petrel lecture must be given in Gladwyn Hall. That eliminates **(B)**.

If the oystercatcher lecture is fifth, it merely has to be preceded by the sandpiper lecture. The sandpiper lecture could be fourth, allowing the oystercatcher to be fifth at either location. Therefore, **(A)** is possible, making it the correct answer. Note: This question could have been answered immediately by looking at the first sketch for the previous question, which depicts this very scenario.

For the record, **(C)** is tempting because the rail lecture is a Floater and thus is frequently the correct answer to a Could Be True question. However, this answer makes the last lecture in Howard Auditorium. With the fourth lecture also in Howard Auditorium (Rule 2), the first three lectures are all left to be in Gladwyn Hall (Rule 3). By Rule 4, the sandpiper lecture would have to be the fourth lecture, leaving the fifth lecture for oystercatchers—not rails. Thus, this answer is impossible.

23. (D) "If" / Could Be True

For this question, the third lecture is on sandpipers. That lecture must take place in Howard Auditorium (Rule 4). With the fourth lecture also in Howard Auditorium (Rule 2), the remaining three lectures must all take place in Gladwyn Hall (Rule 3). Furthermore, the sandpiper lecture must be held before the oystercatcher lecture, so the oystercatcher lecture must be given either fourth or fifth.

		s	o ↙↘	
1	2	3	4	5
G	G	H	H	G

That eliminates **(A)**, **(B)**, and **(C)**, because the oystercatcher cannot be given before the sandpiper lecture, and the second and fifth lectures have to be in Gladwyn Hall.

The tern lecture has to be given before the petrel lecture (Rule 5). With the third lecture filled and the oystercatcher lecture being given in one of the last two spots, the tern lecture can only be given first or second. After all, if it were given fourth, the petrel lecture would have to fifth, leaving no room for the oystercatcher lecture. Therefore, **(E)** is impossible, leaving **(D)** as the only possible answer—and thus the correct answer.

Section IV: Logical Reasoning

Q#	Question Type	Correct	Difficulty
1	Principle (Identify/Strengthen)	A	★
2	Inference	C	★
3	Flaw	A	★
4	Strengthen	C	★
5	Point at Issue (Agree)	B	★
6	Assumption (Necessary)	A	★
7	Paradox	C	★
8	Method of Argument	E	★★
9	Flaw	E	★
10	Assumption (Necessary)	B	★
11	Flaw	C	★★
12	Weaken	B	★★★
13	Paradox	E	★★
14	Inference	B	★★
15	Principle (Identify/Strengthen)	C	★★
16	Main Point	C	★
17	Parallel Reasoning	B	★★★★
18	Inference	E	★★★
19	Weaken	D	★★★
20	Assumption (Necessary)	A	★★
21	Inference	E	★★★★
22	Assumption (Sufficient)	D	★★
23	Parallel Flaw	D	★★★
24	Role of a Statement	C	★★★
25	Assumption (Necessary)	D	★★★
26	Method of Argument	D	★★★★

1. (A) Principle (Identify/Strengthen)

Step 1: Identify the Question Type

Because the correct answer is a principle, this is an Identify the Principle question. Additionally, because the correct answer "helps to justify" the stimulus, this Principle question closely resembles a Strengthen question. The correct answer will likely be phrased more generally than the correct answer to a Strengthen question normally is.

Step 2: Untangle the Stimulus

Break down the argument into evidence and conclusion, just as you would a Strengthen question. The conclusion comes at the end of the stimulus. Basically, the identity of the polluter is not certain enough for the penalty to be imposed. The evidence is that the penalty is extremely severe.

Step 3: Make a Prediction

Start by finding the author's assumption. The evidence is about how extreme the penalty is, while the conclusion is about not imposing the penalty due to uncertainty. Therefore, the assumption is that if a penalty is extreme, it should only be imposed when the identity of the perpetrator is sufficiently clear. The correct answer will state a principle that supports the argument.

Step 4: Evaluate the Answer Choices

(A) matches the prediction.

(B) is a 180 and Out of Scope. The author indicates unwillingness to impose the penalty, which this answer choice argues against. Additionally, this choice introduces the Out of Scope idea of deterrence.

(C) goes Out the Scope by introducing the idea of proportionality between a crime and its penalty. The author never discusses how much harm the pollution caused and therefore it is impossible to tell if this principle would apply.

(D) may be true, but doesn't do anything to justify the argument that the penalty should not be imposed. This choice means the perpetrator is less likely to admit responsibility, so the penalty is less *likely* to be imposed based on the argument's reasoning. But that doesn't strengthen the argument that it *shouldn't* be imposed.

(E) is a Distortion. In the stimulus, an adequate level of certainty of the perpetrator's identity has not yet been achieved, but the argument gives no reason to believe that such a level of certainty would be *impossible* to achieve. The stimulus argues for making sure the identity of the guilty party is sufficiently known before doling out a penalty; it does not argue that penalties should be decreased in order to lower the threshold of certainty for identifying the guilty party.

2. (C) Inference

Step 1: Identify the Question Type

Because the correct answer is the one "supported by the information above," this is an Inference question. The correct answer must be true based on the statements in the stimulus.

Step 2: Untangle the Stimulus

Paraphrase each statement as you read, looking for ideas that are discussed in more than one statement. First, those who live in nursing homes can have trouble with depression. Second, a study shows that people in nursing homes who have connected to pets have lower rates of depression than those who haven't connected to pets.

Step 3: Make a Prediction

Since nursing home residents who enjoy "personal bonds" with pets are less likely to be depressed, this suggests something about the personal bonds *may help* residents avoid depression. Notice the tentative phrasing and keep an eye out for extreme answers.

Step 4: Evaluate the Answer Choices

(C) matches the prediction. While the stimulus would not support a stronger inference, **(C)** is phrased very cautiously. Because personal bonds with pets lead to less depression among nursing home residents, it must be true that depression "*may* result at least in part from a lack of companionship." After all, those residents who enjoy personal bonds with pets are certainly getting one form of companionship that residents without personal bonds with pets are not getting.

(A) makes an Irrelevant Comparison of residents of nursing homes to the population at large. The stimulus only discusses residents of nursing homes.

(B) is Extreme because it jumps to the conclusion that access to pets is the "best method" for helping residents with depression. The stimulus suggests that this method seems to help residents with depression, but it does not suggest that this method is better than all other methods.

(D) is both Out of Scope and Extreme. First, it focuses on psychological well-being in general, rather than on depression among people who live in nursing homes. Also, **(D)** asserts that animal companionship is *essential* for well-being. At most, the stimulus supports the inference that animal companionship appears to aid psychological well-being in some cases.

(E) is also Extreme. It suggests that access to pets will *eliminate* depression in nursing homes. This actually contradicts the stimulus, because personal bonds with pets resulted in only *lower* rates of depression, not a complete elimination of depression.

3. (A) Flaw

Step 1: Identify the Question Type

This question stem straightforwardly asks for the flaw in the argument, which makes this a Flaw question.

Step 2: Untangle the Stimulus

Analyze the argument's evidence and conclusion. The conclusion is the first sentence. Basically, the author believes that a TV ad needs to be humorous in order to be effective. The main piece of evidence comes immediately after the conclusion, following the evidence Keyword *for*: humorous ads attract attention and hold it long enough to convey a message.

Step 3: Make a Prediction

Start by predicting the assumption. The evidence suggests that humor is one way to hold attention. The conclusion goes further, suggesting that humor is the *only* effective way to advertise. Therefore, the author assumes nothing except humor can hold attention. This argument overlooks the possibility that there are potentially many ways besides humor to hold consumers' attention long enough to convey a message.

Step 4: Evaluate the Answer Choices

(A) matches the prediction. The author makes the faulty assumption that humor is the only thing that can hold a person's attention long enough to convey a message.

(B) is a Distortion of the argument's evidence. The evidence explicitly distinguishes between merely catching attention and holding attention long enough to convey a message. It says humor does both.

(C) is tempting, because it describes a necessary versus sufficient flaw, which this argument does commit. However, it gets the argument's problematic logic backward. The author assumes that something sufficient to attract attention (humor) is necessary to attract attention (i.e., the *only* thing that does). This answer choice says the author takes something necessary and says it's sufficient. So, if the words *necessary* and *sufficient* were flipped in this answer choice, it would accurately describe the flaw.

(D) accuses the argument of committing an equivocation flaw. This simply never happens in the stimulus. *Effective* in the conclusion means the same thing as *effective* in the evidence.

(E) doesn't accurately describe the argument. The argument says the purpose of an ad is to both be effective *and* convey its message. Additionally, the argument doesn't include any language that limits an ad's purpose to just those two goals.

4. (C) Strengthen

Step 1: Identify the Question Type

The correct answer will "strengthen the physician's argument," so this is a Strengthen question.

Step 2: Untangle the Stimulus

Break down the argument into evidence and conclusion. Following the contrast Keyword *[b]ut*, the conclusion is that stories of people getting sick after being vaccinated are no reason to be concerned. The physician points out that millions of people get vaccinated, and some of those people are bound to coincidently get sick soon after.

Step 3: Make a Prediction

The physician argues that health problems will sometimes occur merely by coincidence after vaccinations. In other words, she makes an anti-causal argument. This argument overlooks the possibility that any link between vaccinations and illness is more than just a coincidence. The correct answer will need to make it even more likely that vaccinations are not causing health problems. In other words, the argument could be weakened by pointing out that something about vaccinations cause illness. To strengthen the argument, the correct answer will suggest that nothing about vaccinations causes illness.

Step 4: Evaluate the Answer Choices

(C) suggests that vaccinations do not cause health problems by pointing out that people are just as likely to get health problems before vaccinations as they are after vaccinations. If vaccinations were the cause, one would expect people to develop health problems far more frequently *after* getting vaccinations.

(A) is Out of Scope. The physician says the stories about vaccinations are no cause for concern across the board, regardless of which vaccines they discuss. If anything, this weakens the argument because it shows this is a recent problem; i.e., the stories are not outdated and no longer relevant. Most importantly, however, this doesn't lessen the link between the vaccinations and subsequent health problems.

(B) goes Out of Scope by focusing on the likelihood of whether someone that does not get vaccinated for a rare illness could still contract that illness. However, the argument focuses on what happens to those people who *do* get vaccinated.

(D) makes an Irrelevant Comparison between the severity of illnesses which follow vaccinations and the illnesses that vaccinations are supposed to prevent. It doesn't actually address whether or not vaccinations *cause* the illnesses that follow, regardless of how serious they are. Although, if that connection were made, this choice would weaken the physician's argument, making stories of health problems following vaccinations definitely something to cause concern.

(E) is Out of Scope because it introduces medications, not vaccinations.

5. (B) Point at Issue (Agree)

Step 1: Identify the Question Type

Because the correct answer is the claim that two speakers "agree about," this is a Point at Issue (Agree) question.

Step 2: Untangle the Stimulus

Paraphrase each speaker's argument. Sharita believes that those people who are not willing to take care of a cat's offspring need to have their cats spayed or neutered. Her evidence is that there are lots of stray cats because people do not do so. Chad believes that stray cats are annoying and dangerous. He says feeding stray cats worsens the problem, unless those cats then are captured and adopted.

Step 3: Make a Prediction

Both Sharita and Chad discuss stray cats, but in quite different ways. Sharita focuses on what domestic cat owners can do to reduce the number of stray cats. Chad focuses on how people worsen the situation by feeding stray cats. Because their statements are so different in terms of specifics, the point of agreement between them will be about a general issue. Sharita wants to reduce the number of stray cats, and Chad straight out calls stray cats a nuisance. Therefore, both must think that the stray cat situation is troublesome and in need of improvement.

Step 4: Evaluate the Answer Choices

(B) matches the prediction. Both Sharita and Chad look for ways to reduce problems associated with the number of stray cats. Therefore, Sharita and Chad must agree that there are too many stray cats.

(A) is incorrect because Sharita fails to mention anything about feeding stray cats. Only Chad discusses this.

(C) is incorrect because Sharita fails to mention anything about the risk stray cats pose to humans. Only Chad mentions this.

(D) is incorrect because Sharita fails to mention anything about how stray cats spread diseases. Only Chad mentions this.

(E) is incorrect because Sharita fails to mention anything about feeding stray cats or kindness. Once again, only Chad discusses this.

6. (A) Assumption (Necessary)

Step 1: Identify the Question Type

Because the correct answer is the "assumption required by" the argument in the stimulus, this is a Necessary Assumption question. You can use the Denial Test to check your answer.

Step 2: Untangle the Stimulus

Break down the argument into evidence and conclusion. The conclusion follows "therefore" in the last sentence. Basically, the detective believes that most embezzlers and bribers will get caught. The main evidence comes in two pieces. First, people who *repeatedly* embezzle and bribe get more confident as they get away with more crimes. Next, the more crimes a criminal commits, the more likely the criminal will get caught.

Step 3: Make a Prediction

Find the matched and mismatched concepts in the argument. Because both the evidence and conclusion discuss people getting caught, that is the matched idea. The evidence mentions "people who repeatedly commit crimes like embezzlement or bribery." However, the conclusion is about "most people who commit embezzlement or bribery." While these ideas look superficially similar, because they use many of the same words, they are actually quite distinct. Just because those first time embezzlers have gained confidence by getting away with the act doesn't mean they will act on that confidence and embezzle again. The group of criminals who repeatedly commit embezzlement or bribery might be a very small portion of the larger group of people who at some point commit embezzlement or bribery. Thus, in order for the conclusion to follow, the author must assume that *most* people who commit embezzlement or bribery do so repeatedly.

Step 4: Evaluate the Answer Choices

(A) matches the prediction.

(B) doesn't bridge the gap to the conclusion about people who commit embezzlement or bribery being caught. Use the Denial Test. Negated, this choice says such people don't tend to be confident. That doesn't hurt the detective's argument, and therefore the original version is not required.

(C) makes an Irrelevant Comparison of embezzlement and bribery to other crimes. The argument in the stimulus focuses only on embezzlement and bribery.

(D) explains what might cause repeat embezzlers or bribers to eventually be caught. However, this answer choice is only about those who repeatedly commit crimes. It doesn't make that essential connection and explain why most people who commit embezzlement or bribery will be caught. While **(D)** might make the detective's conclusion more likely to be true, it is not necessary for the argument. The Denial Test can help to demonstrate this. The denial of **(D)** is as follows: People who repeatedly commit embezzlement or bribery *do not* become more and more careless the longer they avoid detection. Adding the denied version of **(D)**, the detective's argument could still stand. Criminals could remain careful but still get caught. Because the denied version of **(D)** does not destroy the argument, **(D)** is not the argument's necessary assumption.

(E) is Extreme. It is not necessarily assumed by the detective. The detective's conclusion is what "eventually" happens to embezzlers or bribers; that could include people being caught on their first go. Denied, **(E)** would be that "someone who has committed embezzlement or bribery could be caught the first time." Just because one person can be caught initially wouldn't destroy the detective's whole argument.

7. (C) Paradox

Step 1: Identify the Question Type

The correct answer would "contribute to an explanation" of the phenomenon in the stimulus, so this is a Paradox question. The correct answer will make sense of something that initially seems not to fit together.

Step 2: Untangle the Stimulus

Start by identifying the paradoxical phenomenon. On the one hand, when grain prices double, bread prices only go up a bit. On the other hand, when grain prices double, grain-fed beef nearly doubles as well.

Step 3: Make a Prediction

Both bread and grain-fed beef have grain as their main ingredient. So, if doubled grain prices barely affect bread prices, while grain-fed beef prices nearly double, something besides grain costs must contribute to the overall prices of both products. Additionally, grain costs must account for a smaller percentage of the total cost of bread than of grain-fed beef. The correct answer will point this out.

Step 4: Evaluate the Answer Choices

(C) matches the prediction by pointing out differences in the labor and marketing costs for bread and grain-fed beef. If most of the cost of producing bread comes from labor and marketing, then if the cost of its main ingredient goes up, the price of bread might not change much. On the other hand, if the main cost of producing grain-fed beef comes from its main ingredient, then we would expect grain-fed beef prices to nearly double when grain prices double.

(A) focuses only on beef, rather than on beef and bread. Additionally, while it would make sense for farmers to try to keep their costs low, this answer choice isn't specific enough about how much such labor costs influence the price of grain-fed beef.

(B) is an Irrelevant Comparison. The stimulus is interested in the difference between the *change* in price of the two products, not the difference between the products' *actual* prices. This choice doesn't explain why those percentage increases are so different.

(D) goes Outside the Scope by introducing grass-fed beef. Additionally, **(D)** neglects to include anything related to bread.

(E) is Out of Scope. It focuses on where retail grocery stores get their bread and beef, rather than on how the cost of grain affects the costs of bread and beef. If anything, this makes the paradox stronger, since it would be likely that small independent bakers would have a harder time handling price fluctuations in grain than would wholesale processing operations.

8. (E) Method of Argument

Step 1: Identify the Question Type

Because the correct answer describes the "technique of reasoning" that Kathy uses to respond to Mark, this is a Method of Argument question.

Step 2: Untangle the Stimulus

Start by simply paraphrasing Mark's argument. Mark argues that Qualzan probably causes an increased risk of heart attack because it works on the same physiological mechanism as Zokaz, another drug that increases the risk of heart attack. Turning to Kathy, paraphrase her argument sentence by sentence, in order to focus on *how* she responds to Mark. First, Kathy acknowledges that one aspect of Zokaz and Qualzan is similar: Their beneficial properties come from the same physiological mechanism. Next, following the contrast Keyword *[b]ut*, Kathy points out that the two drugs are chemically different. Because of this, Kathy concludes that Zokaz and Qualzan probably do not have the same side effects.

Step 3: Make a Prediction

Kathy's response to Mark begins by accepting a similarity between Zokaz and Qualzan. Next, she points out a crucial difference between them.

Step 4: Evaluate the Answer Choices

(E) matches the prediction. Mark's argument is an analogy, because it is based on the similarity of physiological mechanisms in Qualzan and Zokaz. Kathy's challenge to the validity of Mark's analogy is based on the chemical difference between Qualzan and Zokaz.

(A) is Out of Scope. Kathy never discusses the overall safety record for Qualzan.

(B) is incorrect because although Kathy does attempt to discredit Mark's argument, she does not do so by pointing out another flawed argument that is similar to Mark's argument. She points out a difference between the two drugs.

(C) is a Distortion because Kathy never questions the validity of the studies cited by Mark.

(D) is Out of Scope because Kathy never mentions any fundamental principle of medicine.

9. (E) Flaw

Step 1: Identify the Question Type

The correct answer describes flawed reasoning in the CEO's argument. Therefore, this is a Flaw question. Keep classic flaws in mind.

Step 2: Untangle the Stimulus

Start by breaking down the argument into evidence and conclusion. The conclusion is the opening sentence. Basically, the CEO suggests that his corporation is environmentally responsible because they do all they can to pollute less. The CEO's evidence is that his corporation's production methods pollute less than they used to and that all existing production methods result in some pollution.

Step 3: Make a Prediction

Identify the CEO's assumption. The CEO's evidence is about how the corporation pollutes less than it used to and that all production methods result in some pollution. The CEO's conclusion is that the corporation is doing everything it can to pollute less. But polluting "less than our old methods" is not necessarily the same as polluting as little as possible. The CEO assumes that there is nothing else the corporation could do to pollute less. The CEO overlooks the possibility that some other production method would pollute less than the method they currently use.

Step 4: Evaluate the Answer Choices

(E) matches the prediction.

(A) is not a flaw in the argument. In the evidence, the CEO does mention that *currently* there are no pollution-free methods, but the CEO does not necessarily assume such methods are impossible to develop.

(B) describes a causal flaw, which is not at play here. The CEO doesn't introduce any sort of cause or effect.

(C) incorrectly describes the argument. The CEO mentions a specific criticism (not being environmentally responsible) and then argues against that criticism only. He doesn't expand his argument to other criticisms.

(D) is a Distortion. The CEO cites as evidence that the company has, in fact, reduced the amount of pollution produced. Therefore, the company's success at reducing pollution is not something the CEO takes for granted. The real question, which **(D)** doesn't address, is whether or not the corporation is doing as much as possible to reduce pollution.

10. (B) Assumption (Necessary)

Step 1: Identify the Question Type

Because the correct answer is the assumption that "the argument requires," this is a Necessary Assumption question. You can use the Denial Test to check your answer.

Step 2: Untangle the Stimulus

Analyze the argument's evidence and conclusion. The conclusion comes at the end. Suppression of the immune system causes or worsens some types of gum disease. The evidence is twofold. First, stress hurts the immune system. Second, people who take care of problems efficiently are less likely to have gum disease than are those who ignore problems.

Step 3: Make a Prediction

This argument is a little difficult to take apart. Working backward, the author creates a chain in the evidence and conclusion. Stress hurts the immune system, and a hurt immune system can aggravate or cause gum disease. In other words, stress can aggravate or cause gum disease. There is nothing wrong with this logic chain, so you need to look elsewhere in the evidence for the gap. The author also says that people who deal with problems are less likely to have gum disease than people who don't. But then he jumps to stress. Stress is not mentioned in the evidence elsewhere and so must be the unique concept. What is the author assuming causes stress? Well, if stress causes gum disease and those who don't deal with their problems are more likely to have gum disease, the author must be assuming that not dealing with one's problems leads to stress. If that chain was difficult to follow, you can always use the Denial Test to check your answer. The negated version of the correct answer will make the argument fall apart.

Step 4: Evaluate the Answer Choices

(B) matches the prediction.

(A) is Out of Scope by bringing up "painful conditions." Even if those are meant to be synonymous with gum disease, the answer still reverses the logic. The stimulus says that not addressing problems quickly and directly can lead to gum disease. However, this answer says that painful conditions can lead to interference with addressing problems.

(C) is a 180, associating high stress with efficient problem solving. This goes against the findings of the recent study, which shows that efficient problem solvers have less gum disease.

(D) is a Distortion. While the stimulus does provide reason to think that efficient problem solvers have fewer dental problems, the reason why has to do with the effect of stress on the immune system, not with the rapid pursuit of dental care.

(E) is Out of Scope, focusing on the reason why people might ignore problems. The argument is about the effect that follows from ignoring problems, not on potential *causes* of why people ignore problems. Additionally, this choice would indicate that people who avoid problems have less stress (because addressing problems is stressful for them). That's the opposite of the author's assumption, which would make this a 180.

11. (C) Flaw

Step 1: Identify the Question Type

Because the correct answer describes the flawed reasoning in the stimulus, this is a Flaw question.

Step 2: Untangle the Stimulus

Identify the argument's evidence and conclusion. The conclusion is that the cooler the storage temperature, the longer fruit will stay fresh. The evidence is the experiment conducted by the science class. Basically, the class stored fruits at three different temperatures, and the fruits stored at the coolest temperature stayed fresh the longest.

Step 3: Make a Prediction

Start by finding the assumption. Here, the evidence is about three specific temperatures. But the conclusion is about temperature in general, suggesting that "the cooler the temperature … the longer they will stay fresh." Thus, the class assumes that the three specific temperatures studied are representative of the entire range of temperatures. This is a gigantic scope shift. Just because the coolest of the three temperatures studied led to the best fruit storage does not mean that no matter how cool the temperature is that it will lead to better fruit storage. The class overlooks the possibility that temperatures below 10 degrees might lead to very poor fruit storage. For example, 50 degrees below 0 may not be good for keeping fruit fresh.

Step 4: Evaluate the Answer Choices

(C) matches the prediction by pointing out the students' improper shift from a narrow range of temperatures (the three tested) to the entire range of temperatures.

(A) is a Distortion of the argument by suggesting that the fruits in the evidence are different from the fruits in the conclusion. Although the stimulus never says which fruits the class studied, the conclusion is specifically about the *same* fruits, as indicated by the phrase "these varieties of fruits."

(B) is Out of Scope, introducing other factors that may lead to fruit spoilage besides temperature. While it is true that the science experiment does not consider these factors, the purpose of the experiment is to determine the effect of temperature on storage. Thus, ignoring the other potential factors is not a flaw in the argument's reasoning. No scientific

experiment can be expected to test all potential factors simultaneously.

(D) incorrectly focuses on the thermometer used in the experiment. You must accept the evidence as true in a Flaw question, and here the evidence is based on knowing the storage temperature. Therefore, you must accept that the class was able to accurately determine the temperature. **(D)** simply fails to mention anything about the argument's conclusion that coolness has a direct effect on the lasting freshness of fruits.

(E) is a Distortion of the argument because the conclusion *does* attempt to explain the results of the experiment. The conclusion that cooler temperatures are preferred for freshness is based off of the evidence the science class gathered.

12. (B) Weaken

Step 1: Identify the Question Type

The correct answer "weakens the argument" in the stimulus, so this is a Weaken question.

Step 2: Untangle the Stimulus

Analyze the argument's evidence and conclusion. The conclusion comes after *[t]hus* at the end of the stimulus. Basically, the author believes that even if population growth trends continue, water shortages will not be a problem. The evidence is that humanity currently uses a small fraction of the Earth's fresh water supply.

Step 3: Make a Prediction

Start by finding the assumption. The evidence is that a lot of additional fresh water is available. The conclusion is that water shortages will not cause problems. Thus, the assumption is that because there is a large total amount of fresh water available, there will be no water shortage problems. This overlooks the possibility that even though there is plenty of fresh water over the entire Earth as a whole, humans may not be able to effectively access that water to avoid shortages. Additionally, this conclusion, like many predictions, assumes that present conditions remain the same in the future. So, the author also assumes that the current amount of fresh water will not significantly decrease.

Step 4: Evaluate the Answer Choices

(B) matches the prediction, suggesting that the fresh water supply is not evenly distributed over the Earth. Thus, even though the total supply is large, some places might be likely to suffer a water shortage. Although **(B)** certainly does not prove that there will be problems caused by water shortages, it does make it more likely to be true that there will be.

(A) doesn't affect the argument. The conclusion suggests that knowledge of population growth trends is not significant for forecasting water shortages, at least in the near future.

(C) goes Out of Scope by introducing water conservation methods. The stimulus states there is enough fresh water that water shortages will not be a problem in the near future. No condition is made that there will only be enough fresh water if conservation methods are used.

(D) addresses a time frame that is too vague. The conclusion focuses on the near future, while **(D)** discusses the potentially much longer period of what "will eventually" happen.

(E) makes an Irrelevant Comparison between growth in water usage in agriculture versus industry. The stimulus focuses on total water use and does not distinguish *how* water is used.

13. (E) Paradox

Step 1: Identify the Question Type

Because the correct answer will "resolve the apparent paradox" in the stimulus, this is a Paradox question. Identify the two statements that appear to conflict.

Step 2: Untangle the Stimulus

Start by finding the apparent paradox, the situation that does not quite seem to fit together. Here, the contrast Keyword *[y]et* marks the paradox. On the one hand, standardization and centralization caused big gains in productivity during the Industrial Revolution. On the other hand, more recently, already productive companies have further increased productivity by letting individual employees make more decisions.

Step 3: Make a Prediction

If already productive companies are increasing productivity through a very different method than was used during the Industrial Revolution (arguably the opposite method), then there must be some significant difference in the situation between these present-day companies and those of the Industrial Revolution. The correct answer will demonstrate how giving employees influence on decision making could actually lead to more productivity in already productive companies.

Step 4: Evaluate the Answer Choices

(E) matches the prediction, pointing out that in already very productive companies, further increases in productivity do not come from more standardization and centralization, but rather from the application of innovative ideas. These ideas, which can be used company-wide to further increase productivity, stem from giving employees more autonomy.

(A) may be true, but it focuses on what most companies do, rather than focusing on what "many already productive companies" do. "Most companies" could include many

companies that are not already productive. Additionally, it describes increasing productivity following the lead of the Industrial Revolution, not reversing it, which is the crux of this paradox.

(B) is a good reason why companies should give individuals more control, but the focus on job satisfaction is Out of Scope. Additionally, it fails to explain *how or why* giving individual employees greater control over their work can lead to more productivity. This choice merely says it does, which is what the stimulus says as well.

(C) is a 180, deepening the paradox. It shows productivity has recently increased due to technology like robots, which would arguably give individuals less control over their work. Additionally, **(C)** discusses *industrial* productivity, while the stimulus is about productive companies, which are not necessarily in the industrial arena. This answer does not explain how some companies have seen their productivity increase by granting more autonomy.

(D) is Out of Scope. It focuses on those companies in which employees have been making decisions as individuals all along, and now the company is taking lessons from the Industrial Revolution. The stimulus is about those companies that have *recently* increased individual influence on decision making. So, this choice does not explain why those companies granting employees greater influence on decision making have seen an increase in productivity.

14. (B) Inference

Step 1: Identify the Question Type

The correct answer is a statement that must be true based on statements in the stimulus. The direction of support flows downward from the stimulus to the answer choices. Therefore, this is an Inference question.

Step 2: Untangle the Stimulus

Make an inventory of the statements, paraphrasing as you read. First, the most important thing about epic poetry is that it spreads social values. Second, epic poetry spreads social values by telling stories about heroic role models. Third, people who hear epic poetry find significance by acting like those role models.

Step 3: Make a Prediction

The first and second statements of the stimulus are connected. Because the most important thing about epic poetry is how it spreads values, and because epic poetry spreads those values by telling stories about heroic role models, it must be true that the most important thing about epic poetry is accomplished through stories about heroic role models.

Step 4: Evaluate the Answer Choices

(B) directly matches the prediction.

(A) is Extreme. While the stimulus says people get meaning and direction from epic poetry, it does not indicate if that is an *important* function of epic poetry. The only thing the stimulus describes as an *important* function of epic poetry is that it spreads values. Furthermore, this answer is not limited to epic poetry, but broadly talks about poetry in general.

(C), like **(A)**, is too broad, focusing on poetry in general, rather than specifically on epic poetry.

(D) is Extreme. Just because epic poetry presents heroic figures as role models, that doesn't necessarily mean *many*, if any, groups actually embrace those heroic figures.

(E) is Extreme by asserting that epic poetry is the *only* place that presents heroic role models. It is possible that other genres not discussed in the stimulus might have a similar effect.

15. (C) Principle (Identify/Strengthen)

Step 1: Identify the Question Type

Because the correct answer is the principle that supports the argument in the stimulus, this is an Identify the Principle question that resembles a Strengthen question. A specific situation will be presented in the stimulus, and your task is to identify the principle that strengthens the author's argument.

Step 2: Untangle the Stimulus

Attack this question as you would a Strengthen question; break down the argument into evidence and conclusion. The conclusion is that confiscating part of convicted burglars' wages after they reenter the workforce is justified. The evidence is that confiscated wages would be used to pay back victims of burglary.

Step 3: Make a Prediction

Start by finding the assumption. The conclusion is that *stealing* from convicted burglars is acceptable. The evidence is about paying back burglary victims. Thus, the author assumes that the government can steal from a former offender, so long as it intends to pay back victims of the same type of offense. In other words, the ends justify the means. The correct answer will be a general principle that suggests that noble intentions behind a questionable act can make it acceptable to do the questionable act.

Step 4: Evaluate the Answer Choices

(C) matches the prediction by suggesting that the motive behind an action determines whether or not it is acceptable.

(A) incorrectly focuses on what should happen to money stolen from a burglar rather than on whether stealing money from a burglar is acceptable in the first place. Additionally, the argument is that the fund will compensate burglary victims in general, not that it will go specifically to the victims of that particular burglar.

(B) goes Out of Scope, focusing on what a burglar is obliged to do rather than on what would be acceptable for the government to do to a burglar. Additionally, this answer choice focuses too specifically on burglars paying back their particular victims, rather than on victims in general.

(D) is a reverse of the Formal Logic. The stimulus says that if stealing from burglars compensates victims, then it is justified. This answer choice says that if a crime is justified, then it compensates people who deserve compensation. Additionally, the stimulus never actually describes burglary victims as deserving compensation.

(E) is a 180. The thrust of the conclusion is that stealing *is* sometimes justified.

16. (C) Main Point

Step 1: Identify the Question Type

The correct answer "expresses the overall conclusion" in the stimulus's argument, so this is a Main Point question. Keep an eye out for the most opinionated statement.

Step 2: Untangle the Stimulus

Read for Keywords, and think especially about the structure of the stimulus. First, the stimulus gives us the point of view of some ads for heartburn medicine. Second, the stimulus provides an unattributed opinion that suggests the heartburn ads are wrong. Third, the stimulus provides facts about heartburn and the esophagus.

Step 3: Make a Prediction

Finding opinions is the key to predicting in a Main Point question. In this question, there are two opinions. First, there is the opinion presented in medicine ads. Second, there is the unattributed opinion. The unattributed opinion must be the author's opinion. The author believes "[t]his is false." Don't leave vague words like *this* in your prediction. Fill them in with information from the stimulus. Thus, the author believes heartburn ads are wrong. In other words, the author believes unrelieved heartburn is *not* likely to cause esophageal cancer.

Step 4: Evaluate the Answer Choices

(C) matches the prediction exactly.

(A) is a piece of the evidence, rather than the conclusion.

(B) is also a piece of evidence, rather than the conclusion.

(D) captures the point of view that the author opposes, rather than the author's own point of view.

(E) paraphrases the author's evidence nicely but does not convey the author's main point. The author's strongest opinion is about the misleading nature of the advertisements, not the actual number of people that will be affected by the dangers described in the ads.

17. (B) Parallel Reasoning

Step 1: Identify the Question Type

Because the correct answer is "most similar in its reasoning" to the argument in the stimulus, this is a Parallel Reasoning question.

Step 2: Untangle the Stimulus

Break down the argument into evidence and conclusion. The conclusion is the opening statement, that at least one halogen lamp must be well crafted. The evidence is that some halogen lamps are on display at Furniture Labyrinth, and all items on display at Furniture Labyrinth are well crafted.

Step 3: Make a Prediction

Because the stimulus is brief and uses Formal Logic, the best strategy is to work with the stimulus as a whole, translating it into Formal Logic algebra. Here, the evidence is: some lamps are on display; if on display → well crafted. The conclusion is: some lamps are well crafted. Algebraically, you're looking for an argument that says: some X are Y; if Y then Z; so some X are Z.

Step 4: Evaluate the Answer Choices

(B) matches the prediction. It turns into: some sonnets were written by Melinda (some X are Y), and all things written by Melinda are disturbing (if Y then Z), so some sonnets are disturbing (so some X are Z).

(A)'s evidence is too weak. There is only a *chance* of storms on some days this week. From just a *chance*, the argument can't conclude that there *will be* a temperature drop on some days.

(C)'s evidence fails to match that in the stimulus. In the stimulus, the evidence is in the form of one "some" statement and one "if-then" statement, but **(C)**'s evidence contains two "if-then" statements. **(C)**'s evidence translates to: "if car shop → can have car worked on there; if car shop → can do good mechanical work."

(D)'s evidence fails to match that in the stimulus. Just because every lake is teeming with healthy fish does not prove that some minnows are healthy, because there could be lots of other healthy fish in the lakes, but no healthy minnows. **(D)**'s evidence would match the stimulus if it said, "Many different species of minnow can be found in the lakes nearby, and every fish in the lakes nearby is healthy."

(E)'s conclusion fails to match the stimulus because it is too definitive. Translated into Formal Logic, **(E)**'s conclusion is, "If cornmeal used at Matteo's Trattoria → healthful and organic." **(E)**'s conclusion would come closer to matching the conclusion of the stimulus if it said, "We can be confident

that *some* of the cornmeal used at Matteo's Trattoria is healthful and organic."

18. (E) Inference

Step 1: Identify the Question Type

Because the correct answer is "supported by" the statements in the stimulus, this is an Inference question. The correct answer must be true based on the stimulus.

Step 2: Untangle the Stimulus

Create an inventory of statements, paraphrasing as you read. First, psychologists have discovered managers do not usually gain job satisfaction or efficiency when companies institute policies allowing managers to choose their own work schedules. Second, psychologists explain this finding by suggesting managers usually have the freedom to choose their own work schedules before these policies are begun. Third, employees besides managers *do* gain job satisfaction and productivity when they get to choose their own schedules. Fourth, there are some limitations to the benefits gained from flexible-schedule policies: benefits decrease over time, and too much flexibility further minimizes benefits.

Step 3: Make a Prediction

The effects of flexible work schedules differ between managers and nonmanagers. Managers showed little improvement, but nonmanagers showed some improvement, with some caveats. The correct answer will not be worded more strongly than the stimulus and will not introduce new information.

Step 4: Evaluate the Answer Choices

(E) must be true based on the stimulus. Policies affect managers and nonmanagers in different ways, as demonstrated by the findings of the stimulus. Therefore, you cannot determine the typical benefits of policies just by looking at managers.

(A) may be true, but it isn't supported by the stimulus. It says flexible schedules have little effect on managers as a group because most already have autonomy, but it doesn't actually distinguish between the effects on managers with and without autonomy. Such an improvement in satisfaction and efficiency is likely based on the result among nonmanagers, but it doesn't have to be true.

(B) is Out of Scope. The stimulus discusses a distinction between effects on individual managers and individual nonmanagers, but it never discusses the effect on an entire workforce. You can't extrapolate from individuals (which seem to have a relatively positive response) to the workforce as a whole. Additionally, even if you were to make that jump, this answer wouldn't make sense. The stimulus suggests that flexible schedules have a neutral or positive effect, which would indicate an overall improvement in morale, not a stagnant state.

(C) is Extreme. When discussing nonmanagers, the stimulus suggests that in the long run, the positive effects of flexible schedules diminish. Additionally, the stimulus never suggests that the positive effects of flexible scheduling would *substantially* improve productivity and satisfaction, even when the policies are first initiated.

(D) is unsupported. The stimulus suggests only that adding flexible schedule policies does not typically increase managers' job satisfaction. But then, most managers already have autonomy. So really, there is no way to know what sort of correlation—small or strong—exists between managers' job satisfaction and flexible schedules.

19. (D) Weaken

Step 1: Identify the Question Type

Because the correct answer "undermines" the argument in the stimulus, this is a Weaken question.

Step 2: Untangle the Stimulus

Analyze the argument's evidence and conclusion. The conclusion follows the contrast Keyword *but* in the middle of the stimulus. Basically, the author believes that the survey respondents who preferred Lopez may have been positively biased toward Lopez. The evidence follows the Keywords "[a]fter all." The reason the author thinks the respondents were biased toward Lopez is that Lopez won the election.

Step 3: Make a Prediction

Start by finding the assumption. Here, the evidence is that Lopez eventually won the election. The conclusion is that survey respondents who preferred her arguments were possibly biased because it's possible that they were among those who were planning to vote for her all along. The argument can be rephrased as follows: Lopez won the election, so survey respondents may have already preferred her when stating they preferred Lopez's debate performance. Thus, the author claims that the bias is what *caused* the survey respondents to prefer Lopez. To weaken a causal argument, it is most likely that an alternative cause is responsible. Thus, the author's assumption is that there was no other reason for them to prefer Lopez, except their preconceived notions. The argument overlooks the possibility that people preferred Lopez's arguments on their merits, rather than simply because she was the candidate who they planned to vote for all along. Additionally, a case of reverse causation seems plausible. Perhaps one reason why Lopez won the election is because people preferred his arguments in the debate. The correct answer will provide an additional reason to believe that the survey respondents were not

actually biased toward Lopez, but genuinely preferred her arguments.

Step 4: Evaluate the Answer Choices

(D) suggests that the respondents genuinely preferred Lopez's arguments. If the respondents said they preferred Tanner immediately before the debate, but changed their preference to Lopez immediately after the debate, then it is likely that the respondents' preference is actually reflective of Lopez's performance in the debate.

(A) is Out of Scope. It incorrectly focuses on people who did not watch the debate, rather than on the survey respondents who did. Those who were surveyed may still have been part of the group that contributed to Lopez's victory, so this does not weaken the argument that bias was present.

(B) is also Out of Scope. It discusses viewers in the live audience, while the stimulus is about viewers in general. At most, **(B)** simply suggests that Tanner looks better than Lopez to a live audience. This fact has little to do with whether or not the people who preferred Lopez were biased or if they genuinely preferred Lopez's arguments.

(C) makes an Irrelevant Comparison between those who watched the debate and those who didn't. The stimulus is only about those who did. Additionally, even if those who watched the debate were more likely to vote for Tanner than were those who didn't watch, that doesn't mean that those who watched preferred Tanner to Lopez. For example, of those who watched the debate, perhaps 30 percent voted for Tanner, but of those who didn't watch the debate, only 20 percent vote for Tanner. So, **(C)** would not definitively weaken the argument that the respondents were already biased toward Lopez.

(E) is Out of Scope. The margin of victory doesn't affect the likelihood that survey respondents were biased.

20. (A) Assumption (Necessary)

Step 1: Identify the Question Type

Because the correct answer is the "assumption required by the argument," this is a Necessary Assumption question. You can use the Denial Test to check your answer.

Step 2: Untangle the Stimulus

Identify the argument's evidence and conclusion. Following *[b]ut* in the middle of the stimulus, the conclusion is that recent research findings that food prohibitions were important in ancient cultures cannot explain the origins of those prohibitions. The evidence is that the ancient peoples who followed the food prohibitions did not have access to the same data that informed the recent research findings.

Step 3: Make a Prediction

The conclusion says that the data at hand cannot explain the origins of food prohibitions. The reasoning is that the data was not available to those in the ancient cultures who followed the prohibitions. Therefore, the author must be assuming that any explanation of a food prohibition's origin must stem only from knowledge accessible to those who followed the prohibition. In other words, knowing why a food was initially prohibited requires looking through the eyes of the members of the ancient culture.

Step 4: Evaluate the Answer Choices

(A) matches the prediction. It essentially says that the explanation of a prohibition's origin must be based on the knowledge available to those who abided by it. The denied version of this answer says that the origin of a food prohibition can be explained using knowledge other than that available to the people who adopted the prohibition. If that's the case, then the data that the researchers used may be able to explain the origin, and the author's argument falls apart.

(B) is Out of Scope. The author never mentions anything about contradictory food prohibitions. Additionally, this answer choice doesn't say anything about the origins of prohibitions, which is the unique concept in the conclusion.

(C) is also Out of Scope. Nutritional value is never mentioned. Additionally, while the stimulus says the prohibitions served social functions, it doesn't mention social *importance* in relation to the origins of the prohibition.

(D) is also Out of Scope. How long it takes to forget the original purpose is immaterial. It may be true that it takes a few generations, but it doesn't have to be true for the author's conclusion to be true. Even if the purpose isn't forgotten after a few generations, the author may still be correct in saying that the medical and anthropological data available to the medical researchers can't explain the origin.

(E) doesn't have to be true for the argument to be true. Even if the people who followed the food prohibitions didn't have a nontechnical (or had a technical) understanding of the prohibitions' medical functions, it wouldn't hurt the author's argument that the prohibitions' origins can only be explained through the understanding of those who abided by them.

21. (E) Inference

Step 1: Identify the Question Type

Because the correct answer "can be properly inferred" from the stimulus, this is an Inference question. The correct answer must be true based on the statements in the stimulus.

Step 2: Untangle the Stimulus

Make an inventory of the statements, paraphrasing as you read. First, more than half of the fiction books the editor has published came from agents. Second, the rest of the fiction books the editor has published came directly from fiction writers from whom the publisher requested manuscripts. Third, if a nonfiction manuscript was seriously looked at or published, then it came from a well-known person, or the editor requested the manuscript from the author after reviewing a proposal.

Step 3: Make a Prediction

While there are some differences in terms of how the editor got the fiction and nonfiction manuscripts that were published, there is also a notable similarity. For both fiction and nonfiction, the editor requested some manuscripts directly from authors. For published fiction, when the editor did not request a submission, the manuscript came from a literary agent. For published nonfiction, when the editor did not request a submission, the manuscript came from a well-known person.

Step 4: Evaluate the Answer Choices

(E) must be true. There are only two types of unrequested manuscripts that the editor has published. First, for fiction, unrequested manuscripts were submitted by literary agents. Second, for nonfiction, unrequested manuscripts were written by well-known people. **(E)** describes the nonfiction manuscripts that were neither requested by the editor nor submitted by literary agents, but that were written by well-known people.

(A) isn't supported by the stimulus. Other than those from renowned figures, unrequested *nonfiction* manuscripts wouldn't get serious attention, but the stimulus doesn't say how many of those there are. Additionally, the editor doesn't say if unrequested *fiction* manuscripts get serious attention or no. Those coming from literary agents are likely unrequested and may very well get thoughtful review. Furthermore, information is only given on fiction manuscripts that were published, which means there could be others that received attention but were not published. With all the uncertainty, it is impossible to say if "most" (more than 50 percent) unrequested manuscripts don't get serious attention.

(B) doesn't have to be true. First of all, the renowned authors in the answer choice (doesn't specify whether they're fiction or nonfiction) are not necessarily the same as the renowned figures in the stimulus (nonfiction authors only). Second, it's possible that most of the books published (other than those by renowned authors) are nonfiction books whose manuscript the editor requested after reviewing the proposal. The stimulus gives two Formal Logic statements that list the four sources for the editor's published books; no information is provided that lets you infer anything about which source type contributes the *most*.

(C) is a Distortion of the Formal Logic. The argument says that if a *nonfiction* book is given serious attention, then it is from a renowned figure *or* was solicited. So, **(C)** fails to consider those requested nonfiction manuscripts.

(D) makes an Irrelevant Comparison between the level of care the publisher uses in considering manuscripts directly submitted versus those submitted by a literary agent. The stimulus discusses careful consideration ("serious attention") only in the context of nonfiction manuscripts, not in the context of manuscripts in general. Additionally, no information is provided in the stimulus about what *levels* of care are given to each type of manuscript. For example, it is not known if the fiction manuscripts that are requested or those that come from literary agents receive more attention. Additionally, only published works of fiction are discussed in the stimulus; careful consideration may also be given to other unpublished works of fiction.

22. (D) Assumption (Sufficient)

Step 1: Identify the Question Type

Because the correct answer is the assumption that allows the conclusion in the stimulus to follow logically, this is a Sufficient Assumption question.

Step 2: Untangle the Stimulus

Analyze the argument's evidence and conclusion. The conclusion follows *[c]onsequently* at the end of the stimulus. Basically, the author concludes that most of the drinking water in the district will probably get polluted. The evidence is that because the budget does not allow for more dairy inspectors to be hired, most of the large dairies will not meet government standards of waste disposal.

Step 3: Make a Prediction

The conclusion suggests that most of the drinking water will probably get polluted. The evidence, on the other hand, only suggests that most dairies will not follow federal standards of waste disposal. You need an answer choice that, when added to the evidence in the stimulus, leads to the conclusion. The logic looks like this:

Evidence:

	If	no new inspectors	→	most large dairies won't meet standards

Conclusion: *Most drinking water is likely polluted.*

You know that the sufficient condition in the evidence has been met. Therefore, the necessary condition of the evidence will follow. To get from the evidence to the conclusion, the author must assume that if most large dairies do not meet the government standards, then most of the drinking water will probably get polluted.

Step 4: Evaluate the Answer Choices

(D) matches the prediction.

(A) is a Distortion. The author is attempting to show that the laxness of most dairies will result in most of the drinking water becoming polluted. This answer choice reverses the logic by showing what would result in the water *not* becoming polluted. Translated into Formal Logic, this choice says:

	If	most dairies meet standards	→	~ most drinking water likely polluted

Even if you contrapose this statement, it doesn't bridge the gap from the evidence to the conclusion. A correct sufficient assumption should negate both of those terms above. There may be other sources of pollution besides just the dairies, so nothing they do can guarantee the safety of the drinking water.

(B) is not sufficient to guarantee the conclusion. Translated, this choice says:

	If	all drinking water clean	→	more dairy inspectors

The contrapositive would be:

	If	~ more dairy inspectors	→	~ all drinking water clean

The stimulus says that the sufficient condition will be met—there won't be more inspectors. But even if not all of the drinking water will stay clean, that doesn't prove *most* drinking water would become polluted, which is what the conclusion of the stimulus predicts. Note that this could be construed as a necessary assumption of the argument, but not a sufficient one. Using the Denial Test, **(B)** becomes "to keep all the drinking water clean *does not* require more inspectors." If that's true, then there's no reason for the author to conclude that a failure to hire more inspectors *will* result in most of the drinking water becoming polluted. There are still some gaps in that construction, but be mindful that even if the correct mismatched concepts are connected, a sufficient assumption must guarantee the conclusion. This answer does not.

(C) doesn't allow the conclusion to follow. Translated into Formal Logic, **(C)** becomes:

	If	all drinking water likely polluted	→	all large dairies ~ meet standards

If you contrapose this choice, you get the result that not all drinking water will likely become polluted. This doesn't contradict the author's conclusion (which is about *most* drinking water), but it doesn't prove it either. Even, if it was found that all the water was polluted, it cannot be guaranteed that the cause was from the dairies not meeting the standards. This answer, like **(A)**, mixes up the Formal Logic expected in the correct answer. A correct sufficient assumption should reverse the two terms above and change the statement "all large dairies won't meet standards" to simply "most large dairies won't meet standards." Otherwise, it would not get triggered based on the evidence.

(E) is Extreme. The evidence says that most large dairies won't meet standards. That means some might. If some dairies do meet standards, then this answer choice wouldn't be triggered by the evidence and therefore the conclusion wouldn't be guaranteed.

23. (D) Parallel Flaw

Step 1: Identify the Question Type

Because the correct answer is the argument that demonstrates "by parallel reasoning" the flaw in the argument in the stimulus, this is a Parallel Flaw question. The correct answer will contain the same flaw as that in the stimulus.

Step 2: Untangle the Stimulus

Break down the argument into evidence and conclusion. The conclusion follows *[s]o* at the end of the stimulus. It is the cautious prediction that Vegetaste Burger will probably be very successful. The evidence is that nearly all successful products were introduced with massive TV ad campaigns, and the company is using a massive TV ad campaign for the Vegetaste Burger.

Step 3: Make a Prediction

The company president makes the error of confusing sufficiency and necessity. It may be true for most products that if it was successful, then it was launched with a massive TV ad campaign. But it does not follow that if a product is launched with a massive TV ad campaign, then it will be successful, even with the qualification of *probably*. In this case, it is possible, even probable, for Vegetaste to be launched with a massive TV ad campaign and still end up unsuccessful. The correct answer will make the same error. Look for a choice that says this: "Almost all X (successful products) are Y (launched with a massive TV campaign), so because Z (Vegetaste) is Y, it will probably become X."

Step 4: Evaluate the Answer Choices

(D) matches the prediction. Having a PhD is usually a necessary requirement for being a president of Sifton University, and Robinson meets that necessary requirement. On that basis alone, the author concludes that Robinson will likely become the president of Sifton University. Just like the stimulus, **(D)** confuses sufficiency and necessity and can be mapped out as "almost all X (presidents of Sifton) are Y (a PhD), so because Z (Robinson) is Y, he will probably become X.

(A) is not parallel because its conclusion is not a prediction and the conclusion is too strong. The conclusion in the stimulus is that Vegetaste Burger will *probably* be successful, whereas this choice says the president's office *is* not in

Corbin's headquarters. Additionally, it fails to match the stimulus because it does not improperly assume that a sufficient condition will be satisfied just because a necessary condition is. **(A)** would match the stimulus if it said, "The president's office will likely be in Corbin's headquarters because almost all of the offices in Corbin's headquarters are small, and the president's office is small."

(B), like **(A)**, gives a conclusion that is too strong. Rather than stating that Donna *likely* has at least 10 years of experience, it states that she definitely has that experience. The first piece of evidence is consistent with the stimulus: almost all X (programmers at Coderight) have Y (at least 10 years of experience). But then it says, "So because Z (Donna) will probably be X, she has Y." **(B)** would match the stimulus if it had kept the first piece of evidence (almost all X have Y), and then said, "Donna has Y (at least 10 years of experience), so she will probably become X (hired at Coderight)."

(C) is not parallel because it fails to have a prediction as its conclusion. Additionally, its evidence also fails to match that in the stimulus. In **(C)**, the evidence includes two conditional statements. In the stimulus, the evidence includes only one conditional statement, plus one concrete statement. **(C)** would match the stimulus if it said, "Almost all X (factory workers) are Y (in opposition to the merger), so because Z (Acme workers) are Y, they will probably become X."

(E) cannot be correct because it doesn't make a necessity versus sufficiency error; it just makes an unwarranted assumption. The conditional statement in the evidence translates to: "Most novels, if published by Peninsula → profitable." **(E)** concludes that because *Safekeeping* is published by Peninsula, it will likely be profitable. That logically follows provided *Safekeeping* was published over the last 10 years and is otherwise similar to Peninsula Press's other published works. **(E)** would match the stimulus if it said, "*Safekeeping* will probably be published by Peninsula Press because almost every novel published by Peninsula has been profitable, and this novel is profitable."

24. (C) Role of a Statement

Step 1: Identify the Question Type

This is a Role of a Statement question because the correct answer "describes the role played" in the argument by the claim about how fossilized bacteria must have had a long evolutionary history.

Step 2: Untangle the Stimulus

Paraphrase the entire stimulus. First, scientists found fossils of old bacteria. Second, the old bacteria were complex, so the bacteria must have already evolved over a long period of time. Third, the Earth is not that much older than the fossils of the old bacteria. Therefore, life on Earth must have started shortly after Earth's formation when conditions were harsh.

Finally, this all leads to the conclusion that life may be able to start under harsh conditions elsewhere in the universe.

Step 3: Make a Prediction

Notice the chain of conclusion Keywords: *so, so,* and "[t]his suggests." The author presents a long chain of logic. The claim in question is that the bacteria in the fossils already had a long evolutionary history. This claim is supported by the piece of evidence that the fossilized bacteria were quite complex. The claim, in turn, supports the subsidiary conclusion that life on Earth must have started shortly after Earth's formation. That subsidiary conclusion is itself evidence for the biologist's main conclusion that life might be able to start under harsh conditions elsewhere in the universe. Therefore, the correct answer will suggest that the claim in question is supported by some evidence (they're complex), but in turn is used to support a subsidiary conclusion (life on Earth began shortly after formation) that ultimately supports the main conclusion (life may arise under harsh conditions elsewhere in the universe).

Step 4: Evaluate the Answer Choices

(C) matches the prediction.

(A) incorrectly states that there is no support given for the claim in question. The fact that the bacteria are quite complex supports the idea that they must have a long evolutionary history.

(B) makes the same error as **(A)** by incorrectly stating that there is no support given for the claim in question.

(D) incorrectly states that the claim in question is not used as support for another claim in the argument. The fact that the bacteria have a long evolutionary history is used to support the idea that the first life on Earth must have appeared soon after Earth's formation.

(E) incorrectly states that the claim in question supports two distinct conclusions that are unrelated to each other. While it is true that the claim in question does support two distinct conclusions, the subsidiary conclusion (that life must have appeared on Earth soon after Earth's formation) is used to then support the main conclusion (that life may be able to arise under harsh conditions elsewhere in the universe).

25. (D) Assumption (Necessary)

Step 1: Identify the Question Type

The correct answer is "an assumption required" by the argument in the stimulus, so this is a Necessary Assumption question.

Step 2: Untangle the Stimulus

Break down the argument into evidence and conclusion. The conclusion is that the stars are not more than a few million miles from Earth. The evidence following the Keywords "reasoned that" comes in the form of a Formal Logic statement: If the stars were more than a few million miles away from Earth, then the stars would have to move at tremendously great speeds.

Step 3: Make a Prediction

Both the evidence and the conclusion discuss the distance of the stars from Earth. However, only the evidence discusses the speed at which stars move. Therefore, the assumption will say something about the speed at which stars move. The logic looks like this:

Evidence:

$$\textbf{If} \quad \begin{array}{c} \textbf{stars more than few} \\ \textbf{million miles from} \\ \textbf{Earth} \end{array} \quad \rightarrow \quad \begin{array}{c} \textbf{stars move} \\ \textbf{tremendously fast} \end{array}$$

Conclusion: *Stars are not more than a few million miles from Earth.*

Notice that if you contrapose the evidence, the necessary result would be the conclusion. Therefore, the author must be assuming that the sufficient condition of the contraposed evidence is being satisfied. In other words, the author must be assuming that the stars do *not* move tremendously fast. Using the Denial Test to test the prediction, if the stars *did* move at tremendously great speeds, then they could be very far from Earth and still circle it in order to appear at roughly the same positions each night. That would crush the old astronomers' conclusion.

Step 4: Evaluate the Answer Choices

(D) matches the prediction.

(A) goes Out of Scope, suggesting that the stars do not revolve around Earth. The argument is about the time when astronomers believed the stars revolved around Earth.

(B) is Extreme. The assumption is that no stars move at tremendously fast speeds, but that does not mean all the stars move at the exact *same* speeds. There could be a variety of different speeds, all less than tremendously fast, at which the stars move. The fact that **(B)** starts with the word *[a]ll* is a clue that it is very unlikely the correct answer to a necessary Assumption question.

(C), like **(A)**, incorrectly contradicts the premise of the argument.

(E) weakens the argument. The astronomers believed that the stars were not more than a few million miles away from Earth. If it were true that a star more than a million miles away could appear in roughly the same position each night, that would make it more likely to be true that stars were, in fact, able to move at tremendously great speeds, and thus be more than a few million miles from Earth.

26. (D) Method of Argument

Step 1: Identify the Question Type

Because the correct answer describes how the argument "proceeds," this is a Method of Argument question. Pay attention to Keywords and structure.

Step 2: Untangle the Stimulus

Paraphrase the stimulus as you read, focusing especially on the structure of the argument. First, the author introduces what people may generally think about two types of painters: people might praise realistic painters and dismiss abstract painters. The author, however, asserts that people must care about something in paintings besides simply the replication of reality. The author's reason is that, were this not true, photography would have already ousted painting.

Step 3: Make a Prediction

The author introduces two types of feelings about paintings. The author then makes a conclusion about what people like in paintings, which is supported by the historical fact that photography has not replaced paintings to show that people don't just want an exact copy of reality. So, abstractly, the author supports his conclusion with evidence that something that would have occurred if he were wrong has not occurred.

Step 4: Evaluate the Answer Choices

(D) matches the prediction. The historical fact is that painting continues to exist alongside photography. The claim about people's artistic preferences is that they like more than just an exact replica.

(A) is Extreme because it discusses a claim about what *most* people appreciate. The stimulus never specifies how many people appreciate something. Even if you assume that the first statement of the stimulus is about most people instead of about some people, (A) still fails to capture the role of the statement regarding photography. That statement is neither a claim about what most people appreciate nor an aesthetic principle.

(B) is a Distortion. The author doesn't present the argument to *defend* the tastes people have. Additionally, like (A), no part of (B) accounts for the role as evidence that the statement about photography plays. That statement is not an aesthetic principle, so it has no match in this answer.

(C) reverses the author's argument because the author uses the historical fact to help explain people's artistic preferences, not the other way around.

(E), like (B), distorts the author's conclusion because the author is not defending people's artistic preferences. Rather, the author argues that there is something about people's artistic preferences that the opening statement of the stimulus fails to capture. In other words, the author is not suggesting that people have the right or wrong artistic preferences, merely that people's artistic preferences have to do with more than just exact replication. Additionally, the statement about photography is brought in as historical fact, but not historical *context*.

PrepTest 71

The Inside Story

PrepTest 71 was administered in December 2013. It challenged 28,363 test takers. What made this test so hard? Here's a breakdown of what Kaplan students who were surveyed after taking the official exam considered PrepTest 71's most difficult section.

Hardest PrepTest 71 Section as Reported by Test Takers

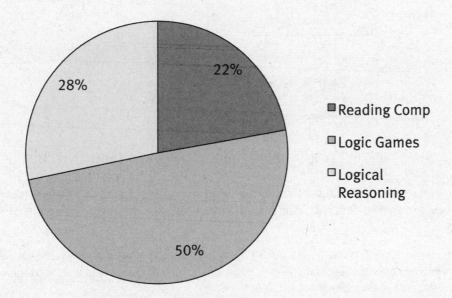

Based on these results, you might think that studying Logic Games is the key to LSAT success. Well, Logic Games is important, but test takers' perceptions don't tell the whole story. For that, you need to consider students' actual performance. The following chart shows the average number of students to miss each question in each of PrepTest 71's different sections.

Percentage Incorrect by PrepTest 71 Section Type

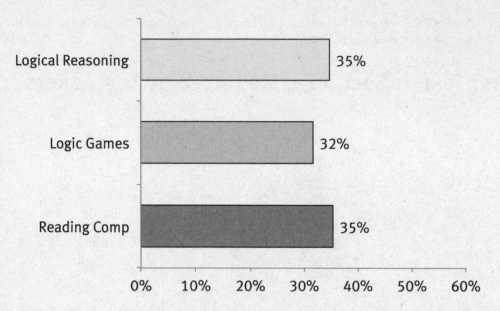

Actual student performance tells quite a different story. On average, students were almost equally likely to miss questions in all three of the different section types, and on PrepTest 71, Reading Comprehension and Logical Reasoning were somewhat higher than Logic Games in actual difficulty.

Maybe students overestimate the difficulty of the Logic Games section because it's so unusual, or maybe it's because a really hard Logic Game is so easy to remember after the test. But the truth is that the testmaker places hard questions throughout the test. Here were the locations of the 10 hardest (most missed) questions in the exam.

Location of 10 Most Difficult Questions in PrepTest 71

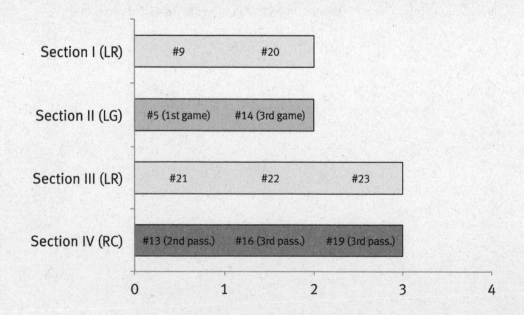

The takeaway from this data is that, to maximize your potential on the LSAT, you need to take a comprehensive approach. Test yourself rigorously, and review your performance on every section of the test. Kaplan's LSAT explanations provide the expertise and insight you need to fully understand your results. The explanations are written and edited by a team of LSAT experts, who have helped thousands of students improve their scores. Kaplan always provides data-driven analysis of the test, ranking the difficulty of every question based on actual student performance. The 10 hardest questions on every test are highlighted with a 4-star difficulty rating, the highest we give. The analysis breaks down the remaining questions into 1-, 2-, and 3-star ratings so that you can compare your performance to that of thousands of other test takers on all LSAC material.

Don't settle for wondering whether a question was really as hard as it seemed to you. Analyze the test with real data, and learn the secrets and strategies that help top scorers master the LSAT.

8 Can't–Miss Features of PrepTest 71

- In Logical Reasoning, PrepTest 71 was exceptionally representative of recent trends: Every LR question type came in within 1.1 questions of the expected number of questions for that type.
- Logical Reasoning was also very balanced in terms of the answers; each answer choice—(A) through (E)—appeared as the correct answer between 9 and 11 times.
- Not everything in Logical Reasoning was predictable here: PrepTest 71 was the first LSAT administration in over 13 years to feature both a Strengthen EXCEPT question *and* a Weaken EXCEPT question.
- PrepTest 71's Logic Games section has a big stunner: It was the first ever (and, at the time of this book's release, still the only one ever) to have *two* Rule Substitution questions.
- PrepTest 71 was the first LSAT in two years to feature a Loose Sequencing game. The last Loose Sequencing game had been on the December 2011 test, and PrepTest 71 was administered in December 2013.
- Choice (D) was the least popular correct answer in Logic Games—showing up only twice—but it was the most popular answer in Reading Comprehension -showing up seven times.
- Speaking of Reading Comp, PrepTest 71 marked the fifth time in seven tests that the Comparative Reading passage was a Law passage, but only the third time since 2009 that Comparative Reading was the second passage in the section.
- It's common to hear test takers refer to success on the LSAT as "slaying the dragon"; this was never more appropriate than on PrepTest 71, which was administered when *The Hobbit: The Desolation of Smaug* was the country's #1 movie!

PrepTest 71 in Context

As much fun as it is to find out what makes a PrepTest unique or noteworthy, it's even more important to know just how representative it is of other LSAT administrations (and, thus, how likely it is to be representative of the exam you will face on Test Day). The following charts compare the numbers of each kind of question and game on PrepTest 71 to the average numbers seen on all officially released LSATs administered over the past five years (from 2012 through 2016).

Number of LR Questions by Type: PrepTest 71 vs. 2012-2016 Average

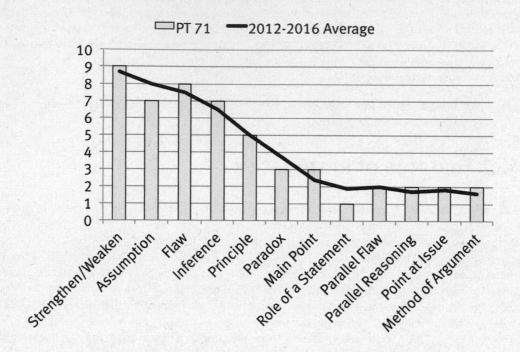

Number of LG Games by Type: PrepTest 71 vs. 2012-2016 Average

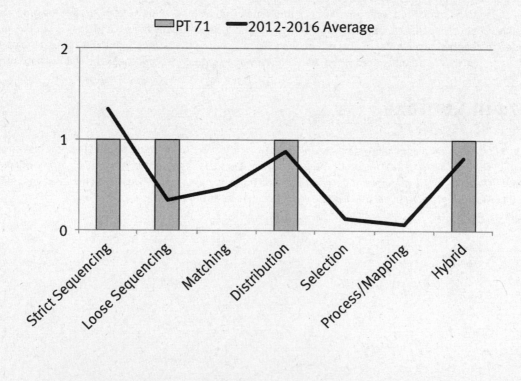

Number of RC Questions by Type: PrepTest 71 vs. 2012-2016 Average

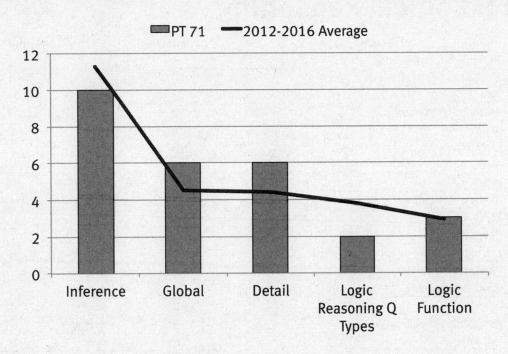

There isn't usually a huge difference in the distribution of questions from LSAT to LSAT, but if this test seems harder (or easier) to you than another you've taken, compare the number of questions of the types on which you, personally, are strongest and weakest. And then, explore within each section to see if your best or worst question types came earlier or later.

Students in Kaplan's comprehensive LSAT courses have access to every released LSAT, and to an online Q-Bank with thousands of officially released questions, games, and passages. If you are studying on your own, you have to do a bit more work to identify your strengths and your areas of opportunity. Quantitative analysis (like that in the charts shown here) is an important tool for understanding how the test is constructed, and how you are performing on it.

Section I: Logical Reasoning

Q#	Question Type	Correct	Difficulty
1	Assumption (Sufficient)	E	★
2	Method of Argument	D	★
3	Flaw	D	★
4	Assumption (Necessary)	D	★
5	Main Point	E	★★
6	Strengthen	D	★★
7	Main Point	E	★
8	Inference	D	★★
9	Method of Argument	A	★★★
10	Point at Issue	C	★
11	Role of a Statement	E	★★
12	Strengthen	B	★★★
13	Weaken	A	★★★
14	Parallel Reasoning	C	★★
15	Inference	B	★
16	Assumption (Necessary)	B	★★★
17	Inference	B	★★
18	Flaw	C	★
19	Principle (Apply/Inference)	A	★★★★
20	Paradox	C	★★★★
21	Flaw	C	★★
22	Assumption (Necessary)	E	★★★
23	Parallel Flaw	C	★★
24	Flaw	E	★
25	Principle (Apply/Inference)	D	★

1. (E) Assumption (Sufficient)

Step 1: Identify the Question Type

This question is a new twist on two common question types. The LSAT Logical Reasoning section has long had questions that ask you to fill in the blank at the end of the stimulus, but typically with a conclusion. This question asks you to fill in an unstated piece of evidence that would allow the already stated conclusion to logically follow. Even though the LSAT does not typically provide a blank for where the missing piece of evidence would go in the argument, Assumption questions ask for that overlooked link. The phrasing "conclusion ... is properly drawn if which one ... completes the passage" makes this a Sufficient Assumption question. This exact question format has appeared as the first question on both PrepTest 70 and PrepTest 71.

Step 2: Untangle the Stimulus

The argument concludes that "the agency is unlikely to achieve its goal." Don't leave vague terms in the conclusion when you analyze an argument. What agency and what goal? The first two sentences in the stimulus define those terms. So, paraphrase the conclusion as follows: The government agency that took over most of the country's large banks is unlikely to strengthen the banking system. The contrast Keyword *but* highlights the primary evidence: the banking system will not be strengthened if the banks' former owners buy them back. The evidence Keyword *since* reaffirms that the question wants you to fill in the blank with another piece of evidence.

Step 3: Make a Prediction

Because this is a Sufficient Assumption question, the new piece of evidence must guarantee the conclusion. The only evidence given that would lead to the banks not being strengthened is about previous owners buying back the banks. The critical aspect to note about this existing evidence is that it is a conditional Formal Logic rule. If the trigger in the Formal Logic statement gets pulled, then the conclusion is guaranteed to follow logically. According to the rule, if the former owners of the banks buy them back, then the banking system will not be strengthened. So, anything that guarantees that the former owners will repurchase the banks would also guarantee the conclusion. The correct answer will indicate that the sufficient condition will be met.

Step 4: Evaluate the Answer Choices

(E) is correct. This fact would make it highly likely, if not definite, that former owners will buy back the banks, which in turn, based on the evidence in the stimulus, will guarantee that the goal of strengthening the banking system is unlikely to be achieved.

(A) is incorrect. Even if the agency fails to sell some of the banks, the evidence does not indicate that that failure would

assure it was *unlikely* that the effort to strengthen the banking system would fail. The stimulus indicates that previous owners shouldn't buy back the banks, but it doesn't mention what would happen if some remained in the government's hands.

(B) is Out of Scope. The author is not concerned by a monopoly, but by former owners retaking their banks. This would only be relevant if the single company is one of the former owners, which the answer choice does not specify.

(C) Is an Irrelevant Comparison. A sluggish economy *may* be something that would make the banking system unlikely to be strengthened. However, the only condition the stimulus provides as sufficient to guarantee that the government agency would not strengthen the banking system is if the previous owners bought the banks back. Introducing other possible sufficient conditions (like the overall economic prognosis) would strengthen the argument, but would not guarantee the conclusion.

(D) is an Irrelevant Comparison between the salvaged banks and other banks. This choice does not necessarily indicate that the agency's efforts to strengthen the overall banking system will be unlikely to succeed. Even if a resold bank will be weaker than the country's other banks, it might well be healthier than it was before, which would be positive movement for the overall system.

2. (D) Method of Argument

Step 1: Identify the Question Type

The phrase "argument proceeds by" indicates a Method of Argument question, which asks *how* the author constructs the argument. Focus on the step-by-step structure of the argument.

Step 2: Untangle the Stimulus

The accountant begins by citing the newspaper industry's usual explanation for falling profits: the rising cost of newsprint. The contrast Keyword [b]*ut* signals the accountant's disagreement and highlights the accountant's refutation of the industry's evidence. The third sentence is a more emphatic restatement of the prior sentence. Finally, the accountant provides an alternative explanation for the newspaper industry's problems (falling circulation and advertising).

Step 3: Make a Prediction

The correct answer will describe how the accountant identifies an explanation put forth by others, disproves it, and then provides an alternative explanation. The correct answer need not include a description of everything in the argument, but you must be able to match each piece of the answer to something in the stimulus.

Step 4: Evaluate the Answer Choices

(D) is an accurate description of how the accountant constructs the argument. The accountant challenges the newspaper industry's explanation for its falling profits (newsprint costs) and provides a different explanation (falling circulation and advertising). Each piece of this answer accurately matches the argument.

(A) cannot be correct as the stimulus does not contain any analogies.

(B) is not correct. Although the accountant does use economic data to raise doubts, the accountant does not attack the *effectiveness* of an *approach* by the newspaper industry. Rather, the accountant addresses the accuracy of an explanation.

(C) is not an accurate description of the argument. The accountant is not criticizing a method or strategy of the newspaper industry, but rather refuting the industry's explanation for declining profits. Also, at a general level this answer is a 180, as the accountant criticizes the conventional explanation and presents a new idea, not vice versa.

(E) has two problems. First, while the accountant does call into question a justification (or reason) for falling profits, he does not criticize a "justification for a *practice*." Moreover, the author does not show how the industry's justification could support a different, disagreeable practice.

3. (D) Flaw

Step 1: Identify the Question Type

The question stem explicitly asks you to identify the flaw in the argument. Identify any disconnect between the evidence and conclusion, and keep common LSAT flaws in mind.

Step 2: Untangle the Stimulus

The author concludes that alcohol consumption is beneficial. The evidence is that alcohol creates an inhospitable environment in the body for certain harmful bacteria.

Step 3: Make a Prediction

Two important LSAT argument patterns are involved in this argument. First, a logical recommendation must balance the potential pros and cons, yet most authors on the LSAT overlook one side or the other. This argument concludes that "on balance" alcohol consumption is beneficial, but Peter only mentions certain beneficial effects of alcohol. He doesn't consider any downsides that might tips the scales against alcohol consumption.

Second, this argument varies in scope. When reading stimuli, notice any qualifications or limitations on the evidence that are not carried over to the conclusion. In this case, the evidence is limited to "*moderate* alcohol consumption," but

the conclusion is not so restricted. The correct answer choice will mention one of these two patterns.

Step 4: Evaluate the Answer Choices

(D) accurately describes how the argument relies on evidence about moderate alcohol consumption yet reaches a conclusion about alcohol consumption generally. A common scope shift or flaw on the LSAT occurs when an author jumps from limited or restricted evidence to a broad, sweeping conclusion.

(A) is not something Peter assumes. This answer is Outside the Scope of the argument, because Peter doesn't address the motivations of those who drink alcohol.

(B) is a 180. Peter bases his argument on scientific evidence, not "popular belief."

(C) is not a flaw. Peter does not conclude that alcohol consumption is the only or the best way to achieve these health benefits. Peter asserts merely that alcohol consumption is beneficial. The fact that he doesn't consider other ways to get the same benefits doesn't hurt his argument and therefore cannot be a flaw.

(E) is similar to **(C)** in that it mentions something Peter does in fact overlook. However, just as in **(C)**, Peter is not wrong in failing to consider this possibility. Peter cites evidence that alcohol has an effect on *certain* harmful bacteria. His conclusion does not depend on alcohol affecting *all* harmful bacteria. An overlooked possibility is a flaw only when, if true, it would weaken the author's argument.

4. (D) Assumption (Necessary)

Step 1: Identify the Question Type

A question that asks you to fill in a blank is usually an Inference question, asking for the logical conclusion. However, this blank follows *because*, which means that the question wants you to provide additional evidence to shore up the already stated conclusion. A question that asks for unstated evidence is an Assumption question. The question stem doesn't immediately indicate whether this is a Sufficient or Necessary Assumption question, but that shouldn't change your general approach. Break down the argument into the evidence and conclusion, and then look for the gap between them.

If you interpreted this as an Inference question, that's also fine because the correct answer will directly follow from the stimulus—the author will supply evidence that bridges the gap to reach the conclusion. In theory, every Assumption question calls for an inference about the relationship between the author's evidence and conclusion. Don't get flustered on categorization of the question though. As long as you know what your task is from the question stem, you're prepared for Step 2. In this case, the correct answer logically *completes* the argument. The part that's missing is the author's reason for his recommendation. Untangle the stimulus to determine what would make a good reason.

Step 2: Untangle the Stimulus

The argument concludes that Grodex should probably conduct its employee-training seminars using innovative new educational methods. The evidence is that the new methods have been effective in training children to think more creatively, though not in teaching them to memorize large amounts of information. Grodex employees need to think creatively, but do not need to be able to effectively memorize information.

Step 3: Make a Prediction

The consultant's argument contains mismatched concepts, from evidence about education methods for children to a conclusion about training methods for adult employees at Grodex Corporation. Thus, the consultant assumes her evidence is relevant. To complete the argument, the author must assume there is some similarity between the training of children and the training of adult employees at Grodex.

Step 4: Evaluate the Answer Choices

(D) is correct. For the author to conclude that Grodex should use innovative methods in its training seminars, it must be true that the results they achieve in children will be similar to those they will achieve in adults. Use the Denial Test to check that assumption. "If the effects of teaching adults were generally *not* similar to teaching children," then the consultant would have no reason to probably recommend the methods, and her conclusion would fall apart. That also means this question could arguably be considered a Necessary Assumption question, because the consultant *needs* this statement in order for her conclusion to be valid. As mentioned in Step 1, though, nothing in the question stem indicates whether this is a Necessary or Sufficient Assumption question, so the test maker would not include a sufficient and a necessary assumption in the answers. There is just one answer that connects the mismatched concepts in the argument—**(D)**.

(A) is Out of Scope. That most Grodex employees began to learn their skills in high school doesn't provide a reason why Grodex should use innovative educational methods. If anything, this choice undermines the utility of the training seminars, since it indicates that most Grodex employees already have creative thinking skills. Additionally, this choice doesn't bridge the gap between the training of children and the training of adults.

(B) is an Irrelevant Comparison. It says corporations using innovative training methods are more successful than companies that don't provide training seminars *at all*. While that might indicate Grodex should provide training seminars,

it doesn't indicate that those seminars should necessarily use the innovative methods. Additionally, this choice doesn't bridge the gap between the training of children and the training of adults.

(C) minimizes the importance of the seminars. However, the seminars' importance or unimportance doesn't affect the argument over which methods should be used to most benefit those who do attend. Additionally, this choice doesn't bridge the gap between the training of children and the training of adults.

(E) is Out of Scope. Even if knowing how to think creatively helps people compensate for deficient memorization skills, this doesn't add a reason why Grodex should use the innovative methods, which foster creative thinking. The stimulus states Grodex employees don't need to be strong in memorization skills, so this benefit is irrelevant.

5. (E) Main Point

Step 1: Identify the Question Type

The question stem explicitly asks you to identify the conclusion, or the main point, of the argument. The correct answer should match the meaning of the argument that you bracket as the conclusion.

Step 2: Untangle the Stimulus

On the LSAT, in both Reading Comprehension and Logical Reasoning, when the author refutes another's point of view, the author's conclusion will usually be the refutation of that view. Here, the essayist says some have claimed overpopulation will likely not be a problem because humans will be able to colonize other planets in the future. The essayist then concludes, "This would, however, be a temporary solution at best." The information after the colon is the essayist's evidence.

Step 3: Make a Prediction

The correct answer should match the meaning of the claim that "[t]his would, however, be a temporary solution at best." However, paraphrasing the conclusion's meaning requires defining the vague term *this*. *This* refers back to what came previously: the claim of others that humans will be able to colonize other planets. So, the essayist's conclusion is that colonizing other planets is at best a temporary solution to the problem of population growth. Avoid answers that drift into the evidence, summarize the entire argument, or extrapolate beyond the argument.

Step 4: Evaluate the Answer Choices

(E) is an accurate match.

(A) references an introductory fact that sets up the central debate as to whether colonizing other planets is a viable solution to overpopulation.

(B) is Extreme and extrapolates beyond the argument. The essayist concludes that colonizing other planets is not a long-term solution to overpopulation, but does not indicate whether there are other potential solutions or how effective their implementation would likely be.

(C) is the author's primary evidence for the conclusion that colonization of other planets is not a long-term solution to overpopulation. Remember that punctuation can act as Keywords. A colon is often an evidence Keyword, indicating that what follows will expand on what was just said.

(D) is implicit in the argument, but is not the explicitly stated conclusion. The essayist's evidence consists of a conditional statement about the population geometrically growing. In order for the essayist's conclusion to follow, she must assume that the sufficient condition will be met, i.e., that population growth will continue. But while this answer bridges a gap between the evidence and the conclusion, it is not itself the conclusion of the argument.

6. (D) Strengthen

Step 1: Identify the Question Type

The questions stem explicitly asks you to strengthen the argument. Identify the assumption, and firm up the bridge between the evidence and conclusion.

Step 2: Untangle the Stimulus

Defining the vague phrase ("this complexity") yields the following paraphrase of the conclusion: the complexity of chocolate's flavor probably masks any difference in taste between full-fat and low-fat chocolate ice cream. The evidence is twofold. First, chocolate has a very complex flavor. Second, taste tests have shown that people dislike low-fat versions of vanilla ice cream but not low-fat versions of chocolate ice cream.

Step 3: Make a Prediction

This argument contains a recurring LSAT argument pattern: the author identifies an interesting phenomenon and then provides an explanation. The usual assumption is that there is no other explanation for the phenomenon. A weakener will likely provide an alternative explanation. A strengthener will likely either discount an alternative explanation or provide additional support for the author's explanation. In this case, the interesting phenomena are the different results in taste tests for low-fat vanilla versus low-fat chocolate ice cream. The author's explanation is that the complexity of chocolate's flavor masks the effects of reduced fat. The author assumes that there is no other explanation for the different taste test results. The correct answer will eliminate an alternative reason or will add to the connection between the complex flavor and the favorable taste test results.

Step 4: Evaluate the Answer Choices

(D) is correct. Notice that the stimulus mentions that chocolate's flavor is complex but says nothing about vanilla. If vanilla were similarly complex, the author's argument would fall apart. This choice proves there is a difference between the complexity of vanilla and chocolate and therefore increases the chances that the author's explanation is correct.

(A) is an Irrelevant Comparison because the stimulus is concerned with the difference in preference between full-fat and low-fat ice cream, not the difference in preference across flavors. Arguably, this choice is also a 180 because it provides an alternative explanation for the disparity in the taste tests. Notice that the stimulus never actually says whether people like high-fat vanilla ice cream, just that they dislike low-fat vanilla ice cream. This answer suggests that the explanation for the difference in preference is simply that people prefer the taste of chocolate over vanilla regardless of fat content.

(B) indicates that the study was conducted well, because it is generally considered best to conduct "blind" taste tests. However, as long as the tests were conducted the same for vanilla and chocolate, whether or not subjects were told of the difference in fat content would not explain their different reactions to low-fat vanilla as compared to low-fat chocolate ice cream.

(C) veers slightly off track. While this choice would support a conclusion that chocolate's complex flavor explains its popularity in general, it does not support the author's conclusion that chocolate's complex flavor masks the difference in taste between full-fat chocolate ice cream and low-fat chocolate ice cream. Additionally, this choice does not rule out the possibility that vanilla's flavor also requires many distinct compounds.

(E) is Out of Scope. People's awareness is irrelevant to the author's conclusion.

7. (E) Main Point

Step 1: Identify the Question Type

The question stem explicitly asks you to identify the conclusion, or the main point, of the argument. The correct answer should match the meaning of the argument that you bracket as the conclusion.

Step 2: Untangle the Stimulus

The ethicist begins by presenting an argument put forth by Robert Gillette. As often seen in both Reading Comprehension and Logical Reasoning, the contrast Keyword *however* indicates the ethicist's opposing conclusion. The ethicist believes that "Gillette's argument is not persuasive." The evidence Keyword *because* indicates that the ethicist's evidence follows.

Step 3: Make a Prediction

Usually, on the LSAT, when the author introduces an alternative point of view, the author's conclusion is that that view is wrong in some way. Here, the ethicist says Gillette's argument is not persuasive. However, don't let your paraphrase end there; make sure you define Gillette's argument. In total, the ethicist is not persuaded by Gillette's argument that thoroughly understanding genetics would benefit humanity. Notice that the ethicist does not argue that Gillette is *wrong*, just that he isn't *convincing*.

Step 4: Evaluate the Answer Choices

(E) is the correct answer because it is the only choice that indicates that Gillette's argument is unconvincing, or unpersuasive. Unusual for a Main Point question, this answer also accurately paraphrases the ethicist's evidence. However, the use of the evidence Keyword *because* indicates that this choice does not confuse a piece of evidence as the conclusion. While this choice is not limited to only the conclusion, it is the only one of the five that is not demonstrably wrong.

(A) goes wrong in two ways. First, it describes *why* the ethicist would draw her conclusion that Gillette is unconvincing but does not express the conclusion itself. Second, the ethicist's evidence is that Gillette isn't persuasive because he fails to *consider cons*, not because his evidence of benefits is wrong.

(B) is incorrect because it mentions what Gillette fails to consider, which is the ethicist's supporting evidence, not her conclusion. While the correct answer includes this evidence, it explicitly identifies it as evidence (by using the Keyword "because"), but **(B)** does not make that distinction.

(C) is Extreme. The ethicist merely says Gillette isn't convincing because he ignores possible cons. The ethicist doesn't go further to say those possible cons mean genetic research should stop.

(D) is similar to **(A)** in that it states that the ethicist's conclusion is a rejection of Gillette's evidence. The ethicist's conclusion is that Gillette's argument isn't convincing, not that his evidence is wrong.

8. (D) Inference

Step 1: Identify the Question Type

A question stem that asks you to use information from the stimulus to support an answer that follows logically (direction of support flowing downward) indicates an Inference question. Accept all statements as true, focus on the most concrete and emphasized facts, and look for any deductions that come from combining facts, especially Formal Logic statements.

Step 2: Untangle the Stimulus

In the first sentence, the author says people have claimed that hypnosis has many uses. The author then describes an experiment involving hypnosis that, according to the author, sheds light on the *supposed* connection between hypnosis and recall. In the experiment, subjects listened to a piece of music and were then hypnotized. Half the subjects under hypnosis were asked to describe the film they had just seen, despite not actually having seen a film. Those subjects were just as detailed and confident in their descriptions as those in the other half, who were asked about the music that they had just heard.

Step 3: Make a Prediction

The correct answer is unlikely to relate to the first sentence, which introduces other claimed uses of hypnosis, but will likely touch on the connection between hypnosis and recall, since the experiment focuses on that aspect. The correct answer will most likely be a modestly worded implication of the experiment. Assess whether each choice must be true, and prioritize answers with safe sounding, modestly phrased wording.

Step 4: Evaluate the Answer Choices

(D) is a modestly phrased implication of the experiment. The subjects had not seen a movie, but when asked under hypnosis to describe "the film they had just viewed," they provided detailed and confident descriptions. This indicates that the leading question affected their recall to "at least some extent."

(A) is Extreme. Though the author mentions many uses have been claimed for hypnosis, she only discusses one: "the supposed connection between hypnosis and increased power of recall." Though the experiment casts some doubt on that particular connection, that's not enough to infer the author believes *many* claims *are* overstated.

(B) is also Extreme. The experiment indicates that in at least some instances, hypnotic suggestion can distort recall, but that does not necessarily imply that hypnosis *cannot* significantly increase recall in other instances.

(C) is Extreme as well. Just because the single experiment apparently triggered false memories in some subjects, that does not imply that hypnotic recall *inevitably* results in false memories. Indeed, there is no indication that those who were asked about the musical piece experienced any false memories. Moreover, the subjects who described movies may have been drawing on real memories from the more distant past.

(E) is an Irrelevant Comparison. The experiment does not compare visual memory and auditory memory. Only auditory memory was actually tested.

9. (A) Method of Argument

Step 1: Identify the Question Type

The phrase "argument proceeds by" indicates a Method of Argument question, which asks you to describe in general terms *how* an author makes her point. Focus on the argument's structure.

Step 2: Untangle the Stimulus

The first sentence provides evidence of a correlation between years with more successful crops and babies with higher birth weights. The second sentence provides the author's conclusion that the health of a newborn depends in large part on the amount of food available to the mother in pregnancy.

Step 3: Make a Prediction

This argument introduces mistaken causality, a common focus of the LSAT. The author uses evidence of a correlation to reach a causal conclusion. The correct answer will describe this type of reasoning without distorting the argument. Notice also that the author makes subtle scope shifts from the evidence to the conclusion. The author equates babies' birth weight with babies' health and successful crops with the amount of food available to the pregnant mother. The correct answer might also call out these scope shifts. In any case, make sure each piece of your answer matches a piece in the stimulus.

Step 4: Evaluate the Answer Choices

(A) is correct. It accurately describes the author's evidence and conclusion. The evidence consists of a claimed correlation between two phenomena (crop success and birth weights), and the conclusion indicates a causal connection between two *other* phenomena (health and food availability).

(B) is Extreme. The author concludes that food availability "to a large extent" determines the health of a newborn, but does not assert that it is the *sole* factor affecting newborn health. Additionally, this answer does not reflect the different phenomena described in the evidence versus those in the conclusion.

(C) is a Distortion. First, this choice does not accurately reflect that the conclusion indicates a causal connection between two phenomena, rather than merely a correlation. Second, while the author asserts a relationship between crops yields and birth weights, he does not necessarily assert that that exact relationship still exists. Finally, this answer does not indicate that the phenomena in the evidence and the conclusion are different, as the correct answer does.

(D) is a Distortion. The author does not assert that a common phenomenon caused both higher birth weights and successful crops, nor does he present a hypothesis about that cause. The author instead uses the correlation between

those two to assert that a causal relationship exists between two related, but different, phenomena.

(E) is a Distortion on two accounts. While the author does infer the existence of a causal connection, he does so based on a separate *correlated* relationship, not from another *causal* relationship. More definitively, this answer cannot be correct because the argument does not include a further explanation for the existence of these two relationships.

10. (C) Point at Issue

Step 1: Identify the Question Type

A question stem that asks what two people disagree over indicates a Point at Issue question. The correct answer will identify an issue that both people address and about which they disagree.

Step 2: Untangle the Stimulus

Vincent asserts that science can only study that which can be measured. He further asserts that happiness cannot be measured because it is entirely subjective. It can be deduced that Vincent further believes that happiness or any other subjective experience cannot be the subject of scientific study.

Yolanda analogizes happiness research to optometry, as both rely on subjects' reports of what they feel and see respectively. She asserts that optometry is a scientific discipline. It can be deduced that Yolanda believes happiness research is also a scientific discipline.

Step 3: Make a Prediction

The correct answer will likely relate to whether happiness research can be a scientific discipline. Or, it might discuss the use of subjective experience in scientific disciplines. Since only Yolanda mentions optometry, that cannot be the subject of the disagreement.

Step 4: Evaluate the Answer Choices

(C) is correct. Yolanda would agree with this answer while Vincent would not. Yolanda asserts that optometry is a scientific discipline despite its reliance on patients' reports, which are by definition subjective. According to Vincent, because subjective experiences cannot be measured, they cannot be studied by any scientific discipline.

(A) is incorrect because, while Vincent explicitly states this, Yolanda's view is not fully discernible. At best, because Yolanda indicates that happiness research relies on subjects' reports of how they feel, it is quite possible that she agrees with Vincent that happiness is an entirely subjective experience.

(B) cannot be correct because Vincent does not give any opinions on optometry.

(D) is implicit in Yolanda's statements, but whether or not Vincent considers optometry a scientific discipline is not discernible.

(E) is a Distortion of Vincent's assertion that subjective experiences cannot be measured. Because this statement is an incorrect contrapositive of Vincent's evidence (it reverses without negating), it's not clear whether or not even Vincent would agree with it. More obviously, Yolanda does not mention experiences that can't be measured, so this can't be the point at issue.

11. (E) Role of a Statement

Step 1: Identify the Question Type

The phrase "role played in the argument" indicates a Role of a Statement question. This question type reproduces a statement from the stimulus and asks you to identify its argumentative purpose. Underline the statement in the stimulus, and then break down the stimulus.

Step 2: Untangle the Stimulus

The claim in question is located at the end of the first sentence. The contrast Keyword [*a*]*lthough* at the beginning of the stimulus highlights a paradox: while cities are more polluted, urbanization might reduce overall pollution. The rest of the paragraph provides reasons why concentrating a population in cities could produce less pollution overall.

Step 3: Make a Prediction

There are two important Keywords that are helpful in understanding this argument's structure. First, the contrast Keyword [*a*]*lthough*. Contrast Keywords always highlight important pieces of an argument: either the conclusion or an important piece of evidence. Second, the conclusion Keyword [*t*]*hus*. Conclusion Keywords will indicate either the ultimate conclusion or a subsidiary conclusion.

In this case, you need to determine which Keyword indicates the author's actual conclusion. Two different methods can help you here. First, look for the most opinionated piece. The last clause of the first sentence is the author's subjective opinion ("may actually"), which goes against the expectation set up in the first clause of the sentence. The second and third sentences are presented as established facts. Second, look for which part of the argument supports the rest. Both the second and third sentences function as reasons to believe that "increasing urbanization may actually reduce the total amount of pollution generated nationwide." It would not make sense to say that the first sentence supports the third. So, the relevant statement is the conclusion of the argument.

Step 4: Evaluate the Answer Choices

(E) correctly describes the relevant statement's role as the argument's conclusion. The conclusion is by definition what the rest of the argument is designed to establish.

(A) is incorrect because it both inaccurately identifies the relevant statement as a piece of evidence and misidentifies the conclusion as a recommendation ("people should live in large cities") that is never actually stated.

(B) is incorrect for two reasons. First, and most importantly, this choice does not mention the statement's vital role as the conclusion. Second, the author does not dispute that "large cities are generally more polluted than the countryside." Rather, the author states it as fact. The contrast Keyword "[a]lthough" functions as an acknowledgement of the paradoxical nature of the two claims in the first sentence. The author accepts both as true and then provides supporting reasons for why the second claim can be true, despite the first claim.

(C) is incorrect. Rarely, if ever, will an author's own opinion (indicated by the opinion word *may*) serve as mere background. Also, ideas highlighted by a contrast Keyword (*[a]lthough*) tend to be significant components of an argument.

(D) is incorrect because the contrast Keyword [*a*]*lthough* indicates a *contrasting* relationship between the two clauses of the first sentence, not a supporting one. Additionally, the claim that large cities are more polluted than the countryside is not the conclusion.

12. (B) Strengthen

Step 1: Identify the Question Type

The question's stem explicitly asks you to strengthen the argument. Identify the assumption and firm up the bridge between the evidence and conclusion.

Step 2: Untangle the Stimulus

The climatologist concludes that the mountain snowpack will probably melt earlier and more rapidly, triggering the negative consequences of greater spring flooding and less storable water. The evidence is that increasing winter temperatures, due to global warming, will cause a greater percentage of precipitation to fall as rain instead of snow.

Step 3: Make a Prediction

The climatologist essentially presents a causal argument. Normally, on the LSAT, authors see a result and identify a likely cause; here, the climatologist sees a changing condition and then predicts a result. She assumes, basically, that there will not be a different result. The correct answer should strengthen the connection between the evidence and conclusion, making it more likely that the result the climatologist predicts will come to pass. That is, that a greater percentage of winter precipitation falling as rain instead of snow will cause mountain snowpack to melt earlier and more rapidly, resulting in greater spring flooding and less storable waters.

Step 4: Evaluate the Answer Choices

(B) is correct. This answer supports the connection between warmer winters and greater spring flooding and less storable water by bringing in analogous evidence from past results in similar regions.

(A) does not bridge the gap between the author's evidence and conclusion. It does indicate that there will be more precipitation (either snow or rain), which might explain higher floods (if it's rain rather than snow, such that the snowpack would melt). But that doesn't explain why there would be less storable water. The change the climatologist points out is the change in proportion of rain to snow. Somehow the correct answer needs to show that that proportion shift will cause the effects the climatologist describes. This answer doesn't address the ratio of snow to rain, just the overall combined amount.

(C) is an Irrelevant Comparison. The quantity of storable water in different locations does not increase the author's causal claim that increased rain will prematurely melt the snowpack forcing flooding and a decrease in the water supply. That difference in water supply may be from other causes than those cited by the author, and thus isn't sufficient to strengthen the overall argument.

(D) is another Irrelevant Comparison. While correct answer **(B)** provides evidence from comparable geography, this answer choice does not. The global scope of this choice means that the Rocky Mountains are being compared to locations with the mildest winters—tropical jungles and the Sahara Desert, for example. Those areas aren't comparable to the Rocky Mountains, so their increased flooding and lack of storable water is irrelevant. Although the Rocky Mountain winters may be getting milder, **(D)** does not provide further evidence that there will be more rain or that the winter snowpack will melt earlier.

(E) is a 180. The climatologist claims that global warming would mean more rain, which means a quickly melting snowpack. More rain would also mean less snow, which would mean a smaller mountain snowpack to begin with. The climatologist claims that that scenario would lead to greater spring flooding, but this choice says a larger mountain snowpack would mean greater spring flooding, so it contradicts the stimulus.

13. (A) Weaken

Step 1: Identify the Question Type

The question stem explicitly asks you to weaken the argument. Identify the assumption and attack it.

Step 2: Untangle the Stimulus

The conclusion is the author's negative recommendation that "animal feed should not include genetically modified plants."

The evidence comes from a study in which some lab rats were fed genetically modified potatoes and others were fed a normal diet of non-genetically modified foods. The first group of rats developed health problems, while the second group of rats did not.

Step 3: Make a Prediction

There are two common problems in this argument. First, there is a scope shift from a study on rats to a conclusion about animal feed, presumably for pets or livestock. Second, the author implies that genetic modifications were responsible for the rats' health problems, which means the author assumes there is no other cause. For that to be likely, the study would need to control for all other factors. Yet the two groups were not necessarily fed equivalent diets in this study: one group got genetically modified potatoes while the other got "a normal diet." Unless "a normal diet" is *non*-genetically modified potatoes, the author's conclusion is unsupported; an alternative cause of the rats' health problems is possible. The correct answer will likely indicate some complication resulting from the study group getting a potato-only diet compared to the control group getting a normal diet, which is unrelated to any genetic modification.

Step 4: Evaluate the Answer Choices

(A) is correct. It raises the possibility that the rats' health problems were caused by eating a single food that is not a normal part of their diet.

(B) is consistent with the argument. The rats may have lost their appetites as the study progressed (likely due to the developing intestinal deformities), but this choice does not lessen the likelihood that the genetic modifications in the potatoes were the cause of the health problems.

(C) is Out of Scope. The evidence indicates that the study group *developed* intestinal deformities over the course of the experiment. Additionally, because all the rats in the study were "lab rats" and therefore likely bred in laboratory conditions, any rate of existing intestinal deformities would be consistent between both groups.

(D) is an Irrelevant Comparison. The author assumes that the genetic modifications cause the health problems, but does not assume that a nutritional deficiency was at fault. Moreover, we don't know what the control group of rats ate; their *normal* diet may not have included non-genetically modified potatoes at all. Also, if anything, this strengthens the argument by removing any suspicion that a difference in nutritional value caused the problems.

(E) is incorrect. The inability of those researchers to provide an explanation of how the genetic modifications to the potatoes would cause the health problems is not evidence that the genetic modifications did not cause the health problems. The absence of evidence supporting a claim does not constitute evidence against that claim.

14. (C) Parallel Reasoning

Step 1: Identify the Question Type

The phrase "similar ... reasoning" indicates a Parallel Reasoning question, which asks you to find the answer that uses the same type of evidence to reach the same type of conclusion as the argument in the stimulus.

Step 2: Untangle the Stimulus

The author begins by describing a claim made by some philosophers: that we visually perceive an object by forming a mental image of that object in our mind. The author concludes that the hypothesis cannot be correct. The author's evidence is the *absurd* series of endless mental images within mental images that follows from the hypothesis.

Step 3: Make a Prediction

You should initially approach Parallel Reasoning questions by characterizing the conclusion. Here, the conclusion that the philosophers' hypothesis cannot be correct is an assertion of fact. When more than one conclusion in the answer choices matches the conclusion in the stimulus, then you need to incorporate the evidence. Here, the author's evidence is that the philosophers' hypothesis would require endless repetition of a mental image and inner self, which is *absurd*. (Think of the infinite image that occurs when you stand between two mirrors.) The correct answer will similarly conclude that a hypothesis cannot be correct based on the absurd necessary implications of that hypothesis.

Step 4: Evaluate the Answer Choices

(C) is a match. The argument concludes that the historians' claim must be false because it would necessitate a similar endless chain of precedent theories within precedent theories deemed to be impossible or absurd.

(A) is not an accurate match. First, in the conclusion, the author doesn't actually reject the linguists' claim. Some linguists say many languages can be traced back to Indo-European. That's different and less extreme than what the author rejects, which is that Indo-European is the *earliest* language. Additionally, the author's evidence is overwhelming contrary evidence, rather than a resultant impossible chain of implications.

(B) is not an accurate match based on the evidence. The argument concludes that a particular claim cannot be correct, but the evidence is based on an infinite number of theories that can't possibly all be true, rather than a single infinite chain that is impossible in itself. Even though the reference to an infinite number of theories is appealing, these are different independent theories, not a self-perpetuating

infinite chain, as contained in the stimulus and the correct answer.

(D) is not correct due to its conclusion. This argument merely concludes that a claim is *unfortunate*, not that it *cannot* be correct. Additionally, the evidence does not contain a similar endless sequence resulting from the rejected claim.

(E) is not an accurate match based on the evidence. The argument concludes that a claim cannot be correct, but the evidence does not contain a similar endless sequence of libraries within libraries that would be required in order to match the stimulus.

15. (B) Inference

Step 1: Identify the Question Type

A question stem that asks you to use information from the stimulus to support an answer that follows logically (direction of support flowing downward) indicates an Inference question. Accept all statements as true, focus on the most concrete and emphasized facts, and look for any deductions to be made by combining statements, especially Formal Logic statements.

Step 2: Untangle the Stimulus

According to the stimulus, greatly exceeding the recommended intake of vitamins A and D is dangerous. Some vitamin-fortified foods have 100 percent of the recommended daily amount of these vitamins in a single serving. But many people consume two to three times the standard serving of vitamin-fortified foods.

Step 3: Make a Prediction

Contrast Keywords such as *but* typically highlight critical information. In this case, combining the last two sentences yields a deduction that at least some people are consuming more than the recommended amounts of vitamins A and D. However, without knowing what constitutes "greatly exceeding" the recommended levels, it cannot be deduced that anybody is consuming dangerous or toxic levels.

Step 4: Evaluate the Answer Choices

(B) matches the prediction from Step 3. It is tentative enough to be correct.

(A) is a Distortion. The stimulus indicates that many people misjudge what constitutes a "serving," but there is no indication as to whether people are aware of the recommended intake levels of vitamins A and D.

(C) is a Distortion. The stimulus indicates that some people exceed the recommended levels because they misjudge the serving size, but there is no indication that they believe it is healthy to do so.

(D) is Out of Scope and Extreme. The stimulus is limited to vitamins A and D and does not indicate whether other vitamin supplements might be advisable. Also, the words *most* and *any* are stronger than the language in the stimulus.

(E) is Out of Scope. The stimulus does not indicate whether manufacturers are aware of people's propensity to exceed the serving size.

16. (B) Assumption (Necessary)

Step 1: Identify the Question Type

A question that asks for the assumption that an argument requires is a Necessary Assumption question. Build the basic bridge between the evidence and conclusion. You can use the Denial Test to check your answer.

Step 2: Untangle the Stimulus

The author concludes that most of the nations that said their oil reserves were unchanged are likely wrong. The evidence provides two scenarios that cause oil reserves to fluctuate: reserves gradually drop as old fields run out, and they rise suddenly with new discoveries of oil. The author then offers a subsidiary conclusion that is functionally the same as the ultimate conclusion.

Step 3: Make a Prediction

The author presents situations in which oil reserves would change, and then concludes that oil reserves probably changed. In order for the conclusion to follow, therefore, the author must be assuming that those situations occurred. The correct answer will say the nations in question probably had oil fields dry up, found new oil, or both.

Step 4: Evaluate the Answer Choices

(B) matches the prediction. Negated, it says it's *unlikely* those nations drained or found oil fields. If the events that cause reserves to fluctuate didn't happen, then the conclusion would no longer make any sense.

(A) is Extreme and a Distortion. First, it applies to *any* nation with oil reserves, while the argument focuses only on several that had reported unchanged oil reserves. Second, the author does not *need* it to be more likely that any single nation was mistaken, just that there were more nations that were mistaken than were not. **(A)** fails the Denial Test because if there was one nation with oil resources that *was* more likely to be correct about their unchanged reserves, that would not undo the strength of the author's conclusion.

(C) is possible based on the argument, but isn't required for the author's point. First, the author doesn't argue that nations necessarily experienced both, and the example of "at least one" nation is too small to be required to conclude that most of those who stated their reserves didn't change were wrong. Negated, this choice says that during 1997, the oil reserves of at least one nation didn't both drop and rise. That

doesn't break the author's conclusion in any way, so it cannot be a necessary assumption.

(D) is Extreme. This choice indicates that the *only* way a nation could be incorrect in claiming unchanged oil reserves is if it *both* drained old oil fields and discovered new ones. So this choice further restricts the author's argument, rather than merely stating something required by the argument as written. The argument's conclusion could be true even if nations' oil reserves had changed due to only one of the two potential causes.

(E) is Out of Scope. The argument is concerned with whether the statements are factually correct, not whether nations are *obligated* to be factually correct.

17. (B) Inference

Step 1: Identify the Question Type

The phrase "must be true" indicates an Inference question. Not only does the phrase articulate the basic test for the correct answer, but its use in the question stem increases the likelihood that the stimulus will contain Formal Logic statements. Diagram the Formal Logic statements and look for deductions that come from combining the statements.

Step 2: Untangle the Stimulus

The stimulus presents three separate Formal Logic statements:

If	sound-insulated	→	quiet enough for home appliances
If	quiet enough for home appliances	→	appropriate for institutional settings
If	EM motor	→	~ quiet enough for home appliances

Step 3: Make a Prediction

As written, the first two statements can be combined to yield the following deduction:

If	sound-insulated	→	appropriate for institutional settings

However, another link can be made between the first and third statements. If you contrapose the first statement, you get:

If	~ quiet enough for home appliances	→	~ sound-insulated

That can be combined with the third statement to yield:

If	EM motor	→	~ sound insulated

The correct answer should match one of these two deductions (or their contrapositives). Some wrong answers will likely be incomplete contrapositives of these deductions or of the original statements.

Step 4: Evaluate the Answer Choices

(B) matches the second deduction.

(A) is an incomplete contrapositive of the first deduction. It reverses without negating.

(C) could be true, as there may be a lower noise standard for institutional settings. So even though EM motors aren't suitable for home appliances, it is possible that some could be used in institutional settings. However, this is not something that must be true.

(D) is an incomplete contrapositive of the first statement in the stimulus. It reverses without negating.

(E) could be true, but does not have to be. Based on the stimulus, motors that *can* be used in homes can also be used in industrial settings; however, the stimulus does not indicate whether or not motors that *can't* be used in homes (such as EM motors) can be used in industrial settings.

18. (C) Flaw

Step 1: Identify the Question Type

The question stem explicitly asks you to identify a flaw in the argument. Notice any disconnect between the evidence and conclusion, and keep the common LSAT flaws in mind.

Step 2: Untangle the Stimulus

The mayor's conclusion appears after the contrast Keyword [*b*]*ut*. Once you replace the vague terms, you can see the mayor concludes that the worry that the factory could cause health problems can be dismissed. In other words, the factory is not likely to cause health problems. The mayor's evidence is that most of the protesters were paid to attend the protest by developers who have a financial interest in stopping the factory's construction.

Step 3: Make a Prediction

The mayor dismisses the protesters' argument simply because many of them were paid to protest. But that doesn't address the actual issue of whether the factory could cause health problems or not. While in real life it may seem like the mayor has a reasonable point, on the LSAT he merely has flawed logic. The ad hominem attack—pointing out a bias in someone's argument rather than addressing the substance of the argument—is a recurring flaw on the LSAT.

Step 4: Evaluate the Answer Choices

(C) describes the classic LSAT flaw committed in this argument.

(A) is not an accurate description of the argument, as nothing in the stimulus indicates that the mayor mischaracterizes the protesters' views. The mayor questions the *sincerity* of the protesters, but that is different from mischaracterizing their views.

(B) is a 180. The mayor actually seeks to *dismiss* fears of potential health problems resulting from building the factory. The mayor never raises a specter of negative consequences resulting from a *failure* to build the factory.

(D) describes a representativeness flaw, which is not at play here. The mayor doesn't draw a conclusion based on an unrepresentative sample; indeed, the mayor's evidence encompasses *most* protestors. The problem is that the motives of those protestors have nothing to do with the safety of the factory.

(E) suggests that the mayor takes a tentative claim ("could cause health problems") and says that it's certain ("will cause health problems"). This doesn't match the argument, because the mayor actually implies that the factory definitively *won't* cause health problems.

19. (A) Principle (Apply/Inference)

Step 1: Identify the Question Type

The question stem explicitly identifies this as a Principle question. Further, it indicates that the stimulus contains the principle or general rule, which means you will need to apply the principle to the answer choices. The correct answer will contain an action that *violates* the principle in the stimulus.

Step 2: Untangle the Stimulus

The stimulus is short and sweet. The word *unless* indicates Formal Logic, although it may not really be necessary to translate it here, because the statement is pretty straightforward: misrepresenting someone else's views is acceptable only when it's done to benefit that person. If you were to diagram this and its contrapositive, it would look like this:

If	*intentionally misrepresent another's beliefs*	→	*should be acting in the interest of that other person*
If	*~ acting in the interest of that other person*	→	*should ~ intentionally misrepresent another's beliefs*

Step 3: Make a Prediction

The correct answer will describe someone who intentionally misrepresents another's beliefs without purposefully acting in that person's interest.

Step 4: Evaluate the Answer Choices

(A) is correct. Ann intentionally misrepresented Bruce's beliefs in order to make him look ridiculous, which is not in his interest.

(B) does not violate the principle. Although Claude intentionally misrepresented Thelma's beliefs, he did so with the purpose of keeping someone from bothering her, which is likely in her interest.

(C) does not violate the principle for two reasons. First, although John violated Maria's confidence, he did not misrepresent her beliefs. Second, he spoke with the purpose of getting others to think highly of her, which could be in her interest.

(D) does not violate the principle because although Harvey lied to Josephine about his *own* beliefs, he did not misrepresent hers.

(E) does not violate the principle because although Wanda was not acting in George's interest, she did not necessarily misrepresent his beliefs. This answer choice doesn't provide any information about George's actual beliefs concerning Egypt's location.

20. (C) Paradox

Step 1: Identify the Question Type

The question stem explicitly asks you to resolve the paradox. Identify the two apparently inconsistent facts, and find the explanation or factor that allows both to be true.

Step 2: Untangle the Stimulus

After an extensive description of the background facts, the last sentence sums up the two paradoxical facts concisely: even though a sheep farming family made more money from selling their wool, their overall prosperity did not increase.

Step 3: Make a Prediction

There are a plethora of potential specific resolutions to this paradox that one might imagine: increased taxes or other farming expenses or some natural disaster. So, as with most Paradox questions, a general prediction is best. The correct answer should indicate some factor that increased their expenses or otherwise held down their overall prosperity, despite their greater revenue from selling wool. The correct answer must accept the facts in the stimulus as true; avoid answers that seem to call the evidence into question.

Step 4: Evaluate the Answer Choices

(C) resolves the paradox. It indicates that the family's income from *other* products, besides wool, would have decreased. *All* Australian sheep famers produced these products, so the decrease in price would have affected this particular family for sure. This might have evened out their overall income.

(A) is Out of Scope. The paradox pertains to the family's prosperity in the *mid*-1800s, which would not be affected by inflation at the *end* of the 1800s. This would have resolved the paradox if it had been in the proper time frame.

(B) is an important type of wrong answer for Paradox questions; it tries to resolve the paradox by undermining one of the facts. Granted, the stimulus merely indicates that international prices were higher than domestic prices, so a dramatic decline in domestic prices might have occurred, offsetting gains from international sales. However, the stimulus also says that "the family generated more income from selling their wool" during this period. The relative prices of the domestic and international markets are irrelevant, since the family's *overall* wool sales increased.

(D), like **(B)**, cannot resolve the paradox because it must be true that the family generated more income from wool sales during that period. Competition or no, the family's wool sales were higher than previously. This choice wouldn't explain why the family's prosperity did not increase as well.

(E) is too uncertain. It's not clear whether the family in question was one of those whose living came exclusively from international wool sales, so this answer may not be pertinent. Additionally, like the other wrong answers, this choice focuses too much on wool sales. Even if this family made their living exclusively on international wool sales, this choice doesn't explain why, if their wool sales went up, their prosperity didn't. This choice would make sense *only* if it meant the family gave up other means of income. But this answer doesn't actually state that, and it would require an unwarranted assumption on your part, so it cannot be correct.

21. (C) Flaw

Step 1: Identify the Question Type

The question stem explicitly asks you to identify the flaw in the argument. Notice any disconnect between the evidence and conclusion, and keep the common LSAT flaws in mind.

Step 2: Untangle the Stimulus

The lawyer concludes that Meyers was not wrong to take the compost in the public garden. The primary reason, highlighted by the contrast Keyword *[h]owever*, is that Meyers had no reason to think the compost was anyone else's property. The lawyer also presents a Formal Logic chain:

| If | you take something you have reason to believe belongs to someone else | → | stealing | → | wrong |

Step 3: Make a Prediction

Compare the Formal Logic chain to the lawyer's additional evidence and conclusion. The lawyer says the sufficient condition was not met: Meyers took something with *no* reason to believe it belonged to someone else. The lawyer uses that to conclude that therefore the necessary condition was not met—Meyers didn't do anything wrong:

$$\text{If} \quad \begin{array}{c} \textit{take something you} \\ \textit{~ have reason to} \\ \textit{believe belongs to} \\ \textit{someone else} \end{array} \quad \rightarrow \quad \textit{~ wrong}$$

The lawyer's argument is an incomplete contrapositive, because she negates the Formal Logic rule without reversing. In other words, the lawyer confuses sufficient and necessary conditions, which is a common flaw on the LSAT. According to the rule, taking something with good reason to believe it belongs to another is *sufficient* to make the act wrong, but the lawyer's logic assumes that for Meyer's thievery to be wrong, it is *necessary* that he had good reason to believe the object belonged to someone else.

Step 4: Evaluate the Answer Choices

(C) accurately describes the flaw. A confusion of sufficient versus necessary commonly appears in Flaw questions that involve Formal Logic. Here the "condition that by itself is enough to make an action wrong" is the "good reason to think (it) is someone else's property."

(A) is not an accurate description of the argument. The lawyer uses a factual claim (Meyers had no good reason to think the compost belonged to another) to reach a moral judgment (Meyers was not wrong), but there is no indication that the lawyer confuses fact and morality.

(B) is irrelevant, because the argument is concerned (rightly) with the circumstances at hand, not with what might have happened under different circumstances. How Meyers would have responded if he *did* have good reason to believe the compost was someone else's property doesn't matter in terms of whether or not he was wrong to act when he *didn't* have good reason to believe that.

(D) is not a plausible ignored possibility answer. To legitimately be a flaw, an overlooked possibility, if true, would have to weaken the author's argument. To the contrary, if the compost belonged to Meyers, it would support the lawyer's contention that Meyers did nothing wrong.

(E) doesn't accurately describe the argument. The lawyer never asserts that if there is *good* evidence that an object is someone else's property, then that means it is *certainly* someone else's property. There is no evidence regarding the ownership of the compost beyond the premise that Meyers had no good reason to think the compost was someone else's property. The author does not conclude, or even necessarily assume, that it was certainly someone else's property.

22. (E) Assumption (Necessary)

Step 1: Identify the Question Type

A question that asks for an assumption on which the argument *depends* is a Necessary Assumption question. Build the basic bridge between the evidence and conclusion. Use the Denial Test to check your answer, if necessary.

Step 2: Untangle the Stimulus

The author concludes that "this practice," i.e., predatory pricing, should be acceptable. The evidence is that even after a company drives its competitors out of business by underselling them, the threat of future competition will prevent the company from raising its prices to unreasonable levels.

Step 3: Make a Prediction

Boiled down, the author's argument is that a company that practices predatory pricing won't raise prices to unreasonable levels, so predatory pricing is acceptable. Oftentimes, necessary assumptions on the LSAT are as simple as the author thinking, "If I have this evidence, I can reasonably reach this conclusion." Therefore, the correct answer will often merely restate the argument in slightly broader Formal Logic terms. Thus, in this case, the author assumes at a basic level that if prices will not become unreasonable, then the practice is okay. Another way of stating that assumption is that aside from the threat of a company raising its prices to unreasonable levels, there is nothing else about engaging in predatory pricing to drive competition out of business that would be unacceptable.

Step 4: Evaluate the Answer Choices

(E) matches the prediction. *Any* is a Formal Logic word that substitutes for *if*. So this choice properly indicates that if a pricing practice does not result in unreasonable prices, then it should be acceptable. Based on the evidence in the stimulus, predator pricing would fall into this category.

(A) is Extreme. The argument says companies that are successful in driving competitors out of business will face a *threat* of renewed competition, but not that the threat will necessarily always materialize. So, the word *inevitably* overreaches. Also, the argument does not cover all successful companies, as this choice does.

(B) is Out of Scope. Whether or not several companies concurrently attempt to engage in predatory pricing is irrelevant to the argument, which is only about what occurs when one company emerges victorious. The author assumes that in at least some instances, a single company will emerge victorious from a predatory pricing war and be able to drive its competitors out of business. But this does not preclude the possibility that some of its competitors attempted to employ the same strategy.

(C) is Out of Scope. The argument does not make any mention of the types of companies that successfully engage in predatory pricing.

(D) is Extreme. The argument indicates that the threat of competition keeps companies from raising prices to *unreasonable* levels, but does not indicate that it is the *only* thing that keeps companies from raising prices at all.

23. (C) Parallel Flaw

Step 1: Identify the Question Type

The phrase "pattern of reasoning … is most similar" indicates a Parallel Reasoning question. This question stem further specifies that you are to match flawed reasoning, so it's a Parallel Flaw question. Understand the flaw in the stimulus and seek out that same flaw in one of the answers.

Step 2: Untangle the Stimulus

An argument that consists of a Formal Logic rule, a factual piece of evidence, and a conclusion can be diagrammed as follows. The Formal Logic rule is in the top row, and the evidence and conclusion turned into a trigger and result, respectively, are in the bottom row:

If	prosecutor wanted to charge Frank as an embezzler (believe X)	→	already indicted (Y)
If	~ already indicted (~ Y)	→	~ an embezzler (~ X)

Step 3: Make a Prediction

When Formal Logic appears in a Parallel Flaw question, the argument usually messes up the contrapositive. However, that's not the case here. At first glance, the author's evidence and conclusion seem to properly map out as the rule's contrapositive. But, at second glance, you might notice that the author doesn't actually set up equivalent terms. The author shifts scope from whether or not the prosecutor *wants* to indict Frank as an embezzler to whether or not Frank *is* an embezzler. This is a classic LSAT belief-versus-fact scope shift.

The correct answer must have the right pieces: a Formal Logic rule, a factual piece of evidence, and a conclusion. Also, the factual evidence and the conclusion should generally map out as the contrapositive of the Formal Logic rule, but with a similar belief-versus-fact scope shift: If "believe X" → Y ; If ~ Y → ~ X.

Step 4: Evaluate the Answer Choices

(C) is a match. It translates algebraically as: If "believe X" → Y; If ~ Y → ~ X.

If	believed left on oven (believe X)	→	rush home
If	at work (~ rush home) (~ Y)	→	~ left on oven (~ X)

The top and bottom rows are in the form of a statement and its contrapositive, except that there is the same belief-to-fact scope shift regarding whether the oven was left on.

(A) is not a match. It translates algebraically as: If X → ~ Y; If ~ Y → X.

If	knew 9:00 appointment would cancel (X)	→	~ come to work until 10:00 (~ Y)
If	~ come to work until 10:00 (~ Y)	→	knew 9:00 appointment would cancel (X)

This argument contains an incomplete contrapositive (reversing without negating), while the stimulus does not. Additionally, this argument does not contain the belief-versus-fact scope shift found in the stimulus.

(B) is not a match. It translates algebraically as: If X → Y; If ~ X → ~ Y.

If	wins lottery (X)	→	stays home to celebrate (Y)
If	~ win lottery (~ X)	→	go to work (~ stay home to celebrate) (~ Y)

Similar to **(A)**, this choice contains an incomplete contrapositive. Additionally, this argument does not contain the belief-versus-fact scope shift found in the stimulus.

(D) is not a match. It translates algebraically as: If "believe X" → Y; If Y → X.

If	believes getting promotion (believe X)	→	come to work early (Y)
If	come to work early (Y)	→	getting a promotion (X)

This choice *does* contain the belief-versus-fact scope shift found in the stimulus. However, this choice *also* contains an incomplete contrapositive, so it is not parallel.

(E) is not a match, it translates algebraically as: If "believe X" → ~ Y; If X → ~ Y.

If	believes getting fired (believe X)	→	~ come to work today (~ Y)
If	getting fired (X)	→	~ coming to work today (~ Y)

This is the most difficult to eliminate because it *does* contain a belief-to-fact scope shift *and* does not contain an incomplete contrapositive, as the other wrong answers all do. However, it also is not set up as a proper contrapositive, while the argument in the stimulus is. So, it is not parallel.

24. (E) Flaw

Step 1: Identify the Question Type

The phrase "vulnerable to the criticism" indicates a Flaw question. Notice any disconnect between the evidence and conclusion, and keep in mind the common LSAT flaws.

Step 2: Untangle the Stimulus

The pediatrician concludes that removing children's tonsils will ensure that they do not have breathing problems during sleep. The evidence is that swollen tonsils give rise to breathing problems and removing children's swollen tonsils has been shown to alleviate such problems.

Step 3: Make a Prediction

Recognizing extremeness or absoluteness in an argument's conclusion can be helpful in recognizing the flaw. The pediatrician asserts that removing tonsils "*will ensure* that children do not experience *any* breathing problems during sleep." Sure, swollen tonsils cause breathing problems during sleep, and removing the tonsils will alleviate that. However, to conclude that removing the tonsils will *guarantee* that a child will never have any breathing problems during sleep makes a big assumption that nothing else can cause breathing problems.

Step 4: Evaluate the Answer Choices

(E) is correct. To be correct, a Flaw answer that is phrased as an ignored possibility, must, if true, weaken the argument. If breathing problems during sleep can be caused by something other than swollen tonsils, then removing the tonsils will *not* ensure that a child does not experience any breathing problems during sleep.

(A) does not answer the baseline question for a Flaw answer choice: Does the author do this? The pediatrician simply does not refer to an authoritative source or expert, or even her own credentials.

(B) sounds profound, but this is merely a variation on circular reasoning, such as "presupposes what it seeks to establish." Here, the author does not have interchangeable evidence and conclusion, so **(B)** is not a flaw committed by the author.

(C) does not accurately describe the evidence and conclusion. The pediatrician states that swollen tonsils cause breathing problems during sleep. Removing the tonsils is intended to achieve the effect of eliminating those problems that are the caused by the tonsils. So, the author is not flawed in stating that removing the swollen tonsils will produce the effect of eliminating tonsil-related breathing issues during sleep. However, the author *is* flawed in drawing the extreme conclusion that *any* breathing problems during sleep would be fixed by the tonsillectomy. Nothing in the stimulus indicates the intent of the surgery was to fix all breathing problems during sleep.

(D) is not correct. To be correct, a Flaw answer that is phrased as an ignored possibility must, if true, weaken the argument. The existence of other medical reasons for removing a child's tonsils would in no way undermine the efficacy of doing so to eliminate breathing problems.

25. (D) Principle (Apply/Inference)

Step 1: Identify the Question Type

The question stem explicitly indicates that this is a Principle question and, moreover, that the stimulus contains a principle or general rule about ethics that must be matched to a specific action in the answers. Apply the Principle questions often contain Formal Logic, so keep an eye out for that.

Step 2: Untangle the Stimulus

The stimulus consists of a Formal Logic rule that can be diagrammed as follows:

If	knowledge of impending policies ~ available to public	→	unethical for gov't officials to use that knowledge for personal financial gain

Step 3: Make a Prediction

It can be advisable to take the contrapositive before trying to match an answer to a Formal Logic statement. However, the question stem specifies that you are looking for an action that would trigger a conclusion that the action is unethical. Thus, this is the correct form of the statement to work with, not its contrapositive. The correct answer will describe an action by a government official to use knowledge of impending policies, which is not available to the public, for personal financial gain.

Step 4: Evaluate the Answer Choices

(D) is correct as it describes a government official (Finance Department) using knowledge of an impending policy (plan to tax luxury cars) to financially benefit (avoid paying the tax), despite the information not being available to the public. Based on the Formal Logic principle, this would be unethical.

(A) does not trigger the rule because there is no reference to any impending policy. Also, the government official no longer works for the bidding company, so it is not clear that the official would personally benefit financially.

(B) does not trigger the rule because the former officer is no longer a government official. Additionally, there is no reference to any impending policies.

(C) does not trigger the rule because the official is using provisions of a previously enacted law, which would be available to the public, rather than inside knowledge of an impending policy.

(E) does not trigger the rule because the information was not only about an impending policy, but it was already made public.

Section II: Logic Games

Game 1: Film Releases

Q#	Question Type	Correct	Difficulty
1	Must Be False (CANNOT Be True)	E	★
2	Must Be True	A	★
3	"If" / Could Be True EXCEPT	E	★
4	"If" / Could Be True	D	★
5	Rule Substitution	A	★★★★

Game 2: Application Evaluation

Q#	Question Type	Correct	Difficulty
6	Acceptability	A	★
7	"If" / Could Be True	B	★
8	"If" / Must Be True EXCEPT	C	★★
9	"If" / Must Be True	B	★★
10	"If" / Could Be True EXCEPT	C	★★
11	"If" / How Many	E	★★★

Game 3: Literature Course

Q#	Question Type	Correct	Difficulty
12	Acceptability	A	★
13	"If" / Could Be True	A	★★
14	"If" / Must Be False (CANNOT Be True)	C	★★★★
15	"If" / Could Be True	B	★★
16	Rule Substitution	D	★★★

Game 4: Paintings in a Museum

Q#	Question Type	Correct	Difficulty
17	Acceptability	C	★
18	"If" / Could Be True	A	★
19	"If" / Must Be True	C	★
20	Could Be True EXCEPT	E	★★
21	"If" / Could Be True	A	★★
22	"If" / Must Be True	E	★★★
23	"If" / Must Be True	B	★★★

Game 1: Film Releases

Step 1: Overview

Situation: A movie studio scheduling film releases

Entities: Six films (*Fiesta, Glaciers, Hurricanes, Jets, Kangaroos, Lovebird*)

Action: Loose Sequencing. Determine the order in which the films are released. A quick glance at the three rules tells you that all the rules are about relative relationships between the entities, so it is Loose rather than Strict.

Limitations: No two films will be released at the same time. So, one film will be released first, one second, one third, and so on.

Step 2: Sketch

Because this is a Loose Sequencing game, no series of slots is needed. The opening sketch can just be a list of the films by initial. As you go through the rules, you'll build the sketch based on the relative relationships.

Step 3: Rules

Rule 1 sets up two relationships: *Fiesta* will be released before *Jets*, and *Fiesta* will be released before *Lovebird*. *Jets* and *Lovebird* can be released in either order.

```
      J
     /
    F
     \
      L
```

Rule 2 sets up a sequence of three films: *Kangaroos* will be released before *Jets*, which will be released before *Hurricanes*.

```
    K — J — H
```

The first two rules can be combined immediately:

```
      K
       \
        J — H
       /
      F
       \
        L
```

Rule 3 sets up a single relationship: *Lovebird* will be released before *Glaciers*. Add this to the sketch.

```
      K
       \
        J — H
       /
      F
       \
        L — G
```

Step 4: Deductions

As with most Loose Sequencing games, the key to making Deductions is to combine the rules using Duplicates. In this case, the combinations have already been made during Step 3.

However, the exact release of the entities still cannot be determined. For example, by Rule 1, *Fiesta* must be released before *Lovebird*, which in turn must be released before *Glaciers* (Rule 3). While these two films must be released after *Fiesta*, there is no relationship between them and the remaining films (*Kangaroos, Jets,* and *Hurricanes*). *Lovebird*

and *Glaciers* can be released before, after, or anywhere amid those three films—as long as they are released after *Fiesta*.

```
      K
       \
        J — H
       /
      F
       \
        L — G
```

Every rule is combined in this one sketch, and every film is included; there are no Floaters. Before proceeding to the questions, consider which films could be released first and last. The first film released could be *Fiesta* or *Kangaroos* because they are the only films that do not have to be released later than another film. Similarly, the last film released could be *Glaciers* or *Hurricanes* because they are the only films that do not have to be released earlier than another film.

Step 5: Questions

1. (E) Must Be False (CANNOT Be True)
The correct answer here must be false. The remaining four answers will all be possible, if not definitely true.

If *Kangaroos* is released first, then *Fiesta* could be released second before the remaining four films. That eliminates **(A)**.

Glaciers has to be released after *Lovebird*, which has to be released after *Fiesta*. If *Fiesta* and *Lovebird* were the first two films released, *Glaciers* could be third. That eliminates **(B)**.

Hurricanes has to be released after *Jets*, which has to be released after both *Fiesta* and *Kangaroos*. If *Fiesta*, *Kangaroos*, and *Jets* were the first three films released, *Hurricanes* could be the fourth. That eliminates **(C)**.

Kangaroos has to be released before *Jets*, which must be released before *Hurricanes*. That means if *Jets* and *Hurricanes* were pushed to the end, the latest *Kangaroos* could be released is fourth. That means it could be fourth, which eliminates **(D)**. However, *Kangaroos* must always have at least two films after it (*Jets* and *Hurricanes*), thus *Kangaroos* cannot be fifth, which makes **(E)** the correct answer.

2. (A) Must Be True
The correct answer here must be true. The four incorrect answers will either be possible or definitely false.

By Rule 1, *Fiesta* must be released earlier than *Jets*. Because *Jets* has to be released before *Hurricanes* (Rule 2), *Fiesta* must also be released before *Hurricanes*. That makes **(A)** the correct answer. The remaining answers all list two films that have no defined relationship between them. Therefore, they are all possible, but none of them *must* be true.

3. (E) "If" / Could Be True EXCEPT
For this question, *Glaciers* will be released before *Hurricanes*. Before *Glaciers*, *Lovebird* must be released (Rule 3), and

Fiesta must be released before that (Rule 1). That creates a loose sequence starting with *Fiesta* and ending with *Hurricanes*. *Jets* must be released at some point in the middle, after *Fiesta* (Rule 1) and before *Hurricanes* (Rule 2). *Kangaroos* merely has to be released at some point before *Jets*.

$$
\begin{array}{c}
K \\[-4pt]
\diagdown \\
\quad J \text{———} H \\
F \diagup \qquad \diagup \\
\diagdown \\
L \text{—} G
\end{array}
$$

The correct answer here must be false. Because *Lovebird* has to be released before *Glaciers* and *Hurricanes*, it cannot be released fifth. That makes **(E)** the correct answer. The remaining answers are all possible.

4. (D) "If" / Could Be True

For this question, *Lovebird* will be released before *Kangaroos*. *Kangaroos* must be released before *Jets* (Rule 2), which must be released before *Hurricanes* (Rule 2). And before *Lovebirds*, *Fiesta* must be released (Rule 1). That creates a string of releases starting with *Fiesta* and ending with *Hurricanes*. The only film left is *Glaciers*, which must be released at some point after *Lovebird*.

$$
F \text{—} L \diagup \begin{array}{c} K \text{—} J \text{—} H \\ \diagdown \\ G \end{array}
$$

That means *Fiesta* must be released first and *Lovebird* second. The schedule of the remaining films is dependent on *Glaciers*, which can be released at any time from third to sixth. The correct answer will be the only one that could be true. Because *Glaciers* can be the last film released, *Jets* could certainly be released before it. That makes **(D)** the correct answer. For the record, all of the remaining answers mention *Lovebird*, which must be released second. The remaining answers all must be false because *Lovebird* is released earlier than every other film except for *Fiesta*.

5. (A) Rule Substitution

This question removes Rule 1 from the game. The correct answer will be a rule that establishes *all* of the restrictions set up by Rule 1 without adding any new restrictions. In other words, the correct answer will force *Fiesta* to be released earlier than *Jets* and *Lovebird*, without adding restrictions that were not originally in place.

Starting with **(A)**, if *Kangaroos* were the only film that could be released before *Fiesta*, then *Fiesta* would definitely be released before *Jets* and *Lovebird*. So, that would reestablish the original restrictions. This may appear to be more restrictive, because it would also force *Fiesta* to be released before *Glaciers* and *Hurricanes*. However, while those restrictions were never *directly* set by the rules, they would not be new. After all, *Glaciers* and *Hurricanes* have to be released after *Lovebird* and *Jets*, respectively (Rule 2 and 3). So, *Fiesta* always had to be released before them, too.

Therefore, because this situation would establish all of the original restrictions without adding anything new, **(A)** is the correct answer. For the record:

If *Kangaroos* were released before *Lovebird*, it would add a restriction that was never in place *and* it would have no effect on when *Fiesta* is released. That eliminates **(B)**.

By the original rules, *Fiesta* had to be released before *Jets*, *Lovebird*, *Hurricanes*, and *Glaciers*. That means it could only be released first or second. However, simply adding that restriction back In does not restore everything. It would also allow *Lovebird* to be released before or after *Fiesta*, which was not allowed by the original rules. That eliminates **(C)**.

Fiesta never had to be released earlier than *Kangaroos*. That eliminates **(D)**.

By the original rules, only *Fiesta* or *Kangaroos* could be released first. However, again, simply adding that restriction back is not enough. If *Kangaroos* were first, this answer would allow *Fiesta* to be released at any other time—even after *Jets* and *Lovebird*. That was not allowed by the original rules. That eliminates **(E)**.

Game 2: Application Evaluation

~~Step 1: Overview~~

Step 1: Overview

Situation: Human resource officers evaluating job applications

Entities: Seven candidates (Farrell, Grant, Hong, Inman, Kent, Lopez, Madsen); four human resource officers (Rao, Smith, Tipton, Ullman)

Action: Distribution. Determine which candidates' applications each officer evaluates.

Limitations: Each application is evaluated by only one officer, and each officer evaluates at least one application. Because there are only four officers and seven applications, at least one officer will have to evaluate multiple applications. Numbers will be crucial in this game.

Step 2: Sketch

Because each application will be evaluated only once, this is classified as a Distribution game as opposed to a Matching game—distributing the seven applications among the four officers. However, even if you considered it a Matching game, it would likely be immaterial as long as you set up a useful sketch. One effective sketch is to set up a column for each officer. List the candidates by initial to the side, and start the sketch with one slot in each column. That sets up four slots, with three more to be added based on the rules and/or the questions.

F G H I K L M

Rao	Smi	Tip	Ull

Step 3: Rules

Rule 1 establishes that Ullman will evaluate Grant's application. Add "G" to the slot under Ullman, but leave the column open. It's still possible that Ullman evaluates other applications.

Rule 2 creates a block. Farrell's and Lopez's applications will be evaluated by the same officer. That could be any officer at this point, so jot this down to the side in shorthand:

F
L

Rule 3 prevents Hong's and Madsen's applications from being evaluated by the same officer that evaluates Inman's application. That does not mean Hong's and Madsen's applications will be evaluated by the same officer, but the officer who evaluates Inman's application will not evaluate either of theirs. Jot this down in shorthand.

NEVER
I
H/M

Rule 4 establishes Kent's application as the *only* application evaluated by one of the officers. That means at least one officer will evaluate a single application, but which one is still unknown. For now, make a shorthand note to the side.

Rule 5 sets up a numeric restriction: Smith has to evaluate more applications than Tipton. That means Smith has to evaluate at least two, so add a second slot under Smith's column. However, Tipton and Smith can still evaluate more, so note this rule in shorthand for continued reference.

Smi > Tip

Step 4: Deductions

There is a lot to consider here, but only a few concrete deductions can be made. The questions hint that deductions will be scarce because each one (except for the Acceptability question) requires additional information (i.e., an "If") to answer it.

Start with the block: the same officer must evaluate Farrell's and Lopez's applications. Without working out the scenarios fully, it appears that any officer could handle both applications. (It can be shown that Tipton cannot, but that would require more testing than is needed at this point.)

There is one Established Entity: Grant's application is evaluated by Ullman. However, with no additional information about Grant or Ullman, nothing more can be determined there.

Numbers are important, especially because of Rule 5. By that rule, Tipton could only evaluate one or two applications. After all, if Tipton evaluated three, Smith would have to evaluate the other four, which would leave no applications for Rao and Ullman, and the Limitations require each human resource officer to review at least one application. Likewise, Smith must evaluate between two to four. If she only does one, then she can't have more than Tipton (Rule 5). To evaluate four, she'd have to review applications from Farrell, Grant, Hong, and Madsen.

Rao	Smi	Tip	Ull
K/I	F	I/K	G
	L		
	H		
	M		

The deduction that Tipton must review either one or two may seem like a case for Limited Options. In this game, though, Limited Options is ultimately unnecessary. The first option would limit Tipton to one application. However, Smith could still evaluate two, three, or four applications. Furthermore, no application could be assigned with certainty. It's a dead-end option. The second option would give Tipton two applications. In that case, Smith would have to evaluate three, and Rao and Ullman would get one each. In that case, every application could be assigned with certainty. However, this scenario is the basis for the third question. So, if you did not set it up now, you would still set it up then.

Neither choice would be more or less effective. The option could be set up now (and will be explained more fully later) or for the third question. It will require the same amount of time and effort either way.

The one concrete deduction that could be made before heading to the questions is based on Numbers. Because Smith has to evaluate at least two applications, Smith cannot evaluate Kent's application, which must be evaluated by itself (Rule 4). Also, Ullman cannot evaluate Kent's application because she already evaluates Grant's. With Kent's application limited to just Rao or Tipton, this would appear to be another potential source for Limited Options. However, neither option leads to anything concrete.

Ultimately the Master Sketch looks like this:

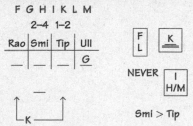

Step 5: Questions

6. (A) Acceptability

As with any Acceptability question, go through the rules one at a time and eliminate answers as they violate the rules.

By Rule 1, Ullman must evaluate Grant's application. That eliminates **(E)**. By Rule 2, the same officer must evaluate Farrell's and Lopez's applications. That eliminates **(B)**. By Rule 3, the officer that evaluates Inman's application cannot also evaluate Hong's or Madsen's. That eliminates **(C)**. By Rule 4, Kent's application must be evaluated by itself. That eliminates **(D)**, which leaves **(A)** as the correct answer.

7. (B) "If" / Could Be True

For this question, Rao will evaluate Hong's application. That means Rao cannot evaluate Inman's application (Rule 3). Kent's application still needs to be evaluated by itself. Rao and Ullman are already evaluating other applications, and Smith needs to evaluate at least two (Rule 5). So, only Tipton can evaluate Kent's application, and that will be Tipton's only application. That leaves four applications: those of Farrell, Inman, Lopez, and Madsen. Smith needs to evaluate at least two of them. However, Smith cannot evaluate both Inman's

and Madsen's applications together (Rule 3). So, even if Smith evaluates one of theirs, she must also evaluate Farrell's or Lopez's—which means she must evaluate them both (Rule 2).

Smith could still evaluate either Inman's or Madsen's application. However, Inman's application could also be evaluated by Ullman, and Madsen's could be evaluated by either Rao or Ullman.

Because Smith could still evaluate Inman's application, **(B)** is the correct answer. The remaining answers all must be false.

8. (C) "If" / Must Be True EXCEPT

For this question, Tipton will evaluate exactly two applications. That means Smith must evaluate three applications (Rule 5), leaving just one each for Rao and Ullman. Ullman already evaluates Grant's application. Kent's application needs to be evaluated by itself, so that must be done by Rao. The remaining applications must be evaluated by Smith and Tipton. The same officer must evaluate Farrell's and Lopez's. However, if that were Tipton, then Smith would evaluate Hong's, Inman's, and Madsen's. But that would violate Rule 3. So, Farrell's and Lopez's applications must be evaluated by Smith.

That leaves Inman's, Hong's, and Madsen's applications. Tipton must evaluate two of them, but Inman's cannot be evaluated with either of the remaining two. So, Inman's must be evaluated by Smith, and Tipton will evaluate Hong's and Madsen's.

Rao	Smi	Tip	Ull
K	F	H	G
	L	M	
	I		

The correct answer here is the one that does not *have* to be true. Because Farrell's application is evaluated by Smith, not Tipton, that makes **(C)** the correct answer. The remaining answers are all confirmed as must be true by the new "If" sketch for this question.

9. (B) "If" / Must Be True

For this question, Madsen's application will be evaluated by itself. This is also true of Kent's application (Rule 4). Ullman already evaluates Grant's application (Rule 1), and Smith has to evaluate at least two (Rule 5). So, the only two officers that can evaluate Madsen's and Kent's applications are Rao and Tipton in either order. That leaves Farrell's, Hong's, Inman's, and Lopez's applications. Smith needs to evaluate at least two of them. However, Smith cannot evaluate both Inman's and Lopez's applications together (Rule 3). So, even if Smith evaluates one of theirs, she must also evaluate Farrell's or Lopez's, which means she must evaluate them both (Rule 2). That leaves just Inman and Hong, who can't be both reviewed together (Rule 3), so one will be reviewed by Smith and the other by Ullman.

Rao	Smi	Tip	Ull
M/K	F	K/M	G
	L		I/H
	H/I		

Either Madsen's or Kent's application could be evaluated by Rao, but either one could also be evaluated by Tipton. That eliminates **(A)** and **(C)**. Either Inman's or Hong's application could be evaluated by Smith, but either one could also be evaluated by Ullman. That eliminates **(D)** and **(E)**. However, Smith *must* evaluate Lopez's application. That makes **(B)** the correct answer.

10. (C) "If" / Could Be True EXCEPT
For this question, Farrell's application will be evaluated along with Inman's. This block also has to include Lopez's application (Rule 2), but cannot include Madsen's and Hong's (Rule 3). This block cannot be evaluated by Tipton because that would give Tipton three applications, giving Smith four and leaving none for the other officers. This block also cannot be evaluated by Ullman because that would give Ullman four applications, leaving only one each for Rao, Smith, and Tipton—and Smith cannot have just one (Rule 5). So, only Rao or Smith can evaluate Farrell's, Inman's, and Lopez's applications. That leads to Limited Options for this question—one with the block under Rao and one with the block under Smith.

However, as it turns out the deduction that the block must be under Rao or Smith already leads to the correct answer. This question is looking for the one answer that must be false, and because Ullman cannot evaluate Lopez's application, that makes **(C)** the correct answer without the need for drawing out the Limited Options. For the record, sketches from other questions can help eliminate the remaining answers.

In the second question, Inman's application could be evaluated along with Farrell's by Smith. In that case, Kent's is evaluated by Tipton and Madsen's could be evaluated by Ullman. That eliminates **(B)** and **(E)**. In the fourth question, Inman's application could be evaluated along with Farrell's by Smith. In that case, Hong's would be evaluated by Ullman. That eliminates **(A)**. And in the final question, Inman's application could be evaluated along with Farrell's by Rao. In that case, Madsen's application is evaluated by Smith. That eliminates **(D)**.

11. (E) "If" / How Many
For this question, Farrell's application will be evaluated by Rao. That means Lopez's will be too (Rule 2). Kent's application still needs to be evaluated by itself. Because Ullman already evaluates Grant's (Rule 1), and Smith needs to evaluate at least two, Kent's application must be evaluated by Tipton. Tipton is closed off. That leaves Hong's, Inman's, and Madsen's applications. Smith needs to evaluate at least two of them. Because Inman's cannot be evaluated with either of the other two, Smith must evaluate Hong's and Madsen's.

Rao	Smi	Tip	Ull
F	H	K	G
L	M		↑

Inman's application could still be evaluated by either Rao or Ullman. Reading the question carefully, the correct answer will state how many applications *other than Farrell's* can be assigned with certainty. Other than Farrell, it's known who's evaluating Grant's, Hong's, Kent's, Lopez's, and Madsen's. That's five people, making **(E)** the correct answer.

Game 3: Literature Course

Step 1: Overview

Situation: Scheduling books to be discussed as part of a literature course

Entities: Six books (F, K, N, O, R, T)

Action: Matching/Sequencing Hybrid. Primarily, determine the order in which the books will be discussed—Sequencing. However, the overview also mentions that some books will be summarized and others will not. Because this is a characteristic of the books, it is considered Matching. However, the game could also be perceived as a Selection/Sequencing Hybrid in which the books are sequenced and at least one books is selected to be summarized.

Limitations: For the Sequencing, the books are discussed one at a time, one per week for six weeks. As for the Matching, at least one book will be summarized, but there's no defined limit.

Step 2: Sketch

The primary action is Sequencing, so list the entities and set up six slots to place them in order. You can notate below each slot whether a book is summarized ("s") or not ("x").

$$\begin{array}{ccccccc} & 1 & 2 & 3 & 4 & 5 & 6 \\ \text{FKNORT} & \underline{} & \underline{} & \underline{} & \underline{} & \underline{} & \underline{} \\ & & & s/x & & & \end{array}$$

Note: To notate whether a book is summarized, you could also use symbols such as Xs and check marks. Or, as mentioned earlier, you could treat the secondary action like a Selection component and circle books that are summarized and cross out those that are not.

Step 3: Rules

Rule 1 states that two books cannot be summarized in consecutive weeks. Shorthand a note to the side.

$$\text{NEVER} \; \underline{}_s \; \underline{}_s$$

Rule 2 provides some Formal Logic: If N is not summarized, then both R and T are summarized. Be sure to draw out the contrapositive: If either R or T is not summarized, then N is summarized.

$$\frac{N}{x} \to \frac{R}{s} \text{ AND } \frac{T}{s}$$

$$\frac{R}{x} \text{ OR } \frac{T}{x} \to \frac{N}{s}$$

Rule 3 sets up some loose sequencing: N is discussed some time before T, which is discussed some time before O.

$$N - T - O$$

Rule 4 sets up more loose sequencing: F is discussed some time before O, which is discussed some time before both K and R (in either order).

$$F - O \overset{K}{\underset{R}{<}}$$

That can be added right to the loose sequencing of Rule 3 right away.

$$N - T \overset{K}{\underset{\substack{\diagdown \\ F \quad R}}{<}} O$$

Step 4: Deductions

Once the final two rules have been combined, all the entities are included into a loose sequencing sketch. Before O is discussed, N and T are discussed, in that order (Rule 3). Also, F is discussed before O (Rule 3), but it could be anywhere before, after, or in between N and T. After O is discussed, K and R are discussed (Rule 4), but in either order.

From that, O must be discussed in week 4. F, N, and T will be discussed in the first three weeks (in some order), and R and K will be discussed in the last two weeks (in either order).

As for which books are summarized, that cannot be determined with certainty. Any of the six books can still be summarized—just not consecutive ones. And the logic of Rule 2 allows for too many possibilities (N by itself could be summarized, as could any combination of N, R, and T—even all three). It's enough to have established O and determined the relative placement of all of the other books.

$$\begin{array}{ccccccc} & 1 & 2 & 3 & 4 & 5 & 6 \\ \text{FKNORT} & \underline{} & \underline{} & \underline{} & O & K/R & R/K \\ & & \underbrace{}_{\text{N--T; F}} & & & & \end{array}$$

$$\begin{array}{c} s/x \\ \text{NEVER} \; \underline{}_s \; \underline{}_s \quad\quad \frac{N}{x} \to \frac{R}{s} \text{ AND } \frac{T}{s} \end{array}$$

$$\frac{R}{x} \text{ OR } \frac{T}{x} \to \frac{N}{s}$$

Step 5: Questions

12. (A) Acceptability

A standard Acceptability question. Go through the rules one at a time, eliminating answers as they violate the rules.

By Rule 1, no two books can be summarized consecutively. That eliminates **(C)**, which states that T and O are summarized, but lists them next to one another. By Rule 2, if N is not summarized, then both R and T must be. That eliminates **(D)**, in which N is not summarized, but only T (along with O) is summarized—not R. By Rule 3, N must be discussed before T. That eliminates **(B)**, which has T before N. By Rule 4, F must be discussed before O. That eliminates **(E)**, which has O before F. That leaves **(A)** as the only answer that does not violate the rules—and thus the correct answer.

13. (A) "If" / Could Be True

For this question, N will be the second book discussed *and* it will not be summarized. Start with the Sequencing. N has to be discussed before T, which must be discussed before O (Rule 3). With N discussed second and O discussed fourth, T must be discussed third. Because F also has to be discussed before O (Rule 4), it must be discussed first. R and K could still be discussed in either order after O.

As for the Matching, because N is not summarized, R and T must both be summarized (Rule 2). With T summarized in week 3, the books in weeks 2 and 4 (N and O) cannot be summarized (Rule 1). R could still be summarized in either week 5 or 6. In either case, it will be consecutive with K, so K cannot be summarized. F may or may not be summarized.

$$\frac{F}{\quad} \; \frac{N}{x} \; \frac{T}{s} \; \frac{O}{x} \; \frac{K/R}{\quad} \; \frac{R/K}{\quad}$$
1 2 3 4 5 6

$$\frac{R}{s} ; \frac{K}{x}$$

In that case, **(A)** is the only answer that could be true, making it the correct answer.

14. (C) "If" / Must Be False (CANNOT Be True)

For this question, O is summarized. Because O is discussed fourth, that means the books discussed third and fifth cannot be summarized (Rule 1). Unfortunately, that's the only concrete deduction that can be made.

$$\frac{\quad}{\quad} \; \frac{\quad}{\quad} \; \frac{\quad}{x} \; \frac{O}{s} \; \frac{\quad}{x} \; \frac{\quad}{\quad}$$
1 2 3 4 5 6

At this point, you could use trial and error for each answer choice, but it might be easier to use the answers as a guide for what to test and try to eliminate multiple answers simultaneously.

The correct answer will be false no matter what. The remaining answers will all be possible. Starting at the top, could F be the first book discussed? If it were, because N and T—in that order—have to be discussed before O, they will be discussed second and third. In that case, T is not summarized. By Rule 2, that means N must be. With N summarized, F cannot be (because they are consecutive).

$$\frac{F}{x} \; \frac{N}{s} \; \frac{T}{x} \; \frac{O}{s} \; \frac{K/R}{x} \; \frac{R/K}{\quad}$$
1 2 3 4 5 6

This is certainly possible, so **(A)** can be eliminated. Also, K and R could still be discussed in either order. K could be sixth, which makes **(B)** possible. And K could be fifth and not summarized, which makes **(D)** possible. That leaves only two answers remaining.

If F is summarized, it cannot be discussed third for this question. It must be discussed either first or second. In either case, N would also be first or second, with T being discussed third. That means T will not be summarized. By Rule 2, that

means N must be. However, N and F are consecutive. Therefore, it is impossible for F to be summarized, too. Because there is no way for F to be summarized, **(C)** is the correct answer.

$$\frac{F/N}{s} \; \frac{N/F}{s} \; \frac{T}{x} \; \frac{O}{s} \; \frac{K/R}{x} \; \frac{R/K}{\quad}$$
1 2 3 4 5 ~~6~~

For the record, here's a sketch that shows how N can be not summarized, eliminating **(E)**:

$$\frac{N}{x} \; \frac{T}{s} \; \frac{F}{x} \; \frac{O}{s} \; \frac{K}{x} \; \frac{R}{s}$$
1 2 3 4 5 6

15. (B) "If" / Could Be True

For this question, the last two books discussed will not be summarized.

$$\frac{\quad}{\quad} \; \frac{\quad}{\quad} \; \frac{\quad}{\quad} \; \frac{O}{\quad} \; \frac{K/R}{x} \; \frac{R/K}{x}$$
1 2 3 4 5 6

The last two books are K and R, so those two books will not be summarized. That eliminates **(A)** and **(C)** immediately. Because R is not summarized, N must be summarized (Rule 2). That eliminates **(E)**. With N summarized, it's impossible for F and T to both be summarized—otherwise, the first three books would all be summarized consecutively, violating Rule 1. That eliminates **(D)**, leaving **(B)** as the correct answer. For the record, O could certainly be summarized, with N summarized as the second book and no other book summarized.

$$\frac{F}{x} \; \frac{N}{s} \; \frac{T}{x} \; \frac{O}{s} \; \frac{K/R}{x} \; \frac{R/K}{x}$$
1 2 3 4 5 6

16. (D) Rule Substitution

For this question, Rule 4 will be removed and must be replaced by a new rule. The correct answer will be a rule that restores all of the original restrictions without adding any new restrictions. More specifically, the correct answer will reestablish that F precedes O and that O precedes K and R—in either order.

By the original rules, there was no need for T to be discussed third—it could also be discussed second, as it was in the sketch for **(E)** in the third question. That means **(A)** adds a new restriction, so it can be eliminated.

Also, T never had to be discussed before F. F could be the first book discussed, as was shown in the sketch for the fourth question. That means **(B)** adds a new restriction, so it can be eliminated.

If K and R were two of the last three books, that would still allow O to be discussed later than either one or both. That does not restore the restriction that O must be discussed before K and R, so **(C)** can be eliminated.

Establishing O as the fourth book discussed does restore one original condition. By Rule 3, N and T will still be discussed before O. That leaves only one space before O. If K and R are discussed consecutively, they could only be discussed in the last two weeks, after O. That restores the second half of the original Rule 4. With K and R in the last two spots and O discussed in week 4, that forces F to be discussed in one of the first three weeks, at any point before O. That completely restores the original rule without adding any new restrictions. That makes **(D)** the correct answer.

For the record, **(E)** establishes F as the third book discussed, which is a restriction that was never required originally. The sketch from the fourth question shows that F could be first, so it need not be third. That eliminates **(E)**.

Game 4: Paintings in a Museum

Step 1: Overview

Situation: A curator arranging paintings in a museum

Entities: Seven paintings (Morisot, Pissarro, Renoir, Sisley, Turner, Vuillard, Whistler)

Action: Strict Sequencing. Determine the order in which the paintings are arranged. The rules contain information about exact distances between entities and information about specific slots, so this is Strict Sequencing rather than Loose Sequencing.

Limitations: The pictures are hung in a horizontal row, so no two paintings will be placed above or below one another (i.e., equally distant from the entrance). In short, this is standard one-to-one Strict Sequencing.

Step 2: Sketch

The arrangement is described as a horizontal row, so it makes sense to set up a horizontal row of seven numbered slots. And because positions 1 and 7 are explicitly referred to as "closest to" and "furthest from" the entrance, respectively, it would be prudent to label your sketch appropriately. The paintings can be listed as the artists' initials.

```
        M P R S T V W
Close  ―――――――――――――――  Far
        1  2  3  4  5  6  7
```

Step 3: Rules

Rule 1 sets up some basic sequencing: the Turner will be closer to the entrance than the Whistler (i.e., in some spot before).

$$T \ldots W$$

That means T cannot be in position farthest from the entrance (7), and W cannot be closest (1). Draw "~ T" and "~ W" under the appropriate spaces.

Rule 2 sets up a stricter sequence: the Renoir must be closer to the entrance than the Morisot, but there must exactly one painting between them. Draw out this Block of Entities.

$$R \underline{\quad} M$$

Because at least two paintings (M and one other) have to be farther from the entrance than R, R cannot be in position 6 or 7. Similarly, M cannot be in either of the first two positions. Add "~ M" and "~ R" under the appropriate slots.

Rule 3 creates another Block of Entities: The Pissarro and the Sisley will be next to one another. However, there's no indication which one is closer to the entrance. Be sure to account for both possibilities.

$$\boxed{PS} \text{ or } \boxed{SP}$$

Rule 4 limits the placement of the Vuillard. If it isn't in position 3, then it must be in position 4. In other words, it can only be in one of those two positions. Build this into the sketch by putting arrows from V to positions 3 and 4.

Step 4: Deductions

Other than labeling where certain paintings cannot go based on Rules 1 and 2, there are no deductions to be had here. - Neither block from Rule 2 nor 3 is limited in its placement. And every entity is mentioned just once in the rules, so there is no way to combine the rules using Duplicates, and there are no Floaters. As for Rule 4, there is no use setting up Limited Options based on where the Vuillard goes. Either position allows for numerous arrangements with no concrete deductions.

With five "If" questions in a batch of seven questions, that's a sign that deductions will be minimal and that the questions will provide the information needed to complete the game. The Master Sketch should look something like this:

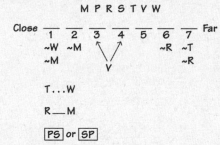

It is personal preference and continual practice that will help you determine whether or not writing all the negative deductions (for example the "~ R" under positions 6 and 7) is helpful for you or whether it unnecessarily crowds the sketch. Some test takers will want them there to remind them of the restrictions, but for others the shorthand of the rules (R __ M; T ... W) will be sufficient.

Step 5: Questions

17. (C) Acceptability

As with any Acceptability question, go through the rules and eliminate answers that violate them.

By Rule 1, the Turner must be closer to the entrance than the Whistler. That eliminates **(B)**, which has the Whistler closer to the entrance. By Rule 2, the Renoir must be closer to the entrance than the Morisot. That eliminates **(A)**, which has the Morisot closer to the entrance. By Rule 3, the Pissarro and the Sisley must be next to one another. That eliminates **(D)**, which places the Turner in between them. By Rule 4, the Vuillard could only be in position 3 or 4. That eliminates **(E)**, which places it second. That leaves **(C)** as the correct answer.

18. (A) "If" / Could Be True

For this question, the Sisley will be in the seventh position, which is farthest from the entrance. By Rule 3, that means the Pissarro must be in the sixth position.

$$\frac{}{1} \quad \frac{}{2} \quad \frac{}{3} \quad \frac{}{4} \quad \frac{}{5} \quad \frac{P}{6} \quad \frac{S}{7}$$

The question is asking for a possible position for the Turner. Because the Pissarro is in the sixth position, that eliminates **(E)**. And the Turner still has to be closer to the front than the Whistler, so it cannot be fifth. That eliminates **(D)**.

The Vuillard could still be in the third or fourth position, and there are three possible placements for the block of Renoir and Morisot. This question will require a little more testing.

The block will be more restrictive, so start by testing that out. The first possibility is to place the Renoir first and the Morisot third. That would mean the Vuillard would be fourth (Rule 4). That would leave the Turner to be second and the Whistler to be fifth.

$$\frac{R}{1} \quad \frac{T}{2} \quad \frac{M}{3} \quad \frac{V}{4} \quad \frac{W}{5} \quad \frac{P}{6} \quad \frac{S}{7}$$

That means the Turner could be second, making **(A)** the correct answer. For the record, if the Turner were third or fourth, then it and the Vuillard would be third and fourth, in some order. That would put the Whistler fifth (Rule 1), forcing the Renoir and the Morisot to be next to one another in the first two positions, violating Rule 2. That eliminates **(B)** and **(C)**.

$$\frac{R}{1} \quad \frac{M}{2} \quad \frac{T/V}{3} \quad \frac{V/T}{4} \quad \frac{W}{5} \quad \frac{P}{6} \quad \frac{S}{7}$$

19. (C) "If" / Must Be True

For this question, the Pissarro will be in the fifth position. That means the Sisley will be in either the fourth or sixth position (Rule 3). However, if the Sisley were in the fourth position, the Vuillard would be in the third position (Rule 4). That would leave positions 1 and 2 as well as 6 and 7 open. There would be no way to place the Renoir and the Morisot with only one painting in between. So, the Sisley cannot be placed in the fourth position.

I) $$\frac{}{1} \quad \frac{}{2} \quad \frac{V}{3} \quad \frac{S}{4} \quad \frac{P}{5} \quad \frac{}{6} \quad \frac{}{7}$$

II) $$\frac{}{1} \quad \frac{}{2} \quad \frac{}{3} \quad \frac{}{4} \quad \frac{P}{5} \quad \frac{S}{6} \quad \frac{}{7}$$

The Sisley must be placed in the sixth position. That makes **(C)** the correct answer.

For the record, if you did not spot that answer immediately, once Sisley is determined to be in the sixth position, there are two ways to place the Renoir and the Morisot. That would lead to the following two arrangements:

$$\frac{R}{1} \quad \frac{T}{2} \quad \frac{M}{3} \quad \frac{V}{4} \quad \frac{P}{5} \quad \frac{S}{6} \quad \frac{W}{7}$$

$$\frac{T}{1} \quad \frac{R}{2} \quad \frac{V}{3} \quad \frac{M}{4} \quad \frac{P}{5} \quad \frac{S}{6} \quad \frac{W}{7}$$

These options show why the remaining answers are all - possible, but none of them *must* be true.

20. (E) Could Be True EXCEPT

The correct answer to this question will be a painting that cannot be placed in the third position. The remaining answers all could be third.

There is no clear way to deduce this information, so answers will have to be tested. However, it is valuable to notice that none of these answers list the Vuillard. So, if any of these paintings are third, the Vuillard would have to fourth. That's a good place to start.

In that case, there are three possible ways to place the block of the Renoir and the Morisot. They could be placed in the first and third positions, which would make the Morisot third.

I) $$\frac{R}{1} \quad \frac{}{2} \quad \frac{M}{3} \quad \frac{V}{4} \quad \frac{}{5} \quad \frac{}{6} \quad \frac{}{7}$$

There's still room for the block of the Pissarro and the Sisley. So, the Morisot could be third, which eliminates **(A)**. (Note that this could also be determined easily by looking at sketches in any of the previous three questions).

The second way to place the Renoir and the Morisot is third and fifth, respectively:

II) $$\frac{}{1} \quad \frac{}{2} \quad \frac{R}{3} \quad \frac{V}{4} \quad \frac{M}{5} \quad \frac{}{6} \quad \frac{}{7}$$

This also allows the block of the Pissarro and the Sisley to be placed. So the Renoir could be third, which eliminates **(B)**.

Finally, the Renoir and the Morisot could be fifth and seventh.

III) $$\frac{}{1} \quad \frac{}{2} \quad \frac{}{3} \quad \frac{V}{4} \quad \frac{R}{5} \quad \frac{}{6} \quad \frac{M}{7}$$

In that case, the Pissarro and the Sisley would have to be two of the first three paintings. If they were second and third, then the Turner would be first and the Whistler sixth. If the Pissarro and Sisley were the first two, that would leave the Turner third and the Whistler sixth.

$$\frac{T}{1} \quad \frac{P/S}{2} \quad \frac{S/P}{3} \quad \frac{V}{4} \quad \frac{R}{5} \quad \frac{W}{6} \quad \frac{M}{7}$$

$$\frac{P/S}{1} \quad \frac{S/P}{2} \quad \frac{T}{3} \quad \frac{V}{4} \quad \frac{R}{5} \quad \frac{W}{6} \quad \frac{M}{7}$$

With that, either the Sisley or the Turner could be third, which eliminates **(C)** and **(D)**. In all of these cases, the Whistler can never be third. That makes **(E)** the correct answer.

While sketches from other questions can help a little, this is undoubtedly a time-consuming question. The best strategy may be to save this until the end and work on the remaining "If" questions first.

21. (A) "If" / Could Be True

For this question, the block of the Renoir and the Morisot will be placed in between the Turner and the Whistler, with the Turner closer to the entrance and the Whistler farther from the entrance (Rule 1).

T...R—M...W

Because the Pissarro and the Sisley must be next to one another, neither one of those could fill the single space between the Renoir and the Morisot. That leaves one painting that could fill that space: the Vuillard.

T...RVM...W

Because the Vuillard can only be placed third or fourth (Rule 4), consider both possibilities. If Vuillard was in the fourth position, then the Renoir and the Morisot would be in the third and fifth positions. The Turner would be in one of the first two positions, and the Whistler would be in one of the last two. However, that would leave no place for the Pissarro and the Sisley to be next to one another, violating Rule 3.

Thus, the only way to set this up is to place the Vuillard in the third position, with the Renoir and the Morisot in the second and fourth positions. In that case, the Turner will be in the first position, with the remaining paintings filling out the last three positions.

II) $\frac{T}{1} \quad \frac{R}{2} \quad \frac{V}{3} \quad \frac{M}{4} \quad \frac{}{5} \quad \frac{}{6} \quad \frac{}{7}$

With that, **(B)**, **(C)**, and **(D)** are observably false. While **(E)** may look possible, placing the Whistler sixth would split up the remaining two paintings—the Pissarro and the Sisley. That would violate Rule 3, making that answer impossible. Only **(A)** is possible, making it the correct answer.

22. (E) "If" / Must Be True

This question sets up a new Block of Entities: the Turner and the Whistler, in that order (Rule 1), must have exactly one painting in between them.

T—W

The painting in between cannot be the Pissarro or the Sisley (Rule 3). And it cannot be the Vuillard, because that would leave no independent painting that could be placed between the Renoir and the Morisot. So, the only paintings that could be placed between the Turner and the Whistler are the Renoir or the Morisot. Either one would set up a larger block of four paintings, like so:

TRWM or RTMW

To place such a large block, the Vuillard could no longer be in the fourth position. Otherwise, there would only be three consecutive positions on either side of it—not enough to

accommodate this block of four paintings. So, the Vuillard would have to be in the third position (Rule 4), making **(E)** the correct answer. For the record, once Vuillard is placed, there are two possible sketches:

I) $\frac{P/S}{1} \quad \frac{S/P}{2} \quad \frac{V}{3} \quad \frac{T}{4} \quad \frac{R}{5} \quad \frac{W}{6} \quad \frac{M}{7}$

II) $\frac{P/S}{1} \quad \frac{S/P}{2} \quad \frac{V}{3} \quad \frac{R}{4} \quad \frac{T}{5} \quad \frac{M}{6} \quad \frac{W}{7}$

These sketches show that **(D)** is impossible. **(A)**, **(B)**, and **(C)** are all possible, but only **(E)** *must* be true.

23. (B) "If" / Must Be True

For this question, the Turner is next to the Vuillard. By Rule 1, the Whistler must be placed in some position farther from the entrance than both of these. With two consecutive blocks (the Turner and the Vuillard, and the Pissarro and the Sisley by Rule 3), there is only one painting that could fill the single space between the Renoir and the Morisot: the Whistler. Therefore, this entire block must be placed farther from the entrance than the block of the Turner and the Vuillard.

T/V V/T ... R W M

The question asks for two paintings in which the first one listed *must* be closer to the entrance than the second one listed. Because the Renoir will certainly be closer to the entrance than the Whistler, **(B)** is the correct answer. For the record, the Pissarro and the Sisley could be in either order, which eliminates **(A)**. The Vuillard and the Turner could also be in either order, which eliminates **(C)** and **(D)**. And the Renoir must be placed closer to the entrance than the Whistler, not the other way around as it is in **(E)**. The following sketch shows enough possibilities to demonstrate why the remaining answers could all be false.

$\frac{P/S}{1} \quad \frac{S/P}{2} \quad \frac{V/T}{3} \quad \frac{T/V}{4} \quad \frac{R}{5} \quad \frac{W}{6} \quad \frac{M}{7}$

Section III: Logical Reasoning

Q#	Question Type	Correct	Difficulty
1	Flaw	C	★
2	Point at Issue	D	★
3	Paradox	B	★
4	Strengthen	E	★
5	Inference	C	★
6	Principle (Identify/Strengthen)	D	★
7	Flaw	A	★
8	Strengthen	C	★
9	Principle (Identify/Strengthen)	D	★★
10	Inference	A	★★
11	Assumption (Sufficient)	A	★★★
12	Main Point	A	★
13	Principle (Identify/Inference)	E	★
14	Assumption (Sufficient)	B	★★★
15	Parallel Flaw	A	★★
16	Strengthen (EXCEPT)	B	★★
17	Inference	C	★★★
18	Flaw	D	★★
19	Assumption (Necessary)	D	★★★
20	Flaw	B	★★
21	Weaken (EXCEPT)	A	★★★★
22	Strengthen	B	★★★★
23	Inference	E	★★★★
24	Parallel Reasoning	A	★★★
25	Strengthen	A	★★★
26	Paradox	E	★★★

1. (C) Flaw

Step 1: Identify the Question Type

The stem calls this argument's reasoning *misleading*, so this is a Flaw question. Identify what's interesting about the gap between the evidence and conclusion, and keep common flaws in mind.

Step 2: Untangle the Stimulus

The author concludes that banking with TekBank is more expensive than with GreenBank. The evidence is that TekBank charges a quarter for ATM transactions, while GreenBank ATM transactions are free.

Step 3: Make a Prediction

The flaw with this argument contains mismatched concepts: the conclusion makes a claim about banking in general, but the evidence talks about only one aspect of banking. Just because TekBank charges more for ATMs doesn't mean it's more expensive overall—there may be other services for which GreenBank charges more than TekBank does.

Step 4: Evaluate the Answer Choices

(C) matches the prediction by highlighting the difference between "overall cost" and "cost of one component."

(A) is Out of Scope. "Other factors" don't matter to a conclusion limited only to cost. Additionally, the conclusion isn't a recommendation, but merely an incorrect deduction.

(B) is a Distortion. While the argument's evidence is inadequate, it's not *irrelevant*. The evidence talks about cost, which is also what the conclusion references. Additionally, the advertisement is not trying to divert attention away from cost; if anything, it's trying to draw attention to it.

(D) describes a classic reasoning flaw—a parts-versus-whole flaw—but it's not the one you want. The author doesn't assume that everything at TekBank costs 25 cents, nor that everything at GreenBank is free.

(E) describes another classic flaw, the idea that the lack of evidence is evidence of the alternative. Unfortunately, that doesn't match the prediction. The author provides evidence, so an "absence of evidence" isn't part of the argument.

2. (D) Point at Issue

Step 1: Identify the Question Type

The stem asks you to identify the point on which Klein and Brown disagree. Both speakers must have an opinion about the correct answer, and those opinions must differ.

Step 2: Untangle the Stimulus

Klein thinks Einstein's theory is wrong because we've only been able to find one-tenth of the matter that the theory predicts. Brown thinks that Einstein's theory is likely right and that we just haven't found all of the matter in the galaxy yet.

Step 3: Make a Prediction

You can sometimes predict the point at issue by comparing the two speakers' conclusions. Klein thinks Einstein was wrong, while Brown thinks Einstein was right. This is where they disagree.

Step 4: Evaluate the Answer Choices

(D) matches the prediction. Klein wants to *abandon* Einstein's theory; Brown does not.

(A) is a 180. Both speakers agree on how much matter has been found.

(B) is Out of Scope. Klein never mentions the theory's successes, so he has no known opinion on this point.

(C) is Out of Scope. Klein indicates that Einstein's theory is not a good predictor, but he gives no information on whether he believes there are other theories that would provide that information. Likewise, although Brown is not ready to abandon Einstein's theory, that doesn't mean he might not think there are other theories that could also predict the amount of matter in the galaxy.

(E) is a Distortion. Because the speakers accept the amount of matter that has been found, they both implicitly accept scientists' accuracy.

3. (B) Paradox

Step 1: Identify the Question Type

The word *explain* signals the Paradox question type. Additionally, the question stem directs you to the paradox: the relationship between threat gestures and physical attacks.

Step 2: Untangle the Stimulus

When chimps get angry, they make threat gestures. But when they make threat gestures, they rarely attack. And when they attack, they rarely make threat gestures.

Step 3: Make a Prediction

The right answer should explain why chimps don't usually attack after making threat gestures, or vice versa, even though anger can give rise to both.

Step 4: Evaluate the Answer Choices

(B) matches the prediction. If threat gestures vent hostile feelings, then that would explain why chimps don't usually attack after making them.

(A) explains why chimps make threat gestures. However, it doesn't explain why chimps don't attack after making the gestures, so it's Out of Scope.

(C) is also Out of Scope. Other means of displaying aggression don't matter. The paradox is between the two: gestures and attacks.

(D) is another Out of Scope answer. Whether chimps respond to other chimps' threat gestures still doesn't explain why threat gestures don't escalate into attacks.

(E) is a 180.Instead of explaining the paradox, **(E)** deepens it by showing that chimps that make threat gestures the most are especially nonviolent.

4. (E) Strengthen

Step 1: Identify the Question Type

Because you need to find the choice that supports the stimulus (support flowing upward), this Is a Strengthen question. Find the answer choice that, if added to the evidence, would make the conclusion more likely to be true.

Step 2: Untangle the Stimulus

The author thinks the Magno-Blanket would likely help relieve arthritic pain in older dogs. The evidence is a hospital study, done on humans, in which a great deal of participants reported reduced joint pain after being treated with magnets. The study seems reliable because dogs and humans are physiologically similar and because the Magno-Blanket would mimic the conditions in the study.

Step 3: Make a Prediction

Any time an LSAT argument relies on a study, examine the study's parameters. Here, you're not told anything about the control group (that is, the participants who did *not* get treated with magnets). Thus, it's possible that everyone in the study saw improvement and that the use of magnets had nothing to do with it.

Step 4: Evaluate the Answer Choices

(E) matches the prediction. If people who were treated with magnets got better, while people who weren't didn't get better, then it's more likely that magnets actually had something to do with alleviating joint pain.

(A) is Out of Scope. This answer takes the argument further, *if* it's proved true. But it doesn't help strengthen the connection between the study and the effectiveness on dogs.

(B) is a 180. If it were true that magnets intensify pain signals, then that would weaken, not strengthen, the author's claim that magnets help reduce pain.

(C) is an Irrelevant Comparison. It doesn't matter how many other ways there are of alleviating pain for either dogs or humans; what matters is whether or not magnets alleviate pain.

(D) is Out of Scope. The study covers "severe joint pain" in general. Whether those who did not see reduced pain were at the low or high end of the severe scale doesn't affect the

argument that the magnets helped reduce pain for the group in general.

5. (C) Inference

Step 1: Identify the Question Type

Questions that ask you to fill in a blank with an argument's conclusion are Inference questions. The correct answer choice must stay within the scope of what you know is true based on the rest of the stimulus.

Step 2: Untangle the Stimulus

Some people argue that ads are bad because they change people's preferences. At the same time, classes in music and art appreciation change people's preferences, yet nobody would say that those classes are bad.

Step 3: Make a Prediction

The author presents an analogy that suggests ads aren't bad—or at least, that the mere fact that they change people's preferences doesn't make them bad.

Step 4: Evaluate the Answer Choices

(C) matches the prediction.

(A) is a 180. It contradicts the argument by implying that ads don't change consumers' preferences.

(B) is Out of Scope. The effects of ads on something other than changing people's preferences are not discussed.

(D) is Out of Scope. You don't know from the stimulus whether people's preferences are changed for better or worse. The stimulus is about whether the act of changing preferences *at all* (regardless of whether it's in a positive or negative way) is wrong or not.

(E) is another 180. The stimulus accepts, rather than denies, the fact that ads change people's preferences.

6. (D) Principle (Identify/Strengthen)

Step 1: Identify the Question Type

Your goal in this Principle question is to identify the general rule or idea that, if true, would make the argument stronger. Approach it like a Strengthen question.

Step 2: Untangle the Stimulus

The author recommends high school career counselors tell aspiring journalists what life is like for *typical* local newspaper reporters. The evidence is that students think of journalism as an international career, when in fact most journalists work on local stories for local papers.

Step 3: Make a Prediction

The argument's conclusion is targeted toward high school career counselors, who appear nowhere in the evidence. The evidence, meanwhile, is about students' misconceptions.

Thus, the author takes for granted that high school career counselors are obligated to correct students' expectations. Supporting this assumption would strengthen the argument.

Step 4: Evaluate the Answer Choices

(D) tasks counselors with disabusing students' "unrealistic conceptions," so it matches the prediction.

(A) is a Distortion. The author wants counselors to paint an accurate picture of journalism, not to *discourage* students from pursuing journalism entirely.

(B) is Extreme and Out of Scope. Nowhere does it say that becoming a journalist, even an international one, is *unattainable* nor does the stimulus discuss the irrelevant concept of maximizing happiness.

(C) is Out of Scope. The stimulus doesn't say what the "top level" of journalism is. Even if the author assumes that local reporters are on a lower level than international ones, then this would *counter* the stimulus, which wants counselors to *not* necessarily encourage students in their unrealistic, glamorous expectations.

(E) is also Out of Scope. The stimulus doesn't say that a career in journalism is "initially appealing" and later regrettable, just that the career in general doesn't match common conceptions.

7. (A) Flaw

Step 1: Identify the Question Type

The phrase "vulnerable to criticism" signals a Flaw question. Find the disconnect between the evidence and conclusion, and keep common flaws in mind.

Step 2: Untangle the Stimulus

The author thinks that marking crosswalks with roadway stripes and flashing lights is a waste of money. The evidence is that more injuries occur at crosswalks with these safety features than at crosswalks without them.

Step 3: Make a Prediction

The author overlooks the possibility that roadway stripes and flashing lights were installed at crosswalks that had a record of higher injuries. It's possible that without such safety features, injury rates at these dangerous crosswalks would be even higher.

Step 4: Evaluate the Answer Choices

(A) matches the prediction.

(B) is a Faulty Use of Detail. The author does indeed imply that safety features that don't work ("so-called safety features") are a waste of money. But that assumption is reasonable. That the author assumes ineffective safety devices are a waste of money is not the problem with the argument; the problem is that the author thinks the devices

are ineffective in the first place. Watch out for answer choices that describe the argument correctly without hitting on an actual flaw.

(C) is Out of Scope. The argument cares only about roadway stripes and flashing lights; the cost and efficacy of other safety features is irrelevant.

(D) is also Out of Scope. While the author doesn't mention other safety features, that lack is not a flaw in the argument. Whether those other features exist or no, the author's argument could still be valid.

(E) is an Irrelevant Comparison. The severity of injuries is unimportant to this argument, which is about the *number* of injuries only. Additionally, the argument is not concerned about injuries to the occupants of cars. The relevant information is about whether the safety features are effective at reducing pedestrian injuries and whether the features are worth the cost.

8. (C) Strengthen

Step 1: Identify the Question Type

This is a classic Strengthen question stem. Find the answer choice that, if added to the evidence, makes the author's conclusion more likely to be true.

Step 2: Untangle the Stimulus

The author concludes that the sighting of an aurora borealis in Korea helps confirm John of Worcester's earlier sighting of two large sunspots. The evidence is that the aurora borealis happened five days after John sighted the sunspots and that sunspot activity typically precedes an aurora borealis by an average of five days.

Step 3: Make a Prediction

Based on the stimulus, you know that sunspots are usually followed by an aurora borealis, but you *don't* know if an aurora borealis only occurs after sunspot activity. (Take care never to bring outside information to the LSAT, no matter how much science you know.) The author takes for granted that nothing other than sunspots caused the aurora borealis in Korea. The correct choice will strengthen the argument by supporting this assumption.

Step 4: Evaluate the Answer Choices

(C) strengthens the argument by confirming that sunspots, and only sunspots, could have caused the aurora borealis in Korea.

(A) is a 180. If the Korean aurora borealis might have just randomly appeared, then the argument is weakened.

(B) is an Irrelevant Comparison. Ancient sunspot sightings don't matter to this argument, which only cares about the sunspots sighted by John of Worcester on December 8, 1128, and their relationship to the Korean aurora borealis.

(D) is Out of Scope. This information is interesting but not logically relevant to the argument, because "unusual weather conditions" don't help discern whether John's sightings were accurate or not. Additionally, this choice doesn't strengthen the connection between the sunspots and the aurora borealis in Korea.

(E) is also interesting but irrelevant. John's drawings don't matter, only the accuracy of his sightings and whether the Korean aurora borealis acted as affirmative proof or no.

9. (D) Principle (Identify/Strengthen)

Step 1: Identify the Question Type

The phrase "following principles" signals an Identify the Principle question. Additionally, because it will *justify* the argument, you need to pick the one that makes the conclusion more likely.

Step 2: Untangle the Stimulus

This stimulus is extremely abstract and wordy and therefore a possible candidate for initially skipping. The author concludes that if you want to make society better, then you shouldn't believe that society's future will be defined solely by things that people can't change. The evidence is that if you think a single person can't affect the future of society, then you'll feel too helpless to do anything to make society better.

Step 3: Make a Prediction

Because this Principle question emulates a Strengthen question, look for mismatched concepts in the argument to zero in on the assumption. The conclusion talks about people who "want to improve society," but the evidence doesn't. The evidence, meanwhile, talks about "feeling helpless," while the conclusion doesn't. The belief that an individual can't affect society's future appears in both the evidence and conclusion, though it's phrased slightly differently in each.

The assumption, then, is that if you want to improve society, then you shouldn't do anything that would make you feel helpless. The right choice will be a principle that props up this assumption.

Another way to spot the mismatched concepts is through Formal Logic.

Evidence:

If	~ believe in individual	→	feel helpless

Conclusion:

If	want to improve society	→	reject belief that future entirely determined by forces individuals are powerless to change

The conclusion can be rewritten as:

Conclusion:

If	want to improve society	→	believe in individual

Then upon taking the contrapositive of the evidence, you can get the same term on the necessary side of both the evidence and conclusion:

Evidence:

If	~ feel helpless	→	believe in individual

Conclusion:

If	want to improve society	→	believe in individual

That leads to the assumption that:

If	want to improve society	→	~ feel helpless

Step 4: Evaluate the Answer Choices

(D) can be restated as "If you want to improve society, then you shouldn't accept a belief that makes you feel helpless," which matches the prediction. Remember, a statement in the form "No one who X should Y" translates into "If X → ~ Y."

(A) is Out of Scope. The author's conclusion is about what people should do *if* they want to improve society, but she makes no statement that people *should* act to change to society. Additionally, **(A)** doesn't mention the mismatched concept from the evidence about beliefs that make a person feel helpless.

(B) is a Faulty Use of Detail. It recycles concepts from the evidence without properly connecting them to the conclusion. **(B)** can be rephrased as "If one rejects the belief that society's future will be determined by vast historical forces, then one should believe individuals *can* have an effect on it." That makes no connection to either wanting to improve society or to feeling helpless.

(C) is a Distortion. It tells you what happens *after* a person already feels helpless, not what may or may not make a person feel helpless in the first place.

(E), like **(A)**, is Out of Scope. It makes a recommendation that individuals *should* act to improve society, as opposed to making a recommendation about what to do *if* they want to improve society. **(E)** can also be seen as a Distortion. The Step 3 prediction was "If one wants to improve society, then one should reject beliefs that make one feel helpless," whereas **(E)** says, "If one feels helpless, then one should act to improve society." So it reverses and distorts the terms.

10. (A) Inference

Step 1: Identify the Question Type

The word *inferred* points to an Inference question. Inventory the facts and make any possible deductions. Choose the answer that stays within the scope of the stimulus.

Step 2: Untangle the Stimulus

The company president says that subcontracting leads to a loss of control over quality. The company does some subcontracting, but only with companies that maintain complete control over quality.

Step 3: Make a Prediction

It isn't always possible to make an exact prediction on Inference questions, but you should do so any time the opportunity presents itself. Here, you can deduce that the companies that are subcontracted must not do any subcontracting of their own. If they did, they'd lose some control, and the company president states that those companies maintain complete control.

Step 4: Evaluate the Answer Choices

(A) matches the prediction.

(B) is Out of Scope. The stimulus says companies who subcontract lose some control over quality, but not that they are necessarily "often disappointed" in the quality.

(C) is a 180. The company president admits that subcontracting work means some control is lost. The president also admits that the company subcontracts. If the president insisted on having as much control as possible, then, by definition, the company wouldn't subcontract.

(D) is Out of Scope. The stimulus gives no information about consumers.

(E) is a Distortion. Just because a company that subcontracts has less control over a product's quality doesn't mean the quality will be inferior. It's possible that the subcontractor has a higher commitment to quality than does the original company.

11. (A) Assumption (Sufficient)

Step 1: Identify the Question Type

The words *if* and *assumed* signal a Sufficient Assumption question. You need to find the choice that, if true, would guarantee the truth of the conclusion. Keep an eye out for Formal Logic, which often appears in Sufficient Assumption questions.

Step 2: Untangle the Stimulus

The author concludes that if students don't achieve broad mastery of the curriculum, then they must not be getting taught by the appropriate methods. In Formal Logic, the conclusion is:

If	~ broad mastery	→	~ appropriate methods

The evidence is that students who devote significant effort and are taught with appropriate methods will achieve broad mastery. In Formal Logic, that is:

If	significant effort AND appropriate methods	→	broad mastery

The contrapositive of this evidence is:

If	~ broad mastery	→	~ significant effort OR ~ appropriate methods

Step 3: Make a Prediction

To see the gap in the argument, compare the conclusion to the contrapositive of the evidence, because they both have the same trigger:

Evidence:

If	~ broad mastery	→	~ significant effort OR ~ appropriate methods

Conclusion:

If	~ broad mastery	→	~ appropriate methods

According to the evidence, a lack of mastery implies a lack of methods OR a lack of effort. The conclusion, however, claims that the result must be a lack of methods. The author ignores the possibility that some students are simply not working hard. To guarantee the conclusion, the right choice must remove the possibility that a lack of mastery could be caused by a lack of effort.

Step 4: Evaluate the Answer Choices

(A) matches the prediction. This choice guarantees that students who have the appropriate methods work hard.

If	appropriate methods	→	significant effort

If that is the case, then any student who doesn't work hard must lack the appropriate methods. If you add this to the evidence, it guarantees the conclusion because anytime the appropriate methods are there, the effort is sure to follow.

(B) is a Distortion of the Formal Logic in the evidence. The evidence says that appropriate methods together with effort are *sufficient* to guarantee broad mastery, not that the two of them are both *necessary*.

(C), like **(B)**, distorts the Formal Logic of the evidence. **(C)** would translate as:

If	~ appropriate methods	→	~ broad mastery

Or contraposed:

If	broad mastery	→	appropriate methods

Both of which are an incorrect contrapositive of the conclusion. This would indicate that appropriate methods are necessary to have broad mastery, but they don't help prove appropriate methods are sufficient, as the conclusion claims.

(D) is a Faulty Use of Detail. It follows from the evidence that appropriate methods are not sufficient by themselves to guarantee broad mastery (students also need to devote significant effort). Additionally, **(D)** actually contradicts the conclusion. The contrapositive of the conclusion says that appropriate methods *are* sufficient to guarantee broad mastery. Formal Logic that contradicts the conclusion certainly cannot guarantee it.

(E), like **(D)**, follows from the evidence. Effort alone is not sufficient to guarantee broad mastery. The first sentence indicates that it takes both effort *and* appropriate methods. Unlike **(D)** though, **(E)** does not contradict the conclusion, but it still does not provide a sufficient assumption.

12. (A) Main Point

Step 1: Identify the Question Type

The stem asks you to identify the argument's conclusion, so this is a Main Point question. Ask yourself which part of the argument is supported by the rest, and be wary of conclusion Keywords.

Step 2: Untangle the Stimulus

The first sentence contains the argument's conclusion: Just because one can is heavier than another doesn't mean it holds more food. Though there are no Keywords to indicate structure, the rest of the stimulus answers *why* that is the case. Basically, it's because the amount of water in the can will affect the overall weight.

Step 3: Make a Prediction

Since this is a Main Point question, finding the conclusion is all you have to do. Make sure that you don't pick a choice that strays beyond the argument's conclusion: Heavier food cans may not contain more food.

Step 4: Evaluate the Answer Choices

(A) is a paraphrase of the first sentence, which is the argument's conclusion.

(B) is a piece of evidence, not the conclusion. It supports the idea that a can's weight is not based solely on the amount of food in it.

(C) has an emphasis Keyword (*unscrupulous*), but it is just another piece of evidence. The information about the amount of food in a can does not support this statement. On the contrary, this statement is used to support the notion that the ratio of food and water in cans is not standardized.

(D) is implied by the last sentence of the argument, which is a piece of evidence.

(E) is implied by the conclusion, but is not the conclusion itself. **(E)** mentions the quantity of water but not the quantity of food, which is a central part of the conclusion.

13. (E) Principle (Identify/Inference)

Step 1: Identify the Question Type

Principles are illustrated by examples. Additionally, the word *proposition* is sometimes used in Principle question stems. This stem indicates that the choices are principles while the stimulus is an example, so this is an Identify the Principle question. The correct answer will be broader than the specific situation in the stimulus.

Step 2: Untangle the Stimulus

Under normal conditions, nobody in a group of three-year-olds could memorize his or her phone number, despite knowing the names of all the digits. When their phone numbers were taught to them as part of a song, however, all of the kids were able to remember their numbers.

Step 3: Make a Prediction

The stimulus provides a single instance in which music served as an effective mnemonic device. Look for an answer choice that says the same, without becoming too extreme.

Step 4: Evaluate the Answer Choices

(E) fits the stimulus without overstating it. It says that songs help kids remember the order of words. (Note that numbers are words.)

(A) is Extreme. The stimulus shows songs can help improve children's memory, not that songs are the *only* thing that will help children learn some things.

(B) is a Distortion. The children knew all the words they needed; they just couldn't remember a specific sequence of words. Note that this choice mentions neither sequences nor music, while also introducing the Out of Scope term *concept*.

(C) is Extreme. The stimulus shows that songs are effective in one case, not that they are more effective than anything else.

(D) is Out of Scope. Counting is mentioned in the stimulus, but *meaning* is not. Even if you believe the ability to count implies understanding the meaning of the numbers, like **(B)**, this choice fails to mention both sequences and music. Those things were central to the author's narrative, whereas counting was only mentioned as background information to indicate the kids knew enough about numbers to memorize a phone number.

14. (B) Assumption (Sufficient)

Step 1: Identify the Question Type

The words "if ... assumed" signal a Sufficient Assumption question. The right choice is an assumption whose truth would guarantee the truth of the conclusion.

Step 2: Untangle the Stimulus

Thus in the final sentence signals the conclusion: some theorists have picked an inappropriate goal for literary criticism. This goal is stated in the first sentence, which is that literary critics should try to be value-neutral. The author thinks this is a bad goal because criticism can't be *completely* value-neutral.

Note that the second sentence of the argument, which takes up the bulk of the stimulus, merely provides the reasoning of some theorists. It ends up having nothing to do with the logical content of the author's argument.

Step 3: Make a Prediction

This argument hinges on subtle mismatched concepts. The theorists say that critics should *strive* to be value-neutral. The author's counter-evidence is that being *completely* value-neutral is impossible. Just because something is impossible doesn't mean someone shouldn't strive for it, but for some reason, the author thinks differently. In other words, the author assumes that impossible goals are inappropriate.

Step 4: Evaluate the Answer Choices

(B) matches the prediction. It's the only choice that even tries to connect the two halves of the author's scope shift: whether something is possible and whether it should be pursued.

(A) is a 180. The author doesn't think that any literary critic should try to be value-neutral.

(C) is an Irrelevant Comparison. In no way does a critic's likelihood of providing criticism figure into the argument.

(D) is a Faulty Use of Detail. It deals with the second sentence of the stimulus, which isn't part of the author's argument.

(E), like **(D)**, talks about readers, which are mentioned in the second sentence, but are irrelevant to the author's argument. So it is an Irrelevant Comparison to discuss whether one group of critics influences readers more than another group of critics. While some theorists are concerned with literary criticism's effect on readers, the author is only concerned with literary criticism itself.

15. (A) Parallel Flaw

Step 1: Identify the Question Type

The phrase "most similar" signals a Parallel Reasoning question, and since the stimulus exhibits "flawed reasoning," it is a Parallel Flaw question.

Step 2: Untangle the Stimulus

The author concludes that all microscopic organisms can feel pain. The evidence is that amoebas and humans both withdraw from stimuli that cause damage, and humans do this because they feel pain.

Step 3: Make a Prediction

The reasoning is flawed for two reasons. First, amoebas might withdraw from stimuli that cause damage for other reasons. Just because pain happens to be the thing that causes humans to avoid damage doesn't mean other reasons don't exist. Second, the author incorrectly generalizes from amoebas to all microscopic organisms—it's possible that amoebas are unique in some way.

Since this is a Parallel Flaw question, it may be helpful to outline the structure of the argument:

P and Q both do X. M do it because of Y. Therefore, R can also do Y.

The correct choice will have the same structure.

Step 4: Evaluate the Answer Choices

(A) has the same flawed structure: Poets (P) and hypnotized people (Q) both use language oddly (X). Q do it because of lower inhibitions (Y). Therefore, artists (R) also have Y. This choice not only has the same structure, but also generalizes from poets to artists.

(B) doesn't have the same scope shift as the stimulus: the evidence and conclusion both talk about corporations. Furthermore, the conclusion is about "most" corporations, whereas the conclusion in the stimulus is about *all* microscopic organisms. Numeric qualifiers such as *most* and *all* must match in Parallel Reasoning questions. Finally, the conclusion states that something is *probably* true, whereas the stimulus's conclusion states that something *must* be true. Qualifiers such as *probably* and *must* need to match in Parallel Reasoning questions as well.

(C) also has qualifications that are absent in the stimulus. The evidence is about *most* athletes; the conclusion states that something is *probably* the case. The stimulus, by contrast, is all certainty. Additionally, rather than discussing two dissimilar groups (like humans and amoebas), this choice compares two types of a larger group: boxers and skaters are both professional athletes.

(D) also has extra qualifiers. The evidence says that *some* predators have a feature; the conclusion says that something is *probably* true. The stimulus's argument always uses *all* and *must.* Additionally, in the stimulus, the group in the conclusion is broader than that in the evidence (microscopic organisms versus amoebas). In this choice, the scope shift is reversed; it shrinks from predatory birds to hawks. Finally, unlike the stimulus, this choice doesn't attribute to hawks the *reason* mammals hunt alone (there is not enough food to support a pack in one area), but rather attributes the *action* (hunting alone).

(E) has one qualifier that the stimulus lacks: *partly.* In the stimulus, humans don't avoid damage *partly* because of pain—pain is the entire reason. Additionally, *hikers* is not a broad group that includes British Columbian hiking trails, so **(E)** does not contain the same scope shift as that in the stimulus.

16. (B) Strengthen (EXCEPT)

Step 1: Identify the Question Type

The structure "if true, supports ... EXCEPT" signals a Strengthen EXCEPT question. The right choice will either weaken the argument or have no effect.

Step 2: Untangle the Stimulus

Although the stimulus is very long and involved, the vast majority of it is background information that isn't directly part of the argument. Narrow in on the conclusion to help direct your analysis. The author concludes that cyclical sunspot activity is a causal factor of the cyclical nature of the snowshoe hare population. The evidence is that sunspots and the hare's population cycle are well correlated.

Step 3: Make a Prediction

Any time an author argues that one thing causes another, the assumption is always the same: that nothing else could be the cause. Any fact that rules out an alternate cause or reinforces the connection between sunspots and hares would strengthen the argument; any fact that introduces a possible alternate cause would weaken the argument.

Step 4: Evaluate the Answer Choices

(B) introduces an alternate cause (local weather patterns) that could affect the hare population. This answer doesn't help explain why the hare populations everywhere behave cyclically simultaneously, so it's not a very good weakener, but it doesn't need to be good in order to be correct. Your requirements are a choice that weakens or does nothing. This choice certainly doesn't strengthen the argument, so it's the right choice.

(A) strengthens the argument by connecting sunspots to a critical element of the population cycle (predator reproduction).

(C) supports the argument by showing how sunspots can cause the hare population to decline.

(D) supports the argument by tightening the correlation between sunspot cycles and hare population cycles. Not only are the cycles correlated, but the extent of those highs and lows are correlated.

(E) also strengthens the argument. If sunspots affect how much nutrition the hares are receiving from their food, then that would affect how many of the hares are able to survive.

17. (C) Inference

Step 1: Identify the Question Type

The stimulus supports the answer choices, so this is an Inference question. Take care not to mistake this for a Strengthen question, in which the right choice would support the stimulus. Inventory the statements and keep an eye out for Formal Logic, making any possible deductions.

Step 2: Untangle the Stimulus

This stimulus is full of Formal Logic. Use the words that indicate necessity—*essential*, *requires*, and *necessary*—to ensure that you translate the statements correctly:

If	successful economy	→	flourishing national science community
If	flourishing national science community	→	young people excited
If	young people excited	→	good communication

Step 3: Make a Prediction

Connect the chain of Formal Logic statements to produce the following:

If	successful economy	→	flourishing national science community	→	young people excited	→	good communication

Deduction:

If	successful economy	→	good communication

You can deduce, therefore, that good communication between scientists and the public is necessary for a successful economy. Likewise, you can deduce the contrapositive that if there is not good communication, there will not be a successful economy.

Step 4: Evaluate the Answer Choices

(C), when translated into Formal Logic, states the prediction exactly.

(A) incorrectly reverses the Formal Logic of Sentence 3.

(B) is Extreme. While the stimulus provides necessary conditions, it never describes the *extent* to which one thing depends on another, nor does it argue that anything depends *principally* on anything else. Degrees of dependence are never discussed in the stimulus.

(D) is also Extreme. The stimulus shows that *many* (at least 1) young people need to get excited about science, not *most* (more than half). Additionally, although more subtle, the stimulus only addresses what is essential for a *successful* economy, whereas **(D)** indicates what is essential for a nation's economy in general, whether successful or not.

(E) is Out of Scope. The stimulus never talks about the success of scientific endeavors. So although communication was mentioned as a requirement for sparking interest in young people, it was not mentioned as a requirement for the success of scientific endeavors.

18. (D) Flaw

Step 1: Identify the Question Type

The stem asks you to identify why the argument is flawed. Keep common flaws in mind.

Step 2: Untangle the Stimulus

The author concludes that, contrary to a recent article, businesses that don't already have videoconferencing equipment wouldn't be wasting their money if they bought it. As evidence, the author puts forward the results of a survey: most of the survey's respondents, all of whom worked for businesses that *did* buy the equipment, said that the equipment was worth the money.

Step 3: Make a Prediction

Any time you see a survey used as evidence on the LSAT, consider whether the survey group is representative of the conclusion group. Here it's not even close: the conclusion makes a claim about businesses that *don't* have the equipment, while the survey only covered businesses that *do* have the equipment. There may be reasons it was previously worthwhile to buy but no longer is.

Step 4: Evaluate the Answer Choices

(D) matches the prediction by pointing out the argument's flaw of representativeness.

(A) is a Distortion. The author does not base the conclusion *merely* on the fact that many businesses bought it. The author's evidence is that most businesses that bought the equipment really liked it (at least according to the survey, it was "well worth the cost.")

(B) describes a classic reasoning flaw: confusing necessary with sufficient. However, the flaw in the stimulus is one of representativeness, not necessity and sufficiency. Additionally, the argument doesn't discuss what conditions (regardless of whether they're sufficient or necessary) would justify the purchase of videoconferencing equipment.

(C) does not describe the argument correctly. The author does not accuse the magazine article of providing insufficient evidence. On the contrary, the author offers counterevidence of a recent survey.

(E) is another inaccurate description. The author maintains a clear distinction between what the equipment costs and whether that cost is worth it for its purchasers.

19. (D) Assumption (Necessary)

Step 1: Identify the Question Type

The phrase "assumption required" signals a Necessary Assumption question. You can use the Denial Test to check your answer.

Step 2: Untangle the Stimulus

The auditor concludes that none of the 20 trucks that XYZ purchased three years ago were diesel-powered. The evidence is that XYZ sold every diesel truck the company owned last year, but none of the 20 trucks purchased three years ago were sold last year.

Step 3: Make a Prediction

Note the subtle gap in this argument: the trucks were bought three years ago, but the sales figures in the evidence only cover last year. This leaves a two-year gap. The auditor assumes, therefore, that none of the trucks in question were sold two or more years ago.

Step 4: Evaluate the Answer Choices

(D) matches the prediction. If some of the trucks were sold two years ago, for example, then they could have been diesel-powered.

(A) is Extreme. What matters is that *every* diesel truck was sold last year; it doesn't matter if other types of trucks were sold as well.

(B) is Out of Scope. This argument cares only about how the trucks were powered, not whether they were new or used.

(C) is also Out of Scope. The purchase history of other trucks besides the 20 under discussion is irrelevant as to whether those 20 were diesel-powered or not.

(E) is another Out of Scope answer. The trucks under discussion were bought three years ago; what trucks, if any, were bought *more* than three years ago makes no difference to this argument.

20. (B) Flaw

Step 1: Identify the Question Type

The phrase "most vulnerable to criticism" signals a Flaw question. Identify what's wrong with the gap between the evidence and conclusion, and keep common flaws in mind.

Step 2: Untangle the Stimulus

Taylor concludes that telepathy is possible. Her evidence is the *amazing* frequency with which good friends and family members know each other's thoughts.

Step 3: Make a Prediction

Whenever an author claims that one thing is the reason or explanation for another, the assumption is always the same: that there are no alternative explanations. In this argument, that assumption is a bad one. Good friends and family members probably know each other's thoughts because they know each other well, not because of telepathy.

Step 4: Evaluate the Answer Choices

(B) hits the nail on the head by pointing out that Taylor has overlooked a "highly plausible alternative explanation." Specifically that explanation is that good friends and family members know each other well enough that they can anticipate one another's thoughts and feelings.

(A) is Out of Scope. It describes a representativeness flaw, which is not at play here. The stimulus gives no indication as to the size of the author's sample.

(C) is a Distortion. The evidence talks about feelings, but the argument isn't based on them. It's based on the high frequency of a particular phenomenon.

(D) is Out of Scope. Taylor says friends' and family members' feelings can be knowable, not that strangers' feelings cannot be.

(E) describes a circular argument, that is, one whose evidence and conclusion are the same. While this is a classic flaw, it is not the flaw here. The argument's conclusion is different from its evidence.

21. (A) Weaken (EXCEPT)

Step 1: Identify the Question Type

This is a classic Weaken question stem with EXCEPT tacked on to the end. The correct answer will either strengthen the argument or have no effect.

Step 2: Untangle the Stimulus

The author concludes that sulfur fumes permanently damage one's sense of smell. The evidence is an experiment in which workers from sulfur-emitting factories did much worse at identifying scents than workers from other occupations did.

Step 3: Make a Prediction

Whenever you see an experiment used as evidence on the LSAT, examine its parameters to make sure it was properly designed and conducted. Here, you don't know anything about the test groups besides the fact that one group worked with sulfur and the other didn't. For the results to be valid,

the two groups must have been identical in all other respects, but the stimulus doesn't confirm this.

Hence, any indication that the sulfur group was at a disadvantage (for reasons other than sulfur exposure) or that the control group had an advantage would weaken the argument. Because this is a Weaken EXCEPT question, the right choice will provide no such indication.

Step 4: Evaluate the Answer Choices

(A) has no effect on the argument, so it's the right answer. If the scents were imprecisely reproduced, that wouldn't necessarily give either group an advantage or a disadvantage in the experiment.

(B) weakens the argument by pointing out a major difference between the two groups: The sulfur group had to distinguish smells in the presence of sulfur fumes, while the other group did not.

(C) weakens the argument by pointing out an advantage for the control group. If most of the non-sulfur workers had prior experience distinguishing smells, then that might explain why they performed better in the experiment.

(D) weakens the argument by pointing out that other fumes, not sulfur, might be the cause of the sulfur workers' damaged sense of smell.

(E) points out a possible disadvantage for the sulfur group. If they were unfamiliar with some of the smells to begin with, then that might explain why they did worse in the experiment.

22. (B) Strengthen

Step 1: Identify the Question Type

The word *principle* and the fact that the principle is in the stimulus, not the answer choices, indicates this may be an Apply the Principle question. However, the principle is also already applied in the Application part of the stimulus. So, the combination of a Principle/Application stimulus and the question stem calling for an answer choice that *justifies* the specific application of the principle makes this a variant on a Strengthen question. Treat the Application as a conclusion and the stated Principle as evidence. The correct answer will strengthen the assumption that ties the two together.

Step 2: Untangle the Stimulus

The Principle outlines a set of conditions under which a person would have to pay a fine: the person has more than one overdue book, at least one of the overdue books is not a children's book, and the person has previously been fined for overdue books.

The Application concludes that Kessler, who has three overdue books, must be fined.

Step 3: Make a Prediction

Kessler meets only the first of the three conditions. Thus, to justify the Application, you'd have to know that Kessler meets the other two as well: that at least one of the overdue books is not a children's book and that Kessler has previously been fined.

Step 4: Evaluate the Answer Choices

(B) matches the prediction by confirming that the other two conditions apply to Kessler.

(A) may initially look right, but on close examination it is slightly off from the prediction. **(A)** says Kessler has a non-children's book out on loan, but doesn't say for sure whether it is one of the overdue books. Based on the conditions in the principle, the non-children's book would need to be one of the overdue books in order for a fine to be necessary.

(C) fails to confirm the third condition—that Kessler has been fined for overdue books in the past.

(D) says nothing about Kessler's *current* overdue books, so it fails to confirm the second condition.

(E) is a 180. By stating that Kessler has never before been fined, **(E)** guarantees that the third condition doesn't apply to Kessler. Thus, it does not justify the Application that Kessler should now be fined for his current overdue books.

23. (E) Inference

Step 1: Identify the Question Type

The stimulus supports the answer choices, so this is an Inference question. Take care not to mistake this for a Strengthen question, in which the right choice would support the stimulus. Inventory the facts and make any deductions possible.

Step 2: Untangle the Stimulus

The professor takes a grim view of the current state of medicine. Patients' feelings that doctors are negligent or careless spur most malpractice suits. Meanwhile, doctors are uncompassionate and rude to their patients, due to both how doctors perceive medicine (as a science) and stress. Sadly, economic incentives encourage doctors to continue being rude.

Step 3: Make a Prediction

No prediction leaps out from this stimulus, which will sometimes be the case on Inference questions. Keep the information from the stimulus firmly in mind as you read the choices, and only pick a choice if it absolutely must be true.

Step 4: Evaluate the Answer Choices

(E) paraphrases the stimulus, which says that doctors " ... now regard medicine as a science ... and are less compassionate as a result." So, many doctors *have* taken an action (regarding medicine as science) that has led to the perception that they care less about people, which is akin to lacking compassion.

(A) is Extreme. You know that economic incentives are a cause for rude behavior, not that they are the *main* cause of that behavior, let alone the main cause of malpractice suits.

(B) is a Distortion, combining two unrelated parts of the stimulus. The incentives encourage doctors to act rudely; the stimulus doesn't say what causes doctors to view medicine as a science rather than an art.

(C) is Out of Scope. The stimulus doesn't say how many of the malpractice suits are justified or not.

(D) is Extreme. The author suggests that viewing medicine as a science is problematic, but doesn't go so far as to recommend that the ideal approach should be "entirely different."

24. (A) Parallel Reasoning

Step 1: Identify the Question Type

The phrase "most closely parallel in its reasoning" signals a Parallel Reasoning question.

Step 2: Untangle the Stimulus

The several instances of the word *if* calls out that this is a Formal Logic stimulus. Map out the Formal Logic sentence by sentence:

| If | poured while wet | → | ~ solid foundation |

| If | ~ solid foundation | → | settle unevenly OR crack |

Conclusion:

| If | settle evenly | → | ~ poured while wet OR crack |

Step 3: Make a Prediction

Notice that the two pieces of evidence set up a chain. Combined, they indicate:

| If | poured while wet | → | settle unevenly OR crack |

The conclusion, however, doesn't state this deduction. Instead, it says that if one of the necessary conditions does *not* occur (settle evenly), then either the sufficient condition (poured while wet) or the other necessary condition (crack) must occur.

The right choice will have the same structure.

Algebraically it is:

| If | W (wet) | → | ~ X (solid foundation) | → | Y (settle unevenly) OR Z (crack) |

$$\text{If} \quad \sim Y \quad \rightarrow \quad \sim W \text{ (dry) or } Z$$

(Note: This argument is not sound, as the Formal Logic in the evidence does not allow you to deduce anything from just the fact that concrete settles evenly. If it settled unevenly *and* didn't crack, then you would know the concrete was poured in while the ground was dry.)

Step 4: Evaluate the Answer Choices

(A) has the same Formal Logic structure as the stimulus.

$$\text{If} \quad W \text{ (camera not working)} \quad \rightarrow \quad \sim X \text{ (properly exposed)} \quad \rightarrow \quad Y \text{ (blurred) OR } Z \text{ (dark)}$$

$$\text{If} \quad \sim Y \quad \rightarrow \quad \sim W \text{ (camera is working) OR } Z$$

(B) can't be right because neither the evidence nor the conclusion matches. The evidence lines up like this:

$$\text{If} \quad \text{working properly} \quad \rightarrow \quad \sim \text{blurred} \quad \rightarrow \quad \text{properly exposed AND properly developed}$$

It incorrectly includes an *and* instead of an *or*. Also, the conclusion reintroduces the original sufficient condition (working properly), rather than negating one of the necessary conditions. The conclusion also includes an *and* statement rather than an *or* statement. Finally, unlike the original stimulus, **(B)** is unflawed so it can't be parallel.

(C) doesn't match because the conclusion is a basic Formal Logic statement without an *or*, whereas the stimulus's conclusion is a compound Formal Logic statement ending with an *or*. Additionally, the evidence doesn't link up into a chain: there are only three items in **(C)**: working properly, blurred, and dark. The stimulus, however, has four items.

(D), like **(C)**, ends with a conclusion that lacks an *or* in its necessary condition. Additionally, the evidence does not line up in the correct manner. Here, the algebraic structure is this:

$$\text{If} \quad W \text{ (working properly)} \quad \rightarrow \quad X \text{ (exposed)}$$

$$\text{If} \quad X \text{ OR } Y \text{ (corrections made)} \quad \rightarrow \quad \sim Z \text{ (developed)}$$

$$\text{If} \quad X \quad \rightarrow \quad \sim Z$$

(E) is the closest of the wrong choices. The evidence lays out nearly exactly like the evidence of the stimulus, except the final term in the chain has an *and* instead of an *or*. Also, the conclusion translates to:

$$\text{If} \quad \text{too much light OR too little light} \quad \rightarrow \quad \sim \text{work properly}$$

Note that the *or* occurs in the sufficient condition rather than in the necessary condition like the stimulus. Also, this answer, unlike the stimulus, does use proper Formal Logic:

$$\text{If} \quad W \text{ (work properly)} \quad \rightarrow \quad X \text{ (properly exposed)} \quad \rightarrow \quad Y \text{ (not too much light) and } Z \text{ (not too little light}$$

$$\text{If} \quad \sim Y \text{ or } \sim Z \quad \rightarrow \quad \sim W$$

Hence, this choice doesn't match the structure of the stimulus and is wrong.

25. (A) Strengthen

Step 1: Identify the Question Type

Strengthen stems don't get any more classic than this. Look for the answer choice that makes the conclusion more likely to be true.

Step 2: Untangle the Stimulus

The author's conclusion, indicated by the phrase "[n]ew evidence indicates that," is that recent property development hasn't hurt the wildlife population of a nearby park. The evidence is a pair of surveys, one conducted before the development and one after. The newer survey found more wildlife than the earlier one. Additionally, the author says, the park's resources are enough to easily support the increased wildlife population.

Step 3: Make a Prediction

Whenever an LSAT argument uses surveys as evidence, check their parameters to make sure that the author hasn't committed an error of representativeness. In this argument, you actually aren't told anything about the parameters of either survey at all. It's possible that they counted different animals or had other differences that would skew the results. The right choice, then, should support the argument by reassuring you that the surveys were comparable.

Step 4: Evaluate the Answer Choices

(A) supports the argument by confirming that both surveys examined the same species and that the species they had in common increased in number from the first survey to the second.

(B) is a 180. It weakens the argument by showing how the recent survey might have inflated the amount of wildlife in the park.

(C) is Out of Scope. It doesn't matter whether the park could have supported the numbers a decade ago; what matters is whether the park can support those numbers now.

(D) is a 180 because it weakens the argument. If the new survey was better at finding hard-to-find animals than the old one, then it's less likely that there are truly more animals living in the park than there used to be. The new survey simply might have done a better job at counting animals that were there all along.

(E) is either another 180 or Out of Scope. If the new survey introduced extra categories of wildlife—plant life— compared to the old one, then that would likely explain the increased numbers, not that the wildlife is actually thriving. If the plant life is not actually included in the *wildlife* count anyway, then simply adding more things to count wouldn't affect the argument one way or another.

26. (E) Paradox

Step 1: Identify the Question Type

Resolving discrepancies is within the realm of Paradox questions. Identify the apparent discrepancy, and pick the answer choice that would allow the two facts to coexist harmoniously.

Step 2: Untangle the Stimulus

Medicine has gotten better and life expectancy has increased. At the same time, the number of serious infections has increased as well. This is the paradox.

Step 3: Make a Prediction

The correct answer will explain why medical advances have helped people live longer but not helped them avoid an increasing rate of serious infections.

Step 4: Evaluate the Answer Choices

(E) explains the paradox. If life-saving treatments make patients more vulnerable to infection, then that would explain why prolonging life also makes infections more common.

(A) is a 180. If doctors prescribe ineffective medications, then that only makes the paradox more puzzling. This fact does not at all explain a rise in infection rates and if anything works against an overall increase in life spans and health.

(B) is a Distortion. It needlessly combines the two effects of advanced medical care, and it doesn't address the increasing rate of serious infections, which is central to the paradox.

(C) is a 180. If serious infections are now curable, that would deepen the mystery why they're occurring at an increasing rate. **(C)** doesn't reconcile an advance in medical care with an increase in infections.

(D) is a Distortion. First, it's not clear if the population has increased and, in any case, this choice contradicts the stimulus. The stimulus says the *rate* has increased, while this answer would indicate the *number* has increased but the rate has remained the same. Finally, even though **(D)** would explain an increase in the *number* of infections, it still wouldn't reconcile why that number is increasing in the face of improved medical care.

Section IV: Reading Comprehension
Passage 1: Sam Gilliam's Approach to Art

Q#	Question Type	Correct	Difficulty
1	Global	A	★
2	Inference	E	★
3	Logic Function	D	★
4	Inference	B	★
5	Detail (EXCEPT)	E	★★
6	Inference	D	★★

Passage 2: Online Gaming and the Virtual Economy

Q#	Question Type	Correct	Difficulty
7	Global	B	★
8	Inference	B	★
9	Inference	C	★
10	Logic Reasoning (Parallel Reasoning)	D	★★
11	Inference	A	★
12	Logic Reasoning (Method of Argument)	A	★★
13	Detail	D	★★★★

Passage 3: Outstanding Performance—Nature or Nurture?

Q#	Question Type	Correct	Difficulty
14	Global	D	★
15	Logic Function	E	★★
16	Inference	A	★★★★
17	Detail	A	★
18	Global	C	★★
19	Detail	D	★★★★

Passage 4: The Science Behind Mirror Images

Q#	Question Type	Correct	Difficulty
20	Global	A	★★★
21	Detail	B	★
22	Detail	B	★★
23	Inference	E	★★
24	Global	D	★★★
25	Inference	C	★★
26	Inference	B	★★★
27	Logic Function	C	★★★

Passage 1: Sam Gilliam's Approach to Art

Step 1: Read the Passage Strategically

Sample Roadmap

line #	Keyword/phrase	¶ Margin notes
2	foremost	Gilliam, well known painter of Wash. Color School
6	important	
8		Evolution of Color Field style
13	motivated	Why Gilliam joined Color Field
17	conservative ... ":"	G's view of contemp artists
18	unmistakable ... felt ... little room	
19	more	
20	importantly	Example
21	For example	
27	Though ... quite popular	
28	impatient	G's reaction to contemp art
30	In its place ... sought ... more	
32	more	
33	in ...	G's goal
34	particular	
35	rare	
36	highly experimental	
37	epitomizes ... refusal to conform	Public expectation
41		Features of G's paintings
42	first	
43		Innovation: unsupp. canvas
48	therefore	Effect of G's technique
49	demonstrate	
50	as well as	
53	helped advance	Emotional impact of G's work
55	could not	
56	but ... more	
57	effectively	

Discussion

The first lines of the passage introduce the **Topic**—the artist Sam Gilliam—and locates him within an artistic movement known as the Washington Color School, which was an offshoot of the Color Field movement. The remainder of paragraph 1 describes how the Color Field movement arose and how it evolved.

Paragraph 2 describes the motivation behind Gilliam's alignment with this artistic movement, which is the **Scope** of the passage. Gilliam was reacting to the work of his African American contemporaries, which he found too conservative and too limited to strictly representational and political concerns. The author then provides an extended example of the work to which Gilliam reacted. Paragraph 2 ends by discussing Gilliam's artistic goals.

In paragraph 3, the author describes how these goals were realized in Gilliam's own work. The author gives a detailed account of Gilliam's innovative unsupported canvas. The author ends the passage by discussing how Gilliam's technique conveyed the emotional complexity of the African American experience.

The **Purpose** of the passage is to describe Gilliam's work, its effects, and the ideas behind it. The **Main Idea** is that Gilliam responded to the literal, representational work of his colleagues by developing a more expressive technique that better captured the range of emotions and tensions felt by African Americans.

1. (A) Global

Step 2: Identify the Question Type

Any question that asks what the author is "primarily concerned" with is a Global question because you need to determine the author's primary purpose.

Step 3: Research the Relevant Text

Instead of researching a specific part of the passage to predict your answer, base your prediction on the Purpose you determined during Step 1.

Step 4: Make a Prediction

The Purpose of the passage is to describe Gilliam's approach to his art and the features of that art.

Step 5: Evaluate the Answer Choices

(A) is therefore correct.

(B) is a Distortion. The author only mentions political themes insofar as they permeate the work of Gilliam's contemporaries in paragraph 2.

(C) is also a Distortion. The style of the Color Field in general evolved, but the author doesn't trace the evolution of Gilliam's work specifically.

(D) blows up a detail from the end of paragraph 2. This detail is in service of the author's overall explanation of Gilliam's reaction to his contemporaries; it is not what the author is *primarily* concerned with.

(E) is Outside the Scope. No technical limitations are mentioned at all with regard to Gilliam's work.

2. (E) Inference

Step 2: Identify the Question Type

This is an Inference question because it asks you to take the characteristics described in the passage and extrapolate to an answer consistent with them.

Step 3: Research the Relevant Text

The characteristics of Gilliam's work are described in paragraph 3.

Step 4: Make a Prediction

Gilliam's creations are characterized by the folding and draping of canvases to create a three-dimensional surface. The correct answer will be consistent with this and any other features of the Color Field style as described in paragraph 1.

Step 5: Evaluate the Answer Choices

(E) is therefore a match.

(A) is a 180. Lines 27–31 express Gilliam's dissatisfaction with literal representation. The passage even says that Gilliam wanted to make art more expressive than a painted figure (line 31).

(B)'s depiction of war scenes would also strike Gilliam as too literal and too nakedly political.

(C) describes more painted figures, the representation of which Gilliam wasn't interested in (lines 30–31).

(D) is too representational to suit Gilliam as it depicts images of the seas and clouds. Also, Gilliam preferred to fold canvases onto themselves, and the canvas in **(D)** is merely unframed and *hanging* from a balcony, whereas Gilliam sought the "unsupported canvas" (lines 42–48).

3. (D) Logic Function

Step 2: Identify the Question Type

This is a Logic Function question because it asks *why* the author mentioned the collage artist, not what the author mentions about the artist.

Step 3: Research the Relevant Text

The collage artist is discussed in lines 22–27.

Step 4: Make a Prediction

The sentence discussing the collage artist begins with the Keywords "for example." Whenever you see these Keywords, look to the previous sentence(s) to see what the example is intended to illustrate. In this case, the author is illustrating the explicitly political art that Gilliam thought was aesthetically conservative and left "little room" for experimentation with new artistic territory.

Step 5: Evaluate the Answer Choices

(D) is therefore correct.

(A) is a 180. Gilliam joined the Washington Color School, and by extension the Color Field movement, because he was - dissatisfied with the work of artists like the collage artist from paragraph 2.

(B) is Extreme. While Gilliam was dissatisfied with the kind of art that his contemporaries created, there is nothing in the passage that supports any notion of *animosity*.

(C) is a Faulty Use of Detail. The author doesn't describe the work of the collage artist in order to establish the popularity of representational art. The Keywords "[f]or example" in line 21 indicate the purpose comes before the actual example. The popularity of representational art is not mentioned until line 27, and then it is done in contrast with Gilliam's attitude toward such art.

(E) is a 180. Gilliam's art was a direct reaction to the explicitly political art of his contemporaries (lines 30–34).

4. (B) Inference

Step 2: Identify the Question Type

Two clues make this an Inference question: the phrase "most strongly suggests" and the focus on Gilliam's *attitude*.

Step 3: Research the Relevant Text

Gilliam's reaction to the art of his contemporaries is discussed in paragraph 2. Look for where the author details Gilliam's view.

Step 4: Make a Prediction

Lines 16–21 say that Gilliam found his contemporaries' approach to be aesthetically conservative and not accommodating of subtlety, ambiguity, or innovation. Lines 28–29 say that Gilliam was impatient with the straightforward, literal approach of his contemporaries. The correct answer will be consistent with these statements.

Step 5: Evaluate the Answer Choices

(B) is therefore a correct characterization of Gilliam's attitude.

(A) is Extreme. Nothing in paragraph 2 indicates that Gilliam was derisive or condescending toward his contemporaries.

(C) is unsupported. *Whimsical* suggests that Gilliam's attitude was playful or fanciful, but the passage suggests that Gilliam was quite serious and deliberate in his reaction to his contemporaries.

(D) is incorrect because someone who was neutral toward his contemporaries would have no reason to be *impatient* (line 28).

(E) is a 180. Lines 12–13 indicate Gilliam was *motivated* to participate in the Color Field Movement in reaction to his contemporaries. Gilliam's reasons for motivation make it clear he did not approve of their techniques, including that he was *impatient* (line 28) with their literal representations.

5. (E) Detail (EXCEPT)

Step 2: Identify the Question Type

This is a Detail question because it asks about what the passage says, not what it implies or suggests. In this case, you must choose the answer that the passage *doesn't* say.

Step 3: Research the Relevant Text

This question stem doesn't have any content clues to help you research, so you'll need to save your research for Step 5 as you evaluate the answer choices.

Step 4: Make a Prediction

The list of things not mentioned in the passage could go on forever. So instead of predicting the answer, eliminate each answer choice that you find stated or paraphrased in the passage.

Step 5: Evaluate the Answer Choices

(E) is a Distortion that's not stated directly in the passage. The image of laundry hanging out to dry did partially inspire some of Gilliam's work, but the passage does not say that this means such images are "most likely" to inspire artists.

(A) is stated in lines 45–48.

(B) is stated in lines 36–39.

(C) is stated in lines 30–35.

(D) is stated in lines 12–21.

6. (D) Inference

Step 2: Identify the Question Type

Any question asking for what the author or anyone in the passage "would be most likely to agree with" is an Inference question.

Step 3: Research the Relevant Text

Gilliam's views on art are described primarily in paragraph 2.

Step 4: Make a Prediction

Paragraph 2 says that Gilliam reacted to the literal, representational approach of his contemporaries. He wanted to convey a more complex depiction of human experience through more expressionistic works. The correct answer will be consistent with these ideas. Remember that a valid LSAT

Inference is a statement that *must* be true based on the passage.

Step 5: Evaluate the Answer Choices

(D) is correct. He wanted to express the complexity of the human experience (lines 30–33), and this desire in part motivated his participation in the Color Field movement (lines 12–16), so **(D)** must be true.

(A) is Extreme. Nothing in the passage suggests that Gilliam is against all aesthetic restrictions of *any* kind.

(B) is a Distortion. The folded and crumpled canvases described in paragraph 3 were partially inspired by the image of clothes drying on a line (lines 43–44), but this doesn't mean that Gilliam saw "real-life images" as a requirement.

(C) is a 180. Gilliam's contemporaries were preoccupied with addressing political issues, and it's this preoccupation that Gilliam reacted against.

(E) is also a 180. Gilliam refused to conform to the public's expectations (lines 36–39).

Passage 2: Online Gaming and the Virtual Economy

Step 1: Read the Passage Strategically

Sample Roadmap

line #	Keyword/phrase	¶ Margin notes
Passage A		
3		Multiplayer online games popular
7	noticed	Castronova discovers economy within game
8	curious	
13	even more interesting	
14		Further discovery: auctions
18	recognized ... shock	Auctions—currency trading
19	!	
23	Moreover ... since	Virtual converted to real
25	in effect	
Passage B		
26	prohibit	
27	but	Some games encourage real trade
28	encourage ... for example	
30	Although ... seems	
32	should	Should virtual items be taxed? Qs raised
34	?	
35	?	
36	?	
37	important ... given	Gov'ts pressed to answer
39	given	
42	should not	
44	will argue	
45	support	Auth: don't tax items that stay in virtual world
46	should not	
47	but rather ... should	
48	such ...	
49	as ... only	
50	Moreover	
51	should not	
52	By contrast ... counsel	
54	and	Auth: tax when virtual items sold for real $
55	even ... regardless	

Discussion

Passage A begins by introducing the world of multiplayer online gaming. Paragraph 1 details some of the activities gamers undertake. Paragraph 2 introduces an economist, Edward Castronova, who made a discovery while playing one such online game. The players had created their own economy. In paragraph 3, the author shares another of Castronova's discoveries: Players were taking their possessions from the virtual economy and auctioning them off in the real economy. By participating in the activities of the game—killing monsters, skinning animals—the players were creating commodities and, by extension, generating wealth.

Passage B begins by saying that some online games encourage real-world trade of virtual items by granting intellectual property rights. Paragraph 2 of the passage gets into the issue raised by this trade. How should tax law respond to the trade of virtual items within the world of an online game? LSAT passages rarely ask rhetorical questions, so not surprisingly, the author of passage B spends paragraph 3 detailing the answers: property acquired in a virtual online gaming world should not be taxed, even when it's traded for other virtual property. The last paragraph draws a contrast, though, with virtual property that gets traded for money in the real world. The author feels that such trades are subject to taxation, lest a tax shelter be created.

The **Topic** of both passages is multiplayer online games, but as is common in Comparative Reading, the passages diverge with respect to Scope. The **Scope** of passage A is the new economic activity generated by the players, and the **Scope** of passage B is the taxing of virtual property within these online games. The **Purpose** of passage A is to describe the discovery Castronova made of the currency trading within the games, and its **Main Idea** is that Castronova discovered a form of currency trading within the virtual world of online gaming.

As for passage B, its **Purpose** is to describe and offer solutions to an issue with trading in virtual property. The **Main Idea** is that virtual property that stays within the world of the game should be exempt from taxation, but that when the property is traded for real money, then it should be subject to taxation.

When you're tackling Comparative Reading, always finish Step 1 by determining the relationship between the passages—the questions are sure to focus on this relationship. Here, the relationship is that passage A recounts the discovery of a new economic phenomenon, and passage B deals with a practical legal issue arising from that phenomenon.

7. (B) Global

Step 2: Identify the Question Type

Any question asking for an appropriate title for a passage is a Global question.

Step 3: Research the Relevant Text

Instead of rereading specific parts of the text, use the work you did in Step 1—namely Topic and Scope—to predict your answer.

Step 4: Make a Prediction

Passage A concerns Castronova's discoveries in the online gaming world. Passage B concerns the tax ramifications of trading in virtual items. The correct answer will reflect these Scopes.

Step 5: Evaluate the Answer Choices

(B) is therefore correct.

(A) misrepresents passage A. All you know about Castronova from passage A is what he discovered through playing online games; his own "economic theories" are never discussed.

(C) is also Outside the Scope of passage A. Nothing in passage A indicates that multiplayer online games have grown at all, much less that that growth was surprising.

(D) overemphasizes the last few lines of each passage. Lines 20–22 say that online gamers are making money, but passage A does not provide a process to make money in online games. Lines 56–58 say that the passage's approach doesn't create a tax shelter, but passage B doesn't target tax shelters overall.

(E) is a Distortion. The economic activity Castronova observed was recognizable as currency trading, so it can't be said that it was a brand new paradigm. Passage B does say that tax revenues are a factor in questions about taxation, but the aim of passage B is not to highlight the revenue that could be made from taxing virtual property.

8. (B) Inference

Step 2: Identify the Question Type

This is an Inference question because it asks you to determine what certain phrases refer to and, in this case, combine references from both passages to get to your answer.

Step 3: Research the Relevant Text

Lines 24 and 49 are relevant, but you must read around these lines for context, so you can see how the authors are using these particular references.

Step 4: Make a Prediction

Skinning animals in the virtual game and pulling fish from a real ocean are both activities requiring effort on one's part. The only difference is that the animal skins are then sold for virtual currency, but the fish are presumably then sold in the real world.

Step 5: Evaluate the Answer Choices

(B) is therefore correct. "Skinning animals" (the former) is discussed virtually, whereas as "fish pulled from the ocean" (the latter) is discussed in the real world.

(A) is Half-Right/Half-Wrong. Passage A says that skinning animals in the virtual world is, in effect, creating wealth, but passage B doesn't say that pulling fish from the ocean is not a wealth-generating activity.

(C) is a Distortion. Passage B indicates that acquiring fish from the ocean *should not* be taxed, but the sale of fish *should* be taxed (lines 49–50). Likewise, the author of B thinks actions in an online game like "skinning animals" also *should not* be taxed if they remain in-game, but *should* be taxed if they are sold for real currency (lines 52–53). So, the author of B treats the two activities the same.

(D), like **(C)**, treats the actual fish and the virtual animal pelts as different. The author of B believes neither should be taxed until they are actually sold for real currency.

(E) is Half-Right/Half-Wrong. Passage A says that skinning animals is one way to create wealth in the online game sphere, but passage B mentions fish from the ocean as real property that is taxed upon sale in the real world. So, the fish example is not a way for game-players to create wealth.

9. (C) Inference

Step 2: Identify the Question Type

This is an Inference question because it asks about the authors' attitudes toward something discussed in the passages.

Step 3: Research the Relevant Text

When asked about an author's attitude, skim the passage for any emphasis/opinion Keywords that you identified in your Roadmap.

Step 4: Make a Prediction

Passage A contains Keywords such as *curious* (line 8*)*, interesting (line 13), and *shock* (line 18). These kinds of words are not present in passage B, whose tone is much more scholarly and detached. The correct answer should reflect this difference in tone.

Step 5: Evaluate the Answer Choices

(C) is correct.

(A) is a 180. No criticism or apprehension is displayed in - passage A.

(B) is unsupported. The tone of passage A is, if anything, colloquial. And there's nothing that passage A dismisses.

(D) is a Distortion. Passage A does call one of Castronova's discoveries *curious* (line 8), but passage A's fascination with virtual commerce is clear; the author is not undecided.

(E) is Half-Right/Half-Wrong. Passage A certainly seems enthusiastic (see the exclamation point in line 19), but no skepticism is indicated anywhere.

10. (D) Logic Reasoning (Parallel Reasoning)

Step 2: Identify the Question Type

The phrase "most analogous to" signals a Parallel Reasoning question.

Step 3: Research the Relevant Text

This question focuses on the more global relationship between the passages, so instead of reading specific lines, use your work from Step 1 to help you predict your answer.

Step 4: Make a Prediction

The relationship between the passages is that passage A recounts the discovery of an economic phenomenon and passage B makes a recommendation for the response of tax law to that phenomenon. The correct answer will be consistent with this relationship.

Step 5: Evaluate the Answer Choices

(D) is parallel. The creation of a new species is analogous to the creation of wealth in passage A, and the application of patent law is analogous to passage B's application of tax law.

(A) isn't parallel because the first title discusses artificial intelligence in general, while the second title is specific to robots. Also, the application of human psychology in the second title isn't directly analogous to passage B's legal analysis.

(B) is wrong because the first title has nothing parallel to passage A's focus on a new discovery.

(C) is Half-Right/Half-Wrong. The first title does reflect Castronova's discovery, but the second title suggests that passage B is about a debate between economists over whether or not the trading between players constitutes real economic activity. That's not the focus of passage B.

(E) might be tempting because it deals with taxation, but it mischaracterizes passage A. The author of A does not say anything that would classify him as a *renegade*. Also, nothing about passage B suggests that the tax proposal discussed is *unorthodox*.

11. (A) Inference

Step 2: Identify the Question Type

This is an Inference question because you have to infer the *likely* sources of the passages based on their content.

Step 3: Research the Relevant Text

This Inference question has a Global feel to it, so instead of researching specific lines, get a handle on the overall tone and content of each passage.

Step 4: Make a Prediction

Based on the tone and style of passage A, it seems to have been taken from a layperson's magazine or journal—there isn't any technical jargon or economic theory. As for passage B, the focus is on the legal implications of virtual intellectual property in online gaming. Passage B appears to have a more narrow audience.

Step 5: Evaluate the Answer Choices

(A) is a match for this prediction.

(B) is a 180. There's no technical economic content in passage A. Additionally, passage B's discussion of tax policy is likely too narrow for a general audience.

(C) is also a 180. It's arguable that although passage B is focused on tax law, it may appear in a journal of economics. However, passage A is nonfiction, so it wouldn't appear in a science-fiction novel.

(D) is Outside the Scope of passage A, which doesn't touch on any legal topics. And passage B explicitly refers to itself as an article (line 44), so it must not be a *speech*.

(E) is Outside the Scope of both passages. Passage A contains no legislative content. Passage B has no fictional content.

12. (A) Logic Reasoning (Method of Argument)

Step 2: Identify the Question Type

This question stem asks for the relationship between the two passages, so it's structured like a Method of Argument question. You need to determine what each passage does in relation to the other.

Step 3: Research the Relevant Text

There's no specific place to research the answer. Instead, use your work from Step 1 to predict your answer.

Step 4: Make a Prediction

Passage A describes Castronova's discovery about the economic activity of online gamers, and passage B advocates for a tax policy in response to that economic activity.

Step 5: Evaluate the Answer Choices

(A) is therefore correct.

(B) is Outside the Scope of passage A. None of Castronova's theories are discussed; only his observations are described.

(C) is a Distortion. Even if you characterize the online gaming community from passage A as a *subculture*, passage B is not discussing how *hard* it is to police these gamers. Passage B

just offers a way to tax the sale of items within the gaming community.

(D) is a Distortion. Passage A doesn't have a negative tone or point of view that *challenges* anything, and it doesn't provide any interpretations for passage B to respond to.

(E) misrepresents passage B. Passage B doesn't discuss theory; it proposes a practical solution to the challenge of t-axing virtual economic activity.

13. (D) Detail

Step 2: Identify the Question Type

This is a Detail question because it asks what is true "based on the passage." The correct answer will be stated or paraphrased rather than implied.

Step 3: Research the Relevant Text

Don't assume that the right answer will come only from line 54. The answer can come from anywhere in passage B where the author gives characteristics of these games.

Step 4: Make a Prediction

Around line 54, the author says that sales of virtual items for real currency within intentionally commodified games should be taxed. But don't forget the first paragraph, where the author mentions that some online games encourage "real-world trade in virtual items" (line 27). These games grant "participants intellectual property rights in their creations" (lines 28–29). That sounds like intentional commodification.

Step 5: Evaluate the Answer Choices

(D) is therefore correct.

(A) is a 180. These online games allow selling *virtual* items for *real* currency, not the other way around.

(B) is Outside the Scope, as it is not mentioned in either passage.

(C) isn't mentioned in passage B, but rather in passage A (lines 11–12).

(E) is a Distortion. The exchanges that occur in these games are those of virtual items for real currency, not virtual for virtual.

Passage 3: Outstanding Performance—Nature or Nurture?

Step 1: Read the Passage Strategically

Sample Roadmap

line #	Keyword/phrase	¶ Margin notes
3	so outstanding	
4	so superior … even	Some believe high performance innate
6	believe … must	
8	supported	Support for this view
11	for example	Ex. musicians
12	and	
14		Ex. athletes
17	Until recently … however … little	Auth: relevant research hadn't been done
21	rather than	
24	suggests	Auth: high performance due to acquired skills, not innate
25	predominantly	
27	rather than … For example	
30	only	Ex. athletes
31	not	
32	Similarly	
33	exceptional	Ex. chess players
34	but … only if	
37	not … but	Auth: Exceptional performers trained early
39	Only extremely rarely	
41		and trained a long time
46	shows	Research: training changes anatomy
47	surprisingly	
51	does not … therefore … support	Auth: innate-talent idea not supported by evid.
52	must	
54	since … suggests instead	Evid. suggests training with some talent may account for outstanding perf.
55	together with	
57	Since	
59	and since	
63	more likely	Desire → train, and train → perf, so desire important too
64	than	

Discussion

The passage begins by introducing the belief of "some people" regarding humans capable of superior performance in their fields of endeavor—they were born that way. Whenever an LSAT author offers the belief of "some people," look for someone else (whether it's the author or another person mentioned later) to give an alternate viewpoint. For now, though, the author just introduces some psychologists who support the innate-talent hypothesis and their evidence. By now the **Topic** (superior performance) and the **Scope** (whether innate talent accounts for it) should become clear.

The author uses the contrast Keyword *however* right away in line 17, which hints at his or her own view. The innate-talent theory was developed without the benefit of substantive research into superior performance. This research, once done, actually casts doubt on the innate-talent hypothesis, suggesting that acquired skills and adaptations are more important factors. Supporting examples are then given from the worlds of athletics and chess.

Further support for the acquired-skills hypothesis comes in paragraph 3, where the author points out that most performers who achieve elite status as adults began with intensive instruction and training in early childhood. The author then cites more research results—even those anatomical characteristics that may have seemed innate probably developed from intense training. So, the author's **Purpose** is to challenge the idea that superior performance is due primarily to differences in innate talent.

This author kindly opens paragraph 4 reiterating what emerges as the passage's **Main Idea**: recent research suggests that the superior performance of certain athletes, musicians, and chess players should be attributed to acquired skills and adaptations rather than to innate talent. The passage then ends by pointing out that because people's interest and desire sustains the intense training that feeds their high performance, such desire might be a better indicator of future high performance than is innate talent.

14. (D) Global

Step 2: Identify the Question Type

Any question asking you to determine the "main point of the passage" is a Global question.

Step 3: Research the Relevant Text

Instead of researching, use your Big Picture understanding from Step 1 to form your prediction.

Step 4: Make a Prediction

The Main Idea of the passage is that high performance in various fields of human endeavor should be attributed more to the skills acquired through intense training than to innate

talent. This idea is stated almost verbatim in lines 23–27, but don't always count on LSAT authors to be this generous.

Step 5: Evaluate the Answer Choices

(D) is therefore correct.

(A) is a Faulty Use of Detail. Although the alteration of physical characteristics is discussed in lines 45–50, that detail misses the primary Purpose of the passage, which was to offer an alternative explanation for extraordinary performance. The idea of performance isn't mentioned at all in **(A)**.

(B) is Extreme. The passage isn't arguing that *anyone* can become an exceptional performer through sustained intense training, but rather that such training plays an important role in exceptional performance.

(C) is also Extreme. The research cited by the author doesn't show innate characteristics to be *irrelevant* to differences in performance. In fact, the author mentions "that level of talent common to all reasonably competent performers" (lines 55–56).

(E) is a Distortion. The passage doesn't say that the recent research has caused psychologists to revise their theories about the role of innate talent. The author never mentions these psychologists beyond paragraph 1.

15. (E) Logic Function

Step 2: Identify the Question Type

This is a Logic Function question because it asks for the "primary function" of the final paragraph.

Step 3: Research the Relevant Text

When a Logic Function question asks about the purpose of a whole paragraph, use your Roadmap to help you predict the answer.

Step 4: Make a Prediction

The author spends the first half of paragraph 4 discussing what the research evidence suggests and spends the second half discussing the factors that might be better predictive indicators of outstanding performance.

Step 5: Evaluate the Answer Choices

(E) is a match of the prediction.

(A) is Outside the Scope due to the phrase "proposals for educational reform." The author doesn't advocate for any policy changes based on the research cited.

(B) is unsupported. No contradictory consequences are given in the last paragraph. The author uses the paragraph merely to extend the argument.

(C) is a Distortion. Paragraph 4 doesn't recount or discuss any evidence; it discusses implications of the evidence.

Furthermore, **(C)** is Outside the Scope because the author doesn't recommend any areas for future research.

(D) is Outside the Scope because the author doesn't introduce any potential objections to his or her view.

16. (A) Inference

Step 2: Identify the Question Type

This is an Inference question because it asks for what could "most reasonably be inferred" from the passage.

Step 3: Research the Relevant Text

Without a clear content clue from the question stem, there's no specific part of the passage to research. Any of the author's statements are fair game.

Step 4: Make a Prediction

Instead of trying to predict all of the valid inferences that can be drawn from the passage, go straight to the answer choices. The correct answer is the one that *must* be true based on the passage. You should be able to find direct textual support for the answer you want to select.

Step 5: Evaluate the Answer Choices

(A) is entirely consistent with the author's Main Idea. The beginning of paragraph 4, for example, says that the difference between good and outstanding performance can be accounted for by extended intense training. Therefore, we couldn't know for sure whether a superior performer was "born that way" or just trained hard for many years.

(B) goes wrong when it places emphasis on "the highest level of innate talent." The author doesn't say that exceptional innate talent *and* intense training are necessary for high performance. In fact, lines 55–57 contradict this.

(C) is a 180. The author never introduces a field of human endeavor for which exceptional innate talent is a requirement for superior performance. The entire passage is set up to debunk that idea.

(D) goes Outside the Scope. The author doesn't weigh in on whether exceptional innate talent detracts from superior performance. The author's point is simply that other factors may be more important contributors to performance than innate talent.

(E) is Extreme. The author doesn't set out to demonstrate that innate talent plays no role whatsoever.

17. (A) Detail

Step 2: Identify the Question Type

This is a Detail question because it begins with the direct, categorical phrase "which one of the following does the passage say."

Step 3: Research the Relevant Text

Read closely for content clues so that your research can be as focused and efficient as possible. Intense practice (or training) is discussed in paragraphs 3 and 4, but the elements necessary for keeping up that practice are mentioned in paragraph 4.

Step 4: Make a Prediction

In lines 58–59, the author says that "sustained intense training usually depends on an appropriate level of interest and desire." The correct answer will either restate or paraphrase this.

Step 5: Evaluate the Answer Choices

(A) contains the exact two words of the prediction.

(B) is Outside the Scope. The passage doesn't mention emotional support from other people.

(C) is a Distortion. Paragraph 3 suggests that beginning instruction at an early age helps superior performers circumvent normal limits on ability, but nothing indicates that these performers can't keep up a regimen of training if they don't start by a certain age.

(D) is also Outside the Scope. The passage never mentions leisure time.

(E) may be a reasonable thing to assume, but it is also never stated in the passage.

18. (C) Global

Step 2: Identify the Question Type

Any question asking you to identify the author's "main purpose" is a Global question.

Step 3: Research the Relevant Text

The research necessary for a Global question doesn't involve rereading the passage; it involves consulting your Big Picture understanding of the passage from Step 1.

Step 4: Make a Prediction

The author's Purpose is to demonstrate, with recent research, that superior performance doesn't derive from innate talent as much as it does from intense training.

Step 5: Evaluate the Answer Choices

(C) is a match, even though it's stated in more abstract terms. The "certain views" on earlier research were that innate ability was largely determinative of superior performance. The author argues those views are not applicable "to a particular class of cases," which include activities such as music, chess, and some athletics (lines 1–2).

(A) is Outside the Scope. There is no "revised theoretical model" in the passage, and what *cases* do appear in the passage (those of superior performers) aren't characterized as *problematic* by the author.

(B) is a Distortion. The evidence that was cited to support the innate-talent theory is different from the evidence the author cites to support the training-adaptation theory. Lines 19–23 compare the two sources of evidence.

(D) is Outside the Scope. The author never introduces possible objections to his or her theory, much less defending the theory against those objections.

(E) mentions "a set of … abstract theoretical postulations," which are never discussed in the passage. Also, the body of research data cited by the author in support of the Main Idea is called "recent" multiple times, not "long-standing."

19. (D) Detail

Step 2: Identify the Question Type

The phrase "the passage says" makes this a Detail question.

Step 3: Research the Relevant Text

According to the Roadmap, chess players (and their memory) are discussed in detail in lines 32–35.

Step 4: Make a Prediction

Here, you can actually use a little Formal Logic to predict the answer. Lines 32–35 say that outstanding "chess players have exceptional memory for chess piece configurations, but only if those configurations are typical of chess games." That must mean that if a configuration is not typical of chess pieces, then superior chess players would not demonstrate memory skills that are any better than those of any other player.

Step 5: Evaluate the Answer Choices

(D) is therefore correct. A configuration is nothing but an arrangement.

(A) is Outside the Scope. Sequences of moves aren't - mentioned anywhere in the passage.

(B), like **(A)**, is also Outside the Scope because sequences of moves are never discussed in the passage.

(C) is Outside the Scope. The difficulty of chess games isn't cited as a factor in chess players' memory skills.

(E) is not mentioned. The author never says how superior chess players perform in the absence of competition.

Passage 4: The Science Behind Mirror Images

Step 1: Read the Passage Strategically

Sample Roadmap

line #	Keyword/phrase	¶ Margin notes
1		Q: why is mirror image reversed L-R?
4	simply	A: rotated field of sight
7	That is	
10	Since	
12		Field-of-sight expl
14	However ... completely	Other phys: mirrors work front-to-back
15	different ... suggesting	
21	most notable	
22	clearly ... false	F-B expl based on false idea
26	appeals strongly	
27	however ... because ... quite successful	Why F-B expl appealing
28	—to a point	
29	because	
30	rather than	
34	but	Mental construct of mirrors against fact
36	contrary ... Indeed	
38	Note ... for example	
40	rather	
42	In addition	
43	motivated	Motive behind F-B expl
44	desire	
45	like	
46	should	
48	However	
49	properly ... only	
50	if	Auth: can't remove observer from equation
51	If	
53	because	

Discussion

The author begins with a question often posed to physicists: why is the left-right orientation of an object reversed when we look at it in the mirror? The answer, the physicists say, lies in the reversal of the axis about which we rotate our field of sight. Since that axis is vertical, the image reverses from left to right, hence the field-of-sight explanation.

The Keyword that opens paragraph 2—*however*—signals another viewpoint being introduced. This confirms the **Topic** (mirror images) and the **Scope** (physicists' explanations for their appearance). Another group of physicists claims that mirrors reverse objects not left-to-right, but front-to-back. After describing this competing explanation in greater detail, the author ends paragraph 2 by noting that the front-to-back hypothesis is based on the false idea that the mirror image of an object is as three-dimensional as the object itself.

Paragraph 3 continues the discussion of the front-to-back explanation. It's an appealing explanation because it conforms to our mental constructs of objects. Those mental constructs usually comport with the facts, but not when it comes to mirrors: we look at mirror images as if they have a dimension of depth, even though they clearly don't.

Paragraph 4 begins with another reason why the front-to-back explanation appeals to scientists. It purports to remove the observer from its account of the phenomenon. But here's where the author finally weighs in. If scientists want to properly explain mirror images, they can't just consider what mirrors do to images; they must also consider how people perceive the images. The very concept of an image implies not only an object observed, but a person observing it. Thanks to this authorial point of view, you can determine the **Purpose**, which is to evaluate the front-to-back explanation for mirror images, and the **Main Idea**, which is that despite the appeal of the front-to-back explanation, it's not a total success because it fails to account for the role of the observer in the appearance of the image.

20. (A) Global

Step 2: Identify the Question Type

This is a Global question because it asks for the "main point of the passage."

Step 3: Research the Relevant Text

This Global question stem gives you some help. Here, the question really is "What main point does the author make about an explanation of mirror images?" That helps frame your prediction.

Step 4: Make a Prediction

The key to the answer lies in lines 48–51. According to the author, an adequate explanation of mirror images needs to account for "both what mirrors do and what happens when we look into mirrors."

Step 5: Evaluate the Answer Choices

(A) is a perfect match. The two particular elements are rephrased in lines 53–43: what mirrors do (the image aspect) and what happens when we look in into mirrors (the observer aspect).

(B) is Outside the Scope. You don't know from the passage whether an adequate explanation exists. The author doesn't say it hasn't already been determined.

(C) is Extreme. The author doesn't claim that only a physicist must develop a satisfactory explanation of mirror images.

(D) might be something that can be inferred from the passage, but it isn't the author's main point. If it were, there would be no need for the author to write the last paragraph.

(E) is a Distortion. Just because physicists disagree on the correct explanation of mirror images doesn't automatically mean that the explanation must be very complicated.

21. (B) Detail

Step 2: Identify the Question Type

The phrase "[a]ccording to the passage" indicates a Detail question.

Step 3: Research the Relevant Text

"Left-to-right reversal" is a content clue leading you to paragraph 1, where the author discusses the field-of-sight explanation.

Step 4: Make a Prediction

In paragraph 1, the author says that left-to-right reversal is a reversal about the axis around which we ordinarily turn our field of sight.

Step 5: Evaluate the Answer Choices

(B) is a perfect match.

(A) is a 180. The front-to-back explanation is presented in opposition to the field-of-sight explanation in paragraph 1.

(C) is Outside the Scope. Nothing in the passage indicates that the size of the object reflected in a mirror has anything to do with the orientation of its image.

(D) is a Faulty Use of Detail because the idea of an object's dimensionality isn't discussed until paragraph 3 (lines 37–38).

(E) is a Faulty Use of Detail. It mentions mental constructs, which are not discussed until paragraph 3 (lines 29–31), where the author isn't referring to the field-of-sight explanation.

22. (B) Detail

Step 2: Identify the Question Type

This is a Detail question because it asks for what is true "[a]ccording to the passage."

Step 3: Research the Relevant Text

This question stem gives a long content clue directing you to lines 28–31.

Step 4: Make a Prediction

According to these lines, our custom of dealing with our mental constructs of objects rather than with our primary sense perceptions is why "[i]t seems natural" (line 28). The *it* in question is in the previous sentence: the "front-to-back" explanation of mirror images.

Step 5: Evaluate the Answer Choices

(B) is therefore correct.

(A) is Outside the Scope. There is no "top-to-bottom explanation" cited in the passage.

(C) is also Outside the Scope. The author never characterizes either the field-of-sight or the front-to-back explanation as *complex*, and there's no mention of our ability to challenge those explanations.

(D) is a Distortion and Extreme. Lines 32–34 say that we can usually rely on an equation between perceptions and our mental constructs of those perceptions and that mirrors are less reliable in this regard. However, the author doesn't say that being accustomed to those constructs "facilitates our ability to reject" those equations.

(E) is Outside the Scope. The author never mentions that we're guilty of overemphasizing mirrors' simulation of our sense perceptions.

23. (E) Inference

Step 2: Identify the Question Type

The phrase "can be inferred" indicates an Inference question.

Step 3: Research the Relevant Text

This question asks for the author's attitude toward the front-to-back explanation, so the beginning of paragraph 3 is the relevant text here.

Step 4: Make a Prediction

In lines 26–28, the author says that the front-to-back mirror explanation is successful "to a point" because it comports with our mental constructs of the mirror image rather than the actual sensory processes occurring when we look into mirrors. The correct answer *must* be true based on this.

Step 5: Evaluate the Answer Choices

(E) is the correct match.

(A) is unsupported. According to the author, the limited success of the front-to-back explanation derives from its understandability and its basis in our mental constructs, not from some ability to reconcile incongruous facts.

(B) is a 180. The author says that we latch onto the front-to-back explanation precisely because it conforms to our mental constructs.

(C) is a Faulty Use of Detail. It introduces a detail from the author's description of the field-of-sight explanation (from paragraph 1), which is an entirely different theory than front-to-back.

(D) is Half Right-Half Wrong. It is "successful only to a point," but not because of anything about "traditional explanations." The author says the front-to-back theory is used by some physicists (line 14) but not necessarily that it is the traditional explanation given by the physics community.

24. (D) Global

Step 2: Identify the Question Type

This is a Global question because it asks for what the author is "primarily concerned with doing." In other words, it's asking for the primary Purpose.

Step 3: Research the Relevant Text

To determine the author's primary Purpose, you must revisit your Roadmap and your work from Step 1, when Purpose was one of the things you predicted.

Step 4: Make a Prediction

The author's Purpose was to describe explanations for the phenomenon of mirror images, with more attention paid to the front-to-back hypothesis and a summary of that explanation's shortcomings.

Step 5: Evaluate the Answer Choices

(D) is therefore correct.

(A) is Extreme and Outside the Scope. Nothing in the passage indicates that the field-of-sight and front-to-back explanations are "diametrically opposed." The evidence for and against these explanations is never evaluated by the author.

(B) isn't what the author is doing. The passage never points out differences between the empirical underpinnings of the field-of-sight explanation and those of the front-to-back explanation.

(C) is a Distortion. The author lays out two things that a successful explanation of mirror images needs to include, but doesn't say that these things are necessarily difficult to include.

(E) is also a Distortion. The author doesn't draw a relationship between the theoretical support for the front-to-back explanation and an acceptance of that explanation. According to the author, the appeal of the front-to-back explanation has to do not with theory but with our mental construct of visual perception with regard to mirrors. Furthermore, the author does *not* accept the front-to-back explanation.

25. (C) Inference

Step 2: Identify the Question Type

This is an Inference question because it asks with what the author would "be most likely to agree."

Step 3: Research the Relevant Text

Without a content clue from the question stem, any of the passage's 54 lines is fair game for the answer.

Step 4: Make a Prediction

Prediction is not efficient here, because many valid inferences could be drawn from the whole passage. In cases like this, go directly to Step 5, but make sure you can find support for an answer choice before you select it as correct.

Step 5: Evaluate the Answer Choices

(C) can be inferred. Lines 43–45 say that the front-to-back explanation of mirror images "is motivated in part by the traditional desire in science to separate the observer from the phenomenon."

(A) is Outside the Scope. The author suggests that the front-to-back explanation falls short not because it was derived from experiments using faulty equipment, but because it attempted to remove the observer from consideration.

(B) is Extreme. The author never gives a reason for why explanations of what mirrors do "generally fail." The author only gives the shortcomings of one theory.

(D) is also Outside the Scope. Lines 29–31 say that we are more accustomed to dealing with our mental constructs than with primary sense perceptions. However, nothing says that this custom is more prevalent in scientists as compared to laypeople.

(E) is a Distortion. Although the author says that we construe our sense perceptions of mirror images in a manner contrary to fact (lines 34–36), this isn't necessarily because we consider the objects or their images as mental constructs.

26. (B) Inference

Step 2: Identify the Question Type

Any question asking for what the author "would be most likely to agree" is an Inference question.

Step 3: Research the Relevant Text

The field-of-sight explanation for mirror images is discussed in paragraph 1.

Step 4: Make a Prediction

From paragraph 1, you know that the field-of-sight explanation accounts for the left-to-right reversal of mirror images by saying that we rotate our field of sight about a vertical axis when we turn from the object to its image. The author also says that it's not the only explanation for mirror images—the front-to-back explanation has many adherents as well.

Step 5: Evaluate the Answer Choices

(B) isn't stated directly in the passage, but you know from paragraph 2 that it's the front-to-back explanation, and not the field-of-sight explanation, that depends on the idea that mirror images are three-dimensional. So, **(B)** is a valid inference.

(A) is a Distortion. The author uses the *simply* in line 4 when describing the physicists' explanation, but that doesn't mean that physicists traditionally want to *simplify* the accepted explanation of mirrors.

(C) is a 180. The field-of-sight theory *does* take the position and orientation of the viewer into account. It holds that this position and orientation are reversed when the viewer switches from looking at the object to looking at its mirror image.

(D) is unsupported because the passage never implicates people's failure to understand the reality of their perceptual processes. The accuracy of the field-of-sight theory is unaffected by the viewer's understanding of the reality of what he or she sees.

(E) is a 180 and Outside the Scope. The author indicates that the field-of-sight explanation is accurate, not that it is unsuccessful. Furthermore, although field-of-sight may not appeal to everyone, the author doesn't mention that a successful explanation of mirror images needs to involve claims about what we "can imagine" rather than about how we rotate our line of sight.

27. (C) Logic Function

Step 2: Identify the Question Type

The phrase "in order to" indicates that you have to determine *why* an author makes a particular mention. That makes this a Logic Function question.

Step 3: Research the Relevant Text

Lines 39–40 are relevant, but you need to read around these lines for context. Look out for Keywords that help you determine the author's intentions.

Step 4: Make a Prediction

The sentence in which the author says we rarely focus our eyes on mirrors contains the phrase "for example." These Keywords mean that the author is using this mention as an example of whatever comes before. In this case, the author is trying to support the idea that mirrors are designed to give the illusion of three dimensions.

Step 5: Evaluate the Answer Choices

(C) is therefore correct.

(A) mentions a contrast that the author never draws. Imagination is never set at odds with perception.

(B) is Extreme. It imputes a point to the author that is never made in the passage. The author says that we deal with our mental constructs more often than we deal with our primary sense perceptions, but that's a far cry from saying that it's *impossible* to avoid using mental constructs. Furthermore, the mental construct–primary perception dichotomy isn't relevant to the reference in question.

(D) is a Faulty Use of Detail. It deals with a detail from earlier in the paragraph that has nothing to do with how our eyes focus on mirrors.

(E) goes Outside the Scope with its mention of the psychological state of the observer. The author also never says that the observer's psyche influences the shape of the object in the mirror.

Glossary

Logical Reasoning
Logical Reasoning Question Types

Argument-Based Questions

Main Point Question

A question that asks for an argument's conclusion or an author's main point. Typical question stems:

Which one the following most accurately expresses the conclusion of the argument as a whole?

Which one of the following sentences best expresses the main point of the scientist's argument?

Role of a Statement Question

A question that asks how a specific sentence, statement, or idea functions within an argument. Typical question stems:

Which one of the following most accurately describes the role played in the argument by the statement that automation within the steel industry allowed steel mills to produce more steel with fewer workers?

The claim that governmental transparency is a nation's primary defense against public-sector corruption figures in the argument in which one of the following ways?

Point at Issue Question

A question that asks you to identify the specific claim, statement, or recommendation about which two speakers/authors disagree (or, rarely, about which they agree). Typical question stems:

A point at issue between Tom and Jerry is

The dialogue most strongly supports the claim that Marilyn and Billy disagree with each other about which one of the following?

Method of Argument Question

A question that asks you to describe an author's argumentative strategy. In other words, the correct answer describes *how* the author argues (not necessarily what the author says). Typical question stems:

Which one of the following most accurately describes the technique of reasoning employed by the argument?

Julian's argument proceeds by

In the dialogue, Alexander responds to Abigail in which one of the following ways?

Parallel Reasoning Question

A question that asks you to identify the answer choice containing an argument that has the same logical structure and reaches the same type of conclusion as the argument in the stimulus does. Typical question stems:

The pattern of reasoning in which one of the following arguments is most parallel to that in the argument above?

The pattern of reasoning in which one of the following arguments is most similar to the pattern of reasoning in the argument above?

Assumption-Family Questions

Assumption Question

A question that asks you to identify one of the unstated premises in an author's argument. Assumption questions come in two varieties.

Necessary Assumption questions ask you to identify an unstated premise required for an argument's conclusion to follow logically from its evidence. Typical question stems:

Which one of the following is an assumption on which the argument depends?

Which one of the following is an assumption that the argument requires in order for its conclusion to be properly drawn?

Sufficient Assumption questions ask you to identify an unstated premise sufficient to establish the argument's conclusion on the basis of its evidence. Typical question stems:

The conclusion follows logically if which one of the following is assumed?

Which one of the following, if assumed, enables the conclusion above to be properly inferred?

Strengthen/Weaken Question

A question that asks you to identify a fact that, if true, would make the argument's conclusion more likely (Strengthen) or less likely (Weaken) to follow from its evidence. Typical question stems:

Strengthen

Which one of the following, if true, most strengthens the argument above?

Which one the following, if true, most strongly supports the claim above?

Weaken

Which one of the following, if true, would most weaken the argument above?

Which one of the following, if true, most calls into question the claim above?

Flaw Question

A question that asks you to describe the reasoning error that the author has made in an argument. Typical question stems:

The argument's reasoning is most vulnerable to criticism on the grounds that the argument

Which of the following identifies a reasoning error in the argument?

The reasoning in the correspondent's argument is questionable because the argument

Parallel Flaw Question

A question that asks you to identify the argument that contains the same error(s) in reasoning that the argument in the stimulus contains. Typical question stems:

The pattern of flawed reasoning exhibited by the argument above is most similar to that exhibited in which one of the following?

Which one of the following most closely parallels the questionable reasoning cited above?

Evaluate the Argument Question

A question that asks you to identify an issue or consideration relevant to the validity of an argument. Think of Evaluate questions as "Strengthen or Weaken" questions. The correct answer, if true, will strengthen the argument, and if false, will weaken the argument, or vice versa. Evaluate questions are very rare. Typical question stems:

Which one of the following would be most useful to know in order to evaluate the legitimacy of the professor's argument?

It would be most important to determine which one of the following in evaluating the argument?

Non-Argument Questions

Inference Question

A question that asks you to identify a statement that follows from the statements in the stimulus. It is very important to note the characteristics of the one correct and the four incorrect answers before evaluating the choices in Inference questions. Depending on the wording of the question stem, the correct answer to an Inference question may be the one that

- *must be true* if the statements in the stimulus are true

- is *most strongly supported* by the statements in the stimulus

- *must be false* if the statements in the stimulus are true

Typical question stems:

If all of the statements above are true, then which one of the following must also be true?

Which one of the following can be properly inferred from the information above?

If the statements above are true, then each of the following could be true EXCEPT:

Which one of the following is most strongly supported by the information above?

The statements above, if true, most support which one of the following?

The facts described above provide the strongest evidence against which one of the following?

Paradox Question

A question that asks you to identify a fact that, if true, most helps to explain, resolve, or reconcile an apparent contradiction. Typical question stems:

Which one of the following, if true, most helps to explain how both studies' findings could be accurate?

Which one the following, if true, most helps to resolve the apparent conflict in the spokesperson's statements?

Each one of the following, if true, would contribute to an explanation of the apparent discrepancy in the information above EXCEPT:

Principle Questions

Principle Question

A question that asks you to identify corresponding cases and principles. Some Principle questions provide a principle in the stimulus and call for the answer choice describing a case that corresponds to the principle. Others provide a specific case in the stimulus and call for the answer containing a principle to which that case corresponds.

On the LSAT, Principle questions almost always mirror the skills rewarded by other Logical Reasoning question types. After each of the following Principle question stems, we note the question type it resembles. Typical question stems:

Which one of the following principles, if valid, most helps to justify the reasoning above? (**Strengthen**)

Which one of the following most accurately expresses the principle underlying the reasoning above? (**Assumption**)

The situation described above most closely conforms to which of the following generalizations? (**Inference**)

Which one of the following situations conforms most closely to the principle described above? (**Inference**)

Which one of the following principles, if valid, most helps to reconcile the apparent conflict among the prosecutor's claims? (**Paradox**)

Parallel Principle Question

A question that asks you to identify a specific case that illustrates the same principle that is illustrated by the case described in the stimulus. Typical question stem:

Of the following, which one illustrates a principle that is most similar to the principle illustrated by the passage?

Untangling the Stimulus

Conclusion Types

The conclusions in arguments found in the Logical Reasoning section of the LSAT tend to fall into one of six categories:

1) Value Judgment (an evaluative statement; e.g., Action X is unethical, or Y's recital was poorly sung)

2) "If"/Then (a conditional prediction, recommendation, or assertion; e.g., If X is true, then so is Y, or If you an M, then you should do N)

3) Prediction (X *will* or *will not* happen in the future)

4) Comparison (X is taller/shorter/more common/less common, etc. than Y)

5) Assertion of Fact (X is true or X is false)

6) Recommendation (we *should* or *should not* do X)

One-Sentence Test

A tactic used to identify the author's conclusion in an argument. Consider which sentence in the argument is the one the author would keep if asked to get rid of everything except her main point.

Subsidiary Conclusion

A conclusion following from one piece of evidence and then used by the author to support his overall conclusion or main point. Consider the following argument:

> The pharmaceutical company's new experimental treatment did not succeed in clinical trials. As a result, the new treatment will not reach the market this year. Thus, the company will fall short of its revenue forecasts for the year.

Here, the sentence "As a result, the new treatment will not reach the market this year" is a subsidiary conclusion. It follows from the evidence that the new treatment failed in clinical trials, and it provides evidence for the overall conclusion that the company will not meet its revenue projections.

Keyword(s) in Logical Reasoning

A word or phrase that helps you untangle a question's stimulus by indicating the logical structure of the argument or the author's point. Here are three categories of Keywords to which LSAT experts pay special attention in Logical Reasoning:

Conclusion words; e.g., *therefore, thus, so, as a result, it follows that, consequently,* [evidence] *is evidence that* [conclusion]

Evidence word; e.g, *because, since, after all, for,* [evidence] *is evidence that* [conclusion]

Contrast words; e.g., *but, however, while, despite, in spite of, on the other hand* (These are especially useful in Paradox and Inference questions.)

Experts use Keywords even more extensively in Reading Comprehension. Learn the Keywords associated with the Reading Comprehension section, and apply them to Logical Reasoning when they are helpful.

Mismatched Concepts

One of two patterns to which authors' assumptions conform in LSAT arguments. Mismatched Concepts describes the assumption in arguments in which terms or concepts in the conclusion are different *in kind* from those in the evidence. The author assumes that there is a logical relationship between the different terms. For example:

> Bobby is a **championship swimmer**. Therefore, he **trains every day**.

Here, the words "trains every day" appear only in the conclusion, and the words "championship swimmer" appear only in the evidence. For the author to reach this conclusion from this evidence, he assumes that championship swimmers train every day.

Another example:

> Susan does **not eat her vegetables**. Thus, she will **not grow big and strong**.

In this argument, not growing big and strong is found only in the conclusion while not eating vegetables is found only in the evidence. For the author to reach this conclusion from this evidence, she must assume that eating one's vegetables is necessary for one to grow big and strong.

See also Overlooked Possibilities.

Overlooked Possibilities

One of two patterns to which authors' assumptions conform in LSAT arguments. Mismatched Concepts describes the assumption in arguments in which terms or concepts in the conclusion are different *in degree, scale, or level of certainty* from those in the evidence. The author assumes that there is no factor or explanation for the conclusion other than the one(s) offered in the evidence. For example:

> Samson does not have a ticket stub for this movie showing. Thus, Samson must have sneaked into the movie without paying.

The author assumes that there is no other explanation for Samson's lack of a ticket stub. The author overlooks several possibilities: e.g., Samson had a special pass for this showing of the movie; Samson dropped his ticket stub by accident or threw it away after entering the theater; someone else in Samson's party has all of the party members' ticket stubs in her pocket or handbag.

Another example:

> Jonah's marketing plan will save the company money. Therefore, the company should adopt Jonah's plan.

Here, the author makes a recommendation based on one advantage. The author assumes that the advantage is the company's only concern or that there are no disadvantages that could outweigh it, e.g., Jonah's plan might save money on marketing but not generate any new leads or customers; Jonah's plan might damage the company's image or reputation; Jonah's plan might include illegal false advertising. Whenever the author of an LSAT argument concludes with a recommendation or a prediction based on just a single fact in the evidence, that author is always overlooking many other possibilities.

See also Mismatched Concepts.

Causal Argument

An argument in which the author concludes or assumes that one thing causes another. The most common pattern on the LSAT is for the author to conclude that A causes B from evidence that A and B are correlated. For example:

> I notice that whenever the store has a poor sales month, employee tardiness is also higher that month. Therefore, it must be that employee tardiness causes the store to lose sales.

The author assumes that the correlation in the evidence indicates a causal relationship. These arguments are vulnerable to three types of overlooked possibilities:

1) There could be **another causal factor**. In the previous example, maybe the months in question are those in which the manager takes vacation, causing the store to lose sales and permitting employees to arrive late without fear of the boss's reprimands.

2) Causation could be **reversed**. Maybe in months when sales are down, employee morale suffers and tardiness increases as a result.

3) The correlation could be **coincidental**. Maybe the correlation between tardiness and the dip in sales is pure coincidence.

See also Flaw Types: Correlation versus Causation.

Another pattern in causal arguments (less frequent on the LSAT) involves the assumption that a particular causal mechanism is or is not involved in a causal relationship. For example:

> The airport has rerouted takeoffs and landings so that they will not create noise over the Sunnyside neighborhood. Thus, the recent drop in Sunnyside's property values cannot be explained by the neighborhood's proximity to the airport.

Here, the author assumes that the only way that the airport could be the cause of dropping property values is through noise pollution. The author overlooks any other possible mechanism (e.g., frequent traffic jams and congestion) through which proximity to the airport could be cause of Sunnyside's woes.

Principle

A broad, law-like rule, definition, or generalization that covers a variety of specific cases with defined attributes. To see how principles are treated on the LSAT, consider the following principle:

> It is immoral for a person for his own gain to mislead another person.

That principle would cover a specific case, such as a seller who lies about the quality of construction to get a higher price for his house. It would also correspond to the case of a teenager who, wishing to spend a night out on the town, tells his mom "I'm going over to Randy's house." He knows that his mom believes that he will be staying at Randy's house, when in fact, he and Randy will go out together.

That principle does not, however, cover cases in which someone lies solely for the purpose of making the other person feel better or in which one person inadvertently misleads the other through a mistake of fact.

Be careful not to apply your personal ethics or morals when analyzing the principles articulated on the test.

Flaw Types

Necessary versus Sufficient

This flaw occurs when a speaker or author concludes that one event is necessary for a second event from evidence that the first event is sufficient to bring about the second event, or vice versa. Example:

> If more than 25,000 users attempt to access the new app at the same time, the server will crash. Last night, at 11:15 pm, the server crashed, so it must be case that more than 25,000 users were attempting to use the new app at that time.

In making this argument, the author assumes that the only thing that will cause the server to crash is the usage level (i.e., high usage is *necessary* for the server to crash). The evidence, however, says that high usage is one thing that will cause the server to crash (i.e., that high usage is *sufficient* to crash the server).

Correlation versus Causation

This flaw occurs when a speaker or author draws a conclusion that one thing causes another from evidence that the two things are correlated. Example:

Over the past half century, global sugar consumption has tripled. That same time period has seen a surge in the rate of technological advancement worldwide. It follows that the increase in sugar consumption has caused the acceleration in technological advancement.

In any argument with this structure, the author is making three unwarranted assumptions. First, he assumes that there is no alternate cause, i.e., there is nothing else that has contributed to rapid technological advancement. Second, he assumes that the causation is not reversed, i.e., technological advancement has not contributed to the increase in sugar consumption, perhaps by making it easier to grow, refine, or transport sugar. And, third, he assumes that the two phenomena are not merely coincidental, i.e., that it is not just happenstance that global sugar consumption is up at the same time that the pace of technological advancement has accelerated.

Unrepresentative Sample

This flaw occurs when a speaker or author draws a conclusion about a group from evidence in which the sample cannot represent that group because the sample is too small or too selective, or is biased in some way. Example:

Moviegoers in our town prefer action films and romantic comedies over other film genres. Last Friday, we sent reporters to survey moviegoers at several theaters in town, and nearly 90 percent of those surveyed were going to watch either an action film or a romantic comedy.

The author assumes that the survey was representative of the town's moviegoers, but there are several reasons to question that assumption. First, we don't know how many people were actually surveyed. Even if the number of people surveyed was adequate, we don't know how many other types of movies were playing. Finally, the author doesn't limit her conclusion to moviegoers on Friday nights. If the survey had been conducted at Sunday matinees, maybe most moviegoers would have been heading out to see an animated family film or a historical drama. Who knows?

Scope Shift/Unwarranted Assumption

This flaw occurs when a speaker's or author's evidence has a scope or has terms different enough from the scope or terms in his conclusion that it is doubtful that the evidence can support the conclusion. Example:

A very small percentage of working adults in this country can correctly define collateralized debt obligation securities. Thus, sad to say, the majority of the nation's working adults cannot make prudent choices about how to invest their savings.

This speaker assumes that prudent investing requires the ability to accurately define a somewhat obscure financial term. But prudence is not the same thing as expertise, and

the speaker does not offer any evidence that this knowledge of this particular term is related to wise investing.

Percent versus Number/Rate versus Number

This flaw occurs when a speaker or author draws a conclusion about real quantities from evidence about rates or percentages, or vice versa. Example:

At the end of last season, Camp SunnyDay laid off half of their senior counselors and a quarter of their junior counselors. Thus, Camp SunnyDay must have more senior counselors than junior counselors.

The problem, of course, is that we don't know how many senior and junior counselors were on staff before the layoffs. If there were a total of 4 senior counselors and 20 junior counselors, then the camp would have laid off only 2 senior counselors while dismissing 5 junior counselors.

Equivocation

This flaw occurs when a speaker or author uses the same word in two different and incompatible ways. Example:

Our opponent in the race has accused our candidate's staff members of behaving unprofessionally. But that's not fair. Our staff is made up entirely of volunteers, not paid campaign workers.

The speaker interprets the opponent's use of the word *professional* to mean "paid," but the opponent likely meant something more along the lines of "mature, competent, and businesslike."

Ad Hominem

This flaw occurs when a speaker or author concludes that another person's claim or argument is invalid because that other person has a personal flaw or shortcoming. One common pattern is for the speaker or author to claim the other person acts hypocritically or that the other person's claim is made from self-interest. Example:

Mrs. Smithers testified before the city council, stating that the speed limits on the residential streets near her home are dangerously high. But why should we give her claim any credence? The way she eats and exercises, she's not even looking out for her own health.

The author attempts to undermine Mrs. Smithers's testimony by attacking her character and habits. He doesn't offer any evidence that is relevant to her claim about speed limits.

Part versus Whole

This flaw occurs when a speaker or author concludes that a part or individual has a certain characteristic because the whole or the larger group has that characteristic, or vice versa. Example:

Patient: I should have no problems taking the three drugs prescribed to me by my doctors. I looked them up, and none of the three is listed as having any major side effects.

Here, the patient is assuming that what is true of each of the drugs individually will be true of them when taken together. The patient's flaw is overlooking possible interactions that could cause problems not present when the drugs are taken separately.

Circular Reasoning

This flaw occurs when a speaker or author tries to prove a conclusion with evidence that is logically equivalent to the conclusion. Example:

> All those who run for office are prevaricators. To   see this, just consider politicians: they all prevaricate.

Perhaps the author has tried to disguise the circular reasoning in this argument by exchanging the words "those who run for office" in the conclusion for "politicians" in the evidence, but all this argument amounts to is "Politicians prevaricate; therefore, politicians prevaricate." On the LSAT, circular reasoning is very rarely the correct answer to a Flaw question, although it is regularly described in one of the wrong answers.

Question Strategies

Denial Test

A tactic for identifying the assumption *necessary* to an argument. When you negate an assumption necessary to an argument, the argument will fall apart. Negating an assumption that is not necessary to the argument will not invalidate the argument. Consider the following argument:

> Only high schools which produced a state champion athlete during the school year will be represented at the Governor's awards banquet. Therefore, McMurtry High School will be represented at the Governor's awards banquet.

Which one of the following is an assumption necessary to that argument?

(1) McMurtry High School produced more state champion athletes than any other high school during the school year.

(2) McMurtry High School produced at least one state champion athlete during the school year.

If you are at all confused about which of those two statements reflects the *necessary* assumption, negate them both.

(1) McMurtry High School **did not produce more** state champion athletes than any other high school during the school year.

That does not invalidate the argument. McMurtry could still be represented at the Governor's banquet.

(2) McMurtry High School **did not produce any** state champion athletes during the school year.

Here, negating the statement causes the argument to fall apart. Statement (2) is an assumption *necessary* to the argument.

Point at Issue "Decision Tree"

A tactic for evaluating the answer choices in Point at Issue questions. The correct answer is the only answer choice to which you can answer "Yes" to all three questions in the following diagram.

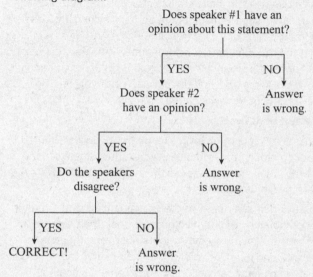

Common Methods of Argument

These methods of argument or argumentative strategies are common on the LSAT:

- Analogy, in which an author draws parallels between two unrelated (but purportedly similar) situations
- Example, in which an author cites a specific case or cases to justify a generalization
- Counterexample, in which an author seeks to discredit an opponent's argument by citing a specific case or cases that appear to invalidate the opponent's generalization
- Appeal to authority, in which an author cites an expert's claim or opinion as support for her conclusion
- Ad hominem attack, in which an author attacks her opponent's personal credibility rather than attacking the substance of her opponent's argument
- Elimination of alternatives, in which an author lists possibilities and discredits or rules out all but one

- Means/requirements, in which the author argues that something is needed to achieve a desired result

Wrong Answer Types in LR

Outside the Scope (Out of Scope; Beyond the Scope)

An answer choice containing a statement that is too broad, too narrow, or beyond the purview of the stimulus, making the statement in the choice irrelevant

180

An answer choice that directly contradicts what the correct answer must say (for example, a choice that strengthens the argument in a Weaken question)

Extreme

An answer choice containing language too emphatic to be supported by the stimulus; often (although not always) characterized by words such as *all*, *never*, *every*, *only*, or *most*

Distortion

An answer choice that mentions details from the stimulus but mangles or misstates what the author said about those details

Irrelevant Comparison

An answer choice that compares two items or attributes in a way not germane to the author's argument or statements

Half-Right/Half-Wrong

An answer choice that begins correctly, but then contradicts or distorts the passage in its second part; this wrong answer type is more common in Reading Comprehension than it is in Logical Reasoning

Faulty Use of Detail

An answer choice that accurately states something from the stimulus, but does so in a manner that answers the question incorrectly; this wrong answer type is more common in Reading Comprehension than it is in Logical Reasoning

Logic Games

Game Types

Strict Sequencing Game

A game that asks you to arrange entities into numbered positions or into a set schedule (usually hours or days). Strict Sequencing is, by far, the most common game type on the LSAT. In the typical Strict Sequencing game, there is a one-to-one matchup of entities and positions, e.g., seven entities to be placed in seven positions, one per position, or six entities to be placed over six consecutive days, one entity per day.

From time to time, the LSAT will offer Strict Sequencing with more entities than positions (e.g., seven entities to be arranged over five days, with some days to receive more than one entity) or more positions than entities (e.g., six entities to be scheduled over seven days, with at least one day to receive no entities).

Other, less common variations on Strict Sequencing include:

Double Sequencing, in which each entity is placed or scheduled two times (there have been rare occurrences of Triple or Quadruple Sequencing). Alternatively, a Double Sequencing game may involve two different sets of entities each sequenced once.

Circular Sequencing, in which entities are arranged around a table or in a circular arrangement (NOTE: When the positions in a Circular Sequencing game are numbered, the first and last positions are adjacent.)

Vertical Sequencing, in which the positions are numbered from top to bottom or from bottom to top (as in the floors of a building)

Loose Sequencing Game

A game that asks you to arrange or schedule entities in order but provides no numbering or naming of the positions. The rules in Loose Sequencing give only the relative positions (earlier or later, higher or lower) between two entities or among three entities. Loose Sequencing games almost always provide that there will be no ties between entities in the rank, order, or position they take.

Circular Sequencing Game

See Strict Sequencing Game.

Selection Game

A game that asks you to choose or include some entities from the initial list of entities and to reject or exclude others. Some Selection games provide overall limitations on the number of entities to be selected (e.g., "choose exactly four of seven students" or "choose at least two of six entrees") while others provide little or no restriction on the number selected ("choose at least one type of flower" or "select from among seven board members").

Distribution Game

A game that asks you to break up the initial list of entities into two, three, or (very rarely) four groups or teams. In the vast majority of Distribution games, each entity is assigned to one and only one group or team. A relatively common variation on Distribution games will provide a subdivided list of entities (e.g., eight students—four men and four women—will form three study groups) and will then require representatives from those subdivisions on each team (e.g., each study group will have at least one of the men on it).

Matching Game

A game that asks you to match one or more members of one set of entities to specific members of another set of entities, or that asks you to match attributes or objects to a set of entities. Unlike Distribution games, in which each entity is placed in exactly one group or team, Matching games usually permit you to assign the same attribute or object to more than one entity.

In some cases, there are overall limitations on the number of entities that can be matched (e.g., "In a school's wood shop, there are four workstations—numbered 1 through 4—and each workstation has at least one and at most three of the following tools—band saw, dremmel tool, electric sander, and power drill"). In almost all Matching games, further restrictions on the number of entities that can be matched to a particular person or place will be found in the rules (e.g., Workstation 4 will have more tools than Workstation 2 has).

Hybrid Game

A game that asks you to do two (or rarely, three) of the standard actions (Sequencing, Selection, Distribution, and Matching) to a set of entities.

The most common Hybrid is Sequencing-Matching. A typical Sequencing-Matching Hybrid game might ask you to schedule six speakers at a conference to six one-hour speaking slots (from 9 am to 2 pm), and then assign each speaker one of two subjects (economic development or trade policy).

Nearly as common as Sequencing-Matching is Distribution-Sequencing. A typical game of this type might ask you to divide six people in a talent competition into either a Dance category or a Singing category, and then rank the competitors in each category.

It is most common to see one Hybrid game in each Logic Games section, although there have been tests with two Hybrid games and tests with none. To determine the type of Hybrid you are faced with, identify the game's action in Step 1 of the Logic Games Method. For example, a game asking you to choose four of six runners, and then assign the four chosen runners to lanes numbered 1 through 4 on a track, would be a Selection-Sequencing Hybrid game.

Mapping Game

A game that provides you with a description of geographical locations and, typically, of the connections among them. Mapping games often ask you to determine the shortest possible routes between two locations or to account for the number of connections required to travel from one location to another. This game type is extremely rare, and as of February 2017, a Mapping game was last seen on PrepTest 40 administered in June 2003.

Process Game

A game that opens with an initial arrangement of entities (e.g., a starting sequence or grouping) and provides rules that describe the processes through which that arrangement can be altered. The questions typically ask you for acceptable arrangements or placements of particular entities after one, two, or three stages in the process. Occasionally, a Process game question might provide information about the arrangement after one, two, or three stages in the process and ask you what must have happened in the earlier stages. This game type is extremely rare, and as of November 2016, a Process game was last seen on PrepTest 16 administered in September 1995. However, there was a Process game on PrepTest 80, administered in December 2016, thus ending a 20-year hiatus.

Game Setups and Deductions

Floater

An entity that is not restricted by any rule or limitation in the game

Blocks of Entities

Two or more entities that are required by rule to be adjacent or separated by a set number of spaces (Sequencing games), to be placed together in the same group (Distribution games), to be matched to the same entity (Matching games), or to be selected or rejected together (Selection games)

Limited Options

Rules or restrictions that force all of a game's acceptable arrangements into two (or occasionally three) patterns

Established Entities

An entity required by rule to be placed in one space or assigned to one particular group throughout the entire game

Number Restrictions

Rules or limitations affecting the number of entities that may be placed into a group or space throughout the game

Duplications

Two or more rules that restrict a common entity. Usually, these rules can be combined to reach additional deductions. For example, if you know that B is placed earlier than A in a sequence and that C is placed earlier than B in that sequence, you can deduce that C is placed earlier than A in the sequence and that there is at least one space (the space occupied by B) between C and A.

Master Sketch

The final sketch derived from the game's setup, rules, and deductions. LSAT experts preserve the Master Sketch for reference as they work through the questions. The Master

Sketch does not include any conditions from New-"If" question stems.

Logic Games Question Types

Acceptability Question

A question in which the correct answer is an acceptable arrangement of all the entities relative to the spaces, groups, or selection criteria in the game. Answer these by using the rules to eliminate answer choices that violate the rules.

Partial Acceptability Question

A question in which the correct answer is an acceptable arrangement of some of the entities relative to some of the spaces, groups, or selection criteria in the game, and in which the arrangement of entities not included in the answer choices could be acceptable to the spaces, groups, or selection criteria not explicitly shown in the answer choices. Answer these the same way you would answer Acceptability questions, by using the rules to eliminate answer choices that explicitly or implicitly violate the rules.

Must Be True/False; Could Be True/False Question

A question in which the correct answer must be true, could be true, could be false, or must be false (depending on the question stem), and in which no additional rules or conditions are provided by the question stem

New-"If" Question

A question in which the stem provides an additional rule, condition, or restriction (applicable only to that question), and then asks what must/could be true/false as a result. LSAT experts typically handle New-"If" questions by copying the Master Sketch, adding the new restriction to the copy, and working out any additional deductions available as a result of the new restriction before evaluating the answer choices.

Rule Substitution Question

A question in which the correct answer is a rule that would have an impact identical to one of the game's original rules on the entities in the game

Rule Change Question

A question in which the stem alters one of the original rules in the game, and then asks what must/could be true/false as a result. LSAT experts typically handle Rule Change questions by reconstructing the game's sketch, but now accounting for the changed rule in place of the original. These questions are rare on recent tests.

Rule Suspension Question

A question in which the stem indicates that you should ignore one of the original rules in the game, and then asks what must/could be true/false as a result. LSAT experts typically handle Rule Suspension questions by reconstructing

the game's sketch, but now accounting for the absent rule. These questions are very rare.

Complete and Accurate List Question

A question in which the correct answer is a list of any and all entities that could acceptably appear in a particular space or group, or a list of any and all spaces or groups in which a particular entity could appear

Completely Determine Question

A question in which the correct answer is a condition that would result in exactly one acceptable arrangement for all of the entities in the game

Supply the "If" Question

A question in which the correct answer is a condition that would guarantee a particular result stipulated in the question stem

Minimum/Maximum Question

A question in which the correct answer is the number corresponding to the fewest or greatest number of entities that could be selected (Selection), placed into a particular group (Distribution), or matched to a particular entity (Matching). Often, Minimum/Maximum questions begin with New-"If" conditions.

Earliest/Latest Question

A question in which the correct answer is the earliest or latest position in which an entity may acceptably be placed. Often, Earliest/Latest questions begin with New-"If" conditions.

"How Many" Question

A question in which the correct answer is the exact number of entities that may acceptably be placed into a particular group or space. Often, "How Many" questions begin with New-"If" conditions.

Reading Comprehension
Strategic Reading

Roadmap

The test taker's markup of the passage text in Step 1 (Read the Passage Strategically) of the Reading Comprehension Method. To create helpful Roadmaps, LSAT experts circle or underline Keywords in the passage text and jot down brief, helpful notes or paragraph summaries in the margin of their test booklets.

Keyword(s) in Reading Comprehension

Words in the passage text that reveal the passage structure or the author's point of view and thus help test takers anticipate and research the questions that accompany the passage. LSAT experts pay attention to six categories of Keywords in Reading Comprehension:

Emphasis/Opinion—words that signal that the author finds a detail noteworthy or that the author has positive or negative opinion about a detail; any subjective or evaluative language on the author's part (e.g., *especially, crucial, unfortunately, disappointing, I suggest, it seems likely*)

Contrast—words indicating that the author finds two details or ideas incompatible or that the two details illustrate conflicting points (e.g., *but, yet, despite, on the other hand*)

Logic—words that indicate an argument, either the author's or someone else's (e.g., *thus, therefore, because, it follows that*)

Illustration—words indicating an example offered to clarify or support another point (e.g., *for example, this shows, to illustrate*)

Sequence/Chronology—words showing steps in a process or developments over time (e.g., *traditionally, in the past, today, first, second, finally, earlier, subsequent*)

Continuation—words indicating that a subsequent example or detail supports the same point or illustrates the same idea as the previous example (e.g., *moreover, in addition, also, further, along the same lines*)

Margin Notes

The brief notes or paragraph summaries that the test taker jots down next to the passage in the margin of the test booklet

Big Picture Summaries: Topic/Scope/Purpose/Main Idea

A test taker's mental summary of the passage as a whole made during Step 1 (Read the Passage Strategically) of the Reading Comprehension Method. LSAT experts account for four aspects of the passage in their big picture summaries:

Topic—the overall subject of the passage

Scope—the particular aspect of the Topic that the author focuses on

Purpose—the author's reason or motive for writing the passage (express this as a verb; e.g., *to refute, to outline, to evaluate, to critique*)

Main Idea—the author's conclusion or overall takeaway; if the passage does not contain an explicit conclusion or thesis, you can combine the author's Scope and Purpose to get a good sense of the Main Idea.

Passage Types

Kaplan categorizes Reading Comprehension passages in two ways, by subject matter and by passage structure.

Subject matter categories

In the majority of LSAT Reading Comprehension sections, there is one passage from each of the following subject matter categories:

Humanities—topics from art, music, literature, philosophy, etc.

Natural Science—topics from biology, astronomy, paleontology, physics, etc.

Social Science—topics from anthropology, history, sociology, psychology, etc.

Law—topics from constitutional law, international law, legal education, jurisprudence, etc.

Passage structure categories

The majority of LSAT Reading Comprehension passages correspond to one of the following descriptions. The first categories—Theory/Perspective and Event/Phenomenon—have been the most common on recent LSATs.

Theory/Perspective—The passage focuses on a thinker's theory or perspective on some aspect of the Topic; typically (though not always), the author disagrees and critiques the thinker's perspective and/or defends his own perspective.

Event/Phenomenon—The passage focuses on an event, a breakthrough development, or a problem that has recently arisen; when a solution to the problem is proposed, the author most often agrees with the solution (and that represents the passage's Main Idea).

Biography—The passage discusses something about a notable person; the aspect of the person's life emphasized by the author reflects the Scope of the passage.

Debate—The passage outlines two opposing positions (neither of which is the author's) on some aspect of the Topic; the author may side with one of the positions, may remain neutral, or may critique both. (This structure has been relatively rare on recent LSATs.)

Comparative Reading

A pair of passages (labeled Passage A and Passage B) that stand in place of the typical single passage exactly one time in each Reading Comprehension section administered since June 2007. The paired Comparative Reading passages share the same Topic, but may have different Scopes and Purposes. On most LSAT tests, a majority of the questions accompanying Comparative Reading passages require the test taker to compare or contrast ideas or details from both passages.

Question Strategies

Research Clues

A reference in a Reading Comprehension question stem to a word, phrase, or detail in the passage text, or to a particular line number or paragraph in the passage. LSAT experts recognize five kinds of research clues:

Line Reference—An LSAT expert researches around the referenced lines, looking for Keywords that indicate why the referenced details were included or how they were used by the author.

Paragraph Reference—An LSAT expert consults her passage Roadmap to see the paragraph's Scope and Purpose.

Quoted Text (often accompanied by a line reference)—An LSAT expert checks the context of the quoted term or phrase, asking what the author meant by it in the passage.

Proper Nouns—An LSAT expert checks the context of the person, place, or thing in the passage, asking whether the author made a positive, negative, or neutral evaluation of it and why the author included it in the passage.

Content Clues—These are terms, concepts, or ideas from the passage mentioned in the question stem but not as direct quotes and not accompanied by line references. An LSAT expert knows that content clues almost always refer to something that the author emphasized or about which the author expressed an opinion.

Reading Comp Question Types

Global Question

A question that asks for the Main Idea of the passage or for the author's primary Purpose in writing the passage. Typical question stems:

> Which one of the following most accurately expresses the main point of the passage?

> The primary purpose of the passage is to

Detail Question

A question that asks what the passage explicitly states about a detail. Typical question stems:

> According to the passage, some critics have criticized Gilliam's films on the grounds that

> The passage states that one role of a municipality's comptroller in budget decisions by the city council is to

> The author identifies which one of the following as a commonly held but false preconception?

> The passage contains sufficient information to answer which of the following questions?

Occasionally, the test will ask for a correct answer that contains a detail *not* stated in the passage:

> The author attributes each of the following positions to the Federalists EXCEPT:

Inference Question

A question that asks for a statement that follows from or is based on the passage but that is not necessarily stated explicitly in the passage. Some Inference questions contain research clues. The following are typical Inference question stems containing research clues:

> Based on the passage, the author would be most likely to agree with which one of the following statements about unified field theory?

> The passage suggests which one of the following about the behavior of migratory water fowl?

> Given the information in the passage, to which one of the following would radiocarbon dating techniques likely be applicable?

Other Inference questions lack research clues in the question stem. They may be evaluated using the test taker's Big Picture Summaries, or the answer choices may make it clear that the test taker should research a particular part of the passage text. The following are typical Inference question stems containing research clues:

> It can be inferred from the passage that the author would be most likely to agree that

> Which one of the following statements is most strongly supported by the passage?

Other Reading Comprehension question types categorized as Inference questions are Author's Attitude questions and Vocabulary-in-Context questions.

Logic Function Question

A question that asks why the author included a particular detail or reference in the passage or how the author used a particular detail or reference. Typical question stems:

> The author of the passage mentions declining inner-city populations in the paragraph most likely in order to

> The author's discussion of Rimbaud's travels in the Mediterranean (lines 23–28) functions primarily to

> Which one of the following best expresses the function of the third paragraph in the passage?

Logic Reasoning Question

A question that asks the test taker to apply Logical Reasoning skills in relation to a Reading Comprehension passage. Logic Reasoning questions often mirror Strengthen or Parallel Reasoning questions, and occasionally mirror Method of Argument or Principle questions. Typical question stems:

> Which one of the following, if true, would most strengthen the claim made by the author in the last sentence of the passage (lines 51–55)?

> Which one of the following pairs of proposals is most closely analogous to the pair of studies discussed in the passage?

Author's Attitude Question

A question that asks for the author's opinion or point of view on the subject discussed in the passage or on a detail mentioned in the passage. Since the correct answer may follow from the passage without being explicitly stated in it, some Author's Attitude questions are characterized as a subset of Inference questions. Typical question stems:

> The author's attitude toward the use of DNA evidence in the appeals by convicted felons is most accurately described as

> The author's stance regarding monetarist economic theories can most accurately be described as one of

Vocabulary-in-Context Question

A question that asks how the author uses a word or phrase within the context of the passage. The word or phrase in question is always one with multiple meanings. Since the correct answer follows from its use in the passage, Vocabulary-in-Context questions are characterized as a subset of Inference questions. Typical question stems:

> Which one of the following is closest in meaning to the word "citation" as it used in the second paragraph of the passage (line 18)?

> In context, the word "enlightenment" (line 24) refers to

Wrong Answer Types in RC

Outside the Scope (Out of Scope; Beyond the Scope)

An answer choice containing a statement that is too broad, too narrow, or beyond the purview of the passage

180

An answer choice that directly contradicts what the correct answer must say

Extreme

An answer choice containing language too emphatic (e.g., *all*, *never*, *every*, *none*) to be supported by the passage

Distortion

An answer choice that mentions details or ideas from the passage but mangles or misstates what the author said about those details or ideas

Faulty Use of Detail

An answer choice that accurately states something from the passage but in a manner that incorrectly answers the question

Half-Right/Half-Wrong

An answer choice in which one clause follows from the passage while another clause contradicts or deviates from the passage

Formal Logic Terms

Conditional Statement ("If"-Then Statement)

A statement containing a sufficient clause and a necessary clause. Conditional statements can be described in Formal Logic shorthand as:

> If [sufficient clause] → [necessary clause]

In some explanations, the LSAT expert may refer to the sufficient clause as the statement's "trigger" and to the necessary clause as the statement's result.

For more on how to interpret, describe, and use conditional statements on the LSAT, please refer to "A Note About Formal Logic on the LSAT" in this book's introduction.

Contrapositive

The conditional statement logically equivalent to another conditional statement formed by reversing the order of and negating the terms in the original conditional statement. For example, reversing and negating the terms in this statement:

> If   A   →   B

results in its contrapositive:

> If   ~B   →   ~A

To form the contrapositive of conditional statements in which either the sufficient clause or the necessary clause has more than one term, you must also change the conjunction *and* to *or*, or vice versa. For example, reversing and negating the terms and changing *and* to *or* in this statement:

> If   M   →   O AND P

results in its contrapositive:

> If   ~O OR ~P   →   ~M